THE BRITISH BOXING BOARD OF CONTROL
BOXING YEARBOOK 2008

Edited by Barry J. Hugman

MAINSTREAM
PUBLISHING

EDINBURGH AND LONDON

First published in Great Britain in 2007 by
MAINSTREAM PUBLISHING COMPANY (EDINBURGH) LTD
7 Albany Street
Edinburgh EH1 3UG

ISBN 9781845962548

A catalogue record for this book is available
from the British Library

Typeset and designed by Typecast (Artwork & Design)

Printed and bound in Great Britain by
William Clowes Ltd, Beccles, Suffolk

Contents

St Andrew's Sporting Club Ltd
The Home of Scottish Boxing

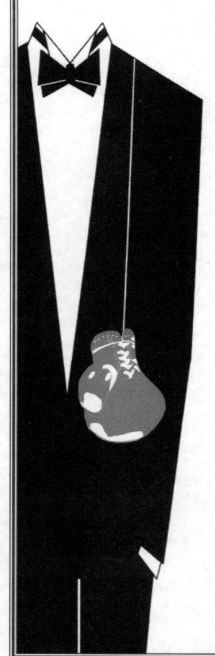

Tommy Gilmour MBE

St Andrew's Sporting Club
Platinum House
120 Carnegie Road
Hillington
Glasgow
G52 4JZ

Tel: 0141 810 5700

Fax: 0141 882 5557

E-Mail: STANDREWSSPORT@AOL.COM

Acknowledgements

Now in its 24th year this publication has always been very much a team effort, with many of the original members still participating, and I would like to thank all those who continue to help establish the *British Boxing Yearbook* as the *'Wisden'* of British boxing.

As in previous years, I am indebted to the BBBoC's General Secretary, Simon Block, along with Lynne Conway, Helen Oakley, Donna Streeter and Sarah Aldridge, for their help and support in placing information at my disposal and being of assistance when required. Simon's assistant, Robert Smith, who is also the Southern, Western and Welsh Area Secretary and a former pro fighter of note, was again extremely helpful, as were Dai Corp and John Carey.

On a business front, I would like to thank the BBBoC for their support and Bernard Hart, the Managing Director of the Lonsdale International Sporting Club, for his efforts in helping to organise the annual British Boxing Board of Control Awards Dinner where the book will be officially launched. The Awards Luncheon or Dinner has been an ongoing function since 1984, when it was established as a vehicle to launch the first *Yearbook*. Following that, Bernard, ably backed up by Kymberley and Chas Taylor, helps to make sure that the standard remains top class. At the same time, I would like to thank all of those who advertised within these pages for their support.

Members of the *Yearbook* 'team' who wrote articles for this year's edition and who have recently been published, or are in the process of publishing their own books are: John Jarrett (whose new book, *Champ in the Corner, The Ray Arcel Story*, published by Tempus, will be available in October); Ralph Oates (as a boxing quiz book specialist, Ralph's latest book, *The Muhammad Ali Quiz Book*, is now on sale. He is also working on another book that will be titled *Aspects of Heavyweight Boxing*); Tracey Pollard (continues to work on a book about the life and times of Brian London, the former British heavyweight champion); Keith Robinson (has recently published *Lanky Bob: The Life, Times and Contemporaries of Bob Fitzsimmons*); and Wynford Jones has recently published *Benny's Boys: The Stable of Benny Jacobs*. By the time you have read this, Melanie Lloyd, who has written several articles for the *Yearbook*, will have published volume two of *Sweet Fighting Man*, a follow up to her successful first venture. Please support all of these authors if you can.

Once again, Wynford, a Class 'A' referee and a big supporter of boxing, came to my aid when travelling to the Board's offices on a regular basis in order to collate vital data required for this publication. Other members of the *Yearbook* 'team' are Bob Yalen, who has covered boxing with ABC across the world and looks after the 'World Title Bouts'' section; Harold Alderman, an unsung hero who has spent over 40 years researching the early days of boxing through to modern times, has extended the 'Early Gloved Boxing' section to take on board the records of two more men who practiced their trade in the period prior to 1909; Eric Armit, the Chairman of the Commonwealth Boxing Council and a leading authority on boxers' records throughout the world, is responsible for the 'A-Z of Current World Champions'; and Derek O'Dell, a former amateur boxer and Chairman of Croydon EBA, produces the 'Obituaries'' section. Following up his excellent article on Victor McLaglen in the 2004 *Yearbook*, the well-known author, Graeme Kent, has presented an interesting article on the rise and fall of Charlie Mitchell, a man who was at his peak immediately prior to the 20th Century. I am also delighted to welcome Ray Caulfield, a former amateur boxer, who is one of the leading lights of the London EBA and a driving force of the EBA movement as a whole. Ray is taking over the 'Directory of Ex-Boxers' Associations' from Ron Olver, a very good friend of boxing, who sadly passed away this year. A tribute to Ron can be found in the 'Obituaries'' section.

Regarding photographs, as in previous years the great majority were produced by Les Clark (Les also puts together 'A Boxing Quiz with a Few Below the Belt' within these pages), who has possibly the largest library of both action shots and poses from British rings over the last 20 years or more. If anyone requires a copy of a photo that has appeared in the *Yearbook* credited to Les, or requires a list, he can be reached at 352 Trelawney Avenue, Langley, Berks SL3 7TS. Other photos were supplied by my good friends, Philip Sharkey and Larry Braysher, the latter being a well-known collector who provided several illustrations for his article on Dick Burge, as well as pictures for the 'Obituaries' and 'World Champions Since Gloves'' sections. I would also like to thank Philip Sharkey, who both wrote and illustrated the Gheto Warriors article and came up with a few shots of current fighters. Another photographer to help us out was Paul Speak, who sent in action shots that we had the right of use for the Ricky Hatton article.

Also, additional input came from Neil Blackburn (in providing added information to make the 'Obituaries'' section as complete as possible); Michael Featherstone (who is always available to help out on birth/death details); Mrs Enza Jacoponi, the Secretary of the European Boxing Union (EBU Championship data covering the past 12 months); Simon Block (Commonwealth and British Championship data); Robert Smith, John Jarrett, Ken Morton and Les Potts (Area Championship data); Patrick Myler (Irish amateur boxing); Malcolm Collins (Welsh amateur boxing); Brian Donald (Scottish amateur boxing); Matthew Bozeat, Steve Brooks, Reece Brotherton, Dave Cockell, Peter Foley, Carl Fox, Dave Goddard, John Homer, Jimmy Lewis, Alan Lynch, Bill Nedley, Keith Nugent, Ted Peate, David Randle and John Shakespeare (English Amateur Boxing). I must also make mention of John Sheppard, of BoxRec.Com, who kindly delivered the update for the Active British-Based Boxers: Career Records' section in the correct order for me to start my audit.

Almost last, but not least, my thanks go to Jean Bastin, who continued to produce a high standard of typesetting and design, and my wife, Jennifer, who looks after the proof reading. It goes without saying that without their input the book wouldn't be the product it is.

Finally, I would like to dedicate this edition of the *British Boxing Yearbook* to my grandchildren, Lukas John Anders Hugman, who was born on 8 August this year, and Daisy May (4 October 1993) and Primrose Anna Ivy (15 February 1998) Kitchener.

Introduction

by Barry J. Hugman

It gives me great pleasure to welcome you to the 24th edition of the British Boxing Yearbook. The format hasn't changed too much over the years, certainly not since the 1993 edition, as myself and the team continue to monitor and update the current goings on, while also continuing to research the past and pass on our findings.

Beginning with the modern era, once again we have decided to stay with the way we produce Active British Based-Boxers: Complete Records. The decision to have one alphabet, instead of separating champions, being taken on the grounds that because there are so many champions these days – British, Commonwealth, European, IBF, WBA, WBC, WBO, and more recently WBU, IBO, WBF, etc, etc, and a whole host of Inter-Continental and International titles – it would cause confusion rather than what was really intended.

If you wish to quickly locate whether or not a boxer fought during the past season (1 July 2006 to 30 June 2007) then the Boxers' Record Index at the back of the book is the place to look. Also, as in the very first edition, we chart the promotions in Britain throughout the season, thus enabling one to refer to the exact venue within a boxer's record.

Regarding our records, if a fighter is counted out standing up we have continued to show it as a stoppage rather than that of a kayo or technical kayo, as in fights where the referee dispenses with the count. Thus fights are recorded as count outs (the count being tolled with the fighter still on the canvas), retirements (where a fighter is retired on his stool) and referee stopped contest. Of course, other types of decisions would take in draws, no contests, and no decisions. In these days of health and safety fears, more and more boxers are being counted out either standing up or when initially floored, especially when a referee feels that the man on the receiving end is unable to defend himself adequately or requires immediate medical attention. One of the reasons that we have yet to discriminate between cut-eye stoppages and other types of finishes, is because a fighter who is stopped because of cuts is often on his way to a defeat in the first place. Thus, if you want to get a true reflection on the fight it is probably better to consult the trade paper, *Boxing News*, rather than rely on a referee's decision to tell you all you want to know; the recorded result merely being a guide.

Continuing the trend, there are always new articles to match the old favourites. Regular features such as Home and Away with British Boxers (John Jarrett), World Title Bouts During the Season (Bob Yalen), A-Z of Current World Champions (Eric Armit), Directory of Ex-Boxers' Associations (Ray Caulfield), Obituaries (Derek O'Dell) and two regular quizzes (Ralph Oates and Les Clark), etc, being supported this year with interesting articles such as Ricky Hatton: The Best of British (Tracey Pollard); Ghetto Warriors (Philip Sharkey); Mick Toomey: A Promoter's Story and Colin McMillan: So Near Yet So Far (Ralph Oates); Joe Erskine: The Classical Heavyweight (Wynford

Jones); Dick Burge: The Lord of the Ring (Larry Braysher); Charlie Mitchell: The Bad Boy of Boxing (Graeme Kent); and Will Jackson's 'Stockton and Thornaby Physical Culture and Boxing Club' (Keith R. Robinson).

Elsewhere, hopefully, you will find all you want to know about British Area, English, Celtic, British, Commonwealth, European and world title bouts that took place in 2006-2007, along with the amateur championships that were held in England, Scotland, Wales and Ireland, as well as being able to access details on champions from the past, both amateur and professional. Last year, I took the decision to drop the amateur international tournaments as they have virtually got lost these days among a welter of multi-nationals, which space, unfortunately, does not allow us to cover.

Historically, what was started several years ago under the heading of 'Early Gloved Championship Boxing', has now been extended to presenting records of some of the leading fighters of the pre-1909 days. Much of this work was due to Harold Alderman painstakingly piecing together results for the pre-Lonsdale Belt and named-weight division period. There are still many who believe as gospel much of what was reported down the ages by 'respected' men such as Nat Fleischer, the owner of *The Ring* magazine and the *Ring Record Book*, and then copied by numerous historians who failed to grasp what the sport was really like before the First World War. Basically, boxing prior to the period in question was a shambles, following bare fists with an assortment of driving gloves, knuckle gloves, and two-ounce gloves, etc, until it arrived at what we recognise today. There were no commissions, with newspapermen becoming all-powerful by naming their own champions at all kinds of weights, and in much of America the sport was illegal, no-decision contests rescuing it from being abolished. If you thought today was dire, then boxing prior to that period was almost impossible in all divisions bar the heavyweights. Because travel was difficult and news travelled slowly, fighters were able to move from town to town proclaiming themselves to be the best and 'ringers' constantly prevailed. With today's research being aided by access to early newspapers, and the use of computers, it is becoming clear that men like Fleischer 'took' the best fighters of the day and then 'fitted' them into the named-weight divisions we now know so well. If that is still as clear as mud, then turn to the pages in question.

Abbreviations and Definitions used in the record sections of the Yearbook:
PTS (Points), CO (Count Out), RSC (Referee Stopped Contest), RTD (Retired), DIS (Disqualification), NC (No Contest), ND (No Decision).

British Boxing Board of Control Ltd: Structure

(Members of the Commonwealth Boxing Council and European Boxing Union)

PRESIDENT	Lord Brooks of Tremorfa DL
CHAIRMAN	Charles Giles
VICE CHAIRMAN	John Handelaar
GENERAL SECRETARY	Simon Block
ADMINISTRATIVE STEWARDS	Baroness Golding* John Rees QC Dave Roden Andrew Vanzie* John Williamson
REPRESENTATIVE STEWARDS	Tony Behan Geoff Boulter Bernard Connolly Ken Honniball Phil Lundgren Ron Pavett Fred Potter
STEWARDS OF APPEAL*	Robin Simpson QC Geoffrey Finn William Tudor John Robert Kidby Prof. Andrew Lees Timothy Langdale QC John Mathew QC Ian Mill QC Colin Ross-Munro QC Peter Richards FRCS Nicholas Valios QC
HONORARY STEWARDS*	Sir Henry Cooper OBE, KSG Mary Peters DBE Leonard Read QPM Bill Sheeran Billy Walker
HONORARY MEDICAL CONSULTANT*	Dr Roger C. Evans FRCP
HONORARY PARLIAMENTARY CONSULTANT*	Jimmy Wray MP Ian Stewart MP
LEGAL CONSULTANT	Michael Boyce DL
MARKETING CONSULTANT	Nicky Piper MBE
HEAD OFFICE	The Old Library Trinity Street Cardiff CF10 1BH Tel: 02920 367000 Fax: 02920 367019 E-mail: sblock@bbbofc.com Website: www.bbbofc.com

* Not directors of the company

AREA COUNCILS - AREA SECRETARIES

AREA NO 1 (SCOTLAND)
Brian McAllister
11 Woodside Crescent, Glasgow G3 7UL
Telephone 0141 3320392. Fax 0141 3312029
E-Mail bmacallister@mcallisters-ca.com

AREA NO 2 (NORTHERN IRELAND)
John Campbell
8 Mount Eden Park, Belfast, Northern Ireland BT9 6RA
Telephone 02890 299 652. Fax 02890 382 906
Mobile 07715 044061

AREA NO 3 (WALES)
Robert Smith
The Old Library, Trinity Street, Cardiff CF10 1BH
Telephone 02920 367000
Fax 02920 367019
E-Mail rsmith@bbbofc.com

AREA NO 4 (NORTHERN)
(Northumberland, Cumbria, Durham, Cleveland, Tyne and Wear, North Yorkshire [north of a line drawn from Whitby to Northallerton to Richmond, including these towns].)
John Jarrett
5 Beechwood Avenue, Gosforth, Newcastle upon Tyne NE3 5DH
Telephone/Fax 01912 856556
E-Mail John.jarrettl@tesco.net

AREA NO 5 (CENTRAL)
(North Yorkshire [with the exception of the part included in the Northern Area - see above], Lancashire, West and South Yorkshire, Greater Manchester, Merseyside and Cheshire, Isle of Man, North Humberside.)
Richard Jones
1 Churchfields, Croft, Warrington, Cheshire WA3 7JR
Telephone/Fax 01925 768132
E-Mail r.m.jones@mmu.ac.uk

AREA NO 6 (SOUTHERN)
(Bedfordshire, Berkshire, Buckinghamshire, Cambridgeshire, Channel Islands, Isle of Wight, Essex, Hampshire, Kent, Hertfordshire, Greater London, Norfolk, Suffolk, Oxfordshire, East and West Sussex.)
Robert W. Smith
The Old Library, Trinity Street, Cardiff CF10 1BH
Telephone 02920 367000. Fax: 02920 367019
E-Mail rsmith@bbbofc.com

AREA NO 7 (WESTERN)
(Cornwall, Devon, Somerset, Dorset, Wiltshire, Avon, Gloucestershire.)
Robert Smith
The Old Library, Trinity Street, Cardiff CF10 1BH
Telephone 02920 367000
Fax 02920 367019
E-Mail rsmith@bbbofc.com

AREA NO 8 (MIDLANDS)
(Derbyshire, Nottinghamshire, Lincolnshire, Salop, Staffordshire, Herefordshire and Worcestershire, Warwickshire, West Midlands, Leicestershire, South Humberside, Northamptonshire.)
Les Potts
1 Sunnyside Villas, Gnosall, Staffordshire
Telephone 01785 823641. Mobile 07973 533835
E-Mail lezpotts@hotmail.com

Foreword

by Simon Block *(General Secretary, British Boxing Board of Control)*

We have started the new season (Autumn 2007) with five world champions holding a title recognised by one of the four major sanctioning organisations - WBC, WBA, IBF and WBO. There is Enzo Maccarinelli (WBO) at cruiserweight, Clinton Woods (WBC) at light-heavyweight, Joe Calzaghe (WBO) at super-middleweight, Junior Witter (WBC) at light-welterweight and Gavin Rees (WBA) at light-welterweight, with one 'Interim' champion at super-featherweight in Alex Arthur (WBO), who, no doubt, will shortly box for the 'full' title.

Britain remains one of the world's strongest boxing countries, both in terms of talent and economic resources. Ricky Hatton and David Haye have world championship opportunities pending and Carl Froch, who has made consistent progress as the British and Commonwealth champion, is waiting for his European title opportunity, success at which will ensure a WBC world championship challenge. Behind these figureheads we have excellent talent coming through, with Amir Khan (who won the Commonwealth lightweight title in July), Jamie Moore (British light-middleweight champion), Kevin Mitchell (Commonwealth super-featherweight champion), John Murray and Derry Matthews still making good progress, while Nathan Cleverly looks to succeed in the very tough super-middleweight division.

The previous 12 months has also had its bizarre moments. Last December I found myself bouncing like a pin-ball off Audley Harrison and Danny Williams as they briefly scuffled after the weigh-in for their contest. The scuffle would normally have led to disciplinary action being taken by the Board, but in view of the good performance both boxers put on and with Board Chairman Charles Giles' approval they were both persuaded by me to make a 'voluntary' donation to the Board's Charity, which the Stewards of the Board felt was an appropriate outcome.

In April, the British light-heavyweight champion, Peter Oboh, inexplicably decided not to proceed with his first British championship defence in three years, against Tony Oakey, despite attending the weigh-in, passing the pre-contest medical and even turning up on the evening to speak to me. No amount of hard talk could persuade a very determined Mr Oboh to reconsider and I still do not understand what got into him, especially as he had appeared before the Stewards of the Board a few months earlier and pleaded with them not to take his licence away for inactivity, on the understanding that he would box before the end of June.

Inevitably, as with any other area of life, we lose friends each year and in this edition, as always, their passing is marked. However, I do feel the need to mention especially the loss of my dear friend and Commonwealth Boxing Council colleague, Ron Olver, who also chaired the Grants Committee of the Board's Benevolent Fund. Ron soldiered on valiantly, despite having both leg and eye disabilities, to produce 'The Old Timers' column each week in *Boxing News*. Congratulations to our Board Inspector, Richard Barber, for taking on this job and filling so well what we thought was an unfillable vacancy. Furthermore, the loss of James Oyebola in a senseless murder touched all who knew him. I had worked closely with James over the last couple of years with regard to his light-welterweight, Ajose Olusegun, and it is a bitter irony that his life should have been cut short so soon after finally obtaining the Commonwealth light-welterweight championship opportunity for which he had fought and argued for so long on behalf of Ajose.

Once again, as with last year, our Awards Committee has had to whittle down the nominations for this year's 'Contest of the Year', but whether it makes the list or not one of the better contests this year was the one for the vacant British and Commonwealth flyweight championship between Dale Robinson and Chris Edwards, both sterling professionals, in Altrincham, Manchester in April. This contest resulted in a draw and at the beginning of this season they were due to be re-matched for the inaugural British super-flyweight championship. As a rule I am among those who prefer not to see a proliferation of championship weight divisions. However, in this case I was an enthusiastic supporter of the motion for an amendment to the Regulations to permit the introduction of this new weight division. When watching Lee Haskins struggle against the Commonwealth bantamweight champion, Tshifhiwa Munyai, and Ian Napa failing valiantly against the European bantamweight champion, Simone Maludrottu, to me they both looked a bit small to be full-blown bantamweights, despite undoubtedly struggling to meet the eight-stone flyweight limit. Although Ian has now bounced back to become the British bantamweight champion with a very creditable win over Jason Booth, it may well be that his best fighting weight is a few pounds below and this new weight division will give more of the British smaller men an opportunity to box at a more comfortable weight. I suspect in this relatively prosperous country of ours we are beginning to see the end of the flyweight division.

This season has started with a bang, with contests lined up such as Junior Witter v Vivian Harris, Joe Calzaghe v Mikkel Kessler and Ricky Hatton v Floyd Mayweather. Ever the optimist, I foresee a continuing future for this wonderful sport of ours.

Congratulations to Barry and the team once again for this compendium of knowledge, now in its 24th year.

EVANS-WATERMAN PROMOTIONS LTD
Licensed to the British Boxing Board of Control

88 WINDSOR ROAD, MAIDENHEAD, BERKS SL6 2DJ
Tel: 01628 623640   Fax: 01628 684633
Mobile: 07768 954643
e-mail: boxevans@yahoo.co.uk

CURRENT LIST

HEAVYWEIGHTS		Rounds	LIGHT-MIDDLEWEIGHTS		Rounds
Roman Greenberg	–	10 or 12	Carl Drake	–	4 or 6
Luke Simpkin	–	4 or 6	George Katsimpas	–	6 or 8
CRUISERWEIGHT			WELTERWEIGHT		
Jim Swindells	–	4 or 6	Patrick Doherty	–	4 or 6
LIGHT-HEAVYWEIGHTS			LIGHT-WELTERWEIGHT		
Nick Okoth	–	6 or 8	Mark McCullough	–	4 or 6
Shpetim Hoti	–	4 or 6			
			LIGHTWEIGHTS		
SUPER-MIDDLEWEIGHTS			Gareth Couch	–	6-8 or 10
Matthew Barr	–	6 or 8	Shane Watson	–	6 or 8
Gary Dawson	–	4 or 6			
MIDDLEWEIGHTS					
Ozzy Adams	–	8 or 10			
Anthony Young	–	6 or 8			

WEST LONDON'S FINEST RISING STABLE
Trainers: Dave Laxen; Darren Whitman; Steve Bernath; Graham Stevenson
EVANS-WATERMAN PROMOTIONS LTD is a member of the P.B.P.A.

British Boxing Board of Control Awards

Now in its 24th year, the BBBoC Awards Ceremony will be held in London later this year and will once again be co-hosted by the Lonsdale International Sporting Club's Bernard Hart. The winners of these prestigious statuettes, designed in the form of a boxer, are selected by a well-informed panel of judges who make a judgement on the season as a whole at an annual meeting.

British Boxer of the Year: The outstanding British Boxer at any weight. 1984: Barrry McGuigan. 1985: Barry McGuigan. 1986: Dennis Andries. 1987: Lloyd Honeyghan. 1988: Lloyd Honeyghan. 1989: Dennis Andries. 1990: Dennis Andries. 1991: Dave McAuley. 1992: Colin McMillan. 1993: Lennox Lewis. 1994: Steve Robinson. 1995: Nigel Benn. 1996: Prince Naseem Hamed. 1997: Robin Reid. 1998: Carl Thompson. 1999: Billy Schwer. 2000: Glenn Catley. 2001: Joe Calzaghe. 2002: Lennox Lewis. 2003: Ricky Hatton. 2004: Scott Harrison. 2005: Ricky Hatton. 2006: Joe Calzaghe.

British Contest of the Year: Although a fight that took place in Europe won the 1984 Award, since that date, the Award, presented to both participants, has applied to the best all-action contest featuring a British boxer in a British ring. 1984: Jimmy Cable v Said Skouma. 1985: Barry McGuigan v Eusebio Pedroza. 1986: Mark Kaylor v Errol Christie. 1987: Dave McAuley v Fidel Bassa. 1988: Tom Collins v Mark Kaylor. 1989: Michael Watson v Nigel Benn. 1990: Orlando Canizales v Billy Hardy. 1991: Chris Eubank v Nigel Benn. 1992: Dennis Andries v Jeff Harding. 1993: Andy Till v Wally Swift Jnr. 1994: Steve Robinson v Paul Hodkinson. 1995: Steve Collins v Chris Eubank. 1996: P. J. Gallagher v Charles Shepherd. 1997: Spencer Oliver v Patrick Mullings. 1998: Carl Thompson v Chris Eubank. 1999: Shea Neary v Naas Scheepers. 2000: Simon Ramoni v Patrick Mullings. 2001: Colin Dunne v Billy Schwer. 2002: Ezra Sellers v Carl Thompson. 2003: David Barnes v Jimmy Vincent. 2004: Michael Gomez v Alex Arthur. 2005: Jamie Moore v Michael Jones. 2006: Kevin Anderson v Young Muttley.

Overseas Boxer of the Year: For the best performance by an overseas boxer in a British ring. 1984: Buster Drayton. 1985: Don Curry. 1986: Azumah Nelson. 1987: Maurice Blocker. 1988: Fidel Bassa. 1989: Brian Mitchell. 1990: Mike McCallum. 1991: Donovan Boucher. 1992: Jeff Harding. 1993: Crisanto Espana. 1994: Juan Molina. 1995: Mike McCallum. 1996: Jacob Matlala. 1997: Ronald Wright. 1998: Tim Austin. 1999: Vitali Klitschko. 2000: Keith Holmes. 2001: Harry Simon. 2002: Jacob Matlala. 2003: Manuel Medina. 2004: In-Jin Chi. 2005: Joshua Okine. 2006: Tshifhiwa Munyai.

Special Award: Covers a wide spectrum, and is an appreciation for services to boxing. 1984: Doctor Adrian Whiteson. 1985: Harry Gibbs. 1986: Ray Clarke. 1987: Hon. Colin Moynihan. 1988: Tom Powell. 1989: Winston Burnett. 1990: Frank Bruno. 1991: Muhammad Ali. 1992: Doctor Oswald Ross. 1993: Phil Martin. 1994: Ron Olver. 1995: Gary Davidson. 1996: Reg Gutteridge and Harry Carpenter. 1997: Miguel Matthews and Pete Buckley. 1998: Mickey Duff and Tommy Miller. 1999: Jim Evans and Jack Lindsay. 2000: Henry Cooper. 2001: John Morris and Leonard 'Nipper' Read. 2002: Roy Francis and Richie Woodhall. 2003: Michael Watson. 2004: Dennie Mancini and Bob Paget. 2005: Barry McGuigan. 2006: Jack Bishop.

Sportsmanship Award: This Award recognises boxers who set a fine example, both in and out of the ring. 1986: Frank Bruno. 1987: Terry Marsh. 1988: Pat Cowdell. 1989: Horace Notice. 1990: Rocky Kelly. 1991: Wally Swift Jnr. 1992: Duke McKenzie. 1993: Nicky Piper. 1994: Francis Ampofo. 1995: Paul Wesley. 1996: Frank Bruno. 1997: Lennox Lewis. 1998: Johnny Williams. 1999: Brian Coleman. 2000: Michael Ayers and Wayne Rigby. 2001: Billy Schwer. 2002: Mickey Cantwell. 2003: Francis Ampofo. 2004: Dale Robinson and Jason Booth. 2005: Ricky Hatton and Kostya Tszyu. 2006: Enzo Maccarinelli and Mark Hobson.

Joe Calzaghe, the 2006 British Boxer of the Year, seen here on the night with Charles Giles, the Chairman of the BBBoC Les Clark

3 Bull Ring
Sedgley, Dudley
West Midlands, DY3 1RU

Telephone: (01902) 670007
Fax: (01902) 665195
Mobile: 07976 283 157

1st team Ltd

Paul (PJ) Rowson Promoter & Manager
Errol Johnson Promoter, Manager, Matchmaker & Trainer

HEAVYWEIGHT
Paul Burton 11-3
Neil Perkins Unboxed

LIGHT-HEAVYWEIGHT
Jonjo Finnegan 10-2-3

SUPER-MIDDLEWEIGHT
Matty Hough 5-2
Richard Collins 1-0-1

MIDDLEWEIGHT
Darren McDermott Midlands Champion 13-0-1
Steve Bendall 26-3
Sam Horton 5-0
Conroy McIntosh 6-21-3
Shane Junior 2-1
Duane Parker Unboxed
Rob Kenney 3-0-1

LIGHT-MIDDLEWEIGHT
Marcus Portman WBF World Champion 17-5-1
Matt Galer 9-7
Wayne Downing 3-5
Mark Lloyd British Masters Champion 8-0

WELTERWEIGHT
Young Muttley Former British Champion 22-3
Stuart Elwell Former Midlands Champion 10-1
Darren Gethin Midlands Champion 8-9-5
Martin Gordon 0-3-1

LIGHT-WELTERWEIGHT
Billy Smith Midlands Champion 9-53
Dean Harrison 7-0
Rob Hunt 6-0
Carl Groombridge Unboxed

LIGHTWEIGHT
Tristan Davies Midlands Champion 10-0
Martin Gethin British Masters Champion 8-0-1
Scott Evans Unboxed

SUPER-FEATHERWEIGHT
Shaun Walton 3-22-3
Steven Gethin 10-32-2

BANTAMWEIGHT
Neil Marston 9-17

FLYWEIGHT
Delroy Spencer 10-53-3

1st Team's Trainer/Cornerman Bob Plant, who is also the proprietor of
TKO (UK) Boxing Supplies, Upper Aston Farm, Aston Lane,
Claverley, near Wolverhampton, West Midlands WV5 7EE
Tel: 07970 035 469

Ricky Hatton: The Best of British

by Tracey Pollard

At the time of writing this article, Ricky Hatton remains undefeated in 43 fights, holds the IBF version of the world light-welterweight title and is on the brink of the most important fight of his career. He is undeniably the nation's favourite boxer, has been acclaimed as one of Britain's greatest fighters ever by past champions and Prince Charles recently presented him with an MBE at Buckingham Palace. Phew!

There are countless other accolades and baubles, amassed during his amateur and professional careers. They filled the Hatton family sideboard to overflowing until he moved into a place of his own just around the corner and created space on the mantelpiece for the trophies of younger brother, Matthew, who is now building his own collection. Some of Ricky's awards won't fit in the display cabinet, like the block of flats in his hometown named Hatton Court in his honour. His most recent fight, in Las Vegas, was attended by celebrities from sport and music, including Robbie Williams and members of the England football team. Although his devotion to his favourite football club, Manchester City, is well documented it was the renowned Manchester United player and good friend, Wayne Rooney, who proudly carried his world title belt into the ring. His other belt was carried in by another friend, fight legend Marco Antonio Barrera, who insisted on escorting Ricky into the ring despite the fact that he was facing a Mexican in front of a crowd expected to be predominantly Mexican. In fact, 10,000 of the 13,000+ in the arena were Brits who had travelled over to support their man. The proposed opponents for his next fight read like a rundown of the biggest names in the sport today, including, Oscar de la Hoya, Shane Mosley, Miguel Cotto, Floyd Mayweather. But, as Richie Woodhall pointed out, would 10,000 fans follow de la Hoya to Manchester to watch him fight? We could soon find out because that fight is on the table, win or lose against Mayweather in December.

So who is the real 'Golden Boy' here? What has made this 29-year-old kid from Hyde (Hyde?). Usually they just say Manchester because no American has heard of Hyde), into this international boxing superstar?

The well-trodden path to boxing glory begins with a talented amateur who attracts attention as he defeats the opposition and has promoters eagerly awaiting his decision to fight for cash. His early victories against men with more experience and less talent or other novices lead to him becoming an exciting prospect. This is rapidly followed by cries of 'yes, but who has he fought?' Which is often accompanied by 'who has he avoided?'. Then there are demands that he step up a level and those demands continue relentlessly until he loses a fight. The victories are obviously because the opponent was past his best or having a bad day, the defeats are because our talented boxer was clearly limited. Few make it to the other side

where veneration awaits as they are recognised as one of Britain's greats. Ricky is already there, having earned the respect of those that have made the journey before him and become recognised as the best of British. His journey isn't over and he will still have to endure the slings and arrows of outrageous cynicism, but he has earned his place in British boxing history.

The journey began, as is so often the case, with a talent for football. A youngster may be destined for success as a sportsman, but it is not always immediately apparent which sport and the Hatton household was always biased towards 'footie'. But it didn't take young Richard too long to identify his calling. His mum, Carol, remembers him bringing home a careers' form when he was 11. He declared that he wanted to be a professional boxer, which must have gone down like a lead balloon in a house where dad and grandad had both played for Manchester City! Ricky had been participating in the sport of kick-boxing from the age of seven, but also played football for his local county team in Tameside. It was

Ricky poses with the prestigious Ring Magazine Belt
Mark Clifford

during this time that he was picked for the Manchester City FA School of Excellence and looked set to follow in the family tradition. Grandad had played for the B team before the War and Dad played under Joe Mercer and Malcolm Allison in the 1960s, firstly as an apprentice then as a pro. It is hardly surprising that Ricky is such a devoted fan, wearing City colours in the ring and entering to the team's 'Blue Moon' theme tune, which has now become just as synonymous with him.

He showed some talent as a kick-boxer but mainly with the use of his fists so, not surprisingly, his trainer (to whom the nation's boxing fans are eternally indebted) advised him to try boxing. His innate boxing ability was immediately apparent. He joined the local amateur boxing club in Hyde and the coach, Ted Peate, left him to have a knock about on the punchbag, but was immediately drawn back by the noise and a strong desire to rescue the club's bag. The kid was undeniably raw, but impressive. He had the same effect on the coach at his next amateur club. Paul Dunne remembers taking Ricky to spar with professionals like Paul Burke and Andy Holligan at the Phoenix Gym in Salford and watching him hold his own against them. In fact, he badly damaged Andy's ribs during sparring for the Shea Neary fight. "He cracked Andy's ribs", remembers the latter's trainer, Billy Graham. "It's a credit to Andy that he still fought Neary with cracked ribs and it shows just how tough he was. Andy is one of my favourite fighters that I have trained, very, very tough. In fact he insisted on sparring with Ricky again, against my advice because Ricky just couldn't help throwing that left hook." Incidentally, Andy lost a close contest with Neary.

Initial impressions proved correct and Ricky won three British schoolboy titles and eight national amateur titles, including two junior ABA titles, a gold in the Golden Gloves and a senior ABA title. He also won a bronze in the world juniors, becoming the first English boxer to beat a Cuban in Cuba. Paul Speak is now Ricky's agent, but he too was a regular visitor to the Phoenix and he remembers the young amateur as a nice quiet lad who never bragged about his achievements. When Ricky was missing from the gym for a few days Paul asked where he was and was surprised to be told he was at the world games in Cuba. Ricky had never even mentioned it. He would like to have fought in the Olympics, but faced with a long wait he decided to turn pro. He visited quite a few gyms, but returned to the Phoenix and Billy Graham. "I knew he would pick me because I had so many great fighters at his weight like Andy Holligan, Paul Burke and Chris Barnett". It was a thriving gym, with British and European champions and limitless sparring plus the body bag, which was the icing on the cake, it being just perfect for his style. He also sparred with Peter Judson, who said Ricky was the best kid he'd sparred with since Naseem Hamed. On the Boxing Monthly Video for June 1997, Billy made ambitious predictions for his fighters. He said: "Michael Brodie will go all the way, Peter Judson will win the British title and a young fighter called Ricky Hatton, who is just turning pro, will become a world champion because he is the most naturally talented kid I've ever had".

"I chose Billy because we are on the same wavelength", says Ricky. "What I am thinking, he says and vice-versa. It's the same when we watch boxing tapes, I'll just be thinking something and Billy says it. It is a relationship that has endured which is rare in this sport, even among families. We have always been friends as much as business," explains Ricky, "He feels for you in the corner and throws each punch with you".

"My favourite fighters used to be tall fighters like Jose Napoles and Bob Foster", says Billy, "but by the time Ricky came I preferred predators, body punchers, so he was made to measure for me. He has a natural talent for picking things up really easily, I soon taught him side-stepping and things like that. He has a natural boxing brain and understanding, he's born for it. He was already a student of boxing when he came. I learnt about boxing by watching and picking it up and Ricky had done the same". Although he is quick to add that he doesn't train Ricky like he used to fight himself. "I don't train fighters like anyone I know or like I fought and would throw them out if they fought like me! I couldn't have put up with me. I was a pain in the ass and feel sorry for my former trainer, Ken Daniels".

It has obviously been a successful partnership, although most people would think that once he had chosen to enter the professional ring, Ricky Hatton was an unstoppable force whoever he had in the corner. "Fighters make fights, trainers just help", is what Billy believes. "I don't think he would have been as good with anyone else. I'm not saying he wouldn't have been a world champion, but he wouldn't have been good as he is. A talented fighter will go far with anyone but you need flair, he would have been a lot more basic with anyone else". "You can't be a great fighter without a great trainer", says Ricky, "plus the dedication and hard work of course. Generally I can figure my opponents out for myself, but in the Kostya Tszyu fight, for example, the tactics during the fight were mostly down to Billy".

Ricky's transition to the paid ranks was rather less than smooth. His debut was scheduled to be on Naseem Hamed's undercard, but unbelievably he failed his medical. Billy had been through a similar disappointment before and thought, oh no, it's just like Danny McCarrick." Danny was a really talented amateur, who Billy believed was a potential world champion, but he failed his medical and couldn't fight in this country. Interestingly, Danny fought and was stopped by Kostya Tszyu as an amateur. Eventually it was discovered that Ricky and Matthew have an unusual heart rate that is actually beneficial in sport, giving them increased stamina. With that drama out of the way, Ricky attempted to make his debut on Robin Reid's undercard on 11 September 1997 in Widnes. Reid successfully defended his WBC title against Hassine Cherifi over 12 rounds, but collapsed because of the heat. Unfortunately this meant that the paramedics were not at ringside. "We had to wait ages", recalls Billy, "but we were unfazed. There was no sign that it affected Ricky and it didn't bother me because I knew what I had got in the corner and couldn't wait to show him off".

The opponent was Kid McAuley and it turned out to

have been a long wait for a very short fight. "Ricky got him with a body shot and the sound was terrible", remembers Billy. "He went to his corner and we were told he was throwing up. I was talking to Ricky in the corner but he was peering round me really upset saying, 'Oh no, they're not going to stop it are they?' He wanted to fight on!" McAuley retired at the end of the first round. "He was always like that. It was the same in Atlantic City with some guy they called 'Dog Pound'," (Ricky fought Kevin Carter in Atlantic City in his ninth contest.). "I was looking at them and I could tell what was going on, he was holding him up because he wanted more of a fight so I shouted 'Stop f...ing about' and he knocked the guy out.

The drama continued into fight two. Nineteen years old, venue - Madison Square Garden! (Might as well start as you mean to go on!). First problem - no trainer. Billy was really disappointed that he couldn't be there but he was in Zambia with Paul Burke, who was fighting for the Commonwealth title against Felix Bwaliya. He then had to rush straight back to London for Ensley Bingham's British title defence, which he won with a 12th-round knockout. Tragically, Bwaliya died during his fight with Burke and there was then some controversy when he was awarded the title. Today, Ricky's second fight is a regular feature in his after-dinner speeches. The way he tells it, he's a million miles from home, without his trainer, frantically trying to communicate his anxiety over the phone. "Billy you should see this guy, he's a monster. He's huge and hairy and covered in tattoos", and so on, roughly along the lines of this guy's massive and I'm small and green and all alone. Billy, the fatherly figure with years of experience and quite a lot on his own mind, consoled his protege with pearls of wisdom and a few words beginning with 'F' and told him: "Stop worrying, if he was any good he wouldn't be fighting you!" In fact, Robert Alvarez managed to survive for four rounds, which was three more than half Ricky's early opponents.

In his first ten fights Ricky stopped five of them in the first round, with only four making it beyond the second, and in his 11th he stopped Tommy Peacock in the second round to become the Central Area light-welterweight champion. His 13th fight was a more leisurely fifth-round stoppage over Dillon Carew for the vacant WBO Inter-Continental light-welterweight title, which he successfully defended six times without venturing further than the fifth round. The fifth of those defences was surprisingly, one of the toughest of his career. "Everybody assumes that my toughest fight was going the distance with Jon Thaxton", Ricky told me back in 2001, "but it was actually this one". Course he's had a few corkers since then, but the worst of them were often caused by his nemesis which first emerged in June 2000 - cuts!

For the fifth defence Ricky made his third trip to the States, to Detroit, where our very own 'Hitman' trained at the legendary Kronk Gym, home to the original 'Hitman', Thomas Hearns. His opponent was Gilbert 'Animal' Quiros, who he described as a massive puncher. Thirty seconds into the first round Ricky suffered a cut over his left eye that

soon left his vision seriously impaired. Back in the corner, he complained that he couldn't see. The doctor told him he could only give him one more round. His cuts man worked on the damage and Ricky declared: "I can see" and launched himself into the second round. A minute and a half later Quiros was felled by a murderous body punch.

In his next fight he unified his title with a fifth-round stoppage of Giuseppe Lauri, adding the WBA Inter-Continental title belt to his collection. Just four weeks later he faced Thaxton at Wembley for the British championship. For the first time in his career he had to stay in the ring for 12 rounds, but he left it with the British title. He didn't think he'd make it past the first round when he suffered a cut that would need 28 stitches and plastic surgery. By the end of the fight they both looked like they'd been in with the surgeon, Thaxton requiring stitches for three cuts of his own. It was a tough and bloody battle and his last contest of 2000, a year that had seen him fight six times, five of them being title fights. They would all be title fights from now on.

He never defended his British title because his subsequent 21 fights have all been for versions of the world title. Five months after becoming the British light-welterweight champion, he fought Tony Pep at Wembley. Four rounds later he had won another title. "Traditionally the hardest body punchers were Mexicans boxing their way out of poverty", said Billy, "but not any more. The hardest body puncher in the world comes from a well-to-do family in Hyde". Ricky was now the WBU light-welterweight champion, a title he would successfully defend 15 times over the next four years. Counted out in four, referee stopped contest in five, counted out in two, ref stopped it in two - there were plenty of those, but Ricky also had to stick around for the verdict a few times too. And his next 12 rounder delivered another shock - his first trip to the canvas. He took on all comers from all corners, but it was a challenge from closer to home that gave the world's light-welters a ray of hope.

In true 'Terminator' fashion, Eamonn Magee has bounced back from many an assault, in and out of the ring. In June 2002 he withstood the best of the 'Hitman' and soaked up a lot of punishment, being pinned on the ropes for long periods of the fight. But he had something that gave him an advantage over most of Ricky's opponents in that he was a southpaw. That would come to rank one rung below cuts on the list of weapons required to dent Ricky's armour. It was a countering right hook to the head, in answer to those formidable lefts to the body, which floored Ricky in the opening round. He wobbled him again in the second round, but Ricky dominated the rest of the fight and kept his title. "Eamonn's a very correct boxer", he said after the fight. "He doesn't waste many shots and they're solid. He was just waiting for me to make that one mistake and fair play to him he nailed me in the first round. I was just disappointed I went down".

The next fight brought another 'first', the only victory by disqualification on his record - W DSC 2. That's 'Dad Stopped Contest'! Before the fight, Ricky's then promoter,

Frank Warren, said: "It's a good domestic fight and you can bet there'll be fireworks on the night". What great foresight and classic understatement. Warren was, of course, referring to the fact that on paper Stephen Smith looked like an ideal challenger with just one loss in 32 wins, half of them finishing early. He was also another of those delightful southpaws, but Ricky felt he would pose a different challenge than Magee. "Magee's shots were pretty basic", he said. "Stephen has more punches in his armoury although Magee perhaps has more power. It should be a very good fight". Smith blamed his one defeat to Bobby Vanzie on dirty tactics but said: "Ricky comes to fight, he doesn't have to cheat". Unfortunately, Stephen's trainer, Darkie Smith, who was also his father, thought otherwise. In the second round he leapt into the ring and pushed referee, Mickey Vann. He was furious because he insisted that Rick had head-butted his son and Vann had failed to take action. Vann had no choice but to take action after that, immediately disqualifying Stephen.

It was widely agreed to be an unfortunate incident and Darkie's impulse to rescue his son cost him dearly. They were still not reconciled many months later when Stephen visited the Phoenix Gym to consult nutritionist, Kerry Kaye. Ricky and Billy embraced him and he asked for Ricky's autograph because he said his young son was a huge fan! That's boxing for you. Ricky was always respectful towards

his opponents and would win a sportsmanship award for the commendable camaraderie between him and Kostya Tszyu, but some people are harder to get along with. Ricky met Floyd Mayweather when he was at ringside for Jermain Taylor/Bernard Hopkins in 2005. He typically held out his hand to say hello, but Mayweather started mouthing off and jabbing his finger in Ricky's face, saying: "I'm gonna get you". Ricky sat down and put his feet up, blocking Mayweather's path. "When he said he wanted to get through I told him to walk round", said Ricky. "The guys from HBO had to intervene. I know some of them are surly when the cameras are on, just for publicity, but not him, there was nobody around. He's just absolutely full of it".

At this time the Phoenix had recently moved to the bodybuilding gym owned by Kerry, who became nutritional adviser and strength coach to Billy's fighters. Billy had always believed in the advantages of weight training, contrary to old-school beliefs. In fact, one of the few rules he imposes on his boxers is that they must be prepared to do weight training and the bar/bag as part of their workout. Also the man who is almost single-handedly keeping the tobacco industry afloat refuses to train boxers who smoke!

This was the last of Ricky's domestic opponents, although Bradford's Junior Witter had mounted a campaign of challenges and taunts in a bid to fight him. Many believed that Witter had yet to earn the right to a rewarding payday,

Ricky (left) looks to work Eamonn Magee over in defence of his WBU light-welter title back in 2002   Tom Casino

many still do. Ricky defended his WBU title a further eight times, usually in Manchester where he drew a capacity crowd of up to 20,000. Only twice did he defend elsewhere. In Newcastle in his next fight he met Joe Hutchinson, who was counted out in the fourth, and in his final defence against Ray Oliveira (w rsc 10) in Canning Town.

Ricky has always expressed his gratitude to his army of supporters and recognises what a tremendous boost it is for him to have those 20,000 fans raise the roof in song when he enters the ring. It probably doesn't do a lot for his opponent's confidence to hear them all booing and is a rather shameful habit of British fans. When Ricky fought Aldo Rios every single opponent on the undercard was greeted with the un-sportsmanlike booing, all except one. Junior Witter's Australian opponent must have been very surprised to be the only visitor to be cheered into the ring, while Witter was booed. As Ricky's popularity soared, Witter's never took off. "The best time to have fought Witter would have been when I was British champion", Ricky told me recently," but the opportunity was lost. Frank Warren built me up but not Witter. I was fighting before big crowds but it was hard to build Witter up because he doesn't put bums on seats. I didn't skip anyone and fought Thaxton at 21, Magee and Smith. Then I left Witter far behind".

Success, fame and fortune have had little effect on Ricky's lifestyle, apart from owning a nice new car. At that time he still lived at home with Mum, Dad and Matthew and still drunk in his local with the same mates. He would also go to as many City matches as he could and spend as much time as possible with his young son, Campbell. People continued to treat him like a familiar face in the street, rather than a celebrity and he was always amiable and approachable. Paul Speak remembers one incident that illustrated Ricky's increasing fame. "We were driving home after a weigh-in and Ricky was feeling a bit sick. He re-hydrates after a weigh-in. We noticed a man who had collapsed at a bus stop and when I checked it turned out he had died. Meanwhile, Ricky was throwing up behind the car. A few people had gathered round and it was almost surreal - they were more interested in Ricky Hatton throwing up than the dying man!" Ricky appears largely unaffected by fame. "I'd like to be remembered as a world champion boxer, not for being famous".

When Ricky fought Vince Phillips, both hoped victory would lead to a match with the undisputed light-welterweight Champion, Kostya Tszyu. Phillips was the only man to have defeated Tszyu and was eager to meet him again now the latter had unified all the world titles, while Ricky's ambition had always been to fight the king of the light-welters. After the Magee fight he said: "My last opponent, Mikhail Krivolapov, was ranked number four by the WBC and Magee was ranked number five. That was the sixth defence of my title and I'll just keep fighting. I don't think Kostya Tszyu is going to fight me unless he has to". But he did think that Tszyu's style might suit him better than Magee's. "Tszyu's shorter than me and he'll probably stand there and fight me at my own game, whereas Eamonn

Magee was a southpaw, backing off all the time". It was of course Ricky who was victorious against Phillips but not before he had endured 12 long rounds marred by a bad cut sustained in the opening session.

Ricky was eager to fight the best in the division and was not only impatient to do so but increasingly dispirited by constant criticism of his level of opponents, which persisted over his next six defences. He was also getting some flak about his eating and drinking habits between fights when he piled on weight. The eye damage sustained in his last fight meant a five-month lay-off before his next fight against Argentina's Aldo Rios, but his now familiar relentless workrate and aggression left no ammunition for the critics. Rios had never been stopped, but in under two minutes he was on the canvas. It looked like it would be another early finish but the Argentinian hardman proved worthy of his reputation, coming back for more again and again. He took many of Ricky's body shots on his elbows and even called him in for more, but by round seven he had soaked up 64 blows to just 16 of his own. He survived the eighth, but they were clearly taking their toll and he finally succumbed in the ninth, dropping to his knees. Although he managed to beat the count before the end of the round, his corner had seen enough.

Ghanaian, Ben Tackie, had never been stopped either and had gone the distance with Tszyu and Sharmba Mitchell. Now he added Ricky to that list, but he was completely outboxed and widely outpointed in a classy performance that was considered by many to be Ricky's best. Ricky soon learned the secret of his survival. "Ben Tackie has got the toughest head I've ever hit in my life!", he said after the fight, nursing his sore hands.

Next up it was a late substitute, Dennis Holbaeck Pederson, who survived for six rounds, while Wilfredo Carlos Vilches stayed until the final bell following that one. The criticism continued as Ricky's frustration mounted. After each victory he hoped that his next fight would be against Tszyu or Mitchell. There were reports that he was becoming disillusioned and rumours of tension between him and his promoter. Critics claimed he was avoiding the division's top fighters, and while Ricky was desperate to prove them wrong the big fights never seemed to materialise. "Don't believe what you read", he told his fans, "I am just itching to show what I can do". He started by showing his next opponent, Mike 'No Joke' Stewart on 7 October 2004. Stewart had appeared on Ricky's undercard in April when he failed to impress against Sharmba Mitchell, but in his defence he came in at late notice. His record showed 20 stoppages in 36 wins, with two losses and two draws, and the IBF declared that the winner would face the victor of the November match between Mitchell and Tszyu. Stewart was confident of bettering his last performance, saying: "I believe that Ricky Hatton is a better fighter than Sharmba Mitchell, but his style will be easier to deal with. I am going to fight until my heart quits".

Stewart paid for every criticism and insult that had been levelled at the champion in recent months. From the opening seconds he struggled to survive under a ferocious and relentless barrage of solid, sickening punches, which saw him being dropped twice in the first round. The fans loved it. He was now living up to his promise to deliver. This was the real Ricky Hatton. They roared with delight as he pummelled the challenger with vicious blows to body and head but, as the punishment continued without respite into the third round, they seemed to wince in sympathy and one particularly crippling body punch brought a collective gasp of pain from the crowd. In the corner Billy tried to soothe the savage beast. "Slowly, slowly Ricky", he cautioned, but the advice bounced off his fighter as surely as Stewart's jab. Ricky was venting all his frustration on the unfortunate, quietly spoken American. The 26-year-old Stewart proved his mettle by surviving another three minutes of a sustained battering in the fourth round before he was floored by the third of three solid left hooks in the fifth and, for the first time in his career, was rescued by the referee.

"Next time we go for the big one", Ricky optimistically told the fans. Victory in this eliminator earned him that right, but he felt he had earned it already. "I beat Tackie as convincingly as Mitchell did and I beat Phillips more convincingly than him". Now he had stopped the previously unstoppable Stewart. "I've been letting things get me down", he admitted. "It hurt me terribly that the boxing fans think that I don't want to come out of Manchester and go to America and fight these guys. The next fight next year, against Tszyu or Mitchell I'll prove it."

He was mostly right and did prove it, but although it was next year it was not his next fight. That proved to be one final defence of his WBU title and this time it was in London, not at the Manchester Evening News Arena, which had become synonymous with his fights. His opponent was another 'unstoppable' in Ray Oliveira. The latter had only been off his feet three times in 58 fights and was the only man to have defeated the WBA champion, Vivian Harris. Two minutes into the fight he was off his feet for the fourth time. He went on to demonstrate the extraordinary toughness which had withstood so many quality opponents, but was stunned by the ferocity of Hattton's opening attack, the short, solid jab finding it's mark every time. In the third he caught Ricky with a right but the man from Hyde just shrugged it off impatiently and his non-stop aggression kept Oliveira on his back foot as caught him repeatedly with short right hooks to the head. The challenger's corner assured him (from behind their rosy spectacles) that his body punches were hurting Hatton, but so far there was little evidence of the record-breaking punch-rate that Oliveira was supposedly famous for.

Although the father of six had indeed broken the record for punches thrown in one of his fights, by the end of the fourth round Ricky had thrown three times as many punches as he had. In frustration he actually lifted Ricky off his feet in the fifth round but stamina was not an issue. There was no sign of exhaustion despite the amount of punishment he was taking, but blood gushed from his nose as a result of a brutal right uppercut and he finished the seventh with a cut over

his left eye. Critics had questioned Ricky's defence but he slipped Oliveira's punches with a flick of the shoulder. His offence is so often his defence, his unrelenting, impenetrable aggression keeping his opponent at full stretch. The sheer volume of punches meant that they couldn't all be textbook, but his style was perfect for the American fight fans, being perpetual motion, no back-pedalling and no coasting. In the corner Oliveira rubbed his ear and complained that he couldn't hear and it was troubling him in the tenth. Now he had eye, ear and nose damage! He dropped to his knees, clutching his ear after a solid right hook to the side of the head and was counted out. His chosen entrance music had been 'My Way', a prophetic choice and an appropriate epitaph for a distinguished career. After the fight he said: "That kid is phenomenal! He's strong and he's smart. No matter what anyone says, Ricky definitely deserves it. He's right up there with Tszyu".

Ricky was prepared to go anywhere in the world to face the undisputed champion, but in the end Tszyu came to him. The fight was set for 4 June 2005 at the MEN Arena in Manchester. Great news for Ricky, right? "Don't get me wrong, I love Manchester", he laughed, "but Sidney and Vegas sounded more appetising". Tszyu was unfazed at the prospect of facing Britain's most popular fighter on his home turf. "It's not going to be easy in Manchester, I've never experienced 22,000 Englishmen booing an Aussie, but I don't want it easy". "It won't bother Tszyu one iota", said Billy and Ricky agreed. "When he fought Julio Cesar Chavez there were a lot of screaming Mexicans but it didn't affect him". They both knew that it would take more than hometown advantage to win this particular fight. "Ricky wants to go down in history as a legendary fighter and he will win because he's the better fighter and nothing else", said Billy. "These are two of the best light-welterweights in the world and the best man is going to win". Tszyu wasn't just one of the best, he was best, but Ricky was undaunted. "Good experienced fighters can get beaten by the new kid on the block. My toughest fights were against Tackie, Phillips and Oliveira, not the cream of the division but good men none the less. We've seen Tszyu at his best, but you still haven't seen what I've got. I've only scraped the surface of what I can do. Having had 38 fights, still unbeaten, selling thousands of tickets - this is just another fight to me, but a tough one".

With that in mind, the usual ten to 12 week training camp had been extended to 15 weeks. For the first time, Ricky was the massive underdog. Only the faithful and the brave believed he could win. Former European champion, Spencer Oliver, described Tszyu as the 'baddest' man on the planet at ten stone. "He is aggression personified and grinds his opponents into the ground", said Angelo Dundee. 'The Thunder From Down Under' was coming to grind down our Ricky, who was described by his Argentinian sparring partner as being very, very nice. Oh dear. Tszyu certainly had the pedigree to do it, having followed up a stunning amateur career by winning the world's premier professional belts, belonging to the IBF, WBC and WBA.

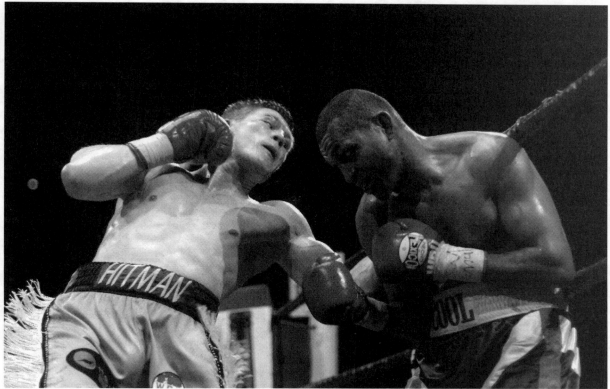

America's Vince Phillips (right), seen here taking a thumping body shot, took Ricky the full 12 rounds in 2003   Tom Casino

He had also been forced out of action for a devastating two years as a result of a recurring shoulder injury and Ricky was not convinced that his three-round victory over Sharmba Mitchell had fully tested that injury. Dundee said: "Anybody challenging Tszyu should be prepared for non-stop aggression", but that could equally apply to Ricky who said: "There is no better fighter than me in terms of stamina, workrate and volume of punches". "He can knock you out with either fist", added Dundee, and he had already done so in 25 of his 34 victories. Ricky had stopped 28 in 38. Tszyu's only defeat was to Vince Phillips, which made Ricky state: "Why is Tszyu fighting me? He has won everything there is to win and has nothing to prove. If I was him I would want to avenge that defeat".

Ricky remained as calm and easy going as he had for each of his other 14 defences and even his family were amazed at his lack of pre-fight nerves. It's a different story for mum and dad. "Me and Carol are up all night talking the night before a fight", his dad, Ray, told me. "And all we can hear is Ricky snoring in the next room". But this fight was different because Ricky had taken that monumental step in a young man's life - he had finally left home. They hardly noticed he had left though because he came home for tea every night! "Ricky kept saying, '32 seconds, 32 seconds', because that's how long it took him to walk from his front door to ours".

Along with his daily six-mile runs, Ricky's workouts were made up of several rounds of bar/bag - one minute leaping over the bar, one minute pounding the bag repeated without rest - then several rounds pounding Billy! Pad sessions where Ricky battered Billy's arthritis-ravaged hands and big fat body bag. Then Billy would limp off to nurse his poor joints and smoke a few ciggies, muttering: "When I die don't anybody get sentimental about that f... .ing bag and bury it with me!" Then Kerry Kaye took over for weight training, consisting of workouts for two different muscle groups on each of four days. Kerry, a former British champion bodybuilder, had trained countless British and international bodybuilding champions but he insisted: "I'm not training these lads to be bodybuilders. Billy said he wanted his lads to be stronger and faster and that's what I train them for". Ricky had noticed an improvement since Kerry had joined 'Team Hatton' and said he felt quicker and more explosive. Sparring partners were brought in for two to three weeks before the lighter sessions in the final week. They were usually top ranked light-welters from around the world and they were invariably impressed by the warm welcome they received. Argentinians, Guillermo Javier Saputo and Victor Hugo Castro, were brought in for this fight. Castro was the Pan-American champion with nine kayos in 19 wins (two losses), Saputo was unbeaten in 14 and had sparred with his promoter, Oscar de la Hoya for his recent fights. He couldn't believe how nice Ricky and his family were to him and was amazed that Ricky chatted to them when they met while they were all out running. In his own experience many boxers would ignore you when they were famous, but even Ricky's mum was nice to them! They were made very welcome and were treated to excursions to a football game (City, of course) and a boxing show.

The press were focussed on Ricky's weight. He was notoriously fond of his grub and a pint or two and there were constant rumours about his condition. He ballooned up between fights, but there was no denying that once he went into training he was soon in condition. Once he stopped over-indulging the excess weight fell off and, with a diet carefully monitored by Kerry, he was always spot on target for the check weights. He was frustrated by the negative press. "Just take a photograph, Tracey", he said in exasperation. "Put it in the paper so everybody can see. Do I honestly look fat?" I'm not sure that my photographic skills did him any favours, but his fitness, speed and power were all there for anyone to see in his workouts, which were always attended by family, friends, members of the press and fans. He despaired of the things he read about himself. "I read in one newspaper that 'Ricky has a good chance if he's fit'. When have I not been fit?" he demanded. "If anybody out there can throw more punches and has a better workrate and stamina I want to meet him and I want his diet!" Billy said: "I'll bet my life that Ricky is going to be the best he's been in his career. He had a couple of fights, Vilchez and Pedersen, that were short notice and the weight came off too quick, but everything is perfect for this fight - the challenge, the opponent, the occasion. This is the thing he's always wanted and the difference this time is that we've both always followed Tszyu and studied him. We know him more than any other opponent and we don't underestimate him. We've been talking about this since he was 17".

There was one dietary hiccup that Kerry discovered some time later. Ricky's biggest weakness is Chinese food. "I'd told him that he could eat as much chicken as he liked. Then I find out he's been eating duck which is just about the worst thing!" "Well, I figured ducks, chickens, they're the same thing, right?", pipes up Ricky. They both have wings of course except that in terms of fat content they're about as compatible as a Big Mac and a lettuce. Kerry just shakes his head in exasperation.

The final workout before a fight has become an occasion in itself, with the gym packed to bursting with supporters and the media. This time it took place on the hottest day in May in 50 years. Ricky pounds Billy for a full and unrelenting 15 rounds and, if the press needed any further convincing, they could witness his rapid recovery. After a dousing with cold water he was leaning on the ropes joking with the onlookers and shouting to his son with barely a trace of breathlessness. Carol often brings Campbell to the gym to see his dad. He runs around, playing, oblivious to the enormity of the task facing his dad. "Campbell, what's going to happen to Kostya Tszyu?" shouts Ricky. "He's going down", is the reply. "Do you want to be a boxer?", I asked him, "No", he answered without hesitiation: "I want to be a spaceman - or superman". An ambitious family, the Hattons.

Matthew Hatton usually trains alongside his brother and has often fought on his undercard. The same is true of the other members of the gym who have come and gone over the years, including Matthew Macklin, who is still trained by Billy. The shows at the MEN were always packed with Manchester fighters and often lasted around six hours. This event was split into two nights of boxing with Michael Brodie's challenge for Scott Harrison's WBO featherweight title topping the bill, while the previous night Matthew Hatton fought on the same bill. Whenever possible Ricky would be in his corner, but obviously not this time. In fact, he couldn't even watch it on TV. Billy had once forbidden him to watch a City match the night before a fight because he got too worked up. "There's no way I can watch Matt's fight if it is shown on TV, not the night before my fight. Often I don't get to see him fight if he is on before me. You just have to shut it out of your mind". Ray believed it was good for Matthew to have Ricky in his corner. "Billy is great in the corner, he stays really calm, but Ricky will shout at Matthew, saying things like, 'Do you want to win this fight or not? It doesn't look like you do!' and that can help as well". Even without his brother's help, Matthew still managed a comfortable points win in an arena that positively crackled with anticipation of the following night's event. Matthew has always been described as having the disadvantage of fighting in his brother's shadow, but then so does every other British fighter. The man casts a very wide shadow. Today, 'Magic' Matthew Hatton's record stands at 31-3-1. He won Central Area titles at welterweight and light-middleweight and holds the IBF Inter-Continental welterweight title and is just one fight away from his own first world title fight of sorts. Victory in his forthcoming fight for the IBO Inter-Continental title in September will give him a shot at the world title.

Very few predicted victory for Ricky against Tszyu. The celebrities were out in force for one of the biggest fights in British boxing history, a British world champion taking on the undisputed world champion in England. The majority of boxing experts thought Ricky was stepping way out of his league. Many felt that his chances were greater the longer the fight lasted, but they didn't expect it to last too long. Jim Watt, former world champion and TV commentator, said he had been compiling a list of Tszyu's weaknesses and got stuck at No.1! Fellow commentator, Ian Darke, told me he would love Ricky to win. "He's a lovely lad, I really like him a lot, but Tszyu is such an intelligent fighter he will have him sussed out". Former British champion, Danny Williams, agreed. "I hate to say it because I'm going against my man, but Tszyu is so good". However, like his trainer, Jim McDonnell, he felt Ricky had a chance if he could last. "Nobody believed in me but we did it", he said, referring to his recent win over Mike Tyson. That aside, he freely admitted that Tyson was not at his best when they fought, unlike Tszyu.

There were not many who could see how the fight

would progress. Former world champion, Frank Bruno, cautioned: "Hopefully it's his (Ricky's) time, but don't get into a war with him (Tszyu) because the guy can punch. He's a legend". Former world champion, Johnny Nelson, thought the opposite to most people. "My head says Tszyu in round eight, my heart says Hatton has to jump on him and do him inside five rounds". Only in Manchester did they realise what our man could do. Manchester promoter, Jack Trickett, who managed Michael Brodie, got it half right when predicting a Manchester double for Brodie and Ricky. Manchester trainer, Bob Shannon, predicted that Ricky's phenomenal workrate would be too much for Tszyu. Odds of a stoppage win for Ricky were given as 30 or 40-1, but he pledged: "Have faith in me, I'm going to do it".

The fight would be in the early hours of the morning to accommodate American television and Ricky had amended his running schedule in preparation for a 2 am fight. He was even stopped by the police one morning, after they had spotted a suspicious hooded figure running through Hyde in the dark. When they realised who it was they gave him a police escort, driving alongside as he ran. He had plenty of support on the night too. A 22,000 sell-out crowd packed the MEN Arena, including celebrities from all over the world. Film star, Russell Crowe, had been training alongside Tszyu in preparation for his role as Jim Braddock in the film:

Cinderella Man. The Australian actor was booed, probably for the first time in his career when he was introduced from the ring by the American MC, Michael Buffer, who had been brought over specially for the occasion. He said that Tszyu was one of the most formidable athletes he had come across and naturally wanted him to win. There was a much warmer welcome for visiting world champions, Ronald 'Winky' Wright, Diego Corrales, Jeff Lacy and our own Frank Bruno and Joe Calzaghe.

The arena became a deafening wall of noise when Ricky's 'Blue Moon' anthem began, heralding his entrance. Little Jamie Bowes, his long-time mascot, helped to hold up a Union Jack in the ring, bearing the message: 'Your support got me here, thanks'. Jamie suffers from hydrocephalus and epilepsy. A tiny cluster of yellow shirts high up in the arena marked out Tszyu's supporters, who bravely sang out their support.

It was no surprise that the fight opened as it was to continue, at a frenetic pace with both fighters surging forward and clinching often. So often in fact, that referee Dave Parris had to separate the two champions over a dozen times in the first round alone. Both landed and withstood solid, accurate shots. Ricky drove Tszyu onto the ropes and followed his trademark left hook to the body with three right uppercuts in succession, which jerked Tszyu's head back. Tszyu made

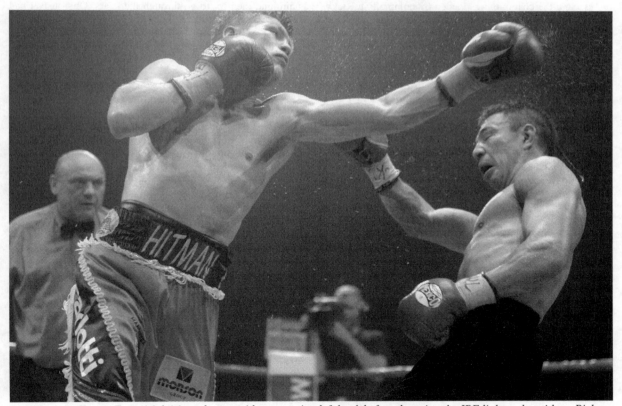

The Big One: Kostya Tszyu (right) just about avoids a sweeping left hook before dropping the IBF light-welter title to Ricky
Tom Casino

use of his right hand, a jab to the head and a solid hook to the body. Ricky shrugged them off as he did with Tszyu's lefts to body and head. It was messy, with constant grappling punctuated by furious exchanges. Ricky was throwing more in the early rounds but Tszyu was perhaps the more accurate. Ricky walked onto that dangerous right hand enough times to earn a rollicking from Billy, but here he was, taking the champion's best shot without flinching and those feared opening rounds were behind him.

Ricky launched himself into the sixth round, driving Tszyu back. He responded with a short left to the jaw. Two left uppercuts from Tszyu, a left-right combination from Ricky, a good right from Tszyu - so it see-sawed. Some felt Tszyu was slightly ahead, including Billy! Ricky had stepped up in class, but he was not being outclassed. There was the worry of cuts with the constant head clashes in the clinches, but as the relentless pace continued it seemed that the exhausting leaning, holding and trading of heavy shots could be taking its toll on Tszyu. Not on Ricky though, his greatest strength, his stamina was never in question. Only a low blow could slow him down, dropping to his knees at the end of the seventh round. In the corner Billy warned: "When he's trading shots you're not slipping and countering".

The excitement in the arena mounted as the rounds progressed. In the eighth Ricky caught Tszyu with a right to the jaw and the champion responded by pummelling Ricky to the ribs, followed by a head shot which was answered with another right to the jaw. Tszyu was now fighting with his mouth hanging open, possibly indicating damage to his jaw. The brawling and aggressive exchanges continued and Ricky was pushed to the canvas. In the ninth, Tszyu scored with a good left, an uppercut on the inside, a right to the head and then another below-the-belt shot that earned him a warning. Ricky's response was to return the low blow, dropping Tszyu to his knees.

By the tenth the excitement of the crowd was at fever pitch. It sounded as if the whole of Manchester was in the arena screaming for their fighter. They traded without respite. Ricky pinned Tszyu on the ropes and piled it on, but Kostya seemed to soak it up and snapped the Englishman's head back with a right cross. Neither boxer had acknowledged a blow with so much as a wince and Billy urged: "You've taken everything he's got". The British always like to kick a man when he's up and critics had repeatedly questioned Ricky's defence. He may not have answered all those questions but what a chin! He had taken the best shots from the best man in the division.

The pace continued unabated in the 11th and Billy said: "We need the last round to make sure, can you do it?" "Course I can", said Ricky. Billy turned to look across at the opposite corner and the unthinkable had happened. Tszyu's trainer had pulled him out. The fight was over. Ricky had won. Collapsing on his back in the ring, sobbing, he got up to hug Tszyu and the crowd sang 'Blue Moon'. Then, as one, they turned and pointed at the small knot of Australians and chanted: "You're not singing now, you're not singing now". After thanking his fans, Ricky said: "I think you'll agree if

I can be half the champion that Kostya Tszyu was I'll be doing well". The former undisputed champion replied: "I am a very, very proud man. I am not saying it is the end of my career, maybe, maybe not, but today I lost to the better fighter. Today Ricky was better than me in every way and I am doing this boxing for 27 years. Ricky, any help from me, always welcome mate". And now perhaps we can see what has made Ricky the phenomenon he is today. He really can do it. So many excellent British fighters are unable to take it to the next level, take on the best in the world. Also, he earns the respect of his opponents as well as the public, not just with his boxing skills but with his people skills - his good nature, treating people with respect and friendliness. He doesn't look down on anybody else, he is simply confident in his own abilities without arrogance.

The judges all had Ricky ahead by five rounds to three rounds, with one even. Tszyu's trainer, Johnny Lewis, said he knew Kostya would need a knockout to win in the 12th and he didn't think he had that in him. He was taken to hospital with a suspected broken jaw. The fight had been for his IBF title, but it was confirmed that Ricky had beaten the man considered to be the undisputed champion and had therefore taken that title. Ricky described how he had done it. "I didn't mind if he won the first four rounds or so, I just wanted to stay close and try and drain his strength, take the speed from him and then try to go through the gears. Obviously I had to take some haymakers, but you're supposed to take shots from Kostya Tszyu. I did it, not necessarily with boxing, but the ability between my ears, being clever and smart and smothering his work. In the last five rounds I went like a 'Trojan', he couldn't keep me off. He made no excuses for the rough nature of the fight, sometimes I hit low, he hit low, back of the head, it's not a tickling contest is it?" Both men met up the next day and Kostya gave Ricky his number in case he ever wanted any advice in his career. "That's not a champion, that's a champion and a half", said Ricky. Not surprisingly, the pair won the BBBoC Sportsmanship Award for 2005.

Accolades followed. Praise was heaped on the Mancunian from all corners of the globe and he became the first British fighter to be named *Ring* magazine's 'Fighter of the Year'. Madame Tussaud's even wanted to add him to their collection. "Hopefully it's the slim Ricky or they'll need to order double wax", he joked. Everybody was talking about his achievement. Sugar Ray Leonard visited England on the after dinner circuit and met up with Ricky a few times. He wanted to know all about the fight and they talked at length, trading air punches. "If anybody is a symbol of what boxing should be about, it's Ricky Hatton", he said. "I've watched him grow and develop for a number of years and I always knew he'd be special. Sometimes it's not just about talent but about what you've got downstairs, if you know what I mean and he had what it takes. What made me an incredible fan was when he kicked Kostya Tszyu's ass! I didn't think the kid had much chance of beating a man like Tszyu, but because he was so focussed, so determined, he beat the man". Of course, that's the glamorous side of the

Luis Collazo (right), pictured ducking under a two-fisted attack from Ricky, took the Englishman to the wire but still lost the
unanimous decision   Ben Duffy

victory. The public don't see the other side as Ricky later pointed out. "After that fight I was peeing blood for a week". Mike Tyson was another visiting celebrity who was full of praise for Ricky. He even phoned him at home to arrange to pop round for a brew. Unfortunately, Ricky was out, having gone Christmas shopping in the Trafford Centre!

So, had he now convinced the critics? Don't be silly. Remember, if you beat the man that everybody agrees is too good for you, then clearly he wasn't that good after all. Witter headed the charge, claiming Tszyu was a shadow of his former self and he could have knocked him out in five rounds. No, it wasn't all good news. It was also the last time Ricky would work with his promoter, Frank Warren as the two split acrimoniously and, in consequence, it was also his last fight (to date) at the MEN Arena. Bitter legal battles ensued, some of which are still unresolved at this time and so cannot be discussed here.

The long pursuit of the Kostya Tszyu goal was over, now a new chase began - to catch Floyd Mayweather. The American, fresh from an impressive victory over Arturo Gatti, made enthusiatic noises. Meanwhile, another likely match for Ricky, against Vivian Harris, was shot down in flames when the latter was trounced by the unfancied and unorthodox, Carlos Maussa. Billy Graham dismissed the

idea of the new WBA champ fighting Ricky with the kind of statement that is guaranteed to come back and bite you in the nether regions. "I honestly don't think anybody would pay to see that".

So, anyway, Ricky's next fight was against Carlos Maussa. It was in Sheffield with new promoter, Dennis Hobson and Fight Academy. Unorthodox was a polite word for Maussa's style of wildly flailing arms and negligible defence. "He's a nightmare!" said Ray Hatton. "It's been impossible to get sparring partners to mimic him". And yet he had stopped 18 of his 22 opponents and never been stopped himself. That was before, but it was indeed a nightmare fight. The legal wrangles nearly prevented the fight from taking place. At a pre-fight press conference, Robert Waterman of Fight Academy, said there had been numerous attempts to stop or sabotage the fight and they had all, including Ricky's family, been vilified in the press and had false accusations levelled at them. Ricky later said: "For the first five or six weeks I wasn't sure if I was training for nothing. It got personal in many ways with regard to my father and my family; that we were dishonest people. That hurt the most. The unification should be top of the agenda, not the rubbish in the courts".

There were further problems on the night. As Ricky

rested in his hotel room, the fire alarm went off. As Paul Speak recalls: "Someone had tampered with the piping in the hotel and they said there was a serious threat that the hotel could explode! Everybody was evacuated, but we ended up the only people left in the hotel. When they told me, I established that it wasn't a hoax and woke Ricky. Then we had to load all the equipment and everything in the car. It was a false alarm, but this is at 5pm on the night of the fight".

The waiting crowd were amazed when 'Blue Moon' didn't ring out as expected. Instead, Ricky had chosen 'Gonna Get Along Without You Now', before the familiar tune was played, heralding fight time. In the very first round Ricky sustained a very bad cut over his left eye. Then, in the third round, another clash of heads gave him one to match over the right eye and though he was winning, he had to do so with blood streaming down his face. Maussa's wild swings were dangerous, if not very accurate. The fight stat's showed that by the sixth round he had thrown 212 punches, of which just 28 had reached their destination. One minute into the ninth, Ricky landed a right followed by a huge, long left hook and the Columbian folded like a rag doll.

After the fight Ricky described it as the sweetest victory. "He's got a cast iron chin. Cotto stopped him on cuts, he didn't knock him flat like that". He then presented the belt to his dad, saying: "I'd like to dedicate this and give this to my dad because this was the hardest period of my career and what my dad's done for me in the build up and the last few months, he deserves this belt more than I do as far as I'm concerned". He already had his eye on the next goal. "I think people thought I was telling 'porkies' when I said I wanted to fight the best. It's been said that I was avoiding this fella and that fella. I think my win against Tszyu and my win tonight proves I want Floyd Mayweather and Miguel Cotto. Obviously, I'll have mandatory defences to deal with, but believe me, look in these eyes, I want those fights and I will get them". He was determined, but it would be costly. Ricky's dream was to emulate his heroes - Hearns, Leonard, Hagler and Duran, to fight the best in his dream venues of Madison Square Garden and Vegas. He wanted to fight in America and impress the Americans. The first step was the hardest - finding the right opponent. The IBF rejected this man, HBO, who were to televise in America, rejected that man and the mandatory's failed to impress anybody. His chosen opponent, Juan Lazcano, 'The Hispanic Causing Panic', then lived up to his name by breaking his finger. To avoid unattractive matches Ricky would be forced to surrender his recently acquired WBA belt and his IBF title in order to satisfy the powers that be, his public and his own ambition.

Then he was offered a fight too tempting to resist, against Luis Collazo for the WBA welterweight title, an opportunity to be world champion at two weights just like his idols. Against Billy's advice, he jumped at it. In every other aspect it was highly unattractive for a fighter wanting an impressive debut in the States. "Style wise, this would not be my first choice", he admitted, "but this is a chance to be a two-weight world champion. I've had 40 fights now and that's a lot. After Kostya Tszyu I need fights for a place in history so this is a good fight. Collazo is very quick, he's a mover and he's a Don King fighter and he usually has the best. He wouldn't have made the match if he thought his fighter would lose". Of course, the infamous American promoter has been known to leave with the winner, even if that man wasn't the same fighter he arrived with.

It was going to be in the Garden, but unfortunately not the Madison Square variety, and it was in the States, but not Las Vegas. They fought at the Bank North Garden in Boston and discovered that King usually has a shrewd idea what he has in the Bank. Collazo had won all but one, with 12 inside from 27 and was a former New York Golden Gloves champion. However, he was relatively unknown even in his home city of New York, whereas Ricky had been voted 'Fighter of the Year' by the American Sportswriters. Collazo would not be receiving any hometown favouritism, Ricky was already the star, but everything was on the line. For the first time in 17 fights he entered the ring as the former world champion, having surrendered both his titles to challenge for this one. He was facing yet another world champion, at a heavier weight and a southpaw to boot. If he lost he would have nothing, not even the bargaining power to challenge other champions. Collazo had nothing to fear. He was confident and used to causing upsets. "I've been the underdog all my life and am known to be the show-stopper, I ruin shows", he said.

This time the imported sparring partner for Ricky was the New York State champion and USA Latin champion, Frankie Figueroa. As usual he soon became a friend and said: "They have shown me a lot of respect, they have been like a second family to me". But unlike his predecessors, he could not say with certainty that he believed Ricky would win. He had prior knowledge of Collazo, having sparred with him two years earlier and been impressed. Figueroa said: "He's got a whole lot better since then". Frankie predicted that the fight would be won on fitness - and it nearly was, but not Ricky's.

It all started so well. Within 12 seconds, Ricky unloaded a superb left hook that knocked Collazo off his feet. He leapt up clear-headed, but Ricky jumped on him with a barrage of shots, without giving him room to work. In frustration, Collazo pushed Ricky at the end of the round. The American struggled again in the second round, but had more success when he found a little range and began to find his rhythm in the third. By the fourth it was becoming apparent that the champion was a skilful boxer with an accurate jab. He became more confident as he continued to catch Ricky and was gloating by the end of the round, while Don King circled the ring, gleefully waving his little American flag. Collazo threw rapid combinations of punches that often missed the mark, but he was landing all too frequently with that southpaw right jab. Ricky answered with a cracking uppercut and it became a ferocious toe-to-toe battle. Caught with a massive right, Ricky came back with two good lefts, cheered on by the 2,000 British fans who had journeyed to

Boston. A furious trade in the ninth ended with another of those right hooks from Collazo.

Ricky had known that this was not the ideal opponent to impress the Americans in his dream Stateside appearance, but this was worse than expected. Billy had made it clear that he was against the move up in weight, while Ricky was the perfect light-welterweight. He certainly didn't look like the perfect welterweight. On this night he didn't even look the perfect Ricky Hatton. Collazo was still bouncing cheerfully and looking alert in the corner, but Ricky looked subdued between rounds and lacked the fire that usually carried him through any number of rounds. As ever he was continually moving forward, but he repeatedly walked onto that right and seemed unable to dominate Collazo as convincingly as his other opponents. He didn't seem to have a big finish in him, unlike Collazo, who caught him early in the final round and wrestled him to the floor. The American suddenly opened up, battering Ricky who didn't seem to have anything left as he hung onto the ropes as we had never seen him before. His speed and reflexes were usually with him to the final bell, but this time pure heart saw him through.

There was a nerve-racking wait for the verdict. Collazo was sure he had won and there was no denying he had been surprisingly good, very good, while Ricky did not look the same 'Hitman' who had steamrolled over Tszyu. Paul Speak recalls the anxiety. "It was his toughest fight, he didn't look his normal self. It's the first time I've thought that Ricky was not completely in control and he was getting hurt. I had an awful gut feeling that he might not get the verdict, especially in America". Then Michael Buffer uttered the immortal words, "And NEW...". The judges saw him winning, 115-112, 115-112, 114-113. Not everybody saw it the same way, but he had won and now he was a world champion again, a two-weight world champion. That would be ample compensation for the barrage of criticism he was about to receive.

He became weary of hearing about his below-par performance. It seemed that his considerable achievements were forgotten as endless inches of print were devoted to his failings. If he wasn't being chastised for putting on too much weight between fights, he was being criticised for failing to impress when he tried to put weight on and move up a division. "Apparently I had an 'off night'", he

Ricky (left) smashes in a left hook to Juan Urango's head, on his way to taking the latter's IBF light-welter crown

Mark Robinson

25

retaliated sarcastically. "Having unanimously beaten a world champion, a quality southpaw, in his own country, in the division above mine, with all that other nonsense hanging over me. Some of my heroes didn't have 41 fights in their whole career". He'd had several changes of venue and opponents before the fight and had to give up his world title belts to avoid unattractive mandatory defences. Souleymane M'baye, now under the management of Frank Warren, even took him to court over the right to fight him. Ricky recently said: "I was due to fight Lazcano and it was only settled seven weeks before. Training camp was rushed and bulking up too quick took my speed. Then again if I hadn't taken the fight I wouldn't have been a two-weight world champion. It was against Billy's wishes, it was a mistake. I got away with it, but I won't do it again".

Ricky readily admitted that it was a rash thing to do, but it had been too exciting an opportunity to pass up. Instead of having a couple of warm-up fights at the new weight, he had gone straight into a world title fight! He believed that it wouldn't be a problem if he'd had more time to work with Kerry and bulk up slowly and sensibly. Ricky also confessed that he had been a little undisciplined with his diet after Kerry gave him the green light to eat extra. Kerry undoubtedly had extra nutritionally sound food in mind, but Ricky had made a beeline for the Chinese take-away! He had only deviated slightly from his rigid pre-fight routine, but he would take no chances next time.

Next time would be in January 2007 at light-welter! The opportunity arose to fight the current holder of his old IBF title, the one he had so gloriously won from Kostya Tszyu and given up to go up to welterweight. HBO had already rejected M'baye, Oktay Urkal and Ben Rabah, but they were suitably impressed with Juan Urango. "HBO are very fussy", said Ricky, "so it shows what they think of Urango. Not many people have heard of him on the world stage, but before the Kostya Tszyu fight not many people had heard of Ricky Hatton". There was of course one small hitch, in that he would have to give up his welterweight title. "It appeals to him to go back to his old weight and get his belt back", said Ray Hatton. "That would be four world title fights and four world champions in four consecutive fights and I think you'd have to check the history books and see if that's a record". There was another great attraction, the fight would be in Las Vegas.

The drawback was that, like many a fighter before him, Ricky would have to sacrifice Christmas. He spent a large part of Christmas, including Christmas Day, in the gym with Billy and Kerry and Matthew, who was also on the bill. Matthew was fighting for his first major title, the IBF Inter-Continental welterweight title. Ricky's girlfriend, Jennifer, discovered the joys of fame when a camera crew followed them everywhere over Christmas as they filmed a day-by-day record in the run up to the fight. On Christmas morning she answered a knock on the door in her nightwear to find, not Santa, but Ray on the doorstep - armed with a film camera. He had been asked to continue the filming on Xmas morning. Fame failed to noticeably alter Ricky. He showed

no sign of becoming conceited and a large photograph of himself and Bernard Manning in nappies looking equally fat hung on the gym wall. "He has no vanity", laughed Billy, "he's only good looking two or three times a year".

Training didn't exactly go to plan. In England Ricky was restricted to a few sparring sessions because of a pulled muscle in his right arm, while in Vegas he was audibly hoarse as he was interviewed, as a result of a bad cold. He played it down and obviously revelled in achieving one of his remaining ambitions - to see his name in lights on the Strip. His old IBF light-welterweight title and the IBO title were at stake, along with a scheduled super-fight with Jose Luis Castillo, who was fighting on the undercard. The last opponent had an iron chin, this one was the 'Iron Twin', so called because of his muscular physique and a matching brother back home in Columbia. He had honed his broad shoulders from an early age when he used to lift boulders from the local river to sell to builders. Couldn't have a paper round like anybody else! Ricky planned to force Urango on to the back foot and said that his muscular physique could be a disadvantage. "Sometimes the muscular mass takes away a bit of speed", he said, ironically echoing the opinions of people who felt that was the reason he had been noticeably slower against Collazo was because he was weighed down by an overcoat of muscle.

Urango didn't usually take a backward step but, then, neither did Ricky, so this could be a real telephone box affair. Ricky was still hoping to impress the American fight fans and silence the critics. Critics aren't that easily silenced though, despite the fact that he won nearly every round, landed the cleaner shots, was clearly the better of the two and never took a backward step during 12 arduous rounds of wrestling the strong, hard hitting Urango. Before the fight the experts expressed concern about how hard a fight this was going to be for Ricky. Urango, with 13 stoppages in 18 fights, would not be easy to beat they agreed. Ricky was the favourite, but they expected the tough Miami-based Columbian to take him the distance. Their predictions proved correct, but even as the fight progressed and their expectations materialised they suddenly began to question why Ricky had failed to stop him. It couldn't be because he was facing the undefeated Urango, who had never been stopped, it must be because of Hatton's lifestyle between fights was affecting his performance.

Three thousand British fans raised the roof of the Paris Hotel, which boasts an Eiffel Tower the size of the real thing. From the first round the two fighters tangled often as Ricky deliberately smothered Urango's punches. The Columbian was very Tyson-like in his appearance and style, but it was immediately apparent that his head could be his most dangerous weapon as he surged forward keeping low. In the opening round an unintentional head clash caught Ricky across the bridge of the nose, but there was no serious damage. Ricky cleverly nipped in with his punches then smothered Urango before he could respond. It wasn't pretty but it was effective. However, it did mean that he would have to spend the fight wrestling with the man described by his former opponent, Miguel Cotto, as the strongest man he had ever fought.

Ricky usually skips out of range and uses his deft head movement to dodge punches but that wasn't as useful here with an opponent who likes a little range for his dangerous swings. Urango caught Ricky with an uppercut in the third round and was clearly confident, raising his hands at the end of each round, even after taking a flush right at the end of the fourth. He landed a couple of good body shots in the fifth, his best round, but then Ricky seemed to step up a gear and Urango acknowledged one of Ricky's own trademark body shots. This was not the crowd-pleasing Vegas debut that Ricky had wanted and in the corner Billy urged him to continue with the strategy that was working for him. "You've not lost a round", he reassured him, "but you'll have to steal it. There's nothing wrong with stealing it". What he knew and the crowd didn't, was that Ricky was running out of steam with another five rounds to go. A bad cold is nothing to someone as fit as a boxer, but not during a fight. If you are just feeling one degree under, that can suddenly catch up with you, especially if your opponent is 100% fit. Billy knew what to expect. And so the holding continued into the eighth round, both fighters swinging as they came out of clinches. Urango constantly moved forward, rarely flinching, throwing solid, heavy shots, which Ricky mostly took on the arms. Then Ricky took a right, possibly while off balance, then another and it looked like Urango was gaining ground. Ricky's offence is usually his defence, his relentless aggression overwhelming his opponent, but he was fighting a different fight here, which prompted the experts to question his fitness, wondering if he had peaked against Tszyu. Billy begged: "Please trust me. He catches you when you stand off". In fact, it was probably Urango's only winning round.

In the 11th there was a bad clash of heads, with Ricky coming off worst, although Urango made all the fuss. Ricky's mouth was bloody as he was wrestled through the ropes. Urango came out for the last round bouncing, hands raised in victory, clearly oblivious to the fact that he'd hardly won a round and didn't win that one either. There was a moment of doubt before the verdict was announced. You can never second-guess Vegas judges but it was a unanimous 119-109 to the reinstated IBF light-welterweight champion. Ricky had his crown back. Castillo had also won his fight that night so the next fight was in the bag, or so they thought.

Meanwhile, Billy was amazed by the barrage of criticism they walked into back in England. They had received compliments and congratulations in America after the fight, but were stunned by the unfavourable press when he returned. The gist seemed to be that Ricky's see-sawing weight had caught up with him and he had fought a negative fight, whereas Billy was immensely proud of his performance. "In actual fact Ricky boxed fantastically. He boxed like a real old pro and should be applauded for that. Don't blame him for clinching, blame me - he was boxing to orders. He had to be restrained and a lot of fighters can't

be restrained, so it just shows how special he is. For the amount of sparring he had for that fight, he was amazing. That fight will make him a better man. Urango was stronger, but Ricky was a mile in front". Ricky recently told me. "I never doubted Billy's advice because I was coughing up in the corner. I went back to the corner and said, 'I don't know what's wrong, my legs are wobbly, I can't breathe'. We both knew why I had to box safe and there's no point being a hero. Despite that, it was actually one of the most comfortable fights I've fought. Urango was strong, but couldn't beat me in any other department. I've never boxed anyone who throws as little and at one point I thought rigor mortis had set in! But when they are throwing nothing it can make it harder to find the target. Against a world champion I only lost two rounds. I don't think that's too bad".

There were immediate cries for Ricky to cut down on the heavy drinking and junk food and spend more time in the gym. A valid point, naturally. After the Tszyu fight his mum, Carol, told me that her boy had promised to mend his ways. It's certainly not an ideal lifestyle for any boxer, never mind one who has to fight at this level, but it had yet to reflect in his results, still unbeaten, still world champion, still capable of fighting 12 rounds at a gruelling pace. Billy admitted: "There will come a day when it will harm him physically. It will shorten his career, but I don't want longevity in his career". Even Sugar Ray Leonard was concerned, warning that Ricky could shoot himself in the foot if he lets his weight increase during his time away from the ring and will struggle to stay at the very top if he over indulges in junk food and alcohol between bouts. "Ricky has been doing it pretty much all his life and it seemed not to bother him but I think what happens is that it eventually catches up with you because, as you get older, you can't continue to abuse your body that way. At some point he will have to stop that yo-yoing".

Ricky was now looking forward to his super-fight with Castillo, but unfortunately the IBF ordered him to face mandatory challenger, Lovemore N'Dou. "Being totally honest, a fight with N'Dou would have been a hard sell to the American fight fans, but I was prepared to explore the possibility", said Dennis Hobson. "Unfortunately, N'Dou's people weren't exactly ringing my phone off the hook trying to make it happen". There was only one thing to do. You guessed it, the belt had to go back. For the second time Ricky surrendered his IBF light-welterweight title. He had made it clear after Tszyu that his ambitions lay in fighting the best opposition in the best venues and he was prepared to make sacrifices to do that. The critics were silent, despite him generally being applauded by a boxing public weary of unappealing contests. He was happy with the decision not to face a lesser-ranked mandatory challenger. "These are the fights you dream of. Jose is one of the best, pound for pound and you become great by fighting the greats". There was one further attraction. "Praise God, no more southpaws", he added wryly.

Castillo had fought the best, including Floyd Mayweather, but he was best known for his two thrilling encounters with Diego Corrales. He said that he felt that Ricky was completely different to Mayweather, who dances and runs, and more comparable to Corrales as both come to fight and can punch and take a punch. The amiable Mexican had come to Manchester in February to promote the June fight. He had brought his wife with him to celebrate their wedding anniversary with a short holiday in England. He also discovered that they make world champions a little differently in Hyde, when Ricky took him for a drink! I bet Mayweather didn't do that. But he soon realised that he couldn't match Ricky's relentless pace and floundered early.

Now, perhaps Ricky would finally get to show the Americans what he could do. "As good as the Tszyu fight was, this could be better style-wise. This is the type of fight that gets me excited. Maussa, Collazo, they were not the type of opponents to look good against. Style-wise, well, I don't know how you would describe Maussa's style! This could be the toughest ever". Billy was equally excited. "This will show everybody what I've been saying for years, that Ricky is the best fighter to come out of this country for years. A lot of my own favourites, like Collins, Benn, McCullough, say that they think he is the best. Maussa was supposed to have a rock-hard chin and Ricky took him out and Collazo was an awkward southpaw. This time he's got a great fighter, not an awkward one".

Ricky was already a regular visitor to Vegas for the big fights. He had always been a huge fight fan and boxing historian and he took time out in March to go over for the fight of his good friend, Marco Antonio Barrera, against Juan Manuel Marquez. They first met when Ricky and Matthew went over for Barrera's second encounter with Eric Morales. After the weigh-in, Barrera was signing autographs and his manager saw Ricky and shouted him over. Barrera invited them up to his room for a drink and said that he had seen the Magee fight and loved it. "He said that when I got shook up in the seventh round anyone else would have slowed down but not me, he thought 'he's a rum f..k.' I've now got to know his family, his mum is really friendly. I was a fan, so to become a friend is marvellous". Barrera came over for the Maussa fight and Ricky was honoured when he asked him to carry his championship belt into the ring. Unfortunately, Barrera lost the fight. Now Ricky asked Barrera to return the favour and carry his belt into the ring. He readily agreed but then Ricky realised that by doing so Barrera might alienate his fellow Mexicans there to support Castillo. He told Barrera he would understand if he didn't want to do it, but his friend said: "No, Ricky, you are family".

Steve Forbes was on the undercard of the Barrera fight and later found himself in England as Ricky's sparring partner for the Castillo fight, along with the Mexican, Enrique Colin. Steve was better known to British' fans for

Ricky wheels away after dropping Jose Luis Castillo for the full count in Las Vegas last June   Mark Robinson

his success in Sugar Ray Leonard's 'Contender' series, where he reached the final. He was trained by Floyd Mayweather senior and had sparred with Floyd, Erik Morales, DeMarcus Corley and Sharmba Mitchell. He was confident of victory for Ricky, possibly by late stoppage. "He is a lot faster than I expected. I always thought he had good speed but he has fast feet and can manoeuvre". Enrique agreed. "He is very strong. I think he is probably faster than Castillo. I could not control him. He is special". Unfortunately, Enrique had to sit out the final sessions after an uppercut dropped him to his knees in agony, his ribs damaged.

Ricky's last workout in England before he flew out to his Las Vegas training camp was, as usual, cheered on by family and friends. Young Campbell, now six, played contentedly with his computer game as Ricky sweated through the gruelling rounds on the pads. Without looking up, he randomly called out: "Uppercut. Body shot. 1,2,3" and then excitedly, "dad, dad, I've reached level two", which was undoubtedly a huge relief to the sweat-drenched Ricky ahead of one of the most crucial fights of his career. He was hoping to impress the American fans, but it looked like they would all be British! Nearly 10,000 British fans were going with him, over 50% of the estimated crowd at the Thomas and Mack Centre where the fight would be held. They would, of course, include the Hatton family and the brothers' girlfriends. Jennifer watched most of his fights with her hands over her eyes. "It's horrible, it's not that nice at all to be honest with you", she admits. Carol is the same, her hand constantly in front of her face. "It's not easy to watch your son in a fight". Not surprisingly, she takes regular sips from her bottle of 'water' (vodka).

Oscar de la Hoya had recently been beaten by Floyd Mayweather, which was a mixed blessing for Ricky because de la Hoya had said that if he won he would come to Manchester to fight Ricky in his next fight. Floyd was the ultimate goal for Ricky, but he wouldn't be if he lost his undisputed pound for pound status. Having won, Mayweather then announced his retirement! Not many people believed him.

Shortly after the de la Hoya fight, Diego Corrales was killed in a motorcycle accident on the Strip. Both Ricky and Castillo would dedicate their fight to his memory.

A crowd-pleasing performance wasn't going to be a problem, considering there were more Brits there than Mexicans, but Ricky was hoping to show America vintage Ricky, and he did. He stopped Castillo with a classic venomous Hatton body shot, dropping him for the first time in a career spanning 63 fights and 47 kayos. Billy had been saying for years that Ricky fights like a Mexican and he was billed as the 'Manchester Mexican', but he managed to out-Mex the real Mexican and surely leave the hard-to-please Americans salivating for more. He burst out of his corner like a Mexican firecracker and between rounds Billy tried unsuccessfully to control him. Neither fighter wanted to give an inch and the referee, Joe Cortez, had his work cut out. Both were throwing uppercuts on the inside during the clinches but Ricky had two or three shots for

every one of Castillo's. In the second round he unloaded those body shots, two right hooks and a left. Castillo was getting through with the jab and Billy urged: "Calm it down, you're smothering your own work". He was well aware of the danger of throwing caution to the wind with a big puncher like Castillo, who did indeed land three good uppercuts early in the third. Ricky hardly seemed to notice, but made a point of complaining about a low blow before the two traded left hooks. He explained later. "He does it all the way through the fight and I wanted the referee to notice and stop it. I expected him to do it, he's known for throwing lots of low blows. It's not a pleasure and it takes its toll over 12 rounds".

Ricky opened the fourth with a left uppercut and right hook. Castillo replied with a right to the jaw and then dropped his punches a wee bit south again, earning a point deduction. Then the 'Hitman' unloaded the rib crusher that had put paid to his Mexican sparring partner two weeks earlier. Castillo turned away then dropped to one knee in agony. He was still unable to rise as he was counted out. Ricky was delighted. "I think the greatest night of my boxing life was 22,000 fans in Manchester at 2am in the morning against Kostya Tszyu, but to beat the best pound-for-pound and come halfway across the world to do it and knock him out in four rounds has to rate alongside it". Billy breathed a sigh of relief. "It was my worst nightmare, him getting in a war with someone like Castillo, but that is the thing about great fighters like Ricky, they get it right even when they get it wrong". "Like Billy said, I went a bit gung-ho", admitted Ricky. "I should have been more cautious, but from the first exchange I felt I could throw him around like a rag doll. Billy was saying, 'Calm down, take it easy, use your boxing ability to break him up from the outside', but I went into the ring frustrated. My last two fights have not been vintage Ricky".

The critics were a lot quieter this time. Prince Charles presented Ricky with his MBE for services to sport a few weeks later at Buckingham Palace and even he said he had enjoyed the fight. "You must be feeling unstoppable. You work hard and deserve all the credit that is coming to you", he said.

So who next? "I want Mayweather, Ricky wants Mayweather", said Billy. "Okay, Mayweather it is then. It's worth going back to welterweight for the dream fight". Whether Floyd was tempted out of 'retirement' by Ricky's taunts after the Castillo fight, who knows? "There was more action in those four rounds than Mayweather's delivered value in his whole career", said Ricky. "My style is his worst nightmare. He will want me like he wants a hole in the head". That did the trick. The two are scheduled to meet in Vegas at the end of 2007 and Oscar de la Hoya has already said that, regardless of the result, he will fight Ricky in Manchester. Ricky said that what he wanted was the right fighters, and the right fights. He wanted to face the best and he's got his wish. As Ricky's mum said: "It's like a big adventure really that we have been living since he was 11".

This article includes extracts from my weekly boxing column, courtesy of the *Tameside Reporter*.

30

Mick Toomey: A Professional Boxing Promoter's Story

by Ralph Oates

This is a story of a man who has spent a lifetime in sport, with a large slice of it in boxing. Now in his 70s, and in poor health, Mick can reflect on his achievements with a sense of satisfaction and in the knowledge that he has almost single-handedly kept boxing going in Hull. It all started for him after retiring from playing Rugby League for 21 years. Finding that he had time on his hands, Mick decided to open an amateur boxing club in amongst the vast housing estate of Bransholme, which at the time was reputed to be the biggest satellite estate in Europe.

With not much for the locals to do, East Hull Catholics ABC soon became a magnet for the youngsters and in a short while had built up a good reputation. It was also developing champions of various ages and weights and, at the same time, keeping kids off the streets. Mick had been an amateur boxer himself at the St Mary's club immediately after the war and it didn't take him too long to become an ABA qualified trainer. All the while, his work was on a voluntary basis, as was that of his helpers, but it was time well spent when the kids appreciated it. However, it wasn't long before Mick found himself getting the 'bug' to go professional and the club was eventually disbanded.

In 1980 he took out a BBBoC trainer's licence, which was followed in 1982 by him becoming a manager, with Stuart Carmichael his first fighter. After helping one or two others to promote dinner shows in the area, Mick set his stall out and co-promoted with Pat Brogan at the Hull City Hall in 1988. This brought Frank Warren and ITV to Hull for the first time and, apart from the revenue engendered, the welcome publicity put Hull on the boxing map. Then, after watching the future undisputed world heavyweight champion, Lennox Lewis, make a winning debut in London Mick was so impressed with the former Olympic gold medallist that he persuaded his manager, Frank Maloney, to bring him to Hull in a joint promotion three fights later. Mick had been at the Royal Albert Hall with one of his boxers on the same bill and had realised what a good ambassador for the sport Lewis would become. With the national media in tow with Lewis, it brought even more publicity to Hull. Mick's next move was to invite Mickey Duff and the National Promotions cable television outfit to Hull in yet another joint promotion.

Thus, in a three-year period, Mick had been responsible for three major promotions in the prestigious Hull City Hall, which was followed by the then Labour Council spending over a million pounds to refurbish the venue. This move, brought about by the massive television and newspaper coverage, was essential in helping Hull in its aim of becoming a top-ten city.

By now Mick really did have the 'bug' and along with two business partners he formed the Hull & District Sporting Club in 1991, which is now the second longest- running club of its kind in British boxing. The main purpose of the club was and still is to be a non-profit making organisation in raising funds for charity, and to date has raised more than £56,000 for many good causes, including hospital wards, medical research, the British Red Cross Blind Institute, handicapped children and local amateur boxing, etc. All the monies raised on the night go to the chosen charity alone, with no expenses or commissions deducted.

These shows have also helped to keep boxing alive in a city that is off the beaten track as far as boxing is concerned. They have also kept boxers from his once large stable busy. With over 40 club shows under his belt, Mick has done his bit for British boxing and has brought many boxers to the city, including big names such as Esham Pickering and Clinton Woods. It's not only boxers who have travelled to Hull, but the BBBoC officials who keep the game up to a high standard, such as referees, timekeepers, managers, matchmakers, trainers, seconds, whips, masters of ceremonies, inspectors and doctors. The list is endless.

There is also no doubt that the punters have a good night out with value-for-money entertainment and a four-course banqueting meal at a quality venue. There is also a top-class cabaret provided and quite often a memorabilia auction for a chosen charity. Supported by local businesses and their clients, all in bib and tucker suits and on their best behaviour, a club rule, the vast majority enjoy a good evening out, which includes a few bouts of professional boxing.

Not only raising money for worthy charities and keeping boxing alive in Hull, many of the current members have been with the club since its inception and get a real kick out of the sport. The club has now promoted at most of the top hotels in and around the city, the most recent being the KC

Henry Cooper (centre) visits the Hull & District Sporting Club

31

Stadium Banqueting Suite, which gives all who attend the opportunity to view this magnificent project for themselves.

Over the years, the Hull & District Sporting Club has brought in leading sports personalities as guest speakers, such as Sir Henry Cooper, Barry McGuigan, John Conteh, John H. Stracey, Frank Maloney, Brendan Ingle, Henry Wharton, Peter Lorimer, Billy Bremner and Norman Hunter, along with many good quality comedians and cabaret acts.

A devout Roman Catholic, with a wife, four grown-up children and two grandsons, Mick is looking for the day when the amateur and professional codes come together and he can actually promote one of his grandsons, who already belongs to a boxing club. Mick is also proud of his son Kevin who, between 1989 and 1996, racked up 29 pro contests. Kevin, who was an undefeated Central Area lightweight champion and boxed 12 times in Hull, looks to eventually take over from Mick.

Not only a manager and promoter of fighters, Mick has also written two books on boxing, which have gone world-wide, containing the only true record of all Hull-born professional boxers. Titled *The Fighting Men of Hull*, the first edition covered the post-war period up until 1994 and the updated version was published in 2004. Those who know him well, including his best friend in boxing, Brendan Ingle, would vouch for the fact that this man puts far more into the sport than he will ever take out. He is Hull boxing through and through.

Mick puts his good fortune in boxing down to teamwork and one of those who has been a main part of the success of the sport in Hull is the matchmaker, John Ingle. Others who have formed part of this reliable team are Steve Butler (whip), Terry Petersen and Nigel Coulton (house seconds), and two great helpers who cover many miles on the night in John Warriner and George Foster, a former professional Rugby League player with Hull KR and Batley.

One of the major milestones in this remarkable man's promotional career was when he set up the 1993 AGM of the British Boxing Board of Control in Hull, in what was one of the few occasions it had been held outside of London. It involved a full weekend of organising accommodation, etc, for over 200 delegates from all over the United Kingdom, amongst them Sir David Hopkin, 'Nipper' Read, John Morris, Simon Block, Robert Smith and all the professional men who make up the Gentlemen of the Board. They were given a Civic reception and a banquet by the Lord Mayor and leading officials of the Council, in yet another event that put boxing on the map in Hull.

Just to give people an idea of what is involved in promoting boxing dinners, many things can change on the day, which can affect the profit/loss margins and leave one in a precarious position. Ticket sales can be cancelled at a late hour, boxers can also pull out at the last minute and substitutes can demand and get more money to keep the show alive. The price of speakers and comedians can vary widely, while ticket prices around the country can fluctuate, dependent on which fighters are appearing. However, with good housekeeping and a combination of hard work the Hull & District SC has survived the pitfalls that many other clubs have succumbed to. It is hardly surprising that so many

clubs have gone to the wall when you consider that in 1991 the total costs per show were between £8/9,000, which have now spiralled to around £14/15,000. Despite this, ticket prices in Hull have been held back by comparison. The club is also considered to be among the best in the country for value and has never once fallen prey to a cancellation.

When Mick first applied for a promoter's licence with the BBBoC, he was invited to appear before the Area Executive Council for questions and assessment of suitability. He also had to declare that he didn't have a criminal record and would be required to lodge a bond at the Board. Without a big-money backer who was willing to look at losing a few thousand pounds just for a 'jolly' or for some publicity in the press, Mick had to settle for the help of a friendly bank manager. He tells the story of the millionaire London promoter, Mike Barrett, being quoted many years ago as saying that people like him would not carry on throwing good money after bad. Following that statement, he never promoted again. Also, sponsors are not easy to come by, especially when you have to contend with an occasionally hostile sporting press. Mind you, if it was that easy everybody would be doing it, a point compounded by the fact that Mick has been the only professional boxing promoter in Hull over the past two or three years.

For nearly 30 years, this former docker and lorry driver trained, managed and promoted many pro boxers (some of whom became champions), while several of his charges appeared in supporting bouts on major title shows and also travelled abroad to fight in Europe and South Africa. Now in the process of winding down his career, he is proud to have rubbed shoulders with many of the leading figures in world boxing and is still in love with the sport. There is no doubt whatsoever that without men like him boxing would be in a much poorer state. Mick Toomey doesn't owe the game a penny and should be seen as a fine example to all those wishing to follow in his footsteps.

Mick seen here with Barry McGuigan (right)

Ghetto Warriors

by Philip Sharkey

One only has to scan the fight schedules listed in *Boxing News* to see names like Rom Krauklis, Sergei Rozhakmens, Kreshnik Qato and Deniss Sirjatovs to know there is a new influx of migrant workers looking to provide extra money for the family budget in a time-honoured way. Where else can you legally earn the equivalent of a month's wages for one night's work than in the boxing ring? Or look at the list of boxers representing Bury Amateur Boxing Club recently. Muideen Ganiyu, Azar Mahmood, and Amraiz Iqbal are all hoping to emulate the Olympic silver medal winner and unbeaten pro, Amir Khan, with each young person bringing respect and pride to their   religious or ethnic community.

While the more educated and qualified newcomers to these shores can find well-paid employment, for the rest hard manual work with long hours and no holiday or sick pay is the only alternative. This is the way it has always been. In what is the first major exhibition in the United Kingdom on our sport, 'Ghetto Warriors- Minority Boxers in Britain' traces how this very English sport has always been popular with ethnic minority groups at the bottom of the socio-economic ladder. Boxers of Jewish, African-Caribbean, African, Romany Traveller, Irish, Asian and now Eastern European origins, have all at one time or another entered the British ring. Boxing has not only been a way out of the ghetto, but also a means of gaining acceptance, respect and even in some cases riches and fame.

The exhibition highlights how boxing has served as a means of social integration by enabling boxers to be proud of their ethnic identity, while also being part of British society. A quick glance at the boxing trunks of Harry Mizler, the Jewish London-born British lightweight champion from the 1930s, shows the Union Jack and the Star of David adorning each leg. Even today, the Bolton-born prospect, Amir Khan, has the Union Jack motif as a background to his name emblazoned on his waistband, reaffirming the surname Khan as a proudly British name.

The starting point of the exhibition is with Daniel Mendoza,1765-1836, the 18th Century popular hero and English-Jewish boxing champion, who changed the public image of Jews in England and is credited as having developed scientific boxing; footwork   and defensive strategies. Mendoza's career seems to capture all the preconceived notions of boxing and his grudge matches with Richard Humphries echo   the great rivalry of 'The Greatest', Muhammad Ali, and 'Smokin' Joe Frazier.

Mendoza was spotted in a street fight by the British champion, Humphries, who was so impressed with his skill and determination that he took him under his wing and turned him into a famed prize-fighter. He was so good that the Prince of Wales became his patron. However, for reasons lost in the mists of time, the great friends became sworn enemies and on 9 January 1788 the two men fought at Odiham, Hampshire. By all accounts, Mendoza, the younger man, was well on top and, as he was about to deliver the finishing blows, Humphries' second, Tom Johnson, a former champion, grabbed his arm, which allowed Humphries to throw some free shots and gain the upper hand to defeat his former pupil. They fought twice more, Mendoza winning both in front of large crowds.

By 1795, Mendoza's colourful life caught up with him when challenged by John Jackson. Jackson was five years younger and 42 lbs heavier, but even then had to resort to dirty tactics, grabbing Mendoza's flowing locks with one hand and pummelling him with the other. Mendoza couldn't return the compliment as Jackson had the foresight to shave his head! After retiring from the ring, Mendoza became the landlord of the Admiral Nelson public house in Whitechapel. I'm not sure if he served Palwin though! He wrote his memoirs and opened a boxing academy at the Lyceum in the Strand, but various battles, both legal and personal, ensured that the fortunes he earned were lost and he died impoverished. This, I am afraid, is often a recurring theme with our revered champions. Chris Finnegan, the former British, Commonwealth and European champion summed it up with his typical sense of humour. "I spent all my money on gambling, women and booze, the rest I just frittered away"!

Also featured are Mendoza's contemporaries, Tom Molineaux and Bill Richmond, black boxers who escaped slavery and achieved fame and success in the ring. The exhibition tells their stories and describes the ways in which wealth and fame proved to be a mixed blessing, as many boxers ended their days poverty ridden or in jail. How opportune that the exhibition should coincide with the bicentenary of the abolition of the slave trade. Richmond, 1763-1829, was born in New York, the son of former slaves. He caught the eye of General Earl Percy who, impressed with his boxing prowess, made him his valet and brought him to England, where he was apprenticed to a cabinet maker. He had his first fight for money at York racecourse after responding to racial insults from local tough guy, George Moore, and had his last professional fight when beating

Jack Carter in three rounds, aged 55! Don't tell Evander Holyfield and George Foreman, please. In retirement he too became a publican and was the landlord of the Horse and Dolphin near Leicester Square.

Echoing former fighters, past and present, Richmond also stayed involved in the sport when running a boxing school and training and seconding aspirant boxers. One such man was Tom Molineaux, who was born a slave on a tobacco plantation in Virginia. He won his freedom by fighting another slave from a neighbouring plantation and travelled to England as he'd heard of the thriving boxing scene there. With Richmond as his trainer/second, he beat all before him until meeting both mens' nemesis, Tom Cribb. Cribb had defeated Richmond five years earlier. The fight was controversial. After Molineaux floored Cribb in the 28th round, the Englishman failed to come to scratch in the 30 seconds allowed, claiming Molineaux was concealing lead in his fists. Following the referee's inspection the fight continued, but Molineaux had lost heart and after 33 rounds he was spent. There was a rematch nine months later, by which time Molineaux had fallen out with Richmond and was not in condition for battle. Having lost a prizefight that is said to have generated £100,000 in wagers, he died in Ireland from the effects of alcoholism, aged 34, and is credited as being the first Black man to contest a title fight.

The exhibition moves on to Dutch Sam (Samuel Elias) and his son, the somewhat obviously named 'Young Dutch Sam', both men being born in London. Dutch Sam, born 1775, is credited with using the uppercut for the first time. Indeed, his nickname was 'The Man with the Iron Hand'. He was sometimes trained by Mendoza, but often boasted that he could train on gin! His hard living caught up with him and he died aged 41. His son had his first professional fight, aged15, and, like his father he has been inducted posthumously into the International Boxing Hall of Fame. He also ran a public house at the end of his boxing career, but died even younger than his father in 1843, aged 35.

Another father and son from the same time was 'The Star of the East', Barney Aaron, 1800-1850, and his son Young Aaron. Barney, the son of a fishmonger from Aldgate, was considered one of the best lightweights of the time and was active from 1819 to 1834. Young Aaron emigrated to America in 1855 and twice held the American lightweight championship.

Yet another east end of London family, the Belascos, were fighting at this time. The most successful was Abraham, 1797-1842, who toured England and Scotland with Daniel Mendoza in 1819 and 1820, doing sparring exhibitions, and was not adverse to taking on any local pugilist who fancied his chances.

In the excellent book, *Fighting Back*, that accompanies the exhibition, it states that of 2,000 active boxers between the 1780s and 1840s, about 36 were Irish, 30 Jews, 22 Blacks and 16 Romany. After 1880, as a result of pogroms and persecution, it is estimated around 150,000 Jewish immigrants arrived in Britain, mainly from Eastern Europe, and settled in the impoverished slums of London's east end as poor immigrants, just like the Huguenots before them and the Bangladeshis of recent times. This kick-started a new wave of Jewish fighters from the area, which would continue until the 1950s.

Considered by many to be Britain's greatest ever boxer, Ted Kid Lewis was born Gershon Mendeloff in Umberston Street, Aldgate, in 1894. His son Morton traced 299 fights from 1909 to December 1929, when, aged 35, he stopped the former welter and middleweight champion, Johnny Basham, in the third round. At only 17 years of age and with over 100 bouts behind him, he became British featherweight champion when stopping Alec Lambert in 17 rounds. Four months later he captured the European title from France's Paul Til and went on to win the world welterweight championship in the first of his 20 battles with the American, Jack Britton. Three of his fights with Britton took place only 19 days apart, two being no-decision ten-rounders and a winning points decision over 20 rounds in Dayton, Ohio to reclaim the title.

Returning to London in 1920 he knocked out Johnny Bee for the British middleweight title and moved back down to welter to bash the aforementioned Johnny Basham in becoming British, European and Empire king. A points win over 20 rounds saw him beat another Jewish champion, Jack Bloomfield, to once again claim the British middleweight crown. Lewis thought nothing of fighting men much bigger and heavier than himself, often taking on heavy weights. So when he fought the French war hero, Georges Carpentier, on 11 May 1922 he saw it as a stepping-stone to challenging the world heavyweight champion, Jack Dempsey! Lewis weighed 147lbs fully clothed, while the world light-heavy champ was on the weight limit of 175lbs. The fight was to end in uproar and controversy after the London referee, Joe Palmer, stopped the action to warn Lewis for holding. Lewis turned to protest that it was the 'Orchid Man' doing the holding and that he'd been butted as well. At that moment, the Frenchman took the opportunity to throw a hard right hand that connected with Lewis's jaw, leaving the latter out for the count and probably lamenting boxing's golden rule - protect yourself at all times! Sally Lewis, the 'Kid's' daughter-in-law, has kindly lent the museum his gym bag, passport, and, of special interest, his gumshield. He is considered to have been the first man to use a gumshield, now of course an essential piece of equipment for any boxer.

Possibly the highlight of the exhibition is the Lonsdale Belt belonging to Johnny Brown. Born Philip Heckman in Mile End, London in 1902, Johnny was providing for his family from the age of 12 following the death of his father and turned pro aged 15. Brown won the British, Empire and European titles from 'Bugler' Harry Lake on points over 20 rounds. After forcing Harry Corbett to retire at the end of 16 rounds and knocking out Mick Hill, he became the only Jewish boxer to win the belt outright. His brother, rather confusingly known as 'Young Johnny' Brown, was a flyweight who challenged Scotland's Elky Clark unsuccessfully for the European title in Glasgow on 30 April 1925. His son, Ronald, an optician, still has his trunks, boots and bag gloves, which are also on display.

Following in the footsteps of Kid Lewis, not only as a Jewish east ender but also taking America by storm was the other famous 'Kid' - Jack 'Kid' Berg. Born Judah Bergman in 1909, the 'Whitechapel Whirlwind' as he was nicknamed, often fought in the USA, beating some of the top fighters of the day in Kid Chocolate, Billy Petrolle and Tony Canzoneri. Berg became the world junior welterweight champion when defeating Mushy Callahan at the Royal Albert Hall, London in 1930. He later moved down five pounds to win the British lightweight title in 1934 from another boxer featured at the museum in Harry Mizler. Seeing two Jewish boxers topping the bill was not uncommon before WW2, although I'm sure it is something we will probably never see again. I believe the last time two Jewish champions shared the Albert Hall ring was when Berg stepped up to congratulate Glasgow's Gary Jacobs, after he won the Commonwealth welterweight championship in 1988.

Berg's nephew, Howard Frederics, who, incidentally, has written an opera on his uncle's life and times, has contributed various items to the exhibition. Amongst which is a cigarette card of Harry Mizler in fighting pose. Mizler was a gold medal winner at the 1930 Empire games and twice an ABA Champion before winning the vacant British lightweight title against Johnny Cuthbert after just six months and 14 contests as a professional.

Of course, it was not only in the ring that the fight game had a strong Jewish influence. Matchmaking managing and promoting being dominated by the likes of Harry Levene and Jack Solomons, followed by the most knowledgeable of them all in Mickey Duff. Born Monek Prager in Krakow, Poland in 1929, Mickey was amongst the last wave of Jewish east-European immigrants escaping religious intolerance. Arriving in London in 1937 with three generations preceding him, all Rabbis, it was no surprise that young Mickey was

Dave Sharkey, the father of Philip, who was an east-end featherweight who boxed between 1945 and 1950

Philip Sharkey

sent to Rabbinical school in Gateshead. However, he was fascinated by boxing and the fight game. Hanging around Klein's gym, trying to earn a couple of shillings when giving Dave Crowley a good few rounds sparring, Mickey was soaking in the knowledge that would see him become the leading authority on all aspects of boxing. He turned pro aged 15, had 69 licensed bouts and many more travelling on the boxing booths with hardened pros such as Ben Valentine, Len 'Davo' Davies and Jackie Rankin. By 1949 he decided his calling was on the other side of the ropes and, during a chance meeting at Ziggy's café in London's east end with fellow pro and boxing booth companion, Dave Sharkey (who, having completed his national service was looking to resume his boxing career), Mickey accompanied Dave to see London promoters, Maurice and Harold Bodinetz. Mickey not only made his first match, but talked his way to becoming Britain's youngest matchmaker. He soon had a managers license, his first signing being the talented Jewish-Canadian stylist, Solly Cantor, a world top-ten rated lightweight. A promoter's license eventually saw him succeed Jack Solomons as British boxing's number-one promoter. Never short of expressing his opinion or giving the press a good quote, his gift of the gab replaced his gift of the jab!

Also on show are recently retired boxers from diverse backgrounds, such as Frank Bruno, Barry McGuigan, Chris Eubank and Lennox Lewis, along with active fighters Roman Greenberg and Martin Power. Greenberg, who was born in Russia, raised in Israel, and training in the USA and the UK, could soon be challenging for a version of the heavyweight crown. He could become the first Jewish heavyweight champion since Max Baer, the champion from the 1930s who fought with a Star of David on his trunks. Baer's claim to be Jewish is somewhat refuted by his trainer Ray Arcel's assertion: "I've seen him in the shower..... he aint Jewish"! Local hero, Power, born and bred just moments from the museum in Camden Town, is a recent British bantamweight champion. His background is from the Irish traveller community, where it is traditional for boys to learn to box from a young age. Martin started at eight and later, with St Pancras ABC, he twice reached the ABA senior finals. He won the vacant 118lbs British professional title against Dale Robinson and defended successfully against Ian Napa and Isaac Ward.

The recent successes of Amir Khan sum up the story of immigrant, minority boxers up to the present time. Khan, British-born of Pakistani parents, is the pride of his community, of the United Kingdom and, I imagine Pakistan.

Moving on, one enters a darkened room that is showing a short film by Elliot Tucker in training for a white-collar fight at the York Hall and is interspersed with interviews with some 'faces' from the London ex-Boxers Association. Duff, Hyman Kern and the Lazar brothers all speak candidly about growing up in poverty and how fighting was not a hobby but a means of survival. The LEBA stalwart, Sam Soraf, along with present day Jewish promoter, Robert Waterman, and Bernard Hart, of the Lonsdale Sporting Club and a former fighter, also added their views on the fight game.

The opening night of the exhibition was a great success, with the guests of honour, Duff, Power and Britain's most experienced and respected boxing journalist, Colin Hart, mixing with the great and the good from the museum and many characters from the world of boxing. Richard Barber, a British Boxing Board of Control official and now writing the 'Old Timers' column in Boxing News, relations of Jack and Joe Bloomfield, Howard Frederics, Kid Berg's nephew and Teddy Baldock's grandson, Martin Sax, both of whom lent many of their photographs, were there, as was Lew Lazar, from probably the last of the great east-end Jewish fighting families. Lew won the Southern Area middleweight title on points against Terence Murphy in Britain's first live televised fight and lost just eight of 60 contests.

Televisions number one master of ceremonies, John MacDonald, was also in attendance. John not only lent some of his photographs, but, through his contacts at Lonsdale, arranged for heavy bags, gloves, head guards, and in the film room, ring posts and ropes, all of which gave the exhibition hall the flavour of real fight arena atmosphere. Matchmaker Roy Hilder, and ex-pro Danny Lutaaya, and promoter/manager, Jonathan Feld, all active in the fight game today were there to cast their eyes on the past. Also there was the UK's most popular ex-boxer, the former British featherweight champion, Sammy McCarthy, who is still fit and trim seemed to be shaking everyone's hands and making them feel like champions as well.

In Colin Hart's excellent speech, he reminisced of growing up, working alongside Sammy on their father's stalls in Watney Street market, usually 'skint', but always talking boxing. To cap a special evening, Martin Power brought along his Lonsdale Belt, which was admired by all present

It was an inspired choice of the museum's Jennifer Marin and Rickie Burman to ask Ruti Ungar to curate the exhibition. Currently completing her dissertation on boxing as a social and cultural phenomenon in late Georgian England, at the Humbolt University in Berlin, she became interested in pugilism after reading about Daniel Mendoza, of whom she is a leading authority. She has promised to make Martin Powers' next fight her first live show!

Accompanying the Ghetto Warriors' exhibition is an excellent book titled *Fighting Back? Jewish and Black Boxers in Britain*, edited by Ruti Ungar and Michael Berkowitz, Professor of Modern Jewish History at University College London. Available from the museum, 020 7284 1997, it contains interesting articles and some rare photographs and prints. It is high time that boxing has been given its own exhibition and it's a pity there was not more room as many great boxing heroes had to be left out. I hear whispers that a Hall Of Fame is being planned and that this exhibition may travel around the country if funding can be raised. Let's hope so, as boxing has many fascinating stories to tell.

Left to Right: Mickey Duff, Martin Power and Colin Hart

Philip Sharkey

Colin McMillan: So Near Yet So Far

by Ralph Oates

When we look back at the many exciting moments in boxing I think we would all agree that the featherweight division has produced its share of thrilling fights over the years. Bouts which have been truly breathtaking, keeping us all on the edge of our seats until the final punch is thrown. Names like Willie Pep and Sandy Saddler, instantly come to mind when we think of the division, class boxers who without doubt can be considered amongst the greats in the sport. These two particular fighting men from the USA helped to keep the poundage in the spotlight during their prime years. Both Pep and Saddler really gave their all on the four occasions they met in the ring. Certainly the term 'No Quarter Given' comes very much to mind when discussing their bouts, which have been well documented throughout the years. Punching power, scientific boxing, pride coupled with a very strong determination to win are attributes which are all associated with these two gladiators and they most certainly set the ring on fire whenever they faced each other.

There have, of course, been many others at the weight who have excelled in reaching the heights from outside the USA. Men like Mexico's Vicente Saldivar who, when at his peak, had a vice like grip on the championship. Those fans who witnessed his three enthralling battles with Wales' Howard Winstone were treated to boxing skills from both, at the highest possible level. Salvador Sanchez was another Mexican fighter who showed every indication in his nine title defences that he was an outstanding ring operator. He looked well on his way to becoming another great at the poundage before he tragically lost his life in a car accident at just 23 years of age.

Another top man was Nicaragua's Alexis Arguello, whose skills not only took him to the WBA championship at the weight but also to the WBC super-featherweight and WBC lightweight crowns. Then there was Panama's Eusebio Pedroza, a long-reigning champion who held the WBA title from 1978-1985 and made 19 successful defences. The exciting emergence of hard-punching Azumah Nelson from Ghana saw him become not only an exceptional WBC featherweight champion but also a WBC ruler at super-featherweight; a true warrior in every sense of the word.

There are really a number of other fighters who can without doubt be named and listed on the role of honour in a division, which is very tough. It should also be proudly noted that on the domestic front the scene has also been very competitive, with a number of outstanding fighters from Britain boxing their way to the very top of the international tree by winning a version of the world title. While there may well be far too many versions of a world championship in any one weight division these days, it's always the WBC, WBA, IBF and WBO title holders who are taken more seriously in boxing. Win one of those championships and you know that you are looked upon, dare I say, as a genuine world champion, the 'Real Deal' so to speak. British fighters who have won versions of these titles at featherweight since the late 1960s include Howard Winstone (WBC), Barry McGuigan (WBA), Paul Hodkinson (WBC), Colin McMillan (WBO), Steve Robinson (WBO), Prince Naseem Hamed (WBO, WBC and IBF), Paul Ingle (IBF) and Scott Harrison (WBO). Certainly a most impressive line up.

One of the said mentioned, Colin McMillan, became the first British holder of the WBO version of the world title in the 126lbs division when defeating the champion, Maurizio Stecca, of Italy over 12 rounds on 16 May 1992. To do so he produced a magical performance of boxing at its very best. Stecca was a fine champion, a man who did not come over to Britain just to give his crown away. When boxing in the amateurs, he had won a gold medal in the 1983 World Cup and been a gold medallist at bantamweight in the 1984 Olympic Games. Maurizio was in his second reign as world title holder, having first won the vacant crown by stopping Pedro Nolasco of the Dominican Republic in round six on 28 January 1989, before losing it in his second defence to the American, Louie Espinosa, when being stopped in round seven on 11 November 1989. However, Stecca regained the title on 26 January 1991 when stopping Armando Reyes of the Dominican Republic in round five.

Posing with the Lonsdale Belt

The defence against McMillan would be his third in his second reign and he fully intended to go back home with the championship. There was no doubt that the British boxer had a difficult night ahead of him against a man with more than just an impressive ring pedigree. Maurizio was having his 46th contest with just one defeat, while McMillan was having his 24th bout, also with the one solitary defeat (due to a cut eye) on his record. When the bell sounded to start the fight Stecca fought the very best he could, calling upon his vast ring experience, but Colin proved to be the better man in all departments, giving British boxing a great boost with his outstanding 12-round points victory over a class champion. Yet, it could be said that McMillan's victory was not really a great surprise, since at the very start of his career he had revealed all the qualities of a potential world beater when fighting his way up towards the British title with his consummate classy, boxing skills which were a joy to watch.

The challenge for the British crown had taken place on 22 May 1991 – this was McMillan's acid test. The defending champion in question was Gary De'Roux, a proud man who would fight anyone at anytime. Gary had won the crown just a few months before meeting Colin, knocking out the then highly-favoured Sean Murphy in five exciting rounds on 5 March. So in Gary, Colin was meeting a man who would come into the ring with a great deal of talent, desire and punching power and one who did not take any prisoners. However, McMillan relieved De'Roux of the title by boxing his way to a seventh-round stoppage.

In the months to follow, Colin confirmed his class by defending his championship on two occasions, stopping Kevin Pritchard on 4 September 1991 in seven rounds and outpointing Sean Murphy over 12 rounds on 29 October 1991 to win the Lonsdale Belt outright in a record time of 160 days. Colin further enhanced his reputation by adding the vacant Commonwealth title to his name when outpointing Ghana's Percy Commey over 12 difficult rounds on 18 January 1992. Prior to contesting the world title, McMillan kept ring sharp by knocking out Tommy Valdez in six rounds on the 25 March 1992. On the same Dagenham show, Stecca also boxed in a non-title bout stopping Roy Muniz in the sixth round. So both champion and future challenger were able to get a close-up view of each other before crossing gloves in the ring.

After his world title victory over the Italian, Colin looked to be in a really tremendous position, with the world appearing to be his oyster and really big international bouts in the offing. A natural looked to be against fellow Briton, Paul Hodkinson of Liverpool, who held the WBC version of the championship. That would have been a money spinner, with both titles on the line just for starters. There were also unification matches against other fellow champions like Mexico's IBF king, Manuel Medina, and the WBA champion, Kyun-Yung Park of South Korea, being mooted. Yet in life the unexpected can arrive as quickly as a left hook to the chin, leaving our plans in tatters. Such a fatal blow, career-wise, happened to McMillan on 26 September 1992 when he made his first defence against Ruben Palacio of Columbia.

While Palacio was a good fighter, every indication was that Colin would retain his crown without too many problems. On the night Palacio knew that this was his big chance and gave it his all, and while McMillan was clearly having difficulty with his challenger his better boxing appeared to be keeping him ahead on the score cards. Then in the eighth round the bout was halted when Colin suffered a dislocated shoulder, which dramatically saw the championship change hands. This was a setback, of that there was no doubt, all the dreams and ambitions had gone in just a moment.

After being out of action for over a year due to the injury, Colin returned to challenge for his old title against the then holder, Steve Robinson of Wales, in Cardiff on 23 October 1993. Robinson had won the vacant WBO world featherweight championship on 17 April 1993 when outpointing John Davison over 12 rounds, Palacio having been forced to relinquish the title due to health problems. Robinson later cemented his claim to the title by knocking out challenger Sean Murphy in round nine on 10 July 1993. So McMillan would be Steve's second defence.

Robinson, who proved in the fullness of time to be an excellent champion, fought his way to a 12-round points victory to keep his crown. This was a further setback for Colin, who duly revealed a fighters' heart when he picked himself up from this defeat to continue his career. After yet another operation on his shoulder, McMillan started to get back on track with a string of six victories before challenging the British champion, Jonjo Irwin, on 14 May 1996. While Colin regained his former title with a 12-round points decision he was later taken to hospital with exhaustion and dehydration. If anything, this contest was a warning sign that the former world champion's skills had sadly erroded and that he had lost that little something, that vital spark, which made him so special.

McMillan later returned to the ring on 3 September 1996 and stopped Trust Ndlovu from Zimbabwe in seven rounds in a final eliminator for the Commonwealth crown. Next up proved to be the curtain closer to the Barking fighter's career when he lost his British title to Paul Ingle, who was coming into the ring undefeated in 14 bouts. The contest was stopped in Ingle's favour in eight rounds on 11 January 1997. This was a double blow for Colin, since at the time there was a very strong possibility that a challenge for Prince Naseem Hamed's WBO world featherweight title might be forthcoming. Unfortunately, this defeat put an end to any plans for such a match. If there was any consolation for Colin he at least lost to a good fighter, since Paul eventually went on to also win European and Commonwealth belts and the IBF version of the world title. However, like many fighters, Colin, who finished his career with a professional record of 35 contests, with 31 wins and four losses, was not lost to the fight game. After he decided to hang up his gloves the former champion turned his attention to management and at this time appears to be making giant strides towards making this venture a successful one. On behalf of the Yearbook I contacted Colin to ask about his career and his views about the sport.

(Ralph Oates) In which year were you born?

(Colin McMillan) I was born on the 12 February 1966.

(RO) Where were you born?

(CM) Hackney Hospital in East London.

(RO) How tall are you?

(CM) Five foot, six inches.

(RO) How old were you when you first started to box?

(CM) I was 15. Some may say that this is a little too late to start, but for me it was an ideal age.

(RO) What made you take up boxing?

(CM) Watching Muhammad Ali and Sugar Ray Leonard boxing on TV. I admired their skills and this, in turn, inspired me to embark on a career in boxing.

(RO) Which amateur club did you box for?

(CM) Barking ABC, which is a very good club. I had a number of happy years there.

(RO) Who was your trainer at the club?

(CM) Terry Davis, an excellent trainer. Sadly, he has now passed away.

(RO) Approximately how many amateur bouts did you have?

(CM) I would say about 75.

(RO) Can you remember how many you actually won?

(CM) I believe I won 62 of these.

(RO) Which titles did you win in the amateur ranks?

(CM) I was PLA champion and London champion on four occasions.

(RO) Do you still attend amateur shows?

(CM) Yes, I often attend amateur shows. It's good to see so many potential champions of the future in action. I also promote a dinner show every year for my former club in Barking.

(RO) In which stance did you box?

(CM) I fought in the orthodox stance, but I was also a switch hitter.

(RO) Many boxers do not like fighting southpaws. How did you feel about meeting them in the ring?

(CM) I must confess that I did not like boxing southpaws. I found them very difficult to cope with.

(RO) Who was your most difficult opponent in the amateurs?

(CM) It had to be Floyd Havard. He was a very clever boxer who defeated me when we met. Floyd, of course, went on to twice win the British super-featherweight title in the pro ranks, defeating the defending champion, Pat Cowdell, in 1988 by way of an eighth-round stoppage and then regaining it in 1994 when stopping Neil Haddock in round ten. Prior to this bout, in the same year Havard challenged for the IBF super-featherweight crown against the excellent champion Juan 'John-John' Molina from Puerto Rico, but failed in his bid when he duly retired in round six.

(RO) What made you decide to turn professional?

(CM) I always intended to go pro from the off. Boxing in the amateurs was a learning curve, an obvious route before going into the paid ranks. I was able to get that vital ring experience by meeting various fighters and hence being able

Colin at home with wife Susan, Amber and Keisha

to come to terms with the different styles and methods which were employed.

(RO) In which year did you have your first professional contest?

(CM) It was 1988 against Mike Chapman, whom I outpointed over six rounds. Mike was having his 11th contest and gave me a good work out. It was a fine introduction to the paid ranks.

(RO) Were you superstitious before you fought?

(CM) Not really, but I always had this ritual whereby I had my haircut before I boxed.

(RO) Who was your manager?

(CM) The former IBF world light-welterweight champion, Terry Marsh, was my manager and later Jonathan Rendell was my advisor.

(RO) Who was your trainer?

(CM) Howard Rainey.

(RO) Who was your most difficult opponent in the professional ranks?

(CM) Dean Phillips. He really came to fight. When we fought, Dean, a super-featherweight, was on a winning streak of four bouts and full of ambition and fire. Let's not forget that he was at the time fighting a former world, British and Commonwealth champion and a victory would have advanced his rating greatly. That really was a great incentive for him. However, I won an eight-round points decision.

(RO) At the British Boxing Board of Control Awards Event in 1992, you received the British boxer of the year award. Would you say that this was one of the highlights of your professional career?

(CM) Yes it was, I was very proud of this award. There were a number of fine boxers in the running at the time, so I felt honoured to be given the vote.

(RO) During your time in the professional ranks you boxed twice in America, winning on both occasions. Did you find that boxing in the USA was beneficial to your career?

(CM) Yes I did. Fighting and training in America gave me vital experience which I was able to call upon in later fights.

(RO) What did you find the most difficult thing to do when boxing?

(CM) Making the weight; this can prove to be an ordeal. Also dealing with the politics within the sport.

(RO) Do you believe that boxing instils discipline and respect to those who participate in the sport?

(CM) I feel it does. From taking part in the sport you gain many values in life, one of which is having respect for yourself and others. That is very important.

(RO) What would you say was your proudest moment when boxing in the professional ranks?

(CM) Winning the British and Commonwealth title and then the world championship. It really was a great moment and gave me a wonderful feeling. There isn't anything quite like it.

(RO) How did your parents feel about your championship wins at the time?

(CM) My mother Maria and father Michael were, needless to say, very proud of my achievement.

(RO) You won the WBO version of the world featherweight title, the British crown twice (winning the Lonsdale Belt outright) and the Commonwealth crown. Was there any reason why you didn't go for the European title?

(CM) It was a career choice. I would liked to have won the European championship, but the opportunity to challenge for the world title came along first and it would have been foolish to turn it down.

(RO) When you held the WBO world title, fellow British fighter, Paul Hodkinson, was a rival champion holding the WBC belt. There was a great deal of speculation at the time that the two of you could eventually meet in a unification match, which would clearly have been a fantastic contest. Sadly, all plans were dashed when you both lost your respective titles to other opponents. Were you sorry that the pair of you did not meet in the ring?

(CM) Yes, it would have been good for British boxing with both our titles on the line. Paul had beaten me in the amateur ranks and I was keen to box him again to put the record straight. I feel certain that we would have both put on a good show, bringing out the very best in each other.

(RO) What was your biggest disappointment in boxing?

(CM) It must be the occasion that I lost the world title to Ruben Palacio due to my injury.

(RO) You attempted to regain your WBO world title from Steve Robinson after being inactive for over a year due to your dislocated shoulder. Why did you not have a warm-up bout first to get rid of ring rust?

(CM) I had to take a chance at the title when it was presented. I could have taken a warm-up bout and lost due to my shoulder injury, then that championship chance and the pay cheque would have gone. I really could not take that risk.

(RO) How do you feel about female involvement in the sport?

(CM) I have no objections so to speak. If women want to box why shouldn't they? Jane Couch has a great deal of ability and often turns in some first-rate performances. So if lady boxers serve the sport well, let them fight.

(RO) Who is your favourite old-time fighter?

(CM) Sugar Ray Robinson, the former world welterweight and middleweight champion. Sugar Ray had it all, a really great fighter. I would add that the word great is not exaggerated when applied to him. His record is full of the top names in boxing and let's not forget that Sugar Ray almost won the world light-heavyweight title on 25 June 1952 when challenging Joey Maxim for the crown. He looked to be on his way to victory until the extreme heat got to him, which duly resulted in a 14th-round retirement defeat. The fight took place on a very hot summer's day. Another favourite of mine is Tony Canzoneri, who won the featherweight, lightweight and light-welterweight world titles – an outstanding fighter. He really was a remarkable ringman, who gave everything when in action and, of course, proved his worth by becoming a world champion in three-weight divisions.

(RO) How do you feel about title fights being held over the duration of 12 rounds rather than 15?

(CM) I think that 12 rounds is more than sufficient and safer.

(RO) How do you feel boxers today compare with those of the past with regard to both their skill and technique?

(CM) I don't really think you can compare with any degree of accuracy, since each period of time calls upon different methods and skills.

(RO) Who is your favourite modern-day fighter?

(CM) I have to go for three-time world heavyweight champion, Muhammad Ali, an extremely talented boxer who not only fought his opponents inside the ring but also racism outside of the roped arena. Ali inspired many to take up the sport and belongs in the history books of boxing.

(RO) Which is your favourite weight division?

(CM) I have two, the featherweights and the welterweights.

(RO) Who in your opinion was the best world heavyweight champion of all time?

(CM) Without a doubt, it has to be Muhammad Ali.

(RO) Which is your favourite world heavyweight title fight?

(CM) The Muhammad Ali–Cleveland Williams bout, which took place in Houston on 14 November 1966. Ali was at his peak in this contest and really took Williams apart in three rounds with his speed of punch and footwork. This was Ali's seventh defence and he gave a staggering performance. He looked unbeatable.

(RO) How do you feel about fighters who continue to box on even when middle-aged?

(CM) I am not happy about it. I feel that every boxer, be it champion or journeyman, should leave the sport before he reaches a certain age. Let's not forget, if you have been boxing for a number of years you will have taken a degree of blows during that period of time and the human body can only take so much punishment. It is wise to walk away from the sport with your health intact.

(RO) What changes would you like to see in the sport?

(CM) When I was formerly with The Professional Boxers Association (PBA), I fully endorsed the need for an insurance policy for boxers – which they could duly call upon when injured, or indeed, if they should ever fall on hard times. I still feel that this is a worthwhile scheme, which should be considered.

(RO) Out of all the boxers in recent years who would you say was an excellent role model for the sport?

(CM) Former three-time world champion, Lennox Lewis. He was a credit to the sport, his behaviour inside and outside of the ring was always first class. Lennox is a fine representative for boxing.

(RO) What annoys you most in the sport?

(CM) The lack of respect some fighters are given from time to time. Boxing is not easy and I find it very annoying to hear some of the harsh criticism aimed at some participants after they have clearly given of their very best in a contest.

(RO) How do you feel about the vast number of world governing bodies in the sport today?

(CM) I have mixed feelings. Too many champions devalue a world title, but on the other hand the vast amount of championships available give more fighters a better chance of winning a crown and in turn a better purse by defending it. So there really is a plus and minus answer to the situation.

It really depends from which perspective you are viewing the problem.

(RO) How do you feel about there being so many weight divisions in the sport at the moment?

(CM) This is a good thing, since many boxers should now be able to find their correct division without the strain of making weight, which can be a problem.

(RO) What would you say to those who would like to ban boxing?

(CM) I would say think again. The sport is a great character builder, giving individuals the chance to aim for something positive in their respective lives. Let's not forget that over the years the sport has developed many fine characters, who have proven to be a credit not just to boxing but to society in general.

(RO) There have been a number of films made about boxing over the years, do you have a particular favourite?

(CM) Yes I do, I am not sure if it was ever released in the cinema, but I once saw a Muhammad Ali video titled *Skill, Brains & Guts*, it was first class.

(RO) How did your nickname 'Sweet C' originate?

(CM) When I started to box in the professional ranks, many said that my style was sweet like Sugar, so the nickname 'Sweet C' came into being.

(RO) What was the best advice you were given when boxing?

(CM) I was advised by Terry Marsh not to give up my day job while boxing, since it is important to keep a regular wage coming in. This really is sound advice.

(RO) Looking at the domestic scene at the moment, who do you tip for the top?

(CM) It is always precarious to make any predictions in boxing, but I feel David Haye has all the attributes to go all the way to the top. He, of course, lost to Carl Thompson by

Colin (right) seen here on his way to regaining the British featherweight title when outpointing Jonjo Irwin in 1996. It was a title he hadn't lost in the ring   Les Clark

way of a fifth-round stoppage in 2004 while bidding for the IBO cruiserweight title, but has since bounced back and at this moment in time is matched to fight Jean-Marc Mormeck for the WBA/WBC cruiserweight titles. The other boxer who I feel is set for a great deal of success is Amir Khan, who has been making steady progress in the professional ranks since winning a silver medal at the 2004 Olympic games in Greece. Amir is an excellent boxer who also has punching power.

(RO) Are you married?

(CM) Yes, I have been married to Susan for 15 years. We have, however, been together for 20 years.

(RO) Do you have any children?

(CM) I have two daughters, Keisha who is 18 and at university and Amber who is 14 years of age.

(RO) I understand that you passed a number of 'A' and 'O' level examinations. What were the subjects?

(CM) I have seven 'O' levels in the following subjects; Mathematics, English Language, English Literature, Physics, History, Economics and Geography. I also have three 'A' levels in English Language, History and Economics.

(RO) You clearly feel that a good education is vital.

(CM) Yes I do, a good education is a must for everyone. It's often said that knowledge is power and that is very true.

(RO) Do you discuss boxing much at home?

(CM) It's a big part of my life, so the sport is discussed at home now and then.

(RO) Do you still attempt to keep fit these days and if so how?

(CM) I go out for a run when time allows.

(RO) Apart from boxing what is your other favourite sport?

(CM) When I was younger I liked a number of sports such as football, cricket, athletics, etc. Boxing of course took all my interest once I got into the game.

(RO) Do you have a favourite football club?

(CM) West Ham and then Arsenal.

(RO) What is your favourite kind of music?

(CM) R' & B' and Soul.

(RO) What advice would you give to anyone embarking on a career in boxing?

(CM) Get a good education, look after your health and look after your money.

(RO) What did you do when you first retired from boxing?

(CM) I was a promotional manager for a club in Barking called Legends. It was very enjoyable.

(RO) Looking back at your professional career, would you do anything different if you had your time over?

(CM) No, I can't say that I would do anything different. I won the British, Commonwealth and world featherweight titles and I am very happy about that.

(RO) You are now a boxing manager, are you enjoying this role?

(CM) I am, but I do not like the political side of the role.

(RO) What are your ambitions for the future?

(CM) I will be getting involved in various different projects both inside and outside of boxing. This includes property development, investment management and organising musical concerts.

When talking to Colin it was obvious to see that he was a man who was more than at ease with life and more than content with his former boxing career. Even when he lost his world title to Ruben Palacio due to a dislocated shoulder, his view on that night is philosophical. Many fighters may well have felt more than just a little bitter over the circumstances of the defeat. Colin was, at the time, on the verge of some big-money fights and when you consider his obvious skills it was more than possible that he could have gone down in history with the greats of the division. However, it wasn't to be, being a case of so near yet so far. Yet Colin is pleased that even if he didn't realise his full potential, he was, even if it was for a short time, a world featherweight champion and his name will be forever etched into the record books.

Clearly Colin still loves the sport, which he served with both honour and dignity. It is, therefore, a plus for boxing that after he retired from the game he duly stayed with the sport and is today a manager. This can only be beneficial, since he can pass on his vast experience to other fighters in his charge. Furthermore, this man is an excellent ambassador for boxing. This is very important since we all know that the sport is always under the microscope of many critics who take every single opportunity to knock the game, so image and presentation is a must these days. A man like Colin who talks intelligently about boxing really helps to nullify the argument to ban the sport whenever presented. It would be a form of justice if Colin was able to take a fighter to a major championship in the next few years. There is no reason why he shouldn't, he has the know how to accomplish this feat. On behalf of the *Yearbook*, I wish Colin, his wife Susan and daughters Keisha and Amber the very best for the future.

Joe Erskine: The Classical Heavyweight

by Wynford Jones

Joe Erskine was born in Angelina Street, Cardiff on 26 January 1934, a street in the docks area of the city also known as Tiger Bay. His birthplace was just a few hundred yards from that of 'Peerless' Jim Driscoll. Also born in the same street was Billy Boston, who would go on to become one of Britain's finest rugby league stars, and as young men they both played in the same local rugby team. Joe was brought up in this fascinating multi-racial community which not only produced a galaxy of sports, stars but also a number of superb jazz musicians and the internationally famous singing star, Shirley Bassey.

Joe's father, John, was a Jamaican and his mother was Welsh. John was determined from the start that Joe would be a champion boxer and his grandmother 'Nana' became one of Joe's staunchest supporters as soon as he was drawn to the ring.

Joe began to box at the age of 11 and won a clutch of titles between six and a half and ten stone before progressing to Cadet boxing and captaining the successful Army team at Wembley in 1951. The following year, he became the Welsh ABA light-heavyweight champion and in 1953 he took the ABA heavyweight championship, with Henry Cooper retaining his title at light-heavyweight.

The names of Cooper and Erskine were to be linked throughout their careers in both the amateur and professional codes and in 1953 they were both members of an ABA squad which went to Germany and Italy with Harry Gibbs as the trainer. Gibbs would later go on to become one of Britain's finest referees in a career spanning 25 years, while the squad also included Dave Charnley, Frankie Jones and Ron Barton, all future champions.

Having impressed in the amateurs, Joe turned professional in 1954 with Cardiff manager, Benny Jacobs, a Romanesque character whose stable included Phil Edwards and David 'Darkie' Hughes. Edwards would eventually challenge Terry Downes for the British middleweight title, while Hughes worked his way through the ranks to challenge Dave Charnley for the British lightweight title. The stable would be further strengthened when Harry Carroll and Lennie 'the Lion' Williams, both of whom would go on to challenge Howard Winstone for the British featherweight title, decided to punch for pay.

Making his professional debut at Hanley less than two months after his 20th birthday, while still in the Army, there was a good deal of support for Joe in the hall as he destroyed Alf Price in less than two rounds. However, celebrations were short-lived as he was due back on guard duty at midnight at Nesscliffe Army Camp, Shrewsbury. He notched up 15 contests in his first year, with three of these taking place on the same night when participating in a 'Novices' heavyweight competition arranged by promoter Jack Solomons, and his record was perfect save for a draw over six rounds in Cardiff with Dinny Powell.

Joe maintained his momentum through 1955, beating Peter Bates in Birmingham in March and outpointing Henry Cooper over ten rounds in London on 15 November in a contest which was an eliminator for the British heavyweight title. It was also his 11th contest of the year. Towards the end of 1955 he was named 'Best Young Boxer' by the Boxing Writers Club, an honour which has meant so much to many of our boxers over the years because it comes from within the sport.

In May 1956, he beat fellow Welshman Dick Richardson on points over ten rounds in Cardiff. Dick, known as the 'Maesglas Marciano', was a tough battler in the ring and Joe was soon in trouble. A cut which he had sustained in training re-opened almost immediately and in the fifth round Joe went to the canvas for the first time in his career. But from that point onwards, Joe showed the qualities of a champion and got up off the floor to take a well-deserved points decision.

Cuts were to remain a huge problem for Joe, but after this injury had healed his big chance came. Joe was still undefeated when he was matched with Johnny Williams at Maindy Stadium in Cardiff on 27 August 1956 for the heavyweight championship of Great Britain. This would be the first time that two Welshmen had met for the heavyweight crown.

Williams, who had taken the title from Jack Gardner in 1952, had lost it to Don Cockell in 1953 and the championship was now vacant following the latter's retirement. The contest against Williams proved to be a hard battle and once more Joe was to be handicapped by cuts, this

time over both eyes. He had to dig deep and survived some desperate moments before emerging with the points decision over 15 rounds. As the Lonsdale Belt was fastened around his waist, torrential rain greeted the new champion. Joe had become the fourth Welshman to win the title, following in the footsteps of Jack Petersen, Tommy Farr and Williams.

On 19 February 1957, Joe was matched with the tough Cuban, Nino Valdes. Valdes had already proved to be more than a match for British heavyweights, forcing Don Cockell into third-round retirement and stopping Dick Richardson in the eighth at Harringay, due to eye injuries which were serious enough to bring about the intervention of the referee.

Valdes totally overwhelmed Joe, knocking him out in the first round and giving him his first taste of defeat, but some of his former stablemates remain convinced that on this occasion Joe was a beaten man before he stepped into the ring. Both Valdes and his manager, Bobby Gleason, were ecstatic after the contest. Nino had warmed up with about half an hour of shadow boxing before the fight and Gleason confirmed that the plan was to win quickly. One of the first visitors to his dressing room after the fight was the Cuban Ambassador, Roberto Mendoza, who gave Valdes a congratulatory hug while the fighter explained in near disbelief that it had only taken two punches.

The Cubans were so impressed by their treatment in London they suggested to the promoter, Jack Solomons, that Valdez would like to challenge Floyd Patterson for the world title in London, though, as always, Jack had been hoping to push the claims of the home fighter. Valdes had boxed Archie Moore in Las Vegas and felt that he had been robbed. This led him to believe that 'the mob' would never let him get near the world title and that Britain provided him with the best opportunity of a level playing field.

For 'Jolting Joe', recovery from this setback was of the utmost importance and he went on to beat Peter Bates once again, this time on points over 12 rounds at Doncaster at the end of May. His next contest came on 17 September when he retained his British title against Henry Cooper at London's Harringay Arena. Joe then beat Joe Bygraves for the Empire title at Leicester, the Welshman taking the decision on points over 15 rounds, while for Cooper it had been a miserable year, losing to Bygraves, Ingemar Johannson and, of course, Erskine.

Quite naturally, Joe now set his sights on the European title, which was held by Sweden's Ingemar Johannson. On 21 February 1958, the pair met at Gothenburg and Joe was retired by his corner after 13 rounds, having been troubled by cuts and taking heavy punishment from the big-hitting Swede. Ingemar went on to win the world title from Floyd Patterson, but then lost the next two contests in their three-fight series.

In June of that year, Joe lost his British and Empire titles to Brian London of Blackpool. He was boxing well until the familiar handicap reared its ugly head. Once Joe's left eyebrow had been opened, London fought like a man possessed and ripped the titles away from the Welshman,

Having won the British heavyweight title, Joe (left) made his first defence a successful one when outpointing Henry Cooper

knocking him out in the eighth round. Victory would have given Joe outright ownership of the Lonsdale Belt but, alas, it was not to be.

The turning point in Joe's career undoubtedly came following a decision to have plastic surgery carried out on his eyebrows. After this, life was somewhat easier for him in the ring and he came back with a win over Max Brianto in Cardiff, before recording the finest victory of his career in February 1959.

On the night when Howard Winstone made his professional debut at Wembley, Joe was matched with the highly regarded American, Willie Pastrano. Willie was fast and skilful, and was considered to be one of the finest boxers in the world. He later confirmed this by going on to win the world light-heavyweight championship. It is some measure of Joe's ability that he was able to outbox a man of Pastrano's calibre. Joe was a clear points winner, moving in to the American at every opportunity and proving to be his master with speedy counterpunching.

Joe took the initiative from the first bell, connecting with his left and pushing Pastrano to the ropes with a right to the body, and he continued to chase the American in the second round. Pastrano began to force the next session, but was caught by a right hook to the body and both men punched away at each other. In the fourth, Joe was scoring with lefts and both boxers were moving quickly around the ring, while in the next round Pastrano was stalking his man almost like a matador. Through the sixth Joe displayed some good work inside, while Pastrano took the seventh with a constant stream of lefts. During this period, the Welshman also showed superb defensive work. The eighth round was

another good one for Pastrano, while in the ninth Joe used his left to good effect, with the American scoring with impeccable counterpunching. Joe was at his best as they came out for the last round, beating Pastrano to the punch with superb left hands, while slipping many of Willie's jabs, and when the final bell sounded the pride of Tiger Bay was a deserving winner of this battle of the purists.

Following the contest, Pastrano commented: "You sports writers sadly underestimate Erskine. He is undoubtedly the best you have and is a difficult man to beat".

Angelo Dundee, Pastrano's manager, was extremely impressed by Joe. He was surprised by the Welshman's skill and felt that if Joe had been bigger and if he could have developed a heavier punch he would have been a world beater. This assessment of Joe comes from Dundee's book, *I Only Talk Winning*.

Pastrano had beaten Dick Richardson on points in London in October 1957 and had also beaten Brian London, but lost their return fight on a controversial cut eye stoppage. Following his defeat by Joe, Dundee decided that Willie's future should be at light-heavyweight and this turned out to be the perfect solution with Pastrano eventually becoming a world champion.

After the win over Pastrano, Joe was once again matched with Dick Richardson, this time at Coney Beach Arena, Porthcawl. Dick was no stranger to the arena, having beaten Hans Kalbfell and Bob Baker and losing to Henry Cooper there in the fifth round of his title challenge. Cooper was bleeding badly and was floored in the fifth round in a neutral corner, but Dick, roared on by the crowd, went all out for victory and was floored by a sucker punch. For the

Joe (right) in training with stablemate, Phil Edwards

Richardson contest, Joe weighed in at 13 stone eight and a half pounds, while Dick came in at 14 stone six and three quarter pounds. However, in spite of Richardson's weight advantage, Joe was a ten-round points winner.

After beating Bruno Scarabellin on points over ten rounds in August, again at Porthcawl, another meeting with Henry Cooper was put in place, with Harry Levene as the promoter and Mickey Duff as matchmaker. Cooper had taken the British and Empire heavyweight titles from Brian London and having gone through a difficult patch himself, Henry would ultimately bring stability to the British heavyweight scene when going on to become the longest-reigning British heavyweight champion.

Over the next few years, Cooper and Erskine met in no less than three title fights, with Henry gaining the upper hand. On 17 November 1959, Joe was stopped in 12 rounds at London's Earls Court Arena and in March 1961 Joe retired in the fifth round, with badly cut eyes bringing the contest to an end. Their final meeting, at Nottingham, came in April 1962 and once more Joe's eyes let him down, with the contest ending in the ninth round.

It was the contest at Earls Court which left the lasting impression on my mind. Joe was floored by a series of punches, which left his body arched over the bottom rope with his head resting on the ring apron, out to the world. There were some worrying moments and Henry feared the worst but, thankfully, Joe recovered.

During the latter stages of his career, Joe beat George Chuvalo on a fifth-round disqualification in Toronto. George was a tough fighter who would later go the full 15 rounds with both Ernie Terrell and Muhammad Ali in contests for the world heavyweight championship. Joe also beat the American, Freddie Mack, at Newtown, mid-Wales, but lost to Karl Mildenberger on points over ten rounds in Dortmund.

The year 1964 saw Joe beat both Jack Bodell and Johnny Prescott, but after losing to the 'Blond Bomber', Billy Walker, on points at Wembley, he announced his retirement. Bodell went on to hold the British title briefly and Walker and Prescott will always be remembered for their two epic battles though, significantly, neither won the British title.

In a ten-year professional career, Joe met many of the big names in the heavyweight division, both at domestic and world level, and could look back on his record with pride. His skills were exquisite, but the paper-thin skin around the eyes proved to be a major problem and I feel sure that had Joe been a bigger man he would have been a serious threat at world level.

From a personal point of view, I shall always remember him as a very quiet, gentle person who accepted the cards dealt to him with dignity. Life was not too kind to him after retirement and the money soon disappeared, some say because of his liking for a bet. His health began to deteriorate as a result of sickle cell anaemia, but he always remained friends with Benny Jacobs and when Benny got to the stage where he was confined to a wheelchair, Joe would often bring his old manager to the ringside on fight night. It was a touching sight, though I doubt that either would have wanted sympathy!

Throughout his life, Joe remained close to his roots and in retirement he was a creature of habit. Each day he would emerge from his house immaculately dressed in a suit and would stroll down to Babs' Bistro in Tiger Bay. This allowed him to have his first pint of the day before official licensing hours clicked in. Later, he would visit his favourite pubs, such as 'The Packet' and would end up at the 'Royal Oak', the pub which for many years was associated with the Driscoll family. Here, Joe would round off the night, occupying a stool in the corner of a room known as the 'office' and when the bell sounded at closing time, his friend Jackie Chambers, himself a boxing trainer, would jokingly warn customers to keep out of Joe's way, but in truth he was the most genial of souls.

Early in 1990, Joe succumbed to illness at the age of 56 and on a cold February day his funeral service was held at the church of St Mary the Virgin on Bute Street. The church was packed with personalities from the world of sport and there were many local people present. On his arrival at the church, Jack Petersen was asked if he would speak and paid handsome tribute to Joe while, earlier that morning, he himself had been diagnosed as suffering from cancer. As well as the tributes, local people sang as the community paid homage to one of its own.

Even though much of the 'Bay' was now being redeveloped, Joe's coffin was carried through the streets and in scenes which were reminiscent of the passing of Jim Driscoll, the headline in the *South Wales Echo* read: "As Great a Grief as Peerless Jim" and this surely reflects the way in which Joe Erskine, a local hero, had touched the lives of so many people. The love, affection and support of his community was the ultimate crown for Joe.

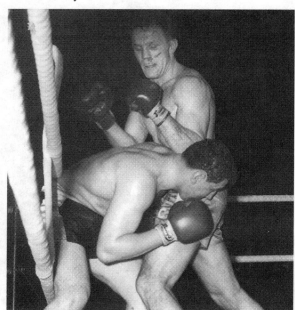

Having beaten Henry Cooper (right) twice, Joe would then lose their next three fights when trying to regain his old British & British Empire heavyweight titles

Dick Burge: The Lord of the Ring

by Larry Braysher

It was 1918, the final year of the Great War, and Germany was bringing the conflict to the 'Home Front' with Zeppelin raids on London. People going about their business were suddenly engulfed in explosions and showered with debris.

This time it was Piccadilly that suffered, with many civilians the innocent victims. Among the rescuers was a soldier in uniform who had been passing. He looked a good deal older than many of his contemporaries, but he was a fit man and he clawed and pulled at the rubble to reach those who were trapped. The combined efforts of the rescuers took many hours and they were hampered by heavy rain. At the finish the soldier was exhausted, his face grimy with brick dust and sweat and his fingers bleeding from digging. Lives were saved that day and he felt with some relief that it was a job well done. It was a fair bet, however, that none of the survivors knew that this rescuer was a former star performer of the ring and one of Britain's great lightweight champions, Dick Burge. Nor did Dick know that tragically his actions that day would ultimately cost him his life. But it had been a life crammed with incident and excitement.

In a relatively short span of 54 years, Dick would have been the first to admit that there was not much that he had not done or tried to do. As well as being a champion boxer, he'd been a promoter, gambler, bookmaker, variety artist, soldier, charity fundraiser, friend and confident of the rich and famous, and even a 'guest' of His Majesty (for several years). Whatever way you looked at it there was never a dull moment for Dick Burge.

Although often thought to be a born and bred 'Geordie', Dick was in fact born in Cheltenham, Gloucestershire in 1865, although his family moved to Newcastle when he was a child. A natural athlete, he was very light on his feet and was a promising sprinter in the local races that were heavily bet on in the north of England at the time. Then in his teens the boxing 'bug' bit, and that was that. Dick gained some valuable experience by travelling with the booths and his natural talent started to push him to the forefront of the country's lightweights. After some good early wins he was matched with fellow 'Geordie', Johnny Robinson, for the 9 stone 12 pounds championship of England. Robinson was a strong puncher, but Dick showed his great promise by getting a draw with the more experienced man. He then gave away a lot of weight, something he was to do many times in his career, to take on Birmingham's Anthony Diamond, one of Britain's best middleweights. He lost a points decision but, nonetheless, gave a good account of himself against the heavier man. Ironically, it was these two bouts, albeit a loss and a draw, which earned Dick a crack at Jem Carney's English (British) lightweight title in 1891. It was a match with no 'love lost' between the two men, which was borne out with Dick's win in the 11th round of a bad tempered affair on a foul.

Now with the English (British) title to his name he started campaigning for a crack at the world crown. However,

it was no easy task and he had to content himself with defences of his own title and other bouts before eventually getting his chance for the vacant world lightweight title against America's Kid Lavigne at the National Sporting Club in 1896. Dick was a worthy challenger and was fancied by many to win, but some stringent weight reducing in a Turkish bath caught up with him in the later rounds and the referee, Bernard Angle, stopped the bout in the 17th round with Burge in no condition to defend himself.

On the same night of his defeat by Lavigne, one of the members of the National Sporting Club, a Colonel North, was so taken with the two boxers that he gave an all-night party at which they were the guests of honour. Not content with that, the next morning the Colonel took the two of them to Leeds, where he was standing in an election to be the local MP. With Lavigne and Burge beside him in his open-topped car they toured the city all day canvassing for 'floating voters'. The three had an uproarious time, even though the Colonel lost the election by just 11 votes.

One of Dick's more irritating traits was his habit of announcing his retirement from the ring at almost regular

Dick in fighting pose

47

intervals. After winning the lightweight title from Jem Carney and returning from a trip to America where he failed to entice Jack McAuliffe, the 140lbs American world champion, into the ring, Dick announced that he would not box again. As a result a substantial collection was made on his behalf and Dick was of course duly grateful. However, he resumed his ring career the following year. Apparently this happened on several occasions. An announcement, followed by a collection, followed by the resumption of his career. It's probably best to assume that Dick was indecisive and any other conclusion that this tendency may have been deemed another source of income, might be an uncharitable one.

Losses were a rarity for Dick because of his speed in the ring. However, twice his record was spoilt when his confidence got the better of him when he challenged Ted Pritchard for the British middleweight title and Jem Smith for the heavyweight version. For the Smith contest he gave away something like three stone. Needless to say he suffered knockout defeats in both of these matches. In his own lightweight class, though, he was still the man to beat and although he lost his title to Tom Causer in 1897 after blatantly fouling him, which in itself almost caused a riot on the night, he made no mistake in the return by knocking the latter out in the first round.

Dick's last important fight was against the famous much-travelled black American, Bobby Dobbs, at the National Sporting Club in Covent Garden. It also turned out to be a most controversial affair, which started a feud between Dick and 'Peggy' Bettinson, the proprietor of the National Sporting Club, which was to last for many years. Right from the off, Dick's bout with Dobbs was the subject of shady dealings that were no doubt instigated by the ringside gamblers that followed the sport. First a money offer was made to Dobbs to take a 'dive'. Then word was filtered back to Dick Burge that it would not be Dobbs in the ring with him on the night, but a 'ringer' of much less ability. As a result, Dick took his training a lot less seriously than he should have. Of course, on the night of the bout Dick discovered that the real Bobby Dobbs was in fact his opponent and was in superb condition. In effect, Dick fell for the 'three card trick' and had to use all his ring skills just to stay out of trouble. By the end of the eighth round Dick was puffing badly and with the prospect of a severe thrashing looming he was retired by his cornerman, Charlie Mitchell. Afterwards, Burge was furious and demanded a return with Dobbs, which he could train properly for and be in proper condition. However, Dobbs and his management showed no interest.

Shortly afterwards Burge and Dobbs ran into one another at a show at the National Sporting Club. Dick challenged him again and when Dobbs declined he lost his head and went for the American there and then before they could be separated. Doing something like this in the hallowed ground of the Sporting Club was close to sacrilege and 'Peggy' Bettinson immediately suspended Dick from the Club. In the subsequent years a lot had happened to Dick Burge, but as the First World War approached he was a well respected promoter and member of the boxing establishment. However,

despite this, Bettinson's ban on him remained in force. Then one day a club member suggested to 'Peggy' that perhaps after such a long time Dick could be re-admitted. This idea was immediately rebuffed by Bettinson, who also stated that he would gladly bet a hundred pounds that Burge would not ever get past the door.

When Dick heard of Bettinson's outburst it was a challenge he could not resist. He told the Sporting Club member concerned to take the bet and that he would cover it if he lost. Therefore, at the next National Sporting Club show Dick paid a visit to a friend who was a professional make-up artist and had a disguise applied, complete with beard and false nose. He then proceeded to waltz into the Club and took a seat by Bettinson himself, even exchanging pleasantries with him, with Bettinson none the wiser who his new acquaintance was. Halfway through the evening Dick whipped off his disguise and confronted Bettinson, who for a moment looked fit to explode. Then his face creased into a smile and the two men started to laugh. He paid his hundred pound bet and welcomed Dick back to the Club. The feud was over.

When Dick's boxing career was at an end he met the person who would become not only his greatest influence but also his best friend, for the rest of his life. Dick was appearing at 'Gatti's' Music Hall doing a boxing training routine and a bit of light sparring for the benefit of the audience. One of the other artists appearing there was one Bella Orchard (her stage name was Ella Lane). The two hit it off immediately, with it being almost love at first sight, and they were married in 1901. But their bliss was to be short-lived as a nightmare for the couple was just about to begin. Dick was arrested and charged with being embroiled in a notorious case that was to become known as 'The Liverpool Bank Frauds'.

The man at the centre of it was a mild-mannered bank clerk called Thomas Gouldie of apparently impeccable character. However, he led a double life and on the other side of the coin he was an inveterate gambler with an addiction to horse racing. He soon got into debt and started stealing from customers' accounts to cover his losses. He then fell in with two dubious racetrack frequenters called Kelly and Styles, to whom he confided that he was stealing from the bank. Realising that they had a source of cash on tap they kidded him that they had cast iron information on potential horseracing winners and urged him to steal the cash to back them, threatening to expose him if he refused. Three other associates of the men became accomplices in the plot, one of them being Dick Burge. Eventually the whole conspiracy was revealed and arrests were made. Dick stood trial at the Old Bailey and pleaded 'Not Guilty'. His explanation was that he thought Gouldie to be a 'rich mug' with more money than sense and that he had no idea that the money was stolen. The prosecution case was that Dick was an active participant in the conspiracy and knew all the circumstances relating to the money. Unfortunately for Dick, out of a total of £160,000 that Gouldie had stolen, he had received £38,000. Also, of the other men involved in the affair, one had since committed suicide and another had absconded.

At the end of the trial, Gouldie and Dick Burge got ten

years apiece, whilst Kelly and Styles, who might have been thought to be the instigators, received only two years each. Dick had every right to feel aggrieved at the result. Not only in the disparity in the sentences, but that he had assisted police to recover £30,000 of his share of the money.

There was one amusing footnote to this depressing episode in Dick's life, which occurred many years later when he was a free man again. Dick was enjoying a bit of relaxation at a London Turkish baths when he recognised the man sitting next to him and asked him if he remembered him. The man replied no and asked him if he should. Whereupon Dick said: "You should do, you gave me ten years once".

Left to right: Dick with Ernest Barry and Pat O'Keefe, the British middleweight champion, 1914-1916 and 1918-1919

The man concerned was none other than the judge from Dick's trial, now Lord Mersey. The old judge was naturally apprehensive at first, but Dick bore him no animosity and the two men chatted amicably before parting. But the almost surreal sight of a judge and his convicted felon standing together in a Turkish Baths, each with nothing but a towel on, must have been a vision to behold.

Dick had served his sentence at Portland Prison and was a model prisoner. On one occasion he even helped out a warder in a life-threatening situation and got a reduction in his sentence for his efforts. Many of his friends stood by him, including Alex Hurley (later to become his business partner) and Robert Watson, a well-known journalist, who penned several sympathetic articles about Dick during his incarceration. Dick ultimately served seven years of his sentence and within months of release decided to return to what he knew best - boxing. Now all he needed was a suitable venue to promote boxing shows in London. Both Dick and Bella felt sure they could make a go of it as long as they could find the right place. Dick toured London without success until fate took a hand when he was travelling on top of double-decker bus in Blackfriars Road, South London and spotted an old looking building called The Surrey Chapel. Despite its name, the clergy had long gone and since then it had failed as a cinema and was now a near derelict warehouse. Dick and Bella, though, could see its enormous potential and with his friend and partner, Alex Hurley, Dick took out a lease on the property. After struggling for a name they called it 'The Ring' after the circular markings on a cat that seemed to come with the fixtures and fittings, which they had adopted. Dick promoted his first show on 14 May 1910, with a top-liner of Ted Newman (Lambeth) versus Jack Roberts (Drury Lane). Prices were one to two shillings and if you came after 9pm it was sixpence. Also, to mark the occasion Dick boxed an exhibition with Young Joseph, although Bella made him promise that he would not entertain any ideas of yet another comeback.

However, it wasn't plain sailing by any means and a few weeks after opening there was a nasty incident when Dick had to virtually single-handedly take on and throw out a pick-pocketing team. He had been around too many racetracks in his time not to recognise a team of 'dips' when he saw them and word soon got out for the likes of them to give 'The Ring' a wide berth. Although business was slow at first, Dick and Bella's enterprise and enthusiasm eventually saw an upturn in their fortunes and attendances started to rise. Dick also lobbied the press and started to get his shows covered in the daily papers as well as the sporting press, which was something of a coup.

Many top fighters got their big break at 'The Ring' as its importance as a fight venue rose. One was the great Jimmy Wilde, although his first encounter with Dick meant his debut there almost never happened. When a very youthful Wilde turned up for his first London appearance, Dick took one look at the frail undernourished looking Welsh lad and was genuinely concerned for his welfare. He demanded that Wilde leave the premises saying: "Look here nipper, I'm having no murder committed here, get!" After much pleading and persuading by Wilde and his manager, Burge relented and allowed him to box. Wilde repaid the vote of confidence by knocking out his opponent in the first round.

Like many of his generation Dick Burge was a patriot and come the First World War, at 49 years of age, he was straight down to the nearest recruiting office to 'do his bit'. Because of his prominence as a former boxer he was enlisted into the Surrey Regiment, who had a 'Sportsman's Battalion', made up of men of sporting prowess. Because of his age Dick was made a recruiting sergeant and carried out this duty along with the British light-heavyweight champion, Pat O'Keefe. Britain's Army at this stage was made up entirely of volunteeers. Later he became a Regimental Policeman and was able to mix his duties, while still promoting shows at 'The Ring'. In fact, the money raised there for War Charities amounted to over £12,000 by the end of the conflict.

At the point of where this article started, Dick took part in rescue operations in Piccadilly shortly after a Zeppelin raid in 1918. He helped pull a number of people from the rubble and also the occupants of a bus who were trapped. Unfortunately, during the rescue the weather turned to heavy rain. When Dick returned home many hours later, he was in a sorry state and Bella took immediate action by getting him into a warm bed. Like a lot of people who are normally very fit, Dick was a bad patient and after showing initial improvement he did a foolhardy thing by going out next day to attend a previous appointment. During the meeting he collapsed and was returned home. Bella sensibly summoned a doctor, but her worst fears were realised when double pneumonia was diagnosed.

After several days, Dick told Bella he knew that he was dying and it was time to put his affairs in order. Most importantly Bella promised him that she would keep his beloved 'Ring' as a going concern.

Dick was buried a few days later and the funeral could only be described as a testament to his popularity. For a man who had once served seven years imprisonment the list of mourners was impressive to say the least. It was a cross section of society, including the aristocracy, with the Marquess of Queensberry and the Duke of Manchester, Union leaders, Scotland Yard detectives, sportsmen and boxers, such as Dick's old friend and opponent, Jem Smith (who only survived Dick by a week), and many friends from show business such as Marie Lloyd. Some other 3,000 people crowded outside the church and joined the cortege with Dick's body on a gun carriage from Marylebone Church to Golders Green Crematorium. Also in a place of honour walking behind her master's coffin was Dick's Bull Terrier bitch, 'Bett'.

Dick Burge was contrary to what many people in those days thought an ex-professional boxer to be like. He had great natural charm and was able to mix at ease in the best of company, although never forgetting his roots. He was articulate, an immaculate dresser, and his aquiline features showed no real sign of his former occupation. Although a confirmed gambler all his life, he accepted his losses with the same good grace that he treated his wins. As I said at the beginning, there never was a dull moment with Dick Burge, and although he came from the humblest of beginnings he really was a 'Lord of the Ring'.

Charlie Mitchell: The Bad Boy of Boxing

by Graeme Kent

Charlie Mitchell was Britain's most successful fighter in the 1880s. He was a handsome, witty, charismatic man, related by marriage to some of the greatest stars of the British and American music halls. He was also an unscrupulous rogue, a hired bully, a fixer of crooked fights and horse-races and a convicted felon. Above all, he was incredibly brave.

He existed at the crossroads of boxing. When Charlie Mitchell started fighting, contests were held in fields with the bare fists. By the time of his retirement the Marquess of Queensberry rules were in effect and matches were held in halls before audiences of the great and the good. But while it lasted, in Mitchell's brief twilight world of the sport anything went. To survive in it a man had to be tough, resourceful and, where necessary, crooked. Mitchell stood up on all three counts.

He was born in Birmingham in 1861, the son of Irish parents. Later, when he had achieved notoriety, his publicity machine claimed that he had been both a medical student and a gymasium proprietor, but in reality the closest he came to either the healing arts or sports administration lay in helping to second various small-time fighters in unrecorded and illegal bouts.

When he was 16 or 17 he had his first fights, defeating two Birmingham men, Bob Cunningham and Charley Smithers. He displayed form, courage and an engaging, cheeky personality, so was encouraged to chance his arm in London. There he drew over ten rounds with Bill Kennedy with the small gloves and defeated Bailey Gray in a bare-knuckle bout. He was doing well but already doubts were being expressed about Mitchell's lack of size. He stood only 5 feet 9 inches tall and weighed under 11 stone.

To dispel the doubts of potential backers, Mitchell, never lacking in self-confidence, took a considerable chance. He allowed himself to be matched in Antwerp with a big Belgian fighter called Caradoff. Mitchell defeated the giant handily and was propelled on to the fringes of the big-time when he fought another up-and-coming youngster, Jack Burke, 'The Irish Lad'.

This bare-knuckle bout took place behind the grandstand at an Ascot race-meeting in 1881 for a purse of £100. It proved to be a scorcher, lasting over an hour. Mitchell appeared to be getting on top, when the police broke up the fight and arrested both protagonists. The doughty Birmingham youth was sentenced to six weeks' imprisonment, the first of a number of similar incarcerations.

Upon his release, Mitchell won a middleweight competition at Chelsea, but then really broke into the big-time when he won a heavyweight tournament in London. This was promoted by a shrewd American called Billy Madden, until recently the manager of the newly-crowned American heavyweight champion John L Sullivan. Madden had fallen out with his bombastic protégé and had journeyed to England to find a local challenger for the title.

Although he weighed less than 11 stone, Mitchell entered the tournament and won it handily. In the process he defeated the well-regarded and burly heavyweight Jack Knifton, known as 'the 81-tonner' for his size. Madden was dubious about the prospects of a lightweight like Mitchell in the USA, but something about the fighter's charisma and utter fearlessness attracted the American, and he signed Mitchell up.

Before crossing the Atlantic, Madden cashed in on the publicity engendered by his tournament and toured Britain with Mitchell in a series of bouts. These were billed as genuine contests, but there is little doubt that the results were all fixed in favour of Mitchell. Madden was not going to risk a possible contest with John L Sullivan by having Mitchell lose to an obscure English fighter at this stage. Mitchell, as always, was perfectly happy to go along with any chicanery, as long as he was paid for it.

Accordingly, the manager dusted off a few former fighters with the remnants of reputations and watched approvingly while Mitchell demonstrated his form, secure in the knowledge that he was not going to get hurt. Among others he defeated were Tug Wilson, who had gone the distance with Sullivan in the USA by falling down every time the champion had hit him, and Alf Greenwood, another English heavyweight who had lost to Sullivan. The English correspondent of the *Police Gazette* commented disapprovingly of this bout: "Both men sparred lightly".

Then Madden sailed for New York with Mitchell, declaring his fighter, with no foundation, to be the English champion. Madden had the press contacts and Mitchell had the mouth. The glib English fighter alternately charmed and amused the newspaper reporters to such an extent that he received acres of newspaper coverage. The *Police Gazette* described the Englishman as "young-looking, smooth-faced and compactly built, with muscles as hard as wood".

After Mitchell secured a convincing victory over Mike Cleary, described as the heavyweight champion of Pennsylvania, there was soon an irrational clamour for him to meet John L Sullivan. The champion, secure in the knowledge that he weighed over 14 stone and that Mitchell was around ten stone, five pounds, had no objection to an apparently easy night's work, and the bout was scheduled for Madison Square Garden on 14 May, 1883.

The two men were due to box four rounds, with gloves under the Marquess of Queensberry Rules. The *Milwaukee Evening Wisconsin* declared: "The immense structure was crowded to its utmost capacity, fully 25,000 persons being present to see the bout between the American and English champions".

To general surprise, Mitchell showed no sign of being overawed by his much bigger and more experienced opponent. Later he told his friend the writer, A.G. Hales: "I felt in my marrow I could whip him, and if I did it meant fistic fame and cartloads of dollars for me".

Sullivan bundled into the Englishman from the opening

bell but Mitchell boxed superbly on the retreat, keeping the champion on the end of his left jab. Towards the end of the round the challenger caused a sensation by crossing his right and knocking Sullivan down.

Sullivan came out for the second round more determined than ever. Gradually his superior weight began to tell. He floored Mitchell and on one occasion bundled his opponent through the ropes, causing the Englishman to hurt his back. In the third round the police intervened to stop the fight with Mitchell in a dazed condition.

It was a loss, but the way in which Mitchell had conducted himself brought him all sorts of plaudits. Madden set to work to persuade Sullivan to fight his man with bare-knuckles anywhere at any time, but the busy champion stalled. This suited Madden and Mitchell just fine. They set off on a lucrative tour of the USA, with the Englishman fighting in New York, Long Island, Colorado and Boston. Mitchell turned in some good victories, but already he was showing signs of involving himself in betting coups and dubious decisions, none of which left him out of pocket.

At Long Island he was awarded a four-round points decision over William Sheriff, only for the referee, without explanation, to change his decision to a draw. A return match with his old adversary Jack Burke was obviously fixed. The *Oregonian* called it "a fiasco", and went on: "A more disgusted crowd than that which left the Garden has rarely been seen in this or any other city".

To make matters worse, in a match with Dominick McCaffrey, which Mitchell was generally expected to win, the Englishman gave a most lacklustre display. *The Scranton Republican* described the closing moments of the bout and the actions of McCormick, the referee: "Everybody yelled and nothing could be understood. The referee tried to make himself undersood, but in vain. He stood at the ropes with the backers at his side, evidently trying to make him do something, whether it was to reverse his decision, call the match a draw, or order another round could only be surmised. At any rate, when McCormick could make himself heard he announced that McCaffrey had won the match and all the gate money".

Even an apparently creditable draw in Boston with the highly-regarded Jake Kilrain was regarded with suspicion by the public, one newspaper dismissing it as "an exhibition affair".

Certainly Mitchell was spending little time in training on his travels. He explained to the *Boston Herald*: "I don't believe in gymnasium work for a boxer. I don't think it is good for him. Walking is good enough for me".

Mitchell and Madden may have been making a lot of money for little effort, but they were also sailing close to the wind. In the midst of their wheeling and dealing they were saved from further scorn when John L Sullivan, simmering like a volcano, announced that he was prepared to fight the Englishman again.

The match was scheduled for Madison Square Garden on 30 June 1884. Another large crowd assembled for the bout and Mitchell entered the ring looking fit and confident. When Sullivan finally turned up it was another matter. The American was still in his street clothes and reeling drunk.

The *Milwaukee Evening Wisconsin* gave an account of the proceedings: "Sullivan, with his hair covering his forehead, and supported by the ropes and stakes, said in a thick voice: 'Gentlemen, I am too sick to spar. I have brought a doctor with me who will tell you I am sick'. He had evidently been drinking hard; his eyes were nearly closed. The immense audience left the structure in disgust".

It was a lifeline for the 23-year-old Mitchell. In two contests with the American champion he had floored Sullivan and frightened the bigger man off, or so Madden and his fighter claimed as they continued their triumphal money-making tour across the continent, incidentally refusing to refund the $2,000 they had been paid for the aborted Sullivan match.

When suitable exhibition partners could not be found Mitchell would spar with Madden. He explained to the *Police News* his reluctance to engage in genuine bare-fist contests: "What is the use of fighting with bare knuckles and running the risk of four or five years in the penitentiary when more money is to be made by sparring with gloves".

Mitchell was still adept at garnering self-publicity. On his tours across the USA he embarked upon a long-running newspaper feud with William Muldoon, trainer of John L Sullivan and a former world heavyweight wrestling champion. Mitchell pretended to be insulted by disparaging remarks made about him by the trainer. "I will give him ample opportunity to show his fighting and wrestling ability," he said to the *Police News* in December, 1885: "I class Muldoon on a par with old women, and feel satisfied I can throw him at any wrestling style, and am dead sure I can whip him".

Finally Mitchell returned to Great Britain. When he left the USA in July 1886 several newspapers described the success he had attained in such a short time. The *Milwaukee Evening Wisconsin* said: "Although he carries away with him $23,500, when he came to this country about three years ago he didn't have a cent". The *Police News* confirmed: "Charlie Mitchell confesses that he is in a position to retire upon his earnings at any time he may choose".

But now Mitchell had even greater plans in mind. The sight of the fat, drunken, out-of-condition Sullivan reeling around the ring in Madison Square Garden had convinced him that if he could keep out of the American's way, he would have a chance against him with bare-knuckles in a large ring.

Smarting from the criticism he had received for his uncouth display, in Madison Square Garden, Sullivan agreed to the match. He arrived in England with his usual entourage and went into training at Windsor. There was a slight hiatus when Mitchell was arrested at his Chertsey training quarters on suspicion of preparing for an illegal prize fight. Eventually he was released, but it was obvious that the proposed bout was too high-profile for England, so it was transferred to the Continent. On 8 March 1888 the *Milwaukee Evening Wisconsin* announced: "Charlie Mitchell, accompanied by Pony Moore, Barnitt, Holske and 14 others, left London at 11 o'clock this morning for France, where, it is supposed, the fight between Mitchell and Sullivan will take place. Mitchell said before leaving that he did not know whether he would win, but he was quite sure he would be able to show that Sullivan was not the fistic wonder that Americans thought".

The bare-knuckle bout took place in the pouring rain near Chantilly, France on 10 March 1888, on the estate of Baron Rothschild. A 24-foot ring on turf was used and the London Prize Ring Rules were in operation.

Despite the awful conditions Mitchell fought the bout of his life, displaying courage, initiative and considerable fitness. He outpaced the big American who plodded around the ring, throwing ponderous right hands. The rain did not abate and the cold wind continued to scream across the field.

Mitchell was caught and floored on a number of occasions, but each time rose jauntily to his feet and trotted confidently back to his corner, waiting for his older opponent to blow up. Throughout he taunted the unhappy Sullivan, who was soon gasping for breath, his teeth chattering with cold.

The bout lasted for 39 rounds, occupying three hours and ten minutes, before both fighters and their handlers agreed to call it a draw as night began to fall. The *Boston Herald* agreed that it seemed a fair verdict: "Sullivan was cold and much weakened by the driving rain. Mitchell was strong at the finish, but his hands were bad".

As if on cue, a party of mounted gendarmes arrived and arrested both contestants. They were held overnight in a grim prison at Senlis. Mitchell described his incarceration with a shudder: "The floors were wet, and the walls slimy, with slugs crawling about". Both fighters were granted bail, forfeited their bonds and departed hastily for the shores of England.

If Mitchell had been popular before, after his contest with Sullivan he was positively idolised. For the rest of his life he resented any intimations that he had spent the Sullivan bout on the retreat. He wrote fiercely to the newspapers: "This is entirely false. I went up and fought him from the start".

True to form, Mitchell looked for the quickest way to profit from his situation. The scam he decided upon was an odd one, even for him. He contacted the famous old bare-knuckle prizefighter, Jem Mace, and suggested that they fight for the British championship. The wily Mitchell had overreached himself here, because Mace was 58 years old! Few took the proposed bout seriously. Nevertheless, the old warhorse accepted Mitchell's challenge and in a very dubious Glasgow contest lost in three rounds. Both men then increased their bank balances by promptly going on a gentle exhibition tour together.

However, the big money lay in the USA and Mitchell was soon on his way back there. He set to work with a will to establish his fortune, appearing in a 'body beautiful' muscle-flexing act, touring with a minstrel show and boxing exhibitions with his former opponent, Jake Kilrain. If he thought he could get away with it Mitchell billed these exhibitions as genuine contests, but he was fooling nobody.

During one of their so-called bouts someone in the discontented audience threw a rotten egg, hitting Mitchell on the forehead and causing the *Ashland Daily News* to comment caustically: "Of course Mitchell and Kilrain are swindling the public. Their exhibitions are disgusting, and are making honest sporting men who like sparring matches sick of boxing".

The two men did take time out for one serious bout, when Kilrain challenged John L Sullivan with the bare-knuckles in New Orleans in 1889. Mitchell acted as his friend's second in Kilrain's gallant 75-round losing battle, the last bare-knuckle bout for the heavyweight title.

Even on this occasion Mitchell managed to upset people around him. The former frontier marshal, Bat Masterson, had been hired as bodyguard for Kilrain and Mitchell. At a hotel celebration after the fight, while Kilrain was recovering in his room, an incensed young man threatened to kill Mitchell for putting on airs. Bloodshed was narrowly averted.

As a result of their participation in the Sullivan-Kilrain bout, Mitchell and another second Mike Donovan had to elude the law rapidly. The *Ashland Daily News* reported from New York: "Charlie Mitchell, with Mike Donovan, has skipped to Canada. Rather than risk himself in the city where he has few friends among the sporting circles who would help him at a pinch, he decided to cross over into Her Majesty's dominions".

There were more problems on this US tour. In the end, on 23 July, Mitchell sailed back to England. Before he left the USA he told a number of newspaper reporters seeing him off: "I'm glad to get out of this blasted country and you can bet I'll never return!"

By this time Billy Madden had departed by the scene. Mitchell was now being managed by his American father-in-law, George Washington 'Pony' Moore, a former minstrel who was now a show-business impresario. Back in England Moore installed Mitchell as the manager of the Washington Music Hall in Battersea.

His new status did not keep the fighter out of trouble. Always quarrelsome and often drunk he began to appear ever more frequently in the docks of law courts. On several occasions he was fined £5 for assault and in 1892 he was sentenced to two months' hard labour for knocking down a man who had intervened in a dispute between Mitchell and two drunken prostitutes. Even in Pentonville Mitchell could not keep out of trouble. He struck a warder who had discovered contraband beef, bread and butter smuggled into Mitchell's cell.

When he was free the fighter also had a profitable sideline in recovering debts from recalcitrant payers, taking 50% of all sums thus recovered. On one occasion he was commissioned to retrieve £50 from an absconding punter on behalf of a Brighton bookmaker. After a suitable interval the worried bookmaker asked Mitchell how he had fared in his mission. "I got my half", explained Mitchell sympathetically, "but I couldn't get yours!"

But Mitchell's disputes had been mere desultory affairs before he linked up with the notorious 'Squire' George Abingdon Baird. Baird was a wealthy drunken reprobate with an affinity with prizefighters. He kept a stable of them on his payroll, including Jem Mace, Mitchell's former opponent. It was the Squire's habit to get roaring drunk and then swagger along Piccadilly or one of London's other popular thoroughfares, picking fights with passers-by. If one of the strangers responded to the challenge, Baird would summon up one of his prizefighters to deal with the unfortunate man.

It was a dissolute way of life which suited Charlie Mitchell admirably. He soon became Baird's senior bodyguard and a close friend of the racehorse owner. He also began to serve quite regular short prison terms for finishing fights that his mischievous patron had started. Mitchell was well paid for his pains and took his resulting brief absences from society almost as a matter of course. When Baird was in his cups he would sometimes take a swing at his bodyguard. When he sobered up he was suitably contrite and generous. Mitchell took such attacks philosophically, reckoning that he was getting paid for them at the rate of almost £20 a punch.

He continued to lose money regularly on those horse races and prizefights he could not fix. In March 1892, Bob Fitzsimmons knocked out Peter Maher in 12 rounds in New Orleans. Mitchell had backed the Irishman heavily to win and was disgusted by Maher's performance. "Maher, I think", he told reporters, "is a terrible cur, quitting before he should have done so. I consider him a disgrace to Ireland".

In an effort to refill their coffers, it was with great hilarity and amid much carousing that Baird took a party, including Mitchell and his father-in-law Pony Moore, to New Orleans in 1893. The object of their journey was to attend the Jem Hall-Bob Fitzsimmons bout. Hall, an Australian, was another protégé of Baird, who had spent a great deal of money on developing the fighter. So much did Hall owe the Squire that Baird was even able to secure the post of second to the Australian when the fight started. The Cornish-born Fitzsimmons was much too good for Hall and knocked him out in a few rounds.

To drown their sorrows and in an attempt to forget the amount of money they had lost in bets on the Australian, Baird, Mitchell and the others went on a monumental drunken spree. In the course of this bender the Squire developed pneumonia, from which he died, far from home, in a short time.

It was a hammer blow for Mitchell. Not only had he lost a meal-ticket in Baird, but in his cups the Squire had often assured the boxer that Mitchell would inherit most of his fortune when his patron died. When the will was read the chagrined fighter was left precisely nothing.

Mitchell had to so something quickly. He had earned a great deal of money but most of it had gone in high living and injudicious gambling. The only way he could make real money quickly was to return to the ring.

By this time James J Corbett, the elegant and skilful former bank-clerk, had defeated John L Sullivan with the gloves for the world heavyweight championship. Although he had been out of the ring for several years and was now in his early 30s, Mitchell at once challenged Corbett. When the champion ignored him Mitchell set out to make the American's life a misery. He conducted a press campaign on both sides of the Atlantic, accusing Corbett of cowardice. He then set out to stalk the champion, turning up at hotels and the foyers of theatres, haranguing Corbett and challenging him to fight.

It was the sort of torment at which Mitchell excelled. He was aided and abetted with enthusiasm by a new friend, Frank 'Pat' Slavin, 'The Sydney Cornstalk', an Australian heavyweight with whom Mitchell had toured the English music halls.

The bout was finally scheduled for the Duval Athletic Club, Jacksonville in Florida on 25 January 1894. The two contestants boxed for a purse of $20,000 and $5,000 a side. The actual fight was an anti-climax. A furious Corbett set about the Englishman from the first bell and administered a sound thrashing to his opponent. Throughout the contest Mitchell continued to mutter insults and obscenities at his opponent through shattered teeth and bloodied lips. Corbett did not let up for a moment. In the third round he battered his game adversary to the canvas. Mitchell did not get up.

Afterwards he made one of the ring's classic utterances. When someone asked Mitchell what happened to his plan to get Corbett mad, the fighter said wryly: "I did, but I got him too mad".

It was Mitchell's last fight. He retired to a life as a prosperous Brighton bookmaker. Until the end of his days he remained in demand as a second at major boxing matches, recruited for his experience and ringwise expertise. In 1915 he was hired as a cornerman for the American, Frank Moran, in his contest with the gifted but temperamental Bombardier Billy Wells. Before the bout started, with both men in the ring, there was an interval for a bulldog to be raffled off in aid of war charities. Always alert, Mitchell utilised the time to direct a flow of vituperation at the nervous English heavyweight. "Look at him!" sneered Mitchell, indicating the quivering Wells. "He wants his mama, doesn't he? Come on now, get the bull pup sold and send for an undertaker and a coffin!" It was enough to undermine the confidence of the fragile Wells. When the bout finally started Moran knocked the home fighter out in ten rounds.

For a time Mitchell guided the fighting affairs of his middleweight son, Charlie junior. When the boy was killed in World War 1, Mitchell was left shattered and died soon afterwards, in 1918.

Graeme Kent has written a number of books on the history of boxing, including *The Great White Hopes*, which was short-listed for the 2005 William Hill Sports Book of the Year competition.

Will Jackson's 'Stockton and Thornaby Physical Culture and Boxing Club'

by K R Robinson

There was no tradition of boxing in the Jackson family – Will Jackson worked in the shipyards as a joiner, his father a left-handed riveter.

Will travelled around the North East in the 1920s and '30s in search of work, but at heart he was a Teeside man. He and his family were forced to settle at 29, Britannia Street, Thornaby on Tees – in an area then known as 'below the steps' or 'below the railway' – after Will was involved in a workplace accident. While working on a ship-side scaffold the structure collapsed. Two workmates died but Will survived, albeit with a fractured skull. Considered unemployable, Will accepted a compensation settlement, which was invested in a small corner shop. In the economic climate of the times this enterprise soon failed under the burden of 'tick' extended to neighbours.

An industrious man with a large family to support – wife Annie and sons Jim (born 1910), George (1911), Billy (1912), Les (1916), Doug (1919) and Des (1925) – Will set about augmenting his benefits. Local industrialist Mr Wrightson of Head Wrightson – a major Thornaby employer – was a personal friend of Will who gave him access to a large allotment, close to the river, for a nominal rental. Pigs and chickens were soon in place and cultivation underway. Annie began regular trips to Stockton market to sell produce until a local busybody informed on them and their benefits were stopped.

Will's trade background and the nearness of the river allowed him to operate a nice little business converting old lifeboats into cabin cruisers. He also began to cast propellers from scrap bronze from the shipyards. Once, when walking home carrying a couple of buckets of moulding sand, he was apprehended by a local bobby and invited to accompany him to the police station. Will set off station bound after advising the policeman to bring the evidence! Shortly after the allotment site was subject to a police raid – all whistles and push bikes – but, forewarned, the scrap and castings had been sunk in the river. Unfortunately the marker buoy broke loose and all was lost.

'Below the railway' was a pretty tough place to live particularly for the Jacksons, who were English Protestants in a largely Irish Catholic area. Billy recalled that they ran the gauntlet every morning to get to school – their respective denominational schools at opposite ends of the borough. In a flash of Les Dawson-like humour Billy said that they were never late for school because you could take a brick out of the wall and see the church clock!

Will stoked up tensions when local MP, Conservative Mr Harold McMillan, dutifully visited at election time with his wife Dorothy. The Labour party supporting Irish majority covered Mac's Bentley with spittle. The staunch Socialist Jacksons hung a Union flag from an upstairs window and cheered vigorously!

The Jacksons were a tight-knit family and every member had to pull their weight. George, known to all as 'Plum', went to sea at the age of 12 as a cabin boy working in the Caribbean/Panama canal area. He sent home his wages in US dollars and Les remembered going to the bank with Annie often returning with one of those big white fivers. This came to an end when the Americans, who held sway in the area, began to insist that sailors on their vessels take out US citizenship.

Les, who called these 'the feast and famine years', sometimes joined the needy outside the dock gates to beg left-over food from the workers. Though many there took their haul home to feed their families, Les' was used to feed the pigs.

Many years later Billy's pal Walter proudly displayed his lobe-less ear to Billy's sons – a relic of Bill's short-lived career as a barber!

When the time come to leave school and go to work Billy signed for a six-year apprenticeship as a shipwright with Richardson Ducks, shipbuilders, on a starting wage of 6/- (30p) a week. The company soon folded and he was sent to work out his indentures with other companies, including three years with Craig Taylor & Co of Thornaby and two years with the Furness Shipbuilding Company in Co Durham. Towards the end of his apprenticeship Billy began to box as a professional – without the benefit of amateur experience. His first recorded bout was in 1931. Billy was then 19-years old, though its pretty certain that he had started fighting earlier at small venues where the bouts attracted little other than local attention and went unreported.

Les was four years younger than Billy. After a few dead-end jobs he was apprenticed to train as a painter and decorator, but he objected to having to drag a barrow load of materials three or four miles a day and quit leaving his mother to placate his irate 'master'. Les had already began to fight for cash and decided that he'd be better off as a full-time pro-aged 14 and weighing 6st 4lb!

Will set up a ring on the allotment for the boys to train. Previously they'd sparred in the front room. Billy said that

Will Jackson's Gym, Parliament Street, Stockton on Tees

he'd knocked out one of his brothers with an uppercut and held him up until he came to so that Annie didn't notice and give him a tousing!

The allotment ring attracted a crowd of locals some of whom fancied their chances and joined in. Will acted as manager and Plum as trainer. With a growing membership Will needed larger facilities so moved over the river to Stockton where he set up a gym above stables in Parliament Street. Photographs show a remarkably well-equipped establishment with punch bags, speed-balls and rowing machines. The walls were papered with boxing posters featuring northern heroes – Mickey McGuire, Benny Sharkey, Jack Casey, etc. Will rather grandly called his new enterprise the 'Stockton and Thornaby Physical Culture and Boxing Club.' Members included both boxers and wrestlers.

On 26 September 1931 Billy scored a two-round stoppage over Londonderry's Joe Quinn at Watson's Arena, Glasgow. Billy was probably working in Scotland at this time – he remembered appearing on the same bill as a young Benny Lynch – but this is the only Scottish bout to have yet come to light.

After finishing his apprenticeship Billy was, like many others on Teeside, unemployed, but he kept busy appearing on Stockton bills. An early stumbling block was Young Simbo of Thornaby, who gained two points verdicts over him. Simbo came under Will's management and was a busy, and winning, performer.

A hand-out survives that Will sent to matchmakers

Billy Jackson aged 19, 5'0", 7st-10lb

and promoters as a boost to Billy's career. He is described as being five feet tall and weighing 7st 10lb, his record is given as 28 wins from 30 contests, with a fair sprinkling of stoppages. His opponents including Kid Hall, Ted Carter and Jim Docherty of Middlesbrough, Alf Hughes, Mickey Rooney and Alex Matherson of Hartlepool and Jack Lindsey of Stockton. The sheet ends with an eight-round draw with Paddy Ross of Bishop Auckland at West Hartlepool on 21 January 1933. This was the first record of many occasions when the brothers appeared on the same bill – Les drawing over six rounds with hometown boy Mushy Regan.

The compilation of Billy's fighting record is greatly hampered by the presence of many other boxers of the same name in the North East during this period. His early billing was usually as 'Young' Jackson, only later becoming Billy Jackson. Being billed as coming from Thornaby or Stockton is understandable, but other billings such as South or North Shields or Newcastle were almost certainly him as well.

Along with Billy and Les, Young Simbo and Tommy Burns of Stockton were the most active of Will's stable. Burns was obviously a class fighter, scoring wins over George Smith, Al Capone (twice), Roy King, George Marsden and Kid Tanner during his career, which seems to have lasted through to 1946.

Jake Johnson, Jackie Green, P.Dodds and Arthur Simpson (not Simbo) were also Will's boys. Despite the lack of promotions in Thornaby there were many fighters who were billed from the borough, including Jack McCleave, Jim McCleary, Jackie and Jim Sullivan, Curley Donn, Jack Bright, Jack Jones, Jimmy Casey and Young Roberts. The two most highly-rated Thornaby men were flyweight Ike Pratt and featherweight Harold Kid Lewis, and though neither were managed by Will both were friendly with the brothers, particularly Les, who often appeared in a supporting role to them at shows.

Billy's name began to be mentioned in ringside reports such as that for a promotion 18 November 1932 at South Shields: "Billy Jackson (South Shields) proved too fast and clever for Young Meecham (Gateshead), the latter surrendering in the fifth". Again, from another South Shields promotion on 3 December: "Billy Jackson (South Shields) and Kid Carter (Newcastle) furnished a clever display. Jackson did well at the start, but the Newcastle boy gradually wore him down, and putting in an extra strong burst at the 'death', Carter gained a points verdict". On 17 February 1933, billed from Jarrow, he appeared at Shiremoor against North Shields' Young Pearson. The newspaper reported: The verdict did not meet with unanimous approval, but Jackson's cleaner hitting and forcing probably influenced the ref".

Billy was on home ground at the Albert Hall, Stockton on 13 March to meet Tommy Knight of Darlington on a bill headed by Peal Bell, who won on a referee's intervention in 12 rounds over Sonny Dokes. "The best bout was an eight rounder between Tommy Knight and Billy Jackson which resulted in a draw. In the fourth round Jackson sent his man down for a count of eight with a right hook to the jaw. Knight made a spirited recovery however".

On 26 March he visited Leeds where he appeared against hometown boy Alan Walls. "Billy Jackson (Thornaby) and Alan Walls gave a capital display over eight rounds,

Jackson gaining a popular win after a clever exhibition. Both boys fought cleanly and intelligently but Jackson was just too good".

Billy then suffered an inside the distance loss against Nipper Nugent of Carlisle at Stockton on 10 May, caused by a cut eye.

The major boxing venue in the North East, and the only one in Newcastle, was the New St James's Hall. Opened in May 1930 the hall was purpose built and had seating for 4,000 and standing room for a further thousand. At least two shows a week were held there, often consisting of ten or 12 four-rounders designed to discover talented newcomers. Popular locals Peter Miller, Billy Charlton, Mickey Steele, Mickey Doyle and Leftie McKie all boxed on these four-round bills and moved on to fight on the more prestigious promotions. Meanwhile, Billy Jackson of Thornaby fought three ten-rounders at the hall over ten days of June 1933.

His first opponent was Willie Sharkey. Billed as the Yiddisher flyweight champion, Willie was a very experienced and hard-punching fighter who had mixed in good company. The *North Mail and Newcastle Chronicle* reported the bout: "In the first round a right swing to the jaw made Jackson drop to his hands on the floor. Jackson scored more frequently with straight leads, while Sharkey was good at close-quarters, and the latter came with his best in the fourth and fifth. Sharkey eased down inexplicably in the sixth and allowed Jackson to take the round easily, while the latter showed greater coolness to show up best later". Willie's younger brother, Benny, the pride of Tyneside, topped the bill defeating Winlaton's Billy Farrell on a fifth-round retirement.

Billy Jackson's performance must have impressed as he returned to top the bill three days later against Gateshead's Peter Miller. Miller's record didn't look too impressive but he was strong and resilient and demanded respect. The *North Mail* reported: "Both weighed just under 8st. Miller was first into the picture with some clever two-handed work, and it was the fourth round before Jackson got into his usual stride. From then on the contest was very even, the boys' efforts bringing applause from all parts of the house. Towards the end Jackson improved, but it was too late and he failed to gain on the margin of points earned in the early part of the contest and the verdict went to Miller".

Invited to top the bill again against Miller, Billy evidently wanted to draw breath as the *North Mail's* humorous columnist, Stroller, noted: "After losing on points to Peter Miller, Billy Jackson consented to box a return if allowed a week to recover his strength and the two meet in Newcastle to-night. Jackson evidently does not think that seven days make one weak! *Boxing* managed a short report on the bout: "Both men boxed in hurricane fashion and although Miller had the best of the early rounds, Jackson pulled up to earn a share of the verdict".

Billed from Newcastle, Billy turned up next at South Shields on 5 July against Newcastle's Jimmy Carr. *Boxing* reported Billy's good form: "Carr was soon in difficulties and sustained a cut to his mouth in the second round. A left floored Carr for nine in the fourth. This was followed by a right to the chin, and this time the game Carr stayed down".

There were a number of good-class Scots active in the North East, chief of them being Bobby McGee – a world class flyweight – Billy McGannon, Tommy Steele and Charlie Smirke were also among their number. Billy was matched against Smirke over 12 rounds at Darlington on 11 August. Charlie was from the famous Glasgow horse racing family and indeed had been a jockey himself before taking to the ring. They fought a draw.

Billy was back at St James's Hall on 14 August pitted against Kid Davies of Rotherham winning over ten rounds.

A return with Charlie Smirke, again over 12 rounds, took place at Norton on Tees on 10 September. On this occasion Billy fought well, running out a deserved points winner mainly through an enterprising use of his left hand. Les appeared on the bill, losing on points over six rounds to Johnny Kilburn of North Shields.

A third bout with Peter Miller was next on the agenda for Billy on 14 September. Miller had suffered somewhat mixed fortunes since their last meeting – losing on points to Ike Pratt and Charlie Smirke, beating Charlie on a sixth-round cut-eye retirement before beating him again on points and losing on a disqualification against Kid Rich. The *North Mail* reported: "Peter Miller beat Billy Jackson on points in the chief ten round contest at the New St James's Hall last night. It was a hard-fought contest throughout. Miller used a good left hand but Jackson came into the limelight from the sixth round and caught Miller with several good right-handed blows. Miller's footwork in the later rounds enabled him to evade several rushes by Jackson".

Billy was back at St James's Hall on 27 October when forcing Mickey Steele of Gateshead to retire in five rounds.

******

Boxing in the North East was in a state of confusion. Though formed in 1929, the British Boxing Board of Control's authority was not accepted throughout the sport. The Northern Area was administrated from Manchester, which, with champions Jackie Brown, Johnny King and Jock McAvoy, was the north's most influential centre of activity. This was argued to be the result of economic depression – the shipbuilding and heavy engineering industry of the Tyne and Tees had suffered to a far greater extent than the cotton textile trade in Lancashire.

The Board's organisation of the sport – then as now – was based on the issue of licenses to all participants – boxers, managers, promoters, etc – and for individual venues, and to prohibit license holders from associating with non-license holders or performing or promoting at non-licensed venues. As licensing spread there was a natural restriction of opportunity at the lower end of the sporting scale as many of the smaller venues were unlicensed.

A Sunday afternoon meeting was held at St James's Hall on 6 August 1933 to discuss the situation. A 100 boxers and others attended and after some lively argument, particularly about the low level of purses, proposals to appoint three Board stewards to lay complaints before the Northern Area Council at Manchester and to form a Newcastle branch were approved by those assembled.

The question of purses was pressing. It was alleged that some men had boxed ten rounds for as little as 25/- (£1.25p).

Preliminary boys boxing six rounders were guaranteed a guinea (£1.05p) under Board rules, though it was argued that this rule was often breached. No such guarantees applied to four rounders and in some instances as little as 6/- (30p) was paid.

Norman Hurst, boxing reporter for the *Sunday Graphic* and a regular contributor to the *North Mail,* published examples of low pay over the following weeks, including a letter from a boxer which clearly pointed to the St James's Hall as a culprit. Hurst also reported that there were too few boxers other than the champions who could be expected to fill a hall and most promoters, including Mr J J Paget of the New St James's Hall, were hard put to make a regular profit.

Hurst often returned to the subject of the poor standard of the current crop of boxers. Only Jackie Brown, Nel Tarleton, Jock McAvoy and Jack Petersen, in his opinion, measured up to the champions of 30 years before. The reason he believed was the prevalence of two-minute rounds. Small-time promoters, he argued, advertised 12-round contests never saying they were two-minute rounds. Young and gullible boxers came to think that they were top of the bill stars when really they couldn't twinkle in third-rate company! A boy builds up a local reputation and when given an opportunity to top a bill of importance over three-minute rounds he falls to pieces after a few rounds. He is disillusioned, disheartened and he becomes just another fighter.

The problem of two-minute rounds had existed since the beginning of boxing under the Queensberry rules. A championship could never be claimed on the strength of a victory gained over two-minutes rounds. No two-minute round matches were recognised in a boxer's record by the Board of Control, when considering his claim to be a championship contender. Hurst asked that the Board dictate that only three-minute round contests be allowed on licensed shows. 'By doing so we shall get a sturdier, hardier breed of fighters and a higher standard of boxers.'

******

Billy's final bout of 1933 was a ten-round decision over Bob Smart of Sheffield at The Stadium, Midland Street, Barnsley, on 26 November.

A copy of the BBB of C 'Articles of Agreement ' between Will and the promoter Robert Nelson shows that Billy and Les were contracted to box ten and eight two-minute rounds, respectively, against selected opponents with six-ounce gloves for the sum of £4, 'both boys all in'.

Billy's first bout of 1934 was on New Year's Day at St James's Hall when he came in as a substitute for Joe Darby of Melton. It was a decision he must have regretted. His opponent was Tommy Burns of Newcastle – not to be confused with Burns of Stockton. The *North Mail* reported: "Tommy Burns proved too strong and forceful for Billy Jackson in the chief contest of ten rounds. Jackson was plucky to a degree, but he had to take severe punishment before the referee stopped the contest in the fifth round after the Teesider had been floored for a long count".

This is the only bout recorded in which Billy took a

beating. Maybe he came in at too short notice and had been out of training over the Christmas holiday. However, he was back in the ring at Redcar on 26 January to face Billy Angel of West Hartlepool, who was knocked out in three rounds. Les outpointed Spider Allen of Hartlepool over eight on the undercard.

On 18 February Billy fought a ten-round draw with Ginger Lawson of Newcastle at Middlesbrough. This is the last bout found for Billy Jackson in 1934.

Talking to Billy many years later he admitted that he had made a name change during this period. He was on the dole at the time and in one bout he found that the referee was a clerk from his local unemployment office. Consequently he lost his dole. This might explain why he seems to have been billed from so many different places – Les was only ever once billed from anywhere other than Thornaby. Billy adopted the name of Cowley. There were fewer Cowleys than Jacksons active at the time and only one Billy from Thurnscoe, South Yorkshire.

The only bout to come to light for Billy Cowley, billed from Gateshead, was against Bill Johnson of Liverpool at Leeds on 4 March 1934. The *North Mail* reported: "Billy Cowley was outpointed over ten rounds by Bill Johnson. It was a spirited affair in which both men used double-handed blows to head and body to useful purpose. Cowley

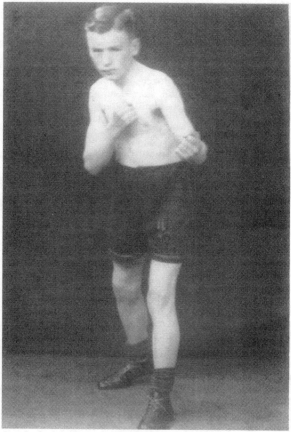

Les Jackson, 14 years old, 6st-4lb

fought well against an elusive opponent, who showed better ringcraft and sounder defensive tactics. Johnson led well with his left which he also used to excellent purpose in defence, while his right crosses were quick and forceful".

The comical Stroller blew Billy's cover in the *North Mail* on 20 April: "Billy Cowley, Thornaby, who opposes Wally Knightly, Sunderland, at the Royal Stadium, Sunderland, tomorrow evening, will be better identified as Billy Jackson; but despite the change of name, his desire to lick Knightly remains the same. What's in an aim?". Peter Miller took Billy's place and won on a four-round retirement.

Billy's name – as Jackson or Cowley – disappeared from the papers for 12 months. He told me that he'd once fought three 15-rounders in a week for 50/- (£2.50) a time. Fifteen rounders were not commonly fought by boys of Billy's standard and were usually reserved for those of contender status. It could be that he was fighting on non-licensed shows, or it might be that he was held to account by the Board for his name change and perhaps suspended.

******

The flyweight division during the 1930s was a hot bed of activity. So intense was the competition and so good the talent that a loss against good opposition could be expunged the following week by a good win. To the eye of a modern ring historian the records of some top-class flyweights appear decidedly spotty. In truth, the British top ten were world class and anyone on his day was a potential champion. Contemporary boxing writers often bemoaned the lack of talent, but viewed in hindsight this period was the interregnum between two of boxing's greatest flyweights – Jimmy Wilde and Benny Lynch. At any other time the British top ten of the '30s would rate as outstanding ring men – near greats.

An idea of the depth of talent is exampled by the proposal in October 1934 that the four leading British flyweights – Benny Lynch, Tommy Pardoe, Mickey Maguire and Bobby McGee – be matched in eliminators to find a challenger to world champion Jackie Brown. McGuire and McGee were matched – to find a challenger for the Northern area champion, Phil Milligan!

A local boxing writer gave his top 18 flyweights in the North East as: (1) Mickey McGuire, (2) Bobby McGee, (3) Teddy Rollins, (4) Johnny Page, (5) Joe Doyle, (6) Ike Pratt, (7) Peter Miller, (8) Willie Sharkey, (9) Tommy Varle, (10) Young Terry, (11) George Smith, (12) Bob Airey, (13) Roy King, (14) Pat Murphy, (15) Johnny O'Donnelly, (16) Ginger Lawson, (17) Lefty McKie, (18) Charlie Ryan. He continued: "Johnny Jones, Les Jackson, Kid Rich and Foster Brown are also worthy of mention. Were I asked whom, because of their precocity, are likely to turn out the best of the bunch I should say George Smith, Les Jackson and Ike Pratt, whose ages are respectively 16, 17 and 19. All three are correct punchers, each can take it, and each uses his grey matter". This listing must date from around early 1934 after Billy's defeat by Tommy Burns, otherwise he would certainly have been rated. Burns' absence might suggest that he was a bantamweight

Though Les began his professional career in 1930, early results are few and far between. His first recorded bout was a six-round points win over Young Hepp of Thornaby at Stockton on 24 August 1931. His second was another six-round decision over Sonny O'Brien, also of Thornaby, again at Stockton on 15 July 1932.

Another bout was more fully reported, having taken place on 2 December 1932 at The Ring, Hartlepool: "Young Jackson (Thornaby) defeated Alec Mathieson (Hartlepool) on points in a rousing six-round contest. Mathieson took a count of seven in the fourth round and was saved by the gong at the end of the round".

Stockton was Les' 'home' arena, the pity is that few promotions were reported. A hand bill from 2 February 1933 advertises two six rounders, two four rounders and a five rounder, which featured a 'Great Return Contest' for a £2 side stake between Young Jackson of Thornaby vs Muldowney of Norton. It was stated that Jackson would fight any 6st 4lb boy in the North. Admission charges were – Ringside 9d, Arena 4d and Standing 2d. The promoter's motto printed at the bottom of the bill was 'NO FIGHT NO PAY'.

Another rare ringside report of Les in action appeared on 27 November 1933 following his appearance at Barnsley, when Billy beat Bob Smart on the same bill: "In a six rounder, Tony Hardcastle (Barnsley) and Les Jackson (Thornaby) provided bright entertainment. Both boys showed skill and were not adverse to a hefty punch. Jackson was rather stronger at close quarters, but Hardcastle levelled matters by his harder hitting and better ringcraft. A draw being a fitting result".

Will always tried hard to get two or three of his boys on a single bill. On 9 March 1934 at The Ring, West Hartlepool, in support of Kid Rocks of Hartlepool against George Hall of Swalwell, Young Simbo outpointed Young Conn, Les outpointed Kid Pearce and Tommy Burns outpointed Young Louis, all over six rounds. Will carried a pocket full of coppers and at the slightest opportunity threw a few pence into the ring to encourage other patrons to contribute 'nobbins' at the end of a good contest.

As a 14-year-old professional Les was not that unusual, indeed he was one of a clutch of talented youngsters, all scaling around the seven-stone mark, who from 1933 onwards were matched and re-matched. Les fought Johnny Kilburn of North Shields, Pat Murphy of Jarrow and Johnny Jones of Consett on 12 occasions so far recorded. His win, loss, draw record against these boys was a creditable – Kilburn 1-2-1, Murphy 1-2-3 and Jones 1-0-1. Another regular opponent was Spider Allen of West Hartlepool, against whom he had a 4-0-1 tally.

On 8 June 1934 Les came in as a substitute, for Willie Sharkey, and made his first appearance at the New St James's Hall when facing Pat Murphy and losing on points over ten rounds. A newspaper item published after this victory, which was mainly concerned with the young George Smith being overworked, concluded: "Another youth to whom this advice is applicable is Les Jackson, the 17-year-old Thornaby fighter. A great kid, this, as Pat Murphy, Jarrow, will concede. Murphy twice outpointed Jackson, but only after a dour struggle each time".

Johnny Jones, described as 'the Consett boy with the old

English style of fighting', gained a ten-round decision over Murphy at the Hall on 22 June, which led to him and Les being matched over ten rounds on 6 July, with Les taking the decision. A return on the 16th resulted in a ten-round draw.

Les' bouts with Murphy and Jones did his reputation a power of good and after scoring a six-round decision over Curly Donn at Middlesbrough on 12 August, he was again matched with Pat Murphy over ten at the NSC, Middlesbrough on 9 September. The comical Stroller commented: "Pat Murphy, Jarrow, hopes to demonstrate his superiority over Les Jackson, Thornaby. More Murphy and Les Jackson!". The result was a draw.

Les returned to St James's Hall on 21 September to meet Johnny Jones over ten. Jones withdrew for whatever reason and Ginger Lawson was substituted. Les suffered the only knockout of his career in one round. He greatly resented this defeat, always maintaining that he was set up, explaining that he had broken a contract – perhaps by accepting the bout with Murphy at Middlesbrough – and the Lawson bout was arranged as his punishment. Lawson was older, bigger, heavier and a rough handful. Ginger was a regular performer throughout the North East. He was always dangerous, which he proved when in February 1935 he scored a two-round knockout over Johnny Kilburn. As said, Ginger had drawn with Billy and later won over Bobby Magee, though Pat Murphy beat him inside the distance.

Amazingly, two days after the Lawson defeat Les again fought Murphy at Middlesbrough, having to settle for another draw over ten rounds. Will's judgement in allowing this bout to go ahead must be questioned. However, this was not an unusual occurrence at that time. On 9 September at Middlesbrough, Ike McGowan was knocked out in three rounds by Les Powell. Later in the evening, Ike returned to the ring and kayoed Kid Leary in three. Stroller previewed the Murphy bout in a more sober than usual manner: "Les Jackson, the smart Thornaby scrapper, will endeavour to teach a few pugilistic tricks to Pat Murphy, Jarrow".

After six week's rest Les scored the only inside-the-distance win of his career, beating Mickey Joyce of Jarrow on a cut eye in three rounds at West Hartlepool on Guy Fawkes Night. On 22 December, Les again faced Pat Murphy at Sunderland and gained the verdict over ten.

New Year's Day 1935 saw Les gaining an eight-round verdict over Spider Allen at Redcar. Three days later he was back at St James's Hall to draw over ten with Pat Murphy, while Les faced Joe Mount of Glasgow over ten rounds at Darlington on 25 February. Stroller's preview showed that he kept his ear to the ground: "The diminutive Thornaby boxer, Les Jackson, who meets Jim Mount, Glasgow, has given up the idea of becoming a jockey. But he can have a mount on Monday! Les won the verdict in a competitive bout. The winner did most of the attacking but Mount fought pluckily and got in some good blows.'

Les was advertised as fighting Tommy Knight on 22 March, but his next bout was against old foe Johnny Kilburn at West Hartlepool, losing on points over ten on the 25th.

The Stockton and Thornaby Physical Culture and Boxing Club, circa 1933
back row: Plum Jackson, (not known), Jake Johnson, (not known), Jackie Green, P.Dodds, Arthur Simpson
front row: (not known), Les Jackson, Will Jackson, Doug Jackson, Billy Jackson, (not known)

Ringside reports show Les as a good boxer who was not afraid to work in close, indeed it seems against other 'boxers' he choose to out work them inside. We should remember the old adage – fight a boxer, box a fighter – he used his grey matter. Not a hard puncher – with but one inside-the-distance win by cuts over Mickey Joyce – he was an accurate puncher who demanded respect.

The small town of Knaresborough near Harrogate ran regular weekly boxing promotions. Young Simbo seems to have been a popular performer there, appearing on five occasions in 1934 with four wins. A local sportsman, Lieut. E.H.Fawcett, sponsored an annual competition and offered a silver cup for the winner. The 1935 competition was set at a limit of 8st 7lb and a Mr I.C.Tetley offered a gold medal for the runner-up. It took place on 29 April, with Les and Billy amongst the entrants. The number of rounds was not reported but Les outpointed Stan Corrigan of Bradford in his first bout and Billy outpointed Young Flynn of Leeds. Les got a bye into the final, while Billy secured his place with a one-round knockout over Harry Cross of Leeds.

The general consensus was that over a short distance Les could outbox his elder brother. And so it proved up to the mid-point of the bout. Les was seconded by Will, while Billy had Plum in his corner. Plum challenged his brother: "Are you letting him win, cos he's winning on points." On hearing this, Billy went out and gave his brother a good hiding. Brother Doug was at ringside and told Billy's son Ian: "Billy just set about Les who didn't stand a chance and you'd not have believed they were brothers." Billy got the decision on points and won the cup. Les was awarded the gold medal, which his daughter Lesley treasures and wears as a pendant.

A week later the pair returned to Knaresborough to appear on a benefit for local boxer Joe Surr and were presented with their prizes. This proved to be the last ring appearance of Billy Jackson of Thornaby.

Three weeks later, on 27 May, Les was matched at Knaresborough against Nipper Grice of Leeds, being stopped in the fifth round. Though billed to fight smart Tom Smith of Sunderland on 2 June, the defeat by Grice was Les' last professional appearance.

The brothers had become disillusioned. Billy was courting Anne and had decided to move south to try and get work in the naval dockyard at Chatham. Another reason was the northern drinking culture. Billy was a deep thinking sort of fellow and the family story is that he once got drunk and asked his brother-in-law Albert to post him through the letter box! So upset was he at the incident that the following Sunday he visited his church and signed the pledge. He didn't preach it but he became teetotal.

Whenever a member of Will's stable fought it was usual for the rest of the boys to go along to give moral support, travelling by train to Leeds, Barnsley or Newcastle. Billy used to tell, with some relish, how on reaching Thornaby as the only one sober he'd start throwing the rest off the train as it pulled into the station and jumped off himself as it pulled out. I've always wondered that having once been drunk and relinquishing control, he was a bit concerned as to what could happen on some subsequent occasion.

Les was only 19 and later told his daughter Lesley that while he was training and travelling about getting his head knocked off his mates were all enjoying themselves camping, going dancing and to the pictures. He also said that as he was getting heavier his fights were becoming tougher. The defeat against Lawson convinced him he had had enough and knew it was time to pack it in.

Billy retired first, much to Will's displeasure, but that made it easier for Les. Will was particularly disappointed as Young Simbo, who he thought would make the big time, had also given up the game.

As previously said boxing was in a confused state in the North East. Preliminary boys probably suffered more than most from the gradual spread of licensing, particularly the youngest and more vulnerable. Billy told of the occasion when one of Will's boys appeared at the New St James's Hall. The old man went to collect the purse only to be told that the gate was poor and there was no money. When Will returned with the rest of his charges, who packed the promoter's office, the cash miraculously appeared.

It would seem that Plum had never been an active boxer, so his role was probably that of a conditioner. None of the press reports of the brothers, Young Simbo nor Tommy Burns mentioned their tiring or lacking in condition and Plum obviously knew his business. Les was a natural boxer. He spent his time training, running – backwards and forwards – for long distances and cycling. Billy was a persistent and aggressive fighter. They were both dedicated and single-minded. Motivation was the least of their needs, they were fighting for bread!

Plum was by trade a steel-fixer. He was employed during the '30s in building airfields and was later involved in the construction of the D-Day Mulberry Harbour. He had a great head for heights. Les said his brother was fearless and like a monkey and while he was clinging on and shuffling along on his bottom, Plum was walking along the narrowest of beams.

Plum always had an interest in boats, his own cruiser in particular, 'The Lady Lily', named after a sister who had died in childhood. On one occasion, Will and a group of his friends set sail for Whitby. The weather was so bad that most of the passengers crowded into the cabin. Plum realised that something was wrong when a couple of them passed out. He dragged them out on the deck and found that fumes from the engine had seeped into the cabin. Luckily no lasting harm was done.

Doug was a regular at the Stockton gym. Les said that he was a good puncher but when hit on the nose his eyes streamed and he couldn't continue. Its not clear if he ever fought competitively. When war broke out Doug, along with Will, Annie, Des and sister Audrey, moved to Gillingham where he and his father gained employment at Chatham Dockyard and would stay until his retirement.

Des was the youngest of the brothers – too young to have been involved with the Club – and joined the Royal Air Force Regiment, doing a bit of boxing there.

Billy's employment at Chatham dockyard gave him 'reserved occupation' status and thus excused him from call-up for the forces. However, in early 1940, which he called 'my bad year', he volunteered for overseas service in Gibraltar where tunnels were being dug into the rock in preparation for an expected siege. Limited space on the peninsular had always been a problem and since the late 18th century Royal Engineers had excavated tunnels to house military stores and, in times of danger, help in defence of the rock.

Billy later jotted down his memories. "The war began to open up, things looked bad for our country. I had moved to Gillingham and Anne had begun to make a home for us. About All Fool's Day – April – I had volunteered to go to Gibraltar. The Italians kept sending the odd plane over. Then the French surrendered and our Navy sunk some of their warships so they couldn't be taken over by the Germans. There were raids on Gibraltar two days running. The place where I was working got a direct hit, but I was in the tunnel. We were without light and heat for a couple of days. In September I was told that we could choose to stay in Gib or be sent home. I choose to be sent home. We left Gib about the beginning of October; the convoy we were with consisted of over 50 ships. I was on a Swedish ship called the 'Belgia'. I sailed west for about five days then swung round to north, north west, then sailed north. The weather was getting colder. One night I could feel some panic around and although I couldn't see anything the next morning I went on deck and we were alone. The mate came and told us that we had run into a U-boat pack and the convoy had scattered. I then knew what loneliness meant. We had a lot of bad weather and a Western Ocean Roll. We managed to connect with other craft and I finally counted 11 ships. We were sailing east and then changed course to south east. One morning a flotilla of our destroyers suddenly came at the

convey, dropping depth charges and putting the wind up me. They were so fast and no doubt we had run into another U-boat pack. After this we were visited by a Fokker-Wolfe Condor – a big four-engined bomber. It flew right over us but did not drop anything. We were flying a Swedish flag. After 21 days at sea we were in home waters and could see Scotland on the port bow. Eventually we turned into the Mersey to see a big passenger liner sticking out of the water. There was an air raid on and we could see pieces of shrapnel hitting the water. We landed and I got to Lime Street station. There was a constant alert. I got a train to London and after 15 hours I arrived at Paddington. I walked to Charing Cross through the rubble and burning buildings and finally I found a train down to Dartford. I was amazed how everything was just going on as usual. I finally got out at Dartford and went to West Terrace were Anne was staying".

Billy didn't talk much about his war-time experiences. Though prevented from joining the forces for a couple of years, he played his part in the Home Guard, sometimes manning a rocket launcher on Gillingham golf course near to home. He probably volunteered for other activities such as Gibraltar. He was certainly at Anzio in 1944, probably on board a Royal Naval ship or Fleet Auxiliary. He also made trips to newly liberated Europe, particularly to Hamburg where he befriended a German family, a friendship which lasted for many years.

Late in 1945, now with a family of two sons, Bill junior and Ian, he obtained his civilian Merchant Navy ticket and joined the liner Orontes, then being used as a troop ship taking Australian servicemen home to Australia. In 1947 the Orontes was docked at Southampton for refitting prior to returning to civilian service. Billy then took ship with the Empire Cedric until January 1948 when, he handed in his merchant ticket and returned to his tools as a carpenter.

******

After retiring from the ring Les tried various jobs before settling down to be a steel fixer, working with Plum on airfield construction near York where he lodged with a local family.

In 1937 he joined the Royal Navy, signing up for 12 years. After initial training as a stoker he found himself posted to HMS Iron Duke, a WW1 battleship converted to a gunnery training ship, in Scapa Flow.

As a small guy and a former boxer, Les found that he was often expected to prove himself when joining a new ship. He entered boxing competitions when given the opportunity and won a few medals and a cup. On one occasion, when on shore leave at Southsea, he took up the challenge and fought in a boxing booth, taking on and beating the booth fighter. He was invited back the following evening but he was only there for beer money.

Les was still at Scapa Flow when war was declared. A month later on the night of 13 October 1939, U-boat U-47 entered the Flow and torpedoed HMS Royal Oak which capsized with the loss of 833 lives. The crew of Iron Duke launched their lifeboats and joined the rescue operations. A short time later, German bombers hit the Iron Duke which was beached, settling on the bottom in shallow water where she remained until 1945 as a depot ship.

Petty Officer Les Jackson in December 1944

In 1941 he was based in Weymouth, manning motor gunboats before joining the destroyer, HMS Ithuriel, in 1942 and taking part in Operation Pedestal, which was an attempt to break the Axis Powers' siege of Malta. Four days into the operation, Ithurial and another destroyer, Pathfinder, were dropping depth charges when a damaged Italian submarine, the Cabalto, surfaced near the Ithurial and was rammed. A boarding party hustled 40 odd crew-members off of the sinking sub on to the Ithurial, which limped back to Gibraltar.

Les was on convoy duty in the Atlantic, Russian Arctic and Mediterranean, but always maintained that the Maltese convoys were the worst. When the Ithurial was leaving the Med the skipper would tell the crew that if they didn't meet up with the next convoy they would steam straight back home to Portsmouth. Crew members on the upper decks scanned the horizon and their hearts would sink when in the distance they saw the flashing lights of ship-to-ship signalling and the destroyer would take up position in the convoy for the return to Malta. When action stations sounded the crew would all shake hands and wish each other good luck. The Ithurial was bombed off the Algerian coast near Bone later in the year and damaged beyond repair. By then Les was back in Blighty on a course.

Les next served on HMS Tuscan, a 'T' class destroyer, which struck a mine off the south coast of Ireland and had to heave to and wait for a tow to take her back to England.

In 1943 Les joined HMS Scurge, an 'S' class destroyer newly built by Cammel Laird, on escort duty, enduring the horrendous seas, weather and ice of the arctic route to Murmansk and Archangel. One of Les's favourite sayings was: "I've skied in Russia and not many can say that!"

HMS Scylla, with Les aboard, was part of the D-Day landings as a flagship of the Eastern Task Group providing fire support for the British beaches of Gold, Sword and Juno. The ship hit a mine off Normandy on 23 June 1944 and was badly damaged, having to retire back to Portsmouth.

HMS Montclare, a former Canadian Pacific Steamship Company passenger ship, had been converted into a Destroyer Depot ship in 1942. Two years later she underwent a second conversion to a Submarine Depot ship. Les joined her in 1944 and went with her to the Far East. In 1945 he joined HMS Oakley a Type II destroyer.

During a spell of shore leave home in the North East, Les had renewed his acquaintance with Irene Pottage, his brother Plum's sister-in-law. Les and Irene married in 1945 before the war ended, though he still had four years left to serve in the navy. Their first born, Lesley, was but ten months old when Les was posted back to the Mediterranean where he served on HMS Fierce, a minesweeper based on Malta.

Les left the navy in 1949, returned north and took up employment in a local power station as a stoker. Having made Petty Officer in the service he had had enough of shovelling coal and moved on to work in the plastics division of ICI. Now settled back into civvy street, his family was completed by the birth of son Desmond in 1951. As a member of the naval reserve, Les was recalled to service at the outbreak of the Korean War, but his previous service overseas meant that he stayed in home waters.

Back home with his family after the war Les rejoined ICI, becoming an assistant process foreman. He helped in an after school boxing club for a while, but shift work and the attitude of some of the teenage lads who required a bit of rough handling cut it short.

Times were good for Les and Irene in the early sixties until 1965 when he began to have trouble with his legs – falling over for no apparent reason. After a series of exhaustive tests – and being told that the problem was all in his mind – Les was operated on in 1966 and again in the following year but to no avail. He left hospital after two years, a paraplegic confined to a wheel chair.

With Irene's support and his own good humour and resilient nature Les came to terms with his disability. His sense of humour always shone through. He often would say: "It's nothing to worry about, it's all in my mind." His family are convinced that his strength of mind and the training he had done in his boxing days allowed him to survive all the traumas that life threw at him. Gradually roles were reversed as Irene succumbed to Alzheimer's disease and Les cared for her for seven years – shopping, cooking, etc – until he could no more.

When Irene went into hospital Les moved in with daughter Lesley and her family. He kept himself busy with model-making and enjoyed visits from Ike Pratt. Ike was a livewire, dancing around his old pal's wheelchair throwing punches and reliving the excitement of their youth.

******

After leaving the merchant service, Billy joined builders Richard Costain as a site carpenter and soon graduated into supervisory roles. He'd obviously enjoyed his wartime experience overseas and worked on construction projects in Nigeria, Persia (Iran), Kuwait and Gan in the Indian Ocean. Daughters Adrienne and Christine completed the family and he and Anne settled in Gillingham where Anne ran a corner grocery store. No doubt remembering his mother's failed business in Thornaby, Billy became a very efficient debt collector when home on leave. Billy returned home permanently in the early '60s and served as a clerk of works for various property developers, usually in the London area.

Billy always maintained an interest in boxing. During the war he occasionally took in one of the popular shows in war-torn London. He remembered seeing Kid Berg on one of these promotions. Asked his opinion of the old 'Whitechapel Whirlwind' he answered with a twinkle in his eye: "The speed of the knee deceives the eye" and left it at that!

His last ring appearance was as 'Sapper Jackson' on an amateur show at the Central Hall, Chatham as a favour to his friend Reverend Newby, a rather dynamic clergyman with whom Billy helped run the Brook Mission Boy's Club, near HM Dockyard. This probably happened in 1945. Who knows when he last used his fists in anger. Billy had a rather robust attitude to industrial relations when confronted by the unruly element – an attitude greatly appreciated by the majority of his site workers.

During the mid-'60s Anne and the girls returned to the North East and Billy lodged in Bromley while continuing to work in London. He often went to the Albert Hall – Joe Bugner was a favourite – and was at Highbury Stadium to see Henry Cooper's attempt at Muhammad Ali's world championship. He was a member of Harry Mullan's 'British Boxing Supporters Club' and attended the club's rather swish dinner at the Café Royal, presided over by the President, Terry Downes. Les had been released from hospital around this time and received a letter of encouragement from the 'Paddington Express'.

Billy enjoyed the odd riot or demonstration and attended the big, London anti-Vietnam war demonstrations just to see what was going on, often intervening on behalf of a policemen knocked down and threatened with a kicking. He said that he had often joined marches and protest meetings against unemployment up north in the '30s and being a little fellow found himself arrested on occasion!

In the mid-'70s he returned north but retirement was far from his mind. Finding his bungalow was lacking an effective damp proof course he got a few quotes, which convinced him that he'd discovered a lucrative little hobby. Having purchased the equipment and done his own property he virtually damp proofed the whole street! Moving back home brought the Jackson boys together again, with only Doug remaining in the south at Gillingham. Lesley vividly remembers her dad and uncle Billy reminiscing about their lives when in their 80s. How they lived near the river and spent a lot of their youth messing about in boats. Getting a free meal when fighting on Jewish charity promotions at Leeds. Les getting a ten bob note (50p) from that great comedian, Jimmy James, in appreciation of a good performance. Will giving vent to his frustration at a poor performance by buffeting them with their gloves. How Les's son Des worked on the North Sea oil rigs and Lesley's son Mike followed his grandfather in to the Royal Navy where he serves still as a Chief Petty Officer.

Billy's son Bill, like his dad, was a tearaway flyweight who was a Kent schoolboy boxing champion. Bill won his title before his own school supporters, who chanted "Knock 'im out, Bill, knock 'im out!" His poor opponent's mother pleaded: "Lay down Godfrey, lay down!"

After serving an engineering apprenticeship at Chatham dockyard, Bill did a stint in the merchant navy as an engineer, then worked in North Sea oil, mostly in Norway. During those long, dark winter nights Bill gained an Open University degree in mathematics.

Billy's second son Ian had a few schoolboy bouts. Blessed with the Jackson sense of humour he describes his last bout when, with Billy in his corner, he was told to jab, jab, jab. In the other corner his opponent, also supported by his father, received the same instruction. The two lads, tears streaming down their faces, stood just in range jabbing for all they were worth while the crowd cheered them on.

Ian served his apprenticeship as a carpenter and joiner and worked as a clerk of works before becoming a building surveyor working for London-based architects, local government and Shell Research. His son, Jim, competed in the British Army of the Rhine Minor Units Boxing Competition as a member of the Royal Engineers 14th Topographical Squadron. Now back in civvies, Jim works as a land surveyor.

******

The Jackson family were not unique in using boxing as a means of avoiding unemployment and alleviating the poverty of the 1930s. Billy and Les used their natural skills and resilience to put together solid records at a time when competition at their weight in the North East was probably unequalled. Though many of their early bouts remain untraced, the brothers' ring records show Billy with a total of 56 bouts, 38-11-7, and Les with 32, 16-6-10. Each fought regularly at the New St James's Hall, then unrivalled as a boxing arena in the area, with Billy topping the bill. What is undeniable, and proven by their later careers, is that the brothers were particularly determined and single-minded individuals. Neither stayed too long in the ring, each achieved responsible positions in their later careers and created close, tight-knit families.

Plum, Billy, Les and Doug, along with all the other members, no doubt benefited greatly from their involvement with Will Jackson's 'Stockton and Thornaby Physical Culture and Boxing Club'.

Billy's sons Ian, aged eight, and Bill, aged 13, 1953

Home and Away with British Boxers, 2006-2007

by John Jarrett

JULY

If he were to be truly honest, 'Joe Fightfan' would just as soon not sit through a 15-fight mega-bill, wherever. In fact he rarely does. People don't go to watch boxing these days; they go to watch a boxer and if they can find out what time his fight goes on, so much the better. And that is where we find the people who are happy to work these mammoth shows; they run the bars and the hamburger stands! Because not many punters turn up at three in the afternoon with a packet of sandwiches and a bottle of water, hoping it will see them through to midnight, or maybe longer!

Promoter Frank Warren loves the mega-show. Probably because he has so many fighters on his books, it is a way of giving them a job. Fifteen fights at the Millennium Stadium in Cardiff; I can remember when that would have been enough for three promotions! Well, that's boxing today.

Warren's super-champ Joe Calzaghe was to have starred on this show but injury put him in a ringside seat instead of a corner stool. The re-scheduled main event saw Bedford's Matt Skelton take revenge on Danny Williams and regain the Commonwealth heavyweight title over 12 rounds. Williams had prevailed in a rather bad-tempered battle, which saw the former K-1 fighter perform as though he had forgotten the Marquess of Queensberry rules. This time around, Skelton actually used his limited boxing skills to come out with the unanimous decision. Williams was unable to pin Matt down with his bigger punches, probably because he was carrying 20st 8lbs around the ring. It was his heaviest ever weight and it was too much.

Talking of big punchers, Enzo Maccarinelli will do for me. Former WBC cruiser-weight champion Marcelo Dominguez had never been stopped in 47 fights over 15 years, that is until he met the Swansea cruiserweight. It was a thunderous right uppercut in the ninth round that sent the Argentine hard man crashing to the floor and although he managed to get up at six the referee called it off, and Maccarinelli added the WBO Interim belt to his WBU strap. It was a sensational win for Enzo, taking his pro log to 24-1 with 18 inside schedule. Serious punching!

Sheffield's former British light-middleweight champion, Ryan Rhodes, showed he still had something to offer when he pushed the WBU middleweight titleholder, Gary Lockett, all the way and the Welshman had to get off the deck in the tenth round and finish strongly to hold on to his belt. Rhodes was happy to be back. Colin Bain came down from Scotland to test former Olympic hero, Amir Khan, and was left wondering if his journey was really necessary. As Khan breezed to win number eight, six inside, Colin was down in rounds one and two before it was called off. Newbridge's Gavin Rees stayed unbeaten after 24 fights as he took a six rounds decision off Martin Watson, but after eight years in the pro game where is he going? Another unbeaten young fighter is Kevin Mitchell, 20 straight wins and too much for French visitor, Imad Ben Khalifa, who was rescued in the second round. As midnight approached, Bradley Pryce took to the ring to defend his Commonwealth light-middleweight title against Tanzania's Hassan Matumla. Pryce had too much of everything for the visitor and the referee saw no point in letting it go on, calling a halt in round four. It was already past bedtime for these lads anyway.

Colorado Springs is over 6,000 feet above sea level, but in the sixth round of a welterweight fight at the Civic Auditorium it was Jerome Ellis who was still flying high as the former British champion, Neil Sinclair, was sent crashing to the floor from a left hook to the body that surely must have had the 32-year-old Belfast veteran thinking there were better things to do on a visit to America. Visit Disneyland for instance, or Las Vegas to play the slots.

It was a hot night at the old York Hall in London and it was even hotter inside the ring as Carl Johanneson hammered his way to a fourth-round victory over Billy Corcoran to take the vacant British super-featherweight title. The Leeds man had too much power for the Wembley Irishman and turned it on in the fourth to have Billy reeling against the ropes. Billy's supporters thought the stoppage premature when it was called off, but Corcoran had sustained a nasty cut on his right eye and was shipping punishment from a man who had stopped 17 of his 24 victims.

Manchester's 21-year-old lightweight comer, John Murray, warmed up for a British title eliminator against Ricky Burns when he stopped Billy Smith in the last round of a six rounder on the York Hall bill. Taking his record to 17-0 with 9 inside, Murray won no medals for beating the Stourport man, as Smith had won only three of his 43 contests, but Billy usually goes the distance. He almost made it this night, but not quite.

They say the toughest thing in this game is the training; the miles on the road and the rounds in the gym, skipping, bag-punching, exercises and sparring. The best part comes on fight night – pay night! Well, for David Haye, his defence of the European cruiserweight title against a dismal Belgian challenger, Ismael Abdoul, was nothing more than a further 12 rounds sparring session with spectators walking out of the Altrincham Sports Centre long before the final bell. It was an unforgivable performance from a champion who even admitted afterwards that he had limited himself to throwing just three right hands per round!

Juliette Winter and Shanee Martin will probably never get paid anything like what Mr Haye took home, but at least they went home with a clear conscience. They gave the fans a helluva fight at Dagenham, as Derby's Winter became the first women's British Masters super-flyweight champion.

AUGUST

British boxers took a holiday this month, which wasn't always a good idea. Ricky Hatton had reason to rue going to Shanghai to watch his favourite football team, Manchester City, play. An evening stroll on his first night in the city turned out to be a walk on the wild side, when Ricky was mugged by four local citizens who absconded with his

£4,000 Rolex watch. Fancy mugging a world champion fighter! Don't they get *Boxing News* in Shanghai? Ricky could probably have flattened the four gentlemen in question but he figured discretion was the better part of valour. "One said, 'Give us your watch.' My first reaction was to say, 'Bleep off! Then I realised they could have had knives. I was angry at the time, but I wasn't beaten up or mugged. It could have been worse". When he got back home, Ricky was about to have something else taken from him, his WBA welterweight title, as that sanctioning body had ordered him to defend against his mandatory challenger, Oktay Urkal. So Hatton relinquished the championship to concentrate on a light-welterweight mega-fight with Jose Luis Castillo. There's boxing, and there's business. This was business.

Another champion to give up his belt was the British middleweight titleholder, Scott Dann, recurring back problems being the cause. The Plymouth puncher had already cleaned up the division to make the Lonsdale Belt his own property, manager Chris Sanigar telling the press: "In fairness to all we decided to free up the title".

At 35, Allan Gray announced his retirement from boxing to concentrate on his heating and plumbing business. Gray was a former undefeated WBF Inter-Continental and Southern Area middleweight champion and put together 28 professional contests, finishing with a 17-2-9 tally. The bottom fell out of Allan's world when his father died in 2003, followed by his manager, Dennie Mancini, a year later. "I miss them terribly", he said.

It was not a good time for Scott Harrison. Battling with alcohol and depression and facing charges of breach of the peace and police assault, the WBO featherweight champion, feeling he had to get out of Scotland, relocated to Belfast where he started training at John Breen's gym. The World Boxing Organisation had earlier given Scott an extension of his defence against mandatory challenger, Juan Manuel Marquez, in order to deal with his personal problems, but was now pushing for the fight to take place. Frank Warren still had faith in Harrison and made a winning bid of $748,000 for the Marquez fight as news broke that Scott had severed his ten-year relationship with Frank Maloney to sign up with Barry Hughes and his Braveheart Promotions. Harrison's future as a fighter was still hanging in the balance.

SEPTEMBER

The Bolton Arena was a seething cauldron in the ninth round of the IBF light-heavyweight championship fight between the titleholder, Clinton Woods, and his old foe, Glengoffe Johnson. It had been a hard, gruelling match with the veteran American looking well on the way to victory. In that ninth session, Woods was hammered around the ring and the referee, Howard Foster, kept a close eye on the Yorkshire gladiator as he reeled before Johnson's sustained attack. Clinton made it to the bell and Johnson's corner were jubilant as the title looked safely back home. But in the opposite corner, a spark still burned in Clinton Woods and at the bell he came out with both guns blazing and never stopped firing. Now Johnson looked in dire straits and the place erupted as Woods, tempered with Sheffield

steel, refused to let his title go. He set up a two-fisted attack that threatened to blow Johnson out of the ring and now the veteran was hanging on. At the final bell, Clinton had to sweat through the scores as they were announced; the American judge was for Woods, Mickey Vann went for Johnson and the Puerto Rican judge saw Woods the winner and still IBF light-heavyweight champion of the world! It was third time lucky for Clinton, after a draw and a defeat. Couldn't happen to a nicer fellow!

A new king was crowned at the Palace, as Bradford's Junior Witter finally got his hands on some serious hardware when lifting the vacant WBC light-welterweight title with a one-sided victory over America's DeMarcus Corley at Alexandra Palace. Now, maybe they should call him Senior Witter! At 32, Witter had lost only one of his 36 fights (two draws) and that was to the IBF champion, Zab Judah, six years ago. He made no mistake against the American southpaw, hurting his man in rounds five and six, and surviving a Corley rally in the eighth to come home free.

Challenging Jamie Moore for his British light-middleweight title in Manchester, Matthew Macklin set a ferocious if hectic pace for three rounds. But this was scheduled for 12 rounds, the championship distance. Over the long haul, Jamie punched his way back into the lead and in the tenth round, a savage left cross brought Macklin down on his face, out for the count. The Birmingham man had given his all in a superb effort, but it just wasn't enough this night, against this champion.

At the venerable York Hall, Ted Bami won the vacant European light-welterweight title with a unanimous decision over Italy's Giuseppe Lauri in a so-so fight that rarely reached the heights. Bami, from the Congo via Brixton, worked harder than the other fellow and that was the deciding factor.

Two days later, on a warm Sunday afternoon at the same venue, Jamaica's Ovill McKenzie blasted his way to the vacant Commonwealth light-heavyweight title with a two-round annihilation of Enfield's Peter Haymer. Peter barely survived the opening round and was felled three times in round two before it was called off. On the same bill, two ladies had a cat-fight as Cathy 'The Bitch' Brown used her experience to defeat Juliette Winter for the inaugural English women's bantamweight title and gain sweet revenge for a previous defeat.

British and Commonwealth cruiserweight champion and Lonsdale Belt winner, Mark Hobson, punched out a lop-sided win over the Czech southpaw, Pavol Polakovic, at the Grosvenor House in Mayfair to add the vacant WBU bauble to his collection. Walking around at 14½ stones and standing six-five, Hobson shouldn't have any problems in his day job – collecting unpaid council tax and business rates for Leeds City Council. Curtis Woodhouse made a winning pro debut against Dean Marcantonio over four rounds. The former footballer (Sheffield United, Birmingham City and Grimsby Town) hopes to do with the gloves what he did with his boots.

On his hometown bill (Woods-Johnson), Amir Khan, still only 19, stormed to a first- round victory over the Thamesmead southpaw, Ryan Barrett, to take his pro log to 9-0 (7) and underline his tremendous potential. This boy can go all the way! Barrett had never been stopped, until this night, when he was floored three times before it was ended at 1.51 of round one. Former British welterweight champion, Michael Jennings, came back to knock out the Czech southpaw, Ratislav Kovac, in round three, body shots doing the damage.

Dagenham's super-featherweight, Kevin Mitchell, retained his IBF Inter-Continental title with an 11th-round stoppage of Belarus' Andrey Isaev in Mayfair. The visitor, also unbeaten going in, suffered a cut on his left eye after a clash of heads in the ninth and protested when the third man called it off two rounds later. Mitchell posted his record to 21-0 and is learning his trade.

Boxing returned to Middlesbrough with Darlington's Isaac (Argy) Ward getting back on the winning trail after losing to Martin Power in a British bantamweight title challenge, when punching out a six-rounds win over Shrewsbury southpaw, Neil Marston. Local lightweight, Paul Truscott, scored his second pro win in his first fight at home and his fans raised the roof as he survived a flash knockdown to beat Steve Gethin over four.

British boxers had mixed success on their travels abroad with victory for the London-born Irishman, Andy Lee, in Las Vegas, where he dumped Jess Salway in round six to take his record to 5-0 (3). Jane Couch had a tough time with the IBA light-welterweight champion, Holly Holm, in Albuquerque and the local favourite had too much of everything for Jane who finished with a cut and a unanimous defeat. At Fort Smith, Arkansas, the former heavyweight champion, Herbie Hide, swung back into action after two-and-a-half years out. Fighting at cruiserweight, the 34-year-old Hide dropped Mitch Hicks four times in just 84 seconds of the first round. All over!

Irish middleweight John Duddy survived his toughest test in his unbeaten 18-fight career when he scraped through to a unanimous decision over twelve rounds against the Mexican veteran, Yori Boy Campas, at the Theatre in Madison Square Garden. At stake was the IBA middleweight title. Duddy's New York fans filled the arena and he gave them a fight, and so did the former IBF light-middleweight champion. Duddy had to dig deep for his win and came out of the ring needing 20 stitches to repair cuts on both eyes. On the undercard, the Galway-born Londoner, Simon O'Donnell, got his second pro win with a fourth-round disqualification victory over Terrance Miller. Two weeks previously, in Philadelphia, O'Donnell had made his debut with a four- rounds decision over Cuba's Andres Larrinaga in a middleweight bout.

The stop-start pro career of Richard Williams moved forward again at the York Hall, as the Stockwell middleweight turned in a fine performance to outbox and outpunch Croatia's Vedran Akrap, who was stopped for the first time when the referee called a halt in round five. Williams, the former IBO light-middleweight champion and undefeated Commonwealth and WBF champion, moved to 21-1-3 and was looking forward to meeting Howard Eastman for the vacant British middleweight title.

On the Witter bill at Ally-Pally, the unheralded bantamweight, Shinny Bayaar, ruined the British debut of Kettering-born Andrew Kooner, who had kicked off his career in Canada after winning Commonwealth Games gold. Kooner had won four fights prior to coming back to Kettering, but he didn't win this one. Shinny uncorked a terrific right hook to drop his man in the third and when he got up it was waved off. Still shaken, Kooner was also badly cut on the forehead.

OCTOBER

At 34, with a perfect record of 41-0 (31), Joe Calzaghe was still looking for the BIG fight, the career-defining contest, the Pay-per-View punch-up against a star name like Bernard Hopkins, or even a jaded Roy Jones. The Welshman has made a career out of defending the WBO title, which is lightly-regarded in the land of the dollar. Joe did get his hands on the more prestigious IBF title when he outclassed Jeff Lacy, but in retrospect the American proved to be an overrated fighter who failed to live up to his press notices. At the MEN Arena in Manchester, Calzaghe faced the unheralded Sakio Bika, from Cameroon via Australia, and came out of the ring looking like he had done 12 rounds with Hopkins or Jones. A nasty cut on his left eye took half-a-dozen stitches to repair, his face was bruised and swollen, and his left hand was knocked up. Sure, he had the win, taking his log to 42-0, but it looked as though the champion, like most everyone else, figured Bika an easy touch. He wasn't, being rough and tough and making Calzaghe look bad when he needed to look good for the HBO cameras.

One Welshman who did look sensational on the bill was the WBO cruiserweight champion, Enzo Maccarinelli. If you drop your programme while this guy is on, just leave it. Don't take your eyes off the ring. If you did, you might have missed Enzo's 71-second blow-out of former victim, Mark Hobson. One big right hand crashed behind Mark's ear and he was on his face. Although the Huddersfield man beat the count he was still stunned and it was stopped. Maccarinelli racked up his 19th early win in 25 fights and is a dangerous man!

WBU featherweight champion, Steve Foster, was undefeated (21-0-1) and so was his challenger, Derry Matthews (16-0), so something had to give. In the event, Derry looked the champ and after 12 one-sided rounds he was.

Liverpool's middleweight, Paul Smith, continued his unbeaten run, now 17-0, when he hammered Dean Walker to a third-round defeat to take the vacant Central Area title. The Sheffield man was on a hiding to nothing, having lost seven of his last eight fights, and he never looked like beating the former Commonwealth Games silver medallist, who dropped Dean three times before it was stopped in round three. A bad match on paper, and in the ring. Smith is a good fighter and is ready for good fights.

Another unbeaten fighter on the Manchester bill was the Sheffield welterweight, Kell Brook. He took his record to 12-0 when Duncan Cotter was stopped in three rounds due to a cut right eye. There was also a victory in his pro debut for the former Commonwealth Games gold medal winner, Kenny Anderson, as he stopped Nick Okoth in four rounds of a light-heavyweight bout.

You never know what you've got with an undefeated fighter. The test for Scott Gammer would have come in the defence of his British heavyweight title against the former champion, Danny Williams, at Aberavon. But Williams pulled out as the date clashed with Ramadan and the Welshman found himself facing Micky Steeds, a guy he had already beaten. There was not much bite in the man from the Isle of Dogs who pinned everything on his right hand and Gammer cruised to a decision victory, taking his pro log to 18-0.

At the Don Valley Stadium in Sheffield, the local veteran John 'Buster' Keeton realised his dream when he stopped Lee Swaby in round seven of their fight for the vacant British cruiserweight championship. With a bad cut over his left eye, the Lincoln southpaw was cornered and beaten into the canvas with a barrage of blows as the third man jumped between them to crown the new champion. At 34, in his fourth challenge for this title, Keeton had lost 14 of his 39 pro fights. He made sure he wasn't going to lose this one.

The Manchester welterweight, Matthew Hatton, forgot his manners in his British title eliminator with an old pro in Alan Bosworth and it cost him a victory he had all but wrapped up. By the tenth and final round, Hatton's miscellaneous misdemeanours had exhausted the patience of Howard Foster and when he hit on the break again it was enough for the referee to rule him out.

Graham Earl had been British and Commonwealth lightweight champion in a nine-year career that saw him beaten only once in 25 fights, and now he was going for the vacant WBU title at the York Hall against Angel Ramirez, from the Argentine via Spain. It was a cracking fight and the visitor was left shaking his head at the final bell as the Luton lad collected all three votes from the officials. To many on press row, Ramirez looked to have done enough to take the belt, but it was not to be. One the same bill, Kevin Mitchell moved to 22-0 and turned in one of his best performances to take the unanimous decision over Ghana's George Ashie and with it the vacant Commonwealth super-featherweight

Graham Earl (left) hammers the oncoming Angel Ramirez with a solid left on his way to winning the WBU lightweight title   Les Clark

title. On the eve of his 22nd birthday, Mitchell came through some rough waters to sail into port with another trophy for his growing collection. The former WBU light-heavyweight champion, Tony Oakey, warmed up for his scheduled British title fight with Peter Oboh by taking a six-rounds decision over shifty Simeon Cover. At 32, Tony showed he still has a few shots left in his locker.

Commonwealth bantamweight champion, Tshifhiwa Munyai, has been a revelation since landing in Britain. Maybe he just likes the York Hall. In June he had dismantled the British champion, Martin Power, inside nine rounds to take the vacant title and this time, back at Bethnal Green, the lanky South African retained against the former flyweight champion, Lee Haskins, who was stopped in six rounds. At 5` 9", Munyai really is a tall order for our little fellows.

NOVEMBER

The Michael Hunter roller coaster came off the rails in devastating fashion as the Hartlepool hero crashed out of the world title picture in round five against Steve Molitor before a packed, and stunned, Borough Hall crowd. Taking his 23rd straight victory, the Canadian Kid collected the vacant IBF super-bantamweight championship and left Hunter shaking his head and wondering where it all went wrong.

Like his southpaw opponent, Michael was undefeated in 27 fights (1 draw) and had hammered his way to the Northern Area, WBF, British, Commonwealth and European championships, winning a Lonsdale Belt along the way. The world title was next, and for three rounds in front of his adoring hometown fans Hunter was in with a shout. But by round four, Molitor had overcome the hostile crowd and was about to overcome their favourite. A sizzling left hand stuck Michael on his backside and although he beat the count, the seeds of doubt were planted. They grew in the fifth as the Canadian whipped in punches from both hands and Hunter was down by the ropes, visibly stunned, shaking his head as he looked across to his trainer, Neil Fannan, in the corner. The dream was ended; Steve Molitor was the new champ!

Over in Dublin the next night, a former Hunter victim, Esham Pickering, tried to recapture the European title he had left in Hartlepool, when going up against the unbeaten Bernard Dunne for the vacant crown. But 'Brown Sugar' was not sweet enough this night as the Irishman boxed and punched his way to a unanimous decision to send the packed crowd into party mood that lasted until a new day dawned in Dublin. Dunne took his pro log to 22-0 (13) as he capped a brilliant amateur career (119 bouts) and a professional campaign that kicked off in the United States under Sugar Ray Leonard and top trainer Freddie Roach. When Steve Molitor gets around to defending his new belt, Dunne and Dublin are ready for the challenge.

Some two years after they were due to fight each other, Carl Froch and Tony Dodson finally got it on at the Nottingham Arena. Originally, Dodson was the British super-middleweight champion when injury forced him to pull out of a defence against the Midlander. Then the Liverpool man hurt his back in a car accident and the fight was off again. Further injury forced him to give the belt up and Froch won the vacant title, but there was bad blood between them and this was a fight that just had to happen. Tony had come back after almost two years out, going 4-0 up to fight time, but Froch in the meantime had developed into a good fighter, defending the British title twice and the Commonwealth six times, and was a winner in all 19 pro fights. Victory over Dodson would give him the Lonsdale Belt to keep. It took Carl just three rounds to bring Dodson to his knees with a devastating left hook to the body and make a lot of people think maybe Froch was as good as he always said he was.

It looked bad for David Haye in the seventh round of his European cruiserweight title defence against the Italian hard man, Giacobbe Fragomeni, at the York Hall in London. The challenger backed Haye to the ropes and two cracking right hands opened a bad cut over his left eye. The Londoner was suddenly in serious trouble, but he kept his cool and in round nine, blood still streaming down his face, he smashed Fragomeni on to the bottom rope and when the Italian stood up his second was on the apron waving his arms. It was over, and David Haye was still on course for a world title shot.

Also looking for a crack at a major title was Alex Arthur. The Edinburgh man retained his European super-featherweight belt against an unbeaten Spaniard, Sergio Palomo, at the Kelvin Hall in Glasgow. After sending Sergio to the canvas three times, the referee called it off in round five. Taking his record to 24-1, the Scot racked up his 18th stoppage victory and, at 28, is a solid performer ready to step on to the big stage.

On the Glasgow bill, one of Britain's best-kept secrets, Nigel Wright, retained his English light-welterweight title against Gary Reid of Stoke, whose forcing tactics were thwarted by the classic boxing of the County Durham southpaw. Nigel took his pro log to 17-2 and looks better every time out. Willie Limond picked up the vacant Commonwealth lightweight title with a sound points win over Kpako Allotey after the Ghanian recovered from a first-round knockdown to take the Scot all the way. Willie had lost only to Alex Arthur in 28 fights going in.

It was Leeds versus Bradford at the Barnsley Metrodome when the British super-feather-weight champion, Carl Johanneson, put his title on the line for Femi Fehintola. After going unbeaten in 13 fights, Femi found the champion too much of a handful and he was rescued in round six after visiting the canvas four times.

At Newport, the Commonwealth light-middleweight champion, Bradley Pryce, finally settled down to his boxing after a ragged start against lanky 34-year-old Andrew Facey, from the Ingle factory in Sheffield, and ran out a unanimous points winner to take his pro log to 23-6.

Former British heavyweight champion Michael Sprott must have been impressive when he retained his European Union title in Mulheim/Ruhr, for he came out with a split decision over the undefeated German Rene Dettweiler. Time was when our lads had to knock them out to get a draw over there! Damaen Kelly was not so fortunate on his trip to Sardinia for the rematch with European bantamweight champion, Simone Maludrottu. The Irishman had lost their Belfast battle in what Tommy Gilmour called: "The biggest robbery I've seen in 35 years of boxing." But Maludrottu

made no mistake this time, punishing Kelly until his corner called it off in the third round. "That's me finished", said Kelly, who won a boatload of titles at fly and super-flyweight in a 22-4 pro record.

David Haye successfully defended his European cruiserweight crown when crushing Italy's Giacobbe Fragomeni in the ninth round   Les Clark

DECEMBER

Maybe we should forget the 'A-Force' and start calling him 'Hot-and-Cold' Harrison. Audley was hot again at the ExCel Arena in London when he demolished his old foe, Danny Williams, inside three rounds to gain revenge for a dismal points defeat by the former British heavyweight champion in the same ring 12 months ago. To be fair to Danny, he took the fight at a week's notice when Matt Skelton pulled out claiming injury, but for once it was a positive performance from the former Olympic gold medallist. It started to go bad for Williams in the first round when a big left uppercut opened a gash on his nose. After the referee called the doctor to the ring to look at the cut, which took seven stitches, Danny stepped up a gear but Harrison knew he was close to a stoppage and was unusually aggressive. Round three saw the finish. It was the left uppercut again and it put Williams on the floor. Danny struggled upright but Harrison pounced and smashed him down again and it was stopped. Taking his record to 21-2, Audley talked a good fight, as usual. "My goal is still to be champ of the world – undisputed champion. Today, you saw it all come together. I was ready for anyone". The jury was still out on this one.

There is a world champion called Harrison, Scott from Glasgow, and in his second reign as WBO featherweight king after six defences he was slated for the ExCel bill against Nicky Cook. But Mr Harrison's professional career had started to unravel of late with reported drink and depression problems and extra-curricular bouts outside the ring, which had come to the attention of the local constabulary. Three days before his title defence against Cook, Harrison pulled out of the show and relinquished his title. The unbeaten Cook was left to box eight rounds with the British Masters champion, Harry Ramogoadi, taking the points and his record to 27-0. Anti-climax!

Wonderboy Amir Khan was last on the big show, but he was worth waiting for, taking what will surely be the first of many titles. The vacant IBF Inter-Continental light-welterweight belt will not get you to Las Vegas, but it will get you on the right bus. The Bolton boy boxed and punched his way to a ten-rounds unanimous decision over the tough Frenchman, Rachid Drilzane, to take his pro log to 10-0, with seven inside. Drilzane was an excellent test and Khan passed with flying colours. Serge Vigne had better luck than his countryman as the French light-middleweight shocked Wayne Alexander in just 70 seconds of round one.

Wythenshawe's Andy Morris had beaten Scotland's John Simpson just over a year previously and he looked on course to retain his British featherweight title in the rematch, for five rounds anyway. But a cut over Andy's left eye, suffered late in the fourth, brought about a stoppage in round five, much to the champion's anguish. Unlucky for Morris, third time lucky for the man from Greenock.

It was also third time lucky for Jonathon Thaxton, beaten in British light-welterweight title challenges against Ricky Hatton and Jason Rowland, but now crowned British lightweight champion after taking a unanimous decision over Salford's Lee Meager at Dagenham. It was Meager's first defence and second defeat in 23 fights and he didn't go

Lee Meager (left) lost his British lightweight title to Jonathan Thaxton, seen here missing with a clubbing right

Les Clark

quietly. In a tremendous contest, both men were bloodied and the Norwich veteran floored Lee in the final round to seal his victory.

At the York Hall, Battersea Bomber, Howard Eastman, had to go through 12 rounds (almost) before detonating a right hand on the 35-year-old chin of former IBO light-middleweight champion, Richard Williams, to bring the curtain down with 54 seconds left in the fight. Victory put the veteran Eastman back on the British middleweight throne, but at 36 his options are limited. His four defeats (41 wins) were all at world title level and he isn't likely to get another shot now.

It was comeback time as the former British welterweight champion, David Barnes, got back in the groove at Sheffield with an easy six-rounds win over Vadzim Astapuk of Belarus. The Manchester southpaw had been idle for nine months and was rusty.

At Birmingham, heavyweight Pele Reid showed he still had enough juice to flatten the likes of Paul King who was stopped in round six. The former British and Commonwealth title challenger had been out four years and it showed. Another fighter needing a shot of WD-40 was the former champion, Matthew Barney, who struggled to beat Varuzhan Davtyan over four rounds after 18 months out. The Southampton boxer has collected titles like some people collect stamps; former undefeated WBU light-heavy champ, former undefeated British, IBO Inter-Continental, Southern Area and British Masters super-middleweight titleholder.

Colin McNeil won the Scottish light-middleweight title when he beat the champion, Barrie Lee, inside four rounds at Glasgow, but had a fright when a nasty cut opened on his right eyebrow in round three. Fearing a stoppage, Colin opened up in the fourth to hammer the Arbroath man with thudding lefts and rights to bring the referee's intervention. The Fauldhouse southpaw was looking forward to boxing Ross Minter in a British welterweight title eliminator.

The Gethin brothers from Walsall are a bonny pair. At Wolverhampton, light-welterweight Martin (8-0) won the vacant British Masters title with a three-rounds stoppage over Judex Meemea, a Mauritian fighting out of Walthamstow. Six days later, older brother Darren had to fight a hard ten rounder to beat Birmingham's Simon Sherrington for the vacant British Masters light-middleweight title. A fine family double!

JANUARY

Manchester 'Hitman' Ricky Hatton has no need of braces to keep his pants up. Every time this guy goes to work it is for some belt or other. In fact, since Ricky stopped Tommy Peacock in two rounds at Oldham in February 1999 for the vacant Central Area light-welterweight title, only three of his subsequent 32 fights have not involved a title of some sort, and that was seven years ago! Give the other kids a break, Ricky.

He was at it again this month in Las Vegas, beating on some unfortunate Columbian to regain the IBF light-welterweight championship and pick up the vacant IBO belt to add to his collection. In taking the unanimous decision over Juan Urango, Hatton strung his pro log out to 42-0, and he's still only 28. The Columbian southpaw was tough and strong, but although undefeated going in after only 18 contests, including one draw, he was limited. He had some success but was always running second, as Hatton had too much of everything, and at the final bell they gave Ricky another couple of belts, the sort he likes.

Apparently it runs in the family. Younger brother Matthew, already a winner of Central Area welterweight and light-middleweight trophies, collected the vacant IBF Inter-Continental welterweight belt on Ricky's show when he outclassed Frank Houghtaling from Albany, New York, the veteran retiring after round seven having survived a fourth-round knockdown. It was Hatton's 30th win in 34 bouts. Ricky's manager Dennis Hobson took two of his new kids from Sheffield along for the ride and the experience, but only Jon Ibbotson, a light-heavy, saw real action. Well, for all 95 seconds. That was how long it took him to blast Shannon Anderson out of the picture. Light-welter Nicki Smedley was ready to face Juan Pablo Montes de Oca, but the Mexican came in too heavy and the fight was cancelled. They did square off, but only in a three-rounds exhibition.

On the same day that Hatton fought in Las Vegas, his domestic rival, Junior Witter, was in action at Alexandra Palace in London, defending his WBC light-welterweight title against Mexico's Arturo Morua. Time was when Hatton and Witter were always mentioned in the same sentence and a fight between them looked a natural. But it hasn't happened yet and it may never happen, Witter probably needing the fight more than the Manchester Hitman. Junior gave a senior performance in beating his Mexican challenger, who showed himself lacking in ambition and, ultimately, stamina. When Witter decided to close the show in the ninth round, Senor Morua couldn't stay with him and was rescued by the referee. Junior took his pro log to 35-1-2 and I think he'll grow old waiting for Hatton. And at 32, Witter shouldn't wait around too long.

Another veteran from the Ingle gym is the former champion, Esham Pickering, now 30 with an excellent resume after ten years in the hardest game. He has been the former undefeated British super-bantamweight, former Commonwealth and European super-bantamweight and former undefeated British Masters bantamweight champion. Having lost the big bouts against Michael Hunter and Bernard Dunne, the man from Newark started again with a lop-sided six-rounds decision over a fat Frenchman, Frederic Gosset. Did I say fat? Monsieur Gosset was 18 pounds heavier than Pickering! When you accept an opponent like that, losing doesn't come into the equation.

Best fight on the Muswell Hill bill saw Scotland's Barry Morrison box and punch his way to a split decision over Lenny Daws to take the unbeaten champion's British light-welterweight title over a hotly contested 12 rounds. The man from Motherwell became the first Scot to hold this title since it was introduced in 1968 and he was a worthy, if narrow, winner. Lenny hurt Morrison in the eighth but in doing so Barry's gumshield came out. When it was replaced, Morrison had recovered.

Darlington super-bantamweight, Isaac (Argy) Ward, brought the Commonwealth title back to Neil Fannan's gym

when he dropped Tanzania's Francis Miyeyusho to his knees with a crushing right hook to the body in round two of their fight at Yarm in Cleveland. His stablemate, Michael Hunter, had recently relinquished the title.

There were mixed fortunes for two Brits in Milan. Former British and Commonwealth light-middleweight champion, Michael Jones, gave the European champion, Michele Piccirillo, a stubborn argument before a thudding right to the head in the last minute of the fight rocked the Englishman and the Italian veteran poured it on to leave Jones on the deck to be counted out. In a six-rounder on the bill, Young Mutley, loudly supported by a travelling section of Black Country fans, boxed well enough to take a unanimous decision over Pole Arek Malek.

British bantamweight champion Martin Power is a glutton for punishment. Having been stopped in nine rounds by Tshifhiwa Munyai for the vacant Commonwealth title, the Londoner stepped back into the lion's den to challenge the South African sensation, this time at the Goresbrook Leisure Centre in Dagenham. It was the same result, only quicker. Munyai was better than he was the first fight and that was good enough. This time around his slashing punches convinced Power's corner that four rounds would do for this night. Make a note of the name. Munyai!

Well beaten inside the first round when challenging Matt Skelton for the British title last time out, big John McDermott got the idea and stopped Vitaly Shkraba of Belarus in just 2.24 of round one on the Dagenham bill. Fight one round, get paid for six! The unbeaten record of Gary Woolcombe was history after his fifth-round defeat by lanky Andrew Facey, who retained his English light-middleweight title. The man from the Ingle factory was all

Having won the WBC light-welter title in September, Junior Witter (right) defended it with some relish when stopping Mexico's Arturo Morua in the ninth round some four months later   Les Clark

71

legs and arms and poor Gary didn't know where the punches were coming from. Dropped in the fifth, he got up but it was stopped soon after.

FEBRUARY

Audley Harrison's dream of winning the undisputed world heavyweight championship may never be more than that. He awoke from a nightmare in the Wembley ring after Michael Sprott exploded a tremendous left hook on his jaw to leave the former Olympic gold medallist stretched out like a rug in the third round. Sprott's European Union and the vacant English titles were on the line but there is always much more than that at stake when top heavyweights clash. The future for Harrison looked bleak indeed as the big man left the ring, now a loser in three of his last five fights, his overall record now being 21-3. If his fists could talk as eloquently as his tongue, his dream would become a reality. Unfortunately, his fists are tongue-tied when they should be speaking volumes. Harrison was heading for Las Vegas after the Sprott fight, but only because he lives there.

Amir Khan had to be content with silver at the last Olympics, but his future looks gold-plated as he rolls up victories in the professional ranks, 11-0 (8) since discarding his vest in July 2005. He was awesome on the Wembley bill as he blew away France's Mohammed Medjadji in just 55 seconds of round one with a cracking right hand to the chin. Medjadji was on his feet at six but still shaky and it was stopped. Khan is ready for stronger opposition.

Fight of the night, indeed of many nights, was the contest for the vacant interim WBO lightweight title between the former British and Commonwealth champion, Graham Earl, and Australia's undefeated Michael Katsidis. This developed into what Americans used to term a 'Pier Six' brawl, with both fighters on the deck before Katsidis prevailed when Earl's corner pulled him out after five punishing rounds. The Greek-Aussie was just too strong and powerful for the lad from Luton, who was floored three times before putting Katsidis down. Michael got up and gave Earl more trouble before the end. Going into that fight, Graham Earl had lost only to Scotland's Ricky Burns, who went on to make a heroic challenge against super-featherweight champion, Alex Arthur. The title had since been won by Carl Johanneson after Arthur vacated and the Leeds man was now making his second defence, against Mr Burns. The champion had home advantage with Leeds Town Hall the battle site, however, Carl didn't need any help in this one. Fighting before a capacity crowd, Johanneson fought like a man inspired to retain the British title with a unanimous decision over a gutsy challenger who was still trying at the final bell. Ricky had been floored in round seven and twice in the ninth, but the champion couldn't keep him down. Still only 23, Ricky will be heard from again.

On the comeback trail at Leeds was the former British and Commonwealth flyweight champion and former IBO super-flyweight titleholder, Jason Booth. Having his second fight at bantamweight, he took a six-rounds decision over Huddersfield's Jamil Hussain. Looking to work his way back to title contention, the Nottingham man took his pro log to 27-4 and at 29 still has some mileage left in him.

Arctic conditions all but knocked out promoter Tony Hay's show at the Central Marriott Hotel in Bristol as snow blanketed the city, and Tony was left with one fight out of a scheduled four. Luckily, the one fight left was the main attraction, the Commonwealth light-heavyweight title bout between the champion, Ovill McKenzie, and former British and European super-middleweight champion, Dean Francis.

As if the Derby-based Jamaican wasn't cold enough, the Basingstoke banger iced him in a sensational 1.47 of the opening round. McKenzie failed to make use of his height and reach advantages as Francis, with father-trainer Trevor in his corner, decked him with a thudding left hook. He took the eight but was flattened soon after and it was stopped. One fight, one round, and nobody asked for their money back!

Ali Nuumbembe, a soldier in the Namibian army, would probably be due a promotion after becoming his country's first Commonwealth boxing champion when he defeated Kevin Anderson for the welterweight title at the Fife Ice Arena in Kirkcaldy. It was a tactical battle all the way and the split decision awarded to Ali could easily have gone the other way. It was that kind of fight, with a big eighth round putting Nuumbembe on the winning trail.

The snow had shifted but it was still freezing cold in Bristol when the local favourite, Glenn Catley, took to the ring at Filton College to box Sergey Kharchenko, from Russia via Spain. The action soon hotted up as the visitor roughed up the local hero and by the third round Glen had a cut over his right eye and had been rocked several times. Sergey rocked him again in the fourth to cop another round and Catley was given a wake-up call by his manager, Chris Sanigar, before coming up for round five. It did the trick. A

In a contest for the vacant WBO interim lightweight title, Graham Earl (left) was forced to retire at the end of the fifth round, but only after giving Australia's Michael Katsidis a tremendous battle   Les Clark

big right hand landed on Sergey's chin and the Russian was flat on his back. He beat the count, but Catley was all over him and the referee waved it off. It was the second comeback win for the 34-year-old former WBC super-middleweight champion and he was now looking for something big.

After suffering a shock knockout in his American debut, the former British welterweight champion, Neil Sinclair, was back home and back in the winning groove when stopping Poland's Arek Malek in four rounds at Cork. Another Irishman chasing a title fight was Eamonn Magee, the former WBU titleholder and mandatory challenger for the British welterweight championship. At Letterkenny in Donegal, the Belfast southpaw took a six-rounds decision over Hungary's Janos Petrovics to satisfy trainer John Breen. "It's up to Eamonn now", said Breen.

MARCH
At the Metroradio Arena in Newcastle it was John Bull versus Uncle Sam in a unique team-match fronted by Barry McGuigan and Sugar Ray Leonard. The Yanks won four-two in the six bouts proper to the competition, a pity really as the Brits won the first two fights that didn't count. So overall it was a four-four draw and everybody went home happy.

Fight of the night saw Ross Minter go down in the eighth round (all contests were over eight-threes) against Freddie Curiel, the American making sure of victory in a see-saw battle with a terrific right to the jaw. Minter went down, struggled upright, then toppled over again as concerned father Alan appeared at the ringside. Ross recovered okay as his record dropped to 17-2-1, but he'd been in a war; a rib injury, right hand swollen, cut on nose and right eye. Curiel also bore the marks of a tough scrap, but he also had the winner's medal around his neck.

At light-middleweight, Anthony Small got the UK off to a winning start with his herky-jerky style, but was lucky to survive the final round as Walter Wright came too late with his big attack. Leicester's Martin Concepcion fought gallantly at light-middle against Alfonso Gomez before two left hooks finished him in round seven. Local middleweight, Paul Buchanan, had the Geordie crowd with him in his bout with rangy Jerson Ravelo, but 16 months inactivity showed in his work and a third-round knockdown clinched victory for the visitor. Veteran former WBC super-middleweight champion, Robin Reid, was also rusty after 20 months on the shelf, but he still had enough to beat Jesse Brinkley in a bad-tempered bout. Scottish southpaw Colin McNeil found Cornelius Bundrage too strong for him and the Detroit man was a winner in round seven of their light-middle bout.

In the fights that didn't count, except to the fighters of course, the Liverpool middle-weight, Paul Smith, boxed smartly to beat Jonathan Reid on a seventh-round stoppage and southpaw Nigel Wright had too much of everything for Jonathan Nelson, who pulled out after two rounds, two cuts, and two knockdowns. An excellent show that went on too long. I got home at 2.15 am and there was another fight and I lost that one!

In Dublin, the undefeated local hero, Bernard Dunne, moved to 23-0 when he defended his European super-bantamweight title against Yersin Jailauov in a punch-perfect three-rounds victory, the challenger from Kazakhstan being floored twice before it was stopped. The former Irish amateur star is headed for a world title shot.

Norwich fans turned out in force to see their favourite son, Jon Thaxton, defend his British lightweight championship against the gutsy challenge of Leicester's Scott Lawton and their boy didn't let them down. The taller Lawton boxed well, but Thaxton is a power-house and he ground his man down until round seven when a tremendous right hook sent Scott into the arms of Richie Davies, who had seen enough. In a companion bout, Esham Pickering regained the vacant British super-bantam title with a lop-sided unanimous decision over Barking's Marc Callaghan.

Britain's smallest fighter, Ian Napa (5'1"), gave himself a big job when he tackled Italy's Simone Maludrottu for his European bantamweight title at Dagenham, the task proving too much for him as the champion punched his way to a unanimous decision to retain for the seventh time.

In the British heavyweight title fight between the undefeated champion, Scott Gammer, and the former titleholder, Danny Williams, the first shock came at the weigh-in when Danny hit just inside 16st 5lbs, lightest since his debut in 1995. Gammer received the second shock when Williams knocked him out in round nine.

Another unbeaten record looked in danger when Derry Matthews defended his WBU featherweight title against the British champion, John Simpson, in his native Liverpool. A right hand from the Scot dumped Derry on his derriere in the very first round and he looked glad of the mandatory eight count. Simpson took the third also, but a clash of heads in round six left the Scot's face a mask of blood and Derry boxed his way to his 18th straight victory. Simpson's title was not at stake.

On the Liverpool show, Kevin Mitchell kept his undefeated slate (23-0), along with his Commonwealth super-featherweight belt, when Harry Ramogoadi had to be rescued in round six after surviving a knockdown. The Coventry-based South African led Kevin a merry dance for three rounds, but Mitchell came on strong to close the show.

Esham Pickering (right) seen here outpointing the game Marc Callaghan to win the vacant British super-bantam title at Dagenham last March   Les Clark

If John Duddy ran for mayor of New York City, he would be a shoo-in. He'd get the Irish vote anyway. Once again he packed them in at Madison Square Garden's smaller arena (Okay it was the St Patrick's Day weekend) as he beat Anthony Bonsante on a technical decision after nine rounds, with the man from Minnesota bleeding from a bad cut on his forehead caused by an accidental clash of heads early in the fight. Victory gave the Irishman the vacant WBC Continental Americas championship and he also retained his IBA belt. That would probably keep your pants up, but I would be sticking with the braces. There was an Irish band and some dancing girls and everybody had a good time. Everybody except Anthony Bonsante, of course!

British cruiserweight champion John Keeton didn't have a very good time when he went to Montreal to contest the vacant Commonwealth title with the Canadian southpaw, Troy Ross. Keeton was dropped by a left cross in the second round, misjudged the count, and got up too late. Knockout!

Marking time for bigger things, the British and Commonwealth super-middleweight champion, Carl Froch, wasted no time getting rid of Sergei Tatevosyan; two rounds!

APRIL

Joe Calzaghe could have phoned this one in. America's Peter Manfredo came to Cardiff with the ringing endorsements of the ace trainer, Freddie Roach, and all-time great, Sugar Ray Leonard, but when the first bell rang in the Millenium Stadium, Manfredo couldn't cut the mustard. He was the victim of what many saw as a premature stoppage in round three, but he was nevertheless a victim; victim number 43 on Calzaghe's unbeaten hit parade and number 20 in WBO title defences.

Young Peter was in over his head, literally, as champion Joe towered a good three inches above him and looked much heavier, although it was only 1¾ pounds on the scales. In the third round, Calzaghe opened up to back Manfredo against the ropes, covering up as Joe's hands flew like those of a drummer whose sticks had flown out of his hands. It was the sheer quantity of Calzaghe's blows rather than the quality, but the attack was enough for Terry O'Connor to wave his arms, thus signifying the end 90 seconds into the round. The Americans around the ring were more stunned than Manfredo and a lot of Brits agreed with them that this contest could have gone on; gone on to a subsequent stoppage no doubt, but at least the challenger would have been a happier victim, if you get what I mean.

For this mammoth bill which started at 2.15 pm, they had closed the roof on this magnificent stadium. They should have closed the door at the tradesmen's entrance when Bobby Gunn showed up for his fight with Enzo Maccarinelli. If Manfredo was 'The Contender', this guy was 'The Pretender'. Billed as Bobby 'Machine' Gunn, the Canadian was firing blanks, not that he had much time to pull the trigger. Maccarinelli blasted him out of there inside 2.35 of round one to retain his WBO cruiserweight title and take his record to 26-1, 20 inside schedule.

Jamie Moore (left), the British light-middleweight champion, was far too good for Argentina's Sebastian Andres Lujan, the 12-round points decision in his favour being a formality

Les Clark

Fortunately for this crowd of 35,000, there were some decent contests on the bill. Bradley Pryce retained his Commonwealth light-middleweight title against the challenge of the tough Ghanaian, Thomas Awinbono. Fighting out of the Calzaghe gym, Bradley had the skill and speed to contain his man and take his pro log to 24-6.

And there was Amir Khan, the Bolton wonderboy, who is Britain's best prospect for my money. Khan was too good for the Doncaster southpaw, Stefy Bull, who was on his way to an early shower; dropped and stopped at 1.45 of round three. Another unbeaten fighter to keep his certificate (now 20-0) was Pontypool's Tony Doherty, who retained his Celtic welterweight title in a rematch with Taz Jones. Doherty won the title with a controversial decision over the boy from Abercynon, but made no mistake this time, a big right hand putting Taz on the deck in round seven. He beat the count but it was stopped.

Former British champion, Michael Jennings, outboxed and outpunched Takaloo over 12 rounds to take his WBU welterweight title in a bloody encounter, both being cut in a fourth-round clash of heads. The Margate man kept trying to unload a big punch but Jennings kept his boxing together to come out with the unanimous decision. In another WBU title bout, at middleweight, Gary Lockett saw off the challenge of Wigan southpaw, Lee Blundell, who was stopped in the third after three knockdowns.

At Altrincham, Dale Robinson and Chris Edwards found themselves in a no-win situation when they boxed 12 rounds for the vacant British and Commonwealth flyweight titles. After the final bell, the titles were still vacant; one judge saw Robinson the winner, another went for Edwards, the third went for a draw. It was an excellent contest so the fans wouldn't mind seeing it again, whenever. This was a rematch, Edwards having stopped the former Commonwealth champion in an eight- rounds upset.

Argentine hard man Sebastian Lujan had been in a few wars, notably against the WBO champion, Antonio Margarito, when his left ear almost parted company from his head! But against the Salford southpaw, Jamie Moore, on the Altrincham bill, Lujan sleep-walked through 12 rounds to leave the British light-middleweight champion a one-sided winner.

Another disappointing performer was Howard Eastman who, having regained the British middleweight title, claimed the vacant Commonwealth title once again in a lack-lustre display against Evans Ashira, from Kenya via Denmark. The 36-year-old Battersea veteran was maybe jet-lagged after a trip to his native Guyana, but his work was negative as he spoiled and held Ashira, breaking up his attacks in a not very edifying spectacle. The decision was unanimous, but by that time the Dudley crowd couldn't have cared less.

In stark contrast was the explosive 105-second blast-out of Polish tough guy, Tomasz Bonin, by David Haye at the Wembley Arena. Bonin had lost only to big Audley Harrison in 38 fights, and that a controversial stoppage, but he was never at the races against the European cruiserweight champion, who was testing the water at heavyweight. He'll swim no bother on this performance! Bonin was smashed to the deck four times before the referee saved him. Haye weighed a sculpted 15st 7lbs yet still talked of going for a world title at cruiserweight against WBC/WBA champion, Jean-Marc Mormeck.

Big shock on the Wembley bill was the sudden walkout of the British light-heavyweight champion, Peter Oboh, one hour before he was due in the ring to defend his title against Tony Oakey. Oboh hadn't boxed in three years and was favourite to win and pick up a £9,000 purse. But before he reached home that night, he had been stripped by the Board, his fight future behind him.

MAY

Portsmouth puncher Tony Oakey could well have said to himself: "I don't understand it. I had a shower this morning. Maybe it was something I said", after the British light-heavyweight champion, Peter Oboh, walked out of Wembley an hour before stepping into the ring with him to defend his title. Whatever, Oboh was now history, his title now vacant and on the line for Tony and Steven Spartacus to sort out a few weeks later at London's ExCel Arena. Sort it out they did in a blistering battle that went into the final round before Steven was hung out to dry over the top rope, prompting the third man's intervention. Spartacus came prepared to go out on his shield and Oakey had a fight on his hands from the opening bell. But the former WBU champion loves nothing more than a toe-to-toe punch-up and he joined in with obvious relish, his attacks taking more and more out of the gutsy guy coming from the other corner. And in the 12th and final session, the man from Portsmouth prevailed, taking his record to 24-2.

Peter Haymer was probably not in the right frame of mind for his eight rounder with Northampton's Paul David as he had been matched with Spartacus in a defence of his English title on this same bill at the ExCel. But Steve got the call from the Board to fight Oakey and Haymer got a guy from the Ingle gym. Haymer should have ignored David's stats, 4-3. As it was he couldn't get untracked and Paul got the decision and a big name on his record. That's show business!

Canada's Troy Ross had destroyed John Keeton for the vacant Commonwealth cruiserweight title back home and he showed how in his British debut, taking out Tony Booth in a fight that saw the Hull journeyman veteran decked four times before it was stopped after 1.52 of the second round.

Eamonn Magee is a fighter. When they picked him up off the road after a vicious street attack in 2004, he was lucky to be still alive. The doctors said he would probably never be able to walk again. Boxing? Forget it, son. That was all he needed to hear. The will to win that had pulled him through 29 professional fights and 11 championship contests, pulled him through three major operations and saw him back in the ring within a year to defend his WBU welterweight crown earlier. But at 35, the Belfast southpaw had to bow to Father Time as the British welterweight champion, Kevin Anderson, fighting on 24-year-old legs, retained his title with a unanimous decision at the Concert Hall in Aberdeen. To seal his victory, Kevin sent Eamonn down with a right hand in round 11. The only other time he had been decked it took a baseball bat to bring him down.

Over in New York, at the Beacon Theatre, Ireland's John Duddy was less than impressive in taking a ten-rounds decision from Dupre Strickland from Louisiana, who was not as good as his stats, 18-1-1. The crowd favourite looked to have an early night when a smashing left hook dumped Dupre on his backside in the opening round. Strickland beat the count and thereafter explored the outer perimeter of the ring, stopping just long enough to inflict two cuts over Duddy's right eye. The Irish middleweight came out with his undefeated slate still intact, now 20-0.

Way down in Memphis on the same night, Duddy's fellow countryman, Andy Lee, preserved his unbeaten record with his ninth-straight victory, over Clinton Bonds from Arkansas who was on his way to the showers inside the first round.

Shanee Martin travelled to Hungary to box for the GBU flyweight title against the champion, Viktoria Milo. She decked Milo in the first round, but Viktoria got up to win a split decision over ten rounds. Experience told over the distance.

Two British lads lived the dream out in Las Vegas, sparring with Shane Mosley and fighting on the Floyd Mayweather-Oscar de la Hoya card at the MGM Grand. But the dream ended for John O'Donnell, who was undefeated on 15 going in, when Christian Solano floored the London welterweight twice on his way to a second-round stoppage. Manchester's John Murray evened the score when he punched Lorenzo Bethea to a standstill inside seven rounds, taking his unbeaten record to 21-0 with 11 stoppages. This light-welter is a lad to watch.

The merry month of May was comeback time. At Altrincham, Michael Gomez, Manchester's former British and WBU super-featherweight champion, got back in harness after 16 months out and stopped Daniel Thorpe at 2.45 of round three to take his record to 33-7. In Glasgow before his 'ain folk' the former Commonwealth super-featherweight champion, Craig Docherty, was back in business, taking a six-threes decision over Billy Smith in a lightweight bout. As he always does, the Stourport journeyman gave the Scot a run for his money, so it was a good pipe-opener for Craig, out since September 2005, who took his pro log to 20-3-1.

At Bradford, the local favourite, Nadeem Siddique, boxed like he'd never been away (13 months) when knocking out Tye Williams in the fourth round to collect the vacant Central Area and British Masters welterweight titles. Taking his record to 19-0, the Ingle fighter punched sharply to drop the Dewsbury southpaw twice for the finish.

At the Beach Ballroom in his native Aberdeen, Lee McAllister led Ghana's Ben Odamattey a merry dance for ten rounds to take the lop-sided decision and the WBF Inter-Continental lightweight championship. With his record now at 24-1, the Ingle-trained fighter was looking for bigger things.

JUNE

The veteran American promoter, Bob Arum, called it one of the five best body punches he'd seen in 42 years in the business. It was a thudding left hook to the rib cage of Arum's man Jose Luis Castillo and it sent the Mexican to the canvas by the ropes in the fourth round, suddenly out of the fight and possibly out of boxing. Castillo hadn't been on the deck before in 63 professional fights, but he'd never met Ricky Hatton before. Unfortunately for Castillo, he was in there with possibly the best Ricky Hatton boxing has seen in his undefeated 43-fight career. The Manchester hitman was fit, focused, and fired up for this fight at the Thomas and Mack Centre in Las Vegas, ostensibly for Ricky's IBO light-welterweight title but mainly for bragging rights in the division. Bring on Floyd Mayweather! The plan was for Hatton to work his way into the fight after four or five rounds, but there would be no fifth round this night. Ricky had a date with an ice-cold Guinness. His mantra was the search and destroy philosophy of the legendary Marvin Hagler and the 33-year-old former two-time WBC lightweight champion never looked like winning, apart from a decent third round. Looking and listening to the 13,044 fans in the arena, Hatton could have been forgiven for thinking he was at home in the MEN Arena. The place was a sea of British flags and football tops with an estimated 8,000 fans having made the trip to this glittering oasis in the Nevada desert.

Also in Vegas was Ricky's younger brother Matthew, defending his IBF Inter-Continental welterweight belt against Puerto Rica's Edwin Vazquez. Matthew was a unanimous winner after a competitive 12 rounds, taking his pro log to 31-3-1, and was looking for a fight with the British champion, Kevin Anderson.

At the 1998 European Amateur Championships in Belarus, Ireland's Bernard Dunne was beaten on points by Norway's Reidar Walstad who went on to take the bronze medal. But when they clashed for the professional title at The Point in Dublin, Ireland's Golden Boy Dunne retained his European super-bantamweight title with an easy unanimous decision over Walstad, who came out with a nasty gash over his left eye to show he'd been in a fight. Dunne remained unbeaten after 24 bouts. On the undercard, Darlington's Franny Jones put his name in the frame with a fifth-round knockout of the former British welterweight champion, Neil Sinclair, who promptly announced his retirement. Jones snatched victory from the jaws of defeat with a big attack as the round was ending. The Belfast man finished with a 25-6 record and a Lonsdale Belt to show the grandchildren.

Colin Lynes went into the lion's den, Motherwell, to fight the big local favourite, Barry Morrison, for his British light-welterweight title. Colin had been stopped by Lenny Dawes who then dropped his title to Morrison, so Lynes was chancing his arm in this one. The gamble paid off as the Hornchurch man stamped his class on the fight early and was never headed, winning the title on a unanimous decision. At 29, after nine years putting together a 29-3 record, they fastened a Lonsdale Belt around his waist.

At the Millennium Hotel in Mayfair, the British featherweight champion, John Simpson, took the measure of his southpaw challenger, Ryan Barrett, who was cut down by a scything left hook to the body in round five. Barrett dropped by the ropes and he didn't get up. He did eventually, but it was too late.

Gary Reid was up against it fighting Ajose Olusegun

for the vacant Commonwealth light-welterweight title at Crystal Palace. The London-based Nigerian won an easy decision to stay undefeated at 20-0. The best is yet to come.

Still going at 38, Jane Couch keeps doing what she loves doing – fighting! She was off in the wilds of Connecticut for a return meeting with a gal called Clampitt, determined to come home still wearing her WIBF light-welterweight belt. Jane had beaten Jaime Clampitt three year ago, but she was three years older and Jaime was three years better and took the decision and the title.

At the end of the fight, Dean Francis was a happy man. He had beaten Ayittey Powers on a ninth-round knockout to add the IBO Inter-Continental belt to his Commonwealth light-heavyweight title, and his dickey right shoulder was just fine. Fighting at Bristol, the Basingstoke battler floored the London-based African in the fifth and brought the curtain down in round nine. Now 33, Francis has held British, EBU and WBO Inter-Continental titles at super-middle, and he is still hungry for more, now at light-heavy.

Another former champ hunting further glory was Ryan Rhodes, the Sheffield southpaw who holds the record for winning one of the current Lonsdale Belts outright in 90 days! That was when Ryan was the undefeated British and IBF Inter-Continental light-middle champ and undefeated WBO Inter-Continental middleweight ruler. There were no titles at stake in the Barnsley ring when Rhodes despatched Paul Buchanan, sending the Geordie down twice before it was stopped at the 89-seconds mark of round one. Ryan Rhodes was back!

At the Eston Sports Academy in Middlesbrough, one of the new kids on the block, Sedgefield's Mark Dawes, had a six-twos light-welter tutorial from one of the senior members on the circuit in Birmingham's Karl Taylor, who showed how he is still going at 41 after 122 fights. Winning his second pro fight, young Mark handed Taylor his 100th defeat and hopefully learned something from one of the old school.

Facts and Figures, 2006-2007

There were 650 (632 in 2005-2006) British-based boxers who were active between 1 July 2006 and 30 June 2007, spread over 205 (190 in 2005-2006) promotions held in Britain, not including the republic of Ireland, during the same period. Those who were either already holding licenses or had been re-licensed amounted to 467, while there were 168 (128 in 2005-2006) new professionals, plus eight non-nationals who began their careers elsewhere and seven women.

Unbeaten During Season (Minimum Qualification: 6 Contests)

7: Dean Harrison. 6: Scott Belshaw, Mark Hastie, James McKinley, Alex Matvienko (1 draw), Anthony Small, Paul Truscott.

Longest Unbeaten Sequence (Minimum Qualification: 10 Contests)

43: Joe Calzaghe, Ricky Hatton. 27: Nicky Cook. 26: Gavin

Rees. 25: Roman Greenberg. 23: Enzo Maccarinelli, Kevin Mitchell. 21: Tony Doherty (nc), Carl Froch, John Murray. 20: Ajose Olusegun, Paul Smith, Junior Witter. 19: Nadeem Sidique. 18: Derry Matthews. 17: Lee McAllister, Anthony Small. 16: Matthew Hall. 14: Darren Barker, Steve Bell (2 draws), Kell Brook, John Fewkes, Darren McDermott (1 draw). 13: Amer Khan, Gary Lockett. 12: Barrie Jones, Amir Khan, Patrick J. Maxwell (1 draw). 11: Garry Buckland, Danny Goode, Michael Lomax (1 draw), Steve McGuire (1 draw), Muhsen Nasser, Mark Thompson. 10: Gareth Couch, Tristan Davies, Michael Grant (1 draw), Darren Johnstone, Willie Limond, Paul McCloskey, Kreshnik Qato, Sam Rukundo (1 draw), Ashley Theophane (1 draw), Joey Vegas.

Most Wins During Season (Minimum Qualification: 6 Contests)

7: Dean Harrison, Lee Noble. 6: Prince Arron, Scott Belshaw, Mark Hastie, James McKinlay, Anthony Small, Billy Smith, Paul Truscott.

Most Contests During Season (Minimum Qualification: 10 Contests)

24: Peter Dunn. 20: Shaun Walton. 19: Billy Smith. 17: Rocky Muscus. 16: Pete Buckley. 15: Steve Cooper, Duncan Cottier, Delroy Spencer. 14: Ben Hudson, Ernie Smith. 13: Kristian Laight, Sergei Rozhakmens, Daniel Thorpe. 12: Mark Phillips. 11: Tony Booth. 10: Paul King, Rom Krauklis, Lee Noble, Deniss Sirjatovs.

Most Contests During Career (Minimum Qualification: 50 Contests)

286: Pete Buckley. 157: Tony Booth. 134: Ernie Smith. 122: Karl Taylor. 109: Howard Clarke. 99: Ojay Abrahams. 98: Anthony Hanna. 93: Peter Dunn. 87: Daniel Thorpe. 81: Carl Allen. 80: Jason Nesbitt. 76: David Kirk. 64: Delroy Spencer. 62: Billy Smith, Chris Woollas. 54: Henry Akinwande. 53: Mark Phillips. 52: Simeon Cover, David Kehoe.

Stop Press: Results for July/August 2007 (British-Based Fighters' Results Only)

Hippodrome Nightclub, Colchester – 1 July (Promoter: Burns)

Tom Glover w pts 10 John Baguley (Vacant British Masters Lightweight Title), Lee Purdy w pts 6 Ben Hudson, Leonard Lothian w pts 4 Matthew Martin Lewis.

Robin Park Arena, Wigan – 6 July (Promoters: Maloney/ Woods)

Ian Napa w pts 12 Jason Booth (Vacant British Bantamweight Title), Vincent Vuma w rsc 8 Mark Thompson (Vacant WBC International L.Middleweight Title), Craig Watson w pts 8 Michael Lomax, Ali Nuumbembe w pts 8 Vladimir Borovski, Tony Dodson w pts 4 Nick Okoth, Brett Flournoy w rsc 4 Yassine El Maachi, Scott Mitchell w pts 4 David Ingleby, Stuart McFadyen w pts 4 Tasif Khan, Alex Matvienko drew 4 Martin Marshall.

Metrodome Leisure Centre, Barnsley – 13 July (Promoter: Maloney)
Leva Kirakosyan w rsc 4 Carl Johanneson (European S.Featherweight Title Defence), John Fewkes w pts 8 Tontcho Tontchev, Geard Ajetovic w rsc 3 Patrick J. Maxwell, Rendall Munroe w rsc 5 Dai Davies, Akaash Bhatia w rsc 5 Steve Gethin, Danny Wallace w rtd 3 Dwayne Hill, Ross Burkinshaw w co 3 Iordan Vasilev, Rod Anderton w pts 4 Carl Wild, Gary Sykes w rsc 2 Deniss Sirjatovs.

Rama, Ontario – 13 July
Martin Lindsay w pts 6 Jose Silviera.

Holiday Inn Hotel, Birmingham – 13 July (Promoter: Purchase)
Gatis Skuja w rtd 5 Dee Mitchell, James McKinley w pts 6 Ernie Smith, Ben Murphy w rsc 2 Neal McQuade, Thomas Costello w pts 4 Jason Nesbitt, Tom Owens w pts 4 Tony Booth.

02 Arena, Greenwich – 14 July (Promoter: Warren)
Steve Luevano w co 11 Nicky Cook (Vacant WBO Featherweight Title), Matthew Marsh w pts 10 Rocky Dean (Vacant Southern Area S.Bantamweight Title), Jamie Cox w pts 4 Johnny Greaves, Amir Khan w rtd 8 Willie Limond (Commonwealth Lightweight Title Challenge), Kevin Mitchell w co 2 Alexander Hrulev (Vacant Inter-Continental S.Featherweight Title), Matt Skelton w pts 12 Michael Sprott (Commonwealth Heavyweight Title Defence), Steve Foster w rsc 3 Vladimir Borov, Vinny Mitchell w rsc 3 Sergei Rozhakmens, Bradley Pryce w rsc 7 Anthony Small (Commonwealth L.Middleweight Title Defence), Martin Concepcion w rsc 1 Matthew Hall.

Dublin, Ireland – 14 July
Paul McCloskey w co 4 Ivan Orlando Bustos, Stephen Haughian w rsc 6 Gary O'Connor, Eugene Heagney w pts 8 Colin Moffett, Patrick Hyland w rsc 1 Roman Rafael.

The Mayfair, Seaton Carew – 15 July (Promoter: Garside)
Craig Denton w pts 6 Matt Scriven, James McElvaney w pts 6 John Baguley, Paul Malcolm w pts 6 David Ingleby, Gavin Reid w pts 6 Delroy Spencer, Mark Dawes w pts 6 Carl Allen.

Civic Hall, Wolverhampton – 20 July (Promoter: Hearn)
Colin Lynes w rsc 8 Young Muttley (British L.Welterweight Title Defence. Vacant European L.Welterweight Title), Marcus Portman w rsc 6 Jozsef Matolcsi (WBF L.Middleweight Title Challenge), Matthew Macklin w co 1 Anatoliy Udalov, Stuart Elwell w pts 6 Alex Matviechuk, Steven Bendall w rtd 2 Davey Jones, Ricky Owen w rsc 5 Anthony Hanna, Kevin Buckley w pts 4 Tony McQuade, Rob Hunt w pts 4 Karl Taylor, Dennis Corpe w rsc 3 Wayne Downing.

The Indoor Arena, Cardiff – 21 July (Promoter: Warren)
Enzo Maccarinelli w pts 12 Wayne Braithwaite (WBO Cruiserweight Title Defence), Gavin Rees w pts 12 Souleymane M'Baye (WBA L.Welterweight Title Challenge), Alex Arthur w rsc 10 Koba Gogoladze (Vacant Interim WBO S.Featherweight Title), Kevin McIntyre w pts 10 Tony Doherty (Celtic Welterweight Title Challenge), Andy Morris w rsc 2 Daniel Thorpe, Nathan Cleverly w co 6 Ayitey Powers, Hari Miles w co 4 Matthew Lloyd, Don Broadhurst w pts 4 Kakhaber Toklikishvili, Kerry Hope w pts 6 Sherman Alleyne, Kenny Anderson w rsc 2 Dean Walker, Barrie Jones w pts 4 Billy Smith.

Debdale Lane Sports Ground, Mansfield – 22 July (Promoter: Scriven)
Andy Bell w pts 6 Delroy Spencer, Darren Broomhall w pts 6 Jonathan Whiteman, Karl Chiverton w pts 6 Lance Verallo, Charlie Chiverton w rsc 1 Ricky Strike.

West Rainton Arena, Houghton le Spring – 27 July (Promoter: Dunn)
David Dolan w rsc 6 Luke Simpkin, Muhsen Nasser w pts 6 Peter Dunn, James Dolan w pts 4 David Ingleby.

Olympia, Liverpool – 11 August (Promoter: Dixon)
Lee Murtagh w pts 6 Graham Delehedy, Joey Ainscough w pts 6 Ernie Smith, Rhys Roberts w pts 6 Delroy Spencer, Scott Quigg w pts 6 Shaun Walton, Shaun Farmer w pts 6 Paddy Pollock, Amir Unsworth w rsc 4 Mark Bett, Denton Vassell w pts 4 Gatis Skuja, Stephen Burke w rsc 1 Craig Tomes, John Watson w pts 4 Johnny Greaves, Tony Quigley w pts 4 Jevgenijs Andrejevs.

Stockholm, Sweden – 18 August
Sam Rukundo w pts 4 Araik Sachbazjan.

Cork, Ireland – 18 August
Jason McKay w pts 8 Mugurel Sebe, Ciaran Healy w pts 6 Martins Kukuls, Neil Sinclair w pts 6 Sergejis Savrinovics.

Salt Lake City, USA – 18 August
Roman Greenberg w rsc 9 Damon Reed.

Dublin, Ireland – 25 August
Tony Oakey drew 12 Brian Magee (British L.Heavyweight Title Defence), Andy Lee w rtd 4 Ciaran Healy, Paul McCloskey w pts 8 Alfredo di Feto, Matthew Macklin w co 4 Darren Rhodes, Nicki Smedley w pts 4 Surinder Sekhon, Willie Thompson w pts 4 Artur Jashkul.

Diary of British Boxing Tournaments, 2006-2007

Tournaments are listed by date, town, venue and named promoter, as licensed by the BBBoC, and cover the period 1 July 2006 to 30 June 2007.

Code: SC = Sporting Club

Date	Town	Venue	Promoters
08.07.06	Cardiff	Millennium Stadium	Warren
10.07.06	Manchester	Midland Hotel	I. Robinson
12.07.06	Bethnal Green	York Hall	Hennessy
21.07.06	Altrincham	Leisure Centre	Maloney
23.07.06	Dagenham	Goresbrook Leisure Centre	Feld
02.09.06	Bolton	Reebok Stadium	Warren
08.09.06	Birmingham	International Convention Centre	Purchase
08.09.06	Mayfair	Grosvenor House Hotel	Warren
09.09.06	Inverurie	Thainstone Centre	T. Gilmour
11.09.06	Manchester	Midland Hotel	I. Robinson
15.09.06	Newport	Leisure Centre	J. Sanigar
15.09.06	Muswell Hill	Alexandra Palace	Hennessy
16.09.06	Burton	Meadowside Leisure Centre	Rowson
18.09.06	Glasgow	Holiday Inn	T. Gilmour
22.09.06	Bethnal Green	York Hall	Hearn
23.09.06	Coventry	Leofric Hotel	Coventry SC
24.09.06	Bethnal Green	York Hall	Feld
24.09.06	Southampton	Guildhall	Bishop
29.09.06	Cardiff	Holland House	Boyce
29.09.06	Motherwell	Concert Hall	C. Gilmour
29.09.06	Manchester	George Carnall Leisure Centre	Maloney
30.09.06	Middlesbrough	Eston Sports Academy	Rowson
30.09.06	Stoke	King's Hall	Carney
01.10.06	Rotherham	Thurcroft Consort Hotel	Goodall
05.10.06	Sunderland	Roker Hotel	Conroy
06.10.06	Mexborough	Empress Ballroom	Hobson
06.10.06	Wolverhampton	Dunstall Racetrack Suite	Rowson
06.10.06	Mansfield	Civic Centre	Scriven
06.10.06	Bethnal Green	York Hall	Maloney
07.10.06	Walsall	Town Hall	Rowson
07.10.06	Weston super Mare	Hutton Moor Leisure Centre	Hay
07.10.06	Belfast	Holiday Inn	Hobson
08.10.06	Swansea	Brangwyn Hall	Hodges
09.10.06	Birmingham	Holiday Inn	Cowdell
09.10.06	Bedworth	Civic Hall	Coventry SC
13.10.06	Doncaster	Dome Leisure Centre	Rushton
13.10.06	Aberavon	Afan Lido	Hearn
13.10.06	Irvine	Magnum Centre	T. Gilmour
14.10.06	Manchester	MEN Arena	Warren
15.10.06	Norwich	Mercy Premier Nightclub	Featherby
18.10.06	Bayswater	Royal Lancaster Hotel	Evans/Waterman
20.10.06	Sheffield	Don Valley Stadium	Hobson
21.10.06	Southwark	Elephant & Castle Leisure Centre	D. Williams
21.10.06	Glasgow	Thistle Hotel	Morrison
23.10.06	Glasgow	Holiday Inn	T. Gilmour
26.10.06	Dudley	Town Hall	Rowson
26.10.06	Wolverhampton	Civic Hall	Purchase
26.10.06	Belfast	Anderstown Leisure Centre	Hobson
27.10.06	Glasgow	Hilton Hotel	Braveheart Promotions
28.10.06	Sheffield	Grosvenor House Hotel	Rhodes
28.10.06	Aberdeen	Beach Ballroom	Ingle

28.10.06	Bethnal Green	York Hall	Warren
03.11.06	Barnsley	Metrodome Leisure Complex	Hobson/Feld
03.11.06	Glasgow	Holiday Inn	T. Gilmour
03.11.06	Bristol	Dolman Exhibition Centre	C. Sanigar
04.11.06	Glasgow	Kelvin Hall	Warren
04.11.06	Mansfield	Civic Centre	Scriven
07.11.06	Leeds	Elland Road Conference & Exhibition Centre	Bateson
10.11.06	Newport	Leisure Centre	J. Sanigar
10.11.06	Telford	Oakengates Theatre	Rowson
10.11.06	Hartlepool	Borough Hall	Hearn
11.11.06	Sutton in Ashfield	Leisure Centre	Calow
12.11.06	Manchester	George Carnall Leisure Centre	Wood
17.11.06	Brierley Hill	Civic Hall	Alton
17.11.06	Bethnal Green	York Hall	Maloney
18.11.06	Newport	Leisure Centre	Warren
20.11.06	Glasgow	Holiday Inn	T. Gilmour
23.11.06	Manchester	Midland Hotel	I. Robinson
24.11.06	Hull	KC Stadium	Hull & District SC
24.11.06	Stoke	King's Hall	Carney
24.11.06	Nottngham	Ice Arena	Hennessy
25.11.06	Belfast	Holiday Inn	Wilton
30.11.06	Piccadilly	Café Royal	Helliet
01.12.06	Doncaster	Dome Leisure Centre	Rushton
01.12.06	Birmingham	Aston Villa Leisure Centre	Purchase
01.12.06	Tower Hill	Grange City Hotel	Merton
02.12.06	Coventry	Leofric Hotel	Coventry SC
02.12.06	Clydebank	Play Drome	C. Gilmour
02.12.06	Southwark	Elephant & Castle Leisure Centre	D. Williams
02.12.06	Longford	Thistle Heathrow Park Hotel	Carman
03.12.06	Wakefield	Lightwaves Leisure Centre	Johnson
03.12.06	Bethnal Green	York Hall	Feld
03.12.06	Bristol	Central Marriott Hotel	Couch
05.12.06	Wolverhampton	Civic Hall	Rowson
06.12.06	Rotherham	Thurcroft Consort Hotel	Goodall
06.12.06	Stoke	Moat House Hotel	Dixon
07.12.06	Bradford	Hilton Hotel	Garber
07.12.06	Sunderland	Roker Hotel	Conroy
07.12.06	Peterborough	Holiday Inn	Pauly
08.12.06	Dagenham	Goresbrook Leisure Centre	Hennessy
09.12.06	Canning Town	ExCel Arena	Warren
09.12.06	Chigwell	Prince Regent Hotel	Burns
10.12.06	Sheffield	Octagon Centre	Hobson
10.12.06	Glasgow	Thistle Hotel	Morrison
11.12.06	Birmingham	Holiday Inn	Cowdell
11.12.06	Cleethorpes	Winter Gardens	Frater
13.12.06	Strand	Savoy Hotel	Helliet
14.12.06	Leicester	Ramada Jarvis Hotel	Griffin
15.12.06	Bethnal Green	York Hall	Hearn
17.12.06	Bolton	Reebok Stadium	Woods
22.12.06	Coventry	Mercia Park Leisure Centre	Hollier
20.01.07	Muswell Hill	Alexandra Palace	Hennessy
22.01.07	Glasgow	Radisson Hotel	T. Gilmour
26.01.07	Glasgow	Hilton Hotel	Braveheart Promotions
26.01.07	Dagenham	Goresbrook Leisure Centre	Maloney
28.01.07	Yarm	Tall Trees Hotel	Garside
01.02.07	Piccadilly	Café Royal	Helliet
09.02.07	Leeds	Town Hall	Maloney
09.02.07	Bristol	Central Marriott Hotel	Hay
15.02.07	Dudley	Town Hall	Rowson
16.02.07	Merthyr	Rhydycar Leisure Centre	Hodges
16.02.07	Sunderland	Roker Hotel	Conroy

16.02.07	Kirkcaldy	Fife Ice Arena	Hearn
17.02.07	Wembley	Arena	Warren
18.02.07	Bethnal Green	York Hall	Feld
19.02.07	Glasgow	Radisson Hotel	T. Gilmour
22.02.07	Leeds	Elland Road Marquee	Spratt
23.02.07	Doncaster	Dome Leisure Centre	Rushton
23.02.07	Birmingham	Aston Villa Leisure Centre	Purchase
23.02.07	Manchester	Midland Hotel	I. Robinson
23.02.07	Peterborough	East of England Showground	Sanders
24.02.07	Bracknell	Leisure Centre	Carman
24.02.07	Bristol	Filton College	C. Sanigar
24.02.07	Stoke	King's Hall	Carney
24.02.07	Manchester	Piccadilly Hotel	Dixon
25.02.07	Manchester	George Carnall Leisure Centre	Woods
25.02.07	Southampton	Guildhall	Bishop
26.02.07	Birmingham	Holiday Inn	Cowdell
02.03.07	Neath	Sports Centre	Hearn
02.03.07	Coventry	Mercia Park Leisure Centre	Hollier
02.03.07	Irvine	Assembly Rooms	T. Gilmour
03.03.07	Newport	Leisure Centre	J. Sanigar
03.03.07	Burton	Meadowside Leisure Centre	Rowson
03.03.07	Alfreton	Leisure Centre	Scriven
09.03.07	Dagenham	Goresbrook Leisure Centre	Maloney
10.03.07	Liverpool	Olympia	Warren
11.03.07	Shaw	Tara Leisure Centre	Doughty
16.03.07	Norwich	Norfolk Showground	Hennessy
16.03.07	Glasgow	Thistle Hotel	Morrison
17.03.07	Birmingham	International Convention Centre	Purchase
18.03.07	Bristol	Central Marriott Hotel	Couch
23.03.07	Nottingham	Ice Arena	Hennessy
24.03.07	Coventry	Leofric Hotel	Coventry SC
26.03.07	Glasgow	Radisson Hotel	T. Gilmour
30.03.07	Newcastle	Metro Radio Arena	Warren
30.03.07	Crawley	K2 Leisure Centre	Hearn
30.03.07	Peterborough	Holiday Inn	Pauly
31.03.07	Derby	Pride Park Toyota Suite	Mitchell
01.04.07	Shrewsbury	Lord Hill Hotel	Scriven
07.04.07	Cardiff	Millennium Stadium	Warren
13.04.07	Rugby	Benn Hall	Hollier
13.04.07	Houghton le Spring	Rainton Meadows Arena	Dunn
13.04.07	Altrincham	Leisure Centre	Woods
14.04.07	Wakefield	Light Waves Leisure Centre	Rowson
15.04.07	Barnsley	Metrodome Leisure Complex	Coldwell
18.04.07	Strand	Savoy Hotel	Helliet
20.04.07	Sheffield	Grosvenor House Hotel	Rhodes
20.04.07	Dudley	Concert Hall	Hennessy
21.04.07	Manchester	Jarvis Piccadilly Hotel	Dixon
23.04.07	Glasgow	Radisson Hotel	T. Gilmour
26.04.07	Manchester	Midland Hotel	I. Robinson
27.04.07	Wembley	Arena	Maloney
27.04.07	Hull	KC Stadium	Hull & District SC
28.04.07	Clydebank	Play Drome	T. Gilmour
28.04.07	Newark	Showground	Calow
29.04.07	Birmingham	Aston Villa Leisure Centre	Purchase
03.05.07	Sheffield	Don Valley Stadium	Hobson
05.05.07	Glasgow	Hilton Hotel	Braveheart Promotions
06.05.07	Darlington	Dolphin Centre	Garside
06.05.07	Altrincham	Leisure Centre	Woods
06.05.07	Leeds	Elland Road Conference & Exhibition Centre	Bateson
11.05.07	Motherwell	Concert Hall	Hearn
11.05.07	Sunderland	Roker Hotel	Conroy

12.05.07	Stoke	Fenton Manor Sports Complex	Carney
13.05.07	Birmingham	Burlington Hotel	Cowdell
14.05.07	Cleethorpes	Beachcomber	Frater
18.05.07	Canning Town	ExCel Arena	Hennessy
19.05.07	Nottingham	Victoria Leisure Centre	Scriven
25.05.07	Glasgow	Thistle Hotel	Morrison
26.05.07	Aberdeen	Beach Ballroom	Ingle
27.05.07	Bradford	Hilton Hotel	Hobson
31.05.07	Manchester	Old Trafford North Stand Suite	Jones
01.06.07	Birmingham	Holiday Inn	Purchase
01.06.07	Peterborough	East of England Showground	Sanders
02.06.07	Bristol	Ashton Gate Conference Centre	Hay
03.06.07	Barnsley	Metrodome Leisure Centre	Coldwell
05.06.07	Glasgow	Radisson Hotel	T. Gilmour
07.06.07	Bayswater	Royal Lancaster Hotel	Evans/Waterman
08.06.07	Motherwell	Concert Hall	T. Gilmour
08.06.07	Mayfair	Millennium Hotel	Feld
09.06.07	Middlesbrough	Eston Sports Academy	Rowson
10.06.07	Neath	Sports Centre	Boyce
14.06.07	Leeds	Elland Road Conference & Leisure Centre	Bateson
15.06.07	Crystal Palace	National Sports Centre	Maloney
16.06.07	Newport	Leisure Centre	C. Sanigar
16.06.07	Bolton	De Vere White's Hotel	Woods
16.06.07	Chigwell	Prince Regent Hotel	Burns
17.06.07	Mansfield	Leisure Centre	Scriven
21.06.07	Peterborough	Holiday Inn	Pauly
24.06.07	Wigan	Robin Park Centre	Woods
24.06.07	Sunderland	Stadium of Light Marquee	Conroy
28.06.07	Dudley	Town Hall	Rowson
29.06.07	Manchester	Midland Hotel	I. Robinson
30.06.07	Belfast	Holiday Inn	Wilton
30.06.07	Manchester	George Carnall Leisure Centre	Dixon

Active British-Based Boxers: Career Records

Shows the complete record for all British-based boxers who have been active between 1 July 2006 and 30 June 2007. Names in brackets are real names, where they differ from ring names, and the first place name given is the boxer's domicile. The given weight class for each boxer is based on the weights made for their last three contests and boxers are either shown as being self-managed or with a named manager, the information being supplied by the BBBoC shortly before going to press. Also included are foreign-born fighters who made their pro debuts in Britain, along with others like Shinny Bayaar (Mongolia), Karl David (Poland), Varuzhan Davtyan (Armenia), Istvan Kecskes (Hungary), Harry Ramogoadi (South Africa), Hastings Rasani (Zimbabwe), Sergei Rozhakmens (Latvia) and Choi Tseveenpurev (Mongolia), who, although starting their careers elsewhere, now hold BBBoC licenses. Former champions, such as Henry Akinwande, Herbie Hide and Neil Sinclair, who continue their careers elsewhere are also included.

Ojay Abrahams
Watford. *Born* Lambeth, 17 December, 1964
S.Middleweight. Former British Masters
Middleweight Champion. *Ht* 5'8½"
Manager Self

21.09.91	Gordon Webster W RSC 3 Tottenham
26.10.91	Mick Reid W RSC 5 Brentwood
26.11.91	John Corcoran W PTS 6 Bethnal Green
21.01.92	Dave Andrews DREW 6 Norwich
31.03.92	Marty Duke W RSC 2 Norwich
19.05.92	Michael Smyth L PTS 6 Cardiff
16.06.92	Ricky Mabbett W PTS 6 Dagenham
13.10.92	Vince Rose L RSC 3 Mayfair
30.01.93	Vince Rose DREW 6 Brentwood
19.05.93	Ricky Mabbett L RSC 4 Leicester
18.09.93	Ricky Mabbett L PTS 6 Leicester
09.12.93	Nick Appiah W PTS 6 Watford
24.01.94	Errol McDonald W RSC 2 Glasgow
09.02.94	Vince Rose W PTS 6 Brentwood
23.05.94	Spencer McCracken L PTS 6 Walsall
11.06.94	Darren Dyer W RSC 1 Bethnal Green
29.09.94	Gary Logan L PTS 10 Bethnal Green
	(Southern Area Welterweight Title Challenge)
13.12.94	Geoff McCreesh L PTS 6 Potters Bar
11.02.95	Gary Murray L PTS 8 Hamanskraal, South Africa
17.07.95	Andreas Panayi L PTS 8 Mayfair
02.10.95	Larbi Mohammed L RTD 5 Mayfair
08.12.95	Jason Beard W CO 2 Bethnal Green
09.04.96	Kevin Thompson W RSC 3 Stevenage
07.05.96	Harry Dhami L RSC 5 Mayfair
	(Vacant Southern Area Welterweight Title)
12.11.96	Spencer McCracken L PTS 8 Dudley
22.04.97	Paul King W RSC 4 Bethnal Green
29.05.97	Paul Ryan L RSC 3 Mayfair
30.06.97	Ahmet Dottuev L RSC 4 Bethnal Green
08.11.97	Anthony McFadden L PTS 8 Southwark
24.03.98	Leigh Wicks W PTS 6 Bethnal Green
28.04.98	Jim Webb W RSC 2 Belfast
10.09.98	Delroy Leslie L PTS 10 Acton
	(Vacant Southern Area L. Middleweight Title)
19.12.98	Michael Jones L PTS 6 Liverpool
23.01.99	Wayne Alexander L DIS 1 Cheshunt
	(Vacant Southern Area L. Middleweight Title)
01.05.99	Wayne Alexander L RSC 3 Crystal Palace
26.06.99	Geoff McCreesh L PTS 8 Millwall
05.10.99	Hussain Osman L PTS 4 Bloomsbury
23.10.99	Paul Samuels L PTS 8 Telford
18.01.00	Howard Eastman L RSC 2 Mansfield
23.03.00	Pedro Thompson DREW 6 Bloomsbury
08.04.00	Anthony Farnell L PTS 8 Bethnal Green
16.05.00	Ryan Rhodes L PTS 6 Warrington
23.05.00	Alexandru Andrei L PTS 6 Paris, France
04.07.00	Lester Jacobs L PTS 4 Tooting
21.09.00	Harry Butler W PTS 6 Bloomsbury
07.10.00	Kofi Jantuah L RTD 3 Doncaster
25.11.00	Donovan Smillie W RSC 2 Manchester
16.12.00	Marlon Hayes L RTD 6 Sheffield
15.01.01	Gordon Behan DREW 6 Manchester
24.02.01	Ruben Groenewald L PTS 6 Bethnal Green
22.04.01	Harry Butler W PTS 6 Streatham
17.05.01	Lee Murtagh W RSC 2 Leeds
	(Vacant British Masters L. Middleweight Title)
21.06.01	Charden Ansoula L PTS 4 Earls Court
28.07.01	Gary Logan L RSC 4 Wembley
10.12.01	Jimmy Vincent L PTS 10 Birmingham
	(British Masters L. Middleweight Title Challenge)
28.01.02	Ian Cooper W PTS 6 Barnsley
16.03.02	John Humphrey L PTS 10 Bethnal Green
	(Vacant Southern Area L.Middleweight Title)
13.04.02	Mihaly Kotai L PTS 6 Liverpool
20.04.02	Freeman Barr L PTS 8 Cardiff
10.05.02	Carl Froch L RSC 1 Bethnal Green
15.06.02	Sam Soliman L PTS 4 Tottenham
17.08.02	Wayne Elcock L PTS 4 Cardiff
17.09.02	David Starie L RSC 4 Bethnal Green
25.10.02	Gilbert Eastman L PTS 4 Bethnal Green
12.12.02	Allan Gray L PTS 10 Leicester Square
	(Southern Area Middleweight Title Challenge. Vacant WBF International Middleweight Title)
05.03.03	David Walker L PTS 6 Bethnal Green
19.04.03	Geard Ajetovic L PTS 4 Liverpool
12.05.03	Jason Collins L PTS 10 Birmingham
	(Vacant British Masters S.Middleweight Title)
05.07.03	Allan Foster L PTS 4 Brentwood
18.09.03	Steve Roache W CO 2 Mayfair
18.10.03	Michael Jones L PTS 6 Manchester
22.11.03	Jason McKay L PTS 4 Belfast
01.12.03	Omar Gumati L PTS 6 Leeds
10.02.04	Daniel Teasdale L PTS 6 Barnsley
23.02.04	Matt Galer L PTS 4 Nottingham
08.03.04	Hamed Jamali L PTS 8 Birmingham
02.04.04	Scott Dann L RSC 6 Plymouth
06.05.04	Daniel Teasdale L PTS 4 Barnsley
13.05.04	Conroy McIntosh L RSC 2 Bethnal Green
12.06.04	Matthew Macklin L PTS 4 Manchester
10.09.04	Paul Smith L PTS 4 Liverpool
29.10.04	Tom Cannon L PTS 4 Renfrew
12.11.04	Matthew Hall L RSC 1 Halifax
27.01.05	Eder Kurti L PTS 6 Piccadilly
27.05.05	Paul Buchanan L PTS 6 Spennymoor
04.06.05	Ricardo Samms L PTS 4 Manchester
18.06.05	Jon Ibbotson L PTS 4 Barnsley
25.10.05	Ricardo Samms L PTS 4 Preston
24.11.05	Jason McKay L PTS 4 Lurgan
04.03.06	Tony Quigley L PTS 4 Manchester
20.03.06	Danny Thornton L PTS 6 Leeds
01.04.06	Richard Horton L PTS 4 Bethnal Green
14.05.06	Rod Anderton L PTS 6 Derby
27.05.06	Andrew Facey L PTS 6 Aberdeen
09.10.06	Neil Tidman L PTS 4 Bedworth
27.10.06	Ali Mateen L PTS 6 Glasgow
11.11.06	Adie Whitmore L PTS 6 Sutton in Ashfield
24.11.06	Darren Barker L RTD 1 Nottingham
02.03.07	Grzegorz Proksa L RTD 2 Neath

Career: 99 contests, won 20, drew 4, lost 75.

Terry Adams
Birmingham. *Born* Birmingham, 1 November, 1978
L.Middleweight. *Ht* 5'8½"
Manager Self

19.02.04	Neil Addis W CO 2 Dudley
15.04.04	Geraint Harvey W PTS 6 Dudley
08.07.04	Geraint Harvey W RSC 6 Birmingham
15.10.04	Jamie Coyle L RSC 5 Glasgow
13.02.05	Michael Lomax L RSC 1 Brentwood
07.04.05	Keith Jones W PTS 6 Birmingham
24.07.05	Gavin Smith W PTS 6 Sheffield
30.09.05	Matt Galer L PTS 10 Burton
	(Vacant Midlands Area L.Middleweight Title)
24.02.06	Gatis Skuja DREW 4 Birmingham
05.03.06	Danny Goode L PTS 8 Southampton
30.03.06	Cello Renda L PTS 4 Peterborough
06.05.06	Ernie Smith W PTS 6 Birmingham
28.05.06	Danny Reynolds L RSC 1 Wakefield
06.10.06	Mark Lloyd L RSC 7 Wolverhampton
	(Vacant British Masters L.Middleweight Title)
11.12.06	Davey Jones L PTS 6 Cleethorpes

Career: 15 contests, won 6, drew 1, lost 8.

Usman Ahmed
Derby. *Born* Derby, 21 November, 1981
Flyweight. *Ht* 5'6"
Manager M.Shinfield

30.09.06	Chris Edwards L PTS 6 Stoke

11.12.06 Delroy Spencer DREW 6 Cleethorpes
03.03.07 Gary Sheil W PTS 6 Alfreton
Career: 3 contests, won 1, drew 1, lost 1.

Joey Ainscough

Liverpool. *Born* Liverpool, 16 August, 1979
L.Heavyweight. *Ht* 6'0"
Manager D. Powell

27.11.99 Mark Dawson W PTS 4 Liverpool
05.02.00 Hussain Osman L PTS 4 Bethnal Green
25.03.00 Chris Crook W PTS 4 Liverpool
06.05.07 Mark Phillips W PTS 6 Altrincham
Career: 4 contests, won 3, lost 1.

Geard Ajetovic

Liverpool. *Born* Beocin, Yugoslavia, 28
February, 1981
S.Middleweight. *Ht* 5'8½"
Manager Self

19.04.03 Ojay Abrahams W PTS 4 Liverpool
17.05.03 Jason Samuels W PTS 4 Liverpool
26.09.03 Gary Beardsley W RSC 3 Reading
07.11.03 Joel Ani W RTD 1 Sheffield
06.02.04 Tomas da Silva W RSC 4 Sheffield
12.05.04 Dmitry Donetskiy W PTS 6 Reading
10.12.04 Conroy McIntosh W PTS 6 Sheffield
21.01.05 Dmitry Yanushevich W RSC 4
Brentford
24.07.05 Conroy McIntosh W PTS 6 Sheffield
14.10.05 Jason Collins W RSC 6 Huddersfield
26.11.05 Magid Ben Driss W PTS 8 Sheffield
18.03.06 Christophe Canclaux L PTS 8 Monte
Carlo, Monaco
13.05.06 Manoocha Salari W RSC 4 Sheffield
27.04.07 Patrick J. Maxwell DREW 6 Wembley
29.05.07 Robert Roselia W PTS 10 Pont
Audemer, France
Career: 15 contests, won 13, drew 1, lost 1.

Henry Akinwande

Dulwich. *Born* London, 12 October, 1965
Heavyweight. Former IBF Inter-
Continental Heavyweight Champion.
Former Undefeated WBN & WBC
FeCarBox Heavyweight Champion.
Former Undefeated WBO, European &
Commonwealth Heavyweight Champion.
Ht 6'7"
Manager Self

04.10.89 Carlton Headley W CO 1 Kensington
08.11.89 Dennis Bailey W RSC 2 Wembley
06.12.89 Paul Neilson W RSC 1 Wembley
10.01.90 John Fairbairn W RSC 1 Kensington
14.03.90 Warren Thompson W PTS 6
Kensington
09.05.90 Mike Robinson W CO 1 Wembley
10.10.90 Tracy Thomas W PTS 6 Kensington
12.12.90 Francois Yrius W RSC 1 Kensington
06.03.91 J. B. Williamson W RSC 2 Wembley
06.06.91 Ramon Voorn W PTS 8 Barking
28.06.91 Marshall Tillman W PTS 8 Nice,
France
09.10.91 Gypsy John Fury W CO 3 Manchester
(Elim. British Heavyweight Title)
06.12.91 Tim Bullock W CO 3 Dussledorf,
Germany
28.02.92 Young Joe Louis W RSC 3 Issy les
Moulineaux, France
26.03.92 Tucker Richards W RSC 2 Telford

10.04.92 Lumbala Tshimba W PTS 8 Carquefou,
France
05.06.92 Kimmuel Odum W DIS 6 Marseille,
France
18.07.92 Steve Garber W RTD 2 Manchester
19.12.92 Axel Schulz DREW 12 Berlin,
Germany
(Vacant European Heavyweight Title)
18.03.93 Jimmy Thunder W PTS 12 Lewisham
*(Vacant Commonwealth Heavyweight
Title)*
01.05.93 Axel Schulz W PTS 12 Berlin,
Germany
(Vacant European Heavyweight Title)
06.11.93 Frankie Swindell W PTS 10 Sun City,
South Africa
01.12.93 Biagio Chianese W RSC 4 Kensington
(European Heavyweight Title Defence)
05.04.94 Johnny Nelson W PTS 10 Bethnal
Green
23.07.94 Mario Schiesser W CO 7 Berlin,
Germany
(European Heavyweight Title Defence)
08.04.95 Calvin Jones W CO 2 Las Vegas,
Nevada, USA
22.07.95 Stanley Wright W RSC 2 Millwall
16.12.95 Tony Tucker W PTS 10 Philadelphia,
Pennsylvania, USA
27.01.96 Brian Sergeant W RSC 1 Phoenix,
Arizona, USA
23.03.96 Gerard Jones W DIS 7 Miami, Florida,
USA
29.06.96 Jeremy Williams W CO 3 Indio,
California, USA
(Vacant WBO Heavyweight Title)
09.11.96 Alexander Zolkin W RSC 10 Las
Vegas, Nevada, USA
(WBO Heavyweight Title Defence)
11.01.97 Scott Welch W PTS 12 Nashville,
Tennessee, USA
(WBO Heavyweight Title Defence)
12.07.97 Lennox Lewis L DIS 5 Stateline,
Nevada, USA
(WBC Heavyweight Title Challenge)
13.12.97 Orlin Norris W PTS 12 Pompano
Beach, Florida, USA
(Final Elim. WBA Heavyweight Title)
06.03.99 Reynaldo Minus W RSC 2 St Paul,
Minnesota, USA
15.05.99 Najeed Shaheed W RSC 9 Miami,
Florida, USA
22.02.00 Chris Serengo W RSC 1 Capetown,
South Africa
25.05.00 Russull Chasteen W CO 5 Tunica,
Mississippi, USA
08.12.00 Ken Craven W CO 1 Tallahassee,
Florida, USA
*(Vacant WBC FeCarBox Heavyweight
Title)*
17.03.01 Peter McNeeley W CO 2 Tallahassee,
Florida, USA
16.06.01 Maurice Harris W CO 1 Cincinnati,
USA
17.11.01 Oliver McCall L CO 10 Las Vegas,
Nevada, USA
08.03.02 Curt Paige W RSC 1 Kissimmee,
Florida, USA
29.10.02 Sam Ubokane W RSC 7 Capetown,
South Africa
10.12.02 Roman Sukhoterin W PTS 12
Constanta, Romania
*(WBN Inter-Continental Heavyweight
Title Challenge)*

31.05.03 Timo Hoffmann W PTS 12 Frankfurt,
Germany
*(IBF Inter-Continental Heavyweight
Title Challenge)*
10.04.04 Anton Nel W RSC 10 Carabas, Nigeria
*(IBF Inter-Continental Heavyweight
Title Defence)*
14.05.05 Alex Vasiliev W PTS 8 Bayreuth,
Germany
24.09.05 Tipton Walker W RSC 2 Atlantic City,
New Jersey, USA
10.12.05 Ed Mahone W PTS 12 Leipzig,
Germany
*(Vacant IBF Inter-Continental
Heavyweight Title)*
04.03.06 Cisse Salif W PTS 12 Oldenburg,
Germany
*(IBF Inter-Continental Heavyweight
Title Defence)*
04.11.06 Oleg Platov L PTS 12 Mülheim an der
Ruhr, Germany
*(IBF Inter-Continental Heavyweight
Title Defence)*
30.06.07 Andriy Oleinyk W PTS 10 Moscow,
Russia
Career: 54 contests, won 50, drew 1, lost 3.

Mark Alexander

Hackney. *Born* Hackney, 18 November,
1975
L.Welterweight. *Ht* 5'9½"
Manager Self

10.04.01 Steve Hanley W PTS 4 Wembley
31.07.01 Damien Dunnion W PTS 4 Bethnal
Green
19.12.01 Dazzo Williams L PTS 6 Coventry
15.05.03 Buster Dennis W PTS 4 Mayfair
01.08.03 Arv Mittoo W PTS 4 Bethnal Green
25.09.03 Henry Castle L PTS 6 Bethnal Green
01.11.03 John Simpson L PTS 4 Glasgow
19.11.05 Graeme Higginson W PTS 4
Southwark
21.05.06 Steve Gethin W PTS 4 Bethnal Green
21.10.06 Shaun Walton W PTS 6 Southwark
Career: 10 contests, won 7, lost 3.

Wayne Alexander

Croydon. *Born* Tooting, 17 July, 1973
Middleweight. Former Undefeated British,
European & WBU L.Middleweight
Champion. Former Undefeated Southern
Area L.Middleweight Champion. *Ht* 5'8¾"
Manager Self

10.11.95 Andrew Jervis W RTD 3 Derby
13.02.96 Paul Murray W PTS 4 Bethnal Green
11.05.96 Jim Webb W RSC 2 Bethnal Green
13.07.96 John Janes W RSC 3 Bethnal Green
05.06.97 Prince Kasi Kaihau W CO 4 Bristol
29.11.97 John Janes W RSC 1 Norwich
21.03.98 Darren Covill W RSC 2 Bethnal Green
09.05.98 Pedro Carragher W CO 2 Sheffield
14.07.98 Lindon Scarlett W RSC 5 Reading
05.12.98 Jimmy Vincent W RSC 3 Bristol
23.01.99 Ojay Abrahams W DIS 1 Cheshunt
*(Vacant Southern Area
L. Middleweight Title)*
01.05.99 Ojay Abrahams W RSC 3 Crystal
Palace
07.08.99 George Richards W RSC 2 Dagenham
19.02.00 Paul Samuels W RSC 3 Dagenham

(Vacant British L. Middleweight Title)
12.08.00 Paul Denton W RSC 1 Wembley
10.02.01 Harry Simon L RSC 5 Widnes
(WBO L. Middleweight Title Challenge)
28.07.01 Viktor Fesetchko W PTS 8 Wembley
17.11.01 Joe Townsley W RSC 2 Glasgow
(British L. Middleweight Title Defence)
19.01.02 Paolo Pizzamiglio W RSC 3 Bethnal Green
(Vacant European L. Middleweight Title)
18.01.03 Viktor Fesetchko W PTS 6 Preston
06.12.03 Delroy Mellis L RSC 8 Cardiff
07.02.04 Howard Clarke W RSC 2 Bethnal Green
10.09.04 Takaloo W RSC 2 Bethnal Green
(Vacant WBU L. Middleweight Title)
11.12.04 Delroy Mellis W PTS 10 Canning Town
04.06.05 Christian Bladt W CO 5 Manchester
04.03.06 Thomas McDonagh W PTS 12 Manchester
(WBU L.Middleweight Title Defence)
09.12.06 Serge Vigne L RSC 1 Canning Town
Career: 27 contests, won 24, lost 3.

Youssef Al Hamidi
Dewsbury. *Born* Syria, 16 December, 1977
Lightweight. *Ht* 5'5"
Manager C.Aston

05.10.06 Paul Holborn L PTS 6 Sunderland
28.10.06 Dwayne Hill W RSC 3 Sheffield
17.11.06 Akaash Bhatia L PTS 4 Bethnal Green
03.12.06 Paul Halpin W PTS 4 Bethnal Green
26.01.07 Clifford Smith DREW 4 Dagenham
09.03.07 Lee Cook L PTS 6 Dagenham
24.06.07 Michael Gomez L RTD 3 Wigan
Career: 7 contests, won 2, drew 1, lost 4.

Carl Allen
Wolverhampton. *Born* Wolverhampton, 20 November, 1969
L.Welterweight. Former Undefeated Midlands Area S. Bantamweight Champion.
Ht 5'7¼"
Manager Self

26.11.95 Gary Jenkinson W PTS 6 Birmingham
29.11.95 Jason Squire L PTS 6 Solihull
17.01.96 Andy Robinson L PTS 6 Solihull
13.02.96 Ervine Blake W RSC 5 Wolverhampton
21.02.96 Ady Benton L PTS 6 Batley
29.02.96 Chris Jickells W PTS 6 Scunthorpe
27.03.96 Jason Squire DREW 6 Whitwick
26.04.96 Paul Griffin L RSC 3 Cardiff
30.05.96 Roger Brotherhood W RSC 5 Lincoln
26.09.96 Matthew Harris W PTS 10 Walsall
(Midlands Area S. Bantamweight Title Challenge)
07.10.96 Emmanuel Clottey L RTD 3 Lewisham
21.11.96 Miguel Matthews W PTS 8 Solihull
30.11.96 Floyd Havard L RTD 3 Tylorstown
29.01.97 Pete Buckley W PTS 8 Stoke
11.02.97 David Morris DREW 8 Wolverhampton
28.02.97 Ian McLeod L RTD 3 Kilmarnock
21.05.97 David Burke L PTS 4 Liverpool
30.06.97 Duke McKenzie L PTS 8 Bethnal Green
12.09.97 Brian Carr L PTS 8 Glasgow
04.10.97 Sergei Devakov L PTS 6 Muswell Hill
03.12.97 Chris Lyons W PTS 8 Stoke

21.05.98 Roy Rutherford L PTS 6 Solihull
09.06.98 Scott Harrison L RSC 6 Hull
30.11.98 Gary Hibbert L PTS 4 Manchester
09.12.98 Chris Jickells W RSC 3 Stoke
04.02.99 Mat Zegan L PTS 4 Lewisham
17.03.99 Craig Spacie W PTS 8 Stoke
08.05.99 Phillip Ndou L RSC 2 Bethnal Green
14.06.99 Pete Buckley W PTS 6 Birmingham
22.06.99 David Lowry L PTS 4 Ipswich
11.10.99 Lee Williamson L PTS 6 Birmingham
19.10.99 Tontcho Tontchev L CO 2 Bethnal Green
20.12.99 Nicky Cook L CO 3 Bethnal Green
08.02.00 Lee Williamson W PTS 8 Wolverhampton
29.02.00 Bradley Pryce L PTS 4 Widnes
28.03.00 Lee Williamson W PTS 8 Wolverhampton
16.05.00 Bradley Pryce L RSC 3 Warrington
24.06.00 Michael Gomez L CO 2 Glasgow
10.10.00 Steve Hanley W PTS 8 Brierley Hill
05.02.01 Lee Meager DREW 6 Hull
12.03.01 Pete Buckley W PTS 6 Birmingham
27.03.01 Pete Buckley W PTS 8 Brierley Hill
15.09.01 Esham Pickering L PTS 6 Derby
17.11.01 Steve Conway L PTS 8 Dewsbury
08.12.01 Esham Pickering L PTS 8 Chesterfield
07.02.02 Mark Bowen L PTS 6 Stoke
20.04.02 Esham Pickering L PTS 6 Derby
21.07.02 Eddie Nevins L PTS 4 Salford
07.09.02 Colin Toohey DREW 6 Liverpool
26.10.02 Dazzo Williams W RSC 2 Maesteg
02.12.02 Esham Pickering L PTS 6 Leicester
28.01.03 Lee Meager L PTS 8 Nottingham
09.05.03 Jeff Thomas DREW 6 Doncaster
08.11.03 Baz Carey W RSC 2 Coventry
28.11.03 Carl Greaves L PTS 4 Derby
28.02.04 Michael Kelly L PTS 4 Bridgend
03.04.04 Andy Morris L PTS 4 Manchester
16.04.04 Dave Stewart L PTS 6 Bradford
17.06.04 Scott Lawton L PTS 10 Sheffield
(Vacant Midlands Area Lightweight Title)
03.09.04 Gavin Rees L PTS 6 Newport
22.10.04 Craig Johnson L PTS 6 Mansfield
12.11.04 Billy Corcoran L RSC 5 Wembley
13.12.04 Jonathan Thaxton L RSC 1 Birmingham
05.03.05 Ryan Barrett L PTS 4 Dagenham
15.05.05 Scott Lawton L PTS 6 Sheffield
18.06.05 Joe McCluskey L PTS 6 Coventry
16.09.05 Stefy Bull L PTS 10 Doncaster
(Vacant WBF Inter-Continental Lightweight Title)
13.11.05 Carl Johanneson L RTD 2 Leeds
17.02.06 Dwayne Hill L PTS 6 Sheffield
25.02.06 Damian Owen L PTS 6 Bristol
10.03.06 Martin Gethin L PTS 4 Walsall
25.03.06 Haider Ali DREW 4 Burton
21.05.06 Andrew Murray L PTS 4 Bethnal Green
01.06.06 Tristan Davies L PTS 6 Birmingham
22.09.06 Ben Jones L PTS 4 Bethnal Green
13.10.06 Stefy Bull L PTS 6 Doncaster
10.11.06 Tristan Davies L PTS 10 Telford
(Vacant Midlands Area Lightweight Title)
09.02.07 Henry Castle L RSC 4 Leeds
20.04.07 Martin Gethin DREW 6 Dudley
27.05.07 Femi Fehintola L PTS 6 Bradford
16.06.07 Garry Buckland L PTS 6 Newport
Career: 81 contests, won 18, drew 7, lost 56.

Jay Allen
Coventry. *Born* Coventry, 27 August, 1985
Middleweight. *Ht* 5'11½"
Manager P. Carpenter

09.10.06 Rocky Muscas W PTS 6 Bedworth
Career: 1 contest, won 1.

Peter Allen
Birkenhead. *Born* Birkenhead, 13 August, 1978
Lightweight. *Ht* 5'5½"
Manager Self

30.04.98 Sean Grant L PTS 6 Pentre Halkyn
21.06.98 Garry Burrell W PTS 6 Liverpool
20.09.98 Simon Chambers L PTS 6 Sheffield
16.11.98 Stevie Kane W PTS 6 Glasgow
07.12.98 Simon Chambers L PTS 6 Bradford
28.02.99 Amjid Mahmood L PTS 6 Shaw
12.03.99 Marc Callaghan L PTS 4 Bethnal Green
15.09.99 Steve Brook L PTS 6 Harrogate
07.10.99 Nicky Wilders L PTS 6 Sunderland
18.10.99 Mark Hudson L PTS 6 Bradford
15.11.99 Craig Docherty L RSC 1 Glasgow
09.12.01 Jeff Thomas L PTS 6 Blackpool
01.03.02 Andrew Ferrans L PTS 8 Irvine
15.03.02 Ricky Burns L PTS 6 Glasgow
17.04.02 Andrew Smith W PTS 6 Stoke
24.06.02 Tasawar Khan L PTS 6 Bradford
14.09.02 Carl Greaves L PTS 6 Newark
08.10.02 Andrew Ferrans L PTS 8 Glasgow
21.10.02 Tony McPake L PTS 6 Glasgow
17.11.02 Choi Tseveenpurev L RSC 4 Shaw
16.02.03 Darryn Walton L PTS 6 Salford
31.05.03 Mally McIver L PTS 6 Barnsley
29.08.03 Steve Mullin L PTS 6 Liverpool
25.04.04 Craig Johnson L PTS 6 Nottingham
08.05.04 Michael Graydon L PTS 6 Bristol
30.05.04 Willie Valentine W PTS 4 Dublin
10.09.04 Steve Mullin L PTS 4 Liverpool
05.11.04 Damian Owen L RSC 1 Hereford
04.03.05 Isaac Ward DREW 6 Hartlepool
10.04.05 Lloyd Otte L PTS 6 Brentwood
30.04.05 Eddie Nevins W PTS 6 Wigan
25.09.05 Carl Johanneson L RTD 9 Leeds
(Vacant Central Area S.Featherweight Title)
16.06.06 David Appleby DREW 4 Liverpool
21.07.06 Chris Pacy L RSC 2 Altrincham
24.09.06 Henry Castle L RSC 6 Southampton
Career: 35 contests, won 5, drew 2, lost 28.

Sherman Alleyne
Bedford. *Born* London, 3 October, 1976
Middleweight. *Ht* 5'5"
Manager J. Feld

24.09.06 Greg Barton L RSC 3 Bethnal Green
17.03.07 Max Maxwell L PTS 6 Birmingham
15.04.07 Jon Musgrave L PTS 6 Barnsley
26.04.07 Prince Arron L PTS 6 Manchester
01.06.07 Rocky Muscas W PTS 6 Peterborough
Career: 5 contests, won 1, lost 4.

Leigh Alliss
Stroud. *Born* Stroud, 11 September, 1975
Western Area L.Heavyweight Champion.
Ht 5'9½"
Manager C. Sanigar

06.03.03 Ovill McKenzie L PTS 4 Bristol
12.05.03 Mark Phillips W PTS 6 Southampton
13.06.03 Egbui Ikeagbu W PTS 6 Bristol

09.10.03	Mark Phillips W PTS 4 Bristol
05.12.03	Dale Nixon W RSC 2 Bristol
13.02.04	Hastings Rasani W PTS 6 Bristol
08.05.04	Michael Pinnock W PTS 4 Bristol
03.07.04	Karl Wheeler W PTS 4 Bristol
01.10.04	Shane White W RSC 2 Bristol
	(Vacant Western Area L.Heavyweight Title)
03.12.04	Valery Odin L RSC 5 Bristol
29.04.05	Varuzhan Davtyan W PTS 4 Plymouth
16.09.05	Neil Simpson W RSC 3 Plymouth
17.11.05	Varuzhan Davtyan W PTS 4 Bristol
07.04.06	Peter Haymer L RSC 9 Bristol
	(English L.Heavyweight Title Challenge)
03.11.06	Tony Booth W PTS 4 Bristol
24.02.07	Enoch Quaye W RSC 4 Bristol

Career: 16 contests, won 13, lost 3.

Wayne Alwan Arab

Hackney. *Born* Zimbabwe, 28 February, 1982
Middleweight. *Ht* 5'10"
Manager M. Helliet

01.02.07	Peter Dunn W PTS 6 Piccadilly

Career: 1 contest, won 1.

Wayne Alwan Arab   Philip Sharkey

Adnan Amar

Nottingham. *Born* Nottingham, 17 February, 1983
Middleweight. Former Undefeated British Masters L.Middleweight Champion.
Ht 5'9½"
Manager J. Ingle

11.06.01	Steve Hanley W PTS 4 Nottingham
13.11.01	Duncan Armstrong W PTS 6 Leeds
21.10.02	Jason Gonzales W PTS 6 Cleethorpes
23.02.03	Arv Mittoo W PTS 6 Shrewsbury
16.03.03	Gareth Wiltshaw W PTS 6 Nottingham
16.04.03	Dave Cotterill W PTS 4 Nottingham
28.04.03	Ernie Smith W PTS 6 Cleethorpes
12.05.03	Pedro Thompson W RSC 4 Birmingham
08.06.03	David Kirk W PTS 6 Nottingham
06.09.03	Chris Duggan W PTS 4 Aberdeen
23.02.04	Wayne Shepherd W RSC 5 Nottingham
10.05.04	Ernie Smith W PTS 6 Birmingham

04.06.04	Dean Hickman L RSC 8 Dudley
	(Vacant Midlands Area L.Welterweight Title)
29.10.04	Daniel Thorpe W PTS 4 Worksop
25.06.05	Ernie Smith W PTS 6 Melton Mowbray
28.01.06	Ben Hudson W PTS 4 Nottingham
27.02.06	Simon Sherrington W RSC 6 Birmingham
	(Vacant British Masters L.Middleweight Title)
23.03.07	Ben Hudson W PTS 4 Nottingham

Career: 18 contests, won 17, lost 1.

Jamie Ambler

Aberystwyth. *Born* Aberystwyth, 16 January, 1985
L.Heavyweight. *Ht* 6'2½"
Manager N. Hodges

12.11.05	Liam Stinchcombe W RTD 3 Bristol
12.12.05	Jason Welborn L RSC 1 Birmingham
10.02.06	Jon Harrison L PTS 4 Plymouth
07.04.06	Danny Goode L PTS 4 Longford
21.04.06	Scott Jordan L PTS 4 Belfast
16.09.06	Jonjo Finnegan L PTS 6 Burton
24.09.06	Paul Morby L PTS 4 Southampton
03.11.06	Kenny Davidson W PTS 6 Glasgow
10.12.06	Stuart Brookes L RSC 1 Sheffield
16.02.07	Shon Davies L PTS 6 Merthyr Tydfil
26.03.07	Ricky Strike W CO 6 Glasgow
07.04.07	Kerry Hope L PTS 6 Cardiff

Career: 12 contests, won 3, lost 9.

James Ancliff

Fettercairn. *Born* Perth, 26 February, 1984
Featherweight. *Ht* 5'5"
Manager A. Morrison/F. Warren

22.04.06	Mickey Coveney L PTS 6 Glasgow
28.10.06	John Baguley W PTS 6 Aberdeen
10.12.06	Neil Marston W PTS 6 Glasgow
26.05.07	John Baguley W PTS 6 Aberdeen

Career: 4 contests, won 3, lost 1.

Kenny Anderson

Edinburgh. *Born* 5 January, 1983
L.Heavyweight. *Ht* 5'11½"
Manager Barry Hughes

14.10.06	Nick Okoth W RSC 4 Manchester
07.04.07	Jorge Gomez W RSC 3 Cardiff

Career: 2 contests, won 2.

Kevin Anderson

Buckhaven. *Born* Kirkcaldy, 26 April, 1980
British Welterweight Champion. Former Commonwealth Welterweight Champion. Former Undefeated Celtic Welterweight Champion. *Ht* 5'8¾"
Manager T. Gilmour

12.04.03	Paul McIlwaine W RSC 2 Bethnal Green
19.04.03	Piotr Bartnicki W RSC 2 Liverpool
17.05.03	Georges Dujardin W RSC 1 Liverpool
05.07.03	Mohamed Bourhis W CO 2 Brentwood
06.09.03	Sergei Starkov W PTS 6 Huddersfield
01.11.03	Alban Mothie W PTS 8 Glasgow
14.02.04	Andrei Napolskikh W PTS 8 Nottingham
13.03.04	Lance Hall W RSC 1 Huddersfield
22.04.04	Dmitri Yanushevich W RSC 2 Glasgow
27.05.04	Danny Moir W RSC 1 Huddersfield

15.10.04	Stephane Benito W RSC 6 Glasgow
26.11.04	Tagir Rzaev W PTS 6 Altrincham
31.01.05	Glenn McClarnon W RSC 4 Glasgow
	(Vacant Celtic Welterweight Title)
11.06.05	Vladimir Borovski W PTS 10 Kirkcaldy
30.09.05	Joshua Okine W PTS 12 Kirkcaldy
	(Commonwealth Welterweight Title Challenge)
17.03.06	Craig Dickson W RSC 7 Kirkcaldy
	(Commonwealth Welterweight Title Defence)
01.06.06	Young Muttley W RSC 10 Birmingham
	(British Welterweight Title Challenge. Commonwealth Welterweight Title Defence)
10.11.06	Anthony Guillet W PTS 8 Hartlepool
16.02.07	Ali Nuumbembe L PTS 12 Kirkcaldy
	(Commonwealth Welterweight Title Defence)
11.05.07	Eamonn Magee W PTS 12 Motherwell
	(British Welterweight Title Defence)

Career: 20 contests, won 19, lost 1.

Kevin Anderson   Les Clark

Rod Anderton

Nottingham. *Born* Nottingham, 17 August, 1978
L.Heavyweight. *Ht* 5'11¾"
Manager M. Shinfield

22.04.05	Michael Pinnock W PTS 6 Barnsley
18.06.05	Nicki Taylor W RSC 4 Barnsley
02.09.05	Paul Billington W RTD 1 Derby
08.12.05	Gary Thompson W PTS 6 Derby
28.01.06	Nick Okoth W PTS 4 Nottingham
14.05.06	Ojay Abrahams W PTS 6 Derby
06.10.06	Richard Turba L RSC 2 Mansfield
24.11.06	Phillip Callaghan W RSC 4 Nottingham
03.03.07	Michael Monaghan L PTS 10 Alfreton
	(Vacant Midlands Area L.Heavyweight Title)
23.03.07	Phillip Callaghan DREW 4 Nottingham

Career: 10 contests, won 7, drew 1, lost 2.

Csaba Andras
Langport. *Born* Hungary, 9 September, 1979
L.Heavyweight. *Ht* 6'0¾"
Manager Self

25.02.05	Billy McClung L PTS 6 Irvine
12.06.05	Coleman Barrett L RSC 1 Leicester Square
17.11.05	Tommy Eastwood L PTS 4 Piccadilly
25.11.05	Tony Moran L PTS 4 Liverpool
16.12.05	Vadim Usenko L RSC 1 Bracknell
02.03.06	Richard Turba L RSC 3 Blackpool
24.04.06	Tyrone Wright L CO 2 Cleethorpes
24.09.06	Danny Couzens W PTS 6 Southampton
03.11.06	Tony Salam L RSC 2 Barnsley

Career: 9 contests, won 1, lost 8.

Steve Anning
Barry. *Born* Cardiff, 24 September, 1980
Welterweight. *Ht* 5'6½"
Manager B. Coleman

02.04.06	Paul Porter DREW 4 Bethnal Green
01.06.06	Pietro Luigi Zara L PTS 6 Porto Torres, Italy
15.09.06	Ian Clyde W RSC 1 Newport
07.10.06	James Gorman L PTS 6 Belfast
10.11.06	Rocky Chakir W PTS 6 Newport
16.02.07	Amir Nadi W PTS 4 Merthyr Tydfil
03.03.07	Steve Cooper W PTS 6 Newport
11.05.07	Willie Bilan L PTS 4 Motherwell

Career: 8 contests, won 4, drew 1, lost 3.

John Anthony
Doncaster. *Born* Doncaster, 16 October, 1974
Cruiserweight. *Ht* 5'11½"
Manager D. Coldwell

22.04.05	Gary Thompson W PTS 4 Barnsley
18.06.05	Lee Mountford W RSC 5 Barnsley
04.11.05	Sandy Robb L PTS 6 Glasgow
12.02.06	Lee Kellett W RSC 1 Manchester
03.06.06	Andrew Lowe L PTS 6 Chigwell
01.10.06	Clint Johnson W PTS 6 Rotherham
02.03.07	Andrew Young W RSC 1 Irvine
17.03.07	Alexander Alexeev L RSC 5 Stuttgart, Germany
15.04.07	JJ Ojuederie L PTS 6 Barnsley
27.04.07	Tony Salam L PTS 4 Wembley
18.05.07	Micky Steeds L PTS 6 Canning Town

Career: 11 contests, won 5, lost 6.

John Anthony   Les Clark

Adil Anwar
Leeds. *Born* Leeds, 6 July, 1987
L.Welterweight. *Ht* 5'9¾"
Manager M. Bateson

14.06.07	Craig Tomes W PTS 6 Leeds

Career: 1 contest, won 1.

Paul Appleby
Edinburgh. *Born* Edinburgh, 22 July, 1987
S.Featherweight. *Ht* 5'9"
Manager T. Gilmour

23.01.06	Graeme Higginson W RTD 3 Glasgow
17.03.06	Ian Reid W RSC 3 Kirkcaldy
28.04.06	Andy Davis W RSC 1 Hartlepool
01.06.06	Graeme Higginson W RSC 2 Birmingham
22.09.06	Mickey Coveney W PTS 6 Bethnal Green
15.12.06	Rakhim Mingaleev W PTS 4 Bethnal Green
16.02.07	Buster Dennis W PTS 8 Kirkcaldy
11.05.07	Istvan Nagy W RSC 5 Motherwell

Career: 8 contests, won 8.

Prince Arron
Droylsden. *Born* Crumpsall, 27 December, 1987
British Masters Middleweight Champion.
Ht 6'3"
Manager W. Barker

28.04.06	Tommy Jones W PTS 6 Manchester
18.06.06	Karl Taylor W PTS 6 Manchester
10.07.06	Geraint Harvey W PTS 6 Manchester
11.09.06	Martin Marshall W PTS 6 Manchester
21.10.06	Anthony Small L RSC 2 Southwark
23.11.06	Rocky Muscas W PTS 6 Manchester
03.12.06	Danny Reynolds L PTS 6 Wakefield
18.02.07	George Katsimpas W PTS 8 Bethnal Green
26.04.07	Sherman Alleyne W PTS 6 Manchester
29.06.07	Cello Renda W PTS 10 Manchester *(Vacant British Masters Middleweight Title)*

Career: 10 contests, won 8, lost 2.

Prince Arron   Les Clark

Alex Arthur
Edinburgh. *Born* Edinburgh, 26 June, 1978
S.Featherweight. Former Undefeated
British, Commonwealth, European, WBO
Inter-Continental, WBA Inter-Continental
& IBF Inter-Continental S.Featherweight

Champion. Former British S.Featherweight
Champion. *Ht* 5'9"
Manager Self

25.11.00	Richmond Asante W RSC 1 Manchester
10.02.01	Eddie Nevins W RSC 1 Widnes
26.03.01	Woody Greenaway W RTD 2 Wembley
28.04.01	Dafydd Carlin W PTS 4 Cardiff
21.07.01	Rakhim Mingaleev W PTS 4 Sheffield
15.09.01	Dimitri Gorodetsky W RSC 1 Manchester
27.10.01	Alexei Slyautchin W RSC 1 Manchester
17.11.01	Laszlo Bognar W RSC 3 Glasgow
19.01.02	Vladimir Borov W RSC 2 Bethnal Green
11.03.02	Dariusz Snarski W RSC 10 Glasgow *(Vacant IBF Inter-Continental S.Featherweight Title)*
08.06.02	Nikolai Eremeev W RTD 5 Renfrew *(Vacant WBO Inter-Continental S.Featherweight Title)*
17.08.02	Pavel Potipko W CO 1 Cardiff
19.10.02	Steve Conway W CO 4 Renfrew *(Vacant British S. Featherweight Title)*
14.12.02	Carl Greaves W RSC 6 Newcastle *(British S.Featherweight Title Defence)*
22.03.03	Patrick Malinga W RSC 6 Renfrew *(Vacant WBA Inter-Continental S.Featherweight Title)*
12.07.03	Willie Limond W RSC 8 Renfrew *(British S.Featherweight Title Defence)*
25.10.03	Michael Gomez L RSC 5 Edinburgh *(British S.Featherweight Title Defence)*
27.03.04	Michael Kizza W CO 1 Edinburgh *(Vacant IBF Inter-Continental S.Featherweight Title)*
22.10.04	Eric Odumasi W RSC 6 Edinburgh *(IBF Inter-Continental S.Featherweight Title Defence)*
03.12.04	Nazareno Ruiz W PTS 12 Edinburgh *(IBF Inter-Continental S.Featherweight Title Defence)*
08.04.05	Craig Docherty W CO 9 Edinburgh *(Vacant British S.Featherweight Title. Commonwealth S.Featherweight Title Challenge)*
23.07.05	Boris Sinitsin W PTS 12 Edinburgh *(European S.Featherweight Title Challenge)*
18.02.06	Ricky Burns W PTS 12 Edinburgh *(British, Commonwealth & European S.Featherweight Title Defences)*
29.04.06	Sergey Gulyakevich W TD 7 Edinburgh *(European S.Featherweight Title Defence)*
04.11.06	Sergio Palomo W RSC 5 Glasgow *(European S.Featherweight Title Defence)*

Career: 25 contests, won 24, lost 1.

Ryan Ashworth
Scarborough. *Born* Stockton, 20 March, 1984
Middleweight. *Ht* 5'8¼"
Manager T. Gilmour/C. Aston

05.12.05	Omar Gumati W PTS 6 Leeds
24.02.06	Jak Hibbert L PTS 6 Scarborough
09.05.06	Peter Dunn W PTS 6 Leeds
13.04.07	Alex Matvienko DREW 4 Altrincham

Career: 4 contests, won 2, drew 1, lost 1.

Chris P. Bacon

Manchester. *Born* Australia, 8 October, 1969
Cruiserweight. Former Undefeated WBF European S.Cruiserweight Champion. Former Undefeated Central Area Cruiserweight Champion. *Ht* 6'0"
Manager S. Foster

21.12.97	Tim Brown W PTS 6 Salford
23.02.98	Tim Brown W PTS 6 Salford
08.05.98	Lee Swaby W RSC 3 Manchester
30.05.98	Phill Day W RSC 4 Bristol
17.07.98	Lee Swaby W PTS 6 Mere
18.09.98	Kevin Mitchell W RSC 1 Manchester
16.10.98	Luke Simpkin W PTS 6 Salford
16.11.98	Paul Bonson W PTS 8 Glasgow
25.02.99	Israel Ajose W PTS 10 Kentish Town
	(Vacant WBF European
	S. Cruiserweight Title)
19.06.99	Kelly Oliver L PTS 8 Dublin
09.10.99	Chris Woollas W PTS 4 Manchester
03.02.01	Collice Mutizwa W RSC 1 Manchester
14.07.01	Garry Delaney L RSC 10 Liverpool
	(British Masters Cruiserweight Title
	Challenge)
12.11.06	Oneal Murray W RSC Manchester
25.02.07	Tony Moran W RSC 7 Manchester
	(Vacant Central Area Cruiserweight
	Title)

Career: 15 contests, won 13, lost 2.

John Baguley

Sheffield. *Born* Rotherham, 13 March, 1988
Lightweight. *Ht* 5'9"
Manager J. Ingle

13.10.06	Wez Miller W PTS 4 Doncaster
28.10.06	James Ancliff L PTS 6 Aberdeen
07.11.06	Matthew Martin Lewis L PTS 6 Leeds
01.12.06	Deniss Sirjatovs W PTS 4 Doncaster
17.12.06	James Brown W PTS 6 Bolton
09.02.07	Stuart McFadyen L PTS 4 Leeds
27.04.07	Chris Hooper W RSC 1 Hull
26.05.07	James Ancliff L PTS 6 Aberdeen
10.06.07	Henry Jones W RSC 4 Neath

Career: 9 contests, won 5, lost 4.

Colin Bain

Glasgow. *Born* Hawick, 10 August, 1978
L.Welterweight. *Ht* 5'8½"
Manager A. Morrison

14.03.03	Dafydd Carlin W PTS 6 Glasgow
16.05.03	Martin Hardcastle W PTS 6 Glasgow
12.07.03	Gareth Wiltshaw W PTS 4 Renfrew
25.10.03	Dave Hinds W PTS 4 Edinburgh
27.03.04	Dave Hinds W PTS 4 Edinburgh
23.04.04	Pete Buckley W PTS 6 Glasgow
19.06.04	Henry Jones W PTS 4 Renfrew
29.10.04	Pete Buckley W PTS 4 Renfrew
12.12.04	Ricky Burns L PTS 6 Glasgow
12.11.05	Gavin Deacon W PTS 6 Glasgow
27.05.06	Mark Bett DREW 6 Glasgow
08.07.06	Amir Khan L RSC 2 Cardiff
10.12.06	Mark Bett W PTS 6 Glasgow

Career: 13 contests, won 10, drew 1, lost 2.

Vince Baldassara

Clydebank. *Born* Clydebank, 6 November, 1978
Scottish Middleweight Champion.
Ht 5'11½"
Manager Self

14.03.03	George Telfer L PTS 4 Glasgow
28.02.04	Rob MacDonald W PTS 6 Manchester
08.10.04	Barrie Lee DREW 6 Glasgow
09.12.04	Eddie Haley W PTS 6 Sunderland
21.02.05	Cafu Santos W CO 2 Glasgow
08.04.05	Barrie Lee L PTS 4 Edinburgh
25.04.05	Ciaran Healy W RSC 4 Glasgow
20.05.05	Mark Wall W PTS 6 Glasgow
17.06.05	Jak Hibbert W RSC 1 Glasgow
12.11.05	Craig Lynch W PTS 10 Glasgow
	(Vacant Scottish Area Middleweight
	Title)
09.03.06	Ryan Kerr DREW 6 Sunderland
08.09.06	Wayne Elcock L CO 6 Birmingham
	(Vacant WBF Inter-Continental
	Middleweight Title)
23.02.07	Cello Renda L CO 3 Birmingham

Career: 13 contests, won 7, drew 2, lost 4.

Ted Bami (Minsende)

Brixton. *Born* Zaire, 2 March, 1978
European L.Welterweight Champion.
Former WBF L.Welterweight Champion.
Ht 5'7"
Manager Self

26.09.98	Des Sowden W RSC 1 Southwark
11.02.99	Gary Reid W RSC 2 Dudley
10.03.00	David Kehoe W PTS 4 Bethnal Green
08.09.00	Jacek Bielski L RSC 4 Hammersmith
29.03.01	Keith Jones W PTS 4 Hammersmith
05.05.01	Francis Barrett W PTS 6 Edmonton
31.07.01	Lance Crosby W PTS 6 Bethnal Green
19.03.02	Michael Smyth W CO 4 Slough
23.06.02	Keith Jones W RSC 4 Southwark
17.08.02	Bradley Pryce W RSC 6 Cardiff
26.10.02	Adam Zadworny W PTS 4 Maesteg
07.12.02	Sergei Starkov W PTS 4 Brentwood
08.03.03	Andrei Devyataykin W RSC 1 Bethnal Green
12.04.03	Laszlo Herczeg W RSC 9 Bethnal Green
	(Vacant WBF L.Welterweight Title)
26.07.03	Samuel Malinga L RSC 3 Plymouth

Ted Bami

Les Clark

(WBF L.Welterweight Title Defence)
09.10.03 Zoltan Surman W RSC 3 Bristol
31.01.04 Jozsef Matolcsi W PTS 6 Bethnal Green
08.05.04 Viktor Baranov W RSC 2 Dagenham
08.10.04 Rafal Jackiewicz W PTS 8 Brentwood
13.02.05 Ricardo Daniel Silva W CO 2 Brentwood
21.10.05 Silence Saheed W PTS 6 Bethnal Green
24.02.06 Maurycy Gojko W CO 4 Dagenham
22.09.06 Giuseppe Lauri W PTS 12 Bethnal Green
(Vacant European L.Welterweight Title)
30.03.07 Giuseppe Lauri W PTS 12 Crawley
(European L.Welterweight Title Defence)
Career: 24 contests, won 22, lost 2.

Darren Barker

Barnet. *Born* Harrow, 19 May, 1982
Southern Area Middleweight Champion.
Ht 6'0½"
Manager Self

24.09.04 Howard Clarke W PTS 6 Nottingham
12.11.04 David White W RSC 2 Wembley
26.03.05 Leigh Wicks W RTD 4 Hackney
10.04.05 Andrei Sherel W RSC 3 Brentwood
09.07.05 Ernie Smith W PTS 6 Nottingham
16.07.05 Dean Walker W PTS 6 Chigwell
02.12.05 John-Paul Temple W RSC 6 Nottingham
20.01.06 Richard Mazurek W PTS 8 Bethnal Green
17.02.06 Louis Mimoune W RSC 2 Bethanl Green
12.05.06 Danny Thornton W RSC 6 Bethnal Green
12.07.06 Conroy McIntosh W RSC 7 Bethnal Green
15.09.06 Hussain Osman W PTS 10 Muswell Hill
(Vacant Southern Area Middleweight Title)
24.11.06 Ojay Abrahams W RTD 1 Nottingham
08.12.06 Paul Samuels W RSC 1 Dagenham
Career: 14 contests, won 14.

Darren Barker   Les Clark

James Barker

Droylsden. *Born* Salford, 17 July, 1985
Welterweight. *Ht* 5'9"
Manager W. Barker

23.02.07 Ali Hussain W PTS 6 Manchester
Career: 1 contest, won 1.

David Barnes (Smith)

Manchester. *Born* Manchester, 16 January, 1981
Welterweight. Former Undefeated British Welterweight Champion. *Ht* 5'8½"
Manager J. Trickett

07.07.01 Trevor Smith W RSC 2 Manchester
15.09.01 Karl Taylor W PTS 4 Manchester
27.10.01 Mark Sawyers W RSC 2 Manchester
15.12.01 James Paisley W RTD 2 Wembley
09.02.02 David Kirk W RTD 1 Manchester
04.05.02 David Baptiste W CO 3 Bethnal Green
01.06.02 Dimitri Protkunas W RSC 1 Manchester
28.09.02 Sergei Starkov W PTS 6 Manchester
12.10.02 Rusian Ashirov W PTS 6 Bethnal Green
14.12.02 Rozalin Nasibulin W RSC 3 Newcastle
18.01.03 Brice Faradji W PTS 6 Preston
05.04.03 Viktor Fesetchko W PTS 8 Manchester
17.07.03 Jimmy Vincent W PTS 12 Dagenham
(Vacant British Welterweight Title)
13.12.03 Kevin McIntyre W RTD 8 Manchester
(British Welterweight Title Defence)
03.04.04 Glenn McClarnon W PTS 12 Manchester
(British Welterweight Title Defence)
12.11.04 James Hare W RSC 6 Halifax
(British Welterweight Title Defence)
28.01.05 Juho Tolppola W PTS 10 Renfrew
22.04.05 Ali Nuumbembe DREW 12 Barnsley
(Vacant WBO Inter-Continental Welterweight Title)
04.06.05 Joshua Okine L RSC 12 Manchester
(Commonwealth Welterweight Title Challenge)
28.01.06 Fabrice Colombel W RSC 4 Nottingham
04.03.06 Silence Saheed W PTS 4 Manchester
10.12.06 Vadzim Astapuk W PTS 6 Sheffield
03.05.07 Jay Morris W RSC 1 Sheffield
Career: 23 contests, won 21, drew 1, lost 1.

Matthew Barney

Southampton. *Born* Fareham, 25 June, 1974
Cruiserweight. Former Undefeated WBU L.Heavyweight Champion. Former Undefeated British, IBO Inter-Continental, Southern Area & British Masters S.Middleweight Champion. *Ht* 5'10¾"
Manager J. Bishop

04.06.98 Adam Cale W PTS 6 Barking
23.07.98 Adam Cale W PTS 6 Barking
02.10.98 Dennis Doyley W PTS 4 Cheshunt
22.10.98 Kevin Burton W PTS 6 Barking
07.12.98 Freddie Yemofio W PTS 4 Acton
17.03.99 Simon Andrews W RTD 4 Kensington
09.05.99 Gareth Hogg W PTS 4 Bracknell
20.05.99 Bobby Banghar W RSC 5 Kensington
(British Masters S. Middleweight Final)
05.06.99 Paul Bowen DREW 10 Cardiff
(Southern Area S. Middleweight Title Challenge)

20.08.99 Adam Cale W PTS 4 Bloomsbury
05.10.99 Delroy Leslie L PTS 10 Bloomsbury
(Vacant Southern Area Middleweight Title)
15.04.00 Mark Dawson W PTS 6 Bethnal Green
06.05.00 Jason Hart W PTS 10 Southwark
(Vacant Southern Area S. Middleweight Title)
30.09.00 Neil Linford L PTS 10 Peterborough
(Elim. British S. Middleweight Title)
02.02.01 Darren Covill W PTS 6 Portsmouth
16.03.01 Matt Mowatt W RSC 1 Portsmouth
(British Masters S. Middleweight Title Defence)
14.07.01 Robert Milewics W PTS 8 Wembley
20.10.01 Jon Penn W RSC 4 Portsmouth
26.01.02 Hussain Osman L RTD 9 Dagenham
(Vacant IBO Inter-Continental S.Middleweight Title. Southern Area S.Middleweight Title Defence)
08.04.02 Hussain Osman W PTS 12 Southampton
(IBO Inter-Continental & Southern Area S. Middleweight Title Challenges)
22.09.02 Paul Owen W CO 7 Southwark
(Vacant British Masters S.Middleweight Title)
20.10.02 Chris Nembhard W PTS 10 Southwark
(Southern Area S. Middleweight Title Defence)
29.03.03 Dean Francis W PTS 12 Wembley
(Vacant British S.Middleweight Title)
01.08.03 Charles Adamu L PTS 12 Bethnal Green
(Vacant Commonwealth S.Middleweight Title)
11.10.03 Tony Oakey W PTS 12 Portsmouth
(WBU L.Heavyweight Title Challenge)
10.09.04 Simeon Cover W PTS 4 Wembley
26.03.05 Thomas Ulrich L PTS 12 Riesa, Germany
(European L.Heavyweight Title Challenge)
09.07.05 Carl Froch L PTS 12 Nottingham
(British & Commonwealth S.Middleweight Title Challenges)
01.12.06 Varuzhan Davtyan W PTS 4 Tower Hill
23.02.07 Ayitey Powers W PTS 6 Peterborough
Career: 30 contests, won 23, drew 1, lost 6.

Ryan Barrett

Thamesmead. *Born* London, 27 December, 1982
British Masters Featherweight Champion. *Ht* 5'10"
Manager Self

13.06.02 Gareth Wiltshaw W PTS 4 Leicester Square
06.09.02 Jason Gonzales W PTS 4 Bethnal Green
12.12.02 Martin Turner W RSC 1 Leicester Square
08.03.03 David Vaughan DREW 4 Bethnal Green
04.10.03 Dafydd Carlin L PTS 4 Belfast
01.05.04 Marty Kayes W RSC 2 Gravesend
19.06.04 Kristian Laight W PTS 4 Muswell Hill
16.10.04 Daniel Thorpe W PTS 4 Dagenham
19.12.04 James Paisley W DIS 5 Bethnal Green
21.01.05 Peter McDonagh W PTS 8 Brentford
05.03.05 Carl Allen W PTS 4 Dagenham
23.03.05 Pete Buckley W PTS 6 Leicester Square

20.06.05	Anthony Christopher W RSC 1 Longford	
01.04.06	Martin Watson L PTS 10 Bethnal Green	

(Elim. British Lightweight Title)

23.07.06	Baz Carey W PTS 6 Dagenham
02.09.06	Amir Khan L RSC 1 Bolton
21.10.06	Steve Gethin W PTS 6 Southwark
03.12.06	Riaz Durgahed W PTS 6 Bethnal Green
18.02.07	Jamie McKeever W PTS 10 Bethnal Green

(Vacant British Masters Featherweight Title)

08.06.07	John Simpson L CO 5 Mayfair

(British Featherweight Title Challenge)

Career: 20 contests, won 15, drew 1, lost 4.

(Alex) Sandy Bartlett

Inverness. *Born* Dingwall, 20 April, 1976
S.Featherweight. *Ht* 5'7"
Manager Self

15.03.04	Marty Kayes W PTS 6 Glasgow
19.04.04	Abdul Mougharbel L PTS 6 Glasgow
11.10.04	Abdul Mougharbel W PTS 6 Glasgow
05.11.04	Ricky Owen L RSC 2 Hereford
19.09.05	Neil Marston W PTS 6 Glasgow
04.11.05	Craig Bromley L RSC 2 Glasgow
20.02.06	Kevin Townsley L PTS 4 Glasgow
25.03.06	John Bothwell L RSC 2 Irvine
02.12.06	Brian Murphy W RSC 5 Clydebank
02.03.07	Furhan Rafiq L PTS 6 Irvine

Career: 10 contests, won 4, lost 6.

Greg Barton

Southend. *Born* , Rochford, 4 April, 1982
Middleweight. *Ht* 5'11½"
Manager J. Eames/J. Feld

26.02.06	Leon Owen L RSC 1 Dagenham
24.09.06	Sherman Alleyne W RSC 3 Bethnal Green
15.12.06	Scott Jordan L PTS 4 Bethnal Green
18.02.07	Eder Kurti W PTS 4 Bethnal Green
08.06.07	Anthony Young L PTS 4 Mayfair

Career: 5 contests, won 2, lost 3.

Colin Baxter

Fauldhouse. *Born* Broxburn, 9 November, 1982
Middleweight. *Ht* 5'10½"
Manager A. Morrison

16.03.07	Tony Stones W PTS 6 Glasgow
25.05.07	Rocky Muscas W PTS 6 Glasgow

Career: 2 contests, won 2.

(Shinebayer) Shinny Bayaar (Sukhbaatar)

Carlisle. *Born* Mongolia, 27 August, 1977
Bantamweight. *Ht* 5'5½"
Manager J. Doughty

25.02.00	Yura Dima DREW 10 Erdene, Mongolia
28.06.00	Manny Melchor L PTS 12 Manila, Philippines

(WBC International M.Flyweight Title Challenge)

10.10.01	Damien Dunnion L PTS 8 Stoke
09.12.01	Delroy Spencer W PTS 4 Shaw
17.11.02	Anthony Hanna W PTS 6 Shaw
20.03.03	Sunkanmi Ogunbiyi L PTS 4 Queensway
08.06.03	Darren Cleary W RSC 2 Shaw
19.10.03	Delroy Spencer W PTS 6 Shaw
21.02.04	Reidar Walstad W RSC 1 Cardiff
31.10.04	Delroy Spencer W PTS 6 Shaw
11.12.04	Martin Power L PTS 10 Canning Town
20.11.05	Abdul Mougharbel W PTS 4 Shaw
02.04.06	Delroy Spencer W PTS 6 Shaw
15.09.06	Andrew Kooner W RSC 3 Muswell Hill
11.03.07	Pete Buckley W PTS 6 Shaw

Career: 15 contests, won 10, drew 1, lost 4.

Andy Bell (Langley)

Nottingham. *Born* Doncaster, 16 July, 1985
Midlands Area & British Masters
Bantamweight Champion. *Ht* 5'8"
Manager Self

22.10.04	Steve Gethin W RSC 5 Mansfield
10.12.04	Dean Ward W PTS 6 Mansfield
06.03.05	Abdul Mougharbel W PTS 4 Mansfield
24.04.05	Wayne Bloy L PTS 4 Askern
13.05.06	Steve Gethin L RSC 2 Sutton in Ashfield
06.10.06	Shaun Walton W PTS 6 Mansfield
01.12.06	Jamie McDonnell L RSC 3 Doncaster
01.04.07	Neil Marston W RSC 8 Shrewsbury

(Vacant Midlands Area Bantamweight Title)

19.05.07	Delroy Spencer W PTS 4 Nottingham
17.06.07	Mo Khaled W PTS 10 Mansfield

(Vacant British Masters Bantamweight Title)

Career: 10 contests, won 7, lost 3.

Ryan Barrett   Philip Sharkey

Steve Bell   Les Clark

Steve Bell

Manchester. *Born* Manchester, 11 June, 1975
Central Area S.Featherweight Champion.
Ht 5'10"
Manager F. Warren

08.05.03	Jus Wallie DREW 4 Widnes
27.09.03	Jaz Virdee W RSC 1 Manchester
13.12.03	Fred Janes W PTS 4 Manchester

03.04.04 Pete Buckley W PTS 4 Manchester
22.05.04 Haider Ali W PTS 6 Widnes
01.10.04 Daniel Thorpe W PTS 6 Manchester
11.02.05 Henry Janes W RTD 3 Manchester
03.06.05 Buster Dennis DREW 6 Manchester
04.03.06 Pete Buckley W PTS 4 Manchester
01.04.06 Jason Nesbitt W PTS 6 Bethnal Green
02.09.06 Daniel Thorpe W RTD 4 Bolton
28.10.06 Steve Gethin W RTD 5 Bethnal Green
10.03.07 Jamie McKeever W RSC 7 Liverpool
          (Vacant Central Area S.Featherweight
          Title)
31.05.07 Rom Krauklis W PTS 6 Manchester
Career: 14 contests, won 12, drew 2.

Scott Belshaw
Lisburn N.Ireland. *Born* Aghalee, N.Ireland,
8 July, 1985
Heavyweight. *Ht* 6'7¼"
Manager F. Maloney/A. Wilton
07.10.06 Lee Webb W RSC 1 Belfast
11.11.06 Anatoliy Kusenko W RSC 1 Dublin
25.11.06 Alexander Subin W RSC 2 Belfast
26.01.07 Makhmud Otazhanov W RSC 2
          Dagenham
09.03.07 Paul King W PTS 4 Dagenham
30.06.07 Chris Woollas W CO 1 Belfast
Career: 6 contests, won 6.

Steven Bendall
Coventry. *Born* Coventry, 1 December,
1973
Middleweight. Former English
Middleweight Champion. Former
Undefeated IBO Inter-Continental &WBU
Inter-Continental Middleweight Champion.
Ht 6'0"
Manager Self
15.05.97 Dennis Doyley W RSC 2 Reading
13.09.97 Gary Reyniers W PTS 4 Millwall
27.02.99 Israel Khumalo W PTS 4 Oldham
02.07.99 Darren Covill W RTD 3 Bristol
24.09.99 Sean Pritchard W PTS 6 Merthyr
03.12.99 Ian Toby W PTS 6 Peterborough
07.04.00 Des Sowden W RSC 3 Bristol
02.06.00 Simon Andrews W RSC 5 Ashford
08.09.00 Jason Barker W PTS 6 Bristol
03.11.00 Eddie Haley W RSC 1 Ebbw Vale
01.12.00 Peter Mitchell W PTS 8 Peterborough
22.08.01 Bert Bado W RSC 1 Hammanskraal,
          South Africa
29.09.01 Alan Gilbert W RTD 3 Southwark
08.12.01 Jason Collins W PTS 12 Dagenham
          (Vacant WBU Inter-Continental
          Middleweight Title)
02.03.02 Ahmet Dottouev W RTD 4 Brakpan,
          South Africa
          (WBU Inter-Continental Middleweight
          Title Defence)
26.04.02 Viktor Fesetchko W RSC 10 Coventry
          (Vacant IBO Inter-Continental
          Middleweight Title)
13.07.02 Phillip Bystrikov W RSC 5 Coventry
06.09.02 Tomas da Silva W RSC 8 Bethnal
          Green
24.01.03 Lee Blundell W RSC 2 Sheffield
          (IBO Inter-Continental Middleweight
          Title Defence)
26.04.03 Mike Algoet W PTS 12 Brentford
          (IBO Inter-Continental Middleweight
          Title Defence)

14.11.03 Kreshnik Qato W PTS 8 Bethnal Green
17.09.04 Scott Dann L RSC 6 Plymouth
          (Vacant British Middleweight Title)
18.06.05 Ismael Kerzazi W PTS 8 Coventry
22.10.05 Magid Ben Driss W PTS 6 Coventry
15.12.05 Donovan Smillie W RSC 5 Coventry
          (English Middleweight Title Challenge)
22.04.06 Sebastian Sylvester L RSC 3
          Mannheim, Germany
          (European Middleweight Title
          Challenge)
07.10.06 Conroy McIntosh W PTS 6 Weston
          super Mare
01.12.06 Wayne Elcock L RSC 8 Birmingham
          (English Middleweight Title Defence)
Career: 28 contests, won 25, lost 3.

Mark Bett
Larkhall. *Born* Lanark, 30 September, 1982
Welterweight. *Ht* 5'7"
Manager A. Morrison
22.04.06 Marco Cittadini DREW 6 Glasgow
27.05.06 Colin Bain DREW 6 Glasgow
21.10.06 Marco Cittadini W PTS 6 Glasgow
10.12.06 Colin Bain L PTS 6 Glasgow
16.02.07 Ali Hussain DREW 6 Sunderland
16.03.07 Ali Hussain W RSC 3 Glasgow
24.06.07 Davey Watson L RTD 5 Sunderland
Career: 7 contests, won 2, drew 3, lost 2.

Akaash Bhatia
Harrow. *Born* Loughborough, 1 May, 1983
S.Featherweight. *Ht* 5'7"
Manager F. Maloney
30.05.06 Kristian Laight W PTS 4 Bethnal Green
29.06.06 Nikita Lukin W PTS 4 Bethnal Green
06.10.06 Rakhim Mingaleev W PTS 4 Bethnal
          Green
17.11.06 Youssef Al Hamidi W PTS 4 Bethnal
          Green
26.01.07 Sergii Tertii W RSC 2 Dagenham
27.04.07 Dai Davies W PTS 4 Wembley
Career: 6 contests, won 6.

Akaash Bhatia   Les Clark

Willie Bilan
Fife. *Born* Kirkcaldy, 17 April, 1986
Welterweight. *Ht* 5'11¼"
Manager T. Gilmour

23.10.06 Steve Cooper W PTS 6 Glasgow
16.02.07 David Kehoe W RSC 1 Kirkcaldy
11.05.07 Steve Anning W PTS 4 Motherwell
Career: 3 contests, won 3.

(Joe John) JJ Bird
Peterborough. *Born* Peterborough, 9
September, 1986
Middleweight. *Ht* 6'1½"
Manager G. De'Roux/D. Powell
23.02.07 Frank Celebi W PTS 4 Peterborough
01.06.07 Duncan Cottier W PTS 4 Peterborough
Career: 2 contests, won 2.

JJ Bird   Philip Sharkey

Chris Black
Coatbridge. *Born* Bellshill, 19 November,
1979
Middleweight. *Ht* 5'7½"
Manager A. Morrison/R. Bannan
22.10.04 Brian Coleman W PTS 4 Edinburgh
12.12.04 Jak Hibbert W RSC 2 Glasgow
28.01.05 Geraint Harvey W PTS 4 Renfrew
01.04.05 Tony Randell W PTS 6 Glasgow
17.06.05 Ciaran Healy DREW 4 Glasgow
22.04.06 Barrie Lee L PTS 10 Glasgow
          (Scottish L.Middleweight Title
          Challenge)
28.10.06 Tyan Booth L PTS 6 Aberdeen
Career: 7 contests, won 4, drew 1, lost 2.

Wayne Bloy
Grimsby. *Born* Grimsby, 30 November,
1982
Bantamweight. *Ht* 5'5"
Manager Self
14.06.04 Neil Read DREW 6 Cleethorpes
20.09.04 Gary Ford W PTS 6 Cleethorpes
24.04.05 Andy Bell W PTS 4 Askern
23.05.05 Neil Marston W PTS 6 Cleethorpes
24.02.06 Abdul Mougharbel W PTS 6
          Scarborough
13.10.06 Jamie McDonnell L PTS 4 Doncaster
23.02.07 Jamie McDonnell L RSC 3 Doncaster
          (Vacant English Bantamweight Title)
Career: 7 contests, won 4, drew 1, lost 2.

91

Lee Blundell

Wigan. *Born* Wigan, 11 August, 1971
Middleweight. Former Undefeated WBF
Inter-Continental & British Masters
Middleweight Champion. Former
Undefeated Central Area L.Middleweight
Champion. *Ht* 6'2"
Manager L. Veitch/J. Gill

25.04.94	Robert Harper W RSC 2 Bury
20.05.94	Freddie Yemofio W RSC 6 Acton
08.09.94	Gordon Blair DREW 6 Glasgow
07.12.94	Kesem Clayton W RTD 2 Stoke
18.02.95	Glenn Catley L RSC 6 Shepton Mallet
11.12.95	Martin Jolley W PTS 6 Morecambe
16.03.97	Martin Jolley W PTS 6 Shaw
08.05.97	Paul Jones L RSC 4 Mansfield
19.09.99	Dean Ashton W RSC 4 Shaw
28.10.99	Jason Collins DREW 6 Burnley
06.12.99	Danny Thornton W PTS 6 Bradford
05.03.00	Ian Toby W RTD 3 Shaw
21.05.00	Phil Epton W RSC 2 Shaw
30.11.00	Danny Thornton W RSC 8 Blackpool
	(Vacant Central Area L.Middleweight Title)
08.03.01	Paul Wesley W RSC 3 Blackpool
03.04.01	Spencer Fearon W PTS 6 Bethnal Green
26.07.01	Harry Butler W RSC 4 Blackpool
15.09.01	Anthony Farnell L RSC 2 Manchester
	(Vacant WBO Inter-Continental L.Middleweight Title)
09.12.01	Neil Bonner W RSC 3 Blackpool
16.03.02	Ryan Rhodes W RSC 3 Bethnal Green
	(Vacant WBF Inter-Continental Middleweight Title)
03.08.02	Alan Gilbert W RSC 6 Blackpool
	(WBF Inter-Continental Middleweight Title Defence)
26.10.02	Darren McInulty W RSC 1 Wigan
	(WBF Inter-Continental Middleweight Title Defence)
24.01.03	Steven Bendall L RSC 2 Sheffield
	(IBO Inter-Continental Middleweight Title Challenge)
19.12.04	Michael Pinnock W PTS 6 Bolton
06.03.05	Howard Clarke W PTS 6 Shaw
30.04.05	Simeon Cover W PTS 10 Wigan
	(Vacant British Masters Middleweight Title)
13.05.05	Michael Pinnock W PTS 4 Liverpool
02.03.06	Hamid Jamali W PTS 6 Blackpool
06.05.06	Conroy McIntosh W PTS 6 Blackpool
07.04.07	Gary Lockett L RSC 3 Cardiff
	(WBU Middleweight Title Challenge)

Career: 30 contests, won 23, drew 2, lost 5.

Robert Boardman

Bristol. *Born* London, 9 September, 1987
L.Heavyweight. *Ht* 5'10"
Manager T. Gilmour

02.06.07	Mark Phillips W PTS 6 Bristol

Career: 1 contest, won 1.

Neil Bonner

Abergele. *Born* Enfield, 13 October, 1975
L.Middleweight. *Ht* 5'9"
Manager Self

22.09.00	Drea Dread W RSC 4 Wrexham
03.11.00	James Lee L PTS 4 Ebbw Vale
04.02.01	Richard Inquieti W PTS 6 Queensferry
26.08.01	Colin McCash W RSC 1 Warrington

09.09.01	Peter Jackson L PTS 6 Hartlepool
21.10.01	Matt Scriven NC 1 Glasgow
09.12.01	Lee Blundell L RSC 3 Blackpool
08.03.02	Paul Buchanan L PTS 6 Ellesmere Port
19.04.02	Lee Murtagh L PTS 6 Darlington
11.05.02	Darrell Grafton L PTS 6 Chesterfield
08.06.02	Joe Townsley L PTS 6 Renfrew
06.10.02	Wayne Shepherd W PTS 6 Rhyl
01.11.02	Dean Cockburn L RSC 2 Preston
24.05.03	Dean Walker L PTS 6 Sheffield
07.04.06	Kevin Phelan L RSC 2 Longford
28.06.07	Mark Lloyd L PTS 4 Dudley

Career: 16 contests, won 4, lost 11, no contest 1.

Jason Booth

Nottingham. *Born* Nottingham, 7
November, 1977
Bantamweight. Former IBO S.Flyweight
Champion. Former Undefeated British
Flyweight Champion. Former Undefeated
Commonwealth Flyweight Champion.
Ht 5'4"
Manager J. Gill/T. Harris

13.06.96	Darren Noble W RSC 3 Sheffield
24.10.96	Marty Chestnut W PTS 6 Lincoln
27.11.96	Jason Thomas W PTS 4 Swansea
18.01.97	David Coldwell W PTS 4 Swadlincote
07.03.97	Pete Buckley W PTS 6 Northampton
20.03.97	Danny Lawson W RSC 3 Newark
10.05.97	Anthony Hanna W PTS 6 Nottingham
19.05.97	Chris Lyons W PTS 6 Cleethorpes
31.10.97	Mark Reynolds W PTS 6 Ilkeston
31.01.98	Anthony Hanna W PTS 6 Edmonton
20.03.98	Louis Veitch W CO 2 Ilkeston
	(Elim. British Flyweight Title)
09.06.98	Dimitar Alipiev W RSC 2 Hull
17.10.98	Graham McGrath W RSC 4 Manchester
07.12.98	Louis Veitch W RSC 5 Cleethorpes
08.05.99	David Guerault L PTS 12 Grande Synthe, France
	(European Flyweight Title Challenge)
12.07.99	Mark Reynolds W RSC 3 Coventry
16.10.99	Keith Knox W RSC 10 Belfast
	(British &Commonwealth Flyweight Title Challenges)
22.01.00	Abie Mnisi W PTS 12 Birmingham
	(Commonwealth Flyweight Title Defence)
01.07.00	John Barnes W PTS 6 Manchester
13.11.00	Ian Napa W PTS 12 Bethnal Green
	(British & Commonwealth Flyweight Title Defences)
26.02.01	Nokuthula Tshabangu W CO 2 Nottingham
	(Commonwealth Flyweight Title Defence)
30.06.01	Alexander Mahmutov L PTS 12 Madrid, Spain
	(European Flyweight Title Challenge)
23.02.02	Jason Thomas W PTS 6 Nottingham
01.06.02	Mimoun Chent L TD 8 Le Havre, France
	(Vacant European Flyweight Title)
16.11.02	Kakhar Sabitov W RSC 6 Nottingham
28.04.03	Lindi Memani W PTS 8 Nottingham
20.09.03	Lunga Ntontela W PTS 12 Nottingham
	(IBO S.Flyweight Title Challenge)
13.03.04	Dale Robinson W PTS 12 Huddersfield
	(IBO S.Flyweight Title Defence)
17.12.04	Damaen Kelly L PTS 12 Huddersfield
	(IBO S.Flyweight Title Defence)
03.11.06	Abdul Mougharbel W PTS 6 Barnsley
09.02.07	Jamil Hussain W PTS 6 Leeds

Career: 31 contests, won 27, lost 4.

Tony Booth

Hull. *Born* Hull, 30 January, 1970
Heavyweight. Former Undefeated British
Masters L.Heavyweight Champion. Former
Undefeated British Masters & Central Area
Cruiserweight Champion. *Ht* 5'11½"
Manager Self

08.03.90	Paul Lynch L PTS 6 Watford
11.04.90	Mick Duncan W PTS 6 Dewsbury
26.04.90	Colin Manners W PTS 6 Halifax
16.05.90	Tommy Warde W PTS 6 Hull
05.06.90	Gary Dyson W PTS 6 Liverpool
05.09.90	Shaun McCrory L PTS 6 Stoke
08.10.90	Bullit Andrews W RSC 3 Cleethorpes
23.01.91	Darron Griffiths DREW 6 Stoke
06.02.91	Shaun McCrory L PTS 6 Liverpool
06.03.91	Billy Brough L PTS 6 Glasgow
18.03.91	Billy Brough W PTS 6 Glasgow
28.03.91	Neville Brown L PTS 6 Alfreton
17.05.91	Glenn Campbell L RSC 2 Bury
	(Central Area S. Middleweight Title Challenge)
25.07.91	Paul Murray W PTS 6 Dudley
01.08.91	Nick Manners DREW 8 Dewsbury
11.09.91	Jim Peters L PTS 8 Hammersmith
28.10.91	Eddie Smulders L RSC 6 Arnhem, Holland
09.12.91	Steve Lewsam L PTS 8 Cleethorpes
30.01.92	Serg Fame W PTS 6 Southampton
12.02.92	Tenko Ernie W RSC 4 Wembley
05.03.92	John Beckles W RSC 6 Battersea
26.03.92	Dave Owens W PTS 6 Hull
08.04.92	Michael Gale L PTS 8 Leeds
13.05.92	Phil Soundy W PTS 6 Kensington
02.06.92	Eddie Smulders L RSC 1 Rotterdam, Holland
18.07.92	Maurice Core L PTS 6 Manchester
07.09.92	James Cook L PTS 8 Bethnal Green
30.10.92	Roy Richie DREW 6 Istrees, France
18.11.92	Tony Wilson DREW 8 Solihull
25.12.92	Francis Wanyama L PTS 6 Izegem, Belgium
09.02.93	Tony Wilson W PTS 8 Wolverhampton
01.05.93	Ralf Rocchigiani DREW 8 Berlin, Germany
03.06.93	Victor Cordoba L PTS 8 Marseille, France
23.06.93	Tony Behan W PTS 6 Gorleston
01.07.93	Michael Gale L PTS 8 York
17.09.93	Ole Klemetsen L PTS 8 Copenhagen, Denmark
07.10.93	Denzil Browne DREW 8 York
02.11.93	James Cook L PTS 8 Southwark
12.11.93	Carlos Christie W PTS 6 Hull
28.01.94	Francis Wanyama L RSC 2 Waregem, Belgium
	(Vacant Commonwealth Cruiserweight Title)
26.03.94	Torsten May L PTS 6 Dortmund, Germany
21.07.94	Mark Prince L RSC 3 Battersea
24.09.94	Johnny Held L PTS 8 Rotterdam, Holland
07.10.94	Dirk Wallyn L PTS 6 Waregem, Belgium
27.10.94	Dean Francis L CO 1 Bayswater
23.01.95	Jan Lefeber L PTS 8 Rotterdam, Holland
07.03.95	John Foreman L PTS 6 Edgbaston
27.04.95	Art Stacey W PTS 10 Hull
	(Vacant Central Area Cruiserweight Title)
04.06.95	Montell Griffin L RSC 2 Bethnal Green
06.07.95	Nigel Rafferty W RSC 7 Hull

22.07.95 Mark Prince L RSC 2 Millwall
06.09.95 Leif Keiski L PTS 8 Helsinki, Finland
25.09.95 Neil Simpson W PTS 8 Cleethorpes
06.10.95 Don Diego Poeder L RSC 2 Waregem, Belgium
11.11.95 Bruce Scott L RSC 3 Halifax
16.12.95 John Marceta L RSC 2 Cardiff
20.01.96 Johnny Nelson L RSC 2 Mansfield
15.03.96 Slick Miller W PTS 6 Hull
27.03.96 Neil Simpson L PTS 6 Whitwick
17.05.96 Mark Richardson W RSC 2 Hull
13.07.96 Bruce Scott L PTS 8 Bethnal Green
03.09.96 Paul Douglas L PTS 4 Belfast
14.09.96 Kelly Oliver L RSC 2 Sheffield
06.11.96 Martin Jolley W PTS 4 Hull
22.11.96 Slick Miller W RSC 5 Hull
11.12.96 Crawford Ashley L RSC 1 Southwark
18.01.97 Kelly Oliver L RSC 4 Swadlincote
27.02.97 Kevin Morton L PTS 6 Hull
25.03.97 Nigel Rafferty DREW 8 Wolverhampton
04.04.97 John Wilson L PTS 6 Glasgow
16.04.97 Robert Norton L RSC 4 Bethnal Green
15.05.97 Phill Day W PTS 4 Reading
11.09.97 Steve Bristow L PTS 4 Widnes
22.09.97 Martin Langtry W PTS 6 Cleethorpes
04.10.97 Bruce Scott W PTS 8 Muswell Hill
28.11.97 Martin Jolley W PTS 6 Hull
15.12.97 Nigel Rafferty W PTS 6 Cleethorpes
06.03.98 Peter Mason W RSC 3 Hull
09.06.98 Crawford Ashley L RSC 6 Hull
(British L. Heavyweight Title Challenge. Vacant Commonwealth L. Heavyweight Title)
18.07.98 Omar Sheika W PTS 8 Sheffield
26.09.98 Toks Owoh L PTS 6 Norwich
29.10.98 Nigel Rafferty W PTS 8 Bayswater
14.12.98 Sven Hamer W PTS 6 Cleethorpes
05.01.99 Ali Saidi W RSC 4 Epernay, France
17.05.99 Darren Ashton W PTS 6 Cleethorpes
12.07.99 Neil Simpson L PTS 10 Coventry
(Elim. British L. Heavyweight Title)
27.09.99 Adam Cale W PTS 6 Cleethorpes
16.10.99 Cathal O'Grady L CO 4 Belfast
18.01.00 Michael Sprott L PTS 6 Mansfield
12.02.00 Thomas Hansvoll L PTS 6 Sheffield
29.02.00 John Keeton L RSC 2 Widnes
09.04.00 Greg Scott-Briggs W PTS 10 Alfreton
(Vacant British Masters L. Heavyweight Title)
15.05.00 Michael Pinnock W PTS 6 Cleethorpes
19.06.00 Toks Owoh L RSC 3 Burton
08.09.00 Dominic Negus W PTS 6 Bristol
30.09.00 Robert Norton L RSC 2 Peterborough
31.10.00 Firat Aslan L RSC 2 Hammersmith
11.12.00 Mark Krence L PTS 6 Sheffield
05.02.01 Denzil Browne L RSC 5 Hull
(Vacant Central Area Cruiserweight Title)
01.04.01 Kenny Gayle DREW 4 Southwark
10.04.01 Mark Baker L PTS 4 Wembley
16.06.01 Butch Lesley L RSC 3 Dagenham
09.09.01 Tommy Eastwood L PTS 4 Southwark
22.09.01 Peter Haymer L PTS 4 Bethnal Green
15.10.01 Colin Kenna L PTS 6 Southampton
01.11.01 Terry Morrill W RSC 7 Hull
24.11.01 Matt Legg L PTS 4 Bethnal Green
16.12.01 Blue Stevens L PTS 4 Southwark
19.01.02 John McDermott L RSC 1 Bethnal Green
20.04.02 Enzo Maccarinelli L PTS 4 Cardiff
28.04.02 Scott Lansdowne L RSC 4 Southwark
10.05.02 Paul Buttery L PTS 4 Preston
23.06.02 Neil Linford L RSC 5 Southwark
03.08.02 Mark Krence L PTS 4 Derby

17.08.02 Enzo Maccarinelli L RTD 2 Cardiff
23.09.02 Slick Miller W PTS 6 Cleethorpes
05.10.02 Phill Day W PTS 4 Coventry
19.10.02 James Zikic L PTS 4 Norwich
27.10.02 Hughie Doherty L PTS 4 Southwark
21.11.02 Jamie Warters W PTS 8 Hull
28.11.02 Roman Greenberg L PTS 4 Finchley
08.12.02 David Haye L RTD 2 Bethnal Green
30.01.03 Mohammed Benguesmia L RTD 4 Algiers, Algeria
05.04.03 Jason Callum L PTS 6 Coventry
17.05.03 Tony Moran L PTS 6 Liverpool
26.07.03 Kelly Oliver L PTS 4 Plymouth
26.09.03 Radcliffe Green W PTS 6 Millwall
14.11.03 Paul Bonson W PTS 6 Hull
14.02.04 Oneal Murray W PTS 8 Holborn
01.05.04 Elvis Michailenko L RTD 4 Gravesend
15.08.04 Bash Ali L RSC 4 Lagos, Nigeria
(WBF Cruiserweight Title Challenge)
26.11.04 Paul Bonson W PTS 6 Hull
11.12.04 Hovik Keuchkerian L CO 1 Madrid, Spain
05.03.05 Junior MacDonald L PTS 4 Southwark
15.04.05 Johny Jensen L PTS 6 Copenhagen, Denmark
04.06.05 Martin Rogan L RSC 2 Manchester
24.07.05 Coleman Barrett L PTS 4 Leicester Square
10.09.05 Darren Morgan L PTS 4 Cardiff
24.09.05 Carl Wright L PTS 4 Coventry
06.10.05 Tommy Eastwood L PTS 4 Longford
25.11.05 Dave Clarke DREW 6 Hull
26.02.06 Ovill McKenzie L PTS 4 Dagenham
05.03.06 Jon Ibbotson L PTS 4 Sheffield
30.03.06 Ervis Jegeni L RSC 1 Piccadilly
13.05.06 Paul Souter L PTS 4 Bethnal Green
26.05.06 Lee Mountford W PTS 6 Hull
12.07.06 Ervis Jegeni L PTS 4 Bethnal Green
23.07.06 Tommy Eastwood L PTS 4 Dagenham
24.09.06 Mervyn Langdale W RSC 1 Southampton
09.10.06 Oneal Murray W PTS 4 Bedworth
21.10.06 Danny Tombs W PTS 4 Southwark
03.11.06 Leigh Alliss L PTS 4 Bristol
03.12.06 JJ Ojuederie L PTS 4 Bethnal Green
23.02.07 Billy Wilson W RSC 5 Doncaster
07.04.07 Derek Chisora L PTS 4 Cardiff
21.04.07 Paulie Silva L PTS 6 Manchester
18.05.07 Troy Ross L RSC 2 Canning Town
Career: 157 contests, won 50, drew 9, lost 98.

Tyan Booth

Sheffield. *Born* Nottingham, 20 March, 1983
Welterweight. *Ht* 6'2½"
Manager J. Ingle

29.10.05 Jimi Hendricks W PTS 6 Aberdeen
08.11.05 Jimi Hendricks W PTS 6 Leeds
27.02.06 Jason Welborn W CO 4 Birmingham
06.05.06 Richard Turba W PTS 6 Blackpool
17.05.06 Alexis Callero L PTS 6 Lanzarote, Canary Islands, Spain
22.09.06 George Hillyard W PTS 6 Bethnal Green
13.10.06 Karl David W PTS 6 Aberavon
28.10.06 Chris Black W PTS 6 Aberdeen
24.11.06 Peter Dunn W PTS 4 Nottingham
02.12.06 Nathan Graham W PTS 6 Southwark
23.03.07 Darren Gethin L RSC 10 Nottingham
(Vacant Midlands Area Welterweight Title)
Career: 11 contests, won 9, lost 2.

Tyan Booth   Les Clark

Alan Bosworth

Northampton. *Born* Northampton, 31 December, 1967
L.Welterweight. Former Undefeated English Lightweight Champion. Former Undefeated British Masters L.Welterweight Champion. *Ht* 5'7"
Manager Self

17.10.95 Simon Hamblett W RSC 2 Wolverhampton
29.10.95 Shaun Gledhill W PTS 6 Shaw
16.11.95 Brian Coleman W PTS 6 Evesham
23.11.95 David Thompson W RSC 4 Tynemouth
13.01.96 Jason Blanche W PTS 6 Halifax
31.01.96 Arv Mittoo W PTS 6 Stoke
16.02.96 John Docherty W PTS 6 Irvine
24.03.96 Scott Walker DREW 6 Shaw
16.05.96 Yifru Retta W PTS 6 Dunstable
07.03.97 Wayne Rigby L RSC 5 Northampton
09.09.97 Colin Dunne L RSC 8 Bethnal Green
31.10.98 Alan Temple L PTS 6 Basingstoke
26.02.99 Des Sowden W PTS 6 Longford
13.03.99 Paul Burke L PTS 6 Manchester
24.04.99 Jan Bergman L RSC 6 Munich, Germany
02.07.99 Keith Jones W PTS 6 Bristol
24.09.99 Woody Greenaway L PTS 6 Merthyr
03.12.99 Darren Underwood W CO 5 Peterborough
20.01.00 Brian Coleman W PTS 6 Piccadilly
24.03.00 Allan Vester L PTS 12 Aarhus, Denmark
(IBF Inter-Continental L. Welterweight Title Challenge)
28.04.00 George Scott L PTS 8 Copenhagen, Denmark
02.06.00 Mohamed Helel W PTS 6 Ashford
25.07.00 Shea Neary L PTS 10 Southwark
01.12.00 David Kirk DREW 8 Peterborough
13.03.01 Eamonn Magee L RSC 5 Plymouth
23.06.01 Keith Jones W PTS 6 Peterborough
23.11.01 Daniel James W RSC 7 Bethnal Green
(Elim. British L.Welterweight Title)
16.03.02 Junior Witter L RSC 3 Northampton
(Vacant British L.Welterweight Title)
28.09.02 Eamonn Magee L RSC 5 Manchester
28.01.03 Oscar Hall L PTS 10 Nottingham
(Elim. British L. Welterweight Title)
25.07.03 Gavin Down W RSC 5 Norwich

(British Masters L.Welterweight Title Challenge. Elim. British L.Welterweight Title)

11.12.03	Stephen Smith W PTS 10 Bethnal Green	

(Vacant English L.Welterweight Title)

12.11.04 Francis Barrett L PTS 10 Wembley
(European Union L.Welterweight Title Challenge)
27.05.05 Nigel Wright L PTS 10 Spennymoor
(English L.Welterweight Title Challenge)
25.02.06 Jus Wallie W RSC 1 Canning Town
13.05.06 James Paisley W PTS 4 Bethnal Green
20.10.06 Matthew Hatton W DIS 10 Sheffield
(Elim. British Welterweight Title)
20.01.07 Ashley Theophane L RSC 7 Muswell Hill
(Elim. British L.Welterweight Title)

Career: 38 contests, won 20, drew 2, lost 16.

John Bothwell
Ballieston. *Born* Glasgow, 8 August, 1981
Featherweight. *Ht* 5'5"
Manager T. Gilmour

17.10.03 Marty Kayes W PTS 6 Glasgow
30.10.03 Colin Moffett DREW 4 Belfast
07.12.03 Ian Reid W PTS 6 Glasgow
06.03.04 Fred Janes DREW 4 Renfrew
08.04.04 Chris Hooper L CO 2 Peterborough
28.05.04 Jason Nesbitt L RSC 3 Glasgow
01.04.05 Michael Crossan L PTS 6 Glasgow
20.05.05 Buster Dennis L RTD 4 Glasgow
14.10.05 Paul Griffin L RSC 1 Dublin
25.03.06 Sandy Bartlett W RSC 2 Irvine
05.06.06 Neil Marston W PTS 6 Glasgow
20.11.06 Jimmy Gilhaney L RSC 1 Glasgow
(Vacant Scottish Area Featherweight Title)

Career: 12 contests, won 4, drew 2, lost 6.

Omid Bourzo
Sheffield. *Born* Tehran, Iran, 1 September, 1979
Cruiserweight. *Ht* 6'1"
Manager J. Ingle

11.10.04 Peter McCormack L PTS 6 Birmingham
09.04.05 Danny McIntosh L PTS 6 Norwich
24.04.05 Jonjo Finnegan W PTS 6 Derby
15.12.05 Neil Tidman L RSC 3 Coventry
22.05.06 Peter McCormack W PTS 6 Birmingham
16.03.07 Paul Davis L RSC 4 Norwich

Career: 6 contests, won 2, lost 4.

Billy Boyle
Sheffield. *Born* Sheffield, 8 July, 1976
Cruiserweight. *Ht* 5'11½"
Manager G. Rhodes

20.04.07 David Ingleby W PTS 4 Sheffield
02.06.07 John Smith W RSC 3 Bristol

Career: 2 contests, won 2.

Ryan Brawley
Irvine. *Born* Irvine, 2 February, 1986
Lightweight. *Ht* 5'10½"
Manager T. Gilmour

19.09.05 Pete Buckley W PTS 6 Glasgow
14.10.05 Lance Verallo W PTS 6 Motherwell

20.02.06 Gavin Deacon W PTS 4 Glasgow
25.03.06 Chris Long W PTS 8 Irvine
06.05.06 Dariusz Snarski W PTS 6 Irvine
28.04.07 Rom Krauklis W PTS 8 Clydebank
11.05.07 Zsolt Jonas W PTS 6 Motherwell

Career: 7 contests, won 7.

Gordon Brennan
Dunfermline. *Born* Dunfermline, 1 August, 1982
L.Heavyweight. *Ht* 5'11"
Manager T. Gilmour

31.03.06 Jimi Hendricks W PTS 6 Inverurie
11.11.06 Tyrone Wright L PTS 6 Sutton in Ashfield
16.02.07 Simon Wood W PTS 4 Kirkcaldy
11.05.07 Leon Owen W PTS 4 Motherwell

Career: 4 contests, won 3, lost 1.

Tommy Broadbent
Leeds. *Born* Leeds, 13 July, 1986
L.Middleweight. *Ht* 5'10¾"
Manager M. Bateson

07.11.06 Steve Cooper W PTS 6 Leeds

Career: 1 contest, won 1.

Don Broadhurst
Birmingham. *Born* Birmingham, 2 February, 1984
Bantamweight. *Ht* 5'2½"
Manager F. Warren

02.09.06 Delroy Spencer W PTS 4 Bolton
18.11.06 Kemal Plavci W PTS 4 Newport
17.02.07 Ravil Mukhamadiarov W PTS 4 Wembley
07.04.07 Delroy Spencer W PTS 4 Cardiff

Career: 4 contests, won 4.

Don Broadhurst — Les Clark

Craig Bromley
Sheffield. *Born* Sheffield, 28 June, 1986
S.Featherweight. *Ht* 5'5"
Manager D. Coldwell

10.12.04 Darren Broomhall L PTS 6 Mansfield
19.12.04 Paddy Folan DREW 6 Bolton
13.02.05 Paddy Folan W PTS 6 Bradford

15.04.05 Neil Marston W RSC 1 Shrewsbury
24.07.05 Neil Read W PTS 4 Sheffield
16.09.05 Dave Hinds W PTS 4 Doncaster
14.10.05 Shaun Walton W PTS 4 Huddersfield
04.11.05 Sandy Bartlett W RSC 2 Glasgow
14.12.06 Rom Krauklis W PTS 6 Leicester

Career: 9 contests, won 7, drew 1, lost 1.

(Ezekiel) Kell Brook
Sheffield. *Born* Sheffield, 3 May, 1986
L.Middleweight. *Ht* 5'9"
Manager F. Warren

17.09.04 Pete Buckley W PTS 6 Sheffield
29.10.04 Andy Cosnett W CO 1 Worksop
09.11.04 Lee Williamson W RSC 2 Leeds
10.12.04 Brian Coleman W RSC 1 Sheffield
19.12.04 Karl Taylor W PTS 6 Bolton
04.03.05 Lea Handley W PTS 6 Rotherham
15.05.05 Ernie Smith W PTS 6 Sheffield
09.07.05 Jonathan Whiteman W RSC 2 Nottingham
10.09.05 Ernie Smith W PTS 4 Cardiff
29.04.06 Ernie Smith W PTS 6 Edinburgh
01.06.06 Geraint Harvey W RSC 3 Barnsley
14.10.06 Duncan Cottier W RSC 3 Manchester
09.12.06 David Kirk W RSC 1 Canning Town
07.04.07 Karl David W RSC 3 Cardiff

Career: 14 contests, won 14.

Scott Brookes
Mexborough. *Born* Rotherham, 16 November, 1987
Cruiserweight. *Ht* 6'2"
Manager D. Hobson

06.10.06 Nicki Taylor W PTS 6 Mexborough
03.05.07 David Ingleby W PTS 6 Sheffield

Career: 2 contests, won 2.

Stuart Brookes
Mexborough. *Born* Mexborough, 31 August, 1982
Middleweight. Former Undefeated British Masters L.Middleweight Champion. *Ht* 5'9"
Manager Self

15.05.05 Geraint Harvey W PTS 6 Sheffield
24.07.05 Tony Randell W PTS 6 Sheffield
09.09.05 Tony Randell W RSC 3 Sheffield
26.11.05 Howard Clarke W PTS 6 Sheffield
05.03.06 Magic Kidem W RSC 1 Sheffield
06.10.06 Eder Kurti W PTS 6 Mexborough
10.12.06 Jamie Ambler W RSC 1 Sheffield
03.05.07 Lee Noble W PTS 10 Sheffield
(Vacant British Masters L.Heavyweight Title)
23.06.07 Taronze Washington W PTS 6 Las Vegas, Nevada, USA

Career: 9 contests, won 9.

Wayne Brooks
Cardiff. *Born* Cardiff, 13 October, 1986
Cruiserweight. *Ht* 6'1"
Manager P. Boyce

13.10.06 Marko Doknic W RSC 3 Aberavon
15.12.06 Simon Wood W RSC 1 Bethnal Green
02.03.07 Nick Okoth DREW 4 Neath
10.06.07 Danny Couzens W PTS 4 Neath

Career: 4 contests, won 3, drew 1.

Wayne Brooks   Les Clark

Chris Brophy

Swansea. *Born* Preston, 28 January, 1979
L.Middleweight. *Ht* 5'10"
Manager Self

29.10.03	Aidan Mooney L RSC 5 Leicester Square
30.11.03	Casey Brooke W PTS 6 Swansea
21.12.03	Gary O'Connor L PTS 6 Bolton
21.02.04	Tony Doherty L RSC 2 Cardiff
02.04.04	Tommy Marshall DREW 6 Plymouth
26.04.04	Scott Haywood L RSC 5 Cleethorpes
05.06.04	Ashley Theophane L RSC 3 Bethnal Green
17.09.04	Tommy Marshall W PTS 6 Plymouth
21.11.04	Jay Morris L RSC 1 Bracknell
31.01.05	George McIlroy L RSC 6 Glasgow
16.09.05	Garry Buckland L PTS 4 Plymouth
24.10.05	Mike Reid L RSC 2 Glasgow
26.02.06	Freddie Luke L PTS 4 Dagenham
11.03.06	Stephen Burke L PTS 4 Newport
13.05.06	Grant Skehill L PTS 4 Bethnal Green
08.09.06	Dee Mitchell L RSC 2 Birmingham
03.12.06	Danny Butler L PTS 4 Bristol
16.02.07	Barrie Jones L PTS 4 Merthyr Tydfil
24.02.07	Jimmy Doherty L PTS 6 Stoke
18.03.07	Chris Long DREW 6 Bristol
07.06.07	Patrick Doherty L CO 4 Kensington

Career: 21 contests, won 2, drew 2, lost 17.

Nathan Brough

Liverpool. *Born* Liverpool, 18 May, 1984
Welterweight. *Ht* 6'0"
Manager T. Gilmour

08.06.07	Billy Smith W PTS 4 Motherwell

Career: 1 contest, won 1.

Barrington Brown

Nottingham. *Born* Nottingham, 11 May, 1982
S.Featherweight. *Ht* 5'7"
Manager J. Gill/T. Harris

06.03.05	Paddy Folan W RSC 6 Shaw
30.09.05	Craig Morgan L PTS 6 Carmarthen
09.10.05	Vinesh Rungea W PTS 6 Hammersmith
18.02.06	Mick Abbott W PTS 6 Stoke
24.04.06	Kevin Townsley L PTS 6 Glasgow
30.05.06	Lloyd Otte W RSC 1 Bethnal Green

30.09.06	Gary Davis DREW 6 Stoke
03.11.06	Danny Wallace L PTS 4 Barnsley

Career: 8 contests, won 4, drew 1, lost 3.*

Barrington Brown   Les Clark

Cathy Brown

Peckham. *Born* Leeds, 28 July, 1970
English Womens Bantamweight Champion.
Former Undefeated Womens BF European
Flyweight Champion. *Ht* 5'2"
Manager J. Feld

31.10.99	Veerle Braspenningsx W PTS 5 Raynes Park
05.02.00	Veerle Braspenningsx W RSC 6 Sint-Truiden, Belgium
01.07.00	Jan Wild W PTS 6 Southwark *(Vacant Womens BF European Flyweight Title)*
31.10.00	Viktoria Vargal W RSC 3 Hammersmith
28.02.01	Marietta Ivanova W PTS 4 Kensington
26.04.01	Oksana Vasilieva L PTS 4 Kensington
16.06.01	Romona Gughie W RSC 3 Wembley
22.11.01	Audrey Guthrie W PTS 6 Mayfair *(Womens BF European Flyweight Title Defence)*
13.12.01	Ilina Boneva W RSC 5 Leicester Square
13.03.02	Svetla Taskova W PTS 4 Mayfair
13.06.02	Alina Shaternikova L PTS 10 Leicester Square *(Vacant Womens BF Flyweight Title)*
30.10.02	Monica Petrova W PTS 6 Leicester Square
20.03.03	Juliette Winter L PTS 4 Queensway
26.04.03	Regina Halmich L PTS 10 Schwerin, Germany *(Womens IBF Flyweight Title Challenge)*
17.12.03	Stefania Bianchini L PTS 10 Bergamo, Italy *(Womens BF European Flyweight Title Challenge)*
06.11.04	Bettina Csabi L PTS 10 Szentes, Hungary *(Womens BF/GBU Bantamweight Title Challenges)*
02.12.04	Viktoria Varga W RSC 3 Crystal Palace
12.06.05	Svetla Taskova W RSC 6 Leicester Square

07.08.05	Stefania Bianchini L PTS 10 Rimini, Italy *(Vacant Womens IBF Interim Flyweight Title)*
08.04.06	Julia Sahin L PTS 10 Kiel, Germany *(Vacant Womens IBF L.Flyweight Title)*
24.09.06	Juliette Winter W PTS 10 Bethnal Green *(Vacant Womens English Bantamweight Title)*

Career: 21 contests, won 13, lost 8.

Cathy Brown   Les Clark

James Brown

Salford. *Born* Salford, 15 August, 1986
S.Featherweight. *Ht* 5'10"
Manager S. Wood

18.06.06	Pete Buckley W PTS 6 Manchester
21.07.06	Graeme Higginson L PTS 4 Altrincham
17.12.06	John Baguley L PTS 6 Bolton

Career: 3 contests, won 1, lost 2.

Paul Buchanan

West Denton. *Born* Newcastle, 23 October, 1981
S.Middleweight. *Ht* 5'10"
Manager G. Robinson

31.01.01	Gary Jones W RTD 1 Piccadilly
26.04.01	Lee Woodruff W PTS 6 Gateshead
08.03.02	Neil Bonner W PTS 6 Ellesmere Port
25.03.02	Dean Cockburn W PTS 6 Sunderland
06.03.04	Davey Jones W PTS 4 Renfrew
01.05.04	Gareth Lawrence W PTS 4 Gravesend
05.11.04	Jason McKay W PTS 6 Hereford
27.05.05	Ojay Abrahams W PTS 6 Spennymoor
25.11.05	Wayne Pinder DREW 6 Liverpool
30.03.07	Jerson Ravelo L PTS 8 Newcastle
03.06.07	Ryan Rhodes L RSC 1 Barnsley

Career: 11 contests, won 8, drew 1, lost 2.

Garry Buckland

Cardiff. *Born* Cardiff, 12 June 1986
Welsh L.Welterweight Champion. *Ht* 5'7"
Manager B. Powell

05.03.05	Warren Dunkley W PTS 4 Dagenham
24.07.05	Danny Gwilym W RSC 2 Leicester Square
16.09.05	Chris Brophy W PTS 4 Plymouth

17.11.05	Bheki Moyo W RSC 3 Bristol
10.02.06	Anthony Christopher W RSC 4 Plymouth
07.04.06	Judex Meemea W RSC 5 Bristol
14.07.06	Ubadel Soto W PTS 4 Alicante, Spain
15.09.06	Karl Taylor W PTS 6 Newport
10.11.06	Judex Meemea W PTS 6 Newport
03.03.07	Stuart Phillips W PTS 10 Newport (Vacant Welsh Area L.Welterweight Title)
16.06.07	Carl Allen W PTS 6 Newport

Career: 11 contests, won 11.

Kevin Buckley

Chester. *Born* Chester, 20 April, 1986
Lightweight. *Ht* 5'7½"
Manager S. Goodwin

03.03.07	Shaun Walton W PTS 6 Burton
20.04.07	Pete Buckley W PTS 4 Dudley

Career: 2 contests, won 2.

Pete Buckley

Birmingham. *Born* Birmingham, 9 March, 1969
Welterweight. Former Undefeated Midlands Area S. Featherweight Champion. Former Midlands Area S. Bantamweight Champion. *Ht* 5'8"
Manager Self

04.10.89	Alan Baldwin DREW 6 Stafford
10.10.89	Ronnie Stephenson L PTS 6 Wolverhampton
30.10.89	Robert Braddock W PTS 6 Birmingham
14.11.89	Neil Leitch W PTS 6 Evesham
22.11.89	Peter Judson W PTS 6 Stafford
11.12.89	Stevie Woods W PTS 6 Bradford
21.12.89	Wayne Taylor W PTS 6 Kings Heath
10.01.90	John O'Meara W PTS 6 Kensington
19.02.90	Ian McGirr L PTS 6 Birmingham
27.02.90	Miguel Matthews DREW 6 Evesham
14.03.90	Ronnie Stephenson DREW 6 Stoke
04.04.90	Ronnie Stephenson L PTS 8 Stafford
23.04.90	Ronnie Stephenson W PTS 6 Birmingham
30.04.90	Chris Clarkson L PTS 8 Mayfair
17.05.90	Johnny Bredahl L PTS 6 Aars, Denmark
04.06.90	Ronnie Stephenson W PTS 8 Birmingham
28.06.90	Robert Braddock W RSC 5 Birmingham
01.10.90	Miguel Matthews W PTS 8 Cleethorpes
09.10.90	Miguel Matthews L PTS 8 Wolverhampton
17.10.90	Tony Smith W PTS 6 Stoke
29.10.90	Miguel Matthews W PTS 8 Birmingham
21.11.90	Drew Docherty L PTS 8 Solihull
10.12.90	Neil Leitch W PTS 8 Birmingham
10.01.91	Duke McKenzie L RSC 5 Wandsworth
18.02.91	Jamie McBride L PTS 8 Glasgow
04.03.91	Brian Robb W RSC 7 Birmingham
26.03.91	Neil Leitch DREW 8 Wolverhampton
01.05.91	Mark Geraghty W PTS 8 Solihull
05.06.91	Brian Robb W PTS 10 Wolverhampton (Vacant Midlands Area S. Featherweight Title)
09.09.91	Mike Deveney L PTS 8 Glasgow
24.09.91	Mark Bates W RTD 5 Basildon
29.10.91	John Armour L PTS 6 Kensington
14.11.91	Mike Deveney L PTS 6 Edinburgh
28.11.91	Craig Dermody L PTS 6 Liverpool
19.12.91	Craig Dermody L PTS 6 Oldham
18.01.92	Alan McKay DREW 8 Kensington
20.02.92	Brian Robb W RSC 10 Oakengates (Midlands Area S. Featherweight Title Defence)
27.04.92	Drew Docherty L PTS 8 Glasgow
15.05.92	Ruben Condori L PTS 10 Augsburg, Germany
29.05.92	Donnie Hood L PTS 8 Glasgow
07.09.92	Duke McKenzie L RTD 3 Bethnal Green
12.11.92	Prince Naseem Hamed L PTS 6 Liverpool
19.02.93	Harald Geier L PTS 12 Vienna, Austria (Vacant WBA Penta-Continental S. Bantamweight Title)
26.04.93	Bradley Stone L PTS 8 Lewisham
18.06.93	Eamonn McAuley L PTS 6 Belfast
01.07.93	Tony Silkstone L PTS 8 York
06.10.93	Jonjo Irwin L PTS 8 Solihull
25.10.93	Drew Docherty L PTS 8 Glasgow
06.11.93	Michael Alldis L PTS 8 Bethnal Green
30.11.93	Barry Jones L PTS 4 Cardiff
19.12.93	Shaun Anderson L PTS 6 Glasgow
22.01.94	Barry Jones L PTS 6 Cardiff
29.01.94	Prince Naseem Hamed L RSC 4 Cardiff
10.03.94	Tony Falcone L PTS 4 Bristol
29.03.94	Conn McMullen W PTS 6 Bethnal Green
05.04.94	Mark Bowers L PTS 6 Bethnal Green
13.04.94	James Murray L PTS 6 Glasgow
06.05.94	Paul Lloyd L RTD 4 Liverpool
03.08.94	Greg Upton L PTS 6 Bristol
26.09.94	John Sillo L PTS 6 Liverpool
05.10.94	Matthew Harris L PTS 6 Wolverhampton
07.11.94	Marlon Ward L PTS 4 Piccadilly
23.11.94	Justin Murphy L PTS 4 Piccadilly
29.11.94	Neil Swain L PTS 4 Cardiff
13.12.94	Michael Brodie L PTS 6 Potters Bar
20.12.94	Michael Alldis L PTS 6 Bethnal Green
10.02.95	Matthew Harris W RSC 6 Birmingham (Midlands Area S. Bantamweight Title Challenge)
23.02.95	Paul Ingle L PTS 8 Southwark
20.04.95	John Sillo L PTS 6 Liverpool
27.04.95	Paul Ingle L PTS 8 Bethnal Green
09.05.95	Ady Lewis L PTS 4 Basildon
23.05.95	Spencer Oliver L PTS 4 Potters Bar
01.07.95	Dean Pithie L PTS 4 Kensington
21.09.95	Patrick Mullings L PTS 6 Battersea
29.09.95	Marlon Ward L PTS 4 Bethnal Green
25.10.95	Matthew Harris L PTS 10 Telford (Midlands Area S. Bantamweight Title Defence)
08.11.95	Vince Feeney L PTS 8 Bethnal Green
28.11.95	Barry Jones L PTS 6 Cardiff
15.12.95	Patrick Mullings L PTS 4 Bethnal Green
05.02.96	Patrick Mullings L PTS 8 Bexleyheath
09.03.96	Paul Griffin L PTS 4 Millstreet
21.03.96	Colin McMillan L RSC 3 Southwark
14.05.96	Venkatesan Deverajan L PTS 4 Dagenham
29.06.96	Matt Brown W RSC 1 Erith
03.09.96	Vince Feeney L PTS 4 Bethnal Green
28.09.96	Fabrice Benichou L PTS 8 Barking
09.10.96	Gary Marston DREW 8 Stoke
06.11.96	Neil Swain L PTS 4 Tylorstown
29.11.96	Alston Buchanan L PTS 8 Glasgow
22.12.96	Brian Carr L PTS 6 Glasgow
11.01.97	Scott Harrison L PTS 4 Bethnal Green
29.01.97	Carl Allen L PTS 8 Stoke
12.02.97	Ronnie McPhee L PTS 6 Glasgow
25.02.97	Dean Pithie L PTS 4 Sheffield
07.03.97	Jason Booth L PTS 6 Northampton
20.03.97	Thomas Bradley W PTS 6 Newark
08.04.97	Sergei Devakov L PTS 6 Bethnal Green
25.04.97	Matthew Harris L PTS 6 Cleethorpes
08.05.97	Gregorio Medina L RTD 2 Mansfield
13.06.97	Mike Deveney L PTS 6 Paisley
19.07.97	Richard Evatt L PTS 4 Wembley
30.08.97	Michael Brodie L PTS 8 Cheshunt
06.10.97	Brendan Bryce W PTS 6 Piccadilly
20.10.97	Kelton McKenzie L PTS 6 Leicester
20.11.97	Ervine Blake L PTS 8 Solihull
06.12.97	Danny Adams L PTS 4 Wembley
13.12.97	Gary Thornhill L PTS 6 Sheffield
31.01.98	Scott Harrison L PTS 4 Edmonton
05.03.98	Steve Conway L PTS 6 Leeds
18.03.98	Ervine Blake L PTS 4 Stoke
26.03.98	Graham McGrath W RTD 4 Solihull
11.04.98	Salim Medjkoune L PTS 6 Southwark
18.04.98	Tony Mulholland L PTS 4 Manchester
27.04.98	Alston Buchanan L PTS 8 Glasgow
11.05.98	Jason Squire W RTD 2 Leicester
21.05.98	Lee Armstrong L PTS 6 Bradford
06.06.98	Tony Mulholland L PTS 6 Liverpool
14.06.98	Lee Armstrong L PTS 6 Shaw
21.07.98	David Burke L PTS 6 Widnes
05.09.98	Michael Gomez L PTS 6 Telford
17.09.98	Brian Carr L PTS 6 Glasgow
03.10.98	Justin Murphy L PTS 6 Crawley
05.12.98	Lehlohonolo Ledwaba L PTS 8 Bristol
19.12.98	Acelino Freitas L RTD 3 Liverpool
09.02.99	Chris Jickells L PTS 6 Wolverhampton
16.02.99	Franny Hogg L PTS 6 Leeds
26.02.99	Richard Evatt L RSC 5 Coventry
17.04.99	Martin O'Malley L RSC 3 Dublin
29.05.99	Richie Wenton L PTS 6 Halifax
14.06.99	Carl Allen L PTS 6 Birmingham
26.06.99	Paul Halpin L PTS 4 Millwall
15.07.99	Salim Medjkoune L PTS 6 Peterborough
07.08.99	Steve Murray L PTS 6 Dagenham
12.09.99	Kevin Gerowski L PTS 6 Nottingham
20.09.99	Mat Zegan L PTS 6 Peterborough
02.10.99	Jason Cook L PTS 4 Cardiff
09.10.99	Brian Carr L PTS 6 Manchester
19.10.99	Gary Steadman L PTS 4 Bethnal Green
27.10.99	Miguel Matthews W PTS 8 Birmingham
20.11.99	Carl Greaves L PTS 10 Grantham (British Masters S. Featherweight Title Challenge)
11.12.99	Gary Thornhill L PTS 6 Liverpool
29.01.00	Bradley Pryce L PTS 4 Manchester
19.02.00	Gavin Rees L PTS 4 Dagenham
29.02.00	Tony Mulholland L PTS 4 Widnes
20.03.00	Carl Greaves L PTS 4 Mansfield
27.03.00	James Rooney L PTS 4 Barnsley
08.04.00	Delroy Pryce L PTS 4 Bethnal Green
17.04.00	Franny Hogg L PTS 8 Glasgow
11.05.00	Craig Spacie L PTS 4 Newark
25.05.00	Jimmy Phelan DREW 6 Hull
19.06.00	Delroy Pryce L PTS 4 Burton
01.07.00	Richard Evatt L PTS 4 Manchester
16.09.00	Lee Meager L PTS 4 Bethnal Green
23.09.00	Gavin Rees L PTS 4 Bethnal Green
02.10.00	Brian Carr L PTS 4 Glasgow
14.10.00	Gareth Jordan L PTS 4 Wembley
13.11.00	Kevin Lear L PTS 6 Bethnal Green
24.11.00	Lee Williamson L PTS 6 Hull
09.12.00	Leo O'Reilly L PTS 4 Southwark
15.01.01	Eddie Nevins L PTS 4 Manchester
23.01.01	David Burke L PTS 4 Crawley
31.01.01	Tony Montana L PTS 6 Piccadilly

19.02.01	Kevin England W PTS 6 Glasgow
12.03.01	Carl Allen L PTS 6 Birmingham
19.03.01	Duncan Armstrong L PTS 6 Glasgow
27.03.01	Carl Allen L PTS 8 Brierley Hill
05.05.01	Danny Hunt L PTS 4 Edmonton
09.06.01	Gary Thornhill L PTS 4 Bethnal Green
21.07.01	Scott Miller L PTS 4 Sheffield
28.07.01	Kevin Lear L PTS 4 Wembley
25.09.01	Ricky Eccleston L PTS 4 Liverpool
07.10.01	Nigel Senior L PTS 6 Wolverhampton
31.10.01	Woody Greenaway L PTS 6 Birmingham
16.11.01	Jimmy Beech L PTS 6 West Bromwich
01.12.01	Chill John L PTS 4 Bethnal Green
09.12.01	Nigel Senior W PTS 6 Shaw
26.01.02	Scott Lawton L PTS 4 Bethnal Green
09.02.02	Sam Gorman L PTS 4 Coventry
23.02.02	Alex Moon L PTS 4 Nottingham
04.03.02	Leo Turner L PTS 6 Bradford
11.03.02	Martin Watson L PTS 4 Glasgow
26.04.02	Scott Lawton L PTS 4 Coventry
10.05.02	Lee Meager L PTS 6 Bethnal Green
08.06.02	Bradley Pryce L RSC 1 Renfrew
20.07.02	Jeff Thomas L PTS 4 Bethnal Green
23.08.02	Ben Hudson DREW 4 Bethnal Green
06.09.02	Dave Stewart L PTS 6 Bethnal Green
14.09.02	Peter McDonagh L PTS 4 Bethnal Green
20.10.02	James Paisley L PTS 4 Southwark
12.11.02	Martin Hardcastle DREW 6 Leeds
29.11.02	Daniel Thorpe L PTS 6 Hull
09.12.02	Nicky Leech L PTS 6 Nottingham
16.12.02	Joel Viney L PTS 6 Cleethorpes
28.01.03	Billy Corcoran L PTS 6 Nottingham
08.02.03	Colin Toohey L PTS 6 Liverpool
15.02.03	Terry Fletcher L PTS 4 Wembley
22.02.03	Dean Lambert L PTS 4 Huddersfield
05.03.03	Billy Corcoran L PTS 6 Bethnal Green
18.03.03	Nathan Ward L PTS 4 Reading
05.04.03	Baz Carey L PTS 4 Manchester
15.05.03	Mike Harrington W PTS 4 Clevedon
27.05.03	Dave Stewart L PTS 4 Dagenham
07.06.03	Rimell Taylor DREW 4 Coventry
12.07.03	George Telfer L PTS 4 Renfrew
22.07.03	Chas Symonds L PTS 6 Bethnal Green
01.08.03	Jas Malik W PTS 4 Bethnal Green
06.09.03	John Murray L PTS 4 Huddersfield
13.09.03	Isaac Ward L PTS 6 Wakefield
25.09.03	Gary Woolcombe L PTS 6 Bethnal Green
06.10.03	Scott Haywood L PTS 6 Barnsley
20.10.03	Joel Viney W PTS 6 Bradford
29.10.03	David Kehoe L PTS 6 Leicester Square
07.11.03	Femi Fehintola L PTS 6 Sheffield
14.11.03	Dave Stewart L PTS 4 Bethnal Green
21.11.03	Henry Castle L PTS 4 Millwall
28.11.03	Lee Meager L PTS 4 Derby
13.12.03	Derry Matthews L PTS 4 Manchester
21.12.03	Daniel Thorpe L PTS 6 Bolton
16.01.04	Nadeem Siddique L PTS 4 Bradford
16.02.04	Scott Haywood L PTS 6 Scunthorpe
29.02.04	Gary O'Connor L PTS 6 Shaw
03.04.04	Steve Bell L PTS 4 Manchester
16.04.04	Isaac Ward L PTS 6 Hartlepool
23.04.04	Colin Bain L PTS 6 Glasgow
06.05.04	Amir Ali L PTS 4 Barnsley
13.05.04	Lee Beavis L PTS 4 Bethnal Green
04.06.04	Tristan Davies L PTS 6 Dudley
03.07.04	Barrie Jones L PTS 4 Newport
03.09.04	Stefy Bull L PTS 6 Doncaster
10.09.04	Tiger Matthews L PTS 4 Liverpool
17.09.04	Kell Brook L PTS 6 Sheffield
24.09.04	Ceri Hall L PTS 6 Dublin
11.10.04	Darren Johnstone L PTS 6 Glasgow
22.10.04	Jonathan Whiteman L PTS 6 Mansfield

29.10.04	Colin Bain L PTS 4 Renfrew
09.11.04	Tom Hogan L PTS 4 Leeds
21.11.04	Chris McDonagh L PTS 4 Bracknell
10.12.04	Craig Johnson L PTS 6 Mansfield
17.12.04	Steve Mullin L PTS 4 Liverpool
12.02.05	Jay Morris L PTS 6 Portsmouth
21.02.05	Stuart Green L PTS 6 Glasgow
05.03.05	Paul Buckley L PTS 6 Southwark
23.03.05	Ryan Barrett L PTS 6 Leicester Square
09.04.05	Nadeem Siddique L PTS 6 Norwich
25.04.05	Jimmy Gilhaney L PTS 6 Glasgow
14.05.05	James Gorman L PTS 6 Dublin
27.05.05	Alan Temple L PTS 4 Spennymoor
04.06.05	Patrick Hyland L PTS 4 Dublin
25.06.05	Sean Hughes DREW 6 Wakefield
24.07.05	Scott Lawton L PTS 6 Sheffield
03.09.05	Jackson Williams L PTS 6 Norwich
19.09.05	Ryan Brawley L PTS 6 Glasgow
14.10.05	Jimmy Gilhaney L PTS 6 Motherwell
23.11.05	Shane Watson L PTS 6 Mayfair
02.12.05	Billy Corcoran L PTS 4 Nottingham
14.12.05	Stephen Burke L PTS 4 Blackpool
23.01.06	David Appleby L PTS 6 Glasgow
02.02.06	Michael Grant L PTS 4 Holborn
18.02.06	Jimmy Doherty L PTS 6 Stoke
04.03.06	Steve Bell L PTS 4 Manchester
13.03.06	Gary McArthur L PTS 6 Glasgow
25.03.06	Brian Murphy L PTS 6 Irvine
02.04.06	Barry Downes L PTS 6 Shaw
13.04.06	Paul Newby L PTS 4 Leeds
28.04.06	Gary O'Connor L PTS 6 Manchester
06.05.06	Ian Clyde L PTS 6 Stoke
20.05.06	Stephen Haughian L PTS 4 Belfast
09.06.06	Wez Miller L PTS 6 Doncaster
18.06.06	James Brown L PTS 6 Manchester
29.06.06	Rob Hunt L PTS 6 Dudley
10.07.06	Calvin White L PTS 6 Manchester
09.09.06	Stuart Green L PTS 8 Inverurie
18.09.06	Stuart Green L PTS 6 Glasgow
29.09.06	Mitch Prince L PTS 6 Motherwell
03.11.06	Mitch Prince L PTS 6 Glasgow
12.11.06	Danny Harding L PTS 6 Manchester
24.11.06	Adam Kelly L PTS 6 Hull
06.12.06	Daniel Thorpe L PTS 6 Rotherham
19.02.07	Mark Hastie L PTS 6 Glasgow
03.03.07	Wayne Downing L PTS 4 Burton
11.03.07	Shinny Bayaar L PTS 6 Shaw
26.03.07	Charles Paul King L PTS 6 Glasgow
20.04.07	Kevin Buckley L PTS 4 Dudley
28.04.07	Furhan Rafiq L PTS 6 Clydebank
03.06.07	Andrew Ward L PTS 4 Barnsley
24.06.07	Jon Kays L PTS 6 Wigan

Career: 286 contests, won 31, drew 11, lost 244.

(Andrew) Stefy Bull (Bullcroft)

Doncaster. *Born* Doncaster, 10 May, 1977
Central Area Lightweight Champion.
Former Undefeated WBF Inter-Continental
Lightweight Champion. Former Undefeated
Central Area Featherweight Champion.
Ht 5'10"
Manager J. Rushton

30.06.95	Andy Roberts W PTS 4 Doncaster
11.10.95	Michael Edwards W PTS 6 Stoke
18.10.95	Alan Hagan W RSC 1 Batley
28.11.95	Kevin Sheil W RSC 6 Wolverhampton
26.01.96	Robert Grubb W PTS 6 Doncaster
12.09.96	Benny Jones W PTS 6 Doncaster
15.10.96	Kevin Sheil DREW 6 Wolverhampton
24.10.96	Graham McGrath W PTS 6 Birmingham
17.12.96	Robert Braddock W RSC 4 Doncaster

	(Vacant Central Area Featherweight Title)
10.07.97	Carl Greaves W PTS 6 Doncaster
11.10.97	Dean Pithie L RSC 11 Sheffield
	(Vacant WBO Inter-Continental S. Featherweight Title)
19.03.98	Chris Lyons W RSC 4 Doncaster
08.04.98	Alex Moon L RSC 3 Liverpool
31.07.99	Jason Dee L RSC 4 Carlisle
09.05.03	Joel Viney W RTD 3 Doncaster
02.06.03	Jason Nesbitt W PTS 6 Cleethorpes
05.09.03	Dave Hinds W PTS 6 Doncaster
20.02.04	Anthony Christopher W PTS 6 Doncaster
07.05.04	Daniel Thorpe W PTS 10 Doncaster
	(Central Area Lightweight Title Challenge)
03.09.04	Pete Buckley W PTS 6 Doncaster
29.10.04	Haroon Din W RSC 2 Doncaster
	(Central Area Lightweight Title Defence)
04.02.05	Gwyn Wale W PTS 10 Doncaster
	(Central Area Lightweight Title Defence)
11.03.05	Jimmy Beech W PTS 4 Doncaster
20.05.05	Billy Smith W PTS 6 Doncaster
16.09.05	Carl Allen W PTS 10 Doncaster
	(Vacant WBF Inter-Continental Lightweight Title)
02.12.05	David Kehoe W PTS 6 Doncaster
03.03.06	Baz Carey W PTS 10 Doncaster
	(WBF Inter-Continental Lightweight Title Defence)
09.06.06	Scott Lawton L RSC 8 Doncaster
	(Vacant English Lightweight Title)
13.10.06	Carl Allen W PTS 6 Doncaster
07.04.07	Amir Khan L RSC 3 Cardiff

Career: 30 contests, won 24, drew 1, lost 5.

Robert Bunford

Llanelli. *Born* Carmarthen, 28 May, 1982
Featherweight. *Ht* 5'6"
Manager D. Davies

03.11.06	Ross Burkinshaw L CO 1 Barnsley
03.12.06	Robert Nelson L PTS 4 Wakefield
26.01.07	Kris Hughes L PTS 6 Glasgow

Career: 3 contests, lost 3.

Craig Bunn

Manchester. *Born* Tameside, 1 April, 1986
Middleweight. *Ht* 6'1"
Manager S. Wood

18.12.05	Gary Round W PTS 6 Bolton
12.02.06	Howard Clarke W PTS 6 Manchester
18.06.06	Ryan Rowlinson W PTS 6 Manchester
12.11.06	Dean Walker DREW 6 Manchester
17.12.06	Shaun Farmer W PTS 6 Bolton

Career: 5 contests, won 4, drew 1.

Stephen Burke

Liverpool. *Born* Liverpool, 18 March, 1979
Welterweight. *Ht* 5'8"
Manager Self

13.05.05	Imad Khamis W RSC 3 Liverpool
14.12.05	Pete Buckley W PTS 4 Blackpool
11.03.06	Chris Brophy W PTS 4 Newport
02.09.06	Billy Smith W PTS 4 Bolton
10.03.07	Daniel Thorpe W PTS 4 Liverpool

Career: 5 contests, won 5.

Ross Burkinshaw
Sheffield. *Born* Sheffield, 10 August, 1986
Bantamweight. *Ht* 5'8"
Manager G. Rhodes

03.11.06	Robert Bunford W CO 1 Barnsley
09.02.07	Delroy Spencer W PTS 4 Leeds

Career: 2 contests, won 2.

Paul Burns
Uddingston. *Born* Rutherglen, 5 January, 1983
L.Middleweight. *Ht* 6'2"
Manager T. Gilmour

06.06.05	Terry Carruthers DREW 6 Glasgow
14.10.05	Surinder Sekhon W PTS 6 Motherwell
21.11.05	Malik Khan W RTD 2 Glasgow
13.03.06	David Kehoe W PTS 6 Glasgow
29.09.06	Peter Dunn W PTS 6 Motherwell
20.11.06	Steve Cooper DREW 6 Glasgow
28.04.07	Danny Gwilym W PTS 6 Clydebank

Career: 7 contests, won 5, drew 2.

Ricky Burns
Coatbridge. *Born* Bellshill, 13 April, 1983
S.Featherweight. *Ht* 5'10"
Manager F. Warren/A. Morrison

20.10.01	Woody Greenaway W PTS 4 Glasgow
15.03.02	Peter Allen W PTS 6 Glasgow
08.06.02	Gary Harrison W RSC 1 Renfrew
06.09.02	Ernie Smith W PTS 6 Glasgow
19.10.02	Neil Murray W RSC 2 Renfrew
08.12.02	No No Junior W PTS 8 Glasgow
08.10.04	Daniel Thorpe W PTS 6 Glasgow
29.10.04	Jeff Thomas W PTS 4 Renfrew
12.12.04	Colin Bain W PTS 6 Glasgow
25.02.05	Graham Earl W PTS 8 Wembley
08.04.05	Buster Dennis W PTS 6 Edinburgh
17.06.05	Haider Ali W PTS 8 Glasgow
23.07.05	Alan Temple W PTS 4 Edinburgh
18.02.06	Alex Arthur L PTS 12 Edinburgh
	(British, Commonwealth & European S.Featherweight Title Challenges)
01.04.06	Adolph Avadja W RSC 5 Bethnal Green
04.11.06	Wladimir Borov W PTS 8 Glasgow
09.02.07	Carl Johanneson L PTS 12 Leeds
	(British S.Featherweight Title Challenge)

Career: 17 contests, won 15, lost 2.

Chris Burton   Les Clark

Chris Burton
Darlington. *Born* Darlington, 27 February, 1981
Heavyweight. *Ht* 6'5"
Manager D. Garside

02.06.05	David Ingleby W RSC 3 Yarm
03.03.06	Istvan Kecskes W PTS 4 Hartlepool
28.04.06	Istvan Kecskes W PTS 4 Hartlepool
23.06.06	Simon Goodwin W RSC 3 Blackpool
30.09.06	Istvan Kecskes W RSC 5 Middlesbrough
05.12.06	Paul Butlin W RSC 4 Wolverhampton
28.01.07	Chris Woollas W RSC 3 Yarm
06.05.07	Paul King W PTS 4 Darlington

Career: 8 contests, won 8.

Robert Burton
Barnsley. *Born* Barnsley, 1 April, 1971
L.Heavyweight. Former Central Area L.Middleweight Champion. Former Central Area Welterweight Champion. *Ht* 5'9"
Manager Self

05.02.01	Gavin Pearson W RSC 3 Bradford
23.02.01	Scott Millar W CO 5 Irvine
20.03.01	Peter Dunn W PTS 6 Leeds
08.05.01	Arv Mittoo W PTS 4 Barnsley
10.06.01	Martyn Bailey DREW 6 Ellesmere Port
08.10.01	Gavin Pearson W RSC 2 Barnsley
16.11.01	Martyn Bailey DREW 4 Preston
24.11.01	Peter Dunn L PTS 6 Wakefield
28.01.02	Peter Dunn W RSC 8 Barnsley
	(Vacant Central Area Welterweight Title)
23.08.02	David Walker L RSC 2 Bethnal Green
19.10.02	John Humphrey L RTD 4 Norwich
09.02.03	Donovan Smillie L PTS 6 Bradford
24.03.03	Andy Halder L PTS 6 Barnsley
31.05.03	David Keir W RSC 9 Barnsley
	(Central Area Welterweight Title Defence)
01.11.03	Scott Dixon L PTS 6 Glasgow
08.12.03	Jed Tytler W PTS 6 Barnsley
10.02.04	Paul Lomax W PTS 6 Barnsley
06.05.04	Matthew Hatton L PTS 10 Barnsley
	(Central Area Welterweight Title Defence)
08.06.04	Lee Murtagh W CO 3 Sheffield
	(Vacant Central Area L.Middleweight Title)
12.11.04	Matthew Hatton L PTS 10 Halifax
	(Central Area L.Middleweight Title Defence)
11.02.05	Paul Smith L CO 1 Manchester
22.04.05	John Marshall L RTD 4 Barnsley
23.07.05	Craig Lynch L PTS 4 Edinburgh
30.09.05	Jonjo Finnegan DREW 4 Burton
22.10.05	Richard Mazurek W PTS 6 Coventry
25.11.05	Matthew Hough L PTS 4 Walsall
12.12.05	Cello Renda L CO 1 Peterborough
11.03.06	Matthew Hall L CO 1 Newport
13.04.06	Donovan Smillie DREW 6 Leeds
29.04.06	Craig Lynch L PTS 4 Edinburgh
01.06.06	Ryan Rowlinson W PTS 4 Barnsley
22.06.06	Jon Ibbotson DREW 6 Sheffield
15.09.06	Daniel Cadman L RSC 5 Muswell Hill
20.10.06	Jon Ibbotson L CO 2 Sheffield
24.11.06	Ricardo Samms L PTS 4 Nottingham
03.12.06	Darren Rhodes L PTS 6 Wakefield
16.03.07	Danny McIntosh L PTS 4 Norwich
15.04.07	Dean Walker W PTS 6 Barnsley

Career: 38 contests, won 13, drew 5, lost 20.

Danny Butler
Bristol. *Born* Bristol, 10 November, 1987
Middleweight. *Ht* 5'10½"
Manager T. Woodward

25.02.06	Magic Kidem W PTS 6 Bristol
07.04.06	Tommy Jones W PTS 4 Bristol
21.05.06	Martin Sweeney W PTS 6 Bristol
03.12.06	Chris Brophy W PTS 4 Bristol
24.02.07	Rocky Chakir W PTS 6 Bristol
18.03.07	Pawel Jas W PTS 6 Bristol
01.06.07	Surinder Sekhon W PTS 6 Birmingham

Career: 7 contests, won 7.

Andrew Butlin
Huddersfield. *Born* Huddersfield, 31 January, 1982
Middleweight. *Ht* 5'10"
Manager Self

12.11.04	Martin Concepcion L RSC 1 Halifax
22.02.07	Steve Cooper W PTS 6 Leeds
14.04.07	Rocky Muscas W PTS 6 Wakefield

Career: 3 contests, won 2, lost 1.

Paul Butlin
Oakham. *Born* Oakham, 16 March, 1976
Heavyweight. *Ht* 6'1½"
Manager Self

05.10.02	Dave Clarke W PTS 4 Coventry
16.11.02	Gary Williams W RSC 1 Coventry
09.12.02	Slick Miller W PTS 6 Nottingham
08.03.03	Dave Clarke W PTS 6 Coventry
19.04.03	Paul Buttery L RSC 3 Liverpool
27.04.04	Ebrima Secka W PTS 6 Leeds
26.09.04	Lee Mountford W PTS 6 Stoke
06.12.04	David Ingleby W CO 5 Leicester
30.04.05	David Ingleby L PTS 6 Coventry
25.06.05	Mal Rice W PTS 4 Melton Mowbray
22.10.05	Jason Callum W PTS 4 Coventry
18.03.06	David Ingleby W PTS 6 Coventry
05.12.06	Chris Burton L RSC 4 Wolverhampton
03.03.07	Luke Simpkin W PTS 4 Burton

Career: 14 contests, won 11, lost 3.

Paul Butlin   Les Clark

Lewis Byrne
Cambridge. *Born* Gravesend, 28 December, 1984
L.Middleweight. *Ht* 5'11¼"
Manager D. Currivan

16.06.07	Robbie James L PTS 4 Newport

Career: 1 contest, lost 1.

C

Daniel Cadman
Waltham Abbey. *Born* Harlow, 25 June, 1980
S.Middleweight. *Ht* 5'10"
Manager Self

25.07.03	Leigh Wicks W PTS 4 Norwich
04.10.03	Patrick Cito W PTS 6 Muswell Hill
28.11.03	Harry Butler W PTS 4 Derby
30.01.04	Mike Duffield W RSC 1 Dagenham
02.06.04	Joel Ani W CO 2 Nottingham
12.11.04	Howard Clarke W PTS 6 Wembley
26.03.05	Lee Williamson W PTS 4 Hackney
10.04.05	Howard Clarke W PTS 4 Brentwood
16.07.05	Michael Banbula W PTS 6 Chigwell
02.12.05	Jason Collins W PTS 6 Nottingham
20.01.06	Magid Ben Driss L RSC 2 Bethnal Green
12.05.06	Paul David L RSC 6 Bethnal Green
15.09.06	Robert Burton W RSC 5 Muswell Hill
09.12.06	Joe Mitchell L PTS 4 Chigwell

Career: 14 contests, won 11, lost 3.

Nobby Cain
Aylesbury. *Born* Perivale, 5 February, 1987
L.Middleweight. *Ht* 5'8"
Manager G. Carman

24.02.07	Rocky Muscas W PTS 4 Bracknell

Career: 1 contest, won 1.

Marc Callaghan
Barking. *Born* Barking, 13 November, 1977
English S.Bantamweight Champion.
Former Undefeated Southern Area
S.Bantamweight Champion. *Ht* 5'6"
Manager Self

08.09.98	Kevin Sheil W PTS 4 Bethnal Green
31.10.98	Nicky Wilders W RSC 1 Southend
12.01.99	Nicky Wilders W RTD 2 Bethnal Green
12.03.99	Peter Allen W PTS 4 Bethnal Green
25.05.99	Simon Chambers L RSC 1 Mayfair
16.10.99	Nigel Leake W PTS 4 Bethnal Green
20.12.99	Marc Smith W PTS 4 Bethnal Green
05.02.00	Steve Brook W RSC 2 Bethnal Green
01.04.00	John Barnes W PTS 4 Bethnal Green
19.08.00	Anthony Hanna W PTS 4 Brentwood
09.10.00	Jamie McKeever L PTS 6 Liverpool
04.11.00	Nigel Senior W RSC 4 Bethnal Green
03.03.01	Anthony Hanna W PTS 6 Wembley
26.05.01	Roy Rutherford L RSC 3 Bethnal Green
01.12.01	Nigel Senior L CO 1 Bethnal Green
26.01.02	Richmond Asante W PTS 4 Dagenham
18.03.02	Michael Hunter DREW 6 Crawley
11.05.02	Andrew Ferrans W PTS 6 Dagenham
21.09.02	Steve Gethin W PTS 6 Brentwood
07.12.02	Stevie Quinn L PTS 4 Brentwood
08.03.03	Dazzo Williams L PTS 8 Bethnal Green
05.07.03	Mark Payne L PTS 6 Brentwood
08.05.04	Baz Carey W PTS 6 Dagenham
27.05.04	Steve Gethin W PTS 6 Huddersfield
20.09.04	John Simpson L PTS 8 Glasgow
19.11.04	Michael Hunter L RSC 10 Hartlepool
	(British S.Bantamweight Title Challenge)
16.06.05	Ian Napa W PTS 10 Dagenham

	(Vacant Southern Area S.Bantamweight Title)
18.11.05	Jackson Asiku L RSC 1 Dagenham
	(Vacant Commonwealth Featherweight Title)
03.03.06	Sean Hughes W PTS 10 Hartlepool
	(Vacant English S.Bantamweight Title)
15.12.06	Dariusz Snarski W PTS 4 Bethnal Green
16.03.07	Esham Pickering L PTS 12 Norwich
	(Vacant British S.Bantamweight Title)

Career: 31 contests, won 19, drew 1, lost 11.

Phillip Callaghan
Leeds. *Born* Leeds, 16 May, 1973
L.Heavyweight. *Ht* 5'11"
Manager T. O'Neill

15.10.06	Paul Davis L RSC 4 Norwich
24.11.06	Rod Anderton L RSC 4 Nottingham
23.02.07	Lee Jones L PTS 4 Birmingham
23.03.07	Rod Anderton DREW 4 Nottingham
20.04.07	Carl Wild L RSC 1 Sheffield

Career: 5 contests, drew 1, lost 4.

Joe Calzaghe
Newbridge. *Born* Hammersmith, 23 March, 1972
WBO S.Middleweight Champion. Former Undefeated British & IBF S.Middleweight Champion. *Ht* 5'11"
Manager F. Warren

01.10.93	Paul Hanlon W RSC 1 Cardiff
10.11.93	Stinger Mason W RSC 1 Watford
16.12.93	Spencer Alton W RSC 2 Newport
22.01.94	Martin Rosamond W RSC 1 Cardiff
01.03.94	Darren Littlewood W RSC 1 Dudley
04.06.94	Karl Barwise W RSC 1 Cardiff
01.07.94	Mark Dawson W RSC 1 Cardiff
30.11.94	Trevor Ambrose W RSC 2 Wolverhampton
14.02.95	Frank Minton W CO 1 Bethnal Green
22.02.95	Bobbi Joe Edwards W PTS 8 Telford
19.05.95	Robert Curry W RSC 1 Southwark
08.07.95	Tyrone Jackson W RSC 4 York
30.09.95	Nick Manners W RSC 4 Basildon
28.10.95	Stephen Wilson W RSC 8 Kensington
	(Vacant British S. Middleweight Title)
13.02.96	Guy Stanford W RSC 1 Cardiff
13.03.96	Anthony Brooks W RSC 2 Wembley
20.04.96	Mark Delaney W RSC 5 Brentwood
	(British S. Middleweight Title Defence)
04.05.96	Warren Stowe W RTD 2 Dagenham
15.05.96	Pat Lawlor W RSC 2 Cardiff
21.01.97	Carlos Christie W CO 2 Bristol
22.03.97	Tyler Hughes W CO 1 Wythenshawe
05.06.97	Luciano Torres W RSC 3 Bristol
11.10.97	Chris Eubank W PTS 12 Sheffield
	(Vacant WBO S. Middleweight Title)
24.01.98	Branco Sobot W RSC 3 Cardiff
	(WBO S. Middleweight Title Defence)
25.04.98	Juan Carlos Gimenez W RTD 9 Cardiff
	(WBO S. Middleweight Title Defence)
13.02.99	Robin Reid W PTS 12 Newcastle
	(WBO S. Middleweight Title Defence)
05.06.99	Rick Thornberry W PTS 12 Cardiff
	(WBO S. Middleweight Title Defence)
29.01.00	David Starie W PTS 12 Manchester
	(WBO S.Middleweight Title Defence)
12.08.00	Omar Sheika W RSC 5 Wembley
	(WBO S.Middleweight Title Defence)
16.12.00	Richie Woodhall W RSC 10 Sheffield

	(WBO S. Middleweight Title Defence)
28.04.01	Mario Veit W RSC 1 Cardiff
	(WBO S. Middleweight Title Defence)
13.10.01	Will McIntyre W RSC 4 Copenhagen, Denmark
	(WBO S. Middleweight Title Defence)
20.04.02	Charles Brewer W PTS 12 Cardiff
	(WBO S. Middleweight Title Defence)
17.08.02	Miguel Jimenez W PTS 12 Cardiff
	(WBO S.Middleweight Title Defence)
14.12.02	Tocker Pudwill W RSC 2 Newcastle
	(WBO S. Middleweight Title Defence)
28.06.03	Byron Mitchell W RSC 2 Cardiff
	(WBO S.Middleweight Title Defence)
21.02.04	Mger Mkrtchian W RSC 7 Cardiff
	(WBO S.Middleweight Title Defence)
22.10.04	Kabary Salem W PTS 12 Edinburgh
	(WBO S.Middleweight Title Defence)
07.05.05	Mario Veit W RSC 6 Braunschweig, Germany
	(WBO S.Middleweight Title Defence)
10.09.05	Evans Ashira W PTS 12 Cardiff
	(WBO S.Middleweight Title Defence)
04.03.06	Jeff Lacy W PTS 12 Manchester
	(IBF S.Middleweight Title Challenge. WBO S.Middleweight Title Defence)
14.10.06	Sakio Bika W PTS 12 Manchester
	(IBF & WBO S.Middleweight Title Defences)
07.04.07	Peter Manfredo W RSC 3 Cardiff
	(WBO S.Middleweight Title Defence)

Career: 43 contests, won 43.

Peter Cannon
Bradford. *Born* Bradford, 20 January, 1981
S.Middleweight. *Ht* 6'1"
Manager C. Aston

20.04.07	Jezz Wilson L RSC 5 Sheffield

Career: 1 contest, lost 1.

(Barry) Baz Carey
Coventry. *Born* Coventry, 11 March, 1971
L.Welterweight. *Ht* 5'4½"
Manager P. Carpenter

19.12.01	J.J. Moore L PTS 4 Coventry
18.01.02	J.J. Moore DREW 4 Coventry
25.02.02	Chris McDonagh L PTS 6 Slough
19.03.02	Ilias Miah W PTS 6 Slough
21.09.02	Jackson Williams L PTS 6 Norwich
10.10.02	Dean Scott W RSC 2 Stoke
19.10.02	Lee McAllister L PTS 4 Renfrew
21.11.02	Chris Hooper L RTD 3 Hull
22.03.03	Dave Hinds W PTS 6 Coventry
05.04.03	Pete Buckley W PTS 4 Manchester
12.05.03	Matthew Marshall L PTS 6 Southampton
07.06.03	Joel Viney W PTS 6 Coventry
26.07.03	Andrew Ferrans DREW 4 Plymouth
13.09.03	Paul McIlwaine W RTD 2 Coventry
12.10.03	Daniel Thorpe DREW 6 Sheffield
08.11.03	Carl Allen L RSC 2 Coventry
15.03.04	Andrew Ferrans L PTS 10 Glasgow
	(Vacant British Masters S.Featherweight Title)
17.04.04	Michael Kelly L PTS 4 Belfast
26.04.04	Rendall Munroe L PTS 6 Cleethorpes
08.05.04	Marc Callaghan L PTS 6 Dagenham
06.11.04	Daniel Thorpe L PTS 6 Coventry
20.11.04	Dave Hinds W RSC 4 Coventry
17.12.04	Kristian Laight W PTS 6 Coventry
30.04.05	Billy Smith W PTS 6 Coventry

99

26.05.05	Daniel Thorpe L PTS 6 Mayfair	
10.09.05	Amir Khan L PTS 4 Cardiff	
24.09.05	Billy Smith NC 5 Coventry	
03.12.05	Billy Smith W PTS 6 Coventry	
14.12.05	Jeff Thomas W PTS 6 Blackpool	
03.03.06	Stefy Bull L PTS 10 Doncaster	
	(WBF Inter-Continental Lightweight	
	Title Challenge)	
06.05.06	Scott Lawton L PTS 10 Stoke	
	(Midlands Area Lightweight Title	
	Challenge)	
01.06.06	Martin Gethin L PTS 4 Birmingham	
23.07.06	Ryan Barrett L PTS 6 Dagenham	
09.10.06	Kristian Laight L PTS 6 Coventry	
04.11.06	Barry Hughes L PTS 4 Glasgow	
05.12.06	Dean Harrison L PTS 4 Wolverhampton	
09.02.07	Chris Pacy L PTS 4 Leeds	
23.02.07	Lewis Smith L PTS 6 Manchester	
24.03.07	Billy Smith L PTS 10 Coventry	
	(Vacant Midlands Area L.Welterweight	
	Title)	

Career: 39 contests, won 11, drew 4, lost 23, no contest 1.

Terry Carruthers

Birmingham. *Born* Birmingham, 4 February, 1986
L.Middleweight. *Ht* 5'8"
Manager Self

21.02.05	Andy Cosnett L PTS 6 Birmingham
06.03.05	Jonathan Whiteman DREW 6 Mansfield
25.04.05	Darren Gethin W RSC 3 Cleethorpes
16.05.05	Andy Cosnett DREW 6 Bedworth
06.06.05	Paul Burns DREW 6 Glasgow
26.06.05	Justin Murphy L RSC 1 Southampton
18.02.06	Danny Johnston W PTS 6 Stoke
11.03.06	Barrie Jones L RSC 1 Newport
26.02.07	Sean McKervey W PTS 6 Birmingham

Career: 9 contests, won 3, drew 3, lost 3.

Henry Castle seen stopping Wladimir Borov last December   Les Clark

Henry Castle

Salisbury. *Born* Southampton, 7 February, 1979
Lightweight. *Ht* 5'6¾"
Manager R. Davies/F. Maloney

29.01.01	Jason Nesbitt W CO 6 Peterborough
26.03.01	Eddie Nevins W RSC 2 Peterborough
23.11.01	Jimmy Beech W PTS 4 Bethnal Green
11.03.02	David Lowry W RSC 1 Glasgow
20.04.02	Jason Nesbitt W PTS 4 Cardiff
25.05.02	Jimmy Beech W PTS 4 Portsmouth
17.08.02	Joel Viney W RSC 1 Cardiff
23.11.02	John Mackay L RTD 8 Derby
29.03.03	Jus Wallie L RSC 2 Portsmouth
25.09.03	Mark Alexander W PTS 6 Bethnal Green
21.11.03	Pete Buckley W PTS 4 Millwall
20.02.04	Daleboy Rees W RSC 4 Bethnal Green
26.06.05	Karl Taylor W PTS 6 Southampton
04.12.05	Gareth Couch L PTS 6 Portsmouth
24.09.06	Peter Allen W RSC 6 Southampton
03.12.06	Wladimir Borov W RSC 4 Bethnal Green
09.02.07	Carl Allen W RSC 4 Leeds
09.03.07	Ian Wilson L RSC 5 Dagenham

Career: 18 contests, won 14, lost 4.

Glenn Catley

Bristol. *Born* Sodbury, 15 March, 1972
S.Middleweight. Former WBC S.Middleweight Champion. Former Undefeated IBF &WBO Inter-Continental S.Middleweight Champion. Former Undefeated British Middleweight Champion. Former WBC International Middleweight Champion. *Ht* 5'8"
Manager C. Sanigar

27.05.93	Rick North W PTS 4 Bristol
26.06.93	Chris Vassiliou W CO 2 Keynsham
31.08.93	Marty Duke W RSC 2 Croydon
13.09.93	Barry Thorogood W PTS 4 Bristol
03.11.93	Marty Duke W RSC 1 Bristol
13.12.93	Shamus Casey W PTS 4 Bristol
10.03.94	Mark Cichocki W PTS 6 Bristol
23.03.94	Carlo Colarusso L RSC 5 Cardiff
25.05.94	Chris Davies W RSC 1 Bristol
02.07.94	Martin Jolley W RSC 1 Keynsham
22.11.94	Kirkland Laing W RSC 5 Bristol
18.02.95	Lee Blundell W RSC 6 Shepton Mallet
06.05.95	Mark Dawson W RSC 5 Shepton Mallet
28.07.95	Kevin Adamson W CO 1 Bristol
02.09.95	Quinn Paynter W RSC 1 Wembley
30.09.95	John Duckworth W RSC 3 Cardiff
28.10.95	Carlos Christie W PTS 8 Bristol
10.11.95	Carlos Christie W CO 3 Bristol
16.12.95	Peter Vosper W RSC 2 Cardiff
26.04.96	Lee Crocker W RSC 2 Cardiff
19.10.96	Paul Wesley W RSC 7 Bristol
21.01.97	George Bocco W RTD 4 Bristol
	(Vacant WBC International Middleweight Title)
05.06.97	Andras Galfi L RSC 7 Bristol
	(WBC International Middleweight Title Defence)
17.01.98	Neville Brown W RTD 8 Bristol
	(British Middleweight Title Challenge)
05.09.98	Richie Woodhall L PTS 12 Telford
	(WBC S. Middleweight Title Challenge)
24.10.98	Andras Galfi W PTS 12 Bristol
	(Vacant WBO Inter-Continental S.Middleweight Title)

05.12.98	Andrew Flute W RSC 5 Bristol
	(Vacant IBF Inter-Continental S. Middleweight Title)
10.12.99	Eric Lucas W RSC 12 Montreal, Canada
	(Final Elim. WBC S. Middleweight Title)
06.05.00	Markus Beyer W RSC 12 Frankfurt, Germany
	(WBC S. Middleweight Title Challenge)
01.09.00	Dingaan Thobela L CO 12 Brakpan, South Africa
	(WBC S.Middleweight Title Defence)
10.07.01	Eric Lucas L RSC 7 Montreal, Canada
	(Vacant WBC S.Middleweight Title)
09.03.02	Danilo Haeussler L PTS 12 Frankfurt, Germany
	(European S. Middleweight Title Challenge)
10.07.02	Vage Kocharyan W PTS 8 Wembley
01.02.03	Danilo Haussler L TD 5 Chemnitz, Germany
	(European S. Middleweight Title Challenge)
03.11.06	Hussain Osman W RSC 3 Bristol
24.02.07	Sergey Kharchenko W RSC 5 Bristol

Career: 36 contests, won 29, lost 7.

(Fatih) Frank Celebi

Bristol. *Born* Kelkit, Turkey, 1 January, 1983
Middleweight. *Ht* 5'8"
Manager C. Sanigar

23.02.07	JJ Bird L PTS 4 Peterborough

Career: 1 contest, lost 1.

(Yuvuzer) Rocky Chakir (Cakir)

Bristol. *Born* Trabzon, Turkey, 12 April, 1982
L.Middleweight. *Ht* 5'7¼"
Manager C. Sanigar

03.11.06	Pawel Jas W PTS 6 Bristol
10.11.06	Steve Anning L PTS 6 Newport
03.12.06	Chris Long L PTS 6 Bristol
24.02.07	Danny Butler L PTS 6 Bristol

Career: 4 contests, won 1, lost 3.

Derek Chisora   Les Clark

Derek Chisora

Finchley. *Born* Zimbabwe, 29 December, 1983
Heavyweight. Ht. 6' 1¼"
Manager F. Maloney

17.02.07 Istvan Kecskes W RSC 2 Wembley
07.04.07 Tony Booth W PTS 4 Cardiff
Career: 2 contests, won 2.

Karl Chiverton
Mansfield. *Born* Sutton in Ashfield, 1 March, 1986
Middleweight. *Ht* 5'9¾"
Manager S. Calow

18.09.04 Karl Taylor W PTS 6 Newark
10.12.04 Cafu Santos L RSC 4 Mansfield
13.05.06 Mark Wall W PTS 6 Sutton in Ashfield
16.09.06 Tony Randell W PTS 6 Burton
11.11.06 Ernie Smith W PTS 6 Sutton in Ashfield
19.05.07 Peter Dunn W PTS 4 Nottingham
Career: 6 contests, won 5, lost 1.

Anthony Christopher
Aberystwyth. *Born* Aberystwyth, 18 August, 1981
Welterweight. *Ht* 5'8¼"
Manager Self

23.09.01 Arv Mittoo DREW 6 Shaw
29.09.02 Ernie Smith W PTS 6 Shrewsbury
03.12.02 Ernie Smith L PTS 6 Shrewsbury
23.02.03 Dean Larter L PTS 6 Aberystwyth
20.02.04 Stefy Bull L PTS 6 Doncaster
06.03.04 Gary Young L CO 1 Renfrew
08.05.05 Dwayne Hill L PTS 6 Sheffield
20.06.05 Ryan Barrett L RSC 1 Longford
01.10.05 Jeff Thomas L PTS 6 Wigan
24.10.05 Jimmy Gilhaney L PTS 6 Glasgow
04.11.05 Peter McDonagh L PTS 4 Bethnal Green
12.12.05 Gary Coombes W RSC 2 Birmingham
10.02.06 Garry Buckland L RSC 4 Plymouth
07.04.06 Shane Watson L RSC 1 Longford
20.05.06 Jason Nesbitt L RSC 4 Bristol
08.10.06 James Lilley L RSC 1 Swansea
Career: 16 contests, won 2, drew 1, lost 13.

Marco Cittadini
Glasgow. *Born* Glasgow, 12 September, 1977
L.Welterweight. *Ht* 5'7¾"
Manager Self

17.06.05 Barrie Jones L RSC 2 Glasgow
22.04.06 Mark Bett DREW 6 Glasgow
21.10.06 Mark Bett L PTS 6 Glasgow
Career: 3 contests, drew 1, lost 2.

Howard Clarke
Warley. *Born* London, 23 September, 1967
S.Middleweight. *Ht* 5'10"
Manager Self

15.10.91 Chris Mylan W PTS 4 Dudley
09.12.91 Claude Rossi W RSC 3 Brierley Hill
04.02.92 Julian Eavis W PTS 4 Alfreton
03.03.92 Dave Andrews W RSC 3 Cradley Heath
21.05.92 Richard O'Brien W CO 1 Cradley Heath
29.09.92 Paul King W PTS 6 Stoke
27.10.92 Gordon Blair L RSC 4 Cradley Heath
16.03.93 Paul King W PTS 6 Edgbaston
07.06.93 Dean Bramhald W RTD 2 Walsall
29.06.93 Paul King W PTS 6 Edgbaston
06.10.93 Julian Eavis L PTS 8 Solihull
30.11.93 Julian Eavis W PTS 8 Wolverhampton

08.02.94 Nigel Bradley W RTD 6 Wolverhampton
18.04.94 Andy Peach W PTS 6 Walsall
28.06.94 Dennis Berry L RSC 3 Edgbaston
12.10.94 Julian Eavis W PTS 8 Stoke
25.10.94 Andy Peach W RSC 3 Edgbaston
02.11.94 Julian Eavis W PTS 8 Birmingham
29.11.94 Julian Eavis W PTS 6 Cannock
07.12.94 Peter Reid W PTS 8 Stoke
25.01.95 Dennis Berry L PTS 8 Stoke
08.03.95 Andrew Jervis W PTS 6 Solihull
11.05.95 David Bain W RSC 1 Dudley
20.09.95 Michael Smyth DREW 6 Ystrad
02.10.95 Nigel Wenton L PTS 6 Mayfair
02.12.96 Martin Smith L PTS 8 Birmingham
29.01.97 Gary Beardsley W PTS 6 Stoke
11.02.97 Prince Kasi Kaihau L RSC 4 Wolverhampton
19.03.97 Mark Cichocki W PTS 6 Stoke
15.04.97 Prince Kasi Kaihau W PTS 6 Edgbaston
30.04.97 Allan Gray W PTS 8 Acton
22.05.97 Michael Alexander W RSC 3 Solihull
21.06.97 Paul Samuels L PTS 8 Cardiff
09.09.97 Harry Dhami L PTS 8 Bethnal Green
05.11.97 Andras Galfi W PTS 8 Tenerife
27.01.98 Mack Razor L PTS 8 Hammanskraal, South Africa
23.03.98 Lindon Scarlett DREW 6 Crystal Palace
18.07.98 Jason Papillion W PTS 8 Sheffield
13.03.99 Fernando Vargas L RSC 4 NYC, New York, USA
(IBF L. Middleweight Title Challenge)
05.11.99 Michael Rask L PTS 12 Aalberg, Denmark
(WBA Inter-Continental L. Middleweight Title Challenge)
29.05.00 Anthony Farnell L PTS 12 Manchester
(WBO Inter-Continental L. Middleweight Title Challenge)
12.08.00 Takaloo L PTS 12 Wembley
(Vacant IBF Inter-Continental L.Middleweight Title)
04.11.00 Richard Williams L CO 4 Bethnal Green
16.12.00 Ryan Rhodes L PTS 6 Sheffield
03.02.01 Michael Jones L PTS 4 Manchester
26.02.01 Jawaid Khaliq L PTS 6 Nottingham
07.04.01 Gary Lockett L RSC 2 Wembley
06.05.01 Ian Cooper L PTS 6 Hartlepool
04.06.01 James Docherty L PTS 6 Hartlepool
14.07.01 Gary Lockett L CO 1 Wembley
15.09.01 Thomas McDonagh L PTS 6 Manchester
10.11.01 Ossie Duran L PTS 6 Wembley
26.11.01 Wayne Pinder L PTS 6 Manchester
16.12.01 Erik Teymour L PTS 6 Southwark
27.01.02 Paul Samuels L PTS 6 Streatham
03.02.02 Lee Murtagh NC 2 Shaw
20.04.02 Wayne Elcock L PTS 4 Cardiff
25.05.02 Ross Minter W RSC 2 Portsmouth
08.06.02 Alexander Vetoux L RSC 4 Renfrew
27.07.02 Mihaly Kotai L RSC 1 Nottingham
08.12.02 Matthew Tait L PTS 6 Bethnal Green
21.12.02 Matthew Thirlwall L PTS 6 Dagenham
25.01.03 Paul Samuels L PTS 6 Bridgend
08.02.03 Michael Jones L PTS 6 Liverpool
05.03.03 Gilbert Eastman L PTS 6 Bethnal Green
05.04.03 Paul Smith L PTS 4 Manchester
21.06.03 Wayne Pinder L PTS 4 Manchester
01.08.03 Arthur Shekhmurzov L PTS 6 Bethnal Green

17.10.03 Scott Dixon L PTS 6 Glasgow
25.10.03 Lawrence Murphy L PTS 6 Edinburgh
14.11.03 Sonny Pollard L PTS 6 Hull
07.02.04 Wayne Alexander L RSC 2 Bethnal Green
03.04.04 Paul Smith L PTS 4 Manchester
10.04.04 Wayne Pinder L PTS 4 Manchester
08.05.04 Allan Foster L PTS 4 Dagenham
04.06.04 Andrew Facey L PTS 6 Hull
17.06.04 Patrick J. Maxwell L RSC 1 Sheffield
24.09.04 Darren Barker L PTS 4 Nottingham
01.10.04 Matthew Hall L RSC 5 Manchester
12.11.04 Daniel Cadman L PTS 6 Wembley
20.11.04 Jason Collins L DIS 3 Coventry
10.12.04 Anthony Small L PTS 4 Sheffield
17.12.04 Paul Smith L CO 1 Liverpool
04.02.05 Jason Rushton L PTS 4 Doncaster
12.02.05 Gary Woolcombe L PTS 6 Portsmouth
20.02.05 Michael Monaghan L PTS 6 Sheffield
06.03.05 Lee Blundell L PTS 6 Shaw
23.03.05 Gareth Lawrence L PTS 6 Leicester Square
10.04.05 Daniel Cadman L PTS 4 Brentwood
21.04.05 Darren McDermott L RTD 1 Dudley
27.05.05 Andrew Buchanan L PTS 4 Spennymoor
16.06.05 Anthony Small L PTS 6 Mayfair
09.07.05 David Walker L PTS 4 Nottingham
03.09.05 Danny McIntosh L PTS 4 Norwich
25.09.05 Darren Rhodes L PTS 6 Leeds
16.10.05 Cello Renda L PTS 4 Peterborough
29.10.05 Andrew Facey L PTS 6 Aberdeen
08.11.05 Ady Clegg L PTS 6 Leeds
26.11.05 Stuart Brookes L PTS 6 Sheffield
03.12.05 Andy Halder L PTS 8 Coventry
16.12.05 Matthew Barr L PTS 4 Bracknell
12.02.06 Craig Bunn L PTS 6 Manchester
23.02.06 Danny Thornton L PTS 6 Leeds
02.04.06 Darren Stubbs L PTS 6 Shaw
23.06.06 Cello Renda L PTS 8 Birmingham
08.12.06 Matthew Thirlwall L PTS 4 Dagenham
24.02.07 Danny Johnston L PTS 6 Stoke
20.04.07 Lee Edwards L PTS 6 Sheffield
28.04.07 Brian Wood L PTS 6 Newark
Career: 109 contests, won 27, drew 2, lost 79, no contest 1.

Nathan Cleverly
Cefn Forest. *Born* Caerphilly, 17 February, 1987
L.Heavyweight. *Ht* 6'1½"
Manager E. Calzaghe

23.07.05 Ernie Smith W PTS 4 Edinburgh
10.09.05 Darren Gethin W PTS 4 Cardiff
04.12.05 Lance Hall W RSC 3 Telford
04.03.06 Jon Foster W PTS 4 Manchester
01.06.06 Brendan Halford W PTS 4 Barnsley
08.07.06 Mark Phillips W PTS 4 Cardiff
14.10.06 Tony Quigley W RSC 5 Manchester
18.11.06 Varuzhan Davtyan W PTS 4 Newport
07.04.07 Nick Okoth W PTS 8 Cardiff
Career: 9 contests, won 9.

Ian Clyde
Crewe. *Born* Ashington, 25 June, 1972
Welterweight. *Ht* 6'0"
Manager M. Carney

06.05.06 Pete Buckley W PTS 6 Stoke
18.05.06 Rob Hunt L RSC 1 Walsall
15.09.06 Steve Anning L RSC 1 Newport
Career: 3 contests, won 1, lost 2.

Richard Collins

Brierley Hill. *Born* Wordsley, 29 November, 1985
L.Heavyweight. *Ht* 6'3"
Manager D. Powell

24.02.07 Justin Jones DREW 6 Stoke
28.06.07 Mark Phillips W PTS 4 Dudley
Career: 2 contests, won 1, drew 1.

Kevin Concepcion

Leicester. *Born* Leicester, 22 February, 1980
S.Middleweight. *Ht* 5'10¾"
Manager P. Carpenter

23.09.06 Ben Hudson W PTS 6 Coventry
09.10.06 Ryan Rowlinson W PTS 6 Bedworth
02.12.06 Rocky Muscas W PTS 6 Coventry
24.03.07 Davey Jones W RSC 1 Coventry
13.05.07 Mark Phillips W PTS 6 Birmingham
Career: 5 contests, won 5.

Martin Concepcion

Leicester. *Born* Leicester, 11 August, 1981
Middleweight. *Ht* 5'9"
Manager F. Warren

06.12.03 Danny Gwilym W RSC 2 Cardiff
07.02.04 Jed Tytler W RSC 2 Bethnal Green
27.03.04 Joel Ani W RTD 3 Edinburgh
05.06.04 William Webster W RSC 1 Bethnal Green
30.07.04 Brian Coleman W RSC 1 Bethnal Green
10.09.04 Rob MacDonald W RSC 2 Bethnal Green
12.11.04 Andrew Butlin W RSC 1 Halifax
03.12.04 David Kirk W PTS 4 Edinburgh
11.12.04 Bertrand Souleyras W RSC 1 Canning Town
25.02.05 Craig Lynch W PTS 6 Wembley
03.06.05 Ernie Smith W PTS 4 Manchester
16.07.05 Ivor Bonavic L RSC 2 Bolton
28.01.06 Manoocha Salari L RSC 2 Nottingham
14.10.06 Thomas McDonagh L PTS 6 Manchester
30.03.07 Alfonso Gomez L RSC 7 Newcastle
Career: 15 contests, won 11, lost 4.

Steve Conway

Dewsbury. *Born* Hartlepool, 6 October, 1977
L.Middleweight. Former IBO L.Middleweight Champion. *Ht* 5'8"
Manager M. Marsden

21.02.96 Robert Grubb W PTS 6 Batley
24.04.96 Ervine Blake W PTS 6 Solihull
20.05.96 Chris Lyons W PTS 6 Cleethorpes
30.05.96 Ram Singh W PTS 6 Lincoln
03.02.97 Jason Squire W PTS 6 Leicester
11.04.97 Marc Smith W PTS 4 Barnsley
22.09.97 Arv Mittoo W PTS 6 Cleethorpes
09.10.97 Arv Mittoo W PTS 6 Leeds
01.11.97 Brian Carr L PTS 6 Glasgow
14.11.97 Brendan Bryce W PTS 6 Mere
04.12.97 Kid McAuley W RSC 5 Doncaster
15.12.97 Nicky Wilders W PTS 6 Cleethorpes
05.03.98 Pete Buckley W PTS 6 Leeds
25.04.98 Dean Phillips W PTS 6 Cardiff
09.05.98 Gary Flear W PTS 4 Sheffield
18.05.98 Brian Coleman W PTS 6 Cleethorpes

05.09.98 Benny Jones W PTS 4 Telford
19.12.98 Gary Thornhill L RSC 9 Liverpool
(WBO Inter-Continental S. Featherweight Title Challenge)
04.06.99 Brian Coleman W PTS 6 Hull
27.09.99 Brian Coleman W PTS 6 Leeds
27.02.00 Chris Price W RTD 3 Leeds
21.03.00 Pedro Miranda L RSC 3 Telde, Gran Canaria
15.07.00 Arv Mittoo W PTS 6 Norwich
20.10.00 Junior Witter L RTD 4 Belfast
25.02.01 Ram Singh W RSC 2 Derby
02.06.01 Jimmy Phelan W PTS 4 Wakefield
18.08.01 Keith Jones W PTS 8 Dewsbury
17.11.01 Carl Allen W PTS 8 Dewsbury
27.04.02 Steve Robinson W PTS 8 Huddersfield
05.10.02 Rakheem Mingaleev W RSC 4 Huddersfield
19.10.02 Alex Arthur L CO 4 Renfrew
(Vacant British S. Featherweight Title)
05.07.03 Dariusz Snarski W RSC 4 Brentwood
05.10.03 Brian Coleman W PTS 6 Bradford
06.11.03 Yuri Romanov L PTS 8 Dagenham
23.11.03 Gareth Wiltshaw W RSC 5 Rotherham
16.04.04 Norman Dhalie W CO 3 Hartlepool
23.10.04 Ernie Smith W PTS 6 Wakefield
25.09.05 Lee Williamson W PTS 6 Leeds
02.12.05 Mihaly Kotai W PTS 10 Nottingham
03.03.06 Mihaly Kotai W PTS 12 Hartlepool
(IBO L.Middleweight Title Challenge)
03.06.06 Attila Kovacs L PTS 12 Szolnok, Hungary
(IBO L.Middleweight Title Defence)
15.12.06 Grzegorz Proksa L PTS 6 Bethnal Green
Career: 42 contests, won 34, lost 8.

Lee Cook

Morden. *Born* London, 26 June, 1981
Lightweight. *Ht* 5'8"
Manager D. Powell/F.Maloney

24.09.04 Jus Wallie W RSC 2 Bethnal Green
26.11.04 Willie Valentine W PTS 4 Bethnal Green
05.03.05 Billy Smith W PTS 4 Southwark
29.04.05 Eddie Anderson W RSC 2 Southwark
20.05.05 Ian Reid W PTS 4 Southwark
04.11.05 Buster Dennis DREW 4 Bethnal Green
11.02.06 David Kehoe W RTD 2 Bethnal Green
02.04.06 Rakhim Mingaleev W PTS 4 Bethnal Green
09.03.07 Youssef Al Hamidi W PTS 6 Dagenham
15.06.07 Rom Krauklis W PTS 4 Crystal Palace
Career: 10 contests, won 9, drew 1.

Nicky Cook

Dagenham. *Born* Stepney, 13 September, 1979
Featherweight. Former Undefeated British, European & Commonwealth Featherweight Champion. Former Undefeated WBF Inter-Continental S. Featherweight Champion. *Ht* 5'6½"
Manager J. Harding

11.12.98 Sean Grant W CO 1 Cheshunt
26.02.99 Graham McGrath W CO 2 Coventry
27.04.99 Vasil Paskelev W CO 1 Bethnal Green
25.05.99 Wilson Acuna W PTS 4 Mayfair
12.07.99 Igor Sakhatarov W PTS 4 Coventry
20.08.99 Vlado Varhegyi W PTS 4 Bloomsbury

27.11.99 John Barnes W PTS 6 Liverpool
20.12.99 Carl Allen W CO 3 Bethnal Green
10.03.00 Chris Jickells W RSC 1 Bethnal Green
27.05.00 Anthony Hanna W PTS 6 Mayfair
16.06.00 Salem Bouaita W PTS 6 Bloomsbury
04.11.00 Vladimir Borov W RSC 1 Bethnal Green
08.12.00 Rakhim Mingaleev W PTS 8 Crystal Palace
19.05.01 Foudil Madani W RSC 1 Wembley
28.11.01 Woody Greenaway W RSC 3 Bethnal Green
19.12.01 Marcelo Ackermann W RSC 3 Coventry
(Vacant WBF Inter-Continental S.Featherweight Title)
20.04.02 Jackie Gunguluza W RTD 4 Wembley
(WBF Inter-Continental S.Featherweight Title Defence)
10.07.02 Andrei Devyataykin W PTS 8 Wembley
05.10.02 Gary Thornhill W RSC 7 Liverpool
(WBF Inter-Continental S.Featherweight Title Defence)
08.02.03 Mishek Kondwani W RSC 12 Brentford
(Vacant Commonwealth Featherweight Title)
31.05.03 David Kiilu W CO 2 Bethnal Green
(Commonwealth Featherweight Title Defence)
24.10.03 Anyetei Laryea W PTS 12 Bethnal Green
(Commonwealth Featherweight Title)
20.03.04 Cyril Thomas W CO 9 Wembley
(European Featherweight Title Challenge)
08.10.04 Johny Begue W PTS 12 Brentwood
(European Featherweight Title Defence)
16.06.05 Dazzo Williams W CO 2 Dagenham
(European &Commonwealth Featherweight Title Defences. British Featherweight Title Challenge)
24.02.06 Yuri Voronin W PTS 12 Dagenham
(European Featherweight Title Defence)
09.12.06 Harry Ramogoadi W PTS 8 Canning Town
Career: 27 contests, won 27.

Steve Cooper

Worcester. *Born* Worcester, 19 November, 1977
L.Middleweight. *Ht* 5'8½"
Manager E. Johnson

09.12.02 Darren Goode W CO 3 Birmingham
16.09.06 Dale Miles L PTS 6 Burton
29.09.06 Mark Hastie L PTS 6 Motherwell
09.10.06 Sean McKervey DREW 6 Birmingham
23.10.06 Willie Bilan L PTS 6 Glasgow
07.11.06 Tommy Broadbent L PTS 6 Leeds
20.11.06 Paul Burns DREW 6 Glasgow
11.12.06 Sean McKervey L PTS 6 Birmingham
22.02.07 Andrew Butlin L PTS 6 Leeds
03.03.07 Steve Anning L PTS 6 Newport
10.03.07 Denton Vassell L RSC 2 Liverpool
28.04.07 Andrew Alan Lowe L PTS 6 Newark
12.05.07 Jimmy Doherty L PTS 6 Stoke
25.05.07 Eamonn Goodbrand L PTS 6 Glasgow
03.06.07 Paul Royston W PTS 6 Barnsley
16.06.07 Jamie Way L PTS 6 Newport
Career: 16 contests, won 2, drew 2, lost 12.

Steve Cooper   Les Clark

Billy Corcoran

Wembley. *Born* Galway, 18 November, 1980
S.Featherweight. Former Undefeated English S.Featherweight Champion. *Ht* 5'7¾"
Manager Self

23.08.02	Jason Nesbitt W PTS 4 Bethnal Green
25.10.02	Jason Nesbitt W RSC 2 Bethnal Green
21.12.02	Daniel Thorpe W CO 2 Dagenham
28.01.03	Pete Buckley W PTS 6 Nottingham
05.03.03	Pete Buckley W PTS 6 Bethnal Green
16.04.03	Mark Payne DREW 4 Nottingham
27.05.03	Jimmy Beech L PTS 6 Dagenham
04.10.03	Martin Hardcastle W PTS 6 Muswell Hill
28.11.03	Haroon Din W RSC 3 Derby
30.01.04	Rakhim Mingaleev W PTS 6 Dagenham
16.04.04	Anthony Hanna W PTS 4 Bradford
12.11.04	Carl Allen W RSC 5 Wembley
09.07.05	Steve Gethin W PTS 6 Nottingham
21.10.05	Roy Rutherford W RTD 4 Bethnal Green
	(*English S.Featherweight Title Challenge*)
02.12.05	Pete Buckley W PTS 4 Nottingham
20.01.06	Frederic Bonifai W PTS 8 Bethnal Green
12.07.06	Carl Johanneson L RSC 4 Bethnal Green
	(*Vacant British S.Featherweight Title*)
15.09.06	Riaz Durgahed W CO 3 Muswell Hill
24.11.06	Sean Hughes W RSC 8 Nottingham
20.04.07	Steve Gethin W PTS 8 Dudley

Career: 20 contests, won 17, drew 1, lost 2.

Eddie Corcoran

Neasden. *Born* Manchester, 5 October, 1985
L.Welterweight. *Ht* 5'11½"
Manager J. Eames/F. Warren

09.12.06	David Kehoe W RSC 3 Canning Town
17.02.07	Karl Taylor W PTS 4 Wembley

Career: 2 contests, won 2.

Eddie Corcoran   Les Clark

Dennis Corpe

Nottingham. *Born* Nottingham, 6 May, 1976
L.Middleweight. *Ht* 5'9¾"
Manager M. Scriven

22.10.04	Joe Mitchell L PTS 6 Mansfield
16.09.05	Mark Lloyd L PTS 6 Telford
01.10.05	Tiger Matthews L PTS 4 Wigan
19.05.07	Wayne Downing W PTS 4 Nottingham

Career: 4 contests, won 1, lost 3.

Thomas Costello

Chelmsley Wood. *Born* Birmingham, 9 January, 1989
L.Middleweight. *Ht* 5'11"
Manager R. Woodhall

29.04.07	Deniss Sirjatovs W RSC 1 Birmingham

Career: 1 contest, won 1.

Duncan Cottier

Woodford. *Born* Isleworth, 10 October, 1977
Welterweight. *Ht* 5'7½"
Manager Self

05.03.05	Geraint Harvey W PTS 4 Dagenham
10.04.05	John O'Donnell L PTS 4 Brentwood
28.04.05	Stuart Phillips DREW 4 Clydach
13.05.05	David Burke L PTS 6 Liverpool
20.05.05	Colin McNeil L PTS 6 Glasgow
16.06.05	Robert Lloyd-Taylor L RSC 1 Mayfair
30.10.05	Aaron Balmer L PTS 4 Bethnal Green
19.11.05	Ashley Theophane L PTS 6 Southwark
04.12.05	Shane Watson L PTS 4 Portsmouth
19.12.05	Gilbert Eastman L RTD 3 Longford
28.01.06	Stephen Haughian L PTS 4 Dublin
18.02.06	Paul McCloskey L PTS 6 Edinburgh
26.02.06	Nathan Graham L PTS 4 Dagenham
05.03.06	Jay Morris W RSC 2 Southampton
30.03.06	Jamal Morrison DREW 4 Bloomsbury
06.04.06	Ben Hudson W PTS 4 Piccadilly
22.04.06	Paddy Pollock L PTS 6 Glasgow
12.05.06	John O'Donnell L RTD 3 Bethnal Green
08.07.06	Ross Minter L PTS 6 Cardiff
24.09.06	Jay Morris L PTS 4 Southampton
14.10.06	Kell Brook L RSC 3 Manchester
23.11.06	Lewis Smith L PTS 6 Manchester
02.12.06	Joe McCluskey L PTS 6 Coventry
09.12.06	Denton Vassell L PTS 4 Canning Town

17.02.07	Grant Skehill L PTS 4 Wembley
25.02.07	Danny Goode L PTS 6 Southampton
16.03.07	Eamonn Goodbrand L PTS 6 Glasgow
25.03.07	Scott Jordan L PTS 6 Dublin
15.04.07	Curtis Woodhouse L PTS 4 Barnsley
26.04.07	Olufemi Moses L PTS 4 Manchester
11.05.07	Tibor Dudas L PTS 4 Motherwell
01.06.07	JJ Bird L PTS 4 Peterborough
16.06.07	Lee Purdy L PTS 4 Chigwell

Career: 33 contests, won 3, drew 2, lost 28.

Gareth Couch

High Wycombe. *Born* High Wycombe, 11 September, 1982
L.Welterweight. *Ht* 5'7½"
Manager J. Evans

19.12.04	Oscar Milkitas W PTS 6 Bethnal Green
23.03.05	Ian Reid W RSC 6 Leicester Square
16.06.05	David Pereira W PTS 4 Mayfair
01.07.05	Silence Saheed W PTS 4 Fulham
23.11.05	Kyle Taylor W PTS 6 Mayfair
04.12.05	Henry Castle W PTS 6 Portsmouth
18.03.06	Martino Ciano W PTS 6 Monte Carlo, Monaco
18.10.06	Daniel Thorpe W PTS 4 Bayswater
04.11.06	Tony Jourda W PTS 6 Monte Carlo, Monaco
07.06.07	Rom Krauklis W PTS 8 Kensington

Career: 10 contests, won 10.

Jane Couch

Fleetwood. *Born* Fleetwood, 12 August, 1968
L.Welterweight. Former Undefeated Womens IBF Welterweight Champion. Former Undefeated Womens BF Welterweight Champion. Former Undefeated Womens IBF Lightweight Champion. Former Womens BF L.Welterweight Champion. *Ht* 5'7"
Manager T. Woodward

30.10.94	Kalpna Shah W RSC 2 Wigan
29.01.95	Fosteres Joseph W PTS 6 Fleetwood
18.04.95	Jane Johnson W RSC 4 Fleetwood
01.07.95	Julia Shirley W PTS 6 Fleetwood
24.05.96	Sandra Geiger W PTS 10 Copenhagen, Denmark
	(*Womens IBF Welterweight Title Challenge*)
01.03.97	Andrea Deshong W RSC 7 New Orleans, Louisiana, USA
	(*Womens IBF Welterweight Title Defence*)
24.08.97	Leah Mellinger W PTS 10 Ledyard, Connecticut, USA
	(*Womens IBF Welterweight Title Defence*)
24.10.97	Dora Webber L PTS 6 Lula, Mississippi, USA
10.01.98	Dora Webber L PTS 10 Atlantic City, New Jersey, USA
	(*Vacant Womens BF L.Welterweight Title*)
25.11.98	Simone Lukic W RSC 2 Streatham
20.02.99	Marisch Sjauw W PTS 10 Thornaby
	(*Womens IBF Welterweight Title Defence. Vacant Womens BF Welterweight Title*)
01.04.99	Heike Noller W PTS 8 Birmingham
31.10.99	Sharon Anyos W PTS 10 Raynes Park
	(*Vacant Womens IBF Lightweight Title*)

09.03.00 Michelle Straus W RSC 3 Bethnal Green
01.07.00 Galina Gumliska W RSC 6 Southwark
(Womens IBF Lightweight Title Defence)
19.08.00 Liz Mueller L PTS 6 Mashantucket, Connecticut, USA
16.06.01 Viktoria Oleynikov W PTS 4 Wembley
31.07.01 Shakurah Witherspoon W PTS 4 Montego Bay, Jamaica
16.12.01 Tzanka Karova W RSC 3 Bristol
21.06.02 Sumya Anani L RSC 4 Waco, Texas, USA
(Vacant Womens IBA L.Welterweight Title)
03.08.02 Borislava Goranova W PTS 6 Blackpool
08.12.02 Borislava Goranova W PTS 10 Bristol
(Vacant Womens BF L.Welterweight Title)
26.02.03 Borislava Goranova W RSC 7 Bristol
15.05.03 Larisa Berezenko W PTS 8 Clevedon
21.06.03 Lucia Rijker L PTS 8 Los Angeles, California, USA
21.09.03 Brenda Bell-Drexel W PTS 10 Bristol
21.12.03 Brenda Bell-Drexel W PTS 8 Bristol
29.02.04 Borislava Goranova W PTS 8 Bristol
03.04.04 Nathalie Toro L PTS 10 Vise, Belgium
(Vacant Womens European L.Welterweight Title)
12.06.04 Jaime Clampitt W PTS 10 Mashantucket, Connecticut, USA
(Womens BF L.Welterweight Title Defence)
02.12.04 Larisa Berezenko W PTS 6 Bristol
21.07.05 Jessica Rakoczy L RSC 6 Lemoore, California, USA
(Vacant Womens WBC Lightweight Title. Womens IBA Lightweight Title Challenge)
12.11.05 Oksana Chernikova W PTS 6 Bristol
05.12.05 Myriam Lamare L RSC 3 Paris, France
(Vacant Womens IBF L.Welterweight Title)
25.02.06 Galina Gumliiska W RSC 3 Bristol
06.05.06 Viktoria Oleynik W PTS 6 Birmingham
23.09.06 Holly Holm L PTS 10 Albuquerque, New Mexico, USA
(Womens IBA L.Welterweight Title Challenge)
20.06.07 Jaime Clampitt L PTS 10 Mashantucket, Connecticut, USA
(Vacant Womens IBF L.Welterweight Title)
Career: 38 contests, won 28, lost 10.

Danny Couzens
Titchfield. *Born* Portsmouth, 29 August, 1984
Cruiserweight. *Ht* 6'0¾"
Manager J. Bishop

24.09.06 Csaba Andras L PTS 6 Southampton
10.06.07 Wayne Brooks L PTS 4 Neath
Career: 2 contests, lost 2.

Mickey Coveney
West Ham. *Born* London, 26 November, 1981
Featherweight. *Ht* 5'4"
Manager Self

12.06.00 Stevie Quinn W PTS 4 Belfast
30.11.00 Gareth Wiltshaw W PTS 4 Peterborough
24.02.01 Dazzo Williams L CO 1 Bethnal Green
03.06.01 Gareth Wiltshaw W PTS 4 Southwark
09.09.01 Richmond Asante W PTS 4 Southwark

28.11.01 Steve Gethin W PTS 4 Bethnal Green
24.03.02 Anthony Hanna W PTS 4 Streatham
25.06.04 David Bailey W PTS 4 Bethnal Green
05.03.05 Rocky Dean L PTS 10 Dagenham
(Vacant Southern Area Featherweight Title)
30.04.05 Jim Betts W CO 4 Dagenham
23.09.05 Andy Morris L RSC 4 Mayfair
22.04.06 James Ancliff W PTS 6 Glasgow
01.06.06 Derry Matthews L PTS 8 Barnsley
22.09.06 Paul Appleby L PTS 6 Bethnal Green
Career: 14 contests, won 9, lost 5.

Simeon Cover
Worksop. *Born* Clapton, 12 March, 1978
S.Middleweight. Former British Masters S.Middleweight Champion. *Ht* 5'11"
Manager D. Ingle

28.03.01 Danny Smith L PTS 6 Piccadilly
18.08.01 Rob Stevenson W PTS 6 Dewsbury
24.09.01 Colin McCash L PTS 6 Cleethorpes
01.11.01 Rob Stevenson L PTS 6 Hull
16.11.01 Jon O'Brien L PTS 6 Dublin
24.11.01 Darren Rhodes L RSC 5 Wakefield
31.01.02 Shpetim Hoti W PTS 6 Piccadilly
13.04.02 Earl Ling L CO 4 Norwich
13.05.02 Roddy Doran DREW 8 Birmingham
02.06.02 Gary Dixon W PTS 6 Shaw
03.08.02 Mike Duffield W RSC 2 Derby
14.09.02 Ivan Botton L PTS 6 Newark
05.12.02 Mark Brookes L RSC 3 Sheffield
15.02.03 Peter Jackson W RSC 2 Wolverhampton
23.02.03 Roddy Doran L PTS 10 Shrewsbury
(Vacant British Masters S.Middleweight Title)
22.03.03 Barry Connell L PTS 4 Renfrew
12.04.03 Danny Smith L CO 5 Norwich
08.06.03 Ivan Botton W PTS 6 Nottingham
25.07.03 Steven Spartacus L CO 3 Norwich
(Vacant British Masters L.Heavyweight Title)
06.10.03 Hamed Jamali L PTS 6 Birmingham
17.10.03 Barry Connell L PTS 6 Glasgow
14.11.03 Terry Morrill W PTS 6 Hull
01.12.03 Clint Johnson L PTS 6 Leeds
15.12.03 Lee Nicholson W RSC 4 Cleethorpes
06.02.04 Mark Brookes L RSC 4 Sheffield
12.03.04 Hastings Rasani L CO 6 Irvine
07.05.04 Dean Cockburn L PTS 6 Doncaster
15.05.04 Gary Thompson W PTS 6 Aberdeen
04.06.04 Danny Norton L RSC 3 Dudley
10.09.04 Matthew Barney L PTS 4 Wembley
05.10.04 Andrew Flute W PTS 4 Dudley
04.11.04 Gary Thompson W PTS 6 Piccadilly
13.12.04 Hamed Jamali W PTS 10 Birmingham
(Vacant British Masters S.Middleweight Title)
21.01.05 Jamie Hearn L PTS 4 Brentford
23.03.05 Jamie Hearn W CO 7 Leicester Square
(Vacant British Masters S.Middleweight Title)
30.04.05 Lee Blundell L PTS 10 Wigan
(Vacant British Masters Middleweight Title)
14.05.05 Danny Thornton DREW 6 Aberdeen
03.06.05 Paul Smith L PTS 6 Manchester
20.06.05 Ryan Walls L RSC 8 Longford
16.09.05 Dean Cockburn W PTS 10 Doncaster
(British Masters S.Middleweight Title Defence)
25.09.05 Danny Thornton L PTS 6 Leeds
03.11.05 Ryan Kerr L PTS 10 Sunderland

(English S.Middleweight Title Challenge)
02.02.06 Jimi Hendricks W PTS 4 Holborn
26.02.06 JJ Ojuederie L PTS 4 Dagenham
30.03.06 Joey Vegas L PTS 10 Piccadilly
(British Masters S.Middleweight Title Defence)
01.06.06 Tony Quigley L PTS 4 Barnsley
16.06.06 Steve McGuire L PTS 6 Liverpool
12.07.06 Joey Vegas L PTS 4 Bethnal Green
15.09.06 Kreshnik Qato L PTS 6 Muswell Hill
06.10.06 Michael Monaghan W PTS 6 Mansfield
28.10.06 Tony Oakey L PTS 6 Bethnal Green
08.12.06 Kreshnik Qato L PTS 10 Dagenham
(Vacant Southern Area S.Middleweight Title)
Career: 52 contests, won 16, drew 2, lost 34.

Andy Cox
Cleethorpes. *Born* Grimsby, 22 February, 1986
L.Welterweight. *Ht* 5'11"
Manager D. Coldwell

14.05.07 Amir Nadi W PTS 6 Cleethorpes
Career: 1 contest, won 1.

Jamie Coyle
Bannockburn. *Born* Stirling, 24 August, 1976
L. Middleweight. *Ht* 6'0"
Manager Self

02.06.03 Richard Inquieti W RSC 2 Glasgow
20.10.03 Jed Tytler W RSC 2 Glasgow
04.12.03 George Robshaw DREW 6 Huddersfield
28.02.04 Geraint Harvey W PTS 4 Bridgend
22.04.04 Peter Dunn W PTS 6 Glasgow
15.10.04 Terry Adams W RSC 5 Glasgow
17.12.04 Arv Mittoo W RSC 5 Huddersfield
25.04.05 Tony Montana W RSC 3 Glasgow
16.06.05 Michael Lomax L PTS 6 Dagenham
30.09.05 Arek Malek W PTS 6 Kirkcaldy
04.11.05 Arek Malek W PTS 6 Glasgow
17.03.06 Karl David L RSC 1 Kirkcaldy
23.06.06 Ben Hudson W PTS 6 Blackpool
10.11.06 Franny Jones L RSC 2 Hartlepool
23.04.07 Rocky Muscas W PTS 8 Glasgow
08.06.07 Graham Delehedy W RSC 4 Motherwell

Career: 16 contests, won 12, drew 1, lost 3.

Anthony Crolla
Manchester. *Born* Manchester, 16 November, 1986
Lightweight. *Ht* 5'8¾"
Manager T. Jones/F. Warren

14.10.06 Abdul Rashid W PTS 4 Manchester
09.12.06 Arial Krasnopolski W RSC 3 Canning Town
31.05.07 Neal McQuade W RSC 1 Manchester
Career: 3 contests, won 3.

Sean Crompton
Wigan. *Born* Wigan, 24 August, 1984
S.Middleweight. *Ht* 5'9"
Manager S. Wood

16.06.07 Ernie Smith W PTS 6 Bolton
24.06.07 Irfan Malik W RSC 3 Wigan
Career: 2 contests, won 2.

Tomas da Silva

Canning Town. *Born* Sao Luiz Maranhao, Brazil, 19 May, 1976
S.Middleweight. *Ht* 5'11"
Manager Self

22.09.01	Conroy McIntosh W PTS 4 Canning Town
03.11.01	Ryan Kerr L PTS 4 Glasgow
16.11.01	Tommy Tolan W RSC 6 Dublin
08.12.01	Darren Covill W PTS 4 Millwall
16.12.01	Duje Postenjak L PTS 6 Glasgow
09.02.02	Thomas McDonagh DREW 4 Manchester
18.02.02	Biagio Falcone W RSC 3 Glasgow
19.04.02	Mark Graversen L PTS 6 Aarhus, Denmark
06.09.02	Steven Bendall L RSC 8 Bethnal Green
27.10.02	Matthew Tait L PTS 6 Southwark
03.12.02	Dean Powell L PTS 4 Bethnal Green
18.01.03	Thomas McDonagh L PTS 4 Preston
05.04.03	Ciaran Healy L PTS 4 Belfast
13.09.03	Michael Monaghan L PTS 6 Newport
02.10.03	Carl Wall DREW 4 Liverpool
06.11.03	Gokhan Kazaz L PTS 4 Dagenham
18.11.03	Matthew Tait L PTS 8 Bethnal Green
13.12.03	Anthony Farnell L PTS 6 Manchester
06.02.04	Geard Ajetovic L RSC 4 Sheffield
01.04.04	Daniel Teasdale L PTS 4 Bethnal Green
16.04.04	Ryan Rhodes L RSC 4 Bradford
24.02.07	Ryan Walls L RSC 2 Bracknell
21.04.07	Mark Nilsen L RSC 5 Manchester

Career: 23 contests, won 4, drew 2, lost 17.

(David) Karl David (Kowalski)

Cardiff. *Born* Wroclaw, Poland, 16 November, 1978
Welterweight. *Ht* 5'6"
Manager P. Boyce

18.05.01	Jozef Kubovsky W RSC 1 Warsaw, Poland
09.06.01	Mariusz Glowacki W RSC 1 Kolobrzeg, Poland
11.08.01	William Gdula W RSC 1 Jaworzno, Poland
10.11.01	Karoly Koos W RSC 4 Wloclawek, Poland
24.11.01	Grzegorz Lewandowski W PTS 4 Lodz, Poland
23.02.02	Vasile Herteg L PTS 6 Wloclawek, Poland
04.05.02	Marian Bunea W PTS 6 Wroclaw, Poland
24.05.02	Rafal Jackiewicz L CO 3 Plonsk, Poland
27.07.02	Cenk Ulug W PTS 6 Kolobrzeg, Poland
18.10.02	Dimitriu Razvan W PTS 6 Kozienice, Poland
21.02.03	Artur Drinaj L PTS 6 Radom, Poland
30.05.03	Marcen Gierke W PTS 6 Lublin, Poland
02.08.03	Abdelilah Benabbou W RSC 5 Wladyslawowo, Poland
14.11.03	Rastislav Kovac W RSC 1 Slupsk, Poland
06.12.03	Virgil Meleg W PTS 6 Tarnow, Poland
28.02.04	Zsolt Botos W PTS 6 Warsaw, Poland
04.06.04	Mircea Lurci W PTS 10 Warsaw, Poland
26.11.04	Virgil Meleg W PTS 6 Warsaw, Poland
10.12.04	Ondra Skala W RSC 4 Jaworzno, Poland
25.02.05	Slawomir Ziemlewicz DREW 8 Wloclawek, Poland
	(Vacant Polish L.Welterweight Title)
29.04.05	Luciano Abis L PTS 12 Cagliari, Italy
	(Vacant IBF Inter-Continental Welterweight Title)
30.09.05	Silence Saheed L PTS 6 Carmarthen
16.12.05	Robert Lloyd-Taylor L PTS 4 Bracknell
17.03.06	Jamie Coyle W RSC 1 Kirkcaldy
16.06.06	David Kehoe W RSC 1 Carmarthen
29.09.06	John-Paul Temple W PTS 6 Cardiff
13.10.06	Tyan Booth L PTS 6 Aberavon
02.03.07	Alex Stoda W PTS 6 Neath
07.04.07	Kell Brook L RSC 3 Cardiff
09.06.07	Slawomir Ziemlewicz L PTS 10 Katowice, Poland

Career: 30 contests, won 20, drew 1, lost 9.

Paul David

Sheffield. *Born* Northampton, 2 September, 1984
Cruiserweight. *Ht* 6'0½"
Manager J. Ingle

27.02.06	Peter McCormack W RTD 2 Birmingham

17.03.06	Steve McGuire L PTS 6 Kirkcaldy
25.03.06	Duane Reid W RSC 3 Burton
12.05.06	Daniel Cadman W RSC 6 Bethnal Green
23.06.06	Richard Turba W PTS 6 Blackpool
21.10.06	Gary Thompson W PTS 6 Glasgow
03.11.06	Brian Magee L PTS 6 Barnsley
26.01.07	Tony Salam L PTS 4 Dagenham
18.05.07	Peter Haymer W PTS 8 Canning Town

Career: 9 contests, won 6, lost 3.

Kenny Davidson

Wishaw. *Born* Motherwell, 11 July, 1981
S.Middleweight. *Ht* 6'0¾"
Manager T. Gilmour

03.11.06	Jamie Ambler L PTS 6 Glasgow
23.04.07	Mark Phillips W PTS 6 Glasgow

Career: 2 contests, won 1, lost 1.

Dai Davies

Merthyr Tydfil. *Born* Merthyr Tydfil, 20 April, 1983
Welsh S.Featherweight Champion. *Ht* 5'6"
Manager D. Gardiner

08.07.04	Neil Marston W PTS 6 Birmingham
01.10.04	Riaz Durgahed W PTS 4 Bristol
02.12.04	Martin Lindsay L RSC 1 Crystal Palace
25.02.05	Matthew Marsh L PTS 4 Wembley
16.07.05	Derry Matthews L RSC 2 Bolton

Paul David   Les Clark

12.12.05	Riaz Durgahed L PTS 6 Peterborough
13.04.06	Gary Sykes L CO 3 Leeds
09.06.06	Jamie McDonnell DREW 4 Doncaster
29.06.06	Jed Syger W PTS 6 Bethnal Green
08.10.06	Henry Jones W PTS 10 Swansea
	(Vacant Welsh Area S.Featherweight
	Title)
16.02.07	Riaz Durgahed W PTS 8 Merthyr
	Tydfil
27.04.07	Akaash Bhatia L PTS 4 Wembley

Career: 12 contests, won 5, drew 1, lost 6.

Sara Davies

Nottingham. *Born* Stockton, 24 August, 1971
L.Middleweight. *Ht* 5'8"
Manager C. Mitchell

31.03.07	Borislava Goranova W PTS 4 Derby

Career: 1 contest, won 1.

Shon Davies

Llanelli. *Born* Carmarthen, 6 September, 1986
L.Heavyweight. *Ht* 5'1½"
Manager D. Davies

23.07.06	Richard Horton W RSC 1 Dagenham
08.10.06	Mark Phillips W PTS 4 Swansea
26.10.06	Nicki Taylor W RSC 1 Wolverhampton
16.02.07	Jamie Ambler W PTS 6 Merthyr Tydfil
03.03.07	Tyrone Wright L PTS 6 Alfreton

Career: 5 contests, won 4, lost 1.

Tristan Davies

Telford. *Born* Shrewsbury, 13 October, 1978
Welterweight. Former Undefeated Midlands Area Lightweight Champion. *Ht* 5'10"
Manager E. Johnson

04.06.04	Pete Buckley W PTS 6 Dudley
05.10.04	Gavin Tait W PTS 6 Dudley
17.02.05	Stuart Phillips W PTS 6 Dudley
16.09.05	Karl Taylor W PTS 4 Telford
04.12.05	Jonathan Whiteman W PTS 4 Telford
14.04.06	Kristian Laight W PTS 6 Telford
01.06.06	Carl Allen W PTS 6 Birmingham
09.10.06	Peter Dunn W PTS 6 Birmingham
10.11.06	Carl Allen W PTS 10 Telford
	(Vacant Midlands Area Lightweight
	Title)
01.04.07	Peter Dunn W PTS 6 Shrewsbury

Career: 10 contests, won 10.

Andy Davis

Abercynon. *Born* Aberdare, 28 December, 1985
Featherweight. *Ht* 5'7"
Manager B. Coleman

10.03.06	Shaun Walton W PTS 6 Walsall
28.04.06	Paul Appleby L RSC 1 Hartlepool
15.09.06	Sergei Rozhakmens W RSC 4 Newport

Career: 3 contests, won 2, lost 1.

Gary Davis (Harding)

St Helens. *Born* Liverpool, 17 October, 1982
Central Area & British Masters S.Bantamweight Champion. *Ht* 5'6"
Manager Self

01.06.02	Steve Gethin L RSC 2 Manchester
05.10.02	Jason Thomas W RSC 5 Liverpool
29.11.02	Simon Chambers W RSC 2 Liverpool
15.11.04	Furhan Rafiq W PTS 6 Glasgow
18.09.05	Rocky Dean L RSC 4 Bethnal Green
24.02.06	Chris Hooper W RSC 1 Scarborough
	(Vacant Central Area S.Bantamweight
	Title. Vacant British Masters
	S.Bantamweight Title)
30.09.06	Barrington Brown DREW 6 Stoke
24.02.07	Abdul Mougharbel W PTS 6 Stoke

Career: 8 contests, won 5, drew 1, lost 2.

Paul Davis

Lowestoft. *Born* Dublin, 10 August, 1979
L.Heavyweight. *Ht* 6'1"
Manager G. Everett

15.10.06	Phillip Callaghan W RSC 4 Norwich
16.03.07	Omid Bourzo W RSC 4 Norwich

Career: 2 contests, won 2.

Varuzhan Davtyan

Birmingham. *Born* Armenia, 11 August, 1972
Cruiserweight. *Ht* 5'8½"
Manager Self

17.04.93	Teymuraz Kekelidze L CO 5 Tbilisi, Georgia
09.03.02	Tony Dodson W PTS 6 Manchester
09.05.02	Rasmus Ojemaye W RSC 3 Leicester Square
29.06.02	Elvis Michailenko L PTS 6 Brentwood
08.09.02	Paul Bonson W PTS 4 Wolverhampton
05.10.02	Mark Hobson L RSC 3 Huddersfield
30.11.02	Eric Teymour L PTS 6 Liverpool
14.12.02	Tomasz Adamek L RTD 4 Newcastle
05.03.03	Carl Froch L RSC 5 Bethnal Green
17.05.03	Jason McKay L PTS 6 Liverpool
24.05.03	Eric Teymour L PTS 4 Bethnal Green
28.06.03	Nathan King L PTS 4 Cardiff
26.07.03	Tony Dodson L RTD 3 Plymouth
20.09.03	Adrian Dodson W PTS 4 Nottingham
20.03.04	Andrew Lowe L PTS 6 Wembley
30.03.04	Jamie Hearn W PTS 4 Southampton
02.06.04	Steven Spartacus L RSC 1 Nottingham
28.10.04	Sam Price L PTS 6 Sunderland
08.12.04	Ryan Walls L PTS 4 Longford
17.12.04	Courtney Fry L RTD 2 Liverpool
12.02.05	Tony Oakey L RTD 5 Portsmouth
10.04.05	Andrew Lowe L PTS 6 Brentwood
29.04.05	Leigh Allis L PTS 4 Plymouth
03.06.05	Tony Quigley L PTS 4 Manchester
11.06.05	Steve McGuire L PTS 6 Kirkcaldy
23.09.05	Tony Dodson L PTS 4 Manchester
14.10.05	Brian Magee L RSC 2 Dublin
17.11.05	Leigh Alliss L PTS 4 Bristol
11.12.05	Steven Spartacus L RSC 1 Chigwell
18.03.06	Neil Simpson L RSC 1 Coventry
21.05.06	Peter Haymer L RSC 4 Bethnal Green
07.10.06	John Smith L DIS 6 Weston super Mare
28.10.06	Tommy Saunders L PTS 4 Bethnal Green
18.11.06	Nathan Cleverly L PTS 4 Newport
01.12.06	Matthew Barney L PTS 4 Tower Hill
13.12.06	Joey Vegas L RSC 1 Strand

Career: 36 contests, won 5, lost 31.

Mark Dawes

Sedgefield. *Born* Stockton, 9 April, 1981
L.Welterweight. *Ht* 5'9"
Manager D. Garside

06.05.07	Peter Dunn W PTS 6 Darlington
09.06.07	Karl Taylor W PTS 6 Middlesbrough

Career: 2 contests, won 2.

Lenny Daws

Morden. *Born* Carshalton, 29 December, 1978
L.Welterweight. Former British L.Welterweight Champion. Former Undefeated Southern Area L.Welterweight Champion. *Ht* 5'10½"
Manager Self

16.04.03	Danny Gwilym W RSC 2 Nottingham
27.05.03	Ben Hudson W RSC 2 Dagenham
25.07.03	Karl Taylor W RTD 2 Norwich
04.10.03	Ernie Smith W PTS 4 Muswell Hill
28.11.03	Tony Montana W PTS 6 Derby
11.12.03	Keith Jones W PTS 6 Bethnal Green
30.01.04	Denis Alekseev W CO 3 Dagenham
24.09.04	Ernie Smith W PTS 6 Nottingham
12.11.04	Keith Jones W PTS 8 Wembley
10.04.05	Silence Saheed W PTS 6 Brentwood
09.07.05	Ivor Bonavic W PTS 6 Nottingham
28.10.05	Oscar Hall W RTD 7 Hartlepool
	(Elim. English L.Welterweight Title)
20.01.06	Colin Lynes W RTD 9 Bethnal Green
	(Elim. British L.Welterweight Title.
	Vacant Southern Area L.Welterweight
	Title)
12.05.06	Nigel Wright W PTS 12 Bethnal Green
	(Vacant British L.Welterweight Title)
20.01.07	Barry Morrison L PTS 12 Muswell Hill
	(British L.Welterweight Title Defence)
18.05.07	Billy Smith W PTS 6 Canning Town

Career: 16 contests, won 15, lost 1.

Gavin Deacon

Northampton. *Born* Northampton, 5 June, 1982
Welterweight. *Ht* 5'9¼"
Manager J. Cox

12.11.05	Colin Bain L PTS 6 Glasgow
12.02.06	Danny Harding L PTS 6 Manchester
20.02.06	Ryan Brawley L PTS 4 Glasgow
03.03.06	Wez Miller L PTS 4 Doncaster
17.03.06	David Appleby L PTS 4 Kirkcaldy
15.10.06	Neal McQuade W PTS 6 Norwich
07.12.06	Tony McQuade DREW 6 Peterborough
14.12.06	Daniel Thorpe L PTS 6 Leicester
23.02.07	Waz Hussain W PTS 4 Birmingham
03.03.07	Deniss Sirjatovs W PTS 4 Alfreton
30.03.07	Neal McQuade W PTS 6 Peterborough
13.04.07	Rendall Munroe L PTS 6 Altrincham
11.05.07	George Watson L PTS 6 Sunderland
08.06.07	Charles Paul King L PTS 4 Motherwell

Career: 14 contests, won 4, drew 1, lost 9.

Robin Deakin

Crawley. *Born* Crawley, 19 April, 1986
Lightweight. *Ht* 5'8½"
Manager F. Warren

28.10.06	Shaun Walton W PTS 4 Bethnal Green
17.02.07	Rom Krauklis L PTS 4 Wembley

Career: 2 contests, won 1, lost 1.

Robin Deakin   Les Clark

Rocky Dean

Thetford. *Born* Bury St Edmonds, 17 June, 1978
Featherweight. Former Southern Area Featherweight Champion. *Ht* 5'5"
Manager Self

14.10.99	Lennie Hodgkins W PTS 6 Bloomsbury
30.10.99	Lennie Hodgkins W PTS 6 Southwark
18.05.00	Danny Lawson W RSC 1 Bethnal Green
29.09.00	Anthony Hanna W PTS 4 Bethnal Green
10.11.00	Chris Jickells L RSC 1 Mayfair
19.04.02	Peter Svendsen W PTS 6 Aarhus, Denmark
19.10.02	Sean Grant W RSC 3 Norwich
21.12.02	Darren Cleary W PTS 4 Millwall
08.02.03	Steve Gethin DREW 4 Norwich
11.07.03	Isaac Ward DREW 4 Darlington
26.07.03	Michael Hunter L RSC 1 Plymouth
10.10.03	Isaac Ward L PTS 6 Darlington
06.11.03	Martin Power L PTS 6 Dagenham
07.12.03	Michael Crossan L PTS 6 Glasgow
24.09.04	Simon Wilson W PTS 4 Millwall
19.12.04	Jim Betts W PTS 8 Bethnal Green
05.03.05	Mickey Coveney W PTS 10 Dagenham *(Vacant Southern Area Featherweight Title)*
20.05.05	Andy Morris L PTS 10 Southwark *(Vacant English Featherweight Title)*
18.09.05	Gary Davis W RSC 4 Bethnal Green
21.10.05	Andrey Isaev L RSC 12 Kharkov, Ukraine *(Vacant WBF Inter-Continental Featherweight Title)*
26.02.06	Vinesh Rungea W PTS 6 Dagenham
09.12.06	Matthew Marsh L PTS 10 Canning Town *(Southern Area Featherweight Title Defence)*

Career: 22 contests, won 12, drew 2, lost 8.

Tony Delaney

Mossley. *Born* Tameside, 29 July, 1983
L.Welterweight. *Ht* 5'7¼"
Manager T. Jones

04.03.06	Jason Nesbitt W PTS 4 Manchester
14.10.06	Jaz Virdee W PTS 6 Manchester

Career: 2 contests, won 2.

Graham Delehedy

Liverpool. *Born* Liverpool, 7 October, 1978
L.Middleweight. *Ht* 5'8"
Manager T. Gilmour

17.05.03	Joel Ani W RSC 4 Liverpool
27.10.03	Rocky Muscus W RSC 2 Glasgow
01.12.03	Gary Cummings W RSC 1 Bradford
27.05.04	Ernie Smith W RSC 3 Huddersfield
08.10.04	David Kehoe W RSC 2 Brentwood
26.11.04	Tony Montana W PTS 6 Altrincham
30.04.05	Cafu Santos W RSC 1 Wigan
23.09.05	Arek Malek W PTS 6 Manchester
28.04.06	Taz Jones L CO 6 Hartlepool
30.03.07	Martin Marshall W CO 2 Crawley
08.06.07	Jamie Coyle L RSC 4 Motherwell

Career: 11 contests, won 9, lost 2.

Jon Dennington

Bexleyheath. *Born* London, 3 July, 1984
Middleweight. *Ht* 5'9¼"
Manager J. Eames

09.03.07	Pawel Jas W PTS 4 Dagenham

Career: 1 contest, won 1.

(Dennis) Buster Dennis (Mwanze)

Canning Town. *Born* Mawokota, Uganda, 31 December, 1981
Featherweight. *Ht* 5'0"
Manager Self

28.03.03	Vitali Makarov W RSC 2 Millwall
03.04.03	Chris Hooper L RSC 1 Hull
15.05.03	Mark Alexander L PTS 4 Mayfair
24.05.03	Haider Ali L PTS 4 Bethnal Green
21.11.03	Anthony Hanna W PTS 6 Millwall
30.11.03	Daleboy Rees W PTS 6 Swansea
20.02.04	Chris Hooper W RSC 2 Bethnal Green
01.04.04	Kevin O'Hara L PTS 4 Bethnal Green
19.06.04	Riaz Durgahed L PTS 4 Muswell Hill
03.09.04	Jamie Arthur L PTS 6 Newport
10.09.04	Derry Matthews L PTS 6 Liverpool
26.11.04	Eddie Hyland L PTS 4 Altrincham
13.12.04	Matt Teague W PTS 6 Cleethorpes
11.02.05	Andy Morris L PTS 6 Manchester
08.04.05	Ricky Burns L PTS 6 Edinburgh
20.05.05	John Bothwell W RTD 4 Glasgow
03.06.05	Steve Bell DREW 6 Manchester
18.06.05	Musa Njue W RSC 7 Kampala, Uganda
18.09.05	Paul Griffin W PTS 6 Bethnal Green
04.11.05	Lee Cook DREW 4 Bethnal Green
10.12.05	Steve Foster DREW 8 Canning Town
24.03.06	Jadgar Abdulla DREW 4 Bethnal Green
18.10.06	Harry Ramogoadi L RSC 9 Bayswater *(Vacant British Masters Featherweight Title)*
16.02.07	Paul Appleby L PTS 8 Kirkcaldy
30.03.07	Martin Lindsay L PTS 6 Crawley

Career: 25 contests, won 8, drew 4, lost 13.

Craig Denton

Hartlepool. *Born* Hartlepool, 7 April, 1981
Middleweight. *Ht* 6'1"
Manager D. Garside

13.04.07	Jeff Hamilton W PTS 6 Houghton le Spring
06.05.07	Jon Foster W PTS 6 Darlington

Career: 2 contests, won 2.

Craig Dickson

Glasgow. *Born* Glasgow, 6 March, 1979
L.Middleweight. *Ht* 5'11"
Manager T. Gilmour

21.10.02	Paul Rushton W RSC 2 Glasgow
18.11.02	Ernie Smith W PTS 6 Glasgow
17.02.03	Jon Hilton W RSC 2 Glasgow
14.04.03	Richard Inquieti W PTS 4 Glasgow
20.10.03	Danny Moir W RSC 3 Glasgow
19.01.04	Dean Nicholas W RSC 5 Glasgow
19.04.04	Ernie Smith W PTS 6 Glasgow
30.09.04	Taz Jones DREW 6 Glasgow
15.11.04	Tony Montana W PTS 8 Glasgow
21.03.05	David Keir W RTD 3 Glasgow
30.09.05	Vadzim Astapuk W RSC 4 Kirkcaldy
21.11.05	David Kehoe W PTS 8 Glasgow
20.02.06	Arek Malek W RSC 5 Glasgow
17.03.06	Kevin Anderson L RSC 7 Kirkcaldy *(Commonwealth Welterweight Title Challenge)*
01.06.06	Darren Gethin L PTS 6 Birmingham
23.10.06	Martin Marshall W RTD 4 Glasgow
02.12.06	Franny Jones L RSC 6 Clydebank

Career: 17 contests, won 13, drew 1, lost 3.

Carl Dilks

Liverpool. *Born* Liverpool, 29 September, 1983
L.Heavyweight. *Ht* 5'11"
Manager S. Wood

06.05.07	Carl Wild W PTS 6 Altrincham
16.06.07	Carl Wild W PTS 6 Bolton

Career: 2 contests, won 2.

Craig Docherty

Glasgow. *Born* Glasgow, 27 September, 1979
Lightweight. Former Commonwealth S.Featherweight Champion. *Ht* 5'7"
Manager T. Gilmour

16.11.98	Kevin Gerowski W PTS 6 Glasgow
22.02.99	Des Gargano W PTS 6 Glasgow
19.04.99	Paul Quarmby W RSC 4 Glasgow
07.06.99	Simon Chambers W PTS 6 Glasgow
20.09.99	John Barnes W PTS 6 Glasgow
15.11.99	Peter Allen W RSC 1 Glasgow
24.01.00	Lee Williamson W PTS 6 Glasgow
19.02.00	Steve Hanley W PTS 6 Prestwick
05.06.00	Sebastian Hart W RSC 1 Glasgow
23.10.00	Lee Armstrong DREW 8 Glasgow
22.01.01	Nigel Senior W RSC 4 Glasgow
20.03.01	Jamie McKeever W RSC 3 Glasgow
11.06.01	Rakhim Mingaleev W PTS 8 Nottingham
27.10.01	Michael Gomez L RSC 2 Manchester *(British S.Featherweight Title Challenge)*
18.03.02	Joel Viney W CO 1 Glasgow
13.07.02	Dariusz Snarski W PTS 6 Coventry
25.01.03	Nikolai Eremeev W PTS 6 Bridgend
12.04.03	Dean Pithie W CO 8 Bethnal Green *(Commonwealth S. Featherweight Title Challenge)*
01.11.03	Abdul Malik Jabir W PTS 12 Glasgow *(Commonwealth S.Featherweight Title Defence)*
22.04.04	Kpakpo Allotey W RSC 6 Glasgow *(Commonwealth S.Featherweight Title Defence)*
15.10.04	Boris Sinitsin L PTS 12 Glasgow *(European S.Featherweight Title Challenge)*

08.04.05 Alex Arthur L CO 9 Edinburgh
*(Vacant British S.Featherweight Title.
Commonwealth S.Featherweight Title
Defence)*
30.09.05 John Mackay W RSC 7 Kirkcaldy
25.05.07 Billy Smith W PTS 6 Glasgow
Career: 24 contests, won 20, drew 1, lost 3.

Tony Dodson

Liverpool. *Born* Liverpool, 2 July, 1980
English S.Middleweight Champion.
Former Undefeated British S.Middleweight
Champion. Former Undefeated Central
Area S.Middleweight Champion. Former
WBF Inter-Continental S.Middleweight
Champion. *Ht* 6'0½"
Manager Self

31.07.99 Michael McDermott W RTD 1 Carlisle
02.10.99 Sean Pritchard W RSC 3 Cardiff
22.01.00 Mark Dawson W PTS 4 Birmingham
11.03.00 Paul Bonson W PTS 4 Kensington
19.08.00 Jimmy Steel W RSC 3 Brentwood
09.09.00 Danny Southam W RSC 2 Manchester
09.10.00 Elvis Michailenko DREW 6 Liverpool
03.02.01 Paul Bonson W PTS 4 Manchester
25.09.01 Paul Wesley W PTS 6 Liverpool
13.10.01 Roman Divisek W CO 1 Budapest,
Hungary
10.11.01 Valery Odin W RSC 4 Wembley
10.12.01 Jon Penn W RSC 2 Liverpool
*(Vacant Central Area S.Middleweight
Title)*
23.02.02 Jason Hart W RSC 2 Nottingham
09.03.02 Varuzhan Davtyan L PTS 6 Manchester
13.04.02 Brian Barbosa W PTS 8 Liverpool
07.09.02 Mike Algoet W PTS 10 Liverpool
*(Vacant WBF Inter-Continental
S.Middleweight Title)*
26.10.02 Albert Rybacki L RSC 9 Maesteg
*(WBF Inter-Continental
S.Middleweight Title Defence)*
19.04.03 Pierre Moreno L RSC 9 Liverpool
*(Vacant WBF Inter-Continental
S.Middleweight Title)*
26.07.03 Varuzhan Davtyan W RTD 3 Plymouth
22.11.03 Allan Foster W RSC 11 Belfast
(Vacant British S.Middleweight Title)
23.09.05 Varuzhan Davtyan W PTS 4
Manchester
25.11.05 Szabolcs Rimovszky W RSC 3
Liverpool
03.03.06 Dmitry Adamovich W PTS 4
Hartlepool
16.06.06 Jamie Hearn W RSC 4 Liverpool
(Vacant English S.Middleweight Title)
24.11.06 Carl Froch L CO 3 Nottingham
*(British & Commonwealth
S.Middleweight Title Challenges)*
Career: 25 contests, won 20, drew 1, lost 4.

(Bernard) Barney Doherty

St.Albans. *Born* Hackney, 19 October, 1985
Lightweight. *Ht* 5'10"
Manager P. Rees/M. Helliet

24.09.06 Tony Jourda L PTS 4 Bethnal Green
Career: 1 contest, lost 1.

Jimmy Doherty

Stoke. *Born* Stafford, 15 August, 1985
L.Middleweight. *Ht* 5'11"
Manager M. Carney

12.11.05 Surinder Sekhon W PTS 6 Stoke
18.02.06 Pete Buckley W PTS 6 Stoke
06.05.06 Jason Nesbitt W PTS 6 Stoke
30.09.06 Aldon Stewart W PTS 6 Stoke
24.02.07 Chris Brophy W PTS 6 Stoke
12.05.07 Steve Cooper W PTS 6 Stoke
Career: 6 contests, won 6.

Patrick Doherty

Kingston. *Born* Greenwich, 24 September,
1984
Welterweight. *Ht* 5'6¾"
Manager J. Evans

07.06.07 Chris Brophy W CO 4 Kensington
Career: 1 contest, won 1.

Shaun Doherty

Bradford. *Born* Bradford, 15 November,
1982
S.Bantamweight. *Ht* 5'7"
Manager C. Aston

23.11.05 Eylon Kedem DREW 6 Mayfair
24.02.06 Neil Marston L PTS 6 Birmingham
27.10.06 Stephen Russell L PTS 6 Glasgow
07.12.06 Anthony Hanna W PTS 6 Bradford
12.05.07 Imran Khan W PTS 6 Stoke
Career: 5 contests, won 2, drew 1, lost 2.

Tony Doherty

Pontypool. *Born* London, 8 April, 1983
Celtic Welterweight Champion. *Ht* 5'8"
Manager F. Warren/B. Hughes

08.05.03 Karl Taylor W PTS 4 Widnes
28.06.03 Paul McIlwaine W RSC 1 Cardiff
13.09.03 Darren Covill W PTS 4 Newport
06.12.03 James Paisley W RSC 3 Cardiff
21.02.04 Chris Brophy W RSC 2 Cardiff
24.04.04 Keith Jones W PTS 6 Reading
22.05.04 Karl Taylor W RTD 2 Widnes
03.07.04 David Kirk W PTS 4 Newport
30.07.04 Ernie Smith W PTS 6 Bethnal Green
03.09.04 Keith Jones W PTS 6 Newport
10.09.04 Peter Dunn W RSC 2 Bethnal Green
19.11.04 Karl Taylor W RSC 2 Bethnal Green
21.01.05 Emmanuel Fleury W RSC 2 Bridgend
22.04.05 Belaid Yahiaoui W PTS 8 Barnsley
16.07.05 Ernie Smith NC 2 Bolton
10.09.05 Taz Jones W PTS 10 Cardiff
(Vacant Celtic Welterweight Title)
28.01.06 Ernie Smith W PTS 6 Nottingham
13.05.06 Andrzej Butowicz W PTS 6 Bethnal
Green
08.07.06 Ihar Filonau W CO 1 Cardiff
18.11.06 Gary O'Connor W PTS 6 Newport
07.04.07 Taz Jones W RSC 7 Cardiff
(Celtic Welterweight Title Defence)
Career: 21 contests, won 20, no contest 1.

Marko Doknic

Liverpool. *Born* Novi Sad, 1 February, 1982
Cruiserweight. *Ht* 6'0"
Manager J. Evans

17.11.05 Dan Guthrie L PTS 4 Bristol
13.10.06 Wayne Brooks L RSC 3 Aberavon
Career: 2 contests, lost 2.

David Dolan

Sunderland. *Born* Sunderland, 7 October,
1979
Heavyweight. *Ht* 6'2"
Manager Self

13.05.06 Nabil Haciani W PTS 4 Sheffield
03.11.06 Paul King W PTS 4 Barnsley
13.04.07 Paul King W PTS 4 Houghton le
Spring
Career: 3 contests, won 3.

John Donnelly

Croxteth. *Born* Liverpool, 15 July, 1984
Featherweight. *Ht* 5'4½"
Manager T. Gilmour

05.06.07 Shaun Walton W PTS 6 Glasgow
Career: 1 contest, won 1.

Barry Downes

Rochdale. *Born* Rochdale, 10 December,
1984
Welterweight. *Ht* 5'10½"
Manager C. Aston

20.11.05 Kristian Laight DREW 6 Shaw
02.04.06 Pete Buckley W PTS 6 Shaw
13.04.06 Sujad Elahi W RSC 3 Leeds
28.05.06 Ruben Giles L PTS 4 Longford
18.06.06 Jonathan Hussey L PTS 6 Manchester
24.02.07 Andrew Alan Lowe L PTS 6 Stoke
09.03.07 Jamie Radford L PTS 4 Dagenham
29.04.07 Ben Murphy L RSC 1 Birmingham
Career: 8 contests, won 2, drew 1, lost 5.

Wayne Downing

West Bromwich. *Born* Sandwell, 30
December, 1979
L.Middleweight. *Ht* 5'9"
Manager E. Johnson

16.02.06 Peter Dunn L PTS 4 Dudley
18.05.06 Malik Khan L RSC 3 Walsall
18.09.06 Tye Williams L RSC 2 Glasgow
17.11.06 Peter Dunn W PTS 6 Brierley Hill
06.12.06 Martin Gordon W PTS 6 Stoke
03.03.07 Pete Buckley W PTS 4 Burton
19.05.07 Dennis Corpe L PTS 4 Nottingham
Career: 7 contests, won 3, lost 4.

Philip Dowse

Aberystwyth. *Born* Aberystwyth, 31 March,
1984
Middleweight. *Ht* 5'10½"
Manager N. Hodges

16.02.07 Ernie Smith W PTS 6 Merthyr Tydfil
10.06.07 Paul Morby W RSC 4 Neath
Career: 2 contests, won 2.

Carl Drake

Plymouth. *Born* Plymouth, 22 February,
1975
L.Middleweight. *Ht* 5'8"
Manager J. Evans

02.06.07 Tommy Marshall W RSC 4 Bristol
Career: 1 contest, won 1.

Ciaran Duffy

Glasgow. *Born* Donegal, 11 September,
1980
L. Middleweight. *Ht* 5'11"
Manager Self

03.11.01 Wayne Shepherd W PTS 6 Glasgow
03.12.01 Pedro Thompson W PTS 6 Leeds
22.04.02 Richard Inquieti W PTS 6 Glasgow

20.11.02	Dave Pearson DREW 6 Leeds
17.03.03	Danny Moir W PTS 6 Glasgow
10.12.06	Paddy Pollock L PTS 6 Glasgow
10.02.07	Rocky Muscas W PTS 4 Letterkenny

Career: 7 contests, won 5, drew 1, lost 1.

Peter Dunn

Pontefract. *Born* Doncaster, 15 February, 1975
Middleweight. *Ht* 5'8"
Manager Self

08.12.97	Leigh Daniels W PTS 6 Bradford
15.05.98	Peter Lennon W PTS 6 Nottingham
18.09.98	Jan Cree L RSC 5 Belfast
23.10.98	Bobby Lyndon W PTS 6 Wakefield
03.12.98	Craig Smith L RSC 3 Sunderland
17.03.99	Des Sowden W PTS 6 Kensington
15.05.99	Ray Wood DREW 4 Blackpool
29.05.99	Dean Nicholas L PTS 6 South Shields
01.10.99	Jon Honney L PTS 4 Bethnal Green
18.10.99	Jan Cree W PTS 6 Glasgow
26.11.99	Gavin Pearson DREW 6 Wakefield
18.02.00	John T. Kelly L PTS 6 Pentre Halkyn
11.03.00	Iain Eldridge L RSC 2 Kensington
18.09.00	Joe Miller L PTS 6 Glasgow
26.10.00	Ram Singh W PTS 6 Stoke
27.11.00	Young Muttley L RSC 3 Birmingham
22.02.01	Darren Spencer W PTS 6 Sunderland
03.03.01	Glenn McClarnon L PTS 4 Wembley

20.03.01	Robert Burton L PTS 6 Leeds
08.04.01	Martyn Bailey L PTS 6 Wrexham
17.05.01	Gavin Pearson L PTS 6 Leeds
25.09.01	Darren Spencer L PTS 4 Liverpool
06.10.01	Lee Byrne L RSC 4 Manchester
13.11.01	Richard Inquieti DREW 6 Leeds
24.11.01	Robert Burton W PTS 6 Wakefield
28.01.02	Robert Burton L RSC 8 Barnsley
	(Vacant Central Area Welterweight Title)
23.03.02	Colin Lynes L PTS 4 Southwark
19.04.02	Oscar Hall L PTS 6 Darlington
28.05.02	Matt Scriven L PTS 8 Leeds
29.06.02	Darren Bruce L PTS 6 Brentwood
28.09.02	Surinder Sekhon L PTS 6 Wakefield
13.09.03	Wayne Shepherd W PTS 6 Wakefield
20.09.03	Michael Lomax L PTS 4 Nottingham
04.10.03	Andy Gibson L PTS 6 Belfast
25.10.03	Gary Young L PTS 6 Edinburgh
13.12.03	Michael Jennings L PTS 6 Manchester
19.02.04	Young Muttley L PTS 6 Dudley
26.02.04	Matthew Hatton L PTS 6 Widnes
06.03.04	Jason Rushton L PTS 6 Renfrew
10.04.04	Ali Nuumembe L PTS 6 Manchester
22.04.04	Jamie Coyle L PTS 6 Glasgow
06.05.04	Jason Rushton L PTS 4 Barnsley
19.06.04	Chris Saunders L PTS 4 Muswell Hill
03.07.04	Oscar Hall L PTS 6 Blackpool
10.09.04	Tony Doherty L RSC 2 Bethnal Green
09.10.04	Steve Russell W PTS 6 Norwich
23.10.04	Geraint Harvey L PTS 6 Wakefield

Barry Downes   Les Clark

11.12.04	Gary Woolcombe L PTS 4 Canning Town
19.12.04	Freddie Luke L PTS 4 Bethnal Green
25.02.05	Chas Symonds L PTS 4 Wembley
07.04.05	Jonjo Finnegan L PTS 6 Birmingham
26.04.05	Tyrone McInerney L RSC 6 Leeds
03.06.05	Oscar Hall L PTS 6 Hull
19.06.05	Gary Woolcombe L RSC 6 Bethnal Green
21.09.05	Danny Moir L PTS 6 Bradford
30.09.05	Paul McInnes L PTS 6 Burton
10.10.05	Joe Mitchell L PTS 6 Birmingham
13.11.05	Khurram Hussain L PTS 4 Leeds
21.11.05	Muhsen Nasser L RSC 4 Glasgow
16.02.06	Wayne Downing W PTS 4 Dudley
23.02.06	Darren Rhodes L PTS 6 Leeds
05.03.06	Muhsen Nasser L PTS 4 Sheffield
30.03.06	Oscar Milkitas L PTS 6 Bloomsbury
14.04.06	Gary Round L PTS 6 Telford
21.04.06	Jason Rushton L PTS 6 Doncaster
29.04.06	Lee McAllister L PTS 6 Edinburgh
09.05.06	Ryan Ashworth L PTS 6 Leeds
18.05.06	Stuart Elwell L PTS 6 Walsall
29.06.06	Marcus Portman L PTS 6 Dudley
18.09.06	Marcus Portman L PTS 6 Glasgow
29.09.06	Paul Burns L PTS 6 Motherwell
09.10.06	Tristan Davies L PTS 6 Birmingham
27.10.06	Lee Noble L PTS 6 Glasgow
04.11.06	Matt Scriven L PTS 6 Mansfield
17.11.06	Wayne Downing L PTS 6 Brierley Hill
24.11.06	Tyan Booth L PTS 4 Nottingham
05.12.06	Rob Kenney DREW 4 Wolverhampton
14.12.06	Simon Fleck L PTS 6 Leicester
22.12.06	Abul Taher L PTS 6 Coventry
01.02.07	Wayne Alwan Arab L PTS 6 Piccadilly
15.02.07	Rob Kenney L PTS 4 Dudley
23.02.07	Max Maxwell L PTS 6 Birmingham
02.03.07	Mark Hastie L PTS 6 Irvine
17.03.07	James McKinley L PTS 6 Birmingham
24.03.07	Sean McKervey L PTS 6 Coventry
01.04.07	Tristan Davies L PTS 6 Shrewsbury
14.04.07	Rob Kenney L PTS 4 Wakefield
06.05.07	Mark Dawes L PTS 6 Darlington
19.05.07	Karl Chiverton L PTS 4 Nottingham
27.05.07	Khurram Hussain L PTS 4 Bradford
03.06.07	Curtis Woodhouse L PTS 4 Barnsley
21.06.07	Clint Smith L PTS 6 Peterborough
30.06.07	Lee Murtagh L PTS 6 Belfast

Career: 93 contests, won 11, drew 4, lost 78.

Riaz Durgahed

Bristol. *Born* Mauritius, 4 May, 1977
S.Featherweight. *Ht* 5'6"
Manager Self

29.02.04	Jason Thomas W RSC 1 Bristol
19.06.04	Buster Dennis W PTS 4 Muswell Hill
01.10.04	Dai Davies L PTS 4 Bristol
02.12.04	Lloyd Otte L PTS 6 Crystal Palace
08.04.05	Scott Flynn L PTS 4 Edinburgh
02.06.05	Jason Nesbitt W PTS 6 Peterborough
02.09.05	Rendall Munroe L PTS 6 Derby
16.10.05	Dave Hinds W PTS 6 Peterborough
18.11.05	Lloyd Otte DREW 4 Dagenham
12.12.05	Dai Davies W PTS 6 Peterborough
03.03.06	Jamie McKeever L PTS 6 Hartlepool
15.09.06	Billy Corcoran L CO 3 Muswell Hill
10.11.06	Sean Hughes W PTS 6 Hartlepool
03.12.06	Ryan Barrett L PTS 6 Bethnal Green
16.02.07	Dai Davies L PTS 8 Merthyr Tydfil
20.04.07	Paul Truscott L PTS 4 Dudley

Career: 16 contests, won 6, drew 1, lost 9.

Graham Earl

Luton. *Born* Luton, 26 August, 1978
Lightweight. Former Undefeated British &
Commonwealth Lightweight Champion.
Former Undefeated Southern Area
Lightweight Champion. *Ht* 5'5¾"
Manager F. Warren

02.09.97	Mark O'Callaghan W RSC 2 Southwark
06.12.97	Mark McGowan W PTS 4 Wembley
11.04.98	Danny Lutaaya W RSC 2 Southwark
23.05.98	David Kirk W PTS 4 Bethnal Green
12.09.98	Brian Coleman W PTS 4 Bethnal Green
10.12.98	Marc Smith W RSC 1 Barking
16.01.99	Lee Williamson W RSC 4 Bethnal Green
08.05.99	Benny Jones W PTS 6 Bethnal Green
15.07.99	Simon Chambers W CO 6 Peterborough
04.03.00	Ivo Golakov W RSC 1 Peterborough
29.04.00	Marco Fattore W PTS 6 Wembley
21.10.00	Lee Williamson W RSC 3 Wembley
10.03.01	Brian Gentry W RSC 8 Bethnal Green *(Vacant Southern Area Lightweight Title)*
22.09.01	Liam Maltby W CO 1 Bethnal Green *(Southern Area Lightweight Title Defence)*
15.12.01	Mark Winters W PTS 10 Wembley *(Elim. British Lightweight Title)*
12.10.02	Chill John W PTS 10 Bethnal Green *(Southern Area Lightweight Title Defence)*
15.02.03	Steve Murray W RSC 2 Wembley *(Southern Area Lightweight Title Defence. Final Elim. British Lightweight Title)*
24.05.03	Nikolai Eremeev W PTS 8 Bethnal Green

Graham Earl   Philip Sharkey

17.07.03	Bobby Vanzie W PTS 12 Dagenham *(British Lightweight Title Challenge)*
11.10.03	Jon Honney W PTS 8 Portsmouth
05.06.04	Bobby Vanzie W PTS 12 Bethnal Green *(Vacant British Lightweight Title)*
30.07.04	Steve Murray W RSC 6 Bethnal Green *(British Lightweight Title Defence)*
25.02.05	Ricky Burns L PTS 8 Wembley
19.06.05	Kevin Bennett W RSC 9 Bethnal Green *(Commonwealth Lightweight Title Challenge. British Lightweight Title Defence)*
27.01.06	Yuri Romanov W PTS 12 Dagenham
28.10.06	Angel Hugo Ramirez W PTS 12 Bethnal Green *(Vacant WBU Lightweight Title)*
17.02.07	Michael Katsidis L RTD 5 Wembley *(Vacant Interim WBO Lightweight Title)*

Career: 27 contests, won 25, lost 2.

Howard Eastman

Battersea. *Born* New Amsterdam, Guyana,
8 December, 1970
British & Commonwealth Middleweight
Champion. Former Undefeated European,
IBO Inter-Continental, WBA Inter-
Continental & Southern Area Middleweight
Champion. *Ht* 5'11"
Manager Self

06.03.94	John Rice W RSC 1 Southwark
14.03.94	Andy Peach W PTS 6 Mayfair
22.03.94	Steve Phillips W RSC 5 Bethnal Green
17.10.94	Barry Thorogood W RSC 6 Mayfair
06.03.95	Marty Duke W RSC 1 Mayfair
20.04.95	Stuart Dunn W RSC 2 Mayfair
23.06.95	Peter Vosper W RSC 1 Bethnal Green
16.10.95	Carlo Colarusso W RSC 1 Mayfair
29.11.95	Brendan Ryan W RSC 2 Bethnal Green
31.01.96	Paul Wesley W RSC 1 Birmingham
13.03.96	Steve Goodwin W RSC 5 Wembley
29.04.96	John Duckworth W RSC 5 Mayfair
11.12.96	Sven Hamer W RSC 10 Southwark *(Vacant Southern Area Middleweight Title)*
18.02.97	John Duckworth W CO 7 Cheshunt
25.03.97	Rachid Serdjane W RSC 7 Lewisham
14.02.98	Vitali Kopitko W PTS 8 Southwark
28.03.98	Terry Morrill W RTD 4 Hull
23.05.98	Darren Ashton W RSC 4 Bethnal Green
30.11.98	Steve Foster W RSC 7 Manchester *(Vacant British Middleweight Title)*
04.02.99	Jason Barker W RSC 6 Lewisham
06.03.99	Jon Penn W RSC 3 Southwark *(Vacant IBO Inter-Continental S. Middleweight Title)*
22.05.99	Roman Babaev W RSC 6 Belfast *(WBA Inter-Continental Middleweight Title Challenge)*
10.07.99	Teimouraz Kikelidze W RSC 6 Southwark *(WBA Inter-Continental Middleweight Title Defence)*
13.09.99	Derek Wormald W RSC 3 Bethnal Green *(British Middleweight Title Defence)*
13.11.99	Mike Algoet W RSC 8 Hull *(WBA Inter-Continental Middleweight Title Defence)*
18.01.00	Ojay Abrahams W RSC 2 Mansfield
04.03.00	Viktor Fesetchko W RTD 4 Peterborough

29.04.00	Anthony Ivory W RTD 6 Wembley
25.07.00	Ahmet Dottouev W RTD 5 Southwark *(WBA Inter-Continental Middleweight Title Defence)*
16.09.00	Sam Soliman W PTS 12 Bethnal Green *(Commonwealth Middleweight Title Challenge)*
05.02.01	Mark Baker W RTD 5 Hull
10.04.01	Robert McCracken W RSC 10 Wembley *(British & Commonwealth Middleweight Title Defences. Vacant European Middleweight Title)*
17.11.01	William Joppy L PTS 12 Las Vegas, Nevada, USA *(Vacant WBA Interim Middleweight Title)*
25.10.02	Chardan Ansoula W RSC 1 Bethnal Green
21.12.02	Hussain Osman W RTD 4 Dagenham
28.01.03	Christophe Tendil W RTD 4 Nottingham *(Vacant European Middleweight Title)*
05.03.03	Gary Beardsley W RSC 2 Bethnal Green
16.04.03	Scott Dann W RSC 3 Nottingham *(British, Commonwealth & European Middleweight Title Defences)*
25.07.03	Hacine Cherifi W RTD 8 Norwich *(European Middleweight Title Defence)*
30.01.04	Sergei Tatevosyan W PTS 12 Dagenham *(European Middleweight Title Defence)*
24.09.04	Jerry Elliott W PTS 10 Nottingham
19.02.05	Bernard Hopkins L PTS 12 Los Angeles, California, USA *(WBC, WBA, IBF & WBO Middleweight Title Challenges)*
16.07.05	Arthur Abraham L PTS 12 Nuremburg, Germany *(WBA Inter-Continental Middleweight Title Challenge)*
24.03.06	Edison Miranda L RSC 7 Hollywood, Florida, USA *(Final Elim. IBF Middleweight Title)*
15.12.06	Richard Williams W CO 12 Bethnal Green *(Vacant British Middleweight Title)*
20.04.07	Evans Ashira W PTS 12 Dudley *(Vacant Commonwealth Middleweight Title)*

Career: 46 contests, won 42, lost 4.

Tommy Eastwood

Epsom. *Born* Epsom, 16 May, 1979
Southern Area Cruiserweight Champion.
Ht 5'11½"
Manager Self

09.09.01	Tony Booth W PTS 4 Southwark
16.12.01	Paul Bonson W PTS 4 Southwark
12.02.02	Adam Cale W PTS 4 Bethnal Green
24.03.02	Dave Clarke W PTS 6 Streatham
23.06.02	Brodie Pearmaine W PTS 4 Southwark
24.01.03	Lee Swaby L PTS 6 Sheffield
26.11.03	Brian Gascoigne W RSC 2 Mayfair
10.09.04	Ovill McKenzie W PTS 8 Wembley
06.10.05	Tony Booth W PTS 4 Longford
17.11.05	Csaba Andras W PTS 4 Piccadilly
25.02.06	Dean Francis L PTS 10 Bristol *(Vacant English Cruiserweight Title)*
28.05.06	Paul King W PTS 4 Longford
23.07.06	Tony Booth W PTS 4 Dagenham

06.10.06 Junior MacDonald W RSC 2 Bethnal Green
(Vacant Southern Area Cruiserweight Title)
02.12.06 Hastings Rasani W PTS 6 Longford
02.03.07 Robert Norton L RSC 8 Coventry
(Vacant English Cruiserweight Title)
Career: 16 contests, won 13, lost 3.

Steve Ede
Gosport. *Born* Southampton, 22 June,1976
Middleweight. Former Undefeated British Masters Middleweight Champion. *Ht* 5'10"
Manager Self
06.02.05 Jed Tytler W RSC 4 Southampton
26.06.05 Mark Wall W PTS 6 Southampton
25.09.05 Rocky Muscus W PTS 6 Southampton
16.12.05 Lee Hodgson W PTS 4 Bracknell
05.03.06 Anthony Young W RSC 3 Southampton
26.05.06 Jake Guntert W RSC 2 Bethnal Green
24.09.06 Lee Hodgson W RSC 3 Southampton
25.02.07 Conroy McIntosh W PTS 10 Southampton
(Vacant British Masters Middleweight Title)
Career: 8 contests, won 8.

Matthew Edmonds
Newport. *Born* Newport, 12 February, 1984
International Masters Bantamweight Champion. *Ht* 5'6"
Manager C. Sanigar
15.09.06 Delroy Spencer W PTS 4 Newport
07.10.06 Colin Moffett W PTS 4 Belfast
10.11.06 Mo Khaled W PTS 6 Newport
03.03.07 Sumaila Badu W PTS 6 Newport
16.06.07 Jamil Hussain W RTD 3 Newport
(Vacant International Masters Bantamweight Title)
Career: 5 contests, won 5.

Chris Edwards
Stoke. *Born* Stoke, 6 May, 1976
English Flyweight Champion.
Former Undefeated British Masters S.Bantamweight Champion. *Ht* 5'3"
Manager M. Carney
03.04.98 Chris Thomas W RSC 2 Ebbw Vale
21.09.98 Russell Laing L PTS 6 Glasgow
26.02.99 Delroy Spencer L PTS 6 West Bromwich
17.04.99 Stevie Quinn L RSC 4 Dublin
19.10.99 Lee Georgiou L RSC 2 Bethnal Green
03.12.99 Daniel Ring L PTS 4 Peterborough
15.05.00 Paddy Folan L PTS 6 Bradford
07.10.00 Andy Roberts W PTS 4 Doncaster
27.11.00 Levi Pattison W PTS 4 Birmingham
16.03.01 Jamie Evans L PTS 6 Portsmouth
03.06.01 Darren Taylor DREW 6 Hanley
08.10.01 Levi Pattison L PTS 4 Barnsley
06.12.01 Neil Read W PTS 8 Stoke
10.10.02 Neil Read W PTS 6 Stoke
13.06.03 Lee Haskins L PTS 6 Bristol
23.04.04 Delroy Spencer DREW 6 Leicester
26.09.04 Neil Read W RSC 2 Stoke
(Vacant British Masters S.Bantamweight Title)
28.10.04 Colin Moffett L PTS 4 Belfast
12.11.05 Delroy Spencer W PTS 4 Stoke
18.02.06 Gary Ford L PTS 6 Stoke
10.03.06 Andrea Sarritzu L CO 4 Bergamo, Italy

06.05.06 Gary Sheil W PTS 6 Stoke
30.09.06 Usman Ahmed W PTS 6 Stoke
24.11.06 Dale Robinson W RSC 8 Stoke
(Vacant English Flyweight Title)
13.04.07 Dale Robinson DREW 12 Altrincham
(Vacant British & Commonwealth Flyweight Titles)
Career: 25 contests, won 10, drew 3, lost 12.

Lee Edwards
Sheffield. *Born* Huntingdon, 25 May, 1984
Middleweight. *Ht* 5'11"
Manager G. Rhodes
08.05.05 Sergey Haritonov W PTS 6 Sheffield
24.07.05 Lee Williamson W PTS 6 Sheffield
30.10.05 Joe Mitchell L RSC 2 Sheffield
17.02.06 Malik Khan W RSC 6 Sheffield
20.04.07 Howard Clarke W PTS 6 Sheffield
Career: 5 contests, won 4, lost 1.

Sujad Elahi
Bradford. *Born* Bradford, 13 October, 1982
L.Welterweight. *Ht* 5'11"
Manager G. Rhodes
23.09.04 David Pinkney L PTS 6 Gateshead
09.12.04 Gary Connolly W RSC 2 Sunderland
20.02.05 Scott Conway DREW 6 Sheffield
08.05.05 Lance Verallo W PTS 6 Sheffield
25.06.05 Andy Cosnett W CO 2 Wakefield
13.04.06 Barry Downes L RSC 3 Leeds
28.10.06 Tom Hogan W RSC 2 Sheffield
Career: 7 contests, won 4, drew 1, lost 2.

Wayne Elcock
Birmingham. *Born* Birmingham, 12 February, 1974
English Middleweight Champion. Former WBU Middleweight Champion. *Ht* 5'9½"
Manager Self
02.12.99 William Webster W PTS 6 Peterborough
04.03.00 Sonny Pollard W RSC 3 Peterborough
07.07.01 Darren Rhodes W PTS 4 Manchester
09.10.01 Valery Odin W PTS 4 Cardiff
02.03.02 Charles Shodiya W RSC 1 Bethnal Green
20.04.02 Howard Clarke W PTS 4 Cardiff
01.06.02 Jason Collins W RSC 2 Manchester
17.08.02 Ojay Abrahams W PTS 4 Cardiff
23.11.02 Jason Collins W RSC 1 Derby
15.02.03 Yuri Tsarenko W PTS 10 Wembley
05.04.03 Anthony Farnell W PTS 12 Manchester
(WBU Middleweight Title Challenge)
29.11.03 Lawrence Murphy L CO 1 Renfrew
(WBU Middleweight Title Defence)
07.02.04 Farai Musiiwa W PTS 6 Bethnal Green
05.06.04 Michael Monaghan W PTS 4 Bethnal Green
07.04.05 Darren Rhodes W CO 1 Birmingham
16.09.05 Scott Dann L PTS 12 Plymouth
(British Middleweight Title Challenge)
06.05.06 Lawrence Murphy W RSC 5 Birmingham
(Elim. British Middleweight Title)
08.09.06 Vince Baldassara W CO 6 Birmingham
(Vacant WBF Inter-Continental Middleweight Title)
01.12.06 Steven Bendall W RSC 8 Birmingham
(English Middleweight Title Challenge)
Career: 19 contests, won 17, lost 2.

Matthew Ellis
Blackpool. *Born* Oldham, 12 April, 1974
Heavyweight. *Ht* 5'11¾"
Manager Self
03.02.96 Laurent Rouze W CO 1 Liverpool
01.04.96 Ladislav Husarik W RTD 4 Den Bosch, Holland
06.09.96 Darren Fearn W RSC 6 Liverpool
26.10.96 Daniel Beun W RSC 1 Liverpool
01.03.97 Yuri Yelistratov L RSC 5 Liverpool
20.07.97 Ricardo Phillips W PTS 4 Indio, California, USA
26.09.97 Albert Call DREW 6 Liverpool
12.03.98 Yuri Yelistratov W RSC 1 Liverpool
21.07.98 Chris Woollas W RSC 5 Widnes
24.10.98 Peter Hrivnak W RSC 1 Liverpool
12.12.98 Harry Senior W PTS 8 Southwark
27.02.99 Michael Murray W PTS 8 Bethnal Green
15.05.99 Biko Botowamungu W PTS 8 Blackpool
27.05.00 Alex Vasiliev W CO 4 Southwark
16.09.00 Dimitri Bakhtov W PTS 4 Bethnal Green
18.11.00 Chris Woollas W PTS 4 Dagenham
17.02.01 Alexei Osokin W PTS 8 Bethnal Green
12.07.01 Ronnie Smith W PTS 6 Houston, Texas, USA
22.09.01 Colin Abelson W CO 1 Bethnal Green
02.03.02 Dennis Bakhtov L RSC 5 Bethnal Green
(WBC International Heavyweight Title Challenge)
29.03.03 Derek McCafferty W PTS 4 Wembley
31.05.03 Audley Harrison L RSC 2 Bethnal Green
27.10.03 Tony Moran L RSC 4 Glasgow
26.10.06 Chris Woollas W PTS 4 Dudley
Career: 24 contests, won 19, drew 1, lost 4.

Stuart Elwell
Darlaston. *Born* Walsall, 14 December, 1977
L.Middleweight. Former Undefeated Midlands Area Welterweight Champion. *Ht* 5'9"
Manager E. Johnson
06.11.00 Ernie Smith W PTS 6 Wolverhampton
28.01.01 Arv Mittoo W PTS 6 Wolverhampton
01.04.01 Richard Inquieti W PTS 6 Wolverhampton
06.10.05 Ernie Smith W PTS 6 Dudley
25.11.05 Ben Hudson W PTS 4 Walsall
10.03.06 David Kirk W PTS 10 Walsall
(Vacant Midlands Area Welterweight Title)
18.05.06 Peter Dunn W PTS 6 Walsall
23.06.06 Franny Jones W RSC 1 Blackpool
10.11.06 Ben Hudson W PTS 4 Telford
23.03.07 John O'Donnell L PTS 10 Nottingham
(Vacant English Welterweight Title)
Career: 10 contests, won 9, lost 1.

Johnny Enigma (Nelson)
Bolton. *Born* Farnworth, 12 July, 1973
Middleweight. *Ht* 5'11"
Manager S. Wood/A. Penarski
06.05.07 Paul Royston W PTS 6 Altrincham
24.06.07 Tony Randell L RSC 5 Wigan
Career: 2 contests, won 1, lost 1.

Andrew Facey

Sheffield. *Born* Wolverhampton, 20 May, 1972
English L.Middleweight Champion. Former Undefeated Central Area Middleweight Champion. *Ht* 6'0"
Manager D. Ingle

06.12.99	Peter McCormack W CO 2 Birmingham	
09.06.00	Matthew Pepper W RSC 1 Hull	
04.11.00	Earl Ling W PTS 6 Derby	
11.12.00	Gary Jones W PTS 6 Cleethorpes	
10.02.01	Louis Swales W RSC 3 Widnes	
17.03.01	Darren Rhodes L PTS 4 Manchester	
24.03.01	Matthew Tait W PTS 4 Chigwell	
16.06.01	Earl Ling DREW 6 Derby	
09.12.01	Michael Pinnock W PTS 6 Shaw	
02.03.02	Darren Rhodes W RSC 6 Wakefield	
	(Vacant Central Area Middleweight Title)	
20.04.02	Darren Ashton W PTS 6 Derby	
13.04.02	Leigh Wicks W PTS 6 Norwich	
03.08.02	Damon Hague L CO 5 Derby	
	(Final Elim. WBF Middleweight Title)	
25.10.02	William Webster W PTS 4 Cotgrave	
16.04.03	Gilbert Eastman W RSC 3 Nottingham	
06.11.03	Matthew Macklin W PTS 10 Dagenham	
	(Vacant English L.Middleweight Title)	
22.11.03	Jamie Moore L RSC 7 Belfast	
	(British & Commonwealth L.Middleweight Title Challenges)	
04.06.04	Howard Clarke W PTS 6 Hull	
17.09.04	Jason Collins W PTS 4 Sheffield	
03.09.05	Jason Collins W PTS 4 Norwich	
29.10.05	Howard Clarke W PTS 6 Aberdeen	
27.05.06	Ojay Abrahams W PTS 6 Aberdeen	
18.11.06	Bradley Pryce L PTS 12 Newport	
	(Commonwealth L.Middleweight Title Challenge)	
26.01.07	Gary Woolcombe W RSC 5 Dagenham	
	(English L.Middleweight Title Defence)	

Career: 24 contests, won 19, drew 1, lost 4.

Shaun Farmer

Hartlepool. *Born* Hull, 7 March, 1977
L.Middleweight. *Ht* 6'0"
Manager T. Conroy

05.10.06	Lee Noble W PTS 6 Sunderland	
17.12.06	Craig Bunn L PTS 6 Bolton	
25.02.07	Alex Matvienko L PTS 6 Manchester	
11.05.07	Matt Scriven W PTS 6 Sunderland	
25.05.07	Paddy Pollock L PTS 6 Glasgow	
24.06.07	Jon Foster W PTS 6 Sunderland	

Career: 6 contests, won 3, lost 3.

Femi Fehintola

Bradford. *Born* Bradford, 1 July, 1982
Lightweight. *Ht* 5'7"
Manager D. Hobson

26.09.03	John-Paul Ryan W PTS 6 Reading	
07.11.03	Pete Buckley W PTS 6 Sheffield	

10.12.03	Jason Nesbitt W PTS 6 Sheffield	
06.02.04	Jason Nesbitt W PTS 6 Sheffield	
20.04.04	Kristian Laight W PTS 6 Sheffield	
17.06.04	Anthony Hanna W PTS 6 Sheffield	
24.10.04	John-Paul Ryan W PTS 6 Sheffield	
10.12.04	Philippe Meheust W PTS 6 Sheffield	
04.03.05	Daniel Thorpe W PTS 6 Rotherham	
24.07.05	Jason Nesbitt W PTS 6 Sheffield	
14.10.05	Rakhim Mingaleev W PTS 8 Huddersfield	
16.12.05	Frederic Gosset W PTS 8 Bracknell	
18.03.06	Ivo Golakov W RSC 2 Monte Carlo, Monaco	
13.05.06	Nikita Lukin W PTS 8 Sheffield	
03.11.06	Carl Johanneson L RSC 6 Barnsley	
	(British S.Featherweight Title Challenge)	
27.05.07	Carl Allen W PTS 6 Bradford	
23.06.07	Barbaro Zepeda W PTS 4 Las Vegas, Nevada, USA	

Career: 17 contests, won 16, lost 1.

Dave Ferguson

Wallsend. *Born* North Shields, 28 February, 1976
Heavyweight. *Ht.* 6'4"
Manager T. Conroy

16.02.07	David Ingleby W PTS 4 Sunderland	
24.06.07	David Ingleby W PTS 4 Sunderland	

Career: 2 contests, won 2.

Andrew Ferrans

New Cumnock. *Born* Irvine, 4 February, 1981
Welterweight. Former Undefeated British Masters S.Featherweight Champion. *Ht* 5'9"
Manager T. Gilmour

19.02.00	Chris Lyons W PTS 6 Prestwick	
03.03.00	Gary Groves W RSC 1 Irvine	
20.03.00	John Barnes DREW 6 Glasgow	
06.06.00	Duncan Armstrong W PTS 6 Motherwell	
18.09.00	Steve Brook W PTS 6 Glasgow	
20.11.00	Duncan Armstrong W PTS 6 Glasgow	
23.02.01	Dave Cotterill L RSC 2 Irvine	
30.04.01	Dave Cotterill W RSC 1 Glasgow	
04.06.01	Jason Nesbitt W RSC 2 Glasgow	
17.09.01	Gary Flear W PTS 8 Glasgow	
10.12.01	Jamie McKeever L PTS 6 Liverpool	
21.01.02	Joel Viney W PTS 8 Glasgow	
01.03.02	Peter Allen W PTS 8 Irvine	
13.04.02	Tony Mulholland L PTS 4 Liverpool	
11.05.02	Marc Callaghan L PTS 6 Dagenham	
23.09.02	Greg Edwards W RTD 4 Glasgow	
08.10.02	Peter Allen W PTS 8 Glasgow	
18.11.02	Joel Viney W PTS 6 Glasgow	
30.11.02	Colin Toohey L PTS 6 Liverpool	
28.02.03	Simon Chambers W RSC 7 Irvine	
28.04.03	Craig Spacie L PTS 6 Nottingham	
26.07.03	Baz Carey DREW 4 Plymouth	
01.11.03	Anthony Hanna W PTS 4 Glasgow	
19.01.04	Dariusz Snarski W PTS 6 Glasgow	
15.03.04	Baz Carey W PTS 10 Glasgow	
	(Vacant British Masters S.Featherweight Title)	
08.05.04	Carl Johanneson L RSC 6 Bristol	
	(WBF S.Featherweight Title Challenge)	
26.02.05	Stephen Chinnock W RTD 5 Burton	
24.10.05	Kristian Laight W PTS 8 Glasgow	
23.02.06	Carl Johanneson L RSC 2 Leeds	

	(Final Elim. British S.Featherweight Title)	
06.05.06	Sergii Tertii W PTS 6 Irvine	
13.10.06	Frederic Gosset W PTS 6 Irvine	
19.02.07	Billy Smith W PTS 6 Glasgow	
05.06.07	Jay Morris W RSC 3 Glasgow	

Career: 33 contests, won 23, drew 2, lost 8.

John Fewkes

Sheffield. *Born* Sheffield, 16 July, 1985
Central Area L.Welterweight Champion. *Ht* 5'8"
Manager T. Gilmour/G. Rhodes

17.09.04	Mark Dane W RSC 2 Sheffield	
24.10.04	Lea Handley W PTS 6 Sheffield	
10.12.04	Jason Nesbitt W PTS 6 Sheffield	
04.03.05	Jason Nesbitt W PTS 6 Rotherham	
08.05.05	Chris Long W PTS 8 Sheffield	
25.06.05	Billy Smith W PTS 6 Wakefield	
24.07.05	Karl Taylor W PTS 6 Sheffield	
09.09.05	Rakhim Mingaleev W PTS 4 Sheffield	
30.10.05	Tony Montana W PTS 6 Sheffield	
17.02.06	Tony Montana W PTS 10 Sheffield	
	(Central Area L.Welterweight Title Challenge)	
21.07.06	Kristian Laight W RSC 5 Altrincham	
29.09.06	Thomas Mazurkiewicz W PTS 4 Manchester	
03.11.06	Scott Haywood W PTS 8 Barnsley	
09.02.07	Craig Watson W PTS 8 Leeds	

Career: 14 contests, won 14.

(John Joseph) Jonjo Finnegan

Burton on Trent. *Born* Burton on Trent, 25 April, 1980
S.Middleweight. *Ht* 6'1"
Manager E. Johnson

08.07.04	Paul Billington W PTS 6 Birmingham	
25.11.04	Nick Okoth DREW 6 Birmingham	
26.02.05	Arv Mittoo W PTS 4 Birmingham	
07.04.05	Peter Dunn W PTS 6 Birmingham	
24.04.05	Omid Bourzo L PTS 6 Derby	
30.09.05	Robert Burton DREW 4 Burton	
25.11.05	Paul Billington W PTS 6 Walsall	
28.01.06	Dave Pearson W PTS 4 Nottingham	
25.03.06	Dave Pearson W PTS 8 Burton	
13.05.06	Ernie Smith W PTS 6 Sutton in Ashfield	
01.06.06	Mark Phillips W PTS 4 Birmingham	
16.09.06	Jamie Ambler W PTS 6 Burton	
30.09.06	Dave Pearson W PTS 6 Middlesbrough	
24.11.06	Dean Walker DREW 4 Nottingham	
03.03.07	Neil Tidman L PTS 10 Burton	
	(Vacant Midlands Area S.Middleweight Title)	

Career: 15 contests, won 10, drew 3, lost 2.

Simon Fleck

Leicester. *Born* Leicester, 26 March, 1979
Middleweight. *Ht* 6'0"
Manager M. Shinfield

22.10.05	Simone Lucas W RSC 5 Mansfield	
08.12.05	Tommy Jones W PTS 6 Derby	
02.03.06	Mark Thompson L CO 3 Blackpool	
24.04.06	Karl Taylor W PTS 6 Cleethorpes	
14.12.06	Peter Dunn W PTS 6 Leicester	
14.05.07	Rocky Muscas W PTS 6 Cleethorpes	

Career: 6 contests, won 5, lost 1.

Brett Flournoy

Bromborough. Born Birkenhead, 7 August, 1979
L.Middleweight. *Ht* 5'10"
Manager D. Waul/F. Maloney

21.07.06	Tommy Jones W RSC 1 Altrincham	
29.09.06	Gatis Skuja W PTS 4 Manchester	
09.02.07	Ernie Smith W PTS 4 Leeds	
13.04.07	Alexander Spitjo W PTS 4 Altrincham	

Career: 4 contests, won 4.

Brett Flournoy   Les Clark

Thomas Flynn

Darwin. Born Blackburn, 23 February, 1977
S.Middleweight. *Ht* 5'11½"
Manager T. Schofield

22.06.06	Jak Hibbert L RSC 3 Sheffield
06.10.06	Muhsen Nasser L PTS 4 Mexborough
26.10.06	James McKinley L PTS 4 Wolverhampton
15.04.07	Paul Royston L RSC 3 Barnsley

Career: 4 contests, lost 4.

Jon Foster

Oldham. Born Nottingham, 18 October, 1979
Middleweight. *Ht* 6'1"
Manager M. Scriven

31.10.97	David Thompson W RSC 4 Ilkeston
26.11.97	Billy McDougall W RSC 2 Stoke
20.03.98	Phil Molyneux W PTS 6 Ilkeston
03.04.98	Harry Butler W PTS 6 Ebbw Vale
23.04.98	Hughie Davey L PTS 6 Newcastle
11.09.98	Brian Dunn W RTD 3 Cleethorpes
07.12.98	Darren Christie W RSC 6 Cleethorpes
06.06.99	Jason Collins DREW 6 Nottingham
20.09.99	Joe Townsley L PTS 6 Glasgow
11.12.99	Jacek Bielski L PTS 6 Merthyr
12.02.00	Zoltan Sarossy L RSC 1 Sheffield
06.06.00	James Docherty L PTS 6 Motherwell
24.09.00	Lee Murtagh L PTS 6 Shaw
25.04.05	Jed Tytler L RSC 2 Cleethorpes
28.01.06	Matthew Hall L RSC 3 Nottingham
04.03.06	Nathan Cleverly L PTS 4 Manchester
13.04.06	Brendan Halford L PTS 6 Leeds
14.05.06	Adie Whitmore L RSC 6 Derby
08.09.06	Leigh Hallet L PTS 6 Birmingham
29.09.06	Alex Matvienko L RTD 3 Manchester
04.11.06	Davey Jones W DIS 6 Mansfield
17.11.06	Sam Horton L PTS 6 Brierley Hill

22.02.07	Franny Jones L CO 3 Leeds
23.03.07	Adie Whitmore L RTD 4 Nottingham
29.04.07	James McKinley L PTS 6 Birmingham
06.05.07	Craig Denton L PTS 6 Darlington
24.06.07	Shaun Farmer L PTS 6 Sunderland

Career: 27 contests, won 7, drew 1, lost 19.

Steve Foster

Salford. Born Salford, 16 September, 1980
Featherweight. Former WBU Featherweight Champion. Former Undefeated English Featherweight Champion. *Ht* 5'6"
Manager S.Foster/S.Wood/F.Warren

15.09.01	Andy Greenaway W PTS 4 Manchester
27.10.01	Gareth Wiltshaw W PTS 4 Manchester
02.03.02	Andy Greenaway W RSC 1 Bethnal Green
04.05.02	Gareth Wiltshaw W PTS 4 Bethnal Green
08.07.02	Ian Turner W RSC 1 Mayfair
20.07.02	Paddy Folan W CO 1 Bethnal Green
28.09.02	Jason White W RSC 3 Manchester
14.12.02	Sean Green W RSC 3 Newcastle
22.03.03	David McIntyre W PTS 4 Renfrew
24.05.03	Henry Janes W PTS 6 Bethnal Green
12.07.03	David McIntyre W RTD 3 Renfrew
18.09.03	Alexander Abramenko W RTD 4 Dagenham
06.11.03	Vladimir Borov W RSC 8 Dagenham
13.12.03	Steve Gethin W RTD 3 Manchester
26.02.04	Sean Hughes W RSC 6 Widnes
	(Vacant English Featherweight Title)
30.07.04	Jean-Marie Codet W PTS 8 Bethnal Green
01.10.04	Gary Thornhill W RSC 9 Manchester
	(English Featherweight Title Defence)
11.02.05	Livinson Ruiz W CO 10 Manchester
	(Vacant WBU Featherweight Title)
16.07.05	Jim Betts W RTD 5 Bolton
10.12.05	Buster Dennis DREW 8 Canning Town
01.04.06	John Simpson W PTS 12 Bethnal Green
	(WBU Featherweight Title Defence)
08.07.06	Frederic Bonifai W RSC 2 Cardiff
14.10.06	Derry Matthews L PTS 12 Manchester
	(WBU Featherweight Title Defence)

Career: 23 contests, won 21, drew 1, lost 1.

Dean Francis

Basingstoke. Born Basingstoke, 23 January, 1974
Commonwealth & IBO Inter-Continental L.Heavyweight Champion. Former Undefeated English Cruiserweight Champion. Former Undefeated British, European & WBO Inter-Continental S.Middleweight Champion. *Ht* 5'10½"
Manager Self

28.05.94	Darren Littlewood W PTS 4 Queensway
17.06.94	Martin Jolley W PTS 6 Plymouth
21.07.94	Horace Fleary W RSC 4 Tooting
02.09.94	Steve Osborne W RTD 4 Spitalfields
27.10.94	Tony Booth W CO 1 Bayswater
22.11.94	Darron Griffiths W RTD 1 Bristol
30.03.95	Paul Murray W RSC 2 Bethnal Green
25.05.95	Hunter Clay W RSC 8 Reading
16.06.95	Paul Murray W RTD 3 Southwark
20.10.95	Zafarou Ballogou L RSC 10 Ipswich
	(WBC International S. Middleweight Title Challenge)

16.12.95	Kid Milo W RSC 3 Cardiff
13.02.96	Mike Bonislawski W RSC 2 Bethnal Green
26.04.96	Neil Simpson W RSC 3 Cardiff
08.06.96	John Marceta W RSC 8 Newcastle
14.09.96	Larry Kenny W RSC 2 Sheffield
19.10.96	Rolando Torres W RSC 4 Bristol
	(Vacant WBO Inter-Continental S. Middleweight Title)
14.03.97	Cornelius Carr W RSC 7 Reading
	(WBO Inter-Continental S. Middleweight Title Defence)
15.05.97	Kit Munro W RSC 2 Reading
	(WBO Inter-Continental S. Middleweight Title Defence)
19.07.97	David Starie W RSC 6 Wembley
	(British S. Middleweight Title Challenge)
19.12.97	Frederic Seillier W RSC 9 Millwall
	(Vacant European S. Middleweight Title)
07.03.98	Mark Baker W RSC 12 Reading
	(British & WBO Inter-Continental S. Middleweight Title Defences)
22.08.98	Xolani Ngemntu W CO 2 Hammanskraal, South Africa
	(WBO Inter-Continental S. Middleweight Title Defence)
31.10.98	Undra White L RTD 4 Basingstoke
	(Vacant IBO Inter-Continental S. Middleweight Title)
20.04.02	Mondili Mbonambi W PTS 8 Wembley
29.03.03	Matthew Barney L PTS 12 Wembley
	(Vacant British S. Middleweight Title)
09.07.05	Paul Bonson W PTS 6 Bristol
12.11.05	Hastings Rasani W RSC 6 Bristol
25.02.06	Tommy Eastwood W PTS 10 Bristol
	(Vacant English Cruiserweight Title)
07.10.06	Hastings Rasani W CO 2 Weston super Mare
09.02.07	Ovill McKenzie W RSC 1 Bristol
	(Commonwealth L.Heavyweight Title Challenge)
02.06.07	Ayitey Powers W CO 9 Bristol
	(Vacant IBO Inter-Continental L.Heavyweight Title)

Career: 31 contests, won 28, lost 3.

Mark Franks (Whitemore)

Wakefield. Born Hannover, Germany, 29 September, 1975
L. Middleweight. *Ht* 5'7¾"
Manager Self

06.12.04	Tommy Marshall L PTS 6 Leeds
18.04.05	Kaye Rehman DREW 6 Bradford
30.04.05	Rob MacDonald W RSC 6 Wigan
01.06.05	Geraint Harvey W PTS 6 Leeds
21.09.05	Malik Khan W RSC 1 Bradford
05.12.05	Simone Lucas W RSC 1 Leeds
20.03.06	Omar Gumati L RTD 4 Leeds
24.09.06	Danny Goode L RSC 3 Southampton
07.12.06	Gavin Pearson L RSC 6 Bradford

Career: 9 contests, won 4, drew 1, lost 4.

Carl Froch

Nottingham. Born Nottingham, 2 July, 1977
British S.Middleweight Champion. Former Undefeated Commonwealth & English S.Middleweight Champion. *Ht* 6'4"
Manager Self

16.03.02	Michael Pinnock W RSC 4 Bethnal Green

10.05.02 Ojay Abrahams W RSC 1 Bethnal Green
23.08.02 Darren Covill W RSC 1 Bethnal Green
25.10.02 Paul Bonson W PTS 6 Bethnal Green
21.12.02 Mike Duffield W RSC 1 Dagenham
28.01.03 Valery Odin W RSC 6 Nottingham
05.03.03 Varuzhan Davtyan W RSC 5 Bethnal Green
16.04.03 Michael Monaghan W RSC 3 Nottingham
04.10.03 Vage Kocharyan W PTS 8 Muswell Hill
28.11.03 Alan Page W RSC 7 Derby
(*Vacant English S.Middleweight Title. Elim. British S.Middleweight Title*)
30.01.04 Dmitri Adamovich W RSC 2 Dagenham

12.03.04 Charles Adamu W PTS 12 Nottingham
(*Commonwealth S.Middleweight Title Challenge*)
02.06.04 Mark Woolnough W RSC 11 Nottingham
(*Commonwealth S.Middleweight Title Defence*)
24.09.04 Damon Hague W RSC 1 Nottingham
(*Vacant British S.Middleweight Title. Commonwealth S.Middleweight Title Defence*)
21.04.05 Henry Porras W RSC 8 Hollywood, California, USA
09.07.05 Matthew Barney W PTS 12 Nottingham
(*British & Commonwealth S.Middleweight Title Defences*)

02.12.05 Ruben Groenewald W RSC 5 Nottingham
(*Commonwealth S.Middleweight Title Defence*)
17.02.06 Dale Westerman W RSC 9 Bethnal Green
(*Commonwealth S.Middleweight Title Defence*)
26.05.06 Brian Magee W RSC 11 Bethnal Green
(*British & Commonwealth S.Middleweight Title Defences*)
24.11.06 Tony Dodson W CO 3 Nottingham
(*British & Commonwealth S.Middleweight Title Defences*)
23.03.07 Sergei Tatevosyan W RSC 2 Nottingham
Career: 21 contests, won 21.

Carl Froch

Les Clark

G

Matt Galer

Burton. *Born* Burton, 15 December, 1973
L.Middleweight. Former Midlands Area
L.Middleweight Champion. *Ht* 5'8"
Manager E. Johnson

30.09.97	Martin Cavey W CO 1 Edgbaston	
18.11.97	Chris Pollock W PTS 6 Mansfield	
16.03.98	Mike Duffield W PTS 6 Nottingham	
14.05.98	Freddie Yemofio W RSC 4 Acton	
14.10.98	Carlton Williams L PTS 6 Stoke	
25.03.99	Gordon Behan L RSC 9 Edgbaston	
	(Midlands Area Middleweight Title Challenge)	
15.08.99	Jason Collins L PTS 6 Derby	
13.11.01	Danny Thornton W RSC 4 Leeds	
09.02.02	Anthony Farnell L RSC 3 Manchester	
23.02.04	Ojay Abrahams W PTS 4 Nottingham	
12.06.04	Gary Lockett L RSC 4 Manchester	
24.09.04	Jim Rock L PTS 6 Dublin	
26.02.05	Mark Phillips W PTS 6 Burton	
30.09.05	Terry Adams W PTS 10 Burton	
	(Vacant Midlands Area L.Middleweight Title)	
16.09.06	Simon Sherrington W RSC 5 Burton	
	(Midlands Area L.Middleweight Title Defence)	
03.03.07	Manoocha Salari L RSC 8 Burton	
	(Midlands Area L.Middleweight Title Defence)	

Career: 16 contests, won 9, lost 7.

Matt Galer   Les Clark

Luke Gallear

Derby. *Born* Derby, 20 December, 1984
L.Middleweight. *Ht* 5'9"
Manager C. Mitchell

31.03.07	Surinder Sekhon L PTS 6 Derby	

Career: 1 contest, lost 1.

Scott Gammer

Pembroke Dock. *Born* Pembroke Dock, 24
October, 1976
Heavyweight. Former British Heavyweight
Champion. *Ht* 6'2"
Manager P. Boyce

15.09.02	Leighton Morgan W RSC 1 Swansea	
26.10.02	James Gilbert W RSC 1 Maesteg	
08.01.03	Dave Clarke W PTS 4 Aberdare	
25.01.03	Ahmad Cheleh W CO 1 Bridgend	
28.06.03	Dave Clarke W RSC 1 Cardiff	
13.09.03	Derek McCafferty W PTS 6 Newport	
08.11.03	Mendauga Kulikauskas DREW 6 Bridgend	
28.02.04	James Zikic W PTS 6 Bridgend	
01.05.04	Paul Buttery W CO 1 Bridgend	
02.06.04	Paul King W RSC 3 Hereford	
17.09.04	Carl Baker W PTS 4 Plymouth	
05.11.04	Roman Bugaj W RSC 2 Hereford	
18.02.05	Micky Steeds W PTS 6 Brighton	
15.05.05	Mark Krence W RSC 8 Sheffield	
	(Elim. British Heavyweight Title)	
30.09.05	Julius Francis W PTS 8 Carmarthen	
10.12.05	Suren Kalachyan W PTS 6 Canning Town	
16.06.06	Mark Krence W RSC 9 Carmarthen	
	(Vacant British Heavyweight Title)	
13.10.06	Micky Steeds W PTS 12 Aberavon	
	(British Heavyweight Title Defence)	
02.03.07	Danny Williams L CO 9 Neath	
	(British Heavyweight Title Defence)	
10.06.07	Paul King W PTS 6 Neath	

Career: 20 contests, won 18, drew 1, lost 1.

Darren Gethin

Walsall. *Born* Walsall, 19 August, 1976
Midlands Area Welterweight Champion.
Former Undefeated British Masters
L.Middleweight Champion. *Ht* 5'8"
Manager E. Johnson

08.07.04	Joe Mitchell DREW 6 Birmingham	
12.09.04	Joe Mitchell W PTS 6 Shrewsbury	
12.11.04	Tyrone McInerney L PTS 4 Halifax	
26.02.05	Tye Williams DREW 4 Burton	
18.04.05	Joe Mitchell W PTS 6 Bradford	
25.04.05	Terry Carruthers L RSC 3 Cleethorpes	
02.06.05	Franny Jones L PTS 8 Yarm	
02.09.05	Scott Conway W RSC 1 Derby	
10.09.05	Nathan Cleverly L PTS 4 Cardiff	
01.10.05	Jonathan Hussey L PTS 6 Wigan	
22.10.05	Joe McCluskey DREW 6 Coventry	
12.02.06	Mark Thompson L PTS 4 Manchester	
23.02.06	Khurram Hussain DREW 4 Leeds	
03.03.06	Jason Rushton W PTS 6 Doncaster	
24.04.06	Gary McArthur L PTS 6 Glasgow	
09.05.06	Danny Reynolds DREW 4 Leeds	
18.05.06	Lance Hall W PTS 6 Walsall	
01.06.06	Craig Dickson W PTS 6 Birmingham	

Darren Gethin   Les Clark

12.07.06	John O'Donnell L PTS 8 Bethnal Green
11.12.06	Simon Sherrington W PTS 10 Birmingham
	(Vacant British Masters L.Middleweight Title)
19.02.07	Lee Noble L PTS 6 Glasgow
23.03.07	Tyan Booth W RSC 10 Nottingham
	(Vacant Midlands Area Welterweight Title)

Career: 22 contests, won 8, drew 5, lost 9.

Martin Gethin

Walsall. *Born* Walsall, 16 November, 1983
British Masters L.Welterweight Champion.
Ht 5'6"
Manager E. Johnson

18.11.04	Kristian Laight W RSC 4 Shrewsbury
15.04.05	Jason Nesbitt W PTS 6 Shrewsbury
06.10.05	John-Paul Ryan W RSC 2 Dudley
25.11.05	Michael Medor W PTS 4 Walsall
10.03.06	Carl Allen W PTS 4 Walsall
01.06.06	Baz Carey W PTS 4 Birmingham
07.11.06	Kristian Laight W PTS 6 Leeds
05.12.06	Judex Meemea W RSC 3 Wolverhampton
	(Vacant British Masters L.Welterweight Title)

Martin Gethin   Les Clark

20.04.07	Carl Allen DREW 6 Dudley

Career: 9 contests, won 8, drew 1.

Steve Gethin

Walsall. *Born* Walsall, 30 July, 1978
Lightweight. *Ht* 5'9"
Manager Self

03.09.99	Ike Halls W RSC 3 West Bromwich
24.10.99	Ricky Bishop W RSC 4 Wolverhampton
22.01.00	Sebastian Hart L PTS 4 Birmingham
10.09.00	Nigel Senior DREW 6 Walsall
03.06.01	Richmond Asante L PTS 4 Southwark
28.11.01	Mickey Coveney L PTS 4 Bethnal Green
09.12.01	Gary Groves W PTS 6 Shaw
17.02.02	Gary Groves W PTS 6 Wolverhampton
01.06.02	Gary Davis W RSC 2 Manchester
21.09.02	Marc Callaghan L PTS 6 Brentwood
02.12.02	Neil Read W RTD 3 Leicester
14.12.02	Isaac Ward L PTS 4 Newcastle
08.02.03	Rocky Dean DREW 4 Norwich
15.02.03	Anthony Hanna W PTS 6 Wolverhampton
08.05.03	Derry Matthews L RSC 3 Widnes
07.09.03	Henry Janes L PTS 4 Shrewsbury
02.10.03	Mark Moran L PTS 4 Liverpool
20.10.03	John Simpson L PTS 8 Glasgow
30.10.03	Gareth Payne W PTS 6 Dudley
13.12.03	Steve Foster L RTD 3 Manchester
05.03.04	Isaac Ward L PTS 6 Darlington
27.05.04	Marc Callaghan L PTS 6 Huddersfield
30.07.04	Chris Hooper L PTS 4 Bethnal Green
08.10.04	Ian Napa L PTS 6 Brentwood
22.10.04	Andy Bell L RSC 5 Mansfield
17.12.04	Mark Moran L PTS 4 Liverpool
13.02.05	Patrick Hyland L PTS 4 Brentwood
24.04.05	Darren Broomhall W CO 5 Derby
09.07.05	Billy Corcoran L PTS 6 Nottingham
05.11.05	Amir Khan L RSC 3 Renfrew
24.03.06	Ian Wilson L PTS 4 Bethnal Green
06.05.06	Paul Newby L PTS 4 Birmingham
13.05.06	Andy Bell W RSC 2 Sutton in Ashfield
21.05.06	Mark Alexander L PTS 4 Bethnal Green
30.09.06	Paul Truscott L PTS 4 Middlesbrough
13.10.06	Gary McArthur L PTS 6 Irvine
21.10.06	Ryan Barrett L PTS 6 Southwark
28.10.06	Steve Bell L RTD 5 Bethnal Green
02.12.06	Mitch Prince L PTS 6 Clydebank
15.12.06	Ben Jones L PTS 4 Bethnal Green
22.01.07	Darren Johnstone L PTS 10 Glasgow
	(British Masters S.Featherweight Title Challenge)
30.03.07	David Mulholland L PTS 4 Crawley
20.04.07	Billy Corcoran L PTS 8 Dudley

Career: 43 contests, won 10, drew 2, lost 31.

Ruben Giles

Virginia Water. *Born* Woking, 1 April, 1987
L.Middleweight. *Ht* 5'7½"
Manager G. Carman

28.05.06	Barry Downes W PTS 4 Longford
17.11.06	Bheki Moyo W RSC 4 Bethnal Green
24.02.07	Mahamadou Traore W RSC 3 Bracknell
27.04.07	Kristian Laight W PTS 4 Wembley

Career: 4 contests, won 4.

Jimmy Gilhaney

Newmains. *Born* Lanark, 8 April, 1982
Scottish Featherweight Champion. *Ht* 5'7"
Manager T. Gilmour

25.04.05	Pete Buckley W PTS 6 Glasgow
14.10.05	Pete Buckley W PTS 6 Motherwell
24.10.05	Anthony Christopher W PTS 6 Glasgow
20.02.06	Sergei Rozhakmens W PTS 6 Glasgow
29.09.06	Brian Murphy W RSC 1 Motherwell
23.10.06	Neil Marston W PTS 6 Glasgow
20.11.06	John Bothwell W RSC 1 Glasgow
	(Vacant Scottish Area Featherweight Title)

Career: 7 contests, won 7.

Martin Gillick

Airdrie. *Born* Bellshill, 13 April, 1980
L.Heavyweight. *Ht* 5'10¼"
Manager D. Coldwell

30.06.07	Mick Jenno L RSC 1 Manchester

Career: 1 contest, lost 1.

Tom Glover

Maldon, Essex. *Born* Maldon, 21 June, 1981
Welterweight. *Ht* 5'6½"
Manager A. Sims

11.02.06	Billy Smith W PTS 4 Bethnal Green
24.03.06	Gavin Tait L PTS 4 Bethnal Green
03.06.06	Ben Hudson W PTS 4 Chigwell
26.10.06	James Gorman DREW 6 Belfast
09.12.06	Rocky Muscas W PTS 4 Chigwell
26.01.07	Nathan Weise DREW 4 Dagenham

Career: 6 contests, won 3, drew 2, lost 1.

Tom Glover   Les Clark

Wayne Goddard

Bordon. *Born* Portsmouth, 10 March, 1986
Welterweight. *Ht* 5'8¾"
Manager Self

30.10.05	Ben Hudson W PTS 4 Bethnal Green
27.01.06	James Gorman W PTS 4 Dagenham
26.05.06	Omar Gumati W PTS 4 Bethnal Green
02.12.06	Pawel Jas W PTS 4 Longford
24.02.07	Djim Lakli W PTS 4 Bracknell

Career: 5 contests, won 5.

Jorge Gomez

Peterborough. *Born* Portugal, 10 February, 1981
L.Heavyweight. *Ht* 5'11½"
Manager D. Powell

23.02.07	Ricky Strike W PTS 4 Peterborough
07.04.07	Kenny Anderson L RSC 3 Cardiff
01.06.07	Danny Thornton L PTS 4 Peterborough

Career: 3 contests, won 1, lost 2.

Michael Gomez (Armstrong)

Manchester. *Born* Dublin, 21 June, 1977
Lightweight. Former WBU S.Featherweight
Champion. Former Undefeated WBO Inter-
Continental & British S.Featherweight
Champion. Former WBO Inter-Continental
S.Featherweight Champion. Former
Undefeated Central Area & IBF Inter-
Continental Featherweight Champion.
Ht 5'5"
Manager S. Wood

10.06.95	Danny Ruegg W PTS 6 Manchester
15.09.95	Greg Upton L PTS 4 Mansfield
24.11.95	Danny Ruegg L PTS 4 Manchester
19.09.96	Martin Evans W RSC 1 Manchester
09.11.96	David Morris W PTS 4 Manchester
22.03.97	John Farrell W RSC 2 Wythenshawe
03.05.97	Chris Williams L PTS 4 Manchester

11.09.97	Wayne Jones W RSC 2 Widnes
18.04.98	Benny Jones W PTS 4 Manchester
16.05.98	Craig Spacie W RSC 3 Bethnal Green
05.09.98	Pete Buckley W PTS 6 Telford
14.11.98	David Jeffrey W RSC 1 Cheshunt
19.12.98	Kevin Sheil W RSC 4 Liverpool
13.02.99	Dave Hinds W PTS 6 Newcastle
27.02.99	Chris Jickells W RSC 5 Oldham
	(Vacant Central Area Featherweight Title)
29.05.99	Nigel Leake W RSC 2 Halifax
	(Vacant IBF Inter-Continental Featherweight Title)
07.08.99	William Alverzo W PTS 6 Atlantic City, New Jersey, USA
04.09.99	Gary Thornhill W RSC 2 Bethnal Green
	(Vacant British S. Featherweight Title)
06.11.99	Jose Juan Manjarrez W PTS 12 Widnes
	(WBO Inter-Continental S. Featherweight Title Defence)
11.12.99	Oscar Galindo W RSC 11 Liverpool
	(WBO Inter-Continental S. Featherweight Title Defence)
29.01.00	Chris Jickells W RSC 4 Manchester
29.02.00	Dean Pithie W PTS 12 Widnes
	(British S. Featherweight Title Defence)
24.06.00	Carl Allen W CO 2 Glasgow
08.07.00	Carl Greaves W CO 2 Widnes
	(British S. Featherweight Title Defence)
19.10.00	Awel Abdulai W PTS 8 Harrisburg, USA
11.12.00	Ian McLeod W PTS 12 Widnes
	(British S.Featherweight Title Defence)
10.02.01	Laszlo Bognar L RSC 9 Widnes
	(WBO Inter-Continental S. Featherweight Title Defence)
07.07.01	Laszlo Bognar W RSC 3 Manchester
	(WBO Inter-Continental S. Featherweight Title Challenge)
27.10.01	Craig Docherty W RSC 2 Manchester
	(British S.Featherweight Title Defence)
01.06.02	Kevin Lear L RTD 8 Manchester
	(Vacant WBU S. Featherweight Title)
28.09.02	Jimmy Beech W RSC 4 Manchester
18.01.03	Rakhim Mingaleev W RTD 4 Preston
05.04.03	Vladimir Borov W RSC 3 Manchester
25.10.03	Alex Arthur W RSC 5 Edinburgh
	(British S.Featherweight Title Challenge)
03.04.04	Ben Odamattey W RSC 3 Manchester
	(Vacant WBU S.Featherweight Title)
22.05.04	Justin Juuko W RSC 2 Widnes
	(WBU S.Featherweight Title Defence)
01.10.04	Leva Kirakosyan W RTD 6 Manchester
	(WBU S.Featherweight Title Defence)
11.02.05	Javier Osvaldo Alvarez L RSC 6 Manchester
	(WBU S.Featherweight Title Defence)
28.01.06	Peter McDonagh L RSC 5 Dublin
	(Vacant All-Ireland Lightweight Title)
06.05.07	Daniel Thorpe W RSC 3 Altrincham
24.06.07	Youssef Al Hamidi W RTD 3 Wigan

Career: 41 contests, won 34, lost 7.

Eamonn Goodbrand

Birkenshaw. *Born* Bellshill, 2 June 1988
L.Middleweight. Ht. 6' 1¼"
Manager A. Morrison

26.01.07	Rocky Muscas W PTS 6 Glasgow
16.03.07	Duncan Cottier W PTS 6 Glasgow
25.05.07	Steve Cooper W PTS 6 Glasgow

Career: 3 contests, won 3.

Danny Goode

New Milton. *Born* Wimbledon, 15 January, 1980
Middleweight. *Ht* 5'8"
Manager Self

16.10.04	Geraint Harvey W PTS 4 Dagenham
06.02.05	Neil Jarmolinski W PTS 4 Southampton
23.03.05	Tony Randell W PTS 6 Leicester Square
30.04.05	John-Paul Temple W PTS 4 Dagenham
26.06.05	John-Paul Temple W PTS 4 Southampton
18.09.05	Rocky Muscus W PTS 4 Bethnal Green
05.03.06	Terry Adams W PTS 8 Southampton
07.04.06	Jamie Ambler W PTS 4 Longford
23.07.06	Ben Hudson W PTS 4 Dagenham
24.09.06	Mark Franks W RSC 3 Southampton
25.02.07	Duncan Cottier W PTS 6 Southampton

Career: 11 contests, won 11.

Chris Goodwin

Chester. *Born* Chester, 31 October, 1988
Welterweight. *Ht* 5'7½"
Manager S. Goodwin

07.12.06	Chris Mullen L PTS 6 Sunderland
24.02.07	Kristian Laight W PTS 6 Stoke
12.05.07	James Lilley W PTS 4 Stoke

Career: 3 contests, won 2, lost 1.

Martin Gordon

Brierley Hill. *Born* Wordsley, 23 July, 1982
Welterweight. *Ht* 5'9"
Manager E. Johnson

26.10.06	Bheki Moyo DREW 6 Dudley
17.11.06	Billy Smith L PTS 6 Brierley Hill
06.12.06	Wayne Downing L PTS 6 Stoke
20.04.07	Kristian Laight L PTS 4 Dudley

Career: 4 contests, drew 1, lost 3.

Martin Gordon   Les Clark

James Gorman

Belfast. *Born* Belfast, 1 August, 1979
L.Welterweight. *Ht* 5'8"
Manager Self

28.06.03	Jamie Arthur L PTS 4 Cardiff
11.10.03	Lee Beavis L PTS 4 Portsmouth

117

25.10.03	George Telfer L PTS 4 Edinburgh	
22.11.03	Peter McDonagh W PTS 4 Belfast	
28.02.04	Ceri Hall L PTS 6 Bridgend	
01.04.04	Lee Beavis L RTD 2 Bethnal Green	
24.09.04	Silence Saheed L PTS 6 Millwall	
12.11.04	Jas Malik W RTD 2 Belfast	
18.03.05	Stephen Haughian L PTS 4 Belfast	
14.05.05	Pete Buckley W PTS 6 Dublin	
24.06.05	Daniel Thorpe W PTS 6 Belfast	
30.09.05	George Hillyard L RSC 1 Kirkcaldy	
24.11.05	Stephen Haughian L PTS 6 Lurgan	
27.01.06	Wayne Goddard L PTS 4 Dagenham	
07.10.06	Steve Anning W PTS 6 Belfast	
26.10.06	Tom Glover DREW 6 Belfast	
25.11.06	Jonathan Whiteman W RSC 2 Belfast	
17.02.07	Chris Long W RSC 3 Cork	

Career: 18 contests, won 7, drew 1, lost 10.

Sam Gorman
Alfreton. Born Nuneaton, 19 October, 1981
Middleweight. Ht 5'9"
Manager P. Carpenter

17.11.01	Shaune Danskin W RSC 3 Coventry
09.02.02	Pete Buckley W PTS 6 Coventry
22.03.02	Brian Coleman W PTS 6 Coventry
25.06.02	Pedro Thompson W PTS 6 Rugby
17.11.02	Wayne Shepherd L PTS 6 Shaw
18.03.06	Tony Randell L PTS 6 Coventry
23.09.06	Magic Kidem L PTS 6 Coventry

Career: 7 contests, won 4, lost 3.

Nathan Graham
Aylesbury. Born Aylesbury, 21 September, 1982
L.Middleweight. Ht 5'9"
Manager Self

24.04.04	Tom Price W RSC 2 Reading
02.12.04	David Payne W RSC 3 Crystal Palace
26.03.05	Gatis Skuja W RSC 1 Hackney
19.11.05	Geraint Harvey W PTS 4 Southwark
26.02.06	Duncan Cottier W PTS 4 Dagenham
21.10.06	Imad Khamis W RSC 2 Southwark
02.12.06	Tyan Booth L PTS 6 Southwark

Career: 7 contests, won 6, lost 1.

Michael Grant
Tottenham. Born London, 2 November, 1983
Welterweight. Ht 5'7"
Manager C. Hall

24.07.05	David Kehoe W PTS 4 Leicester Square
16.09.05	Judex Meemea W RSC 3 Plymouth
09.10.05	Ali Wyatt DREW 4 Hammersmith
13.01.06	Patrik Prokopecz W PTS 4 Torrevieja, Spain
02.02.06	Pete Buckley W PTS 4 Holborn
30.03.06	Franck Aiello W PTS 4 Piccadilly
19.05.06	Lubos Priehradnik W PTS 6 Torrevieja, Spain
03.06.06	Ali Wyatt W PTS 4 Chigwell
24.09.06	Jav Jerome W PTS 4 Bethnal Green
13.10.06	Ceri Hall W PTS 6 Aberavon

Career: 10 contests, won 9, drew 1.

Johnny Greaves
East Ham. Born Forest Gate, 4 March, 1979
L.Welterweight. Ht 5'9"
Manager C. Greaves

09.06.07	Rob Hunt L PTS 6 Middlesbrough
28.06.07	Dean Harrison L PTS 6 Dudley

Career: 2 contests, lost 2.

Stuart Green
Glenrothes. Born Kirkcaldy, 13 December, 1984
L.Welterweight. Ht 5'6"
Manager Self

17.11.03	Chris Long W PTS 6 Glasgow
12.03.04	Jason Nesbitt W PTS 8 Irvine
07.06.04	Gavin Tait W PTS 6 Glasgow
11.10.04	Paul Holborn L PTS 6 Glasgow
21.02.05	Pete Buckley W PTS 6 Glasgow
11.06.05	Dave Hinds W PTS 6 Kirkcaldy
30.09.05	Fred Janes W PTS 4 Kirkcaldy
17.03.06	Adam Kelly W PTS 4 Kirkcaldy
21.04.06	Michael Kelly L PTS 4 Belfast
27.05.06	Lee McAllister L RSC 8 Aberdeen (Vacant Scottish Area Lightweight Title)
09.09.06	Pete Buckley W PTS 8 Inverurie
18.09.06	Pete Buckley W PTS 6 Glasgow
06.10.06	Dean Hickman L PTS 6 Wolverhampton
03.11.06	Martin Kristjansen L PTS 6 Skive, Denmark
13.12.06	Chris Long W PTS 6 Strand
01.02.07	Sam Rukundo L PTS 6 Piccadilly
02.03.07	Ceri Hall L RSC 9 Neath (Vacant Celtic L.Welterweight Title)

Career: 17 contests, won 10, lost 7.

Stuart Green   Philip Sharkey

Roman Greenberg
Finchley. Born Russia, 18 May, 1982
IBO Inter-Continental Heavyweight
Champion. Ht 6'2½"
Manager J. Evans

22.11.01	Dave Clarke W RSC 5 Paddington
25.02.02	Paul Bonson W PTS 6 Slough
25.04.02	Jakarta Nakyru W RSC 4 Las Vegas, Nevada, USA
28.11.02	Tony Booth W PTS 4 Finchley
05.12.02	Dave Clarke W RSC 1 Sheffield
20.12.02	Derek McCafferty W PTS 4 Bracknell
24.01.03	Piotr Jurczk W CO 1 Sheffield
04.03.03	Calvin Miller W RSC 2 Miami, Florida, USA
18.03.03	Gary Williams W RSC 1 Reading
15.05.03	Tracy Williams W RTD 2 Miami, Florida, USA
29.05.03	Troy Beets W RSC 3 Miami, Florida, USA
05.09.03	Luke Simpkin W RTD 4 Sheffield
18.09.03	Konstanin Prizyuk W RSC 1 Mayfair
26.11.03	Mendauga Kulikauskas W RSC 5 Mayfair
15.04.04	Jason Gethers W RSC 6 NYC, New York, USA
10.09.04	Vitaly Shkraba W PTS 6 Wembley
10.12.04	Julius Francis W PTS 10 Sheffield
28.01.05	Marcus McGee W RSC 4 NYC, New York, USA
11.06.05	Josh Gutcher W RSC 4 Las Vegas, Nevada, USA
20.07.05	Mamadou Sacko W PTS 8 Monte Carlo, Monaco
16.12.05	Kendrick Releford W PTS 10 Bracknell
18.03.06	Alex Vassilev W RSC 6 Monte Carlo, Monaco (Vacant IBO Inter-Continental Heavyweight Title)
04.11.06	Alexei Varakin W CO 6 Monte Carlo, Monaco (IBO Inter-Continental Heavyweight Title Defence)
09.12.06	Steve Pannell W RSC 3 Hollywood, Florida, USA
10.03.07	Michael Simms W PTS 10 NYC, New York, USA

Career: 25 contests, won 25.

Carl Griffiths
Oakham. Born Leicester, 4 July, 1984
Lightweight. Ht 5'5¾"
Manager D. Cowland

30.03.07	Tony McQuade L PTS 6 Peterborough
21.06.07	Sergei Rozhakmens W PTS 6 Peterborough

Career: 2 contests, won 1, lost 1.

Danny Gwilym
Bristol. Born Bristol, 15 January, 1975
L.Middleweight. Ht 5'7"
Manager Self

16.12.01	Wayne Wheeler L RSC 2 Bristol
11.02.02	James Lee L PTS 6 Southampton
12.07.02	Mo W PTS 6 Southampton
26.02.03	Wasim Hussain W PTS 6 Bristol
17.03.03	Danny Cooper L PTS 6 Southampton
16.04.03	Lenny Daws L RSC 2 Nottingham
26.09.03	Darren Covill W PTS 6 Millwall
12.10.03	Mo L PTS 6 Sheffield
06.12.03	Martin Concepcion L RSC 2 Cardiff
09.07.05	Arv Mittoo W RSC 4 Bristol
24.07.05	Garry Buckland L RSC 2 Leicester Square
12.11.05	Kristian Laight W PTS 6 Bristol
28.04.07	Paul Burns L PTS 6 Clydebank
06.05.07	Chris Johnson L RSC 4 Altrincham

Career: 14 contests, won 5, lost 9.

H

Ceri Hall

Loughor. *Born* Swansea, 25 March, 1980
L.Welterweight. Former Celtic
L.Welterweight Champion. *Ht* 5'10"
Manager Self

15.09.02	Martin Turner W RSC 1 Swansea	
10.04.03	Silence Saheed DREW 4 Clydach	
08.11.03	Peter McDonagh W PTS 4 Bridgend	
28.02.04	James Gorman W PTS 6 Bridgend	
19.06.04	Chris Long W PTS 4 Muswell Hill	
24.09.04	Pete Buckley W PTS 6 Dublin	
25.11.04	Dean Hickman L PTS 4 Birmingham	
19.02.05	Robbie Murray L PTS 8 Dublin	
28.04.05	Jason Nesbitt W RTD 2 Clydach	
30.09.05	David Kehoe W PTS 6 Carmarthen	
24.11.05	Silence Saheed W PTS 6 Clydach	
25.03.06	Giorgio Marinelli L PTS 10 Rome, Italy	
	(Vacant European Union L.Welterweight Title)	
16.06.06	Billy Smith W PTS 6 Carmarthen	
29.09.06	Chill John DREW 4 Cardiff	
13.10.06	Michael Grant L PTS 6 Aberavon	
02.03.07	Stuart Green W RSC 9 Neath	
	(Vacant Celtic L.Welterweight Title)	
10.06.07	Stuart Phillips L PTS 10 Neath	
	(Celtic L.Welterweight Title Defence)	

Career: 17 contests, won 10, drew 2, lost 5.

Matthew Hall

Manchester. *Born* Manchester, 5 July, 1984
Middleweight. *Ht* 5'7¾"
Manager F. Warren/B. Hughes

28.09.02	Pedro Thompson W RSC 1 Manchester	
14.12.02	Pedro Thompson W PTS 4 Newcastle	
18.01.03	Clive Johnson W PTS 4 Preston	
05.04.03	Brian Coleman W RSC 1 Manchester	
08.05.03	Patrick Cito W PTS 4 Widnes	
06.05.04	Craig Lynch W PTS 6 Barnsley	
12.06.04	Isidro Gonzalez W RSC 3 Manchester	
01.10.04	Howard Clarke W RSC 5 Manchester	
12.11.04	Ojay Abrahams W RSC 1 Halifax	
03.12.04	Jason Collins W PTS 6 Edinburgh	
21.01.05	Leigh Wicks W PTS 4 Bridgend	
11.02.05	Sylvestre Marianini W CO 1 Manchester	
04.06.05	Matt Scriven W RSC 2 Manchester	
28.01.06	Jon Foster W RSC 3 Nottingham	
11.03.06	Robert Burton W CO 1 Newport	
08.07.06	Kevin Phelan W RSC 1 Cardiff	

Career: 16 contests, won 16.

Leigh Hallet

Walsall. *Born* Sutton Coldfield, 29 July, 1980
Middleweight. *Ht* 5'10"
Manager R. Woodhall

08.09.06	Jon Foster W PTS 6 Birmingham	

Career: 1 contest, won 1.

Paul Halpin

Brighton. *Born* Brighton, 4 August, 1974
L.Welterweight. Former Undefeated
Southern Area Featherweight Champion.
Ht 5'5"
Manager J. Feld

04.04.97	Graham McGrath W PTS 6 Brighton	
20.05.97	David Jeffrey W PTS 6 Gillingham	
11.07.97	Wayne Jones W RSC 5 Brighton	
08.10.97	Greg Upton DREW 4 Poplar	
27.02.98	Taffy Evans W RSC 3 Brighton	
16.05.98	Chris Lyons W PTS 6 Chigwell	
26.02.99	Justin Murphy W RSC 2 Bethnal Green	
	(Vacant Southern Area Featherweight Title)	
26.06.99	Pete Buckley W PTS 4 Millwall	
15.11.99	Chris Jickells W PTS 6 Bethnal Green	
19.06.00	Chris Jickells W RSC 4 Burton	
12.08.00	Eddie Nevins W PTS 6 Wembley	
02.03.02	Gary Reid W RSC 3 Bethnal Green	
11.12.05	Karl Taylor W PTS 4 Chigwell	
03.12.06	Youssef Al Hamidi L PTS 4 Bethnal Green	
08.06.07	Tony Jourda W PTS 6 Mayfair	

Career: 15 contests, won 13, drew 1, lost 1.

Darren Hamilton

Bristol. *Born* Bristol, 6 September, 1978
L.Welterweight. *Ht* 5'9"
Manager C. Sanigar

03.11.06	Neal McQuade W PTS 6 Bristol	
07.12.06	Jaz Virdee W PTS 6 Peterborough	
24.02.07	James Lilley W PTS 6 Bristol	

Career: 3 contests, won 3.

Jeff Hamilton

Blackburn. *Born* Blackburn, 24 December, 1975
S.Middleweight. *Ht* 5'11¼"
Manager T. Schofield

13.04.07	Craig Denton L PTS 6 Houghton le Spring	
06.05.07	Dave Sadler W PTS 6 Leeds	

Career: 2 contests, won 1, lost 1.

Anthony Hanna

Birmingham. *Born* Birmingham, 22 September, 1974
Lightweight. Former Undefeated Midlands Area Flyweight Champion. *Ht* 5'6"
Manager N. Nobbs

19.11.92	Nick Tooley L PTS 6 Evesham	
10.12.92	Daren Fifield L RSC 6 Bethnal Green	
11.05.93	Tiger Singh W PTS 6 Norwich	
24.05.93	Lyndon Kershaw L PTS 6 Bradford	
16.09.93	Chris Lyons W PTS 6 Southwark	
06.10.93	Tiger Singh W PTS 6 Solihull	
03.11.93	Mickey Cantwell L PTS 8 Bristol	
25.01.94	Marty Chestnut W PTS 4 Picaddilly	
10.02.94	Allan Mooney W RTD 1 Glasgow	
13.04.94	Allan Mooney L PTS 6 Glasgow	
22.04.94	Jesper Jensen L PTS 6 Aalborg, Denmark	
03.08.94	Paul Ingle L PTS 6 Bristol	
01.10.94	Mark Hughes L PTS 4 Cardiff	
30.11.94	Shaun Norman W PTS 10 Solihull	
	(Vacant Midlands Area Flyweight Title)	
24.02.95	Darren Greaves W RSC 5 Weston super Mare	
06.03.95	Mark Hughes L PTS 6 Mayfair	
27.04.95	Mickey Cantwell L PTS 6 Bethnal Green	
05.05.95	Mark Cokely W RSC 4 Swansea	
04.06.95	Mark Reynolds L PTS 10 Bethnal Green	
	(Elim. British Flyweight Title)	
02.07.95	Mickey Cantwell L PTS 6 Dublin	
02.11.95	Shaun Norman DREW 10 Mayfair	
	(Midlands Area Flyweight Title Defence)	
31.01.96	Marty Chestnut DREW 6 Stoke	
20.03.96	Harry Woods L PTS 6 Cardiff	
22.04.96	Neil Parry W PTS 6 Manchester	
14.05.96	Dharmendra Singh Yadav L PTS 4 Dagenham	
08.10.96	Marty Chestnut W PTS 6 Battersea	
11.12.96	Mark Reynolds DREW 8 Southwark	
28.01.97	Colin Moffett L PTS 4 Belfast	
28.02.97	Paul Weir L PTS 8 Kilmarnock	
14.03.97	Jesper Jensen L PTS 6 Odense, Denmark	
30.04.97	Clinton Beeby DREW 6 Acton	
10.05.97	Jason Booth L PTS 6 Nottingham	
02.06.97	Keith Knox L PTS 6 Glasgow	
14.10.97	Louis Veitch L PTS 6 Kilmarnock	
27.10.97	Russell Laing W PTS 4 Musselburgh	
13.11.97	Noel Wilders L PTS 6 Bradford	
24.11.97	Shaun Anderson L PTS 8 Glasgow	
20.12.97	Damaen Kelly L PTS 4 Belfast	

Paul Halpin　　　　　　　　　　　Philip Sharkey

31.01.98	Jason Booth L PTS 6 Edmonton
23.02.98	David Coldwell W PTS 6 Salford
19.03.98	Andy Roberts L PTS 6 Doncaster
18.05.98	Chris Emanuele W RSC 3 Cleethorpes
11.09.98	Nicky Booth DREW 6 Cleethorpes
18.09.98	Colin Moffett DREW 4 Belfast
29.10.98	Nick Tooley W RTD 6 Bayswater
25.11.98	Nicky Booth W PTS 6 Clydach
21.01.99	Ola Dali W PTS 6 Piccadilly
13.03.99	Damaen Kelly L PTS 12 Manchester
	(Vacant British Flyweight Title.
	Commonwealth Flyweight Title
	Challenge)
24.04.99	Noel Wilders L PTS 6 Peterborough
07.06.99	Alston Buchanan W RSC 3 Glasgow
29.06.99	Tommy Waite L PTS 4 Bethnal Green
16.10.99	Stevie Quinn W PTS 4 Belfast
22.11.99	Frankie DeMilo L PTS 6 Piccadilly
04.12.99	Ady Lewis L PTS 6 Manchester
19.02.00	Ian Napa L PTS 6 Dagenham
13.03.00	Mzukisi Sikali L PTS 6 Bethnal Green
27.05.00	Nicky Cook L PTS 6 Mayfair
25.07.00	David Lowry L PTS 4 Southwark
19.08.00	Marc Callaghan L PTS 4 Brentwood
29.09.00	Rocky Dean L PTS 4 Bethnal Green
07.10.00	Oleg Kiryukhin L PTS 6 Doncaster
14.10.00	Danny Costello DREW 4 Wembley
31.10.00	Dmitri Kirilov L PTS 6 Hammersmith
10.02.01	Tony Mulholland L PTS 4 Widnes
19.02.01	Alex Moon L PTS 6 Glasgow
03.03.01	Marc Callaghan L PTS 6 Wembley
24.04.01	Silence Mabuza L PTS 6 Liverpool
06.05.01	Michael Hunter L PTS 4 Hartlepool
26.05.01	Mickey Bowden L PTS 4 Bethnal Green
04.06.01	Michael Hunter L PTS 4 Hartlepool
01.11.01	Nigel Senior L PTS 6 Hull
24.11.01	Martin Power L PTS 4 Bethnal Green
08.12.01	Faprakob Rakkiatgym L PTS 8 Dagenham
24.03.02	Mickey Coveney L PTS 4 Streatham
23.06.02	Johannes Maisa L PTS 4 Southwark
30.10.02	Mickey Bowden L PTS 4 Leicester Square
08.11.02	Sean Green L PTS 6 Doncaster
17.11.02	Shinny Bayaar L PTS 6 Shaw
14.12.02	Michael Hunter L PTS 8 Newcastle
15.02.03	Steve Gethin L PTS 6 Wolverhampton
24.02.03	Jackson Williams W PTS 6 Birmingham
08.06.03	Darryn Walton L PTS 6 Shaw
25.09.03	Rob Jeffries L PTS 6 Bethnal Green
01.11.03	Andrew Ferrans L PTS 4 Glasgow
14.11.03	Mickey Bowden L PTS 4 Bethnal Green
21.11.03	Buster Dennis L PTS 6 Millwall
29.11.03	Willie Limond L PTS 4 Renfrew
09.04.04	Rendall Munroe L PTS 6 Rugby
16.04.04	Billy Corcoran L PTS 4 Bradford
24.04.04	Lee Beavis L PTS 4 Reading
12.05.04	Chris McDonagh L PTS 4 Reading
02.06.04	John Murray L PTS 4 Nottingham
17.06.04	Femi Fehintola L PTS 6 Sheffield
03.07.04	Jeff Thomas L PTS 6 Blackpool
12.11.06	Stuart McFadyen L PTS 6 Manchester
07.12.06	Shaun Doherty L PTS 6 Bradford
15.04.07	Josh Wale L PTS 6 Barnsley
02.06.07	Darryl Mitchell W RTD 5 Bristol

Career: 98 contests, won 20, drew 7, lost 71.

Danny Harding
Stockport. *Born* Stockport, 5 January, 1981
L.Welterweight. *Ht* 5'8"
Manager S. Wood

12.02.06	Gavin Deacon W PTS 6 Manchester
21.07.06	Neal McQuade W PTS 4 Altrincham
29.09.06	Chris Pacy W PTS 4 Manchester
12.11.06	Pete Buckley W PTS 6 Manchester
25.02.07	Jason Nesbitt W PTS 6 Manchester
13.04.07	Chris Pacy W PTS 6 Altrincham

Career: 6 contests, won 6.

James Hare   Philip Sharkey

James Hare
Robertown. *Born* Dewsbury, 16 July, 1976
L.Middleweight. Former WBF
Welterweight Champion. Former
Undefeated Commonwealth & European
Union Welterweight Champion. *Ht* 5'6"
Manager C. Aston

20.01.96	Brian Coleman W PTS 6 Mansfield
25.06.96	Mike Watson W PTS 4 Mansfield
13.07.96	Dennis Griffin W RSC 4 Bethnal Green
14.09.96	Paul Salmon W RSC 4 Sheffield
14.12.96	Jon Harrison W PTS 4 Sheffield
25.02.97	Kid McAuley W PTS 4 Sheffield
12.04.97	Andy Peach W RSC 1 Sheffield
13.12.97	Costas Katsantonis W RSC 3 Sheffield
09.05.98	Peter Nightingale W PTS 4 Sheffield
18.07.98	Karl Taylor W PTS 4 Sheffield
28.11.98	Peter Nightingale W PTS 6 Sheffield
15.05.99	Lee Williamson W RSC 2 Sheffield
23.10.99	Mark Winters DREW 6 Sheffield
23.10.00	Dean Nicholas W RSC 1 Glasgow
23.01.01	Mark Ramsey W PTS 6 Crawley
26.02.01	Paul Denton W PTS 4 Nottingham
08.05.01	Jessy Moreaux W RSC 3 Barnsley
26.05.01	John Humphrey W RSC 7 Bethnal Green
	(Elim. British Welterweight Title)
08.10.01	John Ameline W PTS 8 Telford
26.11.01	Paul Denton W RTD 4 Manchester
28.01.02	Monney Seka W PTS 10 Barnsley
	(Vacant European Union Welterweight Title)
27.04.02	Julian Holland W RSC 6 Huddersfield
	(Commonwealth Welterweight Title Challenge)
15.06.02	Abdel Mehidi W PTS 8 Leeds
05.10.02	Farai Musiiwa W RSC 8 Huddersfield
	(Commonwealth Welterweight Title Defence)

30.11.02	Earl Foskin W RSC 1 Liverpool
	(Commonwealth Welterweight Title Defence)
22.02.03	Frans Hantindi W RSC 1 Huddersfield
	(Commonwealth Welterweight Title Defence)
21.06.03	Roman Dzuman W PTS 12 Manchester
	(Vacant WBF Welterweight Title)
06.09.03	Jan Bergman W RSC 2 Huddersfield
	(WBF Welterweight Title Defence)
18.10.03	Jozsef Matolcsi W RSC 10 Manchester
	(WBF Welterweight Title Defence)
04.12.03	Cosme Rivera L RSC 10 Huddersfield
	(WBF Welterweight Title Defence)
01.05.04	Jason Williams W RSC 2 Bridgend
27.05.04	Moise Cherni W RSC 5 Huddersfield
12.11.04	David Barnes L RSC 6 Halifax
	(British Welterweight Title Challenge)
09.09.05	Sergey Starkov W PTS 6 Sheffield
14.10.05	Oscar Milkitas W RTD 5 Huddersfield
01.06.06	Ernie Smith W CO 5 Barnsley
17.11.06	Robert Lloyd-Taylor L PTS 6 Bethnal Green

Career: 37 contests, won 33, drew 1, lost 3.

Chris Harman
Barry. *Born* Cardiff, 20 April, 1980
L.Heavyweight. *Ht* 5'11"
Manager P. Boyce

29.09.06	Nick Okoth L PTS 4 Cardiff
26.10.06	Mark Nilsen L PTS 6 Dudley

Career: 2 contests, lost 2.

Audley Harrison
Wembley. *Born* Park Royal, 26 October, 1971
Heavyweight. Former Undefeated WBF
Heavyweight Champion. *Ht* 6'4¾"
Manager Self

19.05.01	Michael Middleton W RSC 1 Wembley
22.09.01	Derek McCafferty W PTS 6 Newcastle
20.10.01	Piotr Jurczyk W RSC 2 Glasgow
20.04.02	Julius Long W CO 2 Wembley
21.05.02	Mark Krence W PTS 6 Custom House
10.07.02	Dominic Negus W PTS 6 Wembley
05.10.02	Wade Lewis W RSC 2 Liverpool
23.11.02	Shawn Robinson W RSC 1 Atlantic City, New Jersey, USA
08.02.03	Rob Calloway W RSC 5 Brentford
29.03.03	Ratko Draskovic W PTS 8 Wembley
31.05.03	Matthew Ellis W RSC 2 Bethnal Green
09.09.03	Quinn Navarre W RSC 3 Miami, Florida, USA
03.10.03	Lisandro Diaz W RSC 4 Las Vegas, Nevada, USA
12.12.03	Brian Nix W RSC 3 Laughlin, Nevada, USA
20.03.04	Richel Hersisia W CO 4 Wembley
	(WBF Heavyweight Title Challenge)
08.05.04	Julius Francis W PTS 12 Bristol
	(WBF Heavyweight Title Defence)
19.06.04	Tomasz Bonin W RSC 9 Muswell Hill
	(WBF Heavyweight Title Defence)
09.06.05	Robert Davis W RSC 7 Temecula, California, USA
18.08.05	Robert Wiggins W RTD 4 San Jose, California, USA
10.12.05	Danny Williams L PTS 12 Canning Town
	(Vacant Commonwealth Heavyweight Title)
14.04.06	Dominick Guinn L PTS 10 Rancho Mirage, California, USA

09.06.06 Andrew Greeley W CO 3 Atlantic City, New Jersey, USA
09.12.06 Danny Williams W RSC 3 Canning Town
17.02.07 Michael Sprott L RSC 3 Wembley
(European Union Heavyweight Title Challenge.Vacant English Heavyweight Title)
Career: 24 contests, won 21, lost 3.

Dean Harrison
Wolverhampton. *Born* Wolverhampton, 9 August, 1983
Welterweight. *Ht* 5'8"
Manager E. Johnson

06.10.06 Joe Mitchell W PTS 4 Wolverhampton
26.10.06 Kristian Laight W PTS 4 Dudley
05.12.06 Baz Carey W PTS 4 Wolverhampton
15.02.07 Daniel Thorpe W PTS 4 Dudley
23.03.07 Kristian Laight W PTS 4 Nottingham
20.04.07 Judex Meemea W RSC 6 Dudley
28.06.07 Johnny Greaves W PTS 6 Dudley
Career: 7 contests, won 7.

Jon Harrison
Plymouth. *Born* Scunthorpe, 18 March, 1977
L.Middleweight. *Ht* 5'11½"
Manager Self

13.01.96 Mark Haslam L PTS 6 Manchester
13.02.96 Paul Samuels L CO 1 Cardiff
16.05.96 Dave Fallon W RSC 4 Dunstable
03.07.96 Allan Gray L PTS 6 Wembley
01.10.96 Cam Raeside L PTS 6 Birmingham
07.11.96 Nicky Bardle L PTS 6 Battersea
14.12.96 James Hare L PTS 4 Sheffield
19.04.97 Jason Williams W PTS 6 Plymouth
11.07.97 Pat Larner L PTS 6 Brighton
07.10.97 Paul Salmon L PTS 6 Plymouth
23.02.98 Alan Gilbert L PTS 6 Windsor
24.03.98 Brian Coleman DREW 6 Wolverhampton
14.07.98 Jason Williams L RTD 2 Reading
12.05.01 Ernie Smith W PTS 4 Plymouth
15.09.01 Darren Williams L PTS 6 Swansea
02.04.04 Nathan Wyatt W PTS 6 Plymouth
27.05.04 Ady Clegg W PTS 4 Huddersfield
17.09.04 Geraint Harvey W PTS 6 Plymouth
13.12.04 Simon Sherrington L RSC 5 Birmingham
04.02.05 Joe Mitchell W PTS 6 Plymouth
29.04.05 Neil Jarmolinski W PTS 6 Plymouth
10.02.06 Jamie Ambler W PTS 4 Plymouth
15.09.06 Taz Jones L PTS 6 Newport
Career: 23 contests, won 9, drew 1, lost 13.

Geraint Harvey
Mountain Ash. *Born* Pontypridd, 1 September, 1979
L.Middleweight. *Ht* 5'9"
Manager Self

22.09.03 Steve Scott W PTS 6 Cleethorpes
29.10.03 Darren Covill W PTS 4 Leicester Square
21.12.03 Danny Moir L PTS 6 Bolton
14.02.04 Arek Malek L PTS 4 Nottingham
28.02.04 Jamie Coyle L PTS 4 Bridgend
15.04.04 Terry Adams L PTS 6 Dudley
24.04.04 Chas Symonds L PTS 4 Reading
08.07.04 Terry Adams L RSC 6 Birmingham
17.09.04 Jon Harrison L PTS 6 Plymouth

24.09.04 Gary Woolcombe L PTS 4 Bethnal Green
16.10.04 Danny Goode L PTS 4 Dagenham
23.10.04 Peter Dunn W PTS 6 Wakefield
21.11.04 Robert-Lloyd Taylor L PTS 4 Bracknell
03.12.04 Colin McNeil L PTS 6 Edinburgh
28.01.05 Chris Black L PTS 4 Renfrew
17.02.05 Young Muttley L PTS 6 Dudley
05.03.05 Duncan Cottier L PTS 4 Dagenham
29.04.05 Courtney Thomas L PTS 6 Plymouth
15.05.05 Stuart Brookes L PTS 6 Sheffield
01.06.05 Mark Franks L PTS 6 Leeds
16.06.05 George Hillyard L RSC 1 Dagenham
23.09.05 Mark Thompson L PTS 4 Manchester
07.10.05 Sam Webb L CO 1 Bethnal Green
19.11.05 Nathan Graham L PTS 4 Southwark
14.12.05 Brian Rose L PTS 6 Blackpool
20.03.06 Danny Reynolds L RTD 2 Leeds
06.05.06 Jonathan Hussey L PTS 6 Blackpool
21.05.06 Jamal Morrison L PTS 4 Bethnal Green
01.06.06 Kell Brook L RSC 3 Barnsley
10.07.06 Prince Arron L PTS 6 Manchester
11.09.06 George Katsimpas L RSC 2 Manchester
25.11.06 Scott Jordan L PTS 4 Belfast
02.12.06 Mark Hastie L PTS 6 Clydebank
17.12.06 Chris Johnson L PTS 6 Bolton
23.02.07 Dee Mitchell L PTS 4 Birmingham
03.03.07 Jamie Way L PTS 6 Newport
Career: 36 contests, won 3, lost 33.

Lee Haskins
Bristol. *Born* Bristol, 29 November, 1983
Bantamweight. Former Undefeated Commonwealth & English Flyweight Champion. *Ht* 5'5"
Manager C. Sanigar

06.03.03 Ankar Miah W RSC 1 Bristol
13.06.03 Chris Edwards W PTS 6 Bristol
09.10.03 Neil Read W PTS 4 Bristol
05.12.03 Jason Thomas W PTS 6 Bristol
13.02.04 Marty Kayes W PTS 6 Bristol
08.05.04 Colin Moffett W RSC 2 Bristol
03.07.04 Sergei Tasimov W RSC 5 Bristol
01.10.04 Junior Anderson W CO 3 Bristol
03.12.04 Delroy Spencer W RTD 3 Bristol
(Vacant English Flyweight Title)
18.02.05 Hugo Cardinale W CO 1 Torrevieja, Spain
08.04.05 Moses Kinyua W PTS 10 Bristol
29.04.05 Andrzej Ziora W RSC 1 Plymouth
16.09.05 Delroy Spencer W RTD 2 Plymouth
10.02.06 Anthony Mathias W RSC 2 Plymouth
(Vacant Commonwealth Flyweight Title)
07.04.06 Zolile Mbityi W PTS 12 Bristol
(Commonwealth Flyweight Title Defence)
06.10.06 Tshifhiwa Munyai L RSC 6 Bethnal Green
(Commonwealth Bantamweight Title Challenge)
24.02.07 Sumaila Badu W PTS 6 Bristol
Career: 17 contests, won 16, lost 1.

Mark Hastie
Motherwell. *Born* Bellshill, 28 July, 1981
Welterweight. *Ht* 5'10¾"
Manager T. Gilmour

29.09.06 Steve Cooper W PTS 6 Motherwell
03.11.06 Surinder Sekhon W RSC 1 Glasgow
02.12.06 Geraint Harvey W PTS 6 Clydebank

19.02.07 Pete Buckley W PTS 6 Glasgow
02.03.07 Peter Dunn W PTS 6 Irvine
08.06.07 Alex Stoda W PTS 4 Motherwell
Career: 6 contests, won 6.

Matthew Hatton   Mark Robinson

Matthew Hatton
Manchester. *Born* Stockport, 15 May, 1981
IBF Inter-Continental Welterweight Champion. Former Undefeated Central Area Welterweight Champion. Former Undefeated Central Area L.Middleweight Champion. *Ht* 5'8½"
Manager Self

23.09.00 David White W PTS 4 Bethnal Green
25.11.00 David White W PTS 4 Manchester
11.12.00 Danny Connelly W PTS 4 Widnes
15.01.01 Keith Jones W PTS 4 Manchester
10.02.01 Karl Taylor W PTS 4 Widnes
17.03.01 Assen Vassilev W RSC 5 Manchester
09.06.01 Brian Coleman W RTD 2 Bethnal Green
21.07.01 Ram Singh W RSC 2 Sheffield
15.09.01 Marcus Portman W RSC 3 Manchester
15.12.01 Dafydd Carlin W PTS 6 Wembley
09.02.02 Paul Denton W PTS 6 Manchester
04.05.02 Karl Taylor W RSC 3 Bethnal Green
20.07.02 Karl Taylor W RTD 2 Bethnal Green
28.09.02 David Kirk L PTS 6 Manchester
14.12.02 Paul Denton W PTS 6 Newcastle
15.02.03 David Keir L RSC 4 Wembley
08.05.03 Jay Mahoney W PTS 6 Widnes
17.07.03 Jay Mahoney W RSC 1 Dagenham
27.09.03 Taz Jones W PTS 6 Manchester
13.12.03 Franny Jones DREW 6 Manchester
26.02.04 Peter Dunn W PTS 6 Widnes
06.05.04 Robert Burton W PTS 10 Barnsley
(Central Area Welterweight Title Challenge)
12.06.04 Matt Scriven W RSC 4 Manchester
01.10.04 Lee Armstrong W PTS 8 Manchester
12.11.04 Robert Burton W PTS 10 Halifax
(Central Area L.Middleweight Title Challenge)
11.03.05 Franny Jones W RTD 6 Doncaster

03.06.05	Adnan Hadoui W PTS 8 Manchester
09.09.05	Dmitry Yanushevich W RSC 4 Sheffield
26.11.05	Sergey Starkov W PTS 10 Sheffield
18.03.06	Alexander Abramenko W RTD 6 Monte Carlo, Monaco
13.05.06	Jose Medina W PTS 8 Boston, Massachusetts, USA
20.10.06	Alan Bosworth L DIS 10 Sheffield
	(Elim. British Welterweight Title)
10.12.06	Vladimir Borovski W PTS 6 Sheffield
20.01.07	Frank Houghtaling W RTD 7 Las Vegas, Nevada, USA
	(Vacant IBF Inter-Continental Welterweight Title)
23.06.07	Edwin Vazquez W PTS 12 Las Vegas, Nevada, USA
	(IBF Inter-Continental Welterweight Title Defence)

Career: 35 contests, won 31, drew 1, lost 3.

Ricky Hatton

Manchester. *Born* Stockport, 6 October, 1978
IBO & WBC International L.Welterweight Champion. Former Undefeated WBA Welterweight Champion. Former Undefeated WBA, IBF & WBU L.Welterweight Champion. Former Undefeated British, WBO Inter-Continental & Central Area L.Welterweight Champion.
Ht 5'7½"
Manager Self

11.09.97	Kid McAuley W RTD 1 Widnes
19.12.97	Robert Alvarez W PTS 4 NYC, New York, USA
17.01.98	David Thompson W RSC 1 Bristol
27.03.98	Paul Salmon W RSC 1 Telford
18.04.98	Karl Taylor W RSC 1 Manchester
30.05.98	Mark Ramsey W PTS 6 Bristol
18.07.98	Anthony Campbell W PTS 6 Sheffield
19.09.98	Pascal Montulet W CO 2 Oberhausen, Germany
31.10.98	Kevin Carter W RSC 1 Atlantic City, New Jersey, USA
19.12.98	Paul Denton W RSC 6 Liverpool
27.02.99	Tommy Peacock W RSC 2 Oldham
	(Vacant Central Area L.Welterweight Title)
03.04.99	Brian Coleman W CO 2 Kensington
29.05.99	Dillon Carew W RSC 5 Halifax
	(Vacant WBO Inter-Continental L. Welterweight Title)
17.07.99	Mark Ramsey W PTS 6 Doncaster
09.10.99	Bernard Paul W RTD 4 Manchester
	(WBO Inter-Continental L. Welterweight Title Defence)
11.12.99	Mark Winters W RSC 4 Liverpool
	(WBO Inter-Continental L. Welterweight Title Defence)
29.01.00	Leoncio Garces W RSC 3 Manchester
25.03.00	Pedro Teran W RSC 4 Liverpool
	(WBO Inter-Continental L. Welterweight Title Defence)
16.05.00	Ambioris Figuero W RSC 4 Warrington
	(WBO Inter-Continental L. Welterweight Title Defence)
10.06.00	Gilbert Quiros W CO 2 Detroit, Michigan, USA
	(WBO Inter-Continental L. Welterweight Title Defence)
23.09.00	Giuseppe Lauri W RSC 5 Bethnal Green

	(WBO Inter-Continental L.Welterweight Title Defence. WBA Inter-Continental L.Welterweight Title Challenge)
21.10.00	Jonathan Thaxton W PTS 12 Wembley
	(Vacant British L.Welterweight Title)
26.03.01	Tony Pep W CO 4 Wembley
	(Vacant WBU L. Welterweight Title)
07.07.01	Jason Rowland W CO 4 Manchester
	(WBU L.Welterweight Title Defence)
15.09.01	John Bailey W RSC 5 Manchester
	(WBU L.Welterweight Title Defence)
27.10.01	Fred Pendleton W CO 2 Manchester
	(WBU L.Welterweight Title Defence)
15.12.01	Justin Rowsell W RSC 2 Wembley
	(WBU L.Welterweight Title Defence)
09.02.02	Mikhail Krivolapov W RSC 9 Manchester
	(WBU L. Welterweight Title Defence)
01.06.02	Eamonn Magee W PTS 12 Manchester
	(WBU L.Welterweight Title Defence)
28.09.02	Stephen Smith W DIS 2 Manchester
	(WBU L.Welterweight Title Defence)
14.12.02	Joe Hutchinson W CO 4 Newcastle
	(WBU L. Welterweight Title Defence)
05.04.03	Vince Phillips W PTS 12 Manchester
	(WBU L.Welterweight Title Defence)
27.09.03	Aldi Rios W RTD 9 Manchester
	(WBU L.Welterweight Title Defence)
13.12.03	Ben Tackie W PTS 12 Manchester
	(WBU L.Welterweight Title Defence)
03.04.04	Dennis Holbaek Pedersen W RSC 6 Manchester
	(WBU L.Welterweight Title Defence)
12.06.04	Wilfredo Carlos Vilches W PTS 12 Manchester
	(WBU L.Welterweight Title Defence)
01.10.04	Michael Stewart W RSC 5 Manchester
	(WBU L.Welterweight Title Defence. Final Elim. IBF L.Welterweight Title)
11.12.04	Ray Oliveira W CO 10 Canning Town
	(WBU L.Welterweight Title Defence)
04.06.05	Kostya Tszyu W RSC 11 Manchester
	(IBF L.Welterweight Title Challenge)
26.11.05	Carlos Maussa W CO 9 Sheffield
	(IBF L.Welterweight Title Challenge. WBA L.Welterweight Title Defence)
13.05.06	Luis Collazo W PTS 12 Boston, Massachusetts, USA
	(WBA Welterweight Title Challenge)
20.01.07	Juan Urango W PTS 12 Las Vegas, Nevada, USA
	(IBF L.Welterweight Title Challenge. Vacant IBO L.Welterweight Title)
23.06.07	Jose Luis Castillo W CO 4 Las Vegas, Nevada, USA
	(IBO L.Welterweight Title Defence. Vacant WBC International L.Welterweight Title)

Career: 43 contests, won 43.

Stephen Haughian

Lurgan Co. Armagh. *Born* Craigavon, 20 November, 1984
L.Welterweight. *Ht* 5'10½"
Manager J. Breen/F. Warren

18.03.05	James Gorman W PTS 4 Belfast
14.10.05	Imad Khamis W RSC 4 Dublin
24.11.05	James Gorman W PTS 6 Lurgan
28.01.06	Duncan Cottier W PTS 4 Dublin
20.05.06	Pete Buckley W PTS 4 Belfast
26.10.06	Denis Alekseevs W RSC 1 Belfast
11.11.06	Silence Saheed W PTS 6 Dublin
17.02.07	Dwayne Hill W RSC 2 Cork
25.03.07	Chill John W PTS 6 Dublin

Career: 9 contests, won 9.

David Haye

Bermondsey. *Born* London, 13 October, 1980
Cruiserweight. Former Undefeated European & English Cruiserweight Champion. *Ht* 6'3"
Manager Self

08.12.02	Tony Booth W RTD 2 Bethnal Green
24.01.03	Saber Zairi W RSC 4 Sheffield
04.03.03	Roger Bowden W RSC 2 Miami, Florida, USA
18.03.03	Phill Day W RSC 2 Reading
15.07.03	Vance Wynn W RSC 1 Los Angeles, California, USA
01.08.03	Greg Scott-Briggs W CO 1 Bethnal Green
26.09.03	Lolenga Mock W RSC 4 Reading
14.11.03	Tony Dowling W RSC 1 Bethnal Green
	(Vacant English Cruiserweight Title)
20.03.04	Hastings Rasani W RSC 1 Wembley
12.05.04	Arthur Williams W RSC 3 Reading
10.09.04	Carl Thompson L RSC 5 Wembley
	(IBO Cruiserweight Title Challenge)
10.12.04	Valery Semishkur W RSC 1 Sheffield
21.01.05	Garry Delaney W RTD 3 Brentford
04.03.05	Glen Kelly W CO 2 Rotherham
14.10.05	Vincenzo Rossitto W RSC 2 Huddersfield
16.12.05	Alexander Gurov W CO 1 Bracknell
	(European Cruiserweight Title Challenge)
24.03.06	Lasse Johansen W RSC 8 Bethnal Green
	(European Cruiserweight Title Defence)
21.07.06	Ismail Abdoul W PTS 12 Altrincham
	(European Cruiserweight Title Defence)
17.11.06	Giacobbe Fragomeni W RSC 9 Bethnal Green
	(European Cruiserweight Title Defence)
27.04.07	Tomasz Bonin W RSC 1 Wembley

Career: 20 contests, won 19, lost 1.

Peter Haymer

Enfield. *Born* London, 10 July, 1978
English L.Heavyweight. Champion.
Ht 6'1¼"
Manager C. Hall

25.11.00	Adam Cale W RSC 1 Manchester
27.01.01	Darren Ashton W PTS 4 Bethnal Green
10.03.01	Daniel Ivanov W CO 2 Bethnal Green
26.03.01	Radcliffe Green W PTS 4 Wembley
05.05.01	Terry Morrill W PTS 4 Edmonton
22.09.01	Tony Booth W PTS 4 Bethnal Green
24.11.01	Nathan King L PTS 4 Bethnal Green
12.02.02	Nathan King L PTS 4 Bethnal Green
09.05.02	Mark Snipe W PTS 4 Leicester Square
15.06.02	Paul Bonson W PTS 4 Tottenham
30.10.02	Jimmy Steel W PTS 4 Leicester Square
18.03.03	Mark Brookes W PTS 6 Reading
18.09.03	Ovill McKenzie W PTS 4 Mayfair
10.12.03	Mark Brookes DREW 6 Sheffield
12.11.04	Steven Spartacus W PTS 10 Wembley
	(English L.Heavyweight Title Challenge)
10.12.04	Mark Brookes W RSC 10 Sheffield
	(English L.Heavyweight Title Defence)
24.04.05	Ryan Walls W PTS 6 Leicester Square
19.06.05	Tony Oakey W PTS 10 Bethnal Green
	(English L.Heavyweight Title Defence)

07.04.06 Leigh Alliss W RSC 9 Bristol
          (English L.Heavyweight Title Defence)
21.05.06 Varuzhan Davtyan W RSC 4 Bethnal
          Green
24.09.06 Ovill McKenzie L RSC 2 Bethnal
          Green
          (Vacant Commonwealth L.Heavyweight
          Title)
18.05.07 Paul David L PTS 8 Canning Town
Career: 22 contests, won 17, drew 1, lost 4.

Scott Haywood

Derby. *Born* Derby, 5 June, 1981
L.Welterweight. *Ht* 6'0"
Manager Self
06.10.03 Pete Buckley W PTS 6 Barnsley
23.11.03 Arv Mittoo W PTS 6 Rotherham
16.02.04 Pete Buckley W PTS 6 Scunthorpe
26.04.04 Chris Brophy W RSC 5 Cleethorpes
27.09.04 Judex Meemea W PTS 6 Cleethorpes
16.12.04 Tony Montana L PTS 6 Cleethorpes
26.02.05 Jimmy Beech W PTS 6 Burton
24.04.05 Chris Long W PTS 6 Derby
02.09.05 Kristian Laight W PTS 6 Derby
08.12.05 Dave Hinds W RTD 3 Derby
28.01.06 Jus Wallie W PTS 4 Nottingham
25.03.06 Billy Smith W PTS 6 Burton
14.05.06 Surinder Sekhon W RSC 1 Derby
03.11.06 John Fewkes L PTS 8 Barnsley
09.02.07 Billy Smith W PTS 4 Leeds
13.04.07 Gary O'Connor W PTS 6 Altrincham
11.05.07 Billy Smith W PTS 4 Motherwell
Career: 17 contests, won 15, lost 2.

Scott Haywood   Les Clark

Eugene Heagney

Huddersfield. *Born* Dublin, 4 April, 1983
Featherweight. *Ht* 5'8"
Manager M. Marsden
29.06.06 Neil Marston W PTS 6 Dudley
11.11.06 Delroy Spencer W PTS 4 Dublin
03.12.06 Neil Read W PTS 6 Wakefield
14.04.07 Delroy Spencer W PTS 6 Wakefield
14.06.07 Shaun Walton W PTS 6 Leeds
Career: 5 contests, won 5.

Ciaran Healy

Belfast. *Born* Belfast, 25 December, 1974
Middleweight. *Ht* 5'11"
Manager Self
05.04.03 Tomas da Silva W PTS 4 Belfast
18.09.03 Patrick Cito W PTS 4 Mayfair
04.10.03 Joel Ani W PTS 4 Belfast
22.11.03 Neil Addis W RSC 1 Belfast
26.06.04 Jason McKay L PTS 6 Belfast
25.04.05 Vince Baldassara L RSC 4 Glasgow
17.06.05 Chris Black DREW 4 Glasgow
18.02.06 Karoly Domokos W PTS 4 Dublin
21.04.06 George Hillyard L CO 6 Belfast
18.11.06 Anthony Small L RSC 3 Newport
23.06.07 Lukasz Wawrzyczek L PTS 8 Dublin
Career: 11 contests, won 5, drew 1, lost 5.

(Jack) Jak Hibbert

Sheffield. *Born* Sheffield, 21 September, 1985
Middleweight. *Ht* 6'0"
Manager D. Hobson
12.12.04 Chris Black L RSC 2 Glasgow
04.03.05 Neil Jarmolinski W PTS 6 Rotherham
17.06.05 Vince Baldassara L RSC 1 Glasgow
24.02.06 Ryan Ashworth W PTS 6 Scarborough
22.06.06 Thomas Flynn W RSC 3 Sheffield
20.10.06 Lee Noble L RSC 6 Sheffield
10.12.06 Lee Noble L PTS 6 Sheffield
Career: 7 contests, won 3, lost 4.

Dean Hickman

West Bromwich. *Born* West Bromwich, 24 November, 1979
L.Welterweight. Former Undefeated Midlands Area L.Welterweight Champion. *Ht* 5'7"
Manager E. Johnson
17.02.02 Wayne Wheeler DREW 6
          Wolverhampton
13.04.02 Wayne Wheeler W PTS 6
          Wolverhampton
13.07.02 Dai Bando W RSC 1 Wolverhampton
02.11.02 Darren Goode W RSC 2
          Wolverhampton
15.02.03 Gareth Wiltshaw W PTS 6
          Wolverhampton
21.03.03 David Vaughan W PTS 6 West
          Bromwich
30.06.03 Dave Hinds W RSC 4 Shrewsbury
17.07.03 Lee McAllister W PTS 6 Walsall
30.10.03 John-Paul Ryan W PTS 6 Dudley
15.04.04 Tony Montana W PTS 6 Dudley
04.06.04 Adnan Amar W RSC 8 Dudley
          (Vacant Midlands Area L.Welterweight
          Title)
25.11.04 Ceri Hall W PTS 4 Birmingham
17.02.05 Gary Reid W PTS 10 Dudley
          (Midlands Area L.Welterweight Title
          Defence)
11.03.05 Nigel Wright L CO 7 Doncaster
          (Vacant English L.Welterweight Title)
16.02.06 Ernie Smith W PTS 4 Dudley
17.03.06 Barry Morrison L RSC 1 Kirkcaldy
          (Elim. British L.Welterweight Title)
29.06.06 Tom Hogan W RSC 2 Dudley
06.10.06 Stuart Green W PTS 6 Wolverhampton
20.04.07 Gary Reid L RSC 5 Dudley
          (Vacant Midlands Area L.Welterweight
          Title)
Career: 19 contests, won 15, drew 1, lost 3.

Herbie Hide

Norwich. *Born* Nigeria, 27 August, 1971
Heavyweight. Former WBO Heavyweight Champion. Former Undefeated British, WBC International & Penta-Continental Heavyweight Champion. *Ht* 6'1½"
Manager Self
24.10.89 L. A. Williams W CO 2 Bethnal Green
05.11.89 Gary McCrory W RTD 1 Kensington
19.12.89 Steve Osborne W RSC 6 Bethnal Green
27.06.90 Alek Penarski W RSC 3 Kensington
05.09.90 Steve Lewsam W RSC 4 Brighton
26.09.90 Jonjo Greene W RSC 1 Manchester
17.10.90 Gus Mendes W RSC 2 Bethnal Green
18.11.90 Steve Lewsam W RSC 1 Birmingham
29.01.91 Lennie Howard W RSC 1 Wisbech
09.04.91 David Jules W RSC 1 Mayfair
14.05.91 John Westgarth W RTD 4 Dudley
03.07.91 Tucker Richards W RSC 3 Brentwood
15.10.91 Eddie Gonzalez W CO 2 Hamburg,
          Germany
29.10.91 Chris Jacobs W RSC 1 Cardiff
21.01.92 Conroy Nelson W RSC 2 Norwich
          (Vacant WBC International
          Heavyweight Title)
03.03.92 Percell Davis W CO 1 Amsterdam,
          Holland
08.09.92 Jean Chanet W RSC 7 Norwich
06.10.92 Craig Peterson W RSC 7 Antwerp,
          Belgium
          (WBC International Heavyweight Title
          Defence)
12.12.92 James Pritchard W RSC 2 Muswell Hill
30.01.93 Juan Antonio Diaz W RSC 3
          Brentwood
          (Vacant Penta-Continental
          Heavyweight Title)
27.02.93 Michael Murray W RSC 5 Dagenham
          (Vacant British Heavyweight Title)
11.05.93 Jerry Halstead W RSC 4 Norwich
          (Penta-Continental Heavyweight Title
          Defence)
18.09.93 Everett Martin W PTS 10 Leicester
06.11.93 Mike Dixon W RSC 9 Bethnal Green
          (Penta-Continental Heavyweight Title
          Defence)
04.12.93 Jeff Lampkin W RSC 2 Sun City, South
          Africa
          (WBC International Heavyweight Title
          Defence)
19.03.94 Michael Bentt W CO 7 Millwall
          (WBO Heavyweight Title Challenge)
11.03.95 Riddick Bowe L CO 6 Las Vegas,
          Nevada, USA
          (WBO Heavyweight Title Defence)
06.07.96 Michael Murray W RSC 6 Manchester
09.11.96 Frankie Swindell W CO 1 Manchester
28.06.97 Tony Tucker W RSC 2 Norwich
          (Vacant WBO Heavyweight Title)
18.04.98 Damon Reed W RSC 1 Manchester
          (WBO Heavyweight Title Defence)
26.09.98 Willi Fischer W RSC 2 Norwich
          (WBO Heavyweight Title Defence)
26.06.99 Vitali Klitschko L CO 2 Millwall
          (WBO Heavyweight Title Defence)
14.07.01 Alexei Osokin W RSC 3 Liverpool
22.09.01 Joseph Chingangu L RSC 2 Newcastle
16.04.03 Derek McCafferty W RSC 7
          Nottingham
27.05.03 Joseph Chingangu W CO 1 Dagenham
04.10.03 Alex Vasiliev W RSC 5 Muswell Hill
12.03.04 Mendauga Kulikauskas L RSC 4
          Nottingham

23.09.06	Mitch Hicks W RSC 1 Fort Smith, Arkansas, USA	
24.03.07	Valery Semishkur W CO 1 Hamburg, Germany	
27.04.07	Pavol Polakovic W CO 6 Hamburg, Germany	
16.06.07	Aleh Dubiaha W CO 1 Ankara, Turkey	

Career: 43 contests, won 39, lost 4.

Graeme Higginson

Blackburn. *Born* Blackburn, 31 July, 1982
L.Welterweight. *Ht* 5'8¼"
Manager Self

14.10.05	Darren Johnstone L PTS 6 Motherwell
03.11.05	Tom Hogan L PTS 6 Sunderland
19.11.05	Mark Alexander L PTS 4 Southwark
23.01.06	Paul Appleby L RTD 3 Glasgow
04.03.06	Dougie Walton DREW 6 Coventry
27.05.06	Omar Akram W RSC 2 Glasgow
01.06.06	Paul Appleby L RSC 2 Birmingham
21.07.06	James Brown W PTS 4 Altrincham
06.12.06	Andrew Ward W PTS 6 Rotherham
28.01.07	Paul Truscott L PTS 4 Yarm

Career: 10 contests, won 3, drew 1, lost 6.

Dwayne Hill

Sheffield. *Born* Sheffield, 31 January, 1986
Lightweight. *Ht* 5'8"
Manager G. Rhodes

08.05.05	Anthony Christopher W PTS 6 Sheffield
24.07.05	Gary Coombes W RSC 3 Sheffield
30.10.05	Gavin Tait W PTS 6 Sheffield
12.11.05	Lance Verallo W PTS 6 Sheffield
17.02.06	Carl Allen W PTS 6 Sheffield
16.06.06	Daniel Thorpe W PTS 4 Liverpool
28.10.06	Youssef Al Hamidi L RSC 3 Sheffield
17.02.07	Stephen Haughian L RSC 2 Cork

Career: 8 contests, won 6, lost 2.

George Hillyard

Canning Town. *Born* Forest Gate, 19
November, 1984
British Masters L.Middleweight Champion.
Ht 5'9¼"
Manager A. Sims

16.06.05	Geraint Harvey W RSC 1 Dagenham
30.09.05	James Gorman W RSC 1 Kirkcaldy
21.10.05	Ernie Smith L PTS 4 Bethnal Green
18.11.05	Richard Mazurek W PTS 6 Dagenham
24.02.06	Gary Harrison W RTD 4 Dagenham
21.04.06	Ciaran Healy W CO 6 Belfast
22.09.06	Tyan Booth L PTS 6 Bethnal Green
15.12.06	Marcus Portman L PTS 8 Bethnal Green
20.01.07	Tony Randell DREW 4 Muswell Hill
18.05.07	Matt Scriven W PTS 4 Canning Town
16.06.07	Dave Wakefield W PTS 10 Chigwell *(Vacant British Masters L.Middleweight Title)*

Career: 11 contests, won 7, drew 1, lost 3.

Mark Hobson

Huddersfield. *Born* Workington, 7 May,
1976
WBU Cruiserweight Champion. Former
Undefeated British & Commonwealth
Cruiserweight Champion. *Ht* 6'5"
Manager C. Aston

09.06.97	Michael Pinnock W PTS 6 Bradford
06.10.97	P. R. Mason W PTS 6 Bradford
13.11.97	P. R. Mason W PTS 6 Bradford
27.02.98	Colin Brown DREW 6 Irvine
21.05.98	Paul Bonson W PTS 6 Bradford
15.06.98	Martin Jolley W RSC 3 Bradford
25.10.98	Mark Snipe W RSC 3 Shaw
26.11.98	Danny Southam W RSC 5 Bradford
19.04.99	Mark Levy L PTS 8 Bradford
11.09.99	Paul Bonson W PTS 4 Sheffield
06.12.99	Brian Gascoigne W RSC 3 Bradford
11.03.00	Nikolai Ermenkov W RSC 3 Kensington
27.03.00	Luke Simpkin W PTS 4 Barnsley
13.05.00	Paul Bonson W PTS 4 Barnsley
25.09.00	Mark Dawson W CO 1 Barnsley
26.02.01	Billy Bessey W PTS 4 Nottingham
24.04.01	Sebastiaan Rothmann L RTD 9 Liverpool *(WBU Cruiserweight Title Challenge)*
08.10.01	Firat Arslan L RSC 7 Barnsley
10.12.01	Luke Simpkin W RTD 3 Liverpool
23.02.02	Valery Semishkur W PTS 6 Nottingham
27.04.02	Lee Swaby W PTS 10 Huddersfield *(Final Elim. British Cruiserweight Title)*
05.10.02	Varuzhan Davtyan W RSC 3 Huddersfield
25.01.03	Abdul Kaddu W RSC 4 Bridgend *(Vacant Commonwealth Cruiserweight Title)*
10.05.03	Muslim Biarslanov W RSC 2 Huddersfield
05.09.03	Robert Norton W PTS 12 Sheffield *(Commonwealth Cruiserweight Title Defence. Vacant British Cruiserweight Title)*
13.03.04	Tony Moran W RSC 3 Huddersfield *(British & Commonwealth Cruiserweight Title Defences)*
27.05.04	Lee Swaby W RSC 6 Huddersfield *(British & Commonwealth Cruiserweight Title Defences)*
17.12.04	Bruce Scott W PTS 12 Huddersfield *(British & Commonwealth Cruiserweight Title Defences)*
04.03.06	Enzo Maccarinelli L PTS 12 Manchester *(WBU Cruiserweight Title Challenge)*
01.06.06	John Keeton W RSC 4 Barnsley *(British & Commonwealth Cruiserweight Title Defences)*
08.09.06	Pavol Polakovic W PTS 12 Mayfair *(Vacant WBU Cruiserweight Title)*
14.10.06	Enzo Maccarinelli L RSC 1 Manchester *(WBO Cruiserweight Title Challenge)*

Career: 32 contests, won 26, drew 1, lost 5.

Lee Hodgson

Hayes. *Born* Hammersmith, 28 June, 1973
Middleweight. *Ht* 5'9½"
Manager D. Currivan

27.09.02	Kevin Phelan W RSC 1 Bracknell
03.12.02	Leigh Wicks W PTS 4 Bethnal Green
08.02.03	Dean Powell W PTS 4 Brentford
21.03.03	Elroy Edwards W RSC 3 Longford
29.03.03	Matthew Barr L RSC 1 Wembley
20.03.04	Rob MacDonald W RSC 3 Wembley
07.04.04	Conroy McIntosh L RSC 3 Leicester Square
25.09.05	Mark Phillips W PTS 6 Southampton
16.12.05	Steve Ede L PTS 4 Bracknell
24.09.06	Steve Ede L RSC 3 Southampton

Career: 10 contests, won 6, lost 4.

Tom Hogan

Carlisle. *Born* Wigan, 2 May, 1977
Welterweight. *Ht* 5'9½"
Manager T. Conroy

09.11.04	Pete Buckley W PTS 6 Leeds
21.02.05	Mike Reid L PTS 6 Glasgow
06.10.05	Kristian Laight W PTS 6 Sunderland
03.11.05	Graeme Higginson W PTS 6 Sunderland
08.12.05	Adam Kelly W PTS 6 Sunderland
09.03.06	David Pinkney W PTS 6 Sunderland
31.03.06	Mike Reid W PTS 6 Inverurie
29.06.06	Dean Hickman L RSC 2 Dudley
05.10.06	Gary O'Connor L PTS 6 Sunderland
28.10.06	Sujad Elahi L RSC 2 Sheffield
16.03.07	Paddy Pollock L RSC 3 Glasgow

Career: 11 contests, won 6, lost 5.

Paul Holborn

Sunderland. *Born* Sunderland, 1 March,
1984
L.Welterweight. *Ht* 5'8½"
Manager Self

11.10.04	Stuart Green W PTS 6 Glasgow
15.12.04	Amir Ali L PTS 6 Sheffield
06.10.05	Daniel Thorpe W PTS 6 Sunderland
03.11.05	Haroon Din DREW 6 Sunderland
28.04.06	Billy Smith W PTS 4 Hartlepool
11.05.06	Kristian Laight W PTS 6 Sunderland
05.10.06	Youssef Al Hamidi W PTS 6 Sunderland

Career: 7 contests, won 5, drew 1, lost 1.

Jon Honney

Basingstoke. *Born* Basingstoke, 6 August,
1975
Southern Area L.Welterweight Champion.
Ht 5'7"
Manager Self

01.10.99	Peter Dunn W PTS 4 Bethnal Green
18.12.99	Marco Fattore W PTS 4 Southwark
21.02.00	Costas Katsantonis L RSC 1 Southwark
13.07.00	Mickey Yikealo L PTS 4 Bethnal Green
29.09.00	Manzo Smith L PTS 4 Bethnal Green
06.11.00	Jimmy Gould L PTS 6 Wolverhampton
16.03.01	Woody Greenaway W PTS 6 Portsmouth
07.09.01	Young Muttley L RSC 1 West Bromwich
20.10.01	Martin Watson L RSC 3 Glasgow
23.02.02	Darrell Grafton L RTD 1 Nottingham
28.11.02	Henry Jones W PTS 4 Finchley
20.12.02	Martin Hardcastle W PTS 4 Bracknell
05.03.03	Francis Barrett L PTS 10 Bethnal Green *(Vacant Southern Area L.Welterweight Title)*
27.05.03	Stephen Smith L PTS 8 Dagenham
26.07.03	Michael Ayers W PTS 6 Plymouth
11.10.03	Graham Earl L PTS 8 Portsmouth
07.04.04	Peter McDonagh L PTS 10 Leicester Square *(Vacant Southern Area Lightweight Title)*
12.05.04	John Alldis W PTS 6 Reading
22.05.04	Nigel Wright L RSC 2 Widnes
26.11.04	Rob Jeffries L PTS 8 Bethnal Green
25.02.05	Lee Beavis L PTS 4 Wembley
25.09.05	Daniel Thorpe L PTS 4 Southampton
04.11.05	Danny Hunt L PTS 8 Bethnal Green
27.01.06	Leo O'Reilly L PTS 6 Dagenham

11.02.06	Dean Phillips L RSC 2 Bethnal Green
26.05.06	Tontcho Tontchev L PTS 6 Bethnal Green
24.09.06	Ashley Theophane L PTS 6 Bethnal Green
20.10.06	Nicki Smedley L PTS 6 Sheffield
24.02.07	Nathan Ward W PTS 10 Bracknell
	(Vacant Southern Area L.Welterweight Title)

Career: 29 contests, won 8, lost 21.

Chris Hooper
Scarborough. *Born* Barking, 28 September, 1977
S.Featherweight. *Ht* 5'9"
Manager Self

01.11.01	Jason Nesbitt W RSC 6 Hull
28.01.02	Greg Edwards W RSC 2 Barnsley
27.07.02	John Mackay L PTS 4 Nottingham
26.09.02	Sid Razak W PTS 6 Hull
21.11.02	Baz Carey W RTD 3 Hull
03.04.03	Buster Dennis W RSC 1 Hull
20.02.04	Buster Dennis L RSC 2 Bethnal Green
08.04.04	John Bothwell W CO 2 Peterborough
30.07.04	Steve Gethin W PTS 4 Bethnal Green
01.10.04	Andy Morris L RSC 3 Manchester
24.02.06	Gary Davis L RSC 1 Scarborough
	(Vacant Central Area S.Bantamweight Title. Vacant British Masters S.Bantamweight Title)
21.04.06	Martin Lindsay L RSC 1 Belfast
24.11.06	Jason Nesbitt DREW 6 Hull
09.02.07	Danny Wallace L PTS 4 Leeds
27.04.07	John Baguley L RSC 1 Hull

Career: 15 contests, won 7, drew 1, lost 7.

Kerry Hope
Merthyr Tydfil. *Born* Merthyr Tydfil, 21 October, 1981
Middleweight. *Ht* 5'10"
Manager F. Warren

21.01.05	Brian Coleman W PTS 4 Bridgend
08.04.05	Ernie Smith W PTS 4 Edinburgh
27.05.05	Lee Williamson W PTS 4 Spennymoor
10.09.05	John-Paul Temple W PTS 4 Cardiff
04.03.06	Matt Scriven W PTS 4 Manchester
01.06.06	Joe Mitchell W PTS 4 Barnsley
08.07.06	Ryan Rowlinson W PTS 4 Cardiff
18.11.06	Manoocha Salari W RSC 2 Newport
07.04.07	Jamie Ambler W PTS 6 Cardiff

Career: 9 contests, won 9.

Richard Horton
Romford. *Born* Romford, 12 November, 1981
S.Middleweight. *Ht* 6'0¾"
Manager D. Powell

25.02.06	Nick Okoth W CO 3 Canning Town
01.04.06	Ojay Abrahams W PTS 4 Bethnal Green
13.05.06	Mark Phillips W PTS 4 Bethnal Green
23.07.06	Shon Davies L RSC 1 Dagenham
24.09.06	Mark Phillips W PTS 4 Bethnal Green

Career: 5 contests, won 4, lost 1.

Sam Horton
Stourbridge. *Born* Wordsley, 20 August, 1985
S.Middleweight. *Ht* 5'11"
Manager E. Johnson

07.10.06	Tony Randell W PTS 6 Walsall
17.11.06	Jon Foster W PTS 6 Brierley Hill
15.02.07	Dave Pearson W RSC 4 Dudley
20.04.07	Tony Stones W PTS 4 Dudley
28.06.07	Ernie Smith W PTS 4 Dudley

Career: 5 contests, won 5.

Matthew Hough
Walsall. *Born* Walsall, 5 January, 1977
L.Heavyweight. *Ht* 6'2"
Manager E. Johnson

17.02.05	Paddy Ryan W PTS 6 Dudley
21.04.05	Mark Phillips W PTS 4 Dudley
25.11.05	Robert Burton W PTS 4 Walsall
10.03.06	John Ruddock W PTS 6 Walsall
18.05.06	Dean Walker W PTS 6 Walsall
07.10.06	Danny McIntosh L RSC 6 Walsall
15.02.07	Nicki Taylor L RSC 2 Dudley

Career: 7 contests, won 5, lost 2.

Ben Hudson
Cambridge. *Born* Cambridge, 29 March, 1973
L.Middleweight. *Ht* 5'6"
Manager Self

23.08.02	Pete Buckley DREW 4 Bethnal Green
06.09.02	Scott Lawton L PTS 4 Bethnal Green
26.09.02	Jas Malik W CO 3 Fulham
27.10.02	Peter McDonagh W PTS 6 Southwark
08.12.02	Daffyd Carlin W PTS 6 Bethnal Green
18.02.03	Brian Coleman W PTS 6 Bethnal Green
08.04.03	Peter McDonagh L PTS 6 Bethnal Green
26.04.03	Robert Lloyd-Taylor W PTS 4 Brentford
27.05.03	Lenny Daws L RSC 2 Dagenham
25.09.03	Chas Symonds L PTS 6 Bethnal Green
09.07.03	John O'Donnell L RTD 3 Nottingham
30.09.05	Mike Reid L PTS 4 Kirkcaldy
07.10.05	Craig Watson L PTS 4 Bethnal Green
21.10.05	John O'Donnell L PTS 4 Bethnal Green
30.10.05	Wayne Goddard L PTS 4 Bethnal Green
12.11.05	Scott Lawton L PTS 6 Stoke
25.11.05	Stuart Elwell L PTS 4 Walsall
11.12.05	Surinder Sekhon W PTS 6 Chigwell
28.01.06	Adnan Amar L PTS 4 Nottingham
17.02.06	Lee Meager L PTS 4 Bethnal Green
03.03.06	Franny Jones L PTS 6 Hartlepool
24.03.06	Robert Lloyd-Taylor L PTS 6 Bethnal Green
06.04.06	Duncan Cottier L PTS 4 Piccadilly
14.04.06	Mark Lloyd L PTS 4 Telford
12.05.06	Allan Gray W PTS 4 Bethnal Green
03.06.06	Tom Glover L PTS 4 Chigwell
23.06.06	Jamie Coyle L PTS 6 Blackpool
23.07.06	Danny Goode L PTS 4 Dagenham
15.09.06	Grzegorz Proksa L PTS 4 Muswell Hill
23.09.06	Kevin Concepcion L PTS 6 Coventry
30.09.06	Franny Jones L PTS 6 Middlesbrough
07.10.06	Marcus Portman L PTS 6 Walsall
28.10.06	Lee McAllister L PTS 8 Aberdeen
10.11.06	Stuart Elwell L PTS 4 Telford
24.11.06	Aaron Thomas L PTS 6 Stoke
02.12.06	Nathan Ward L PTS 6 Longford
23.03.07	Adnan Amar L PTS 4 Nottingham
27.04.07	Glen Matsell L PTS 6 Hull
06.05.07	Danny Reynolds L PTS 8 Leeds
18.05.07	David Walker L PTS 6 Canning Town
15.06.07	Sam Webb L PTS 4 Crystal Palace

Career: 41 contests, won 7, drew 1, lost 33.

Barry Hughes
Glasgow. *Born* Glasgow, 18 November, 1978
L.Welterweight. *Ht* 5'8"
Manager Self

07.12.98	Woody Greenaway L PTS 6 Acton
18.02.99	Leon Dobbs W RSC 1 Glasgow
09.04.99	Gareth Dooley W PTS 6 Glasgow
26.06.99	Des Sowden W CO 1 Glasgow
04.10.99	Tony Smith W RSC 2 Glasgow
12.11.99	Brendan Ahearne W RSC 5 Glasgow
13.12.99	Jason Vlasman W RSC 2 Glasgow
24.02.00	No No Junior W RSC 1 Glasgow
18.03.00	Gary Flear W RSC 4 Glasgow
07.04.00	Billy Smith W PTS 6 Glasgow
12.08.00	Dave Travers W PTS 4 Wembley
15.03.02	Woody Greenaway W PTS 8 Glasgow
19.10.02	Arsen Vassilev W CO 3 Renfrew
08.12.02	Paul McIlwaine W RSC 2 Glasgow
16.05.03	Martin Watson L RTD 8 Glasgow
	(Vacant Scottish Lightweight Title)
06.03.04	Peter McDonagh W PTS 6 Renfrew
23.04.04	Brian Coleman W PTS 8 Glasgow
28.05.04	Charles Shepherd DREW 12 Glasgow
	(Vacant WBU Inter-Continental Lightweight Title)
19.06.04	Nigel Senior W RSC 3 Renfrew
04.11.06	Baz Carey W PTS 4 Glasgow

Career: 20 contests, won 17, drew 1, lost 2.

Danny Hughes
Sunderland. *Born* Sunderland, 3 March, 1986
Heavyweight. *Ht* 6'5¼"
Manager T. Conroy

24.06.07	Lee Webb W RSC 4 Sunderland

Career: 1 contest, won 1.

Kris Hughes
Bellshill. *Born* Bellshill, 23 November, 1987
Bantamweight. *Ht* 5'11¼"
Manager Barry Hughes/F. O'Connor

27.10.06	Delroy Spencer W PTS 6 Glasgow
26.01.07	Robert Bunford W PTS 6 Glasgow

Career: 2 contests, won 2.

Sean Hughes
Pontefract. *Born* Pontefract, 5 June, 1982
S.Featherweight. Former Undefeated Central Area S.Bantamweight Champion.
Ht 5'9"
Manager Self

02.03.02	Paddy Folan W PTS 6 Wakefield
25.06.02	John Paul Ryan W PTS 6 Rugby
05.10.02	Paddy Folan W PTS 4 Huddersfield
10.02.03	Neil Read W PTS 6 Sheffield
24.05.03	John-Paul Ryan W PTS 6 Sheffield
13.09.03	Daniel Thorpe W PTS 6 Wakefield
05.10.03	Paddy Folan W RSC 4 Bradford
	(Vacant Central Area S.Bantamweight Title)
07.12.03	Marty Kayes W PTS 6 Bradford
26.02.04	Steve Foster L RSC 6 Widnes
	(Vacant English Featherweight Title)
23.10.04	Kristian Laight W PTS 6 Wakefield
04.03.05	Michael Hunter L RSC 6 Hartlepool
	(British S.Bantamweight Title Challenge)

08.05.05 Billy Smith W PTS 6 Bradford
25.06.05 Pete Buckley DREW 6 Wakefield
14.10.05 Bernard Dunne L RSC 2 Dublin
          (Vacant IBC S.Bantamweight Title)
03.03.06 Marc Callaghan L PTS 10 Hartlepool
          (Vacant English S.Bantamweight Title)
28.05.06 Shaun Walton W PTS 6 Wakefield
10.11.06 Riaz Durgahed L PTS 6 Hartlepool
24.11.06 Billy Corcoran L RSC 8 Nottingham
14.04.07 Sergei Rozhakmens W PTS 6
          Wakefield

Career: 19 contests, won 12, drew 1, lost 6.

Sean Hughes   Les Clark

Albi Hunt

Ealing. *Born* Hammersmith, 20 April, 1974
L.Welterweight. *Ht* 5'9"
Manager J. Feld

28.04.02 Jason Gonzales W PTS 6 Southwark
22.09.02 Daniel Thorpe W PTS 6 Southwark
18.02.07 Pawel Jas W PTS 4 Bethnal Green
08.06.07 Daniel Thorpe W PTS 4 Mayfair

Career: 4 contests, won 4.

Rob Hunt

Stafford. *Born* Stafford, 9 November, 1985
Welterweight. *Ht* 6'0"
Manager P. Dykes

18.05.06 Ian Clyde W RSC 1 Walsall
29.06.06 Pete Buckley W PTS 6 Dudley
07.10.06 Karl Taylor W PTS 6 Walsall
15.02.07 Kristian Laight W PTS 6 Dudley
09.06.07 Johnny Greaves W PTS 6
          Middlesbrough

Career: 5 contests, won 5.

Michael Hunter

Hartlepool. *Born* Hartlepool, 5 May, 1978
Featherweight. Former Undefeated British,
European, Commonwealth, WBF &
Northern Area S.Bantamweight Champion.
Ht 5'7½"
Manager Self

23.07.00 Sean Grant W PTS 6 Hartlepool
01.10.00 Chris Emanuele W PTS 6 Hartlepool
24.11.00 Gary Groves W RSC 2 Darlington
09.12.00 Chris Jickells W PTS 4 Southwark

11.02.01 Paddy Folan W RSC 6 Hartlepool
06.05.01 Anthony Hanna W PTS 4 Hartlepool
04.06.01 Anthony Hanna W PTS 4 Hartlepool
09.09.01 John Barnes W RSC 8 Hartlepool
          *(Vacant Northern Area S.Bantamweight
          Title)*
29.11.01 Joel Viney W PTS 6 Hartlepool
26.01.02 Stevie Quinn W CO 2 Dagenham
18.03.02 Marc Callaghan DREW 6 Crawley
18.05.02 Mark Payne W PTS 8 Millwall
18.10.02 Frankie DeMilo W PTS 12 Hartlepool
          (Vacant WBF S. Bantamweight Title)
14.12.02 Anthony Hanna W PTS 8 Newcastle
07.06.03 Afrim Mustafa W RSC 5 Trieste, Italy
26.07.03 Rocky Dean W RSC 1 Plymouth
04.10.03 Nikolai Eremeev W PTS 6 Belfast
08.11.03 Gennadiy Delisandru W PTS 6
          Bridgend
16.04.04 Mark Payne W RSC 7 Hartlepool
          (Vacant British S.Bantamweight Title)
02.06.04 Vladimir Borov W PTS 6 Hereford
19.11.04 Marc Callaghan W RSC 10 Hartlepool
          (British S.Bantamweight Title Defence)
04.03.05 Sean Hughes W RSC 6 Hartlepool
          (British S.Bantamweight Title Defence)
27.05.05 Kamel Guerfi W RSC 6 Spennymoor
28.10.05 Esham Pickering W PTS 12 Hartlepool
          *(European & Commonwealth
          S.Bantamweight Title Challenges.
          British S.Bantamweight Title Defence)*
03.03.06 Yersin Jailauov W RSC 2 Hartlepool
          *(European S.Bantamweight Title
          Defence)*
28.04.06 German Guartos W RTD 3 Hartlepool
          *(European S.Bantamweight Title
          Defence)*
23.06.06 Tuncay Kaya W CO 9 Blackpool
          *(European S.Bantamweight Title
          Defence)*
10.11.06 Steve Molitor L CO 5 Hartlepool
          (Vacant IBF S.Bantamweight Title)
30.03.07 Ben Odamattey W PTS 8 Crawley

Career: 29 contests, won 27, drew 1, lost 1.

Ali Hussain

Bradford. *Born* Bradford, 3 July 1988
L.Welterweight. *Ht* 6'1"
Manager C. Aston

07.12.06 Kristian Laight L PTS 6 Bradford
16.02.07 Mark Bett DREW 6 Sunderland
23.02.07 James Barker L PTS 6 Manchester
16.03.07 Mark Bett L RSC 3 Glasgow

Career: 4 contests, drew 1, lost 3.

Jamil Hussain

Bradford. *Born* Pakistan, 15 September,
1979
Bantamweight. *Ht* 5'7"
Manager C. Aston

08.10.01 Andy Greenaway W RSC 3 Barnsley
28.01.02 Neil Read W CO 2 Barnsley
18.03.02 Darren Cleary DREW 4 Crawley
27.04.02 Darren Cleary DREW 4 Huddersfield
22.02.03 Danny Wallace L RSC 1 Huddersfield
30.03.06 Moses Kinyua W PTS 6 Peterborough
09.02.07 Jason Booth L PTS 6 Leeds
16.06.07 Matthew Edmonds L RTD 3 Newport
          *(Vacant International Masters
          Bantamweight Title)*

Career: 8 contests, won 3, drew 2, lost 3.

Khurram Hussain

Bradford. *Born* Bradford, 11 August, 1980
L.Middleweight. *Ht* 5'10"
Manager J. Ingle

13.11.05 Peter Dunn W PTS 4 Leeds
03.12.05 Kyle Taylor W PTS 6 Coventry
23.02.06 Darren Gethin DREW 4 Leeds
04.03.06 Joe McCluskey W PTS 6 Coventry
28.05.06 Tye Williams W PTS 6 Wakefield
24.02.07 Jonathan Hussey L PTS 6 Manchester
06.05.07 Karl Taylor W PTS 4 Leeds
27.05.07 Peter Dunn W PTS 4 Bradford

Career: 8 contests, won 6, drew 1, lost 1.

(Wajid) Waz Hussain

Sutton Coldfield. *Born* Birmingham, 25
February, 1983
Lightweight. *Ht* 5'9"
Manager R. Woodhall

01.12.06 Neal McQuade DREW 4 Birmingham
23.02.07 Gavin Deacon L PTS 4 Birmingham

Career: 2 contests, drew 1, lost 1.

Jonathan Hussey

Manchester. *Born* Manchester, 18 August,
1982
Welterweight. *Ht* 6'0"
Manager J. Trickett

08.07.05 Joe Mitchell W PTS 4 Altrincham
01.10.05 Darren Gethin W PTS 6 Wigan
18.12.05 Karl Taylor W PTS 6 Bolton
12.02.06 Tye Williams W PTS 6 Manchester
06.05.06 Geraint Harvey W PTS 6 Blackpool
18.06.06 Barry Downes W PTS 6 Manchester
10.07.06 Imad Khamis W PTS 6 Manchester
26.10.06 Billy Smith L PTS 6 Dudley
24.02.07 Khurram Hussain W PTS 6
          Manchester

Career: 9 contests, won 8, lost 1.

Eddie Hyland

Wellingborough. *Born* Dublin, 24 April,
1981
Lightweight. *Ht* 5'6½"
Manager J. Harding

26.11.04 Buster Dennis W PTS 4 Altrincham
04.06.05 Stefan Berza W RSC 1 Dublin
17.09.05 Peter Batora W RSC 1 Dublin
11.03.06 Tibor Rafael W RSC 2 Dublin
16.06.06 Steve Mullin L RTD 4 Liverpool
10.02.07 Gheorghe Ghiompirica W PTS 4
          Letterkenny
30.06.07 Daniel Thorpe W PTS 4 Belfast

Career: 7 contests, won 6, lost 1.

Patrick Hyland

Wellingborough. *Born* Dublin, 16
September, 1983
S.Featherweight. *Ht* 5'7¼"
Manager J. Harding

24.09.04 Dean Ward W PTS 4 Dublin
13.02.05 Steve Gethin W PTS 4 Brentwood
04.06.05 Pete Buckley W PTS 4 Dublin
17.09.05 Imrich Parlagi W PTS 4 Dublin
18.11.05 Craig Morgan W PTS 4 Dagenham
11.03.06 Tibor Besze W CO 1 Dublin
23.06.07 Lajos Beller W RSC 1 Dublin

Career: 7 contests, won 7.

IJ

Jon Ibbotson
Sheffield. *Born* Sheffield, 2 September, 1982
L.Heavyweight. *Ht* 6'3½"
Manager D. Hobson

15.12.04	Paul Billington W PTS 4 Sheffield
20.02.05	Nick Okoth W PTS 6 Sheffield
22.04.05	Daniel Teasdale W RSC 1 Barnsley
18.06.05	Ojay Abrahams W PTS 4 Barnsley
05.03.06	Tony Booth W PTS 4 Sheffield
13.05.06	Magid Ben Driss W RSC 2 Sheffield
22.06.06	Robert Burton DREW 6 Sheffield
20.10.06	Robert Burton W CO 2 Sheffield
20.01.07	Shannon Anderson W RSC 1 Las Vegas, Nevada, USA
03.05.07	Darren Stubbs L RSC 4 Sheffield

Career: 10 contests, won 8, drew 1, lost 1.

Alex Ibbs
Stoke. *Born* Stoke, 17 August, 1985
Heavyweight. *Ht* 6'4"
Manager R. Woodhall

01.12.06	Istvan Kecskes W PTS 4 Birmingham
12.05.07	David Ingleby W PTS 6 Stoke

Career: 2 contests, won 2.

David Ingleby
Lancaster. *Born* Lancaster, 14 June, 1980
Heavyweight. *Ht* 6'3"
Manager Self

09.06.03	Costi Marin L RSC 1 Bradford
01.12.03	Paul Bonson L PTS 6 Leeds
28.02.04	Paul King L RSC 3 Manchester
01.05.04	Jason Callum L PTS 6 Coventry
10.07.04	Scott Lansdowne L RSC 4 Coventry
20.09.04	Dave Clarke W RTD 5 Glasgow
06.12.04	Paul Butlin L CO 5 Leicester
30.04.05	Paul Butlin W PTS 6 Coventry
02.06.05	Chris Burton L RSC 3 Yarm
12.05.05	Scott Lansdowne L RSC 1 Leicester
18.03.06	Paul Butlin L PTS 6 Coventry
06.04.06	Matt Paice L PTS 4 Piccadilly
13.05.06	Carl Baker L RSC 4 Sheffield
07.10.06	Henry Smith W PTS 6 Weston super Mare
16.02.07	Dave Ferguson L PTS 4 Sunderland
20.04.07	Billy Boyle L PTS 4 Sheffield
03.05.07	Scott Brookes L PTS 6 Sheffield
12.05.07	Alex Ibbs L PTS 6 Stoke
24.06.07	Dave Ferguson L PTS 4 Sunderland

Career: 19 contests, won 3, lost 16.

Hamed Jamali
Birmingham. *Born* Iran, 23 November, 1973
S.Middleweight. *Ht* 5'9"
Manager Self

09.12.02	Dale Nixon W CO 1 Birmingham
24.02.03	Harry Butler W PTS 6 Birmingham
06.10.03	Simeon Cover W PTS 6 Birmingham
08.12.03	JJ Ojuederie W PTS 6 Birmingham
08.03.04	Ojay Abrahams W PTS 8 Birmingham
10.05.04	Jason Collins W PTS 8 Birmingham
11.10.04	Hastings Rasani W PTS 8 Birmingham
13.12.04	Simeon Cover L PTS 10 Birmingham *(Vacant British Masters S.Middleweight Title)*
21.02.05	Michael Pinnock W PTS 8 Birmingham
02.03.06	Lee Blundell L PTS 6 Blackpool
07.04.06	Dan Guthrie L RSC 3 Bristol
08.09.06	Cello Renda L RSC 1 Birmingham

Career: 12 contests, won 8, lost 4.

Robbie James
Rhymney. *Born* Merthyr, 23 August, 1984
L.Middleweight. *Ht* 5'11"
Manager C. Sanigar

15.09.06	Jav Jerome W PTS 4 Newport
03.03.07	Gatis Skuja W PTS 6 Newport
16.06.07	Lewis Byrne W PTS 4 Newport

Career: 3 contests, won 3.

Pawel Jas
Wood Green. *Born* Wroclaw, Poland, 11 April, 1979
L.Middleweight. *Ht* 5'11½"
Manager C. Hall

03.11.06	Rocky Chakir L PTS 6 Bristol
10.11.06	Jamie Way L PTS 6 Newport
24.11.06	Andrew Alan Lowe L PTS 6 Stoke
02.12.06	Wayne Goddard L PTS 4 Longford
18.02.07	Albi Hunt L PTS 4 Bethnal Green
09.03.07	Jon Dennington L PTS 4 Dagenham
18.03.07	Danny Butler L PTS 6 Bristol

Career: 7 contests, lost 7.

Pawel Jas   Les Clark

Stuart Jeffrey
Nottingham. *Born* Nottingham, 12 August, 1978
L.Middleweight. *Ht* 5'9¼"
Manager J. Gill/T. Harris

24.02.07	Paul Royston W PTS 6 Manchester

Career: 1 contest, won 1.

Ervis Jegeni
Wood Green. *Born* Albania, 4 May, 1986
Heavyweight. *Ht* 6'1¼"
Manager C. Hall

30.03.06	Tony Booth W RSC 1 Piccadilly
21.05.06	Istvan Kecskes W PTS 4 Bethnal Green
12.07.06	Tony Booth W PTS 4 Bethnal Green
09.03.07	Gabor Gyuris W CO 1 Torrevieja, Spain
15.06.07	Janos Somogyi W RSC 4 Torrevieja, Spain

Career: 5 contests, won 5.

Ervis Jegeni   Les Clark

Michael Jennings
Chorley. *Born* Preston, 9 September, 1977
WBU Welterweight Champion. Former British Welterweight Champion. Former Undefeated English Welterweight Champion. Former Undefeated WBU Inter-Continental Welterweight Champion.
Ht 5'9¼"
Manager F. Warren

15.05.99	Tony Smith W RSC 1 Blackpool
11.12.99	Lee Molyneux W PTS 4 Liverpool
29.02.00	Lee Molyneux W PTS 6 Widnes
25.03.00	Brian Coleman W PTS 6 Liverpool
16.05.00	Brian Coleman W PTS 6 Warrington
29.05.00	William Webster W PTS 6 Manchester
08.07.00	Paul Denton W PTS 6 Widnes
04.09.00	Mark Ramsey W PTS 6 Manchester
25.11.00	Ernie Smith W PTS 4 Manchester
11.12.00	Paul Denton W PTS 4 Widnes
10.02.01	Mark Haslam W RSC 2 Widnes
07.07.01	David Kirk W PTS 6 Manchester
15.09.01	Gary Harrison W PTS 6 Manchester
09.02.02	James Paisley W RSC 3 Manchester
01.06.02	Lee Williamson W PTS 6 Manchester
28.09.02	Karl Taylor W RSC 4 Manchester
01.11.02	Richard Inquieti W RSC 2 Preston
18.01.03	Lee Williamson W RTD 4 Preston
08.05.03	Jimmy Gould W RTD 6 Widnes *(Vacant WBU Inter-Continental Welterweight Title)*
27.09.03	Sammy Smith W RTD 4 Manchester *(WBU Inter-Continental Welterweight Title Defence)*

13.12.03	Peter Dunn W PTS 6 Manchester	
01.04.04	Brett James W RTD 5 Bethnal Green *(WBU Inter-Continental Welterweight Title Defence)*	
22.05.04	Rafal Jackiewicz W PTS 8 Widnes	
01.10.04	Chris Saunders W RTD 5 Manchester *(English Welterweight Title Challenge)*	
11.02.05	Vasile Dragomir W CO 3 Manchester	
03.06.05	Gavin Down W RSC 9 Manchester *(English Welterweight Title Defence)*	
16.07.05	Jimmy Vincent W CO 1 Bolton *(Vacant British Welterweight Title)*	
25.10.05	Bradley Pryce W PTS 12 Preston *(British Welterweight Title Defence)*	
28.01.06	Young Muttley L PTS 12 Nottingham *(British Welterweight Title Defence)*	
02.09.06	Rastislav Kovac W CO 3 Bolton	
07.04.07	Takaloo W PTS 12 Cardiff *(WBU Welterweight Title Challenge)*	

Career: 31 contests, won 30, lost 1.

Mick Jenno

Liverpool. *Born* Liverpool, 16 July, 1977
S.Middleweight. *Ht* 5'11"
Manager W. Dixon

30.06.07 Martin Gillick W RSC 1 Manchester
Career: 1 contest, won 1.

Jav Jerome

Birmingham. *Born* Afghanistan, 1 June, 1982
Middleweight. *Ht* 5'8"
Manager N. Nobbs

23.02.06 Gavin Smith L RSC 5 Leeds
20.05.06 Leon Owen L PTS 6 Bristol
15.09.06 Robbie James L PTS 4 Newport
24.09.06 Michael Grant L PTS 4 Bethnal Green
Career: 4 contests, lost 4.

Jav Jerome   Les Clark

Carl Johanneson

Leeds. *Born* Leeds, 1 August, 1978
British S.Featherweight Champion. Former
Undefeated Central Area S.Featherweight
Champion. Former Undefeated WBF
S.Featherweight Champion. *Ht* 5'5"
Manager F. Maloney

08.07.00 Calvin Sheppard W PTS 3 North
          Carolina, USA

15.09.00	Sean Thomassen W RSC 1 Paterson, New Jersey, USA	
14.10.00	Hiep Bui W RSC 1 Scranton, Pennsylvania, USA	
08.12.00	Walusimbi Kizito W PTS 4 Atlantic City, New Jersey, USA	
12.04.01	Efrain Guzman W PTS 4 Melville, New York, USA	
04.05.01	Calvin Sheppard W RSC 4 Atlantic City, New Jersey, USA	
26.06.01	Joey Figueroa W PTS 6 NYC, New York, USA	
26.10.01	Jose Ramon Disla W RSC 5 Atlantic City, New Jersey, USA	
14.12.01	Angel Rios W PTS 6 Uncasville, Connecticut, USA	
03.03.02	Kema Muse W PTS 6 Scranton, Pennsylvania, USA	
02.07.02	James Baker W RSC 4 Washington DC, USA	

16.01.03	Juan R. Llopis W RSC 5 Philadelphia, Pennsylvania, USA	
05.06.03	Koba Gogoladze L PTS 8 Detroit, Michigan, USA	
18.07.03	Reggie Sanders W PTS 6 Dover, Delaware, USA	
21.08.03	Steve Trumble W RSC 2 Philadelphia, Pennsylvania, USA	
30.01.04	Harold Grey W RSC 5 Philadelphia, Pennsylvania, USA	
20.03.04	Carl Greaves W RTD 3 Wembley *(WBF S.Featherweight Title Challenge)*	
08.05.04	Andrew Ferrans W RSC 6 Bristol *(WBF S.Featherweight Title Defence)*	
19.06.04	Alexander Abramenko W RSC 5 Muswell Hill *(WBF S.Featherweight Title Defence)*	
02.12.04	Leva Kirakosyan L RSC 1 Crystal Palace	
08.05.05	Jimmy Beech W CO 2 Bradford	

Carl Johanneson   Les Clark

09.07.05 Daniel Thorpe W RSC 3 Bristol
25.09.05 Peter Allen W RTD 9 Leeds
   (Vacant Central Area S.Featherweight Title)
13.11.05 Carl Allen W RTD 2 Leeds
23.02.06 Andrew Ferrans W RSC 2 Leeds
   (Final Elim. British S.Featherweight Title)
12.07.06 Billy Corcoran W RSC 4 Bethnal Green
   (Vacant British S.Featherweight Title)
03.11.06 Femi Fehintola W RSC 6 Barnsley
   (British S.Featherweight Title Defence)
09.02.07 Ricky Burns W PTS 12 Leeds
   (British S.Featherweight Title Defence)
Career: 28 contests, won 26, lost 2.

(Garnet) Chill John

Brighton. *Born* St Vincent, 11 August, 1977
L.Welterweight. *Ht* 5'7"
Manager Self

22.10.00 Paul Philpott W PTS 6 Streatham
03.02.01 Dave Travers W PTS 4 Brighton
25.02.01 Scott Hocking W RSC 4 Streatham
05.05.01 Woody Greenaway W PTS 6 Brighton
04.07.01 Steve Hanley W PTS 4 Bloomsbury
20.10.01 Mark Halstead W PTS 4 Portsmouth
01.12.01 Pete Buckley W PTS 4 Bethnal Green
13.04.02 Jonathan Thaxton L RSC 2 Norwich
12.07.02 Daniel Thorpe W PTS 4 Southampton
22.09.02 Jason Hall L PTS 6 Southwark
12.10.02 Graham Earl L PTS 10 Piccadilly
   (Southern Area Lightweight Title Challenge)
21.12.02 Lee Meager L RSC 5 Dagenham
02.10.03 Danny Hunt L PTS 10 Liverpool
   (Vacant English Lightweight Title)
21.02.04 Peter McDonagh L RTD 2 Brighton
05.03.05 Rob Jeffries L PTS 8 Southwark
29.09.06 Ceri Hall DREW 4 Cardiff
18.11.06 Gavin Rees L PTS 8 Newport
17.02.07 Paul McCloskey L PTS 6 Cork
25.03.07 Stephen Haughian L PTS 6 Dublin
23.06.07 Oisin Fagan L PTS 8 Dublin
Career: 20 contests, won 8, drew 1, lost 11.

Chris Johnson

Manchester. *Born* Chorley, 8 March, 1981
L.Middleweight. *Ht* 5'10"
Manager S. Wood

29.09.06 Paul Porter L RSC 2 Manchester
17.12.06 Geraint Harvey W PTS 6 Bolton
11.03.07 Karl Taylor W RTD 3 Shaw
06.05.07 Danny Gwilym W RSC 4 Altrincham
24.06.07 David Kirk W PTS 4 Wigan
Career: 5 contests, won 4, lost 1.

Clint Johnson

Leeds. *Born* Leeds, 13 April, 1974
Cruiserweight. *Ht* 6'2"
Manager Self

11.11.97 Jon Penn W RSC 2 Leeds
04.12.97 John O'Byrne L PTS 6 Sunderland
17.02.98 Rob Galloway W PTS 6 Leeds
20.09.98 Rob Galloway W PTS 6 Sheffield
29.10.98 Mike White L PTS 6 Newcastle
06.11.98 Gerard Zdiarski W PTS 4 Mayfair
07.12.98 Carl Nicholson W PTS 6 Bradford
16.02.99 Danny Southam L RSC 5 Leeds
15.09.99 Steve Loftus W PTS 6 Harrogate
28.03.00 Martin Jolley W PTS 6 Hartlepool

17.04.00 Alex Mason L PTS 6 Birmingham
20.05.00 Jason Barker L RSC 1 Rotherham
23.10.00 Joe Gillon L CO 4 Glasgow
17.05.01 Paul Bonson L PTS 6 Leeds
18.06.01 Mark Brookes L PTS 6 Bradford
13.09.01 Darren Littlewood W PTS 6 Sheffield
03.11.01 Joe Gillon W CO 3 Glasgow
03.12.01 Jimmy Steel DREW 6 Leeds
15.12.01 Mark Brookes L PTS 4 Sheffield
18.02.02 Billy McClung L PTS 6 Glasgow
01.03.02 Billy McClung L PTS 6 Irvine
16.03.02 Clinton Woods L RSC 3 Bethnal Green
08.10.02 Allan Foster L PTS 6 Glasgow
02.12.02 Greg Scott-Briggs W PTS 6 Leeds
08.02.03 Andrew Lowe L PTS 6 Brentford
05.04.03 Darren Corbett L RSC 4 Belfast
12.10.03 Scott Lansdowne L PTS 4 Sheffield
01.12.03 Simeon Cover W PTS 6 Leeds
20.03.04 Courtney Fry L RSC 2 Wembley
28.02.06 Keiran O'Donnell L RSC 1 Leeds
21.04.06 Stewart Mitchell L PTS 4 Doncaster
01.10.06 John Anthony L PTS 6 Rotherham
Career: 32 contests, won 11, drew 1, lost 20.

Craig Johnson

Clay Cross. *Born* Chesterfield, 10 November, 1980
Lightweight. *Ht* 5'7"
Manager M. Shinfield

25.04.04 Peter Allen W PTS 6 Nottingham
18.09.04 David Bailey L PTS 6 Newark
22.10.04 Carl Allen W PTS 6 Mansfield
10.12.04 Pete Buckley W PTS 6 Mansfield
06.03.05 Ian Reid W PTS 6 Mansfield
11.09.05 Billy Smith W PTS 4 Kirkby in Ashfield
12.11.05 Jason Nesbitt W PTS 6 Sheffield
29.04.07 Sergei Rozhakmens W PTS 6 Birmingham
Career: 8 contests, won 7, lost 1.

Danny Johnston

Stoke. *Born* Stoke, 19 May, 1981
Middleweight. *Ht* 5'10"
Manager M. Carney

26.09.04 Karl Taylor W PTS 6 Stoke
12.11.05 Manoocha Salari L RSC 5 Stoke
18.02.06 Terry Carruthers L PTS 6 Stoke
06.05.06 Derrick Grieve W RSC 3 Stoke
24.11.06 Martin Marshall W PTS 6 Stoke
24.02.07 Howard Clarke W PTS 6 Stoke
12.05.07 Thomas Mazurkiewicz L PTS 6 Stoke
Career: 7 contests, won 4, lost 3.

Darren Johnstone

Larkhall. *Born* Motherwell, 30 March, 1982
British Masters S.Featherweight Champion.
Ht 5'9"
Manager T. Gilmour

17.11.03 Jamie Hill W PTS 6 Glasgow
15.03.04 Ian Reid W PTS 6 Glasgow
07.06.04 Joel Viney W PTS 6 Glasgow
11.10.04 Pete Buckley W PTS 6 Glasgow
27.05.05 Gavin Tait W PTS 6 Motherwell
14.10.05 Graeme Higginson W PTS 6 Motherwell
04.11.05 Jonathan Whiteman W RSC 3 Glasgow
21.11.05 Lance Verallo W PTS 6 Glasgow
24.04.06 Henry Jones W CO 4 Glasgow
   (Vacant British Masters S.Featherweight Title)

22.01.07 Steve Gethin W PTS 10 Glasgow
   (British Masters S.Featherweight Title Defence)
Career: 10 contests, won 10.

Barrie Jones

Rhondda. *Born* Tylorstown, South Wales, 1 March, 1985
Welterweight. *Ht* 5'11¼"
Manager D. Powell/F. Warren

03.07.04 Pete Buckley W PTS 4 Newport
03.09.04 Dave Hinds W PTS 4 Newport
21.01.05 Lea Handley W PTS 4 Bridgend
17.06.05 Marco Cittadini W RSC 2 Glasgow
10.09.05 Jas Malik W RSC 1 Cardiff
11.03.06 Terry Carruthers W RSC 1 Newport
29.04.06 David Kehoe W RTD 2 Edinburgh
08.07.06 James Paisley W RSC 2 Cardiff
18.11.06 Ernie Smith W PTS 4 Newport
16.02.07 Chris Brophy W PTS 4 Merthyr Tydfil
07.04.07 Daniel Thorpe W RSC 2 Cardiff
05.05.07 Rocky Muscas W PTS 6 Glasgow
Career: 12 contests, won 12.

Ben Jones

Crawley. *Born*: Crawley, 12 June, 1982
Lightweight. *Ht* 5'8"
Manager M. Alldis

22.09.06 Carl Allen W PTS 4 Bethnal Green
15.12.06 Steve Gethin W PTS 4 Bethnal Green
30.03.07 Rom Krauklis L RSC 1 Crawley
Career: 3 contests, won 2, lost 1.

Davey Jones   Les Clark

Davey Jones

Epworth. *Born* Grimsby, 30 May, 1977
S.Middleweight. *Ht* 5'11"
Manager M. Shinfield

23.09.02 William Webster W PTS 6 Cleethorpes
08.11.02 William Webster W PTS 6 Doncaster
30.11.02 Matt Scriven W PTS 6 Newark
16.12.02 Gary Jones W PTS 6 Cleethorpes
21.02.03 Jimi Hendricks W PTS 6 Doncaster
09.05.03 Wayne Shepherd W PTS 6 Doncaster
22.09.03 Steve Brumant L PTS 6 Cleethorpes
26.02.04 Paul Smith L PTS 4 Widnes
06.03.04 Paul Buchanan L PTS 4 Renfrew

23.05.05	Ernie Smith DREW 6 Cleethorpes
15.12.05	Omar Gumati W PTS 6 Cleethorpes
16.02.06	Mark Lloyd L PTS 6 Dudley
04.11.06	Jon Foster L DIS 6 Mansfield
11.12.06	Terry Adams W PTS 6 Cleethorpes
23.02.07	Jason Rushton L CO 7 Doncaster
	(Vacant Central Area L.Middleweight Title)
24.03.07	Kevin Concepcion L RSC 1 Coventry
28.06.07	Rob Kenney L PTS 4 Dudley

Career: 17 contests, won 8, drew 1, lost 8.

Franny Jones

Darlington. *Born* Burnley, 7 February, 1981
L.Middleweight. *Ht* 5'9¼"
Manager M. Marsden

05.05.02	Surinder Sekhon W PTS 6 Hartlepool
28.09.02	Martin Scotland W PTS 6 Wakefield
18.10.02	Richard Inquieti W PTS 6 Hartlepool
27.02.03	Danny Moir DREW 6 Sunderland
17.03.03	Gary Porter W PTS 6 Glasgow
11.07.03	Gary Cummings W RSC 2 Darlington
10.10.03	Pedro Thompson W PTS 6 Darlington
13.12.03	Matthew Hatton DREW 6 Manchester
05.03.04	Danny Moir NC 3 Darlington
	(Vacant Northern Area L.Middleweight Title)
16.04.04	Brian Coleman W PTS 6 Hartlepool
19.11.04	Paul Lomax W RSC 2 Hartlepool
04.03.05	Ali Nuumbembe L PTS 6 Hartlepool
11.03.05	Matthew Hatton L RTD 6 Doncaster
02.06.05	Darren Gethin W PTS 8 Yarm
28.10.05	Ernie Smith W PTS 4 Hartlepool
03.03.06	Ben Hudson W PTS 6 Hartlepool
28.04.06	Richard Mazurek W PTS 6 Hartlepool
23.06.06	Stuart Elwell L RSC 1 Blackpool
30.09.06	Ben Hudson W PTS 6 Middlesbrough
10.11.06	Jamie Coyle W RSC 2 Hartlepool
02.12.06	Craig Dickson W RSC 6 Clydebank
22.02.07	Jon Foster W CO 3 Leeds
23.06.07	Neil Sinclair W CO 5 Dublin

Career: 23 contests, won 17, drew 2, lost 3, no contest 1.

Henry Jones

Pembroke. *Born* Haverfordwest, 23 December, 1975
Lightweight. *Ht* 5'0¼"
Manager M. Goodall

17.06.95	Abdul Mannon W PTS 6 Cardiff
07.07.95	Harry Woods L PTS 4 Cardiff
07.10.95	Frankie Slane L PTS 4 Belfast
28.11.95	Jason Thomas L PTS 4 Cardiff
20.12.95	Brendan Bryce W PTS 6 Usk
20.03.96	Danny Lawson W CO 1 Cardiff
29.05.96	Ian Turner L PTS 6 Ebbw Vale
02.10.96	Jason Thomas W PTS 4 Cardiff
26.10.96	Danny Costello L RSC 3 Liverpool
29.04.97	Tommy Waite L PTS 4 Belfast
19.05.97	Francky Leroy L RSC 1 Coudekerque, France
02.12.97	Ian Turner L RSC 8 Swansea
	(Vacant Welsh Bantamweight Title)
30.10.98	Tiger Singh W CO 4 Peterborough
05.05.00	Jason Edwards L PTS 6 Pentre Halkyn
28.11.02	Jon Honney L PTS 4 Finchley
23.02.03	David Vaughan L PTS 6 Aberystwyth
10.04.03	Daleboy Rees L PTS 4 Clydach
07.05.03	Jason Nesbitt W PTS 6 Ellesmere Port
15.06.03	Dean Lambert L RSC 4 Bradford
20.04.04	Scott Lawton L PTS 6 Sheffield

19.06.04	Colin Bain L PTS 4 Renfrew
03.07.04	Michael Graydon DREW 6 Bristol
30.09.05	Jason Nesbitt W PTS 6 Carmarthen
24.04.06	Darren Johnstone L CO 4 Glasgow
	(Vacant British Masters S.Featherweight Title)
16.06.06	Furhan Rafiq W PTS 6 Carmarthen
08.10.06	Dai Davies L PTS 10 Swansea
	(Vacant Welsh Area S.Featherweight Title)
10.06.07	John Baguley L RSC 4 Neath

Career: 27 contests, won 8, drew 1, lost 18.

Justin Jones

Burslem. *Born* Burslem, 5 April, 1982
L.Heavyweight. *Ht* 6'3"
Manager M. Carney

24.02.07	Richard Collins DREW 6 Stoke

Career: 1 contest, drew 1.

Lee Jones

Telford. *Born* Northallerton, 31 May, 1983
L.Heavyweight. *Ht* 6'2"
Manager R. Woodhall

01.12.06	Nicki Taylor W PTS 4 Birmingham
23.02.07	Phillip Callaghan W PTS 4 Birmingham
30.06.07	Paulie Silva L PTS 6 Manchester

Career: 3 contests, won 2, lost 1.

Michael Jones

Liverpool. *Born* Liverpool, 14 November, 1974
L.Middleweight. Former British & Commonwealth L.Middleweight Champion. *Ht* 6'0¼"
Manager Self

15.11.97	Harry Butler W PTS 4 Bristol
17.01.98	Martin Cavey W CO 1 Bristol
07.03.98	Darren McInulty W PTS 4 Reading
25.04.98	Koba Kulu W RSC 3 Cardiff
06.06.98	G. L. Booth W RSC 2 Liverpool
10.10.98	Takaloo W PTS 6 Bethnal Green
19.12.98	Ojay Abrahams W PTS 6 Liverpool
26.06.99	Paul King W PTS 6 Glasgow
11.03.00	Alan Gilbert W RTD 3 Kensington
02.06.00	Mohammed Boualleg W PTS 8 Ashford
03.02.01	Howard Clarke W PTS 4 Manchester
24.04.01	Judicael Bedel W PTS 6 Liverpool
06.10.01	Delroy Mellis W PTS 8 Manchester
10.12.01	Piotr Bartnicki W RSC 4 Liverpool
13.04.02	Mark Richards W RSC 1 Liverpool
28.05.02	Joshua Onyango W RSC 4 Liverpool
	(Commonwealth L. Middleweight Title Challenge)
08.02.03	Howard Clarke W PTS 6 Liverpool
19.04.03	Jamie Moore L PTS 12 Liverpool
	(Commonwealth L.Middleweight Title Defence. Vacant British L.Middleweight Title)
18.10.03	Ojay Abrahams W PTS 6 Manchester
13.03.04	Jason Williams W PTS 6 Huddersfield
10.04.04	Darren Rhodes W RSC 3 Manchester
	(Final Elim. British L.Middleweight Title)
26.11.04	Jamie Moore W DIS 3 Altrincham
	(British L.Middleweight Title Challenge)

08.07.05	Jamie Moore L RSC 6 Altrincham
	(British L.Middleweight Title Defence)
03.03.06	Ismael Kerzazi W RSC 6 Hartlepool
23.06.06	Sergey Starkov W PTS 6 Blackpool
10.11.06	Szabolcs Rimovszky W RSC 1 Hartlepool
25.01.07	Michele Piccirillo L RSC 12 Milan, Italy
	(European L.Middleweight Title Challenge)

Career: 27 contests, won 24, lost 3.

(Lee) Taz Jones

Abercynon. *Born* Aberdare, 24 August, 1982
Welterweight. Former Undefeated British Masters L.Middleweight Champion. *Ht* 5'11"
Manager B. Coleman

15.09.02	David White DREW 4 Swansea
02.11.02	Gerard McAuley DREW 4 Belfast
21.12.02	Luke Rudd W RTD 1 Millwall
08.01.03	Elroy Edwards W PTS 6 Aberdare
27.09.03	Matthew Hatton L PTS 6 Manchester
06.12.03	Ernie Smith W PTS 4 Cardiff
21.02.04	Craig Lynch W PTS 4 Cardiff
17.04.04	Andy Gibson W PTS 6 Belfast
03.09.04	Karl Taylor W PTS 4 Newport
30.09.04	Craig Dickson DREW 6 Glasgow
08.12.04	Kevin Phelan W PTS 10 Longford
	(British Masters L.Middleweight Title Challenge)
18.03.05	Neil Sinclair W RSC 1 Belfast
23.07.05	Colin McNeil L PTS 10 Edinburgh
	(Vacant Celtic L.Middleweight Title)
10.09.05	Tony Doherty L PTS 10 Cardiff
	(Vacant Celtic Welterweight Title)
28.04.06	Graham Delehedy W CO 6 Hartlepool
15.09.06	Jon Harrison W PTS 6 Newport
07.04.07	Tony Doherty L RSC 7 Cardiff
	(Celtic Welterweight Title Challenge)

Career: 17 contests, won 10, drew 3, lost 4.

Tommy Jones

Llanelli. *Born* Swansea, 6 July, 1983
Middleweight. *Ht* 5'8"
Manager D. Davies

08.12.05	Simon Fleck L PTS 6 Derby
18.12.05	Alex Matvienko L PTS 6 Bolton
04.03.06	Richard Mazurek L PTS 6 Coventry
07.04.06	Danny Butler L PTS 4 Bristol
28.04.06	Prince Arron L PTS 6 Manchester
13.05.06	Mark Lloyd L PTS 6 Sutton in Ashfield
29.06.06	Mark Lloyd L PTS 6 Dudley
21.07.06	Brett Flournoy L RSC 1 Altrincham
06.10.06	Scott Woolford L PTS 4 Bethnal Green

Career: 9 contests, lost 9.

Scott Jordan

Belfast. *Born* Dundonald, 22 April, 1984
L.Middleweight. *Ht* 5'9¼"
Manager Self

21.04.06	Jamie Ambler W PTS 4 Belfast
25.11.06	Geraint Harvey W PTS 4 Belfast
15.12.06	Greg Barton W PTS 4 Bethnal Green
25.03.07	Duncan Cottier W PTS 6 Dublin
30.06.07	Alexander Spitjo L RSC 5 Belfast

Career: 5 contests, won 4, lost 1.

K

Zahir Kahut
Batley. *Born* Pakistan, 25 September, 1973
Heavyweight. *Ht* 6'6"
Manager C. Aston

16.06.07 Scott Mitchell W PTS 6 Bolton

Career: 1 contest, won 1.

Ysopov Karium
Rugby. *Born* Tblisi, Georgia, 29 January,
1981
L.Middleweight. *Ht* 5'9"
Manager J. Hollier

02.03.07 Olufemi Moses L PTS 4 Coventry
13.04.07 Ferenc Olah W RSC 1 Rugby

Career: 2 contests, won 1, lost 1.

George Katsimpas
Cheddar. *Born* Bristol, 8 June, 1980
Middleweight. *Ht* 5'7¾"
Manager J. Evans

05.03.06 Leon Owen W RSC 2 Southampton
20.05.06 Tony Randell W RSC 1 Bristol
11.09.06 Geraint Harvey W RSC 2 Manchester
26.10.06 Cello Renda W RSC 2 Wolverhampton
18.02.07 Prince Arron L PTS 8 Bethnal Green

Career: 5 contests, won 4, lost 1.

George Katsimpas   Les Clark

Jon Kays
Ashton-under-Lyne. *Born* Tameside, 24
May, 1983
Welterweight. *Ht* 5'8½"
Manager O. Harrison

24.06.07 Pete Buckley W PTS 6 Wigan

Career: 1 contest, won 1.

Istvan Kecskes
Wolverhampton. *Born* Nagykoros, Hungary,
26 January, 1980
Heavyweight. *Ht* 6'1"
Manager E. Johnson

24.11.01 Piotr Scieszka L RSC 2 Lodz, Poland

29.12.01 Karol Nowinski L PTS 6 Konin, Poland
09.02.02 Karoly Farkas W RSC 2 Budapest,
Hungary
01.04.02 Richel Hersisia L RSC 4 Gent, Belgium
20.05.02 Laszlo Virag DREW 4 Budapest,
Hungary
01.06.02 Cengiz Koc L RSC 2 Nurnberg,
Germany
24.11.02 Pavel Vanacek W PTS 4 Bad Honnef,
Germany
21.12.02 Balu Sauer L RSC 4 Cottbus, Germany
14.03.03 Zoltan Petranyi L PTS 4 Budapest,
Hungary
05.07.03 Rene Monse L RSC 2 Dessau,
Germany
07.09.03 Aleh Dubiaha L RSC 4 Prague, Czech
Republic
09.11.03 Josef Jakob L RSC 1 Bad Honnef,
Germany
24.04.04 Volodia Lazebnik L RSC 3 Dabrowa
Gornicza, Poland
03.03.06 Chris Burton L PTS 4 Hartlepool
11.03.06 Darren Morgan L PTS 4 Newport
25.03.06 Luke Simpkin L PTS 4 Burton
28.04.06 Chris Burton L PTS 4 Hartlepool
12.05.06 Sam Sexton L PTS 4 Bethnal Green
21.05.06 Ervis Jegeni L PTS 4 Bethnal Green
16.09.06 Scott Lansdowne L PTS 4 Burton
30.09.06 Chris Burton L RSC 5 Middlesbrough
01.12.06 Alex Ibbs L PTS 4 Birmingham
11.12.06 Chris Woollas L PTS 6 Cleethorpes
17.02.07 Derek Chisora L RSC 2 Wembley

Career: 24 contests, won 2, drew 1, lost 21.

John Keeton
Sheffield. *Born* Sheffield, 19 May, 1972
British Cruiserweight Champion. Former
Undefeated WBF & WBO Inter-Continental
Cruiserweight Champion. *Ht* 6'0"
Manager D. Ingle

11.08.93 Tony Colclough W RSC 1 Mansfield
15.09.93 Val Golding L PTS 6 Ashford
27.10.93 Darren McKenna W RSC 3 Stoke
01.12.93 Julius Francis L PTS 4 Bethnal Green
19.01.94 Dennis Bailey W RTD 2 Stoke
17.02.94 Dermot Gascoyne L RSC 1 Dagenham
09.04.94 Eddie Knight W RTD 5 Mansfield
11.05.94 John Rice W RSC 5 Sheffield
02.06.94 Devon Rhooms W RSC 2 Tooting
06.09.94 Mark Walker W RSC 5 Stoke
24.09.94 Dirk Wallyn L CO 3 Middlekerke,
Belgium
26.10.94 Lee Archer W PTS 6 Stoke
09.12.94 Bruce Scott L CO 2 Bethnal Green
11.02.95 Rudiger May L PTS 6 Frankfurt,
Germany
06.03.95 Simon McDougall W RSC 5 Mayfair
07.07.95 Nicky Piper L RTD 2 Cardiff
15.09.95 Steve Osborne W RSC 4 Mansfield
27.10.95 Nicky Wadman W RSC 1 Brighton
03.11.95 Monty Wright W RSC 4 Dudley
11.11.95 Denzil Browne W RSC 4 Halifax
30.01.96 Cesar Kazadi W RSC 3 Lille, France
11.05.96 Terry Dunstan L RSC 1 Bethnal Green
(British Cruiserweight Title Challenge)
14.09.96 John Pierre W PTS 4 Sheffield
14.12.96 Nigel Rafferty W RTD 3 Sheffield
12.04.97 Nigel Rafferty W RSC 6 Sheffield
11.10.97 Kelly Oliver L RSC 8 Sheffield
*(Vacant WBOInter-Continental
Cruiserweight Title)*
16.05.98 Jacob Mofokeng L RTD 4
Hammanskraal, South Africa

18.07.98 Kelly Oliver W RSC 2 Sheffield
23.01.99 Garry Delaney W PTS 12 Cheshunt
*(Vacant WBO Inter-Continental
Cruiserweight Title)*
15.05.99 William Barima W RTD 3 Sheffield
29.02.00 Tony Booth W RSC 2 Widnes
16.12.00 Bruce Scott L CO 6 Sheffield
(Vacant British Cruiserweight Title)
21.07.01 Radcliffe Green W PTS 4 Sheffield
19.03.02 Butch Lesley W PTS 12 Slough
(Vacant WBF Cruiserweight Title)
16.04.04 Paul Bonson W PTS 4 Bradford
14.05.05 Paul Bonson W PTS 4 Aberdeen
11.06.05 Krzysztof Wlodarczyk L RTD 3
Gorzow Wielkopolski, Poland
*(WBC Youth Cruiserweight Title
Challenge)*
10.09.05 Don Diego Poeder L CO 1 Rotterdam,
Netherlands
01.06.06 Mark Hobson L RSC 4 Barnsley
*(British & Commonwealth
Cruiserweight Title Challenges)*
20.10.06 Lee Swaby W RSC 7 Sheffield
(Vacant British Cruiserweight Title)
19.03.07 Troy Ross L CO 2 Montreal, Canada
*(Vacant Commonwealth Cruiserweight
Title)*

Career: 41 contests, won 26, lost 15.

John Keeton   Les Clark

David Kehoe
Northampton. *Born* Northampton, 24
December, 1972
Welterweight. *Ht* 5'10½"
Manager J. Gill

06.02.96 Simon Frailing W CO 1 Basildon
20.04.96 Paul Salmon W PTS 6 Brentwood
12.11.96 Peter Nightingale L PTS 6 Dudley
28.04.97 Craig Kelley L DIS 3 Enfield
18.11.97 Peter Nightingale DREW 4 Mansfield
27.01.98 Paul Miles L PTS 4 Bethnal Green
11.03.98 Trevor Tacy W RTD 1 Bethnal Green
28.03.98 David Thompson W PTS 6 Crystal
Palace
26.05.98 Dave Hinds W RSC 5 Mayfair

08.09.98	Marc Smith W PTS 6 Bethnal Green
12.01.99	Gary Flear L PTS 4 Bethnal Green
25.01.99	Roger Sampson L PTS 4 Glasgow
12.03.99	Jamie McKeever L RSC 2 Bethnal Green
02.07.99	Mark McGowan L RSC 3 Bristol *(Vacant British Masters Lightweight Title)*
13.09.99	Stephen Smith L DIS 2 Bethnal Green
05.10.99	John Humphrey L PTS 4 Bloomsbury
24.10.99	Young Muttley L RTD 1 Wolverhampton
02.12.99	Liam Maltby L PTS 4 Peterborough
19.02.00	Dariusz Snarski DREW 6 Prestwick
10.03.00	Ted Bami L PTS 4 Bethnal Green
17.04.00	Mark Hawthorne L PTS 4 Birmingham
25.07.00	P.J.Gallagher L PTS 6 Southwark
08.09.00	Dariusz Snarski W PTS 4 Hammersmith
27.11.00	Anthony Maynard L RSC 5 Birmingham
16.03.02	Wayne Wheeler DREW 6 Northampton
28.05.02	Ricky Eccleston L RSC 4 Liverpool
14.09.02	Danny Hunt L RSC 3 Bethnal Green
16.11.02	Gwyn Wale L PTS 4 Nottingham
01.02.03	Mark Winters L RSC 2 Belfast
29.10.03	Pete Buckley W PTS 6 Leicester Square
08.07.04	Rocky Muscus W PTS 6 The Strand
08.10.04	Graham Delehedy L RSC 2 Brentwood
18.03.05	Paul McCloskey L RSC 3 Belfast
24.04.05	Ashley Theophane L PTS 4 Leicester Square
26.06.05	Jay Morris L PTS 4 Southampton
24.07.05	Michael Grant L PTS 4 Leicester Square
30.09.05	Ceri Hall L PTS 6 Carmarthen
09.10.05	Ashley Theophane L PTS 4 Hammersmith
12.11.05	George Telfer L PTS 6 Glasgow
21.11.05	Craig Dickson L PTS 8 Glasgow
02.12.05	Stefy Bull L PTS 6 Doncaster
09.12.05	Grzegorz Proksa L RSC 3 Iver Heath
11.02.06	Lee Cook L RTD 2 Bethnal Green
13.03.06	Paul Burns L PTS 6 Glasgow
01.04.06	Dean Smith L PTS 4 Bethnal Green
13.04.06	Nadeem Siddique L PTS 6 Leeds
29.04.06	Barrie Jones L RTD 2 Edinburgh
30.05.06	Scott Woolford L PTS 4 Bethnal Green
16.06.06	Karl David L RSC 1 Carmarthen
09.12.06	Eddie Corcoran L RSC 3 Canning Town
16.02.07	Willie Bilan L RSC 1 Kirkcaldy
03.05.07	Nicki Smedley L RSC 4 Sheffield

Career: 52 contests, won 9, drew 3, lost 40.

Lee Kellett

Barrow. *Born* Barrow, 28 September, 1978
Cruiserweight. *Ht* 6'2"
Manager M. Helliet

12.02.06	John Anthony L RSC 1 Manchester
23.06.06	Gary Thompson L PTS 4 Blackpool
13.10.06	Gary Neville W RSC 1 Irvine
25.02.07	Mervyn Langdale W RSC 1 Southampton

Career: 4 contests, won 2, lost 2.

Adam Kelly

Sheffield. *Born* Sheffield, 8 August, 1987
L.Welterweight. *Ht* 5'8"
Manager J. Ingle

08.12.05	Tom Hogan L PTS 6 Sunderland
05.03.06	Tye Williams W PTS 4 Sheffield
17.03.06	Stuart Green L PTS 4 Kirkcaldy
27.05.06	Mike Reid DREW 6 Aberdeen
20.10.06	Tye Williams W PTS 4 Sheffield
24.11.06	Pete Buckley W PTS 6 Hull
06.12.06	Rom Krauklis W PTS 6 Stoke
03.05.07	Matt Seawright W PTS 4 Sheffield

Career: 8 contests, won 5, drew 1, lost 2.

Damaen Kelly

Belfast. *Born* Belfast, 3 April, 1973
Bantamweight. Former Undefeated IBO S.Flyweight Champion. Former Undefeated WBF & IBO Flyweight Champion. Former Undefeated European Flyweight Champion. Former Undefeated WBC International S.Flyweight Champion. Former British & Commonwealth Flyweight Champion.
Ht 5'5"
Manager Self

27.09.97	Chris Thomas W RSC 1 Belfast
22.11.97	Bojidar Ivanov W CO 1 Manchester
20.12.97	Anthony Hanna W PTS 4 Belfast
14.02.98	Hristo Lessov W RSC 2 Southwark
14.03.98	Mark Reynolds W RSC 4 Bethnal Green
02.05.98	Krasimir Tcholakov W RSC 3 Kensington
26.09.98	Mike Thomas W PTS 6 Uncasville, Connecticut, USA
12.12.98	Alfonso Zvenyika W PTS 12 Chester *(Commonwealth Flyweight Title Challenge)*
13.03.99	Anthony Hanna W PTS 12 Manchester *(Vacant British Flyweight Title. Commonwealth Flyweight Title Defence)*
22.05.99	Keith Knox L RTD 6 Belfast *(British & Commonwealth Flyweight Title Defences)*
16.10.99	Igor Gerasimov W RSC 4 Belfast *(Vacant WBC International S. Flyweight Title)*
12.02.00	Alexander Mahmutov W PTS 12 Sheffield *(European Flyweight Title Challenge)*
12.06.00	Jose Antonio Lopez Bueno W PTS 12 Belfast *(European Flyweight Title Defence)*
30.09.00	Zolile Mbitye W PTS 12 Peterborough *(IBO Flyweight Title Challenge)*
17.02.01	Paulino Villabos W PTS 12 Bethnal Green *(IBO Flyweight Title Defence)*
31.07.01	Sipho Mantyi W RSC 4 Bethnal Green
18.01.02	Simphewe Xabendini W RSC 1 Coventry
21.05.02	Celso Dangud W PTS 12 Custom House *(Vacant WBF Flyweight Title)*
05.10.02	Jovy Oracion W PTS 8 Liverpool
27.09.03	Irene Pacheco L RSC 7 Barranquilla, Colombia, *(IBF Flyweight Title Challenge)*
17.04.04	Andrei Kostin W RSC 1 Belfast
26.06.04	Delroy Spencer W RSC 4 Belfast
17.12.04	Jason Booth W PTS 12 Huddersfield *(IBO S.Flyweight Title Challenge)*
25.11.05	Ian Napa W PTS 10 Liverpool
21.04.06	Simone Maludrottu L PTS 12 Belfast *(European Bantamweight Title Challenge)*
25.11.06	Simone Maludrottu L RSC 3 Olbia, Sardinia, Italy *(European Bantamweight Title Challenge)*

Career: 26 contests, won 22, lost 4.

Colin Kenna

Southampton. *Born* Dublin, 28 July, 1976
Heavyweight. Former Southern Area Heavyweight Champion. *Ht* 6'1"
Manager Self

25.02.01	Slick Miller W RSC 3 Streatham
22.04.01	Eamonn Glennon W PTS 4 Streatham
15.10.01	Tony Booth W PTS 6 Southampton
11.02.02	Dave Clarke W RSC 4 Southampton
08.04.02	James Gilbert W RSC 1 Southampton
12.07.02	Gary Williams W RSC 3 Southampton
01.11.02	Paul Buttery DREW 6 Preston
17.03.03	Derek McCafferty W PTS 6 Southampton
12.05.03	Paul Bonson W PTS 6 Southampton
01.08.03	Michael Sprott L RSC 1 Bethnal Green *(Southern Area Heavyweight Title Challenge)*
26.10.03	Darren Ashton W CO 1 Longford
20.02.04	Paul Bonson W PTS 6 Southampton
30.03.04	Chris Woollas W PTS 6 Southampton
12.05.04	Mark Krence L RTD 3 Reading
06.02.05	Oneal Murray W RTD 3 Southampton
19.02.05	Paul King DREW 6 Dublin
26.06.05	Julius Francis W PTS 4 Southampton
04.12.05	Wayne Llewelyn W CO 2 Portsmouth *(Vacant Southern Area Heavyweight Title)*
28.01.06	Luke Simpkin W PTS 8 Dublin
05.03.06	Micky Steeds L PTS 10 Southampton *(Southern Area Heavyweight Title Defence)*
22.04.06	Oleg Platov L RSC 5 Mannheim, Germany
25.02.07	Keith Long W PTS 8 Southampton

Career: 22 contests, won 16, drew 2, lost 4.

Rob Kenney

Wolverhampton. *Born* Wolverhampton, 1 August, 1977
Middleweight. *Ht* 5'9"
Manager E. Johnson

05.12.06	Peter Dunn DREW 4 Wolverhampton
15.02.07	Peter Dunn W PTS 4 Dudley
14.04.07	Peter Dunn W PTS 4 Wakefield
28.06.07	Davey Jones W PTS 4 Dudley

Career: 4 contests, won 3, drew 1.

Mo Khaled (Al Saroodi)

Sheffield. *Born* Doha, Qatar, 19 January, 1988
S.Bantamweight. *Ht* 5'4"
Manager J. Ingle

26.05.06	Neil Marston L DIS 5 Hull
12.07.06	Neil Marston W PTS 4 Bethnal Green
29.09.06	Danny Wallace L RSC 1 Manchester
10.11.06	Matthew Edmonds L PTS 6 Newport
11.03.07	Stuart McFadyen L PTS 6 Shaw
27.05.07	Robert Nelson DREW 6 Bradford
17.06.07	Andy Bell L PTS 10 Mansfield *(Vacant British Masters Bantamweight Title)*

Career: 7 contests, won 1, drew 1, lost 5.

Imad Khamis
Manchester. *Born* Egypt, 9 March, 1977
L.Middleweight. *Ht* 5'11½"
Manager W. Barker

13.05.05	Stephen Burke L RSC 3 Liverpool
17.06.05	Martin McDonagh L DIS 4 Glasgow
16.09.05	Michael Medor L PTS 4 Plymouth
14.10.05	Stephen Haughian L RSC 4 Dublin
26.11.05	Billy Dib L PTS 6 Sheffield
26.02.06	James Paisley W RSC 3 Dagenham
23.03.06	Silence Saheed L RSC 5 The Strand
10.07.06	Jonathan Hussey L PTS 6 Manchester
11.09.06	Thomas Mazurkiewicz DREW 6 Manchester
21.10.06	Nathan Graham L RSC 2 Southwark
23.11.06	Thomas Mazurkiewicz L PTS 6 Manchester
10.12.06	Nicki Smedley L RSC 4 Sheffield
18.02.07	Jamal Morrison L RSC 2 Bethnal Green

Career: 13 contests, won 1, drew 1, lost 11.

Amer Khan
Sheffield. *Born* Sheffield, 21 February, 1981
Central Area L.Heavyweight Champion.
Ht 6'2"
Manager D. Ingle

06.06.03	Gary Jones W PTS 6 Hull
31.07.03	Michael Pinnock W PTS 6 Sheffield
05.09.03	Shpetim Hoti W RTD 4 Sheffield
04.12.03	Terry Morrill W PTS 6 Sunderland
06.02.04	Terry Morrill W PTS 6 Sheffield
03.04.04	Michael Pinnock W PTS 6 Sheffield
17.06.04	Hastings Rasani W PTS 6 Sheffield
24.10.04	Paulie Silva W PTS 6 Sheffield
04.03.05	Karl Wheeler W PTS 6 Rotherham
26.11.05	Jimi Hendricks W RSC 4 Sheffield
05.03.06	Paul Bonson W PTS 6 Sheffield
18.06.06	Darren Stubbs W PTS 10 Manchester *(Vacant Central Area L.Heavyweight Title)*
23.03.07	Ayitey Powers W PTS 6 Nottingham

Career: 13 contests, won 13.

Amir Khan
Bolton. *Born* Bolton, 8 December, 1986
Lightweight. *Ht* 5'10"
Manager F. Warren

16.07.05	David Bailey W RSC 1 Bolton
10.09.05	Baz Carey W PTS 4 Cardiff
05.11.05	Steve Gethin W RSC 3 Renfrew
10.12.05	Daniel Thorpe W RSC 2 Canning Town
28.01.06	Vitali Martynov W RSC 1 Nottingham
25.02.06	Jackson Williams W RSC 3 Canning Town
20.05.06	Laszlo Komjathi W PTS 6 Belfast
08.07.06	Colin Bain W RSC 2 Cardiff
02.09.06	Ryan Barrett W RSC 1 Bolton
09.12.06	Rachid Drilzane W PTS 10 Canning Town *Vacant IBF Inter-Continental L.Welterweight Title)*
17.02.07	Mohammed Medjadji W RSC 1 Wembley
07.04.07	Stefy Bull W RSC 3 Cardiff

Career: 12 contests, won 12.

Imran Khan
Shelton. *Born* Stoke, 1 July, 1981
Featherweight. *Ht* 5'5"
Manager M. Carney

24.11.06	Sammy Stewart W RSC 1 Stoke
12.05.07	Shaun Doherty L PTS 6 Stoke

Career: 2 contests, won 1, lost 1.

(Maciej) Magic Kidem (Brzostek)
Birmingham. *Born* Poland,18 June, 1981
S.Middleweight. *Ht* 5'10½"
Manager Self

25.02.06	Danny Butler L PTS 6 Bristol
05.03.06	Stuart Brookes L RSC 1 Sheffield
24.04.06	Dave Pearson L PTS 6 Cleethorpes
23.09.06	Sam Gorman W PTS 6 Coventry
11.03.07	Lee Noble L PTS 4 Shaw

Career: 5 contests, won 1, lost 4.

Charles Paul King
Motherwell. *Born* Bellshill, 26 October, 1982
L.Welterweight. *Ht.* 5'10"
Manager T. Gilmour

Amir Khan   Les Clark

22.01.07   Rom Krauklis W PTS 6 Glasgow
26.03.07   Pete Buckley W PTS 6 Glasgow
28.04.07   Amir Nadi W PTS 6 Clydebank
08.06.07   Gavin Deacon W PTS 4 Motherwell
Career: 4 contests, won 4.

Nathan King

Mountain Ash. *Born* Aberdare, 19 March, 1981
L.Heavyweight. *Ht* 6'3"
Manager B. Coleman

27.01.01   Tony Oakey L PTS 6 Bethnal Green
28.04.01   Pinky Burton W PTS 4 Cardiff
09.06.01   Michael Pinnock W PTS 4 Bethnal Green
09.10.01   Darren Ashton W PTS 6 Cardiff
24.11.01   Peter Haymer W PTS 4 Bethnal Green
12.02.02   Peter Haymer W PTS 4 Bethnal Green
20.04.02   Radcliffe Green W PTS 6 Cardiff
17.08.02   Valery Odin L PTS 6 Cardiff
14.12.02   Paul Bonson L PTS 4 Newcastle
10.04.03   Ovill McKenzie L PTS 4 Clydach
28.06.03   Varuzhan Davtyan W PTS 4 Cardiff
21.02.04   Daniel Sackey L PTS 4 Cardiff
12.03.04   Elvis Michailenko L PTS 6 Millwall
03.07.04   Nick Okoth W PTS 4 Newport
22.10.04   Hastings Rasani W PTS 6 Edinburgh
24.11.04   Eric Teymour L PTS 12 Mayfair
           (*Vacant WBU S.Middleweight Title*)
13.02.05   Malik Dziarra W PTS 6 Brentwood
28.06.05   Malik Dziarra L PTS 8 Cuaxhaven, Germany
13.05.06   Tony Oakey L PTS 6 Bethnal Green
15.09.06   Tyrone Wright W RTD 6 Newport
10.11.06   Neil Tidman W PTS 6 Newport
Career: 21 contests, won 12, lost 9.

Paul King

Sheffield. *Born* Sheffield, 9 August, 1974
Heavyweight. *Ht* 6'3"
Manager Self

10.02.04   Billy Wilson L PTS 6 Barnsley
28.02.04   David Ingleby W RSC 3 Manchester
12.03.04   Micky Steeds L PTS 6 Millwall
03.04.04   Carl Baker W PTS 6 Sheffield
10.04.04   Albert Sosnowski L PTS 4 Manchester
02.06.04   Scott Gammer L RSC 3 Hereford
18.09.04   Luke Simpkin W PTS 6 Newark
30.09.04   Chris Woollas W PTS 4 Glasgow
12.11.04   Leif Larsen L CO 1 Copenhagen, Denmark
06.02.05   Billy Bessey W PTS 6 Southampton
19.02.05   Colin Kenna DREW 6 Dublin
04.03.05   Carl Baker L RSC 2 Rotherham
30.04.05   Wayne Llewelyn L PTS 6 Dagenham
28.05.06   Tommy Eastwood L PTS 4 Longford
07.10.06   Martin Rogan L PTS 6 Belfast
21.10.06   Kelvin Davis L PTS 4 Southwark
03.11.06   David Dolan L PTS 4 Barnsley
01.12.06   Pele Reid L RSC 6 Birmingham
02.03.07   John McDermott L PTS 6 Neath
09.03.07   Scott Belshaw L PTS 4 Dagenham
16.03.07   Sam Sexton L PTS 6 Norwich
13.04.07   David Dolan L PTS 4 Houghton le Spring
06.05.07   Chris Burton L PTS 4 Darlington
10.06.07   Scott Gammer L PTS 6 Neath
Career: 24 contests, won 5, drew 1, lost 18.

David Kirk

Sutton in Ashfield. *Born* Mansfield, 5 October, 1974
Middleweight. Former Undefeated WBF European Welterweight Champion. *Ht* 5'8"
Manager Self

01.11.96   Arv Mittoo W PTS 6 Mansfield
04.12.96   Stuart Rimmer W PTS 6 Stoke
20.02.97   Chris Price W PTS 6 Mansfield
16.03.97   Gary Hibbert L PTS 6 Shaw
25.03.97   Miguel Matthews W PTS 6 Wolverhampton
28.04.97   Mark Breslin L PTS 8 Glasgow
06.10.97   Christian Brady L PTS 6 Birmingham
30.10.97   Trevor Tacy L PTS 6 Newark
08.12.97   Nick Hall L PTS 6 Nottingham
12.01.98   Juha Temonen DREW 6 Helsinki, Finland
24.01.98   Jason Cook L RSC 3 Cardiff
24.02.98   Roy Rutherford L PTS 6 Edgbaston
11.03.98   Patrick Gallagher L PTS 6 Bethnal Green
27.04.98   Tommy Peacock L PTS 6 Manchester
08.05.98   Chris Barnett L PTS 6 Manchester
23.05.98   Graham Earl L PTS 4 Bethnal Green
04.06.98   Mark Richards L PTS 6 Dudley
21.09.98   Steve McLevy L PTS 8 Glasgow
12.10.98   Malcolm Melvin L PTS 10 Birmingham
           (*Midlands Area L. Welterweight Title Challenge*)
31.10.98   Bernard Paul L PTS 6 Southend
28.11.98   Glenn McClarnon L PTS 4 Belfast
11.12.98   Charlie Kane L PTS 8 Prestwick
20.02.99   Dennis Berry L PTS 10 Thornaby
           (*Vacant Continental European Welterweight Title*)
09.05.99   Sammy Smith L PTS 6 Bracknell
20.05.99   Steve Brumant W PTS 4 Kensington
05.06.99   Neil Sinclair L PTS 8 Cardiff
11.09.99   Glenn McClarnon L PTS 6 Sheffield
20.10.99   Dave Gibson W PTS 6 Stoke
18.11.99   Adrian Chase W PTS 10 Mayfair
           (*Vacant WBF European Welterweight Title*)
26.11.99   Gerard Murphy L RTD 3 Hull
25.03.00   Jacek Bielski L PTS 6 Liverpool
29.04.00   Eamonn Magee L RSC 8 Wembley
13.08.00   Ram Singh W PTS 6 Nottingham
09.09.00   Mally McIver L PTS 6 Newark
23.09.00   Steve Murray L PTS 4 Bethnal Green
09.10.00   Steve Saville W PTS 8 Birmingham
19.11.00   Gavin Down L PTS 10 Chesterfield
           (*Vacant British Masters L.Welterweight Title*)
01.12.00   Alan Bosworth DREW 8 Peterborough
04.02.01   Mark Winters L PTS 6 Queensferry
28.02.01   Ossie Duran L PTS 8 Kensington
           (*Vacant WBF European Welterweight Title*)
10.03.01   Junior Witter L RSC 2 Bethnal Green
10.04.01   Colin Lynes L PTS 6 Wembley
20.04.01   Mark Winters L PTS 6 Dublin
16.06.01   Oscar Hall L PTS 6 Derby
07.07.01   Michael Jennings L PTS 6 Manchester
28.07.01   Jonathan Thaxton L PTS 4 Wembley
13.09.01   David Walker DREW 8 Sheffield
17.11.01   Kevin McIntyre L PTS 4 Glasgow
24.11.01   Ivan Kirpa L PTS 4 Bethnal Green
08.12.01   Chris Saunders L CO 2 Chesterfield
26.01.02   Colin Lynes L PTS 6 Dagenham
09.02.02   David Barnes L RTD 1 Manchester

11.03.02   Matthew Macklin L PTS 4 Glasgow
25.05.02   Francis Barrett L PTS 6 Portsmouth
08.06.02   Kevin McIntyre L RTD 4 Renfrew
28.09.02   Matthew Hatton W PTS 6 Manchester
22.03.03   Kevin McIntyre L RSC 1 Renfrew
24.05.03   Nigel Wright L PTS 4 Bethnal Green
31.05.03   Sammy Smith L PTS 4 Bethnal Green
08.06.03   Adnan Amar L PTS 6 Nottingham
04.10.03   Francis Barrett L PTS 6 Muswell Hill
10.04.04   Albert Sosnowski L PTS 4 Manchester
07.05.04   Gary Woolcombe L PTS 4 Bethnal Green
19.06.04   Gary Young L PTS 4 Renfrew
03.07.04   Tony Doherty L PTS 4 Newport
19.11.04   Ross Minter L PTS 6 Bethnal Green
03.12.04   Martin Concepcion L PTS 4 Edinburgh
11.09.05   Gatis Skuja L PTS 6 Kirkby in Ashfield
12.11.05   Joe Mitchell W PTS 6 Sheffield
10.03.06   Stuart Elwell L PTS 10 Walsall
           (*Vacant Midlands Area Welterweight Title*)
04.11.06   Colin McNeil L PTS 6 Glasgow
17.11.06   Sam Webb L PTS 4 Bethnal Green
09.12.06   Kell Brook L RSC 1 Canning Town
06.05.07   Brian Rose L PTS 6 Altrincham
18.05.07   Matthew Thirlwall L PTS 4 Canning Town
24.06.07   Chris Johnson L PTS 4 Wigan
Career: 76 contests, won 11, drew 3, lost 62.

Arial Krasnopolski

Nottingham. *Born* Warsaw, Poland, 8 May, 1987
L.Welterweight. *Ht* 5'6"
Manager J. Gill/T. Harris

15.06.06   Jaz Virdee L PTS 6 Peterborough
09.12.06   Anthony Crolla L RSC 3 Canning Town
Career: 2 contests, lost 2.

Rom Krauklis

Peterborough. *Born* Latvia, 21 September, 1985
Lightweight. *Ht* 5'6½"
Manager I. Pauly

06.12.06   Adam Kelly L PTS 6 Stoke
14.12.06   Craig Bromley L PTS 6 Leicester
22.01.07   Charles Paul King L PTS 6 Glasgow
17.02.07   Robin Deakin W PTS 4 Wembley
30.03.07   Ben Jones W RSC 1 Crawley
28.04.07   Ryan Brawley L PTS 8 Clydebank
31.05.07   Steve Bell L PTS 6 Manchester
07.06.07   Gareth Couch L PTS 8 Kensington
15.06.07   Lee Cook L PTS 4 Crystal Palace
24.06.07   Gary Sykes L PTS 4 Wigan
Career: 10 contests, won 2, lost 8.

Eder Kurti

Kennington. *Born* Albania, 29 August, 1984
S.Middleweight. *Ht* 5'10¾"
Manager B. Baker

04.11.04   Cafu Santos W RSC 1 Piccadilly
02.12.04   Craig Lynch W DIS 4 Crystal Palace
27.01.05   Ojay Abrahams W PTS 6 Piccadilly
19.11.05   JJ Ojuederie L RSC 4 Southwark
06.10.06   Stuart Brookes L PTS 6 Mexborough
02.12.06   Dave Pearson W PTS 6 Southwark
18.02.07   Greg Barton L PTS 4 Bethnal Green
Career: 7 contests, won 4, lost 3.

Kristian Laight

Nuneaton. *Born* Nuneaton, 15 June, 1980
Welterweight. *Ht* 5'10"
Manager J. Gill

26.09.03 James Paisley L PTS 6 Millwall
14.11.03 Matt Teague L PTS 6 Hull
05.12.03 Justin Hicks L PTS 6 Bristol
07.02.04 Kevin Mitchell L PTS 4 Bethnal Green
30.03.04 Chris McDonagh L PTS 6 Southampton
08.04.04 Jaz Virdee W PTS 6 Peterborough
20.04.04 Femi Fehintola L PTS 6 Sheffield
04.06.04 Gary Coombes DREW 6 Dudley
19.06.04 Ryan Barrett L PTS 4 Muswell Hill
23.10.04 Sean Hughes L PTS 6 Wakefield
18.11.04 Martin Gethin L RSC 4 Shrewsbury
17.12.04 Baz Carey L PTS 6 Coventry
08.05.05 Nadeem Siddique L RSC 7 Bradford
25.06.05 John-Paul Ryan DREW 6 Melton
          Mowbray
09.07.05 Chris Long L PTS 6 Bristol
02.09.05 Scott Haywood L PTS 6 Derby
06.10.05 Tom Hogan L PTS 6 Sunderland
24.10.05 Andrew Ferrans L PTS 8 Glasgow
12.11.05 Danny Gwilym L PTS 6 Bristol
20.11.05 Barry Downes DREW 6 Shaw
02.12.05 Charlie Thompson DREW 6 Doncaster
18.12.05 Gary O'Connor L PTS 6 Bolton
16.02.06 Haider Ali L PTS 4 Dudley
02.03.06 Jeff Thomas L PTS 6 Blackpool
30.03.06 Jaz Virdee L PTS 6 Peterborough
14.04.06 Tristan Davies L PTS 6 Telford
21.04.06 Wez Miller W PTS 6 Doncaster
11.05.06 Paul Holborn L PTS 6 Sunderland
21.05.06 Chris Long L PTS 6 Bristol
30.05.06 Akaash Bhatia L PTS 4 Bethnal Green
15.06.06 Neal McQuade W PTS 6 Peterborough
21.07.06 John Fewkes L RSC 5 Altrincham
09.10.06 Baz Carey DREW 6 Bedworth
26.10.06 Dean Harrison L PTS 4 Dudley
07.11.06 Martin Gethin L PTS 6 Leeds
24.11.06 Jack Perry L PTS 4 Nottingham
07.12.06 Ali Hussain W PTS 6 Bradford
15.02.07 Rob Hunt L PTS 6 Dudley
24.02.07 Chris Goodwin L PTS 6 Stoke
16.03.07 Lee Purdy L PTS 4 Norwich
23.03.07 Dean Harrison L PTS 4 Nottingham
13.04.07 Gary Sykes L PTS 4 Altrincham
20.04.07 Martin Gordon W PTS 4 Dudley
27.04.07 Ruben Giles L PTS 4 Wembley
Career: 44 contests, won 5, drew 5, lost 34.

Mervyn Langdale

Southampton. *Born* Hythe, Hull, 11 May, 1977
Cruiserweight. *Ht* 6'4"
Manager J. Bishop

06.02.05 Nick Okoth DREW 6 Southampton
24.09.06 Tony Booth L RSC 1 Southampton
25.02.07 Lee Kellett L RSC 1 Southampton
Career: 3 contests, drew 1, lost 2.

Scott Lansdowne

Leicester. *Born* Leicester, 11 August, 1972
Heavyweight. Former Undefeated
Midlands Area Cruiserweight Champion.
Former Undefeated WBF European
S.Cruiserweight Champion. *Ht* 5'10"
Manager P. Carpenter

15.12.98 Gary Williams W PTS 6 Sheffield
11.09.99 Luke Simpkin W PTS 4 Sheffield
09.12.99 Geoff Hunter W PTS 6 Sheffield
20.05.00 Gary Williams W RSC 1 Leicester
          *(Vacant WBF European
          S. Cruiserweight Title)*
21.10.00 Adam Cale W RSC 5 Sheffield
29.01.01 Nigel Rafferty W PTS 4 Peterborough
28.04.02 Tony Booth L RSC 4 Southwark
23.06.02 Paul Bonson L PTS 4 Southwark
30.11.02 Tony Dowling W RSC 2 Newark
          *(Vacant Midlands Area Cruiserweight
          Title)*
16.03.03 Michael Pinnock W PTS 6 Nottingham
12.10.03 Clint Johnson W PTS 4 Sheffield
11.12.03 Steven Spartacus L RSC 3 Bethnal
          Green
          (Vacant English L.Heavyweight Title)
10.07.04 David Ingleby W RSC 4 Coventry
06.12.04 Jason Callum W CO 1 Leicester
25.06.05 Carl Baker L RSC 8 Melton Mowbray
          *(Vacant British Masters Heavyweight
          Title)*
12.12.05 David Ingleby W RSC 1 Leicester
21.05.06 Julius Francis W PTS 4 Bethnal Green
16.09.06 Istvan Kecskes W PTS 4 Burton
Career: 18 contests, won 14, lost 4.

Scott Lawton

Stoke. *Born* Stoke, 23 September, 1976
English Lightweight Champion. Former
Undefeated Midlands Area Lightweight
Champion. *Ht* 5'10"
Manager M. Carney

29.09.01 Dave Hinds W RSC 2 Southwark
08.12.01 Ilias Miah W PTS 4 Dagenham
26.01.02 Pete Buckley W PTS 4 Bethnal Green
26.04.02 Pete Buckley W PTS 4 Coventry
06.09.02 Ben Hudson W PTS 4 Bethnal Green
30.01.03 Dave Stewart L PTS 6 Piccadilly
26.04.03 Chris McDonagh W RSC 2 Brentford
13.06.03 Jason Nesbitt W PTS 6 Queensway
14.11.03 Jimmy Beech W RSC 5 Bethnal Green
20.04.04 Henry Jones W PTS 6 Sheffield
17.06.04 Carl Allen W PTS 10 Sheffield
          *(Vacant Midlands Area Lightweight
          Title)*
17.09.04 Silence Saheed W PTS 6 Sheffield
10.12.04 Roger Sampson W PTS 6 Sheffield
04.03.05 Peter McDonagh W PTS 6 Rotherham
15.05.05 Carl Allen W PTS 6 Sheffield
24.07.05 Pete Buckley W PTS 6 Sheffield
09.09.05 Alan Temple L PTS 6 Sheffield
12.11.05 Ben Hudson W PTS 6 Stoke
18.02.06 Surinder Sekhon DREW 8 Stoke
06.05.06 Baz Carey W PTS 10 Stoke
          *(Midlands Area Lightweight Title
          Defence)*
09.06.06 Stefy Bull W RSC 8 Doncaster
          (Vacant English Lightweight Title)
30.09.06 Judex Meemea W DIS 7 Stoke
24.11.06 Karl Taylor W PTS 4 Stoke
16.03.07 Jonathan Thaxton L RSC 7 Norwich
          (British Lightweight Title Challenge)
Career: 24 contests, won 20, drew 1, lost 3.

Barrie Lee

Arbroath. *Born* Arbroath, 29 March, 1982
L.Middleweight. Former Scottish
L.Middleweight Champion. *Ht* 5'8"
Manager A. Morrison/K. Morrison

25.10.03 Dave Wakefield W PTS 4 Edinburgh
29.11.03 Brian Coleman W PTS 4 Renfrew
27.03.04 Arv Mittoo W PTS 4 Edinburgh
23.04.04 William Webster W PTS 6 Glasgow
28.05.04 Brian Coleman W PTS 6 Glasgow
19.06.04 Craig Lynch W PTS 6 Renfrew
08.10.04 Vince Baldassara DREW 6 Glasgow
22.10.04 Craig Lynch W PTS 10 Edinburgh
          (Vacant Scottish L.Middleweight Title)
03.12.04 John-Paul Temple W PTS 4 Edinburgh
08.04.05 Vince Baldassara W PTS 4 Edinburgh
03.06.05 Thomas McDonagh L RSC 7
          Manchester
          *(WBU Inter-Continental
          L.Middleweight Title Challenge)*
22.04.06 Chris Black W PTS 10 Glasgow
          (Scottish L.Middleweight Title Defence)
27.05.06 Kevin Phelan W PTS 6 Glasgow
10.12.06 Colin McNeil L RSC 4 Glasgow
          *(Scottish Area L.Middleweight Title
          Defence)*
Career: 14 contests, won 11, drew 1, lost 2.

Dwayne Lewis

Canning Town. *Born* London, 12 June, 1979
S.Middleweight. Ht. 5'11¼"
Manager B. Ajayi

18.02.07 Nick Okoth DREW 4 Bethnal Green
Career: 1 contest, drew 1.

Dwayne Lewis   Les Clark

Matthew Martin Lewis

Colchester. *Born* Colchester, 13 October, 1974
Lightweight. *Ht* 5'7½"
Manager A. Sims

07.11.06 John Baguley W PTS 6 Leeds
17.11.06 Ian Wilson L PTS 4 Bethnal Green
16.03.07 Leonard Lothian DREW 4 Norwich
Career: 3 contests, won 1, drew 1, lost 1.

James Lilley

Swansea. *Born* Swansea, 14 November, 1986
L.Welterweight. *Ht* 5'10"
Manager N. Hodges

08.10.06 Anthony Christopher W RSC 1
          Swansea

24.02.07 Darren Hamilton L PTS 6 Bristol
12.05.07 Chris Goodwin L PTS 4 Stoke
Career: 3 contests, won 1, lost 2.

Willie Limond

Glasgow. *Born* Glasgow, 2 February, 1979
Commonwealth Lightweight Champion.
Former Undefeated Celtic & European
Union S.Featherweight Champion. *Ht* 5'7"
Manager F. Warren/A. Morrison

12.11.99 Lennie Hodgkins W RTD 1 Glasgow
13.12.99 Steve Hanley W PTS 6 Glasgow
24.02.00 Nigel Senior W RSC 6 Glasgow
18.03.00 Phil Lashley W RSC 1 Glasgow
07.04.00 Jimmy Beech W RSC 2 Glasgow
26.05.00 Billy Smith W PTS 4 Glasgow
24.06.00 Haroon Din W PTS 4 Glasgow
10.11.00 Danny Connelly W PTS 6 Glasgow
17.12.00 Billy Smith W PTS 6 Glasgow
15.02.01 Marcus Portman W PTS 6 Glasgow
03.04.01 Trevor Smith W PTS 4 Bethnal Green
27.04.01 Choi Tseveenpurev W PTS 6 Glasgow
07.09.01 Gary Reid W PTS 8 Glasgow
03.11.01 Rakhim Mingaleev W PTS 6 Glasgow
17.11.01 Keith Jones W PTS 4 Glasgow
11.03.02 Dave Hinds W PTS 6 Glasgow
06.09.02 Assen Vassilev W RSC 3 Glasgow
22.03.03 Jimmy Beech W CO 4 Renfrew
12.07.03 Alex Arthur L RSC 8 Renfrew
         (British S.Featherweight Title
         Challenge)
01.11.03 Dariusz Snarski W RSC 1 Glasgow
29.11.03 Anthony Hanna W PTS 4 Renfrew
06.03.04 Dafydd Carlin W RSC 1 Renfrew
19.06.04 Youssouf Djibaba W PTS 10 Renfrew
         (Vacant European Union
         S.Featherweight Title)
29.10.04 Frederic Bonifai W PTS 8 Glasgow
03.12.04 Alberto Lopez W PTS 10 Edinburgh
         (European Union S.Featherweight Title
         Defence)
20.05.05 John Mackay W RSC 5 Glasgow
17.06.05 Kevin O'Hara W PTS 10 Glasgow
         (Vacant Celtic S.Featherweight Title)
05.11.05 Jus Wallie W PTS 6 Renfrew
04.11.06 Kpakpo Allotey W PTS 12 Glasgow
         (Vacant Commonwealth Lightweight
         Title)
Career: 29 contests, won 28, lost 1.

Martin Lindsay   Les Clark

Martin Lindsay

Belfast. *Born* Belfast, 10 May, 1982
S.Featherweight. *Ht* 5'7"
Manager J. Rooney

02.12.04 Dai Davies W RSC 1 Crystal Palace
24.04.05 Rakhim Mingaleev W PTS 4 Leicester
         Squar
02.07.05 Henry Janes W RSC 2 Dundalk
17.09.05 Peter Feher W PTS 4 Dublin
21.04.06 Chris Hooper W RSC 1 Belfast
13.10.06 Nikita Lukin W PTS 6 Aberavon
30.03.07 Buster Dennis W PTS 6 Crawley
Career: 7 contests, won 7.

Mark Lloyd

Telford. *Born* Walsall, 21 October, 1975
Middleweight. Former Undefeated British
Masters L.Middleweight Champion.
Ht 5'10"
Manager E. Johnson

16.09.05 Dennis Corpe W PTS 6 Telford
04.12.05 Gatis Skuja W PTS 4 Telford
16.02.06 Davey Jones W PTS 6 Dudley
14.04.06 Ben Hudson W PTS 4 Telford
13.05.06 Tommy Jones W PTS 6 Sutton in
         Ashfield
29.06.06 Tommy Jones W PTS 6 Dudley
06.10.06 Terry Adams W RSC 7 Wolverhampton
         (Vacant British Masters L.Middleweight
         Title)
28.06.07 Neil Bonner W PTS 4 Dudley
Career: 8 contests, won 8.

Robert Lloyd-Taylor (Lloyd)

Northolt. *Born* Perivale, 1 September, 1980
Welterweight. *Ht* 5'11¼"
Manager Self

27.09.02 Wayne Wheeler W PTS 6 Bracknell
25.10.02 Nicky Leech L PTS 6 Cotgrave
20.12.02 Dean Larter W PTS 4 Bracknell
26.04.03 Ben Hudson L PTS 4 Brentford
31.05.03 Aidan Mooney W PTS 4 Bethnal Green
26.10.03 Arv Mittoo W PTS 6 Longford
14.11.03 Michael Lomax L PTS 6 Bethnal Green
07.04.04 Joe Mitchell W RSC 5 Leicester Square
07.05.04 Chas Symonds L RTD 5 Bethnal Green
08.07.04 Ivor Bonavic W PTS 4 The Strand
18.09.04 Matt Scriven W RTD 4 Newark
21.11.04 Geraint Harvey W PTS 4 Bracknell
21.01.05 Ivor Bonavic W CO 2 Brentford
16.06.05 Duncan Cottier W RSC 1 Mayfair
16.12.05 Karl David W PTS 4 Bracknell
24.03.06 Ben Hudson W PTS 6 Bethnal Green
17.11.06 James Hare W PTS 6 Bethnal Green
27.04.07 Craig Watson L PTS 8 Wembley
Career: 18 contests, won 13, lost 5.

Gary Lockett

Cwmbran. *Born* Pontypool, 25 November,
1976
WBU Middleweight Champion. Former
WBO Inter-Continental L.Middleweight
Champion. *Ht* 5'10"
Manager Self

06.09.96 Ernie Loveridge W PTS 4 Liverpool
26.10.96 Charlie Paine W RSC 4 Liverpool
24.10.98 Lee Bird W RSC 2 Liverpool
27.02.99 Carl Smith W RSC 2 Bethnal Green
15.05.99 Mike Whittaker W RSC 2 Blackpool

19.06.99 Kid Halls W CO 1 Dublin
09.03.00 Kevin Thompson W CO 2 Liverpool
04.11.00 David Baptiste W PTS 4 Bethnal Green
23.01.01 Abdul Mehdi W RSC 2 Crawley
03.03.01 Hussain Osman W CO 3 Wembley
07.04.01 Howard Clarke W RSC 2 Wembley
08.05.01 Mike Algoet W PTS 6 Barnsley
14.07.01 Howard Clarke W CO 1 Wembley
25.09.01 Denny Dalton W RSC 1 Liverpool
24.11.01 Chris Nembhard W RSC 2 Bethnal
         Green
09.02.02 Kevin Kelly W CO 4 Manchester
         (Vacant WBO Inter-Continental
         L.Middleweight Title)
20.04.02 Youri Tsarenko L PTS 12 Cardiff
         (WBO Inter-Continental
         L.Middleweight Title Defence)
23.11.02 Viktor Fesetchko W PTS 8 Derby
29.03.03 Jason Collins W CO 1 Portsmouth
08.05.03 Yuri Tsarenko W PTS 10 Widnes
28.06.03 Michael Monaghan W PTS 10 Cardiff
21.02.04 Kreshnik Qato W RSC 2 Cardiff
12.06.04 Matt Galer W RSC 4 Manchester
03.09.04 Michael Monaghan W RSC 3 Newport
10.09.05 Allan Gray W CO 2 Cardiff
26.11.05 Victor Kpadenue W PTS 8 Rome, Italy
11.03.06 Gilbert Eastman W RSC 1 Newport
         (Vacant WBU Middleweight Title)
08.07.06 Ryan Rhodes W PTS 12 Cardiff
         (WBU Middleweight Title Defence)
18.11.06 Ayitey Powers W PTS 10 Newport
07.04.07 Lee Blundell W RSC 3 Cardiff
         (WBU Middleweight Title Defence)
Career: 30 contests, won 29, lost 1.

Michael Lomax

Chingford. *Born* London, 25 September,
1978
Welterweight. *Ht* 6'0"
Manager Self

05.07.03 Ernie Smith W PTS 4 Brentwood
20.09.03 Peter Dunn W PTS 4 Nottingham
14.11.03 Robert Lloyd-Taylor W PTS 6 Bethnal
         Green
16.01.04 Craig Lynch W PTS 6 Bradford
31.01.04 Steve Brumant W PTS 6 Bethnal Green
08.05.04 David Keir W RTD 4 Dagenham
13.02.05 Terry Adams W RSC 1 Brentwood
16.06.05 Jamie Coyle W PTS 6 Dagenham
18.11.05 Kevin Phelan W PTS 8 Dagenham
15.12.06 Billy Smith W PTS 6 Bethnal Green
30.03.07 Silence Saheed DREW 6 Crawley
Career: 11 contests, won 10, drew 1.

Chris Long

Calne. *Born* Gloucester, 5 March, 1980
L.Welterweight. *Ht* 5'9"
Manager Self

15.05.03 Darren Goode W RSC 1 Clevedon
21.09.03 Daniel Thorpe L PTS 6 Bristol
17.11.03 Stuart Green L PTS 6 Glasgow
13.02.04 Justin Hicks W RSC 4 Bristol
29.02.04 Gareth Perkins L PTS 6 Bristol
12.03.04 Ivor Bonavic W PTS 6 Millwall
01.05.04 Stuart Phillips W RSC 1 Bridgend
19.06.04 Ceri Hall L PTS 4 Muswell Hill
12.09.04 Ernie Smith DREW 6 Shrewsbury
24.09.04 John O'Donnell L RSC 4 Nottingham
02.12.04 Gavin Tait W PTS 6 Bristol
27.01.05 Sam Rukundo L PTS 4 Piccadilly
24.04.05 Scott Haywood L PTS 6 Derby

08.05.05 John Fewkes L PTS 8 Sheffield
09.07.05 Kristian Laight W PTS 6 Bristol
25.02.06 Muhsen Nasser L PTS 4 Bristol
05.03.06 Shane Watson L PTS 4 Southampton
25.03.06 Ryan Brawley L PTS 8 Irvine
21.05.06 Kristian Laight W PTS 6 Bristol
08.10.06 Stuart Phillips L PTS 4 Swansea
03.12.06 Rocky Chakir W PTS 6 Bristol
13.12.06 Stuart Green L PTS 6 Strand
17.02.07 James Gorman L RSC 3 Cork
18.03.07 Chris Brophy DREW 6 Bristol
30.03.07 Tibor Dudas L PTS 4 Crawley
28.04.07 Gary McArthur L PTS 10 Clydebank
(Vacant British Masters Lightweight Title)
Career: 26 contests, won 8, drew 2, lost 16.

Keith Long
Brixton. *Born* Greenwich, 30 July, 1968
Heavyweight. *Ht* 5'11½"
Manager B. Baker

15.02.97 Steve Cranston W PTS 4 Tooting
04.02.99 Gordon Minors W PTS 6 Lewisham
24.04.99 Derek McCafferty L PTS 4 Peterborough
07.08.99 Israel Ajose DREW 6 Dagenham
29.11.99 Mark Potter W PTS 8 Wembley
13.04.00 Harry Senior W PTS 10 Holborn
18.11.00 Luke Simpkin W RSC 3 Dagenham
13.09.01 Mike Holden W PTS 10 Sheffield
(Elim.British Heavyweight Title)
08.07.02 Alexei Varakin W RSC 4 Mayfair
17.09.02 Danny Williams L PTS 12 Bethnal Green
(British & Commonwealth Heavyweight Title Challenges)
15.02.03 Slick Miller W RSC 1 Wembley
24.01.04 Denis Bakhtov L PTS 12 Wembley
(WBC International Heavyweight Title Challenge)
19.11.04 Matt Skelton L RSC 11 Bethnal Green
(British & Commonwealth Heavyweight Title Challenges)
25.02.07 Colin Kenna L PTS 8 Southampton
Career: 14 contests, won 8, drew 1, lost 5.

Leonard Lothian   Les Clark

Leonard Lothian
Sheffield. *Born* Northampton, 11 February, 1988
Welterweight. *Ht* 5'6"
Manager J. Ingle

16.03.07 Matthew Martin Lewis DREW 4 Norwich
19.05.07 Dave Ryan L PTS 6 Nottingham
26.05.07 Mike Reid W PTS 6 Aberdeen
Career: 3 contests, won 1, drew 1, lost 1.

Andrew Lowe
Hackney. *Born* Hackney, 23 June, 1974
Southern Area L. Heavyweight Champion.
Ht 5'10"
Manager Self

19.05.01 Rob Stevenson W PTS 4 Wembley
16.06.01 William Webster W RSC 2 Dagenham
20.10.01 Tom Cannon W PTS 4 Glasgow
24.11.01 Paul Wesley W PTS 4 Bethnal Green
15.12.01 Mark Snipe W PTS 4 Chigwell
12.02.02 Ali Forbes W PTS 4 Bethnal Green
04.05.02 Radcliffe Green W PTS 4 Bethnal Green
12.10.02 Paul Bonson W PTS 4 Bethnal Green
08.02.03 Clint Johnson W PTS 6 Brentford
29.03.03 Radcliffe Green W PTS 10 Wembley
(Vacant Southern Area L.Heavyweight Title)
31.05.03 Neil Linford W PTS 10 Bethnal Green
(Elim. British L. Heavyweight Title)
07.11.03 Radcliffe Green W PTS 6 Sheffield
20.03.04 Varuzhan Davtyan W PTS 6 Wembley
12.05.04 Peter Oboh L RTD 10 Reading
(British & Commonwealth L.Heavyweight Title Challenges)
10.04.05 Varuzhan Davtyan W PTS 6 Brentwood
03.06.06 John Anthony W PTS 6 Chigwell
09.12.06 Neil Tidman W PTS 6 Chigwell
26.01.07 Brian Magee L PTS 10 Dagenham
(Final Elim.British L.Heavyweight Title)
Career: 18 contests, won 16, lost 2.

Andrew Alan Lowe
Newark *Born* Newark, 28 February, 1980
L.Middleweight. *Ht* 5'11¾"
Manager C. Greaves

30.09.06 Jon Musgrave L PTS 6 Stoke
24.11.06 Pawel Jas W PTS 6 Stoke
24.02.07 Barry Downes W PTS 6 Stoke
28.04.07 Steve Cooper W PTS 6 Newark
Career: 4 contests, won 3, lost 1.

Simone Lucas
Nottingham. *Born* Burundi, 6 August, 1978
S.Middleweight. *Ht* 5'10"
Manager J. Gill/T. Harris

22.10.05 Simon Fleck L RSC 5 Mansfield
20.11.05 Rob MacDonald W RSC 4 Shaw
05.12.05 Mark Franks L RSC 6 Leeds
25.02.06 Matthew Crouch W PTS 6 Bristol
02.04.06 Marvyn Wallace L CO 4 Bethnal Green
26.05.06 Kreshnik Qato L PTS 4 Bethnal Green
21.07.06 Alex Matvienko L PTS 4 Altrincham
Career: 7 contests, won 2, lost 5.

Colin Lynes
Hornchurch. *Born* Whitechapel, 26 November, 1977
British L.Welterweight Champion.
Former Undefeated IBO L.Welterweight Champion. Former IBO Inter-Continental L.Welterweight Champion. *Ht* 5'7½"
Manager Self

04.06.98 Les Frost W CO 1 Barking
23.07.98 Ram Singh W CO 1 Barking
22.10.98 Brian Coleman W RSC 2 Barking
31.10.98 Marc Smith W PTS 4 Basingstoke
10.12.98 Trevor Smith W RSC 1 Barking
25.02.99 Dennis Griffin W PTS 6 Kentish Town
20.05.99 Mark Haslam W PTS 4 Barking
18.05.00 Jason Vlasman W RSC 2 Bethnal Green
16.09.00 Karl Taylor W PTS 6 Bethnal Green
14.10.00 Brian Coleman W PTS 6 Wembley
09.12.00 Jimmy Phelan W PTS 6 Southwark
17.02.01 Mark Ramsey W PTS 6 Bethnal Green
10.04.01 David Kirk W PTS 6 Wembley
10.11.01 Keith Jones W PTS 6 Wembley
01.12.01 Leonti Voronchuk W PTS 6 Bethnal Green
26.01.02 David Kirk W PTS 6 Dagenham
23.03.02 Peter Dunn W PTS 6 Southwark
18.05.02 Kevin Bennett W RSC 4 Millwall
29.06.02 Ian Smith W RSC 7 Brentwood
21.09.02 Abdelilah Touil W CO 7 Brentwood
07.12.02 Richard Kiley W RSC 9 Brentwood
(Vacant IBO Inter-Continental L.Welterweight Title)
08.03.03 Samuel Malinga L RTD 8 Bethnal Green
(IBO Inter-Continental L.Welterweight Title Defence)
18.10.03 Brian Coleman W PTS 4 Manchester
22.11.03 Fabrice Colombel W PTS 6 Belfast
31.01.04 Cesar Levia W PTS 8 Bethnal Green
08.05.04 Pablo Sarmiento W PTS 12 Dagenham
(IBO L.Welterweight Title Challenge)
13.02.05 Juaquin Gallardo W PTS 12 Brentwood
(IBO L.Welterweight Title Defence)
21.10.05 Junior Witter L PTS 12 Bethnal Green
(British, Commonwealth & European L.Welterweight Title Challenges)
20.01.06 Lenny Daws L RTD 9 Bethnal Green
(Elim. British L.Welterweight Title. Vacant Southern Area L.Welterweight Title)
15.12.06 Janos Petrovics W RSC 6 Bethnal Green
30.03.07 Arek Malek W RTD 2 Crawley
08.06.07 Barry Morrison W PTS 12 Motherwell
(British L.Welterweight Title Challenge)
Career: 32 contests, won 29, lost 3.

Colin Lynes   Les Clark

137

Lee McAllister

Aberdeen. *Born* Aberdeen, 5 October, 1982
Scottish & WBF Inter-Continental
Lightweight Champion. Former Undefeated
British Masters L.Welterweight Champion.
Ht 5'9"
Manager Self

19.10.02	Baz Carey W PTS 4 Renfrew
17.11.02	Arv Mittoo W PTS 6 Bradford
23.02.03	Lee Williamson W PTS 6 Shrewsbury
13.04.03	Ernie Smith W PTS 4 Bradford
12.05.03	Ernie Smith W PTS 6 Birmingham
15.06.03	Brian Coleman W PTS 6 Bradford
11.07.03	John-Paul Ryan W RTD 2 Darlington
17.07.03	Dean Hickman L PTS 6 Walsall
03.08.03	Brian Coleman W PTS 4 Stalybridge
06.09.03	Jeff Thomas W PTS 10 Aberdeen
	(Vacant British Masters L.Welterweight Title)
28.11.03	Ernie Smith W PTS 6 Hull
30.01.04	Karl Taylor W PTS 4 Dagenham
08.03.04	Lee Williamson W PTS 6 Birmingham
15.05.04	Martin Hardcastle W PTS 8 Aberdeen
13.02.05	Daniel Thorpe W PTS 4 Bradford
26.04.05	Mark Wall W PTS 6 Leeds
14.05.05	Karl Taylor W RTD 3 Aberdeen
23.07.05	Billy Smith W PTS 4 Edinburgh
29.10.05	Jackson Williams W RSC 5 Aberdeen
18.02.06	Silence Saheed W PTS 4 Edinburgh
29.04.06	Peter Dunn W PTS 6 Edinburgh
12.05.06	Billy Smith W PTS 4 Bethnal Green
27.05.06	Stuart Green W RSC 8 Aberdeen
	(Vacant Scottish Area Lightweight Title)
28.10.06	Ben Hudson W PTS 8 Aberdeen
26.05.07	Ben Odamattey W PTS 10 Aberdeen
	(Vacant WBF Inter-Continental Lightweight Title)

Career: 25 contests, won 24, lost 1.

Gary McArthur

Clydebank. *Born* Glasgow, 27 July, 1982
British Masters Lightweight Champion.
Ht 5'9"
Manager T. Gilmour

23.01.06	Lance Verallo W PTS 6 Glasgow
13.03.06	Pete Buckley W PTS 6 Glasgow
24.04.06	Darren Gethin W PTS 6 Glasgow
18.09.06	Billy Smith W PTS 8 Glasgow
13.10.06	Steve Gethin W PTS 6 Irvine
02.12.06	Frederic Gosset W PTS 6 Clydebank
28.04.07	Chris Long W PTS 10 Clydebank
	(Vacant British Masters Lightweight Title)
08.06.07	Egon Szabo W PTS 6 Motherwell

Career: 8 contests, won 8.

Enzo Maccarinelli

Swansea. *Born* Swansea, 20 August, 1980
WBO Cruiserweight Champion. Former
Undefeated WBU Cruiserweight Champion.
Ht 6'4"
Manager F. Warren

02.10.99	Paul Bonson W PTS 4 Cardiff
11.12.99	Mark Williams W RSC 1 Merthyr

26.02.00	Nigel Rafferty W RSC 3 Swansea
12.05.00	Lee Swaby L CO 3 Swansea
11.12.00	Chris Woollas W PTS 4 Widnes
28.04.01	Darren Ashton W CO 1 Cardiff
09.10.01	Eamonn Glennon W RSC 2 Cardiff
15.12.01	Kevin Barrett W RSC 2 Wembley
12.02.02	James Gilbert W RSC 2 Bethnal Green
20.04.02	Tony Booth W PTS 4 Cardiff
17.08.02	Tony Booth W RTD 2 Cardiff
12.10.02	Dave Clarke W RSC 2 Bethnal Green
18.01.03	Paul Bonson W PTS 4 Preston
29.03.03	Valery Shemishkur W RSC 1 Portsmouth
28.06.03	Bruce Scott W RSC 4 Cardiff
	(Vacant WBU Cruiserweight Title)
13.09.03	Andrei Kiarsten W CO 1 Newport
	(WBU Cruiserweight Title Defence)
06.12.03	Earl Morais W RSC 1 Cardiff
	(WBU Cruiserweight Title Defence)
21.02.04	Garry Delaney W RSC 8 Cardiff
	(WBU Cruiserweight Title Defence)
03.07.04	Ismail Abdoul W PTS 12 Newport
	(WBU Cruiserweight Title Defence)
03.09.04	Jesper Kristiansen W CO 3 Newport
	(WBU Cruiserweight Title Defence)
21.01.05	Rich LaMontagne W RSC 4 Bridgend
	(WBU Cruiserweight Title Defence)

04.06.05	Roman Bugaj W RSC 1 Manchester
26.11.05	Marco Heinichen W RSC 1 Rome, Italy
04.03.06	Mark Hobson W PTS 12 Manchester
	(WBU Cruiserweight Title Defence)
08.07.06	Marcelo Dominguez W RSC 9 Cardiff
	(Vacant WBO Interim Cruiserweight Title)
14.10.06	Mark Hobson W RSC 1 Manchester
	(WBO Cruiserweight Title Defence)
07.04.07	Bobby Gunn W RSC 1 Cardiff
	(WBO Cruiserweight Title Defence)

Career: 27 contests, won 26, lost 1.

Paul McCloskey

Dungiven. *Born* Londonderry, 3 August,
1979
L. Welterweight. *Ht* 5'8½"
Manager J. Breen/F. Warren

18.03.05	David Kehoe W RSC 3 Belfast
17.06.05	Oscar Milkitas W PTS 4 Glasgow
05.11.05	Billy Smith W PTS 4 Renfrew
24.11.05	Henry Janes W RSC 3 Lurgan
18.02.06	Duncan Cottier W PTS 6 Edinburgh
11.03.06	Surinder Sekhon W RSC 1 Newport
04.11.06	Daniel Thorpe W RTD 3 Glasgow

Enzo Maccarinelli

Les Clark

138

09.12.06   Silence Saheed W PTS 4 Canning Town
10.02.07   Eugen Stan W PTS 6 Letterkenny
17.02.07   Chill John W PTS 6 Cork
Career: 10 contests, won 10.

Joe McCluskey

Coventry. *Born* Coventry, 26 November, 1977
Welterweight. *Ht* 5'9"
Manager Self

01.05.04   John-Paul Ryan W RTD 2 Coventry
10.07.04   Declan English W RSC 4 Coventry
20.11.04   Judex Meemea DREW 6 Coventry
18.06.05   Carl Allen W PTS 6 Coventry
22.10.05   Darren Gethin DREW 6 Coventry
04.03.06   Khurram Hussain L PTS 6 Coventry
23.09.06   Thomas Mazurkiewicz L RSC 2 Coventry
02.12.06   Duncan Cottier W PTS 6 Coventry
26.02.07   Ali Wyatt L RSC 5 Birmingham
13.05.07   Ali Wyatt DREW 8 Birmingham
Career: 10 contests, won 4, drew 3, lost 3.

Darren McDermott   Les Clark

Darren McDermott

Dudley. *Born* Dudley, 17 July, 1978
Midlands Area Middleweight Champion.
Former Undefeated British Masters
Middleweight Champion. *Ht* 6'1"
Manager D. Powell

26.04.03   Leigh Wicks W PTS 4 Brentford
13.06.03   Gary Jones W RSC 1 Queensway
30.10.03   Harry Butler W PTS 4 Dudley
21.02.04   Freddie Yemofio W RSC 3 Cardiff
15.04.04   Mark Phillips W PTS 4 Dudley
03.07.04   Neil Addis W PTS 4 Newport
11.12.04   Gokhan Kazaz DREW 4 Canning Town
21.04.05   Howard Clarke W RTD 1 Dudley
06.10.05   Andy Halder W RTD 5 Dudley
         (Midlands Area Middleweight Title Challenge)
16.02.06   Michael Monaghan W RTD 9 Dudley
         (Midlands Area Middleweight Title Defence)
29.06.06   Andrzej Butowicz W RSC 3 Dudley

26.10.06   Hussain Osman W PTS 10 Dudley
         (Vacant British Masters Middleweight Title)
15.02.07   Darren Rhodes W RSC 5 Dudley
         (Elim.British Middleweight Title)
28.06.07   Conroy McIntosh W RSC 2 Dudley
         (Midlands Area Middleweight Title Defence)
Career: 14 contests, won 13, drew 1.

John McDermott

Horndon. *Born* Basildon, 26 February, 1980
Heavyweight. *Ht* 6'3"
Manager J. Branch

23.09.00   Slick Miller W RSC 1 Bethnal Green
21.10.00   Gary Williams W PTS 4 Wembley
13.11.00   Geoff Hunter W RSC 1 Bethnal Green
27.01.01   Eamonn Glennon W RSC 1 Bethnal Green
24.02.01   Alexei Osokin W PTS 4 Bethnal Green
26.03.01   Mal Rice W RSC 2 Wembley
09.06.01   Luke Simpkin W PTS 6 Bethnal Green
22.09.01   Gary Williams W RSC 4 Bethnal Green
24.11.01   Gordon Minors W RSC 3 Bethnal Green
19.01.02   Tony Booth W RSC 1 Bethnal Green
04.05.02   Martin Roothman W RSC 1 Bethnal Green
14.09.02   Alexander Mileiko W RSC 2 Bethnal Green
12.10.02   Mendauga Kulikauskas W PTS 6 Bethnal Green
14.12.02   Jason Brewster W RSC 1 Newcastle
15.02.03   Derek McCafferty W PTS 4 Wembley
08.05.03   Konstantin Prizyuk W PTS 8 Widnes
18.09.03   Nicolai Popov L RSC 2 Dagenham
13.05.04   James Zikic W RSC 4 Bethnal Green
30.07.04   Suren Kalachyan W CO 7 Bethnal Green
11.12.04   Mark Krence L PTS 10 Canning Town
         (Vacant English Heavyweight Title)
08.04.05   Slick Miller W RSC 1 Edinburgh
10.12.05   Matt Skelton L RSC 1 Canning Town
         (British Heavyweight Title Challenge)
26.01.07   Vitaly Shkraba W RSC 1 Dagenham
02.03.07   Paul King W PTS 6 Neath
15.06.07   Luke Simpkin W RSC 2 Crystal Palace
Career: 25 contests, won 22, lost 3.

Peter McDonagh

Bermondsey. *Born* Galway, 21 December, 1977
L.Welterweight. All-Ireland Lightweight
Champion. Former Southern Area
Lightweight Champion. *Ht* 5'9"
Manager Self

28.04.02   Arv Mittoo W PTS 6 Southwark
23.06.02   Dave Hinds W PTS 6 Southwark
14.09.02   Pete Buckley W PTS 4 Bethnal Green
27.10.02   Ben Hudson L PTS 6 Southwark
18.02.03   Daffyd Carlin L PTS 4 Bethnal Green
08.04.03   Ben Hudson W PTS 4 Bethnal Green
08.11.03   Ceri Hall L PTS 4 Bridgend
22.11.03   James Gorman L PTS 4 Belfast
21.02.04   Chill John W RTD 2 Brighton
06.03.04   Barry Hughes L PTS 6 Renfrew
07.04.04   Jon Honney W PTS 10 Leicester Square
         (Vacant Southern Area Lightweight Title)
19.11.04   David Burke L PTS 8 Bethnal Green

21.01.05   Ryan Barrett L PTS 8 Brentford
04.03.05   Scott Lawton L PTS 6 Rotherham
30.04.05   Rob Jeffries L PTS 10 Dagenham
         (Southern Area Lightweight Title Defence)
14.05.05   Robbie Murray L PTS 10 Dublin
         (Vacant Irish L.Welterweight Title)
07.08.05   Brunet Zamora L PTS 6 Rimini, Italy
04.11.05   Anthony Christopher W PTS 4 Bethnal Green
28.01.06   Michael Gomez W RSC 5 Dublin
         (Vacant All-Ireland Lightweight Title)
24.09.06   Jason Nesbitt W PTS 4 Bethnal Green
01.12.06   Karl Taylor W PTS 4 Tower Hill
Career: 21 contests, won 10, lost 11.

Thomas McDonagh

Manchester. *Born* Manchester, 8 December, 1980
Middleweight. Former Undefeated
WBU Inter-Continental L.Middleweight
Champion. *Ht* 6'0"
Manager F. Warren/B. Hughes

09.10.99   Lee Molyneux W PTS 4 Manchester
06.11.99   Lee Molyneux W PTS 4 Widnes
11.12.99   Arv Mittoo W RSC 2 Liverpool
29.01.00   Emmanuel Marcos W PTS 4 Manchester
29.02.00   William Webster W RTD 2 Widnes
25.03.00   Lee Molyneux W PTS 6 Liverpool
16.05.00   Richie Murray W PTS 4 Warrington
29.05.00   David Baptiste W PTS 6 Manchester
04.09.00   Colin Vidler W PTS 6 Manchester
11.12.00   Richie Murray W PTS 6 Widnes
15.01.01   Kid Halls W RSC 4 Manchester
10.02.01   Harry Butler W PTS 6 Widnes
17.03.01   David Baptiste W PTS 4 Manchester
07.07.01   Paul Denton W PTS 6 Manchester
15.09.01   Howard Clarke W PTS 6 Manchester
27.10.01   Mark Richards DREW 4 Manchester
09.02.02   Tomas da Silva DREW 4 Manchester
01.06.02   Delroy Mellis W PTS 4 Manchester
28.09.02   Brian Coleman W RSC 1 Manchester
18.01.03   Tomas da Silva W PTS 4 Preston
05.04.03   Paul Wesley W PTS 6 Manchester
08.05.03   Marcus Portman W PTS 6 Widnes
27.09.03   Eugenio Monteiro W PTS 12 Manchester
         (Vacant WBU Inter-Continental L.Middleweight Title)
26.02.04   Bobby Banghar W CO 2 Widnes
         (WBU Inter-Continental L.Middleweight Title Defence)
03.04.04   Craig Lynch W PTS 6 Manchester
06.05.04   Bradley Pryce W PTS 12 Barnsley
         (WBU Inter-Continental L.Middleweight Title Defence)
12.11.04   Darren Rhodes W PTS 10 Halifax
         (Elim. British L.Middleweight Title)
03.06.05   Barrie Lee W RSC 7 Manchester
         (WBU Inter-Continental L.Middleweight Title Defence)
25.10.05   Dean Walker W PTS 6 Preston
04.03.06   Wayne Alexander L PTS 12 Manchester
         (WBU L.Middleweight Title Challenge)
14.10.06   Martin Concepcion W PTS 6 Manchester
21.04.07   Vladimir Borovski W PTS 6 Manchester
30.06.07   Alexander Matviechuk W PTS 6 Manchester
Career: 33 contests, won 30, drew 2, lost 1.

(Stephen) Junior MacDonald

Lewisham. *Born* Lewisham, 9 August, 1979
Cruiserweight. *Ht* 6'2½"
Manager F. Maloney

05.03.05	Tony Booth W PTS 4 Southwark
29.04.05	Gary Thompson W RSC 1 Southwark
19.06.05	Radcliffe Green W RTD 1 Bethnal Green
07.10.05	Paul Bonson W PTS 4 Bethnal Green
27.01.06	Sergey Voron W RSC 2 Dagenham
30.05.06	Julien Perriaux W RSC 5 Bethnal Green
06.10.06	Tommy Eastwood L RSC 2 Bethnal Green
	(Vacant Southern Area Cruiserweight Title)

Career: 7 contests, won 6, lost 1.

Nick McDonald

Moreton. *Born* Birkenhead, 24 February, 1984
S.Featherweight. *Ht* 5'6"
Manager F. Maloney

06.10.06	Nikita Lukin L RSC 2 Bethnal Green

Career: 1 contest, lost 1.

Jamie McDonnell

Doncaster. *Born* Doncaster, 3 March, 1986
English Bantamweight Champion. *Ht* 5'8"
Manager J. Rushton

16.09.05	Neil Read W PTS 6 Doncaster
02.12.05	Delroy Spencer W PTS 6 Doncaster
03.03.06	Gary Sheil W PTS 6 Doncaster
21.04.06	Neil Marston W PTS 4 Doncaster
09.06.06	Dai Davies DREW 4 Doncaster
13.10.06	Wayne Bloy W PTS 4 Doncaster
01.12.06	Andy Bell W RSC 3 Doncaster
23.02.07	Wayne Bloy W RSC 3 Doncaster
	(Vacant English Bantamweight Title)

Career: 8 contests, won 7, drew 1.

James McElvaney

Middlesbrough. *Born* Middlesbrough, 30 December, 1986
Lightweight. *Ht* 5'8"
Manager D. Garside

06.05.07	Shaun Walton W PTS 6 Darlington
09.06.07	Sergei Rozhakmens W PTS 6 Middlesbrough

Career: 2 contests, won 2.

Stuart McFadyen

Colne. *Born* Burnley, 27 January, 1982
S.Bantamweight. *Ht* 5'4"
Manager S. Wood

21.07.06	Neil Read W RSC 1 Altrincham
29.09.06	Abdul Mougharbel W PTS 4 Manchester
12.11.06	Anthony Hanna W PTS 6 Manchester
09.02.07	John Baguley W PTS 4 Leeds
11.03.07	Mo Khaled W PTS 6 Shaw

Career: 5 contests, won 5.

Steve McGuire

Glenrothes. *Born* Kirkcaldy, 1 June, 1981
L.Heavyweight. *Ht* 6'2¼"
Manager T. Gilmour

17.11.03	Shane White W CO 2 Glasgow
22.04.04	Paul Billington W RTD 3 Glasgow
15.10.04	Karl Wheeler W PTS 4 Glasgow
11.06.05	Varuzhan Davtyan W PTS 6 Kirkcaldy
30.09.05	Marcin Radola W RSC 1 Kirkcaldy
17.03.06	Paul David W PTS 6 Kirkcaldy
28.04.06	Valery Odin W PTS 6 Hartlepool
16.06.06	Simeon Cover W PTS 6 Liverpool
10.11.06	Richard Turba DREW 6 Hartlepool
16.02.07	Roman Vanicky W RSC 1 Kirkcaldy
11.05.07	Neil Tidman W PTS 8 Motherwell

Career: 11 contests, won 10, drew 1.

Jamie McIlroy

Stevenston. *Born* Irvine, 14 September, 1985
S.Featherweight. *Ht* 5'8"
Manager T. Gilmour

25.02.05	John-Paul Ryan W PTS 6 Irvine
21.03.05	Rocky Flanagan W PTS 6 Glasgow
06.05.06	Sergei Rozhakmens W PTS 6 Irvine
13.10.06	Shaun Walton W PTS 6 Irvine

Career: 4 contests, won 4.

Tyrone McInerney

Huddersfield. *Born* Huddersfield, 24 March, 1978
L.Middleweight. *Ht* 5'6"
Manager Self

08.06.04	Judex Meemea DREW 6 Sheffield
12.11.04	Darren Gethin W PTS 4 Halifax
26.04.05	Peter Dunn W RSC 6 Leeds
21.10.06	Paddy Pollock DREW 6 Glasgow
15.06.07	Scott Woolford L PTS 4 Crystal Palace

Career: 5 contests, won 2, drew 2, lost 1.

Conroy McIntosh

Wolverhampton. *Born* Wolverhampton, 5 December, 1973
Middleweight. *Ht* 5'7"
Manager E. Johnson

31.01.01	Ross Murray W CO 1 Piccadilly
23.06.01	Francie Doherty L PTS 4 Peterborough
22.09.01	Tomas da Silva L PTS 4 Canning Town
11.02.02	Ty Browne DREW 4 Southampton
03.03.02	Wayne Shepherd DREW 6 Shaw
21.05.02	Ty Browne DREW 4 Custom House
13.07.02	Darren Covill W PTS 4 Wolverhampton
17.11.02	Gary Dixon W RSC 2 Shaw
30.11.02	Andy Halder L PTS 4 Coventry
22.02.03	George Robshaw L PTS 4 Huddersfield
08.03.03	Andy Halder L PTS 4 Coventry
20.06.03	Michael Thomas W CO 2 Gatwick
07.09.03	Roddy Doran L PTS 10 Shrewsbury
	(Vacant Midlands Area Middleweight Title)
07.11.03	Patrick J. Maxwell L RSC 4 Sheffield
07.04.04	Lee Hodgson W RSC 3 Leicester Square
13.05.04	Ajay Abrahams W RSC 2 Bethnal Green
10.07.04	Andy Halder L PTS 10 Coventry
	(Vacant Midlands Area Middleweight Title)
10.12.04	Geard Ajetovic L PTS 6 Sheffield
24.07.05	Geard Ajetovic L PTS 6 Sheffield
21.09.05	Patrick J. Maxwell L RSC 2 Bradford
17.11.05	Joey Vegas L RSC 3 Piccadilly
10.02.06	Cello Renda L RSC 1 Plymouth
06.05.06	Lee Blundell L PTS 6 Blackpool
20.05.06	Jason McKay L PTS 6 Belfast
01.06.06	Paul Smith L PTS 8 Barnsley
12.07.06	Darren Barker L RSC 7 Bethnal Green
07.10.06	Steven Bendall L PTS 6 Weston super Mare
25.02.07	Steve Ede L PTS 10 Southampton
	(Vacant British Masters Middleweight Title)
25.03.07	Lukasz Wawrzyczek L PTS 8 Dublin
28.06.07	Darren McDermott L RSC 2 Dudley
	(Midlands Area Middleweight Title Challenge)

Career: 30 contests, won 6, drew 3, lost 21.

Danny McIntosh

Norwich. *Born* Norwich, 1 March, 1980
L. Heavyweight. *Ht* 6'2"
Manager J. Ingle

09.04.05	Omid Bourzo W PTS 6 Norwich
03.09.05	Howard Clarke W PTS 4 Norwich
06.10.05	Michael Banbula W PTS 6 Longford
07.10.06	Matthew Hough W RSC 6 Walsall
16.03.07	Robert Burton W PTS 4 Norwich

Career: 5 contests, won 5.

Danny McIntosh   Les Clark

Kevin McIntyre

Paisley. *Born* Paisley, 5 May, 1978
Scottish Welterweight Champion.
Ht 5'10½"
Manager Self

13.11.98	Ray Wood W RSC 4 Glasgow
18.02.99	Gareth Dooley W RSC 3 Glasgow
21.05.99	Mohamed Helel W PTS 6 Glasgow
26.06.99	Karim Bouali L RTD 1 Glasgow
18.03.00	Chris Hall W RSC 3 Glasgow
07.04.00	Dave Travers W RSC 4 Glasgow
26.05.00	Tommy Peacock W RSC 5 Glasgow
24.06.00	Lee Williamson W PTS 4 Glasgow
02.10.00	Paul Denton W PTS 6 Glasgow
10.11.00	Mark Ramsey W RSC 4 Glasgow
17.12.00	Ernie Smith W PTS 6 Glasgow
15.02.01	John Humphrey L RSC 4 Glasgow
27.04.01	Michael Smyth W PTS 6 Glasgow
17.11.01	David Kirk W PTS 4 Glasgow
16.12.01	Manzo Smith W PTS 6 Glasgow
11.03.02	Karl Taylor W PTS 4 Glasgow
26.04.02	Craig Lynch W PTS 10 Glasgow
	(Vacant Scottish Welterweight Title)
08.06.02	David Kirk W RTD 5 Renfrew
19.10.02	Nigel Wright W PTS 6 Renfrew

22.03.03	David Kirk W RSC 1 Renfrew	
12.07.03	Paul Denton W PTS 4 Renfrew	
25.10.03	Karim Hussine W PTS 6 Edinburgh	
13.12.03	David Barnes L RTD 8 Manchester	
	(British Welterweight Title Challenge)	
02.06.04	Keith Jones W PTS 6 Hereford	
17.12.04	Sergey Starkov W PTS 6 Huddersfield	
05.11.05	Nigel Wright L RSC 1 Renfrew	
	(Final Elim. British L.Welterweight Title)	
06.05.06	Gary Reid L RSC 6 Stoke	
	(Vacant British Masters L.Welterweight Title)	
05.05.07	Dave Wakefield W PTS 6 Glasgow	

Career: 28 contests, won 23, lost 5.

Jason McKay
Banbridge. *Born* Craigavon, NI, 11 October, 1977
S.Middleweight. All-Ireland L.Heavyweight Champion. *Ht* 6'1"
Manager F. Warren/J. Breen

18.02.02	Jimmy Steel W PTS 4 Glasgow
11.05.02	Harry Butler W PTS 4 Dagenham
27.07.02	Simon Andrews W RSC 3 Nottingham
08.10.02	Dean Cockburn W PTS 4 Glasgow
08.02.03	William Webster W RSC 1 Liverpool
12.04.03	Marcin Radola W RSC 1 Bethnal Green
17.05.03	Varuzhan Davtyan W PTS 6 Liverpool
04.10.03	Jamie Hearn W PTS 8 Belfast
22.11.03	Ojay Abrahams W PTS 4 Belfast
17.04.04	Alan Gilbert W PTS 6 Belfast
26.06.04	Ciaran Healy W PTS 6 Belfast
05.11.04	Paul Buchanan L PTS 6 Hereford
24.11.05	Ojay Abrahams W PTS 4 Lurgan
18.02.06	Dean Walker W RTD 1 Edinburgh
20.05.06	Conroy McIntosh W PTS 6 Belfast
26.10.06	Sandris Tomson W RSC 6 Belfast
11.11.06	Michael Monaghan W PTS 10 Dublin
	(Vacant All-Ireland L.Heavyweight Title)
25.03.07	Darren Rhodes W PTS 6 Dublin

Career: 18 contests, won 17, lost 1.

Jamie McKeever
Birkenhead. *Born* Birkenhead, 7 July, 1979
S.Featherweight. Former British Featherweight Champion. Former Undefeated Central Area Featherweight Champion. *Ht* 5'6½"
Manager Self

12.03.98	Dave Hinds W PTS 4 Liverpool
08.04.98	Kid McAuley W RTD 1 Liverpool
06.06.98	Brian Coleman W PTS 4 Liverpool
21.07.98	Stuart Rimmer W PTS 4 Widnes
31.10.98	John T. Kelly L PTS 6 Southend
22.01.99	Garry Burrell W RSC 2 Carlisle
12.03.99	David Kehoe W RSC 2 Bethnal Green
28.05.99	Arv Mittoo W PTS 6 Liverpool
02.10.99	Lee Armstrong DREW 6 Cardiff
27.11.99	Nigel Leake W RSC 2 Liverpool
01.07.00	Gary Flear L PTS 4 Manchester
09.10.00	Marc Callaghan W PTS 6 Liverpool
20.03.01	Craig Docherty L RSC 3 Glasgow
25.09.01	Sebastian Hart W PTS 4 Liverpool
10.12.01	Andrew Ferrans W PTS 6 Liverpool
09.03.02	James Rooney W PTS 6 Manchester
13.04.02	Barry Hawthorne W PTS 6 Liverpool
07.09.02	Tony Mulholland W PTS 10 Liverpool
	(Vacant Central Area Featherweight Title)

08.02.03	Tony Mulholland W RSC 6 Liverpool
	(Vacant British Featherweight Title)
17.05.03	Roy Rutherford L PTS 12 Liverpool
	(British Featherweight Title Defence)
28.02.04	Dazzo Williams L PTS 12 Bridgend
	(British Featherweight Title Challenge)
23.09.05	Jim Betts W RSC 4 Manchester
25.11.05	Dariusz Snarski W PTS 6 Liverpool
03.03.06	Riaz Durgahed W PTS 6 Hartlepool
16.06.06	Jackson Asiku L RSC 1 Liverpool
	(Commonwealth Featherweight Title Challenge)
18.02.07	Ryan Barrett L PTS 10 Bethnal Green
	(Vacant British Masters Featherweight Title)
10.03.07	Steve Bell L RSC 7 Liverpool
	(Vacant Central Area S.Featherweight Title)

Career: 27 contests, won 18, drew 1, lost 8.

(Helen) Angel McKenzie (Hobbs)
Thornton Heath. *Born* Russia, 10 June, 1973
L.Welterweight. *Ht* 5'7"
Manager Self

26.02.06	Alena Kokavcova W PTS 4 Dagenham
01.10.06	Elena Schmitt W PTS 4 Bruchsal, Germany
11.11.06	Galina Gumliiska L PTS 4 Rheinstetten, Germany
31.03.07	Ramona Kuehne L PTS 6 Berlin, Germany
23.06.07	Jill Emery L PTS 8 Dublin

Career: 5 contests, won 2, lost 3.

Ovill McKenzie
Canning Town. *Born* Jamaica, 26 November, 1979
L.Heavyweight. Former Commonwealth L.Heavyweight Champion. *Ht* 5'9"
Manager C. Mitchell

06.03.03	Leigh Alliss W PTS 4 Bristol
10.04.03	Nathan King W PTS 4 Clydach
02.06.03	Pinky Burton L PTS 8 Glasgow
18.09.03	Peter Haymer L PTS 4 Mayfair
24.10.03	Courtney Fry L PTS 4 Bethnal Green
15.11.03	Edwin Cleary W PTS 4 Coventry
30.01.04	Steven Spartacus W PTS 6 Dagenham
12.03.04	Harry Butler W RSC 2 Millwall
03.04.04	Denis Inkin L PTS 8 Manchester
10.09.04	Tommy Eastwood L PTS 8 Wembley
04.12.04	Stipe Drews L PTS 8 Berlin, Germany
06.02.05	Paul Bonson W PTS 4 Southampton
13.02.05	Gyorgy Hidvegi W RSC 3 Brentwood
13.05.05	Courtney Fry W PTS 4 Liverpool
01.07.05	Hastings Rasani W PTS 6 Fulham
26.02.06	Tony Booth W PTS 4 Dagenham
23.03.06	Paul Bonson W PTS 6 The Strand
30.03.06	Paul Bonson W RSC 3 Bloomsbury
24.09.06	Peter Haymer W RSC 2 Bethnal Green
	(Vacant Commonwealth L.Heavyweight Title)
09.02.07	Dean Francis L RSC 1 Bristol
	(Commonwealth L.Heavyweight Title Defence)

Career: 20 contests, won 13, lost 7.

Sean McKervey
Coventry. *Born* Coventry, 17 July, 1983
L.Middleweight. *Ht* 5'8½"
Manager O. Delargy

04.03.06	Ernie Smith W PTS 6 Coventry
09.10.06	Steve Cooper DREW 6 Birmingham
11.12.06	Steve Cooper W PTS 6 Birmingham
26.02.07	Terry Carruthers L PTS 6 Birmingham
24.03.07	Peter Dunn W PTS 6 Coventry

Career: 5 contests, won 3, drew 1, lost 1.

James McKinley
Birmingham. *Born* Birmingham, 21 August, 1981
Middleweight. *Ht* 6'0"
Manager R. Woodhall

08.09.06	Mark Phillips W PTS 4 Birmingham
26.10.06	Thomas Flynn W PTS 4 Wolverhampton
01.12.06	Jon Musgrave W PTS 4 Birmingham
23.02.07	Matt Scriven W PTS 6 Birmingham
17.03.07	Peter Dunn W PTS 6 Birmingham
29.04.07	Jon Foster W PTS 6 Birmingham

Career: 6 contests, won 6.

Matthew Macklin
Birmingham. *Born* Birmingham, 14 May, 1982
L.Middleweight. All-Ireland Middleweight Champion. *Ht* 5'10"
Manager Self

17.11.01	Ram Singh W RSC 1 Glasgow
15.12.01	Christian Hodorogea W CO 1 Wembley
09.02.02	Dimitri Protkunas W RTD 3 Manchester
11.03.02	David Kirk W PTS 4 Glasgow
20.04.02	Illia Spassov W CO 3 Cardiff
01.06.02	Guy Alton W RSC 3 Manchester
28.09.02	Leonti Voronchuk W RSC 5 Manchester
15.02.03	Ruslan Yakupov W PTS 6 Wembley
24.05.03	Paul Denton W PTS 6 Bethnal Green
06.11.03	Andrew Facey L PTS 10 Dagenham
	(Vacant English L.Middleweight Title)
21.02.04	Dean Walker W CO 1 Cardiff
24.04.04	Scott Dixon W RTD 5 Reading
12.06.04	Ojay Abrahams W PTS 3 Manchester
14.05.05	Michael Monaghan W CO 5 Dublin
	(Vacant All-Ireland Middleweight Title)
04.08.05	Leo Laudat W RSC 3 Atlantic City, New Jersey, USA
28.10.05	Anthony Little W RSC 2 Philadelphia, Pennsylvania, USA
26.11.05	Alexey Chirkov W CO 1 Sheffield
01.06.06	Marcin Piatkowski W RSC 4 Birmingham
29.09.06	Jamie Moore L RSC 10 Manchester
	(British L.Middleweight Title Challenge)

Career: 19 contests, won 17, lost 2.

Matthew Macklin   Les Clark

Gary McMillan

Edinburgh. *Born* Edinburgh, 12 January, 1987
Welterweight. *Ht* 5'10"
Manager F. Maloney

17.11.06	Scott Woolford L PTS 4 Bethnal Green
16.02.07	Thomas Mazurkiewicz DREW 4 Kirkcaldy

Career: 2 contests, drew 1, lost 1.

Gary McMillan   Les Clark

Joe McNally

Liverpool. *Born* Liverpool, 30 October, 1984
Middleweight. *Ht* 5'9¾"
Manager L. Maloney

10.03.07	Rocky Muscas W PTS 4 Liverpool

Career: 1 contest, won 1.

Colin McNeil

Fauldhouse. *Born* Lanark, 21 December, 1972
Scottish L.Middleweight Champion. Former Undefeated Celtic L.Middleweight Champion. *Ht* 5'8"
Manager A. Morrison/F. Warren

06.03.04	Arv Mittoo W PTS 4 Renfrew
27.03.04	Lee Williamson W PTS 4 Edinburgh
19.06.04	Andrei Ivanov W RSC 2 Renfrew
22.10.04	Ivor Bonavic W PTS 4 Edinburgh
03.12.04	Geraint Harvey W PTS 6 Edinburgh
28.01.05	Matt Scriven W PTS 4 Renfrew
20.05.05	Duncan Cottier W PTS 6 Glasgow
23.07.05	Taz Jones W PTS 10 Edinburgh
	(Vacant Celtic L.Middleweight Title)
23.09.05	Ossie Duran L PTS 12 Mayfair
	(Commonwealth L.Middleweight Title Challenge)
29.04.06	Gary Young W CO 1 Edinburgh
	(Elim.British Welterweight Title)
04.11.06	David Kirk W PTS 6 Glasgow
10.12.06	Barrie Lee W RSC 4 Glasgow
	(Scottish Area L.Middleweight Title Challenge)
30.03.07	Cornelius Bundrage L RSC 7 Newcastle

Career: 13 contests, won 11, lost 2.

Neal McQuade

Peterborough. *Born* London, 17 November, 1977
L.Welterweight. *Ht* 5'4½"
Manager I. Pauly

15.06.06	Kristian Laight L PTS 6 Peterborough
21.07.06	Danny Harding L PTS 4 Altrincham
15.10.06	Gavin Deacon L PTS 6 Norwich
03.11.06	Darren Hamilton L PTS 6 Bristol
01.12.06	Waz Hussain DREW 4 Birmingham
24.02.07	Abdul Rashid W PTS 6 Peterborough
30.03.07	Gavin Deacon L PTS 6 Peterborough
31.05.07	Anthony Crolla L RSC 1 Manchester
29.06.07	Lewis Smith L PTS 6 Manchester

Career: 9 contests, won 1, drew 1, lost 7.

Tony McQuade

Peterborough. *Born* Peterborough, 2 June, 1988
S.Featherweight. *Ht* 5'5½"
Manager I. Pauly

07.12.06	Gavin Deacon DREW 6 Peterborough
30.03.07	Carl Griffiths W PTS 6 Peterborough
18.04.07	Leroy Smedley L PTS 6 Strand
21.06.07	Shaun Walton W PTS 6 Peterborough

Career: 4 contests, won 2, drew 1, lost 1.

Brian Magee

Belfast. *Born* Lisburn, 9 June, 1975
L.Heavyweight. Former IBO S.Middleweight Champion. Former Undefeated IBO Inter-Continental S.Middleweight Champion. *Ht* 6'0"
Manager P. Magee

13.03.99	Dean Ashton W RSC 2 Manchester
22.05.99	Richard Glaysher W RSC 1 Belfast
22.06.99	Chris Howarth W RSC 1 Ipswich
13.09.99	Dennis Doyley W RSC 3 Bethnal Green
16.10.99	Michael Pinnock W RSC 3 Belfast
12.02.00	Terry Morrill W RTD 4 Sheffield
21.02.00	Rob Stevenson W RSC 5 Southwark
20.03.00	Darren Ashton W RTD 5 Mansfield
15.04.00	Pedro Carragher W CO 2 Bethnal Green
12.06.00	Jason Barker W PTS 8 Belfast
11.00.00	Teimouraz Kikelidze W RSC 4 Belfast
29.01.01	Neil Linford W PTS 12 Peterborough
	(Vacant IBO Inter-Continental S. Middleweight Title)
31.07.01	Chris Nembhard W RSC 6 Bethnal Green
10.12.01	Ramon Britez W CO 1 Liverpool
	(IBO S.Middleweight Title Challenge)
18.03.02	Vage Kocharyan W PTS 8 Crawley
15.06.02	Mpush Makambi W RSC 7 Leeds
	(IBO S. Middleweight Title Defence)
09.11.02	Jose Spearman W PTS 12 Altrincham
	(IBO S.Middleweight Title Defence)
22.02.03	Miguel Jimenez W PTS 12 Huddersfield
	(IBO S. Middleweight Title Defence)
21.06.03	Andre Thysse W PTS 10 Manchester
	(IBO S.Middleweight Title Defence)
04.10.03	Omar Eduardo Gonzalez W RSC 1 Belfast
	(IBO S.Middleweight Title Defence)
22.11.03	Hacine Cherifi W RTD 8 Belfast
	(IBO S.Middleweight Title Defence)

17.04.04	Jerry Elliott W PTS 12 Belfast
	(IBO S.Middleweight Title Defence)
26.06.04	Robin Reid L PTS 12 Belfast
	(IBO S.Middleweight Title Defence)
26.11.04	Neil Linford W RSC 7 Altrincham
16.07.05	Vitali Tsypko L PTS 12 Nurnberg, Germany
	(Vacant European S.Middleweight Title)
14.10.05	Varuzhan Davtyan W RSC 2 Dublin
28.01.06	Daniil Prakapsou W RSC 2 Dublin
26.05.06	Carl Froch L RSC 11 Bethnal Green
	(British & Commonwealth S.Middleweight Title Challenges)
03.11.06	Paul David W PTS 6 Barnsley
26.01.07	Andrew Lowe W PTS 10 Dagenham
	(Final Elim.British L.Heavyweight Title)
08.06.07	Danny Thornton W RTD 2 Motherwell

Career: 31 contests, won 28, lost 3.

Eamonn Magee

Belfast. *Born* Belfast, 13 July, 1971
Welterweight. Former WBU Welterweight Champion. Former Undefeated Commonwealth L.Welterweight Champion. *Ht* 5'9"
Manager Self

25.11.95	Pete Roberts W CO 4 Dublin
09.03.96	Steve McGovern W PTS 4 Millstreet
28.05.96	John Stovin W RSC 2 Belfast
03.09.96	Kevin McKillan W RTD 4 Belfast
05.11.96	Shaun Stokes W RSC 2 Belfast
28.01.97	Karl Taylor W PTS 6 Belfast
03.03.97	Troy Townsend W RSC 1 Austin, Texas, USA
28.03.97	Teddy Reid L PTS 6 Boston, Mass, USA
29.04.97	Peter Nightingale W RTD 2 Belfast
02.06.97	Kevin McKillan W RSC 3 Belfast
	(Elim. All-Ireland L. Welterweight Title)
14.02.98	Dennis Griffin W RSC 2 Southwark
26.09.98	Allan Hall W RSC 7 York
30.11.98	Paul Burke L PTS 12 Manchester
	(Vacant Commonwealth L. Welterweight Title)
22.05.99	Alan Temple W CO 3 Belfast
10.07.99	Karl Taylor W RTD 3 Southwark
13.09.99	Paul Burke W RSC 6 Bethnal Green
	(Commonwealth L. Welterweight Title Challenge)
16.10.99	Radoslav Gaidev W RSC 1 Belfast
04.03.00	Joseph Miyumo W RSC 1 Peterborough
	(Commonwealth L. Welterweight Title Defence)
29.04.00	David Kirk W RSC 8 Wembley
16.09.00	Pavel Melnikov W PTS 8 Bethnal Green
11.11.00	Shea Neary W PTS 12 Belfast
	(Commonwealth L. Welterweight Title Defence)
13.03.01	Alan Bosworth W RSC 5 Plymouth
12.05.01	Harrison Methula W RSC 7 Plymouth
	(Commonwealth L. Welterweight Title Defence)
27.10.01	Matthews Zulu W PTS 12 Manchester
	(Commonwealth L.Welterweight Title Defence)
09.02.02	Jonathan Thaxton W RSC 6 Manchester
	(Commonwealth L. Welterweight Title Defence)

01.06.02	Ricky Hatton L PTS 12 Manchester	
	(WBU L. Welterweight Title Challenge)	
28.09.02	Alan Bosworth W RSC 5 Manchester	
14.06.03	Otkay Urkal L PTS 12 Magdeburg, Germany	
	(European L.Welterweight Title Challenge)	
06.12.03	Jimmy Vincent W PTS 12 Cardiff	
	(Vacant WBU Welterweight Title)	
18.03.05	Allan Vester W RSC 3 Belfast	
	(WBU Welterweight Title Defence)	
20.05.06	Takaloo L PTS 12 Belfast	
	(WBU Welterweight Title Defence)	
10.02.07	Janos Petrovics W PTS 6 Letterkenny	
11.05.07	Kevin Anderson L PTS 12 Motherwell	
	(British Welterweight Title Challenge)	

Career: 33 contests, won 27, lost 6.

(Jebrael) Jimmy Maile

Nottingham. *Born* Iran, 2 February, 1982
L.Middleweight. *Ht* 5'11"
Manager M. Shinfield

15.09.06	Jamie Way L RSC 4 Newport
11.11.06	Dale Miles L RSC 5 Sutton in Ashfield

Career: 2 contests, lost 2.

Irfan Malik

Bradford. *Born* Pakistan, 23 August, 1972
S.Middleweight. *Ht* 5'9"
Manager C. Aston

24.06.07	Sean Crompton L RSC 3 Wigan

Career: 1 contest, lost 1.

Dean Marcantonio (Springate)

Eltham. *Born* Isle of Sheppey, 8 August, 1976
L.Middleweight. *Ht* 5'5"
Manager M. Roe

26.02.06	Dave Wakefield L RSC 3 Dagenham
23.07.06	Rocky Muscas W PTS 4 Dagenham
08.09.06	Curtis Woodhouse L PTS 4 Mayfair
03.12.06	Jamal Morrison L RSC 2 Bethnal Green

Career: 4 contests, won 1, lost 3.

Matthew Marsh

West Ham. *Born* Sidcup, 1 August, 1982
Southern Area Featherweight Champion.
Ht 5'5¾"
Manager F. Warren/F. Maloney

Matthew Marsh   Les Clark

10.09.04	Fred Janes W PTS 4 Bethnal Green	
19.11.04	Dean Ward W PTS 4 Bethnal Green	
11.12.04	Abdul Mougharbel W PTS 4 Canning Town	
25.02.05	Dai Davies W PTS 4 Wembley	
10.12.05	Darren Cleary W PTS 4 Canning Town	
29.06.06	Frederic Gosset W PTS 6 Bethnal Green	
09.12.06	Rocky Dean W PTS 10 Canning Town	
	(Southern Area Featherweight Title Challenge)	

Career: 7 contests, won 7.

Martin Marshall

Sunderland. *Born* Sunderland, 28 January, 1983
Middleweight. *Ht* 6'1"
Manager Self

14.05.04	Richard Mazurek DREW 6 Sunderland
23.09.04	Richard Inquieti W PTS 6 Gateshead
28.10.04	Richard Inquieti W PTS 6 Sunderland
09.12.04	Gary Porter L PTS 6 Sunderland
19.12.04	John Marshall L CO 5 Bolton
12.05.05	Muhsen Nasser L PTS 6 Sunderland
27.05.05	Gary Porter L PTS 6 Motherwell
11.06.05	Keith Ellwood W PTS 6 Kirkcaldy
06.10.05	Alex Stoda W PTS 6 Sunderland
03.11.05	Malik Khan W PTS 6 Sunderland
08.12.05	Brendan Halford L RSC 5 Sunderland
09.03.06	Omar Gumati DREW 6 Sunderland
11.09.06	Prince Arron L PTS 6 Manchester
23.10.06	Craig Dickson L RTD 4 Glasgow
24.11.06	Danny Johnston L PTS 6 Stoke
07.12.06	Thomas Mazurkiewicz W PTS 6 Sunderland
16.02.07	Paddy Pollock W PTS 4 Sunderland
30.03.07	Graham Delehedy L CO 2 Crawley
24.06.07	Matt Scriven W PTS 6 Sunderland

Career: 19 contests, won 8, drew 2, lost 9.

Tommy Marshall

Plymouth. *Born* Aberystwyth, 22 August, 1984
Middleweight. *Ht* 6'0"
Manager Self

02.04.04	Chris Brophy DREW 6 Plymouth
03.07.04	Arv Mittoo W PTS 6 Bristol
17.09.04	Chris Brophy L PTS 6 Plymouth
06.12.04	Mark Franks W PTS 6 Leeds
18.02.05	William Imoro L PTS 4 Torrevieja, Spain
02.06.07	Carl Drake L RSC 4 Bristol

Career: 6 contests, won 2, drew 1, lost 3.

Neil Marston

Shrewsbury. *Born* Shrewsbury, 8 February, 1977
Featherweight. *Ht* 5'7"
Manager E. Johnson

08.07.04	Dai Davies L PTS 6 Birmingham
12.09.04	Paddy Folan W PTS 6 Shrewsbury
18.11.04	Paddy Folan W PTS 6 Shrewsbury
06.12.04	Paddy Folan W PTS 6 Bradford
28.01.05	Scott Flynn L RSC 2 Renfrew
15.04.05	Craig Bromley L RSC 1 Shrewsbury
23.05.05	Wayne Bloy L PTS 6 Cleethorpes
19.09.05	Sandy Bartlett L PTS 6 Glasgow
13.11.05	Robert Nelson L PTS 6 Leeds
24.02.06	Shaun Doherty W PTS 6 Birmingham

ACTIVE BRITISH-BASED BOXERS: CAREER RECORDS

04.03.06	Darren Cleary L PTS 4 Manchester
14.04.06	Neil Read W PTS 6 Telford
21.04.06	Jamie McDonnell L PTS 4 Doncaster
14.05.06	Pete Walkman W RSC 6 Derby
26.05.06	Mo Khaled W DIS 5 Hull
05.06.06	John Bothwell L PTS 6 Glasgow
29.06.06	Eugene Heagney L PTS 6 Dudley
12.07.06	Mo Khaled L PTS 4 Bethnal Green
30.09.06	Isaac Ward L PTS 6 Middlesbrough
09.10.06	Dougie Walton L PTS 6 Birmingham
23.10.06	Jimmy Gilhaney L PTS 6 Glasgow
10.11.06	Furhan Rafiq W PTS 6 Telford
30.11.06	Sergei Rozhakmens W PTS 6 Piccadilly
10.12.06	James Ancliff L PTS 6 Glasgow
01.04.07	Andy Bell L RSC 8 Shrewsbury (Vacant Midlands Area Bantamweight Title)
09.06.07	Gavin Reid L CO 2 Middlesbrough

Career: 26 contests, won 9, lost 17.

Shanee Martin

Colchester. *Born* Dagenham, 31 January, 1982
Bantamweight. *Ht* 5'2"
Manager Self

16.10.04	Iliana Boneva W RSC 4 Dagenham
05.03.05	Svetla Taskova W PTS 6 Dagenham
18.09.05	Albena Atseva W RSC 3 Bethnal Green
19.11.05	Valerie Rangeard W PTS 6 Southwark
26.02.06	Maya Frenzel W RSC 5 Dagenham
23.07.06	Juliette Winter L PTS 8 Dagenham
21.10.06	Tatiana Puchkova W RSC 2 Southwark
03.12.06	Rebekka Herrmann W PTS 8 Bethnal Green
18.02.07	Oksana Romanova L RSC 7 Bethnal Green
04.05.07	Viktoria Milo L PTS 10 Szombathely, Hungary (Womens IBF-GBU Flyweight Title Challenge)
29.06.07	Svetla Taskova W PTS 6 Manchester

Career: 11 contests, won 8, lost 3.

Ali Mateen

Sheffield. *Born* Sheffield, 2 June, 1986
S.Middleweight. *Ht* 5'11½"
Manager J. Ingle

15.11.04	Keith Ellwood W PTS 6 Glasgow
26.11.04	Glen Matsell L RTD 3 Hull
06.03.05	Rob MacDonald W PTS 6 Shaw
15.12.05	Richard Mazurek L PTS 6 Coventry
26.05.06	Jimi Hendricks W CO 2 Hull
27.10.06	Ojay Abrahams W PTS 6 Glasgow

Career: 6 contests, won 4, lost 2.

Glen Matsell

Hull. *Born* Hull, 24 March, 1975
L.Middleweight. *Ht* 5'9"
Manager K. Toomey

26.11.04	Ali Mateen W RTD 3 Hull
27.04.07	Ben Hudson W PTS 6 Hull

Career: 2 contests, won 2.

Derry Matthews

Liverpool. *Born* Liverpool, 23 September, 1983
WBU Featherweight Champion. Former Undefeated English Featherweight Champion. *Ht* 5'8½"
Manager F. Warren/S. Vaughan

18.01.03	Sergei Tasimov W CO 1 Preston
05.04.03	Jus Wallie W PTS 4 Manchester
08.05.03	Steve Gethin W RSC 3 Widnes
20.06.03	Henry Janes W RSC 1 Liverpool
29.08.03	Marty Kayes W RTD 2 Liverpool
02.10.03	Alexei Volchan W RSC 2 Liverpool
13.12.03	Pete Buckley W PTS 4 Manchester
26.02.04	Gareth Payne W RSC 4 Widnes
03.04.04	Henry Janes W PTS 4 Manchester
10.09.04	Buster Dennis W PTS 6 Liverpool
17.12.04	Dean Ward W RSC 1 Liverpool
13.05.05	John Mackay W PTS 6 Liverpool
16.07.05	Dai Davies W RSC 2 Bolton
25.10.05	Frederic Bonifai W PTS 6 Preston
28.01.06	Stephen Chinnock W RTD 6 Nottingham (Vacant English Featherweight Title)
01.06.06	Mickey Coveney W PTS 8 Barnsley
14.10.06	Steve Foster W PTS 12 Manchester (WBU Featherweight Title Challenge)
10.03.07	John Simpson W PTS 12 Liverpool (WBU Featherweight Title Defence)

Career: 18 contests, won 18.

Alex Matvienko

Bolton. *Born* Bolton, 9 May, 1978
Middleweight. *Ht* 5'11"
Manager S. Wood

18.12.05	Tommy Jones W PTS 6 Bolton
02.04.06	Tony Randell W PTS 6 Shaw
21.07.06	Simone Lucas W PTS 4 Altrincham
29.09.06	Jon Foster W RTD 3 Manchester
12.11.06	Thomas Flynn W RSC 5 Manchester
25.02.07	Shaun Farmer W PTS 6 Manchester
13.04.07	Ryan Ashworth DREW 4 Altrincham
24.06.07	Ronnie Daniels W PTS 6 Wigan

Career: 8 contests, won 7, drew 1.

Kevin Maxwell

Belfast. *Born* Belfast, 4 April, 1984
L.Welterweight. *Ht* 5'6"
Manager B. Hearn

30.06.07	Deniss Sirjatovs W PTS 4 Belfast

Career: 1 contest, won 1.

Max Maxwell

Birmingham. *Born* Jamaica, 26 July, 1979
Middleweight. *Ht* 5'10"
Manager R. Woodhall

26.10.06	Anthony Young L PTS 4 Wolverhampton
01.12.06	Ernie Smith W PTS 6 Birmingham
23.02.07	Peter Dunn W PTS 6 Birmingham
17.03.07	Sherman Alleyne W PTS 6 Birmingham
29.04.07	Matt Scriven W PTS 4 Birmingham

Career: 5 contests, won 4, lost 1.

Patrick J. Maxwell

Sheffield. *Born* USA, 20 March, 1979
S.Middleweight. *Ht* 5'8¼"
Manager Frank Joseph

17.03.98	Danny Thornton W PTS 6 Sheffield
12.08.00	Matthew Ashmole W RSC 3 Wembley
26.03.01	Jason Collins L PTS 4 Wembley
27.10.01	Prince Kasi Kaihau W CO 4 Manchester
09.02.02	Leigh Wicks W PTS 4 Manchester
09.03.03	Surinder Sekhon W RSC 1 Shaw
10.06.03	Andy Halder W RSC 1 Sheffield

05.09.03	Isidro Gonzalez W RSC 6 Sheffield
07.11.03	Conroy McIntosh W RSC 4 Sheffield
17.06.04	Howard Clarke W RSC 1 Sheffield
21.09.05	Conroy McIntosh W RSC 2 Bradford
14.10.06	Anthony Little W RSC 3 Philadelphia, Pennsylvania, USA
17.11.06	Charden Ansoula W PTS 6 Cabazon, California, USA
09.03.07	Kevin Phelan W RSC 2 Dagenham
27.04.07	Geard Ajetovic DREW 6 Wembley

Career: 15 contests, won 13, drew 1, lost 1.

Anthony Maynard

Birmingham. *Born* Birmingham, 12 January, 1972
L.Welterweight. Former Undefeated Midlands Area Lightweight Champion. *Ht* 5'8"
Manager Self

17.10.94	Malcolm Thomas W PTS 6 Birmingham
02.11.94	Dean Phillips W PTS 6 Birmingham
25.01.95	Neil Smith L PTS 6 Stoke
07.02.95	Anthony Campbell W PTS 8 Wolverhampton
08.03.95	Scott Walker W PTS 6 Solihull
28.03.95	Kid McAuley W PTS 8 Wolverhampton
11.05.95	Gary Hiscox W RSC 4 Dudley
06.06.95	Richard Swallow L RSC 2 Leicester
02.10.95	Jay Mahoney W PTS 8 Birmingham
26.10.95	Ray Newby W PTS 8 Birmingham
17.01.96	Tom Welsh W RSC 8 Solihull
06.03.96	G. G. Goddard W RSC 3 Solihull
20.03.97	Richard Swallow W PTS 6 Solihull
24.10.97	Brian Coleman W CO 1 Birmingham
27.03.98	Gary Flear W RSC 9 Telford (Vacant Midlands Area Lightweight Title)
30.05.98	Michael Ayers W PTS 8 Bristol
21.11.98	Stephen Smith L PTS 10 Southwark
27.11.00	David Kehoe W RSC 5 Birmingham
07.04.01	Alfred Kotey L RTD 6 Wembley (Vacant WBF Inter-Continental Lightweight Title)
11.06.01	Woody Greenaway W PTS 4 Nottingham
08.10.01	Bobby Vanzie L RSC 1 Barnsley (British Lightweight Title Challenge)
09.03.02	David Burke L PTS 6 Manchester
09.11.02	Chris Barnett W PTS 6 Altrincham
08.02.03	Gary Hibbert DREW 6 Liverpool
18.10.03	Gary Hibbert L PTS 6 Manchester
07.02.04	Danny Hunt L PTS 10 Bethnal Green (English Lightweight Title Challenge)
07.04.05	Tony Montana W PTS 4 Birmingham
23.06.06	Daniel Thorpe W PTS 4 Birmingham
01.12.06	Silence Saheed W PTS 6 Birmingham

Career: 29 contests, won 20, drew 1, lost 8.

Thomas Mazurkiewicz

Manchester. *Born* Poland, 11 May, 1984
L.Middleweight. *Ht* 5'9"
Manager S. Wood

11.09.06	Imad Khamis DREW 6 Manchester
23.09.06	Joe McCluskey W RSC 2 Coventry
29.09.06	John Fewkes L PTS 4 Manchester
23.11.06	Imad Khamis W PTS 6 Manchester
07.12.06	Martin Marshall L PTS 6 Sunderland
16.02.07	Gary McMillan DREW 4 Kirkcaldy
09.03.07	Paul Porter W PTS 4 Dagenham
12.05.07	Danny Johnston W PTS 6 Stoke

Career: 8 contests, won 4, drew 2, lost 2.

Lee Meager
Salford. *Born* Salford, 18 January, 1978
Lightweight. Former British Lightweight
Champion. *Ht* 5'8"
Manager Self

16.09.00	Pete Buckley W PTS 4 Bethnal Green	
14.10.00	Chris Jickells W PTS 4 Wembley	
18.11.00	Billy Smith W RSC 1 Dagenham	
09.12.00	Jason Nesbitt W RSC 2 Southwark	
05.02.01	Carl Allen DREW 6 Hull	
13.03.01	Lennie Hodgkins W RSC 3 Plymouth	
12.05.01	Jason White W PTS 4 Plymouth	
31.07.01	Steve Hanley W PTS 6 Bethnal Green	
13.09.01	Arv Mittoo W PTS 6 Sheffield	
16.03.02	Jason Nesbitt W PTS 8 Bethnal Green	
10.05.02	Pete Buckley W PTS 6 Bethnal Green	
25.10.02	Iain Eldridge W RSC 5 Bethnal Green	
21.12.02	Chill John W RSC 5 Dagenham	
28.01.03	Carl Allen W PTS 8 Nottingham	
28.11.03	Pete Buckley W PTS 4 Derby	
11.12.03	Charles Shepherd W RTD 7 Bethnal Green	
02.06.04	Michael Muya W PTS 8 Nottingham	
19.11.04	Danny Hunt L PTS 10 Bethnal Green	
	(English Lightweight Title Challenge)	
09.07.05	Martin Watson W PTS 10 Nottingham	
02.12.05	Tony Montana W PTS 8 Nottingham	
17.02.06	Ben Hudson W PTS 4 Bethnal Green	
12.05.06	Dave Stewart W RSC 6 Bethnal Green	
	(Vacant British Lightweight Title)	
08.12.06	Jonathan Thaxton L PTS 12 Dagenham	
	(British Lightweight Title Defence)	

Career: 23 contests, won 20, drew 1, lost 2.

Michael Medor
London. *Born* Mauritius, 23 May, 1982
Welterweight. *Ht* 5'10¾"
Manager C. Sanigar

16.09.05	Imad Khamis W PTS 4 Plymouth
16.10.05	Jason Nesbitt W PTS 6 Peterborough
25.11.05	Martin Gethin L PTS 4 Walsall
29.09.06	Craig Watson L RSC 1 Manchester

Career: 4 contests, won 2, lost 2.

Judex Meemea
Walthamstow. *Born* Mauritius, 24
November, 1973
L.Welterweight. *Ht* 5'10"
Manager C. Sanigar

21.02.04	Jay Morris DREW 4 Brighton
08.06.04	Tyrone McInerney DREW 6 Sheffield
27.09.04	Scott Haywood L PTS 6 Cleethorpes
20.11.04	Joe McCluskey DREW 6 Coventry
26.03.05	Ashley Theophane W PTS 6 Hackney
02.06.05	Andy Cosnett W PTS 6 Peterborough
18.06.05	Gwyn Wale L RSC 5 Barnsley
24.07.05	Bheki Moyo W PTS 4 Leicester Square
16.09.05	Michael Grant L RSC 3 Plymouth
21.10.05	Dave Stewart L RSC 4 Bethnal Green
12.12.05	Billy Smith W PTS 6 Peterborough
07.04.06	Garry Buckland L RSC 5 Bristol
15.06.06	Lea Handley W PTS 6 Peterborough
30.09.06	Scott Lawton L DIS 7 Stoke
10.11.06	Garry Buckland L PTS 6 Newport
05.12.06	Martin Gethin L RSC 3 Wolverhampton
	(Vacant British Masters L.Welterweight Title)
20.04.07	Dean Harrison L RSC 6 Dudley

Career: 17 contests, won 5, drew 3, lost 9.

Dale Miles
Alfreton. *Born* Mansfield, 19 November,
1984
L.Middleweight. *Ht* 5'11"
Manager S. Calow

13.05.06	Karl Taylor W RSC 3 Sutton in Ashfield
16.09.06	Steve Cooper W PTS 6 Burton
11.11.06	Jimmy Maile W RSC 5 Sutton in Ashfield

Career: 3 contests, won 3.

Ian Millarvie
Hamilton. *Born* Bellshill, 7 April, 1980
Heavyweight. *Ht* 6'5¾"
Manager T. Gilmour

31.01.05	Mal Rice W RTD 3 Glasgow
21.02.05	Luke Simpkin W PTS 6 Glasgow
27.05.05	Sergey Voron W RSC 1 Motherwell
17.03.06	Jason Callum W CO 3 Kirkcaldy
11.04.07	Sean McClain W PTS 4 NYC, New York, USA

Career: 5 contests, won 5.

(Wesley) Wez Miller
Doncaster. *Born* Doncaster, 24 April, 1986
Lightweight. *Ht* 5'8"
Manager J. Rushton

03.03.06	Gavin Deacon W PTS 4 Doncaster
21.04.06	Kristian Laight L PTS 6 Doncaster
09.06.06	Pete Buckley W PTS 6 Doncaster
13.10.06	John Baguley L PTS 4 Doncaster

Career: 4 contests, won 2, lost 2.

Ross Minter
Crawley. *Born* Crawley, 10 November, 1978
Welterweight. Former Undefeated Southern
Area & English Welterweight Champion.
Ht 5'7¾"
Manager F. Warren

26.03.01	Brian Coleman W PTS 4 Wembley
05.05.01	Trevor Smith W RTD 3 Edmonton
28.07.01	Lee Williamson W PTS 4 Wembley
24.11.01	Karl Taylor W PTS 4 Bethnal Green
15.12.01	Ernie Smith W RSC 2 Wembley
02.03.02	Paul Denton W PTS 6 Bethnal Green
25.05.02	Howard Clarke L RSC 2 Portsmouth
12.10.02	Dafydd Carlin W RSC 1 Bethnal Green
15.02.03	Karl Taylor W PTS 6 Wembley
29.03.03	Jay Mahoney W RSC 2 Portsmouth
24.05.03	Jay Mahoney W PTS 6 Bethnal Green
18.09.03	John Marshall DREW 6 Dagenham
19.11.04	David Kirk W PTS 6 Bethnal Green
25.02.05	Ernie Smith W PTS 4 Wembley
29.04.05	Chas Symonds W RSC 3 Southwark
	(Southern Area Welterweight Title Challenge)
23.09.05	Sammy Smith W RSC 3 Mayfair
	(Southern Area Welterweight Title Defence)
10.12.05	Brett James W RSC 4 Canning Town
	(Vacant English Welterweight Title. Southern Area Welterweight Title Defence)
08.07.06	Duncan Cottier W PTS 6 Cardiff
17.02.07	Sasha Shnip W RSC 2 Wembley
30.03.07	Freddy Curiel L RSC 8 Newcastle

Career: 20 contests, won 17, drew 1, lost 2.

Darryl Mitchell
Plymouth. *Born* Ballymena, 7 November,
1983
S.Featherweight. *Ht* 5'7½"
Manager T. Gilmour

13.12.06	Shaun Walton W PTS 4 Strand
02.06.07	Anthony Hanna L RTD 5 Bristol

Career: 2 contests, won 1, lost 1.

(Delroy) Dee Mitchell
Birmingham. *Born* Birmingham, 16
November, 1976
L.Middleweight. *Ht* 5'9"
Manager R. Woodhall

08.09.06	Chris Brophy W RSC 2 Birmingham
26.10.06	Tony Randell W PTS 4 Wolverhampton
01.12.06	Billy Smith W PTS 4 Birmingham
23.02.07	Geraint Harvey W PTS 4 Birmingham
17.03.07	Matt Scriven W RSC 2 Birmingham
29.04.07	Tye Williams W PTS 8 Birmingham

Career: 6 contests, won 6.

Joe Mitchell
Birmingham. *Born* Birmingham, 8
February, 1971
L.Middleweight. *Ht* 5'9"
Manager Self

20.02.04	Steve Scott W PTS 6 Doncaster
07.04.04	Robert Lloyd-Taylor L RSC 5 Leicester Square
08.07.04	Darren Gethin DREW 6 Birmingham
12.09.04	Darren Gethin L PTS 6 Shrewsbury
05.10.04	Mark Wall DREW 6 Dudley
22.10.04	Dennis Corpe W PTS 6 Mansfield
25.11.04	Ernie Smith L PTS 6 Birmingham
04.02.05	Jon Harrison L PTS 6 Plymouth
18.04.05	Darren Gethin L PTS 6 Bradford
18.06.05	Scott Conway W RSC 5 Barnsley
08.07.05	Jonathan Hussey L PTS 4 Altrincham
16.09.05	Gary Round L PTS 6 Telford
10.10.05	Peter Dunn W PTS 6 Birmingham
30.10.05	Lee Edwards W RSC 2 Sheffield
12.11.05	David Kirk L PTS 6 Sheffield
02.12.05	Jason Rushton L PTS 6 Doncaster
24.02.06	Ernie Smith W PTS 6 Birmingham
23.04.06	Omar Gumati L PTS 4 Chester
01.06.06	Kerry Hope L PTS 4 Barnsley
23.06.06	Dave Wakefield L PTS 6 Birmingham
06.10.06	Dean Harrison L PTS 4 Wolverhampton
09.12.06	Daniel Cadman W PTS 4 Chigwell

Career: 22 contests, won 7, drew 2, lost 13.

Kevin Mitchell
Dagenham. *Born* Dagenham, 29 October,
1984
Commonwealth & IBF Inter-Continental
S.Featherweight Champion. *Ht* 5'8"
Manager F. Warren

17.07.03	Stevie Quinn W CO 1 Dagenham
18.09.03	Csabi Ladanyi W RSC 1 Dagenham
06.11.03	Vlado Varhegyi W RSC 3 Dagenham
24.01.04	Jaz Virdee W RSC 1 Wembley
07.02.04	Kristian Laight W RSC 4 Bethnal Green
24.04.04	Eric Patrac W RSC 1 Reading
13.05.04	Slimane Kebaili W RSC 1 Bethnal Green
05.06.04	Jason Nesbitt W RSC 3 Bethnal Green
10.09.04	Arpad Toth W RSC 3 Bethnal Green
22.10.04	Mounir Guebbas W PTS 6 Edinburgh

19.11.04	Alain Rakow W CO 1 Bethnal Green
11.12.04	Henry Janes W PTS 4 Canning Town
08.04.05	Frederic Bonifai W PTS 6 Edinburgh
29.04.05	Karim Chakim W PTS 8 Southwark
23.09.05	Wladimir Borov W RSC 2 Mayfair
25.10.05	Daniel Thorpe W RSC 4 Preston
10.12.05	Mohammed Medjadji W RSC 6 Canning Town
	(Vacant IBF Inter-Continental S.Featherweight Title)
25.02.06	Youssef Djibaba W PTS 12 Canning Town
	(IBF Inter-Continental S.Featherweight Title Defence)
13.05.06	Kirkor Kirkorov W RTD 2 Bethnal Green
	(IBF Inter-Continental S.Featherweight Title Defence)
08.07.06	Imad Ben Khalifa W RSC 2 Cardiff
08.09.06	Andrey Isaev W RSC 11 Mayfair
	(IBF Inter-Continental S.Featherweight Title Defence)
28.10.06	George Ashie W PTS 12 Bethnal Green
	(Vacant Commonwealth S.Featherweight Title)
10.03.07	Harry Ramogoadi W RSC 6 Liverpool
	(Commonwealth S.Featherweight Title Defence)

Career: 23 contests, won 23.

Kevin Mitchell   Les Clark

Scott Mitchell

Bolton. *Born* Bolton, 3 February, 1979
Heavyweight. *Ht.* 6'3"
Manager A. Penarski

16.06.07	Zahir Kahut L PTS 6 Bolton

Career: 1 contest, lost 1.

Vinny Mitchell

Dagenham. *Born* Dagenham, 1 May, 1987
Lightweight. Ht. 5'7¼"
Manager F. Warren

17.02.07	Shaun Walton W PTS 4 Wembley

Career: 1 contest, won 1.

Colin Moffett

Belfast. *Born* Belfast, 15 April, 1975
S.Bantamweight. *Ht* 5'6"
Manager Self

05.11.96	Shane Mallon W RSC 2 Belfast
28.01.97	Anthony Hanna W PTS 4 Belfast
29.04.97	Gary Hickman W PTS 4 Belfast
02.06.97	Jason Thomas L RSC 3 Belfast
20.12.97	Graham McGrath DREW 4 Belfast
18.09.98	Anthony Hanna DREW 4 Belfast
28.11.98	Shaun Norman W PTS 4 Belfast
31.07.99	Waj Khan W CO 1 Carlisle
16.10.99	Delroy Spencer L PTS 4 Bethnal Green
31.03.00	Steffen Norskov L PTS 4 Esbjerg, Denmark
05.06.00	Keith Knox L RSC 3 Glasgow
02.12.00	Dale Robinson L PTS 4 Bethnal Green
15.09.01	Chris Emanuele L RSC 4 Nottingham
27.04.02	Levi Pattison L RSC 2 Huddersfield
27.07.02	Jim Betts L RSC 3 Nottingham
30.10.03	John Bothwell DREW 4 Belfast
08.05.04	Lee Haskins L RSC 2 Bristol
19.06.04	Michael Crossan DREW 4 Renfrew
28.10.04	Chris Edwards W PTS 4 Belfast
20.05.06	Delroy Spencer W PTS 4 Belfast
07.10.06	Matthew Edmonds L PTS 4 Belfast

Career: 21 contests, won 7, drew 4, lost 10.

Michael Monaghan

Lincoln. *Born* Nottingham, 31 May, 1976
L.Heavyweight. Former Midlands Area L.Heavyweight Champion. *Ht* 5'10¾"
Manager M. Scriven

23.09.96	Lee Simpkin W PTS 6 Cleethorpes
24.10.96	Lee Bird W RSC 6 Lincoln
09.12.96	Lee Simpkin W PTS 6 Chesterfield
16.12.96	Carlton Williams W PTS 6 Cleethorpes
20.03.97	Paul Miles W PTS 6 Newark
26.04.97	Paul Ryan L RSC 2 Swadlincote
05.07.97	Ali Khattab W PTS 4 Glasgow
18.08.97	Trevor Meikle W PTS 6 Nottingham
12.09.97	Willie Quinn L PTS 6 Glasgow
19.09.97	Roy Chipperfield W PTS 6 Salford
30.09.97	George Richards L PTS 6 Edgbaston
10.03.98	Anthony van Niekirk L RTD 6 Hammanskraal, South Africa
23.04.98	Darren Sweeney L PTS 10 Edgbaston
	(Midlands Area Middleweight Title Challenge)
19.09.98	Jim Rock L PTS 12 Dublin
	(Vacant WAA Inter-Continental S. Middleweight Title)
27.11.98	Mark Dawson W PTS 6 Nottingham
07.12.98	Mike Whittaker L PTS 6 Manchester
14.09.02	Paul Billington W RSC 4 Newark
30.11.02	Gary Beardsley W PTS 6 Newark
24.02.03	Jason Collins W PTS 8 Birmingham
16.04.03	Carl Froch L RSC 3 Nottingham
28.06.03	Gary Lockett L PTS 10 Cardiff
13.09.03	Tomas da Silva W PTS 6 Newport
25.04.04	Jason Collins W PTS 6 Nottingham
05.06.04	Wayne Elcock L PTS 4 Bethnal Green
03.09.04	Gary Lockett L RSC 3 Newport
29.10.04	Lawrence Murphy L PTS 6 Renfrew
20.02.05	Howard Clarke W PTS 6 Sheffield
18.03.05	Jim Rock L PTS 8 Belfast
27.03.05	Michal Bilak W PTS 6 Prague, Czech Republic
30.04.05	John Humphrey L PTS 6 Dagenham
14.05.05	Matthew Macklin L CO 5 Dublin
	(Vacant All-Ireland Middleweight Title)
16.02.06	Darren McDermott L RTD 9 Dudley
	(Midlands Area Middleweight Title Challenge)
06.10.06	Simeon Cover L PTS 6 Mansfield
11.11.06	Jason McKay L PTS 10 Dublin
	(Vacant Irish L.Heavyweight Title)
30.11.06	Joey Vegas L PTS 10 Piccadilly
	(British Masters S.Middleweight Title Challenge)
03.03.07	Rod Anderton W PTS 10 Alfreton
	(Vacant Midlands Area L.Heavyweight Title)

19.05.07	Tyrone Wright L RSC 10 Nottingham

(Midlands Area L.Heavyweight Defence. Vacant British Masters L.Heavyweight Title)

Career: 37 contests, won 17, lost 20.

Jamie Moore

Salford. *Born* Salford, 4 November, 1978
British L.Middleweight Champion.
Former Commonwealth L.Middleweight
Champion. *Ht* 5'8"
Manager S. Wood

09.10.99	Clive Johnson W RSC 3 Manchester
13.11.99	Peter Nightingale W PTS 4 Hull
19.12.99	Paul King W PTS 6 Salford
29.02.00	David Baptiste W RSC 3 Manchester
20.03.00	Harry Butler W RSC 2 Mansfield
14.04.00	Jimmy Steel W PTS 6 Manchester
27.05.00	Koba Kulu W RTD 3 Southwark
07.10.00	Leigh Wicks W PTS 4 Doncaster
12.11.00	Prince Kasi Kaihau W RSC 2 Manchester
25.11.00	Wayne Shepherd W RSC 3 Manchester
17.03.01	Richie Murray W RSC 1 Manchester
27.05.01	Paul Denton W RSC 3 Manchester
07.07.01	Scott Dixon L CO 5 Manchester
	(Vacant WBO Inter-Continental L.Middleweight Title)
26.01.02	Harry Butler W RSC 3 Dagenham
09.03.02	Andrzej Butowicz W RSC 5 Manchester
07.09.02	Delroy Mellis W CO 6 Liverpool
08.02.03	Akhmed Oligov W PTS 6 Liverpool
19.04.03	Michael Jones W PTS 12 Liverpool
	(Vacant British L. Middleweight Title. Commonwealth L. Middleweight Title Challenge)
18.10.03	Gary Logan W CO 5 Manchester
	(British & Commonwealth L.Middleweight Title Defences)
22.11.03	Andrew Facey W RSC 7 Belfast
	(British & Commonwealth L.Middleweight Title Defences)
10.04.04	Adam Katumwa W RSC 5 Manchester
	(Vacant Commonwealth L.Middleweight Title)
26.06.04	Ossie Duran L RSC 3 Belfast
	(Commonwealth L.Middleweight Title Defence)
26.11.04	Michael Jones L DIS 3 Altrincham
	(British L.Middleweight Title Defence)
08.07.05	Michael Jones W RSC 6 Altrincham
	(British L.Middleweight Title Challenge)
23.09.05	David Walker W RSC 4 Manchester
	(British L.Middleweight Title Defence)
27.01.06	Vladimir Borovski W RSC 3 Dagenham
21.07.06	Mike Algoet W RSC 5 Altrincham
29.09.06	Matthew Macklin W RSC 10 Manchester
	(British L.Middleweight Title Defence)
09.03.07	Mugurel Sebe W PTS 8 Dagenham
13.04.07	Sebastian Andres Lujan W PTS 12 Altrincham

Career: 30 contests, won 27, lost 3.

Thomas Moran

Edinburgh. *Born* Edinburgh, 5 June, 1985
L.Middleweight. *Ht* 5'11¾"
Manager T. Gilmour

31.03.06	Lance Verallo W PTS 6 Inverurie

10.11.06	Lukasz Wawrzyczek L PTS 4 Hartlepool

Career: 2 contests, won 1, lost 1.

Tony Moran

Liverpool. *Born* Liverpool, 4 July, 1973
Cruiserweight. *Ht* 6'6"
Manager Self

26.04.01	Shaun Bowes L PTS 6 Gateshead
13.11.01	Paul Bonson L PTS 6 Leeds
19.03.02	Graham Nolan W PTS 6 Slough
10.05.02	Eamonn Glennon W RTD 1 Preston
03.06.02	Dave Clarke W PTS 6 Glasgow
07.09.02	Adam Cale W PTS 4 Liverpool
05.10.02	Jason Brewster W PTS 4 Liverpool
29.11.02	Adam Cale W RSC 1 Liverpool
08.02.03	Michael Pinnock W PTS 4 Liverpool
17.02.03	Brian Gascoigne W RSC 1 Glasgow
19.04.03	Paul Bonson W PTS 4 Liverpool
17.05.03	Tony Booth W PTS 6 Liverpool
27.10.03	Matthew Ellis W RSC 4 Glasgow
13.03.04	Mark Hobson L RSC 3 Huddersfield
	(British & Commonwealth Cruiserweight Title Challenges)
30.04.05	Paul Bonson W PTS 6 Wigan
13.05.05	Lee Mountford W RSC 1 Liverpool
08.07.05	Neil Dawson L RSC 4 Altrincham
25.11.05	Csaba Andras W PTS 4 Liverpool
17.03.06	Gyorgy Hidvegi L RSC 5 Kirkcaldy
	(Vacant WBF Cruiserweight Title)
25.02.07	Chris P. Bacon L RSC 7 Manchester
	(Vacant Central Area Cruiserweight Title)

Career: 20 contests, won 14, lost 6.

Paul Morby

Portsmouth. Born Portsmouth, 15 October, 1979
Middleweight. *Ht* 5'11"
Manager J. Bishop

24.09.06	Jamie Ambler W PTS 4 Southampton
25.02.07	Dave Wakefield W PTS 6 Southampton
10.06.07	Philip Dowse L RSC 4 Neath

Career: 3 contests, won 2, lost 1.

Paul Morby   Les Clark

Andy Morris

Wythenshawe. *Born* Manchester, 10 March, 1983
Featherweight. Former British
Featherweight Champion. Former

Undefeated English Featherweight
Champion. *Ht* 5'6½"
Manager F. Warren

18.01.03	Jason Nesbitt W PTS 4 Preston
05.04.03	Haroon Din W RSC 1 Manchester
08.05.03	Daniel Thorpe W PTS 4 Widnes
06.11.03	Dave Hinds W PTS 4 Dagenham
13.12.03	Henry Janes W PTS 4 Manchester
26.02.04	Daniel Thorpe W RSC 3 Widnes
03.04.04	Carl Allen W PTS 4 Manchester
12.06.04	Jus Wallie W PTS 6 Manchester
01.10.04	Chris Hooper W RSC 3 Manchester
11.02.05	Buster Dennis W PTS 6 Manchester
20.05.05	Rocky Dean W PTS 10 Southwark
	(Vacant English Featherweight Title)
23.09.05	Mickey Coveney W RSC 4 Mayfair
05.11.05	John Simpson W PTS 12 Renfrew
	(Vacant British Featherweight Title)
29.04.06	Rendall Munroe W PTS 12 Edinburgh
	(British Featherweight Title Defence)
09.12.06	John Simpson L RSC 5 Canning Town
	(British Featherweight Title Defence)

Career: 15 contests, won 14, lost 1.

Jay Morris

Newport, IoW. *Born* Newport, IoW, 8 May, 1978
Welterweight. *Ht* 5'7"
Manager Self

21.02.04	Judex Meemea DREW 4 Brighton
30.03.04	Casey Brooke W RSC 1 Southampton
21.11.04	Chris Brophy W RSC 1 Bracknell
12.02.05	Pete Buckley W PTS 6 Portsmouth
26.06.05	David Kehoe W PTS 4 Southampton
25.09.05	Ivor Bonavic L PTS 6 Southampton
04.12.05	Ivor Bonavic W PTS 6 Portsmouth
05.03.06	Duncan Cottier L RSC 2 Southampton
24.09.06	Duncan Cottier W PTS 4 Southampton
02.12.06	Alex Stoda L RSC 4 Southwark
03.05.07	David Barnes L RSC 1 Sheffield
05.06.07	Andrew Ferrans L RSC 3 Glasgow

Career: 12 contests, won 6, drew 1, lost 5.

Barry Morrison

Motherwell. *Born* Bellshill, 8 May, 1980
L.Welterweight. Former British
L.Welterweight Champion. Former
Undefeated British Masters L.Welterweight
Champion. *Ht* 5'7"
Manager T. Gilmour

12.04.03	Keith Jones W PTS 4 Bethnal Green
28.04.03	Arv Mittoo W RSC 3 Nottingham
05.07.03	Cristian Hodorogea W RSC 3 Brentwood
06.09.03	Jay Mahoney W RSC 2 Huddersfield
04.10.03	Sergei Starkov W PTS 6 Belfast
01.11.03	Tarik Amrous W PTS 8 Glasgow
28.02.04	Zoltan Surman W RSC 3 Bridgend
22.04.04	Andrei Devyataykin W PTS 8 Glasgow
15.10.04	Adam Zadworny W RSC 2 Glasgow
27.05.05	Gary Reid W RTD 8 Motherwell
	(British Masters L.Welterweight Title Challenge)
14.10.05	Tony Montana W PTS 10 Motherwell
	(British Masters L.Welterweight Title Defence)
17.03.06	Dean Hickman W RSC 1 Kirkcaldy
	(Elim. British L.Welterweight Title)
21.04.06	Mihaita Mutu L PTS 8 Belfast
22.09.06	Mounir Guebbas W PTS 6 Bethnal Green

20.01.07 Lenny Daws W PTS 12 Muswell Hill
          *(British L.Welterweight Title
          Challenge)*
08.06.07 Colin Lynes L PTS 12 Motherwell
          (British L.Welterweight Title Defence)
Career: 16 contests, won 14, lost 2.

Barry Morrison   Les Clark

Jamal Morrison

Kilburn. *Born* London, 17 February, 1981
L.Middleweight. *Ht* 5'8¾"
Manager J. Tiftik

24.07.05 Casey Brooke W PTS 4 Leicester
          Square
30.03.06 Duncan Cottier DREW 4 Bloomsbury
21.05.06 Geraint Harvey W PTS 4 Bethnal
          Green
03.12.06 Dean Marcantonio W RSC 2 Bethnal
          Green
18.02.07 Imad Khamis W RSC 2 Bethnal Green
Career: 5 contests, won 4, drew 1.

(Moses) Olufemi Moses (Ajayi)

Droylsden. *Born* Nigeria, 28 May, 1985
Welterweight. *Ht* 5'10"
Manager W. Barker

23.02.07 Silence Saheed W PTS 4 Manchester
02.03.07 Ysopov Karium W PTS 4 Coventry
26.04.07 Duncan Cottier W PTS 4 Manchester
Career: 3 contests, won 3.

Abdul Mougharbel (Almgharbel)

Dewsbury. *Born* Syria, 10 November, 1975
S.Bantamweight. *Ht* 5'4"
Manager C. Aston

15.03.04 Hussain Nasser W RTD 3 Bradford
19.04.04 Sandy Bartlett W PTS 6 Glasgow
11.10.04 Sandy Bartlett L PTS 6 Glasgow
22.10.04 Scott Flynn L PTS 4 Edinburgh
19.11.04 Isaac Ward L PTS 4 Hartlepool
11.12.04 Matthew Marsh L PTS 4 Canning
          Town
06.03.05 Andy Bell L PTS 4 Mansfield
18.04.05 Neil Read W PTS 6 Bradford
27.05.05 Kevin Townsley L PTS 6 Motherwell
06.06.05 Gary Ford W PTS 6 Glasgow
16.09.05 Shaun Walton DREW 6 Telford

28.10.05 Isaac Ward L PTS 6 Hartlepool
20.11.05 Shinny Bayaar L PTS 4 Shaw
04.12.05 Shaun Walton DREW 6 Telford
24.02.06 Wayne Bloy L PTS 6 Scarborough
29.09.06 Stuart McFadyen L PTS 4 Manchester
03.11.06 Jason Booth L PTS 6 Barnsley
26.01.07 Stephen Russell L PTS 6 Glasgow
24.02.07 Gary Davis L PTS 6 Stoke
Career: 19 contests, won 4, drew 2, lost 13.

Lee Mountford

Pudsey. *Born* Leeds, 1 September, 1972
Heavyweight. *Ht* 6'2"
Manager Self

19.04.02 Gary Thompson DREW 4 Darlington
24.06.02 Eamonn Glennon L PTS 6 Bradford
20.11.02 Nate Joseph W PTS 6 Leeds
03.02.03 Eamonn Glennon DREW 6 Bradford
28.02.03 Gary Thompson W PTS 6 Irvine
13.05.03 Nate Joseph L PTS 6 Leeds
01.12.03 Dave Clarke W PTS 6 Bradford
15.03.04 Greg Scott-Briggs DREW 6 Bradford
09.04.04 Carl Wright L PTS 4 Rugby
20.04.04 Lee Swaby L RSC 1 Sheffield
26.09.04 Paul Butlin L PTS 6 Stoke
28.10.04 Martin Rogan L RSC 1 Belfast
13.02.05 Nate Joseph L PTS 6 Bradford
13.05.05 Tony Moran L RSC 1 Liverpool
18.06.05 John Anthony L RSC 5 Barnsley
25.09.05 Dave Clarke W PTS 4 Leeds
22.10.05 Tyrone Wright L CO 3 Mansfield
03.03.06 Stewart Mitchell L PTS 4 Doncaster
26.05.06 Tony Booth L PTS 6 Hull
15.10.06 Sam Sexton L RSC 2 Norwich
Career: 20 contests, won 4, drew 3, lost 13.

Bheki Moyo

Earls Court. *Born* Pretoria, South Africa, 6
October, 1974
L.Welterweight. *Ht* 5'7"
Manager J. Gill

24.07.05 Judex Meemea L PTS 4 Leicester
          Square
28.10.05 Damian Owen L PTS 6 Hartlepool
17.11.05 Garry Buckland L RSC 3 Bristol
21.05.06 Ali Wyatt L RSC 3 Bristol
29.06.06 Nathan Weise L PTS 4 Bethnal Green
26.10.06 Martin Gordon DREW 6 Dudley
17.11.06 Ruben Giles L RSC 4 Bethnal Green
Career: 7 contests, drew 1, lost 6.

David Mulholland

Liverpool. *Born* Liverpool, 11 December,
1979
Lightweight. *Ht* 5'9"
Manager J. Evans

13.05.06 Frederic Gosset W PTS 4 Sheffield
30.03.07 Steve Gethin W PTS 4 Crawley
Career: 2 contests, won 2.

Chris Mullen

South Shields. *Born* South Shields, 24 May,
1986
Welterweight. *Ht* 5'9"
Manager M. Gates

07.12.06 Chris Goodwin W PTS 6 Sunderland
13.04.07 Martin Sweeney W RSC 6 Houghton le
          Spring
Career: 2 contests, won 2.

Rendall Munroe

Leicester. *Born* Leicester, 1 June, 1980
Featherweight. *Ht* 5'7"
Manager M. Shinfield/D. Coldwell

20.09.03 Joel Viney W RTD 3 Nottingham
23.11.03 John-Paul Ryan W PTS 6 Rotherham
14.02.04 Neil Read W RSC 1 Nottingham
09.04.04 Anthony Hanna W PTS 6 Rugby
26.04.04 Baz Carey W PTS 6 Cleethorpes
27.09.04 David Bailey W PTS 6 Cleethorpes
08.10.04 David Killu W PTS 6 Brentwood
18.06.05 Darren Broomhall W RSC 3 Barnsley
02.09.05 Riaz Durgahed W PTS 6 Derby
28.01.06 Jonathan Whiteman W RSC 2
          Nottingham
29.04.06 Andy Morris L PTS 12 Edinburgh
          (British Featherweight Title Challenge)
13.04.07 Gavin Deacon W PTS 6 Altrincham
Career: 12 contests, won 11, lost 1.

Ben Murphy

Hove. *Born* Hove, 11 March, 1980
L.Welterweight. *Ht* 5'3¾"
Manager R. Woodhall

17.03.07 Deniss Sirjatovs W PTS 4 Birmingham
29.04.07 Barry Downes W RSC 1 Birmingham
Career: 2 contests, won 2.

Brian Murphy

Cambuslang. *Born* Rutherglen, 16 August,
1987
Lightweight. *Ht* 5'8½"
Manager T. Gilmour

25.03.06 Pete Buckley W PTS 6 Irvine
29.06.06 Ian Wilson L RTD 1 Bethnal Green
29.09.06 Jimmy Gilhaney L RSC 1 Motherwell
20.11.06 Sergei Rozhakmens W PTS 6 Glasgow
02.12.06 Sandy Bartlett L RSC 5 Clydebank
23.04.07 Shaun Walton L RSC 5 Glasgow
Career: 6 contests, won 2, lost 4.

John Murray

Manchester. *Born* Manchester, 20
December, 1984
WBC Youth Lightweight Champion.
Ht 5'8"
Manager S. Wood

06.09.03 Pete Buckley W PTS 4 Huddersfield
18.10.03 Matthew Burke W RSC 1 Manchester
21.12.03 Jason Nesbitt W PTS 6 Bolton
30.01.04 Norman Dhalie W CO 2 Dagenham
12.03.04 John-Paul Ryan W RSC 1 Nottingham
02.06.04 Anthony Hanna W PTS 4 Nottingham
24.09.04 Dariusz Snarski W RSC 2 Nottingham
31.10.04 Ernie Smith W PTS 4 Shaw
26.11.04 Daniel Thorpe W RSC 2 Altrincham
09.12.04 Harry Ramogoadi W RSC 4 Stockport
06.03.05 Karl Taylor W PTS 6 Shaw
08.07.05 Mounir Guebbas W PTS 8 Altrincham
06.08.05 Johnny Walker W PTS 6 Tampa,
          Florida, USA
23.09.05 Azad Azizov W RSC 3 Manchester
29.10.05 Tyrone Wiggins W RSC 4 Gatineau,
          Canada
02.12.05 Nacho Mendoza W TD 8 Nottingham
          (Vacant WBC Youth Lightweight Title)
12.07.06 Billy Smith W RSC 6 Bethnal Green
15.09.06 Moebi Sarouna W PTS 10 Muswell
          Hill
          (WBC Youth Lightweight Title Defence)

08.12.06 Billy Smith W PTS 6 Dagenham
20.01.07 Ben Odamattey W RSC 5 Muswell Hill
05.05.07 Lorenzo Bethea W RSC 7 Las Vegas, Nevada, USA
Career: 21 contests, won 21.

John Murray   Les Clark

Oneal Murray

Brixton. *Born* Jamaica, 8 March, 1973
Heavyweight. *Ht* 6'0"
Manager B. Baker

29.03.01 Oddy Papantoniou L PTS 4 Hammersmith
04.10.01 Michael Pinnock W PTS 6 Finsbury
15.10.01 Joe Brame W RSC 2 Southampton
15.12.01 Steven Spartacus L RSC 4 Chigwell
27.01.02 Adam Cale W PTS 6 Streatham
23.02.03 Brodie Pearmaine L PTS 4 Streatham
13.04.03 Dave Clarke L PTS 4 Streatham
14.02.04 Tony Booth L PTS 8 Holborn
06.02.05 Colin Kenna L RTD 3 Southampton
28.06.05 Denis Boytsov L RSC 1 Cuaxhaven, Germany
11.12.05 Earl Ling W RSC 3 Norwich
09.10.06 Tony Booth L PTS 4 Bedworth
12.11.06 Chris P. Bacon L RSC 1 Manchester
Career: 13 contests, won 4, lost 9.

Lee Murtagh

Leeds. *Born* Leeds, 30 September, 1973
Middleweight. Former Undefeated Central Area L.Middleweight Champion. Former Undefeated Central Area Middleweight Champion. Former British Masters Middleweight Champion. Former British Masters L.Middleweight Champion.
Ht 5'9¼"
Manager Self

12.06.95 Dave Curtis W PTS 6 Bradford
25.09.95 Roy Gbasai W PTS 6 Bradford
30.10.95 Cam Raeside L PTS 6 Bradford
11.12.95 Donovan Davey W PTS 6 Bradford
13.01.96 Peter Varnavas W PTS 6 Halifax
05.02.96 Shamus Casey W PTS 6 Bradford
20.05.96 Shaun O'Neill W PTS 6 Bradford
24.06.96 Michael Alexander W PTS 6 Bradford
28.10.96 Jimmy Vincent L RSC 2 Bradford

14.04.97 Lee Simpkin W PTS 6 Bradford
09.10.97 Brian Dunn W PTS 6 Leeds
05.03.98 Wayne Shepherd W PTS 6 Leeds
08.08.98 Alan Gilbert W PTS 4 Scarborough
13.03.99 Keith Palmer DREW 6 Manchester
27.09.99 Jawaid Khaliq L RSC 5 Leeds
          (Vacant WBF European L. Middleweight Title)
27.02.00 Gareth Lovell W PTS 6 Leeds
24.09.00 Jon Foster W PTS 6 Shaw
03.12.00 Michael Alexander W PTS 6 Shaw
17.05.01 Ojay Abrahams L RSC 2 Leeds
          (Vacant British Masters L. Middleweight Title)
03.03.02 Howard Clarke NC 2 Shaw
19.04.02 Neil Bonner W PTS 6 Darlington
21.06.02 Wayne Shepherd W PTS 10 Leeds
          (Vacant British Masters Middleweight Title)
02.12.02 Martyn Bailey L RSC 6 Leeds
          (British Masters Middleweight Title Defence)
10.05.03 Darren Rhodes L PTS 6 Huddersfield
15.09.03 Matt Scriven W DIS 9 Leeds
          (British Masters L.Middleweight Title Challenge)
01.12.03 Gary Beardsley L RSC 6 Leeds
          (British Masters L.Middleweight Title Defence)
08.06.04 Robert Burton L CO 3 Sheffield
          (Vacant Central Area L.Middleweight Title)
15.12.04 Dean Walker W PTS 10 Sheffield
          (Vacant Central Area Middleweight Title)
20.05.05 Jason Rushton W PTS 10 Doncaster
          (Central Area L.Middleweight Title Challenge)
27.01.06 Gary Woolcombe L RSC 4 Dagenham
03.06.07 John Musgrave L PTS 6 Barnsley
30.06.07 Peter Dunn W PTS 6 Belfast
Career: 32 contests, won 21, drew 1, lost 9, no contest 1.

(Nikos) Rocky Muscus (Agrapidis Israel)

Chertsey. *Born* Athens, Greece, 5 August, 1983
S.Middleweight. *Ht* 5'6½"
Manager Self

12.05.03 Danny Cooper L PTS 6 Southampton
18.09.03 Wayne Wheeler L PTS 6 Mayfair
27.10.03 Graham Delehedy L RSC 2 Glasgow
08.07.04 David Kehoe L PTS 6 The Strand
30.09.04 Richard Inquieti W PTS 4 Glasgow
23.10.04 Tye Williams L PTS 6 Wakefield
24.11.04 Ivor Bonavic L PTS 4 Mayfair
18.09.05 Danny Goode L PTS 4 Bethnal Green
25.09.05 Steve Ede L PTS 6 Southampton
23.07.06 Dean Marcantonio L PTS 4 Dagenham
09.10.06 Jay Allen L PTS 6 Bedworth
18.10.06 Anthony Young L PTS 4 Bayswater
11.11.06 Billy Walsh L PTS 4 Dublin
23.11.06 Prince Arron L PTS 6 Manchester
02.12.06 Kevin Concepcion L PTS 6 Coventry
09.12.06 Tom Glover L PTS 4 Chigwell
26.01.07 Eamonn Goodbrand L PTS 6 Glasgow
10.02.07 Ciaran Duffy L PTS 4 Letterkenny
24.02.07 Nobby Cain L PTS 4 Bracknell
10.03.07 Joe McNally L PTS 4 Liverpool
14.04.07 Andrew Butlin L PTS 6 Wakefield

23.04.07 Jamie Coyle L PTS 8 Glasgow
05.05.07 Barrie Jones L PTS 6 Glasgow
14.05.07 Simon Fleck L PTS 6 Cleethorpes
25.05.07 Colin Baxter L PTS 6 Glasgow
01.06.07 Sherman Alleyne L PTS 6 Peterborough
Career: 26 contests, won 1, lost 25.

Jon Musgrave

Barnsley. *Born* Barnsley, 26 July, 1982
L.Middleweight. *Ht* 5'11"
Manager T. Schofield

30.09.06 Andrew Alan Lowe W PTS 6 Stoke
01.12.06 James McKinley L PTS 4 Birmingham
26.03.07 Paul Royston W PTS 6 Glasgow
15.04.07 Sherman Alleyne W PTS 6 Barnsley
03.06.07 Lee Murtagh L PTS 6 Barnsley
Career: 5 contests, won 3, lost 2.

(Lee) Young Muttley (Woodley)

West Bromwich. *Born* West Bromwich, 17 May, 1976
L.Welterweight. Former British Welterweight Champion. Former Undefeated WBF Inter-Continental, English & Midlands Area L.Welterweight Champion. *Ht* 5'8½"
Manager Self

03.09.99 Dave Hinds W RSC 4 West Bromwich
24.10.99 David Kehoe W RTD 1 Wolverhampton
22.01.00 Wahid Fats L PTS 4 Birmingham
18.02.00 Stuart Rimmer W RSC 1 West Bromwich
27.11.00 Peter Dunn W RSC 3 Birmingham
07.09.01 Jon Honney W RSC 1 West Bromwich
16.11.01 Tony Montana W PTS 6 West Bromwich
26.11.01 Lee Byrne W RSC 1 Manchester
23.02.02 Brian Coleman W PTS 4 Nottingham
23.03.02 Adam Zadworny W RSC 3 Southwark
02.11.02 Tony Montana W PTS 4 Wolverhampton
21.03.03 Gary Reid W RSC 7 West Bromwich
          (Vacant Midlands Area L.Welterweight Title)
28.04.03 John Marshall W RSC 5 Nottingham
17.07.03 Tony Montana W PTS 4 Walsall
19.02.04 Peter Dunn W PTS 4 Dudley
08.05.04 Sammy Smith W RSC 1 Bristol
          (Vacant English L.Welterweight Title)
05.10.04 Gavin Down W RSC 6 Dudley
          (English L.Welterweight Title Defence. Vacant WBF Inter-Continental L.Welterweight Title)
17.02.05 Geraint Harvey W PTS 6 Dudley
21.04.05 Oscar Hall W PTS 10 Dudley
          (WBF Inter-Continental L.Welterweight Title Defence)
30.09.05 Surinder Sekhon W PTS 4 Burton
28.01.06 Michael Jennings W PTS 12 Nottingham
          (British Welterweight Title Challenge)
01.06.06 Kevin Anderson L RSC 10 Birmingham
          (British Welterweight Title Defence. Commonwealth Welterweight Title Challenge)
22.09.06 Alexander Abramenko W CO 1 Bethnal Green
25.01.07 Arek Malek W PTS 6 Milan, Italy
Career: 24 contests, won 22, lost 2.

Amir Nadi

Birmingham. *Born* Iraq, 21 November, 1981
L.Welterweight. *Ht* 5'10"
Manager N. Nobbs

16.02.07	Steve Anning L PTS 4 Merthyr Tydfil
02.03.07	Abul Taher L PTS 6 Coventry
28.04.07	Charles Paul King L PTS 6 Clydebank
14.05.07	Andy Cox L PTS 6 Cleethorpes

Career: 4 contests, lost 4.

Ian Napa

Hackney. *Born* Zimbabwe, 14 March, 1978
Bantamweight. Former Undefeated
Southern Area Flyweight Champion.
Ht 5'1"
Manager B. Lawrence

06.06.98	Nick Tooley W PTS 6 Liverpool
14.07.98	Nicky Booth W PTS 6 Reading
10.10.98	Sean Green W PTS 6 Bethnal Green
30.01.99	Delroy Spencer W PTS 6 Bethnal Green
15.11.99	Mark Reynolds W PTS 10 Bethnal Green *(Southern Area Flyweight Title Challenge)*
19.02.00	Anthony Hanna W PTS 6 Dagenham
08.04.00	Delroy Spencer W PTS 8 Bethnal Green
15.07.00	Jamie Evans W PTS 4 Millwall
13.11.00	Jason Booth L PTS 12 Bethnal Green *(British & Commonwealth Flyweight Title Challenges)*
24.02.01	Oleg Kiryukhin W PTS 6 Bethnal Green
09.06.01	Peter Culshaw L RSC 8 Bethnal Green *(WBU Flyweight Title Challenge)*
08.05.04	Danny Costello W PTS 4 Dagenham
08.10.04	Steve Gethin W PTS 6 Brentwood
13.02.05	Alexey Volchan W PTS 4 Brentwood
16.06.05	Marc Callaghan L PTS 10 Dagenham *(Vacant Southern Area S.Bantamweight Title)*
04.11.05	Martin Power L PTS 12 Bethnal Green *(British Bantamweight Title Challenge)*
25.11.05	Damaen Kelly L PTS 10 Liverpool
06.10.06	Delroy Spencer W PTS 6 Bethnal Green
09.03.07	Simone Maludrottu L PTS 12 Dagenham *(European Bantamweight Title Challenge)*

Career: 19 contests, won 13, lost 6.

Muhsen Nasser

Sheffield. *Born* Yemen, 10 April, 1986
L.Middleweight. *Ht* 5'11"
Manager J. Ingle

11.10.04	Andy Cosnett W PTS 6 Birmingham
26.11.04	Rocky Flanagan W PTS 6 Hull
27.01.05	Ernie Smith W PTS 6 Piccadilly
12.05.05	Martin Marshall W PTS 6 Sunderland
30.10.05	Lance Verallo W PTS 6 Sheffield
12.11.05	Dave Hinds W PTS 6 Sheffield
21.11.05	Peter Dunn W RSC 4 Glasgow
25.02.06	Chris Long W PTS 4 Bristol
05.03.06	Peter Dunn W PTS 4 Sheffield
06.10.06	Thomas Flynn W PTS 4 Mexborough
10.12.06	Karl Taylor W PTS 6 Sheffield

Career: 11 contests, won 11.

Muhsen Nasser　　　　Les Clark

Robert Nelson

Bradford. *Born* Bradford, 15 January, 1980
S.Bantamweight. *Ht* 5'5"
Manager M. Marsden

27.05.05	Delroy Spencer W PTS 4 Spennymoor
25.06.05	Delroy Spencer W PTS 6 Wakefield
13.11.05	Neil Marston W PTS 6 Leeds
09.05.06	Delroy Spencer DREW 6 Leeds
28.05.06	Neil Read W PTS 6 Wakefield
03.12.06	Robert Bunford W PTS 4 Wakefield
14.04.07	Shaun Walton W PTS 8 Wakefield
27.05.07	Mo Khaled DREW 6 Bradford

Career: 8 contests, won 6, drew 2.

Jason Nesbitt

Nuneaton. *Born* Birmingham, 15 December, 1973
Welterweight. *Ht* 5'9"
Manager Self

06.11.00	Stephen Chinnock L PTS 6 Wolverhampton
09.12.00	Lee Meager L RSC 2 Southwark
29.01.01	Henry Castle L CO 6 Peterborough
27.03.01	Billy Smith W PTS 6 Brierley Hill
21.05.01	Sid Razak L PTS 6 Birmingham
04.06.01	Andrew Ferrans L RSC 2 Glasgow
07.07.01	Colin Toohey L PTS 4 Manchester
15.09.01	Colin Toohey L PTS 4 Manchester
22.09.01	John Mackay L PTS 4 Canning Town
01.11.01	Chris Hooper L RSC 6 Hull
16.03.02	Lee Meager L PTS 6 Bethnal Green
27.03.02	Greg Edwards W RSC 5 Mayfair
20.04.02	Henry Castle L PTS 4 Cardiff
04.05.02	Danny Hunt L PTS 4 Bethnal Green
15.06.02	Jesse James Daniel L PTS 4 Leeds
27.07.02	Craig Spacie L PTS 4 Nottingham
23.08.02	Billy Corcoran L PTS 4 Bethnal Green
25.10.02	Billy Corcoran L RSC 2 Bethnal Green
03.12.02	Mark Bowen L PTS 6 Shrewsbury
11.12.02	Matt Teague L PTS 6 Hull
20.12.02	Chris McDonagh L PTS 6 Bracknell
18.01.03	Andy Morris L PTS 4 Preston
09.02.03	Mally McIver L PTS 6 Bradford
09.03.03	Choi Tseveenpurev L PTS 8 Shaw
29.03.03	Kevin O'Hara L RSC 3 Portsmouth
07.05.03	Henry Jones L PTS 6 Ellesmere Port
02.06.03	Stefy Bull L PTS 6 Cleethorpes
13.06.03	Scott Lawton L PTS 6 Queensway
17.07.03	Haider Ali L PTS 4 Dagenham
29.08.03	Gary Thornhill L CO 1 Liverpool
05.10.03	Nadeem Siddique L PTS 6 Bradford
08.11.03	Harry Ramogoadi L PTS 6 Coventry
23.11.03	Amir Ali L PTS 6 Rotherham
10.12.03	Femi Fehintola L PTS 6 Sheffield
21.12.03	John Murray L PTS 6 Bolton
06.02.04	Femi Fehintola L PTS 6 Sheffield
23.02.04	Carl Greaves L PTS 6 Nottingham
05.03.04	Haroon Din L PTS 6 Darlington
12.03.04	Stuart Green L PTS 8 Irvine
03.04.04	Daniel Thorpe L PTS 6 Sheffield
16.04.04	John O'Donnell L PTS 4 Bradford
27.04.04	Jim Betts L PTS 6 Leeds
07.05.04	Jus Wallie L PTS 6 Bethnal Green
28.05.04	John Bothwell W RSC 3 Glasgow
05.06.04	Kevin Mitchell L RSC 3 Bethnal Green
30.07.04	Lee Beavis L PTS 4 Bethnal Green
20.09.04	Matt Teague L PTS 6 Cleethorpes
30.09.04	Eddie Nevins L PTS 6 Hull
18.11.04	Joel Viney W PTS 6 Blackpool
26.11.04	John Davidson W RSC 1 Altrincham
10.12.04	John Fewkes L PTS 6 Sheffield
17.12.04	Gwyn Wale L PTS 4 Huddersfield
13.02.05	Nadeem Siddique L PTS 6 Bradford
04.03.05	John Fewkes L PTS 6 Rotherham
01.04.05	Martin McDonagh L PTS 6 Glasgow
15.04.05	Martin Gethin L PTS 6 Shrewsbury
28.04.05	Ceri Hall L RTD 2 Clydach
02.06.05	Riaz Durgahed L PTS 6 Peterborough
24.07.05	Femi Fehintola L PTS 6 Sheffield
09.09.05	Nicki Smedley L PTS 4 Sheffield
30.09.05	Henry Jones L PTS 6 Carmarthen
16.10.05	Michael Medor L PTS 6 Peterborough
12.11.05	Craig Johnson L PTS 6 Sheffield
25.11.05	Nadeem Siddique L RSC 6 Hull
17.02.06	Dave Stewart L PTS 4 Bethnal Green
04.03.06	Tony Delaney L PTS 4 Manchester
01.04.06	Steve Bell L PTS 6 Bethnal Green
28.04.06	Davis Kamara L PTS 6 Manchester
06.05.06	Jimmy Doherty L PTS 6 Stoke
20.05.06	Anthony Christopher W RSC 4 Bristol
05.06.06	Mitch Prince L PTS 6 Glasgow
24.09.06	Peter McDonagh L PTS 4 Bethnal Green
01.10.06	Andrew Ward DREW 6 Rotherham
24.11.06	Chris Hooper DREW 6 Hull
02.12.06	Shane Watson L PTS 6 Longford
25.02.07	Danny Harding L PTS 6 Manchester
10.03.07	John Watson L PTS 4 Liverpool
28.04.07	Jonathan Whiteman W RTD 5 Newark
18.05.07	Dave Stewart L PTS 4 Canning Town
09.06.07	Davey Watson L PTS 6 Middlesbrough

Career: 80 contests, won 7, drew 2, lost 71.

Gary Neville

Irvine. *Born* Irvine, 4 September, 1981
Cruiserweight. *Ht* 6'4"
Manager T. Gilmour

13.10.06	Lee Kellett L RSC 1 Irvine

Career: 1 contest, lost 1.

Lee Nicholson

Doncaster. *Born* Mexborough, 10 November, 1976
Cruiserweight. *Ht* 5'11"
Manager Self

24.09.01	Jason Brewster L PTS 6 Cleethorpes
17.02.02	Jason Brewster L PTS 6 Wolverhampton

11.05.02	Fola Okesola L RSC 1 Dagenham
07.09.03	Stewart West L RSC 2 Shrewsbury
01.12.03	Mike Duffield W PTS 6 Barnsley
15.12.03	Simeon Cover L RSC 4 Cleethorpes
29.10.04	Dean Cockburn L RSC 2 Doncaster
13.12.04	Dean Cockburn L RSC 3 Cleethorpes
23.05.05	Slick Miller W PTS 6 Cleethorpes
03.03.06	Jimmy Harrington DREW 4 Doncaster
21.04.06	Jimmy Harrington L RTD 3 Doncaster
13.10.06	Billy Wilson L RSC 5 Doncaster

Career: 12 contests, won 2, drew 1, lost 9.

Mark Nilsen

Sale. *Born* Manchester, 26 July, 1978
L.Heavyweight. *Ht* 6'0"
Manager W. Dixon

17.02.02	Kenroy Lambert W PTS 6 Salford
26.10.06	Chris Harman W PTS 6 Dudley
06.12.06	Simon Wood W PTS 4 Stoke
24.02.07	Carl Wild W PTS 6 Manchester
21.04.07	Tomas Da Silva W RSC 5 Manchester
30.06.07	Nicki Taylor W CO 4 Manchester

Career: 6 contests, won 6.

Lee Noble

Sheffield. *Born* Barnsley, 23 April, 1987
Middleweight. *Ht* 6'0"
Manager J. Ingle

05.10.06	Shaun Farmer L PTS 6 Sunderland
13.10.06	Jason Rushton W PTS 6 Doncaster
20.10.06	Jak Hibbert W RSC 6 Sheffield

Mark Nilsen   Les Clark

27.10.06	Peter Dunn W PTS 6 Glasgow
10.12.06	Jak Hibbert W PTS 6 Sheffield
09.02.07	Mark Thompson L PTS 6 Leeds
19.02.07	Darren Gethin W PTS 6 Glasgow
11.03.07	Magic Kidem W PTS 4 Shaw
03.05.07	Stuart Brookes L PTS 10 Sheffield
	(Vacant British Masters L.Heavyweight Title)
17.06.07	Alexander Spitjo W PTS 4 Mansfield

Career: 10 contests, won 7, lost 3.

Robert Norton

Stourbridge. *Born* Dudley, 20 January, 1972
English Cruiserweight Champion. Former
Undefeated British Masters Cruiserweight
Champion. Former WBU Cruiserweight
Champion. *Ht* 6'2"
Manager Self

30.09.93	Stuart Fleet W CO 2 Walsall
27.10.93	Kent Davis W PTS 6 West Bromwich
02.12.93	Eddie Pyatt W RSC 2 Walsall
26.01.94	Lennie Howard W PTS 6 Birmingham
17.05.94	Steve Osborne W PTS 6 Kettering
05.10.94	Chris Woollas DREW 6 Wolverhampton
30.11.94	L. A. Williams W RSC 2 Wolverhampton
10.02.95	Newby Stevens W RSC 3 Birmingham
22.02.95	Steve Osborne W PTS 6 Telford
21.04.95	Cordwell Hylton W PTS 6 Dudley
25.10.95	Nigel Rafferty W RSC 6 Telford
31.01.96	Gary Williams W RSC 2 Birmingham
25.04.96	Steve Osborne W RSC 5 Mayfair
01.10.96	Andrew Benson W RSC 6 Birmingham
12.11.96	Nigel Rafferty W PTS 8 Dudley
11.02.97	Touami Benhamed W RSC 5 Bethnal Green
16.04.97	Tony Booth W RSC 4 Bethnal Green
20.12.97	Darren Corbett L PTS 12 Belfast
	(Commonwealth Cruiserweight Title Challenge)
03.04.98	Adrian Nicolai W RSC 2 West Bromwich
03.10.98	Tim Brown W CO 3 West Bromwich
01.04.99	Jacob Mofokeng W PTS 12 Birmingham
	(WBU Cruiserweight Title Challenge)
24.09.99	Sebastiaan Rothmann L RSC 8 Merthyr
	(WBU Cruiserweight Title Defence)
30.09.00	Tony Booth W RSC 3 Peterborough
18.11.00	Darron Griffiths W PTS 10 Dagenham
	(Elim. British Cruiserweight Title)
05.02.01	Lee Swaby W PTS 8 Hull
30.11.02	Paul Bonson W PTS 6 Coventry
05.09.03	Mark Hobson L PTS 12 Sheffield
	(Commonwealth Cruiserweight Title Challenge. Vacant British Cruiserweight Title)
09.04.04	Greg Scott-Briggs W CO 1 Rugby
10.07.04	Chris Woollas W RSC 4 Coventry
06.12.04	Paul Bonson W CO 6 Leicester
	(Vacant British Masters Cruiserweight Title)
22.10.05	Dmitry Adamovich W CO 2 Coventry
09.10.06	Roland Horvath W RSC 3 Bedworth
02.03.07	Tommy Eastwood W RSC 8 Coventry
	(Vacant English Cruiserweight Title)

Career: 33 contests, won 29, drew 1, lost 3.

(Paulus) Ali Nuumbembe

Glossop. *Born* Oshakati, Namibia, 24 June, 1978
Commonwealth Welterweight Champion.
Ht 5'8½"
Manager S. Wood

16.04.03	Dai Bando W PTS 4 Nottingham
15.06.03	Ernie Smith W PTS 4 Bradford
03.08.03	Lee Williamson W PTS 6 Stalybridge
29.08.03	Ernie Smith W PTS 6 Liverpool
05.10.03	Keith Jones W PTS 6 Bradford
07.12.03	Brian Coleman W RTD 2 Bradford
16.01.04	Wayne Wheeler W RSC 1 Bradford
29.02.04	William Webster W RSC 3 Shaw
10.04.04	Peter Dunn W PTS 6 Manchester
09.10.04	Bethuel Ushona L PTS 10 Windhoek, Namibia
	(Vacant Namibian Welterweight Title)
09.12.04	Lee Armstrong W PTS 6 Stockport
04.03.05	Franny Jones W PTS 6 Hartlepool
22.04.05	David Barnes DREW 12 Barnsley
	(Vacant WBO Inter-Continental Welterweight Title)
08.07.05	Dmitry Yanushevich W RSC 2 Altrincham
23.09.05	Gavin Down W RSC 3 Manchester
18.12.05	Ernie Smith W CO 4 Bolton
12.02.06	Sergey Starkov W PTS 8 Manchester
29.06.06	Ajose Olusegun L CO 6 Bethnal Green
29.09.06	Vladimir Borovski W PTS 6 Manchester
16.02.07	Kevin Anderson W PTS 12 Kirkcaldy
	(Commonwealth Welterweight Title Challenge)

Career: 20 contests, won 17, drew 1, lost 2.

Tony Oakey   Les Clark

Tony Oakey

Havant. *Born* Portsmouth, 2 January, 1976
British L.Heavyweight Champion. Former
WBU L.Heavyweight Champion. Former
Undefeated Commonwealth & Southern
Area L.Heavyweight Champion. *Ht* 5'8"
Manager Self

12.09.98	Smokey Enison W RSC 2 Bethnal Green	
21.11.98	Zak Chelli W RSC 1 Southwark	
16.01.99	Jimmy Steel W PTS 4 Bethnal Green	
06.03.99	Mark Dawson W PTS 4 Southwark	
10.07.99	Jimmy Steel W PTS 4 Southwark	
01.10.99	Michael Pinnock W PTS 4 Bethnal Green	
21.02.00	Darren Ashton W PTS 4 Southwark	
13.03.00	Martin Jolley W PTS 6 Bethnal Green	
21.10.00	Darren Ashton W PTS 4 Wembley	
27.01.01	Nathan King W PTS 6 Bethnal Green	
26.03.01	Butch Lesley W PTS 10 Wembley *(Southern Area L. Heavyweight Title Challenge)*	
08.05.01	Hastings Rasani W RSC 10 Barnsley *(Vacant Commonwealth L. Heavyweight Title)*	
09.09.01	Konstantin Ochrej W RSC 4 Southwark	
20.10.01	Chris Davies W PTS 12 Portsmouth *(Commonwealth L.Heavyweight Title Defence)*	
02.03.02	Konstantin Shvets W PTS 12 Bethnal Green *(Vacant WBU L. Heavyweight Title)*	
25.05.02	Neil Simpson W PTS 12 Portsmouth *(WBU L. Heavyweight Title Defence)*	
12.10.02	Andrei Kaersten W PTS 12 Bethnal Green *(WBU L. Heavyweight Title Defence)*	
29.03.03	Neil Linford W PTS 12 Portsmouth *(WBU L. Heavyweight Title Defence)*	
11.10.03	Matthew Barney L PTS 12 Portsmouth *(WBU L.Heavyweight Title Defence)*	
12.02.05	Varuzhan Davtyan W RTD 5 Portsmouth	

19.06.05	Peter Haymer L PTS 10 Bethnal Green *(English L.Heavyweight Title Challenge)*	
01.04.06	Radek Seman W PTS 8 Bethnal Green	
13.05.06	Nathan King W PTS 6 Bethnal Green	
28.10.06	Simeon Cover W PTS 6 Bethnal Green	
09.03.07	Josip Jalusic W PTS 6 Dagenham	
18.05.07	Steven Spartacus W RSC 12 Canning Town *(Vacant British L.Heavyweight Title)*	

Career: 26 contests, won 24, lost 2.

(David) Dezzie O'Connor

Plymouth. *Born* Plymouth, 26 September, 1984
L.Welterweight. *Ht* 5'6"
Manager C. Sanigar

23.02.07	Jamie Spence L RSC 3 Peterborough	

Career: 1 contest, lost 1.

Gary O'Connor

Manchester. *Born* Manchester, 29 August, 1978
L.Welterweight. *Ht* 5'10"
Manager Self

21.12.03	Chris Brophy W PTS 6 Bolton	
29.02.04	Pete Buckley W PTS 6 Shaw	
18.12.05	Kristian Laight W PTS 6 Bolton	
12.02.06	Lance Verallo W RSC 4 Manchester	
28.04.06	Pete Buckley W PTS 6 Manchester	
10.07.06	Silence Saheed W PTS 6 Manchester	
05.10.06	Tom Hogan W PTS 6 Sunderland	
18.11.06	Tony Doherty L PTS 6 Newport	
13.04.07	Scott Haywood L PTS 6 Altrincham	

Career: 9 contests, won 7, lost 2.

John O'Donnell   Les Clark

John O'Donnell

Shepherds Bush. *Born* Croydon, 13 November, 1985
English Welterweight Champion. *Ht* 5'11"
Manager Self

16.04.04	Jason Nesbitt W PTS 4 Bradford	
02.06.04	Dave Hinds W PTS 4 Nottingham	
24.09.04	Chris Long W RSC 4 Nottingham	
12.11.04	Ernie Smith W PTS 6 Wembley	
10.04.05	Duncan Cottier W PTS 4 Brentwood	
09.07.05	Ben Hudson W RTD 3 Nottingham	
21.10.05	Ben Hudson W PTS 4 Bethnal Green	
20.01.06	Matt Scriven W RSC 4 Bethnal Green	
28.01.06	Zaid Bediouri W PTS 6 Dublin	
17.02.06	Karl Taylor W PTS 4 Bethnal Green	
12.05.06	Duncan Cottier W RTD 3 Bethnal Green	
12.07.06	Darren Gethin W PTS 8 Bethnal Green	
15.09.06	Silence Saheed W PTS 6 Muswell Hill	
08.12.06	Ernie Smith W CO 2 Dagenham	
23.03.07	Stuart Elwell W PTS 10 Nottingham *(Vacant English Welterweight Title)*	
05.05.07	Christian Solano L RSC 2 Las Vegas, Nevada, USA	

Career: 16 contests, won 15, lost 1.

Kevin O'Hara

Belfast. *Born* Belfast, 21 September, 1981
Welterweight. *Ht* 5'6"
Manager J.Breen/F.Warren

02.11.02	Mike Harrington W RSC 1 Belfast	
01.02.03	Jus Wallie W RSC 2 Belfast	
29.03.03	Jason Nesbitt W RSC 3 Portsmouth	
14.06.03	Piotr Niesporek W PTS 4 Magdeburg, Germany	
02.10.03	Vladimir Borov W PTS 6 Liverpool	
30.10.03	Henry Janes W PTS 6 Belfast	
29.11.03	Gareth Payne W PTS 4 Renfrew	
06.03.04	Henry Janes W PTS 6 Renfrew	
01.04.04	Buster Dennis W PTS 4 Bethnal Green	
06.05.04	Choi Tsveenpurev L PTS 8 Barnsley	
28.10.04	Jean-Marie Codet W PTS 8 Belfast	
17.06.05	Willie Limond L PTS 10 Glasgow *(Vacant Celtic S.Featherweight Title)*	
24.11.05	Damian Owen W PTS 6 Lurgan	
20.05.06	Daniel Thorpe W PTS 6 Belfast	
26.10.06	Eric Patrac W PTS 6 Belfast	

Career: 15 contests, won 13, lost 2.

Daley Ojuederie

Watford. *Born* Watford, 16 May, 1985
Middleweight. *Ht* 5'11¼"
Manager C. Hall

03.12.06	Gatis Skuja DREW 4 Bethnal Green	

Career: 1 contest, drew 1.

(Gary) JJ Ojuederie

Watford. *Born* Watford, 13 September, 1979
Cruiserweight. *Ht* 6'0"
Manager C. Sanigar

29.09.00	Chris Nembhard L RSC 1 Bethnal Green	
08.12.03	Hamid Jamali L PTS 6 Birmingham	
13.02.04	Jason Samuels L DIS 3 Bristol	
28.02.04	Mike Allen W RSC 1 Bridgend	
16.10.05	Karl Wheeler DREW 4 Peterborough	
19.11.05	Eder Kurti W RSC 4 Southwark	
16.12.05	Sam Price W PTS 6 Bracknell	
26.02.06	Simeon Cover W PTS 4 Dagenham	
23.07.06	Carl Wright W PTS 4 Dagenham	
03.12.06	Tony Booth W PTS 4 Bethnal Green	
15.04.07	John Anthony W PTS 6 Barnsley	

Career: 11 contests, won 7, drew 1, lost 3.

Nick Okoth

Battersea. *Born* Camden Town, 19 July, 1973
L. Heavyweight. *Ht* 5'11"
Manager J. Evans

18.09.03 Mark Phillips W PTS 4 Mayfair
28.02.04 Paulie Silva L PTS 6 Manchester
08.04.04 Karl Wheeler L PTS 6 Peterborough
24.04.04 Daniel Sackey L RSC 2 Reading
03.07.04 Nathan King L PTS 4 Newport
31.10.04 Darren Stubbs L PTS 6 Shaw
25.11.04 Jonjo Finnegan DREW 6 Birmingham
03.12.04 Paul Henry W RSC 5 Bristol
21.01.05 Sam Price L PTS 6 Brentford
06.02.05 Mervyn Langdale DREW 6
Southampton
20.02.05 Jon Ibbotson L PTS 6 Sheffield
08.04.05 Dan Guthrie L RSC 2 Bristol
09.09.05 Steven Birch W PTS 4 Sheffield
28.01.06 Rod Anderton L PTS 4 Nottingham
25.02.06 Richard Horton L CO 3 Canning Town
29.09.06 Chris Harman W PTS 4 Cardiff
14.10.06 Kenny Anderson L RSC 4 Manchester
18.02.07 Dwayne Lewis DREW 4 Bethnal Green
02.03.07 Wayne Brooks DREW 4 Neath
07.04.07 Nathan Cleverly L PTS 8 Cardiff
15.06.07 Tony Salam L PTS 4 Crystal Palace
Career: 21 contests, won 4, drew 4, lost 13.

Dean O'Loughlin

Hull. *Born* Beverley, 25 September, 1982
Heavyweight. Ht. 6'5"
Manager J. Rushton/J. Griffin
01.12.06 Lee Webb W RSC 3 Doncaster
23.02.07 Lee Webb W RSC 2 Doncaster
Career: 2 contests, won 2.

Ajose Olusegun

Kentish Town. *Born* Nigeria, 6 December,
1979
Commonwealth L.Welterweight Champion.
Former Undefeated ABU L.Welterweight
Champion. *Ht* 5'9"
Manager Self
24.05.01 Tony Montana W RSC 1 Kensington
21.06.01 Woody Greenaway W RSC 1 Earls
Court
09.09.01 Sunni Ajayi W PTS 6 Lagos, Nigeria
04.10.01 Stuart Rimmer W RTD 2 Finsbury
13.03.02 Gary Flear W PTS 4 Mayfair
13.06.02 Keith Jones W PTS 6 Leicester Square
30.10.02 Martin Holgate W RSC 7 Leicester
Square
27.11.02 Vladimir Kortovski W RSC 1 Tel Aviv,
Israel
15.12.02 Adewale Adegbusi W RSC 6 Lagos,
Nigeria
20.03.03 Cristian Hodorogea W PTS 4
Queensway
26.04.03 Keith Jones W PTS 6 Brentford
29.10.03 Karl Taylor W PTS 6 Leicester Square
10.04.04 Victor Kpadenue W PTS 12 Carabas,
Nigeria
(ABU L.Welterweight Title Challenge)
03.09.04 Bradley Pryce W RSC 4 Newport
26.03.05 Vasile Dragomir W PTS 8 Hackney
26.05.06 Alexander Abramenko W RSC 2
Bethnal Green
29.06.06 Ali Nuumbembe W CO 6 Bethnal
Green
17.11.06 Franck Aiello W RSC 2 Bethnal Green
09.03.07 Vladimir Khodokovski W PTS 6
Dagenham
15.06.07 Gary Reid W PTS 12 Crystal Palace
*(Vacant Commonwealth L.Welterweight
Title)*
Career: 20 contests, won 20.

Ajose Olusegun   Les Clark

Hussain Osman

Paddington. *Born* Syria, 25 July, 1973
Middleweight. Former IBO Inter-
Continental & Southern Area
S.Middleweight Champion. Former
Undefeated WBO Inter-Continental
Southern Area Middleweight Champion.
Ht 5'9½"
Manager J. Feld
09.05.99 Wayne Asker W PTS 4 Bracknell
20.05.99 Karim Bouali W PTS 4 Barking
15.07.99 Neil Linford W RSC 5 Peterborough
05.10.99 Ojay Abrahams W PTS 4 Bloomsbury
05.02.00 Joey Ainscough W PTS 4 Bethnal
Green
01.04.00 George Foreman W PTS 4 Bethnal
Green
22.05.00 Steve Timms W RSC 2 Coventry
25.09.00 James Lowther L PTS 8 Barnsley
03.03.01 Gary Lockett L CO 2 Wembley
26.05.01 Lee Molloy W RSC 1 Bethnal Green
04.06.01 Richard Williams L PTS 10 Hartlepool
28.10.01 Gary Logan W PTS 10 Southwark
*(Southern Area Middleweight Title
Challenge)*
26.01.02 Matthew Barney W RTD 9 Dagenham
*(Vacant IBO Inter-Continental
S.Middleweight Title. Southern Area
S.Middleweight Title Challenge)*
08.04.02 Matthew Barney L PTS 12
Southampton
*(IBO Inter-Continental & Southern
Area S. Middleweight Title Defences)*
21.05.02 Darren Rhodes W PTS 10 Custom
House
20.07.02 Gary Logan W PTS 12 Bethnal Green
*(Vacant WBO Inter-Continental
Middleweight Title)*
21.12.02 Howard Eastman L RTD 4 Dagenham
31.05.03 Gary Beardsley W RSC 5 Bethnal
Green
09.10.03 Scott Dann L PTS 8 Bristol
01.04.04 Eric Teymour L RSC 8 Bethnal Green
18.09.05 John Humphrey L PTS 10 Bethnal
Green

*(Vacant Southern Area Middleweight
Title)*
30.09.05 Jason Samuels L PTS 4 Carmarthen
25.10.05 Ryan Rhodes L RTD 4 Preston
11.03.06 Paul Smith L RSC 4 Newport
01.06.06 Albert Rybacki L PTS 6 Birmingham
15.09.06 Darren Barker L PTS 10 Muswell Hill
*(Vacant Southern Area Middleweight
Title)*
06.10.06 Ryan Walls W RSC 2 Bethnal Green
26.10.06 Darren McDermott L PTS 10 Dudley
*(Vacant British Masters Middleweight
Title)*
03.11.06 Glenn Catley L RSC 3 Bristol
07.12.06 Cello Renda L RSC 4 Peterborough
20.01.07 Matthew Thirlwall L RSC 5 Muswell
Hill
Career: 31 contests, won 14, lost 17.

Damian Owen

Swansea. *Born* Swansea, 7 May, 1985
Welsh Lightweight Champion. *Ht* 5'7"
Manager T. Gilmour
01.10.04 Darren Payne W RSC 4 Bristol
05.11.04 Peter Allen W RSC 1 Hereford
08.04.05 Jus Wallie W PTS 4 Bristol
28.10.05 Bheki Moyo W PTS 6 Hartlepool
24.11.05 Kevin O'Hara L PTS 6 Lurgan
25.02.06 Carl Allen W PTS 6 Bristol
21.04.06 Steve Mullin W RSC 6 Belfast
13.10.06 Yauhen Kruhlik W PTS 6 Aberavon
02.03.07 Dean Phillips W CO 4 Neath
(Vacant Welsh Area Lightweight Title)
08.06.07 Pedro Verdu L RSC 3 Motherwell
Career: 10 contests, won 8, lost 2.

Leon Owen

Swansea. *Born* Mountain Ash, 7 October,
1983
S.Middleweight. *Ht* 6'1"
Manager N. Hodges
26.02.06 Greg Barton W RSC 1 Dagenham
05.03.06 George Katsimpas L RSC 2
Southampton
20.05.06 Jav Jerome W PTS 6 Bristol
08.10.06 Dave Pearson W PTS 4 Swansea
11.05.07 Gordon Brennan L PTS 4 Motherwell
Career: 5 contests, won 3, lost 2.

Ricky Owen

Swansea. *Born* Swansea, 10 May, 1985
Featherweight. *Ht* 5'6"
Manager Self
05.11.04 Sandy Bartlett W RSC 2 Hereford
16.06.05 Billy Smith W PTS 4 Dagenham
30.09.05 Rakhim Mingaleev W PTS 4
Carmarthen
03.03.06 Alexander Vladimirov W PTS 6
Hartlepool
02.03.07 Egon Szabo W PTS 6 Neath
Career: 5 contests, won 5.

Tom Owens

Birmingham. *Born* Birmingham, 1 May,
1983
Cruiserweight. *Ht* 6'4"
Manager R. Woodhall
01.06.07 Gary Thompson L RTD 1 Birmingham
Career: 1 contest, lost 1.

Chris Pacy

Bridlington. *Born* Doncaster, 17 May, 1983
Lightweight. *Ht* 5'6"
Manager F. Maloney

30.05.06	Billy Smith W PTS 4 Bethnal Green
21.07.06	Peter Allen W RSC 2 Altrincham
29.09.06	Danny Harding L PTS 4 Manchester
09.02.07	Baz Carey W PTS 4 Leeds
13.04.07	Danny Harding L PTS 6 Altrincham

Career: 5 contests, won 3, lost 2.

Chris Pacy   Les Clark

James Paisley

Belfast. *Born* Ballymena, 4 January, 1980
Welterweight. *Ht* 5'8"
Manager Self

09.09.01	Babatunde Ajayi L PTS 4 Southwark
28.10.01	Carl Walton W PTS 4 Southwark
15.12.01	David Barnes L RTD 2 Wembley
31.01.02	Tony Montana L PTS 6 Piccadilly
09.02.02	Michael Jennings L RSC 3 Manchester
11.03.02	Nigel Wright L PTS 4 Glasgow
23.06.02	Jason Gonzales W PTS 6 Southwark
17.09.02	Dave Stewart L RSC 5 Bethnal Green
20.10.02	Pete Buckley W PTS 4 Southwark
27.10.02	Elvis Mbwakongo L RSC 2 Southwark
22.02.03	Gwyn Wale L RSC 1 Huddersfield
26.09.03	Kristian Laight W PTS 6 Millwall
06.12.03	Tony Doherty L RSC 3 Cardiff
20.02.04	Justin Hudson W PTS 4 Bethnal Green
24.09.04	Nathan Ward L PTS 4 Bethnal Green
19.12.04	Ryan Barrett L DIS 5 Bethnal Green
19.06.05	Nathan Ward L RSC 4 Bethnal Green
	(Vacant British Masters Welterweight Title)
26.02.06	Imad Khamis L RSC 3 Dagenham
13.05.06	Alan Bosworth L PTS 4 Bethnal Green
08.07.06	Barrie Jones L RSC 2 Cardiff

Career: 20 contests, won 5, lost 15.

Dave Pearson

Middlesbrough. *Born* Middlesbrough, 1
April, 1974
L.Heavyweight. *Ht* 6'2¾"
Manager M. Shinfield

15.04.02	Ian Thomas L CO 3 Shrewsbury
03.10.02	Gary Firby W CO 3 Sunderland
21.10.02	Gary Jones L RSC 3 Cleethorpes
05.12.02	Chris Steele W PTS 6 Sunderland
24.03.03	Reagan Denton L PTS 6 Barnsley
31.05.03	Gary Jones L RSC 2 Barnsley
11.07.03	Ben Coward L PTS 6 Darlington
16.02.04	Brian Coleman L PTS 6 Scunthorpe
26.02.04	Tony Quigley L RSC 1 Widnes
26.04.04	Mark Phillips L RSC 6 Cleethorpes
25.06.04	Gerard London L PTS 4 Bethnal Green
06.11.04	Brian Coleman W PTS 6 Coventry
16.12.04	Peter McCormack W PTS 6 Cleethorpes
25.04.05	Peter McCormack W PTS 6 Cleethorpes
02.09.05	Mark Phillips L PTS 6 Derby
15.12.05	Ryan Rowlinson L PTS 6 Cleethorpes
28.01.06	Jonjo Finnegan L PTS 4 Nottingham
25.03.06	Jonjo Finnegan L PTS 8 Burton
24.04.06	Magic Kidem W PTS 6 Cleethorpes
30.09.06	Jonjo Finnegan L PTS 6 Middlesbrough
08.10.06	Leon Owen L PTS 4 Swansea
02.12.06	Eder Kurti L PTS 6 Southwark
15.02.07	Sam Horton L RSC 4 Dudley
14.05.07	Tony Stones DREW 6 Cleethorpes

Career: 24 contests, won 6, drew 1, lost 17.

Gavin Pearson

Bradford. *Born* Bradford, 10 March, 1977
Middleweight. *Ht* 5'10"
Manager C. Aston

26.11.98	Bobby Lyndon W PTS 6 Bradford
07.12.98	Dale Lowe L PTS 6 Cleethorpes
21.02.99	Les Frost W PTS 6 Bradford
12.03.99	Piotr Banicki DREW 4 Bethnal Green
03.04.99	Piotr Banicki DREW 4 Carlisle
06.05.99	Paul Swindles W PTS 6 Sunderland
29.05.99	Craig Smith L RSC 1 South Shields
12.09.99	Mike Watson W PTS 6 Nottingham
14.11.99	Chris Steele W PTS 6 Bradford
26.11.99	Peter Dunn DREW 6 Wakefield
09.12.99	John Marsden W PTS 6 Sunderland
06.03.00	John Marsden W PTS 6 Bradford
20.03.00	Joe Miller L PTS 6 Glasgow
17.04.00	Arv Mittoo W PTS 6 Glasgow
15.05.00	John Marsden W CO 5 Bradford
25.06.00	Robbie Sivyer L PTS 6 Wakefield
04.12.00	Dave Hinds W PTS 6 Bradford
05.02.01	Robert Burton L RSC 3 Bradford
17.05.01	Peter Dunn W PTS 6 Leeds
08.10.01	Robert Burton L RSC 2 Barnsley
18.03.02	Richard Inquieti W PTS 6 Glasgow
25.03.02	Danny Moir W PTS 6 Sunderland
29.04.02	Richard Inquieti W PTS 6 Bradford
09.05.02	Mark Paxford W PTS 6 Sunderland
20.11.02	Ciaran Duffy DREW 6 Leeds
02.12.02	Richie Murray W RTD 4 Bradford
07.12.06	Mark Franks W RSC 6 Bradford

Career: 27 contests, won 17, drew 4, lost 6.

Gareth Perkins

Swansea. *Born* Swansea, 17 December,
1982
Welterweight. *Ht* 5'5"
Manager Self

Dave Pearson — continued

29.02.04	Chris Long W PTS 6 Bristol
17.11.06	Paul Porter DREW 4 Bethnal Green

Career: 2 contests, won 1, drew 1.

Jack Perry

Derby. *Born* Derby, 20 June, 1987
L.Welterweight. *Ht* 6'1"
Manager J. Ingle

16.09.06	Deniss Sirjatovs W PTS 6 Burton
24.11.06	Kristian Laight W PTS 4 Nottingham
03.03.07	Matt Seawright W RSC 2 Burton

Career: 3 contests, won 3.

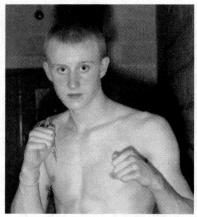

Jack Perry   Les Clark

Kevin Phelan

Slough. *Born* Slough, 11 June, 1977
Middleweight. Former British Masters
L.Middleweight Champion. *Ht* 6'1"
Manager Self

27.09.02	Lee Hodgson L RSC 1 Bracknell
21.03.03	Jimi Hendricks W RSC 6 Longford
12.04.03	Steve Russell W PTS 4 Norwich
26.04.03	Dave Wakefield W PTS 4 Brentford
09.05.03	Leigh Wicks W PTS 6 Longford
26.10.03	Brian Coleman W PTS 6 Longford
27.11.03	Dave Wakefield W PTS 6 Longford
25.03.04	Danny Moir L PTS 10 Longford
	(Vacant British Masters L.Middleweight Title)
02.06.04	David Walker L PTS 6 Nottingham
23.09.04	Danny Moir W RTD 3 Gateshead
	(British Masters L.Middleweight Title Challenge)
08.12.04	Taz Jones L PTS 10 Longford
	(British Masters L.Middleweight Title Defence)
06.10.05	John-Paul Temple W PTS 6 Longford
18.11.05	Michael Lomax L PTS 8 Dagenham
19.12.05	Danny Moir W CO 4 Longford
07.04.06	Neil Bonner W RSC 2 Longford
27.05.06	Barrie Lee L PTS 6 Glasgow
03.06.06	Jim Rock L RTD 7 Dublin
	(Vacant All-Ireland Middleweight Title)
08.07.06	Matthew Hall L RSC 1 Cardiff
06.10.06	Jackson Osei Bonsu L RSC 4 Bethnal Green
09.12.06	Anthony Small L RSC 1 Canning Town
09.03.07	Patrick J. Maxwell L RSC 2 Dagenham

Career: 21 contests, won 10, lost 11.

Dean Phillips

Llanelli. *Born* Swansea, 1 February, 1976
Lightweight. *Ht* 5'6"
Manager Self

10.03.94	Paul Richards L PTS 6 Bristol
23.03.94	Phil Janes W RSC 1 Cardiff
27.08.94	Craig Kelley W RSC 4 Cardiff
21.09.94	Steve Edwards W RTD 4 Cardiff
02.11.94	Anthony Maynard L PTS 6 Birmingham
04.02.95	Greg Upton W PTS 6 Cardiff
04.03.95	Mike Deveney W PTS 8 Livingston
24.03.95	Bamana Dibateza W PTS 6 Swansea
16.06.95	Danny Luutaya W RSC 2 Southwark
22.07.95	Colin McMillan L PTS 8 Millwall
20.09.95	Mervyn Bennett W PTS 6 Ystrad
16.03.96	Mike Anthony Brown W RSC 6 Glasgow
26.04.96	Bamana Dibateza W PTS 6 Cardiff
19.09.96	Peter Judson L RSC 10 Manchester *(Vacant IBF Inter-Continental S. Featherweight Title)*
24.01.98	Jimmy Phelan W PTS 6 Cardiff
25.04.98	Steve Conway L PTS 6 Cardiff
30.11.03	Nigel Senior W CO 1 Swansea
28.02.04	Gary Hibbert W RSC 5 Bridgend
01.05.04	Michael Muya W PTS 8 Bridgend
19.11.04	Kevin Bennett L PTS 12 Hartlepool *(Commonwealth Lightweight Title Challenge)*
11.02.06	Jon Honney W RSC 2 Bethnal Green
02.04.06	Tontcho Tontchev L RSC 1 Bethnal Green
02.03.07	Damian Owen L CO 4 Neath *(Vacant Welsh Area Lightweight Title)*

Career: 23 contests, won 15, lost 8.

Mark Phillips

St Clare's. *Born* Carmarthen, 28 April, 1975
L.Heavyweight. *Ht* 6'0"
Manager Self

26.10.00	Shayne Webb W PTS 6 Clydach
12.12.00	Tommy Matthews W PTS 6 Clydach
13.03.01	William Webster W RTD 1 Plymouth
07.10.01	Danny Norton L PTS 6 Wolverhampton
12.12.01	Simon Andrews W PTS 6 Clydach
25.04.02	Mark Ellwood L PTS 6 Hull
10.05.02	Scott Dann L PTS 6 Bethnal Green
23.06.02	Gareth Hogg L PTS 6 Southwark
10.07.02	Scott Dann L PTS 4 Wembley
03.12.02	Jamie Hearn L PTS 4 Bethnal Green
20.12.02	Ryan Walls L PTS 4 Bracknell
06.03.03	Darren Dorrington L PTS 8 Bristol
21.03.03	Steve Timms L PTS 6 West Bromwich
05.04.03	Dale Nixon L PTS 6 Coventry
13.04.03	Donovan Smillie L PTS 6 Bradford
12.05.03	Leigh Alliss L PTS 6 Southampton
27.05.03	Steven Spartacus L RSC 2 Dagenham
30.06.03	Roddy Doran L PTS 6 Shrewsbury
06.09.03	Alan Page L PTS 6 Huddersfield
18.09.03	Nick Okoth L PTS 4 Mayfair
09.10.03	Leigh Alliss L PTS 4 Bristol
30.11.03	Jimi Hendricks W PTS 6 Swansea
16.01.04	Donovan Smillie L PTS 4 Bradford
07.04.04	Christian Imaga L PTS 6 Leicester Square
15.04.04	Darren McDermott L PTS 4 Dudley
26.04.04	Dave Pearson W RSC 6 Cleethorpes
04.06.04	Steve Timms L PTS 6 Dudley
03.12.04	Dan Guthrie L RSC 1 Bristol
26.02.05	Matt Galer L PTS 6 Burton
21.04.05	Matthew Hough L PTS 4 Dudley
09.07.05	Liam Stinchcombe L PTS 4 Bristol
02.09.05	Dave Pearson W PTS 6 Derby
25.09.05	Lee Hodgson L PTS 6 Southampton
10.10.05	Peter McCormack W PTS 6 Birmingham
04.11.05	Gary Woolcombe L PTS 4 Bethnal Green
24.11.05	Glenn McClarnon L PTS 4 Lurgan
04.03.06	James Davenport L PTS 4 Manchester
30.03.06	Danny Tombs L PTS 4 Bloomsbury
13.05.06	Richard Horton L PTS 4 Bethnal Green
01.06.06	Jonjo Finnegan L PTS 4 Birmingham
09.06.06	Jason Rushton L PTS 6 Doncaster
08.07.06	Nathan Cleverly L PTS 4 Cardiff
08.09.06	James McKinley L PTS 4 Birmingham
24.09.06	Richard Horton L PTS 4 Bethnal Green
08.10.06	Shon Davies L PTS 4 Swansea
28.10.06	Carl Wild L PTS 6 Sheffield
02.12.06	Neil Tidman L PTS 6 Coventry
17.12.06	Robin White L PTS 4 Bolton
23.04.07	Kenny Davidson L PTS 6 Glasgow
06.05.07	Joey Ainscough L PTS 6 Altrincham
13.05.07	Kevin Concepcion L PTS 6 Birmingham
02.06.07	Robert Boardman L PTS 6 Bristol
28.06.07	Richard Collins L PTS 4 Dudley

Career: 53 contests, won 8, lost 45.

Stuart Phillips

Port Talbot. *Born* Abergavenny, 24 January, 1981
Celtic L.Welterweight Champion. *Ht* 5'8"
Manager N. Hodges

08.11.03	Lance Hall W PTS 4 Bridgend
30.11.03	Wayne Wheeler W PTS 4 Swansea
01.05.04	Chris Long L RSC 1 Bridgend
17.02.05	Tristan Davies L PTS 6 Dudley
28.04.05	Duncan Cottier DREW 4 Clydach
17.11.05	Ali Wyatt W PTS 4 Bristol
08.10.06	Chris Long W PTS 4 Swansea
03.03.07	Garry Buckland L PTS 10 Newport *(Vacant Welsh Area L.Welterweight Title)*
10.06.07	Ceri Hall W PTS 10 Neath *(Celtic L.Welterweight Title Challenge)*

Career: 9 contests, won 5, drew 1, lost 3.

Esham Pickering

Newark. *Born* Newark, 7 August, 1976
British S.Bantamweight Champion.
Former European & Commonwealth
S.Bantamweight Champion. Former
Undefeated British Masters Bantamweight
Champion. *Ht* 5'5"
Manager Self

23.09.96	Brendan Bryce W RSC 5 Cleethorpes
24.10.96	Kevin Sheil W PTS 6 Lincoln
22.11.96	Amjid Mahmood W RSC 2 Hull
09.12.96	Des Gargano W RTD 2 Chesterfield
16.12.96	Graham McGrath W PTS 6 Cleethorpes
20.03.97	Robert Braddock W RSC 6 Newark
12.04.97	Graham McGrath W PTS 4 Sheffield
26.04.97	Mike Deveney W PTS 4 Swadlincote
16.05.97	Chris Price W PTS 6 Hull
26.06.97	Graham McGrath W PTS 6 Salford
01.11.97	Mike Deveney W RSC 8 Glasgow *(Elim. British Featherweight Title)*
09.05.98	Jonjo Irwin L PTS 12 Sheffield *(Vacant British Featherweight Title)*
11.09.98	Louis Veitch W PTS 6 Newark

15.08.99	Chris Lyons W RSC 2 Derby
23.10.99	Ian Turner W PTS 6 Telford
20.11.99	Marc Smith W PTS 6 Grantham
19.02.00	Kevin Gerowski W PTS 10 Newark *(Vacant British Masters Bantamweight Title. Elim. British Bantamweight Title)*
13.08.00	Lee Williamson W PTS 6 Nottingham
16.12.00	Mauricio Martinez L RSC 1 Sheffield *(WBO Bantamweight Title Challenge)*
15.09.01	Carl Allen W PTS 6 Derby
08.12.01	Carl Allen W PTS 6 Chesterfield
20.04.02	Carl Allen W PTS 6 Derby
24.09.02	Alejandro Monzon L PTS 12 Gran Canaria, Spain *(Vacant WBA Inter-Continental S.Featherweight Title)*
02.12.02	Carl Allen W PTS 6 Leicester
08.02.03	Duncan Karanja W CO 5 Brentford *(Vacant Commonwealth S.Bantamweight Title)*
12.07.03	Brian Carr W RSC 4 Renfrew *(Vacant British S.Bantamweight Title. Commonwealth S.Bantamweight Title Defence)*
24.10.03	Alfred Tetteh W RSC 7 Bethnal Green *(Commonwealth S.Bantamweight Title Defence)*
16.01.04	Vincenzo Gigliotti W CO 10 Bradford *(Vacant European S.Bantamweight Title)*
12.05.04	Juan Garcia Martin W RSC 8 Reading *(European S.Bantamweight Title Defence)*
08.05.05	Noel Wilders W PTS 8 Bradford
09.06.05	Miguel Mallon W RSC 10 Alcobendas, Madrid, Spain *(European S.Bantamweight Title Defence)*
28.10.05	Michael Hunter L PTS 12 Hartlepool *(European & Commonwealth S.Bantamweight Title Defences. British S.Bantamweight Title Challenge)*
02.12.05	Frederic Bonifai W PTS 6 Nottingham
11.11.06	Bernard Dunne L PTS 12 Dublin *(Vacant European S.Bantamweight Title)*
20.01.07	Frederic Gosset W PTS 6 Muswell Hill
16.03.07	Marc Callaghan W PTS 12 Norwich *(Vacant British S.Bantamweight Title)*

Career: 36 contests, won 31, lost 5.

(Patrick) Paddy Pollock

Wishaw. *Born* Bellshill, 10 October, 1985
L.Middleweight. *Ht* 5'10½"
Manager A. Morrison

22.04.06	Duncan Cottier W PTS 6 Glasgow
21.10.06	Tyrone McInerney DREW 6 Glasgow
10.12.06	Ciaran Duffy W PTS 6 Glasgow
26.01.07	Dave Wakefield L PTS 6 Glasgow
16.02.07	Martin Marshall L PTS 4 Sunderland
16.03.07	Tom Hogan W RSC 3 Glasgow
25.05.07	Shaun Farmer W PTS 6 Glasgow

Career: 7 contests, won 4, drew 1, lost 2.

Paul Porter

Luton. *Born* Luton, 4 October, 1978
L.Middleweight. *Ht* 5'9¼"
Manager F. Maloney

11.02.06	Omar Gumati L RSC 3 Bethnal Green
02.04.06	Steve Anning DREW 4 Bethnal Green
29.09.06	Chris Johnson W RSC 2 Manchester

17.11.06 Gareth Perkins DREW 4 Bethnal Green
09.03.07 Thomas Mazurkiewicz L PTS 4 Dagenham

Career: 5 contests, won 1, drew 2, lost 2.

Marcus Portman   Les Clark

Marcus Portman

West Bromwich. *Born* West Bromwich, 26 September, 1980
L.Middleweight. Former Undefeated British Masters Welterweight Champion. *Ht* 6'0"
Manager E. Johnson

18.02.00 Ray Wood W PTS 6 West Bromwich
28.03.00 Billy Smith W PTS 6 Wolverhampton
10.09.00 Alan Kershaw W RSC 2 Walsall
15.02.01 Willie Limond L PTS 6 Glasgow
01.04.01 Tony Smith W PTS 6 Wolverhampton
20.04.01 Darren Melville L RSC 3 Millwall
07.09.01 Tony Smith W PTS 6 West Bromwich
15.09.01 Matthew Hatton L RSC 3 Manchester
12.12.01 Ross McCord DREW 4 Clydach
18.01.02 Andy Egan W PTS 4 Coventry
25.02.02 Sammy Smith W PTS 6 Slough
27.04.02 Gavin Wake W PTS 4 Huddersfield
08.05.03 Thomas McDonagh L PTS 6 Widnes
17.05.03 Scott Dixon W PTS 6 Liverpool
30.06.03 Wayne Wheeler W RSC 3 Shrewsbury
07.09.03 Jason Williams W PTS 6 Shrewsbury
19.02.04 Richard Swallow W PTS 10 Dudley
           (British Masters Welterweight Title Challenge)
03.04.04 Chris Saunders L RSC 1 Sheffield
           (Vacant English Welterweight Title)
29.06.06 Peter Dunn W PTS 6 Dudley
18.09.06 Peter Dunn W PTS 6 Glasgow
07.10.06 Ben Hudson W PTS 6 Walsall
15.12.06 George Hillyard W PTS 8 Bethnal Green

Career: 22 contests, won 16, drew 1, lost 5.

Martin Power

St Pancras. *Born* London, 14 February, 1980
Bantamweight. Former Undefeated British Bantamweight Champion. *Ht* 5'6"
Manager F. Maloney

09.06.01 Sean Grant W PTS 4 Bethnal Green
28.07.01 Andrew Greenaway W RSC 3 Wembley
22.09.01 Stevie Quinn W RSC 2 Bethnal Green

24.11.01 Anthony Hanna W PTS 4 Bethnal Green
19.01.02 Gareth Wiltshaw W PTS 4 Bethnal Green
08.07.02 Darren Cleary W PTS 4 Mayfair
12.10.02 Stevie Quinn W RSC 4 Bethnal Green
15.02.03 Stevie Quinn W RTD 1 Wembley
29.03.03 Dave Hinds W PTS 4 Portsmouth
17.07.03 Darren Cleary W PTS 6 Dagenham
06.11.03 Rocky Dean W PTS 6 Dagenham
24.01.04 Delroy Spencer W RTD 1 Wembley
01.04.04 Fred Janes W RSC 2 Bethnal Green
13.05.04 Jean-Marie Codet W PTS 8 Bethnal Green
30.07.04 Delroy Spencer W CO 2 Bethnal Green
11.12.04 Shinny Bayaar W PTS 10 Canning Town
20.05.05 Dale Robinson W PTS 12 Southwark
           (Vacant British Bantamweight Title)
04.11.05 Ian Napa W PTS 12 Bethnal Green
           (British Bantamweight Title Defence)
30.05.06 Isaac Ward W RSC 8 Bethnal Green
           (British Bantamweight Title Defence)
29.06.06 Tshifhiwa Munyai L RSC 9 Bethnal Green
           (Vacant Commonwealth Bantamweight Title)

26.01.07 Tshifhiwa Munyai L RTD 5 Dagenham
           (Commonwealth Bantamweight Title Challenge)

Career: 21 contests, won 19, lost 2.

Mitch Prince

Cumbernauld. *Born* Johannesburg, South Africa, 15 March, 1984
L.Welterweight. *Ht* 5'5½"
Manager T. Gilmour

05.06.06 Jason Nesbitt W PTS 6 Glasgow
29.09.06 Pete Buckley W PTS 6 Motherwell
03.11.06 Pete Buckley W PTS 6 Glasgow
02.12.06 Steve Gethin W PTS 6 Clydebank
16.02.07 Dariusz Snarski DREW 6 Kirkcaldy

Career: 5 contests, won 4, drew 1.

Bradley Pryce (Price)

Newbridge. *Born* Newport, 15 March, 1981
Commonwealth L.Middleweight Champion. Former Undefeated Welsh Welterweight Champion. Former Undefeated IBF Inter-Continental L.Welterweight Champion. Former Undefeated WBO Inter-Continental Lightweight Champion. *Ht* 5'11"

Bradley Pryce   Les Clark

Manager F. Warren/E. Calzaghe

17.07.99	Dave Hinds W PTS 4 Doncaster
23.10.99	David Jeffrey W RSC 3 Telford
06.11.99	Eddie Nevins W RSC 2 Widnes
29.01.00	Pete Buckley W PTS 4 Manchester
29.02.00	Carl Allen W PTS 4 Widnes
16.05.00	Carl Allen W RSC 3 Warrington
15.07.00	Gary Flear W RSC 1 Millwall
07.10.00	Gary Reid W RSC 5 Doncaster
27.01.01	Joel Viney W RSC 3 Bethnal Green
17.03.01	Brian Coleman W PTS 4 Manchester
28.04.01	Jason Hall W PTS 12 Cardiff
	(Vacant WBO Inter-Continental Lightweight Title)
21.07.01	Stuart Patterson W RSC 5 Sheffield
09.10.01	Lucky Sambo W PTS 12 Cardiff
	(WBO Inter-Continental Lightweight Title Defence)
12.02.02	Gavin Down W RSC 9 Bethnal Green
	(Vacant IBF Inter-Continental L.Welterweight Title)
20.04.02	Dafydd Carlin W RSC 8 Cardiff
08.06.02	Pete Buckley W RSC 1 Renfrew
17.08.02	Ted Bami L RSC 6 Cardiff
23.11.02	Craig Lynch W CO 4 Derby
01.02.03	Neil Sinclair L RSC 8 Belfast
	(British Welterweight Title Challenge)
08.05.03	Ivan Kirpa W PTS 10 Widnes
21.02.04	Farai Musiiwa L PTS 6 Cardiff
06.05.04	Thomas McDonagh L PTS 12 Barnsley
	(WBU International L.Middleweight Title Challenge)
03.07.04	Keith Jones W RSC 8 Newport
	(Vacant Welsh Welterweight Title)
03.09.04	Ajose Olusegun L RSC 4 Newport
11.12.04	Sergey Styopkin W RSC 10 Canning Town
25.10.05	Michael Jennings L PTS 12 Preston
	(British Welterweight Title Challenge)
11.03.06	Ossie Duran W PTS 12 Newport
	(Commonwealth L.Middleweight Title Challenge)
08.07.06	Hassan Matumla W RSC 4 Cardiff
	(Commonwealth L.Middleweight Title Defence)
18.11.06	Andrew Facey W PTS 12 Newport
	(Commonwealth L.Middleweight Title Defence)
07.04.07	Thomas Awinbono W PTS 12 Cardiff
	(Commonwealth L.Middleweight Title Defence)

Career: 30 contests, won 24, lost 6.

Lee Purdy

Colchester. *Born* Colchester, 29 May, 1987
Welterweight. *Ht* 5'7"
Manager A. Sims

08.12.06	Deniss Sirjatovs W RSC 3 Dagenham
16.03.07	Kristian Laight W PTS 4 Norwich
16.06.07	Duncan Cottier W PTS 4 Chigwell

Career: 3 contests, won 3.

Kreshnik Qato

Wembley. *Born* Albania, 13 August, 1978
European Union EE & Southern Area
S.Middleweight Champion. Former
Undefeated Eastern European Boxing
Association S.Middleweight Champion.
Ht 5'9½"
Manager P. Fondu

28.09.01	Erik Teymour L PTS 6 Millwall
16.12.01	Lawrence Murphy L PTS 6 Glasgow
08.04.02	Ty Browne W PTS 4 Southampton
10.05.02	Paul Jones L PTS 6 Millwall
20.03.03	Jason Collins W PTS 4 Queensway
13.04.03	Mark Thornton W RSC 3 Streatham
13.05.03	Danny Thornton W PTS 6 Leeds
26.07.03	Scott Dann L RSC 2 Plymouth
26.09.03	Joel Ani W PTS 6 Millwall
14.11.03	Steven Bendall L PTS 8 Bethnal Green
21.02.04	Gary Lockett L RSC 2 Cardiff
16.10.04	Vladimir Zavgorodniy W PTS 10 Yalta, Ukraine
	(Vacant Eastern European Boxing Association S.Middleweight Title)
05.03.05	Rizvan Magomedov W PTS 12 Durres, Albania
	(Eastern European Boxing Association S.Middleweight Title Defence)
12.06.05	Dmitry Donetskiy W RSC 6 Leicester Square
09.10.05	Daniil Prakapsou W PTS 8 Hammersmith
02.04.06	Laurent Goury W PTS 6 Bethnal Green
26.05.06	Simone Lucas W PTS 4 Bethnal Green
15.07.06	Sylvain Touzet W PTS 6 Tirana, Albania
15.09.06	Simeon Cover W PTS 6 Muswell Hill
08.12.06	Simeon Cover W PTS 10 Dagenham
	(Vacant Southern Area S.Middleweight Title)
03.03.07	Alexander Zaitsev W PTS 12 Tirana, Albania
	(Vacant European Union-EE S.Middleweight Title)

Career: 21 contests, won 15, lost 6.

Scott Quigg

Bury. *Born* Bury, 9 October, 1988
S.Bantamweight. *Ht* 5'8"
Manager Brian Hughes/W. Dixon

21.04.07	Gary Sheil W PTS 6 Manchester
30.06.07	Shaun Walton W RSC 1 Manchester

Career: 2 contests, won 2.

Tony Quigley

Liverpool. *Born* Liverpool, 1 October, 1984
L.Heavyweight. *Ht* 5'10"
Manager Self

26.02.04	Dave Pearson W RSC 1 Widnes
22.05.04	Patrick Cito W PTS 4 Widnes
01.10.04	Leigh Wicks W PTS 4 Manchester
11.02.05	Shpetim Hoti W CO 1 Manchester
03.06.05	Varuzhan Davtyan W PTS 4 Manchester
04.03.06	Ojay Abrahams W PTS 4 Manchester
01.06.06	Simeon Cover W PTS 4 Barnsley
14.10.06	Nathan Cleverly L RSC 5 Manchester
10.03.07	Dean Walker W RSC 2 Liverpool
26.04.07	Ricky Strike W RSC 3 Manchester

Career: 10 contests, won 9, lost 1.

Kreshnik Qato   Les Clark

Jamie Radford

Woolwich. *Born* Newham, 2 August, 1987
Welterweight. *Ht* 5'7¾"
Manager J. Eames

09.03.07　Barry Downes W PTS 4 Dagenham

Career: 1 contest, won 1.

Jamie Radford　　　　　　　　Les Clark

Furhan Rafiq

Glasgow. *Born* Glasgow, 16 December, 1977
S.Featherweight. *Ht* 5'8"
Manager Self

19.04.04　Paddy Folan W PTS 6 Glasgow
15.11.04　Gary Davis L PTS 6 Glasgow
05.06.06　Shaun Walton W PTS 6 Glasgow
16.06.06　Henry Jones L PTS 6 Carmarthen
09.09.06　Shaun Walton W PTS 6 Inverurie
10.11.06　Neil Marston L PTS 6 Telford
22.01.07　Shaun Walton W PTS 6 Glasgow
02.03.07　Sandy Bartlett W PTS 6 Irvine
28.04.07　Pete Buckley W PTS 6 Clydebank

Career: 9 contests, won 6, lost 3.

Harry Ramogoadi

Coventry. *Born* South Africa, 21 March, 1976
S.Featherweight. Former Undefeated British Masters Featherweight Champion. *Ht* 5'6"
Manager Self

20.11.98　Dan Ngweyna W PTS 4 Thembisa, South Africa
24.01.99　Zachariah Madau W PTS 4 Johannesburg, South Africa
26.03.99　Jan van Rooyen DREW 4 Witbank, South Africa
27.06.99　Kenneth Buhlalu W PTS 4 Durban, South Africa
23.07.99　Bethule Machedi W PTS 4 Johannesburg, South Africa
25.09.99　Malepa Levi W PTS 6 Nelspruit, South Africa
01.12.99　Mandla Mashiane L PTS 6 Johannesburg, South Africa

13.07.00　Martin Mnyandu L PTS 6 Johannesburg, South Africa
28.10.00　Trevor Gouws W PTS 6 Johannesburg, South Africa
18.02.01　Thomas Mashaba DREW 6 Johannesburg, South Africa
15.04.01　Malepa Levi W PTS 8 Johannesburg, South Africa
02.11.01　Malcolm Klaasen W PTS 6 Benoni, South Africa
08.02.02　Takalani Kwinda W PTS 8 Johannesburg, South Africa
09.10.02　Ariel Mathebula W PTS 6 Sandton, South Africa
24.10.03　Stephen Oates W PTS 6 Bethnal Green
08.11.03　Jason Nesbitt W PTS 6 Coventry
09.04.04　Nigel Senior W RSC 1 Rugby
10.07.04　Choi Tseveenpurev L RTD 6 Coventry *(British Masters Featherweight Title Challenge)*
09.12.04　John Murray L RSC 4 Stockport
06.03.05　Choi Tseveenpurev L RSC 5 Shaw *(British Masters Featherweight Title Challenge)*
01.06.05　Danny Wallace W PTS 6 Leeds
23.07.05　Jamie Arthur W RSC 5 Edinburgh
18.10.06　Buster Dennis W RSC 9 Bayswater *(Vacant British Masters Featherweight Title)*
09.12.06　Nicky Cook L PTS 8 Canning Town
22.12.06　Daniel Thorpe W PTS 6 Coventry
10.03.07　Kevin Mitchell L RSC 6 Liverpool *(Commonwealth S.Featherweight Title Challenge)*

13.04.07　Ferenc Szabo W RSC 4 Rugby
15.06.07　Tshifhiwa Munyai L PTS 8 Crystal Palace

Career: 28 contests, won 18, drew 2, lost 8.

Tony Randell (Webster)

Birmingham. *Born* Peterborough, 11 April, 1982
Middleweight. *Ht* 5'11½"
Manager Self

16.12.04　Scott Conway W PTS 6 Cleethorpes
13.02.05　Gavin Smith L PTS 6 Bradford
23.03.05　Danny Goode L PTS 6 Leicester Square
01.04.05　Chris Black L PTS 6 Glasgow
16.05.05　Sergey Haritonov W RSC 4 Birmingham
24.07.05　Stuart Brookes L PTS 6 Sheffield
09.09.05　Stuart Brookes L RSC 3 Sheffield
10.10.05　Simon Sherrington L PTS 6 Birmingham
30.10.05　Jake Guntert L PTS 4 Bethnal Green
18.12.05　Mark Thompson L RSC 2 Bolton
17.02.06　Reagan Denton L PTS 6 Sheffield
18.03.06　Sam Gorman W PTS 6 Coventry
02.04.06　Alex Matvienko L PTS 6 Shaw
13.04.06　Danny Wright L PTS 6 Leeds
20.05.06　George Katsimpas L RSC 1 Bristol
16.09.06　Karl Chiverton L PTS 6 Burton
07.10.06　Sam Horton L PTS 6 Walsall
26.10.06　Dee Mitchell L PTS 4 Wolverhampton
06.12.06　Ryan Rowlinson DREW 6 Rotherham

Tony Randell　　　　　　　　　　　　Les Clark

20.01.07	George Hillyard DREW 4 Muswell Hill
31.05.07	Brian Rose L PTS 6 Manchester
24.06.07	Johnny Enigma W RSC 5 Wigan

Career: 22 contests, won 4, drew 2, lost 16.

Hastings Rasani

Birmingham. *Born* Zimbabwe, 16 April, 1974
Cruiserweight. *Ht* 6'2"
Manager Self

21.12.97	Elias Chikwanda W RSC 4 Harare, Zimbabwe
28.02.98	Victor Ndebele W CO 1 Harare, Zimbabwe
04.04.98	William Mpoku W PTS 8 Harare, Zimbabwe
03.05.98	Nightshow Mafukidze W CO 3 Harare, Zimbabwe
30.05.98	Frank Mutiyaya W RSC 4 Harare, Zimbabwe
24.07.98	Ambrose Mlilo L RSC 9 Harare, Zimbabwe
13.01.99	Tobia Wede W RSC 4 Harare, Zimbabwe
27.02.99	Ambrose Mlilo L CO 9 Harare, Zimbabwe
27.03.99	Gibson Mapfumo W CO 1 Harare, Zimbabwe
17.04.99	Eric Sauti W RSC 2 Harare, Zimbabwe
05.06.99	Gibson Mapfumo W RSC 2 Harare, Zimbabwe
18.12.99	Gibson Mapfumo W RSC 3 Harare, Zimbabwe
02.01.01	Neil Simpson L CO 4 Coventry
	(Vacant Commonwealth L.Heavyweight Title)
24.03.01	Gibson Mapfumo W CO 3 Harare, Zimbabwe
28.04.01	Arigoma Chiponda W DIS Harare, Zimbabwe
08.05.01	Tony Oakey L RSC 10 Barnsley
	(Vacant Commonwealth L.Heavyweight Title)
06.10.01	Sipho Moyo L CO 9 Harare, Zimbabwe
15.03.02	Elvis Michailenko L RSC 5 Millwall
24.05.03	Elvis Michailenko L RSC 4 Bethnal Green
31.07.03	Mark Brookes L PTS 6 Sheffield
05.09.03	Carl Thompson L RSC 1 Sheffield
04.10.03	Steven Spartacus L RSC 1 Muswell Hill
11.11.03	Denzil Browne L PTS 6 Leeds
13.02.04	Leigh Alliss L PTS 6 Bristol
21.02.04	Earl Ling DREW 4 Norwich
12.03.04	Simeon Cover W CO 6 Irvine
20.03.04	David Haye L RSC 1 Wembley
12.05.04	Jamie Hearn L RSC 4 Reading
17.06.04	Amer Khan L PTS 6 Sheffield
17.09.04	Mark Brookes L PTS 6 Sheffield
11.10.04	Hamed Jamali L PTS 8 Birmingham
22.10.04	Nathan King L PTS 6 Edinburgh
08.12.04	Sam Price L PTS 6 Longford
17.12.04	Neil Simpson L PTS 6 Coventry
21.02.05	Karl Wheeler L PTS 6 Peterborough
24.04.05	Nicki Taylor W RTD 4 Askern
08.05.05	Nate Joseph W RSC 4 Bradford
15.05.05	Danny Grainger W RSC 5 Sheffield
02.06.05	Karl Wheeler W RSC 5 Peterborough
01.07.05	Ovill McKenzie L PTS 6 Fulham
09.09.05	Lee Swaby L PTS 4 Sheffield
24.09.05	Neil Linford W RSC 5 Coventry
12.11.05	Dean Francis L RSC 6 Bristol
19.12.05	Valery Odin W PTS 4 Longford
11.03.06	Bruce Scott W PTS 8 Newport

07.10.06	Dean Francis L CO 2 Weston super Mare
02.12.06	Tommy Eastwood L PTS 6 Longford
20.01.07	Troy Ross L CO 3 Muswell Hill
11.03.07	Darren Stubbs L RSC 5 Shaw

Career: 49 contests, won 20, drew 1, lost 28.

Abdul Rashid

Manchester. *Born* Manchester, 17 February, 1975
Lightweight. *Ht* 5'7"
Manager G. Hunter

18.06.06	Sergei Rozhakmens W PTS 6 Manchester
14.10.06	Anthony Crolla L PTS 4 Manchester
24.02.07	Neal McQuade L PTS 6 Manchester

Career: 3 contests, won 1, lost 2.

(Shahid) Sid Razak

Birmingham. *Born* Birmingham, 9 March, 1973
Lightweight. *Ht* 5'7"
Manager R. Woodhall

13.02.01	Neil Read W PTS 6 Brierley Hill
27.03.01	Tommy Thomas W RSC 2 Brierley Hill
21.05.01	Jason Nesbitt W PTS 6 Birmingham
08.10.01	Gareth Wiltshaw L PTS 6 Birmingham
14.09.02	J.J.Moore L PTS 6 Newark
26.09.02	Chris Hooper L PTS 6 Hull
08.12.03	Steve Mullin L PTS 6 Birmingham
08.03.04	Steve Mullin L PTS 6 Birmingham
01.06.07	Sergei Rozhakmens L PTS 6 Birmingham

Career: 9 contests, won 3, lost 6.

Neil Read

Bilston. *Born* Wolverhampton, 9 February, 1972
Featherweight. *Ht* 5'4"
Manager P. Bowen

08.02.00	Gary Groves W PTS 6 Wolverhampton
10.09.00	Stephen Chinnock L RSC 5 Walsall
30.11.00	Paddy Folan L RSC 6 Blackpool
13.02.01	Sid Razak L PTS 6 Brierley Hill
08.03.01	John-Paul Ryan W PTS 6 Stoke
26.08.01	Lee Holmes L PTS 6 Warrington
06.12.01	Chris Edwards L PTS 8 Stoke
28.01.02	Jamil Hussain L CO 2 Barnsley
13.04.02	Stephen Chinnock L CO 3 Wolverhampton
	(Midlands Area Featherweight Title Challenge)
29.06.02	Jamie Yelland L PTS 6 Brentwood
03.08.02	Isaac Ward L RSC 1 Blackpool
23.09.02	Andy Roberts L PTS 6 Cleethorpes
10.10.02	Chris Edwards L PTS 6 Stoke
08.11.02	Andy Roberts L PTS 6 Doncaster
02.12.02	Steve Gethin L RTD 3 Leicester
10.02.03	Sean Hughes L PTS 6 Sheffield
17.03.03	Junior Anderson W CO 2 Southampton
07.06.03	Gareth Payne L RSC 5 Coventry
	(Vacant Midlands Area S.Bantamweight Title)
05.09.03	Andy Roberts L PTS 6 Doncaster
09.10.03	Lee Haskins L PTS 4 Bristol
08.11.03	Gareth Payne L PTS 4 Coventry
14.02.04	Rendall Munroe L RSC 1 Nottingham
03.04.04	Mark Moran L RSC 2 Manchester
14.06.04	Wayne Bloy DREW 6 Cleethorpes
26.09.04	Chris Edwards L RSC 2 Stoke

	(Vacant British Masters S.Bantamweight Title)
31.10.04	Gary Ford L PTS 6 Shaw
18.04.05	Abdul Mougharbel L PTS 6 Bradford
24.07.05	Craig Bromley L PTS 4 Sheffield
16.09.05	Jamie McDonnell L PTS 6 Doncaster
12.11.05	Mick Abbott L PTS 6 Stoke
23.02.06	Tasif Khan L RSC 6 Leeds
14.04.06	Neil Marston L PTS 6 Telford
28.05.06	Robert Nelson L PTS 6 Wakefield
21.07.06	Stuart McFadyen L RSC 1 Altrincham
13.10.06	Josh Wale L RSC 1 Doncaster
03.12.06	Eugene Heagney L PTS 6 Wakefield
11.12.06	Dougie Walton L RSC 5 Birmingham

Career: 37 contests, won 3, drew 1, lost 33.

Gavin Rees

Newbridge. *Born* Newport, 10 May, 1980
L.Welterweight. Former Undefeated WBO
Inter-Continental Featherweight Champion.
Ht 5'7"
Manager F. Warren/E. Calzaghe

05.09.98	John Farrell W PTS 4 Telford
05.12.98	Ernie Smith W PTS 4 Bristol
27.03.99	Graham McGrath W RSC 2 Derby
05.06.99	Wayne Jones W RSC 2 Cardiff
11.12.99	Dave Hinds W RSC 2 Liverpool
19.02.00	Pete Buckley W PTS 4 Dagenham
29.05.00	Willie Valentine W RSC 3 Manchester
23.09.00	Pete Buckley W PTS 4 Bethnal Green
13.11.00	Steve Hanley W RSC 1 Bethnal Green
15.01.01	Chris Jickells W RSC 2 Manchester
28.04.01	Vladimir Borov W RSC 4 Cardiff
	(Vacant WBO Inter-Continental Featherweight Title)
21.07.01	Nigel Senior W RSC 2 Sheffield
09.10.01	Nikolai Eremeev W PTS 12 Cardiff
	(WBO Inter-Continental Featherweight Title Defence)
12.02.02	Rakhim Mingaleev W PTS 6 Bethnal Green
20.04.02	Gary Flear W RTD 4 Cardiff
08.07.02	Ernie Smith W RSC 5 Mayfair
17.08.02	Sergei Andreychikov W RTD 1 Cardiff
14.12.02	Jimmy Beech W PTS 4 Newcastle
15.02.03	Andrei Devyataykin W PTS 6 Wembley
28.06.03	Daniel Thorpe W RSC 1 Cardiff
03.07.04	Michael Muya W RSC 2 Newport
03.09.04	Carl Allen W PTS 6 Newport
11.03.06	Daniel Thorpe W RSC 5 Newport
08.07.06	Martin Watson W PTS 6 Cardiff
18.11.06	Chill John W PTS 8 Newport
07.04.07	Billy Smith W PTS 6 Cardiff

Career: 26 contests, won 26.

Gary Reid

Stoke. *Born* Jamaica, 20 November, 1972
L.Welterweight. Former Undefeated
Midlands Area & British Masters
L.Welterweight Champion. *Ht* 5'5½"
Manager M. Carney

09.12.98	Carl Tilley W CO 1 Stoke
11.02.99	Ted Bami L RSC 2 Dudley
23.03.99	Lee Williamson W PTS 6 Wolverhampton
07.10.99	Stuart Rimmer W RSC 2 Mere
19.12.99	No No Junior L PTS 6 Salford
14.04.00	Lee Molyneux W PTS 6 Manchester
18.05.00	Sammy Smith W RSC 1 Bethnal Green
23.07.00	Kevin Bennett L RSC 4 Hartlepool

21.09.00	Karim Bouali L PTS 4 Bloomsbury
07.10.00	Bradley Pryce L RSC 5 Doncaster
07.09.01	Willie Limond L PTS 8 Glasgow
22.09.01	Francis Barrett L PTS 4 Bethnal Green
17.02.02	Richie Caparelli W PTS 6 Salford
02.03.02	Paul Halpin L RSC 3 Bethnal Green
26.04.02	Martin Watson L PTS 6 Glasgow
28.05.02	Gareth Jordan DREW 6 Liverpool
13.07.02	Gary Greenwood L RSC 5 Coventry
05.10.02	Joel Viney W CO 2 Coventry
18.11.02	Martin Watson L RSC 4 Glasgow
21.03.03	Young Muttley L RSC 7 West Bromwich
	(Vacant Midlands Area L.Welterweight Title)
10.10.03	Oscar Hall W RSC 2 Darlington
26.09.04	Tony Montana W PTS 10 Stoke
	(Vacant British Masters L.Welterweight Title)
17.02.05	Dean Hickman L PTS 10 Dudley
	(Midlands Area L.Welterweight Title Challenge)
27.05.05	Barry Morrison L RTD 8 Motherwell
	(British Masters L.Welterweight Title Defence)
25.11.05	Jason Cook L DIS 2 Liverpool
18.02.06	Davis Kamara W PTS 6 Stoke
06.05.06	Kevin McIntyre W RSC 6 Stoke
	(Vacant British Masters L.Welterweight Title)
26.05.06	Leo O'Reilly W RSC 2 Bethnal Green
04.11.06	Nigel Wright L PTS 10 Glasgow
	(English L.Welterweight Title Challenge)
20.04.07	Dean Hickman W RSC 5 Dudley
	(Vacant Midlands Area L.Welterweight Title)
15.06.07	Ajose Olusegun L PTS 12 Crystal Palace
	(Vacant Commonwealth L.Welterweight Title)

Career: 31 contests, won 13, drew 1, lost 17.

Gavin Reid

Redcar. *Born* Aberdeen, 17 November, 1978
S.Bantamweight. *Ht* 5'8½"
Manager M. Marsden

09.06.07	Neil Marston W CO 2 Middlesbrough

Career: 1 contest, won 1.

Mike Reid

Aberdeen. *Born* Inverurie, 4 November, 1983
Welterweight. *Ht* 5'8"
Manager Self

15.11.04	Willie Valentine W PTS 6 Glasgow
21.02.05	Tom Hogan W PTS 6 Glasgow
11.06.05	Lance Verallo W PTS 6 Kirkcaldy
30.09.05	Ben Hudson W PTS 4 Kirkcaldy
24.10.05	Chris Brophy W RSC 2 Glasgow
31.03.06	Tom Hogan L PTS 6 Inverurie
27.05.06	Adam Kelly DREW 6 Aberdeen
09.09.06	Billy Smith L PTS 8 Inverurie
03.11.06	Tye Williams L RSC 6 Glasgow
26.05.07	Leonard Lothian L PTS 6 Aberdeen

Career: 10 contests, won 5, drew 1, lost 4.

Pele Reid

Birmingham. *Born* Birmingham, 11 January, 1973
Heavyweight. Former Undefeated WBO Inter-Continental Heavyweight Champion. *Ht* 6'3"
Manager R. Woodhall

24.11.95	Gary Williams W RSC 1 Manchester
20.01.96	Joey Paladino W RSC 1 Mansfield
26.01.96	Vance Idiens W RSC 1 Brighton
11.05.96	Keith Fletcher W CO 1 Bethnal Green
25.06.96	Andy Lambert W CO 1 Mansfield
12.10.96	Eduardo Carranza W CO 2 Milan, Italy
02.11.96	Ricky Sullivan W RSC 2 Garmisch, Germany
25.02.97	Michael Murray W RSC 1 Sheffield
28.06.97	Ricardo Kennedy W RSC 1 Norwich
	(Vacant WBO Inter-Continental Heavyweight Title)
11.10.97	Eli Dixon W CO 9 Sheffield
	(WBO Inter-Continental Heavyweight Title Defence)
15.11.97	Albert Call W RSC 2 Bristol
06.06.98	Wayne Llewelyn W CO 1 Liverpool
	(Elim. British Heavyweight Title)
19.09.98	Biko Botowamungo W RTD 3 Oberhausen, Germany
30.01.99	Julius Francis L RSC 3 Bethnal Green
	(British & Commonwealth Heavyweight Title Challenges)
26.06.99	Orlin Norris L RSC 1 Millwall
22.01.00	Jacklord Jacobs L RSC 2 Birmingham
04.10.01	Mal Rice W PTS 4 Finsbury
13.12.01	Derek McCafferty W RSC 3 Leicester Square
27.01.02	Luke Simpkin DREW 4 Streatham
09.05.02	Michael Sprott L RSC 7 Leicester Square
	(Vacant WBF European Heavyweight Title)
06.09.02	Derek McCafferty DREW 4 Bethnal Green
15.10.02	Joseph Chingangu W RSC 3 Bethnal Green
01.12.06	Paul King W RSC 6 Birmingham
17.03.07	Roman Suchoterin W PTS 6 Birmingham
01.06.07	Chris Woollas W CO 1 Birmingham

Career: 25 contests, won 19, drew 2, lost 4.

Robin Reid

Runcorn. Liverpool, 19 February, 1971
S.Middleweight. Former IBO S.Middleweight Champion. Former Undefeated WBF S.Middleweight Champion. Former WBC S.Middleweight Champion. *Ht* 5'9"
Manager Self

27.02.93	Mark Dawson W RSC 1 Dagenham
06.03.93	Julian Eavis W RSC 2 Glasgow
10.04.93	Andrew Furlong W PTS 6 Swansea
10.09.93	Juan Garcia W PTS 6 San Antonio, Texas, USA
09.10.93	Ernie Loveridge W PTS 4 Manchester
18.12.93	Danny Juma DREW 6 Manchester
09.04.94	Kesem Clayton W RSC 1 Mansfield
04.06.94	Andrew Furlong W RSC 2 Cardiff
17.08.94	Andrew Jervis W RSC 1 Sheffield
19.11.94	Chris Richards W RSC 3 Cardiff
04.02.95	Bruno Westenberghs W RSC 1 Cardiff
04.03.95	Marvin O'Brien W RSC 6 Livingston
06.05.95	Steve Goodwin W CO 1 Shepton Mallet
10.06.95	Martin Jolley W CO 1 Manchester
22.07.95	John Duckworth W PTS 8 Millwall
15.09.95	Trevor Ambrose W CO 5 Mansfield
10.11.95	Danny Juma W PTS 8 Derby
26.01.96	Stinger Mason W RSC 2 Brighton
16.03.96	Andrew Flute W RSC 7 Glasgow
26.04.96	Hunter Clay W RSC 1 Cardiff
08.06.96	Mark Dawson W RSC 5 Newcastle
31.08.96	Don Pendleton W RTD 4 Dublin
12.10.96	Vincenzo Nardiello W CO 7 Milan, Italy
	(WBC S. Middleweight Title Challenge)
08.02.97	Giovanni Pretorius W RSC 7 Millwall
	(WBC S. Middleweight Title Defence)
03.05.97	Henry Wharton W PTS 12 Manchester
	(WBC S. Middleweight Title Defence)
11.09.97	Hassine Cherifi W PTS 12 Widnes
	(WBC S. Middleweight Title Defence)
19.12.97	Thulani Malinga L PTS 12 Millwall
	(WBC S. Middleweight Title Defence)
18.04.98	Graham Townsend W RSC 6 Manchester
13.02.99	Joe Calzaghe L PTS 12 Newcastle
	(WBO S. Middleweight Title Challenge)
24.06.00	Silvio Branco L PTS 12 Glasgow
	(WBU S. Middleweight Title Challenge)
08.12.00	Mike Gormley W RSC 1 Crystal Palace
	(Vacant WBF S. Middleweight Title)
19.05.01	Roman Babaev W RSC 3 Wembley
	(WBF S. Middleweight Title Defence)
14.07.01	Soon Botes W RSC 4 Liverpool
	(WBF S.Middleweight TitleDefence)
20.10.01	Jorge Sclarandi W CO 3 Glasgow
	(WBF S. Middleweight Title Defence)
19.12.01	Julio Cesar Vasquez W PTS 12 Coventry
	(WBF S. Middleweight Title Defence)
10.07.02	Francisco Mora W PTS 12 Wembley
	(WBF S. Middleweight Title Defence)
29.11.02	Mondili Mbonambi W RSC 2 Liverpool
05.04.03	Enrique Carlos Campos W RSC 8 Leipzig, Germany
04.10.03	Willard Lewis W RSC 6 Zwickau, Germany
24.10.03	Dmitri Adamovich W CO 4 Bethnal Green
13.12.03	Sven Ottke L PTS 12 Nuremberg, Germany
	(WBA & IBF S.Middleweight Title Challenges)
26.06.04	Brian Magee W PTS 12 Belfast
	(IBO S.Middleweight Title Challenge)
13.02.05	Ramdane Serdjane W PTS 6 Brentwood
06.08.05	Jeff Lacy L RTD 8 Tampa, Florida, USA
	(IBF S.Middleweight Title Challenge. IBO S.Middleweight Title Defence)
30.03.07	Jesse Brinkley W PTS 8 Newcastle

Career: 45 contests, won 39, drew 1, lost 5.

(Marcello) Cello Renda

Peterborough. *Born* Peterborough, 4 June, 1985
Middleweight. *Ht* 5'11"
Manager I. Pauly

30.09.04	Mark Ellwood W RSC 2 Hull
04.11.04	Joey Vegas L RSC 3 Piccadilly
12.12.04	Scott Forsyth W RSC 1 Glasgow
21.02.05	Tom Cannon W PTS 6 Peterborough
11.03.05	Ricardo Samms L PTS 4 Doncaster
02.06.05	Michael Banbula DREW 6 Peterborough
16.10.05	Howard Clarke W PTS 4 Peterborough
12.12.05	Robert Burton W CO 1 Peterborough

10.02.06	Conroy McIntosh W RSC 1 Plymouth
30.03.06	Terry Adams W PTS 4 Peterborough
15.06.06	Gatis Skuja W PTS 4 Peterborough
23.06.06	Howard Clarke W PTS 8 Birmingham
08.09.06	Hamed Jamali W RSC 1 Birmingham
26.10.06	George Katsimpas L RSC 2 Wolverhampton
07.12.06	Hussain Osman W RSC 4 Peterborough
23.02.07	Vince Baldassara W CO 3 Birmingham
30.03.07	Ayitey Powers L RSC 2 Peterborough
29.06.07	Prince Arron L PTS 10 Manchester
	(Vacant British Masters Middleweight Title)

Career: 18 contests, won 12, drew 1, lost 5.

Danny Reynolds

Leeds. *Born* Leeds, 12 May, 1978
Middleweight. *Ht* 5'8"
Manager M. Bateson

08.11.05	Karl Taylor W RSC 4 Leeds
28.02.06	Gary Coombes W CO 1 Leeds
20.03.06	Geraint Harvey W RTD 2 Leeds
09.05.06	Darren Gethin DREW 4 Leeds
28.05.06	Terry Adams W RSC 1 Wakefield
03.12.06	Prince Arron W PTS 6 Wakefield
22.02.07	Anthony Young W RSC 4 Leeds
06.05.07	Ben Hudson W PTS 8 Leeds
14.06.07	Surinder Sekhon W PTS 6 Leeds

Career: 9 contests, won 8, drew 1.

Darren Rhodes

Leeds. *Born* Leeds, 16 September, 1975
S.Middleweight. *Ht* 5'11"
Manager Self

18.07.98	Andy Kemp W RSC 1 Sheffield
10.10.98	Perry Ayres W CO 2 Bethnal Green
27.02.99	Gareth Lovell W PTS 4 Oldham
01.05.99	Carlton Williams W RSC 4 Crystal Palace
29.05.99	Sean Pritchard DREW 4 Halifax
09.10.99	Leigh Wicks W PTS 4 Manchester
11.12.99	Leigh Wicks W PTS 4 Liverpool
25.03.00	Leigh Wicks W PTS 4 Liverpool
29.05.00	Dean Ashton W RSC 3 Manchester
08.07.00	Jason Collins DREW 4 Widnes
04.09.00	Jason Collins L PTS 4 Manchester
11.12.00	Paul Wesley W PTS 4 Widnes
17.03.01	Andrew Facey W PTS 4 Manchester
07.07.01	Wayne Elcock L PTS 4 Manchester
24.11.01	Simeon Cover W RSC 5 Wakefield
02.03.02	Andrew Facey L RSC 4 Wakefield
	(Vacant Central Area Middleweight Title)
21.05.02	Hussain Osman L PTS 10 Custom House
15.06.02	Harry Butler W PTS 4 Leeds
28.09.02	Martin Thompson W PTS 8 Wakefield
09.11.02	Wayne Pinder L RSC 4 Altrincham
12.04.03	Mihaly Kotai L PTS 10 Bethnal Green
10.05.03	Lee Murtagh W PTS 6 Huddersfield
05.07.03	Darren Bruce W RSC 3 Brentwood
06.09.03	Scott Dixon DREW 6 Huddersfield
04.12.03	Steve Roberts W CO 6 Huddersfield
10.04.04	Michael Jones L RSC 3 Manchester
	(Final Elim. British L.Middleweight Title)
12.11.04	Thomas McDonagh L PTS 10 Halifax
	(Elim. British L.Middleweight Title)
07.04.05	Wayne Elcock L CO 1 Birmingham
25.09.05	Howard Clarke W PTS 6 Leeds
13.11.05	Ernie Smith W PTS 6 Leeds
23.02.06	Peter Dunn W PTS 6 Leeds

09.09.06	Jozsef Nagy L PTS 12 Szentes, Hungary
	(Vacant IBF Inter-Continental S.Middleweight Title)
03.12.06	Robert Burton W PTS 6 Wakefield
15.02.07	Darren McDermott L RSC 5 Dudley
	(Elim.British Middleweight Title)
25.03.07	Jason McKay L PTS 6 Dublin
06.05.07	Dean Walker W PTS 4 Leeds

Career: 36 contests, won 21, drew 3, lost 12.

Ryan Rhodes

Sheffield. *Born* Sheffield, 20 November, 1976
Middleweight. Former Undefeated WBO Inter-Continental Middleweight Champion. Former Undefeated British & IBF Inter-Continental L.Middleweight Champion. *Ht* 5'8½"
Manager F. Warren/D. Coldwell

04.02.95	Lee Crocker W RSC 2 Cardiff
04.03.95	Shamus Casey W CO 1 Livingston
06.05.95	Chris Richards W PTS 6 Shepton Mallet
15.09.95	John Rice W RSC 2 Mansfield
10.11.95	Mark Dawson W PTS 6 Derby
20.01.96	John Duckworth W RSC 2 Mansfield
26.01.96	Martin Jolley W CO 3 Brighton
11.05.96	Martin Jolley W RSC 2 Bethnal Green
25.06.96	Roy Chipperfield W RSC 1 Mansfield
14.09.96	Del Bryan W PTS 6 Sheffield
14.12.96	Paul Jones W RSC 8 Sheffield
	(Vacant British L. Middleweight Title)
25.02.97	Peter Waudby W CO 1 Sheffield
	(British L. Middleweight Title Defence)
14.03.97	Del Bryan W RSC 7 Reading
	(British L. Middleweight Title Defence)
12.04.97	Lindon Scarlett W RSC 1 Sheffield
	(Vacant IBF Inter-Continental L. Middleweight Title)
02.08.97	Ed Griffin W RSC 2 Barnsley
	(IBF Inter-Continental L. Middleweight Title Defence. Vacant WBO L. Middleweight Title)
11.10.97	Yuri Epifantsev W RSC 2 Sheffield
	(Final Elim. WBO Middleweight Title)
13.12.97	Otis Grant L PTS 12 Sheffield
	(Vacant WBO Middleweight Title)
18.07.98	Lorant Szabo W RSC 8 Sheffield
	(WBO Inter-Continental Middleweight Title Challenge)
28.11.98	Fidel Avendano W RSC 1 Sheffield
	(WBO Inter-Continental Middleweight Title Defence)
27.03.99	Peter Mason W RSC 1 Derby
17.07.99	Jason Matthews L CO 2 Doncaster
	(Vacant WBO Middleweight Title)
15.01.00	Eddie Haley W RSC 5 Doncaster
16.05.00	Ojay Abrahams W PTS 6 Warrington
21.10.00	Michael Alexander W PTS 6 Wembley
16.12.00	Howard Clarke W PTS 6 Sheffield
21.07.01	Youri Tsarenko W PTS 6 Sheffield
27.10.01	Jason Collins W PTS 4 Manchester
16.03.02	Lee Blundell L RSC 3 Bethnal Green
	(Vacant WBF Inter-Continental Middleweight Title)
16.04.03	Paul Wesley W CO 3 Nottingham
25.07.03	Alan Gilbert W RSC 5 Norwich
11.12.03	Peter Jackson W PTS 6 Bethnal Green
12.03.04	Scott Dixon W PTS 8 Nottingham
16.04.04	Tomas da Silva W RSC 4 Bradford
22.04.05	Peter Jackson W PTS 6 Barnsley
03.06.05	Craig Lynch W RSC 3 Manchester

16.07.05	Alan Gilbert W RSC 2 Bolton
25.10.05	Hussain Osman W RTD 4 Preston
01.06.06	Jevgenijs Andrejevs W PTS 8 Barnsley
08.07.06	Gary Lockett L PTS 12 Cardiff
	(WBU Middleweight Title Challenge)
03.06.07	Paul Buchanan W RSC 1 Barnsley

Career: 40 contests, won 36, lost 4.

Rhys Roberts

Manchester. *Born* Manchester, 3 June, 1989
S.Bantamweight. *Ht* 5'6"
Manager Brian Hughes/W. Dixon

30.06.07	Delroy Spencer W PTS 6 Manchester

Career: 1 contest, won 1.

Dale Robinson

Huddersfield. *Born* Huddersfield, 9 April, 1980
Flyweight. Former Undefeated Commonwealth Flyweight Champion. Former Undefeated Central Area Flyweight Champion. *Ht* 5'4"
Manager Self

25.09.00	John Barnes W PTS 4 Barnsley
28.10.00	Delroy Spencer W RSC 4 Coventry
02.12.00	Colin Moffett W PTS 4 Bethnal Green
26.02.01	Christophe Rodrigues W PTS 6 Nottingham
07.04.01	Andrei Kostin W PTS 6 Wembley
08.05.01	Terry Gaskin W RTD 3 Barnsley
	(Central Area Flyweight Title Challenge)
27.04.02	Jason Thomas W RSC 4 Huddersfield
18.05.02	Sergei Tasimov W RSC 3 Millwall
15.06.02	Kakhar Sabitov W PTS 6 Leeds
05.10.02	Alain Bonnel W PTS 8 Huddersfield
30.11.02	Marc Dummett W RSC 3 Liverpool
22.02.03	Spencer Matsangura W PTS 12 Huddersfield
	(Vacant Commonwealth Flyweight Title)
10.05.03	Zolile Mbityi W PTS 12 Huddersfield
	(Commonwealth Flyweight Title Defence)
09.10.03	Emil Stoica W RSC 3 Bristol
04.12.03	Pavel Kubasov W CO 4 Huddersfield
13.03.04	Jason Booth L PTS 12 Huddersfield
	(IBO S.Flyweight Title Challenge)
27.05.04	Moses Kinyau W PTS 6 Huddersfield
17.12.04	Lahcene Zemmouri W RSC 8 Huddersfield
20.05.05	Martin Power L PTS 12 Southwark
	(Vacant British Bantamweight Title)
28.10.05	Moses Kinyua DREW 6 Hartlepool
04.03.06	Delroy Spencer W RSC 3 Manchester
01.06.06	Moses Kinyua W PTS 6 Barnsley
24.11.06	Chris Edwards L RSC 8 Stoke
	(Vacant English Flyweight Title)
13.04.07	Chris Edwards DREW 12 Altrincham
	(Vacant British & Commonwealth Flyweight Titles)

Career: 24 contests, won 19, drew 2, lost 3.

Jim Rock

Dublin. *Born* Dublin, 12 March, 1972
All-Ireland S.Middleweight & Middleweight Champion. IBC Middleweight Champion. Former Undefeated All-Ireland L.Middleweight Champion. Former Undefeated WAA Inter-

Continental S.Middleweight Champion.
Former Undefeated WBF European
L.Middleweight Champion. *Ht* 5'11"
Manager M. O'Callaghan

25.11.95	Craig Lynch W PTS 4 Dublin
09.03.96	Peter Mitchell W PTS 6 Millstreet
03.09.96	Rob Stevenson W PTS 6 Belfast
05.11.96	Danny Quacoe W RSC 4 Belfast
28.01.97	Roy Chipperfield W RTD 2 Belfast
12.04.97	George Richards W PTS 6 Sheffield
13.09.97	Robert Njie W CO 3 Millwall
18.04.98	Ensley Bingham L RSC 7 Manchester
19.09.98	Michael Monaghan W PTS 12 Dublin
	(Vacant WAA Inter-Continental
	S. Middleweight Title)
14.12.98	Perry Ayres W RTD 3 Cleethorpes
22.01.99	Jimmy Vincent W PTS 10 Dublin
20.02.99	Pedro Carragher W RSC 3 Thornaby
	(Vacant WBF European
	L. Middleweight Title)
17.04.99	Michael Alexander W RSC 1 Dublin
	(Vacant All-Ireland S. Middleweight
	Title)
19.06.99	Kevin Thompson W PTS 4 Dublin
15.04.00	Allan Gray W PTS 10 Bethnal Green
	(Vacant All-Ireland L. Middleweight
	Title)
12.06.00	Alan Gilbert W PTS 6 Belfast
20.10.00	Brooke Welby W RSC 3 Belfast
11.11.00	David Baptiste W PTS 4 Belfast
08.12.00	Tommy Attardo W PTS 8 Worcester, Mass, USA
24.03.01	Hollister Elliott W CO 6 Worcester, Mass, USA
20.04.01	Jason Collins W PTS 6 Dublin
01.12.01	Ian Cooper L PTS 6 Bethnal Green
24.04.02	Harry Butler W PTS 6 Dublin
01.02.03	Takaloo L RSC 9 Belfast
	(Vacant WBU L. Middleweight Title)
30.10.03	Alan Jones L PTS 8 Belfast
24.09.04	Matt Galer W PTS 6 Dublin
28.10.04	Sylvestre Marianini W PTS 6 Belfast
19.02.05	Peter Jackson W CO 7 Dublin
	(All-Ireland S.Middleweight Title
	Defence)
18.03.05	Michael Monaghan W PTS 8 Belfast
14.10.05	Alan Jones W PTS 12 Dublin
	(Vacant IBC Middleweight Title)
03.06.06	Kevin Phelan W RTD 7 Dublin
	(Vacant All-Ireland Middleweight Title)
25.03.07	Szabolcs Rimovszky W RSC 2 Dublin

Career: 32 contests, won 28, lost 4.

Martin Rogan

Belfast. *Born* Belfast, 1 May, 1971
Heavyweight. *Ht* 6'3"
Manager J. Breen/F. Warren

28.10.04	Lee Mountford W RSC 1 Belfast
18.03.05	Billy Bessey W PTS 4 Belfast
04.06.05	Tony Booth W RSC 2 Manchester
20.05.06	Darren Morgan W PTS 4 Belfast
07.10.06	Paul King W PTS 6 Belfast
26.10.06	Jevgenijs Stamburskis W RSC 3 Belfast

Career: 6 contests, won 6.

Brian Rose

Blackpool. *Born* Birmingham, 2 February, 1985
Middleweight. *Ht* 6'0"
Manager D. Powell

14.12.05	Geraint Harvey W PTS 6 Blackpool
25.02.07	Ernie Smith W PTS 6 Manchester
06.05.07	David Kirk W PTS 6 Altrincham
31.05.07	Tony Randell W PTS 6 Manchester
24.06.07	Justin Barnes W RSC 2 Wigan

Career: 5 contests, won 5.

Ryan Rowlinson

Rotherham. *Born* Mexborough, 4 June, 1979
S.Middleweight. *Ht* 6'0"
Manager Self

15.12.05	Dave Pearson W PTS 6 Cleethorpes
18.02.06	Craig Lynch DREW 4 Edinburgh
01.06.06	Robert Burton LPTS 4 Barnsley
18.06.06	Craig Bunn L PTS 6 Manchester
08.07.06	Kerry Hope L PTS 4 Cardiff
01.10.06	Ernie Smith W PTS 6 Rotherham
09.10.06	Kevin Concepcion L PTS 6 Bedworth
06.12.06	Tony Randell DREW 6 Rotherham
16.06.07	Nigel Travis L PTS 6 Bolton

Career: 9 contests, won 2, drew 2, lost 5.

Paul Royston

Sheffield. *Born* Rotherham, 16 January, 1985
L.Middleweight. *Ht* 5'10"
Manager D. Coldwell

24.02.07	Stuart Jeffrey L PTS 6 Manchester
26.03.07	Jon Musgrave L PTS 6 Glasgow
15.04.07	Thomas Flynn W RSC 3 Barnsley
06.05.07	Johnny Enigma L PTS 6 Altrincham
03.06.07	Steve Cooper L PTS 6 Barnsley
30.06.07	Willie Thompson L PTS 4 Belfast

Career: 6 contests, won 1, lost 5.

Sergei Rozhakmens

Sutton in Ashfield. *Born* Riga, Latvia, 6 May, 1979
Lightweight. *Ht* 5'7"
Manager M. Scriven

13.11.02	Sergei Lazarenko W RSC 1 Tallin, Estonia
22.02.03	Leonti Voronchuk L RSC 3 Narva, Estonia
20.02.06	Jimmy Gilhaney L PTS 6 Glasgow
06.05.06	Jamie McIlroy L PTS 6 Irvine
18.06.06	Abdul Rashid L PTS 6 Manchester
15.09.06	Andy Davis L RSC 4 Newport
10.11.06	Shaun Walton L PTS 6 Telford
20.11.06	Brian Murphy L PTS 6 Glasgow
30.11.06	Neil Marston L PTS 6 Piccadilly
01.02.07	Kim Poulsen L RSC 5 Piccadilly
01.04.07	Shaun Walton DREW 6 Shrewsbury
14.04.07	Sean Hughes L PTS 6 Wakefield
29.04.07	Craig Johnson L PTS 6 Birmingham
06.05.07	Davey Watson L PTS 6 Darlington
01.06.07	Sid Razak W PTS 6 Birmingham
09.06.07	James McElvaney L PTS 6 Middlesbrough
21.06.07	Carl Griffiths L PTS 6 Peterborough
30.06.07	Amir Unsworth L PTS 6 Manchester

Career: 18 contests, won 2, drew 1, lost 15.

Sam Rukundo

Tottenham. *Born* Kampala Uganda, 18 May, 1980
L.Welterweight. Former Undefeated British Masters Lightweight Champion. *Ht* 5'7¼"

Manager M. Helliet

04.11.04	Henry Janes W PTS 6 Piccadilly
27.01.05	Chris Long W PTS 4 Piccadilly
23.03.05	Billy Smith W RSC 3 Leicester Square
26.05.05	John-Paul Ryan W RSC 4 Mayfair
14.10.05	Bela Sandor W PTS 6 Struer, Denmark
17.11.05	Haroon Din W RSC 3 Piccadilly
02.02.06	Silence Saheed W PTS 10 Holborn
	(Vacant British Masters Lightweight Title)
08.09.06	Gheorghe Ghiompirica W CO 2 Vejle, Denmark
01.02.07	Stuart Green W PTS 6 Piccadilly
31.03.07	Robert Osiobe DREW 4 Gothenburg, Sweden

Career: 10 contests, won 9, drew 1.

Jason Rushton

Doncaster. *Born* Doncaster, 15 February, 1983
Central Area L.Middleweight Champion. *Ht* 5'10"
Manager J. Rushton/F. Warren

27.10.01	Ram Singh W PTS 6 Manchester
09.02.02	Brian Gifford W RSC 1 Manchester
01.06.02	Tony Smith W PTS 4 Manchester
08.11.02	Gary Hadwin W CO 4 Doncaster
21.02.03	Wayne Shepherd W PTS 6 Doncaster
05.09.03	Harry Butler W PTS 4 Doncaster
27.09.03	Jimi Hendricks W PTS 4 Manchester
06.03.04	Peter Dunn W PTS 6 Renfrew
06.05.04	Peter Dunn W PTS 4 Barnsley
03.09.04	Ernie Smith W PTS 4 Doncaster
29.10.04	Brian Coleman W PTS 6 Doncaster
04.02.05	Howard Clarke W PTS 4 Doncaster
11.03.05	Lee Armstrong W PTS 10 Doncaster
	(Vacant Central Area L.Middleweight Title)
20.05.05	Lee Murtagh L PTS 10 Doncaster
	(Central Area L.Middleweight Title Defence)
02.12.05	Joe Mitchell W PTS 6 Doncaster
03.03.06	Darren Gethin L PTS 6 Doncaster
21.04.06	Peter Dunn W PTS 6 Doncaster
09.06.06	Mark Phillips W PTS 6 Doncaster
13.10.06	Lee Noble L PTS 6 Doncaster
23.02.07	Davey Jones W CO 7 Doncaster
	(Vacant Central Area L.Middleweight Title)

Career: 20 contests, won 17, lost 3.

Stephen Russell

Paisley. *Born* Paisley, 29 December, 1987
Featherweight. *Ht* 5'6"
Manager Barry Hughes

27.10.06	Shaun Doherty W PTS 6 Glasgow
26.01.07	Abdul Mougharbel W PTS 6 Glasgow
05.05.07	Delroy Spencer W PTS 4 Glasgow

Career: 3 contests, won 3.

Dave Ryan

Derby. *Born* Derby, 6 May, 1988
Welterweight. *Ht* 5'10"
Manager C. Mitchell

31.03.07	Deniss Sirjatovs W PTS 6 Derby
19.05.07	Leonard Lothian W PTS 6 Nottingham

Career: 2 contests, won 2.

Dave Sadler

Leeds. *Born* Leeds, 14 December, 1980
S.Middleweight. *Ht* 5'11"
Manager M. Marsden

06.05.07   Jeff Hamilton L PTS 6 Leeds
Career: 1 contest, lost 1.

(Saheed) Silence Saheed (Salawu)

Canning Town. *Born* Ibadan, Nigeria, 1
January, 1978
L.Welterweight. *Ht* 5'6"
Manager D. Lutaaya

28.03.03   Martin Hardcastle W PTS 4 Millwall
10.04.03   Ceri Hall DREW 4 Clydach
27.05.03   Francis Barrett W RSC 1 Dagenham
11.10.03   Wayne Wheeler W RSC 1 Portsmouth
15.11.03   Gary Greenwood W RTD 1 Coventry
21.11.03   Jaz Virdee W RSC 2 Millwall
01.05.04   Alan Temple L DIS 8 Gravesend
          *(Vacant British Masters Lightweight
          Title)*
17.09.04   Scott Lawton L PTS 6 Sheffield
24.09.04   James Gorman W PTS 6 Millwall
09.10.04   Jonathan Thaxton L PTS 6 Norwich
22.10.04   Nigel Wright L PTS 8 Edinburgh
10.04.05   Lenny Daws L PTS 6 Brentwood
01.07.05   Gareth Couch L PTS 4 Fulham
30.09.05   Karl David W PTS 6 Carmarthen
21.10.05   Ted Bami L PTS 6 Bethnal Green
17.11.05   Andrew Murray L PTS 4 Piccadilly
24.11.05   Ceri Hall L PTS 6 Clydach
02.02.06   Sam Rukundo L PTS 10 Holborn
          *(Vacant British Masters Lightweight
          Title)*
18.02.06   Lee McAllister L PTS 4 Edinburgh
04.03.06   David Barnes L PTS 4 Manchester
23.03.06   Imad Khamis W RSC 5 The Strand
02.04.06   Leo O'Reilly DREW 6 Bethnal Green
10.07.06   Gary O'Connor L PTS 6 Manchester
15.09.06   John O'Donnell L PTS 6 Muswell Hill
11.11.06   Stephen Haughian L PTS 6 Dublin
01.12.06   Anthony Maynard L PTS 6 Birmingham
09.12.06   Paul McCloskey L PTS 4 Canning Town
23.02.07   Olufemi Moses L PTS 4 Manchester
30.03.07   Michael Lomax DREW 6 Crawley
Career: 29 contests, won 8, drew 3, lost 18.

Tony Salam   Les Clark

Tony Salam

Romford. *Born* Nigeria, 24 September, 1983
L.Heavyweight. *Ht* 6'0"
Manager J. Oyebola

03.11.06   Csaba Andras W RSC 2 Barnsley
26.01.07   Paul David W PTS 4 Dagenham
09.03.07   Nicki Taylor W RSC 1 Dagenham
27.04.07   John Anthony W PTS 4 Wembley
15.06.07   Nick Okoth W PTS 4 Crystal Palace
Career: 5 contests, won 5.

Manoocha Salari

Worksop. *Born* Iran, 25 May, 1974
Midlands Area L.Middleweight Champion.
Ht 5'9½"
Manager J. Ingle

12.11.05   Danny Johnston W RSC 5 Stoke
25.11.05   Paul McInnes W PTS 6 Walsall
12.12.05   Simon Sherrington DREW 6
          Birmingham
28.01.06   Martin Concepcion W RSC 2
          Nottingham
26.02.06   Gokhan Kazaz DREW 4 Dagenham
13.05.06   Geard Ajetovic L RSC 4 Sheffield
18.11.06   Kerry Hope L RSC 2 Newport
03.03.07   Matt Galer W RSC 8 Burton
          *(Midlands Area L.Middleweight Title
          Challenge)*
13.04.07   Mark Thompson L RSC 1 Altrincham
Career: 9 contests, won 4, drew 2, lost 3.

Ricardo Samms

Nottingham. *Born* Nottingham, 2 June,
1982
L.Heavyweight. *Ht* 6'1"
Manager J. Ingle

11.03.05   Cello Renda W PTS 4 Doncaster
04.06.05   Ojay Abrahams W PTS 4 Manchester
25.10.05   Ojay Abrahams W PTS 4 Preston
24.11.06   Robert Burton W PTS 4 Nottingham
Career: 4 contests, won 4.

Ricardo Samms   Les Clark

Paul Samuels

Newport. *Born* Newport, 23 March, 1973
S.Middleweight. Former Undefeated IBF
Inter-Continental & Welsh L.Middleweight
Champion. *Ht* 6'0"
Manager Self

11.11.95   Wayne Windle W RSC 2 Halifax
13.02.96   Jon Harrison W CO 1 Cardiff
05.03.96   Tom Welsh W RSC 3 Bethnal Green
13.03.96   Brian Coleman W PTS 6 Wembley
15.05.96   Gary Hiscox W RSC 3 Cardiff
12.11.96   Mark Ramsey W RSC 4 Dudley
21.06.97   Howard Clarke W PTS 8 Cariddf
15.11.97   Justin Simmons W CO 1 Bristol
24.01.98   Prince Kasi Kaihau W CO 3 Cardiff
25.04.98   Del Bryan W PTS 8 Cardiff
05.09.98   Spencer McCracken W PTS 8 Telford
05.12.98   Craig Winter W CO 2 Bristol
          (Vacant Welsh L. Middleweight Title)
27.03.99   Pedro Carragher W RSC 2 Derby
05.06.99   Eric Holland W RSC 9 Cardiff
          *(Vacant IBF Inter-Continental
          L. Middleweight Title)*
23.10.99   Ojay Abrahams W PTS 8 Telford
19.02.00   Wayne Alexander L RSC 3 Dagenham
          (Vacant British L. Middleweight Title)
23.01.01   Rob Dellapenna DREW 4 Crawley
27.01.02   Howard Clarke W PTS 4 Streatham
29.06.02   Richard Williams T DRAW 3
          Brentwood
          (IBO L. Middleweight Title Challenge)
07.12.02   Richard Williams L RSC 10 Brentwood
          (IBO L. Middleweight Title Challenge)
25.01.03   Howard Clarke W PTS 6 Bridgend
08.12.06   Darren Barker L RSC 1 Dagenham
Career: 22 contests, won 17, drew 2, lost 3.

Chris Saunders

Barnsley. *Born* Barnsley, 15 August, 1969
Welterweight. Former British & English
Welterweight Champion. *Ht* 5'8"
Manager Self

22.02.90   Malcolm Melvin W PTS 4 Hull
10.04.90   Mike Morrison W PTS 6 Doncaster
20.05.90   Justin Graham W RSC 3 Sheffield
29.11.90   Ross Hale L PTS 6 Bayswater
05.03.91   Rocky Ferrari W PTS 4 Glasgow
19.03.91   Richard Woolgar W RSC 3 Leicester
26.03.91   Felix Kelly L PTS 6 Bethnal Green
17.04.91   Billy Schwer L RSC 1 Kensington
16.05.91   Richard Burton L PTS 6 Liverpool
06.06.91   Mark Tibbs W RSC 6 Barking
30.06.91   Billy Schwer L RSC 3 Southwark
01.08.91   James Jiora W PTS 6 Dewsbury
03.10.91   Gary Flear L PTS 6 Burton
24.10.91   Ron Shinkwin W PTS 6 Dunstable
21.11.91   J. P. Matthews L RSC 4 Burton
30.01.92   John O. Johnson L PTS 6 Southampton
11.02.92   Eddie King W RSC 4 Wolverhampton
27.02.92   Richard Burton L PTS 10 Liverpool
          *(Vacant Central Area L. Welterweight
          Title)*
09.09.92   John O. Johnson DREW 6 Stoke
01.10.92   Mark McCreath L RSC 4 Telford
01.12.92   Shea Neary L PTS 6 Liverpool
22.02.93   Cham Joof L PTS 4 Eltham
16.03.93   Mark Elliot L PTS 6 Wolverhampton
26.04.93   Dean Hollington W RSC 5 Lewisham
23.10.93   Michael Smyth L PTS 6 Cardiff
02.12.93   Rob Stewart L PTS 4 Sheffield
03.03.94   Kevin Lueshing W RSC 4 Ebbw Vale
04.06.94   Jose Varela W CO 2 Dortmund,
          Germany
26.08.94   Julian Eavis W PTS 6 Barnsley
26.09.94   Julian Eavis W PTS 6 Cleethorpes
26.10.94   Lindon Scarlett W PTS 8 Leeds
17.12.94   Roberto Welin W RSC 7 Cagliari, Italy
15.09.95   Del Bryan W PTS 12 Mansfield
          (British Welterweight Title Challenge)

13.02.96 Kevin Lueshing L RSC 3 Bethnal Green
(British Welterweight Title Defence)
25.06.96 Michael Carruth L RSC 10 Mansfield
09.06.97 Derek Roche L RSC 4 Bradford
(Central Area Welterweight Title Challenge. Elim. British Welterweight Title)
27.02.98 Scott Dixon L PTS 10 Glasgow
(Elim. British Welterweight Title)
17.04.99 Michael Carruth L RSC 5 Dublin
08.12.01 David Kirk W CO 2 Chesterfield
15.06.02 Arv Mittoo W PTS 6 Norwich
24.09.02 Robert Pacuraru W RTD 4 Gran Canaria, Spain
09.02.03 Richard Swallow W PTS 4 Bradford
03.04.04 Marcus Portman W RSC 1 Sheffield
(Vacant English Welterweight Title)
19.06.04 Peter Dunn W PTS 4 Muswell Hill
01.10.04 Michael Jennings L RTD 5 Manchester
(English Welterweight Title Defence)
15.04.07 Tye Williams W PTS 6 Barnsley
Career: 46 contests, won 23, drew 1, lost 22.

Tommy Saunders
Hatfield. *Born* Hatfield, 17 February, 1987
Cruiserweight. *Ht* 5'11¼"
Manager J. Eames/F. Warren
28.10.06 Varuzhan Davtyan W PTS 4 Bethnal Green
17.02.07 Gary Thompson W PTS 4 Wembley
Career: 2 contests, won 2.

Tommy Saunders   Les Clark

Lindsay Scragg
Wolverhampton. *Born* Wolverhampton, 19 April, 1979
S.Featherweight. *Ht.* 5'3¼"
Manager E. Johnson
15.02.07 Valerie Rangeard W RSC 2 Dudley
28.06.07 Yarkor Chavez Annan W PTS 4 Dudley
Career: 2 contests, won 2.

Matt Scriven
Nottingham. *Born* Nottingham, 1 September, 1973
Middleweight. Former Undefeated Midlands Area L.Middleweight Champion. Former British Masters L.Middleweight Champion. *Ht* 5'10"

Manager Self
26.11.97 Shamus Casey W PTS 6 Stoke
08.12.97 Shane Thomas W PTS 6 Bradford
20.03.98 C. J. Jackson L PTS 6 Ilkeston
15.05.98 Lee Bird W RSC 5 Nottingham
08.10.98 Stevie McCready L RTD 3 Sunderland
01.04.99 Adrian Houldey W PTS 6 Birmingham
25.04.99 Danny Thornton L RSC 4 Leeds
27.06.99 Shane Junior L RSC 2 Alfreton
11.09.99 David Arundel L RTD 1 Sheffield
20.03.00 James Docherty L PTS 6 Glasgow
27.03.00 Matt Mowatt L PTS 4 Barnsley
09.04.00 David Matthews W PTS 6 Alfreton
06.06.00 Jackie Townsley L RSC 3 Motherwell
04.11.00 Brett James L RTD 1 Bethnal Green
04.02.01 Mark Paxford L PTS 6 Queensferry
26.02.01 Pedro Thompson W RTD 1 Nottingham
12.03.01 Ernie Smith W PTS 6 Birmingham
20.03.01 James Docherty L RSC 1 Glasgow
21.05.01 Christian Brady L RSC 5 Birmingham
(Vacant Midlands Area Welterweight Title)
21.10.01 Neil Bonner NC 1 Glasgow
04.03.02 Danny Parkinson L PTS 6 Bradford
22.04.02 Gary Porter L PTS 6 Glasgow
28.05.02 Peter Dunn W PTS 8 Leeds
14.09.02 Ernie Smith W PTS 6 Newark
29.09.02 James Lee L RTD 4 Shrewsbury
30.11.02 Davey Jones L PTS 6 Newark
16.03.03 Lee Williamson W PTS 10 Nottingham
(Vacant Midlands Area & British Masters L. Middleweight Titles)
08.06.03 Wayne Shepherd W PTS 10 Nottingham
(British Masters L.Middleweight Title Defence)
15.09.03 Lee Murtagh L DIS 9 Leeds
(British Masters L.Middleweight Title Defence)
12.03.04 David Walker L RSC 3 Nottingham
12.06.04 Matthew Hatton L RSC 4 Manchester
18.09.04 Robert Lloyd-Taylor L RTD 4 Newark
28.01.05 Colin McNeil L PTS 4 Renfrew
06.03.05 Mark Wall W PTS 4 Mansfield
29.04.05 Gary Woolcombe L RSC 4 Southwark
04.06.05 Matthew Hall L RSC 2 Manchester
20.01.06 John O'Donnell L RSC 4 Bethnal Green
04.03.06 Kerry Hope L PTS 4 Manchester
04.11.06 Peter Dunn W PTS 6 Mansfield
23.02.07 James McKinley L PTS 6 Birmingham
17.03.07 Dee Mitchell L RSC 2 Birmingham
29.04.07 Max Maxwell L PTS 4 Birmingham
11.05.07 Shaun Farmer L PTS 6 Sunderland
18.05.07 George Hillyard L PTS 4 Canning Town
31.05.07 Dave Wakefield L PTS 6 Manchester
24.06.07 Martin Marshall L PTS 6 Sunderland
Career: 46 contests, won 13, lost 32, no contest 1.

Matt Seawright
Tamworth. *Born* Bathgate, 8 February, 1978
Welterweight. *Ht* 5'7"
Manager N. Nobbs
03.03.07 Jack Perry L RSC 2 Burton
03.05.07 Adam Kelly L PTS 4 Sheffield
Career: 2 contests, lost 2.

Surinder Sekhon
Barnsley. *Born* Birmingham, 4 October, 1979
L.Middleweight. *Ht* 5'9"
Manager T. Schofield/D. Coldwell

05.05.02 Franny Jones L PTS 6 Hartlepool
28.09.02 Peter Dunn W PTS 6 Wakefield
27.02.03 Ryan Kerr L PTS 6 Sunderland
09.03.03 P.J.Maxwell L RSC 1 Shaw
09.09.05 Grzegorz Proksa L PTS 4 Sheffield
30.09.05 Young Muttley L PTS 4 Burton
14.10.05 Paul Burns L PTS 6 Motherwell
12.11.05 Jimmy Doherty L PTS 6 Stoke
11.12.05 Ben Hudson L PTS 6 Chigwell
18.02.06 Scott Lawton DREW 8 Stoke
11.03.06 Paul McCloskey L RSC 1 Newport
14.05.06 Scott Haywood L RSC 1 Derby
03.11.06 Mark Hastie L RSC 1 Glasgow
31.03.07 Luke Gallear W PTS 6 Derby
12.05.07 Aaron Thomas L PTS 4 Stoke
01.06.07 Danny Butler L PTS 6 Birmingham
14.06.07 Danny Reynolds L PTS 6 Leeds
Career: 17 contests, won 2, drew 1, lost 14.

Sam Sexton
Norwich. *Born* Norwich, 18 July, 1984
Heavyweight. *Ht* 6'2"
Manager G. Everett
03.09.05 Paul Bonson W PTS 6 Norwich
11.12.05 Jason Callum W PTS 6 Norwich
12.05.06 Istvan Kecskes W PTS 4 Bethnal Green
15.10.06 Lee Mountford W RSC 2 Norwich
16.03.07 Paul King W PTS 6 Norwich
Career: 5 contests, won 5.

Sam Sexton   Les Clark

Gary Sheil
Chester. *Born* Chester, 29 June, 1983
Bantamweight. *Ht* 5'2¾"
Manager Self
03.03.06 Jamie McDonnell L PTS 6 Doncaster
23.04.06 Delroy Spencer L PTS 6 Chester
06.05.06 Chris Edwards L PTS 6 Stoke
03.03.07 Usman Ahmed L PTS 6 Alfreton
21.04.07 Scott Quigg L PTS 6 Manchester
Career: 5 contests, lost 5.

Simon Sherrington
Birmingham. *Born* Birmingham, 14 July, 1971
L.Middleweight. *Ht* 5'9½"
Manager Self
09.10.00 Paddy Martin W RSC 5 Birmingham
28.11.00 Pedro Thompson W RSC 5 Brierley Hill
13.12.04 Jon Harrison W RSC 5 Birmingham
21.02.05 Lee Williamson DREW 6 Birmingham
16.05.05 Lee Williamson W PTS 8 Birmingham

10.10.05	Tony Randell W PTS 6 Birmingham
12.12.05	Manoocha Salari DREW 6 Birmingham
27.02.06	Adnan Amar L RSC 6 Birmingham
	(Vacant British Masters L.Middleweight Title)
22.05.06	Gatis Skuja DREW 8 Birmingham
16.09.06	Matt Galer L RSC 5 Burton
	(Midlands Area L.Middleweight Title Challenge)
11.12.06	Darren Gethin L PTS 10 Birmingham
	(Vacant British Masters L.Middleweight Title)

Career: 11 contests, won 5, drew 3, lost 3.

Nadeem Siddique

Bradford. *Born* Bradford, 28 October, 1977
Central Area & British Masters
Welterweight Champion. *Ht* 5'8"
Manager J. Ingle

17.11.02	Daniel Thorpe W PTS 4 Bradford
09.02.03	Norman Dhalie W PTS 4 Bradford
13.04.03	Dave Hinds W PTS 4 Bradford
15.06.03	Nigel Senior W PTS 6 Bradford
05.10.03	Jason Nesbitt W PTS 6 Bradford
27.10.03	Daniel Thorpe W PTS 6 Glasgow
07.12.03	Chris Duggan W RSC 2 Bradford
16.01.04	Pete Buckley W PTS 4 Bradford
16.04.04	Arv Mittoo W PTS 6 Bradford
15.05.04	Joel Viney W PTS 6 Aberdeen
24.09.04	Dave Hinds W PTS 4 Nottingham
13.02.05	Jason Nesbitt W PTS 6 Sheffield
09.04.05	Pete Buckley W PTS 6 Norwich
08.05.05	Kristian Laight W RSC 7 Bradford
03.06.05	Daniel Thorpe W PTS 6 Hull
13.11.05	Billy Smith W PTS 6 Leeds
25.11.05	Jason Nesbitt W RSC 6 Hull
13.04.06	David Kehoe W PTS 6 Leeds
27.05.07	Tye Williams W RSC 4 Bradford
	(Vacant Central Area & British Masters Welterweight Titles)

Career: 19 contests, won 19.

(Paulino) Paulie Silva

Droylsden. *Born* Almada, Portugal, 29
April, 1978
L. Heavyweight. *Ht* 5'10"
Manager Self

28.02.04	Nick Okoth W PTS 6 Manchester
02.04.04	Courtney Fry L PTS 4 Plymouth
24.10.04	Amer Khan L PTS 6 Sheffield
16.09.05	Dan Guthrie W RSC 2 Plymouth
21.04.07	Tony Booth W PTS 6 Manchester
30.06.07	Lee Jones W PTS 6 Manchester

Career: 6 contests, won 4, lost 2.

Luke Simpkin

Swadlincote. *Born* Derby, 5 May, 1979
Heavyweight. *Ht* 6'2"
Manager Self

24.09.98	Simon Taylor W CO 3 Edgbaston
16.10.98	Chris P. Bacon L PTS 6 Salford
10.12.98	Jason Flisher W RSC 5 Barking
04.02.99	Danny Watts L CO 3 Lewisham
28.05.99	Tommy Bannister W RSC 4 Liverpool
07.08.99	Owen Beck L PTS 4 Dagenham
11.09.99	Scott Lansdowne L PTS 4 Sheffield
11.03.00	Albert Sosnowski L PTS 4 Kensington
27.03.00	Mark Hobson L PTS 4 Barnsley
29.04.00	Johan Thorbjoernsson L PTS 4 Wembley

23.09.00	Mark Potter L PTS 6 Bethnal Green
30.09.00	Gordon Minors DREW 4 Peterborough
18.11.00	Keith Long L RSC 3 Dagenham
03.02.01	Paul Buttery W RSC 1 Manchester
01.04.01	Wayne Llewelyn L PTS 6 Southwark
24.04.01	Darren Chubbs L PTS 4 Liverpool
06.05.01	Billy Bessey L PTS 6 Hartlepool
09.06.01	John McDermott L PTS 6 Bethnal Green
13.09.01	Mark Krence L PTS 4 Sheffield
10.12.01	Mark Hobson L RTD 3 Liverpool
27,.01.02	Pele Reid DREW 4 Streatham
15.03.02	Mike Holden L PTS 6 Millwall
13.04.02	Fola Okesola W PTS 4 Liverpool
10.05.02	Julius Francis DREW 6 Millwall
23.08.02	Mark Potter L PTS 6 Bethnal Green
10.06.03	Mark Krence L RTD 8 Sheffield
	(Vacant Midlands Area Heavyweight Title)
05.09.03	Roman Greenberg L RTD 4 Sheffield
25.04.04	Dave Clarke W RSC 2 Nottingham
18.09.04	Paul King L PTS 6 Newark
02.12.04	Micky Steeds L RSC 3 Crystal Palace
21.02.05	Ian Millarvie L PTS 6 Glasgow
26.04.05	Carl Baker W RSC 4 Leeds
09.07.05	Henry Smith W RSC 3 Bristol
11.09.05	Carl Baker L PTS 10 Kirkby in Ashfield
	(British Masters Heavyweight Title Challenge)
28.01.06	Colin Kenna L PTS 8 Dublin
25.03.06	Istvan Kecskes W PTS 4 Burton
02.12.06	Micky Steeds L PTS 6 Southwark
03.03.07	Paul Butlin L PTS 4 Burton
15.06.07	John McDermott L RSC 2 Crystal Palace

Career: 39 contests, won 9, drew 3, lost 27.

John Simpson

Greenock. *Born* Greenock, 26 July, 1983
British Featherweight Champion. *Ht* 5'7"
Manager F. Warren/A. Morrison

23.09.02	Simon Chambers W RSC 1 Glasgow
06.10.02	Lee Holmes L PTS 6 Rhyl
07.12.02	Matthew Burke W PTS 4 Brentwood
20.01.03	John-Paul Ryan W PTS 6 Glasgow
17.02.03	Joel Viney W RTD 1 Glasgow
14.04.03	Simon Chambers W PTS 6 Glasgow
20.10.03	Steve Gethin W PTS 8 Glasgow
01.11.03	Mark Alexander W PTS 4 Glasgow
19.01.04	Henry Janes W PTS 8 Glasgow
31.01.04	Gennadiy Delisandru W PTS 4 Bethnal Green
22.04.04	Jus Wallie W PTS 6 Glasgow
02.06.04	Fred Janes W PTS 6 Hereford
20.09.04	Marc Callaghan W PTS 8 Glasgow
05.11.04	Dazzo Williams L PTS 12 Hereford
	(British Featherweight Title Challenge)
06.06.05	Dariusz Snarski W RSC 3 Glasgow
05.11.05	Andy Morris L PTS 12 Renfrew
	(Vacant British Featherweight Title)
01.04.06	Steve Foster L PTS 12 Bethnal Green
	(WBU Featherweight Title Challenge)
09.12.06	Andy Morris W RSC 5 Canning Town
	(British Featherweight Title Challenge)
10.03.07	Derry Matthews L PTS 12 Liverpool
	(WBU Featherweight Title Challenge)
08.06.07	Ryan Barrett W CO 5 Mayfair
	(British Featherweight Title Defence)

Career: 20 contests, won 15, lost 5.

Neil Sinclair

Belfast. *Born* Belfast, 23 February, 1974
L.Middleweight. Former Undefeated British
Welterweight Champion. *Ht* 5'10½"
Manager Self

14.04.95	Marty Duke W RSC 2 Belfast
27.05.95	Andrew Jervis L RSC 3 Belfast
17.07.95	Andy Peach W RSC 1 Mayfair
26.08.95	George Wilson W PTS 4 Belfast
07.10.95	Wayne Shepherd W PTS 6 Belfast
02.12.95	Brian Coleman W RTD 1 Belfast
13.04.96	Hughie Davey W PTS 6 Liverpool
28.05.96	Prince Kasi Kaihau W RSC 2 Belfast
03.09.96	Dennis Berry L PTS 6 Belfast
27.09.97	Trevor Meikle W RSC 5 Belfast
20.12.97	Chris Pollock W RTD 3 Belfast
21.02.98	Leigh Wicks L RSC 1 Belfast
19.09.98	Paul Denton W RSC 1 Dublin
07.12.98	Michael Smyth W CO 1 Acton
22.01.99	Mark Ramsey W CO 3 Dublin
05.06.99	David Kirk W PTS 8 Cardiff
16.10.99	Paul Dyer W RSC 8 Belfast
18.03.00	Dennis Berry W RSC 2 Glasgow
16.05.00	Paul Dyer W RSC 6 Warrington
24.06.00	Chris Henry W RSC 1 Glasgow
12.08.00	Adrian Chase W RSC 2 Wembley
16.12.00	Daniel Santos L CO 2 Sheffield
	(WBO Welterweight Title Challenge)
28.04.01	Zoltan Szilii W CO 2 Cardiff
22.09.01	Viktor Fesetchko W PTS 6 Bethnal Green
19.11.01	Harry Dhami W RSC 5 Glasgow
	(British Welterweight Title Challenge)
20.04.02	Leonti Voronchuk W RSC 4 Cardiff
15.06.02	Derek Roche W CO 1 Leeds
	(British Welterweight Title Defence)
17.08.02	Dmitri Kashkan W RSC 4 Cardiff
02.11.02	Paul Knights W RSC 2 Belfast
	(British Welterweight Title Defence)
01.02.03	Bradley Pryce W RSC 8 Belfast
	(British Welterweight Title Defence)
30.07.04	Craig Lynch W PTS 6 Bethnal Green
18.03.05	Taz Jones L RSC 1 Belfast
05.07.06	Jerome Ellis L CO 6 Colorado Springs, Colorado, USA
17.02.07	Arek Malek W RSC 4 Cork
23.06.07	Franny Jones L CO 5 Dublin

Career: 35 contests, won 29, lost 6.

Deniss Sirjatovs

Sutton in Ashfield. *Born* Riga, Latvia, 14
November, 1984
L.Welterweight. *Ht* 5'10¾"
Manager M. Scriven

06.05.06	George McIlroy L RSC 2 Irvine
16.09.06	Jack Perry L PTS 6 Burton
01.12.06	John Baguley L PTS 4 Doncaster
08.12.06	Lee Purdy L RSC 3 Dagenham
03.03.07	Gavin Deacon L PTS 4 Alfreton
17.03.07	Ben Murphy L PTS 4 Birmingham
31.03.07	Dave Ryan L PTS 6 Derby
15.04.07	Andrew Ward L PTS 6 Barnsley
29.04.07	Thomas Costello L RSC 1 Birmingham
01.06.07	Jamie Spence L RSC 3 Peterborough
30.06.07	Kevin Maxwell L PTS 4 Belfast

Career: 11 contests, lost 11.

Grant Skehill

Wanstead. *Born* London, 1 October, 1985
L.Middleweight. *Ht* 5'11¼"
Manager F. Warren

13.05.06 Chris Brophy W PTS 4 Bethnal Green
28.10.06 Ernie Smith W PTS 4 Bethnal Green
17.02.07 Duncan Cottier W PTS 4 Wembley
Career: 3 contests, won 3.

Matt Skelton

Bedford. *Born* Bedford, 23 January, 1968
Commonwealth Heavyweight Champion.
Former Undefeated British, WBU &
English Heavyweight Champion. *Ht* 6'3"
Manager Self

22.09.02 Gifford Shillingford W RSC 2
          Southwark
27.10.02 Slick Miller W CO 1 Southwark
08.12.02 Neil Kirkwood W RSC 1 Bethnal
          Green
18.02.03 Jacklord Jacobs W RSC 4 Bethnal
          Green
08.04.03 Alexei Varakin W CO 2 Bethnal Green
15.05.03 Dave Clarke W RSC 1 Mayfair
17.07.03 Antoine Palatis W RSC 4 Dagenham
18.09.03 Mike Holden W RSC 6 Dagenham
          (Vacant English Heavyweight Title)
11.10.03 Costi Marin W RSC 1 Portsmouth
25.10.03 Ratko Draskovic W RSC 3 Edinburgh
15.11.03 Patriche Costel W CO 1 Bayreuth,
          Germany
07.02.04 Julius Francis W PTS 10 Bethnal Green

(English Heavyweight Title Defence)
24.04.04 Michael Sprott W CO 12 Reading
          (British & Commonwealth
          Heavyweight Title Challenges)
05.06.04 Bob Mirovic W RTD 4 Bethnal Green
          (Commonwealth Heavyweight Title
          Defence)
19.11.04 Keith Long W RSC 11 Bethnal Green
          (British & Commonwealth
          Heavyweight Title Defences)
25.02.05 Fabio Eduardo Moli W RSC 6
          Wembley
          (Vacant WBU Heavyweight Title)
16.07.05 Mark Krence W RTD 7 Bolton
          (British Heavyweight Title Defence)
10.12.05 John McDermott W RSC 1 Canning
          Town
          (British Heavyweight Title Defence)
25.02.06 Danny Williams L PTS 12 Canning
          Town
          (Commonwealth Heavyweight Title
          Challenge)
01.04.06 Suren Kalachyan W CO 4 Bethnal
          Green
08.07.06 Danny Williams W PTS 12 Cardiff
          (Commonwealth Heavyweight Title
          Challenge)
Career: 21 contests, won 20, lost 1.

Matt Skelton   Les Clark

Gatis Skuja

Bethnal Green. *Born* Latvia, 23 June, 1982
L.Middleweight. *Ht* 5'9"
Manager C. Sanigar

26.03.05 Nathan Graham L RSC 1 Hackney
11.09.05 David Kirk W PTS 6 Kirkby in
          Ashfield
04.12.05 Mark Lloyd L PTS 4 Telford
24.02.06 Terry Adams DREW 4 Birmingham
24.03.06 Sam Webb L PTS 4 Bethnal Green
22.05.06 Simon Sherrington DREW 8
          Birmingham
15.06.06 Cello Renda L PTS 4 Peterborough
14.07.06 Laurent Gomis L RSC 2 Alicante,
          Spain
29.09.06 Brett Flournoy L PTS 4 Manchester
03.11.06 Gavin Smith DREW 6 Barnsley
03.12.06 Daley Oujederie DREW 4 Bethnal
          Green
03.03.07 Robbie James L PTS 6 Newport
Career: 12 contests, won 1, drew 4, lost 7.

Anthony Small

Deptford. *Born* London, 28 June, 1981
L.Middleweight. *Ht* 5'9"
Manager Self

12.05.04 Lance Hall W RSC 1 Reading
10.09.04 Emmanuel Marcos W RSC 1 Wembley
10.12.04 Howard Clarke W PTS 4 Sheffield
21.01.05 Andrei Sherel W RSC 3 Brentford
24.04.05 Dmitry Donetskiy W PTS 4 Leicester
          Square
16.06.05 Howard Clarke W PTS 6 Mayfair
20.07.05 David le Franc W RSC 1 Monte Carlo,
          Monaco
14.10.05 Ismael Kerzazi W RSC 1 Huddersfield
23.11.05 Ernie Smith W PTS 6 Mayfair
24.03.06 Kai Kauramaki W CO 3 Bethnal Green
30.05.06 Alexander Matviechuk W RSC 6
          Bethnal Green
21.07.06 Vladimir Borovski W PTS 6
          Altrincham
21.10.06 Prince Arron W RSC 2 Southwark
18.11.06 Ciaran Healy W RSC 3 Newport
09.12.06 Kevin Phelan W RSC 1 Canning Town
17.02.07 Sergey Starkov W RSC 4 Wembley
30.03.07 Walter Wright W PTS 8 Newcastle
Career: 17 contests, won 17.

Leroy Smedley

Leeds. *Born* Scarborough, 14 January, 1982
Lightweight. Ht. 5'9"
Manager M. Marsden

18.04.07 Tony McQuade W PTS 6 Strand
Career: 1 contest, won 1.

Nicki Smedley

Sheffield. *Born* Sheffield, 3 February, 1986
Welterweight. *Ht* 5'10"
Manager D. Hobson

24.07.05 Lance Verallo W PTS 6 Sheffield
09.09.05 Jason Nesbitt W PTS 4 Sheffield
26.11.05 Rakhim Mingaleev W PTS 4 Sheffield
05.03.06 Davis Kamara W PTS 6 Sheffield
13.05.06 Artak Tsironyan W PTS 4 Sheffield
22.06.06 Martin Sweeney W RSC 3 Sheffield
20.10.06 Jon Honney W PTS 6 Sheffield
10.12.06 Imad Khamis W RSC 4 Sheffield
03.05.07 David Kehoe W RSC 4 Sheffield
Career: 9 contests, won 9.

Billy Smith

Stourport. *Born* Kidderminster, 10 June, 1978
Welterweight. Former Undefeated Midlands Area L.Welterweight Champion. *Ht* 5'7"
Manager Self

28.03.00	Marcus Portman L PTS 6 Wolverhampton
07.04.00	Barry Hughes L PTS 6 Glasgow
18.05.00	Manzo Smith L PTS 4 Bethnal Green
26.05.00	Willie Limond L PTS 4 Glasgow
07.07.00	Gareth Jordan L PTS 6 Chigwell
15.07.00	David Walker L RTD 2 Millwall
09.09.00	Ricky Eccleston L PTS 4 Manchester
24.09.00	Choi Tsveenpurev L RTD 2 Shaw
18.11.00	Lee Meager L RSC 1 Dagenham
17.12.00	Willie Limond L PTS 6 Glasgow
03.02.01	Scott Spencer L PTS 6 Brighton
09.03.01	Darren Melville L PTS 4 Millwall
27.03.01	Jason Nesbitt L PTS 6 Brierley Hill
05.03.05	Lee Cook L PTS 4 Southwark
23.03.05	Sam Rukundo L RSC 3 Leicester Square
30.04.05	Baz Carey L PTS 6 Coventry
08.05.05	Sean Hughes L PTS 6 Bradford
20.05.05	Stefy Bull L PTS 6 Doncaster
02.06.05	Isaac Ward L PTS 8 Yarm
16.06.05	Ricky Owen L PTS 4 Dagenham
25.06.05	John Fewkes L PTS 6 Wakefield
16.07.05	Craig Watson L PTS 8 Blackpool
23.07.05	Lee McAllister L PTS 4 Edinburgh
11.09.05	Craig Johnson L PTS 4 Kirkby in Ashfield
24.09.05	Baz Carey NC 5 Coventry
01.10.05	John Davidson W PTS 6 Wigan
09.10.05	Andrew Murray L PTS 4 Hammersmith
22.10.05	Jonathan Whiteman L PTS 6 Mansfield
05.11.05	Paul McCloskey L PTS 4 Renfrew
13.11.05	Nadeem Siddique L PTS 6 Leeds
25.11.05	Steve Mullin L PTS 4 Liverpool
03.12.05	Baz Carey L PTS 6 Coventry
12.12.05	Judex Meemea L PTS 6 Peterborough
11.02.06	Tom Glover L PTS 4 Bethnal Green
24.02.06	Lance Hall W PTS 6 Birmingham
25.03.06	Scott Haywood L PTS 8 Burton
07.04.06	Michael Graydon W PTS 4 Bristol
28.04.06	Paul Holborn L PTS 4 Hartlepool
12.05.06	Lee McAllister L PTS 4 Bethnal Green
21.05.06	Ashley Theophane L PTS 4 Bethnal Green
30.05.06	Chris Pacy L PTS 4 Bethnal Green
16.06.06	Ceri Hall L PTS 6 Carmarthen
23.06.06	Paul Truscott L PTS 4 Blackpool
12.07.06	John Murray L RSC 6 Bethnal Green
02.09.06	Stephen Burke L PTS 4 Bolton
09.09.06	Mike Reid W PTS 8 Inverurie
18.09.06	Gary McArthur L PTS 8 Glasgow
29.09.06	Gwyn Wale W PTS 6 Motherwell
26.10.06	Jonathan Hussey W PTS 6 Dudley
04.11.06	Jonathan Whiteman W PTS 6 Mansfield
17.11.06	Martin Gordon W PTS 6 Brierley Hill
01.12.06	Dee Mitchell L PTS 4 Birmingham
08.12.06	John Murray L PTS 6 Dagenham
15.12.06	Michael Lomax L PTS 6 Bethnal Green
09.02.07	Scott Haywood L PTS 4 Leeds
19.02.07	Andrew Ferrans L PTS 6 Glasgow
24.03.07	Baz Carey W PTS 10 Coventry
	(Vacant Midlands Area L.Welterweight Title)
07.04.07	Gavin Rees L PTS 6 Cardiff
11.05.07	Scott Haywood L PTS 4 Motherwell
18.05.07	Lenny Daws L PTS 6 Canning Town
25.05.07	Craig Docherty L PTS 6 Glasgow
08.06.07	Nathan Brough L PTS 4 Motherwell

Career: 62 contests, won 9, lost 52, no contest 1.

Clifford Smith

Woking. *Born* Guildford, 28 July, 1987
Lightweight. *Ht* 5'6½"
Manager F. Maloney

30.05.06	Rakhim Mingaleev W PTS 4 Bethnal Green
29.06.06	Kaloyan Stoyanov Dimov W PTS 4 Bethnal Green
06.10.06	Frederic Gosset W PTS 4 Bethnal Green
26.01.07	Youssef Al Hamidi DREW 4 Dagenham

Career: 4 contests, won 3, drew 1.

Clint Smith

Desborough. *Born* Kettering, 1 July, 1981
L.Middleweight. *Ht* 5'11½"
Manager I. Pauly

| 05.03.05 | Lee Williamson W PTS 6 Southwark |
| 21.06.07 | Peter Dunn W PTS 6 Peterborough |

Career: 2 contests, won 2.

Ernie Smith

Stourport. *Born* Kidderminster, 10 June, 1978
S.Middleweight. *Ht* 5'8"
Manager Self

24.11.98	Woody Greenaway L PTS 6 Wolverhampton
05.12.98	Gavin Rees L PTS 4 Bristol
27.01.99	Arv Mittoo DREW 6 Stoke
11.02.99	Tony Smith W PTS 6 Dudley
22.02.99	Liam Maltby W PTS 4 Peterborough
08.03.99	Wayne Jones W PTS 6 Birmingham
18.03.99	Carl Greaves L PTS 6 Doncaster
25.03.99	Brian Coleman L PTS 6 Edgbaston
27.05.99	Brian Coleman W PTS 6 Edgbaston
14.06.99	Dave Gibson W PTS 6 Birmingham
22.06.99	Koba Gogoladze L RSC 1 Ipswich
03.10.99	Gavin Down L RSC 1 Chesterfield
30.11.99	Brian Coleman L PTS 8 Wolverhampton
13.12.99	Richie Murray L RSC 5 Cleethorpes
24.02.00	Brian Coleman L PTS 6 Edgbaston
02.03.00	Oscar Hall L PTS 6 Birkenhead
10.03.00	John Tiftik L PTS 4 Chigwell
18.03.00	Biagio Falcone L PTS 4 Glasgow
07.04.00	Barry Connell L PTS 6 Glasgow
14.04.00	Jose Luis Castro L PTS 6 Madrid, Spain
06.05.00	Matthew Barr L PTS 4 Southwark
15.05.00	Harry Butler L PTS 6 Birmingham
26.05.00	Biagio Falcone L PTS 4 Glasgow
06.06.00	Chris Henry L PTS 8 Brierley Hill
08.07.00	Takaloo L RSC 4 Widnes
13.08.00	Jawaid Khaliq L RSC 4 Nottingham
	(Vacant Midlands Area Welterweight Title)
24.09.00	Shaun Horsfall L PTS 6 Shaw
09.10.00	Dave Gibson W PTS 6 Birmingham
22.10.00	Matthew Barr L PTS 4 Streatham
06.11.00	Stuart Elwell L PTS 6 Wolverhampton
25.11.00	Michael Jennings L PTS 4 Manchester
03.12.00	Shaun Horsfall L PTS 6 Shaw
17.12.00	Kevin McIntyre L PTS 6 Glasgow
20.01.01	David Walker L RTD 1 Bethnal Green
12.03.01	Matt Scriven L PTS 6 Birmingham
24.03.01	Bobby Banghar L PTS 4 Chigwell
12.05.01	Jon Harrison L PTS 4 Plymouth
21.05.01	Brian Coleman W PTS 6 Birmingham
03.06.01	Babatunde Ajayi L PTS 4 Southwark
16.06.01	Bobby Banghar L PTS 4 Dagenham
26.07.01	Andy Abrol L PTS 6 Blackpool
13.09.01	Leo O'Reilly L PTS 6 Sheffield
29.09.01	Brett James L PTS 6 Southwark
01.11.01	Lance Crosby L PTS 6 Hull
17.11.01	Nigel Wright L PTS 4 Glasgow
15.12.01	Ross Minter L RSC 2 Wembley
11.02.02	Tony Montana L PTS 6 Shrewsbury
13.05.02	Martin Scotland W RTD 2 Birmingham
15.06.02	Gavin Wake L PTS 4 Leeds
08.07.02	Gavin Rees L RSC 5 Mayfair
06.09.02	Ricky Burns L PTS 6 Glasgow
14.09.02	Matt Scriven L PTS 6 Newark
29.09.02	Anthony Christopher L PTS 6 Shrewsbury
18.11.02	Craig Dickson L PTS 6 Glasgow
03.12.02	Anthony Christopher W PTS 6 Shrewsbury
23.02.03	Gary Greenwood L PTS 4 Shrewsbury
24.03.03	Darrell Grafton L PTS 6 Barnsley
13.04.03	Lee McAllister L PTS 4 Bradford
28.04.03	Adnan Amar L PTS 6 Cleethorpes
12.05.03	Lee McAllister L PTS 6 Birmingham
31.05.03	Robbie Sivyer L PTS 6 Barnsley
08.06.03	Jonathan Woollins W PTS 4 Nottingham
15.06.03	Ali Nuumembe L PTS 4 Bradford
05.07.03	Michael Lomax L PTS 4 Brentwood
29.08.03	Ali Nuumembe L PTS 6 Liverpool
04.10.03	Lenny Daws L PTS 4 Muswell Hill
18.11.03	Chas Symonds L PTS 6 Bethnal Green
28.11.03	Lee McAllister L PTS 6 Hull
06.12.03	Taz Jones L PTS 4 Cardiff
07.02.04	Gary Woolcombe L PTS 4 Bethnal Green
09.04.04	Richard Swallow L PTS 4 Rugby
19.04.04	Craig Dickson L PTS 6 Glasgow
10.05.04	Adnan Amar L PTS 6 Birmingham
27.05.04	Graham Delehedy L RSC 3 Huddersfield
08.07.04	Steve Brumant L PTS 8 Birmingham
30.07.04	Tony Doherty L PTS 6 Bethnal Green
03.09.04	Jason Rushton L PTS 4 Doncaster
12.09.04	Chris Long DREW 6 Shrewsbury
24.09.04	Lenny Daws L PTS 6 Nottingham
23.10.04	Steve Conway L PTS 6 Wakefield
31.10.04	John Murray L PTS 4 Shaw
12.11.04	John O'Donnell L PTS 6 Wembley
25.11.04	Joe Mitchell W PTS 6 Birmingham
03.12.04	George Telfer L PTS 4 Edinburgh
13.12.04	Luke Teague L PTS 6 Cleethorpes
27.01.05	Muhsen Nasser L PTS 6 Piccadilly
12.02.05	Nathan Ward L PTS 6 Portsmouth
25.02.05	Ross Minter L PTS 4 Wembley
05.03.05	Gary Woolcombe L PTS 6 Southwark
23.03.05	Delroy Mellis L PTS 6 Leicester Square
08.04.05	Kerry Hope L PTS 4 Edinburgh
21.04.05	Jimmy Gould L PTS 4 Dudley
30.04.05	Andy Egan DREW 6 Coventry
08.05.05	Danny Parkinson L PTS 6 Bradford
15.05.05	Kell Brook L PTS 6 Sheffield
23.05.05	Davey Jones DREW 6 Cleethorpes
03.06.05	Martin Concepcion L PTS 4 Manchester
18.06.05	Richard Mazurek W PTS 6 Coventry
25.06.05	Adnan Amar L PTS 6 Melton Mowbray
09.07.05	Darren Barker L PTS 6 Nottingham
16.07.05	Tony Doherty NC 2 Bolton
23.07.05	Nathan Cleverly L PTS 4 Edinburgh

167

10.09.05   Kell Brook L PTS 4 Cardiff
25.09.05   Gavin Smith DREW 6 Leeds
06.10.05   Stuart Elwell L PTS 6 Dudley
21.10.05   George Hillyard W PTS 4 Bethnal Green
28.10.05   Franny Jones L PTS 4 Hartlepool
13.11.05   Darren Rhodes L PTS 6 Leeds
23.11.05   Anthony Small L PTS 6 Mayfair
02.12.05   Matthew Thirlwall L PTS 4 Nottingham
18.12.05   Ali Nuumbembe L CO 4 Bolton
28.01.06   Tony Doherty L PTS 6 Nottingham
16.02.06   Dean Hickman L PTS 4 Dudley
24.02.06   Joe Mitchell L PTS 6 Birmingham
04.03.06   Sean McKervey L PTS 6 Coventry
02.04.06   Mark Thompson L PTS 6 Shaw
29.04.06   Kell Brook L PTS 6 Edinburgh
06.05.06   Terry Adams L PTS 6 Birmingham
13.05.06   Jonjo Finnegan L PTS 6 Sutton in Ashfield
01.06.06   James Hare L CO 5 Barnsley
21.07.06   Mark Thompson L RSC 3 Altrincham
02.09.06   Denton Vassell L RSC 3 Bolton
01.10.06   Ryan Rowlinson L PTS 6 Rotherham
28.10.06   Grant Skehill L PTS 4 Bethnal Green
04.11.06   Gary Young L PTS 6 Glasgow
11.11.06   Karl Chiverton L PTS 6 Sutton in Ashfield
18.11.06   Barrie Jones L PTS 4 Newport
01.12.06   Max Maxwell L PTS 6 Birmingham
08.12.06   John O'Donnell L CO 2 Dagenham
09.02.07   Brett Flournoy L PTS 4 Leeds
16.02.07   Philip Dowse L PTS 6 Merthyr Tydfil
25.02.07   Brian Rose L PTS 6 Manchester
16.06.07   Sean Crompton L PTS 6 Bolton
28.06.07   Sam Horton L PTS 4 Dudley

Career: 134 contests, won 13, drew 5, lost 115, no contest 1.

Gavin Smith

Bradford. *Born* Bradford, 16 December, 1981
L.Middleweight. *Ht* 5'7¾"
Manager Self

23.10.04   Mark Wall W PTS 6 Wakefield
10.12.04   Mark Wall W PTS 4 Sheffield
13.02.05   Tony Randell W PTS 6 Bradford
24.07.05   Terry Adams L PTS 6 Sheffield
25.09.05   Ernie Smith DREW 6 Leeds
23.02.06   Jav Jerome W RSC 5 Leeds
13.05.06   Aleksandr Zhuk W RSC 3 Sheffield
03.11.06   Gatis Skuja DREW 6 Barnsley

Career: 8 contests, won 5, drew 2, lost 1.

Henry Smith

Bristol. *Born* Bristol, 24 September, 1978
Heavyweight. *Ht* 5'11½"
Manager Self

20.02.05   Radcliffe Green W PTS 6 Bristol
21.03.05   Billy McClung L PTS 6 Glasgow
09.07.05   Luke Simpkin L RSC 3 Bristol
07.10.06   David Ingleby L PTS 6 Weston super Mare

Career: 4 contests, won 1, lost 3.

John Smith

Weston super Mare. *Born* Bristol, 2 February, 1980
Cruiserweight. *Ht* 5'11"
Manager T. Gilmour

25.02.05   Sandy Robb L RSC 5 Irvine

09.07.05   Gary Thompson W PTS 4 Bristol
07.10.06   Varuzhan Davtyan W DIS 6 Weston super Mare
02.06.07   Billy Boyle L RSC 3 Bristol

Career: 4 contests, won 2, lost 2.

Lewis Smith

Accrington. *Born* Blackburn, 25 November, 1987
Welterweight. *Ht* 5'8"
Manager W. Barker

23.11.06   Duncan Cottier W PTS 6 Manchester
23.02.07   Baz Carey W PTS 6 Manchester
29.06.07   Neal McQuade W PTS 6 Manchester

Career: 3 contests, won 3.

Paul Smith

Liverpool. *Born* Liverpool, 6 October, 1982
Central Area Middleweight Champion.
Ht 5'11"
Manager F. Warren

05.04.03   Howard Clarke W PTS 4 Manchester
08.05.03   Andrei Ivanov W RSC 2 Widnes
20.06.03   Elroy Edwards W RSC 2 Liverpool
29.08.03   Patrick Cito W PTS 4 Liverpool
02.10.03   Mike Duffield W RSC 1 Liverpool
13.12.03   Joel Ani W PTS 4 Manchester
26.02.04   Davey Jones W PTS 4 Widnes
03.04.04   Howard Clarke W PTS 4 Manchester
12.06.04   Steve Timms W RSC 1 Manchester
10.09.04   Ojay Abrahams W PTS 4 Liverpool
01.10.04   Jason Collins W RSC 1 Manchester
17.12.04   Howard Clarke W CO 1 Liverpool
11.02.05   Robert Burton W CO 1 Manchester
03.06.05   Simeon Cover W PTS 6 Manchester
11.03.06   Hussain Osman W RSC 4 Newport
01.06.06   Conroy McIntosh W PTS 8 Barnsley
14.10.06   Dean Walker W RSC 3 Manchester
      (Vacant Central Area Middleweight Title)
18.11.06   Ryan Walls W RSC 4 Newport
10.03.07   Alexander Polizzi W RSC 8 Liverpool
30.03.07   Jonathan Reid W RSC 7 Newcastle

Career: 20 contests, won 20.

Steven Spartacus (Smith)

Ipswich. *Born* Bury St Edmunds, 3 November, 1976
L.Heavyweight. Former Undefeated British Masters L.Heavyweight Champion Former English L.Heavyweight Champion.
Ht 5'10½"
Manager Self

08.09.00   Michael Pinnock W PTS 4 Hammersmith
30.09.00   Martin Jolley W PTS 6 Chigwell
24.03.01   Calvin Stonestreet W PTS 4 Chigwell
16.06.01   Kevin Burton W RSC 1 Dagenham
07.09.01   Rob Stevenson W RSC 4 Bethnal Green
27.10.01   Darren Ashton W PTS 4 Manchester
24.11.01   Michael Pinnock W PTS 4 Bethnal Green
15.12.01   Oneal Murray W RSC 4 Chigwell
19.01.02   Darren Ashton W PTS 4 Bethnal Green
14.09.02   Calvin Stonestreet W RSC 3 Bethnal Green
08.02.03   Paul Bonson W PTS 6 Norwich
27.05.03   Mark Phillips W RSC 2 Dagenham
25.07.03   Simeon Cover W CO 3 Norwich

      (Vacant British Masters L.Heavyweight Title)
04.10.03   Hastings Rasani W RSC 1 Muswell Hill
11.12.03   Scott Lansdowne W RSC 3 Bethnal Green
      (Vacant English L.Heavyweight Title)
30.01.04   Ovill McKenzie L PTS 6 Dagenham
02.06.04   Varuzhan Davtyan W RSC 1 Nottingham
12.11.04   Peter Haymer L PTS 10 Wembley
      (English L.Heavyweight Title Defence)
10.04.05   Sam Price W RSC 6 Brentwood
      (British Masters L.Heavyweight Title Defence)
11.12.05   Varuzhan Davtyan W RSC 1 Chigwell
17.02.06   Karim Bennama W PTS 6 Bethnal Green
08.12.06   Ayitey Powers L PTS 6 Dagenham
18.05.07   Tony Oakey L RSC 12 Canning Town
      (Vacant British L.Heavyweight Title)

Career: 23 contests, won 19, lost 4.

Jamie Spence

Northampton. *Born* Northampton, 9 June, 1984
L.Welterweight. *Ht.* 5'7¼"
Manager K. Sanders

03.12.06   Gavin Tait L RSC 4 Bethnal Green
23.02.07   Dezzie O'Connor W RSC 3 Peterborough
01.06.07   Deniss Sirjatovs W RSC 3 Peterborough

Career: 3 contests, won 2, lost 1.

Delroy Spencer

Walsall. *Born* Walsall, 25 July, 1968
Bantamweight. British Masters Flyweight Champion. *Ht* 5'4"
Manager Self

30.10.98   Gwyn Evans L PTS 4 Peterborough
21.11.98   Jamie Evans W PTS 4 Southwark
30.01.99   Ian Napa L PTS 6 Bethnal Green
26.02.99   Chris Edwards W PTS 6 West Bromwich
30.04.99   Nicky Booth L PTS 6 Scunthorpe
06.06.99   Nicky Booth L PTS 4 Nottingham
19.06.99   Willie Valentine L PTS 4 Dublin
16.10.99   Colin Moffett W PTS 4 Bethnal Green
31.10.99   Shane Mallon W PTS 6 Raynes Park
29.11.99   Lee Georgiou L PTS 4 Wembley
19.02.00   Steffen Norskov L PTS 4 Aalborg, Denmark
08.04.00   Ian Napa L PTS 8 Bethnal Green
15.04.00   Lee Georgiou L PTS 4 Bethnal Green
04.07.00   Ankar Miah W RSC 3 Tooting
13.07.00   Darren Hayde W PTS 4 Bethnal Green
30.09.00   Paul Weir L PTS 8 Chigwell
28.10.00   Dale Robinson L RSC 4 Coventry
02.12.00   Keith Knox W PTS 6 Bethnal Green
08.05.01   Levi Pattison L PTS 4 Barnsley
22.05.01   Mimoun Chent L DIS 5 Telde, Gran Canaria
16.06.01   Sunkanmi Ogunbiyi L PTS 4 Wembley
22.11.01   Darren Taylor W PTS 8 Paddington
      (Vacant British Masters Flyweight Title)
09.12.01   Shinny Bayaar L PTS 4 Shaw
19.12.01   Gareth Payne L PTS 4 Coventry
18.01.02   Gareth Payne W PTS 4 Coventry
28.01.02   Levi Pattison L RSC 5 Barnsley
19.10.03   Shinny Bayaar L PTS 6 Shaw

13.12.03	Mark Moran L PTS 4 Manchester
24.01.04	Martin Power L RTD 1 Wembley
23.04.04	Chris Edwards DREW 6 Leicester
26.06.04	Damaen Kelly L RSC 4 Belfast
30.07.04	Martin Power L CO 2 Bethnal Green
31.10.04	Shinny Bayaar L PTS 6 Shaw
12.11.04	Stevie Quinn L PTS 6 Belfast
03.12.04	Lee Haskins L RTD 3 Bristol
	(Vacant English Flyweight Title)
27.05.05	Robert Nelson L PTS 4 Spennymoor
25.06.05	Robert Nelson L PTS 6 Wakefield
16.09.05	Lee Haskins L RTD 2 Plymouth
16.10.05	Moses Kinyua L PTS 6 Peterborough
30.10.05	Lee Fortt L PTS 4 Bethnal Green
12.11.05	Chris Edwards L PTS 4 Stoke
02.12.05	Jamie McDonnell L PTS 6 Doncaster
11.02.06	John Armour L PTS 6 Bethnal Green
04.03.06	Dale Robinson L RSC 3 Manchester
02.04.06	Shinny Bayaar L PTS 6 Shaw
23.04.06	Gary Sheil W PTS 6 Chester
09.05.06	Robert Nelson DREW 6 Leeds
20.05.06	Colin Moffett L PTS 4 Belfast
28.05.06	Tasif Khan L PTS 6 Wakefield
02.09.06	Don Broadhurst L PTS 4 Bolton
15.09.06	Matthew Edmonds L PTS 4 Newport
06.10.06	Ian Napa L PTS 6 Bethnal Green
27.10.06	Kris Hughes L PTS 6 Glasgow
11.11.06	Eugene Heagney L PTS 4 Dublin
11.12.06	Usman Ahmed DREW 6 Cleethorpes
09.02.07	Ross Burkinshaw L PTS 4 Leeds
26.02.07	Dougie Walton L PTS 6 Birmingham
07.04.07	Don Broadhurst L PTS 4 Cardiff
14.04.07	Eugene Heagney L PTS 4 Wakefield
05.05.07	Stephen Russell L PTS 4 Glasgow
19.05.07	Andy Bell L PTS 4 Nottingham
03.06.07	Josh Wale L PTS 6 Barnsley
16.06.07	Rob Turley L PTS 6 Newport
30.06.07	Rhys Roberts L PTS 6 Manchester

Career: 64 contests, won 10, drew 3, lost 51.

Alexander Spitjo
Mansfield. *Born* Riga, Latvia, 21 February, 1986
L.Middleweight. *Ht* 5'10½"
Manager M. Scriven

13.04.07	Brett Flournoy L PTS 4 Altrincham
27.04.07	Sam Webb L RSC 1 Wembley
17.06.07	Lee Noble L PTS 4 Mansfield
30.06.07	Scott Jordan W RSC 5 Belfast

Career: 4 contests, won 1, lost 3.

Michael Sprott
Reading. *Born* Reading, 16 January, 1975
European Union & English Heavyweight Champion. Former British &Commonwealth Heavyweight Champion. Former Undefeated Southern Area & WBF European Heavyweight Champion.
Ht 6'0¾"
Manager D. Powell/F. Warren

20.11.96	Geoff Hunter W RSC 1 Wembley
19.02.97	Johnny Davison W CO 2 Acton
17.03.97	Slick Miller W CO 1 Mayfair
16.04.97	Tim Redman W CO 2 Bethnal Green
20.05.97	Waldeck Fransas W PTS 6 Edmonton
02.09.97	Gary Williams W PTS 6 Southwark
08.11.97	Darren Fearn W PTS 6 Southwark
06.12.97	Nick Howard W RSC 1 Wembley
10.01.98	Johnny Davison W RSC 2 Bethnal Green
14.02.98	Ray Kane W RTD 1 Southwark

14.03.98	Michael Murray W PTS 6 Bethnal Green
12.09.98	Harry Senior L RSC 6 Bethnal Green
	(Vacant Southern Area Heavyweight Title)
16.01.99	Gary Williams W PTS 6 Bethnal Green
10.07.99	Chris Woollas W RTD 4 Southwark
18.01.00	Tony Booth W PTS 6 Mansfield
14.10.00	Wayne Llewelyn L RSC 3 Wembley
17.02.01	Timo Hoffmann W PTS 8 Bethnal Green
24.03.01	Timo Hoffmann L PTS 8 Magdeburg, Germany
03.11.01	Corrie Sanders L RSC 1 Brakpan, South Africa
20.12.01	Jermell Lamar Barnes W PTS 8 Rotterdam, Holland
12.02.02	Danny Williams L RTD 8 Bethnal Green
	(British & Commonwealth Heavyweight Title Challenges)
09.05.02	Pele Reid W RSC 7 Leicester Square
	(Vacant WBF European Heavyweight Title)
10.07.02	Garing Lane W PTS 6 Wembley
17.09.02	Derek McCafferty W PTS 8 Bethnal Green
12.12.02	Tamas Feheri W RSC 2 Leicester Square
24.01.03	Mike Holden W RSC 4 Sheffield
18.03.03	Mark Potter W RSC 3 Reading
	(Southern Area Heavyweight Title Challenge. Elim. British Heavyweight Title)
10.06.03	Petr Horacek W CO 1 Sheffield
01.08.03	Colin Kenna W RSC 1 Bethnal Green
	(Southern Area Heavyweight Title Defence)
26.09.03	Danny Williams L RSC 5 Reading
	(British & Commonwealth Heavyweight Title Challenges)
24.01.04	Danny Williams W PTS 12 Wembley
	(British & Commonwealth Heavyweight Title Challenges)
24.04.04	Matt Skelton L CO 12 Reading
	(British & Commonwealth Heavyweight Title Defences)
10.09.04	Robert Sulgan W RSC 1 Bethnal Green
23.04.05	Cengiz Koc W PTS 10 Dortmund, Germany
	(Vacant European Union Heavyweight Title)
01.10.05	Paolo Vidoz L PTS 12 Oldenburg, Germany
	(European Heavyweight Title Challenge)
13.12.05	Vladimir Virchis L PTS 12 Solden, Austria
	(WBO Inter-Continental Heavyweight Title Challenge)
18.02.06	Antoine Palatis W PTS 10 Edinburgh
	(Vacant European Union Heavyweight Title)
15.07.06	Ruslan Chagaev L RSC 8 Hamburg, Germany
	(Vacant WBO Asia-Pacific Heavyweight Title)
04.11.06	Rene Dettweiler W PTS 12 Mülheim an der Ruhr, Germany
	(European Union Heavyweight Title Defence)
17.02.07	Audley Harrison W RSC 3 Wembley
	(European Union Heavyweight Title Defence. Vacant English Heavyweight Title)

Career: 40 contests, won 30, lost 10.

Micky Steeds
Isle of Dogs. *Born* London, 14 September, 1983
Cruiserweight. Former Undefeated Southern Area Heavyweight Champion.
Ht 6'0"
Manager Self

18.09.03	Slick Miller W PTS 4 Mayfair
21.02.04	Brodie Pearmaine W RSC 1 Brighton
12.03.04	Paul King W PTS 6 Millwall
02.12.04	Luke Simpkin W RSC 3 Crystal Palace
18.02.05	Scott Gammer L PTS 6 Brighton
24.04.05	Julius Francis W PTS 8 Leicester Square
12.06.05	Mal Rice W PTS 6 Leicester Square
24.07.05	Garry Delaney W PTS 6 Leicester Square
05.03.06	Colin Kenna W PTS 10 Southampton
	(Southern Area Heavyweight Title Challenge)
13.10.06	Scott Gammer L PTS 12 Aberavon
	(British Heavyweight Title Challenge)
02.12.06	Luke Simpkin W PTS 6 Southwark
18.05.07	John Anthony W PTS 6 Canning Town

Career: 12 contests, won 10, lost 2.

Aldon Stewart
Nottingham. *Born* Nottingham, 27 November, 1982
Welterweight. *Ht* 5'10"
Manager J. Gill/T. Harris

30.09.06	Jimmy Doherty L PTS 6 Stoke
05.12.06	Jason Welborn L RSC 3 Wolverhampton

Career: 2 contests, lost 2.

Dave Stewart   Les Clark

Dave Stewart
Ayr. *Born* Irvine, 5 September, 1975
Welterweight. Former Undefeated British Masters Lightweight Champion. *Ht* 6'0¼"
Manager Self

15.02.01	Danny Connelly W PTS 6 Glasgow
27.04.01	Woody Greenaway W PTS 6 Glasgow
07.09.01	John Marshall W PTS 6 Glasgow
15.06.02	Dave Hinds W PTS 6 Tottenham
06.09.02	Pete Buckley W PTS 6 Bethnal Green
17.09.02	James Paisley W RSC 5 Bethnal Green
30.01.03	Scott Lawton W PTS 6 Piccadilly
26.04.03	Nigel Senior W RSC 2 Brentford

(British Masters Lightweight Title Challenge)
27.05.03 Pete Buckley W PTS 4 Dagenham
01.08.03 Norman Dhalie W RTD 2 Bethnal Green
26.09.03 Jimmy Beech W RTD 2 Reading
14.11.03 Pete Buckley W PTS 4 Bethnal Green
16.04.04 Carl Allen W PTS 6 Bradford
10.09.04 Bobby Vanzie W PTS 4 Wembley
10.04.05 Daniel Thorpe W RSC 3 Brentwood
16.07.05 Anthony Mezaache W PTS 8 Chigwell
21.10.05 Judex Meemea W PTS 6 Bethnal Green
17.02.06 Jason Nesbitt W PTS 4 Bethnal Green
12.05.06 Lee Meager L RSC 6 Bethnal Green
(Vacant British Lightweight Title)
24.11.06 Kpakpo Allotey W PTS 10 Nottingham
(Elim. Commonwealth Lightweight Title)
18.05.07 Jason Nesbitt W PTS 4 Canning Town
Career: 21 contests, won 20, lost 1.

Sammy Stewart
Leeds. *Born* Leeds, 10 July, 1984
Featherweight. *Ht* 5'8"
Manager T. O'Neill
24.11.06 Imran Khan L RSC 1 Stoke
Career: 1 contest, lost 1.

(Alexei) Alex Stoda
Wisbech. *Born* Venemaa, Estonia, 21 February, 1978
L.Middleweight. *Ht* 5'10"
Manager B. Lee
06.10.05 Martin Marshall L PTS 6 Sunderland
30.10.05 Anthony Young L PTS 6 Bethnal Green
30.05.06 Sam Webb W RSC 3 Bethnal Green
18.06.06 Mark Thompson L RSC 1 Manchester
03.11.06 Gary Woolcombe L DIS 4 Barnsley
02.12.06 Jay Morris W RSC 4 Southwark
02.03.07 Karl David L PTS 6 Neath
08.06.07 Mark Hastie L PTS 4 Motherwell
Career: 8 contests, won 2, lost 6.

Tony Stones
Bradford. *Born* Manchester, 18 February, 1978
S.Middleweight. *Ht* 5'10"
Manager M. Marsden
16.03.07 Colin Baxter L PTS 6 Glasgow
20.04.07 Sam Horton L PTS 4 Dudley
14.05.07 Dave Pearson DREW 6 Cleethorpes
Career: 3 contests, drew 1, lost 2.

Ricky Strike
Sheffield. *Born* Rotherham, 28 November, 1978
L.Heavyweight. *Ht* 5'9"
Manager D. Coldwell
23.02.07 Jorge Gomez L PTS 4 Peterborough
26.03.07 Jamie Ambler L CO 6 Glasgow
26.04.07 Tony Quigley L RSC 3 Manchester
Career: 3 contests, lost 3.

Darren Stubbs
Oldham. *Born* Manchester, 16 October, 1971
Cruiserweight. *Ht* 5'10"
Manager J. Doughty

02.06.02 Adam Cale W RSC 6 Shaw
21.06.02 Dean Cockburn L RSC 1 Leeds
17.11.02 Shpetim Hoti W RTD 2 Shaw
29.11.02 Jamie Wilson W PTS 6 Hull
09.03.03 Martin Thompson W RSC 3 Shaw
18.03.03 Jamie Hearn W RSC 3 Reading
08.06.03 Danny Grainger L RSC 2 Shaw
19.10.03 Paul Wesley W PTS 6 Shaw
29.02.04 Patrick Cito W PTS 6 Shaw
10.04.04 Alan Page L PTS 4 Manchester
20.04.04 Paul Owen W PTS 6 Sheffield
31.10.04 Nick Okoth W PTS 6 Shaw
20.11.05 Paul Bonson W PTS 6 Shaw
02.04.06 Howard Clarke W PTS 6 Shaw
18.06.06 Amer Khan L PTS 10 Manchester
(Vacant Central Area L.Heavyweight Title)
11.03.07 Hastings Rasani W RSC 5 Shaw
03.05.07 Jon Ibbotson W RSC 4 Sheffield
Career: 17 contests, won 13, lost 4.

Lee Swaby
Lincoln. *Born* Lincoln, 14 May, 1976
Cruiserweight. Former Undefeated British Masters Cruiserweight Champion. *Ht* 6'2"
Manager Self
29.04.97 Naveed Anwar W PTS 6 Manchester
19.06.97 Liam Richardson W RSC 4 Scunthorpe
30.10.97 Phil Ball W RSC 3 Newark
17.11.97 L. A. Williams W PTS 6 Manchester
02.02.98 Tim Redman L PTS 6 Manchester
27.02.98 John Wilson W CO 3 Glasgow
07.03.98 Phill Day L PTS 4 Reading
08.05.98 Chris P. Bacon L RSC 3 Manchester
17.07.98 Chris P. Bacon L PTS 6 Mere
19.09.98 Cathal O'Grady L RSC 1 Dublin
20.12.98 Mark Levy L RTD 5 Salford
23.06.99 Lee Archer W PTS 6 West Bromwich
04.09.99 Garry Delaney L PTS 8 Bethnal Green
03.10.99 Brian Gascoigne DREW 6 Chesterfield
11.12.99 Owen Beck L PTS 4 Liverpool
05.03.00 Kelly Oliver L PTS 10 Peterborough
(Vacant British Masters Cruiserweight Title)
15.04.00 Mark Levy L PTS 4 Bethnal Green
12.05.00 Enzo Maccarinelli W CO 3 Swansea
26.05.00 Steffen Nielsen L PTS 4 Holbaek, Denmark
09.09.00 Tony Dowling W RSC 9 Newark
(Vacant British Masters Cruiserweight Title)
05.02.01 Robert Norton L PTS 8 Hull
24.03.01 Crawford Ashley L PTS 8 Sheffield
30.04.01 Eamonn Glennon W PTS 6 Glasgow
02.06.01 Denzil Browne DREW 8 Wakefield
31.07.01 Stephane Allouane W PTS 4 Bethnal Green
13.09.01 Kevin Barrett W PTS 4 Sheffield
15.12.01 Chris Woollas W RSC 4 Sheffield
27.04.02 Mark Hobson L PTS 10 Huddersfield
(Final Elim. British Cruiserweight Title)
03.08.02 Greg Scott-Briggs W RSC 4 Derby
05.12.02 Eamonn Glennon W PTS 4 Sheffield
24.01.03 Tommy Eastwood W PTS 6 Sheffield
10.06.03 Paul Bonson W PTS 4 Sheffield
05.09.03 Brodie Pearmaine W RTD 4 Sheffield
20.04.04 Lee Mountford W RSC 1 Sheffield
27.05.04 Mark Hobson L RSC 6 Huddersfield
(British & Commonwealth Cruiserweight Title Challenges)

24.10.04 Denzil Browne W RSC 7 Sheffield
(Elim. British Cruiserweight Title)
09.09.05 Hastings Rasani W PTS 4 Sheffield
26.11.05 Vitaly Shkraba W RSC 3 Sheffield
04.03.06 Marco Huck L RTD 6 Oldenburg, Germany
20.10.06 John Keeton L RSC 7 Sheffield
(Vacant British Cruiserweight Title)
02.12.06 Alexander Alexeev L RSC 5 Berlin, Germany
Career: 41 contests, won 22, drew 2, lost 17.

Martin Sweeney
Darwen. *Born* Rochdale, 19 August, 1981
L.Middleweight. *Ht* 5'7¾"
Manager Self
11.05.06 Zahoor Hussain L PTS 6 Sunderland
21.05.06 Danny Butler L PTS 6 Bristol
22.06.06 Nicki Smedley L RSC 3 Sheffield
30.09.06 Aaron Thomas L CO 2 Stoke
13.04.07 Chris Mullen L RSC 6 Houghton le Spring
Career: 5 contests, lost 5.

James Swindells
Aldershot. *Born* Aylesbury, 24 July, 1975
Cruiserweight. Height. 5'10½"
Manager J. Evans
05.06.07 Andrew Young L RSC 2 Glasgow
Career: 1 contest, lost 1.

Gary Sykes
Dewsbury. *Born* Dewsbury, 13 February, 1984
Lightweight. *Ht* 5'8"
Manager C. Aston/S. Wood
23.02.06 Dave Hinds W PTS 6 Leeds
13.04.06 Dai Davies W CO 3 Leeds
13.04.07 Kristian Laight W PTS 4 Altrincham
24.06.07 Rom Krauklis W PTS 4 Wigan
Career: 4 contests, won 4.

Gary Sykes   Les Clark

TUV

(Mohammed) Abul Taher

Coventry. Born Coventry, 17 January, 1987
Welterweight. *Ht* 5'11"
Manager G. Singh

22.12.06 Peter Dunn W PTS 6 Coventry
02.03.07 Amir Nadi W PTS 6 Coventry

Career: 2 contests, won 2.

Gavin Tait

Carmarthen. *Born* Carmarthen, 2 March, 1976
Welterweight. *Ht* 5'7"
Manager Self

07.06.04 Stuart Green L PTS 6 Glasgow
03.07.04 Justin Hicks W RSC 5 Bristol
05.10.04 Tristan Davies L PTS 6 Dudley
24.11.04 David Pereira L PTS 6 Mayfair
02.12.04 Chris Long L PTS 6 Bristol
07.04.05 Gary Coombes W RSC 3 Birmingham
27.05.05 Darren Johnstone L PTS 6 Motherwell
30.10.05 Dwayne Hill L PTS 6 Sheffield
24.03.06 Tom Glover W PTS 4 Bethnal Green
21.10.06 Calvin White W PTS 4 Southwark
03.12.06 Jamie Spence W RSC 4 Bethnal Green

Career: 11 contests, won 5, lost 6.

Gavin Tait   Les Clark

(Mehrdud) Takaloo (Takalobigashi)

Margate. *Born* Iran, 23 September, 1975
Welterweight. Former WBU Welterweight
Champion. Former Undefeated WBU
L.Middleweight Champion. Former
Undefeated IBF Inter-Continental
L.Middleweight Champion. *Ht* 5'9"
Manager F. Warren

19.07.97 Harry Butler W RSC 1 Wembley
13.09.97 Michael Alexander W PTS 4 Millwall
15.11.97 Koba Kulu W RSC 3 Bristol
19.12.97 Mark Sawyers W PTS 4 Millwall
07.02.98 Jawaid Khaliq L RSC 4 Cheshunt

16.05.98 Anas Oweida W RSC 1 Bethnal Green
10.10.98 Michael Jones L PTS 6 Bethnal Green
30.01.99 Darren McInulty W RSC 5 Bethnal Green
03.04.99 Gareth Lovell W RSC 6 Kensington
26.06.99 Leigh Wicks W CO 3 Millwall
04.09.99 Carlton Williams W RSC 4 Bethnal Green
23.10.99 Prince Kasi Kaihau W RSC 3 Telford
29.01.00 Paul King W RSC 2 Manchester
08.04.00 Biagio Falcone W RTD 4 Bethnal Green
08.07.00 Ernie Smith W RSC 4 Widnes
12.08.00 Howard Clarke W PTS 12 Wembley
(Vacant IBF Inter-Continental L.Middleweight Title)
13.11.00 Jason Collins W RSC 2 Bethnal Green
24.02.01 James Lowther W PTS 12 Bethnal Green
(IBF Inter-Continental L.Middleweight Title Defence)
07.07.01 Anthony Farnell W RSC 1 Manchester
(Vacant WBU L.Middleweight Title)
22.09.01 Scott Dixon W CO 1 Bethnal Green
(WBU L. Middleweight Title Defence)
04.05.02 Gary Logan W RSC 10 Bethnal Green
(WBU L. Middleweight Title Defence)
17.08.02 Daniel Santos L PTS 12 Cardiff
(WBO L.Middleweight Title Challenge. WBU L.Middleweight Title Defence)
01.02.03 Jim Rock W RSC 9 Belfast
(Vacant WBU L. Middleweight Title)
24.05.03 Jose Rosa W PTS 12 Bethnal Green
(WBU L.Middleweight Title Defence)
13.09.03 Vladimir Borovski W CO 3 Newport
24.01.04 Eugenio Monteiro L PTS 8 Wembley
10.09.04 Wayne Alexander L RSC 2 Bethnal Green
(Vacant WBU L.Middleweight Title)
23.07.05 Delroy Mellis W PTS 8 Edinburgh
25.02.06 Turgay Uzun W PTS 10 Canning Town
20.05.06 Eamonn Magee W PTS 12 Belfast
(WBU Welterweight Title Challenge)
07.04.07 Michael Jennings L PTS 12 Cardiff
(WBU Welterweight Title Defence)

Career: 31 contests, won 25, lost 6.

Karl Taylor

Birmingham. *Born* Birmingham, 5 January, 1966
Welterweight. Former Undefeated Midlands
Area Lightweight Champion. *Ht* 5'5"
Manager Self

18.03.87 Steve Brown W PTS 6 Stoke
06.04.87 Paul Taylor L PTS 6 Southampton
12.06.87 Mark Begley W RSC 1 Leamington
18.11.87 Colin Lynch W RSC 4 Solihull
29.02.88 Peter Bradley L PTS 8 Birmingham
04.10.89 Mark Antony W CO 2 Stafford
30.10.89 Tony Feliciello L PTS 8 Birmingham
06.12.89 John Davison L PTS 8 Leicester
23.12.89 Regilio Tuur L RTD 1 Hoogvliet, Holland
22.02.90 Mark Ramsey L RSC 4 Hull
29.10.90 Steve Walker DREW 6 Birmingham
10.12.90 Elvis Parsley L PTS 6 Birmingham
16.01.91 Wayne Windle W PTS 8 Stoke
02.05.91 Billy Schwer L RSC 2 Northampton
25.07.91 Peter Till L RSC 4 Dudley
(Midlands Area Lightweight Title Challenge)
24.02.92 Charlie Kane L PTS 8 Glasgow

28.04.92 Richard Woolgar W PTS 6 Wolverhampton
29.05.92 Alan McDowall L PTS 6 Glasgow
25.07.92 Michael Armstrong L RSC 3 Manchester
02.11.92 Hugh Forde L PTS 6 Wolverhampton
23.11.92 Dave McHale L PTS 8 Glasgow
22.12.92 Patrick Gallagher L RSC 3 Mayfair
13.02.93 Craig Dermody L RSC 5 Manchester
31.03.93 Craig Dermody W PTS 6 Barking
07.06.93 Mark Geraghty W PTS 8 Glasgow
13.08.93 Giorgio Campanella L CO 6 Arezzo, Italy
05.10.93 Paul Harvey W PTS 6 Mayfair
21.10.93 Charles Shepherd L RTD 5 Bayswater
21.12.93 Patrick Gallagher L PTS 6 Mayfair
09.02.94 Alan Levene W RSC 2 Brentwood
01.03.94 Shaun Cogan L PTS 6 Dudley
15.03.94 Patrick Gallagher L PTS 6 Mayfair
18.04.94 Peter Till W PTS 10 Walsall
(Midlands Area Lightweight Title Challenge)
24.05.94 Michael Ayers DREW 8 Sunderland
12.11.94 P. J. Gallagher L PTS 6 Dublin
29.11.94 Dingaan Thobela W PTS 8 Cannock
31.03.95 Michael Ayers L RSC 8 Crystal Palace
(British Lightweight Title Challenge)
06.05.95 Cham Joof W PTS 8 Shepton Mallet
23.06.95 Poli Diaz L PTS 8 Madrid, Spain
02.09.95 Paul Ryan L RSC 3 Wembley
04.11.95 Carl Wright L PTS 6 Liverpool
15.12.95 Peter Richardson L PTS 8 Bethnal Green
23.01.96 Paul Knights DREW 6 Bethnal Green
05.03.96 Andy Holligan L PTS 6 Barrow
20.03.96 Mervyn Bennett W PTS 8 Cardiff
21.05.96 Malcolm Melvin L PTS 10 Edgbaston
(Midlands Area L. Welterweight Title Challenge)
07.10.96 Joshua Clottey L RSC 2 Lewisham
20.12.96 Anatoly Alexandrov L RSC 7 Bilbao, Spain
28.01.97 Eamonn Magee L PTS 6 Belfast
28.02.97 Mark Breslin L RSC 6 Kilmarnock
30.08.97 Gilbert Eastman L PTS 4 Cheshunt
25.10.97 Tontcho Tontchev L PTS 4 Queensferry
22.11.97 Bobby Vanzie L PTS 6 Manchester
18.04.98 Ricky Hatton L RSC 1 Manchester
18.07.98 James Hare L PTS 4 Sheffield
26.09.98 Oktay Urkal L PTS 8 Norwich
28.11.98 Junior Witter L PTS 6 Sheffield
06.03.99 George Scott L RSC 4 Southwark
15.05.99 Jon Thaxton L PTS 6 Sheffield
10.07.99 Eamonn Magee L RTD 3 Southwark
06.11.99 Alan Sebire W PTS 6 Widnes
15.11.99 Steve Murray L RSC 1 Bethnal Green
19.08.00 Iain Eldridge L PTS 4 Brentwood
04.09.00 Tomas Jansson L PTS 6 Manchester
16.09.00 Colin Lynes L PTS 6 Bethnal Green
09.12.00 David Walker L PTS 6 Southwark
10.02.01 Matthew Hatton L PTS 4 Widnes
10.03.01 Francis Barrett L RSC 3 Bethnal Green
10.04.01 Costas Katsantonis L PTS 4 Wembley
16.06.01 Brett James DREW 4 Wembley
15.09.01 David Barnes L PTS 4 Manchester
28.10.01 Babatunde Ajayi L PTS 4 Southwark
24.11.01 Ross Minter L PTS 4 Bethnal Green
15.12.01 Alexandra Vetoux L PTS 4 Wembley
12.02.02 Brett James DREW 4 Bethnal Green
11.03.02 Kevin McIntyre L PTS 4 Glasgow
04.05.02 Matthew Hatton L RSC 3 Bethnal Green
25.06.02 Rimell Taylor DREW 6 Rugby

20.07.02 Matthew Hatton L RTD 2 Bethnal
Green
28.09.02 Michael Jennings L RSC 4 Manchester
16.11.02 Gavin Wake L PTS 4 Nottingham
30.11.02 Tony Conroy L PTS 4 Coventry
14.12.02 Alexander Vetoux L RTD 3 Newcastle
15.02.03 Ross Minter L PTS 6 Wembley
29.03.03 Alexander Vetoux L RSC 1 Portsmouth
08.05.03 Tony Doherty L PTS 4 Widnes
25.07.03 Lenny Daws L RTD 2 Norwich
06.10.03 Jonathan Woollins W PTS 6
Birmingham
29.10.03 Ajose Olusegun L PTS 6 Leicester
Square
29.11.03 Gary Young L RSC 3 Renfrew
30.01.04 Lee McAllister L PTS 4 Dagenham
05.03.04 Oscar Hall L PTS 6 Darlington
27.03.04 Jamie Arthur L PTS 6 Edinburgh
06.05.04 Ashley Theophane L PTS 4 Barnsley
22.05.04 Tony Doherty L RTD 2 Widnes
03.09.04 Taz Jones L PTS 4 Newport
18.09.04 Karl Chiverton L PTS 6 Newark
26.09.04 Danny Johnston L PTS 6 Stoke
19.11.04 Tony Doherty L RSC 2 Bethnal Green
19.12.04 Kell Brook L PTS 6 Bolton
06.03.05 John Murray L PTS 6 Shaw
14.05.05 Lee McAllister L RTD 3 Aberdeen
26.06.05 Henry Castle L PTS 6 Southampton
24.07.05 John Fewkes L PTS 6 Sheffield
16.09.05 Tristan Davies L PTS 4 Telford
08.11.05 Danny Reynolds L RSC 4 Leeds
11.12.05 Paul Halpin L PTS 4 Chigwell
18.12.05 Jonathan Hussey L PTS 6 Bolton
17.02.06 John O'Donnell L PTS 4 Bethnal Green
01.04.06 Ashley Theophane L PTS 4 Bethnal
Green
24.04.06 Simon Fleck L PTS 6 Cleethorpes
13.05.06 Dale Miles L RSC 3 Sutton in Ashfield
18.06.06 Prince Arron L PTS 6 Manchester
15.09.06 Garry Buckland L PTS 6 Newport
07.10.06 Rob Hunt L PTS 6 Walsall
24.11.06 Scott Lawton L PTS 4 Stoke
01.12.06 Peter McDonagh L PTS 4 Tower Hill
10.12.06 Muhsen Nasser L PTS 6 Sheffield
17.02.07 Eddie Corcoran L PTS 4 Wembley
11.03.07 Chris Johnson L RTD 3 Shaw
06.05.07 Khurram Hussain L PTS 4 Leeds
09.06.07 Mark Dawes L PTS 6 Middlesbrough
Career: 122 contests, won 16, drew 6, lost 100.

Nicki Taylor

Askern. *Born* Doncaster, 6 July, 1979
L.Heavyweight. *Ht* 5'11"
Manager M. Scriven

20.09.04 Sandy Robb L RSC 5 Glasgow
24.04.05 Hastings Rasani L RTD 4 Askern
18.06.05 Rod Anderton L RSC 4 Barnsley
22.10.05 Michael Pinnock W PTS 6 Mansfield
12.11.05 Danny Tombs DREW 4 Sheffield
12.12.05 Karl Wheeler L PTS 4 Peterborough
14.05.06 Duane Reid L RSC 2 Derby
06.10.06 Scott Brookes L PTS 6 Mexborough
26.10.06 Shon Davies L RSC 1 Wolverhampton
01.12.06 Lee Jones L PTS 4 Birmingham
15.02.07 Matthew Hough W RSC 2 Dudley
25.02.07 Robin White L PTS 4 Manchester
09.03.07 Tony Salam L RSC 1 Dagenham
30.06.07 Mark Nilsen L CO 4 Manchester
Career: 14 contests, won 2, drew 1, lost 11.

John-Paul Temple

Brighton. *Born* London, 30 May, 1973
L.Middleweight. *Ht* 5'11"
Manager R. Davies

11.02.97 Mark O'Callaghan W PTS 6 Bethnal
Green
17.03.97 Les Frost W CO 4 Mayfair
24.04.97 Chris Lyons W PTS 6 Mayfair
23.10.97 Chris Lyons W PTS 8 Mayfair
26.03.98 Trevor Smith L RSC 5 Piccadilly
28.04.98 Chris Price L PTS 6 Brentford
05.10.99 Jason Hall L PTS 6 Bloomsbury
25.02.00 Daniel James L PTS 10 Newmarket
(*Vacant Southern Area L.Welterweight
Title*)
21.11.04 Neil Jarmolinski DREW 4 Bracknell
03.12.04 Barrie Lee L PTS 4 Edinburgh
30.04.05 Danny Goode L PTS 4 Dagenham
26.06.05 Danny Goode L PTS 4 Southampton
10.09.05 Kerry Hope L PTS 4 Cardiff
06.10.05 Kevin Phelan L PTS 6 Longford
02.12.05 Darren Barker L RSC 6 Nottingham
29.09.06 Karl David L PTS 6 Cardiff
Career: 16 contests, won 4, drew 1, lost 11.

Jonathan Thaxton

Norwich. *Born* Norwich, 10 September,
1974
British Lightweight Champion. Former

Nicki Taylor   Les Clark

Jonathan Thaxton   Les Clark

Undefeated WBF Lightweight Champion. Former Southern Area, IBF & WBO Inter-Continental L.Welterweight Champion. *Ht 5'6"*
Manager Self

09.12.92	Scott Smith W PTS 6 Stoke
03.03.93	Dean Hiscox W PTS 6 Solihull
17.03.93	John O. Johnson W PTS 6 Stoke
23.06.93	Brian Coleman W PTS 8 Gorleston
22.09.93	John Smith W PTS 6 Wembley
07.12.93	Dean Hollington W RSC 3 Bethnal Green
10.03.94	B. F. Williams W RSC 4 Watford
	(Vacant Southern Area L.Welterweight Title)
18.11.94	Keith Marner L PTS 10 Bracknell
	(Southern Area L.Welterweight Title Defence)
26.05.95	David Thompson W RSC 6 Norwich
23.06.95	Delroy Leslie W PTS 6 Bethnal Green
12.08.95	Rene Prins L PTS 8 Zaandam, Holland
08.12.95	Colin Dunne L RSC 5 Bethnal Green
	(Vacant Southern Area Lightweight Title)
20.01.96	John O. Johnson W RSC 4 Mansfield
13.02.96	Paul Ryan W RSC 1 Bethnal Green
25.06.96	Mark Elliot W CO 5 Mansfield
	(Vacant IBF Inter-Continental L.Welterweight Title)
14.09.96	Bernard Paul W PTS 12 Sheffield
	(Vacant WBO Inter-Continental L.Welterweight Title)
27.03.97	Paul Burke W RSC 9 Norwich
	(IBF & WBO Inter-Continental L.Welterweight Title Defences)
28.06.97	Gagik Chachatrian W RSC 2 Norwich
	(IBF & WBO Inter-Continental L.Welterweight Title Defences)
29.11.97	Rimvidas Billius W PTS 12 Norwich
	(IBF & WBO Inter-Continental L.Welterweight Title Defences)
26.09.98	Emanuel Burton L RSC 7 Norwich
	(IBF & WBO Inter-Continental L.Welterweight Title Defences)
15.05.99	Karl Taylor W PTS 6 Sheffield
07.08.99	Brian Coleman W PTS 6 Dagenham
15.11.99	Jason Rowland L RSC 5 Bethnal Green
	(British L.Welterweight Title Challenge)
15.07.00	Kimoun Kouassi W RSC 3 Norwich
21.10.00	Ricky Hatton L PTS 12 Wembley
	(Vacant British L.Welterweight Title)
26.03.01	Alan Temple W PTS 4 Wembley
28.07.01	David Kirk W PTS 4 Wembley
09.02.02	Eamonn Magee L RSC 6 Manchester
	(Commonwealth L.Welterweight Title Challenge)
13.04.02	Chill John W RSC 2 Norwich
15.06.02	Marc Waelkens W RSC 7 Norwich
21.09.02	Viktor Baranov W RSC 1 Norwich
09.10.04	Silence Saheed W PTS 6 Norwich
13.12.04	Carl Allen W RSC 1 Birmingham
09.04.05	Christophe de Busillet W CO 4 Norwich
	(Vacant WBF Lightweight Title)
03.09.05	Vasile Dragomir W CO 4 Norwich
	(WBF Lightweight Title Defence)
17.02.06	Alan Temple W RSC 5 Bethnal Green
13.05.06	Jorge Daniel Miranda W PTS 10 Sheffield
08.12.06	Lee Meager W PTS 12 Dagenham
	(British Lightweight Title Challenge)
16.03.07	Scott Lawton W RSC 7 Norwich
	(British Lightweight Title Defence)

Career: 39 contests, won 32, lost 7.

Ashley Theophane

Kilburn. *Born* London, 20 August, 1980
L.Welterweight. GBC Welterweight Champion. *Ht 5'7"*
Manager Self

03.06.03	Lee Bedell W RSC 4 Bethnal Green
22.07.03	Brian Coleman W PTS 6 Bethnal Green
25.04.04	David Kirk W PTS 6 Nottingham
06.05.04	Karl Taylor W PTS 4 Barnsley
05.06.04	Chris Brophy W RSC 3 Bethnal Green
19.06.04	Arv Mittoo W PTS 4 Muswell Hill
02.12.04	Keith Jones W PTS 6 Crystal Palace
26.03.05	Judex Meemea L PTS 6 Hackney
24.04.05	David Kehoe W PTS 4 Leicester Square
12.06.05	Jus Wallie W PTS 4 Leicester Square
18.09.05	Oscar Milkitas L PTS 4 Bethnal Green
09.10.05	David Kehoe W PTS 4 Hammersmith
19.11.05	Duncan Cottier W PTS 6 Southwark
25.02.06	Daniel Thorpe DREW 4 Canning Town
17.03.06	Josef Holub W CO 3 Horka, Germany
01.04.06	Karl Taylor W PTS 4 Bethnal Green
21.05.06	Billy Smith W PTS 4 Bethnal Green
24.09.06	Jon Honney W PTS 6 Bethnal Green
07.10.06	Ibrahim Barakat W PTS 6 Horka, Germany
02.12.06	Omar Siala W RSC 11 Berlin, Germany
	(Vacant GBC Welterweight Title)
20.01.07	Alan Bosworth W RSC 7 Muswell Hill
	(Elim. British L.Welterweight Title)

Career: 21 contests, won 18, drew 1, lost 2.

Ashley Theophane   Philip Sharkey

Matthew Thirlwall

Bermondsey. *Born* Middlesbrough, 28 November, 1980
S.Middleweight. *Ht 5'9½"*
Manager Self

16.03.02	William Webster W RSC 1 Bethnal Green

10.05.02	Leigh Wicks W PTS 4 Bethnal Green
23.08.02	Harry Butler W RSC 3 Bethnal Green
25.10.02	Jason Collins W RSC 5 Bethnal Green
21.12.02	Howard Clarke W PTS 6 Dagenham
28.01.03	Gary Beardsley L PTS 6 Nottingham
16.04.03	Gary Beardsley W PTS 6 Nottingham
27.05.03	Leigh Wicks W PTS 6 Dagenham
04.10.03	Dean Powell W RSC 2 Muswell Hill
11.12.03	Harry Butler W PTS 6 Bethnal Green
12.03.04	Patrick Cito W RSC 3 Nottingham
24.09.04	Jason Collins W PTS 4 Nottingham
02.12.05	Ernie Smith W PTS 4 Nottingham
20.01.06	Donovan Smillie W CO 9 Bethnal Green
	(Final Elim. English S.Middleweight Title)
24.03.06	Moises Martinez W RSC 6 Hollywood, Florida, USA
08.12.06	Howard Clarke W PTS 4 Dagenham
20.01.07	Hussain Osman W RSC 5 Muswell Hill
18.05.07	David Kirk W PTS 4 Canning Town

Career: 18 contests, won 16, lost 2.

Aaron Thomas

Stoke. *Born* St Asaph, 11 April, 1980
L.Middleweight. *Ht 5'8"*
Manager C. Sanigar

30.09.06	Martin Sweeney W CO 2 Stoke
24.11.06	Ben Hudson W PTS 6 Stoke
12.05.07	Surinder Sekhon W PTS 4 Stoke

Career: 3 contests, won 3.

Gary Thompson

Lancaster. *Born* Darwen, 22 June, 1981
Cruiserweight. *Ht 5'9"*
Manager D. Coldwell

22.09.01	Michael Thompson L RSC 3 Newcastle
16.11.01	Adam Cale W PTS 6 Preston
10.12.01	Rob Galloway W PTS 6 Bradford
23.12.01	Lee Whitehead L PTS 4 Salford
08.02.02	Shane White DREW 6 Preston
17.02.02	Lee Whitehead DREW 6 Salford
19.04.02	Lee Mountford DREW 4 Darlington
11.05.02	Tony Dowling L RSC 3 Newark
18.10.02	Michael Thompson L PTS 4 Hartlepool
26.10.02	Paul Richardson DREW 6 Wigan
02.12.02	Danny Thornton L PTS 6 Leeds
03.02.03	Nate Joseph L PTS 4 Bradford
28.02.03	Lee Mountford L PTS 6 Irvine
07.06.03	Carl Wright L RTD 2 Coventry
06.05.04	Simon Francis L PTS 4 Barnsley
15.05.04	Simeon Cover L PTS 6 Aberdeen
08.06.04	Simon Francis L RTD 2 Sheffield
04.11.04	Simeon Cover L PTS 6 Piccadilly
06.12.04	Nate Joseph W PTS 6 Bradford
20.02.05	Neil Dawson L PTS 6 Sheffield
11.03.05	Dean Cockburn L RSC 4 Doncaster
22.04.05	John Anthony L PTS 4 Barnsley
29.04.05	Junior MacDonald L RSC 1 Southwark
01.06.05	Danny Thornton L PTS 4 Leeds
09.07.05	John Smith L PTS 4 Bristol
11.09.05	Brian Gascoigne DREW 6 Kirkby in Ashfield
19.09.05	Sandy Robb L PTS 6 Glasgow
09.10.05	Paul Bowen L CO 1 Hammersmith
08.12.05	Rod Anderton L PTS 6 Derby
15.12.05	Tyrone Wright DREW 6 Cleethorpes
23.06.06	Lee Kellett W PTS 4 Blackpool
21.10.06	Paul David L PTS 6 Glasgow

17.02.07 Tommy Saunders L PTS 4 Wembley
01.06.07 Tom Owens W RTD 1 Birmingham
Career: 34 contests, won 5, drew 6, lost 23.

Mark Thompson

Heywood. *Born* Rochdale, 28 May, 1981
L.Middleweight. *Ht* 5'11"
Manager S. Wood

23.09.05 Geraint Harvey W PTS 4 Manchester
20.11.05 Danny Moir W RSC 2 Shaw
18.12.05 Tony Randell W RSC 2 Bolton
12.02.06 Darren Gethin W PTS 4 Manchester
02.03.06 Simon Fleck W CO 3 Blackpool
02.04.06 Ernie Smith W PTS 6 Shaw
18.06.06 Alex Stoda W RSC 1 Manchester
21.07.06 Ernie Smith W RSC 3 Altrincham
29.09.06 Alexander Matviechuk W PTS 8
          Manchester
09.02.07 Lee Noble W PTS 6 Leeds
13.04.07 Manoocha Salari W RSC 1 Altrincham
Career: 11 contests, won 11.

Willie Thompson

Ballyclare. *Born* Larne, 2 January, 1980
L.Middleweight. *Ht* 6'0"
Manager A. Wilton

30.06.07 Paul Royston W PTS 4 Belfast
Career: 1 contest, won 1.

Danny Thornton

Leeds. *Born* Leeds, 20 July, 1978
Cruiserweight. Former Undefeated Central
Area Middleweight Champion. *Ht* 5'10"
Manager Self

06.10.97 Pedro Carragher L PTS 6 Bradford
13.11.97 Shaun O'Neill DREW 6 Bradford
08.12.97 Shaun O'Neill DREW 6 Bradford
09.02.98 Roy Chipperfield W RSC 4 Bradford
17.03.98 Patrick J. Maxwell L PTS 6 Sheffield
30.03.98 Mark Owens W PTS 6 Bradford
15.05.98 Danny Bell W PTS 6 Nottingham
15.06.98 Jimmy Hawk W PTS 6 Bradford
12.10.98 Wayne Shepherd W PTS 6 Bradford
21.02.99 Shaun O'Neill W RSC 5 Bradford
25.04.99 Matt Scriven W RSC 4 Leeds
14.06.99 Martin Thompson W PTS 6 Bradford
18.10.99 Paul Henry W PTS 4 Bradford
14.11.99 Dean Ashton W PTS 4 Bradford
06.12.99 Lee Blundell L PTS 6 Bradford
05.02.00 Steve Roberts L PTS 6 Bethnal Green
25.03.00 Lee Molloy W RSC 2 Liverpool
06.06.00 Joe Townsley L RSC 7 Motherwell
          *(IBO Inter-Continental
          L. Middleweight Title Challenge)*
30.11.00 Lee Blundell L RSC 8 Blackpool
          *(Vacant Central Area L. Middleweight
          Title)*
20.03.01 Ian Toby W PTS 8 Leeds
13.11.01 Matt Galer L RSC 4 Leeds
02.12.02 Gary Thompson W PTS 6 Leeds
13.05.03 Kreshnik Qato L PTS 6 Leeds
06.06.03 Jason Collins W PTS 10 Hull
          *(Vacant Central Area Middleweight
          Title)*
28.11.03 Jason Collins W PTS 10 Hull
          *(Central Area Middleweight Title
          Defence)*
10.02.04 Mo W PTS 6 Barnsley
08.05.04 Scott Dann L RSC 3 Bristol

(Vacant English Middleweight Title)
14.05.05 Simeon Cover DREW 6 Aberdeen
01.06.05 Gary Thompson W PTS 4 Leeds
25.09.05 Simeon Cover W PTS 6 Leeds
29.10.05 Jozsef Nagy L PTS 12 Szentes,
          Hungary
          (Vacant EBA S.Middleweight Title)
23.02.06 Howard Clarke W PTS 6 Leeds
20.03.06 Ojay Abrahams W PTS 6 Leeds
12.05.06 Darren Barker L RSC 6 Bethnal Green
01.06.07 Jorge Gomez W PTS 4 Peterborough
08.06.07 Brian Magee L RTD 2 Motherwell
Career: 36 contests, won 21, drew 3, lost 12.

Daniel Thorpe

Sheffield. *Born* Sheffield, 24 September,
1977
Lightweight. Former Central Area
Lightweight Champion. *Ht* 5'7½"
Manager D. Coldwell

07.09.01 Brian Gifford DREW 4 Bethnal Green
24.09.01 Ram Singh W RSC 4 Cleethorpes
17.11.01 Mally McIver L PTS 6 Dewsbury
10.12.01 Jason Gonzales W RSC 2 Birmingham
17.12.01 Joel Viney L RSC 2 Cleethorpes
11.02.02 Gareth Wiltshaw L PTS 6 Shrewsbury
04.03.02 Dave Travers W PTS 6 Birmingham
13.04.02 Jackson Williams L PTS 6 Norwich
11.05.02 Dean Scott W RSC 1 Chesterfield
21.05.02 Chris McDonagh L PTS 6 Custom
          House
08.06.02 Gary Young L RSC 1 Renfrew
12.07.02 Chill John L PTS 4 Southampton
21.07.02 John Marshall L RSC 1 Salford
22.09.02 Albi Hunt L PTS 6 Southwark
05.10.02 Gavin Down L RSC 2 Chesterfield
17.11.02 Nadeem Siddique L PTS 4 Bradford
29.11.02 Pete Buckley W PTS 6 Hull
21.12.02 Billy Corcoran L CO 2 Dagenham
16.02.03 Eddie Nevins L RSC 8 Salford
          *(Vacant Central Area S.Featherweight
          Title)*
22.03.03 Jamie Arthur L PTS 4 Renfrew
29.03.03 Danny Hunt L PTS 6 Portsmouth
12.04.03 Jackson Williams L PTS 6 Norwich
19.04.03 Steve Mullin W RSC 1 Liverpool
28.04.03 Jeff Thomas L PTS 6 Cleethorpes
08.05.03 Andy Morris L PTS 4 Widnes
08.06.03 Choi Tsveenpurev L PTS 8 Shaw
20.06.03 Colin Toohey L PTS 6 Liverpool
28.06.03 Gavin Rees L RSC 1 Cardiff
03.08.03 Joel Viney L PTS 6 Stalybridge
06.09.03 Joel Viney W PTS 6 Aberdeen
13.09.03 Sean Hughes L PTS 6 Wakefield
21.09.03 Chris Long W PTS 6 Bristol
12.10.03 Baz Carey DREW 6 Sheffield
19.10.03 Charles Shepherd L PTS 6 Shaw
27.10.03 Nadeem Siddique L PTS 6 Glasgow
06.11.03 Lee Beavis L PTS 4 Dagenham
07.12.03 Mally McIver W PTS 10 Bradford
          (Vacant Central Area Lightweight Title)
21.12.03 Pete Buckley W PTS 6 Bolton
26.02.04 Andy Morris L RSC 3 Widnes
03.04.04 Jason Nesbitt W PTS 6 Sheffield
23.04.04 Dave Hinds W PTS 6 Leicester
07.05.04 Stefy Bull L PTS 10 Doncaster
          *(Central Area Lightweight Title
          Defence)*
22.05.04 Gary Thornhill L RSC 4 Manchester
03.07.04 Joel Viney W RSC 1 Blackpool

10.09.04 Mickey Bowden W PTS 6 Wembley
18.09.04 Carl Greaves L PTS 6 Newark
01.10.04 Steve Bell L PTS 6 Manchester
08.10.04 Ricky Burns L PTS 6 Glasgow
16.10.04 Ryan Barrett L PTS 4 Dagenham
29.10.04 Adnan Amar L PTS 4 Worksop
06.11.04 Baz Carey W PTS 6 Coventry
26.11.04 John Murray L RSC 2 Altrincham
13.02.05 Lee McAllister L PTS 4 Bradford
04.03.05 Femi Fehintola L PTS 6 Rotherham
10.04.05 Dave Stewart L RSC 3 Brentwood
14.05.05 Tye Williams W RSC 3 Aberdeen
26.05.05 Baz Carey W PTS 6 Mayfair
03.06.05 Nadeem Siddique L PTS 6 Hull
24.06.05 James Gorman L PTS 6 Belfast
02.07.05 Michael Kelly L PTS 4 Dundalk
09.07.05 Carl Johanneson L RSC 3 Bristol
25.09.05 Jon Honney W PTS 4 Southampton
06.10.05 Paul Holborn L PTS 6 Sunderland
25.10.05 Kevin Mitchell L RSC 4 Preston
25.11.05 Haider Ali W RTD 4 Walsall
10.12.05 Amir Khan L RSC 2 Canning Town
27.01.06 Ian Wilson L PTS 4 Dagenham
25.02.06 Ashley Theophane DREW 4 Canning
          Town
11.03.06 Gavin Rees L RSC 5 Newport
13.05.06 Dean Smith L PTS 4 Bethnal Green
20.05.06 Kevin O'Hara L PTS 6 Belfast
28.05.06 Shane Watson L PTS 6 Longford
16.06.06 Dwayne Hill L PTS 4 Liverpool
23.06.06 Anthony Maynard L PTS 4
          Birmingham
02.09.06 Steve Bell L RTD 4 Bolton
06.10.06 Jonathan Whiteman L PTS 6 Mansfield
18.10.06 Gareth Couch L PTS 4 Bayswater
04.11.06 Paul McCloskey L RTD 3 Glasgow
06.12.06 Pete Buckley W PTS 6 Rotherham
14.12.06 Gavin Deacon W PTS 6 Leicester
22.12.06 Harry Ramogoadi L PTS 6 Coventry
15.02.07 Dean Harrison L PTS 4 Dudley
10.03.07 Stephen Burke L PTS 4 Liverpool
07.04.07 Barrie Jones L RSC 2 Cardiff
06.05.07 Michael Gomez L RSC 3 Altrincham
08.06.07 Albi Hunt L PTS 4 Mayfair
30.06.07 Eddie Hyland L PTS 4 Belfast
Career: 87 contests, won 21, drew 3, lost 63.

Neil Tidman

Bedworth. *Born* Nuneaton, 16 April, 1978
Midlands Area S.Middleweight Champion.
Ht 5'10"
Manager P. Carpenter

18.06.05 Lee Williamson W PTS 6 Coventry
22.10.05 Michael Banbula W PTS 6 Coventry
15.12.05 Omid Bourzo W RSC 3 Coventry
09.10.06 Ojay Abrahams W PTS 4 Bedworth
10.11.06 Nathan King L PTS 6 Newport
02.12.06 Mark Phillips W PTS 6 Coventry
09.12.06 Andrew Lowe L PTS 6 Chigwell
03.03.07 Jonjo Finnegan W PTS 10 Burton
          *(Vacant Midlands Area S.Middleweight
          Title)*
18.04.07 Joey Vegas L PTS 4 Strand
11.05.07 Steve McGuire L PTS 8 Motherwell
Career: 10 contests, won 6, lost 4.

Danny Tombs

Sheffield. *Born* London, 26 May, 1986
L.Heavyweight. *Ht* 5'10½"
Manager D. Hobson (senior)

12.11.05	Nicki Taylor DREW 4 Sheffield
19.11.05	Michael Banbula W RSC 2 Southwark
30.03.06	Mark Phillips W PTS 4 Bloomsbury
21.10.06	Tony Booth L PTS 4 Southwark

Career: 4 contests, won 2, drew 1, lost 1.

Craig Tomes
Barnsley. *Born* Barnsley, 22 November, 1980
Welterweight. *Ht* 5'7"
Manager T. Schofield

14.06.07	Adil Anwar L PTS 6 Leeds

Career: 1 contest, lost 1.

Nigel Travis
Manchester. *Born* Oldham, 5 July, 1972
S.Middleweight. *Ht* 6'0"
Manager S. Wood

16.06.07	Ryan Rowlinson W PTS 6 Bolton

Career: 1 contest, won 1.

Paul Truscott
Middlesbrough. *Born* Middlesbrough, 1 May, 1986
S.Featherweight. *Ht* 5'9"
Manager M. Marsden

23.06.06	Billy Smith W PTS 4 Blackpool
30.09.06	Steve Gethin W PTS 4 Middlesbrough
10.11.06	Rakhim Mingaleev W PTS 4 Hartlepool
28.01.07	Graeme Higginson W PTS 4 Yarm
25.03.07	Peter Feher W RSC 1 Dublin
20.04.07	Riaz Durgahed W PTS 4 Dudley
09.06.07	Ben Odamattey W PTS 6 Middlesbrough

Career: 7 contests, won 7.

Choi Tseveenpurev
Oldham. *Born* Mongolia, 6 October, 1971
WBF Featherweight Champion. Former Undefeated British Masters Featherweight Champion. *Ht* 5'5¾"
Manager J. Doughty

22.11.96	Jeun-Tae Kim W CO 8 Seoul, South Korea
19.08.98	Veerachol Sahaprom L PTS 10 Bangkok, Thailand
02.10.98	Surapol Sithnaruepol W CO 1 Bangkok, Thailand
07.01.99	Ekarat 13Reintower W CO 2 Krabi, Thailand
01.05.99	Bulan Bugiarso L PTS 12 Kalimanton, Indonesia
12.08.99	Jiao Hasabayar W RSC 4 Ulan-Bator, Mongolia
22.08.99	Con Roksa W CO 3 Seinyeng, China
22.08.99	Thongdang Sorvoraphin W CO 4 Seinyeng, China
21.05.00	David Jeffrey W RSC 2 Shaw
24.09.00	Billy Smith W RTD 2 Shaw
03.12.00	Chris Williams W PTS 4 Shaw
27.04.01	Willie Limond L PTS 6 Glasgow
23.09.01	Steve Hanley W PTS 6 Shaw
06.10.01	Livinson Ruiz W PTS 4 Manchester
09.12.01	Kevin Gerowski W RSC 5 Shaw *(Vacant British Masters Featherweight Title)*
22.03.02	Chris Emanuele W PTS 4 Coventry

02.06.02	John Mackay W RSC 5 Shaw
17.11.02	Peter Allen W RSC 4 Shaw
09.03.03	Jason Nesbitt W PTS 8 Shaw
08.06.03	Daniel Thorpe W PTS 8 Shaw
29.02.04	John Mackay W RSC 3 Shaw
13.03.04	Lehlohonolo Ledwaba L PTS 8 Copenhagen, Denmark
06.05.04	Kevin O'Hara W PTS 8 Barnsley
10.07.04	Harry Ramogoadi W RTD 6 Coventry *(British Masters Featherweight Title Defence)*
06.03.05	Harry Ramogoadi W RSC 5 Shaw *(British Masters Featherweight Title Defence)*
20.11.05	Alexey Volchan W RSC 10 Shaw
02.04.06	David Kiilu W RSC 3 Shaw *(Vacant WBF Featherweight Title)*
11.03.07	Nikoloz Berkatsashvili W RSC 4 Shaw *(WBF Featherweight Title Defence)*

Career: 28 contests, won 24, lost 4.

Richard Turba
Blackpool. *Born* Nitra, Slovakia, 21 February, 1985
L.Heavyweight. *Ht* 5'10"
Manager W. Barker

14.12.05	Paul Billington W PTS 6 Blackpool
02.03.06	Csaba Andras W RSC 3 Blackpool
06.05.06	Tyan Booth L PTS 6 Blackpool
16.06.06	Mike Allen W RSC 2 Liverpool
23.06.06	Paul David L PTS 6 Blackpool
06.10.06	Rod Anderton W RSC 2 Mansfield
10.11.06	Steve McGuire DREW 6 Hartlepool

Career: 7 contests, won 4, drew 1, lost 2.

Rob Turley
Cefn Fforest. *Born* Newport, 24 November, 1986
S.Featherweight. *Ht* 5'7"
Manager C. Sanigar

16.06.07	Delroy Spencer W PTS 6 Newport

Career: 1 contest, won 1.

Amir Unsworth (Morshedi)
Sleaford. *Born* Warrington, 12 January, 1981
L.Welterweight. *Ht* 5'7"
Manager C. Greaves

30.06.07	Sergei Rozhakmens W PTS 6 Manchester

Career: 1 contest, won 1.

Denton Vassell
Manchester. *Born* Manchester, 13 September, 1984
L.Middleweight. *Ht* 5'9¾"
Manager F. Warren

02.09.06	Ernie Smith W RSC 3 Bolton
09.12.06	Duncan Cottier W PTS 4 Canning Town
10.03.07	Steve Cooper W RSC 2 Liverpool

Career: 3 contests, won 3.

Joey Vegas (Lubega)
Tottenham. *Born* Namirembe Uganda, 1 January, 1982
Cruiserweight. British Masters S.Middleweight Champion. *Ht* 5'8½"

Manager M. Helliet

04.11.04	Cello Renda W RSC 3 Piccadilly
27.01.05	Egbui Ikeagwo W PTS 4 Piccadilly
26.03.05	Egbui Ikeagwo W PTS 4 Hackney
26.05.05	Gareth Lawrence W PTS 4 Mayfair
17.11.05	Conroy McIntosh W RSC 3 Piccadilly
30.03.06	Simeon Cover W PTS 10 Piccadilly *(British Masters S.Middleweight Title Challenge)*
12.07.06	Simeon Cover W PTS 4 Bethnal Green
30.11.06	Michael Monaghan W PTS 10 Piccadilly *(British Masters S.Middleweight Title Defence)*
13.12.06	Varuzhan Davtyan W RSC 1 Strand
18.04.07	Neil Tidman W PTS 4 Strand

Career: 10 contests, won 10.

Joey Vegas   Philip Sharkey

(Jaspreet) Jaz Virdee
Peterborough. *Born* London, 26 March, 1979
L.Welterweight. *Ht* 5'9"
Manager I. Pauly

22.07.03	Rob Jeffries L PTS 6 Bethnal Green
27.09.03	Steve Bell L RSC 1 Manchester
21.11.03	Silence Saheed L RSC 2 Millwall
24.01.04	Kevin Mitchell L RSC 1 Wembley
08.04.04	Kristian Laight L PTS 6 Peterborough
30.03.06	Kristian Laight W PTS 6 Peterborough
15.06.06	Arial Krasnopolski W PTS 6 Peterborough
14.10.06	Tony Delaney L PTS 6 Manchester
07.12.06	Darren Hamilton L PTS 6 Peterborough

Career: 9 contests, won 2, lost 7.

Dave Wakefield

Tooting. *Born* London, 8 January, 1979
L.Middleweight. *Ht* 5'11"
Manager D. Powell

12.12.02	Mark Thornton L PTS 4 Leicester Square
13.04.03	Jon Hilton W PTS 4 Streatham
26.04.03	Kevin Phelan L PTS 4 Brentford
03.06.03	Justin Hudson L PTS 4 Bethnal Green
13.06.03	William Webster DREW 6 Queensway
25.10.03	Barrie Lee L PTS 4 Edinburgh
27.11.03	Kevin Phelan L PTS 6 Longford
20.02.04	Chas Symonds L RSC 5 Bethnal Green
15.05.04	Alan Campbell DREW 6 Aberdeen
26.02.06	Dean Marcantonio W RSC 3 Dagenham
06.05.06	Lance Hall W PTS 6 Birmingham
23.06.06	Joe Mitchell W PTS 6 Birmingham
26.01.07	Paddy Pollock W PTS 6 Glasgow
25.02.07	Paul Morby L PTS 6 Southampton
05.05.07	Kevin McIntyre L PTS 6 Glasgow
31.05.07	Matt Scriven W PTS 6 Manchester
16.06.07	George Hillyard L PTS 10 Chigwell *(Vacant British Masters L.Middleweight Title)*

Career: 17 contests, won 6, drew 2, lost 9.

Dave Wakefield   Les Clark

Gwyn Wale

Barnsley. *Born* Barnsley, 24 August, 1984
L.Welterweight. *Ht* 5'8"
Manager T. Gilmour

17.09.02	Arv Mittoo W PTS 6 Bethnal Green
05.10.02	Martin Hardcastle W PTS 4 Huddersfield
16.11.02	David Kehoe W PTS 4 Nottingham
22.02.03	James Paisley W RSC 1 Huddersfield
10.05.03	David Vaughan DREW 4 Huddersfield
13.09.03	Gary Cummings L PTS 6 Wakefield
17.12.04	Jason Nesbitt W PTS 4 Huddersfield
04.02.05	Stefy Bull L PTS 10 Doncaster *(Central Area Lightweight Title Challenge)*
18.06.05	Judex Meemea W RSC 5 Barnsley
29.09.06	Billy Smith L PTS 6 Motherwell

Career: 10 contests, won 6, drew 1, lost 3.

Josh Wale

Brampton. *Born* Barnsley, 8 April, 1988
S.Bantamweight. *Ht* 5'7"
Manager D. Coldwell

13.10.06	Neil Read W RSC 1 Doncaster
15.04.07	Anthony Hanna W PTS 6 Barnsley
03.06.07	Delroy Spencer W PTS 6 Barnsley

Career: 3 contests, won 3.

David Walker

Bermondsey. *Born* Bromley, 17 June, 1976
L.Middleweight. Former Undefeated
Southern Area L.Middleweight Champion.
Former Undefeated Southern Area
Welterweight Champion. *Ht* 5'10"
Manager Self

29.04.00	Dave Fallon W RSC 1 Wembley
27.05.00	Stuart Rimmer W RSC 2 Southwark
15.07.00	Billy Smith W RTD 2 Millwall
16.09.00	Keith Jones W PTS 6 Bethnal Green
14.10.00	Jason Vlasman W RSC 1 Wembley
18.11.00	Gary Flear W PTS 4 Dagenham
09.12.00	Karl Taylor W PTS 6 Southwark
20.01.01	Ernie Smith W RTD 1 Bethnal Green
17.02.01	Paul Denton W PTS 4 Bethnal Green
19.05.01	Mark Ramsey W PTS 4 Wembley
14.07.01	David White W PTS 4 Liverpool
13.09.01	David Kirk DREW 8 Sheffield
16.03.02	Paul Dyer W RSC 6 Bethnal Green *(Vacant Southern Area Welterweight Title)*
10.05.02	Pedro Thompson W RSC 3 Bethnal Green
23.08.02	Robert Burton W RSC 2 Bethnal Green
25.10.02	Brett James W RSC 4 Bethnal Green *(Southern Area Welterweight Title Defence)*
21.12.02	Jimmy Vincent L RSC 8 Dagenham *(Final Elim. British Welterweight Title)*
05.03.03	Ojay Abrahams W PTS 6 Bethnal Green
16.04.03	Leigh Wicks W PTS 6 Nottingham
27.05.03	John Humphrey W CO 2 Dagenham *(Southern Area L.Middleweight Title Challenge. Elim. British L.Middleweight Title)*
25.07.03	Spencer Fearon W RSC 4 Norwich *(Southern Area L.Middleweight Title Defence)*
04.10.03	Roman Karmazin L RTD 3 Muswell Hill *(European L.Middleweight Title Challenge)*
12.03.04	Matt Scriven W RSC 3 Nottingham
02.06.04	Kevin Phelan W PTS 6 Nottingham
12.11.04	Danny Moir W RSC 5 Wembley
09.07.05	Howard Clarke W PTS 4 Nottingham
23.09.05	Jamie Moore L RSC 4 Manchester *(British L.Middleweight Title Challenge)*
18.05.07	Ben Hudson W PTS 6 Canning Town

Career: 28 contests, won 24, drew 1, lost 3.

Dean Walker

Sheffield. *Born* Sheffield, 25 April, 1979
L.Heavyweight. *Ht* 5'11"
Manager D. Coldwell

21.10.00	Colin McCash DREW 6 Sheffield
11.12.00	James Lee L PTS 6 Sheffield
27.07.01	Chris Duggan W RSC 4 Sheffield

15.12.01	William Webster W PTS 6 Sheffield
03.03.02	Shaun Horsfall W PTS 6 Shaw
02.06.02	Wayne Shepherd W PTS 6 Shaw
03.08.02	Richard Inquieti W PTS 6 Derby
05.10.02	Martin Scotland W PTS 6 Chesterfield
24.05.03	Neil Bonner W PTS 6 Sheffield
12.10.03	Paul Lomax W PTS 6 Sheffield
10.02.04	Neil Addis W PTS 6 Barnsley
21.02.04	Matthew Macklin L CO 1 Cardiff
08.06.04	Andrei Ivanov W PTS 6 Sheffield
03.09.04	Dean Cockburn L PTS 10 Doncaster *(Vacant Central Area S.Middleweight Title)*
15.12.04	Lee Murtagh L PTS 10 Sheffield *(Vacant Central Central Area Middleweight Title)*
20.02.05	Mo W PTS 6 Sheffield
19.03.05	Jozsef Nagy L RTD 8 Tapolca, Hungary *(IBF Inter-Continental Middleweight Title Challenge)*
16.07.05	Darren Barker L PTS 6 Chigwell
25.10.05	Thomas McDonagh L PTS 6 Preston
18.02.06	Jason McKay L RTD 1 Edinburgh
18.05.06	Matthew Hough L PTS 6 Walsall
14.10.06	Paul Smith L RSC 3 Manchester *(Vacant Central Area Middleweight Title)*
12.11.06	Craig Bunn DREW 6 Manchester
24.11.06	Jonjo Finnegan DREW 4 Nottingham
11.12.06	Tyrone Wright L PTS 6 Cleethorpes
10.03.07	Tony Quigley L RSC 2 Liverpool
15.04.07	Robert Burton L PTS 6 Barnsley
06.05.07	Darren Rhodes L PTS 4 Leeds

Career: 28 contests, won 11, drew 3, lost 14.

Mark Walker

Boldon Colliery. *Born* South Shields, 14
December, 1973
Heavyweight. *Ht.* 6'2"
Manager S. Foster/D. Powell/F. Warren

04.11.06	Chris Woollas DREW 4 Glasgow

Career: 1 contest, drew 1.

Danny Wallace

Leeds. *Born* Leeds, 12 July, 1980
S.Featherweight. *Ht* 5'7"
Manager R. Manners

24.08.01	Roger Glover W PTS 4 Atlantic City, USA
12.04.02	Michael Weaver DREW 4 Philadelphia, USA
22.02.03	Jamil Hussain W RSC 1 Huddersfield
12.04.03	Ian Turner W RSC 4 Bethnal Green
10.05.03	Marcel Kasimov L RSC 3 Huddersfield
06.09.03	Alexei Volchan W PTS 4 Huddersfield
31.01.04	Jamie Yelland W PTS 6 Bethnal Green
13.03.04	Henry Janes L PTS 4 Huddersfield
11.09.04	Joseph Barela W RSC 2 Philadelphia, Pennsylvania, USA
06.12.04	Fred Janes W RSC 2 Leeds
01.06.05	Harry Ramogoadi L PTS 6 Leeds
05.12.05	Matt Teague L PTS 10 Leeds *(Vacant British Masters & Central Area Featherweight Titles)*
29.09.06	Mo Khaled W RSC 1 Manchester
03.11.06	Barrington Brown W PTS 4 Barnsley
09.02.07	Chris Hooper W PTS 4 Leeds

Career: 15 contests, won 10, drew 1, lost 4.

Ryan Walls
Slough. *Born* Reading, 29 January, 1979
L.Heavyweight. Former Undefeated
Southern Area S.Middleweight Champion.
Former British Masters Cruiserweight
Champion. *Ht* 6'0½"
Manager Self

20.12.02	Mark Phillips W PTS 4 Bracknell
23.02.03	Michael Pinnock W PTS 6 Streatham
21.03.03	Jimmy Steel W PTS 6 Longford
12.04.03	Earl Ling W RSC 4 Norwich
09.05.03	Darren Ashton W PTS 6 Longford
01.08.03	Darren Ashton W PTS 4 Bethnal Green
26.10.03	Michael Pinnock W PTS 10 Longford
	(Vacant British Masters Cruiserweight Title)
25.03.04	Pinky Burton L PTS 10 Longford
	(British Masters Cruiserweight Title Defence)
08.05.04	Toks Owoh W PTS 6 Bristol
08.12.04	Varuzhan Davtyan W PTS 4 Longford
24.02.05	Ryan Kerr L PTS 10 Sunderland
	(Vacant English S.Middleweight Title)
24.04.05	Peter Haymer L PTS 6 Leicester Square
08.05.05	Donovan Smillie W PTS 6 Bradford
20.06.05	Simeon Cover W RSC 8 Longford
19.12.05	Gareth Lawrence W RTD 6 Longford
	(Vacant Southern Area S.Middleweight Title)
06.10.06	Hussain Osman L RSC 2 Bethnal Green
18.11.06	Paul Smith L RSC 4 Newport
24.02.07	Tomas Da Silva W RSC 2 Bracknell

Career: 18 contests, won 13, lost 5.

Dougie Walton
Coventry. *Born* Coventry, 9 August, 1981
Featherweight. *Ht* 5'4"
Manager P. Cowdell

04.03.06	Graeme Higginson DREW 6 Coventry
09.10.06	Neil Marston W PTS 6 Birmingham
11.12.06	Neil Read W RSC 5 Birmingham
26.02.07	Delroy Spencer W PTS 6 Birmingham
13.05.07	Shaun Walton W PTS 4 Birmingham

Career: 5 contests, won 4, drew 1.

Shaun Walton
Telford. *Born* West Bromwich, 2 January, 1975
Lightweight. *Ht* 5'10"
Manager E. Johnson

15.04.05	Dave Hinds W PTS 6 Shrewsbury
16.09.05	Abdul Mougharbel DREW 6 Telford
14.10.05	Craig Bromley L PTS 4 Huddersfield
04.12.05	Abdul Mougharbel DREW 6 Telford
10.03.06	Andy Davis L PTS 6 Walsall
28.05.06	Sean Hughes L PTS 6 Wakefield
05.06.06	Furhan Rafiq L PTS 6 Glasgow
09.09.06	Furhan Rafiq L PTS 6 Inverurie
06.10.06	Andy Bell L PTS 6 Mansfield
13.10.06	Jamie McIlroy L PTS 6 Irvine
21.10.06	Mark Alexander L PTS 6 Southwark
28.10.06	Robin Deakin L PTS 4 Bethnal Green
10.11.06	Sergei Rozhakmens W PTS 6 Telford
30.11.06	Kim Poulsen L PTS 6 Piccadilly
13.12.06	Darryl Mitchell L PTS 4 Strand
22.01.07	Furhan Rafiq L PTS 6 Glasgow
17.02.07	Vinny Mitchell L PTS 4 Wembley
03.03.07	Kevin Buckley L PTS 6 Burton
01.04.07	Sergei Rozhakmens DREW 6 Shrewsbury

14.04.07	Robert Nelson L PTS 8 Wakefield
23.04.07	Brian Murphy W RSC 5 Glasgow
06.05.07	James McElvaney L PTS 6 Darlington
13.05.07	Dougie Walton L PTS 4 Birmingham
05.06.07	John Donnelly L PTS 6 Glasgow
14.06.07	Eugene Heagney L PTS 6 Leeds
21.06.07	Tony McQuade L PTS 6 Peterborough
30.06.07	Scott Quigg L RSC 1 Manchester

Career: 27 contests, won 3, drew 3, lost 21.

Andrew Ward
Maltby. *Born* Rotherham, 19 September, 1982
L.Welterweight. *Ht* 5'7"
Manager D. Coldwell

01.10.06	Jason Nesbitt DREW 6 Rotherham
06.12.06	Graeme Higginson L PTS 6 Rotherham
15.04.07	Deniss Sirjatovs W PTS 6 Barnsley
03.06.07	Pete Buckley W PTS 4 Barnsley

Career: 4 contests, won 2, drew 1, lost 1.

Isaac Ward
Darlington. *Born* Darlington, 7 April, 1977
Commonwealth S.Bantamweight
Champion. *Ht* 5'5"
Manager M. Marsden

03.08.02	Neil Read W RSC 1 Blackpool
18.10.02	John-Paul Ryan W PTS 6 Hartlepool
14.12.02	Steve Gethin W PTS 4 Newcastle
11.07.03	Rocky Dean DREW 4 Darlington
13.09.03	Pete Buckley W PTS 6 Wakefield
10.10.03	Rocky Dean W PTS 6 Darlington
04.12.03	Jamie Yelland W PTS 6 Huddersfield
05.03.04	Steve Gethin W PTS 6 Darlington
16.04.04	Pete Buckley W PTS 6 Hartlepool
03.07.04	Dave Hinds W PTS 6 Blackpool
19.11.04	Abdul Mougharbel W PTS 4 Hartlepool
04.03.05	Peter Allen DREW 6 Hartlepool
02.06.05	Billy Smith W PTS 8 Yarm
28.10.05	Abdul Mougharbel W PTS 6 Hartlepool
28.04.06	Rakhim Mingaleev W PTS 4 Hartlepool
30.05.06	Martin Power L RSC 8 Bethnal Green
	(British Bantamweight Title Challenge)
30.09.06	Neil Marston W PTS 6 Middlesbrough
28.01.07	Francis Miyeyusho W CO 2 Yarm
	(Vacant Commonwealth S.Bantamweight Title)

Career: 18 contests, won 15, drew 2, lost 1.

Nathan Ward
Reading. *Born* Reading, 19 July, 1979
L.Welterweight. Former Undefeated British
Masters Welterweight Champion. *Ht* 5'10"
Manager Self

27.09.02	Darren Goode W RSC 1 Bracknell
03.12.02	Dean Larter W PTS 4 Bethnal Green
20.12.02	Arv Mittoo W PTS 6 Bracknell
18.03.03	Pete Buckley W PTS 4 Reading
26.04.03	Cristian Hodorogea L RSC 1 Brentford
26.09.03	Casey Brooke W RSC 1 Reading
26.11.03	Lance Hall L PTS 4 Mayfair
12.05.04	Dave Hinds W PTS 4 Reading
24.09.04	James Paisley W PTS 4 Bethnal Green
26.11.04	Lea Handley W CO 2 Bethnal Green
12.02.05	Ernie Smith W PTS 6 Portsmouth
19.06.05	James Paisley W RSC 4 Bethnal Green
	(Vacant British Masters Welterweight Title)

02.12.06	Ben Hudson W PTS 6 Longford
24.02.07	Jon Honney L PTS 10 Bracknell
	(Vacant Southern Area L.Welterweight Title)

Career: 14 contests, won 11, lost 3.

Craig Watson
Manchester. *Born* Oldham, 7 February, 1983
Welterweight. *Ht* 5'10"
Manager F. Maloney

20.05.05	Willie Valentine W RTD 2 Southwark
19.06.05	Jus Wallie W PTS 4 Bethnal Green
16.07.05	Billy Smith W PTS 4 Bolton
07.10.05	Ben Hudson W PTS 4 Bethnal Green
04.11.05	Sergii Tertii W PTS 6 Bethnal Green
29.09.06	Michael Medor W RSC 1 Manchester
25.11.06	Rakhim Mingaleev W PTS 6 Belfast
09.02.07	John Fewkes L PTS 8 Leeds
27.04.07	Robert Lloyd-Taylor W PTS 8 Wembley

Career: 9 contests, won 8, lost 1.

Davey Watson
Wheatley Hill. *Born* Stockton, 9 September, 1987
L.Welterweight. *Ht* 5'10"
Manager D. Garside

06.05.07	Sergei Rozhakmens W PTS 6 Darlington
09.06.07	Jason Nesbitt W PTS 6 Middlesbrough
24.06.07	Mark Bett W RTD 5 Sunderland

Career: 3 contests, won 3.

George Watson
Newcastle. *Born* Newcastle, 13 December, 1983
Lightweight. *Ht* 6'0"
Manager T. Conroy

11.05.07	Gavin Deacon W PTS 6 Sunderland

Career: 1 contest, won 1.

John Watson
Liverpool. *Born* Whiston, 9 June, 1983
L.Welterweight. *Ht* 5'9¾"
Manager L. Maloney

10.03.07	Jason Nesbitt W PTS 4 Liverpool

Career: 1 contest, won 1.

Martin Watson
Coatbridge. *Born* Bellshill, 12 May, 1981
Celtic Lightweight Champion. Former
Undefeated Scottish Lightweight
Champion. *Ht* 5'8"
Manager R. Bannon/A. Morrison

24.05.01	Shaune Danskin W RSC 3 Glasgow
20.10.01	Jon Honney W RSC 3 Glasgow
16.12.01	Richie Caparelli W PTS 6 Glasgow
11.03.02	Pete Buckley W PTS 4 Glasgow
26.04.02	Gary Reid W PTS 6 Glasgow
08.06.02	Scott Miller W RSC 2 Renfrew
18.11.02	Gary Reid W RSC 4 Glasgow
22.03.03	Joel Viney W RSC 2 Renfrew
16.05.03	Barry Hughes W RTD 8 Glasgow
	(Vacant Scottish Lightweight Title)
30.10.03	Mark Winters DREW 8 Belfast
01.04.04	Steve Murray L PTS 10 Bethnal Green
19.06.04	Jus Wallie W PTS 6 Renfrew

177

29.10.04 Mark Winters W PTS 10 Renfrew
  (Vacant Celtic Lightweight Title)
28.01.05 Jimmy Beech W PTS 4 Renfrew
09.07.05 Lee Meager L PTS 10 Nottingham
01.04.06 Ryan Barrett W PTS 10 Bethnal Green
  (Elim. British Lightweight Title)
29.04.06 George Ashie W PTS 6 Edinburgh
08.07.06 Gavin Rees L PTS 6 Cardiff
Career: 18 contests, won 14, drew 1, lost 3.

Shane Watson
Ruislip. *Born* Hillingdon, 12 August, 1984
L.Welterweight. *Ht* 5'9½"
Manager J. Evans

23.11.05 Pete Buckley W PTS 6 Mayfair
04.12.05 Duncan Cottier W PTS 4 Portsmouth
05.03.06 Chris Long W PTS 4 Southampton
07.04.06 Anthony Christopher W RSC 1
  Longford
28.05.06 Daniel Thorpe W PTS 6 Longford
02.12.06 Jason Nesbitt W PTS 6 Longford
Career: 6 contests, won 6.

Jamie Way
Abercarn. *Born* Newport, 11 December,
1981
Welterweight. *Ht* 5'7"
Manager B. Powell

15.09.06 Jimmy Maile W RSC 4 Newport
10.11.06 Pawel Jas W PTS 6 Newport
03.03.07 Geraint Harvey W PTS 6 Newport
16.06.07 Steve Cooper W PTS 6 Newport
Career: 4 contests, won 4.

Lee Webb
Plymouth. *Born* Plymouth, 25 November,
1971
Heavyweight. *Ht.* 6'4"
Manager N. Christian

07.10.06 Scott Belshaw L RSC 1 Belfast
01.12.06 Dean O'Loughlin L RSC 3 Doncaster
23.02.07 Dean O'Loughlin L RSC 2 Doncaster
24.06.07 Danny Hughes L RSC 4 Sunderland
Career: 4 contests, lost 4.

Sam Webb
Chislehurst. *Born* Sidcup, 11 April, 1981
Middleweight. *Ht* 5'8¾"
Manager F. Maloney

07.10.05 Geraint Harvey W CO 1 Bethnal Green
04.11.05 Vadzim Astapuk W RSC 2 Bethnal
  Green
27.01.06 Aleksandr Zhuk W PTS 4 Dagenham
24.03.06 Gatis Skuja W PTS 4 Bethnal Green
30.05.06 Alex Stoda L RSC 3 Bethnal Green
17.11.06 David Kirk W PTS 4 Bethnal Green
27.04.07 Alexander Spitjo W RSC 1 Wembley
15.06.07 Ben Hudson W PTS 4 Crystal Palace
Career: 8 contests, won 7, lost 1.

Nathan Weise
Thameside. *Born* Bath, 7 July, 1984
Welterweight. *Ht* 5'11½"
Manager F. Maloney

29.06.06 Bheki Moyo W PTS 4 Bethnal Green
26.01.07 Tom Glover DREW 4 Dagenham
Career: 2 contests, won 1, drew 1.

Jason Welborn
Warley. *Born* Sandwell, 9 May, 1986
L.Middleweight. *Ht* 5'10"
Manager D. Powell

12.12.05 Jamie Ambler W RSC 1 Birmingham
27.02.06 Tyan Booth L CO 4 Birmingham
05.12.06 Aldon Stewart W RSC 3
  Wolverhampton
Career: 3 contests, won 2, lost 1.

Calvin White
Lancaster. *Born* Preston, 3 December, 1978
Lightweight. *Ht* 5'9"
Manager J. Pennington

10.07.06 Pete Buckley W PTS 6 Manchester
21.10.06 Gavin Tait L PTS 4 Southwark
Career: 2 contests, won 1, lost 1.

Robin White
Bolton. *Born* Bolton, 26 June, 1980
L.Heavyweight. *Ht* 6'4"
Manager S. Wood

17.12.06 Mark Phillips W PTS 4 Bolton
25.02.07 Nicki Taylor W PTS 4 Manchester
Career: 2 contests, won 2.

Jonathan Whiteman
Mansfield. *Born* Sutton in Ashfield, 1 May,
1984
Welterweight. *Ht* 5'11"
Manager C. Greaves

22.10.04 Pete Buckley W PTS 6 Mansfield
10.12.04 Joel Viney W RSC 4 Mansfield
06.03.05 Terry Carruthers DREW 6 Mansfield
24.04.05 Dave Curran L DIS 2 Askern
09.07.05 Kell Brook L RSC 2 Nottingham
11.09.05 Ian Reid W PTS 4 Kirkby in Ashfield
22.10.05 Billy Smith W PTS 6 Mansfield
04.11.05 Darren Johnstone L RSC 3 Glasgow
04.12.05 Tristan Davies L PTS 4 Telford
28.01.06 Rendall Munroe L RSC 2 Nottingham
06.10.06 Daniel Thorpe W PTS 6 Mansfield
04.11.06 Billy Smith L PTS 6 Mansfield
25.11.06 James Gorman L RSC 2 Belfast
28.04.07 Jason Nesbitt L RTD 5 Newark
Career: 14 contests, won 5, drew 1, lost 8.

Adie Whitmore
Derby. *Born* Alfreton, 28 July, 1987
S.Middleweight. *Ht* 6'2"
Manager M. Shinfield

08.12.05 Jimi Hendricks W RSC 1 Derby
14.05.06 Jon Foster W RSC 6 Derby
11.11.06 Ojay Abrahams W PTS 6 Sutton in
  Ashfield
23.03.07 Jon Foster W RTD 4 Nottingham
Career: 4 contests, won 4.

Carl Wild
Sheffield. *Born* Sheffield, 3 April, 1986
L.Heavyweight. *Ht.* 6'2"
Manager G. Rhodes

28.10.06 Mark Phillips W PTS 6 Sheffield
24.02.07 Mark Nilsen L PTS 6 Manchester
20.04.07 Phillip Callaghan W RSC 1 Sheffield
06.05.07 Carl Dilks L PTS 6 Altrincham
16.06.07 Carl Dilks L PTS 6 Bolton
Career: 5 contests, won 2, lost 3.

Danny Williams
Brixton. *Born* London, 13 July, 1973
British Heavyweight Champion. Former
Commonwealth Heavyweight Champion.
Former Undefeated WBO & WBU Inter-
Continental Heavyweight Champion.
Ht 6'3"
Manager Self

21.10.95 Vance Idiens W CO 2 Bethnal Green
09.12.95 Joey Paladino W RSC 1 Bethnal Green
13.02.96 Slick Miller W RSC 1 Bethnal Green
09.03.96 James Wilder W PTS 4 Millstreet
13.07.96 John Pierre W PTS 4 Bethnal Green
31.08.96 Andy Lambert W RSC 2 Dublin
09.11.96 Michael Murray W CO 1 Manchester
08.02.97 Shane Woollas W RSC 2 Millwall
03.05.97 Albert Call W RSC 4 Manchester
19.07.97 R. F. McKenzie W RSC 2 Wembley
15.11.97 Bruce Douglas W RSC 2 Bristol
19.12.97 Derek Amos W RSC 4 NYC, New
  York, USA
21.02.98 Shane Woollas W RSC 2 Belfast
16.05.98 Antonio Diaz W CO 3 Bethnal Green
10.10.98 Antoine Palatis W PTS 12 Bethnal
  Green
  *(Vacant WBO Inter-Continental
  Heavyweight Title)*
03.04.99 Julius Francis L PTS 12 Kensington
  *(British & Commonwealth
  Heavyweight Title Challenges)*
02.10.99 Ferenc Deak W RTD 1 Namur,
  Belgium
18.12.99 Harry Senior W PTS 12 Southwark
  *(Vacant Commonwealth Heavyweight
  Title)*
19.02.00 Anton Nel W CO 5 Dagenham
06.05.00 Michael Murray W RSC 6 Frankfurt,
  Germany
24.06.00 Craig Bowen-Price W CO 1 Glasgow
23.09.00 Quinn Navarre W RSC 6 Bethnal
  Green
21.10.00 Mark Potter W RSC 6 Wembley
  *(Commonwealth & WBO Inter-
  Continental Heavyweight Title
  Defences. Vacant British Heavyweight
  Title)*
09.06.01 Kali Meehan W RSC 1 Bethnal Green
  *(Commonwealth Heavyweight Title
  Defence)*
28.07.01 Julius Francis W CO 4 Wembley
  *(British & Commonwealth
  Heavyweight Title Defences)*
15.12.01 Shawn Robinson W RSC 2
  Mashantucket Connecticut, USA
12.02.02 Michael Sprott W RTD 7 Bethnal
  Green
  *(British & Commonwealth
  Heavyweight Title Defences)*
17.09.02 Keith Long W PTS 12 Bethnal Green
  *(British & Commonwealth
  Heavyweight Title Defences)*
08.02.03 Sinan Samil Sam L RSC 6 Berlin,
  Germany
  *(European Heavyweight Title
  Challenge)*
26.04.03 Bob Mirovic W RSC 4 Brentford
  *(Commonwealth Heavyweight Title
  Defence)*
26.09.03 Michael Sprott W RSC 5 Reading
  *(British & Commonwealth
  Heavyweight Title Defences)*

24.01.04 Michael Sprott L PTS 12 Wembley
(British & Commonwealth Heavyweight Title Defences)
01.04.04 Ratko Draskovic W RSC 1 Bethnal Green
13.05.04 Augustin N'Gou W RTD 3 Bethnal Green
(Vacant WBU Inter-Continental Heavyweight Title)
30.07.04 Mike Tyson W CO 4 Louisville, Kentucky, USA
11.12.04 Vitali Klitschko L RSC 8 Las Vegas, USA
(WBC Heavyweight Title Challenge)
04.06.05 Zoltan Petranyi W RSC 3 Manchester
10.12.05 Audley Harrison W PTS 12 Canning Town
(Vacant Commonwealth Heavyweight Title)
25.02.06 Matt Skelton W PTS 12 Canning Town
(Commonwealth Heavyweight Title Defence)
20.05.06 Adnan Serin W RTD 3 Belfast
08.07.06 Matt Skelton L PTS 12 Cardiff
(Commonwealth Heavyweight Title Defence)
09.12.06 Audley Harrison L RSC 3 Canning Town
02.03.07 Scott Gammer W CO 9 Neath
(British Heavyweight Title Challenge)
Career: 43 contests, won 37, lost 6.

Richard Williams

Stockwell. *Born* London, 9 May, 1971
Middleweight. Former IBO L.Middleweight Champion. Former Undefeated Commonwealth & WBF L.Middleweight Champion. *Ht* 5'9½"
Manager Self

08.03.97 Marty Duke W RSC 3 Brentwood
30.06.97 Danny Quacoe W PTS 4 Bethnal Green
02.09.97 Michael Alexander L PTS 4 Southwark
16.10.99 Pedro Carragher W RSC 2 Bethnal Green
06.11.99 Lee Bird W RSC 4 Bethnal Green
20.12.99 Harry Butler W RSC 1 Bethnal Green
17.04.00 Kevin Thompson W CO 1 Birmingham
16.06.00 Piotr Bartnicki W RSC 3 Bloomsbury
08.09.00 Dean Ashton W RSC 1 Hammersmith
04.11.00 Howard Clarke W CO 4 Bethnal Green
02.12.00 Aziz Daari W RSC 2 Bethnal Green
23.01.01 Tony Badea W RSC 3 Crawley
(Commonwealth L. Middleweight Title Challenge)
04.06.01 Hussain Osman W PTS 10 Hartlepool
25.09.01 Andrew Murray W RSC 3 Liverpool
(Commonwealth L. Middleweight Title Defence)
20.10.01 Viktor Fesetchko W RSC 6 Portsmouth
01.12.01 Shannan Taylor W RSC 4 Bethnal Green
(Commonwealth L. Middleweight Title Defence. Vacant IBO L. Middleweight Title)
29.06.02 Paul Samuels T DRAW 3 Brentwood
(IBO L. Middleweight Title Defence)
07.12.02 Paul Samuels W RSC 10 Brentwood
(IBO L. Middleweight Title Defence)
08.03.03 Andrei Pestriaev W PTS 12 Bethnal Green
(IBO L. Middleweight Title Defence. WBF L. Middleweight Title Challenge)

21.06.03 Sergio Martinez L PTS 12 Manchester
(IBO L.Middleweight Title Defence)
31.01.04 Ayittey Powers W RSC 7 Bethnal Green
(Vacant Commonwealth L.Middleweight Title)
17.04.04 Sergio Martinez L RTD 9 Belfast
(IBO L.Middleweight Title Challenge)
26.11.04 Szabolcs Rimovszky W RSC 3 Altrincham
24.02.06 Marcin Piatkowski W PTS 8 Dagenham
22.09.06 Vedran Akrap W RSC 5 Bethnal Green
15.12.06 Howard Eastman L CO 12 Bethnal Green
(Vacant British Middleweight Title)
Career: 26 contests, won 21, drew 1, lost 4.

Tye Williams

Dewsbury. *Born* London, 9 June, 1976
Welterweight. *Ht* 5'9"
Manager M. Marsden

23.10.04 Rocky Muscus W PTS 6 Wakefield
09.11.04 Lea Handley L RSC 1 Leeds
26.02.05 Darren Gethin DREW 4 Burton
14.05.05 Daniel Thorpe L RSC 3 Aberdeen
25.06.05 Gary Connolly W CO 4 Wakefield
11.12.05 Jackson Williams L PTS 6 Norwich
12.02.06 Jonathan Hussey L PTS 6 Manchester
05.03.06 Adam Kelly L PTS 4 Sheffield
25.03.06 Scott Conway DREW 4 Burton
14.05.06 Scott Conway W RSC 5 Derby
28.05.06 Khurram Hussain L PTS 6 Wakefield
18.09.06 Wayne Downing W RSC 2 Glasgow
20.10.06 Adam Kelly L PTS 4 Sheffield
03.11.06 Mike Reid W RSC 6 Glasgow
15.04.07 Chris Saunders L PTS 6 Barnsley
29.04.07 Dee Mitchell L PTS 8 Birmingham
27.05.07 Nadeem Siddique L RSC 4 Bradford
(Vacant Central Area & British Masters Welterweight Titles)
Career: 17 contests, won 5, drew 2, lost 10.

Billy Wilson

York. *Born* York, 28 December, 1980
Heavyweight. *Ht* 6'6"
Manager T. O'Neill

15.09.03 Carl Baker L RSC 2 Leeds
11.11.03 Brodie Pearmaine W PTS 6 Leeds
10.02.04 Paul King W PTS 6 Barnsley
06.12.04 Simon Goodwin W PTS 6 Leeds
16.12.04 Chris Woollas L PTS 6 Cleethorpes
13.10.06 Lee Nicholson W RSC 5 Doncaster
23.02.07 Tony Booth L RSC 5 Doncaster
Career: 7 contests, won 4, lost 3.

Ian Wilson

Camden. *Born* London, 9 June, 1981
S.Featherweight. *Ht* 5'10½"
Manager F. Maloney

19.06.05 Lance Verallo W PTS 4 Bethnal Green
07.10.05 Ian Reid W PTS 4 Bethnal Green
27.01.06 Daniel Thorpe W PTS 4 Dagenham
24.03.06 Steve Gethin W PTS 4 Bethnal Green
29.06.06 Brian Murphy W RTD 1 Bethnal Green
17.11.06 Matthew Martin Lewis W PTS 4 Bethnal Green
09.03.07 Henry Castle W RSC 5 Dagenham
Career: 7 contests, won 7.

(Jeremy) Jezz Wilson

Sheffield. *Born* Wolverhampton, 22 June, 1979
S.Middleweight. *Ht* 5'9"
Manager G. Rhodes

20.04.07 Peter Cannon W RSC 5 Sheffield
Career: 1 contest, won 1.

Juliette Winter

Derby. *Born* Whitehaven, 21 February, 1973
Bantamweight. *Ht* 5'6"
Manager Self

16.06.01 Sara Hall L RTD 4 Derby
20.09.01 Claire Cooper L RSC 4 Blackfriars
20.03.03 Cathy Brown W PTS 4 Queensway
24.01.04 Esther Schouten L RTD 3 Amsterdam, Holland
23.07.06 Shanee Martin W PTS 8 Dagenham
24.09.06 Cathy Brown L PTS 10 Bethnal Green
(Vacant Womens English Bantamweight Title)
12.05.07 Yarkor Chavez Annan W PTS 4 Stoke
Career: 7 contests, won 3, lost 4.

Junior Witter

Bradford. *Born* Bradford, 10 March, 1974
WBC L.Welterweight Champion. Former Undefeated British, Commonwealth, European, European Union, WBU Inter-Continental & WBF L.Welterweight Champion. *Ht* 5'7"
Manager J. Ingle

18.01.97 Cam Raeside DREW 6 Swadlincote
04.03.97 John Green W PTS 6 Yarm
20.03.97 Lee Molyneux W RSC 6 Salford
25.04.97 Trevor Meikle W PTS 6 Mere
15.05.97 Andreas Panayi W RSC 5 Reading
02.08.97 Brian Coleman W PTS 4 Barnsley
04.10.97 Michael Alexander W PTS 4 Hannover, Germany
07.02.98 Mark Ramsey DREW 6 Cheshunt
05.03.98 Brian Coleman W PTS 6 Leeds
18.04.98 Jan Bergman W PTS 6 Manchester
05.09.98 Mark Winters W PTS 8 Telford
28.11.98 Karl Taylor W PTS 4 Sheffield
13.02.99 Malcolm Melvin W RSC 2 Newcastle
(Vacant WBF L. Welterweight Title)
17.07.99 Isaac Cruz W PTS 8 Doncaster
06.11.99 Harry Butler W PTS 6 Widnes
21.03.00 Mrhai Iourgh W RSC 1 Telde, Gran Canaria
08.04.00 Arv Mittoo W PTS 4 Bethnal Green
24.06.00 Zab Judah L PTS 12 Glasgow
(IBF L. Welterweight Title Challenge)
20.10.00 Steve Conway W RTD 4 Belfast
25.11.00 Chris Henry W RSC 3 Manchester
10.03.01 David Kirk W RSC 2 Bethnal Green
22.05.01 Fabrice Faradji W RSC 1 Telde, Gran Canaria
21.07.01 Alan Temple W CO 5 Sheffield
27.10.01 Colin Mayisela W RSC 2 Manchester
(Vacant WBU Inter-Continental L.Welterweight Title)
16.03.02 Alan Bosworth W RSC 3 Northampton
(Vacant British L.Welterweight Title)
08.07.02 Laatekwi Hammond W RSC 2 Mayfair
(Vacant Commonwealth L.Welterweight Title)
19.10.02 Lucky Samba W RSC 2 Renfrew

23.11.02 Giuseppe Lauri W RSC 2 Derby
(Final Elim. WBO L. Welterweight Title)
05.04.03 Jurgen Haeck W RTD 4 Manchester
(Vacant European Union L.Welterweight Title)
27.09.03 Fred Kinuthia W RSC 2 Manchester
(Commonwealth L.Welterweight Title Defence)
16.04.04 Oscar Hall W RSC 3 Bradford
02.06.04 Salvatore Battaglia W RSC 2 Nottingham
(Vacant European L.Welterweight Title)
12.11.04 Krzysztof Bienias W RSC 2 Wembley
(European L.Welterweight Title Defence)
19.02.05 Lovemore N'Dou W PTS 12 Los Angeles, California, USA
(Commonwealth L.Welterweight Title Defence)
09.07.05 Andreas Kotelnik W PTS 12 Nottingham
(European L.Welterweight Title Defence)
21.10.05 Colin Lynes W PTS 12 Bethnal Green
(British, Commonwealth & European L.Welterweight Title Defences)

15.09.06 DeMarcus Corley W PTS 12 Muswell Hill
(Vacant WBC L.Welterweight Title)
20.01.07 Arturo Morua W RSC 9 Muswell Hill
(WBC L.Welterweight Title Defence)
Career: 38 contests, won 35, drew 2, lost 1.

Brian Wood

South Normanton. *Born* Sutton in Ashfield, 5 September, 1981
S.Middleweight. *Ht* 5'10"
Manager S. Calow
28.04.07 Howard Clarke W PTS 6 Newark
Career: 1 contest, won 1.

Simon Wood

Brierley Hill. *Born* Wordsley, 6 May, 1975
L.Heavyweight. *Ht* 5'7"
Manager E. Johnson
06.12.06 Mark Nilsen L PTS 4 Stoke
15.12.06 Wayne Brooks L RSC 1 Bethnal Green
16.02.07 Gordon Brennan L PTS 4 Kirkcaldy
Career: 3 contests, lost 3.

Curtis Woodhouse

Hull. *Born* Beverley, 17 April, 1980
L.Middleweight. Ht. 5'8¼"
Manager D. Powell
08.09.06 Dean Marcantonio W PTS 4 Mayfair
15.04.07 Duncan Cottier W PTS 4 Barnsley
03.06.07 Peter Dunn W PTS 4 Barnsley
Career: 3 contests, won 3.

Clinton Woods

Sheffield. *Born* Sheffield, 1 May, 1972
IBF L.Heavyweight Champion.
Former Undefeated British, European, WBC International & Commonwealth L.Heavyweight Champion. Former Commonwealth S.Middleweight Champion. Former Undefeated Central Area S.Middleweight Champion. *Ht* 6'2"
Manager D. Hobson
17.11.94 Dave Proctor W PTS 6 Sheffield
12.12.94 Earl Ling W RSC 5 Cleethorpes
23.02.95 Paul Clarkson W RSC 1 Hull
06.04.95 Japhet Hans W RSC 3 Sheffield
16.05.95 Kevin Burton W PTS 6 Cleethorpes
14.06.95 Kevin Burton W RSC 6 Batley
21.09.95 Paul Murray W PTS 6 Sheffield
20.10.95 Phil Ball W RSC 4 Mansfield
22.11.95 Andy Ewen W RSC 3 Sheffield
05.02.96 Chris Walker W RSC 6 Bradford
16.03.96 John Duckworth W PTS 8 Sheffield
13.06.96 Ernie Loveridge W PTS 6 Sheffield
14.11.96 Craig Joseph W PTS 10 Sheffield
(Vacant Central Area S. Middleweight Title)
20.02.97 Rocky Shelly W RSC 2 Mansfield
10.04.97 Darren Littlewood W RSC 6 Sheffield
(Central Area S. Middleweight Title Defence)
26.06.97 Darren Ashton W PTS 6 Sheffield
25.10.97 Danny Juma W PTS 8 Queensferry
26.11.97 Jeff Finlayson W PTS 8 Sheffield
06.12.97 Mark Baker W PTS 12 Wembley
(Vacant Commonwealth S.Middleweight Title)
28.03.98 David Starie L PTS 12 Hull
(Commonwealth S. Middleweight Title Defence)
18.06.98 Peter Mason W RTD 4 Sheffield
30.11.98 Mark Smallwood W RSC 7 Manchester
13.03.99 Crawford Ashley W RSC 8 Manchester
(British, Commonwealth & European L. Heavyweight Title Challenges)
10.07.99 Sam Leuii W RSC 6 Southwark
(Commonwealth L. Heavyweight Title Defence)
11.09.99 Lenox Lewis W RSC 10 Sheffield
(Commonwealth L. Heavyweight Title Defence)
10.12.99 Terry Ford W RTD 4 Warsaw, Poland
12.02.00 Juan Perez Nelongo W PTS 12 Sheffield
(European L. Heavyweight Title Defence)
29.04.00 Ole Klemetsen W RSC 9 Wembley
(European L. Heavyweight Title Defence)
15.07.00 Greg Scott-Briggs W RSC 3 Millwall
24.03.01 Ali Forbes W RTD 10 Sheffield
(Vacant WBC International L. Heavyweight Title)
27.07.01 Paul Bonson W PTS 6 Sheffield

Junior Witter   Les Clark

13.09.01	Yawe Davis W PTS 12 Sheffield
	(Final Elim.WBC L.Heavyweight Title)
16.03.02	Clint Johnson W RSC 3 Bethnal Green
07.09.02	Roy Jones L RSC 6 Portland, Oregon, USA
	(WBC, WBA & IBF L.Heavyweight Title Challenges)
24.01.03	Sergio Martin Beaz W RSC 3 Sheffield
18.03.03	Arturo Rivera W RSC 2 Reading
10.06.03	Demetrius Jenkins W RSC 7 Sheffield
07.11.03	Glengoffe Johnson DREW 12 Sheffield
	(Vacant IBF L.Heavyweight Title)
06.02.04	Glengoffe Johnson L PTS 12 Sheffield
	(Vacant IBF L.Heavyweight Title)
24.10.04	Jason DeLisle W RSC 12 Sheffield
	(Elim. IBF L.Heavyweight Title)
04.03.05	Rico Hoye W RSC 5 Rotherham
	(Vacant IBF L.Heavyweight Title)
09.09.05	Julio Gonzalez W PTS 12 Sheffield
	(IBF L.Heavyweight Title Defence)
13.05.06	Jason DeLisle W RSC 6 Sheffield
	(IBF L.Heavyweight Title Defence)
02.09.06	Glengoffe Johnson W PTS 12 Bolton
	(IBF L.Heavyweight Title Defence)

Career: 44 contests, won 40, drew 1, lost 3.

Gary Woolcombe

Welling. *Born* London, 4 August, 1982
Southern Area L.Middleweight Champion.
Former Undefeated British Masters
L.Middleweight Champion. *Ht* 5'10¾"
Manager F. Maloney

15.05.03	Paul McIlwaine W RSC 2 Mayfair
22.07.03	Arv Mittoo W PTS 6 Bethnal Green
25.09.03	Pete Buckley W PTS 6 Bethnal Green
18.11.03	John Butler W PTS 4 Bethnal Green
07.02.04	Ernie Smith W PTS 4 Bethnal Green
14.02.04	Lee Williamson W PTS 6 Holborn
07.05.04	David Kirk W PTS 4 Bethnal Green
05.06.04	Ivor Bonavic W PTS 4 Bethnal Green
24.09.04	Geraint Harvey W PTS 4 Bethnal Green
19.11.04	Keith Jones W PTS 4 Bethnal Green
11.12.04	Peter Dunn W PTS 4 Canning Town
12.02.05	Howard Clarke W PTS 6 Portsmouth
05.03.05	Ernie Smith W PTS 6 Southwark
29.04.05	Matt Scriven W RSC 4 Southwark
20.05.05	Danny Parkinson W RSC 3 Southwark
19.06.05	Peter Dunn W RSC 6 Bethnal Green
07.10.05	Delroy Mellis W RTD 8 Bethnal Green

	(Vacant British Masters L.Middleweight Title)
04.11.05	Mark Phillips W PTS 4 Bethnal Green
27.01.06	Lee Murtagh W RSC 4 Dagenham
24.03.06	Eugenio Monteiro W PTS 8 Bethnal Green
26.05.06	Gilbert Eastman W RSC 7 Bethnal Green
	(Southern Area L.Middleweight Title Challenge)
03.11.06	Alex Stoda W DIS 4 Barnsley
26.01.07	Andrew Facey L RSC 5 Dagenham
	(English L.Middleweight Title Challenge)
15.06.07	Anthony Young W RSC 4 Crystal Palace

Career: 24 contests, won 23, lost 1.

Scott Woolford

Ramsgate. *Born* Rush Green, 6 September, 1983
L.Middleweight. *Ht* 5'7"
Manager F. Maloney

30.05.06	David Kehoe W PTS 4 Bethnal Green
06.10.06	Tommy Jones W PTS 4 Bethnal Green
17.11.06	Gary McMillan W PTS 4 Bethnal Green
15.06.07	Tyrone McInerney W PTS 4 Crystal Palace

Career: 4 contests, won 4.

Chris Woollas

Epworth. *Born* Scunthorpe, 22 November, 1973
Heavyweight. Former Undefeated Midlands
Area Cruiserweight Champion. *Ht* 5'11"
Manager M. Shinfield

17.08.94	Darren Littlewood W RSC 4 Sheffield
05.10.94	Robert Norton DREW 6 Wolverhampton
05.12.94	Neil Simpson W PTS 6 Cleethorpes
10.02.95	Monty Wright L RSC 4 Birmingham
30.06.95	Kenny Nevers L RSC 2 Doncaster
25.09.95	Cliff Elden DREW 6 Cleethorpes
08.11.95	Stevie Pettit W PTS 6 Walsall
17.11.95	Markku Salminen L PTS 6 Helsinki, Finland
11.12.95	Cliff Elden DREW 6 Cleethorpes
15.02.96	Pele Lawrence W RSC 6 Sheffield
29.02.96	John Pierre DREW 6 Scunthorpe
16.03.96	David Jules W PTS 6 Sheffield
22.04.96	Jacklord Jacobs DREW 4 Crystal Palace
30.05.96	Martin Langtry L RSC 6 Lincoln
	(Midlands Area Cruiserweight Title Challenge)
03.09.96	Darren Corbett L RSC 7 Belfast
02.10.96	Rocky Shelly W RSC 6 Stoke
09.10.96	Nigel Rafferty W PTS 6 Stoke
28.10.96	Colin Brown L PTS 8 Glasgow
10.11.96	Michael Gale DREW 6 Glasgow
25.11.96	Albert Call L PTS 6 Cleethorpes
17.12.96	Darren Corbett L RSC 1 Doncaster
16.01.97	Mark Smallwood L PTS 8 Solihull
31.01.97	Tim Redman L PTS 6 Pentre Halkyn
14.03.97	Kelly Oliver L PTS 6 Reading
24.03.97	Mikael Lindblad L RSC 7 Helsinki, Finland
19.06.97	Ian Henry W PTS 6 Scunthorpe
02.08.97	Kelly Oliver L RSC 3 Barnsley
15.12.97	Neil Simpson W PTS 6 Cleethorpes

Clinton Woods   Les Clark

26.01.98	Colin Brown W PTS 6 Glasgow
26.03.98	Cliff Elden L PTS 4 Scunthorpe
06.05.98	Simon McDougall W PTS 6 Blackpool
21.07.98	Matthew Ellis L RSC 5 Widnes
11.09.98	Lennox Williams W PTS 6 Cleethorpes
12.03.99	Albert Sosnowski L PTS 4 Bethnal Green
27.05.99	Nigel Rafferty W PTS 10 Edgbaston (*Midlands Area Cruiserweight Title Challenge*)
10.07.99	Michael Sprott L RTD 4 Southwark
13.09.99	Dominic Negus L PTS 10 Bethnal Green (*Elim. British Cruiserweight Title*)
09.10.99	Chris P. Bacon L PTS 4 Manchester
30.10.99	Terry Dunstan L RSC 1 Southwark
08.04.00	Bruce Scott L RSC 2 Bethnal Green
13.07.00	Firat Aslan L RSC 2 Bethnal Green
08.09.00	Petr Horacek L PTS 4 Hammersmith
21.10.00	Danny Percival L PTS 4 Wembley
18.11.00	Matthew Ellis L PTS 4 Dagenham
11.12.00	Enzo Maccarinelli L PTS 4 Widnes
15.12.01	Lee Swaby L RSC 4 Sheffield
21.10.02	Greg Scott-Briggs W PTS 6 Cleethorpes
01.11.02	Spencer Wilding DREW 6 Preston
28.04.03	Eamonn Glennon W PTS 6 Cleethorpes
22.11.03	Albert Sosnowski L RSC 1 Belfast
16.02.04	Dave Clarke W PTS 6 Scunthorpe
30.03.04	Colin Kenna L PTS 6 Southampton
10.07.04	Robert Norton L RSC 4 Coventry
30.09.04	Paul King L PTS 4 Glasgow
06.11.04	Carl Wright L RSC 1 Coventry
16.12.04	Billy Wilson W PTS 6 Cleethorpes
26.10.06	Mathew Ellis L PTS 4 Dudley
04.11.06	Mark Walker DREW 4 Glasgow
11.12.06	Istvan Kecskes W PTS 6 Cleethorpes
28.01.07	Chris Burton L RSC 3 Yarm
01.06.07	Pele Reid L CO 1 Birmingham
30.06.07	Scott Belshaw L CO 1 Belfast

Career: 62 contests, won 18, drew 8, lost 36.

Carl Wright

Rugby. *Born* Rugby, 26 April, 1978
Midlands Area & British Masters
Cruiserweight Champion. *Ht* 6'1¼"
Manager Self

25.06.02	Dave Clarke W PTS 6 Rugby
05.10.02	Adam Cale W PTS 6 Coventry
16.11.02	Jimmy Steel W PTS 6 Coventry
08.03.03	Gary Williams W PTS 6 Coventry
16.03.03	Darren Ashton DREW 6 Nottingham
07.06.03	Gary Thompson W RTD 2 Coventry
13.09.03	Darren Ashton W PTS 6 Coventry
09.04.04	Lee Mountford W PTS 4 Rugby
01.05.04	Paul Bonson W PTS 6 Coventry
06.11.04	Chris Woollas W RSC 1 Coventry
17.12.04	Tony Dowling W PTS 10 Coventry (*Vacant Midlands Area Cruiserweight Title*)
18.06.05	Nate Joseph W CO 1 Coventry (*Vacant British Masters Cruiserweight Title*)
24.09.05	Tony Booth W PTS 4 Coventry
12.12.05	Cafu Santos W RSC 4 Leicester
23.07.06	JJ Ojuederie L PTS 4 Dagenham
13.04.07	Roland Horvath W RSC 2 Rugby

Career: 16 contests, won 14, drew 1, lost 1.

Nigel Wright

Crook. *Born* Bishop Auckland, 22 June, 1979
English L.Welterweight Champion. *Ht* 5'9"

Manager G. Robinson

10.02.01	Keith Jones W PTS 4 Widnes
15.09.01	Tommy Peacock W RSC 1 Manchester
17.11.01	Ernie Smith W PTS 4 Glasgow
19.01.02	Woody Greenaway W CO 2 Bethnal Green
11.03.02	James Paisley W PTS 4 Glasgow
19.10.02	Kevin McIntyre L PTS 6 Renfrew
29.03.03	Darren Melville W PTS 6 Portsmouth
24.05.03	David Kirk W PTS 4 Bethnal Green
02.10.03	Nigel Senior W RSC 5 Liverpool
29.11.03	Jason Hall W PTS 6 Renfrew
06.03.04	George Telfer W RSC 3 Renfrew
22.05.04	Jon Honney W RSC 2 Widnes
22.10.04	Silence Saheed W PTS 8 Edinburgh
11.03.05	Dean Hickman W CO 7 Doncaster (*Vacant English L.Welterweight Title*)
27.05.05	Alan Bosworth W PTS 10 Spennymoor (*English L.Welterweight Title Defence*)
05.11.05	Kevin McIntyre W RSC 1 Renfrew (*Final Elim. British L.Welterweight Title*)
18.02.06	Valery Kharyanov W CO 4 Edinburgh
12.05.06	Lenny Daws L PTS 12 Bethnal Green (*Vacant British L.Welterweight Title*)
04.11.06	Gary Reid W PTS 10 Glasgow (*English L.Welterweight Title Defence*)
30.03.07	Jonathan Nelson W RTD 2 Newcastle

Career: 20 contests, won 18, lost 2.

Tyrone Wright

Nottingham. *Born* Nottingham, 7 September, 1978
Midlands Area & British Masters
L.Heavyweight Champion. *Ht* 6'2"
Manager M. Shinfield

22.10.05	Lee Mountford W CO 3 Mansfield
15.12.05	Gary Thompson DREW 6 Cleethorpes
24.04.06	Csaba Andras W CO 2 Cleethorpes
15.09.06	Nathan King L RTD 3 Newport
11.11.06	Gordon Brennan W PTS 6 Sutton in Ashfield
11.12.06	Dean Walker W PTS 6 Cleethorpes
03.03.07	Shon Davies W PTS 6 Alfreton
19.05.07	Michael Monaghan W RSC 10 Nottingham (*Midlands Area L.Heavyweight Title Challenge. Vacant British Masters L.Heavyweight Title*)

Career: 8 contests, won 6, drew 1, lost 1.

Ali Wyatt

Torquay. *Born* Iran, 15 May, 1977
Welterweight. *Ht* 5'5¾"
Manager C. Sanigar

09.10.05	Michael Grant DREW 4 Hammersmith
17.11.05	Stuart Phillips L PTS 4 Bristol
21.05.06	Bheki Moyo W RSC 3 Bristol
03.06.06	Michael Grant L PTS 4 Chigwell
23.06.06	Lance Hall W RSC 5 Birmingham
26.02.07	Joe McCluskey W RSC 5 Birmingham
13.05.07	Joe McCluskey DREW 8 Birmingham

Career: 7 contests, won 3, drew 2, lost 2.

Andrew Young

Inverness. *Born* Inverness, 6 May, 1980
Cruiserweight. *Ht* 6'2½"
Manager T. Gilmour

02.03.07	John Anthony L RSC 1 Irvine
05.06.07	James Swindells W RSC 2 Glasgow

Career: 2 contests, won 1, lost 1.

Anthony Young

Crawley. *Born* Crawley, 10 April, 1984
S.Middleweight. *Ht* 5'11¼"
Manager G. Earl

30.10.05	Alex Stoda W PTS 6 Bethnal Green
05.03.06	Steve Ede L RSC 3 Southampton
18.10.06	Rocky Muscus W PTS 4 Bayswater
26.10.06	Max Maxwell W PTS 4 Wolverhampton
22.02.07	Danny Reynolds L RSC 4 Leeds
08.06.07	Greg Barton W PTS 4 Mayfair
15.06.07	Gary Woolcombe L RSC 4 Crystal Palace

Career: 7 contests, won 4, lost 3.

Anthony Young   Philip Sharkey

Gary Young

Edinburgh. *Born* Edinburgh, 23 May, 1983
Welterweight. *Ht* 5'7"
Manager Self

11.03.02	Paul McIlwaine W CO 2 Glasgow
08.06.02	Daniel Thorpe W RSC 1 Renfrew
02.11.02	Keith Jones W PTS 4 Belfast
22.03.03	Dean Larter W RSC 2 Renfrew
12.07.03	Lee Williamson W PTS 4 Renfrew
25.10.03	Peter Dunn W PTS 6 Edinburgh
29.11.03	Karl Taylor W RSC 3 Renfrew
06.03.04	Anthony Christopher W CO 1 Renfrew
27.03.04	Keith Jones W PTS 6 Edinburgh
19.06.04	David Kirk W PTS 4 Renfrew
22.10.04	Lionel Saraille W RSC 3 Edinburgh
28.01.05	Thomas Hengstberger W RSC 3 Renfrew
08.04.05	Viktor Baranov W PTS 8 Edinburgh
05.11.05	Ivor Bonavic W RSC 8 Renfrew
18.02.06	Oscar Milkitas W PTS 8 Edinburgh
29.04.06	Colin McNeil L CO 1 Edinburgh (*Elim. British Welterweight Title*)
04.11.06	Ernie Smith W PTS 6 Glasgow

Career: 17 contests, won 16, lost 1.

British Area Title Bouts, 2006-2007

Note that BBBoC Regulations state that any Area champion who wins English, Celtic, British, Commonwealth and European championships have to automatically relinquish their titles.

Central Area

Titleholders at 30 June 2007

Fly: *vacant*. **Bantam:** *vacant*. **S.Bantam:** Gary Davis. **Feather:** Matt Teague. **S.Feather:** Steve Bell. **Light:** Stefy Bull. **L.Welter:** John Fewkes. **Welter:** Nadeem Siddique. **L.Middle:** Jason Rushton. **Middle:** Paul Smith. **S.Middle:** *vacant*. **L.Heavy:** Amer Khan. **Cruiser:** *vacant*. **Heavy:** *vacant*.

Title Bouts Held Between 1 July 2006 and 30 June 2007

14 October	Paul Smith W RSC 3 Dean Walker, Manchester (Vacant Middleweight Title)
23 February	Jason Rushton W CO 7 Davey Jones, Doncaster (Vacant L.Middleweight Title)
25 February	Chris P. Bacon W RSC 7 Tony Moran, Manchester (Vacant Cruiserweight Title)
10 March	Steve Bell W RSC 7 Jamie McKeever, Liverpool (Vacant S.Featherweight Title)
27 May	Nadeem Siddique W RSC 4 Tye Williams, Bradford (Vacant Welterweight Title)

Between 1 July 2006 and 30 June 2007, Carl Johanneson (Feather), Matthew Hatton (Welter) and Lee Murtagh (L.Middle) all relinquished their titles, while Dean Cockburn (S.Middle) and Chris P. Bacon (Cruiser) retired.

Midlands Area

Titleholders at 30 June 2007

Fly: *vacant*. **Bantam:** Andy Bell. **S.Bantam:** *vacant*. **Feather:** *vacant*. **S.Feather:** *vacant*. **Light:** *vacant*. **L.Welter:** *vacant*. **Welter:** Darren Gethin. **L.Middle:** Manoocha Salari. **Middle:** Darren McDermott. **S.Middle:** Neil Tidman. **L.Heavy:** Tyrone Wright. **Cruiser:** Carl Wright. **Heavy:** *vacant*.

Title Bouts Held Between 1 July 2006 and 30 June 2007

16 September	Matt Galer W RSC 5 Simon Sherrington, Burton (L.Middleweight Title Defence)
10 November	Tristan Davies W PTS 10 Carl Allen, Telford (Vacant Lightweight Title)
3 March	Michael Monaghan W PTS 10 Rod Anderton, Alfreton (Vacant L.Heavyweight Title)
3 March	Neil Tidman W PTS 10 Jonjo Finnegan, Burton (Vacant S.Middleweight Title)
3 March	Matt Galer L RSC 8 Manoocha Salari, Burton (L.Middleweight Title Defence)
23 March	Darren Gethin W CO 10 Tyan Booth, Nottingham (Vacant Welterweight Title)
24 March	Billy Smith W PTS 10 Baz Carey, Coventry (Vacant L.Welterweight Title)

1 April	Andy Bell W RSC 8 Neil Marston, Shrewsbury (Vacant Bantamweight Title)
20 April	Gary Reid W RSC 5 Dean Hickman, Dudley (Vacant L.Welterweight Title)
19 May	Michael Monaghan L RSC 10 Tyrone Wright, Nottingham (L.Heavyweight Title Defence)
28 June	Darren McDermott W RSC 2 Conroy McIntosh, Dudley (Middleweight Title Defence)

Between 1 July 2006 and 30 June 2007, Tristan Davies (Light), Dean Hickman (L.Welter), Billy Smith (L.Welter), Gary Reid (L.Welter) and Stuart Elwell (Welter) relinquished their titles, while Gareth Payne (S.Bantam) and Stephen Chinnock (Feather) retired.

Northern Area

Titleholders at 30 June 2007

Fly: *vacant*. **Bantam:** *vacant*. **S.Bantam:** *vacant*. **Feather:** *vacant*. **S.Feather:** *vacant*. **Light:** *vacant*. **L.Welter:** *vacant*. **Welter:** *vacant*. **L.Middle:** *vacant*. **Middle:** *vacant*. **S.Middle:** *vacant*. **L.Heavy:** *vacant*. **Cruiser:** *vacant*. **Heavy:** *vacant*.

Title Bouts Held Between 1 July 2006 and 30 June 2007

None

Between 1 July 2006 and 30 June 2007, Oscar Hall (Welter) and Eddie Haley (Middle) retired.

Northern Ireland Area

Titleholders at 30 June 2007

Fly: *vacant*. **Bantam:** *vacant*. **S.Bantam:** *vacant*. **Feather:** *vacant*. **S.Feather:** *vacant*. **Light:** *vacant*. **L.Welter:** *vacant*. **Welter:** *vacant*. **L.Middle:** *vacant*. **Middle:** *vacant*. **S.Middle:** *vacant*. **L.Heavy:** *vacant*. **Cruiser:** *vacant*. **Heavy:** *vacant*.

Title Bouts Held Between 1 July 2006 and 30 June 2007

None

Scottish Area

Titleholders at 30 June 2007

Fly: *vacant*. **Bantam:** *vacant*. **S.Bantam:** *vacant*. **Feather:** Jimmy Gilhaney. **S.Feather:** *vacant*. **Light:** Lee McAllister. **L.Welter:** *vacant*. **Welter:** Kevin McIntyre. **L.Middle:** Colin McNeil. **Middle:** Vince Baldassara. **S.Middle:** Tom Cannon. **L.Heavy:** *vacant*. **Cruiser:** *vacant*. **Heavy:** *vacant*.

Title Bouts Held Between 1 July 2006 and 30 June 2007

| 20 November | Jimmy Gilhaney W RSC 1 John Bothwell, Glasgow (Vacant Featherweight Title) |
| 10 December | Barrie Lee L RSC 4 Colin McNeil, Glasgow (L.Middleweight Title Defence) |

Southern Area

Titleholders at 30 June 2007

Fly: *vacant.* **Bantam:** *vacant.* **S.Bantam:** *vacant.* **Feather:** Matthew Marsh. **S.Feather:** *vacant.* **Light:** Rob Jeffries. **L.Welter:** Jon Honney. **Welter:** *vacant.* **L.Middle:** Gary Woolcombe. **Middle:** Darren Barker. **S.Middle:** Kreshnik Qato. **L.Heavy:** Andrew Lowe. **Cruiser:** Tommy Eastwood. **Heavy:** *vacant.*

Title Bouts Held Between 1 July 2006 and 30 June 2007

15 September	Darren Barker W PTS 10 Hussain Osman, Muswell Hill (Vacant Middleweight Title)
6 October	Tommy Eastwood W RSC 2 Junior MacDonald, Bethnal Green (Vacant Cruiserweight Title)
8 December	Kreshnik Qato W PTS 10 Simeon Cover, Dagenham (Vacant S.Middleweight Title)
9 December	Rocky Dean L PTS 10 Matthew Marsh, Canning Town (Featherweight Title Defence)
24 February	Jon Honney W PTS 10 Nathan Ward, Bracknell (Vacant L.Welterweight Title)

Between 1 July 2006 and 30 June 2007, Ryan Walls (S.Middle) and Micky Steeds (Heavy) relinquished their titles.

Welsh Area

Titleholders at 30 June 2007

Fly: *vacant.* **Bantam:** *vacant.* **S.Bantam:** *vacant.* **Feather:** *vacant.* **S.Feather:** Dai Davies. **Light:** Damian Owen. **L.Welter:** Garry Buckland. **Welter:** *vacant.* **L.Middle:** *vacant.* **Middle:** *vacant.* **S.Middle:** *vacant.* **L.Heavy:** *vacant.* **Cruiser:** *vacant.* **Heavy:** *vacant.*

Title Bouts Held Between 1 July 2006 and 30 June 2007

8 October	Dai Davies W PTS 10 Henry Jones, Swansea (Vacant S.Featherweight Title)
2 March	Damian Owen W CO 4 Dean Phillips, Neath (Vacant Lightweight Title)
3 March	Garry Buckland W PTS 10 Stuart Phillips, Newport (Vacant L.Welterweight Title)

Western Area

Titleholders at 30 June 2007

Fly: *vacant.* **Bantam:** *vacant.* **S.Bantam:** *vacant.* **Feather:** *vacant.* **S.Feather:** *vacant.* **Light:** *vacant.* **L.Welter:** *vacant.* **Welter:** *vacant.* **L.Middle:** *vacant.* **Middle:** *vacant.* **S.Middle:** *vacant.* **L.Heavy:** Leigh Alliss. **Cruiser:** *vacant.* **Heavy:** *vacant.*

Title Bouts Held Between 1 July 2006 and 30 June 2007

None

A great action shot from the Rocky Dean (right) v Matthew Marsh contest for the Southern Area featherweight title last December

Les Clark

English and Celtic Title Bouts, 2006-2007

English Championships

Titleholders at 30 June 2007

Fly: Chris Edwards. **Bantam:** Jamie McDonnell. **S.Bantam:** Marc Callaghan. **Feather:** vacant. **S.Feather:** vacant. **Light:** Scott Lawton. **L.Welter:** Nigel Wright. **Welter:** John O'Donnell. **L.Middle:** Andrew Facey. **Middle:** Wayne Elcock. **S.Middle:** Tony Dodson. **L.Heavy:** Peter Haymer. **Cruiser:** Robert Norton. **Heavy:** Michael Sprott.

Title bouts held between 1 July 2006 and 30 June 2007

4 November	Nigel Wright W PTS 10 Gary Reid, Glasgow (L.Welterweight Title Defence)
24 November	Chris Edwards W RSC 8 Dale Robinson, Stoke (Vacant Flyweight Title)
1 December	Steven Bendall L RSC 8 Wayne Elcock, Birmingham (Middleweight Title Defence)
26 January	Andrew Facey W RSC 5 Gary Woolcombe, Dagenham (L.Middleweight Title Defence)
17 February	Michael Sprott W RSC 3 Audley Harrison, Wembley (Vacant Heavyweight Title)
23 February	Jamie McDonnell W RSC 3 Wayne Bloy, Doncaster (Vacant Bantamweight Title)
2 March	Robert Norton W RSC 8 Tommy Eastwood, Coventry (Vacant Cruiserweight Title)
23 March	John O'Donnell W PTS 10 Stuart Elwell, Nottingham (Vacant Welterweight Title)

Between 1 July 2006 and 30 June 2007, Derry Matthews (Feather), Billy Corcoran (S.Feather) and Dean Francis (Cruiser) all relinquished their titles

Celtic Championships

Titleholders at 30 June 2007

Fly: vacant. **Bantam:** vacant: **S.Bantam:** vacant. **Feather:** vacant. **S.Feather:** vacant. **Light:** Martin Watson. **L.Welter:** Stuart Phillips. **Welter:** Tony Doherty. **L.Middle:** vacant. **Middle:** vacant. **S.Middle:** vacant. **L.Heavy:** vacant. **Cruiser:** vacant. **Heavy:** vacant.

Title bouts held between 1 July 2006 and 30 June 2007

2 March	Ceri Hall W RSC 9 Stuart Green, Neath (Vacant L.Welterweight Title)
7 April	Tony Doherty W RSC 7 Taz Jones, Cardiff (Welterweight Title Defence)
10 June	Ceri Hall L PTS 10 Stuart Phillips, Neath (L.Welterweight Title Defence)

In a meeting for the vacant English heavyweight title last February, Michael Sprott (left) created the surprise of the season when stopping Audley Harrison in the third round at Wembley

Les Clark

PROFESSIONAL BOXING PROMOTERS' ASSOCIATION

PRESENTS

THE BRITISH MASTERS CHAMPIONS

UNDER BBB OF C RULES

HEAVY:	CARL BAKER
CRUISER:	CARL WRIGHT
LIGHT-HEAVY:	TYRONE WRIGHT
SUPER-MIDDLE:	JOEY VEGAS
MIDDLE:	PRINCE ARRON
LIGHT-MIDDLE:	GEORGE HILLYARD
WELTER:	NADEEM SIDIQUE
LIGHT-WELTER:	MARTIN GETHIN
LIGHT:	GARY McARTHUR
SUPER-FEATHER:	DARREN JOHNSTONE
FEATHER:	RYAN BARRETT
SUPER-BANTAM:	GARY DAVIS
BANTAM:	ANDY BELL
FLY:	DELROY SPENCER

INTERNATIONAL MASTERS BANTAM CHAMPION: MATTHEW EDMONDS

THE ONLY ALL-COMERS TITLE OPERATING IN BRITISH BOXING. OUR CHAMPIONS HAVE TO DEFEND WHEN A VALID CHALLENGE IS MADE WITH MORE THAN 30 DAYS NOTICE. TO CHALLENGE FOR OUR TITLE, PROMOTERS SHOULD APPLY TO:

THE PBPA
P O BOX 25188
LONDON
SW1V 3WL

TEL: 0207 592 0102
FAX: 0207 821 1831
EMAIL: bdbaker@tiscali.co.uk

CHAIRMAN: Bruce Baker
GENERAL SECRETARY: Greg Steene
DIRECTORS: B. Baker, G. Steene, J. Gill, J. Evans, P. Brogan

MEMBERSHIP IS OPEN TO PROMOTERS AND MANAGERS. THOSE INTERESTED PLEASE APPLY

British Title Bouts, 2006-2007

All of last season's title bouts are shown in date order within their weight divisions and give the boxers' respective weights, the names of the referee and judges involved, and the scorecard if going to a decision. Foreign-born boxers, who contest a British title having qualified by being British citizens for more than five years, are shown by domicile/birthplace.

Flyweight

13 April Dale Robinson 7.12 (England) DREW 12 Chris Edwards 7.12 (England), The Leisure Centre, Altrincham. Referee: Terry O'Connor. Scorecards: Phil Edwards 115-113, Mickey Vann 113-115, Dave Parris 114-114. This was the first time that the title had been contested since Jason Booth handed back his belt in December 2003 and still we await a new champion.

Bantamweight

There were no championship fights during the period and Colin Power relinquished his title on 26 June 2007 due to an injured shoulder. Power had been due to defend against Jason Booth in Wigan on 6 July and his place was taken at short notice by Ian Napa, who won on points.

S.Bantamweight

16 March Esham Pickering 8.9½ (England) W PTS 12 Marc Callaghan 8.9½ (England), The Norfolk Showground, Norwich. Referee: John Keane. Scorecards: Richie Davies 120-108, Mark Green 120-108, Ian John-Lewis 120-109. Contested for the vacant title after Michael Hunter

Dale Robinson (left) and Chris Edwards fought a bruising draw last April when trying to decide the vacant British flyweight title

Les Clark

relinquished in September 2006 to concentrate on a crack at the IBF championship.

Featherweight

9 December　Andy Morris 9.0 (England) L RSC 5 John Simpson 8.13 (Scotland), ExCel Arena, Canning Town, London. Referee: John Keane. Judges: Richie Davies, Paul Thomas, Terry O'Connor.

8 June　John Simpson 8.13 (Scotland) W CO 5 Ryan Barrett 8.12 (England), Millennium Hotel, Mayfair, London. Referee: Richie Davies. Judges: Mickey Vann, Dave Parris, John Keane.

S.Featherweight

12 July　Carl Johanneson 9.3½ (England) W RSC 4 Billy Corcoran 9.2 (England), York Hall, Bethnal Green, London. Referee: Ian John-Lewis. Judges: Mickey Vann, Marcus McDonnell, Mark Green. This was a vacant title fight following Alex Arthur's decision to relinquish on 11 April 2006.

3 November　Carl Johanneson 9.4 (England) W RSC 6 Femi Fehintola 9.3 (England), The Metrodome Leisure Complex, Barnsley. Referee: Howard Foster. Judges: Dave Parris, Mickey Vann, Terry O'Connor.

9 February　Carl Johanneson 9.4 (England) W PTS 12 Ricky Burns 9.4 (Scotland), The Town Hall, Leeds. Referee: Howard Foster. Scorecards: Victor Loughlin 118-109, Mickey Vann 117-110, Phil Edwards 116-110.

Lightweight

8 December　Lee Meager 9.8½ (England) L PTS 12 Jonathan Thaxton 9.8½ (England), Goresbrook Leisure Centre, Dagenham. Referee: Ian John-Lewis. Scorecards: Dave Parris 110-119, Mark Green 109-118, Marcus McDonnell 110-118.

16 March　Jonathan Thaxton 9.8½ (England) W RSC 7 Scott Lawton 9.8 (England), The Norfolk Showground, Norwich. Referee: Richie Davies. Judges: John Keane, Mark Green, Ian John-Lewis.

L.Welterweight

20 January　Nicky Daws 9.13½ (England) L PTS 12 Barry Morrison 9.13¾ (Scotland), Alexandra Palace, Muswell Hill, London. Referee: Mickey Vann. Scorecards: Marcus McDonnell 114-115, Phil Edwards 113-115, Dave Parris 117-112.

8 June　Barry Morrison 10.0 (Scotland) L PTS 12 Colin Lynes 9.13¼ (England), The Concert Hall, Motherwell. Referee: Phil Edwards. Scorecards: Mark Green 112-116, Victor Loughlin 113-116, Terry O'Connor 111-117.

Welterweight

11 May　Kevin Anderson 146¾ (Scotland) W PTS 12

Eamonn Magee 10.7 (Northern Ireland), The Concert Hall, Motherwell. Referee: Howard Foster. Scorecards: Victor Loughlin 119-110, John Keane 118-110, Ian John-Lewis 117-110.

L.Middleweight

29 September　Jamie Moore 11.0 (England) W RSC 10 Matthew Macklin 10.13 (England), George Carnall Sports Centre, Manchester. Referee: Victor Loughlin. Judges: Richie Davies, Dave Parris, Phil Edwards.

Middleweight

15 December　Howard Eastman 11.6 (England/Guyana) W CO 12 Richard Williams 11.5¼ (England), York Hall, Bethnal Green, London. Referee: Victor Loughlin. Judges: Richie Davies, John Keane, Mark Green. Billed for the vacant title after Scott Dann relinquished in August 2006 following a car crash.

S.Middleweight

24 November　Carl Froch 11.12½ (England) W CO 3 Tony Dodson 11.12 (England), The Ice Arena, Nottingham. Referee: Phil Edwards. Judges: Ian John-Lewis, Marcus McDonnell, Mark Green.

L.Heavyweight

18 May　Tony Oakey 12.7 (England) W RSC 12 Steven Spartacus 12.6 (England), ExCel Arena, Canning Town, London. Referee: Richie Davies. Judges: Marcus McDonnell, Mark Green, Ian John-Lewis. This was a vacant title fight brought about after the champion, Peter Oboh, pulled out of a defence against Oakey on 27 April an hour before the contest was due to take place. Needless to say, Oboh was then stripped of the belt.

Cruiserweight

20 October　John Keeton 14.3½ (England) W RSC 7 Lee Swaby 14.3½ (England), Don Valley Stadium, Sheffield. Referee: Mickey Vann. Judges: Victor Loughlin, John Keane, Paul Thomas. Billed for the vacant title after Mark Hobson gave up the crown on winning the WBU championship on 8 September 2006.

Heavyweight

13 October　Scott Gammer 16.12 (Wales) W PTS Micky Steeds 16.8 (England), The Afan Lido, Aberavon. Referee: Paul Thomas. Scorecards: Terry O'Connor 118-110, Mark Green 118-110, John Keane 120-108.

2 March　Scott Gammer 17.1¾ (Wales) L CO 9 Danny Williams 16.5 (England), The Sports Centre, Neath. Referee: Victor Loughlin. Judges: Howard Foster, Richie Davies, Terry O'Connor.

Lord Lonsdale Challenge Belts: Outright Winners

Outright Winners of the National Sporting Club's Challenge Belt, 1909-1935 (21)

Under pressure from other promoters with bigger venues, and in an effort to sustain their monopoly – having controlled championship fights in Britain up until that point in time – the National Sporting Club launched the belt in 1909. They did so on the proviso that there should be eight weight divisions – fly, bantam, feather, light, welter, middle, light-heavy, and heavy – and that to win a belt outright a champion must score three title-match victories at the same weight, but not necessarily consecutively. Worth a substantial amount of money, and carrying a £1 a week pension from the age of 50, the President of the NSC, Lord Lonsdale, donated the first of 22 belts struck. Known as the Lonsdale Belt, despite the inscription reading: 'The National Sporting Club's Challenge Belt', the first man to put a notch on a belt was Freddie Welsh, who outpointed Johnny Summers for the lightweight title on 8 November 1909, while Jim Driscoll became the first man to win one outright. The record time for winning the belt is held by Jim Higgins (279 days).

FLYWEIGHT	Jimmy Wilde; Jackie Brown
BANTAMWEIGHT	Digger Stanley; Joe Fox; Jim Higgins; Johnny Brown; Dick Corbett; Johnny King
FEATHERWEIGHT	Jim Driscoll; Tancy Lee; Johnny Cuthbert; Nel Tarleton
LIGHTWEIGHT	Freddie Welsh
WELTERWEIGHT	Johnny Basham; Jack Hood
MIDDLEWEIGHT	Pat O'Keefe; Len Harvey; Jock McAvoy
L. HEAVYWEIGHT	Dick Smith
HEAVYWEIGHT	Bombardier Billy Wells; Jack Petersen

Note: Both Dick Corbett and Johnny King – with one notch apiece on the 'special' British Empire Lonsdale Belt that was struck in 1933 and later presented to the winner of the Tommy Farr v Joe Louis fight – were allowed to keep their Lonsdale Belts with just two notches secured; Freddie Welsh, also with two notches, was awarded a belt due to his inability to defend because of the First World War; the first bantam belt came back into circulation and was awarded to Johnny Brown; Al Foreman, with just one notch on the second lightweight belt, took it back to Canada with him without the consent of the BBBoC; while the second light-heavy belt was awarded to Jack Smith of Worcester for winning a novices heavyweight competition. Having emigrated to New Zealand, Smith later presented the visiting Her Majesty The Queen with the belt and it now hangs in the BBBoC's offices.

Outright Winners of the BBBoC Lord Lonsdale Challenge Belt, 1936-2007 (121)

Re-introduced by the British Boxing Board of Control as the Lord Lonsdale Challenge Belt, but of less intrinsic value, Benny Lynch's eight-round win over Pat Palmer (16 September 1936 at Shawfield Park, Glasgow) got the new version underway, while Eric Boon became the first man to win one outright, in 1939, following victories over Dave Crowley (2) and Arthur Danahar. Since those early days, six further weight divisions have been added and, following on from Henry Cooper's feat of winning three Lonsdale Belts outright, on 10 June 1981 the BBBoC's rules and regulations were amended to read that no boxer shall receive more than one belt as his own property, in any one weight division. A later amendment stated that from 1 September 1999, any boxer putting a notch on a Lonsdale Belt for the first time would require three more notches at the same weight before he could call the belt his own. However, men who already had a notch on the Lonsdale Belt prior to 1 September 1999 could contest it under the former ruling of three winning championship contests at the same weight. Incidentally, the fastest of the modern belt winners is Ryan Rhodes (90 days), while Chris and Kevin Finnegan are the only brothers to have each won a belt outright.

FLYWEIGHT	Jackie Paterson; Terry Allen; Walter McGowan; John McCluskey; Hugh Russell; Charlie Magri; Pat Clinton; Robbie Regan; Francis Ampofo; Ady Lewis
BANTAMWEIGHT	Johnny King; Peter Keenan (2); Freddie Gilroy; Alan Rudkin; Johnny Owen; Billy Hardy; Drew Docherty; Nicky Booth
S. BANTAMWEIGHT	Richie Wenton; Michael Brodie; Michael Alldis; Michael Hunter
FEATHERWEIGHT	Nel Tarleton; Ronnie Clayton (2); Charlie Hill; Howard Winstone (2); Evan Armstrong; Pat Cowdell; Robert Dickie; Paul Hodkinson; Colin McMillan; Sean Murphy; Jonjo Irwin; Dazzo Williams
S. FEATHERWEIGHT	Jimmy Anderson; John Doherty; Floyd Havard; Charles Shepherd; Michael Gomez; Alex Arthur

LIGHTWEIGHT	Eric Boon; Billy Thompson; Joe Lucy; Dave Charnley; Maurice Cullen; Ken Buchanan; Jim Watt; George Feeney; Tony Willis; Carl Crook; Billy Schwer; Michael Ayers; Bobby Vanzie; Graham Earl
L. WELTERWEIGHT	Joey Singleton; Colin Power; Clinton McKenzie; Lloyd Christie; Andy Holligan; Ross Hale; Junior Witter
WELTERWEIGHT	Ernie Roderick; Wally Thom; Brian Curvis (2); Ralph Charles; Colin Jones; Lloyd Honeyghan; Kirkland Laing; Del Bryan; Geoff McCreesh; Derek Roche; Neil Sinclair; David Barnes
L. MIDDLEWEIGHT	Maurice Hope; Jimmy Batten; Pat Thomas; Prince Rodney; Andy Till; Robert McCracken; Ryan Rhodes; Ensley Bingham; Jamie Moore
MIDDLEWEIGHT	Pat McAteer; Terry Downes; Johnny Pritchett; Bunny Sterling; Alan Minter; Kevin Finnegan; Roy Gumbs; Tony Sibson; Herol Graham; Neville Brown; Howard Eastman; Scott Dann
S. MIDDLEWEIGHT	Sammy Storey; David Starie; Carl Froch
L. HEAVYWEIGHT	Randy Turpin; Chic Calderwood; Chris Finnegan; Bunny Johnson; Tom Collins; Dennis Andries; Tony Wilson; Crawford Ashley
CRUISERWEIGHT	Johnny Nelson; Terry Dunstan; Bruce Scott; Mark Hobson
HEAVYWEIGHT	Henry Cooper (3); Horace Notice; Lennox Lewis; Julius Francis; Danny Williams; Matt Skelton

Note: Walter McGowan, Charlie Magri and Junior Witter, with one notch apiece, kept their belts under the three years/no available challengers' ruling, while Johnny King, with two notches, was awarded the belt on the grounds that the Second World War stopped him from making further defences. Incidentally, King and Nel Tarleton are the only men to have won both the NSC and BBBoC belts outright.

Howard Eastman (left), already an outright winner of a Lonsdale Belt at middleweight, punched his way to a 12th-round kayo victory over Richard Williams to put his first notch on another belt at the weight   Les Clark

British Champions Since Gloves, 1878-2007

The listings below show the tenure of all British champions at each weight since gloves (two ounces or more) were introduced to British rings under Queensberry Rules. Although Charley Davis (147 lbs) had beaten Ted Napper (140 lbs) with gloves in 1873, we start with Denny Harrington, who defeated George Rooke for both the English and world middleweight titles in London on 12 March 1878. We also make a point of ignoring competition winners, apart from Anthony Diamond who beat Dido Plumb for the middles title over 12 rounds, basically because full championship conditions or finish fights of three-minute rounds were not applied. Another point worth bearing in mind, is that prior to the 1880s there were only five weights – heavy, middle, light, feather and bantam. Anything above 154 lbs, the middleweight limit, was classified a heavyweight contest, whereas lightweight, feather and bantamweight poundages were much looser. Therefore, to put things into current perspective, in many cases we have had to ascertain the actual poundage of fighters concerned and relate them to the modern weight classes. Another point worth remembering is that men born outside Britain who won international titles in this country, are not recorded for fear of added confusion and, although many of the champions or claimants listed before 1909 were no more than English titleholders, having fought for the 'championship of England', for our purposes they carry the 'British' label.

Prior to 1909, the year that the Lord Lonsdale Challenge Belt was introduced and weight classes subsequently standardised, poundages within divisions could vary quite substantially, thus enabling men fighting at different weights to claim the same 'title' at the same time. A brief history of the weight fluctuations between 1891 and 1909, shows:

Bantamweight   With the coming of gloves, the division did not really take off until Nunc Wallace established himself at 112 lbs on beating (small) Bill Goode after nine rounds in London on 12 March 1889. Later, with Wallace fighting above the weight, Billy Plimmer was generally recognised as the country's leading eight stoner, following victories over Charles Mansford and Jem Stevens, and became accepted as world champion when George Dixon, the number one in America's eyes, gradually increased his weight. In 1895, Pedlar Palmer took the British title at 112 lbs, but by 1900 he had developed into a 114 pounder. Between 1902 and 1904, Joe Bowker defended regularly at 116 lbs and in 1909 the NSC standardised the weight at 118 lbs, even though the USA continued for a short while to accept only 116 lbs.

Featherweight   Between 1886 and 1895, one of the most prestigious championship belts in this country was fought for at 126 lbs and, although George Dixon was recognised in the USA as world featherweight champion – gradually moving from 114 to 122 lbs – no major international contests took place in Britain during the above period at his weight. It was only in 1895, when Fred Johnson took the British title at 120 lbs, losing it to Ben Jordan two years later, that we came into line with the USA. Ben Jordan became an outstanding champion who, between 1898 and 1899, was seen by the NSC as world champion at 120 lbs. However, first Harry Greenfield, then Jabez White and Will Curley, continued to claim the 126 lbs version of the British title and it was only in 1900, when Jack Roberts beat Curley, that the weight limit was finally standardised at nine stone.

Lightweight   Outstanding champions often carried their weights as they grew in size. A perfect example of this was Dick Burge, the British lightweight champion from 1891-1901, who gradually increased from 134 to 144 lbs, while still maintaining his right to the title. It was not until 1902 that Jabez White brought the division into line with the USA. Later, both White, and then Goldswain, carried their weight up to 140 lbs and it was left to Johnny Summers to set the current limit of 135 lbs.

Welterweight   The presence of Dick Burge fighting from 134 to 144 lbs plus up until 1900, explains quite adequately why the welterweight division, although very popular in the USA, did not take off in this country until 1902. The championship was contested between 142 and 146 lbs in those days and was not really supported by the NSC, but by 1909 with their backing it finally became established at 147 lbs.

On 8 September 1970, Bunny Sterling became the first immigrant to win a British title under the ten-year residential ruling, while earlier, on 28 June 1948, Dick Turpin won the British middleweight title and, in doing so, became the first coloured fighter to win the title, thus breaking down the so-called 'colour bar'. On 20 May 1998, the BBBoC passed a ruling allowing fighters from abroad, who take out British citizenship, the opportunity to fight for the British title after five years residency instead of ten.

Note that the Lonsdale Belt notches (title bout wins) relate to NSC, 1909-1935, and BBBoC, 1936-2006.

Champions in **bold** are accorded national recognition.

*Undefeated champions (Does not include men who forfeited titles).

Title Holder	Lonsdale Belt Notches	Tenure	Title Holder	Lonsdale Belt Notches	Tenure	Title Holder	Lonsdale Belt Notches	Tenure
Flyweight (112 lbs)			Joe Symonds		1914	**Elky Clark***	2	1924-1927
Sid Smith		1911	**Tancy Lee**	1	1914-1915	**Johnny Hill***	1	1927-1929
Sid Smith	1	1911-1913	Jimmy Wilde		1914-1915	**Jackie Brown**		1929-1930
Bill Ladbury		1913-1914	**Joe Symonds**	1	1915-1916	**Bert Kirby**	1	1930-1931
Percy Jones	1	1914	**Jimmy Wilde***	3	1916-1923	**Jackie Brown**	3	1931-1935

191

BRITISH CHAMPIONS SINCE GLOVES, 1878-2007

Title Holder	Lonsdale Belt Notches	Tenure
Benny Lynch*	2	1935-1938
Jackie Paterson	4	1939-1948
Rinty Monaghan*	1	1948-1950
Terry Allen	1	1951-1952
Teddy Gardner*	1	1952
Terry Allen*	2	1952-1954
Dai Dower*	1	1955-1957
Frankie Jones	2	1957-1960
Johnny Caldwell*	1	1960-1961
Jackie Brown	1	1962-1963
Walter McGowan*	1	1963-1966
John McCluskey*	3	1967-1977
Charlie Magri*	1	1977-1981
Kelvin Smart	1	1982-1984
Hugh Russell*	3	1984-1985
Duke McKenzie*	2	1985-1986
Dave Boy McAuley*	1	1986-1988
Pat Clinton*	3	1988-1991
Robbie Regan	1	1991
Francis Ampofo	1	1991
Robbie Regan*	2	1991-1992
Francis Ampofo	3	1992-1996
Mickey Cantwell*	1	1996-1997
Ady Lewis*	3	1997-1998
Damaen Kelly	1	1999
Keith Knox	1	1999
Jason Booth*	2	1999-2003

Bantamweight (118 lbs)

Title Holder	Lonsdale Belt Notches	Tenure
Nunc Wallace*		1889-1891
Billy Plimmer		1891-1895
Tom Gardner		1892
Willie Smith		1892-1896
Nunc Wallace		1893-1895
George Corfield		1893-1896
Pedlar Palmer		1895-1900
Billy Plimmer		1896-1898
Harry Ware		1899-1900
Harry Ware		1900-1902
Andrew Tokell		1901-1902
Jim Williams		1902
Andrew Tokell		1902
Harry Ware		1902
Joe Bowker		1902-1910
Owen Moran		1905-1907
Digger Stanley		1906-1910
Digger Stanley	2	1910-1913
Bill Beynon	1	1913
Digger Stanley	1	1913-1914
Curley Walker*	1	1914-1915
Joe Fox*	3	1915-1917
Tommy Noble	1	1918-1919
Walter Ross*	1	1919-1920
Jim Higgins	3	1920-1922
Tommy Harrison		1922-1923
Bugler Harry Lake	1	1923
Johnny Brown	3	1923-1928
Alf Pattenden	2	1928-1929
Johnny Brown		1928
Teddy Baldock		1928-1929
Teddy Baldock*	1	1929-1931
Dick Corbett	1	1931-1932
Johnny King	1	1932-1934
Dick Corbett*	1	1934
Johnny King	1+2	1935-1947
Jackie Paterson	2	1947-1949
Stan Rowan*	1	1949

Title Holder	Lonsdale Belt Notches	Tenure
Danny O'Sullivan	1	1949-1951
Peter Keenan	3	1951-1953
John Kelly	1	1953-1954
Peter Keenan	3	1954-1959
Freddie Gilroy*	4	1959-1963
Johnny Caldwell	1	1964-1965
Alan Rudkin	1	1965-1966
Walter McGowan	1	1966-1968
Alan Rudkin*	4	1968-1972
Johnny Clark*	1	1973-1974
Dave Needham	1	1974-1975
Paddy Maguire	1	1975-1977
Johnny Owen*	4	1977-1980
John Feeney	1	1981-1983
Hugh Russell	1	1983
Davy Larmour	1	1983
John Feeney	1	1983-1985
Ray Gilbody	2	1985-1987
Billy Hardy*	5	1987-1991
Joe Kelly	1	1992
Drew Docherty	4	1992-1997
Paul Lloyd	2	1997-1999
Noel Wilders*	2	1999-2000
Ady Lewis	1	2000
Tommy Waite	1	2000
Nicky Booth	5	2000-2004
Martin Power*	3	2005-2007

S. Bantamweight (122 lbs)

Title Holder	Lonsdale Belt Notches	Tenure
Richie Wenton*	3	1994-1996
Michael Brodie*	3	1997-1999
Patrick Mullings	1	1999
Drew Docherty*	1	1999
Michael Alldis	3	1999-2001
Patrick Mullings	1	2001
Michael Alldis*	1	2002
Esham Pickering*	1	2003-2004
Michael Hunter*	4	2004-2006
Esham Pickering	1	2006-

Featherweight (126 lbs)

Title Holder	Lonsdale Belt Notches	Tenure
Bill Baxter		1884-1891
Harry Overton		1890-1891
Billy Reader		1891-1892
Fred Johnson		1891-1895
Harry Spurden		1892-1895
Jack Fitzpatrick		1895-1897
Fred Johnson		1895-1897
Harry Greenfield		1896-1899
Ben Jordan*		1897-1900
Jabez White		1899-1900
Will Curley		1900-1901
Jack Roberts		1901-1902
Will Curley		1902-1903
Ben Jordan*		1902-1905
Joe Bowker		1905
Johnny Summers		1906
Joe Bowker		1905-1906
Jim Driscoll		1906-1907
Spike Robson		1906-1907
Jim Driscoll*	3	1907-1913
Spike Robson		1907-1910
Ted Kid Lewis*	1	1913-1914
Llew Edwards*	1	1915-1917
Charlie Hardcastle	1	1917
Tancy Lee*	3	1917-1919
Mike Honeyman	2	1920-1921

Title Holder	Lonsdale Belt Notches	Tenure
Joe Fox*	1	1921-1922
George McKenzie	2	1924-1925
Johnny Curley	2	1925-1927
Johnny Cuthbert	1	1927-1928
Harry Corbett	1	1928-1929
Johnny Cuthbert	2	1929-1931
Nel Tarleton	1	1931-1932
Seaman Tommy Watson	2	1932-1934
Nel Tarleton	2	1934-1936
Johnny McGrory	1	1936-1938
Jim Spider Kelly	1	1938-1939
Johnny Cusick	1	1939-1940
Nel Tarleton*	3	1940-1947
Ronnie Clayton	6	1947-1954
Sammy McCarthy	1	1954-1955
Billy Spider Kelly	1	1955-1956
Charlie Hill	3	1956-1959
Bobby Neill	1	1959-1960
Terry Spinks	2	1960-1961
Howard Winstone*	7	1961-1969
Jimmy Revie	2	1969-1971
Evan Armstrong	2	1971-1972
Tommy Glencross	1	1972-1973
Evan Armstrong*	2	1973-1975
Vernon Sollas	1	1975-1977
Alan Richardson	2	1977-1978
Dave Needham	2	1978-1979
Pat Cowdell*	3	1979-1982
Steve Sims*	1	1982-1983
Barry McGuigan*	2	1983-1986
Robert Dickie	3	1986-1988
Peter Harris	1	1988
Paul Hodkinson*	3	1988-1990
Sean Murphy	2	1990-1991
Gary de Roux	1	1991
Colin McMillan*	3	1991-1992
John Davison*	1	1992-1993
Sean Murphy	1	1993
Duke McKenzie*	1	1993-1994
Billy Hardy*	1	1994
Michael Deveney	1	1995
Jonjo Irwin	2	1995-1996
Colin McMillan	1	1996-1997
Paul Ingle*	3	1997-1998
Jonjo Irwin*	2	1998-1999
Gary Thornhill	1	2000
Scott Harrison*	3	2001-2002
Jamie McKeever	1	2003
Roy Rutherford	1	2003
Dazzo Williams	4	2003-2005
Nicky Cook*	1	2005
Andy Morris	2	2005-2006
John Simpson	2	2006-

S. Featherweight (130 lbs)

Title Holder	Lonsdale Belt Notches	Tenure
Jimmy Anderson*	3	1968-1970
John Doherty	1	1986
Pat Cowdell	1	1986
Najib Daho	1	1986-1987
Pat Cowdell	1	1987-1988
Floyd Havard	1	1988-1989
John Doherty	1	1989-1990
Joey Jacobs	1	1990
Hugh Forde	1	1990
Kevin Pritchard	1	1990-1991
Robert Dickie	1	1991
Sugar Gibiliru	1	1991

Title Holder	Lonsdale Belt Notches	Tenure
John Doherty	1	1991-1992
Michael Armstrong	1	1992
Neil Haddock	2	1992-1994
Floyd Havard*	3	1994-1995
P. J. Gallagher	2	1996-1997
Charles Shepherd	3	1997-1999
Michael Gomez*	5	1999-2002
Alex Arthur	3	2002-2003
Michael Gomez	1	2003-2004
Alex Arthur*	2	2005-2006
Carl Johanneson	3	2006-

Lightweight (135 lbs)

Title Holder	Lonsdale Belt Notches	Tenure
Dick Burge		1891-1897
Harry Nickless		1891-1894
Tom Causer		1894-1897
Tom Causer		1897
Dick Burge*		1897-1901
Jabez White		1902-1906
Jack Goldswain		1906-1908
Johnny Summers		1908-1909
Freddie Welsh	1	1909-1911
Matt Wells	1	1911-1912
Freddie Welsh*	1	1912-1919
Bob Marriott*	1	1919-1920
Ernie Rice	1	1921-1922
Seaman Nobby Hall		1922-1923
Harry Mason		1923-1924
Ernie Izzard	2	1924-1925
Harry Mason		1924-1925
Harry Mason*	1	1925-1928
Sam Steward		1928-1929
Fred Webster		1929-1930
Al Foreman*	1	1930-1932
Johnny Cuthbert		1932-1934
Harry Mizler		1934
Jackie Kid Berg		1934-1936
Jimmy Walsh	1	1936-1938
Dave Crowley	1	1938
Eric Boon	3	1938-1944
Ronnie James*	1	1944-1947
Billy Thompson	3	1947-1951
Tommy McGovern	1	1951-1952
Frank Johnson	1	1952-1953
Joe Lucy	1	1953-1955
Frank Johnson	1	1955-1956
Joe Lucy	2	1956-1957
Dave Charnley*	3	1957-1965
Maurice Cullen	4	1965-1968
Ken Buchanan*	2	1968-1971
Willie Reilly*	1	1972
Jim Watt	1	1972-1973
Ken Buchanan*	1	1973-1974
Jim Watt*	2	1975-1977
Charlie Nash*	1	1978-1979
Ray Cattouse	2	1980-1982
George Feeney*	3	1982-1985
Tony Willis	3	1985-1987
Alex Dickson	1	1987-1988
Steve Boyle	2	1988-1990
Carl Crook	5	1990-1992
Billy Schwer	1	1992-1993
Paul Burke	1	1993
Billy Schwer*	2	1993-1995
Michael Ayers*	5	1995-1997
Wayne Rigby	2	1998
Bobby Vanzie	5	1998-2003
Graham Earl	1	2003-2004
Graham Earl*	3	2004-2006
Lee Meager	1	2006
Jonathan Thaxton	2	2006-

L. Welterweight (140 lbs)

Title Holder	Lonsdale Belt Notches	Tenure
Des Rea	1	1968-1969
Vic Andreetti*	2	1969-1970
Des Morrison	1	1973-1974
Pat McCormack	1	1974
Joey Singleton	3	1974-1976
Dave Boy Green*	1	1976-1977
Colin Power*	2	1977-1978
Clinton McKenzie	1	1978-1979
Colin Power	1	1979
Clinton McKenzie	5	1979-1984
Terry Marsh*	1	1984-1986
Tony Laing*	1	1986
Tony McKenzie	2	1986-1987
Lloyd Christie	3	1987-1989
Clinton McKenzie*	1	1989
Pat Barrett*	2	1989-1990
Tony Ekubia	1	1990-1991
Andy Holligan	3	1991-1994
Ross Hale	4	1994-1995
Paul Ryan	1	1995-1996
Andy Holligan*	1	1996-1997
Mark Winters	2	1997-1998
Jason Rowland*	2	1998-2000
Ricky Hatton*	1	2000-2001
Junior Witter*	2	2002-2006
Lenny Daws	1	2006-2007
Barry Morrison	1	2007
Colin Lynes	1	2007-

Welterweight (147 lbs)

Title Holder	Lonsdale Belt Notches	Tenure
Charlie Allum		1903-1904
Charlie Knock		1904-1906
Curly Watson		1906-1910
Young Joseph		1908-1910
Young Joseph	1	1910-1911
Arthur Evernden		1911-1912
Johnny Summers		1912
Johnny Summers	2	1912-1914
Tom McCormick		1914
Matt Wells		1914
Johnny Basham	3	1914-1920
Matt Wells		1914-1919
Ted Kid Lewis		1920-1924
Tommy Milligan*		1924-1925
Hamilton Johnny Brown		1925
Harry Mason		1925-1926
Jack Hood*	3	1926-1934
Harry Mason		1934
Pat Butler*		1934-1936
Dave McCleave		1936
Jake Kilrain	1	1936-1939
Ernie Roderick	5	1939-1948
Henry Hall	1	1948-1949
Eddie Thomas	2	1949-1951
Wally Thom	1	1951-1952
Cliff Curvis*	1	1952-1953
Wally Thom	2	1953-1956
Peter Waterman*	2	1956-1958
Tommy Molloy	2	1958-1960
Wally Swift	1	1960
Brian Curvis*	7	1960-1966
Johnny Cooke	2	1967-1968
Ralph Charles*	3	1968-1972
Bobby Arthur	1	1972-1973
John H. Stracey*	1	1973-1975
Pat Thomas	2	1975-1976
Henry Rhiney	2	1976-1979
Kirkland Laing	1	1979-1980
Colin Jones*	3	1980-1982
Lloyd Honeyghan*	2	1983-1985
Kostas Petrou	1	1985
Sylvester Mittee	1	1985
Lloyd Honeyghan*	1	1985-1986
Kirkland Laing	4	1987-1991
Del Bryan	2	1991-1992
Gary Jacobs*	2	1992-1993
Del Bryan	4	1993-1995
Chris Saunders	1	1995-1996
Kevin Lueshing	1	1996-1997
Geoff McCreesh*	4	1997-1999
Derek Roche	3	1999-2000
Harry Dhami	3	2000-2001
Neil Sinclair*	4	2001-2003
David Barnes	4	2003-2005
Michael Jennings	2	2005-2006
Young Muttley	1	2006
Kevin Anderson	2	2006-

L. Middleweight (154 lbs)

Title Holder	Lonsdale Belt Notches	Tenure
Larry Paul	2	1973-1974
Maurice Hope*	3	1974-1977
Jimmy Batten	3	1977-1979
Pat Thomas	3	1979-1981
Herol Graham*	2	1981-1983
Prince Rodney*	1	1983-1984
Jimmy Cable	2	1984-1985
Prince Rodney	2	1985-1986
Chris Pyatt*	1	1986
Lloyd Hibbert*	1	1987
Gary Cooper	1	1988
Gary Stretch	2	1988-1990
Wally Swift Jnr	2	1991-1992
Andy Till	3	1992-1994
Robert McCracken*	3	1994-1995
Ensley Bingham*	2	1996
Ryan Rhodes*	3	1996-1997
Ensley Bingham	3	1997-1999
Wayne Alexander*	2	2000-2003
Jamie Moore	3	2003-2004
Michael Jones	1	2004-2005
Jamie Moore	3	2005-

Middleweight (160 lbs)

Title Holder	Lonsdale Belt Notches	Tenure
Denny Harrington		1878-1880
William Sheriff*		1880-1883
Bill Goode		1887-1890
Toff Wall*		1890
Ted Pritchard		1890-1895
Ted White		1893-1895
Ted White*		1895-1896
Anthony Diamond*		1898
Dick Burge*		1898-1900
Jack Palmer		1902-1903
Charlie Allum		1905-1906
Pat O'Keefe		1906
Tom Thomas	1	1906-1910
Jim Sullivan*	1	1910-1912
Jack Harrison*	1	1912-1913

Title Holder	Lonsdale Belt Notches	Tenure
Pat O'Keefe	2	1914-1916
Bandsman Jack Blake	1	1916-1918
Pat O'Keefe*	1	1918-1919
Ted Kid Lewis		1920-1921
Tom Gummer	1	1920-1921
Gus Platts		1921
Johnny Basham		1921
Ted Kid Lewis	2	1921-1923
Johnny Basham		1921
Roland Todd		1923-1925
Roland Todd		1925-1927
Tommy Milligan	1	1926-1928
Frank Moody		1927-1928
Alex Ireland		1928-1929
Len Harvey	5	1929-1933
Jock McAvoy	3+2	1933-1944
Ernie Roderick	1	1945-1946
Vince Hawkins	1	1946-1948
Dick Turpin	2	1948-1950
Albert Finch	1	1950
Randy Turpin*	1	1950-1954
Johnny Sullivan	1	1954-1955
Pat McAteer*	3	1955-1958
Terry Downes	1	1958-1959
John Cowboy McCormack	1	1959
Terry Downes	2	1959-1962
George Aldridge	1	1962-1963
Mick Leahy	1	1963-1964
Wally Swift	1	1964-1965
Johnny Pritchett*	4	1965-1969
Les McAteer	1	1969-1970
Mark Rowe	1	1970
Bunny Sterling	4	1970-1974
Kevin Finnegan*	1	1974
Bunny Sterling*	1	1975
Alan Minter	3	1975-1977
Kevin Finnegan	1	1977
Alan Minter*	1	1977-1978
Tony Sibson	1	1979
Kevin Finnegan*	1	1979-1980
Roy Gumbs	3	1981-1983
Mark Kaylor	1	1983-1984
Tony Sibson*	1	1984
Herol Graham*	1	1985-1986
Brian Anderson	1	1986-1987
Tony Sibson*	1	1987-1988
Herol Graham	4	1988-1992
Frank Grant	2	1992-1993
Neville Brown	6	1993-1998
Glenn Catley*	1	1998
Howard Eastman*	4	1998-2004
Scott Dann*	4	2004-2006
Howard Eastman	1	2006-

S. Middleweight (168 lbs)

Title Holder	Lonsdale Belt Notches	Tenure
Sammy Storey	2	1989-1990
James Cook*	1	1990-1991
Fidel Castro	2	1991-1992
Henry Wharton*	1	1992-1993
James Cook	1	1993-1994
Cornelius Carr*	1	1994
Ali Forbes	1	1995
Sammy Storey*	1	1995
Joe Calzaghe*	2	1995-1997
David Starie	1	1997
Dean Francis*	2	1997-1998
David Starie*	5	1998-2003

Title Holder	Lonsdale Belt Notches	Tenure
Matthew Barney*	1	2003
Tony Dodson*	1	2003-2004
Carl Froch	4	2004-

L. Heavyweight (175lbs)

Title Holder	Lonsdale Belt Notches	Tenure
Dennis Haugh		1913-1914
Dick Smith	2	1914-1916
Harry Reeve*	1	1916-1917
Dick Smith*	1	1918-1919
Boy McCormick*	1	1919-1921
Jack Bloomfield*	1	1922-1924
Tom Berry	1	1925-1927
Gipsy Daniels*	1	1927
Frank Moody	1	1927-1929
Harry Crossley	1	1929-1932
Jack Petersen*	1	1932
Len Harvey*	1	1933-1934
Eddie Phillips		1935-1937
Jock McAvoy	1	1937-1938
Len Harvey	2	1938-1942
Freddie Mills*	1	1942-1950
Don Cockell	2	1950-1952
Randy Turpin*	1	1952
Dennis Powell	1	1953
Alex Buxton	2	1953-1955
Randy Turpin*	1	1955
Ron Barton*	1	1956
Randy Turpin*	2	1956-1958
Chic Calderwood	3	1960-1963
Chic Calderwood*	1	1964-1966
Young John McCormack	2	1967-1969
Eddie Avoth	2	1969-1971
Chris Finnegan	2	1971-1973
John Conteh*	2	1973-1974
Johnny Frankham	1	1975
Chris Finnegan*	1	1975-1976
Tim Wood	1	1976-1977
Bunny Johnson*	3	1977-1981
Tom Collins	3	1982-1984
Dennis Andries*	5	1984-1986
Tom Collins*	1	1987
Tony Wilson	3	1987-1989
Tom Collins*	1	1989-1990
Steve McCarthy	1	1990-1991
Crawford Ashley*	3	1991-1992
Maurice Core*	2	1992-1994
Crawford Ashley	3	1994-1999
Clinton Woods*	1	1999-2000
Neil Simpson*	2	2000-2002
Peter Oboh	2	2003-2007
Tony Oakey	1	2007-

Cruiserweight (200 lbs)

Title Holder	Lonsdale Belt Notches	Tenure
Sam Reeson*	1	1985-1986
Andy Straughn	1	1986-1987
Roy Smith	1	1987
Tee Jay	1	1987-1988
Glenn McCrory*	2	1988
Andy Straughn	1	1988-1989
Johnny Nelson*	3	1989-1991
Derek Angol*	2	1991-1992
Carl Thompson*	1	1992-1994
Dennis Andries	1	1995
Terry Dunstan*	3	1995-1996
Johnny Nelson*	1	1996-1998
Bruce Scott	1	1998-1999

Title Holder	Lonsdale Belt Notches	Tenure
Carl Thompson*	1	1999-2000
Bruce Scott	2	2000-2003
Mark Hobson*	5	2003-2006
John Keeton	1	2006-

Heavyweight (200 lbs +)

Title Holder	Lonsdale Belt Notches	Tenure
Tom Allen*		1878-1882
Charlie Mitchell*		1882-1894
Jem Smith		1889-1891
Ted Pritchard		1891-1895
Jem Smith		1895-1896
George Chrisp		1901
Jack Scales		1901-1902
Jack Palmer		1903-1906
Gunner Moir		1906-1909
Iron Hague		1909-1910
P.O. Curran		1910-1911
Iron Hague		1910-1911
Bombardier Billy Wells	3	1911-1919
Joe Beckett		1919
Frank Goddard	1	1919
Joe Beckett*	1	1919-1923
Frank Goddard		1923-1926
Phil Scott*		1926-1931
Reggie Meen		1931-1932
Jack Petersen	3	1932-1933
Len Harvey		1933-1934
Jack Petersen		1934-1936
Ben Foord		1936-1937
Tommy Farr*	1	1937-1938
Len Harvey*	1	1938-1942
Jack London	1	1944-1945
Bruce Woodcock	2	1945-1950
Jack Gardner	1	1950-1952
Johnny Williams	1	1952-1953
Don Cockell*	1	1953-1956
Joe Erskine	2	1956-1958
Brian London	1	1958-1959
Henry Cooper*	9	1959-1969
Jack Bodell	1	1969-1970
Henry Cooper	1	1970-1971
Joe Bugner	1	1971
Jack Bodell	1	1971-1972
Danny McAlinden	1	1972-1975
Bunny Johnson	1	1975
Richard Dunn	2	1975-1976
Joe Bugner*	1	1976-1977
John L. Gardner*	2	1978-1980
Gordon Ferris	1	1981
Neville Meade	1	1981-1983
David Pearce*	1	1983-1985
Hughroy Currie	1	1985-1986
Horace Notice*	4	1986-1988
Gary Mason	2	1989-1991
Lennox Lewis*	3	1991-1993
Herbie Hide*	1	1993-1994
James Oyebola	1	1994-1995
Scott Welch*	1	1995-1996
Julius Francis	4	1997-2000
Mike Holden*	1	2000
Danny Williams	5	2000-2004
Michael Sprott	1	2004
Matt Skelton	4	2004-2006
Scott Gammer	2	2006-2007
Danny Williams	1	2007-

Early Gloved Boxing: Two Leading British Boxers' Records

by Harold Alderman

W PTS = Won Points. W RSF = Won Referee Stopped Fight. W RTD= Won Retired. W DISQ = Won Disqualified. W KO = Won by Knockout (Count Out). DREW = Contest Drawn. L PTS = Lost Points. L RSF = Lost Referee Stopped Fight. L RTD = Lost Retired. L DISQ = Lost Disqualified. L KO = Lost by Knockout (Count Out). EXH = Exhibition Bout.

Charlie 'Toff' Wall

From Hackney. Billed as the English 10st 4lbs champion in February 1885, 10st 8lbs champion in May 1886, 11st champion in August 1886 and 11st 4lbs champion from July 1885. Was the official English 11st 4lbs champion from 8 February 1890 to 19 October 1891. Championship recognition was withdrawn because of Wall's failure to go ahead with proposed bouts and he was so good that others refused to take him on in anything other than exhibition bouts. He claimed that he was never bested even when drunk, although it was alleged that the gentleman amateur, Robert 'Bob' Hare, had the best of their spar of 13 December 1886 when Wall was drunk

1884

28 January Jim Picton EXH 3 Hackney
15 February Jack Donoghue W PTS 3 Shoreditch. The first series of a 10st 4lbs, £5 competition
15 February Arthur Cooper W PTS 3 Shoreditch. The semi-final of a 10st 4lbs, £5 competition
15 February Tom Picton W PTS 3 Shoreditch. The final of a 10st 4lbs, £5 competition
20 February Jim Picton EXH 3 St Lukes
12 March Jim Picton EXH 3 Hackney
27 March Jim Picton EXH 3 Hackney
12 May Jim Picton EXH 3 Hackney
4 September Tommy Hill EXH 4 Shoreditch
22 September Jim Picton EXH 3 Hackney
26 September Charlie Parrish EXH 3 Hackney
6 October Jim Picton EXH 3 Kingsland
6 October Bill Cheese EXH 3 Kingsland. This was the second of two exhibitions on the same show
13 October Tom Symons EXH 3 Shoreditch
27 October H.Bussard EXH 3 Tottenham
18 November Mr Keightley EXH 3 Old Ford
25 November J.Thompson EXH 3 Oxford Street
23 December Bill Cheese EXH 3 Old Ford

1885

5 January Bill Cheese EXH 3 Shoreditch
13 January George 'Rough' Pearson EXH 3 Old Ford
26 January H.Boswell EXH 3 Tottenham
27 January George 'Rough' Pearson EXH 3 Old Ford
2 February Jim Picton EXH 3 Tottenham
2 February Bob Dunbar EXH 3 Shoreditch. This was the second of two exhibitions on the same day
14 February Bill Long EXH 3 Islington
24 February Manning Salmon EXH 3 Enfield Highway. Wall was billed as the English 10st 4lbs champion
16 March Bill Cheese EXH 3 Shoreditch
17 March Bill Cheese EXH 3 Shoreditch
20 April Bill Cheese EXH 3 Shoreditch
22 April Bob Preston EXH 3 Clapton Park
11 May J.'Yorkey' Cashley EXH 3 Shoreditch
14 July George 'Rough' Pearson W RTD 63 Epping Forest (start) and Chingford (finish). This was Wall's debut in a bare-knuckle prize fight under London Prize Ring Rules. The first 42 rounds, lasting 52 minutes, were fought at Epping Forest before being stopped by the police, so the fight moved on three miles to Chingford where 21 more rounds, lasting 30 minutes, were fought. Pearson was reported as being 5'10" and 11st 4lbs, with Wall 5'4½" and 10st 9lbs
22 September Mr McCarthy EXH 3 Tottenham
23 October 'An amateur' EXH 3 Shoreditch

26 October 'A pupil' EXH 3 Bethnal Green
2 November Mr Richardson EXH 3 Bethnal Green
3 November J.Thurgood EXH 3 Bethnal Green
17 November 'A pupil' EXH 3 Shoreditch
26 November 'A pupil' EXH 3 Shoreditch
30 November J.'Yorkey' Cashley EXH 3 Bethnal Green
7 December 'Ching Ghook' EXH 3 Shoreditch
8 December Bob Dunbar EXH 3 Bethnal Green
8 December Jack 'Baby' Partridge EXH 3 Hounsditch. This was the second of two exhibitions given on the same day
30 December 'A pupil' EXH 3 Shoreditch

1886

19 January Tom Smith EXH 3 City Road
21 January Jack 'Baby' Partridge W RTD 2 Shoreditch. The first series of a 10st 4lb competition
21 January Jack Donaghue W PTS 3 Shoreditch. The semi-final of a 10st 4lb competition
21 January Ted Burchell W PTS 3 Shoreditch. The final of a 10st 4lb competition
23 January Bells Life in London stated: "'Toff' Wall one of the regular Saturday night sparrers at the Blue Anchor, Church Street, Shoreditch"
25 January Pat Condon EXH 3 Bethnal Green
26 January Jack 'Baby' Partridge EXH 3 Shoreditch
8 February 'A pupil' EXH 3 Shoreditch
8 February A.Kilbride EXH 3 Islington. This was the second of two exhibitions on the same day
23 February H.Pearson EXH 3 Shoreditch
2 March Jim Picton EXH 3 Shoreditch
5 March Jim Young EXH 3 Piccadilly
13 March Wall challenged 'All England' at 10-8, £50 prize or £200 a side. This was repeated on 17 March
13 March Jack McKay EXH 3 Bethnal Green
25 March Tom Smith EXH 3 Liverpool
27 March Tom Smith EXH 3 Manchester
29 March Tom Smith EXH 3 Manchester. Throughout this tour, Wall was billed as the 10st 8lbs middleweight champion
5 April Bill Cheese EXH 3 Bethnal Green
12 April C.Mellorslip EXH 3 Hackney
13 April Tom Smith EXH 3 Newmarket
15 April William 'Coddy' Middings EXH 3 Newmarket
20 April Tom Smith EXH 3 Lewisham Road
22 April Tom Smith EXH 3 New Cross
28 April Tom Smith EXH 3 Woolwich
3 May Tom Smith EXH 3 Harrow Road
5 May Mr A.F. 'Peggy' Bettison EXH 3 City Road
6 May Challenged world from 10st up to 10st 8lbs
10 May Mr Mackay EXH 3 Bethnal Green
18 May Mr A.F. 'Peggy' Bettison EXH 3 Tufnell Park
19 May Sporting Life stated: "Next week 'Toff' Wall leaves for the USA to take on the so-called 'American 10st 8lbs middleweight champion', Jack Dempsey, to decide the world title"
24 May Jem Smith EXH 3 Shoreditch. Smith, the English 'Prize Ring Rules' heavyweight champion was three stone heavier, but was completely outclassed by 'Toff' Wall, who even floored him during the bout. Smith failed to turn up the following day for another three-round exhibition at this venue
3 June Bill Cheese EXH 3 Shoreditch
28 June Ching Ghook EXH 3 Shoreditch
28 June J.'Yorkey' Cashley EXH 3 Bethnal Green. This was the second of two exhibitions on the same day

16 July Bill Samuels EXH 3 Cardiff
22 July Jack 'Baby' Partridge EXH 3 Lambeth
26 July Mr.T.Evans EXH 3 Cardiff
26 July Bill Samuels EXH 3 Cardiff. This was the second of two exhibitions on the same night
27 July Bill Samuels EXH 3 Cardiff
28 July Bill Samuels EXH 3 Cardiff
29 July Bill Samuels EXH 3 Cardiff
30 July Bill Samuels EXH 3 Cardiff
31 July Bill Samuels EXH 3 Cardiff
August W. 'Coddy' Middings EXH 3 Newport
6 August J. 'Yorkey' Cashley EXH 3 London
11 August Woolf Bendoff EXH 3 Shoreditch
19 October Jim Young EXH 3 Piccadilly
2 December Mr.W.J.King EXH 3 St Johns Wood
7 December Alec Roberts EXH 3 Shoreditch
13 December Robert 'Bob' Hair EXH 3 Blackfriars. It is sometimes claimed that this was the one occasion when Wall, who was stated to be drunk, didn't have it all his own way
16 December James Kendrick EXH 3 Shoreditch

1887
4 January Bill Wall EXH 3 Smithfield
7 February Young McKay EXH 3 Shoreditch
15 February Jack Knifeton EXH 3 Islington. This was the first day of a three-day show, all being exhibitions and was the final of a catchweight competition. The lumbering 6'1" tall Knifeton was completely outclassed, having nothing but size. Knifeton also sparred on the following two days, firstly against Charlie Mitchell (Birmingham) and then versus Alf Greenfield, both of whom completely outclassed him and made him look foolish. Knifeton was often stated to be Scottish born but was, in fact, London-born, albeit of Scottish parents
16 February Jack Wannop EXH 3 Islington
16 February Dick Roberts EXH 3 Islington. This was the second of two exhibitions on the same day
17 February Jem Smith EXH 3 Leeds
18 February Jim Young EXH 3 Mile End Road. Wall was now freely being billed as the English 11st 4lbs middleweight champion
14 April Jem Smith EXH 3 Leeds
15 April Jem Smith EXH 3 Leeds
16 April Jem Smith EXH 3 Leeds
11 May Jem Smith EXH 3 Newmarket
25 May Jem Smith EXH 3 Fleet Street
24 June Jem Smith EXH 3 Piccadilly
2 July Jem Smith EXH 3 Chingford
3 July Jem Smith EXH 3 Chingford
15 August Jem Smith EXH 3 Birmingham
30 September Alf Mitchell EXH 3 Shoreditch
12 December Bill Wall EXH 3 Dalston. 'Toff' Wall still billed as the English 11st 4lbs champion. Bill was his brother

1888
6 January Bill Wall EXH 3 Hackney Road
16 January Bill Wall EXH 3 Woolwich
19 January Bill Wall EXH 3 Hackney Road
20 January Bill Wall EXH 3 Hackney Road
21 January Bill Wall EXH 3 Hackney Road
30 January Jack Hickey EXH 3 Battersea
31 January Jack Hickey EXH 3 Battersea
1 February Jack Hickey EXH 3 Battersea
2 February Jack Hickey EXH 3 Battersea
3 February Jack Hickey EXH 3 Battersea
4 February Jack Hickey EXH 3 Battersea
6 February Jack Hickey EXH 3 Liverpool
24 February Wall was reported to be the 11st 4lbs middleweight champion of the universe
27 February Jack Davis EXH 3 Clerkenwell. It is reported that Wall is to go to the USA to meet Jack Dempsey to decide the undisputed world 11st 4lbs middleweight title
3 March Wall was challenged to a bout for the British 11st middleweight title by Jack Hickey (Ireland), but was unable to accept any serious bouts due to illness

7 April Bill Wall EXH 3 Waltham Cross
23 April Bill Wall EXH 3 Bristol
24 April Bill Wall EXH 3 Bristol
25 April Bill Wall EXH 3 Bristol
8 October Bill Wall EXH 3 Bristol
9 October Bill Wall EXH 3 Bristol
10 October Bill Wall EXH 3 Cadogan
11 October Bill Wall EXH 3 Cadogan
12 October Bill Wall EXH 3 Cadogan
5 November Bill Wall EXH 3 Hackney Road
6 November Bill Wall EXH 3 Hackney Road
7 November Bill Wall EXH 3 Hackney Road
8 November Bill Wall EXH 3 Hackney Road
9 November Bill Wall EXH 3 Hackney Road
10 November Bill Wall EXH 3 Hackney Road
12 November Ted White EXH 3 Holborn
12 November Bill Wall EXH 3 Hackney Road. This was the second of two exhibitions on the same day
13 November Bill Wall EXH 3 Hackney Road
14 November Bill Wall EXH 3 Hackney Road
15 November Bill Wall EXH 3 Hackney Road
16 November Bill Wall EXH 3 Hackney Road
17 November Bill Wall EXH 3 Hackney Road
30 November Bill Wall EXH 3 Mile End Road
3 December Ted Burchell W PTS 3 Westminster. The first series of a catchweight competition and Wall's comeback to serious boxing after a long illness
5 December Wall withdrew from the 11st contest at the same venue as unable to make the weight
6 December Mike Moore W RTD 1 Westminster. The semi-final of a catchweight competition
8 December Alf Mitchell W PTS 4 Westminster. The final of a catchweight competition

1889
22 January 'Toff' Wall, the 11st 4lbs middleweight champion, is willing to defend against anyone
22 January Bill Wall EXH 3 Mile End Road
28 January Bill Wall EXH 3 Clerkenwell
29 January Bill Hatcher EXH 3 Pentonville
16 February Bill Wall EXH 3 Shoreditch
23 February Jack Fenton EXH 3 Shoreditch
25 February Bill Wall EXH 3 Cambridge
6 March Bill Wall EXH 3 Shoreditch
9 March 'Toff' Wall is the English 11st 4lbs champion
19 March Jack 'Baby' Partridge EXH 3 Homerton
12 April Bill Wall EXH 3 Shoreditch
14 May Bill Wall EXH 3 Hackney
14 May Bill Wall EXH 3 Hackney. The second of two exhibitions on the same day
24 May Jack Welland EXH 3 Mile End Road
30 July Bill Wall EXH 3 Shoreditch
30 July Bill Wall EXH 3 Hackney Road
24 August Bill Wall EXH 3 Shoreditch
31 August Bill Wall EXH 3 Shoreditch
2 September Bill Wall EXH 3 Battersea
6 September Bill Wall EXH 3 Shoreditch
12 October Wall challenged any man in the world to decide the 11st 4lbs middleweight title
21 October Jim Young EXH 3 Bristol
22 October Jim Young EXH 3 Bristol
23 October Jim Young EXH 3 Bristol
25 October Jim Young EXH 3 Bath
26 October Jim Young EXH 3 Bath
9 November Jack Welland EXH 3 Clerkenwell
16 December Bill Wall EXH 3 Hackney Road
17 December Bill Wall EXH 3 Hackney Road
18 December Bill Wall EXH 3 Hackney Road
19 December Bill Wall EXH 3 Hackney Road
20 December Bill Wall EXH 3 Hackney Road
21 December Bill Wall EXH 3 Hackney Road

1890

8 February Bill 'Chesterfield' Goode W PTS 12 Soho. Billed for the English 11st 4lbs middleweight title and £225, it was reported to be the greatest glove fight ever seen up to this time. Wall was brilliant, winning every round, and showed no signs of tiring, but did badly injure his arm which, in fact, was to bother him for the rest of his life
14 February Jim Burchell EXH 3 Shoreditch
24 February Bill Wall EXH 3 Bristol
25 February Bill Wall EXH 3 Bristol
26 February Bill Wall EXH 3 Bristol
27 February Bill Wall EXH 3 Bristol
28 February Bill Wall EXH 3 Bristol
1 March Bill Wall EXH 3 Bristol
26 November Jim Burchell EXH 3 Bedford

1891

3 January Ted Burchell EXH 3 Shoreditch
10 January Ted Burchell EXH 3 Shoreditch
15 January Ted Burchell EXH 3 Shoreditch
17 January Ted Burchell EXH 3 Shoreditch
24 February Wall is challenged by Bob Fitzsimmons, the English-born American 11st 4lbs champion, to a bout for world title at that weight
25 February Wall accepted Fitzsimmons' challenge
26 March Jem Porter EXH 3 Waltham Cross
27 April Jem Porter EXH 3 Enfield Highway
23 May Jim Richardson EXH 3 Haymarket
21 December On this date at the NSC, John O'Brien (Cardiff) knocked out Alf Mitchell (Cardiff) in the eighth round to decide the English 11st 4lbs title and championship belt. Wall was not taken into consideration because of his unreliability when going ahead with promised bouts

1892

1 February Bill Wall EXH 3 Shoreditch
15 March Jim Burchell EXH 3 Kentish Town
2 May William 'Cock Robin' Robinson EXH 3 Shoreditch
6 December Jim Young EXH 3 Long Acre

1893

16 January Jim Young EXH 3 Shoreditch
1 February Joe Steers EXH 3 Camden Town
29 September 'Dido' Plumb EXH 3 Soho
23 November 'Dido' Plumb EXH 3 Shoreditch
25 November 'Dido' Plumb EXH 3 Shoreditch

1894

15 January 'Dido' Plumb EXH 3 Shoreditch
3 December 'Dido' Plumb EXH 3 Shoreditch

1895

5 February Mr George Jones EXH 3 Leytonstone
20 March William 'Cock Robin' Robinson EXH 3 Shoreditch
26 April Mr George Jones EXH 3 Canning Town.

1896

26 February Jem Smith EXH 3 Bethnal Green
12 March Mr George Jones EXH 3 Shoreditch
5 December Bill Day EXH 3 Shoreditch
14 December George Pearson EXH 3 Northampton
19 December 'Ginger' Osborne EXH 3 Shoreditch

1897

20 May 'Dido' Plumb EXH 3 Tottenham
27 December 'Dido' Plumb EXH 3 Islington
28 December 'Dido' Plumb EXH 3 Islington
29 December 'Dido' Plumb EXH 3 Islington
30 December 'Dido' Plumb EXH 3 Islington
31 December 'Dido' Plumb EXH 3 Islington

1898

1 January 'Dido' Plumb EXH 3 Islington
26 October 'Dido' Plumb EXH 3 Hounslow

12 December 'Dido' Plumb EXH 3 West Brompton. There were no fights traced for Wall in 1899. On 24 March, 1900, in the *Mirror of Life*, it was stated that early in his career 'Dido' Plumb had lost on points to 'Toff' Wall. However, no such bout has ever been traced or even previously mentioned and Plumb was always stated to have been Wall's pupil

1900

21 June Dido Plumb EXH 3 Bermondsey

1901

28 March Dido Plumb EXH 3 Mildmay AC
1 April Mr William Ligo EXH 3 Stamford Hill
6 May Dido Plumb EXH 3 Ponders End
17 July 'Leader of gang of toughs' W KO 6 Hackney. This was reported in *Mirror of Life*

1916

18 August Bill 'Chesterfield' Goode EXH 3 Lambeth. This was the last traced ring appearance for Wall. Early in his career, Wall supposedly met Herr Kohl (Germany). Still untraced, the 8 December 1897 *Mirror of Life* stated that long ago 'Toff' Wall beat Coll (not Kohl) of Germany. Also a three-round exhibition bout against Jem Mace in Liverpool was reported as having taken place

Career: 228 contests, won 12, 216 exhibitions

Toff Wall

Joe Collins (Alias Tug Wilson)

Born: 3 March 1847
Claimant: English 11st middleweight title, 1880-1882. Claimant: English heavyweight title, 1881-1882. Claimant: World heavyweight title, July-September 1882. Never officially lost a bout, but was mainly a bare-knuckle prize fighter

1864-1865

Tom Kenny 'The Shoe Black' W DIS near Leicester. Round number badly faded in 23 December 1879 *Sporting Life*. Was a bare-knuckle prize fight, lasting one hour, 15 minutes and was stated to be Joe Collins' 'ring debut', aged about 17. The bout has not been traced and there are some doubts about it as it was not listed in *'Fistiana'*

1866

2 July Jack Almey W (70 mins) near Leicester. A bare-knuckle prize fight stopped by police, with the opponent's surname later given variously as Orme, Omey and Ormey
Patsy Gillen W 3 Leeds. Not traced, although claimed

1867

28 March Tom Kenny 'The Shoe Black' DREW 37 Fiskerton, Notts. Lasting two hours 29 minutes (also just 37 minutes given with no mention of rounds), it was a bare-knuckle prize fight that was stopped by the police

1868-1878

The is no record of taking an active part in any bouts

1879

17 January Tompkin Gilbert EXH 3 Nottingham
25 March Alf Greenfield EXH 3 Leicester
25 March Tom Allen EXH 5 Leicester
22 December Teddy Carney W RTD 25 Nottingham. Stated to be Wilson's first bout for several years, having fought Kenny 'The Shoe Black' in his last bout

1880

23 January Teddy Carney EXH 3 Leicester
2 February Jimmy Highland EXH 3 Nottingham. The opponent's surname also given as Ireland. Collins repeatedly challenged the world at 11st during the year and when his challenges went unanswered he formally claimed to be the English 11st champion

1881

18 January George Fryer EXH 3 Leicester
26 May Alf Greenfield DREW 21 near Brighton. Lasting one hour, 35 minutes, it had been billed as being for the English 'bare-knuckle' heavyweight championship and £200. At the request of the Prince of Wales, who was a spectator at the bout, it went unreported in the general sporting press with the exception of *The Sportsman* of 28 May 1881, which although carrying a report didn't name the men. Several weeks later, on 28 July 1881, the *Sporting Life* gave the venue as Leicester and stated that the bout went into the 28th round and lasted one hour, 45 minutes. Greenfield broke a small bone in his right arm in the fifth round, but carried on for a further 16 rounds. The *Sportsman* stated that Greenfield was unable to continue, but had so badly punished Wilson that he too was unable to continue and was in fact the first one to agree to a draw. Wilson later claimed that he was winning easily at the time of stoppage
5 July Alf Greenfield EXH 3 Leicester
8 August Alf Greenfield EXH 3 Birmingham
7 September Tug Wilson is the 11st middleweight champion

1882

6 April William Sherriff 'The Prussian' EXH 3 Shoreditch
24 April William Sherriff 'The Prussian' EXH 3 Leicester
6 April Alf Greenfield, the English bare knuckle heavyweight champion, announced his retirement and Tug Wilson formally claimed the title
21 May William Sherriff 'The Prussian' EXH 3 Leicester
22 May William Sherriff 'The Prussian' EXH 3 Leicester
6 June Sailed for the USA on 'Lord Clive'
17 July John L Sullivan W PTS 4 Madison Square Garden, NYC, New York, USA. Sullivan had agreed to stop Wilson inside the scheduled four rounds or forfeit $1000 to Wilson. Having failed, the referee awarded the decision to Wilson, who had lasted the distance simply by dropping (27 times in all). Wilson stood between rounds and laughed and smiled throughout, while Sullivan sat down between rounds and was puffed out at the end the finish. Wilson was also on half of the gate receipts (attendance was 12,000) and reportedly got $8000 in all from this one bout. He then formally laid claim to the world heavyweight title
11 September Wilson arrived back in England on the 'Indiana', having sailed from the USA on 30 August. Although he had promised to return to the USA on 2 October to fulfil contracts signed, he never did

1883

23 January Charlie Mitchell EXH 3 Leicester. Wilson had all of the best of it, nearly stopping Mitchell in third round
29 January Charlie Mitchell EXH 3 Manchester. Wilson, acting under orders, allowed Mitchell to have the best of it
5 February Charlie Mitchell EXH 3 Sheffield. Bout was sparred even, it being Wilson's third and last spar with Mitchell on this 'Sparring Tour'. In later years, it was stated that Mitchell took on and beat all the top men in England in genuine bouts on this tour. However, other than the spar with Wilson the only two other top men he met were Alf Greenfield (once) and William Sherriff 'The Prussian', both in spars
12 March William Sherriff 'The Prussian' EXH 3 Nottingham
13 March William Sherriff 'The Prussian' EXH 3 Nottingham
16 March William Sherriff 'The Prussian' EXH 3 Edinburgh
17 March William Sherriff 'The Prussian' EXH 3 Edinburgh
19 June William Sherriff 'The Prussian' EXH 3 Leicester
14 July 'Young' Halford EXH 3 near Nottingham. The actual venue was the 'The Boatman Inn', but just where it was is not given
28 November Formally retired from all forms of boxing, having gone into an entirely different business

1886

13 April Alf Greenfield EXH 3 Leicester

1905

12 August Jem Mace EXH 3 Euston Music Hall. This is the final traced ring appearance of Joe Collins' (Tug Wilson's) ring career. On 24 May 1912, in Hamilton, Ohio, USA, a 62-year-old man died, who was stated to be Tug Wilson, the old English heavyweight

Career: 30 contests, won 5, drew 2, 23 exhibitions

Tug Wilson

Commonwealth Title Bouts, 2006-2007

All of last season's title bouts are shown in date order within their weight divisions and give the boxers' respective weights, the names of the British referees and judges involved, along with the scorecard if going to a decision. Where applicable, boxers are recorded by their country of citizenship/birthplace.

Flyweight

13 April   Dale Robinson 7.12 (England) DREW 12 Chris Edwards 7.12 (England), The Leisure Centre, Altrincham, England. Referee: Terry O'Connor. Scorecards: Phil Edwards 115-113, Mickey Vann 113-115, Dave Parris 114-114. Initially billed for the vacant British title, it was also given Commonwealth championship status after Lee Haskins (England) handed in his belt after deciding to move up to bantam on 28 March 2007. Following the result, the title remains vacant.

Bantamweight

6 October   Tshifhiwa Munyai 8.5½ (South Africa) W RSC 6 Lee Haskins 8.6 (England), York Hall, Bethnal Green, London, England. Referee: Mickey Vann. Judges: Richie Davies, Dave Parris, Terry O'Connor.

26 January   Tshifhiwa Munyai 8.5½ (South Africa) W RTD 4 Martin Power 8.5¾ (England), Goresbrook Leisure Centre, Dagenham, England. Referee: Ian John-Lewis. Judges: John Keane, Mark Green, Richie Davies.

Kevin Mitchell (right) won his first major title when outpointing Ghana's George Ashie for the vacant Commonwealth super-featherweight title last October

Les Clark

S.Bantamweight

28 January   Isaac Ward 8.9 (England) W CO 2 Francis Miyeyusho 8.5½ (Tanzania), Tall Trees Hotel, Yarm, England. Referee: Victor Loughlin. Judges: Howard Foster, John Keane, Mark Green. Contested for the vacant title after Michael Hunter (England) relinquished on 21 November, having decided to move up a weight division.

Featherweight

Jackson Asiku (Uganda) failed to defend during the period.

S.Featherweight

28 October   Kevin Mitchell 9.3½ (England) W PTS 12 George Ashie 9.2½ (Ghana), York Hall, Bethnal Green, London, England. Referee: Dave Parris. Judges: Marcus McDonnell 117-113, Ian John-Lewis 116-112, Mickey Vann 116-113. Billed for the vacant title after Scotland's Alex Arthur returned his belt on 27 September 2006 to concentrate on a world title opportunity.

10 March   Kevin Mitchell 9.3½ (England) W RSC 6 Harry Ramogoadi 9.3¾ (South Africa), Olympia, Liverpool, England. Referee: Phil Edwards. Judges: Terry O'Connor, Dave Parris, Mickey Vann.

Lightweight

4 November   Willie Limond 9.8¾ (Scotland) W PTS 12 Kpako Allottey 9.7¼ (Ghana), Kelvin Hall, Glasgow, Scotland. Referee: Howard Foster. Judges: Mickey Vann 116-111, Victor Loughlin 117-112, 116-113. Billed for the vacant title after Graham Earl relinquished on 14 September 2006 to concentrate on getting a world title opportunity. Stop Press: England's Amir Khan became the new champion when stopping Limond in the eighth round in Greenwich on 14 July.

L.Welterweight

15 June   Ajose Olusegun 9.13 (Nigeria) W PTS 12 Gary Reid 10.0 (England), National Sports Centre, Crystal Palace, London, England. Referee: John Keane. Judges: Dave Parris 120-108, Terry O'Connor 119-109, Marcus McDonnell 119-110. Following on from the decision made by Junior Witter on 13 June 2006 to hand in his belt to concentrate on the world title, this was contested for the vacant title.

Welterweight

16 February   Kevin Anderson 10.7 (Scotland) L PTS 12 Ali Nuumbembe 10.6¾ (Namibia), Fife Ice Arena, Kirkcaldy, Scotland. Referee: Phil Edwards. Judges: Victor Loughlin 115-116, Howard Foster 112-116, Terry O'Connor 114-115.

L.Middleweight

8 July   Bradley Pryce 10.13½ (Wales) W RSC 4 Hassan Matumla 10.11 (Tanzania), Millennium Stadium, Cardiff,

Wales. Referee: John Keane. Judges: Howard Foster, Paul Thomas, Terry O'Connor.

18 November   Bradley Pryce 10.13¼ (Wales) W PTS 12 Andrew Facey 10.13½ (England), The Leisure Centre, Newport, Wales. Referee: Paul Thomas. Judges: Terry O'Connor 117-112, Richie Davies 117-113, Dave Parris 116-112.

7 April   Bradley Pryce 10.13 (Wales) W PTS 12 Thomas Awimbono (Ghana), Millennium Stadium, Cardiff, Wales. Referee: Marcus McDonnell. Judges: Terry O'Connor 120-109, Mickey Vann 118-111, Dave Parris 117-111.

Middleweight

20 April   Howard Eastman 11.5½ (England/Guyana) W PTS 12 Evans Ashira 11.5 (Kenya), The Concert Hall, Dudley, England. Referee: John Keane. Scorecards: Ian John-Lewis 116-112, Terry O'Connor 116-113, Howard Foster 116-113. Billed for the vacant title after Scott Dann failed to recover from a back injury sustained in a car crash and retired in March 2007.

S.Middleweight

24 November   Carl Froch 11.12½ (England) W CO 3 Tony Dodson 11.12 (England), The Ice Arena, Nottingham, England. Referee: Phil Edwards: Judges: Ian John-Lewis, Mark Green, Marcus McDonnell. Froch handed in his belt on 12 June 2007 to concentrate on his European and world title aspirations and Jermain Mackey (Bahamas) and Charles Adamu (Ghana) were matched to contest the vacant title.

L.Heavyweight

24 September   Ovill McKenzie 12.5 (Jamaica) W RSC 2 Peter Haymer 12.5½ (England), York Hall, Bethnal Green, London, England. Referee: Marcus McDonnell. Judges: Ian John-Lewis, Mark Green, John Keane. Contested for the vacant title after Peter Oboh (England/Nigeria) returned his belt on 26 April 2006 when in no position to defend.

9 February   Ovill McKenzie 12.4 (Jamaica) L RSC 1 Dean Francis 12.6 (England), Central Marriott Hotel, Bristol, England. Referee: Marcus McDonnell. Judges: Dave Parris, Richie Davies, Terry O'Connor.

Cruiserweight

19 March   Troy Ross 13.12½ (Canada/Guyana) W CO 2 John Keeton 14.4 (England), The Casino, Montreal, Canada. This was the first Commonwealth championship fight at the weight since Mark Hobson (England) relinquished the title on winning the WBU crown on 8 September 2006.

Heavyweight

8 July   Danny Williams 20.8 (England) L PTS 12 Matt Skelton 18.3 (England), The Millennium Stadium, Cardiff, Wales. Referee: Howard Foster. Scorecards: Terry O'Connor 112-117, John Keane 112-117, Paul Thomas 114-115.

Commonwealth Champions, 1887-2007

Since the 1997 edition, Harold Alderman's magnificent research into Imperial British Empire title fights has introduced many more claimants/champions than were shown previously. Prior to 12 October 1954, the date that the British Commonwealth and Empire Boxing Championships Committee was formed, there was no official body as such and the Australian and British promoters virtually ran the show, with other members of the British Empire mainly out in the cold. We have also listed Canadian representatives, despite championship boxing in that country being contested over ten or 12 rounds at most, but they are not accorded the same kind of recognition that their British and Australian counterparts are. Boxers who became Commonwealth champions while being licensed and qualified to contest national titles outside of their country of birth are recorded by domicile/birthplace. Reconstituted as the British Commonwealth Boxing Championships Committee on 22 November 1972, and with a current membership that includes Australia, Bahamas, Barbados, Canada, Ghana, Guyana, Jamaica, Kenya, Namibia, New Zealand, Nigeria, South Africa, Tanzania, Trinidad &Tobago, Uganda and Zambia, in 1989 the 'British' tag was dropped.

COMMONWEALTH COUNTRY CODE
A = Australia; ANT = Antigua; BAH = Bahamas; BAR = Barbados; BER = Bermuda; C = Canada; E = England; F = Fiji; GH = Ghana; GU = Guyana; I = Ireland; J = Jamaica; K = Kenya; MAU = Mauritius; N = Nigeria; NAM = Namibia; NZ = New Zealand; NI = Northern Ireland; PNG = Papua New Guinea; SA = South Africa; SAM = Samoa; S = Scotland; SK = St Kitts; SL = St Lucia; T = Tonga; TR = Trinidad; U = Uganda; W = Wales; ZA = Zambia; ZI = Zimbabwe.

Champions in **bold** denote those recognised by the British Commonwealth and Empire Boxing Championships Committee (1954 to date) and, prior to that, those with the best claims

*Undefeated champions (Does not include men who forfeited titles)

In trying to avenge the only defeat on his record, Martin Power (left) was again beaten by Tshifhiwa Munyai for the Commonwealth bantam title, this time by a fourth-round retirement

Les Clark

Flyweight (112 lbs)

Title Holder	Birthplace/Domicile	Tenure
Elky Clark*	S	1924-1927
Harry Hill	E	1929
Frenchy Belanger	C	1929
Vic White	A	1929-1930
Teddy Green	A	1930-1931
Jackie Paterson	S	1940-1948
Rinty Monaghan*	NI	1948-1950
Teddy Gardner	E	1952
Jake Tuli	SA	1952-1954
Dai Dower*	W	1954-1957
Frankie Jones	S	1957
Dennis Adams*	SA	1957-1962
Jackie Brown	S	1962-1963
Walter McGowan*	S	1963-1969
John McCluskey	S	1970-1971
Henry Nissen	A	1971-1974
Big Jim West*	A	1974-1975
Patrick Mambwe	ZA	1976-1979
Ray Amoo	N	1980
Steve Muchoki	K	1980-1983
Keith Wallace*	E	1983-1984
Richard Clarke	J	1986-1987
Nana Yaw Konadu*	GH	1987-1989
Alfred Kotey*	GH	1989-1993
Francis Ampofo*	E/GH	1993
Daren Fifield	E	1993-1994
Francis Ampofo	E/GH	1994-1995
Danny Ward	SA	1995-1996
Peter Culshaw	E	1996-1997
Ady Lewis*	E	1997-1998
Alfonso Zvenyika	ZI	1998
Damaen Kelly	NI	1998-1999
Keith Knox	S	1999
Jason Booth*	E	1999-2003
Dale Robinson	E	2003-2004
Lee Haskins*	E	2006-2007

Bantamweight (118 lbs)

Title Holder	Birthplace/Domicile	Tenure
Digger Stanley	E	1904-1905
Owen Moran	E	1905
Ted Green	A	1905-1911
Charlie Simpson*	A	1911-1912
Jim Higgins	S	1920-1922
Tommy Harrison	E	1922-1923
Bugler Harry Lake	E	1923
Johnny Brown	E	1923-1928
Billy McAllister	A	1928-1930
Teddy Baldock*	E	1928-1930
Johnny Peters	E	1930
Dick Corbett	E	1930-1932
Johnny King	E	1932-1934
Dick Corbett	E	1934
Frankie Martin	C	1935-1937
Baby Yack	C	1937
Johnny Gaudes	C	1937-1939
Lefty Gwynn	C	1939
Baby Yack	C	1939-1940
Jim Brady	S	1941-1945
Jackie Paterson	S	1945-1949
Stan Rowan	E	1949
Vic Toweel	SA	1949-1952
Jimmy Carruthers*	A	1952-1954
Peter Keenan	S	1955-1959
Freddie Gilroy*	NI	1959-1963
Johnny Caldwell	NI	1964-1965
Alan Rudkin	E	1965-1966
Walter McGowan	S	1966-1968
Alan Rudkin	E	1968-1969
Lionel Rose*	A	1969
Alan Rudkin*	E	1970-1972
Paul Ferreri	A	1972-1977
Sulley Shittu	GH	1977-1978
Johnny Owen*	W	1978-1980
Paul Ferreri	A	1981-1986
Ray Minus*	BAH	1986-1991
John Armour*	E	1992-1996
Paul Lloyd*	E	1996-2000
Ady Lewis	E	2000
Tommy Waite	NI	2000
Nicky Booth	E	2000-2002
Steve Molitor	C	2002-2004
Joseph Agbeko	GH	2004-2006
Tshifhiwa Munyai	SA	2006-

S. Bantamweight (122 lbs)

Title Holder	Birthplace/Domicile	Tenure
Neil Swain	W	1995
Neil Swain	W	1996-1997
Michael Brodie	E	1997-1999
Nedal Hussein*	A	2000-2001
Brian Carr	S	2001-2002
Michael Alldis	E	2002
Esham Pickering	E	2003-2005
Michael Hunter*	E	2005-2006
Isaac Ward	E	2007-

Featherweight (126 lbs)

Title Holder	Birthplace/Domicile	Tenure
Jim Driscoll*	W	1908-1913
Llew Edwards	W	1915-1916
Charlie Simpson*	A	1916
Tommy Noble	E	1919-1921
Bert Spargo	A	1921-1922
Bert McCarthy	A	1922
Bert Spargo	A	1922-1923
Billy Grime	A	1923
Ernie Baxter	A	1923
Leo Kid Roy	C	1923
Bert Ristuccia	A	1923-1924
Barney Wilshur	C	1923
Benny Gould	C	1923-1924
Billy Grime	A	1924
Leo Kid Roy	C	1924-1932
Johnny McGrory	S	1936-1938
Jim Spider Kelly	NI	1938-1939
Johnny Cusick	E	1939-1940
Nel Tarleton	E	1940-1947
Tiger Al Phillips	E	1947
Ronnie Clayton	E	1947-1951
Roy Ankrah	GH	1951-1954
Billy Spider Kelly	NI	1954-1955
Hogan Kid Bassey*	N	1955-1957
Percy Lewis	TR	1957-1960
Floyd Robertson	GH	1960-1967
John O'Brien	S	1967
Johnny Famechon*	A	1967-1969
Toro George	NZ	1970-1972
Bobby Dunne	A	1972-1974
Evan Armstrong	S	1974
David Kotey*	GH	1974-1975
Eddie Ndukwu	N	1977-1980
Pat Ford*	GU	1980-1981
Azumah Nelson*	GH	1981-1985
Tyrone Downes	BAR	1986-1988
Thunder Aryeh	GH	1988-1989
Oblitey Commey	GH	1989-1990
Modest Napunyi	K	1990-1991
Barrington Francis*	C	1991
Colin McMillan*	E	1992
Billy Hardy*	E	1992-1996
Jonjo Irwin	E	1996-1997
Paul Ingle*	E	1997-1999
Patrick Mullings	E	1999-2000
Scott Harrison*	S	2000-2002
Nicky Cook*	E	2003-2005
Jackson Asiku	U	2005-

S. Featherweight (130 lbs)

Title Holder	Birthplace/Domicile	Tenure
Billy Moeller	A	1975-1977
Johnny Aba*	PNG	1977-1982
Langton Tinago	ZI	1983-1984
John Sichula	ZA	1984
Lester Ellis*	A/E	1984-1985
John Sichula	ZA	1985-1986
Sam Akromah	GH	1986-1987
John Sichula	ZA	1987-1989
Mark Reefer*	E	1989-1990
Thunder Aryeh	GH	1990-1991
Hugh Forde	E	1991
Paul Harvey	E	1991-1992
Tony Pep	C	1992-1995
Justin Juuko*	U	1995-1998
Charles Shepherd*	E	1999
Mick O'Malley	A	1999-2000
Ian McLeod*	S	2000
James Armah*	GH	2000-2001
Alex Moon	E	2001-2002
Dean Pithie	E	2002-2003
Craig Docherty	S	2003-2004
Alex Arthur*	S	2004-2006
Kevin Mitchell	E	2006-

Lightweight (135 lbs)

Title Holder	Birthplace/Domicile	Tenure
Jim Burge	A	1890
George Dawson*	A	1890
Harry Nickless	E	1892-1894
Arthur Valentine	E	1894-1895

Title Holder	Birthplace/Domicile	Tenure
Dick Burge*	E	1894-1895
Jim Murphy*	NZ	1894-1897
Eddie Connolly*	C	1896-1897
Jack Goldswain	E	1906-1908
Jack McGowan	A	1909
Hughie Mehegan	A	1909-1910
Johnny Summers*	E	1910
Hughie Mehegan	A	1911
Freddie Welsh*	W	1912-1914
Ernie Izzard	E	1928
Tommy Fairhall	A	1928-1930
Al Foreman	E	1930-1933
Jimmy Kelso	A	1933
Al Foreman*	E	1933-1934
Laurie Stevens*	SA	1936-1937
Dave Crowley	E	1938
Eric Boon	E	1938-1944
Ronnie James*	W	1944-1947
Arthur King	C	1948-1951
Frank Johnson	E	1953
Pat Ford	A	1953-1954
Ivor Germain	BAR	1954
Pat Ford	A	1954-1955
Johnny van Rensburg	SA	1955-1956
Willie Toweel	SA	1956-1959
Dave Charnley	E	1959-1962
Bunny Grant	J	1962-1967
Manny Santos*	NZ	1967
Love Allotey	GH	1967-1968
Percy Hayles	J	1968-1975
Jonathan Dele	N	1975-1977
Lennox Blackmore	GU	1977-1978
Hogan Jimoh	N	1978-1980
Langton Tinago	ZI	1980-1981
Barry Michael	A/E	1981-1982
Claude Noel	T	1982-1984
Graeme Brooke	A	1984-1985
Barry Michael*	A/E	1985-1986
Langton Tinago	ZI	1986-1987
Mo Hussein	E	1987-1989
Pat Doherty	E	1989
Najib Daho	E	1989-1990
Carl Crook	E	1990-1992
Billy Schwer	E	1992-1993
Paul Burke	E	1993
Billy Schwer	E	1993-1995
David Tetteh	GH	1995-1997
Billy Irwin	C	1997
David Tetteh	GH	1997-1999
Bobby Vanzie	E	1999-2001
James Armah*	GH	2001-2002
David Burke*	E	2002
Michael Muya	K	2003
Kevin Bennett	E	2003-2005
Graham Earl*	E	2005-2006
Willie Limond	S	2006-

L. Welterweight (140 lbs)

Title Holder	Birthplace/Domicile	Tenure
Joe Tetteh	GH	1972-1973
Hector Thompson	A	1973-1977
Baby Cassius Austin	A	1977-1978
Jeff Malcolm	A	1978-1979
Obisia Nwankpa	N	1979-1983
Billy Famous	N	1983-1986
Tony Laing	E	1987-1988
Lester Ellis	A/E	1988-1989
Steve Larrimore	BAH	1989
Tony Ekubia	E/N	1989-1991
Andy Holligan	E	1991-1994
Ross Hale	E	1994-1995
Paul Ryan	E	1995-1996
Andy Holligan	E	1996-1997
Bernard Paul	E/MAU	1997-1999
Eamonn Magee	NI	1999-
Paul Burke	E	1997
Felix Bwalya*	ZA	1997
Paul Burke	E	1998-1999
Eamonn Magee*	NI	1999-2002
Junior Witter*	E	2002-2006
Ajose Olusegun	N	2007-

Welterweight (147 lbs)

Title Holder	Birthplace/Domicile	Tenure
Tom Williams	A	1892-1895
Dick Burge	E	1895-1897
Eddie Connolly*	C	1903-1905
Joe White*	C	1907-1909
Johnny Summers	E	1912-1914
Tom McCormick	I	1914
Matt Wells	E	1914-1919
Fred Kay	A	1915
Tommy Uren	A	1915-1916
Fritz Holland	A	1916
Tommy Uren	A	1916-1919
Fred Kay	A	1919-1920
Johnny Basham	W	1919-1920
Bermondsey Billy Wells	E	1922
Ted Kid Lewis	E	1920-1924
Tommy Milligan*	S	1924-1925
Jack Carroll	A	1928
Charlie Purdie	A	1928-1929
Wally Hancock	A	1929-1930
Tommy Fairhall*	A	1930
Jack Carroll	A	1934-1938
Eddie Thomas	W	1951
Wally Thom	E	1951-1952
Cliff Curvis	W	1952
Gerald Dreyer	SA	1952-1954
Barry Brown	NZ	1954
George Barnes	A	1954-1956
Darby Brown	A	1956
George Barnes	A	1956-1958
Johnny van Rensburg	SA	1958
George Barnes	A	1958-1960
Brian Curvis*	W	1960-1966
Johnny Cooke	E	1967-1968
Ralph Charles*	E	1968-1972
Clyde Gray	C	1973-1979
Chris Clarke	C	1979
Clyde Gray*	C	1979-1980
Colin Jones*	W	1981-1984
Sylvester Mittee	E/SL	1984-1985
Lloyd Honeyghan*	E/J	1985-1986
Brian Janssen	A	1987
Wilf Gentzen	A	1987-1988
Gary Jacobs	S	1988-1989
Donovan Boucher	C	1989-1992
Eamonn Loughran*	NI	1992-1993
Andrew Murray*	GU	1993-1997
Kofi Jantuah*	GH	1997-2000
Scott Dixon*	S	2000
Jawaid Khaliq*	E	2000-2001
Julian Holland	A	2001-2002
James Hare*	E	2002-2003
Ossie Duran*	GH	2003-2004
Fatai Onikeke	NI	2004-2005
Joshua Okine	GH	2005
Kevin Anderson	S	2005-2007
Ali Nuumbembe	NAM	2007-

L. Middleweight (154 lbs)

Title Holder	Birthplace/Domicile	Tenure
Charkey Ramon*	A	1972-1975
Maurice Hope*	E/ANT	1976-1979
Kenny Bristol	GU	1979-1981
Herol Graham*	E	1981-1984
Ken Salisbury	A/E	1984-1985
Nick Wilshire	E	1985-1987
Lloyd Hibbert	E	1987
Troy Waters*	A/E	1987-1991
Chris Pyatt*	E	1991-1992
Mickey Hughes	E	1992-1993
Lloyd Honeyghan	E/J	1993-1994
Leo Young	A	1994-1995
Kevin Kelly	A	1995
Chris Pyatt	E	1995-1996
Steve Foster	E	1996-1997
Kevin Kelly	A	1997-1999
Tony Badea	C	1999-2001
Richard Williams*	E	2001
Joshua Onyango	K	2002
Michael Jones	E	2002-2003
Jamie Moore*	E	2003-2004
Richard Williams*	E	2004
Jamie Moore	E	2004
Ossie Duran	GH	2004-2006
Bradley Pryce	W	2006-

Middleweight (160 lbs)

Title Holder	Birthplace/Domicile	Tenure
Chesterfield Goode	E	1887-1890
Toff Wall	E	1890-1891
Jim Hall	A	1892-1893
Bill Heffernan	NZ	1894-1896
Bill Doherty	A	1896-1897
Billy Edwards	A	1897-1898
Dido Plumb*	E	1898-1901
Tom Duggan	A	1901-1903

Title Holder	Birthplace/ Domicile	Tenure
Jack Palmer*	E	1902-1904
Jewey Cooke	E	1903-1904
Tom Dingey	C	1904-1905
Jack Lalor	SA	1905
Ted Nelson	A	1905
Tom Dingey	C	1905
Sam Langford*	C	1907-1911
Ed Williams	A	1908-1910
Arthur Cripps	A	1910
Dave Smith	A	1910-1911
Jerry Jerome	A	1913
Arthur Evernden	E	1913-1914
Mick King	A	1914-1915
Les Darcy*	A	1915-1917
Ted Kid Lewis	E	1922-1923
Roland Todd	E	1923-1926
Len Johnson	E	1926-1928
Tommy Milligan	S	1926-1928
Alex Ireland	S	1928-1929
Len Harvey	E	1929-1933
Del Fontaine	C	1931
Ted Moore	E	1931
Jock McAvoy	E	1933-1939
Ron Richards*	A	1940
Ron Richards*	A	1941-1942
Bos Murphy	NZ	1948
Dick Turpin	E	1948-1949
Dave Sands*	A	1949-1952
Randy Turpin	E	1952-1954
Al Bourke	A	1952-1954
Johnny Sullivan	E	1954-1955
Pat McAteer	E	1955-1958
Dick Tiger	N	1958-1960
Wilf Greaves	C	1960
Dick Tiger*	N	1960-1962
Gomeo Brennan	BAH	1963-1964
Tuna Scanlon*	NZ	1964
Gomeo Brennan	BAH	1964-1966
Blair Richardson*	C	1966-1967
Milo Calhoun	J	1967
Johnny Pritchett*	E	1967-1969
Les McAteer	E	1969-1970
Mark Rowe	E	1970
Bunny Sterling	E/J	1970-1972
Tony Mundine*	A	1972-1975
Monty Betham	NZ	1975-1978
Al Korovou	A	1978
Ayub Kalule	U	1978-1980
Tony Sibson*	E	1980-1983
Roy Gumbs	E/SK	1983
Mark Kaylor	E	1983-1984
Tony Sibson*	E	1984-1988
Nigel Benn	E	1988-1989
Michael Watson*	E	1989-1991
Richie Woodhall	E	1992-1995
Robert McCracken	E	1995-1997
Johnson Tshuma	SA	1997-1998
Paul Jones	E	1998-1999
Jason Matthews*	E	1999

Title Holder	Birthplace/ Domicile	Tenure
Alain Bonnamie*	C	1999-2000
Sam Soliman	A	2000
Howard Eastman*	E/GU	2000-2004
James Obede Toney	GH	2004-2006
Scott Dann*	E	2006-2007
Howard Eastman	E/GU	2007-

S. Middleweight (168 lbs)

Title Holder	Birthplace/ Domicile	Tenure
Rod Carr	A	1989-1990
Lou Cafaro	A	1990-1991
Henry Wharton*	E	1991-1997
Clinton Woods	E	1997-1998
David Starie	E	1998-2003
Andre Thysse	SA	2003
Charles Adamu	GH	2003-2004
Carl Froch*	E	2004-2007

L. Heavyweight (175 lbs)

Title Holder	Birthplace/ Domicile	Tenure
Dave Smith*	A	1911-1915
Jack Bloomfield*	E	1923-1924
Tom Berry	E	1927
Gipsy Daniels*	W	1927
Len Harvey	E	1939-1942
Freddie Mills*	E	1942-1950
Randy Turpin*	E	1952-1955
Gordon Wallace	C	1956-1957
Yvon Durelle*	C	1957-1959
Chic Calderwood	S	1960-1963
Bob Dunlop*	A	1968-1970
Eddie Avoth	W	1970-1971
Chris Finnegan	E	1971-1973
John Conteh*	E	1973-1974
Steve Aczel	A	1975
Tony Mundine	A	1975-1978
Gary Summerhays	C	1978-1979
Lottie Mwale	ZA	1979-1985
Leslie Stewart*	TR	1985-1987
Willie Featherstone	C	1987-1989
Guy Waters*	A/E	1989-1993
Brent Kosolofski	C	1993-1994
Garry Delaney	E	1994-1995
Noel Magee	I	1995
Nicky Piper*	W	1995-1997
Crawford Ashley	E	1998-1999
Clinton Woods*	E	1999-2000
Neil Simpson	E	2001
Tony Oakey*	E	2001-2002
Peter Oboh*	E/N	2002-2006
Ovill McKenzie	J	2006-2007
Dean Francis	E	2007-

Cruiserweight (200 lbs)

Title Holder	Birthplace/ Domicile	Tenure
Stewart Lithgo	E	1984
Chisanda Mutti	ZA	1984-1987
Glenn McCrory*	E	1987-1989
Apollo Sweet	A	1989
Derek Angol*	E	1989-1993
Francis Wanyama	U	1994-1995
Chris Okoh	E	1995-1997
Darren Corbett	NI	1997-1998
Bruce Scott	E/J	1998-1999
Adam Watt*	A	2000-2001
Bruce Scott*	E/J	2001-2003
Mark Hobson*	E	2003-2006
Troy Ross	C	2007-

Heavyweight (200 lbs +)

Title Holder	Birthplace/ Domicile	Tenure
Peter Jackson*	A	1889-1901
Dan Creedon	NZ	1896-1903
Billy McColl	A	1902-1905
Tim Murphy	A	1905-1906
Bill Squires	A	1906-1909
Bill Lang	A	1909-1910
Tommy Burns*	C	1910-1911
P.O. Curran	I	1911
Dan Flynn	I	1911
Bombardier Billy Wells	E	1911-1919
Bill Lang	A	1911-1913
Dave Smith	A	1913-1917
Joe Beckett*	E	1919-1923
Phil Scott	E	1926-1931
Larry Gains	C	1931-1934
Len Harvey	E	1934
Jack Petersen	W	1934-1936
Ben Foord	SA	1936-1937
Tommy Farr	W	1937
Len Harvey*	E	1939-1942
Jack London	E	1944-1945
Bruce Woodcock	E	1945-1950
Jack Gardner	E	1950-1952
Johnny Williams	W	1952-1953
Don Cockell	E	1953-1956
Joe Bygraves	J	1956-1957
Joe Erskine	W	1957-1958
Brian London	E	1958-1959
Henry Cooper	E	1959-1971
Joe Bugner	E	1971
Jack Bodell	E	1971-1972
Danny McAlinden	NI	1972-1975
Bunny Johnson	E/J	1975
Richard Dunn	E	1975-1976
Joe Bugner*	E	1976-1977
John L. Gardner*	E	1978-1981
Trevor Berbick	C/J	1981-1986
Horace Notice*	E	1986-1988
Derek Williams	E	1988-1992
Lennox Lewis*	E	1992-1993
Henry Akinwande	E	1993-1995
Scott Welch	E	1995-1997
Julius Francis*	E	1997-1999
Danny Williams	E	1999-2004
Michael Sprott	E	2004
Matt Skelton*	E	2004-2005
Danny Williams	E	2005-2006
Matt Skelton	E	2006-

European Title Bouts, 2006-2007

All of last season's title bouts are shown in date order within their weight divisions and give the boxers' respective weights, along with the scorecard if going to a decision. British officials are listed where applicable.

Flyweight

27 July Ivan Pozo 7.13 (Spain) L RSC 12 Andrea Sirritzu 7.12¾ (Italy), Vigorelli Velodrome, Milan, Italy.

8 October Andrea Sarritzu 7.13 (Italy) W PTS 12 Christophe Rodrigues 7.13 (France), The Palalido, Milan, Italy. Scorecards: Ian John-Lewis 118-110, 118-110, 117-111.

1 June Andrea Sarritzu 7.12¼ (Italy) DREW 12 Bernard Inom 8.0 (France), The Big Tent, Niort, Ajaccio, Corsica, France. Referee: Mark Green. Scorecards: 115-113, 113-115, 114-114.

Bantamweight

4 August Simone Maludrottu 8.4½ (Italy) W PTS 12 Karim Quibir Lopez 8.6 (Spain), St Theresa of Gallura Sports Palace, Sardinia, Italy. Scorecards: Dave Parris 118-110, 118-109, 117-110.

25 November Simone Maludrottu 8.5½ (Italy) W RSC 3 Damaen Kelly 8.5½ (Northern Ireland), Geovillage Sports Palace, Olbia, Sardinia, Italy.

9 March Simone Maludrottu 8.6 (Italy) W PTS 12 Ian Napa 8.5¼ (England), Goresbrook Leisure Centre, Dagenham, England. Scorecards: 117-112, 116-113, 117-112.

S.Bantamweight

11 November Bernard Dunne 8.9 (Republic of Ireland) W PTS 12 Esham Pickering 8.10 (England), Point Depot, Dublin, Ireland. Scorecards: 117-111, 115-113, 117-111. Contested for the vacant crown after Michael Hunter (England) had vacated on 8 September 2006 in order to concentrate on challenging for the IBF version of the world title.

25 March Bernard Dunne 8.9½ (Republic of Ireland) W RSC 3 Yersin Jailauov 8.9½ (Kazakhstan), Point Depot, Dublin, Ireland.

23 June Bernard Dunne 8.10 (Republic of Ireland) W PTS 12 Reidar Walstad 8.9¼ (Norway), Point Depot, Dublin, Ireland. Scorecards: Richie Davies 116-112, 118-111, 115-113.

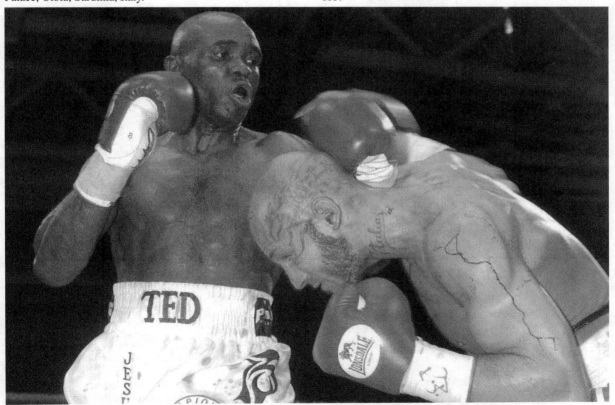

England's Ted Bami (left) made a successful defence of his European light-welter title when winning the return against Giuseppe Lauri (Italy) in March

Les Clark

Featherweight
3 November   Cyril Thomas 8.12 (France) TECH DRAW 3 Yuri Voronin 9.0 (Ukraine), Pierre Ratte Sports Palace, St Quentin, France. Judge: Ian John-Lewis. Thomas relinquished the title on 8 January 2007.
25 May   Alberto Servidei 9.0 (Italy) W PTS 12 Yuri Voronin 8.13 (Ukraine), The Sports Palace, Ravenna, Italy. Scorecards: Terry O'Connor 115-113, 116-113, 116-113.

S.Featherweight
4 November   Alex Arthur 9.4 (Scotland) W RSC 5 Sergio Palomo 9.2¼ (Spain), Kelvin Hall, Glasgow, Scotland. Arthur relinquished on 29 November 2006 to concentrate on a world title shot.
10 March   Leva Kirakosyan 9.4 (Armenia) W RSC 3 Antonio Joao Bento 9.2 (Portugal), Solverde Casino, Algarve, Portugal. Judge: Richie Davies.

Lightweight
11 November   Juan Carlos Diaz Melero 9.8½ (Spain) L CO 3 Yuri Romanov 9.8 (Belarus), The Sports Pavilion, Ciudad Real, Spain.
28 April   Yuri Romanov 9.8¼ (Belarus) W CO 3 Tontcho Tontchev 9.7¾ (Bulgaria), The Sports Palace, Minsk, Belarus. Referee: Terry O'Connor. Judge: Marcus McDonnell.

L.Welterweight
22 September   Ted Bami 9.12½ (England) W PTS 12 Giuseppe Lauri 9.13¼ (Italy), York Hall, Bethnal Green, London, England. Scorecards: 117-112, 117-112, 118-111. Billed for the vacant title after Junior Witter had handed in his belt on 20 June 2006 to progress his world title ambitions.
30 March   Ted Bami 9.13¼ (England) W PTS 12 Giuseppe Lauri 9.13¼ (Italy), The K2 Leisure Centre, Crawley, England. Scorecards: 116-111, 117-112, 116-110.

Welterweight
8 October   Frederic Klose 10.6¼ (France) W PTS 12 Giovanni Parisi 10.7 (Italy), The Palalido, Milan, Italy. Referee: Ian John-Lewis. Scorecards: 116-112, 116-112, 114-114. Klose relinquished the title on 8 November 2006.
25 February   Jackson Osei Bonsu 10.5½ (Belgium) W CO 8 Nordine Mouchi 10.5½ (France), Elancourt Sports Palace, Yvelines, France.
9 June   Jackson Osei Bonsu 10.5½ (Belgium) W CO 12 Cristian de Martinis 10.5½ (Italy), The Sports Palace, Antwerp, Belgium.

L.Middleweight
27 July   Michele Piccirillo 11.0 (Italy) W RSC 11 Lusa Messi 10.11½ (Italy), Vigorelli Velodrome, Milan, Italy.
25 January   Michele Piccirillo 11.0 (Italy) W RSC 12 Michael Jones 11.0 (England), The Palalido, Milan, Italy. Piccirillo relinquished the title on 19 April 2007.

Middleweight
6 October   Amin Asikainen 11.5¼ (Finland) W PTS 12 Alexander Sipos 11.5½ (Germany), Hartwall Arena, Helsinki, Finland. Scorecards: 115-113, 117-111, 117-112.
30 January   Amin Asikainen 11.5¼ (Finland) W PTS 12 Lorenzo di Giacomo 11.5 (Italy), Hartwall Arena, Helsinki, Finland. Scorecards: 118-112, 118-110, 119-110.
23 June   Amin Asikainen 11.5 (Finland) L RSC 11 Sebastian Sylvester 9.5½ (Germany), The Stadium Hall, Zwickau, Germany. Judge: John Keane.

S.Middleweight
12 October   Mger Mkrtchian 12.0 (Armenia) L PTS 12 David Gogoya 11.13 (Georgia), Casino Konti, St Petersburg, Russia. Scorecards: 112-117, 113-115, 116-114.
2 December   David Gogoya 11.12 (Georgia) W PTS 12 Jackson Chanet 11.12 (France), The OmniSports Palace, Paris, France. Scorecards: 116-111, 115-112, 116-112.
1 June   David Gogoya 11.13 (Georgia) L PTS 12 Cristian Sanavia 11.11¼ (Italy), The Big Tent, Niort, Ajaccio, Corsica, France. Scorecards: Mark Green 116-115, 112-117, 114-116.

L.Heavyweight
13 January   Thomas Ulrich 12.6¾ (Germany) W RSC 10 Rachid Kanfouah 12.5¾ (France), Brandberge Arena, Halle, Germany. Judge: Mark Green. Contested for the vacant title after Stipe Drews (Croatia) returned his belt on 7 November 2006 to concentrate on his world title challenge.
19 May   Thomas Ulrich 12.6½ (Germany) W CO 1 Leonardo Turchi 12.5½ (Italy), Color Line Arena, Hamburg, Germany. Judge: Dave Parris.

Cruiserweight
21 July David Haye 14.3½ (England) W PTS 12 Ismail Abdoul 14.2½ (Belgium), The Leisure Centre, Altrincham, England. Scorecards: 120-108, 120-108, 120-108.
17 November   David Haye 14.4 (England) W RSC 9 Giacobe Fragomeni 14.2 (Italy), York Hall, Bethnal Green, London, England. Haye handed his belt in on 28 February 2007 after being made the mandatory challenger for the WBC title.
22 June   Vincenzo Cantatore 14.3 (Italy) W PTS 12 Alexander Gurov 14.2 (Ukraine), The Coliseum, Rome, Italy. Referee: Dave Parris. Scorecards: Marcus McDonnell 116-114, 116-114, 114-114.

Heavyweight
15 July   Paolo Vidoz 17.0 (Italy) L CO 6 Vladimir Virchis 17.11 (Ukraine), Color Line Arena, Hamburg, Germany. Judge: Mickey Vann.
19 May   Vladimir Virchis 17.10 (Ukraine) W PTS 12 Paolo Vidoz 17.4¼ (Italy), Color Line Arena, Hamburg, Germany. Referee: Dave Parris. Scorecards: 119-109, 116-112, 117-111.

European Champions, 1909-2007

Prior to 1946, the championship was contested under the auspices of the International Boxing Union, re-named that year as the European Boxing Union (EBU). The IBU had come into being when Victor Breyer, a Paris-based journalist and boxing referee who later edited the Annuaire du Ring (first edition in 1910), warmed to the idea of an organisation that controlled boxing right across Europe, regarding rules and championship fights between the champions of the respective countries. He first came to London at the end of 1909 to discuss the subject with the NSC, but went away disappointed. However, at a meeting between officials from Switzerland and France in March 1912, the IBU was initially formed and, by June of that year, had published their first ratings. By April 1914, Belgium had also joined the organisation, although it would not be until the war was over that the IBU really took off. Many of the early champions shown on the listings were the result of promoters, especially the NSC, billing their own championship fights. Although the (French dominated) IBU recognised certain champions, prior to being re-formed in May 1920, they did not find their administrative 'feet' fully until other countries such as Italy (1922), Holland (1923), and Spain (1924), produced challengers for titles. Later in the 1920s, Germany (1926), Denmark (1928), Portugal (1929) and Romania (1929) also joined the fold. Unfortunately, for Britain, its representatives (Although the BBBoC, as we know it today, was formed in 1929, an earlier attempt to form a Board of Control had been initiated in April 1918 by the NSC and it was that body who were involved here) failed to reach agreement on the three judges' ruling, following several meetings with the IBU early in 1920 and, apart from Elky Clark (fly), Ernie Rice and Alf Howard (light), and Jack Hood (welter), who conformed to that stipulation, fighters from these shores would not be officially recognised as champions until the EBU was formed in 1946. This led to British fighters claiming the title after beating IBU titleholders, or their successors, under championship conditions in this country. The only men who did not come into this category were Kid Nicholson (bantam), and Ted Kid Lewis and Tommy Milligan (welter), who defeated men not recognised by the IBU. For the record, the first men recognised and authorised, respectively, as being champions of their weight classes by the IBU were: Sid Smith and Michel Montreuil (fly), Charles Ledoux (bantam), Jim Driscoll and Louis de Ponthieu (feather), Freddie Welsh and Georges Papin (light), Georges Carpentier and Albert Badoud (welter), Georges Carpentier and Ercole Balzac (middle), Georges Carpentier and Battling Siki (light-heavy and heavy).

EUROPEAN COUNTRY CODE

ARM = Armenia; AU = Austria; BE = Belarus; BEL = Belgium; BUL = Bulgaria; CRO = Croatia; CZ = Czechoslovakia; DEN = Denmark; E = England; FIN = Finland; FR = France; GEO = Georgia; GER = Germany; GRE = Greece; HOL = Holland; HUN = Hungary; ITA = Italy; KAZ = Kazakhstan; LUX = Luxembourg; NI= Northern Ireland; NOR = Norway; POL = Poland; POR = Portugal; RoI = Republic of Ireland; ROM = Romania; RUS = Russia; S = Scotland; SP = Spain; SWE = Sweden; SWI = Switzerland; TU = Turkey; UK = Ukraine; W= Wales; YUG = Yugoslavia.

Champions in **bold** denote those recognised by the IBU/EBU

*Undefeated champions (Does not include men who may have forfeited titles)

Title Holder	Birthplace/ Domicile	Tenure	Title Holder	Birthplace/ Domicile	Tenure	Title Holder	Birthplace/ Domicile	Tenure
Flyweight (112 lbs)			**Dai Dower**	W	1955	**Andrea Sarritzu**	ITA	2006-
Sid Smith	E	1913	**Young Martin**	SP	1955-1959			
Bill Ladbury	E	1913-1914	**Risto Luukkonen**	FIN	1959-1961	**Bantamweight (118 lbs)**		
Percy Jones	W	1914	**Salvatore Burruni***	ITA	1961-1965	Joe Bowker	E	1910
Joe Symonds	E	1914	**Rene Libeer**	FR	1965-1966	Digger Stanley	E	1910-1912
Tancy Lee	S	1914-1916	**Fernando Atzori**	ITA	1967-1972	**Charles Ledoux**	FR	1912-1921
Jimmy Wilde	W	1914-1915	**Fritz Chervet**	SWI	1972-1973	Bill Beynon	W	1913
Jimmy Wilde*	W	1916-1923	**Fernando Atzori**	ITA	1973	Tommy Harrison	E	1921-1922
Michel Montreuil	BEL	1923-1925	**Fritz Chervet***	SWI	1973-1974	**Charles Ledoux**	FR	1922-1923
Elky Clark*	S	1925-1927	**Franco Udella**	ITA	1974-1979	Bugler Harry Lake	E	1923
Victor Ferrand	SP	1927	**Charlie Magri***	E	1979-1983	Johnny Brown	E	1923-1928
Emile Pladner	FR	1928-1929	**Antoine Montero**	FR	1983-1984	**Henry Scillie***	BEL	1925-1928
Johnny Hill	S	1928-1929	**Charlie Magri***	E	1984-1985	Kid Nicholson	E	1928
Eugene Huat	FR	1929	**Franco Cherchi**	ITA	1985	Teddy Baldock	E	1928-1931
Emile Degand	BEL	1929-1930	**Charlie Magri**	E	1985-1986	**Domenico Bernasconi**	ITA	1929
Kid Oliva	FR	1930	**Duke McKenzie***	E	1986-1988	**Carlos Flix**	SP	1929-1931
Lucien Popescu	ROM	1930-1931	**Eyup Can***	TU	1989-1990	**Lucien Popescu**	ROM	1931-1932
Jackie Brown	E	1931-1935	**Pat Clinton***	S	1990-1991	**Domenico Bernasconi**	ITA	1932
Praxile Gyde	FR	1932-1935	**Salvatore Fanni**	ITA	1991-1992	**Nicholas Biquet**	BEL	1932-1935
Benny Lynch	S	1935-1938	**Robbie Regan***	W	1992-1993	**Maurice Dubois**	SWI	1935-1936
Kid David*	BEL	1935-1936	**Luigi Camputaro**	ITA	1993-1994	**Joseph Decico**	FR	1936
Ernst Weiss	AU	1936	**Robbie Regan***	W	1994-1995	**Aurel Toma**	ROM	1936-1937
Valentin Angelmann*	FR	1936-1938	**Luigi Camputaro***	ITA	1995-1996	**Nicholas Biquet**	BEL	1937-1938
Enrico Urbinati*	ITA	1938-1943	**Jesper Jensen**	DEN	1996-1997	**Aurel Toma**	ROM	1938-1939
Raoul Degryse	BEL	1946-1947	**David Guerault***	FR	1997-1999	**Ernst Weiss**	AU	1939
Maurice Sandeyron	FR	1947-1949	**Alexander Mahmutov**	RUS	1999-2000	**Gino Cattaneo**	ITA	1939-1941
Rinty Monaghan*	NI	1949-1950	**Damaen Kelly***	NI	2000	**Gino Bondavilli***	ITA	1941-1943
Terry Allen	E	1950	**Alexander Mahmutov**	RUS	2000-2002	**Jackie Paterson**	S	1946
Jean Sneyers*	BEL	1950-1951	**Mimoun Chent**	FR	2002-2003	**Theo Medina**	FR	1946-1947
Teddy Gardner*	E	1952	**Alexander Mahmutov***	RUS	2003	**Peter Kane**	E	1947-1948
Louis Skena*	FR	1953-1954	**Brahim Asloum***	FR	2003-2005	**Guido Ferracin**	ITA	1948-1949
Nazzareno Giannelli	ITA	1954-1955	**Ivan Pozo**	SP	2005-2006	**Luis Romero**	SP	1949-1951

Title Holder	Birthplace/Domicile	Tenure
Peter Keenan	S	1951-1952
Jean Sneyers*	BEL	1952-1953
Peter Keenan	S	1953
John Kelly	NI	1953-1954
Robert Cohen*	FR	1954-1955
Mario D'Agata	ITA	1955-1958
Piero Rollo	ITA	1958-1959
Freddie Gilroy	NI	1959-1960
Pierre Cossemyns	BEL	1961-1962
Piero Rollo	ITA	1962
Alphonse Halimi	FR	1962
Piero Rollo	ITA	1962-1963
Mimoun Ben Ali	SP	1963
Risto Luukkonen	FIN	1963-1964
Mimoun Ben Ali	SP	1965
Tommaso Galli	ITA	1965-1966
Mimoun Ben Ali	SP	1966-1968
Salvatore Burruni*	ITA	1968-1969
Franco Zurlo	ITA	1969-1971
Alan Rudkin	E	1971
Agustin Senin*	SP	1971-1973
Johnny Clark*	E	1973-1974
Bob Allotey	SP	1974-1975
Daniel Trioulaire	FR	1975-1976
Salvatore Fabrizio	ITA	1976-1977
Franco Zurlo	ITA	1977-1978
Juan Francisco Rodriguez	SP	1978-1980
Johnny Owen*	W	1980
Valerio Nati	ITA	1980-1982
Giuseppe Fossati	ITA	1982-1983
Walter Giorgetti	ITA	1983-1984
Ciro de Leva*	ITA	1984-1986
Antoine Montero	FR	1986-1987
Louis Gomis*	FR	1987-1988
Fabrice Benichou	FR	1988
Vincenzo Belcastro*	ITA	1988-1990
Thierry Jacob*	FR	1990-1992
Johnny Bredahl*	DEN	1992
Vincenzo Belcastro	ITA	1993-1994
Prince Naseem Hamed*	E	1994-1995
John Armour*	E	1995-1996
Johnny Bredahl	DEN	1996-1998
Paul Lloyd*	E	1998-1999
Johnny Bredahl*	DEN	1999-2000
Luigi Castiglione	ITA	2000-2001
Fabien Guillerme	FR	2001
Alex Yagupov	RUS	2001
Spend Abazi	SWE	2001-2002
Noel Wilders	E	2003
David Guerault	FR	2003-2004
Frederic Patrac	FR	2004
Simone Maludrottu	ITA	2004-

S. Bantamweight (122 lbs)

Title Holder	Birthplace/Domicile	Tenure
Vincenzo Belcastro	ITA	1995-1996
Salim Medjkoune	FR	1996
Martin Krastev	BUL	1996-1997
Spencer Oliver	E	1997-1998
Sergei Devakov	UK	1998-1999
Michael Brodie*	E	1999-2000
Vladislav Antonov	RUS	2000-2001
Salim Medjkoune*	FR	2001-2002
Mahyar Monshipour*	FR	2002-2003
Esham Pickering	E	2003-2005
Michael Hunter*	E	2005-2006
Bernard Dunne	RoI	2006-

Featherweight (126 lbs)

Title Holder	Birthplace/Domicile	Tenure
Young Joey Smith	E	1911
Jean Poesy	FR	1911-1912
Jim Driscoll*	W	1912-1913
Ted Kid Lewis*	E	1913-1914
Louis de Ponthieu*	FR	1919-1920
Arthur Wyns	BEL	1920-1922
Billy Matthews	E	1922
Eugene Criqui*	FR	1922-1923
Edouard Mascart	FR	1923-1924

Title Holder	Birthplace/Domicile	Tenure
Charles Ledoux	FR	1924
Henri Hebrans	BEL	1924-1925
Antonio Ruiz	SP	1925-1928
Luigi Quadrini	ITA	1928-1929
Knud Larsen	DEN	1929
Jose Girones	SP	1929-1934
Maurice Holtzer*	FR	1935-1938
Phil Dolhem	BEL	1938-1939
Lucien Popescu	ROM	1939-1941
Ernst Weiss	AU	1941
Gino Bondavilli	ITA	1941-1945
Ermanno Bonetti*	ITA	1945-1946
Tiger Al Phillips	E	1947
Ronnie Clayton	E	1947-1948
Ray Famechon	FR	1948-1953
Jean Sneyers	BEL	1953-1954
Ray Famechon	FR	1954-1955
Fred Galiana*	SP	1955-1956
Cherif Hamia	FR	1957-1958
Sergio Caprari	ITA	1958-1959
Gracieux Lamperti	FR	1959-1962
Alberto Serti	ITA	1962-1963
Howard Winstone	W	1963-1967
Jose Legra*	SP	1967-1968
Manuel Calvo	SP	1968-1969
Tommaso Galli	ITA	1969-1970
Jose Legra*	SP	1970-1972
Gitano Jiminez	SP	1973-1975
Elio Cotena	ITA	1975-1976
Nino Jimenez	SP	1976-1977
Manuel Masso	SP	1977
Roberto Castanon*	SP	1977-1981
Salvatore Melluzzo	ITA	1981-1982
Pat Cowdell*	E	1982-1983
Loris Stecca*	ITA	1983
Barry McGuigan*	NI	1983-1985
Jim McDonnell*	E	1985-1987
Valerio Nati*	ITA	1987
Jean-Marc Renard*	BEL	1988-1989
Paul Hodkinson*	E	1989-1991
Fabrice Benichou	FR	1991-1992
Maurizio Stecca	ITA	1992-1993
Herve Jacob	FR	1993
Maurizio Stecca	ITA	1993
Stephane Haccoun	FR	1993-1994
Stefano Zoff	ITA	1994
Medhi Labdouni	FR	1994-1995
Billy Hardy	E	1995-1998
Paul Ingle*	E	1998-1999
Steve Robinson	W	1999-2000
Istvan Kovacs*	HUN	2000-2001
Manuel Calvo*	SP	2001-2002
Cyril Thomas	FR	2002-2004
Nicky Cook*	E	2004-2006
Cyril Thomas*	FR	2006-2007
Alberto Servidei	ITA	2007-

S. Featherweight (130 lbs)

Title Holder	Birthplace/Domicile	Tenure
Tommaso Galli	ITA	1971-1972
Domenico Chiloiro	ITA	1972
Lothar Abend	GER	1972-1974
Sven-Erik Paulsen*	NOR	1974-1976
Roland Cazeaux	FR	1976
Natale Vezzoli	ITA	1976-1979
Carlos Hernandez	SP	1979
Rodolfo Sanchez	SP	1979
Carlos Hernandez	SP	1979-1982
Cornelius Boza-Edwards*	E	1982
Roberto Castano	SP	1982-1983
Alfredo Raininger	ITA	1983-1984
Jean-Marc Renard	BEL	1984
Pat Cowdell	E	1984-1985
Jean-Marc Renard*	BEL	1986-1987
Salvatore Curcetti	ITA	1987-1988
Piero Morello	ITA	1988
Lars Lund Jensen	DEN	1988
Racheed Lawal	DEN	1988-1989

Title Holder	Birthplace/Domicile	Tenure
Daniel Londas*	FR	1989-1991
Jimmy Bredahl*	DEN	1992
Regilio Tuur	HOL	1992-1993
Jacobin Yoma	FR	1993-1995
Anatoly Alexandrov*	KAZ	1995-1996
Julian Lorcy*	FR	1996
Djamel Lifa	FR	1997-1998
Anatoly Alexandrov*	RUS	1998
Dennis Holbaek Pedersen	DEN	1999-2000
Boris Sinitsin	RUS	2000
Dennis Holbaek Pedersen*	DEN	2000
Tontcho Tontchev*	BUL	2001
Boris Sinitsin	RUS	2001-2002
Pedro Oscar Miranda	SP	2002
Affif Djelti	FR	2002-2003
Boris Sinitsin	RUS	2003-2005
Alex Arthur*	S	2005-2006
Leva Kirakosyan	ARM	2007-

Lightweight (135 lbs)

Title Holder	Birthplace/Domicile	Tenure
Freddie Welsh	W	1909-1911
Matt Wells	E	1911-1912
Freddie Welsh*	W	1912-1914
Georges Papin	FR	1920-1921
Ernie Rice	E	1921-1922
Seaman Nobby Hall	E	1922-1923
Harry Mason	E	1923-1926
Fred Bretonnel	FR	1924
Lucien Vinez	FR	1924-1927
Luis Rayo*	SP	1927-1928
Aime Raphael	FR	1928-1929
Francois Sybille	BEL	1929-1930
Alf Howard	E	1930
Harry Corbett	E	1930-1931
Francois Sybille	BEL	1930-1931
Bep van Klaveren	HOL	1931-1932
Cleto Locatelli	ITA	1932
Francois Sybille	BEL	1932-1933
Cleto Locatelli*	ITA	1933
Francois Sybille	BEL	1934
Carlo Orlandi*	ITA	1934-1935
Enrico Venturi*	ITA	1935-1936
Vittorio Tamagnini	ITA	1936-1937
Maurice Arnault	FR	1937
Gustave Humery	FR	1937-1938
Aldo Spoldi*	ITA	1938-1939
Karl Blaho	AU	1940-1941
Bruno Bisterzo	ITA	1941
Ascenzo Botta	ITA	1941
Bruno Bisterzo	ITA	1941-1942
Ascenzo Botta	ITA	1942
Roberto Proietti	ITA	1942-1943
Bruno Bisterzo	ITA	1943-1946
Roberto Proietti*	ITA	1946
Emile Dicristo	FR	1946-1947
Kid Dussart	BEL	1947
Roberto Proietti	ITA	1947-1948
Billy Thompson	E	1948-1949
Kid Dussart	BEL	1949
Roberto Proietti*	ITA	1949-1950
Pierre Montane	FR	1951
Elis Ask	FIN	1951-1952
Jorgen Johansen	DEN	1952-1954
Duilio Loi*	ITA	1954-1959
Mario Vecchiatto	ITA	1959-1960
Dave Charnley	E	1960-1963
Conny Rudhof*	GER	1963-1964
Willi Quatuor*	GER	1964-1965
Franco Brondi	ITA	1965
Maurice Tavant	FR	1965-1966
Borge Krogh	DEN	1966-1967
Pedro Carrasco*	SP	1967-1969
Miguel Velazquez	SP	1970-1971
Antonio Puddu	ITA	1971-1974
Ken Buchanan*	S	1974-1975
Fernand Roelandts	BEL	1976
Perico Fernandez*	SP	1976-1977
Jim Watt*	S	1977-1979

Title Holder	Birthplace/ Domicile	Tenure
Charlie Nash*	NI	1979-1980
Francisco Leon	SP	1980
Charlie Nash	NI	1980-1981
Joey Gibilisco	ITA	1981-1983
Lucio Cusma	ITA	1983-1984
Rene Weller	GER	1984-1986
Gert Bo Jacobsen	DEN	1986-1988
Rene Weller*	GER	1988
Policarpo Diaz*	SP	1988-1990
Antonio Renzo	ITA	1991-1992
Jean-Baptiste Mendy*	FR	1992-1994
Racheed Lawal	DEN	1994
Jean-Baptiste Mendy*	FR	1994-1995
Angel Mona	FR	1995-1997
Manuel Carlos Fernandes	FR	1997
Oscar Garcia Cano	SP	1997
Billy Schwer*	E	1997-1999
Oscar Garcia Cano	SP	1999-2000
Lucien Lorcy*	FR	2000-2001
Stefano Zoff*	ITA	2001-2002
Jason Cook	W	2002-2003
Stefano Zoff*	ITA	2003-2005
Juan Carlos Diaz Melero	SP	2005-2006
Yuri Romanov	BE	2006-

L. Welterweight (140 lbs)

Title Holder	Birthplace/ Domicile	Tenure
Olli Maki	FIN	1964-1965
Juan Sombrita-Albornoz	SP	1965
Willi Quatuor*	GER	1965-1966
Conny Rudhof	GER	1967
Johann Orsolics	AU	1967-1968
Bruno Arcari*	ITA	1968-1970
Rene Roque	FR	1970-1971
Pedro Carrasco*	SP	1971-1972
Roger Zami	FR	1972
Cemal Kamaci	TU	1972-1973
Toni Ortiz	SP	1973-1974
Perico Fernandez*	SP	1974
Jose Ramon Gomez-Fouz	SP	1975
Cemal Kamaci*	TU	1975-1976
Dave Boy Green*	E	1976-1977
Primo Bandini	ITA	1977
Jean-Baptiste Piedvache	FR	1977-1978
Colin Power	E	1978
Fernando Sanchez	SP	1978-1979
Jose Luis Heredia	SP	1979
Jo Kimpuani	FR	1979-1980
Giuseppe Martinese	ITA	1980
Antonio Guinaldo	SP	1980-1981
Clinton McKenzie	E	1981-1982
Robert Gambini	FR	1982-1983
Patrizio Oliva*	ITA	1983-1985
Terry Marsh	E	1985-1986
Tusikoleta Nkalankete	FR	1987-1989
Efren Calamati	ITA	1989-1990
Pat Barrett	E	1990-1992
Valery Kayumba	ITA	1992-1993
Christian Merle	FR	1993-1994
Valery Kayumba	FR	1994
Khalid Rahilou*	FR	1994-1996
Soren Sondergaard*	DEN	1996-1998
Thomas Damgaard*	DEN	1998-2000
Oktay Urkal*	GER	2000-2001
Gianluca Branco*	ITA	2001-2002
Oktay Urkal*	GER	2002-2003
Junior Witter*	E	2004-2006
Ted Bami	E	2006-

Welterweight (147 lbs)

Title Holder	Birthplace/ Domicile	Tenure
Young Joseph	E	1910-1911
Georges Carpentier*	FR	1911-1912
Albert Badoud*	SWI	1915-1921
Johnny Basham	W	1919-1920
Ted Kid Lewis	E	1920-1924
Piet Hobin	BEL	1921-1925
Billy Mack	E	1923
Tommy Milligan	S	1924-1925
Mario Bosisio*	ITA	1925-1928

Title Holder	Birthplace/ Domicile	Tenure
Leo Darton	BEL	1928
Alf Genon	BEL	1928-1929
Gustave Roth	BEL	1929-1932
Adrien Aneet	BEL	1932-1933
Jack Hood*	E	1933
Gustav Eder	GER	1934-1936
Felix Wouters	BEL	1936-1938
Saverio Turiello	ITA	1938-1939
Marcel Cerdan*	FR	1939-1942
Ernie Roderick	E	1946-1947
Robert Villemain*	FR	1947-1948
Livio Minelli	ITA	1949-1950
Michele Palermo	ITA	1950-1951
Eddie Thomas	W	1951
Charles Humez*	FR	1951-1952
Gilbert Lavoine	FR	1953-1954
Wally Thom	E	1954-1955
Idrissa Dione	FR	1955-1956
Emilio Marconi	ITA	1956-1958
Peter Waterman*	E	1958
Emilio Marconi	ITA	1958-1959
Duilio Loi*	ITA	1959-1963
Fortunato Manca*	ITA	1964-1965
Jean Josselin	FR	1966-1967
Carmelo Bossi	ITA	1967-1968
Fighting Mack	HOL	1968-1969
Silvano Bertini	ITA	1969
Jean Josselin	FR	1969
Johann Orsolics	AU	1969-1970
Ralph Charles	E	1970-1971
Roger Menetrey	FR	1971-1974
John H. Stracey*	E	1974-1975
Marco Scano	ITA	1976-1977
Jorgen Hansen	DEN	1977
Jorg Eipel	GER	1977
Alain Marion	FR	1977-1978
Jorgen Hansen	DEN	1978
Josef Pachler	AU	1978
Henry Rhiney	E	1978-1979
Dave Boy Green	E	1979
Jorgen Hansen*	DEN	1979-1981
Hans-Henrik Palm	DEN	1982
Colin Jones*	W	1982-1983
Gilles Elbilia	FR	1983-1984
Gianfranco Rosi	ITA	1984-1985
Lloyd Honeyghan*	E	1985-1986
Jose Varela	GER	1986-1987
Alfonso Redondo	SP	1987
Mauro Martelli*	SWI	1987-1988
Nino la Rocca	ITA	1989
Antoine Fernandez	FR	1989-1990
Kirkland Laing	E	1990
Patrizio Oliva*	ITA	1990-1992
Ludovic Proto	FR	1992-1993
Gary Jacobs*	S	1993-1994
Jose Luis Navarro	SP	1994-1995
Valery Kayumba	FR	1995
Patrick Charpentier*	FR	1995-1996
Andrei Pestriaev*	RUS	1997
Michele Piccirillo*	ITA	1997-1998
Maxim Nesterenko	RUS	1998-1999
Alessandro Duran	ITA	1999
Andrei Pestriaev	RUS	1999-2000
Alessandro Duran	ITA	2000
Thomas Damgaard	DEN	2000-2001
Alessandro Duran	ITA	2001-2002
Christian Bladt	DEN	2002
Michel Trabant*	GER	2002-2003
Frederic Klose	FR	2003-2005
Oktay Urkal*	GER	2005
Frederic Klose*	FR	2006
Jackson Osei Bonsu	BEL	2007-

L. Middleweight (154 lbs)

Title Holder	Birthplace/ Domicile	Tenure
Bruno Visintin	ITA	1964-1966
Bo Hogberg	SWE	1966
Yolande Leveque	FR	1966
Sandro Mazzinghi*	ITA	1966-1968

Title Holder	Birthplace/ Domicile	Tenure
Remo Golfarini	ITA	1968-1969
Gerhard Piaskowy	GER	1969-1970
Jose Hernandez	SP	1970-1972
Juan Carlos Duran	ITA	1972-1973
Jacques Kechichian	FR	1973-1974
Jose Duran	SP	1974-1975
Eckhard Dagge	GER	1975-1976
Vito Antuofermo	ITA	1976
Maurice Hope*	E	1976-1978
Gilbert Cohen	FR	1978-1979
Marijan Benes	YUG	1979-1981
Louis Acaries	FR	1981
Luigi Minchillo*	ITA	1981-1983
Herol Graham*	E	1983-1984
Jimmy Cable	E	1984
Georg Steinherr	GER	1984-1985
Said Skouma*	FR	1985-1986
Chris Pyatt	E	1986-1987
Gianfranco Rosi*	ITA	1987
Rene Jacquot*	FR	1988-1989
Edip Secovic	AU	1989
Giuseppe Leto	ITA	1989
Gilbert Dele*	FR	1989-1990
Said Skouma	FR	1991
Mourad Louati	HOL	1991
Jean-Claude Fontana	FR	1991-1992
Laurent Boudouani	FR	1992-1993
Bernard Razzano	FR	1993-1994
Javier Castillejos	SP	1994-1995
Laurent Boudouani*	FR	1995-1996
Faouzi Hattab	FR	1996
Davide Ciarlante*	ITA	1996-1997
Javier Castillejo*	SP	1998
Mamadou Thiam*	FR	1998-2000
Roman Karmazin*	RUS	2000
Mamadou Thiam*	FR	2001
Wayne Alexander*	E	2002
Roman Karmazin*	RUS	2003-2004
Sergei Dzindziruk*	UK	2004-2005
Michele Piccirillo*	ITA	2006-2007

Middleweight (160 lbs)

Title Holder	Birthplace/ Domicile	Tenure
Georges Carpentier*	FR	1912-1918
Ercole Balzac	FR	1920-1921
Gus Platts	E	1921
Willem Westbroek	HOL	1921
Johnny Basham	W	1921
Ted Kid Lewis	E	1921-1923
Roland Todd	E	1923-1924
Ted Kid Lewis	E	1924-1925
Bruno Frattini	ITA	1924-1925
Tommy Milligan	S	1925-1928
Rene Devos	BEL	1926-1927
Barthelemy Molina	FR	1928
Alex Ireland	S	1928-1929
Mario Bosisio	ITA	1928
Leone Jacovacci	ITA	1928-1929
Len Johnson	E	1928-1929
Marcel Thil	FR	1929-1930
Mario Bosisio	ITA	1930-1931
Poldi Steinbach	AU	1931
Hein Domgoergen	GER	1931-1932
Ignacio Ara	SP	1932-1933
Gustave Roth	BEL	1933-1934
Marcel Thil*	FR	1934-1938
Edouard Tenet	FR	1938
Bep van Klaveren	HOL	1938
Anton Christoforidis	GRE	1938-1939
Edouard Tenet	FR	1939
Josef Besselmann*	GER	1942-1943
Marcel Cerdan	FR	1947-1948
Cyrille Delannoit	BEL	1948
Marcel Cerdan*	FR	1948
Cyrille Delannoit	BEL	1948-1949
Tiberio Mitri*	ITA	1949-1950
Randy Turpin	E	1951-1954
Tiberio Mitri	ITA	1954
Charles Humez	FR	1954-1958

EUROPEAN CHAMPIONS, 1909-2007

Title Holder	Birthplace/ Domicile	Tenure
Gustav Scholz*	GER	1958-1961
John Cowboy McCormack	S	1961-1962
Chris Christensen	DEN	1962
Laszlo Papp*	HUN	1962-1965
Nino Benvenuti*	ITA	1965-1967
Juan Carlos Duran	ITA	1967-1969
Tom Bogs	DEN	1969-1970
Juan Carlos Duran	ITA	1970-1971
Jean-Claude Bouttier	FR	1971-1972
Tom Bogs*	DEN	1973
Elio Calcabrini	ITA	1973-1974
Jean-Claude Bouttier	FR	1974
Kevin Finnegan	E	1974-1975
Gratien Tonna*	FR	1975
Bunny Sterling	E	1976
Angelo Jacopucci	ITA	1976
Germano Valsecchi	ITA	1976-1977
Alan Minter	E	1977
Gratien Tonna	FR	1977-1978
Alan Minter*	E	1978-1979
Kevin Finnegan	E	1980
Matteo Salvemini	ITA	1980
Tony Sibson*	E	1980-1982
Louis Acaries	FR	1982-1984
Tony Sibson	E	1984-1985
Ayub Kalule	DEN	1985-1986
Herol Graham	E	1986-1987
Sumbu Kalambay*	ITA	1987
Pierre Joly	FR	1987-1988
Christophe Tiozzo*	FR	1988-1989
Francesco dell'Aquila	ITA	1989-1990
Sumbu Kalambay*	ITA	1990-1993
Agostino Cardamone*	ITA	1993-1994
Richie Woodhall*	E	1995-1996
Alexandre Zaitsev	RUS	1996
Hassine Cherifi*	FR	1996-1998
Agostino Cardamone*	ITA	1998
Erland Betare*	FR	1999-2000
Howard Eastman*	E	2001
Cristian Sanavia	ITA	2001-2002
Morrade Hakkar*	FR	2002
Howard Eastman*	E	2003-2004
Morrade Hakkar	FR	2005
Sebastian Sylvester	GER	2005-2006
Amin Asikainen	FIN	2006-2007
Sebastian Sylvester	GER	2007-

S. Middleweight (168 lbs)

Title Holder	Birthplace/ Domicile	Tenure
Mauro Galvano*	ITA	1990-1991
James Cook	E	1991-1992
Franck Nicotra*	FR	1992
Vincenzo Nardiello	ITA	1992-1993
Ray Close*	NI	1993
Vinzenzo Nardiello	ITA	1993-1994
Frederic Seillier*	FR	1994-1995
Henry Wharton*	E	1995-1996
Frederic Seillier*	FR	1996
Andrei Shkalikov*	RUS	1997
Dean Francis*	E	1997-1998
Bruno Girard*	FR	1999
Andrei Shkalikov	RUS	2000-2001
Danilo Haeussler	GER	2001-2003
Mads Larsen*	DEN	2003-2004
Rudy Markussen*	DEN	2004-2005
Vitali Tsypko	UK	2005
Jackson Chanet	FR	2005-2006
Mger Mkrtchian	ARM	2006
David Gogoya	GEO	2006-2007
Cristian Sanavia	ITA	2007-

L. Heavyweight (175 lbs)

Title Holder	Birthplace/ Domicile	Tenure
Georges Carpentier	FR	1913-1922
Battling Siki	FR	1922-1923
Emile Morelle	FR	1923
Raymond Bonnel	FR	1923-1924
Louis Clement	SWI	1924-1926
Herman van T'Hof	HOL	1926
Fernand Delarge	BEL	1926-1927
Max Schmeling*	GER	1927-1928
Michele Bonaglia*	ITA	1929-1930
Ernst Pistulla*	GER	1931-1932
Adolf Heuser	GER	1932
John Andersson	SWE	1933
Martinez de Alfara	SP	1934
Marcel Thil	FR	1934-1935
Merlo Preciso	ITA	1935
Hein Lazek	AU	1935-1936
Gustave Roth	BEL	1936-1938
Adolf Heuser*	GER	1938-1939
Luigi Musina*	ITA	1942-1943
Freddie Mills*	E	1947-1950
Albert Yvel	FR	1950-1951
Don Cockell*	E	1951-1952
Conny Rux*	GER	1952
Jacques Hairabedian	FR	1953-1954
Gerhard Hecht	GER	1954-1955
Willi Hoepner	GER	1955
Gerhard Hecht	GER	1955-1957
Artemio Calzavara	ITA	1957-1958
Willi Hoepner	GER	1958
Erich Schoeppner	GER	1958-1962
Giulio Rinaldi	ITA	1962-1964
Gustav Scholz*	GER	1964-1965
Giulio Rinaldi	ITA	1965-1966
Piero del Papa	ITA	1966-1967
Lothar Stengel	GER	1967-1968
Tom Bogs*	DEN	1968-1969
Yvan Prebeg	YUG	1969-1970
Piero del Papa	ITA	1970-1971
Conny Velensek	GER	1971-1972
Chris Finnegan	E	1972
Rudiger Schmidtke	GER	1972-1973
John Conteh*	E	1973-1974
Domenico Adinolfi	ITA	1974-1976
Mate Parlov*	YUG	1976-1977
Aldo Traversaro	ITA	1977-1979
Rudi Koopmans	HOL	1979-1984
Richard Caramonolis	FR	1984
Alex Blanchard	HOL	1984-1987
Tom Collins	E	1987-1988
Pedro van Raamsdonk	HOL	1988
Jan Lefeber	HOL	1988-1989
Eric Nicoletta	FR	1989-1990
Tom Collins	E	1990-1991
Graciano Rocchigiani*	GER	1991-1992
Eddie Smulders	HOL	1993-1994
Fabrice Tiozzo*	FR	1994-1995
Eddy Smulders	HOL	1995-1996
Crawford Ashley	E	1997
Ole Klemetsen*	NOR	1997-1998
Crawford Ashley	E	1998-1999
Clinton Woods*	E	1999-2000
Yawe Davis	ITA	2001-2002
Thomas Ulrich*	GER	2002-2003
Stipe Drews*	CRO	2003-2004
Thomas Ulrich*	GER	2004-2005
Stipe Drews*	CRO	2006
Thomas Ulrich	GER	2007-

Cruiserweight (200 lbs)

Title Holder	Birthplace/ Domicile	Tenure
Sam Reeson*	E	1987-1988
Angelo Rottoli	ITA	1989
Anaclet Wamba*	FR	1989-1990
Johnny Nelson*	E	1990-1992
Akim Tafer*	FR	1992-1993
Massimiliano Duran	ITA	1993-1994
Carl Thompson	E	1994
Alexander Gurov	UK	1995
Patrice Aouissi	FR	1995
Alexander Gurov*	UK	1995-1996
Akim Tafer*	FR	1996-1997
Johnny Nelson	E	1997-1998
Terry Dunstan*	E	1998
Alexei Iliin	RUS	1999
Torsten May*	GER	1999-2000
Carl Thompson*	E	2000-2001
Alexander Gurov*	UK	2001-2002
Pietro Aurino*	ITA	2002-2003
Vincenzo Cantatore	ITA	2004
Alexander Gurov	UK	2004-2005
David Haye*	E	2005-2007
Vincenzo Cantatore	ITA	2007-

Heavyweight (200 lbs +)

Title Holder	Birthplace/ Domicile	Tenure
Georges Carpentier	FR	1913-1922
Battling Siki	FR	1922-1923
Erminio Spalla	ITA	1923-1926
Paolino Uzcudun	SP	1926-1928
Harry Persson	SWE	1926
Phil Scott	E	1927
Pierre Charles	BEL	1929-1931
Hein Muller	GER	1931-1932
Pierre Charles	BEL	1932-1933
Paolino Uzcudun	SP	1933
Primo Carnera	ITA	1933-1935
Pierre Charles	BEL	1935-1937
Arno Kolblin	GER	1937-1938
Hein Lazek	AU	1938-1939
Adolf Heuser	GER	1939
Max Schmeling*	GER	1939-1941
Olle Tandberg	SWE	1943
Karel Sys*	BEL	1943-1946
Bruce Woodcock	E	1946-1949
Joe Weidin	AU	1950-1951
Jack Gardner	E	1951
Hein Ten Hoff	GER	1951-1952
Karel Sys	BEL	1952
Heinz Neuhaus	GER	1952-1955
Franco Cavicchi	ITA	1955-1956
Ingemar Johansson*	SWE	1956-1959
Dick Richardson	W	1960-1962
Ingemar Johansson*	SWE	1962-1963
Henry Cooper*	E	1964
Karl Mildenberger	GER	1964-1968
Henry Cooper*	E	1968-1969
Peter Weiland	GER	1969-1970
Jose Urtain	SP	1970
Henry Cooper	E	1970-1971
Joe Bugner	E	1971
Jack Bodell	E	1971
Jose Urtain	SP	1971-1972
Jurgen Blin	GER	1972
Joe Bugner*	E	1972-1975
Richard Dunn	E	1976
Joe Bugner	E	1976-1977
Jean-Pierre Coopman	BEL	1977
Lucien Rodriguez	FR	1977
Alfredo Evangelista	SP	1977-1979
Lorenzo Zanon*	SP	1979-1980
John L. Gardner*	E	1980-1981
Lucien Rodriguez	FR	1981-1984
Steffen Tangstad	NOR	1984-1985
Anders Eklund	SWE	1985
Frank Bruno*	E	1985-1986
Steffen Tangstad	NOR	1986
Alfredo Evangelista	SP	1987
Anders Eklund	SWE	1987
Francesco Damiani	ITA	1987-1989
Derek Williams	E	1989-1990
Jean Chanet	FR	1990
Lennox Lewis*	E	1990-1992
Henry Akinwande*	E	1993-1995
Zeljko Mavrovic*	CRO	1995-1998
Vitali Klitschko*	UK	1998-1999
Vladimir Klitschko*	UK	1999-2000
Vitali Klitschko*	UK	2000-2001
Luan Krasniqi	GER	2002
Przemyslaw Saleta	POL	2002
Sinan Samil Sam	TU	2002-2004
Luan Krasniqi	GER	2004-2005
Paolo Vidoz	ITA	2005-2006
Vladimir Virchis	UK	2006-

A-Z of Current World Champions

by Eric Armit

Shows the record since 1 July 2006, plus career summary and pen portrait, of all men holding IBF, WBA, WBC and WBO titles as at 30 June 2007. The author has also produced the same data for those who first won titles during that period, but were no longer champions on 30 June 2007. World champions belonging to other bodies are shown if they are considered to be the best man at the weight. Incidentally, the place name given is the respective boxer's domicile and may not necessarily be his birthplace, while all nicknames are shown where applicable in brackets. Not included are British fighters, Joe Calzaghe (WBO super-middleweight champion), Ricky Hatton (IBO light-welterweight champion), Enzo Maccarinelli (WBO cruiserweight champion), Junior Witter (WBC light-welterweight champion) and Clinton Woods (IBF light-heavyweight champion). Their full records can be found among the Active British-Based Boxers: Career Records section.

Arthur (King Arthur) Abraham

Yerevan, Armenia. *Born* 20 February, 1980

IBF Middleweight Champion

Major Amateur Honours: Competed in the 200 European Olympic qualifiers
Turned Pro: August 2003
Significant Results: Cristian Zanabria W CO 5, Nader Hamdan W RSC 12, Ian Gardner W PTS 12, Hector Velazco W CO 5, Howard Eastman W PTS 12, Kingsley Ikeke W CO 5, Shannon Taylor W PTS 12, Kofi Jantuah W PTS 12
Type/Style: Is a tough, strong and aggressive fighter
Points of Interest: 5' 10" tall. Arthur's real name is Avetik Abrahamyan and although born in Armenia he received German citizenship in 2006. Is with the Sauerland Group, as is his brother Alex who boxes as a pro at light-middleweight. Has 18 wins by stoppage or kayo after winning his first 14 bouts inside the distance. Won the vacant IBF title by beating Kingsley Ikeke in December 2005 and has made four defences, but suffered a broken jaw against Edison Miranda. He is played into the ring by the Smurf Song from the TV programme which featured a Father Abraham
23.09.06 Edison Miranda W PTS 12 Wetzlar
      (IBF Middleweight Title Defence)
26.05.07 Sebastien Demers W RSC 3 Bamberg
      (IBF Middleweight Title Defence)
Career: 23 contests, won 23.

Alejandro (Naco) Berrio

Cartagena, Colombia. *Born* 7 August, 1976

IBF S.Middleweight Champion

Major Amateur Honours: Competed in the 1997 World Junior Championships
Turned Pro: February 1997
Significant Results: Carl Handy W RSC 8, Eric Mitchell L RSC 1, Syd Vanderpool W CO 9, Robert Stieglitz L RSC 11, Yusef Mack W RSC 6
Type/Style: An aggressive, rangy banger who seems in recent bouts to have banished doubts about his chin
Points of Interest: 6'1" tall. He is now based in South Florida and was once trained by former Jim Watt victim, Howard Davis. Twenty five of his 26 wins and all four of his losses have come inside the distance
03.03.07 Robert Stieglitz W RSC 3 Rostock
      (Vacant IBF S.Middleweight Title)
Career: 30 contests, won 26, lost 4.

Silvio (Il Barbaro) Branco

Civitavecchia, Italy. *Born* 26 August, 1966

Former WBA L.Heavyweight Champion. Former Undefeated Italian Middleweight Champion

Major Amateur Honours: None known, but claims 30 fights with only one defeat
Turned Pro: July 1988
Significant Results: Agostino Cardamone L PTS 12 (twice) & L CO 10, Richie Woodhall L RSC 9, Rodney Toney DREW 12, Thomas Tate W PTS 12, Verno Phillips W PTS 12, Glengoffe Johnson W PTS 12, Robin Reid W PTS 12, Sven Ottke L PTS 12, Stipe Drews L PTS 12, Mehdi Sahnoune W RSC 11, Fabrice Tiozzo L PTS 12, Thomas Ulrich L RSC 11, Sasha Mitrevski W RSC 5
Type/Style: A strong, orthodox boxer with a sound chin and good stamina
Points of Interest: 6'0" tall. Nicknamed the 'Barbarian', his father and two brothers all fought professionally. Failed in challenges for the European middleweight and light-heavyweight titles and IBF super-middleweight title before beating Mehdi Sahnoune for the WBA title in 2003. Lost the title in his first defence to Fabrice Tiozzo in 2004. After winning the WBA 'interim' title by beating Manny Siaca, he was recognised as full champion again at the age of 40 when Tiozzo retired. Has 34 wins inside the distance
27.07.07 Manny Siaca W PTS 12 Milan
      (Vacant WBA 'Interim' L.Heavyweight Title)
28.04.07 Stipe Drews L PTS 12 Oberhausen
      (WBA L.Heavyweight Title Defence)
Career: 66 contests, won 55, drew 2, lost 9.

Shannon (The Cannon) Briggs

New York, USA. Born 4 December, 1971

Former WBO Heavyweight Champion

Major Amateur Honours: Former double New York Golden Gloves champion. Competed in the 1991 National Golden Gloves and won a silver medal in the Pan-American Games in the same year. A wrist injury cost him his place in the Olympic trials in 1992
Turned Pro: July 1992
Significant Results: Darroll Wilson L RSC 3, Lennox Lewis L RSC 5, Frans Botha DREW 10, Sedrick Fields L PTS 8, Jameel McCline L PTS 10, Abraham Okine W RSC 3, Ray Mercer W CO 7
Type/Style: Is a rumbustious hard-punching type, but slow and not strong on stamina
Points of Interest: 6'4" tall. Became a 'Cinderella' figure when winning a version of the world title at the age of 34, eight years after losing to Lennox Lewis in his only previous title attempt back in 1998. An accomplished man, he overcame a poor background in Brownsville, New York and as a homeless person in New Jersey, to get a high school degree, play chess and write poetry. Also issued a rap music album and appeared on MTV. Has 42 wins inside the distance

04.11.06 Sergei Lyakhovich W RSC 12 Phoenix
(WBO Heavyweight Title Challenge)
02.06.07 Sultan Ibragimov L PTS 12 Atlantic
City
(WBO Heavyweight Title Defence)
Career: 54 contests, won 48, drew 1, lost 5.

Celestino (Pelenchin) Caballero

Colon, Panama. *Born* 21 June, 1976
WBA S.Bantamweight Champion
Major Amateur Honours: None known
Turned Pro: November 1998
Significant Results: Jose Rojas L CO 3, Giovanni Andrade W DIS 10, Ricardo Cordoba L PTS 12, Daniel Ponce de Leon W PTS 12, Yober Ortega W PTS 12, Roberto Bonilla W RSC 7
Type/Style: Tall, rangy southpaw
Points of Interest: 5'11" tall. Also known as 'The Towering Inferno', he wanted to be a footballer but took up boxing instead for financial reasons, having started at the age of 14. First won the 'interim' WBA title by beating Yober Ortega in October 2005 and became full champion with his crushing victory over Somsak Sithchatchawal in Thailand. Promoted by Sycuan Ringside promotions, a Native American promotions group, he has 18 wins by stoppage or kayo. His fight with Sithchatchawal was staged at an ancient Temple
04.10.06 Somsak Sithchatchawal W RSC 3
Korat
(WBA S.Bantamweight Title Challenge)
16.03.07 Ricardo Castillo W RSC 9 Hollywood
(WBA S.Bantamweight Title Defence)
Career: 28 contests, won 26, lost 2.

Ivan (Iron Boy) Calderon

Guaynabo, Puerto Rico. *Born* 7 January, 1975
WBO M.Flyweight Champion
Major Amateur Honours: A bronze medallist in the 1999 Pan-American Games, he also competed in the World Championships that year. Won a silver medal in 1999 Central American Games before competing in the 2000 Olympic Games. Claims 110 wins in 130 bouts
Turned Pro: February 2001
Significant Results: Jorge Romero W RTD 4, Alejandro Moreno W PTS 10, Eduardo Marquez W TD 9, Lorenzo Trejo W PTS 12, Alex Sanchez W PTS 12, Edgar Cardenas W CO 11, Roberto Leyva W PTS 12, Carlos Fajardo W PTS 12, Noel Tunacao W RSC 8, Gerard Verde W PTS 12, Daniel Reyes

W PTS 12, Isaac Bustos W PTS 12, Miguel Tellez W RSC 9
Type/ Style: Southpaw. Although an excellent boxer technically and good counter-puncher, he lacks power
Points of Interest: 5' 0" tall. Won the WBO title with a technical verdict over Eduardo Marquez in May 2003 and has made 11 defences. An extrovert who is tremendously popular in Puerto Rico, being voted Boxer of the Year there in 2002, he has only six wins by stoppage or kayo. Revenged an amateur defeat when beating Jose Luis Varela
21.10.06 Jose Luis Varela W PTS 12
Barranquilla
(WBO M.Flyweight Title Defence)
28.04.07 Ronald Barrera W PTS 12 Barranquilla
(WBO M.Flyweight Title Defence)
Career: 28 contests won 28.

Mariano (Adrenalina) Carrera

Cordoba, Argentine. *Born* 22 July, 1980
Former Undefeated WBA Middleweight Champion. Former Undefeated South American & Argentinian Middleweight Champion
Major Amateur Honours: As the Argentinian national champion he competed in the 2000 Olympics
Turned Pro: May 2001
Significant Results: Orlando Acuna L PTS 10, Miguel Angel Arroyo W PTS 10, Jaun Italo Meza W PTS 10 & W RSC 3, Hector Velazco W RSC 10, Jorge Sclarandi W CO 10, Paulo Sanchez L PTS 10 & W PTS 10
Type/Style: A clever, lanky counter-puncher with a good left hook, there may be a question over his chin
Points of Interest: 6'0" tall. Mariano started boxing at the age of 12 and is a stable mate of the WBO flyweight champion Omar Narvaez. Has 20 wins by knockout or stoppage and stopped Javier Castillejo in 11 rounds in his challenge for the WBA title. Was later stripped of the title after testing positive for a banned substance, with the bout being declared a no contest
25.07.06 Luis Parada W CO 10 Buenos Aires
02.12.06 Javier Castillejo W RSC 11 Berlin
(WBA Middleweight Title Challenge)
12.05.07 Oney Valdez W RSF 4 Managua
Career: 35 contests, won 30, lost 4, no contest 1.

Joel (Cepillo) Casamayor

Guantanamo, Cuba. *Born* 12 July, 1971
Former Undefeated WBC

Lightweight Champion. Former WBA S.Featherweight Champion
Major Amateur Honours: The world junior champion in 1989 and a gold medallist in the 1992 Olympics, he won silver medals in the 1993 World Championships, the 1994 World Cup and the Goodwill Games. Claims just 30 losses in over 400 fights
Turned Pro: September 1996
Significant Results: Julio Gervacio W RSC 2, Jose Luis Noyola W PTS 12, Antonio Hernandez W PTS 12, David Santos W PTS 12, Jong-Kwon Baek W RSC 2, Robert Garcia W RSC 9, Edwin Santana W PTS 12, Acelino Freitas L PTS 12, Diego Corrales W RSC 6 & L PTS 12, Jose Luis Castillo L PTS 12
Type/Style: A tall southpaw, he is a classy, slick and clever boxer who lacks a heavy punch
Points of Interest: 6'2" tall. Started boxing at the age of eight. Defected from Cuba in 1996 and was with Main Events before being dropped by them for allegedly drinking and not training hard enough. Won the WBA 'interim' super-featherweight title in June 1999 by beating Antonio Hernandez and gained full recognition with his win over Jong-Kwon Baek in May 2000. Having made three defences he was deposed by Acelino Freitas, whose WBO title was also on the line, and then spent nearly six years in the backwoods before getting a crack at Diego Corrales for the WBC lightweight crown. Although Corrales failed to make the weight, the contest went ahead and on winning Joel was handed the title. However, on looking to meet Freitas instead of making a defence against David Diaz, the 'interim' champion, he was stripped in February 2007 before being given status as the WBC 'interim' lightweight title holder in May. Has 21 wins inside the distance
07.07.06 Lamont Pearson W RSC 9 Phoenix
07.10.06 Diego Corrales W PTS 12 Las Vegas
Career: 38 contests, won 34, drew 1, lost 3.

Javier (The Lynx of Parla) Castillejo

Madrid, Spain. *Born* 22 March, 1968
Former WBA Middleweight Champion. Former WBC L.Middleweight Champion. Former Undefeated European & Spanish L.Middleweight Champion. Former Undefeated Spanish Welterweight Champion

Major Amateur Honours: None known
Turned Pro: July 1988
Significant Results: Julio Cesar Vazquez
L PTS 12, Bernard Razzano W RSC 6,
Laurent Boudouani L RSC 6, Ahmet
Dottuev W RSC 12, Keith Mullings
W PTS 12, Paolo Roberto W RSC 7,
Mikael Rask W RSC 7, Tony Marshall
W PTS 10. Oscar de la Hoya L PTS 12,
Roman Karmazin W PTS 12, Fernando
Vargas L PTS 10
Type/Style: Aggressive, strong and a
heavy puncher
Points of Interest: 5'9" tall. Having
failed in a bid for the WBA light-
middleweight title against Julio Cesar
Vazquez in 1993, he won the WBC
light-middleweight title in January 1999
and made six defences before losing the
title to Oscar de la Hoya in June 2001.
Won the WBC 'interim' title after
beating Roman Karmazin in July 2002
and when Ronald Wright relinquished
the title he was then recognised as the
full champion. However, he was then
stripped of the title for refusing to meet
Ricardo Mayorga in a title defence
and moved up to middleweight. Was
originally declared the loser against
Mariano Carrera on an 11-round
stoppage, but Carrera tested positive for
a banned substance and the bout was
declared a no contest. Following that,
Castillejo was reinstated as champion.
Has 40 wins inside the distance and
was twice European champion at light-
middleweight
15.07.06 Felix Sturm W RSC 10 Hamburg
          *(WBA 'Secondary' Middleweight Title
          Challenge)*
02.12.06 Mariano Carrera L RSC 11 Berlin
          (WBA Middleweight Title Defence)
28.04.07 Felix Sturm L PTS 12 Oberhausen
          (WBA Middleweight Title Defence)
Career: 69 contests, won 61, lost 7, no contest 1.

Hugo (Fidel) Cazares
Los Mochis, Mexico. *Born* 24 March,
1978
WBO L.Flyweight Champion. Former
Undefeated Mexican L.Flyweight
Champion
Major Amateur Honours: None known
Turned Pro: February 1997
Significant Results: Sergio Perez L CO
1, Gerson Guerrero L RSC 5, Rafael
Orozco W CO 6, Eric Jamili W CO 3,
Valentin Leon W RSC 3, Juan Keb-Baas
W CO 9, Miguel del Valle W PTS 10,
Nelson Dieppa W TD 10, Alex Sanchez
W RSC 8, Kaichon Sorvoraphin W CO
6, Domingo Guillen W CO 1

Type/Style: Is a powerful, tough,
aggressive switch-hitter who can also
box a bit
Points of Interest: 5'6" tall. Was
already fighting over ten rounds by his
sixth fight. His record shows 19 wins
by stoppage or kayo and he is unbeaten
in his last 16 fights, with 12 of those
ending inside the distance. Has made
five defences since winning the title
from Nelson Dieppa in April 2005
30.09.06 Nelson Dieppa W RSC 10 Caguas
          (WBO L.Flyweight Title Defence)
04.05.07 Wilfrido Valdez W RSC 2 Las Vegas
          (WBO L.Flyweight Title Defence)
Career: 28 contests, won 24, drew 1, lost 3.

Ruslan (White Tyson) Chagaev
Andizhan, Uzbekistan. *Born* 19
October, 1978
WBA Heavyweight Champion
Major Amateur Honours: Competed
in the 1996 and 2000 Olympic Games.
Won a bronze medal in the 1997 World
Junior Championships and gold medals
in both the 1997 and 2001 World
Championships. Claims 82 wins in 86
amateur fights
Turned Pro: October 1997
Significant Results: Rob Calloway
T DRAW 3 & W CO 2, Sherman
Williams W PTS 8, Marc Krenec W
CO 5, Vladimir Virchis W PTS 12

Type/Style: Stocky, strong southpaw
counter puncher with fast hands and a
good chin
Points of Interest: 6'1" tall with a
74" reach. Having started boxing at
13, his first World Amateur title in
1997 was taken off him when it was
discovered that he had had two fights
as a professional in the United States.
These were later changed to exhibition
bouts so that he could continue as an
amateur, but they were genuine paid
bouts so are included on his record.
Gave away 11" in height and 90lbs in
weight to Nikolai Valuev. Has 17 wins
by stoppage or kayo
15.07.06 Michael Sprott W RSC 8 Hamburg
18.11.06 John Ruiz W PTS 12 Dusseldorf
14.04.07 Nikolai Valuev W PTS 12 Stuttgart
          (WBA Heavyweight Title Challenge)
Career: 24 contests, won 23, drew 1.

In-Jin Chi
Seoul, South Korea. Born 18 July,
1973
WBC Featherweight Champion.
Former Undefeated South Korean
Bantamweight Champion
Major Amateur Honours: None known
Turned Pro: November 1991
Significant Results: Jesse Maca W PTS
10 & W PTS 12, Baby Lorona W PTS
10, Erik Morales L PTS 12, Sammy

Ruslan Chagaev   Les Clark

Duran W RSC 3, Michael Brodie DREW 12 and W CO 9, Eiichi Sugama W PTS, Tommy Browne W PTS 12, Tadashi Koshimoto L PTS 12
Style/Type: Tough, raw and aggressive, he is a good body puncher with a strong chin
Points of Interest: 5'7" tall with a 67" reach. Lost his first paid fight but since then only Erik Morales and Tadashi Koshimoto have beaten him. With 18 wins inside the distance, he won the WBC title for the first time by beating Michael Brodie in April 2004 and made two defences before losing the title to Koshimoto in January 2006. Was then inactive until regaining the title by beating Rodolfo Lopez
17.12.06 Rodolfo Lopez W PTS 12 Seoul
(WBC Featherweight Title Challenge)
Career: 35 contests, won 31, drew 1, lost 3.

In-Jin Chi   Les Clark

Kermit (The Killer) Cintron

Carolina, Puerto Rico. *Born* 22 October, 1979
IBF Welterweight Champion
Major Amateur Honours: He competed in the 1999 PAL Championships and lost in the Eastern Olympic trials in 2000
Turned Pro: October 2000
Significant Results: Ian MacKillop W RSC 2, Humberto Aranda W RSC 5, Elio Ortiz W RSC 6, Teddy Reid W RSC 8, Antonio Margarito L RSC 5, David Estrada W RSC 10
Type/Style: Tall, rangy puncher
Points of Interest: 5'11" tall with a 72" reach. Had a tough early life, which included becoming an orphan by the age of 13, and originally intended to be a wrestler until an injury changed that. His uncle, Benjamin Serrano, boxed as a pro at middleweight. Trained by Manny Stewart, he won the WBO 'interim' title when beating Teddy Reid in July 2004, but was easily beaten by Antonio Margarito when he challenged for the full title. Has 25 wins by stoppage or kayo
28.10.06 Mark Suarez W RSC 5 Palm Beach
(Vacant IBF Welterweight Title)
Career: 28 contests, won 27, lost 1.

Miguel Cotto

Caguas, Puerto Rico. *Born* 29 October, 1980
WBA Welterweight Champion. Former Undefeated WBO L.Welterweight Champion
Major Amateur Honours: He won a gold medal in the 1997 Pan-American Championships, was a bronze medallist in the 1997 Central American Games, picked up silver medals in the 1997 and 1998 World Junior Championships and collected silver medals in the Pan-American Cadet Championships and the Central American Games in 1998. He competed without success in both the World Championships and the Pan-American Games in 1999. Won a gold medal in the 2000 Central American Games, having earlier competed in the 2000 Olympics where he lost to Mohamad Abdulaev
Turned Pro: February 2001
Significant Results: Justin Juuko W RSC 5, John Brown W PTS 10, Cesar Bazan W RSC 11, Joel Perez W CO 4, Demetrio Ceballos W RSC 7, Charles Maussa W RSC 8, Victoriano Sosa W RSC 4, Lovemore Ndou W PTS 12, Kelson Pinto W RSC 6, Randall Bailey W RSC 6, DeMarcus Corley W RSC 5, Mohamad Abdulaev W RSC 9, Ricardo Torres W CO 7, Gianluca Branco W RSC 8, Paul Malignaggi W PTS 12
Type/ Style: Miguel is a classy hard-hitting box puncher with an exciting style, but has been rocked a few times
Points of Interest: 5'8" tall with a 67" reach. His father, uncle and cousin all boxed and his brother Jose Miguel Cotto lost to Juan Diaz in a fight for the IBF lightweight title in April 2006. Is trained by his uncle Evangelista and has 25 wins inside the distance. Won the WBO light-welterweight title in September 2004 by beating Kelson Pinto and made six title defences before moving up to win the WBA welterweight crown

02.12.06 Carlos Quintana W RTD 5 Atlantic City
(Vacant WBA Welterweight Title)
03.03.07 Oktay Urkal W RSC 11 San Juan
(WBA Welterweight Title Defence)
09.06.07 Zab Judah W RSC 11 New York City
(WBA Welterweight Title Defence)
Career: 30 contests, won 30.

Steve (USS) Cunningham

Philadelphia, USA. *Born* 15 July, 1976
IBF Cruiserweight Champion

Major Amateur Honours: A National Golden Gloves champion 1998, he competed in the 2000 US Championships where he lost a box-off for third place
Turned Pro: October 2000
Significant Results: Terry McGroom W PTS 8, Sebastiaan Rothmann W PTS 10, Guillermo Jones W PTS 10, Kelvin Davis W PTS 12
Type/Style: Classy and slick, but not a big puncher
Points of Interest: 6'3" tall with an 82" reach, Steve is trained by Richie Giachetti who also trained Larry Holmes. A reformed street fighter and former sailor who worked as an aircraft refueller, he started his boxing in the Navy in 1996. The loss to Krzysztof Wlodarczyk was a split decision, with the American judge having Steve nine points in front. Has ten wins inside the distance
25.11.06 Krzysztof Wlodarczyk L PTS 12
Warsaw
(Vacant IBF Cruiserweight Title)
26.05.07 Krzysztof Wlodarczyk W PTS 12
Katowice
(IBF Cruiserweight Title Challenge)
Career: 21 contests, won 20, lost 1.

Vic (Raging Bull) Darchinyan

Australia. *Born* Vanadvor, Armenia 7 January, 1976
IBF Flyweight Champion. Former Undefeated Australian Flyweight Champion

Major Amateur Honours: Competed in the 1997 World Championships before winning a bronze medal in the 1998 European Championships. He then participated in the 2000 European Championships and was a quarter-finalist in the 2000 Olympics
Turned Pro: November 2000
Significant Results: Raul Medina W TD 8, Wandee Chor Chareon W CO 4 & W CO 5, Alejandro Montiel W PTS 10, Irene Pacheco W RSC 11, Mzukisi Sikali W RSC 8, Jair Jimenez W RSC 5, Diosdado Gabi W RSC 8, Luis Maldonado W RSC 8
Type/Style: Is a strong, aggressive southpaw and a good boxer with a hard punch in both hands
Points of Interest: 5'5" tall. His real first name is Vakhtang and he stayed and settled in Australia after representing Armenia in the Sydney Olympics. Originally trained by Jeff Fenech, but now by Billy Hussein, he won the Australian title in only his seventh fight. Next came the IBF title in December 2004, stopping the previously unbeaten Irene Pacheco, and he has made six defences. Has stopped or kayoed 22 opponents
07.10.06 Glenn Donaire W TD 6 Las Vegas
(IBF Flyweight Title Defence)
03.03.07 Victor Burgos W RSC 12 Carson
(IBF Flyweight Title Defence)
Career: 28 contests, won 28.

Chad (Bad) Dawson

Hartsville, USA. *Born* 13 July,1983
WBC L.Heavyweight Champion

Major Amateur Honours: Finished as runner up in the 1998 United States Junior Championships and collected a bronze medal in the 2000 World Junior Championships before taking the gold medal in the United States Under-19 Championships
Turned Pro: August 2001
Significant Results: Brett Lally W RSC 4, Darnell Wilson W PTS 10, Carl Daniels W RTD 7, Ian Gardner W RSC 11, Eric Harding W PTS 12
Type/Style: Tall southpaw who has a fast, hard jab and a big right cross
Points of Interest: 6'3" tall. Chad's father was a pro boxer back in the 1980s and he started boxing at the age of 11. Works as a volunteer at the local YMCA and brings his son into the ring before and after each fight. Is trained by Floyd Mayweather (senior) and has 16 wins by stoppage or kayo, but had to climb off the floor to beat Tomasz Adamek
03.02.07 Tomasz Adamek W PTS 12 Kissimmee
(WBC L.Heavyweight Title Challenge)
09.06.07 Jesus Ruiz W RSC 6 Hartford
(WBC L.Heavyweight Title Defence)
Career: 24 contests, won 24.

David Diaz

Chicago, USA. *Born* 7 June, 1976
WBC Lightweight Champion

Major Amateur Honours: Was a silver medallist in the 1992 United States Junior Olympics and in the 1995 United States Championships. A four-time winner of the Chicago Golden Gloves, he also won National Golden Gloves titles in 1993,1994 and 1996, but lost to Oktay Urkal in the 1996 Olympics. Claims 175 wins in 191 amateur contests
Turned Pro: November 1996
Significant Results: Joaquin Gallardo W PTS 8, Emmanuel Augustus W PTS 8, Ener Julio W RSC 10, Jaime Rangel W RSC 10, Kendall Holt W RSC 8, Ramazan Palyani DREW 12, Silverio Ortiz W PTS 10
Type/Style: Despite being a tough, strong, brawling southpaw, he lacks punching power
Points of Interest: 5'6" tall. Became the full WBC champion when Diego Corrales was stripped after failing to make the weight for a defence against Joel Casamayor in October last year. Was unbeaten in his first 26 fights and has stopped or kayoed 17 opponents, but was behind on all three cards before stopping Jose Armando Santa Cruz
12.08.06 Jose Armando Santa Cruz W RSC 10
Las Vegas
(WBC 'Interim' Lightweight Title Challenge)
Career: 34 contests, won 32, lost 1, drew 1.

Juan (Baby Bull) Diaz

Houston, USA. *Born* 17 September, 1983
WBA & WBO Lightweight Champion

Major Amateur Honours: As the Mexican junior and senior champion in 1999, he claims 105 wins in 110 fights, but was too young for the Sydney Olympics
Turned Pro: June 2002
Significant Results: John Bailey W RSC 7, Eleazar Contreras W PTS 10, Joel Perez W RSC 6, Martin O'Malley W CO 2, Lakva Sim W PTS 12, Julien Lorcy W PTS 12, Billy Irwin W RSC 9, Jose Miguel Cotto W PTS 12
Type/Style: A solid, busy fighter with great hand speed, Juan is developing as a puncher
Points of Interest: 5'6" tall. Started boxing when he was eight years old and became the fourth youngest fighter to win a version of the lightweight title, while still a high school student at the time he beat Lakva Sim for the title in July 2004. Now at College taking

Government studies, he is trained by ex-pro Ronnie Shields and has 16 wins by stoppage or kayo. Made four defences of his WBA title before beating Acelino Freitas to unify the WBA and WBO titles

15.07.06 Randy Suico W RSC 9 Las Vegas
(WBA Lightweight Title Defence)
04.11.06 Fernando Angulo W PTS 12 Phoenix
(WBA Lightweight Title Defence)
28.04.07 Acelino Freitas W RTD 8 Ledyard
(WBA Lightweight Title Defence. WBO Lightweight Title Challenge)
Career: 32 contests, won 32.

Julio (The Kid) Diaz
Huiquilpan, Mexico. Born 24 December, 1979
IBF Lightweight Champion

Major Amateur Honours: A silver medallist in the 1995 US Junior Olympics, he also competed in the 1998 US Championships

Turned Pro: December 1999
Significant Results: Justo Sencion W CO 9, Dario Esalas W CO 4, Angel Manfredy L PTS 12, Juan Valenzuela L CO 1, James Crayton W PTS 10, Ernesto Zepeda W RSC 7, Miguel Angel Huerta W RSC 8, Courtney Burton W RSC 11, Javier Jauregui W PTS 12, Jose Luis Castillo L RSC 10, Ricky Quiles W PTS 12
Type/Style: Is a long-limbed box-puncher with an excellent left jab who also switches. There is still a question mark over his chin
Points of Interest: 5'9" tall with a 70" reach. Elder brother Antonio lost in challenges for the WBC and WBO welterweight titles and two other brothers also boxed pro. After losses to Angel Manfredy and Juan Valenzuela, he almost gave up boxing to become a construction worker. Vacated the IBF

title to challenge Jose Luis Castillo for the WBC title in 2005, before winning the vacant IBF 'interim' title by beating Ricky Quiles in May 2006 and the full title when knocking out Jesus Chavez. Has 25 wins inside the distance

03.02.07 Jesus Chavez W CO 3 Kissimmee
(IBF Lightweight Title Challenge)
Career: 37 contests, won 34, lost 3.

Stipe (Spiderman) Drews
Makarska, Croatia. *Born* 8 June, 1973
WBA L.Heavyweight Champion.
Former Undefeated European L.Heavyweight Champion

Major Amateur Honours: Competed in the 1995 World Championships, the 1996 Olympic Games and European Championships and the 1997 World Championships. Won a silver medal in the 1997 Mediterranean Games and was six times a Croatian champion
Turned Pro: May 1999
Significant Results: Massimiliano Saiani W RSC 2, Manuel Lee Osie W PTS 12, Silvio Branco W PTS 12, Kamel Amrane W PTS 12, Konstantin Shvets W PTS 12, Paul Briggs L PTS 12, Ovill McKenzie W PTS 8, Antonio Brancalion W PTS 12, Kai Kurzawa W PTS 12
Type/Style: Is a tall, skinny southpaw with a very long reach and an awkward style
Points of Interest: 6'6" tall. In the amateurs his name was spelt Drvis but has been 'Westernised'. Worked as a car mechanic and loves surfing. Won the vacant European title by beating Silvio Branco in 2003 and made three defences before relinquishing the title. He then regained the title by beating Antonio Brancalion in January 2006 and made one further defence. Was deducted three points and floored three times in his WBC title eliminator against Paul Briggs in 2004. Is a stable mate of Felix Sturm and has stopped or kayoed 13 opponents

28.04.07 Silvio Branco W PTS 12 Oberhausen
(WBA L.Heavyweight Title Challenge)
Career: 33 contests, won 32, lost 1.

Sergei Dzindziruk
Nozewska, Ukraine. *Born* 1 March, 1976
WBO L.Middleweight Champion.
Former Undefeated European L.Middleweight Champion

Major Amateur Honours: He competed in both the 1993 European and

Juan Diaz Les Clark

1994 World Junior Championships. Despite failing at the 1996 Olympics, he went on to win a bronze medal in 1996 European Championships and silver medals in the 1997 World Championships and 1998 European Championships. Also competed in the 1998 Goodwill Games. Claims 195 wins in 220 fights

Turned Pro: February 1999

Significant Results: Ariel Chavez W RSC 7, Andrei Pestriaev W RSC 5, Mamadou Thiam W RTD 3, Hussein Bayram W CO 11, Jimmy Colas W PTS 12, Daniel Santos W PTS 12, Sebastian Lujan W PTS 12

Type/Style: A tall and lean southpaw, he is a good boxer with a hard right hook

Points of Interest: 6'0" tall. Started boxing in 1985 and is based in Germany but three of his first four pro fights were in Britain. However, his first fight, in Poland, was not sanctioned by the Polish federation and so is not included on the record given below. He won the European title by beating Mamadou Thiam in July 2004 and made two defences before landing the WBO title in December 2005 when beating Daniel Santos. Has 23 wins inside the distance, but has made just three defences in 30 months

21.10.06	Alisultan Nadirbegov W PTS 12 Halle	
	(WBO L.Middleweight Title Defence)	
19.05.07	Carlos Nascimento W RSC 11 Hamburg	
	(WBO L.Middleweight Title Defence)	

Career: 33 contests, won 33.

Zsolt (Firebird) Erdei

Budapest, Hungary. *Born* 31 May, 1974

WBO L.Heavyweight Champion

Major Amateur Honours: The European junior champion in 1992, he competed in the 1995 World Championships and 1996 Olympics and won a silver medal in the 1996 European Championships. He went on to win gold medals in the 1997 World Championship, the 1998 and 2000 European Championships and a bronze medal in the 2000 Olympics

Turned Pro: December 2000

Significant Results: Jim Murray W CO 5, Juan Carlos Gimenez W RSC 8, Massimiliano Saiani W RSC 7, Julio Gonzalez W PTS 12, Hugo Garay W PTS 12 (twice), Alejandro Lakatus W PTS 12, Mehdi Sahnoune W RSC 12, Paul Murdoch W RSC 10

Type/Style: Although an excellent, clever technical craftsman and quick combination puncher with a strong, accurate jab, he is not a puncher

Points of Interest: 5' 10" tall with a 72" reach. Based in Germany, in beating Julio Gonzalez in January 2004 he brought the WBO title back to his stable after fellow Universum fighter, Dariusz Michalczewski, had lost it to the same fighter. Floored twice in early fights, he has 17 wins inside the distance and has made eight defences

29.07.06	Thomas Ulrich W PTS 12 Oberhausen	
	(WBO L.Heavyweight Title Defence)	
27.01.07	Danny Santiago W RSC 8 Dusseldorf	
	(WBO L.Heavyweight Title Defence)	
16.06.07	George Blades W RSC 11 Budapest	
	(WBO L.Heavyweight Title Defence)	

Career: 27 contests, won 27.

Mzonke (The Rose of Khayelitsha) Fana

Cape Town, South Africa. *Born* 29 October, 1973

IBF S.Featherweight Champion. Former Undefeated South African S.Featherweight Champion

Major Amateur Honours: None known

Turned Pro: March 1994

Significant Results: Mkhuseli Kondile L PTS 12, Matthews Zulu W PTS 12, Dean Pithie L PTS 12, Irvin Buhalu W PTS 12 (twice), Patrick Malinga W RSC 2, Ali Funeka W PTS 12, Yuri Voronin W PTS 10, Randy Suico W PTS 12, Marco Antonio Barrera L CO 2,

Type/Style: Recognised as a good counter puncher with an excellent left jab and plenty of stamina, but not as a hitter

Points of Interest: 5'7" tall with a 70" reach. His father was a policeman and for many years after he started boxing lived in an old shack. He made 11 defences of his South African super-featherweight title, but had to climb off the floor twice for his win over Randy Suico. Has won only nine times inside the distance

08.12.06	Roberto David Arrieta W PTS 12 Johannesburg	
20.04.07	Malcolm Klassen W PTS 12 Khayelitsha	
	(IBF S.Featherweight Title Challenge)	

Career: 29 contests, won 26, lost 3.

Jhonny Gonzalez

Pachuca, Mexico. *Born* 15 September, 1980

WBO Bantamweight Champion

Former Undefeated Mexican Bantamweight Champion

Major Amateur Honours: Won a bronze medal in the Pan-American Championships in 1997 and was Mexican champion three times

Turned Pro: August 1999

Significant Results: Saul Briseno W RSC 8, Ablorh Sowah W RSC 10, Ricardo Vargas L PTS 10 & L TD 7, Francisco Mateos W RSC 1, Diego Andrade W RSC 1, Francisco Tejedor W RSC 1, Hugo Vargas W CO 3, Gabriel Elizondo W RSC 2, Adonis Rivas W PTS 12, Trini Mendoza W RSC 4, Ratanchai Sorvoraphin W RSC 7, Mark Johnson W CO 8, Fernando Montiel W PTS 12

Type/Style: Although not a stylish boxer, he is a tough, rangy fighter and a very hard puncher

Points of Interest: 5' 7" tall. The spelling of his Christian name is due to his father, who was also a pro boxer, recording the name wrongly when obtaining the birth certificate. His first defence was supposed to be against Marc Johnson, but when the latter failed to make the weight their contest went on as a non-title fight. Lost his first two professional fights, but has 29 wins by kayo or stoppage and is trained by former pro, Miguel Angel 'Raton' Gonzalez

16.09.06	Israel Vazquez L RSC 10 Las Vegas	
	(WBC S.Bantamweight Title Challenge)	
30.03.07	Irene Pacheco W RSC 9 Tucson	
	(WBO Bantamweight Title Defence)	

Career: 39 contests, won 34, lost 5.

Robert (The Ghost) Guerrero

Gilroy, USA. *Born* 27 March,1983

IBF Featherweight Champion

Major Amateur Honours: Won a gold medal in the 1998 United States Junior Championships and a bronze medal in the 1999 PAL Tournament and United States Championships. Competed in the United States trials for the 2000 Olympics

Turned Pro: April 2001

Significant Results: Marcos Badillo W PTS 6, Enrique Sanchez W RSC 8, Cesar Figueroa W CO 4, Adrian Valdez W RSC 12, Gamaliel Diaz L PTS 12 & W CO 6, Sandro Marcos W RSC 3

Type/Style: Is a tall, skinny southpaw

Points of Interest: 5'10" tall. His father was twice San Francisco Golden Gloves champion and Robert started boxing when he was just nine years old, being only 16 when competing in the 2000 Olympic trials. Although Orlando Salido was declared the winner of their IBF title fight he tested positive for Nandrolone and was stripped. Following that, the title was declared vacant. Robert then regained his old crown in Copenhagen, Denmark, in what was his first fight outside the United States as a professional. Has 13 wins by stoppage or kayo

02.09.06 Eric Aiken W RTD 8 Los Angeles
            (IBF Featherweight Title Challenge)
04.11.06 Orlando Salido L PTS 12 Las Vegas
            (IBF Featherweight Title Defence)
23.02.07 Spend Abazi W RTD 8 Copenhagen
            (Vacant IBF Featherweight Title)
Career: 23 contests, won 20, lost 2, drew 1.

Joan (Sycuan Warrior) Guzman

Santo Domingo, Dominican Republic. *Born* 1 May, 1976
WBO S.Featherweight Champion. Former Undefeated WBO S.Bantamweight Champion. Former Undefeated Dominican Featherweight and S.Bantamweight Champion

Major Amateur Honours: Won a gold medal in the 1995 Pan-American Games and competed in the 1996 Olympics. Was a three-time Central American champion and claims 310 wins and just 10 losses
Turned Pro: September 1997
Significant Results: Francisco de Leon W CO 11, Hector Avila W CO 2, Edgar Ruiz W PTS 12, Fabio Oliva W CO 3, Jorge Monsalvo W CO 1, Agapito Sanchez W RSC 7, Fernando Beltran W PTS 12, Terdsak Jandaeng W PTS 12, Javier Jauregui W PTS 10
Type/Style: Compact and powerful, he is a short-armed fighter with good movement and a strong body puncher who could be a star of the future if more active
Points of Interest: 5'7" tall. Having changed his nickname from 'Little Tyson', he started boxing at the age of eight. Won the vacant WBO title in Cardiff in August 2002 by knocking out Fabio Oliva. Due to contract problems and postponed title fights he made only two defences in three years. He then relinquished the super-bantamweight title in 2005 and jumped two divisions to super-featherweight. The WBO title became vacant after Jorge Barrios failed to make the weight for his defence

against Joan, but when the fight went ahead the latter won recognition as champion by winning. Managed by the Sycuan Native American group, he lost to current WBO flyweight champion Omar Narvaez in the 1996 Olympics. Has 17 wins inside the distance, but his last six wins have all been on points

16.09.06 Jorge Barrios W PTS 12 Las Vegas
18.12.06 Antonio Davis W PTS 12 Santo Domingo
            (WBO S.Featherweight Title Defence)
Career: 27 contests, won 27.

Hozumi Hasegawa

Nishiwaki City. Japan. *Born* 16 December, 1980
WBC Bantamweight Champion

Major Amateur Honours: None known
Turned Pro: November 1999
Significant Results: Jess Maca W PTS 12, Gunao Uno W PTS 12, Alvin Felisilda W CO 10, Jun Toriumi W PTS 10, Veerapol Sahaprom W PTS 12 (twice), Gerard Martinez W RSC 7
Type/ Style: He is a tall, fast and stylish southpaw who utilises a counter-punching style
Points of Interest: 5'5" tall. With only seven wins inside the distance, he was once known as the 'Japanese Pernell Whittaker' due to his boxing skills. Lost two of his first five fights but is now unbeaten in 19 bouts and Veerapol Sahaprom had not tasted defeat in his previous 45 fights before Hozumi beat him for the WBC title in April 2005. He has since made four defences

13.11.06 Genaro Garcia W PTS 12 Tokyo
            (WBO Bantamweight Title Defence)
03.05.07 Simpiwe Vetyeka W PTS 12 Tokyo
            (WBO Bantamweight Title Defence)
Career: 24 contests, won 22, lost 2.

Sultan (The Russian Bomber) Ibragimov

Tlyarata, Russia. *Born* 8 March, 1975
WBO Heavyweight Champion

Major Amateur Honours: Won a gold medal in the Four-Nations Championships in Moscow in 2000. In the same year he won silver medals in the European Championships, losing to Jackson Chanet on disqualification in the final, and the Olympic Games, where he beat Chanet but lost to Felix Savon in the final. Was Russian champion in 1999 and 2001
Turned Pro: May 2002
Significant Results: James Walton

W RSC 6, Al Cole W RSC 3, Zuri Lawrence W RSC 11, Friday Ahunanya W TD 9, Lance Whitaker W RSC 7
Type/Style: Aggressive two-fisted southpaw
Points of Interest: 6'2" tall. He turned pro in the United States and is trained by Jeff Mayweather, the brother of Roger Mayweather. Started boxing at the age of 17 and has 17 wins inside the distance, eight of which have come in the first round, but had to climb off the floor to get a draw with Ray Austin. His cousin Timur Ibragimov is also a pro heavyweight

28.07.06 Ray Austin DREW 12 Hollywood
10.03.07 Javier Mora W RSC 1 New York
02.06.07 Shannon Briggs W PTS 12 Atlantic City
            (WBO Heavyweight Title Challenge)
Career: 22 contests, won 21, drew 1.

Chris (The Smiling Dragon) John

Semarang, Indonesia. *Born* 4 September, 1981
WBA Featherweight Champion. Former Undefeated Indonesian Featherweight Champion

Major Amateur Honours: None known
Turned Pro: June 1998
Significant Results: Ratanchai Sorvoraphin W PTS 10, Oscar Leon W PTS 10, Osamu Sato W PTS 12, Jose Rojas TD 4, Derrick Gainer W PTS 12, Tommy Browne W RTD 9, Juan Manuel Marquez W PTS 12
Type/Style: Is a tall, switch-hitting counter-puncher with good footwork
Points of Interest: 5' 7½" tall with a 65" reach. Christened Johannes Christian John, his original nickname was 'Thin Man', which he took as a tribute to Alexis Arguello before eventually deciding that it was no longer suitable for his improved muscular build. His father was a former amateur boxer and Chris has been boxing since he was six, originally training in a garage before being based in a gym in Australia. Is also an international standard competitor at martial arts, winning a gold medal in the South-East Asia Games in 1997. He won the vacant WBA 'interim' title in September 2003 on beating Oscar Leon, and made three defences until he was recognised as full champion when Juan Manuel Marquez was stripped of the title. Has 20 wins inside the distance

09.09.06 Renan Acosta W PTS 12 Jakarta
            (WBA Featherweight Title Defence)

03.03.07 Jose Rojas W PTS 12 Jakarta
(WBA Featherweight Title Defence)
Career: 40 contests, won 39, drew 1.

Koki (Baby) Kameda

Osaka, Japan. *Born* 17 November, 1986
Former Undefeated WBA L.Flyweight Champion. Former Undefeated Orient & Pacific Flyweight Champion
Major Amateur Honours: None known. He had only 17 amateur fights, winning 16
Turned Pro: December 2003
Significant Results: Saman Sorjaturong W CO 1, Wanmeechok Singwangcha W RSC 3, Nohel Arambulet W RTD 7, Carlos Bouchan W CO 6, Carlos Fajardo W RSC 2
Type/Style: Utilises a swarming peek-a-boo style from his southpaw stance and hits hard with both hands
Points of Interest: A flamboyant, shaven-headed mouthy personality, he is the hottest property in Japanese boxing with his title win over Juan Jose Landaeta drawing a TV audience of over 60 million. Koki is one of the three fighting brothers all trained by his father, and his younger brother Daiki, a world rated flyweight, is equally as talented and flamboyant. Turned pro at the age of 17, competing in ten-round bouts by his fourth contest, and had beaten two former world champions, Saman Sorjaturong and Nohel Arambulet, inside the distance in his first nine fights. Having started as a flyweight, his title winning effort against Landaeta was his first fight at light-flyweight. With this victory he became one of only three Japanese fighters to win a world title before their 20th birthday. He relinquished the title in January due to weight problems and moved up to flyweight
02.08.06 Juan Jose Landaeta W PTS 12 Yokohama
(Vacant WBA L.Flyweight Title)
20.12.06 Juan Jose Landaeta W PTS 12 Tokyo
(WBA L.Flyweight Title Defence)
24.03.07 Everardo Morales W PTS 10 Tokyo
23.05.07 Irfan Ogah W RSC 8 Osaka
Career: 15 contests, won 15.

Mikkel (Viking Warrior) Kessler

Copenhagen, Denmark. *Born* 1 March, 1979
WBA & WBC S.Middleweight Champion
Major Amateur Honours: Was the European junior champion in 1996 and the Danish junior champion in 1996 and 1997
Turned Pro: March 1998
Significant Results: Elicier Julio W CO 3, Manny Sobral W RTD 5, Dingaan Thobela W PTS 12, Henry Porras W RSC 9, Julio Cesar Green W CO 1, Andre Thysse W PTS 12, Manny Siaca W RTD 7, Anthony Mundine W PTS 12, Eric Lucas W RSC 10
Type/Style: A tall, strong, quality box fighter with a good jab, he has been unfortunate to have been troubled by hand injuries in the past
Points of Interest: 6'1" tall with a 73" reach. Heavily tattooed, he came in against Manny Siaca in November 2004 for the title as a late substitute when Mads Larsen dropped out and made the most of his opportunity. He made two defences of his WBA title before adding the WBC title to his collection and has 29 wins by stoppage or kayo. Is managed by Team Palle and was voted the Danish 'Fighter of the Year' for 2004
14.10.06 Markus Beyer W CO 3 Copenhagen
(WBA S.Middleweight Title Defence. WBC S.Middleweight Title Challenge)
24.03.07 Librado Andrade W PTS 12 Copenhagen
(WBA & WBC S.Middleweight Title Defences)
Career: 39 contests, won 39.

Malcolm (Stone) Klassen

Toekumsrus, South Africa. *Born* 12 March, 1981
Former IBF S.Featherweight Champion. Former Undefeated South African Featherweight Champion
Major Amateur Honours: None known
Turned Pro: May 1999
Significant Results: Takalani Ndlovu L PTS 6, Harry Ramogoadi L PTS 6, Jeff Mathebula DREW 6, Edward Mpofu W PTS 12, Lindile Tyhali W RSC 3, Willie Mabasa W PTS 12
Type/Style: Is a slick boxer with outstanding hand speed and the best jab in South African boxing
Points of Interest: When he started out as a pro he won only three of his first six fights, having boxed at super-featherweight and even as low as super-bantam. Won the South African featherweight title when beating Edward Mpofu in August 2005 and made three defences before moving up a weight to win the IBF title in the higher division. Has ten wins inside the distance and was voted South African 'Boxer of the Year' for 2006
28.07.06 Momwabesi Mbilase W RSC 4 Johannesburg
(South African Featherweight Title Defence)
04.11.06 Gairy St Clair W PTS 12 Johannesburg
(IBF S.Featherweight Title Challenge)
20.04.07 Mzonke Fana L PTS 12 Khayelitsha
(IBF S.Featherweight Title Defence)
Career: 25 contests, won 19, lost 4, drew 2.

Vladimir Klitschko

Kiev, Ukraine. *Born* 25 March, 1976
IBF Heavyweight Champion. Former WBO Heavyweight Champion. Former Undefeated European Heavyweight Champion
Major Amateur Honours: Having won a gold medal in the 1993 European Junior Championships, a year later he took silver medals in the 1994 World Junior Championships and World Military Championships. He then went one better in the 1995 World Military Championship when winning the gold medal and in 1996 he was the runner-up in the European Championships, prior to picking up a gold medal in the Olympics
Turned Pro: November 1996
Significant Results: Ross Puritty L RSC 11, Axel Schulz W RSC 8, Chris Byrd W PTS 12 & W RSC 7, Frans Botha W RSC 8, Ray Mercer W RSC 6, Jameel McCline W RSC 10, Corrie Sanders L RSC 2, Lamon Brewster L RSC 5, DaVarryl Williamson W TD 5, Eliseo Castillo W RSC 4, Samuel Peter W PTS 12
Type/Style: Although he has a mechanical jab and cross approach, his reach and punching power makes him a difficult opponent. Regardless of him being a champion there are still some questions over his stamina and chin
Points of Interest: 6'6" tall. Despite losing his first amateur fight he was not deterred and has 43 wins inside the distance as a pro. After winning the European title by beating Axel Schulz in September 1999 he made only one defence before handing in his belt and going on to win the WBO title when outpointing Chris Byrd in October 2000. He made five defences before dropping the title in a shock stoppage loss to Corrie Sanders in March 2003. The younger brother of the former WBO and WBC champion, Vitali, he was then stopped by Lamon Brewster

in a fight for the vacant WBO title in April 2004. Now self managed, he won the IBF title by beating Chris Byrd in April 2006 and has made two defences

11.11.06 Calvin Brock W RSC 7 New York City
(IBF Heavyweight Title Defence)
10.03.07 Ray Austin W RSC 2 Mannheim
(IBF Heavyweight Title Defence)
Career: 51 contests, won 48, lost 3.

Eagle Kyowa

Pichit, Thailand. *Born* 4 December, 1978

WBC M.Flyweight Champion
Major Amateur Honours: None known
Turned Pro: January 2000
Significant Results: Nico Thomas W CO 3, Noel Tunacao W PTS 10, Elmer Gejon W PTS 8, Jose Antonio Aguirre W PTS 12, Satoshi Kogumazaka W TD 8, Isaac Bustos L RSC 4, Katsunari Takayama W PTS 12, Ken Nakajima W RSC 7, Rodel Mayol W PTS 12
Type/Style: Short, sturdy and orthodox, he is a good boxer who lacks a big punch
Points of Interest: 5' 3½" tall. A Thai based in Japan, his real name is Den Junlaphan, but he has also boxed as Den Sorjaturong and Eagle Okuda and is now boxing under the name of his current sponsor 'Kyowa' after falling out with his previous sponsor. Starting as a pro in Thailand, he was fighting over ten rounds by his third fight and moved his base to Japan after only five fights. Having won the WBC title by beating Jose Antonio Aguirre in January 2004, he then lost it to Isaac Bustos in his second defence in December 2004 after suffering an injury to his arm. Regained the title by outpointing Katsunari Takayama in August 2005 and has made four further defences, but was on the floor twice in the fight with Lorenzo Trejo. Married to a former boxer, he has won only five fights by stoppage or kayo

13.11.06 Lorenzo Trejo W PTS 12 Tokyo
(WBC M.Flyweight Title Defence)
04.06.07 Akira Yaegashi W PTS 12 Yokohama
(WBC M.Flyweight Title Defence)
Career: 19 contests, won 18, lost 1.

Rodolfo (Rudy) Lopez

Cancun, Mexico. *Born* 18 September, 1983

Former WBC Featherweight Champion
Major Amateur Honours: None known
Turned Pro: October 2000

Significant Results: Tommy Browne L PTS 10, Jesus Perez W CO 4, Humberto Martinez W CO 6, Freddy Blandon W CO 10 (twice), Carlos Garcia L CO 4
Type/Style: Is a stylish box-puncher who sometimes switches to southpaw and has good stamina but not a great chin
Points of Interest: 5'7" tall. Managed and trained by Marco Antonio Barrera, his brother Jorge is also a pro. Had done most of his fighting on the Yucatan Peninsula circuit, being kayoed by Carlos Garcia in a challenge for the Mexican featherweight title only two fights before challenging Takashi Koshimoto for the WBC crown, so his win was a huge upset and he has slipped badly since that peak. Has 13 wins inside the distance

30.07.06 Takashi Koshimoto W RSC 7 Fukuoka
(WBC Featherweight Title Challenge
17.12.06 In-Jin Chi L PTS 12 Seoul
(WBC Featherweight Title Defence)
31.03.07 Naoki Matsuda L CO 5 Cancun
Career: 24 contests, won 19, lost 4, drew 1.

Paul (Magic Man) Malignaggi

Brooklyn, USA. *Born* 23 November, 1980

IBF L.Welterweight Champion
Major Amateur Achievements: Won a gold medal in the 1998 New York Golden Gloves novice category and a silver medal in the 2000 New York Golden Gloves senior division. Having taken a bronze medal in the 2000 PAL Championships, he then failed to win a medal in the 2000 National Golden Gloves. Paul put this right in 2001 when he won the gold medal at the United States Championships
Turned Pro: July 2001
Significant Results: Ray Martinez W PTS 10, Sandro Casamonica W TD 7, Jeremy Yelton W PTS 8, Donald Camarena W PTS 10, Miguel Cotto L PTS 12
Type/Style: Speedy, skilful boxer with a great jab but no real punching power
Points of Interest: 5'8½" tall. Is managed by Lou DiBella and trained by Buddy McGirt, who once held the same IBF title. His parents were Sicilian immigrants, but his father abandoned the family when Paul was six. Plagued by hand trouble until he had an operation in 2005, he climbed off the floor and overcame a fractured orbital eye socket to last the distance

in a challenge to Miguel Cotto for the WBO light-welterweight title in June 2006. With just five wins by stoppage or kayo, he continues to work as a Telemarketer

17.02.07 Edner Cherry W PTS 12 New York
16.06.07 Lovemore Ndou W PTS 12 Uncasville
(IBF L.Welterweight Title Challenge)
Career: 24 contests, won 23, lost 1.

Antonio Margarito

Tijuana, Mexico. *Born* 18 March, 1978
WBO Welterweight Champion
Major Amateur Honours: None known, but he claims 18 wins in 23 contests
Turned Pro: January 1994
Significant Results: Larry Dixon L PTS 10, Rodney Jones L PTS 10, Alfred Ankamah W CO 4, Danny Perez W PTS 8 & W PTS 12, David Kamau W CO 2, Frankie Randall W RSC 4, Daniel Santos NC 1 & L TD 9, Antonio Diaz W RSC 10, Andrew Lewis W RSC 2, Hercules Kyvelos W RSC 2, Sebastien Lujan W RSC 10, Kermit Cintron W RSC 5
Type/Style: Is a tall, strong, aggressive banger. Although a bit one-paced, he has a good jab and a strong chin
Points of Interest: 6'0" tall. Having turned pro at the age of 15 and suffering three early defeats, his first fight with Daniel Santos for the WBO welterweight was stopped and declared a no-contest due to Antonio suffering a bad cut. When Santos handed in the belt, Antonio won the vacant title by beating Antonio Diaz in March 2002. His challenge against Santos for the WBO light-middleweight title also went to a technical decision due to a cut. Has made seven defences and has 24 wins inside the distance

02.12.06 Joshua Clottey W PTS 12 Atlantic City
(WBO Welterweight Title Defence)
Career: 39 contests, won 34, lost 4, no contests 1.

Juan Manuel (Dinamita) Marquez

Mexico City, Mexico. *Born* 23 August, 1973

WBC S.Featherweight Champion.
Former Undefeated IBF, WBA & WBO Featherweight Champion
Major Amateur Honours: None known, but claims 32 wins in 33 bouts
Turned Pro: May 1993
Significant Results: Julian Wheeler W RSC 10, Julio Gervacio W CO 10, Agapito Sanchez W PTS 12, Alfred Kotey W PTS 12, Freddy Norwood

L PTS 12, Daniel Jimenez W RTD 7, Julio Gamboa W RTD 6, Robbie Peden W RSC 10, Manuel Medina W RSC 7, Derrick Gainer W TD 7, Manny Pacquiao DREW 12, Orlando Salido W PTS 12, Victor Polo W PTS 12, Chris John L PTS 12

Type/Style: Is a solid, compact stylist and a hard puncher with either hand

Points of Interest: 5'7" tall. Having originally studied to be an accountant, his father boxed as a pro and he is the elder brother of the former undefeated IBF bantamweight champion and current WBC super-bantamweight champion, Rafael Marquez. Started boxing at the age of 12 and lost his first pro fight on a disqualification. Was defeated by Freddy Norwood in a challenge for the WBA title in September 1999, but then won the IBF title by beating Manuel Medina in February 2003. Never lost either title in the ring, being stripped of the IBF title and then losing WBA recognition because he was no longer a double or 'super' champion. Failed in a challenge for his old WBA title when losing on points to Chris John in Indonesia in March 2006 and then won the 'interim' WBO featherweight crown by beating Terdsak Jandaeng before becoming the full champion when Scott Harrison was stripped. With 33 wins by stoppage or kayo, he was floored three times in the first round of his fight with Manny Pacquiao in May 2004

05.08.06 Terdsak Jandaeng W RSC 7 Stateline
(Vacant WBO 'Interim' Featherweight Title)
25.11.06 Jimrex Jaca W CO 9 Hidalgo
(WBO 'Interim' Featherweight Title Defence)
17.03.07 Marco Antonio Barrera W PTS 12 Las Vegas
(WBC S.Featherweight Title Challenge)
Career: 51contests, won 47, drew 1, lost 3.

Rafael Marquez

Mexico City, Mexico. *Born* 25 March, 1975

WBC S.Bantamweight Champion. Former Undefeated IBF Bantamweight Champion

Major Amateur Honours: None known, but claims only one loss in 57 fights

Turned Pro: September 1995

Significant Results: Victor Rabanales L CO 8, Francisco Mateos L RSC 3, Tomas Rivera W CO 2, Genaro Garcia L RSC 2, Aquiles Guzman W RSC 7,

Gerardo Espinoza W RSC 4, Mark Johnson W PTS 10 & W RSC 8, Tim Austin W RSC 8, Mauricio Pastrana W PTS 12 & W RSC 3, Peter Frissina W RSC 2, Heriberto Ruiz W CO 3, Ricardo Vargas W PTS 12

Type/Style: A compact and solid fighter, he is a big puncher with the right hand. However, his defence is not too sound

Points of Interest: 5'5" tall. Lost his first pro fight against Victor Rabanales, who was a former WBC bantamweight champion with more than 50 fights to his name at the time. Rafael eventually won the IBF title by stopping Tim Austin in February 2003, just two weeks after his brother Juan Manuel Marquez won the IBF featherweight title. Their father, also Rafael, was a pro in the 1950s. With 33 wins by the short route and all of his losses also coming inside the distance, he is trained by the top Mexican, Nacho Beristan. He made five defences of his IBF bantamweight crown before moving up to win the WBC title at super-bantamweight

05.08.06 Silence Mabuza W RTD 9 Stateline
(IBF Bantamweight Title Defence)
03.03.07 Israel Vazquez W RTD 7 Carson
(WBC S.Bantamweight Title Challenge)
Career: 39 contests, won 36, lost 3.

Oleg (The Big O) Maskaev

Zhambul, Kazakhstan. *Born* 2 March, 1969

WBC Heavyweight Champion

Amateur Honours: A former Russian champion, he won a gold medal in the 1990 Russian Army Championships and World Military Championships and competed in the 1993 World Championships. Collected a gold medal again in the 1994 Asian Championships and finished runner-up in the 1994 World Cup

Turned Pro: April 1993

Significant Results: Alex Miroshnichenko W CO 3, Oliver McCall L RSC 1, David Tua L RSC 11, Alex Stewart W RSC 7, Courage Tshabalala W RSC 9, Hasim Rahman W CO 8, Derrick Jefferson W RSC 4, Kirk Johnson L CO 4, Lance Whitaker L CO 2, Corrie Sanders L RSC 8, Julius Francis W RSC 2, David Defiagbon W PTS 10, Sinan Samil Sam W PTS 12

Type/Style: Big and upright, he is a strong fighter. A fair puncher but obviously vulnerable as all of his losses have come inside the distance

Points of Interest: 6'3" tall. He was born in Kazakhstan but to Russian parents and worked on the family farm and in the coal mines before joining the Russian Army and rising to the rank of Lieutenant It was in the Army where he started boxing and included in his list of victims was Vitali Klitschko, whom he stopped inside a round. Married with four children, there are some doubts over whether his 1993 fight with Alex Miroshnichenko, who was then unbeaten in 21 pro fights, should be counted as he continued to fight as an amateur after this. Now has dual United States and Russian citizenship. Has 26 wins by stoppage or kayo and is unbeaten since 2002

12.08.06 Hasim Rahman W RSC 12 Las Vegas
(WBC Heavyweight Title Challenge)
10.12.06 Peter Okhello W PTS 12 Moscow
(WBC Heavyweight Title Defence)
Career: 39 contests, won 34, lost 5.

Floyd (Little Stone) Mayweather

Grand Rapids, USA. *Born* 24 February, 1977

WBC Welterweight Champion. Former Undefeated WBC L.Middleweight Champion. Former Undefeated IBF Welterweight Champion. Former Undefeated WBC L.Welterweight Champion. Former Undefeated WBC Lightweight Champion. Former Undefeated WBC S.Featherweight Champion

Major Amateur Honours: A National Golden Gloves champion in 1993, 1994 and 1996, and US champion in 1995, with that first NGG title being at 106lbs. Competed in the 1995 World Championships and won a bronze medal in the 1996 Olympics. Won 84 of 90 fights

Turned Pro: October 1996

Significant Results: Genaro Hernandez W RTD 8, Angel Manfredy W RSC 2, Carlos Rios W PTS 12, Justin Juuko W RSC 9, Carlos Gerena W RTD 7, Gregorio Vargas W PTS 12, Diego Corrales W RSC 10, Carlos Hernandez W PTS 12, Jesus Chavez W RTD 9, Jose Luis Castillo W PTS 12 (twice), Victoriano Sosa W PTS 12, Phillip Ndou W RSC 7, DeMarcus Corley W PTS 12, Henry Bruseles W RSC 8, Arturo Gatti W RSC 6, Sharmba Mitchell W RSC 6, Zab Judah W PTS 12

Type/Style: Is a talented, flashy fighter

with fast hands, great reflexes and a hard punch

Points of Interest: 5'8" tall with a 72" reach. Floyd's father, also named Floyd, was a good professional and Floyd's uncle, Roger, was WBA super-featherweight and WBC light-welterweight champion and trains Oscar De La Hoya, so boxing is well and truly in the blood. He won the WBC super-featherweight title in October 1998, beating Genaro Hernandez, and made eight defences prior to winning the WBC lightweight title when defeating Jose Luis Castillo in April 2002. Floyd then made two defences before moving up to win the light-welterweight title from Arturo Gatti in June 2005. Not making a defence he moved up again to beat Zab Judah in April 2006 for the IBF welterweight title, although he was lucky not to be disqualified when his trainer climbed into the ring during one of the rounds. Again not making a defence, he went on to win the WBC welterweight and light-middleweight titles to make himself a five-division champion. Has 24 wins by stoppage or kayo

04.11.06 Carlos Baldomir W PTS 12 Las Vegas
             (WBC Welterweight Title Challenge)
05.05.07 Oscar de la Hoya W PTS 12 Las Vegas
             (WBC L.Middleweight Title Challenge)
Career: 38 contests, won 38.

Floyd Mayweather   Les Clark

Souleymane (The Sensation) M'Baye
Clichy, France. *Born* 21 March, 1975
WBA L.Welterweight Champion.
Former Undefeated European & French L.Welterweight Champion
Major Amateur Honours: No major

honours, but he competed in the French Amateur Championships in 1996 and 1997. In 1997 he represented France in international tournaments and also competed in the World Military Championships that year. Claims a 30-5 record
Turned Pro: November 1998
Significant Results: Christophe Carlier W PTS 6, Alan Temple W RTD 7, Nordine Mouchi W PTS 10, Frederic Tripp W PTS 10, Jurgen Hack W RSC 2, Khalid Rahilou W PTS 10, Vivian Harris L PTS 12, Andreas Kotelnik W PTS 12
Type/Style: Tall and slim, he is a long-armed combination puncher with fast hands and a fluid style
Points of Interest: Born to Senegalese parents he is a former member of the French Military and was a European champion at both kick-boxing and savate before turning to boxing. Still working for the Municipal Sports Department, he won the vacant European title by beating Jurgen Haeck in January 2002 but was unsuccessful in a challenge for the WBA title against Vivian Harris in July 2003. Has 20 wins inside the distance, but was almost stopped in the first round of his title win over Raul Balbi

08.07.06 Lazlo Komjathi W RTD 4 Cardiff
02.09.06 Raul Balbi W RSC 4 Bolton
             (Vacant WBA L.Welterweight Title)
10.03.07 Andreas Kotelnik DREW 12 Liverpool
             (WBA L.Welterweight Title Defence)
Career: 37 contests, won 35, lost 1, drew 1.

Christian Mijares
Gomez Palacio, Mexico. *Born* 2 October, 1981
WBC S.Flyweight Champion. Former Undefeated Mexican S.Flyweight Champion
Major Amateur Honours: None known
Turned Pro: August 1997
Significant Results: Tomas Rojas W PTS 12, Gerson Guerrero W RSC 8, Alimi Goitia W RSC 3, Luis Maldonado DREW 12
Type/Style: Lanky, fast, accurate, busy southpaw and an excellent tactical boxer
Points of Interest: 5'6" tall. Trained by his uncle, Vicente Saldivar Mijares, who lost to Esteban DeJesus in a challenge for the WBC lightweight title in 1977, Christian had never fought outside Mexico until he climbed off the floor to beat Katsushige Kawashima

for the vacant WBC 'interim' title. The fight with Reynaldo Lopez was a defence of the 'interim' title and he was recognised as full champion when reigning champion Masamori Tokuyama retired. Has 12 wins inside the distance and is unbeaten since July 2002

18.09.06 Katsushige Kawashima W PTS 12 Yokohama
             (Vacant WBC 'Interim' S.Flyweight Title)
17.11.06 Reynaldo Lopez W PTS 12 Torreon
             (WBC 'Interim' S.Flyweight Title Defence)
03.01.07 Katsushige Kawashima W RSC 10 Tokyo
             (WBC S.Flyweight Title Defence)
14.04.07 Jorge Arce W PTS 12 San Antonio
             (WBC S.Flyweight Title Defence)
Career: 36 contests, won 31, lost 3, drew 2.

Steve Molitor   Les Clark

Steve (The Canadian Kid) Molitor
Sarnia, Canada. *Born* 4 April, 1980
IBF S.Bantamweight Champion.
Former Undefeated Commonwealth Bantamweight Champion
Major Amateur Honours: The Canadian national champion at flyweight in 1999, he competed in the 1998 Americas Championships, the 1999 Pan-American Games and 1999 World Championships, where he lost to the current WBO flyweight champion, Omar Narvaez
Turned Pro: May 2000
Significant Results: Scotty Olson W RSC 5, Nicky Booth W PTS 12, Julio Coronel W PTS 10, John MacKay W PTS 8, Hugo Dianzo W PTS 12, Debind Thapa W RSC 8
Type/Style: Is a tall, skinny southpaw who is a cool, slick and clever boxer
Points of Interest: 5'7" tall. Was

inactive for over a year before beating Michael Hunter, partially due to Gabula Vabaza failing a medical when he and Steve were scheduled to fight for the vacant title in South Africa. His brother Johnny was also an outstanding boxer but has finished up in jail. He is trained by ex-pro, Chris Johnson, who won a bronze medal in the 1992 Olympics, and he has nine wins inside the distance

10.11.06 Michael Hunter W CO 5 Hartlepool
(Vacant IBF S.Bantamweight Title)
Career: 23 contests, won 23.

Fernando (Cochulito) Montiel

Los Mochis, Mexico. *Born* 1 March, 1979
WBO S.Flyweight Champion.
Former Undefeated WBO Flyweight Champion
Major Amateur Honours: Claiming 33 wins in 36 fights, he was a local Golden Gloves champion.
Turned Pro: December 1996
Significant Results: Paulino Villalobos DREW 10 & W PTS 10, Sergio Millan W PTS 10, Cruz Carbajal W RSC 4, Isidro Garcia W RSC 7, Zoltan Lunka W RSC 7, Juan Domingo Cordoba W CO 1, Jose Lopez W PTS 12, Pedro Alcazar W RSC 6, Roy Doliguez W RSC 3, Mark Johnson L PTS 12, Reynaldo Hurtado W CO 7, Ivan Hernandez W RSC 7, Evert Briceno W PTS 12, Pramuansak Posuwan W PTS 12, Jhonny Gonzalez L PTS 12
Type/ Style: Clever and stylish, he has a good uppercut
Points of Interest: 5'4" tall. The youngest of a fighting family, his father and four brothers all being boxers, he won his first 11 bouts inside the distance. Jointly trained by his father Manuel and a Japanese trainer based in Mexico, Fernando has 24 wins by knockout or stoppage. He won the WBO title, stopping Isidro Garcia in December 2000, and made three defences before moving up to win the super-flyweight title when beating Pedro Alcazar in June 2002. Sadly, Alcazar collapsed and died after the fight. Having lost the title in his second defence to Mark Johnson in August 2003, Fernando came back to regain the title by stopping Ivan Hernandez in April 2005 and made two defences before an unsuccessful challenge for the WBO bantamweight title against Jhonny Gonzalez in May 2006

24.02.07 Z Gorres W PTS 12 Cebu City
(WBO S.Flyweight Title Defence)
Career: 36 contests, won 33, drew 1, lost 2.

Fernando Montiel

Jean-Marc Mormeck

Pointe-A-Pitre, Guadeloupe. *Born* 3 June, 1972
WBA & WBC Cruiserweight Champion. Former Undefeated French L.Heavyweight Champion
Major Amateur Honours: None. Claims 13 wins in 15 fights
Turned Pro: March 1995
Significant Results: Lee Manuel Osie L PTS 4, Alain Simon W PTS 10, Pascual Warusfel W PTS 10, Valery Vikhor W RSC 3, Virgil Hill W RTD 8, Dale Brown W RSC 8, Alexander Gurov W RSC 8, Wayne Braithwaite W PTS 12, O'Neil Bell L RSC 10
Type/Style: Is a strong, stocky, aggressive pressure fighter with a hard clubbing right hand who just keeps rumbling forward
Points of Interest: 5'11½" tall. Worked as Security Guard at McDonalds and only took up boxing at the age of 15 after being injured at football. Having had three operations on his right hand, he won the WBA title by beating Virgil Hill in February 2002 and the WBC crown when decisioning Wayne Braithwaite in April 2005. Lost both titles in January 2006 when defeated by O'Neil Bell in a bout that was also a challenge for the IBF title. Has 22 wins by stoppage or kayo and is now based in the USA with Don King as his promoter

08.07.06 Sebastian Hill W RSC 4 St Louis
17.03.07 O'Neil Bell W PTS 12 Paris
(WBC & WBA Cruiserweight Title Challenges)
Career: 36 contests, won 33, lost 3.

Alexander (Explosivo) Munoz

Miranda, Venezuela. *Born* 8 February,1979
WBA S.Flyweight Champion
Major Amateur Honours: Was an outstanding amateur, claiming 129 wins in 158 fights, he competed in the World Junior Championships in 1997 and won a silver medal in the Americas Championships the same year
Turned Pro: October 1998
Significant Results: Ramon Games W RSC 10, Sornpichai Kratchingdaeng W RSC 5, Shoji Kobayashi W RSC 8, Eiji Kojima W CO 2 & W RSC 10, Martin Castillo L PTS 12 (twice)
Type/Style: Has an all-out aggressive style with a punch to match and is deadly with the left hook
Points of Interest: 5'6" tall with a 68" reach. Holds the record for the most consecutive inside the distance wins at the start of a career by a Venezuelan fighter after winning his first 23 fights by kayo or stoppage. Had Shoji Kobayashi on the floor five times when becoming the WBA champion in March 2002, but lost the title in his fourth defence to Martin Castillo in December 2004. He then made an unsuccessful challenge to Castillo in January 2006. Was recently seriously injured by a street mugging when receiving a bullet wound to the knee

27.11.06 Luis Trejo W CO 5 Caracas
03.05.07 Nobuo Nashiro W PTS 12 Tokyo
(WBA S.Flyweight Title Challenge)
Career: 32 contests, won 30, lost 2.

Omar (Huracan) Narvaez

Trelew, Argentina. *Born* 7 October, 1975
WBO Flyweight Champion
Major Amateur Honours: Won a bronze medal in the 1997 World Championships, a silver in the 1999 Championships, and gold medals in the 1999 Pan-American Games and South American Championships. Earlier, he had competed in the 1996 Olympics, where he beat the future double WBO champion, Joan Guzman, and he was also selected for the 2000 Olympics
Turned Pro: December 2000

Significant Results: Carlos Montiveros DREW 4, Wellington Vicente W PTS 10, Marcos Obregon W PTS 10, Adonis Rivas W PTS 12, Luis Lazarate W DIS 10, Andrea Sarritzu W PTS 12 & DREW 12, Everardo Morales W RSC 5, Alexander Mahmutov W RSC 10, Bernard Inom W RSC 11, Dario Azuaga W RSC 6

Type/Style: A stocky and aggressive southpaw, he has fast hands

Points of Interest: 5'3" tall. Became the first of the 2000 Olympians to win a version of a world title when he beat Adolfo Rivas in only his 12th paid fight in July 2002. Was originally trained by the Cuban, Sarbelio Fuentes, but now has a local trainer and has made ten defences. Has 15 wins by stoppage or kayo

05.08.06 Rexon Flores W PTS 12 Cordoba
          (WBO Flyweight Title Defence)
14.10.06 Walberto Ramos W PTS 12 Buenos Aires
          (WBO Flyweight Title Defence)
10.03.07 Brahim Asloum W PTS 12 Le Cannet
          (WBO Flyweight Title Defence)

Career: 26 contests, won 24, drew 2.

Nobuo Nashiro

Nara, Japan. *Born* 12 October, 1981
Former WBA S.Flyweight Champion.
Former Undefeated Japanese S.Flyweight Champion

Major Amateur Honours: None known as he only a mediocre 38-19 record
Turned Pro: July 2003
Significant Results: Hidenobu Honda W PTS 10, Seiji Tanaka W RSC 10, Prosper Matsuura W PTS 10

Type/Style: Short and sturdy, he has an unsophisticated 'Marciano-style' aggression

Points of Interest: 5'4" tall. A University Graduate, he equalled a Japanese record for winning a world title in the least number of contests when becoming the WBC champion in only his eighth fight. Has had to overcome the trauma of Seiji Tanaka dying after their fight in which he won the Japanese title in April 2005. Made only one defence of the Japanese title before winning the WBA title and has five wins inside the distance

22.07.06 Martin Castillo W RSC 10 Osaka
          (WBA S.Flyweight Title Challenge)
02.12.06 Eduardo Garcia W PTS 12 Osaka
          (WBA S.Flyweight Title Defence)
03.05.07 Alexander Munoz L PTS 12 Tokyo
          (WBA S.Flyweight Title Defence)

Career: 10 contests, won 9, lost 1.

Lovemore (The Black Panther) Ndou

Sydney, Australia. *Born* Nacefield, South Africa 16 August, 1971
Former IBF L.Welterweight Champion
Major Amateur Honours: Was a four-time South African champion
Turned Pro: April 1993
Significant Results: Jerry Malinga L PTS 6, Mthobeli Mhlophe DREW 12, Teofilo Tunacao W RSC 3, Justin Rowsell W RSC 6, Guillermo Mosquera L PTS 10, Steve Quinonez L PTS 8, Carlos Rios W CO 5, Sharmba Mitchell L PTS 12, Miguel Cotto L PTS 12, Junior Witter L PTS 12

Type/Style: Has an aggressive, crowding style and although a good puncher he has been floored a few times

Points of Interest: 5'8" tall. Turned pro in South Africa where he was trained by Gerrie Coetzee and Harold Volbrecht in his early days, but moved his base to Australia in May 1996. A member of the Vanda tribe and one of seven children, his brother Ruddock also boxed as a pro. Lost IBF title eliminators to Sharmba Mitchell, Miguel Cotto and Junior Witter before winning the title. Has 30 wins by stoppage or kayo

04.02.07 Naoufel Ben Rabah W RSC 11 Sydney
          (Final Elim. IBF L.Welterweight Title)
16.06.07 Paul Malignaggi L PTS 12 Uncasville
          (IBF L.Welterweight Title Defence)

Career: 55 contests, won 45, lost 9, drew 1.

Yutaka Niida

Kanagawa, Japan. *Born* 2 October, 1978
WBA M.Flyweight Champion.
Undefeated Japanese M.Flyweight Champion

Major Amateur Honours: None known
Turned Pro: November 1996
Significant Results: Makoto Suzuki W RSC 9, Daisuke Iida DREW 10, Chana Porpaoin W PTS 12, Nohel Arambulet L PTS 12 & W PTS 12, Juan Jose Landaeta W PTS 12, Jae-Won Kim W PTS 12, Eriberto Gejon W TD 10, Ronald Barrera W PTS 12

Type/Style: Aggressive, with good speed and a big right-hand punch, he has, however, a suspect chin

Points of Interest: 5'2" tall. Managed by Mitsunori Seki, who failed in five attempts to win versions of the world featherweight title, he climbed off the floor twice in the first round for his draw with Daisuke Iida. Although

surprisingly retiring immediately after winning the WBA title when beating Chana Porpaoin in August 2001, he returned to action in July 2003 and lost to Nohel Arambulet for the WBA title. In a return in July 2004, Arambulet failed to make the weight and Yutaka won the vacant title after outpointing the Venezuelan. Has made five defences

07.04.07 Katsunari Takayama W PTS 12 Tokyo
          (WBA M.Flyweight Title Defence)

Career: 25 contests, won 21, drew 3, lost 1.

Omar (Giant Killer) Nino

Guadalajara, Mexico. *Born* 12 May, 1976
Former Undefeated WBC L.Flyweight Champion

Major Amateur Honours: None known
Turned Pro: May 1995
Significant Results: Jorge Arce W RSC 1, Gilberto Keb-Baas L CO 5, Rafael Orozco T DRAW 3, Edgar Sosa W PTS 10, Juan Alberto Rosas L CO 9, Carlos Bouchan W PTS 10

Type/Style: Is a tough come-forward type with a good right hand, but slow

Points of Interest: 5'3" tall. Although his defence of the title in the return with Brian Viloria was declared a draw, Omar was stripped of the title when he tested positive for amphetamine. He has ten wins inside the distance, including an early career first-round stoppage of Jorge Arce

10.08.06 Brian Viloria W PTS 12 Las Vegas
          (WBC L.Flyweight Title Challenge)
18.11.06 Brian Viloria DREW 12 Las Vegas
          (WBC L.Flyweight Title Defence)

Career: MISSING

Daniel Ponce de Leon

Cuauhtemoc, Mexico. *Born* 27 July, 1980
WBO S.Bantamweight Champion
Major Amateur Honours: He was the Mexican amateur champion five times before winning a bronze medal in the Pan-American Games in 1999 and competing in the 2000 Olympics
Turned Pro: March 2001
Significant Results: Trinidad Mendoza W RSC 2, Francisco Tejedor W RSC 1, Jesus Perez W RSC 1, Cesar Figueroa W CO 6, Ivan Alvarez W RSC 5, Carlos Contreras W PTS 10, Emmanuel Lucero W RSC 3, Julio Gamboa W CO 4, Celestino Caballero L PTS 12, Ricardo Barajas W CO 2,

Sod Looknongyangtoy W PTS 12, Gerson Guerrero W CO 2
Type/Style: Strong but crude, he is a southpaw with a big punch
Points of Interest: 5'5" tall. Started boxing at the age of 13 and was a member of the Mexican national squad at the age of 14. Initially signed up by a local promoter, he is now with Oscar de la Hoya's Golden Boy Promotions. Won the WBO title by beating Sod Looknongyangtoy in October 2005 and has made four defences. Has 28 wins inside the distance

15.07.06 Sod Looknongyangtoy W CO 1 Las Vegas
  (WBO S.Bantamweight Title Defence)
21.10.06 Al Seeger W RSC 8 El Paso
  (WBO S.Bantamweight Title Defence)
17.03.07 Gerry Penalosa W PTS 12 Las Vegas
  (WBO S.Bantamweight Title Defence)
Career: 32 contests, won 31, lost 1.

Muhammad (Rock Breaker) Rachman

Papua, Indonesia. *Born* 23 December, 1972
IBF M.Flyweight Champion. Former Undefeated Indonesian M.Flyweight Champion

Major Amateur Honours: None known
Turned Pro: January 1993
Significant Results: Jin-Ho Kim W PTS 10, Lindi Memani W PTS 12, Patrick Twala W PTS 10, Ernesto Rubillar W PTS 10, Jun Arlos W PTS 10, Noel Tunacao W RSC 2, Daniel Reyes W PTS 12, Fahlan Sakkreerin T DRAW 3, Omar Soto W CO 6
Style/Type: Is a busy southpaw, but not a puncher
Points of Interest: 5'3" tall with a 59" reach. Self-managed, his real name is Mohamed Rachman Sawaludin and he gained his nickname after beating a Filipino boxer known as 'The Rock'. He is unbeaten in his last 37 bouts, with 27 wins by stoppage or kayo, and has made three defences since winning the IBF title by beating Daniel Reyes in September 2004. Has only fought outside Indonesia four times and lost all four. Last year he enrolled in an Indonesian University to study law

23.12.06 Benjie Sorolla W RSC 7 Jakarta
  (IBF M.Flyweight Title Defence)
Career: 68 contests, won 57, drew 4, lost 7.

Juan Carlos (Coton) Reveco

Malargue, Argentina. *Born* 26 April, 1981
WBA L.Flyweight Champion

Major Amateur Honours: The Argentinian champion in 2000 and 2002, he competed in the 2003 Pan-American Championships and 2004 Olympic qualifiers
Turned Pro: April 2004
Significant Results: Bernardo Albornoz W RTD 5, Freddy Beleno W PTS 10,
Type/Style: Although a smart boxer with a fast, accurate jab and good body punching attributes, he has been floored and rocked
Points of Interest: Juan Carlos comes from a big family, being the fifth of 12 children, and started boxing at the age of 17. Had to overcome a bad cut when beating Nethra Sasiprapa, a fight he dedicated to the former world middleweight champion, the late Hugo Corro, who also hailed from Mendoza. Is trained by Ricardo Bracamonte and the former WBO featherweight champion, Juan Pablo Chacon

26.08.06 Juan Francisco Roque W KO 6 Malargue
22.12.06 Ricardo Toledo W PTS 8 Mendoza
24.02.07 Adrian Garzon W KO 7 Mendoza
22.06.07 Nethra Sasiprapa W CO 8 Mendoza
  (Vacant WBA L.Flyweight Title)
Career: 16 contests, won 16.

Gairy (Superman) St Clair

Sydney, Australia. *Born* Guyana, 2 February, 1975
Former IBF S.Featherweight Champion & Former Undefeated Guyanese S.Featherweight Champion

Major Amateur Honours: Competed in the 1993 Central American Championships and the 1994 Commonwealth Games
Turned Pro: October 1994
Significant Results: Alric Johnson W PTS 10, Diego Corrales L PTS 12, Vivian Harris L PTS 10, Leonardo Dorin L PTS 10, Jackson Asiku W PTS 8, Theo Quaye W RSC 11, Shamir Reyes W RSC 12
Type/Style: Is a busy and strong pressure fighter, but his defence is not too good
Points of Interest: 5'6" tall. Missed out most of 1999 due to managerial problems and then moved his base to Australia in 2001, being unbeaten in a run of 23 bouts until losing his title to Malcolm Klassen. Having turned pro as a super-bantamweight and even fighting as high as light-welterweight, he is trained by the legendary

Australian, Johnny Lewis. Has 17 wins by stoppage or kayo

29.07.06 Cassius Baloyi W PTS 12 Johannesburg
  (IBF S.Featherweight Title Challenge)
04.11.06 Malcolm Klassen L PTS 12 Johannesburg
  (IBF S.Featherweight Title Defence)
Career: 44 contests, won 38, lost 4, drew 2.

Takefumi Sakata

Hiroshima, Japan. *Born* 29 January, 1980
WBA Flyweight Champion. Former Undefeated Japanese Flyweight Champion

Major Amateur Honours: None known
Turned Pro: December 1998
Significant Results: Masaki Kawabata W PTS 10, Daisuke Naito DREW 10, Shiro Yahiro W RSC 9, Trash Nakamura L PTS 10 & W PTS 10, Lorenzo Parra L PTS 12 (twice)
Type/Style: Strong and durable with great stamina
Points of Interest: 5'4" tall. Had two spells as Japanese champion, taking part in eight title fights. Lost twice on majority decisions to Lorenzo Parra in title challenges, suffering a broken jaw but going the distance in the first bout in 2004, before being beaten by Roberto Vasquez for the vacant WBA 'interim' title. In the third bout with Parra, the champion failed to make the weight and was stripped of the title before the fight went ahead. Following Parra's second-round retirement, Takefumi dedicated his win to the late founder of his gym, Masaki Kanehira. Has 13 wins by stoppage or kayo

17.07.06 Kisuk Bae W RSC 5 Tokyo
18.09.06 Kyung-Jin Son W RSC 5 Tokyo
02.12.06 Roberto Vasquez L PTS 12 Paris
  (Vacant WBA 'Interim' Flyweight Title)
19.03.07 Lorenzo Parra W RTD 2 Tokyo
Career: 35 contests, won 30, lost 4, drew 1.

Orlando (Siri) Salido

Ciudad Obregon, Mexico. *Born* 16 November, 1980
Former Undefeated IBF Featherweight Champion

Major Amateur Honours: None known
Turned Pro: March 1996
Significant Results: William Abelyan L PTS 6, Mark Burse DREW 8, Regilio Tuur W PTS 8, Lamont Pearson W PTS 10, Alfred Kotey W PTS 10, Juan Manuel Marquez L PTS 12, Cesar Soto W PTS 10

Type/Style: Is a strong and crafty fighter with a good punch in both hands

Points of Interest: 5'6" tall. Started badly when winning only five of his first nine fights, but his only loss since 2001 was against Juan Manuel Marquez in 2004 when he challenged for the IBF and WBA featherweight titles. Although beating Robert Guerrero he was stripped of the IBF title six days later after he tested positive for the anabolic steroid, Nandrolone. Has 18 wins by stoppage or kayo

19.08.06 Franner Trinidad W RSC 1 Ciudad Obregon
04.11.06 Robert Guerrero W PTS 12 Las Vegas
        (IBF Featherweight Title Challenge)
Career: 39 contests, won 27, lost 9, drew 2, no decision 1.

Wladimir Sidorenko

Energodar, Ukraine. *Born* 23 September, 1975
WBA Bantamweight Champion

Major Amateur Honours: Competed in the 1997 and 1999 World Championships and won a silver medal in the 2001 World Championships. Won a World Military Championships title three times and was a gold medallist in both the 1998 and 2000 European Championships before winning a bronze medal in the 2000 Olympics

Turned Pro: November 2001

Significant Results: Giovanni Andrade W RSC 3, Sergey Tasimov W PTS 8, Moises Castro W PTS 12, Joseph Agbeko W PTS 12, Silvio Gamez W PTS 12, Julio Zarate W PTS 12, Jose de Jesus Lopez W PTS 12, Ricardo Cordoba DREW 12

Type/Style: Is a short, sturdy, busy counter-puncher with a tight guard

Points of Interest: 5'4" tall. Starting boxing in 1988, he comes from a boxing family with his brother also having boxed as a pro, and had 310 amateur fights before punching for pay. He won the WBA title by decisioning Julio Zarate in February 2005 and has made five defences, including two draws with Ricardo Cordoba. Not a heavy puncher, he has only six wins inside the distance

15.07.06 Poonsawat Kratingdaengym W PTS 12 Hamburg
        (WBA Bantamweight Title Defence)
17.03.07 Ricardo Cordoba DREW 12 Stuttgart
        (WBA Bantamweight Title Defence)
29.06.07 Jerome Arnould W CO 7 Marseille
        (WBA Bantamweight Title Defence)
Career: 22 contests, won 20, drew 2.

Travis (Tremendous) Simms

Norwalk, USA. Born 1 May, 1971
WBA L.Middleweight Champion

Major Amateur Honours: Won a silver medal in the 1993 National Golden Gloves and a bronze medal in the 1995 US Championships. Also collected gold medals in the 1995 and 1996 PAL Championships. Competed in the 1996 Olympic trials and was the alternative to David Reid for a position on the Olympic team

Turned Pro: February 1998

Significant Results: Kevin Kelly W PTS 8, Antoine Robinson W RSC 8, Alejandro Garcia W CO 5, Bronco McKart W PTS 12

Type/Style: A southpaw who switches, he has fast hands and a solid jab

Points of Interest: 5'9½" tall. From a boxing family, his dad was a pro and his identical twin brother Tarvis is a pro at middleweight, Travis is one of nine children and is managed by a lady. Won the 'secondary' WBA title by beating Alejandro Garcia in December 2003 and achieved full recognition as WBA champion when the WBA 'super' champion Ronald Wright relinquished the title. Made only one defence when beating Bronco McKart in October 2004 before being stripped and designated 'Champion in Recess' after a long period of inactivity due to contractual problems. He did not fight again until defeating Jose Antonio Rivera to regain his title. Has 19 wins inside the distance

06.01.07 Jose Antonio Rivera W RSC 9 Hollywood
        (WBA L.Middleweight Title Challenge)
Career: 25 contests, won 25.

Ulises (Archie) Solis

Guadalajara, Mexico. *Born* 28 August, 1981
IBF L.Flyweight Champion. Former Undefeated Mexican L.Flyweight Champion

Major Amateur Honours: None known, but he claims only two losses in 38 fights.

Turned Pro: April 2000

Significant Results: Omar Soto W PTS 10, Juan Keb-Baas W RSC 9, Edgar Sosa W PTS 6 & W PTS 12, Lee Sandoval W RTD 8, Gabriel Munoz W CO 3, Nelson Dieppa L PTS 12, Carlos Fajardo W RSC 8, Will Grigsby W PTS 12, Erik Ortiz W RSC 9

Type/Style: Although not a big puncher, he is an accomplished stand-up boxer with an excellent jab

Points of Interest: 5'3" tall. Ulises is a member of a fighting family and his elder brother Jorge has lost only once in 34 fights, and that was to Manny Pacquiao. Has 18 wins inside the distance, with his only defeat coming when he lost a majority verdict to Nelson Dieppa in a challenge for the WBO title in July 2004. He then went on to win the IBF title with a win over Will Grigsby in January 2006 and has made four defences

04.08.06 Omar Salado DREW 12 Tijuana
        (IBF L.Flyweight Title Defence)
25.01.07 Will Grigsby W RTD 8 Las Vegas
        (IBF L.Flyweight Title Defence)
19.05.07 Jose Antonio Aguirre W RSC 9 Guadalajara
        (IBF L.Flyweight Title Defence)
Career: 26 contests, won 23, drew 2, lost 1.

Edgar Sosa

Mexico City, Mexico. *Born* 23 August, 1979
WBC L.Flyweight Champion

Major Amateur Honours: None known
Turned Pro: April 2002

Significant Results: Ulises Solis L PTS 6 & L PTS 12, Manuel Vargas L RSC 8, Omar Nino L PTS 10, Isaac Bustos L PTS 12, Domingo Guillen W RSC 6, Francisco Rosas W PTS 12, Gilberto Keb-Baas W PTS 12

Type/Style: A good tactical boxer with a strong jab and plenty of movement, he has a good chin and packs punching power

Points of Interest: A couple of his uncles were boxers and he started boxing at the age of ten. Is trained by Miguel 'Raton' Gonzalez, who is the father of the WBO bantamweight champion, Jhonny Gonzalez, and managed by Haitian businessman, Jacques Deschamps. In late 2003 his record was a mediocre 12-5, but four of the losses were close decisions to fighters who went on to win versions of world titles and Edgar is unbeaten in his last 15 contests. Has 14 wins by stoppage or kayo

02.09.06 Nohel Arambulet W TD 10 Petionville
14.04.07 Brian Viloria W PTS 12 San Antonio
        (Vacant WBC L.Flyweight Title)
Career: 32 contests, won 27, lost 5.

Cory (The Next Generation) Spinks

St Louis, USA. *Born* 20 February, 1978

IBF L.Middleweight Champion. Former WBA, WBC and IBF Welterweight Champion

Major Amateur Honours: Won a gold medal at the 1997 Police Athletic League Championships and claims 78 wins in 81 contests.

Turned Pro: November 1997

Significant Results: Antonio Diaz L PTS 12, Jorge Vaca W RSC 7, Edgar Ruiz W PTS 10, Larry Marks W PTS 12, Michele Piccirillo L PTS 12 & W PTS 12, Rafael Pineda W TD 7, Ricardo Mayorga W PTS 12, Zab Judah W PTS 12 & L RSC 9, Miguel Gonzalez W PTS 12

Type/Style: Is a tall, upright southpaw with good speed and a fine combination puncher

Points of Interest: 5'10" tall. He is the son of former world heavyweight champion Leon Spinks and nephew of Mike. Lost to Michele Piccirillo on a disputed decision in a challenge for the IBF welterweight title in 2002, but then beat the Italian in a return in March

2003 and added the WBA and WBC titles when defeating Ricardo Mayorga in December 2003. Made successful defences against Zab Judah and Miguel Gonzalez, only to lose the titles to Judah in February 2005. He was then inactive until beating Roman Karmazin. Has only 11 wins by stoppage or kayo

08.07.06	Roman Karmazin W PTS 12 St Louis *(IBF L.Middleweight Title Challenge)*
03.02.07	Rodney Jones W PTS 12 Kissimmee *(IBF L.Middleweight Title Defence)*
19.05.07	Jermain Taylor L PTS 12 Memphis *(WBC & WBO Middleweight Title Challenges)*

Career: 40 contests, won 36, lost 4.

Felix (Storm) Sturm

Leverkusen, Germany. *Born* 31 January, 1979

WBA Middleweight Champion. Former WBO Middleweight Champion

Major Amateur Honours: Won a gold medal in the 1997 European Junior Championships and was the German champion in 1995, 1998 and 1999. Felix was a quarter-finalist in both the

1999 World Championships and 2000 Olympics and won a gold medal in the European Championships in 2000. Claims 113 wins in 122 fights

Turned Pro: January 2001

Significant Results: Lorant Szabo W PTS 8, Tshepo Mashego W PTS 10, Hector Velazco W PTS 12, Ruben Varon W PTS 12, Oscar de la Hoya L PTS 12, Robert Frazier W PTS 10, Hassine Cherifi W CO 3, Bert Schenk W CO 2, Jorge Sendra W PTS 12, Maselino Maseo W PTS 12

Type/Style: Is a tall, strong, technically sound box-puncher with a solid jab

Points of Interest: 5'11" tall. Fought in the amateurs under his real name Adnan Catic, but took the name Sturm, which means storm in German, as a pro. Won the WBO title by beating Hector Velazco in September 2003 and made one defence before losing the title on a close decision to Oscar de la Hoya in June 2004. Became the WBA 'secondary' champion when beating Maselino Maseo in March 2006 and was recognised as the full champion when Jermain Taylor was stripped of the 'super' title. Has only 12 wins inside the distance

15.07.06	Javier Castillejo L RSC 10 Hamburg *(WBA 'Secondary' Middleweight Title Defence)*
02.12.06	Gavin Topp W RSC 6 Berlin
28.04.07	Javier Castillejo W PTS 12 Oberhausen *(WBA Middleweight Title Challenge)*
30.06.07	Noe Tulio Gonzalez W PTS 12 Stuttgart *(WBA Middleweight Title Defence)*

Career: 30 contests, won 28, lost 2.

Jermain (Bad Intentions) Taylor

Little Rock, USA. *Born* 11 August, 1978

WBC & WBO Middleweight Champion. Former Undefeated WBA and IBF Middleweight Champion

Major Amateur Honours: A United States junior champion in 1996, he went on to win two National Golden Gloves titles and collected bronze medals in the 1998 Goodwill Games and 2000 Olympics

Turned Pro: January 2001

Significant Results: Sam Hill W PTS 10, Alex Bunema W RSC 7, Raul Marquez W RTD 9, William Joppy W PTS 12, Daniel Edouard W RSC 3, Bernard Hopkins W PTS 12 (twice), Ronald Wright DREW 12

Type/Style: Is a good, stylish boxer with

Cory Spinks   Les Clark

227

an excellent jab, but sometimes seem to lack sparkle

Points of Interest: 6'1" tall. His uncle, who had boxed as an amateur, started Jermain in boxing at the age of 13 before he eventually progressed with a scholarship to the United States Olympic Centre. Although he won all four versions of the world title when beating Bernard Hopkins in July 2005, the IBF stripped him and he relinquished the WBA title when he elected to fight Bernard Hopkins in a return match. Married to an athlete, he has made four defences of his WBC and WBO titles and is trained by Emanuel Stewart

09.12.06 Kassim Ouma W PTS 12 Little Rock
(WBC & WBO Middleweight Title Defences)
19.05.07 Cory Spinks W PTS 12 Memphis
(WBC & WBO Middleweight Title Defences)

Career: 28 contests, won 27, drew 1.

Ricardo (Mochuelo) Torres

Manague, Colombia. *Born* 16 February, 1980
WBO L.Welterweight Champion

Major Amateur Honours: Won a gold medal in the 1998 Pan-American Junior Championships and in the same year competed in the World Junior Championships. Lost to Miguel Cotto in the Americas qualifiers for the 2000 Olympics

Turned Pro: March 2001

Significant Results: Emilio Julio W RSC 3, Ignacio Solar W CO 5, Edwin Vazquez W RSC 3, Miguel Cotto L CO 7, Carlos Donquiz W CO 2

Type/Style: An aggressive come-forward banger who can adapt, there is still a question over his chin

Points of Interest: 5'8" tall. Ricardo won 26 of his first 28 fights by stoppage or kayo, 11 of them in the first round. Had Miguel Cotto on the floor in his challenge for the WBO title in 2005, but was floored four times himself. His brother Jose Miguel Torres is a successful pro light-middleweight

18.11.06 Mike Arnaoutis W PTS 12 Las Vegas
(Vacant WBO L.Welterweight Title)
28.04.07 Arturo Morua W PTS 12 Barranquilla
(WBO L.Welterweight Title Defence)

Career: 32 contests, won 31, lost 1.

Edwin (Dinamita) Valero

Merida, Venezuela. *Born* 3 December, 1981

WBA S.Featherweight Champion

Major Amateur Honours: Three times a Venezuelan amateur champion, he won a gold medal in the 2000 Central American Games and competed in the 2000 Olympics qualifiers. Claims only six losses in 92 fights

Turned Pro: July 2002

Significant Results: Roque Cassiani W CO 1, Esteban Morales W CO 1, Aram Ramazyan W CO 1, Whyber Garcia W CO 1, Genaro Trazancos W RSC 2

Type/Style: A loose-limbed, aggressive southpaw banger with a devastating punch in both hands, he relies on offence rather than defence

Points of Interest: 5'7" tall. Started boxing at the age of 12 and set a record by winning all of his first 18 pro bouts inside the first round. Based in Japan, he is banned from fighting in the United States after failing an MRI scan in New York in 2004 due to a brain injury suffered in a motor-cycle accident in Venezuela. All of his fights have ended inside the distance and only three have gone beyond the first round

05.08.06 Vicente Mosquera W RSC 10 Panama City
(WBA S.Featherweight Title Challenge)
03.01.07 Michael Lozada W RSC 1 Tokyo
(WBA S.Featherweight Title Defence)
03.05.07 Nobuhito Honmo W RSC 8 Tokyo
(WBA S.Featherweight Title Defence)

Career: 22 contests, won 22.

Pongsaklek Wonjongkam

Nakhorn Ratchasima, Thailand. *Born* 11 August, 1977
WBC Flyweight Champion

Major Amateur Honours: None

Turned Pro: December 1994

Significant Results: Jerry Pahayaha L PTS 8 & L CO 5, Randy Mangubat W CO 3 & W PTS 12 (twice), Mzukisi Sikali W RSC 1, Juanito Rubillar W PTS 10, Malcolm Tunacao W RSC 1, Daisuke Naito W CO 1 & W TD 7, Jesus Martinez W PTS 12, Hidenobu Honda W PTS 12, Hussein Hussein W PTS 12, Masaki Nakanuma W PTS 12, Gilbert Keb-Baas W PTS 12, Everardo Morales W RSC 4

Type/Style: A tough, aggressive, pressure fighter, he is also a southpaw with a wicked right hook

Points of Interest: 5' 4". Christened Dongskorn Wonjongkan, Pongsaklek's last loss was in December 1995 and he is unbeaten in his last 55 bouts,

having also boxed under the names of Nakornthong, Parkview and Sithkanongsak. He won the WBC title by halting Malcolm Tunacao in March 2001 and has made 17 defences. With 34 wins by stoppage or kayo, his quickest victory came when he put Daisuke Naito away in just 34 seconds, however, he has lost some of his gloss due to the poor quality of challengers recently. As Lito Sisnorio was not licensed by the Philippines Board at the time of their fight there is some doubt over the validity of the bout

17.11.06 Monelisi Myekeni W PTS 12 Korat
(WBC Flyweight Title Defence)
26.01.07 Lito Sisnorio W RSC 4 Mae Sot
06.04.07 Tomonobu Shimizu W RTD 7 Saraburi
(WBC Flyweight Title Defence)

Career: 67 contests, won 65, lost 2.

Krzysztof (Diablo) Wlodarczyk

Warsaw, Poland. *Born* 19 September, 1981
Former IBF Cruiserweight Champion. Former Undefeated European Union Cruiserweight Champion

Major Amateur Honours: Was twice national junior champion and won a bronze medal in the 1997 European Cadet Championships

Turned Pro: June 2000

Significant Results: Vincenzo Rossitto W RSC 10, Ismael Abdoul W RSC 12, Pavel Melkomian L RTD 4, Alain Simon W RSC 6, Joseph Marwa W PTS 10, Rudiger May W CO 10, John Keeton W RTD 3, Hector Avila W CO 6

Type/Style: An upright stylist, who is tough, strong and a big puncher but a bit on the slow side

Points of Interest: 6'1" tall. Before winning the WBC youth title at cruiserweight, his only loss came against Pavel Melkomian and was due to both fighters being cut. Came in as a substitute when winning the vacant title against Steve Cunningham after Guillermo Jones pulled out. The win over Cunningham was split and controversial, with the American judge having Cunningham ten points ahead. Has 27 wins inside the distance

01.07.06 Mircea Telecan W RSC 1 Kepno
25.11.06 Steve Cunningham W PTS 12 Warsaw
(Vacant IBF Cruiserweight Title)
26.05.07 Steve Cunningham L PTS 12 Katowice
(IBF Cruiserweight Title Defence)

Career: contests 39, won 37, lost 2.

World Title Bouts, 2006-2007

by Bob Yalen

All of last season's title bouts for the IBF, WBA, WBC and WBO are shown in date order within their weight division and give the boxers' respective weights as well as the scorecard if going to a decision. British officials, where applicable, are also listed. Yet again there were no WORLD TITLE FIGHTS as such, just a proliferation of champions recognised by the above four commissions and spread over 17 weight divisions. Below the premier league, come other commissions such as the WBU, IBO, IBC and WBF, etc, etc, which would devalue the world championships even further if one recognised their champions as being the best in the world. Despite that, we have shown the Ricky Hatton v Jose Luis Castillo IBO light-welterweight title fight among the listings as those two were arguably the top men in the division. Right now, the WBA have decided to continue recognising their champions who move on to claim other commissions' titles as super champions – despite vacating the title and creating a new champion, who, for our purposes, is classified as a 'secondary' champion – which if taken up in general could eventually lead to the best man at his weight being recognised universally as a world champion if the fights can be made.

M.Flyweight

21 October   Ivan Calderon 7.6½ (Puerto Rico) W PTS 12 Jose Luis Varela 7.6¾ (Venezuela), Elias Chegwin Coliseum, Barranquilla, Colombia – WBO. Scorecards: 118-109, 118-109, 119-108.

13 November   Eagle Kyowa 7.7 (Thailand) W PTS 12 Lorenzo Trejo 7.7 (Mexico), Nihon Budokan Martial Arts Hall, Tokyo, Japan – WBC. Scorecards: 113-112, 113-112, 114-113.

23 December   Muhammad Rachman 7.7 (Indonesia) W RSC 7 Benjie Sorolla 7.6¾ (Philippines), Bung Kamo Tennis Stadium, Senayan, Jakarta, Indonesia – IBF.

7 April   Yutaka Niida 7.7 (Japan) W PTS 12 Katsunari Takayama 7.6¾ (Japan), Korakuen Hall, Tokyo, Japan – WBA. Scorecards: 115-113, 114-113, 114-115. Earlier, on 7 November in Osaka, Japan, Takayama (Japan) had stopped Panama's Carlos Melo in the ninth round to win the vacant WBA 'interim' title.

28 April   Ivan Calderon 7.6¼ (Puerto Rico) W PTS 12 Ronald Barrera 7.5 (Colombia), North University Coliseum, Barranquilla, Colombia – WBO. Scorecards: 115-113, 115-113, 113-115.

4 June   Eagle Kyowa 7.6¾ (Thailand) W PTS 12 Akira Yaegashi 7.6¼ (Japan), The Pacifico, Yokohama, Japan – WBC. Scorecards: 118-108, 119-107, 119-107.

L.Flyweight

2 August   Koki Kameda 7.10 (Japan) W PTS 12 Juan Jose Landaeta 7.9¾ (Venezuela), The Arena, Yokohama, Japan - WBA. Scorecards: 115-113, 114-113, 112-115. Contested for the vacant title after Roberto Vasquez (Panama) vacated in May 2006.

4 August   Ulises Solis 7.10 (Mexico) DREW 12 Omar Salado 7.10 (Mexico), Rooster Hippodrome, Tijuana, Mexico - IBF. Scorecards: 115-113, 114-114, 114-114.

10 August   Brian Viloria 7.10 (USA) L PTS 12 Omar Nino 7.10 (Mexico), Orleans Hotel & Casino, Las Vegas, Nevada, USA - WBC. Scorecards: Mark Green 112-117, 110-118, 111-117. Earlier, on 18 July 2006, Wandee Chor Chareon (Thailand) outpointed Juanito Rubillar (Philippines) over 12 rounds to win the vacant 'interim' title, an honour he would eventually lose on the scales on 9 October after

being matched to defend against Munetsugu Kayo (Japan). Despite that, the fight went ahead with Chareon outpointing Kayo over 12 rounds in Tokyo, Japan.

30 September   Hugo Cazares 7.10 (Mexico) W RSC 10 Nelson Dieppa 7.10 (Puerto Rico), Hector Sola Bezares Coliseum, Caguas, Puerto Rico – WBO.

18 November   Omar Nino 7.9 (Mexico) DREW 12 Brian Viloria 7.10 (USA), Thomas & Mack Centre, Las Vegas, Nevada, USA – WBC. Scorecards: 115-112, 113-113, 113-113. Nino was stripped early in February 2007 after failing the post-fight drug test.

20 December   Koki Kameda 7.9¾ (Japan) W PTS 12 Juan Jose Landaeta 7.10 (Venezuela), Ariake Coliseum, Tokyo, Japan – WBA. Scorecards: Terry O'Connor 115-113, 116-111, 119-108. Due to having weight problems, Kameda relinquished the title in January 2007 to campaign at flyweight.

25 January   Ulises Solis 7.9 (Mexico) W RTD 8 Will Grigsby 7.10 (USA), Orleans Arena, Las Vegas, Nevada, USA – IBF. Judge: Howard Foster.

14 April   Edgar Sosa 7.10 (Mexico) W PTS 12 Brian Viloria 7.10 (USA), The Alamodome, San Antonio, Texas, USA – WBC. Scorecards: 115-113, 115-113, 114-114.

4 May   Hugo Cazares 7.10 (Mexico) W RSC 2 Wilfrido Valdez 7.10 (Colombia), MGM Grand, Las Vegas, Nevada, USA – WBO.

19 May   Ulises Solis 7.10 (Mexico) W RSC 9 Jose Antonio Aguirre 7.10 (Mexico), Benito Juarez Auditorium, Guadalajara, Mexico – IBF.

22 June   Juan Carlos Reveco 7.9¾ (Argentina) W CO 8 Nethra Sasiprapa 7.9¾ (Thailand), Vicente Polimeni Stadium, Las Heras, Mendoza, Argentina – WBA.

Flyweight

5 August   Omar Narvaez 7.13½ (Argentina) W PTS 12 Rexon Flores 7.11 (Philippines), The Orfeo Superdome, Cordoba, Argentina – WBO. Scorecards: 119-107, 119-107, 120-106.

7 October   Vic Darchinyan 8.0 (Armenia) W TD 6 Glenn Donaire 7.13 (Philippines), Mandalay Bay Resort & Casino, Las Vegas, Nevada, USA – IBF. Referee: Tony Weeks. Scorecards: 60-53, 60-53, 60-53.

14 October Omar Narvaez 8.0 (Argentina) W PTS 12 Walberto Ramos 7.13¾ (Colombia), Luna Park Stadium, Buenos Aires, Argentina – WBO. Scorecards: 115-111, 117-109, 115-112.

17 November Pongsaklek Wonjongkam 8.0 (Thailand) W PTS 12 Monelisi Myekeni 7.13¾ (South Africa), Suranaree Stadium, Korat, Thailand – WBC. Scorecards: 119-108, 117-111, 118-110.

3 March Vic Darchynan 7.13½ (Armenia) W RSC 12 Victor Burgos 7.13¼ (Mexico), Home Depot Centre, Carson, California, USA – IBF.

10 March Omar Narvaez 8.0 (Argentina) W PTS 12 Brahim Asloum 7.13¼ (France), The Sports Palace, Le Cannet, France – WBO. Scorecards: 118-109, 117-110, 116-111.

6 April Pongsaklek Wonjongkam 8.0 (Thailand) W RTD 7 Tomonobu Shimizu 7.13¾ (Japan), Tabkwang District Main Stadium, Saraburi, Thailand – WBC.

Note: Due to defend the WBA title against Roberto Vasquez (Panama) on 21 October 2006, the champion, Lorenzo Parra (Panama), was forced to pull out after suffering injured knee ligaments and Vasquez met Japan's Takefumi Sakata to contest the 'interim' title in Paris, France on 2 December, winning a split points decision after 12 rounds. With Parra still not recovered the WBA tried to bring Vasquez and Sakata together in a return, but negotiations were tenuous and the fight failed to take place. It was then announced that Parra was going to defend his title against Sakata in Tokyo, Japan on 19 March 2007, with the winner giving Vasquez first crack at the title. After all the waiting it was ridiculous for Parra (116¾) to then lose his title on the scales. Although the fight went ahead, only Sakata (112) could win the title and following a three-round stoppage victory over Parra the WBA declared him champion.

S.Flyweight

22 July Martin Castillo 8.3 (Mexico) L RSC 10 Nobuo Nashiro 8.3 (Japan), Higashi Arena, Osaka, Japan – WBA.

2 December Nobuo Nashiro 8.2¾ (Japan) W PTS 12 Eduardo Garcia 8.2¾ (Mexico), Prefectural Gymnasium, Osaka, Japan – WBA. Scorecards: 117-112, 118-110, 117-112.

3 January Cristian Mijares 8.3 (Mexico) W RSC 10 Katsushige Kawashima 8.3 (Japan), Ariake Coliseum, Tokyo, Japan – WBC. Earlier, on 18 September, Mijares had won the vacant 'interim' title when outpointing Kawashima over 12 rounds in Yokohama, Japan and successfully defended it title when defeating Reynaldo Lopez (Colombia) on points over 12 rounds at Torreon, Coahuila, Mexico on 17 November. When Tokuyama relinquished the main title on 10 December, due to weight making difficulties, Mijares was appointed champion.

24 February Fernando Montiel 8.3 (Mexico) W PTS 12 Z Gorres 8.3 (Philippines), The Sports Complex, Cebu City, Philippines – WBO. Scorecards: 115-111, 114-112, 111-115.

14 April Christian Mijares 8.3 (Mexico) W PTS 12 Jorge Arce 8.3 (Mexico), The Alamadome, San Antonio, Texas,

USA – WBC. Scorecards: Mark Green 118-110, 119-109, 117-111.

3 May Nobuo Nashiro 8.3 (Japan) L PTS 12 Alexander Munoz 8.2¾ (Venezuela), Ariake Coliseum, Tokyo, Japan – WBA. Scorecards: 109-118, 112-117, 111-117.

Note: Due to defend the IBF title against Mexico's Ricardo Vargas on 4 November in Phoenix, Arizona, when Luis Perez (Nicaragua) came in over the weight and the fight had to be scrapped he forfeited his belt. The IBF title remains vacant.

Bantamweight

15 July Wladimir Sidorenko 8.5¾ (Ukraine) W PTS 12 Poonsawat Kratingdaengym 8.6 (Thailand), Color Line Arena, Hamburg, Germany - WBA. Scorecards: 120-108, 116-112, 115-113.

5 August Rafael Marquez 8.6 (Mexico) W RTD 9 Silence Mabuza 8.5½ (South Africa), Montbleu Resort Casino, Stateline, Nevada, USA – IBF. Marquez vacated the IBF version of the title within days of becoming the WBC junior featherweight champion on 3 March 2007 and Luis Perez (Nicaragua) and Genaro Garcia were matched to decide the championship on 7 July.

13 November Hozumi Hasegawa 8.5¾ (Japan) W PTS 12 Genaro Garcia 8.5¾ (Mexico), Nihon Budokan Martial Arts Hall, Tokyo, Japan – WBC. Scorecards: 114-110, 114-109, 114-109.

17 March Wladimir Sidorenko 8.6 (Ukraine) DREW 12 Ricardo Cordoba 8.5¼ (Panama), Hanns Martin-Schleyer Hall, Stuttgart, Germany – WBA. Scorecards: 117-111, 114-114, 114-114.

30 March Jhonny Gonzalez 8.5½ (Mexico) W RSC 9 Irene Pacheco 8.6 (Colombia), Desert Diamond Casino, Tucson, Arizona, USA - WBO.

3 May Hozumi Hasegawa 8.6 (Japan) W PTS 12 Simpiwe Vetyeka 8.5¾ (South Africa), Ariake Coliseum, Tokyo, Japan – WBC. Scorecards: 116-112, 116-112, 115-113.

29 June Wladimir Sidorenko 8.5½ (Ukraine) W CO 7 Jerome Arnould 8.5½ (France), The Sports Palace, Marseille, France – WBA.

S.Bantamweight

15 July Daniel Ponce de Leon 8.10 (Mexico) W CO 1 Sod Looknongyangtoy 8.10 (Thailand), MGM Grand, Las Vegas, Nevada, USA - WBO.

16 September Israel Vazquez 8.10 (Mexico) W RSC 10 Jhonny Gonzalez 8.9 (Mexico), MGM Grand, Las Vegas, Nevada, USA – WBC.

4 October Somsak Sithchatchawal 8.10 (Thailand) L RSC 3 Celestino Caballero 8.9 (Panama), Ban Rai Temple, Korat, Thailand – WBA. Referee: John Coyle.

21 October Daniel Ponce de Leon 8.10 (Mexico) W RSC 8 Al Seeger 8.10 (USA), Don Haskins' Centre, El Paso, Texas, USA – WBO.

10 November Steve Molitor 8.9½ (Canada) W CO 5 Michael Hunter 8.9¾ (England), Borough Hall, Hartlepool, England – IBF. Referee: Phil Edwards. Judge: Howard

Foster. Billed for the vacant title after Israel Vazquez (Mexico), who also held the WBC belt, was stripped in March 2006 for failing to agree a defence within the time limit. Following that, Molitor was selected to fight Sergio Medina (Mexico) for the vacant crown. However, for whatever reason, Medina turned the opportunity down and Molitor was set to meet a replacement in Gabula Vabaza in Johannesburg, South Africa on 1 September 2006, only for the fight to called off the day before, due to the South African failing a pre-fight medical. It was then announced that Molitor would meet England's Hunter to decide the vacant title.

3 March Israel Vazquez 8.9¾ (Mexico) L RTD 7 Rafael Marquez 8.9½ (Mexico), Home Depot Centre, Carson, California – WBC.

16 March Celestino Caballero 8.10 (Panama) W RSC 9 Ricardo Castillo 8.9¾ (Mexico), Seminole Hard Rock Live Arena, Hollywood, Florida, USA – WBA.

17 March Daniel Ponce de Leon 8.10 (Mexico) W PTS 12 Gerry Penalosa 8.10 (Philippines), MGM Grand, Las Vegas, Nevada, USA – WBO. Scorecards: 119-109, 119-109, 120-108.

Featherweight

30 July Takashi Koshimoto 9.0 (Japan) L RSC 7 Rodolfo Lopez 9.0 (Mexico), Marine Messe Convention Centre, Fukuoka, Japan – WBC. Referee: Ian John-Lewis. Judge: Larry O'Connell.

2 September Eric Aiken 8.13 (USA) L RTD 8 Robert Guerrero 8.12½ (USA), Staples Centre, Los Angeles, California, USA – IBF.

9 September Chris John 8.12¼ (Indonesia) W PTS 12 Renan Acosta 8.13 (Panama), Soemantri Brodjonegoro Hall, Jakarta, Indonesia – WBA. Scorecards: 119-108, 119-109, 120-107.

4 November Robert Guerrero 9.0 (USA) L PTS 12 Orlando Salido 9.0 (Mexico), Mandalay Bay Hotel, Las Vegas, Nevada, USA – IBF. Scorecards: 110-118, 111-117, 113-115. Having failed the post-fight drug test, Salido was stripped in mid-November.

17 December Rodolfo Lopez 8.13¾ (Mexico) L PTS 12 In-Jin Chi 9.0 (South Korea), Chungmu Art Hall, Seoul, South Korea – WBC. Scorecards: 113-116, 112-116, 111-117.

23 February Robert Guerrero 9.0 (USA) W RTD 8 Spend Abazi 9.0 (Albania), Falconer Centre, Copenhagen, Denmark – IBF.

3 March Chris John 9.0 (Indonesia) W PTS 12 Jose Rojas 8.13½ (Venezuela), Bung Karno Indoor Tennis Stadium, Senayan, Jakarta, Indonesia – WBA. Scorecards: 118-108, 117-109, 116-110.

Note: With the champion, Scott Harrison (Scotland), due to defend the WBO title against Joan Guzman (Dominican Republic) on 25 February 2006, the fight was moved on to 20 May after Harrison had dental surgery to remove a wisdom tooth. Then, in early April, Guzman decided to move up a weight and was replaced as Harrison's opponent by Martin Honorio (Mexico), followed by Gairy St Clair (Australia)

when the latter went missing. In mid-May that fight was also called off after Harrison got himself arrested, prior to going into a clinic suffering from depression and alcohol problems. Bearing in mind that Harrison was only allowed nine months between defences but recognising his situation, the WBO gave him a further three months 'disability leave' to make a defence, while also setting up an 'interim' title fight for 5 August 2006, which was won by Juan Manuel Marquez (Mexico) when he stopped Terdsak Jandaeng (Thailand) in the seventh round at Stateline, Nevada, USA. At the end of September, having been allowed an additional month recuperation and back in training, it was announced that Harrison would be meeting Nicky Cook (England) on 7 December 2006, with the winner to defend against Marquez. Plans for the fight were then thrown into jeopardy on 6 October when Harrison was arrested in Spain for assault, but after being released on bail on 17 November and getting medical clearance from the BBBoC it was confirmed that Harrison v Cook was still going ahead on 7 December. Meanwhile, Marquez successfully defended the 'interim' title when scoring a ninth-round knockout win over Jimrex Jaca (Philippines) at the Dodge Arena, Hidalgo, Texas, USA on 25 November. Shockingly, Harrison was unable to make the weight for the Cook fight and with just three days to go he relinquished the title. Within days of that happening the WBO handed the belt to Marquez, but after the latter moved up to super-feather to capture the WBC title from Marco Antonio Barrera in March 2007 yet again the championship was vacated. It was later announced that Cook and Steve Luevano (USA) would decide the vacant title on 7 July.

S.Featherweight

29 July Cassius Baloyi 9.3¾ (South Africa) L PTS 12 Gairy St Clair 9.3½ (Guyana), Emperors Palace Casino, Johannesburg, South Africa – IBF. Scorecards: Howard Foster 112-116, 113-115, 114-115.

5 August Vicente Mosquera 9.4 (Panama) L RSC 10 Edwin Valero 9.3¾ (Venezuela), Figali Convention Centre, Panama City, Panama – WBA.

16 September Marco Antonio Barrera 9.4 (Mexico) W PTS 12 Rocky Juarez 9.3 (USA), MGM Grand, Las Vegas, Nevada, USA – WBC. Scorecards: 117-111, 115-113, 115-113.

4 November Gairy St Clair 9.3½ (Guyana) L PTS 12 Malcolm Klassen 9.4 (South Africa), Emperor's Palace Conference Centre, Johannesburg, South Africa – IBF. Scorecards: 112-118, 111-117, 115-113.

18 December Joan Guzman 9.4 (Dominican Republic) W PTS 12 Antonio Davis 9.4 (USA), Virgilio Travieso Soto Leisure Centre, Santo Domingo, Dominican Republic – WBO. Earlier, on 16 September 2006, Jorge Barrios (Argentina) forfeited the WBO title when failing to make the weight for a title defence against Guzman at the MGM Grand in Las Vegas, Nevada, USA. Despite that, the fight went ahead and following a 12-round points win, Guzman was proclaimed the new champion.

3 January Edwin Valero 9.4 (Venezuela) W RSC 1 Michael Lozada 9.3½ (Mexico), Ariake Coliseum, Tokyo, Japan – WBA.

17 March   Marco Antonio Barrera 9.4 (Mexico) L PTS 12 Juan Manuel Marquez 9.3 (Mexico), MGM Grand, Las Vegas, Nevada, USA – WBC. Scorecards: 111-116, 111-116, 109-118.

20 April   Malcolm Klassen 9.3¾ (South Africa) L PTS 12 Mzonke Fana 9.3½ (South Africa), Oliver Tambo Hall, Khayelitsha, South Africa – IBF. Scorecards: 112-116, 113-116, 115-114.

3 May   Edwin Valero 9.4 (Venezuela) W RSC 8 Nobuhito Honmo 9.3½ (Japan), Ariake Coliseum, Tokyo, Japan – WBA.

Lightweight

15 July   Juan Diaz 9.9 (USA) W RSC 9 Randy Suico 9.9 (Philippines), MGM Grand, Las Vegas, Nevada, USA - WBA.

4 November   Juan Diaz 9.8 (USA) W PTS 12 Fernando Angulo 9.8 (Venezuela), Chase Field Baseball Stadium, Phoenix, Arizona, USA – WBA. Scorecards: 118-109, 118-109, 116-111.

3 February   Jesus Chavez 9.8 ¾ (Mexico) L CO 3 Julio Diaz 9.9 (USA), Silver Spurs Arena, Kissimmee, Florida, USA – IBF.

28 April   Juan Diaz 9.9 (USA) W RTD 8 Acelino Freitas 9.9 (Brazil), Foxwoods Resort & Casino, Ledyard, Connecticut, USA – WBA/WBO. Earlier, on 4 October, it had been reported that Freitas had retired and that Graham Earl (England) and Michael Katsidis (Australia) would be contesting the vacant WBO title. However, a few weeks later Freitas rescinded his retirement plans and Katsidis met Earl for the vacant WBO 'interim' title at the Wembley Arena in England on 17 February 2007, winning by a fifth-round retirement. A few months later, in a fight that was effectively contesting the 'secondary' WBA title, Prawet Singwangcha (Thailand) and Jose Miguel Cotto (Puerto Rico) drew over 12 rounds at the Angel Espada Coliseum, Salinas, Puerto Rico on 11 May.

Note: Due to defend the WBC version of the title against Joel Casamayor (Cuba) in Las Vegas, Nevada, USA on 7 October 2006, Diego Corrales (USA) failed to make the weight and was stripped of his crown. Despite that, the fight went ahead and on winning via a split decision over 12 rounds the Cuban was confirmed as the new champion. Earlier, on 12 August 2006, David Diaz (USA) had won the WBC 'interim' title when stopping Jose Armando Santa Cruz (Mexico) in the tenth round in Las Vegas, Nevada, USA, which was upgraded to full title status in February 2007 when Casamayor was stripped following an announcement that he would be meeting the WBO champion, Acelino Freitas. After that fight failed to happen, Casamayor was announced as being the WBC 'interim' champion in May, while Diaz looked forward to a defence against Erik Morales.

L.Welterweight

2 September   Souleymane M'Baye 9.13½ (France) W RSC 4 Raul Balbi 10.0 (Argentina), Reebok Stadium, Bolton, England – WBA. Referee: Paul Thomas. Judges:

John Coyle, Dave Parris, Terry O'Connor. Billed for the vacant title after Ricky Hatton (England) handed in his belt on winning the WBA welter crown in May 2006.

15 September   Junior Witter 9.12¼ (England) W PTS 12 DeMarcus Corley 9.13½ (USA), Alexandra Palace, Muswell Hill, London, England – WBC. Scorecards: 117-111, 118-112, 116-113. Floyd Mayweather (USA) relinquished the title in March 2006 on moving up a division to meet Zab Judah for the IBF title, leaving Witter and Corley to contest the vacant crown.

18 November   Ricardo Torres 9.13 (Colombia) W PTS 12 Mike Arnaoutis 9.12 (Greece), Thomas & Mack Centre, Las Vegas, Nevada, USA - WBO. Scorecards: 116-111, 114-113, 113-114. This one was designated as a vacant title bout after Miguel Cotto (Puerto Rico) handed in his belt towards the end of October.

20 January   Junior Witter 9.13¾ (England) W RSC 9 Arturo Morua 9.13¾ (Mexico), Alexandra Palace, Wood Green, London, England – WBC.

20 January   Juan Urango 9.13 (Colombia) L PTS 12 Ricky Hatton 9.13 (England), Paris Hotel, Las Vegas, Nevada, USA – IBF. Scorecards: 109-119, 109-119, 109-119. By mid-February Hatton had relinquished the IBF title when being told that he had to sign for a defence against the South African-born mandatory challenger, Lovemore Ndou, now domiciled in Australia. Ndou had won a final eliminator in Sydney, Australia on 4 February when stopping Naoufel Ben Rabah (Tunisia) at the end of the 11th. As Hatton had already signed for a big fight against Mexico's Jose Luis Castillo to decide the IBO championship his decision was an easy one and following that Ndou was handed the title on a plate.

10 March   Souleymane M'Baye 9.13¾ (France) DREW 12 Andreas Kotelnik 10.0 (Ukraine), Olympia, Liverpool, England – WBA. Referee: Dave Parris. Scorecards: Paul Thomas 115-113, Mickey Vann 112-117, Terry O'Connor 114-114.

28 April   Ricardo Torres 9.13½ (Colombia) W PTS 12 Arturo Morua 9.13¼ (Mexico), North University Coliseum, Barranquilla, Colombia – WBO. Scorecards: 120-109, 120-108, 118-110.

16 June   Lovemore Ndou 9.12¼ (South Africa) L PTS 12 Paul Malignaggi 9.12 (USA), Mohegun Sun Arena, Uncasville, Connecticut, USA – IBF. Scorecards: 108-118, 106-120, 106-120.

23 June   Ricky Hatton 10.0 (England) W CO 4 Jose Luis Castillo 10.0 (Mexico), Thomas & Mack Centre, Las Vegas, Nevada, USA – IBO.

Welterweight

22 July   Carlos Baldomir 10.7 (Argentina) W RSC 9 Arturo Gatti 10.7 (Canada), Boardwalk Hall, Atlantic City, New Jersey, USA – WBC.

28 October   Kermit Cintron 10.6 (Puerto Rico) W RSC 5 Mark Suarez 10.6¼ (USA), The County Convention Centre, Palm Beach, Florida, USA - IBF. Earlier, on 15 August, it was announced that Floyd Mayweather (USA) had relinquished the IBF title in order to challenge Carlos

Baldomir for the WBA crown, rather than defend against the little known Suarez (USA). Following this action, Suarez was booked to meet Puerto Rico's Cintron to contest the vacant title.

4 November   Carlos Baldomir 10.7 (Argentina) L PTS 12 Floyd Mayweather 10.6 (USA), Mandalay Bay Hotel, Las Vegas, Nevada, USA – WBC. Scorecards: John Keane 108-120, 108-120, 110-118. On 10 February 2007, Shane Mosley (USA) outpointed Luis Collazo (USA) over 12 rounds in Las Vegas, Nevada to win the 'interim' title.

2 December   Miguel Cotto 10.7 (Puerto Rico) W RTD 5 Carlos Quintana 10.6 (Puerto Rico), Boardwalk Hall, Atlantic City, New Jersey, USA – WBA. Billed for the vacant title after Ricky Hatton (England) moved back to the light-welter division on 31 August.

2 December   Antonio Margarito 10.7 (Mexico) W PTS 12 Joshua Clottey 10.7 (Ghana), Boardwalk Hall, Atlantic City, New Jersey, USA – WBO. Scorecards: 116-112, 116-112, 118-109.

3 March   Miguel Cotto 10.7 (Puerto Rico) W RSC 11 Oktay Urkal 10.6 (Germany), Roberto Clemente Coliseum, San Juan, Puerto Rico – WBA.

9 June   Miguel Cotto 10.6½ (Puerto Rico) W RSC 11 Zab Judah 10.5 (USA), Madison Square Garden, NYC, New York, USA – WBA.

L.Middleweight

8 July   Roman Karmazin 10.13 (Russia) L PTS 12 Cory Spinks 10.13 (USA), Savvis Centre, St Louis, Missouri, USA – IBF. Scorecards: 113-115, 113-115, 114-114.

21 October   Sergei Dzindziruk 10.13 (Ukraine) W PTS 12 Alisultan Nadirbegov 10.11½ (Russia), Brandberge Arena, Halle, Germany – WBO. Referee: Terry O'Connor. Scorecards: 120-108, 119-108, 119-109.

6 January   Jose Antonio Rivera 10.13 (USA) L RSC 9 Travis Simms 10.13¾ (USA), Seminole Hard Rock Live Arena, Hollywood, Florida, USA – WBA.

3 February   Cory Spinks 10.13¾ (USA) W PTS 12 Rodney Jones 10.13 (USA), Silver Spurs Arena, Kissimmee, Florida, USA – IBF. Scorecards: 120-108, 1180110, 120-108.

5 May   Oscar de la Hoya 11.0 (USA) L PTS 12 Floyd Mayweather 10.10 (USA), MGM Grand, Las Vegas, Nevada, USA – WBC. Scorecards: 112-116, 113-115, 115-113. Mayweather vacated the title in June, preferring to hold on to the WBC welterweight crown.

19 May   Sergei Dzindziruk 10.13¾ (Ukraine) W RSC 11 Carlos Nascimento 10.11½ (Brazil), Color Line Arena, Hamburg, Germany – WBO. Judge: Paul Thomas.

Middleweight

23 September   Arthur Abraham 11.6 (Armenia) W PTS 12 Edison Miranda 11.6 (Colombia), Rittal Arena, Wetzlar, Germany - IBF. Scorecards: Dave Parris 114-109, 115-109, 114-109.

2 December   Javier Castillejo 11.5½ (Spain) L RSC 11 Mariano Carrera 11.5½ (Argentina), Estrel Congress Centre, Berlin, Germany – WBA. Earlier, on 15 July, Javier Castillejo (Spain) stopped Felix Sturm (Germany) in the tenth round to take the latter's WBA 'secondary' title at the Color Line Arena, Hamburg, Germany, prior to being handed full title status in November when the WBA decided not to agree to recognise Taylor as their 'super' champion any longer. The WBA's decision was made after Taylor was matched against Kassim Ouma, an opponent who failed to meet their criteria. Following the Carrera contest, Castillejo was reinstated as champion at the end of February 2007 after a second drug sample taken from the Argentinian tested positive for a banned substance.

9 December   Jermain Taylor 11.5½ (USA) W PTS 12 Kassim Ouma 11.4½ (Uganda), Alltel Arena, Little Rock, Arkansas, USA – WBO/WBC. Scorecards: 118-110, 117-111, 115-113.

28 April   Javier Castillejo 11.4¼ (Spain) L PTS 12 Felix Sturm 11.5½ (Germany), Koenig Pilsener Arena, Oberhausen, Germany – WBA. Scorecards: John Coyle 112-116, 112-116, 114-115.

19 May   Jermain Taylor 11.5¾ (USA) W PTS 12 Cory Spinks 11.5¾ (USA), FedEx Forum, Memphis, Tennessee, USA – WBO/WBC. Scorecards: 117-111, 115-113, 111-117.

26 May   Arthur Abraham 12.0 (Armenia) W RSC 3 Sebastien Demers 11.13 (Canada), JAKO Arena, Bamberg, Germany – IBF.

30 June   Felix Sturm 11.5¾ (Germany) W PTS 12 Noe Tulio Gonzalez 11.5½ (Uruguay), Porsche Arena, Stuttgart, Germany – WBA. Scorecards: 120-108, 118-110, 116-112.

S.Middleweight

14 October   Joe Calzaghe 12.0 (Wales) W PTS 12 Sakio Bika 12.0 (Cameroon), MEN Arena, Manchester, England – IBF/WBO. Referee: Mickey Vann. Scorecards: Phil Edwards 116-111, 117-110, 117-110. On 27 November it was reported that Calzaghe had relinquished the IBF version of the title in order to defend his WBO crown against Peter Manfredo (USA), rather than face Robert Stieglitz (Germany), the IBF's mandatory challenger.

14 October   Mikkel Kessler 11.13¾ (Denmark) W CO 3 Markus Beyer 12.0 (Germany), Parken Stadium, Copenhagen, Denmark – WBC/WBA. With Kessler recognised as the WBA 'super" champion, Anthony Mundine stopped fellow Australian, Sam Soliman, in Sydney on 7 March 2007 to win the vacant WBA 'secondary' title.

3 March   Alejandro Berrio 12.0 (Colombia) W RSC 3 Robert Stieglitz 11.13¼ (Germany), Town Hall, Rostock, Germany – IBF.

24 March   Mikkel Kessler 12.0 (Denmark) W PTS 12 Librado Andrade 12.0 (Mexico), Parken Stadium, Copenhagen, Denmark – WBC/WBA. Scorecards: John Keane 120-108, 120-108, 120-108. On 27 June Anthony Mundine (Australia) outpointed Pablo Daniel Zamora Nievas (Argentina) over 12 rounds at the Broadbeach Leisure Centre on the Australian Gold Coast to retain his WBA 'secondary' title.

7 April   Joe Calzaghe 11.13¾ (Wales) W RSC 3 Peter

Manfredo 11.12 (USA), Millennium Stadium, Cardiff, Wales – WBO. Referee: Terry O'Connor.

L.Heavyweight

29 July   Zsolt Erdei 12.4¼ (Hungary) W PTS 12 Thomas Ulrich 12.6¼ (Germany), Koenig Pilsener Arena, Oberhausen, Germany - WBO. Scorecards: 118-110, 116-112, 120-108.

2 September   Clinton Woods 12.7 (England) W PTS 12 Glengoffe Johnson 12.4 (Jamaica), Reebok Stadium, Bolton, England - IBF. Referee: Howard Foster. Scorecards: Mickey Vann 115-113, 116-112, 113-115.

7 October   Tomasz Adamek 12.6 (Poland) W PTS 12 Paul Briggs 12.7 (Australia), Allstate Arena, Rosemont, Illinois, USA – WBC. Scorecards: 114-112, 115-111, 113-113.

27 January   Zsolt Erdei 12.5 (Hungary) W RSC 8 Danny Santiago 12.4½ (USA), Castle Guard Arena, Dusseldorf, Germany – WBO.

3 February   Tomasz Adamek 12.6 (Poland) L PTS 12 Chad Dawson 12.7 (USA), Silver Spurs Arena, Kissimmee, Florida, USA – WBC. Scorecards: 109-117, 108-118, 110-116.

28 April   Stipe Drews 12.6¼ (Croatia) W PTS 12 Silvio Branco 12.6¼ (Italy), Koenig Pilsener Arena, Oberhausen, Germany – WBA. Scorecards: 116-113, 116-112, 115-113. Earlier, on 27 July 2006, Branco won the vacant WBA 'interim' title when outpointing Manny Siaca (Puerto Rico) over 12 rounds in Milan, Italy. Branco was installed as the champion on 21 October 2006 after Fabrice Tiozzo (France), who had been due to defend against Hugo Garay, announced his retirement from the ring.

9 June   Chad Dawson 12.6 (USA) W RSC 6 Jesus Ruiz 12.6¾ (Mexico), Connecticut Convention Centre, Hartford, Connecticut, USA – WBC.

16 June   Zsolt Erdei 12.4 (Hungary) W RSC 11 George Blades 12.6¼ (USA), SYMA Sports & Leisure Centre, Budapest, Hungary – WBO.

Note: Following his 12-round points win over Antonio Tarver (USA) for the IBO title in Atlantic City, New Jersey, USA on 10 June 2006, Bernard Hopkins announced that he had no plans to stay in the light-heavyweight division and was handing back his belt.

Cruiserweight

14 October   Enzo Maccarinelli 14.3 (Wales) W RSC 1 Mark Hobson 14.4 (England), MEN Arena, Manchester, England – WBO. Referee: Terry O'Connor. Judges: Roy Francis, Mickey Vann, Dave Parris. Earlier, on 8 July 2006, in Cardiff, Wales, Maccarinelli had stopped Marcelo Dominguez (Argentina) in the ninth round to win the vacant WBO 'interim' title. Following Nelson's decision to retire after breaking down in training in September 2006, Maccarinelli was immediately upgraded to full champion proper.

25 November   Krzysztof Wlodarczyk 13.10¼ (Poland) w pts 12 Steve Cunningham 13.11½ (USA), Torwar Sports Hall, Warsaw, Poland – IBF. Scorecards: 116-112, 115-113, 109-119. After O'Neill Bell (Jamaica) was forced to return his IBF belt for not fulfilling his mandatory requirements, a contest to decide the vacant title was made for 6 May 2006 between Cunningham (USA), who had outpointed Kelvin Davis (USA) over 12 rounds in Cleveland, USA on 3 September 2005 in an eliminator, and Guillermo Jones (Panama). The match was called off at the last moment due to a contractual dispute and Cunningham was later matched against Poland's Wlodarczyk, a fighter who had lost just once in 36 contests.

17 March   O'Neil Bell 14.2½ (Jamaica) L PTS 12 Jean-Marc Mormeck 14.2¼ (Guadaloupe), Marcel Cerdan Sports Palace, Paris, France – WBA/WBC. Scorecards: 113-115, 113-115, 112-116. Earlier, on 2 December 2006, in Paris, France, Luis Pineda (Panama) had won the vacant WBA 'interim' title when stopping Russia's Valery Brudov in the 11th round. Following Pineda being stripped, Firat Aslan (Germany) outpointed Brudov over 12 rounds on 16 June to win the vacant 'interim' belt.

7 April   Enzo Maccarinelli 14.4 (Wales) W RSC 1 Bobby Gunn 13.13 (USA), Millennium Stadium, Cardiff, Wales – WBO. Judge: Terry O'Connor.

26 May   Krzysztof Wlodarczyk 14.0 (Poland) L PTS 12 Steve Cunningham 13.12 (USA), Apodek Arena, Katowice, Poland – IBF. Referee: Dave Parris. Scorecards: 112-116, 112-115, 114-114.

Heavyweight

12 August   Hasim Rahman 16.11 (USA) L RSC 12 Oleg Maskaev 17.1 (Kazakhstan), Thomas & Mack Centre, Las Vegas, Nevada, USA – WBC.

7 October   Nikolai Valuev 23.6 (Russia) W RSC 11 Monte Barrett 15.12½ (USA), Allstate Arena, Rosemont, Illinois, USA – WBA.

4 November   Sergei Lyakhovich 17.0 (Belarus) L RSC 12 Shannon Briggs 19.2 (USA), Chase Field Baseball Stadium, Phoenix, Arizona, USA.

11 November   Vladimir Klitschko 17.3 (Ukraine) W RSC 7 Calvin Brock 16.0½ (USA), Madison Square Garden, NYC, New York, USA – IBF.

10 December   Oleg Maskaev 17.2 (Kazaakhstan) W PTS 12 Peter Okhello 18.2½ (Uganda), Olympic Sports Arena, Moscow, Russia – WBC. Scorecards: 120-107, 118-109, 120-107.

20 January   Nikolai Valuev 23.0½ (Russia) W RTD 3 Jameel McCline 19.2½ (USA), St Jacob Hall, Basle, Switzerland – WBA. Referee: John Coyle. Judge: Paul Thomas.

10 March   Vladimir Klitschko 17.8½ (Ukraine) W RSC 2 Ray Austin 17.9 (USA), SAP Arena, Mannheim, Germany – IBF. Judge: Roy Francis.

14 April   Nikolai Valuev 22.11 (Russia) L PTS 12 Ruslan Chagaev 16.4¼ (Uzbekistan), Porsche Arena, Stuttgart, Germany – WBA. Scorecards: 111-117, 113-115, 114-114.

2 June   Shannon Briggs 19.7 (USA) L PTS 12 Sultan Ibragimov 15.11 (Russia), Boardwalk Hall, Atlantic City, New Jersey, USA – WBO. Scorecards: 111-117, 109-119, 113-115.

World Champions Since Gloves, 1889-2007

Since I began to carry out extensive research into world championship boxing from the very beginnings of gloved action, I discovered much that needed to be amended regarding the historical listings as we know them, especially prior to the 1920s. Although yet to finalise my researches, despite making considerable changes, the listings are the most comprehensive ever published. Bearing all that in mind, and using a wide range of American newspapers, the aim has been to discover just who had claims, valid or otherwise. Studying the records of all the recognised champions, supplied by Professor Luckett Davis and his team, fights against all opposition have been analysed to produce the ultimate data. Because there were no boxing commissions as such in America prior to the 1920s, the yardstick used to determine valid claims were victories over the leading fighters of the day and recognition given within the newspapers. Only where that criteria has been met have I adjusted previous information. Please note that weight limits for the bantam (1919), feather (1921), light (1913), welter (1921) and middleweight (1921) divisions were only universally recognised in the years stated in brackets. Prior to that the champions shown would have won title claims at varying weights, which were massaged in later years to fit the modern weight classes.

Championship Status Code:

AU = Austria; AUST = Australia; CALIF = California; CAN = Canada; CLE = Cleveland Boxing Commission; EBU = European Boxing Union; FL = Florida; FR = France; GB = Great Britain; GEO = Georgia; H = Hawaii; IBF = International Boxing Federation; IBU = International Boxing Union; ILL = Illinois; LOUIS = Louisiana; MARY = Maryland; MASS = Massachusetts; MICH = Michigan; NBA = National Boxing Association; NC = North Carolina; NY = New York; PEN = Pennsylvania; SA = South Africa; TBC = Territorial Boxing Commission; USA = United States; WBA = World Boxing Association; WBC = World Boxing Council; WBO = World Boxing Organisation.

Champions in **bold** are accorded universal recognition.

*Undefeated champions (Only relates to universally recognised champions prior to 1962 and thereafter WBA/WBC/IBF/ WBO champions. Does not include men who forfeited titles).

Title Holder	Birthplace	Tenure	Status
M. Flyweight (105 lbs)			
Kyung-Yung Lee*	S Korea	1987	IBF
Hiroki Ioka	Japan	1987-1988	WBC
Silvio Gamez*	Venezuela	1988-1989	WBA
Samuth Sithnaruepol	Thailand	1988-1989	IBF
Napa Kiatwanchai	Thailand	1988-1989	WBC
Bong-Jun Kim	S Korea	1989-1991	WBA
Nico Thomas	Indonesia	1989	IBF
Rafael Torres	Dom Republic	1989-1992	WBO
Eric Chavez	Philippines	1989-1990	IBF
Jum-Hwan Choi	S Korea	1989-1990	WBC
Hideyuki Ohashi	Japan	1990	WBC
Fahlan Lukmingkwan	Thailand	1990-1992	IBF
Ricardo Lopez*	Mexico	1990-1997	WBC
Hi-Yon Choi	S Korea	1991-1992	WBA
Manny Melchor	Philippines	1992	IBF
Hideyuki Ohashi	Japan	1992-1993	WBA
Ratanapol Sowvoraphin	Thailand	1992-1996	IBF
Chana Porpaoin	Thailand	1993-1995	WBA
Paul Weir*	Scotland	1993-1994	WBO
Alex Sanchez	Puerto Rico	1993-1997	WBO
Rosendo Alvarez	Nicaragua	1995-1998	WBA
Ratanapol Sowvoraphin	Thailand	1996-1997	IBF
Ricardo Lopez*	Mexico	1997-1998	WBC/WBO
Zolani Petelo*	S Africa	1997-2000	IBF
Ricardo Lopez*	Mexico	1998	WBC
Eric Jamili	Philippines	1998	WBO
Kermin Guardia*	Colombia	1998-2002	WBO
Ricardo Lopez*	Mexico	1998-1999	WBA/WBC
Wandee Chor Chareon	Thailand	1999-2000	WBC
Nohel Arambulet	Venezuela	1999-2000	WBA
Jose Antonio Aguirre	Mexico	2000-2004	WBC
Jomo Gamboa	Philippines	2000	WBA
Keitaro Hoshino	Japan	2000-2001	WBA
Chana Porpaoin	Thailand	2001	WBA
Roberto Levya	Mexico	2001-2003	IBF
Yutaka Niida*	Japan	2001	WBA
Keitaro Hoshino	Japan	2002	WBA
Jorge Mata	Spain	2002-2003	WBO
Nohel Arambulet	Venezuela	2002-2004	WBA
Miguel Barrera	Colombia	2002-2003	IBF
Eduardo Marquez	Nicaragua	2003	WBO
Ivan Calderon	Puerto Rico	2003-	WBO
Edgar Cardenas	Mexico	2003	IBF
Daniel Reyes	Colombia	2003-2004	IBF
Eagle Kyowa	Thailand	2004	WBC
Muhammad Rachman	Indonesia	2004-	IBF
Yutaka Niida	Japan	2004-	WBA
Isaac Bustos	Mexico	2004-2005	WBC
Katsunari Takayama	Japan	2005	WBC
Eagle Kyowa	Thailand	2005-	WBC
L. Flyweight (108 lbs)			
Franco Udella	Italy	1975	WBC
Jaime Rios	Panama	1975-1976	WBA
Luis Estaba	Venezuela	1975-1978	WBC
Juan Guzman	Dom Republic	1976	WBA
Yoko Gushiken	Japan	1976-1981	WBA
Freddie Castillo	Mexico	1978	WBC
Sor Vorasingh	Thailand	1978	WBC
Sun-Jun Kim	S Korea	1978-1980	WBC
Shigeo Nakajima	Japan	1980	WBC
Hilario Zapata	Panama	1980-1982	WBC
Pedro Flores	Mexico	1981	WBA
Hwan-Jin Kim	S Korea	1981	WBA
Katsuo Tokashiki	Japan	1981-1983	WBA
Amado Ursua	Mexico	1982	WBC
Tadashi Tomori	Japan	1982	WBC
Hilario Zapata	Panama	1982-1983	WBC
Jung-Koo Chang*	S Korea	1983-1988	WBC
Lupe Madera	Mexico	1983-1984	WBA
Dodie Penalosa	Philippines	1983-1986	IBF
Francisco Quiroz	Dom Republic	1984-1985	WBA
Joey Olivo	USA	1985	WBA
Myung-Woo Yuh	S Korea	1985-1991	WBA
Jum-Hwan Choi	S Korea	1986-1988	IBF
Tacy Macalos	Philippines	1988-1989	IBF
German Torres	Mexico	1988-1989	WBC

Title Holder	Birthplace	Tenure	Status
Yul-Woo Lee	S Korea	1989	WBC
Muangchai Kitikasem	Thailand	1989-1990	IBF
Jose de Jesus	Puerto Rico	1989-1992	WBO
Humberto Gonzalez	Mexico	1989-1990	WBC
Michael Carbajal*	USA	1990-1993	IBF
Rolando Pascua	Philippines	1990-1991	WBC
Melchor Cob Castro	Mexico	1991	WBC
Humberto Gonzalez	Mexico	1991-1993	WBC
Hiroki Ioka	Japan	1991-1992	WBA
Josue Camacho	Puerto Rico	1992-1994	WBO
Myung-Woo Yuh*	S Korea	1992-1993	WBA
Michael Carbajal	USA	1993-1994	IBF/WBC
Silvio Gamez	Venezuela	1993-1995	WBA
Humberto Gonzalez	Mexico	1994-1995	WBC/IBF
Michael Carbajal*	USA	1994	WBO
Paul Weir	Scotland	1994-1995	WBO
Hi-Yong Choi	S Korea	1995-1996	WBA
Saman Sorjaturong*	Thailand	1995	WBC/IBF
Jacob Matlala*	South Africa	1995-1997	WBO
Saman Sorjaturong	Thailand	1995-1999	WBC
Carlos Murillo	Panama	1996	WBA
Michael Carbajal	USA	1996-1997	IBF
Keiji Yamaguchi	Japan	1996	WBA
Pichitnoi Chor Siriwat	Thailand	1996-2000	WBA
Mauricio Pastrana	Colombia	1997-1998	IBF
Jesus Chong	Mexico	1997	WBO
Melchor Cob Castro	Mexico	1997-1998	WBO
Mauricio Pastrana	Colombia	1997-1998	IBF
Juan Domingo Cordoba	Argentina	1998	WBO
Jorge Arce	Mexico	1998-1999	WBO
Will Grigsby	USA	1998-1999	IBF
Michael Carbajal*	USA	1999-2000	WBO
Ricardo Lopez*	Mexico	1999-2002	IBF
Yo-Sam Choi	S Korea	1999-2002	WBC
Masibuleke Makepula*	S Africa	2000	WBO
Will Grigsby	USA	2000	WBO
Beibis Mendoza	Colombia	2000-2001	WBA
Rosendo Alvarez	Nicaragua	2001-2004	WBA
Nelson Dieppa	Puerto Rico	2001-2005	WBO
Jorge Arce*	Mexico	2002-2005	WBC
Jose Victor Burgos	Mexico	2003-2004	IBF
Erick Ortiz	Mexico	2005	WBC
Roberto Vasquez*	Panama	2005-2006	WBA
Hugo Cazares	Mexico	2005-	WBO
Will Grigsby	USA	2005-2006	IBF
Brian Viloria	USA	2005-2006	WBC
Ulises Solis	Mexico	2006-	IBF
Koki Kameda*	Japan	2006-2007	WBA
Omar Nino	Mexico	2006-2007	WBC
Edgar Solis	Mexico	2007-	WBC
Juan Carlos Reveco	Argentina	2007-	WBA

Flyweight (112 lbs)

Title Holder	Birthplace	Tenure	Status
Johnny Coulon	Canada	1910	USA
Sid Smith	England	1911-1913	GB
Sid Smith	England	1913	GB/IBU
Bill Ladbury	England	1913-1914	GB/IBU
Percy Jones	Wales	1914	GB/IBU
Tancy Lee	Scotland	1915	GB/IBU
Joe Symonds	England	1915-1916	GB/IBU
Jimmy Wilde	Wales	1916	GB/IBU
Jimmy Wilde	Wales	1916-1923	
Pancho Villa*	Philippines	1923-1925	
Fidel la Barba	USA	1925-1927	NBA/CALIF
Fidel la Barba*	USA	1927	
Pinky Silverberg	USA	1927	NBA
Johnny McCoy	USA	1927-1928	CALIF
Izzy Schwartz	USA	1927-1929	NY
Frenchy Belanger	Canada	1927-1928	NBA
Newsboy Brown	Russia	1928	CALIF
Johnny Hill	Scotland	1928-1929	GB
Frankie Genaro	USA	1928-1929	NBA

Title Holder	Birthplace	Tenure	Status
Emile Pladner	France	1929	NBA/IBU
Frankie Genaro	USA	1929-1931	NBA/IBU
Midget Wolgast	USA	1930-1935	NY
Young Perez	Tunisia	1931-1932	NBA/IBU
Jackie Brown	England	1932-1935	NBA/IBU
Jackie Brown	England	1935	GB/NBA
Benny Lynch	Scotland	1935-1937	GB/NBA
Small Montana	Philippines	1935-1937	NY/CALIF
Valentin Angelmann	France	1936-1938	IBU
Peter Kane*	England	1938-1939	NBA/NY/GB/IBU
Little Dado	Philippines	1938-1939	CALIF
Little Dado	Philippines	1939-1943	NBA/CALIF
Jackie Paterson	Scotland	1943-1947	
Jackie Paterson	Scotland	1947-1948	GB/NY
Rinty Monaghan	Ireland	1947-1948	NBA
Rinty Monaghan*	Ireland	1948-1950	
Terry Allen	England	1950	
Dado Marino	Hawaii	1950-1952	
Yoshio Shirai	Japan	1952-1954	
Pascual Perez	Argentina	1954-1960	
Pone Kingpetch	Thailand	1960-1962	
Fighting Harada	Japan	1962-1963	
Pone Kingpetch	Thailand	1963	
Hiroyuki Ebihara	Japan	1963-1964	
Pone Kingpetch	Thailand	1964-1965	
Salvatore Burruni	Italy	1965	
Salvatore Burruni	Italy	1965-1966	WBC
Horacio Accavallo*	Argentina	1966-1968	WBA
Walter McGowan	Scotland	1966	WBC
Chartchai Chionoi	Thailand	1966-1969	WBC
Efren Torres	Mexico	1969-1970	WBC
Hiroyuki Ebihara	Japan	1969	WBA
Bernabe Villacampo	Philippines	1969-1970	WBA
Chartchai Chionoi	Thailand	1970	WBC
Berkrerk Chartvanchai	Thailand	1970	WBA

Terry Allen

Title Holder	Birthplace	Tenure	Status
Masao Ohba*	Japan	1970-1973	WBA
Erbito Salavarria	Philippines	1970-1971	WBC
Betulio Gonzalez	Venezuela	1971-1972	WBC
Venice Borkorsor*	Thailand	1972-1973	WBC
Chartchai Chionoi	Thailand	1973-1974	WBA
Betulio Gonzalez	Venezuela	1973-1974	WBC
Shoji Oguma	Japan	1974-1975	WBC
Susumu Hanagata	Japan	1974-1975	WBA
Miguel Canto	Mexico	1975-1979	WBC
Erbito Salavarria	Philippines	1975-1976	WBA
Alfonso Lopez	Panama	1976	WBA
Guty Espadas	Mexico	1976-1978	WBA
Betulio Gonzalez	Venezuela	1978-1979	WBA
Chan-Hee Park	S Korea	1979-1980	WBC
Luis Ibarra	Panama	1979-1980	WBA
Tae-Shik Kim	S Korea	1980	WBA
Shoji Oguma	Japan	1980-1981	WBC
Peter Mathebula	S Africa	1980-1981	WBA
Santos Laciar	Argentina	1981	WBA
Antonio Avelar	Mexico	1981-1982	WBC
Luis Ibarra	Panama	1981	WBA
Juan Herrera	Mexico	1981-1982	WBA
Prudencio Cardona	Colombia	1982	WBC
Santos Laciar*	Argentina	1982-1985	WBA
Freddie Castillo	Mexico	1982	WBC
Eleonicio Mercedes	Dom Republic	1982-1983	WBC
Charlie Magri	Tunisia	1983	WBC
Frank Cedeno	Philippines	1983-1984	WBC
Soon-Chun Kwon	S Korea	1983-1985	IBF
Koji Kobayashi	Japan	1984	WBC
Gabriel Bernal	Mexico	1984	WBC
Sot Chitalada	Thailand	1984-1988	WBC
Hilario Zapata	Panama	1985-1987	WBA
Chong-Kwan Chung	S Korea	1985-1986	IBF
Bi-Won Chung	S Korea	1986	IBF
Hi-Sup Shin	S Korea	1986-1987	IBF
Fidel Bassa	Colombia	1987-1989	WBA
Dodie Penalosa	Philippines	1987	IBF
Chang-Ho Choi	S Korea	1987-1988	IBF
Rolando Bohol	Philippines	1988	IBF
Yong-Kang Kim	S Korea	1988-1989	WBC
Duke McKenzie	England	1988-1989	IBF
Elvis Alvarez*	Colombia	1989	WBO
Sot Chitalada	Thailand	1989-1991	WBC
Dave McAuley	Ireland	1989-1992	IBF
Jesus Rojas	Venezuela	1989-1900	WBA
Yukihito Tamakuma	Japan	1990-1991	WBA
Isidro Perez	Mexico	1990-1992	WBO
Yul-Woo Lee	S Korea	1990	WBA
Muangchai Kitikasem	Thailand	1991-1992	WBC
Elvis Alvarez	Colombia	1991	WBA
Yong-Kang Kim	S Korea	1991-1992	WBA
Pat Clinton	Scotland	1992-1993	WBO
Rodolfo Blanco	Colombia	1992	IBF
Yuri Arbachakov	Russia	1992-1997	WBC
Aquiles Guzman	Venezuela	1992	WBA
Pichit Sitbangprachan*	Thailand	1992-1994	IBF
David Griman	Venezuela	1992-1994	WBA
Jacob Matlala	S Africa	1993-1995	WBO
Saen Sorploenchit	Thailand	1994-1996	WBA
Alberto Jimenez	Mexico	1995-1996	WBO
Francisco Tejedor	Colombia	1995	IBF
Danny Romero*	USA	1995-1996	IBF
Mark Johnson*	USA	1996-1998	IBF
Jose Bonilla	Venezuela	1996-1998	WBA
Carlos Salazar	Argentina	1996-1998	WBO
Chatchai Sasakul	Thailand	1997-1998	WBC
Hugo Soto	Argentina	1998-1999	WBA
Ruben Sanchez	Mexico	1998-1999	WBO
Manny Pacquiao	Philippines	1998-1999	WBC
Silvio Gamez	Venezuela	1999	WBA
Irene Pacheco	Colombia	1999-2004	IBF

Title Holder	Birthplace	Tenure	Status
Jose Antonio Lopez	Spain	1999	WBO
Sornpichai Pisanurachan	Thailand	1999-2000	WBA
Medgoen Singsurat	Thailand	1999-2000	WBC
Isidro Garcia	Mexico	1999-2000	WBO
Malcolm Tunacao	Philippines	2000-2001	WBC
Eric Morel	USA	2000-2003	WBA
Fernando Montiel*	Mexico	2000-2002	WBO
Pongsaklek Wonjongkam	Thailand	2001-	WBC
Adonis Rivas	Nicaragua	2002	WBO
Omar Narvaez	Argentina	2002-	WBO
Lorenzo Parra	Venezuela	2003-2007	WBA
Vic Darchinyan	Armenia	2004-	IBF
Takefumi Sakata	Japan	2007-	WBA

S. Flyweight (115 lbs)

Title Holder	Birthplace	Tenure	Status
Rafael Orono	Venezuela	1980-1981	WBC
Chul-Ho Kim	S Korea	1981-1982	WBC
Gustavo Ballas	Argentina	1981	WBA
Rafael Pedroza	Panama	1981-1982	WBA
Jiro Watanabe	Japan	1982-1984	WBA
Rafael Orono	Venezuela	1982-1983	WBC
Payao Poontarat	Thailand	1983-1984	WBC
Joo-Do Chun	S Korea	1983-1985	IBF
Jiro Watanabe	Japan	1984-1986	WBC
Kaosai Galaxy*	Thailand	1984-1992	WBA
Elly Pical	Indonesia	1985-1986	IBF
Cesar Polanco	Dom Republic	1986	IBF
Gilberto Roman	Mexico	1986-1987	WBC
Elly Pical	Indonesia	1986-1987	IBF
Santos Laciar	Argentina	1987	WBC
Tae-Il Chang	S Korea	1987	IBF
Jesus Rojas	Colombia	1987-1988	WBC
Elly Pical	Indonesia	1987-1989	IBF
Gilberto Roman	Mexico	1988-1989	WBC
Jose Ruiz	Puerto Rico	1989-1992	WBO
Juan Polo Perez	Colombia	1989-1990	IBF
Nana Yaw Konadu	Ghana	1989-1990	WBC
Sung-Il Moon	S Korea	1990-1993	WBC
Robert Quiroga	USA	1990-1993	IBF
Jose Quirino	Mexico	1992	WBO
Katsuya Onizuka	Japan	1992-1994	WBA
Johnny Bredahl	Denmark	1992-1994	WBO
Julio Cesar Borboa	Mexico	1993-1994	IBF
Jose Luis Bueno	Mexico	1993-1994	WBC
Hiroshi Kawashima	Japan	1994-1997	WBC
Harold Grey	Colombia	1994-1995	IBF
Hyung-Chul Lee	S Korea	1994-1995	WBA
Johnny Tapia*	USA	1994-1997	WBO
Alimi Goitia	Venezuela	1995-1996	WBA
Carlos Salazar	Argentina	1995-1996	IBF
Harold Grey	Colombia	1996	IBF
Yokthai Sith-Oar	Thailand	1996-1997	WBA
Danny Romero	USA	1996-1997	IBF
Gerry Penalosa	Philippines	1997-1998	WBC
Johnny Tapia*	USA	1997-1998	IBF/WBO
Satoshi Iida	Japan	1997-1998	WBA
In-Joo Cho	S Korea	1998-2000	WBC
Victor Godoi	Argentina	1998-1999	WBO
Jesus Rojas	Venezuela	1998-1999	WBA
Mark Johnson	USA	1999-2000	IBF
Diego Morales	Mexico	1999	WBO
Hideki Todaka	Japan	1999-2000	WBA
Adonis Rivas	Nicaragua	1999-2001	WBO
Felix Machado	Venezuela	2000-2003	IBF
Masamori Tokuyama	Japan	2000-2004	WBC
Silvio Gamez	Venezuela	2000-2001	WBA
Celes Kobayashi	Japan	2001-2002	WBA
Pedro Alcazar	Panama	2001-2002	WBO
Alexander Munoz	Venezuela	2002-2004	WBA
Fernando Montiel	Mexico	2002-2003	WBO
Luis Perez	Nicaragua	2003-2006	IBF
Mark Johnson	USA	2003-2004	WBO

237

Title Holder	Birthplace	Tenure	Status
Katsushige Kawashima	Japan	2004-2005	WBC
Ivan Hernandez	Mexico	2004-2005	WBO
Martin Castillo	Mexico	2004-2006	WBA
Fernando Montiel	Mexico	2005-	WBO
Masamori Tokuyama*	Japan	2005-2006	WBC
Nobuo Nashiro	Japan	2006-2007	WBA
Cristian Mijares	Mexico	2007-	WBC
Alexander Munoz	Venezuela	2007-	WBA

Bantamweight (118 lbs)

Title Holder	Birthplace	Tenure	Status
Tommy Kelly	USA	1889	
George Dixon	Canada	1889-1890	
Chappie Moran	England	1889-1890	
Tommy Kelly	USA	1890-1892	
Billy Plimmer	England	1892-1895	
Pedlar Palmer	England	1895-1899	
Terry McGovern	USA	1899	USA
Pedlar Palmer	England	1899-1900	GB
Terry McGovern*	USA	1899-1900	
Clarence Forbes	USA	1900	
Johnny Reagan	USA	1900-1902	
Harry Ware	England	1900-1902	GB
Harry Harris	USA	1901	
Harry Forbes	USA	1901-1902	
Kid McFadden	USA	1901	
Dan Dougherty	USA	1901	
Andrew Tokell	England	1902	GB
Harry Ware	England	1902	GB
Harry Forbes	USA	1902-1903	USA
Joe Bowker	England	1902-1904	GB
Frankie Neil	USA	1903-1904	USA
Joe Bowker*	England	1904-1905	

Title Holder	Birthplace	Tenure	Status
Frankie Neil	USA	1905	USA
Digger Stanley	England	1905-1907	
Owen Moran	England	1905-1907	
Jimmy Walsh	USA	1905-1908	USA
Owen Moran	England	1907	GB
Monte Attell	USA	1908-1910	
Jimmy Walsh	USA	1908-1911	
Digger Stanley	England	1909-1912	GB
Frankie Conley	Italy	1910-1911	
Johnny Coulon	Canada	1910-1911	
Monte Attell	USA	1910-1911	
Johnny Coulon	Canada	1911-1913	USA
Charles Ledoux	France	1912-1913	GB/IBU
Eddie Campi	USA	1913-1914	
Johnny Coulon	Canada	1913-1914	
Kid Williams	Denmark	1913-1914	
Kid Williams	Denmark	1914-1915	
Kid Williams	Denmark	1915-1917	
Johnny Ertle	USA	1915-1918	
Pete Herman	USA	1917-1919	
Pal Moore	USA	1918-1919	
Pete Herman	USA	1919-1920	
Joe Lynch	USA	1920-1921	
Pete Herman	USA	1921	
Johnny Buff	USA	1921-1922	
Joe Lynch	USA	1922-1923	
Joe Lynch	USA	1923-1924	NBA
Joe Burman	England	1923	NY
Abe Goldstein	USA	1923-1924	NY
Joe Lynch	USA	1924	
Abe Goldstein	USA	1924	
Eddie Martin	USA	1924-1925	
Charley Rosenberg	USA	1925-1926	
Charley Rosenberg	USA	1926-1927	NY
Bud Taylor*	USA	1926-1928	NBA
Bushy Graham*	Italy	1928-1929	NY
Al Brown	Panama	1929-1931	
Al Brown	Panama	1931	NY/IBU
Pete Sanstol	Norway	1931	CAN
Al Brown	Panama	1931-1933	
Al Brown	Panama	1933-1934	NY/NBA/IBU
Speedy Dado	Philippines	1933	CALIF
Baby Casanova	Mexico	1933-1934	CALIF
Sixto Escobar	Puerto Rico	1934	CAN
Sixto Escobar	Puerto Rico	1934-1935	NBA
Al Brown	Panama	1934-1935	NY/IBU
Lou Salica	USA	1935	CALIF
Baltazar Sangchilli	Spain	1935-1938	IBU
Lou Salica	USA	1935	NBA/NY
Sixto Escobar	Puerto Rico	1935-1937	NBA/NY
Harry Jeffra	USA	1937-1938	NY/NBA
Sixto Escobar	Puerto Rico	1938-1939	NY/NBA
Al Brown	Panama	1938	IBU
Sixto Escobar	Puerto Rico	1939	
George Pace	USA	1939-1940	NBA
Lou Salica	USA	1939	CALIF
Tony Olivera	USA	1939-1940	CALIF
Little Dado	Philippines	1940	CALIF
Lou Salica	USA	1940-1941	
Kenny Lindsay	Canada	1941	CAN
Lou Salica	USA	1942	NY
David Kui Kong Young	Hawaii	1941-1943	TBC
Lou Salica	USA	1941-1942	NY/NBA
Manuel Ortiz	USA	1942-1943	NBA
Manuel Ortiz	USA	1943-1945	NY/NBA
David Kui Kong Young	Hawaii	1943	TBC
Rush Dalma	Philippines	1943-1945	TBC
Manuel Ortiz	USA	1945-1947	
Harold Dade	USA	1947	
Manuel Ortiz	USA	1947-1950	
Vic Toweel	S Africa	1950-1952	
Jimmy Carruthers*	Australia	1952-1954	

Pete Herman

PETE HERMAN
LD'S BANTAM CHAMPION

Title Holder	Birthplace	Tenure	Status
Robert Cohen	Algeria	1954	
Robert Cohen	Algeria	1954-1956	NY/EBU
Raton Macias	Mexico	1955-1957	NBA
Mario D'Agata	Italy	1956-1957	NY/EBU
Alphonse Halimi	Algeria	1957	NY/EBU
Alphonse Halimi	Algeria	1957-1959	
Joe Becerra*	Mexico	1959-1960	
Alphonse Halimi	Algeria	1960-1961	EBU
Eder Jofre	Brazil	1960-1962	NBA
Johnny Caldwell	Ireland	1961-1962	EBU
Eder Jofre	Brazil	1962-1965	
Fighting Harada	Japan	1965-1968	
Lionel Rose	Australia	1968-1969	
Ruben Olivares	Mexico	1969-1970	
Chuchu Castillo	Mexico	1970-1971	
Ruben Olivares	Mexico	1971-1972	
Rafael Herrera	Mexico	1972	
Enrique Pinder	Panama	1972	
Enrique Pinder	Panama	1972-1973	WBC
Romeo Anaya	Mexico	1973	WBA
Rafael Herrera	Mexico	1973-1974	WBC
Arnold Taylor	S Africa	1973-1974	WBA
Soo-Hwan Hong	S Korea	1974-1975	WBA
Rodolfo Martinez	Mexico	1974-1976	WBC
Alfonso Zamora	Mexico	1975-1977	WBA
Carlos Zarate	Mexico	1976-1979	WBC
Jorge Lujan	Panama	1977-1980	WBA
Lupe Pintor*	Mexico	1979-1983	WBC
Julian Solis	Puerto Rico	1980	WBA
Jeff Chandler	USA	1980-1984	WBA
Albert Davila	USA	1983-1985	WBC
Richard Sandoval	USA	1984-1986	WBA
Satoshi Shingaki	Japan	1984-1985	IBF
Jeff Fenech*	Australia	1985-1987	IBF
Daniel Zaragoza	Mexico	1985	WBC
Miguel Lora	Colombia	1985-1988	WBC
Gaby Canizales	USA	1986	WBA
Bernardo Pinango*	Venezuela	1986-1987	WBA
Takuya Muguruma	Japan	1987	WBA
Kelvin Seabrooks	USA	1987-1988	IBF
Chang-Yung Park	S Korea	1987	WBA
Wilfredo Vasquez	Puerto Rico	1987-1988	WBA
Kaokor Galaxy	Thailand	1988	WBA
Orlando Canizales*	USA	1988-1994	IBF
Sung-Il Moon	S Korea	1988-1989	WBA
Raul Perez	Mexico	1988-1991	WBC
Israel Contrerras*	Venezuela	1989-1991	WBO
Kaokor Galaxy	Thailand	1989	WBA
Luisito Espinosa	Philippines	1989-1991	WBA
Greg Richardson	USA	1991	WBC
Gaby Canizales	USA	1991	WBO
Duke McKenzie	England	1991-1992	WBO
Joichiro Tatsuyushi*	Japan	1991-1992	WBC
Israel Contrerras	Venezuela	1991-1992	WBA
Eddie Cook	USA	1992	WBA
Victor Rabanales	Mexico	1992-1993	WBC
Rafael del Valle	Puerto Rico	1992-1994	WBO
Jorge Elicier Julio	Colombia	1992-1993	WBA
Il-Jung Byun	S Korea	1993	WBC
Junior Jones	USA	1993-1994	WBA
Yasuei Yakushiji	Japan	1993-1995	WBC
John Michael Johnson	USA	1994	WBA
Daorung Chuwatana	Thailand	1994-1995	WBA
Alfred Kotey	Ghana	1994-1995	WBO
Harold Mestre	Colombia	1995	IBF
Mbulelo Botile	S Africa	1995-1997	IBF
Wayne McCullough	Ireland	1995-1997	WBC
Veeraphol Sahaprom	Thailand	1995-1996	WBA
Daniel Jimenez	Puerto Rico	1995-1996	WBO
Nana Yaw Konadu	Ghana	1996	WBA
Robbie Regan*	Wales	1996-1998	WBO
Daorung Chuwatana	Thailand	1996-1997	WBA

Title Holder	Birthplace	Tenure	Status
Sirimongkol Singmanassak	Thailand	1997	WBC
Nana Yaw Konadu	Ghana	1997-1998	WBA
Tim Austin	USA	1997-2003	IBF
Joichiro Tatsuyoshi	Japan	1997-1998	WBC
Jorge Elicier Julio	Colombia	1998-2000	WBO
Johnny Tapia	USA	1998-1999	WBA
Veeraphol Sahaprom	Thailand	1998-2005	WBC
Paulie Ayala	USA	1999-2001	WBA
Johnny Tapia*	USA	2000	WBO
Mauricio Martinez	Panama	2000-2002	WBO
Eidy Moya	Venezuela	2001-2002	WBA
Cruz Carbajal	Mexico	2002-2004	WBO
Johnny Bredahl*	Denmark	2002-2004	WBA
Rafael Marquez*	Mexico	2003-2007	IBF
Ratanchai Sowvoraphin	Thailand	2004-2005	WBO
Julio Zarate	Mexico	2004-2005	WBA
Wladimir Sidorenko	Ukraine	2005-	WBA
Hozumi Hasegawa	Japan	2005-	WBC
Jhonny Gonzalez	Mexico	2005-	WBO

S. Bantamweight (122 lbs)

Title Holder	Birthplace	Tenure	Status
Rigoberto Riasco	Panama	1976	WBC
Royal Kobayashi	Japan	1976	WBC
Dong-Kyun Yum	S Korea	1976-1977	WBC
Wilfredo Gomez*	Puerto Rico	1977-1983	WBC
Soo-Hwan Hong	S Korea	1977-1978	WBA
Ricardo Cardona	Colombia	1978-1980	WBA
Leo Randolph	USA	1980	WBA
Sergio Palma	Argentina	1980-1982	WBA
Leonardo Cruz	Dom Republic	1982-1984	WBA
Jaime Garza	USA	1983-1984	WBC
Bobby Berna	Philippines	1983-1984	IBF
Loris Stecca	Italy	1984	WBA
Seung-In Suh	S Korea	1984-1985	IBF
Victor Callejas	Puerto Rico	1984-1986	WBA
Juan Meza	Mexico	1984-1985	WBC
Ji-Won Kim*	S Korea	1985-1986	IBF
Lupe Pintor	Mexico	1985-1986	WBC
Samart Payakarun	Thailand	1986-1987	WBC
Louie Espinosa	USA	1987	WBA
Seung-Hoon Lee*	S Korea	1987-1988	IBF
Jeff Fenech*	Australia	1987-1988	WBC
Julio Gervacio	Dom Republic	1987-1988	WBA
Bernardo Pinango	Venezuela	1988	WBA
Daniel Zaragoza	Mexico	1988-1990	WBC
Jose Sanabria	Venezuela	1988-1989	IBF
Juan J. Estrada	Mexico	1988-1989	WBA
Fabrice Benichou	Spain	1989-1990	IBF
Kenny Mitchell	USA	1989	WBO
Valerio Nati	Italy	1989-1990	WBO
Jesus Salud	USA	1989-1990	WBA
Welcome Ncita	S Africa	1990-1992	IBF
Paul Banke	USA	1990	WBC
Orlando Fernandez	Puerto Rico	1990-1991	WBO
Luis Mendoza	Colombia	1990-1991	WBA
Pedro Decima	Argentina	1990-1991	WBC
Kiyoshi Hatanaka	Japan	1991	WBC
Jesse Benavides	USA	1991-1992	WBO
Daniel Zaragoza	Mexico	1991-1992	WBC
Raul Perez	Mexico	1991-1992	WBA
Thierry Jacob	France	1992	WBC
Wilfredo Vasquez	Puerto Rico	1992-1995	WBA
Tracy Harris Patterson	USA	1992-1994	WBC
Duke McKenzie	England	1992-1993	WBO
Kennedy McKinney	USA	1992-1994	IBF
Daniel Jimenez	Puerto Rico	1993-1995	WBO
Vuyani Bungu *	S Africa	1994-1999	IBF
Hector Acero-Sanchez	Dom Republic	1994-1995	WBC
Marco Antonio Barrera	Mexico	1995-1996	WBO
Antonio Cermeno *	Venezuela	1995-1997	WBA
Daniel Zaragoza	Mexico	1995-1997	WBC
Junior Jones	USA	1996-1997	WBO

239

Title Holder	Birthplace	Tenure	Status
Erik Morales*	Mexico	1997-2000	WBC
Kennedy McKinney*	USA	1997-1998	WBO
Enrique Sanchez	Mexico	1998	WBA
Marco Antonio Barrera	Mexico	1998-2000	WBO
Nestor Garza	Mexico	1998-2000	WBA
Lehlohonolo Ledwaba	S Africa	1999-2001	IBF
Erik Morales	Mexico	2000	WBC/WBO
Erik Morales*	Mexico	2000	WBC
Marco Antonio Barrera*	Mexico	2000-2001	WBO
Clarence Adams	USA	2000-2001	WBA
Willie Jorrin	USA	2000-2002	WBC
Manny Pacquiao*	Philippines	2001-2003	IBF
Agapito Sanchez*	Dom Republic	2001-2002	WBO
Yober Ortega	Venezuela	2001-2002	WBA
Yoddamrong Sithyodthong	Thailand	2002	WBA
Osamu Sato	Japan	2002	WBA
Joan Guzman*	Dom Republic	2002-2005	WBO
Salim Medjkoune	France	2002-2003	WBA
Oscar Larios	Mexico	2002-2005	WBC
Mahyar Monshipour	Iran	2003-2006	WBA
Israel Vazquez*	Mexico	2004-2005	IBF
Daniel Ponce de Leon	Mexico	2005-	WBO
Israel Vazquez	Mexico	2005-2006	IBF/WBC
Somsak Sithchatchawal	Thailand	2006	WBA
Israel Vazquez	Mexico	2006-2007	WBC
Celestino Caballero	Panama	2006-	WBA
Steve Molitor	Canada	2006-	IBF
Rafael Marquez	Mexico	2007-	WBC

Featherweight (126 lbs)

Title Holder	Birthplace	Tenure	Status
Ike Weir	Ireland	1889-1890	
Billy Murphy	New Zealand	1890-1893	
George Dixon	Canada	1890-1893	
Young Griffo	Australia	1890-1893	
Johnny Griffin	USA	1891-1893	
Solly Smith	USA	1893	
George Dixon	Canada	1893-1896	
Solly Smith	USA	1896-1898	
Frank Erne	USA	1896-1897	
George Dixon	Canada	1896-1900	
Harry Greenfield	England	1897-1899	
Ben Jordan	England	1897-1899	
Will Curley	England	1897-1899	
Dave Sullivan	Ireland	1898	
Ben Jordan	England	1899-1905	GB
Eddie Santry	USA	1899-1900	
Terry McGovern	USA	1900	
Terry McGovern	USA	1900-1901	USA
Young Corbett II	USA	1901-1903	USA
Eddie Hanlon	USA	1903	
Young Corbett II	USA	1903-1904	
Abe Attell	USA	1903-1904	
Abe Attell	USA	1904-1911	USA
Joe Bowker	England	1905-1907	GB
Jim Driscoll	Wales	1907-1912	GB
Abe Attell	USA	1911-1912	
Joe Coster	USA	1911	
Joe Rivers	Mexico	1911	
Johnny Kilbane	USA	1911-1912	
Jim Driscoll*	Wales	1912-1913	GB/IBU
Johnny Kilbane	USA	1912-1922	USA
Johnny Kilbane	USA	1922-1923	NBA
Johnny Dundee	Italy	1922-1923	NY
Eugene Criqui	France	1923	
Johnny Dundee*	Italy	1923-1924	
Kid Kaplan	Russia	1925	NY
Kid Kaplan*	Russia	1925-1926	
Honeyboy Finnegan	USA	1926-1927	MASS
Benny Bass	Russia	1927-1928	NBA
Tony Canzoneri	USA	1928	
Andre Routis	France	1928-1929	
Bat Battalino	USA	1929-1932	

Title Holder	Birthplace	Tenure	Status
Bat Battalino	USA	1932	NBA
Tommy Paul	USA	1932-1933	NBA
Kid Chocolate*	Cuba	1932-1934	NY
Baby Arizmendi	Mexico	1932-1933	CALIF
Freddie Miller	USA	1933-1936	NBA
Baby Arizmendi	Mexico	1934-1935	NY
Baby Arizmendi	Mexico	1935-1936	NY/MEX
Baby Arizmendi	Mexico	1936	MEX
Petey Sarron	USA	1936-1937	NBA
Henry Armstrong	USA	1936-1937	CALIF/MEX
Mike Belloise	USA	1936	NY
Maurice Holtzer	France	1937-1938	IBU
Henry Armstrong*	USA	1937-1938	NBA/NY
Leo Rodak	USA	1938	MARY
Joey Archibald	USA	1938-1939	NY
Leo Rodak	USA	1938-1939	NBA
Joey Archibald	USA	1939-1940	
Joey Archibald	USA	1940	NY
Petey Scalzo	USA	1940-1941	NBA
Jimmy Perrin	USA	1940	LOUIS
Harry Jeffra	USA	1940-1941	NY/MARY
Joey Archibald	USA	1941	NY/MARY
Richie Lemos	USA	1941	NBA
Chalky Wright	Mexico	1941-1942	NY/MARY
Jackie Wilson	USA	1941-1943	NBA
Willie Pep	USA	1942-1946	NY
Jackie Callura	Canada	1943	NBA
Phil Terranova	USA	1943-1944	NBA
Sal Bartolo	USA	1944-1946	NBA
Willie Pep	USA	1946-1948	
Sandy Saddler	USA	1948-1949	
Willie Pep	USA	1949-1950	
Sandy Saddler*	USA	1950-1957	
Hogan Kid Bassey	Nigeria	1957-1959	
Davey Moore	USA	1959-1963	
Sugar Ramos	Cuba	1963-1964	
Vicente Saldivar*	Mexico	1964-1967	
Raul Rojas	USA	1967	CALIF
Howard Winstone	Wales	1968	WBC
Raul Rojas	USA	1968	WBA
Johnny Famechon	France	1968-1969	AUST
Jose Legra	Cuba	1968-1969	WBC
Shozo Saijyo	Japan	1968-1971	WBA
Johnny Famechon	France	1969-1970	WBC
Vicente Saldivar	Mexico	1970	WBC
Kuniaki Shibata	Japan	1970-1972	WBC
Antonio Gomez	Venezuela	1971-1972	WBA
Clemente Sanchez	Mexico	1972	WBC
Ernesto Marcel*	Panama	1972-1974	WBA
Jose Legra	Cuba	1972-1973	WBC
Eder Jofre	Brazil	1973-1974	WBC
Ruben Olivares	Mexico	1974	WBA
Bobby Chacon	USA	1974-1975	WBC
Alexis Arguello*	Nicaragua	1974-1977	WBA
Ruben Olivares	Mexico	1975	WBC
David Kotey	Ghana	1975-1976	WBC
Danny Lopez	USA	1976-1980	WBC
Rafael Ortega	Panama	1977	WBA
Cecilio Lastra	Spain	1977-1978	WBA
Eusebio Pedroza	Panama	1978-1985	WBA
Salvador Sanchez*	Mexico	1980-1982	WBC
Juan Laporte	Puerto Rico	1982-1984	WBC
Min-Keun Oh	S Korea	1984-1985	IBF
Wilfredo Gomez	Puerto Rico	1984	WBC
Azumah Nelson*	Ghana	1984-1988	WBC
Barry McGuigan	Ireland	1985-1986	WBA
Ki-Yung Chung	S Korea	1985-1986	IBF
Steve Cruz	USA	1986-1987	WBA
Antonio Rivera	Puerto Rico	1986-1988	IBF
Antonio Esparragoza	Venezuela	1987-1991	WBA
Calvin Grove	USA	1988	IBF
Jeff Fenech*	Australia	1988-1989	WBC

Title Holder	Birthplace	Tenure	Status
Jorge Paez*	Mexico	1988-1990	IBF
Maurizio Stecca	Italy	1989	WBO
Louie Espinosa	USA	1989-1990	WBO
Jorge Paez*	Mexico	1990-1991	IBF/WBO
Marcos Villasana	Mexico	1990-1991	WBC
Kyun-Yung Park	S Korea	1991-1993	WBA
Troy Dorsey	USA	1991	IBF
Maurizio Stecca	Italy	1991-1992	WBO
Manuel Medina	Mexico	1991-1993	IBF
Paul Hodkinson	England	1991-1993	WBC
Colin McMillan	England	1992	WBO
Ruben Palacio	Colombia	1992-1993	WBO
Tom Johnson	USA	1993-1997	IBF
Steve Robinson	Wales	1993-1995	WBO
Gregorio Vargas	Mexico	1993	WBC
Kevin Kelley	USA	1993-1995	WBC
Eloy Rojas	Venezuela	1993-1996	WBA
Alejandro Gonzalez	Mexico	1995	WBC
Manuel Medina	Mexico	1995	WBC
Prince Naseem Hamed*	England	1995-1997	WBO
Luisito Espinosa	Philippines	1995-1999	WBC
Wilfredo Vasquez	Puerto Rico	1996-1998	WBA
Prince Naseem Hamed *	England	1997	WBO/IBF
Prince Naseem Hamed*	England	1997-1999	WBO
Hector Lizarraga	Mexico	1997-1998	IBF
Freddie Norwood	USA	1998	WBA
Manuel Medina	Mexico	1998-1999	IBF
Antonio Cermeno	Venezuela	1998-1999	WBA
Cesar Soto	Mexico	1999	WBC
Freddie Norwood	USA	1999-2000	WBA
Prince Naseem Hamed	England	1999-2000	WBC/WBO
Paul Ingle	England	1999-2000	IBF
Prince Naseem Hamed*	England	2000	WBO
Gustavo Espadas	Mexico	2000-2001	WBC
Derrick Gainer	USA	2000-2003	WBA
Mbulelo Botile	S Africa	2000-2001	IBF
Istvan Kovacs	Hungary	2001	WBO
Erik Morales	Mexico	2001-2002	WBC
Frankie Toledo	USA	2001	IBF
Julio Pablo Chacon	Argentina	2001-2002	WBO
Manuel Medina	Mexico	2001-2002	IBF
Johnny Tapia	USA	2002	IBF
Marco Antonio Barrera*	Mexico	2002	WBC
Scott Harrison	Scotland	2002-2003	WBO
Erik Morales*	Mexico	2002-2003	WBC
Juan Manuel Marquez*	Mexico	2003	IBF
Manuel Medina	Mexico	2003	WBO
Juan Manuel Marquez	Mexico	2003-2005	IBF/WBA
Scott Harrison	Scotland	2003-2006	WBO
In-Jin Chi	S Korea	2004-2006	WBC
Juan Manuel Marquez	Mexico	2005-2006	WBA
Valdemir Pereira	Brazil	2005-2006	IBF
Takashi Koshimoto	Japan	2006	WBC
Chris John	Indonesia	2006-	WBA
Eric Aiken	USA	2006	IBF
Rodolfo Lopez	Mexico	2006	WBC
Robert Guerrero	USA	2006	IBF
Orlando Salido	Mexico	2006	IBF
Juan Manuel Marquez*	Mexico	2006-2007	WBO
In-Jin Chi	S Korea	2006-	WBC
Robert Guerrero	USA	2007-	IBF

S. Featherweight (130 lbs)

Title Holder	Birthplace	Tenure	Status
Johnny Dundee	Italy	1921-1923	NY
Jack Bernstein	USA	1923	NY
Jack Bernstein	USA	1923	NBA/NY
Johnny Dundee	Italy	1923-1924	NBA/NY
Kid Sullivan	USA	1924-1925	NBA/NY
Mike Ballerino	USA	1925	NBA/NY
Tod Morgan	USA	1925-1929	NBA/NY
Benny Bass	Russia	1929-1930	NBA/NY
Benny Bass	Russia	1930-1931	NBA

Title Holder	Birthplace	Tenure	Status
Kid Chocolate	Cuba	1931-1933	NBA
Frankie Klick	USA	1933-1934	NBA
Sandy Saddler	USA	1949-1950	NBA
Sandy Saddler	USA	1950-1951	CLE
Harold Gomes	USA	1959-1960	NBA
Flash Elorde	Philippines	1960-1962	NBA
Flash Elorde	Philippines	1962-1967	WBA
Raul Rojas	USA	1967	CALIF
Yoshiaki Numata	Japan	1967	WBA
Hiroshi Kobayashi	Japan	1967-1971	WBA
Rene Barrientos	Philippines	1969-1970	WBC
Yoshiaki Numata	Japan	1970-1971	WBC
Alfredo Marcano	Venezuela	1971-1972	WBA
Ricardo Arredondo	Mexico	1971-1974	WBC
Ben Villaflor	Philippines	1972-1973	WBA
Kuniaki Shibata	Japan	1973	WBA
Ben Villaflor	Philippines	1973-1976	WBA
Kuniaki Shibata	Japan	1974-1975	WBC
Alfredo Escalera	Puerto Rico	1975-1978	WBC
Sam Serrano	Puerto Rico	1976-1980	WBA
Alexis Arguello*	Nicaragua	1978-1980	WBC
Yasutsune Uehara	Japan	1980-1981	WBA
Rafael Limon	Mexico	1980-1981	WBC
Cornelius Boza-Edwards	Uganda	1981	WBC
Sam Serrano	Puerto Rico	1981-1983	WBA
Rolando Navarrete	Philippines	1981-1982	WBC
Rafael Limon	Mexico	1982	WBC
Bobby Chacon	USA	1982-1983	WBC
Roger Mayweather	USA	1983-1984	WBA
Hector Camacho*	Puerto Rico	1983-1984	WBC
Rocky Lockridge	USA	1984-1985	WBA
Hwan-Kil Yuh	S Korea	1984-1985	IBF
Julio Cesar Chavez*	Mexico	1984-1987	WBC
Lester Ellis	England	1985	IBF
Wilfredo Gomez	Puerto Rico	1985-1986	WBA
Barry Michael	England	1985-1987	IBF
Alfredo Layne	Panama	1986	WBA
Brian Mitchell*	S Africa	1986-1991	WBA
Rocky Lockridge	USA	1987-1988	IBF
Azumah Nelson	Ghana	1988-1994	WBC
Tony Lopez	USA	1988-1989	IBF
Juan Molina*	Puerto Rico	1989	WBO
Juan Molina	Puerto Rico	1989-1990	IBF
Kamel Bou Ali	Tunisia	1989-1992	WBO
Tony Lopez	USA	1990-1991	IBF
Joey Gamache*	USA	1991	WBA
Brian Mitchell*	S Africa	1991-1992	IBF
Genaro Hernandez	USA	1991-1995	WBA
Juan Molina*	Puerto Rico	1992-1995	IBF
Daniel Londas	France	1992	WBO
Jimmy Bredahl	Denmark	1992-1994	WBO
Oscar de la Hoya*	USA	1994	WBO
James Leija	USA	1994	WBC
Gabriel Ruelas	USA	1994-1995	WBC
Regilio Tuur*	Surinam	1994-1997	WBO
Eddie Hopson	USA	1995	IBF
Tracy Harris Patterson	USA	1995	IBF
Yong-Soo Choi	S Korea	1995-1998	WBA
Arturo Gatti*	Canada	1995-1997	IBF
Azumah Nelson	Ghana	1996-1997	WBC
Genaro Hernandez	USA	1997-1998	WBC
Barry Jones*	Wales	1997-1998	WBO
Roberto Garcia	USA	1998-1999	IBF
Anatoly Alexandrov	Kazakhstan	1998-1999	WBO
Takenori Hatakeyama	Japan	1998-1999	WBA
Floyd Mayweather*	USA	1998-2002	WBC
Lakva Sim	Mongolia	1999	WBA
Acelino Freitas*	Brazil	1999-2002	WBO
Diego Corrales*	USA	1999-2000	IBF
Jong-Kwon Baek	S Korea	1999-2000	WBA
Joel Casamayor	Cuba	2000-2002	WBA
Steve Forbes	USA	2000-2002	IBF

241

Title Holder	Birthplace	Tenure	Status
Acelino Freitas*	Brazil	2002-2004	WBO/WBA
Sirimongkol Singmanassak	Thailand	2002-2003	WBC
Carlos Hernandez	El Salvador	2003-2004	IBF
Jesus Chavez	Mexico	2003-2004	WBC
Yodesnan Sornontachai	Thailand	2004-2005	WBA
Erik Morales	Mexico	2004	WBC
Diego Corrales*	USA	2004	WBO
Erik Morales	Mexico	2004	IBF
Mike Anchondo	USA	2004-2005	WBO
Marco Antonio Barrera*	Mexico	2004-2005	WBC
Robbie Peden	Australia	2005	IBF
Jorge Barrios	Argentina	2005-2006	WBO
Vincente Mosquera	Panama	2005-2006	WBA
Marco Antonio Barrera*	Mexico	2005-2006	WBC/IBF
Marco Antonio Barrera	Mexico	2006-2007	WBC
Cassius Baloyi	South Africa	2006	IBF
Gairy St Clair	Guyana	2006	IBF
Edwin Valero	Venezuela	2006-	WBA
Malcolm Klassen	S Africa	2006-2007	IBF
Joan Guzman	Dom Republic	2006-	WBO
Juan Manuel Marquez	Mexico	2007-	WBC
Mzonke Fana	S Africa	2007-	IBF

Lightweight (135 lbs)

Title Holder	Birthplace	Tenure	Status
Jack McAuliffe	Ireland	1889-1894	USA
Jem Carney	England	1889-1891	
Jimmy Carroll	England	1889-1891	
Dick Burge	England	1891-1896	GB
George Lavigne	USA	1894-1896	USA
George Lavigne	USA	1896	
George Lavigne	USA	1896-1897	
Eddie Connolly	Canada	1896-1897	
George Lavigne	USA	1897-1899	
Frank Erne	Switzerland	1899-1902	
Joe Gans	USA	1902	
Joe Gans	USA	1902-1906	
Jabez White	England	1902-1905	GB
Jimmy Britt	USA	1902-1905	
Battling Nelson	Denmark	1905-1907	
Joe Gans	USA	1906-1908	
Battling Nelson	Denmark	1908-1910	
Ad Wolgast	USA	1910-1912	
Willie Ritchie	USA	1912	
Freddie Welsh	Wales	1912-1914	GB
Willie Ritchie	USA	1912-1914	USA
Freddie Welsh	Wales	1914-1917	
Benny Leonard*	USA	1917-1925	
Jimmy Goodrich	USA	1925	NY
Rocky Kansas	USA	1925-1926	
Sammy Mandell	USA	1926-1930	
Al Singer	USA	1930	
Tony Canzoneri	USA	1930-1933	
Barney Ross*	USA	1933-1935	
Tony Canzoneri	USA	1935-1936	
Lou Ambers	USA	1936-1938	
Henry Armstrong	USA	1938-1939	
Lou Ambers	USA	1939-1940	
Sammy Angott	USA	1940-1941	NBA
Lew Jenkins	USA	1940-1941	NY
Sammy Angott*	USA	1941-1942	
Beau Jack	USA	1942-1943	NY
Slugger White	USA	1943	MARY
Bob Montgomery	USA	1943	NY
Sammy Angott	USA	1943-1944	NBA
Beau Jack	USA	1943-1944	NY
Bob Montgomery	USA	1944-1947	NY
Juan Zurita	Mexico	1944-1945	NBA
Ike Williams	USA	1945-1947	NBA
Ike Williams	USA	1947-1951	
Jimmy Carter	USA	1951-1952	
Lauro Salas	Mexico	1952	
Jimmy Carter	USA	1952-1954	

Title Holder	Birthplace	Tenure	Status
Paddy de Marco	USA	1954	
Jimmy Carter	USA	1954-1955	
Wallace Bud Smith	USA	1955-1956	
Joe Brown	USA	1956-1962	
Carlos Ortiz	Puerto Rico	1962-1963	
Carlos Ortiz*	Puerto Rico	1963-1964	WBA/WBC
Kenny Lane	USA	1963-1964	MICH
Carlos Ortiz	Puerto Rico	1964-1965	
Ismael Laguna	Panama	1965	
Carlos Ortiz	Puerto Rico	1965-1966	
Carlos Ortiz*	Puerto Rico	1966-1967	WBA
Carlos Ortiz	Puerto Rico	1967-1968	
Carlos Teo Cruz	Dom Republic	1968-1969	
Mando Ramos	USA	1969-1970	
Ismael Laguna	Panama	1970	
Ismael Laguna	Panama	1970	WBA
Ken Buchanan*	Scotland	1970-1971	WBA
Ken Buchanan	Scotland	1971	
Ken Buchanan	Scotland	1971-1972	WBA
Pedro Carrasco	Spain	1971-1972	WBC
Mando Ramos	USA	1972	WBC
Roberto Duran*	Panama	1972-1978	WBA
Chango Carmona	Mexico	1972	WBC
Rodolfo Gonzalez	Mexico	1972-1974	WBC
Guts Ishimatsu	Japan	1974-1976	WBC
Esteban de Jesus	Puerto Rico	1976-1978	WBC
Roberto Duran*	Panama	1978-1979	
Jim Watt	Scotland	1979-1981	WBC
Ernesto Espana	Venezuela	1979-1980	WBA
Hilmer Kenty	USA	1980-1981	WBA
Sean O'Grady	USA	1981	WBA
Alexis Arguello*	Nicaragua	1981-1983	WBC
Claude Noel	Trinidad	1981	WBA

Tony Canzoneri

Title Holder	Birthplace	Tenure	Status	Title Holder	Birthplace	Tenure	Status
Arturo Frias	USA	1981-1982	WBA	Mushy Callahan	USA	1927-1930	NBA/NY
Ray Mancini	USA	1982-1984	WBA	Mushy Callahan	USA	1930	NBA
Edwin Rosario	Puerto Rico	1983-1984	WBC	Jackie Kid Berg	England	1930-1931	NBA
Charlie Choo Choo Brown	USA	1984	IBF	Tony Canzoneri	USA	1931-1932	NBA
Harry Arroyo	USA	1984-1985	IBF	Johnny Jadick	USA	1932	NBA
Livingstone Bramble	USA	1984-1986	WBA	Johnny Jadick	USA	1932-1933	PEN
Jose Luis Ramirez	Mexico	1984-1985	WBC	Battling Shaw	Mexico	1933	LOUIS
Jimmy Paul	USA	1985-1986	IBF	Tony Canzoneri	USA	1933	LOUIS
Hector Camacho*	Puerto Rico	1985-1987	WBC	Barney Ross*	USA	1933-1935	ILL
Edwin Rosario	Puerto Rico	1986-1987	WBA	Maxie Berger	Canada	1939	CAN
Greg Haugen	USA	1986-1987	IBF	Harry Weekly	USA	1941-1942	LOUIS
Vinny Pazienza	USA	1987-1988	IBF	Tippy Larkin	USA	1946-1947	NY/NBA
Jose Luis Ramirez	Mexico	1987-1988	WBC	Carlos Ortiz	Puerto Rico	1959-1960	NBA
Julio Cesar Chavez*	Mexico	1987-1988	WBA	Duilio Loi	Italy	1960-1962	NBA
Greg Haugen	USA	1988-1989	IBF	Duilio Loi	Italy	1962	WBA
Julio Cesar Chavez*	Mexico	1988-1989	WBA/WBC	Eddie Perkins	USA	1962	WBA
Mauricio Aceves	Mexico	1989-1990	WBO	Duilio Loi*	Italy	1962-1963	WBA
Pernell Whitaker*	USA	1989	IBF	Roberto Cruz	Philippines	1963	WBA
Edwin Rosario	Puerto Rico	1989-1990	WBA	Eddie Perkins	USA	1963-1965	WBA
Pernell Whitaker*	USA	1989-1990	IBF/WBC	Carlos Hernandez	Venezuela	1965-1966	WBA
Juan Nazario	Puerto Rico	1990	WBA	Sandro Lopopolo	Italy	1966-1967	WBA
Pernell Whitaker*	USA	1990-1992	IBF/WBC/WBA	Paul Fujii	Hawaii	1967-1968	WBA
Dingaan Thobela*	S Africa	1990-1992	WBO	Nicolino Loche	Argentina	1968-1972	WBA
Joey Gamache	USA	1992	WBA	Pedro Adigue	Philippines	1968-1970	WBC
Miguel Gonzalez*	Mexico	1992-1996	WBC	Bruno Arcari*	Italy	1970-1974	WBC
Giovanni Parisi*	Italy	1992-1994	WBO	Alfonso Frazer	Panama	1972	WBA
Tony Lopez	USA	1992-1993	WBA	Antonio Cervantes	Colombia	1972-1976	WBA
Fred Pendleton	USA	1993-1994	IBF	Perico Fernandez	Spain	1974-1975	WBC
Dingaan Thobela	S Africa	1993	WBA	Saensak Muangsurin	Thailand	1975-1976	WBC
Orzubek Nazarov	Kyrghyzstan	1993-1998	WBA	Wilfred Benitez	USA	1976	WBA
Rafael Ruelas	USA	1994-1995	IBF	Miguel Velasquez	Spain	1976	WBC
Oscar de la Hoya*	USA	1994-1995	WBO	Saensak Muangsurin	Thailand	1976-1978	WBC
Oscar de la Hoya*	USA	1995	WBO/IBF	Antonio Cervantes	Colombia	1977-1980	WBA
Oscar de la Hoya*	USA	1995-1996	WBO	Wilfred Benitez*	USA	1977-1978	NY
Phillip Holiday	S Africa	1995-1997	IBF	Sang-Hyun Kim	S Korea	1978-1980	WBC
Jean-Baptiste Mendy	France	1996-1997	WBC	Saoul Mamby	USA	1980-1982	WBC
Artur Grigorian	Uzbekistan	1996-2004	WBO	Aaron Pryor*	USA	1980-1984	WBA
Steve Johnston	USA	1997-1998	WBC	Leroy Haley	USA	1982-1983	WBC
Shane Mosley*	USA	1997-1999	IBF	Bruce Curry	USA	1983-1984	WBC
Jean-Baptiste Mendy	France	1998-1999	WBA	Johnny Bumphus	USA	1984	WBA
Cesar Bazan	Mexico	1998-1999	WBC	Bill Costello	USA	1984-1985	WBC
Steve Johnston	USA	1999-2000	WBC	Gene Hatcher	USA	1984-1985	WBA
Julien Lorcy	France	1999	WBA	Aaron Pryor	USA	1984-1985	IBF
Stefano Zoff	Italy	1999	WBA	Ubaldo Sacco	Argentina	1985-1986	WBA
Paul Spadafora*	USA	1999-2003	IBF	Lonnie Smith	USA	1985-1986	WBC
Gilberto Serrano	Venezuela	1999-2000	WBA	Patrizio Oliva	Italy	1986-1987	WBA
Takanori Hatakeyama	Japan	2000-2001	WBA	Gary Hinton	USA	1986	IBF
Jose Luis Castillo	Mexico	2000-2002	WBC	Rene Arredondo	Mexico	1986	WBC
Julien Lorcy	France	2001	WBA	Tsuyoshi Hamada	Japan	1986-1987	WBC
Raul Balbi	Argentina	2001-2002	WBA	Joe Manley	USA	1986-1987	IBF
Leonardo Dorin	Romania	2002-2003	WBA	Terry Marsh*	England	1987	IBF
Floyd Mayweather*	USA	2002-2004	WBC	Juan M. Coggi	Argentina	1987-1990	WBA
Javier Jauregui	Mexico	2003-2004	IBF	Rene Arredondo	Mexico	1987	WBC
Acelino Freitas	Brazil	2004	WBO	Roger Mayweather	USA	1987-1989	WBC
Lakva Sim	Mongolia	2004	WBA	James McGirt	USA	1988	IBF
Julio Diaz*	Mexico	2004-2005	IBF	Meldrick Taylor	USA	1988-1990	IBF
Jose Luis Castillo	Mexico	2004-2005	WBC	Hector Camacho	Puerto Rico	1989-1991	WBO
Juan Diaz*	USA	2004-2007	WBA	Julio Cesar Chavez*	Mexico	1989-1990	WBC
Diego Corrales*	USA	2004-2005	WBO	Julio Cesar Chavez*	Mexico	1990-1991	IBF/WBC
Diego Corrales	USA	2005-2006	WBC/WBO	Loreto Garza	USA	1990-1991	WBA
Leavander Johnson	USA	2005	IBF	Greg Haugen	USA	1991	WBO
Jesus Chavez	Mexico	2005-2007	IBF	Hector Camacho	Puerto Rico	1991-1992	WBO
Diego Corrales	USA	2006	WBC	Edwin Rosario	Puerto Rico	1991-1992	WBA
Acelino Freitas	Brazil	2006-2007	WBO	Julio Cesar Chavez	Mexico	1991-1994	WBC
Joel Casamayor	Cuba	2006-2007	WBC	Rafael Pineda	Colombia	1991-1992	IBF
Julio Diaz	USA	2007-	IBF	Akinobu Hiranaka	Japan	1992	WBA
David Diaz	USA	2007-	WBC	Carlos Gonzalez	Mexico	1992-1993	WBO
Juan Diaz	USA	2007-	WBA/WBO	Pernell Whitaker*	USA	1992-1993	IBF
				Morris East	Philippines	1992-1993	WBA
L. Welterweight (140 lbs)				Juan M. Coggi	Argentina	1993-1994	WBA
Pinkey Mitchell	USA	1922-1926	NBA	Charles Murray	USA	1993-1994	IBF
Mushy Callahan	USA	1926-1927	NBA	Zack Padilla*	USA	1993-1994	WBO

243

Title Holder	Birthplace	Tenure	Status
Frankie Randall	USA	1994	WBC
Jake Rodriguez	USA	1994-1995	IBF
Julio Cesar Chavez	Mexico	1994-1996	WBC
Frankie Randall	USA	1994-1996	WBA
Konstantin Tszyu	Russia	1995-1997	IBF
Sammy Fuentes	Puerto Rico	1995-1996	WBO
Juan M. Coggi	Argentina	1996	WBA
Giovanni Parisi	Italy	1996-1998	WBO
Oscar de la Hoya*	USA	1996-1997	WBC
Frankie Randall	USA	1996-1997	WBA
Khalid Rahilou	France	1997-1998	WBA
Vince Phillips	USA	1997-1999	IBF
Carlos Gonzalez	Mexico	1998-1999	WBO
Sharmba Mitchell	USA	1998-2001	WBA
Terron Millett	USA	1999	IBF
Randall Bailey	USA	1999-2000	WBO
Kostya Tszyu*	Russia	1999-2001	WBC
Zab Judah	USA	2000-2001	IBF
Ener Julio	Colombia	2000-2001	WBO
Kostya Tszyu*	Russia	2001	WBA/WBC
DeMarcus Corley	USA	2001-2003	WBO
Kostya Tszyu*	Russia	2001-2004	WBA/WBC/IBF
Zab Judah*	USA	2003-2004	WBO
Kostya Tszyu	Russia	2004-2005	IBF
Arturo Gatti	Canada	2004-2005	WBC
Vivien Harris	Guyana	2004-2005	WBA
Miguel Cotto*	Puerto Rico	2004-2006	WBO
Ricky Hatton*	England	2005	IBF
Carlos Maussa	Colombia	2005	WBA
Floyd Mayweather*	USA	2005-2006	WBC
Ricky Hatton*	England	2005-2006	IBF/WBA
Juan Urango	Colombia	2006-2007	IBF
Souleymane M'Baye	France	2006-	WBA
Junior Witter	England	2006-	WBC
Ricardo Torres	Colombia	2006-	WBO
Ricky Hatton*	England	2007	IBF
Lovemore Ndou	S Africa	2007	IBF
Paul Malignaggi	USA	2007-	IBF
Ricky Hatton	England	2007-	IBO

Welterweight (147 lbs)

Title Holder	Birthplace	Tenure	Status
Paddy Duffy	USA	1889-1890	
Tommy Ryan	USA	1891-1894	
Mysterious Billy Smith	USA	1892-1894	
Tommy Ryan	USA	1894-1897	USA
Tommy Ryan	USA	1897-1899	
Dick Burge	GB	1897	
George Green	USA	1897	
Tom Causer	GB	1897	
Joe Walcott	Barbados	1897	
George Lavigne	USA	1897-1899	
Dick Burge	GB	1897-1898	
Mysterious Billy Smith	USA	1898-1900	
Bobby Dobbs	USA	1898-1902	
Rube Ferns	USA	1900	
Matty Matthews	USA	1900	
Eddie Connolly	Canada	1900	
Matty Matthews	USA	1900-1901	
Rube Ferns	USA	1901	
Joe Walcott	Barbados	1901-1906	
Eddie Connolly	Canada	1902-1903	GB
Matty Matthews	USA	1902-1903	
Rube Ferns	USA	1903	
Martin Duffy	USA	1903-1904	
Honey Mellody	USA	1904	
Jack Clancy	USA	1904-1905	GB
Dixie Kid	USA	1904-1905	
Buddy Ryan	USA	1904-1905	
Sam Langford	Canada	1904-1905	
George Petersen	USA	1905	
Jimmy Gardner	USA	1905	
Mike Twin Sullivan	USA	1905-1906	

Title Holder	Birthplace	Tenure	Status
Joe Gans	USA	1906	
Joe Walcott	Barbados	1906	USA
Honey Mellody	USA	1906	USA
Honey Mellody	USA	1906-1907	
Joe Thomas	USA	1906-1907	
Mike Twin Sullivan	USA	1907-1911	
Jimmy Gardner	USA	1907-1908	
Frank Mantell	USA	1907-1908	
Harry Lewis	USA	1908-1910	
Jack Blackburn	USA	1908	
Jimmy Gardner	USA	1908-1909	
Willie Lewis	USA	1909-1910	
Harry Lewis	USA	1910-1911	GB/FR
Jimmy Clabby	USA	1910-1911	
Dixie Kid	USA	1911-1912	GB/FR
Ray Bronson	USA	1911-1914	
Marcel Thomas	France	1912-1913	FR
Wildcat Ferns	USA	1912-1913	
Spike Kelly	USA	1913-1914	
Mike Glover	USA	1913-1915	
Mike Gibbons	USA	1913-1914	
Waldemar Holberg	Denmark	1914	
Tom McCormick	Ireland	1914	
Matt Wells	England	1914-1915	AUSTR
Kid Graves	USA	1914-1917	
Jack Britton	USA	1915	
Ted Kid Lewis	England	1915-1916	
Jack Britton	USA	1916-1917	
Ted Kid Lewis	England	1917	
Ted Kid Lewis	England	1917-1919	
Jack Britton	USA	1919-1922	
Mickey Walker	USA	1922-1923	
Mickey Walker	USA	1923-1924	NBA
Dave Shade	USA	1923	NY
Jimmy Jones	USA	1923	NY/MASS
Mickey Walker	USA	1924-1926	
Pete Latzo	USA	1926-1927	
Joe Dundee	Italy	1927-1928	
Joe Dundee	Italy	1928-1929	NY
Jackie Fields	USA	1929	NBA
Jackie Fields	USA	1929-1930	
Young Jack Thompson	USA	1930	
Tommy Freeman	USA	1930-1931	
Young Jack Thompson	USA	1930	
Lou Brouillard	Canada	1931-1932	
Jackie Fields	USA	1932-1933	
Young Corbett III	Italy	1933	
Jimmy McLarnin	Ireland	1933-1934	
Barney Ross	USA	1934	
Jimmy McLarnin	Ireland	1934-1935	
Barney Ross	USA	1935-1938	
Barney Ross	USA	1938	NY/NBA
Felix Wouters	Belgium	1938	IBU
Henry Armstrong	USA	1938-1940	
Fritzie Zivic	USA	1940	
Fritzie Zivic	USA	1940-1941	NY/NBA
Izzy Jannazzo	USA	1940-1942	MARY
Red Cochrane	USA	1941-1942	NY/NBA
Red Cochrane	USA	1942-1946	
Marty Servo	USA	1946	
Sugar Ray Robinson*	USA	1946-1951	
Johnny Bratton	USA	1951	NBA
Kid Gavilan	Cuba	1951-1952	NBA/NY
Kid Gavilan	Cuba	1952-1954	
Johnny Saxton	USA	1954-1955	
Tony de Marco	USA	1955	
Carmen Basilio	USA	1955-1956	
Johnny Saxton	USA	1956	
Carmen Basilio*	USA	1956-1957	
Virgil Akins	USA	1957-1958	MASS
Virgil Akins	USA	1958	
Don Jordan	Dom Republic	1958-1960	

Title Holder	Birthplace	Tenure	Status
Benny Kid Paret	Cuba	1960-1961	
Emile Griffith	Virgin Islands	1961	
Benny Kid Paret	Cuba	1961-1962	
Emile Griffith	Virgin Islands	1962-1963	
Luis Rodriguez	Cuba	1963	
Emile Griffith*	Virgin Islands	1963-1966	
Willie Ludick	S Africa	1966-1968	SA
Curtis Cokes*	USA	1966	WBA
Curtis Cokes*	USA	1966-1967	WBA/WBC
Charley Shipes	USA	1966-1967	CALIF
Curtis Cokes	USA	1968-1969	
Jose Napoles	Cuba	1969-1970	
Billy Backus	USA	1970-1971	
Jose Napoles	Cuba	1971-1972	
Jose Napoles*	Cuba	1972-1974	WBA/WBC
Hedgemon Lewis	USA	1972-1974	NY
Jose Napoles	Cuba	1974-1975	
Jose Napoles	Cuba	1975	WBC
Angel Espada	Puerto Rico	1975-1976	WBA
John H. Stracey	England	1975-1976	WBC
Carlos Palomino	Mexico	1976-1979	WBC
Pipino Cuevas	Mexico	1976-1980	WBA
Wilfred Benitez	USA	1979	WBC
Sugar Ray Leonard	USA	1979-1980	WBC
Roberto Duran	Panama	1980	WBC
Thomas Hearns	USA	1980-1981	WBA
Sugar Ray Leonard	USA	1980-1981	WBC
Sugar Ray Leonard*	USA	1981-1982	
Don Curry*	USA	1983-1984	WBA
Milton McCrory	USA	1983-1985	WBC
Don Curry*	USA	1984-1985	WBA/IBF
Don Curry	USA	1985-1986	
Lloyd Honeyghan	Jamaica	1986	
Lloyd Honeyghan	Jamaica	1986-1987	WBC/IBF
Mark Breland	USA	1987	WBA
Marlon Starling	USA	1987-1988	WBA
Jorge Vaca	Mexico	1987-1988	WBC
Lloyd Honeyghan	Jamaica	1988-1989	WBC
Simon Brown*	Jamaica	1988-1991	IBF
Tomas Molinares	Colombia	1988-1989	WBA
Mark Breland	USA	1989-1990	WBA
Marlon Starling	USA	1989-1990	WBC
Genaro Leon*	Mexico	1989	WBO
Manning Galloway	USA	1989-1993	WBO
Aaron Davis	USA	1990-1991	WBA
Maurice Blocker	USA	1990-1991	WBC
Meldrick Taylor	USA	1991-1992	WBA
Simon Brown*	Jamaica	1991	WBC/IBF
Simon Brown	Jamaica	1991	WBC
Maurice Blocker	USA	1991-1993	IBF
James McGirt	USA	1991-1993	WBC
Crisanto Espana	Venezuela	1992-1994	WBA
Gert Bo Jacobsen*	Denmark	1993	WBO
Pernell Whitaker	USA	1993-1997	WBC
Felix Trinidad*	Puerto Rico	1993-2000	IBF
Eamonn Loughran	Ireland	1993-1996	WBO
Ike Quartey	Ghana	1994-1998	WBA
Jose Luis Lopez	Mexico	1996-1997	WBO
Michael Loewe*	Romania	1997-1998	WBO
Oscar de la Hoya	USA	1997-1999	WBC
Ahmed Kotiev	Russia	1998-2000	WBO
James Page	USA	1998-2000	WBA
Oscar de la Hoya	USA	2000	WBC
Daniel Santos*	Puerto Rico	2000-2002	WBO
Shane Mosley	USA	2000-2002	WBC
Andrew Lewis	Guyana	2001-2002	WBA
Vernon Forrest	USA	2001	IBF
Vernon Forrest	USA	2002-2003	WBC
Antonio Margarito	Mexico	2002-	WBO
Ricardo Mayorga*	Nicaragua	2002-2003	WBA
Michele Piccirillo	Italy	2002-2003	IBF
Ricardo Mayorga	Nicaragua	2003	WBA/WBC

Title Holder	Birthplace	Tenure	Status
Cory Spinks*	USA	2003	IBF
Cory Spinks	USA	2003-2005	IBF/WBA/WBC
Zab Judah	USA	2005-2006	IBF/WBA/WBC
Carlos Baldomir	Argentina	2006	WBC
Zab Judah	USA	2006	IBF
Luis Collazo	USA	2006	WBA
Floyd Mayweather*	USA	2006	IBF
Ricky Hatton*	England	2006	WBA
Kermin Cintron	Puerto Rico	2006-	IBF
Floyd Mayweather	USA	2006-	WBC
Miguel Cotto	Puerto Rico	2006-	WBA

L. Middleweight (154 lbs)

Title Holder	Birthplace	Tenure	Status
Emile Griffith*	USA	1962-1963	AU
Denny Moyer	USA	1962-1963	WBA
Ralph Dupas	USA	1963	WBA
Sandro Mazzinghi	Italy	1963-1965	WBA
Nino Benvenuti	Italy	1965-1966	WBA
Ki-Soo Kim	S Korea	1966-1968	WBA
Sandro Mazzinghi	Italy	1968-1969	WBA
Freddie Little	USA	1969-1970	WBA
Carmelo Bossi	Italy	1970-1971	WBA
Koichi Wajima	Japan	1971-1974	WBA
Oscar Albarado	USA	1974-1975	WBA
Koichi Wajima	Japan	1975	WBA
Miguel de Oliveira	Brazil	1975	WBC
Jae-Do Yuh	S Korea	1975-1976	WBA
Elisha Obed	Bahamas	1975-1976	WBC
Koichi Wajima	Japan	1976	WBA
Jose Duran	Spain	1976	WBA
Eckhard Dagge	Germany	1976-1977	WBC
Miguel Castellini	Argentina	1976-1977	WBA
Eddie Gazo	Nicaragua	1977-1978	WBA
Rocky Mattioli	Italy	1977-1979	WBC
Masashi Kudo	Japan	1978-1979	WBA
Maurice Hope	Antigua	1979-1981	WBC
Ayub Kalule	Uganda	1979-1981	WBA
Wilfred Benitez	USA	1981-1982	WBC
Sugar Ray Leonard*	USA	1981	WBA
Tadashi Mihara	Japan	1981-1982	WBA
Davey Moore	USA	1982-1983	WBA
Thomas Hearns*	USA	1982-1986	WBC
Roberto Duran*	Panama	1983-1984	WBA
Mark Medal	USA	1984	IBF
Mike McCallum*	Jamaica	1984-1987	WBA
Carlos Santos	Puerto Rico	1984-1986	IBF
Buster Drayton	USA	1986-1987	IBF
Duane Thomas	USA	1986-1987	WBC
Matthew Hilton	Canada	1987-1988	IBF
Lupe Aquino	Mexico	1987	WBC
Gianfranco Rosi	Italy	1987-1988	WBC
Julian Jackson*	Virgin Islands	1987-1990	WBA
Don Curry	USA	1988-1989	WBC
Robert Hines	USA	1988-1989	IBF
John David Jackson*	USA	1988-1993	WBO
Darrin van Horn	USA	1989	IBF
Rene Jacqot	France	1989	WBC
John Mugabi	Uganda	1989-1990	WBC
Gianfranco Rosi	Italy	1989-1994	IBF
Terry Norris	USA	1990-1993	WBC
Gilbert Dele	France	1991	WBA
Vinny Pazienza*	USA	1991-1992	WBA
Julio Cesar Vasquez	Argentina	1992-1995	WBA
Verno Phillips	USA	1993-1995	WBO
Simon Brown	USA	1993-1994	WBC
Terry Norris	USA	1994	WBC
Vince Pettway	USA	1994-1995	IBF
Luis Santana	Dom Republic	1994-1995	WBC
Pernell Whitaker*	USA	1995	WBA
Gianfranco Rosi	Italy	1995	WBO
Carl Daniels	USA	1995	WBA
Verno Phillips	USA	1995	WBO

WORLD CHAMPIONS SINCE GLOVES, 1889-2007

Title Holder	Birthplace	Tenure	Status
Paul Vaden	USA	1995	IBF
Terry Norris*	USA	1995	WBC
Paul Jones	England	1995-1996	WBO
Terry Norris	USA	1995-1997	IBF/WBC
Julio Cesar Vasquez	Argentina	1995-1996	WBA
Bronco McKart	USA	1996	WBO
Ronald Wright	USA	1996-1998	WBO
Laurent Boudouani	France	1996-1999	WBA
Terry Norris	USA	1997	WBC
Raul Marquez	USA	1997	IBF
Luis Campas	Mexico	1997-1998	IBF
Keith Mullings	USA	1997-1999	WBC
Harry Simon*	Namibia	1998-2001	WBO
Fernando Vargas	USA	1998-2000	IBF
Javier Castillejo	Spain	1999-2001	WBC
David Reid	USA	1999-2000	WBA
Felix Trinidad*	Puerto Rico	2000	WBA
Felix Trinidad*	Puerto Rico	2000-2001	IBF/WBA
Oscar de la Hoya*	USA	2001-2002	WBC
Fernando Vargas	USA	2001-2002	WBA
Ronald Wright*	USA	2001-2004	IBF
Daniel Santos	Puerto Rico	2002-2005	WBO
Oscar de la Hoya	USA	2002-2003	WBA/WBC
Shane Mosley	USA	2003-2004	WBA/WBC
Ronald Wright	USA	2004	IBF/WBA/WBC
Ronald Wright	USA	2004-2005	WBA/WBC
Verno Phillips	USA	2004	IBF
Kassim Ouma	Uganda	2004-2005	IBF
Ronald Wright*	USA	2005	WBC
Travis Simms	USA	2005	WBA
Javier Castillejo	Spain	2005	WBC
Alejandro Garcia	Mexico	2005-2006	WBA
Roman Karmazin	Russia	2005-2006	IBF
Ricardo Mayorga	Nicaragua	2005-2006	WBC
Sergei Dzindziruk	Ukraine	2005-	WBO
Jose Antonio Rivera	USA	2006-2007	WBA
Oscar de la Hoya	USA	2006-2007	WBC
Cory Spinks	USA	2006-	IBF
Travis Simms	USA	2007-	WBA
Floyd Mayweather*	USA	2007	WBC

Middleweight (160 lbs)

Title Holder	Birthplace	Tenure	Status
Nonpareil Jack Dempsey	Ireland	1889-1891	USA
Bob Fitzsimmons	England	1891-1893	USA
Jim Hall	Australia	1892-1893	GB
Bob Fitzsimmons	England	1893-1894	
Bob Fitzsimmons	England	1894-1899	
Frank Craig	USA	1894-1895	GB
Dan Creedon	New Zealand	1895-1897	GB
Tommy Ryan	USA	1895-1896	
Kid McCoy	USA	1896-1898	
Tommy Ryan	USA	1898-1905	
Charley McKeever	USA	1900-1902	
George Gardner	USA	1901-1902	
Jack O'Brien	USA	1901-1905	
George Green	USA	1901-1902	
Jack Palmer	England	1902-1903	GB
Hugo Kelly	USA	1905-1908	
Jack Twin Sullivan	USA	1905-1908	
Sam Langford	Canada	1907-1911	
Billy Papke	USA	1908	
Stanley Ketchel	USA	1908	
Billy Papke	USA	1908	
Stanley Ketchel	USA	1908-1910	
Billy Papke	USA	1910-1913	
Stanley Ketchel*	USA	1910	
Hugo Kelly	USA	1910-1912	
Cyclone Johnny Thompson	USA	1911-1912	
Harry Lewis	USA	1911	
Leo Houck	USA	1911-1912	
Georges Carpentier	France	1911-1912	
Jack Dillon	USA	1912	

Title Holder	Birthplace	Tenure	Status
Frank Mantell	USA	1912-1913	
Frank Klaus	USA	1912-1913	
Georges Carpentier	France	1912	IBU
Jack Dillon	USA	1912-1915	
Eddie McGoorty	USA	1912-1913	
Frank Klaus	USA	1913	IBU
Jimmy Clabby	USA	1913-1914	
George Chip	USA	1913-1914	
Joe Borrell	USA	1913-1914	
Jeff Smith	USA	1913-1914	
Eddie McGoorty	USA	1914	AUSTR
Jeff Smith	USA	1914	AUSTR
Al McCoy	USA	1914-1917	
Jimmy Clabby	USA	1914-1915	
Mick King	Australia	1914	AUSTR
Jeff Smith	USA	1914-1915	AUSTR
Young Ahearn	England	1915-1916	
Les Darcy*	Australia	1915-1917	AUSTR
Mike Gibbons	USA	1916-1917	
Mike O'Dowd	USA	1917-1920	
Johnny Wilson	USA	1920-1921	
Johnny Wilson	USA	1921-1922	NBA/NY
Bryan Downey	USA	1921-1922	OHIO
Johnny Wilson	USA	1922-1923	NBA
Dave Rosenberg	USA	1922	NY
Jock Malone	USA	1922-1923	OHIO
Mike O'Dowd	USA	1922-1923	NY
Johnny Wilson	USA	1923	
Harry Greb	USA	1923-1926	
Tiger Flowers	USA	1926	
Mickey Walker	USA	1926-1931	
Gorilla Jones	USA	1932	NBA
Marcel Thil	France	1932-1933	NBA/IBU
Marcel Thil	France	1933-1937	IBU
Ben Jeby	USA	1933	NY
Lou Brouillard	Canada	1933	NY
Lou Brouillard	Canada	1933	NY/NBA
Vearl Whitehead	USA	1933	CALIF
Teddy Yarosz	USA	1933-1934	PEN
Vince Dundee	USA	1933-1934	NY/NBA
Teddy Yarosz	USA	1934-1935	NY/NBA
Babe Risko	USA	1935-1936	NY/NBA
Freddie Steele	USA	1936-1938	NY/NBA
Fred Apostoli	USA	1937-1938	IBU
Edouard Tenet	France	1938	IBU
Young Corbett III	Italy	1938	CALIF
Freddie Steele	USA	1938	NBA
Al Hostak	USA	1938	NBA
Solly Krieger	USA	1938-1939	NBA
Fred Apostoli	USA	1938-1939	NY
Al Hostak	USA	1939-1940	NBA
Ceferino Garcia	Philippines	1939-1940	NY
Ken Overlin	USA	1940-1941	NY
Tony Zale	USA	1940-1941	NBA
Billy Soose	USA	1941	NY
Tony Zale	USA	1941-1947	
Rocky Graziano	USA	1947-1948	
Tony Zale	USA	1948	
Marcel Cerdan	Algeria	1948-1949	
Jake la Motta	USA	1949-1950	
Jake la Motta	USA	1950-1951	NY/NBA
Sugar Ray Robinson	USA	1950-1951	PEN
Sugar Ray Robinson	USA	1951	
Randy Turpin	England	1951	
Sugar Ray Robinson*	USA	1951-1952	
Randy Turpin	England	1953	GB/EBU
Carl Bobo Olson	Hawaii	1953-1955	
Sugar Ray Robinson	USA	1955-1957	
Gene Fullmer	USA	1957	
Sugar Ray Robinson	USA	1957	
Carmen Basilio	USA	1957-1958	
Sugar Ray Robinson	USA	1958-1959	

Title Holder	Birthplace	Tenure	Status	Title Holder	Birthplace	Tenure	Status
Sugar Ray Robinson	USA	1959-1960	NY/EBU	Nigel Benn	England	1990	WBO
Gene Fullmer	USA	1959-1962	NBA	Chris Eubank*	England	1990-1991	WBO
Paul Pender	USA	1960-1961	NY/EBU	Julian Jackson	Virgin Islands	1990-1993	WBC
Terry Downes	England	1961-1962	NY/EBU	James Toney*	USA	1991-1993	IBF
Paul Pender	USA	1962	NY/EBU	Gerald McClellan*	USA	1991-1993	WBO
Dick Tiger	Nigeria	1962-1963	NBA	Reggie Johnson	USA	1992-1993	WBA
Dick Tiger	Nigeria	1963		Gerald McClellan*	USA	1993-1995	WBC
Joey Giardello	USA	1963-1965		Chris Pyatt	England	1993-1994	WBO
Dick Tiger	Nigeria	1965-1966		Roy Jones*	USA	1993-1994	IBF
Emile Griffith	Virgin Islands	1966-1967		John David Jackson	USA	1993-1994	WBA
Nino Benvenuti	Italy	1967		Steve Collins*	Ireland	1994-1995	WBO
Emile Griffith	Virgin Islands	1967-1968		Jorge Castro	Argentina	1994	WBA
Nino Benvenuti	Italy	1968-1970		Julian Jackson	Virgin Islands	1995	WBC
Carlos Monzon	Argentina	1970-1974		Bernard Hopkins*	USA	1995-2001	IBF
Carlos Monzon*	Argentina	1974-1976	WBA	Lonnie Bradley*	USA	1995-1998	WBO
Rodrigo Valdez	Colombia	1974-1976	WBC	Quincy Taylor	USA	1995-1996	WBC
Carlos Monzon*	Argentina	1976-1977		Shinji Takehara	Japan	1995-1996	WBA
Rodrigo Valdez	Colombia	1977-1978		Keith Holmes	USA	1996-1998	WBC
Hugo Corro	Argentina	1978-1979		William Joppy	USA	1996-1997	WBA
Vito Antuofermo	Italy	1979-1980		Julio Cesar Green	Dom Republic	1997-1998	WBA
Alan Minter	England	1980		William Joppy	USA	1998-2001	WBA
Marvin Hagler	USA	1980-1987		Hassine Cherifi	France	1998-1999	WBC
Marvin Hagler	USA	1987	WBC/IBF	Otis Grant*	Canada	1998	WBO
Sugar Ray Leonard	USA	1987	WBC	Bert Schenk	Germany	1999	WBO
Frank Tate	USA	1987-1988	IBF	Keith Holmes	USA	1999-2001	WBC
Sumbu Kalambay	Zaire	1987-1989	WBA	Jason Matthews	England	1999	WBO
Thomas Hearns	USA	1987-1988	WBC	Armand Krajnc	Slovenia	1999-2002	WBO
Iran Barkley	USA	1988-1989	WBC	Bernard Hopkins*	USA	2001	WBC/IBF
Michael Nunn	USA	1988-1991	IBF	Felix Trinidad	Puerto Rico	2001	WBA
Roberto Duran	Panama	1989-1990	WBC	Bernard Hopkins*	USA	2001-2004	WBC/WBA/IBF
Doug de Witt	USA	1989-1990	WBO	Harry Simon	Namibia	2002-2003	WBO
Mike McCallum	Jamaica	1989-1991	WBA	Hector Javier Velazco	Argentina	2003	WBO
				Felix Sturm	Germany	2003-2004	WBO
				Oscar de la Hoya	USA	2004	WBO
				Bernard Hopkins	USA	2004-2005	IBF/WBA/WBC/WBO
				Jermain Taylor*	USA	2005	IBF/WBA/WBC/WBO
				Jermain Taylor*	USA	2005-	WBA/WBC/WBO
				Arthur Abraham	Armenia	2005-	IBF
				Jermain Taylor	USA	2006-	WBC/WBO
				Javier Castillejo	Spain	2006	WBA
				Mariano Carrera	Argentina	2006-2007	WBA
				Javier Castillejo	Spain	2007	WBA
				Felix Sturm	Germany	2007-	WBA

S. Middleweight (168 lbs)

Title Holder	Birthplace	Tenure	Status
Murray Sutherland	Scotland	1984	IBF
Chong-Pal Park*	S Korea	1984-1987	IBF
Chong-Pal Park	S Korea	1987-1988	WBA
Graciano Rocchigiani*	Germany	1988-1989	IBF
Fully Obelmejias	Venezuela	1988-1989	WBA
Sugar Ray Leonard*	USA	1988-1990	WBC
Thomas Hearns*	USA	1988-1991	WBO
In-Chul Baek	S Korea	1989-1990	WBA
Lindell Holmes	USA	1990-1991	IBF
Christophe Tiozzo	France	1990-1991	WBA
Mauro Galvano	Italy	1990-1992	WBC
Victor Cordoba	Panama	1991-1992	WBA
Darrin van Horn	USA	1991-1992	IBF
Chris Eubank	England	1991-1995	WBO
Iran Barkley	USA	1992-1993	IBF
Michael Nunn	USA	1992-1994	WBA
Nigel Benn	England	1992-1996	WBC
James Toney	USA	1993-1994	IBF
Steve Little	USA	1994	WBA
Frank Liles	USA	1994-1999	WBA
Roy Jones*	USA	1994-1997	IBF
Steve Collins*	Ireland	1995-1997	WBO
Thulani Malinga	S Africa	1996	WBC
Vincenzo Nardiello	Italy	1996	WBC
Robin Reid	England	1996-1997	WBC

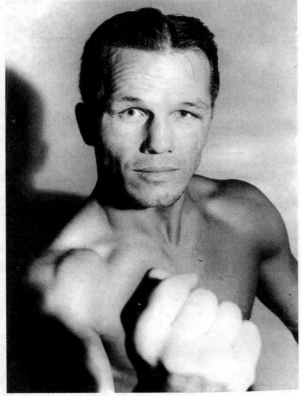

Tony Zale

Title Holder	Birthplace	Tenure	Status
Charles Brewer	USA	1997-1998	IBF
Joe Calzaghe*	Wales	1997-2006	WBO
Thulani Malinga	S Africa	1997-1998	WBC
Richie Woodhall	England	1998-1999	WBC
Sven Ottke*	Germany	1998-2003	IBF
Byron Mitchell	USA	1999-2000	WBA
Markus Beyer	Germany	1999-2000	WBC
Bruno Girard	France	2000-2001	WBA
Glenn Catley	England	2000	WBC
Dingaan Thobela	S Africa	2000	WBC
Dave Hilton	Canada	2000-2001	WBC
Byron Mitchell	USA	2001-2003	WBA
Eric Lucas	Canada	2001-2003	WBC
Sven Ottke*	Germany	2003-2004	IBF/WBA
Markus Beyer	Germany	2003-2004	WBC
Anthony Mundine	Australia	2004	WBA
Manny Sica	Puerto Rico	2004	WBA
Cristian Sanavia	Italy	2004	WBC
Jeff Lacy	USA	2004-2006	IBF
Markus Beyer	Germany	2004-2006	WBC
Mikkel Kessler*	Denmark	2004-2006	WBA
Joe Calzaghe*	Wales	2006	WBO/IBF
Mikkel Kessler	Denmark	2006-	WBC/WBA
Joe Calzaghe	Wales	2006-	WBO
Alejandro Berrio	Colombia	2007-	IBF

L. Heavyweight (175 lbs)

Title Holder	Birthplace	Tenure	Status
Jack Root	Austria	1903	
George Gardner	Ireland	1903	
George Gardner	Ireland	1903	USA
Bob Fitzsimmons	England	1903-1905	USA
Jack O'Brien	USA	1905-1911	
Sam Langford	Canada	1911-1913	
Georges Carpentier	France	1913-1920	IBU
Jack Dillon	USA	1914-1916	USA
Battling Levinsky	USA	1916-1920	USA
Georges Carpentier	France	1920-1922	
Battling Siki	Senegal	1922-1923	
Mike McTigue	Ireland	1923-1925	
Paul Berlenbach	USA	1925-1926	
Jack Delaney*	Canada	1926-1927	
Jimmy Slattery	USA	1927	NBA
Tommy Loughran	USA	1927	NY
Tommy Loughran*	USA	1927-1929	
Jimmy Slattery	USA	1930	NY
Maxie Rosenbloom	USA	1930-1931	
Maxie Rosenbloom	USA	1931-1933	NY
George Nichols	USA	1932	NBA
Bob Godwin	USA	1933	NBA
Maxie Rosenbloom	USA	1933-1934	
Maxie Rosenbloom	USA	1934	NY
Joe Knight	USA	1934-1935	FL/NC/GEO
Bob Olin	USA	1934-1935	NY
Al McCoy	Canada	1935	CAN
Bob Olin	USA	1935	NY/NBA
John Henry Lewis	USA	1935-1938	NY/NBA
Gustav Roth	Belgium	1936-1938	IBU
Ad Heuser	Germany	1938	IBU
John Henry Lewis	USA	1938	
John Henry Lewis	USA	1938-1939	NBA
Melio Bettina	USA	1939	NY
Len Harvey	England	1939-1942	GB
Billy Conn	USA	1939-1940	NY/NBA
Anton Christoforidis	Greece	1941	NBA
Gus Lesnevich	USA	1941	NBA
Gus Lesnevich	USA	1941-1946	NY/NBA
Freddie Mills	England	1942-1946	GB
Gus Lesnevich	USA	1946-1948	
Freddie Mills	England	1948-1950	
Joey Maxim	USA	1950-1952	
Archie Moore	USA	1952-1960	
Archie Moore	USA	1960-1962	NY/EBU

Title Holder	Birthplace	Tenure	Status
Harold Johnson	USA	1961-1962	NBA
Harold Johnson	USA	1962-1963	
Willie Pastrano	USA	1963	
Willie Pastrano*	USA	1963-1964	WBA/WBC
Eddie Cotton	USA	1963-1964	MICH
Willie Pastrano	USA	1964-1965	
Jose Torres	Puerto Rico	1965-1966	
Dick Tiger	Nigeria	1966-1968	
Bob Foster	USA	1968-1970	
Bob Foster*	USA	1970-1972	WBC
Vicente Rondon	Venezuela	1971-1972	WBA
Bob Foster*	USA	1972-1974	
John Conteh	England	1974-1977	WBC
Victor Galindez	Argentina	1974-1978	WBA
Miguel Cuello	Argentina	1977-1978	WBC
Mate Parlov	Yugoslavia	1978	WBC
Mike Rossman	USA	1978-1979	WBA
Marvin Johnson	USA	1978-1979	WBC
Victor Galindez	Argentina	1979	WBA
Matt Saad Muhammad	USA	1979-1981	WBC
Marvin Johnson	USA	1979-1980	WBA
Mustafa Muhammad	USA	1980-1981	WBA
Michael Spinks	USA	1981-1983	WBA
Dwight Muhammad Qawi	USA	1981-1983	WBC
Michael Spinks*	USA	1983-1985	
J. B. Williamson	USA	1985-1986	WBC
Slobodan Kacar	Yugoslavia	1985-1986	IBF
Marvin Johnson	USA	1986-1987	WBA
Dennis Andries	Guyana	1986-1987	WBC

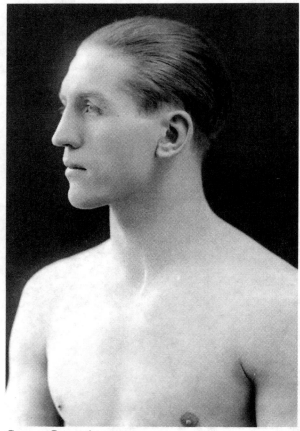

Georges Carpentier

Bobby Czyz	USA	1986-1987	IBF
Thomas Hearns*	USA	1987	WBC
Leslie Stewart	Trinidad	1987	WBA
Virgil Hill	USA	1987-1991	WBA
Charles Williams	USA	1987-1993	IBF
Don Lalonde	Canada	1987-1988	WBC
Sugar Ray Leonard*	USA	1988	WBC
Michael Moorer*	USA	1988-1991	WBO
Dennis Andries	Guyana	1989	WBC
Jeff Harding	Australia	1989-1990	WBC
Dennis Andries	Guyana	1990-1991	WBC
Leonzer Barber	USA	1991-1994	WBO
Thomas Hearns	USA	1991-1992	WBA
Jeff Harding	Australia	1991-1994	WBC
Iran Barkley*	USA	1992	WBA
Virgil Hill*	USA	1992-1996	WBA
Henry Maske	Germany	1993-1996	IBF
Mike McCallum	Jamaica	1994-1995	WBC
Dariusz Michalczewski*	Poland	1994-1997	WBO
Fabrice Tiozzo	France	1995-1997	WBC
Virgil Hill	USA	1996-1997	IBF/WBA
Roy Jones	USA	1997	WBC
Montell Griffin	USA	1997	WBC
Dariusz Michalczewski*	Poland	1997	WBO/IBF/WBA
Dariusz Michalczewski	Poland	1997-2003	WBO
William Guthrie	USA	1997-1998	IBF
Roy Jones*	USA	1997-1998	WBC
Lou del Valle	USA	1997-1998	WBA
Reggie Johnson	USA	1998-1999	IBF
Roy Jones*	USA	1998-1999	WBC/WBA
Roy Jones*	USA	1999-2002	WBC/WBA/IBF
Roy Jones*	USA	2002-2003	WBA/WBC
Mehdi Sahnoune	France	2003	WBA
Antonio Tarver*	USA	2003	IBF/WBC
Silvio Branco	Italy	2003-2004	WBA
Julio Gonzalez	Mexico	2003-2004	WBO
Antonio Tarver*	USA	2003-2004	WBC
Zsolt Erdei	Hungary	2004-	WBO
Glengoffe Johnson*	Jamaica	2004	IBF
Antoine Tarver	USA	2004-2006	IBO
Fabrice Tiozzo*	France	2004-2006	WBA
Clinton Woods	England	2005-	IBF
Tomasz Adamek	Poland	2005-2007	WBC
Bernard Hopkins*	USA	2006	IBO
Silvio Branco	Italy	2006-2007	WBA
Chad Dawson	USA	2006-	WBC
Stipe Drews	Croatia	2007-	WBA

Cruiserweight (200 lbs)

Marvin Camel	USA	1979-1980	WBC
Carlos de Leon	Puerto Rico	1980-1982	WBC
Ossie Ocasio	Puerto Rico	1982-1984	WBA
S. T. Gordon	USA	1982-1983	WBC
Marvin Camel	USA	1983-1984	IBF
Carlos de Leon	Puerto Rico	1983-1985	WBC
Lee Roy Murphy	USA	1984-1986	IBF
Piet Crous	S Africa	1984-1985	WBA
Alfonso Ratliff	USA	1985	WBC
Dwight Muhammad Qawi	USA	1985-1986	WBA
Bernard Benton	USA	1985-1986	WBC
Carlos de Leon	Puerto Rico	1986-1988	WBC
Evander Holyfield*	USA	1986-1987	WBA
Rickey Parkey	USA	1986-1987	IBF
Evander Holyfield*	USA	1987-1988	WBA/IBF
Evander Holyfield*	USA	1988	
Taoufik Belbouli*	France	1989	WBA
Carlos de Leon	Puerto Rico	1989-1990	WBC
Glenn McCrory	England	1989-1990	IBF
Robert Daniels	USA	1989-1991	WBA
Boone Pultz	USA	1989-1990	WBO
Jeff Lampkin*	USA	1990-1991	IBF
Magne Havnaa*	Norway	1990-1992	WBO
Masimilliano Duran	Italy	1990-1991	WBC
Bobby Czyz	USA	1991-1993	WBA

Anaclet Wamba	Congo	1991-1995	WBC
James Warring	USA	1991-1992	IBF
Tyrone Booze	USA	1992-1993	WBO
Al Cole*	USA	1992-1996	IBF
Marcus Bott	Germany	1993	WBO
Nestor Giovannini	Argentina	1993-1994	WBO
Orlin Norris	USA	1993-1995	WBA
Dariusz Michalczewski*	Poland	1994-1995	WBO
Ralf Rocchigiani	Germany	1995-1997	WBO
Nate Miller	USA	1995-1997	WBA
Marcelo Dominguez	Argentina	1995-1998	WBC
Adolpho Washington	USA	1996-1997	IBF
Uriah Grant	USA	1997	IBF
Carl Thompson	England	1997-1999	WBO
Imamu Mayfield	USA	1997-1998	IBF
Fabrice Tiozzo	France	1997-2000	WBA
Juan Carlos Gomez*	Cuba	1998-2002	WBC
Arthur Williams	USA	1998-1999	IBF
Johnny Nelson*	England	1999-2006	WBO
Vassily Jirov	Kazakhstan	1999-2003	IBF
Virgil Hill	USA	2000-2002	WBA
Jean-Marc Mormeck*	Guadeloupe	2002-2005	WBA
Wayne Braithwaite	Guyana	2002-2005	WBC
James Toney*	USA	2003-2004	IBF
Kelvin Davis	USA	2004-2005	IBF
Jean-Marc Mormeck	Guadaloupe	2005-2006	WBA/WBC
O'Neil Bell*	USA	2005-2006	IBF
O'Neil Bell	USA	2006	IBF/WBA/WBC
O'Neil Bell	USA	2006-2007	WBA/WBC
Enzo Maccarinelli	Wales	2006-	WBO
Krzysztof Wlodarczyk	Poland	2006-2007	IBF
Jean-Marc Mormeck	Guadaloupe	2007-	WBA/WBC
Steve Cunningham	USA	2007-	IBF

Heavyweight (200 lbs+)

John L. Sullivan	USA	1889-1892	USA
Peter Jackson	Australia	1889-1892	
Frank Slavin	Australia	1890-1892	GB/AUST
Peter Jackson	Australia	1892-1893	GB/AUST
James J. Corbett	USA	1892-1894	USA
James J. Corbett	USA	1894-1895	
James J. Corbett	USA	1895-1897	
Peter Maher	Ireland	1895-1896	
Bob Fitzsimmons	England	1896-1897	
Bob Fitzsimmons	England	1897-1899	
James J. Jeffries	USA	1899-1902	
James J. Jeffries	USA	1902-1905	
Denver Ed Martin	USA	1902-1903	
Jack Johnson	USA	1902-1908	
Bob Fitzsimmons	England	1905	
Marvin Hart	USA	1905-1906	
Jack O'Brien	USA	1905-1906	
Tommy Burns	Canada	1906-1908	
Jack Johnson	USA	1908-1909	
Jack Johnson	USA	1909-1915	
Sam Langford	USA	1909-1911	
Sam McVey	USA	1911-1912	
Sam Langford	USA	1912-1914	
Luther McCarty	USA	1913	
Arthur Pelkey	Canada	1913-1914	
Gunboat Smith	USA	1914	
Harry Wills	USA	1914	
Georges Carpentier	France	1914	
Sam Langford	USA	1914-1915	
Jess Willard	USA	1915-1919	
Joe Jeannette	USA	1915	
Sam McVey	USA	1915	
Harry Wills	USA	1915-1916	
Sam Langford	USA	1916-1917	
Bill Tate	USA	1917	
Sam Langford	USA	1917-1918	
Harry Wills	USA	1918-1926	
Jack Dempsey	USA	1919-1926	
Gene Tunney*	USA	1926-1928	

WORLD CHAMPIONS SINCE GLOVES, 1889-2007

Max Schmeling	Germany	1930-1932	
Jack Sharkey	USA	1932-1933	
Primo Carnera	Italy	1933-1934	
Max Baer	USA	1934-1935	
James J. Braddock	USA	1935	
James J. Braddock	USA	1935-1936	NY/NBA
George Godfrey	USA	1935-1936	IBU
James J. Braddock	USA	1936-1937	
Joe Louis*	USA	1937-1949	
Ezzard Charles	USA	1949-1950	NBA
Lee Savold	USA	1950-1951	GB/EBU
Ezzard Charles	USA	1950-1951	NY/NBA
Joe Louis	USA	1951	GB/EBU
Jersey Joe Walcott	USA	1951	NY/NBA
Jersey Joe Walcott	USA	1951-1952	
Rocky Marciano*	USA	1952-1956	
Floyd Patterson	USA	1956-1959	
Ingemar Johansson	Sweden	1959-1960	
Floyd Patterson	USA	1960-1962	
Sonny Liston	USA	1962-1964	
Muhammad Ali	USA	1964	
Muhammad Ali*	USA	1964-1967	WBC
Ernie Terrell	USA	1965-1967	WBA
Muhammad Ali	USA	1967	
Muhammad Ali	USA	1967-1968	WBC
Joe Frazier*	USA	1968-1970	NY/MASS
Jimmy Ellis	USA	1968-1970	WBA
Joe Frazier	USA	1970-1973	
George Foreman	USA	1973-1974	
Muhammad Ali	USA	1974-1978	
Leon Spinks	USA	1978	
Leon Spinks	USA	1978	WBA
Ken Norton	USA	1978	WBC
Larry Holmes*	USA	1978-1983	WBC
Muhammad Ali*	USA	1978-1979	WBA
John Tate	USA	1979-1980	WBA
Mike Weaver	USA	1980-1982	WBA
Michael Dokes	USA	1982-1983	WBA
Gerrie Coetzee	S Africa	1983-1984	WBA
Larry Holmes	USA	1983-1985	IBF
Tim Witherspoon	USA	1984	WBC
Pinklon Thomas	USA	1984-1986	WBC
Greg Page	USA	1984-1985	WBA
Tony Tubbs	USA	1985-1986	WBA
Michael Spinks	USA	1985-1987	IBF
Tim Witherspoon	USA	1986	WBA
Trevor Berbick	Jamaica	1986	WBC
Mike Tyson*	USA	1986-1987	WBC
James Smith	USA	1986-1987	WBA
Mike Tyson*	USA	1987	WBA/WBC
Tony Tucker	USA	1987	IBF
Mike Tyson	USA	1987-1989	
Mike Tyson	USA	1989-1990	IBF/WBA/WBC
Francesco Damiani	Italy	1989-1991	WBO
James Douglas	USA	1990	IBF/WBA/WBC
Evander Holyfield	USA	1990-1992	IBF/WBA/WBC
Ray Mercer	USA	1991-1992	WBO
Michael Moorer*	USA	1992-1993	WBO
Riddick Bowe	USA	1992	IBF/WBA/WBC
Riddick Bowe	USA	1992-1993	IBF/WBA
Lennox Lewis	England	1992-1994	WBC
Tommy Morrison	USA	1993	WBO
Michael Bentt	England	1993-1994	WBO
Evander Holyfield	USA	1993-1994	WBA/IBF
Herbie Hide	England	1994-1995	WBO
Michael Moorer	USA	1994	WBA/IBF
Oliver McCall	USA	1994-1995	WBC
George Foreman	USA	1994-1995	WBA/IBF
Riddick Bowe*	USA	1995-1996	WBO
George Foreman*	USA	1995	IBF
Bruce Seldon	USA	1995-1996	WBA
Frank Bruno	England	1995-1996	WBC
Frans Botha	S Africa	1995-1996	IBF
Mike Tyson	USA	1996	WBC
Michael Moorer	USA	1996-1997	IBF
Henry Akinwande*	England	1996-1997	WBO
Mike Tyson	USA	1996	WBA
Evander Holyfield*	USA	1996-1997	WBA
Lennox Lewis*	England	1997-1999	WBC
Herbie Hide	England	1997-1999	WBO
Evander Holyfield	USA	1997-1999	IBF/WBA
Vitali Klitschko	Ukraine	1999-2000	WBO
Lennox Lewis*	England	1999-2000	IBF/WBA/WBC
Chris Byrd	USA	2000	WBO
Lennox Lewis	England	2000-2001	IBF/WBC
Evander Holyfield	USA	2000-2001	WBA
Vladimir Klitschko	Ukraine	2000-2003	WBO
John Ruiz	USA	2001-2003	WBA
Hasim Rahman	USA	2001	WBC/IBF
Lennox Lewis*	England	2001-2002	WBC/IBF
Lennox Lewis*	England	2002-2006	WBC
Chris Byrd	USA	2002-2006	IBF
Roy Jones*	USA	2003	WBA
Corrie Sanders*	S Africa	2003	WBO
Lamon Brewster	USA	2004-2006	WBO
John Ruiz	Puerto Rico	2004-2005	WBA
Vitali Klitschko*	Ukraine	2004-2005	WBC
James Toney	USA	2005	WBA
John Ruiz	Puerto Rico	2005	WBA
Nikolai Valuev	Russia	2005-2007	WBA
Hasim Rahman	USA	2005-2006	WBC
Sergei Lyakhovich	Belarus	2006	WBO
Vladimir Klitschko	Ukraine	2006-	IBF
Oleg Maskaev	Kazakhstan	2006-	WBC
Shannon Briggs	USA	2006-2007	WBO
Ruslan Chagaev	Uzbekistan	2007-	WBA
Sultan Ibragimov	Russia	2007-	WBO

Jack Dempsey

ABA National Championships, 2006-2007

Note: Only men who fought at some stage of the competition are included.

Combined Services

Nelson Barracks Gymnasium, Portsmouth – 2 November
L.Fly: no entries. **Fly:** *final*: A.Whitfield (Army) w pts G.Smith (RN). **Bantam:** *final*: J.Allen (Army) wo. **Feather:** *final*: J.Evans (Army) w pts M.Travis (RN). **Light:** *final*: A.Urritia (RN) w pts J.Elfidh (Army). **L.Welter:** *final*: M.Stead (Army) w pts K.Sheen (RN). **Welter:** *final*: S.Briggs (Army) w pts D.Robinson (RN). **Middle:** *final*: J.Summers (Army) w pts S.Tighe (RN). **L.Heavy:** *final*: T.Richardson (Army) w pts N.McGarry (RN). **Cruiser:** *final*: S.McDonald (RN) w pts C.Dilks (Army). **Heavy:** *final*: S.O'Connor (RN) w pts D.Frost (Army). **S.Heavy:** no entries.

Eastern Counties

Broadside ABC, Norwich – 20 October, Abercrombie Way Centre, Harlow – 21 October, The Civic Hall, Grays – 27 October
L.Fly: no entries. **Fly:** *final*: M.Walsh (Kingfisher) wo. **Bantam:** *final*: R.Walsh (Kingfisher) wo. **Feather:** *final*: L.Walsh (Kingfisher) wo. **Light:** *final*: M.Poston (Harwich) wo. **L.Welter:** *final*: S.Crompton (Kingfisher) w rsc 3 K.Allen (Eastgate). **Welter:** *semi-finals:* D.Brown (Berry Boys) wo, A.Ogogo (Triple A) w pts P.McAleese (New Astley); *final:* A.Ogogo w rsc 2 D.Brown. **Middle:** *quarter-finals:* L.Pizzey (Norwich Lads) wo, L.Byrne (Icini) wo, S.Kobiessi (New Astley) wo, K.Wootton (Harlow) w pts R.Warman (Berry Boys); *semi-final:* K.Wootton w pts L.Pizzey, L.Byrne w pts S.Kobiessi; *final:* K.Wootton w pts L.Byrne. **L.Heavy:** *final*: C.Brodie (Arena) wo. **Cruiser:** *final*: M.Redhead (Kingfisher) wo. **Heavy:** *final*: P.Wright (Chatteris) wo. **S.Heavy:** no entries.

Home Counties

Albury Ride Gymnasium, Cheshunt – 27 October, The Sports Centre, Thame – 4 November
L.Fly: no entries. **Fly:** *final*: A.Sexton (Cheshunt) wo. **Bantam:** no entries. **Feather:** *final*: I.Bailey (Slough) w pts L.Lewis (Wolvercote). **Light:** *final*: G.Jones (Reading) w pts L.Shinkwin (Bushey). **L.Welter:** *semi-finals:* M.Maisey (Wolvercote) wo, L.Gray (Stevenage) w pts M.McCullough (Chalfont); *final:* L.Gray w pts M.Maisey. **Welter:** no entries. **Middle:** *final*: T.Skipper (Stevenage) wo. **L.Heavy:** *semi-finals:* H.Sessegnon (Wolvercote) wo, M.Shinkwin (Bushey) w pts A.Dennis (Luton Shamrock); *final*: V.Sessegnon w co 2 M.Shinkwin. **Cruiser:** *final*: L.Howkins (Pinewood Starr) wo. **Heavy:** no entries. **S.Heavy:** no entries.

Midland Counties v Tyne, Tees & Wear

Midland Counties
Northern Zone Heritage Hotel, Derby – 22 October & Triumph Social Club, Coventry – 29 October
L.Fly: *final*: K.Saeed (Birmingham City Police) wo. **Fly:** *final*: U.Malik (Merlin Youth) wo. **Bantam:** *final*: L.Wood (Phoenix)

wo. **Feather:** *final*: J.Spring (Terry Allen Unique) w pts A.Brennan (Triumph). **Light:** *final*: R.Bennett (Belgrave) wo. **L.Welter:** no entries. **Welter:** *final*: D.Watson (Boston) w rsc 3 C.Broomhead (Buxton). **Middle:** *semi-finals:* J.Easy (Huthwaite) wo, A.Johnson (St George) w pts G.Khang (Belgrave); *final:* A.Johnson w pts J.Easy. **L.Heavy:** *semi-finals:* E.Dube (Merlin Youth) wo, V.Petkovic (One Nation) w pts L.Spare (Bulkington); *final:* E.Dube w pts V.Petkovic. **Cruiser:** *final*: D.Ward (Belgrave) wo. **Heavy:** *final*: R.Wilson (Trinity) wo. **S.Heavy:** *final*: S.McPhilbin (St George) wo.

Southern Zone Castle Vale Residents Club, Birmingham – 20 October & Triumph Social Club, Coventry – 29 October
L.Fly: *final*: S.Smith (Kingsthorpe Boys) wo. **Fly:** no entries. **Bantam:** *final*: S.King (Ironworks) wo. **Feather:** *final*: J.Bray (Lions) wo. **Light:** *final*: F.Gavin (Hall Green) wo. **L.Welter:** *final*: T.Walker (Tamworth) w pts C.Trueman (Aston Police). **Welter:** *semi-finals:* S.Miller (Hulton Abbey) wo, J.Jeavons (Aston Police) w pts J.Connelly (Ironworks); *final:* J.Jevons w pts S.Miller. **Middle:** *final*: B.Murphy (Aston Police) wo. **L.Heavy:** *final*: J.Ingram (Aston Police) w pts E.Clayton (Donnington Ex-Servicemen). **Cruiser:** no entries. **Heavy:** no entries. **S.Heavy:** *final*: T.Cope (Tamworth) wo.

Midland Counties Finals – Marstons Stadium, Hinckley – 2 November
L.Fly: K.Saeed (Birmingham City Police) w pts S.Smith (Kingsthorpe Boys). **Fly:** U.Malik (Merlin Youth) wo. **Bantam:** L.Wood (Phoenix) w pts S.King (Ironworks). **Feather:** J.Bray (Lions) w pts J.Spring (Terry Allen Unique). **Light:** F.Gavin (Hall Green) w pts R.Bennett (Belgrave). **L.Welter:** T.Walker (Tamworth) wo. **Welter:** J.Jeavons (Aston Police) w pts D.Watson (Boston). **Middle:** A.Johnson (St George) w pts B.Murphy (Aston Police). **L.Heavy:** J.Ingram (Aston Police) w pts E.Dube (Merlin Youth). **Cruiser:** D.Ward (Belgrave) wo. **Heavy:** R.Wilson (Trinity) wo. **S.Heavy:** T.Cope (Tamworth) w pts S.McPhilbin (St George).

Tyne, Tees & Wear
Eldon Square, Newcastle – 26 October & 1 November
L.Fly: no entries. **Fly:** no entries. **Bantam:** *final*: S.Hall (Spennymoor) wo. **Feather:** *final*: M.Ward (Birtley Boys) w rsc 2 C.Elgey (Shildon). **Light:** *quarter-finals:* G.Bainbridge (Chester Moor) wo, J.Watson (Grainger Park) wo, R.Boyle (Birtley Boys) wo, G.Reay (East Durham & Houghall) w rsc 2 T.Ratcliffe (Sunderland); *semi-finals:* R.Boyle w rsc 3 G.Bainbridge, J.Watson w pts G.Reay; *final:* J.Watson w pts R.Boyle. **L.Welter:** *semi-finals:* B.Saunders (South Durham) wo, C.Dixon (Birtley Boys) w pts P.Boyle (Halfpenny); *final:* B.Saunders w pts C.Dixon. **Welter:** *semi-finals:* M.Hogarth (Bishop Auckland) wo, M.Clauzel (Northumbria) w rsc 2 T.Whitfield (Birtley Boys), M.Hogarth (Bishop Auckland); *final:* M.Clauzel w pts M.Hogarth. **Middle:** *final*: I.Turnbull (Hylton Castle) w pts T.Grange (Phil Thomas SoB). **L.Heavy:** *final*: S.McCrone (Spennymoor) w rsc 4 G.Barr (Birtley Boys). **Cruiser:** *final*: J-L.Dickinson (Birtley Boys) wo. **Heavy:** *final*: W.Baister (Marley Potts) wo. **S.Heavy:** *final*: D.Hughes (Hylton Castle) wo.

Midland Counties v Tyne, Tees & Wear   Triumph Social Club, Coventry – 12 November
L.Fly: K.Saeed (Birmingham City Police) wo. **Fly:** U.Malik

(Merlin Youth) wo. **Bantam:** S.Hall (Spennymoor) w pts L.Wood (Phoenix). **Feather:** M.Ward (Birtley Boys) w rsc 2 J.Bray (Lions). **Light:** F.Gavin (Hall Green) w pts J.Watson (Grainger Park). **L.Welter:** B.Saunders (South Durham) w pts C.Trueman (Aston Police) – replaced T.Walker (Tamworth). **Welter:** M.Clauzel (Northumbria) w rsc 3 J.Jeavons (Aston Police). **Middle:** A.Johnson (St George) w pts I.Turnbull (Hylton Castle). **L.Heavy:** S.McCrone (Spennymoor) w pts J.Ingram (Aston Police). **Cruiser:** J-L.Dickinson (Birtley Boys) w pts D.Ward (Belgrave). **Heavy:** W.Baister (Marley Potts) w rsc 3 R.Wilson (Trinity). **S.Heavy:** D.Hughes (Hylton Castle) w rsc 2 T.Cope (Tamworth).

North-West Counties

East Lancs & Cheshire Division   Audley Community Centre, Blackburn – 20 October
L.Fly: no entries. **Fly:** *final*: J.Wilkinson (Fox) wo. **Bantam:** *final*: K.De'ath (Northside) w pts J.Murray (Boarshaw). **Feather:** *final*: B.Cunliffe (Sharples) wo. **Light:** *semi-finals:* J.Kays (Arrow) wo, J.Cosgrove (Barton) w pts C.Conwell (Northside); *final*: J.Kays w rtd 2 J.Cosgrove. **L.Welter:** *quarter-finals:* S.Rampling (Northside) wo, D.Wolfendon (Fox) wo, M.Ganiyu (Bury) w pts T.Bradford (Paramount), D.Askew (Workington) w pts T.Dwyer (Barton); *semi-finals:* D.Askew w pts S.Rampling; M.Ganyu w pts D.Wolfenden; *final*: M.Ganyu w D.Askew. **Welter:** *semi-finals:* M.King (Cleator) wo, K.Kirkham (Northside) w rsc 3 T.Sidlow (Collyhurst & Moston); *final*: K.Kirkham w pts M.King. **Middle:** *semi-finals:* J.Cropper (Roche) wo, K.Connelly (Collyhurst & Moston) w disq 3 D.Wilson (Centurians); *final*: K.Connolly w pts J.Cropper. **L.Heavy:** *final*: K.Borucki (Manx) wo. **Cruiser:** *final*: G.Whitehouse (Barrow) wo. **Heavy:** no entries. **S.Heavy:** *final*: T.Fury (Jimmy Egan's) wo.

West Lancs & Cheshire Division The Gymnasium, Kirkby – 18 October, Everton Park Sports Centre, Liverpool – 21 October
L.Fly: *final*: P.Butler (Vauxhall Motors) w pts P.Lowe (Golden Gloves). **Fly:** *semi-finals:* P.Edwards (Salisbury) w pts A.Bridge (Croxteth), P.Smith (Stockbridge) w pts J.Gilbertson (St Aloysius); *final*: P.Edwards w pts P.Smith. **Bantam:** *final*: J.Donnelly (Croxteth) w pts C.Farrelly (Higherside). **Feather:** *final*: S.Smith (Rotunda) wo. **Light:** *final*: T.Stalker (St Aloysius) w pts L.Jennings (Tower Hill). **L.Welter:** *final*: N.Brough (Salisbury) wo. **Welter:** *final*: J.Selkirk (Rotunda) w rsc 1 D.Angus (Salisbury). **Middle:** *semi-finals:* M.Phillips (Vauxhall Motors) wo, M.Bebbington (Warrington) w pts L.Andrews (Croxteth); *final*: M.Phillips w rsc 1 M.Bebbington. **L.Heavy:** *final*: J.Ainscough (Kirkdale) wo. **Cruiser:** *final*: J.Ward (Kirkby) wo. **Heavy:** *final*: T.Bellew (Rotunda) wo. **S.Heavy:** *final*: D.Price (Salisbury) wo.

North-West Counties Finals   The Forum, Wythenshawe – 3 November
L.Fly: P.Butler (Vauxhall Motors) wo. **Fly:** P.Edwards (Salisbury) w pts J.Wilkinson (Fox). **Bantam:** K.De'ath (Northside) w pts J.Donnelly (Croxteth). **Feather:** S.Smith (Rotunda) w pts B.Cunliffe (Sharples). **Light:** T.Stalker (St Aloysius) w pts J.Kays (Arrow). **L.Welter:** N.Brough (St Aloysius) w pts M.Ganiyu (Bury). **Welter:** J.Selkirk (Rotunda) w pts K.Kirkham (Northside). **Middle:** M.Phillips (Vauxhall Motors) w pts K.Connelly (Collyhurst & Moston). **L.Heavy:** J.Ainscough (Kirkdale) w pts K.Borucki (Manx). **Cruiser:** J. Ward (Kirkby) w rsc 1 G.Whitehouse (Barrow). **Heavy:** T.Bellew (Rotunda) wo. **S.Heavy:** D.Price (Salisbury) w pts T.Fury (Jimmy Egan's).

Southern Counties

Shinewater Sports Centre, Eastbourne – 29 October, Effingham Park Hotel, Copthorne – 3 November
L.Fly: no entries. **Fly:** no entries. **Bantam:** *final*: S.Goff (St Mary's) w pts R.Smart (Southampton). **Feather:** *semi-finals:* P.Adamczew (Crawley) wo, A.Dingsdale (Brompton) w pts P.Barney (Golden Ring); *final*: A.Dingsdale w rsc 2 P.Adamczew. **Light:** *final*: J.Dean (Waterside) wo. **L.Welter:** *quarter-finals:* M.Page (Golden Ring) wo, L.Ellett (Hove) w rsc 1 J.Verlander (Hastings West Hill), A.Battle (Warriors) w pts A.Swan (Faversham), A.Leigh (Moneyfields) w pts M.Tew (Southampton); *semi-finals:* M.Page w pts L.Ellett, A.Leigh w pts A.Battle; *final*: M.Page w pts A.Leigh. **Welter:** *semi-finals:* S.Ayres (Guildford) wo, J.Leigh (Moneyfields) w pts B.Buchanan (Hastings West Hill); *final*: J.Leigh w pts S.Ayres. **Middle:** *quarter-finals:* T.Hill (Golden Ring) wo, A.Watson (Crawley) wo, A.Gibbens (Bognor) wo, M.Coombs (Moneyfields) w pts M.Jenman (Moulescombe); *semi-finals:* T.Hill w pts A.Watson, A.Gibbens w rtd 2 M.Coombs; *final*: A.Watson – replaced T.Hill – w pts A.Gibbens. **L.Heavy:** *final*: A.Hanniver (Hastings West Hill) wo. **Heavy:** *final*: D.Reed (Moneyfields) w rsc 3 B.Frankham (Westree). **S.Heavy:** *semi-finals:* D.Taylor (Southampton) wo, T.Dallas (St Mary's) w pts N.Baker (Hove); *final*: T.Dallas w rsc 1 D.Taylor.

Western Counties

Northern Division   Town Hall, Lydney – 21 October, The Leisure Centre, Yate – 28 October
L.Fly: no entries. **Fly:** no entries. **Bantam:** *final*: D.Webb (Broad Plain) wo. **Feather:** *final*: C.Higgs (Lydney) wo. **Light:** *final*: J.Jameson (Yeovil) w pts P.Leworthy (Downend). **L.Welter:** *final*: J.Cox (Walcot Boys) wo. **Welter:** *final*: J.Taylor (Broad Plain) w pts J.Hicks (Yeovil). **Middle:** *quarter-finals:* C.Wood (Malmesbury/Wolvercote) wo, M.Robins (Downend) wo, M.Reid (Walcot Boys) wo, G.Morgan (Forest Oaks) w pts D.Devaine (Weston super Mare); *semi-finals:* C.Wood w rsc 1 M.Robins, M.Reid w rsc 3 G.Morgan; *final*: M.Reid w pts C.Wood. **L.Heavy:** *final*: M.Jennings (Amalgamated, Guernsey) wo. **Cruiser:** no entries. **Heavy:** no entries. **S.Heavy:** *final*: M.Elkins (Barnstaple) wo.

Southern Division (no title bouts, just walkovers)
L.Fly: no entries. **Fly:** no entries. **Bantam:** no entries. **Feather:** no entries. **Light:** *final*: B.Murray (Leonis) wo. **L.Welter:** no entries. **Welter:** *final*: A.Coles (Camborne & Redruth) wo. **Middle:** *final*: C.Culkin (Leonis) wo. **L.Heavy:** *final*: M.Spooner (Devonport) wo. **Cruiser:** no entries. **Heavy:** no entries. **S.Heavy:** no entries.

Western Counties Finals   Town Hall, Launceston – 4 November
L.Fly: no entries. **Fly:** no entries. **Bantam:** D.Webb (Broad Plain) wo. **Feather:** C.Higgs (Lydney) wo. **Light:** B.Murray (Leonis) w J.Jameson (Yeovil). **L.Welter:** J.Cox (Walcot Boys) wo. **Welter:** A.Coles (Camborne & Redruth) w J.Taylor (Broad Plain). **Middle:** M.Reid (Walcot Boys) w pts C.Culkin (Leonis). **L.Heavy:** M.Spooner (Devonport) w M.Jennings (Amalgamated, Guernsey). **Cruiser:** no entries. **Heavy:** no entries. **S.Heavy:** M.Elkins (Barnstaple) wo.

Yorkshire v London

Yorkshire
The Sports Centre, Havercroft – 27 October
L.Fly: no entries. **Fly:** *final*: A.Al-Fadil (Unity) w pts C.Robinson

(St Paul's). **Bantam:** *final*: l.Campbell (St Paul's) wo. **Feather:** *final*: S.Mounieme (St Paul's) w pts J.Dyer (Burmantofts). **Light:** no entries. **L.Welter:** *final*: A.Anwar (Bateson's) w pts P.Smith (Airedale). **Welter:** *final*: J.Wilson (Steel City) wo. **Middle:** *final*: R.Taylor (Handsworth Police) w pts T.Coward (Wombwell). **L.Heavy:** *final*: P.Goodwin (St Paul's) wo. **Cruiser:** *final*: C.Owen (Sheffield Boxing Centre) w pts D.Slaney (Conisborough). **Heavy:** *final*: D.Price (Westway) w rtd 2 B.Atkin (St Vincent's). **S.Heavy:** no entries.

London
North-East Division   York Hall, Bethnal Green – 18 October
L.Fly: no entries. **Fly:** no entries. **Bantam:** *final*: J.Cole (West Ham) wo. **Feather:** no entries. **Light:** *final*: L.Turner (West Ham) w pts M.Idress (Repton). **L.Welter:** *final*: G.Barker (Repton) wo. **Welter:** *final*: D.Herdman (Repton) w rsc 2 D.Miller (Peacock). **Middle:** *final*: R.Pickard (Repton) w pts J.Bishop (Dagenham). **L.Heavy:** *final*: D.Orwell (Dagenham) wo. **Cruiser:** *final*: T.Conquest (Hornchurch & Elm Park) T.Lodhi (Repton). **Heavy:** *final*: W.Camacho (Peacock) w pts O.Ossai (Repton). **S.Heavy:** *final*: D.Campbell (Repton) wo.

North-West Division   Brent Town Hall, Wembley – 19 October, York Hall, Bethnal Green – 21 October
L.Fly: no entries. **Fly:** no entries. **Bantam:** no entries. **Feather:** no entries. **Light:** *final*: B.Puddle (Dale Youth) w pts P.Liggins

(Trojan). **L.Welter:** *final*: C.Evangelou (Haringey Police) w pts B. Zarakani (Haringey Police). **Welter:** *quarter-finals:* O.Ekundayo (Haringey Police) w pts N.Cain (Dale Youth), H.Sidiqzai (Dale Youth) w pts T.Grublys (Hayes), S.O'Meara (Dale Youth) w pts A.Neunie (Haringey Police), A.Reid (Dale Youth) w pts E.Ochieng (Haringey Police); *semi-finals:* O.Ekundayo w pts H.Sidiqzai, S.O'Meara w pts A.Reid; *final:* O.Ekundayo w pts S.O'Meara. **Middle:** *semi-finals:* J.Degale (Dale Youth) wo, G.Groves (Dale Youth) w pts L.Reid (Dale Youth); *final:* G.Groves w pts J.Degale. **L.Heavy:** no entries. **Cruiser:** *final:* D.Mohseni (All Stars) wo. **Heavy:** no entries. **S.Heavy:** *final*: A.Al-Sady (All Stars) wo.

South-East & South-West Divisions   National Sports Centre, Crystal Palace – 17 October, York Hall, Bethnal Green – 21 October
L.Fly: no entries. **Fly:** *final*: S.Langley (Hollington) wo. **Bantam:** *final*: M.Casey (Fisher) w pts D.Pettitt (Nemesis). **Feather:** *final*: J.Saeed (Lynn) wo. **Light:** *final*: C.Morales (Fitzroy Lodge) w pts G.Boden (New Addington). **L.Welter:** *final*: D.Davis (Fitzroy Lodge) w pts G.Gardner (New Addington). **Welter:** *quarter-finals:* M.Welsh (Fitzroy Lodge) wo, M.Barber (Fitzroy Lodge) wo, D.Wright (Lynn) wo, F.Mankenda (Hollington) w pts M.White-Dowe (Marvels Lane); *semi-finals:* M.Welsh w pts M.Barber, F.Mankenda w pts D.Wright; *final:* M.Welsh w pts F.Mankenda. **Middle:** *final*: T.McDonagh (South Norwood & Victory) w pts L.Keating (Honour Oak). **L.Heavy:** *final*: O.Mbwakongo (Fisher) w rsc 4 B.Aird (Honour Oak). **Cruiser:** *final*: L.Williams

Khalid Saeed (Birmingham City Police), seen here outpointing Vauxhall Motor's Paul Butler (left) to win the 2006 ABA light-flyweight title, needed only two tournament contests to become champion
Les Clark

(Fitzroy Lodge) w rsc 3 D.Burton (Honour Oak). **Heavy:** *final*: M.McDonagh (Hollington) w pts S.Karpenko (Lynn). **S.Heavy:** *final*: D.Akinlade (Fitzroy Lodge) wo.

London Finals   National Sports Centre, Crystal Palace – 28 October

L.Fly: no entries. **Fly:** *final*: S.Langley (Hollington) wo. **Bantam:** *final*: J.Cole (West Ham) w pts M.Casey (Fisher). **Feather:** *final*: J.Saeed (Lynn) wo. **Light:** *semi-finals*: B.Puddle (Dale Youth) wo, L.Turner (West Ham) w pts C.Morales (Fitzroy Lodge); *final*: L.Turner w pts B.Puddle. **L.Welter:** *semi-finals*: D.Davis (Fitzroy Lodge) wo, G.Barker (Repton) w pts C.Evangelou (Haringey Police); *final*: G.Barker w pts D.Davis. **Welter:** *semi-finals*: M.Welsh (Fitzroy) wo, O.Ekundayo (Haringey Police) w pts D.Herdman (Repton); *final*: O.Ekundayo w pts M.Welsh. **Middle:** *semi-finals*: R.Pickard (Repton) wo, G.Groves (Dale Youth) w pts T.McDonagh (South Norwood & Victory); *final*: G.Groves w co 3 R.Pickard. **L.Heavy:** *final*: O.Mbwakongo (Fisher) w pts D.Orwell (Dagenham). **Cruiser:** *semi-finals*: L.Williams (Fitzroy Lodge) wo, T.Conquest (Hornchurch & Elm Park) w pts D.Mohseni (All Stars); *final*: L.Williams w rsc 1 T.Conquest. **Heavy:** *final*: M.McDonagh (Hollington) wo W.Camach (Peacock). **S.Heavy:** *semi-finals*: D.Alinlade (Fitzroy Lodge) wo, D.Campbell (Repton) w pts A.Al-Sady (All Stars); *final*: S.Heavy: D.Campbell w pts D.Akinlade.

Yorkshire v London   The Working Mens' Club, Birdwell – 10 November

L.Fly: no entries. **Fly:** S.Langley (Hollington) w pts A.Al-Fadil (Unity). **Bantam:** L.Campbell (St Paul's) w rsc 3 J.Cole (West Ham). **Feather:** S.Mounieme (St Paul's) w pts J.Saeed (Lynn). **Light:** L.Turner (West Ham) wo. **L.Welter:** G.Barker (Repton) w pts A.Anwar (Bateson's). **Welter:** O.Ekundayo (Haringey Police) w pts J.Wilson (Steel City). **Middle:** G.Groves (Dale Youth) w rtd 3 R.Taylor (Handsworth Police). **L.Heavy:** O.Mbwakongo (Fisher) w pts P.Goodwin (St Paul's). **Cruiser:** L.Williams (Fitzroy Lodge) w pts C.Owen (Sheffield Boxing Centre). **Heavy:** D.Price (Westway) w pts M.McDonagh (Hollington). **S.Heavy:** D.Campbell (Repton) wo.

English ABA Quarter-Finals, Semi-Finals & Finals

Olympia, Liverpool – 15 & 16 November, York Hall, Bethnal Green – 1 December

L.Fly: *final*: K.Saeed (Birmingham City Police) w pts P.Butler (Vauxhall Motors). **Fly:** *quarter-finals*: M.Walsh (Norwich Lads) wo, G.Smith (RN) wo, P.Edwards (Salisbury) w pts A.Sexton (Cheshunt), S.Langley (Hollington) w pts U.Malik (Merlin Youth); *semi-finals*: M.Walsh w pts P.Edwards, S.Langley (Hollington) w pts G.Smith (RN); *final*: M.Walsh w pts S.Langley. **Bantam:** *quarter-finals*: K.De'ath (Northside) wo, R.Walsh (Kingfisher) w pts D.Webb (Broad Plain), S.Goff (St Mary's) w pts J.Allen (Army), L.Campbell (St Paul's) w pts S.Hall (Spennymoor); *semi-finals*: R.Walsh w pts K.De'ath, L.Campbell w pts S.Goff; *final*: L.Campbell w pts R.Walsh. **Feather:** *quarter-finals*: L.Walsh (Kingfisher) w pts C.Higgs (Lydney), S.Smith (Rotunda) w pts I.Bailey (Slough), A.Dingsdale (Brompton) w pts M.Travis (RN), S.Mounieme (St Paul's) w pts M.Ward (Birtley Boys); *semi-finals*: S.Smith w pts L.Walsh, S.Mounieme w pts A.Dingsdale; *final*: S.Smith w pts S.Mounieme. **Light:** *quarter-finals*: M.Poston (Harwich) w pts B.Murray (Leonis), T.Stalker (St Aloysius) w pts G.Jones (Reading), J.Dean (Waterside) w pts A.Urritia, F.Gavin

(Hall Green) w pts L.Turner (West Ham); *semi-finals*: T.Stalker w pts M.Poston, F.Gavin w pts J.Dean; *final*: F.Gavin w pts T.Stalker. **L.Welter:** *quarter-finals*: J.Cox (Walcot Boys) w rsc 4 S.Crompton (Kingfisher), N.Brough (St Aloysius) w rsc 3 L.Gray (Stevenage), M.Stead (Army) w pts M.Page (Golden Ring), B.Saunders (South Durham) w pts G.Barker (Repton); *semi-finals*: N.Brough w pts J.Cox, B.Saunders w pts M.Stead; *final*: B.Saunders w disq 4 N.Brough. **Welter:** *quarter-finals*: J.Selkirk (Rotunda) wo, A.Ogogo (Triple A) w rsc 3 A.Coles (Camborne & Redruth), D.Robinson (RN) w pts J.Leigh (Moneyfields), M.Clauzel (Northumbria) w pts O.Ekundayo (Haringey Police); *semi-finals*: J.Selkirk w rsc 4 A.Ogogo, M.Clauzel w rsc 4 D.Robinson; *final*: J.Selkirk w pts M.Clauzel. **Middle:** *quarter-finals*: M.Reid (Walcot Boys) w pts K.Wootton (Harlow), M.Phillips (Vauxhall Motors) w rsc 4 T.Skipper (Stevenage), J.Summers (Army) w pts A.Watson (Crawley), G.Groves (Dale Youth) w rsc 3 A.Johnson (St George's); *semi-finals*: M.Reid w pts M.Phillips, G.Groves w rsc 2 J.Summers; *final*: G.Groves w pts M.Reid. **L.Heavy:** *quarter-finals*: C.Brodie (Arena) w rsc 2 M.Spooner (Devonport), J.Ainscough (Kirkdale) w pts H.Sessegnon (Wolvercote), A.Richardson (Army) w pts A.Hanniver (West Hill Hastings), O.Mbwakongo (Fisher) w pts S.McCrone (Spennymoor); *semi-finals*: J.Ainscough w pts C.Brodie, O.Mbwakongo w pts A.Richardson; *final*: O.Mbwakongo w pts J.Ainscough. **Cruiser:** *quarter-finals*: M.Redhead (Kingfisher) wo, J-L.Dickinson (Birtley Boys) wo, J.Ward (Kirkby) w pts L.Howkins (Pinewood Starr), T.Watson (Golden Ring) w pts S.McDonald (RN); *semi-finals*: M.Redhead w pts J.Ward, J-L.Dickinson w rsc 3 T.Watson; *final*: J-L.Dickinson w rsc 3 M.Redhead. **Heavy:** *quarter-finals*: T.Bellew (Rotunda) wo, P.Wright (Chatham) wo, D.Reed (Moneyfields) wo, D.Price (Westway) w pts W.Baister (Marley Potts); *semi-finals*: T.Bellew w rtd 2 P.Wright, D.Price w pts D.Reed; *final*: D.Price w pts T.Bellew. **S.Heavy:** *quarter-finals*: T.Dallas (St Mary's) wo, D.Price (Salisbury) wo, D.Hughes (Hylton Castle) w pts D.Campbell (Repton); *semi-finals*: D.Price (Salisbury) wo M.Elkins (Barnstaple), T.Dallas w rsc 3 D.Hughes; *final*: D.Price w pts T.Dallas.

South Durham's Bradley Saunders (left) won the 2006 ABA light-welter title when Nathan Brough (St Aloysius) was disqualified in the fourth round. Saunders was 24-7 ahead at the finish   Les Clark

ABA Champions, 1881-2007

Please note that despite the most recent champions being crowned in 2006, as the championships were held during the 2006-2007 season it is the latter year which is shown.

L. Flyweight

1971 M. Abrams
1972 M. Abrams
1973 M. Abrams
1974 C. Magri
1975 M. Lawless
1976 P. Fletcher
1977 P. Fletcher
1978 J. Dawson
1979 J. Dawson
1980 T. Barker
1981 J. Lyon
1982 J. Lyon
1983 J. Lyon
1984 J. Lyon
1985 M. Epton
1986 M. Epton
1987 M. Epton
1988 M. Cantwell
1989 M. Cantwell
1990 N. Tooley
1991 P. Culshaw
1992 D. Fifield
1993 M. Hughes
1994 G. Jones
1995 D. Fox
1996 R. Mercer
1997 I. Napa
1998 J. Evans
1999 G. Jones
2000 J. Mulherne
2001 C. Lyon
2002 D. Langley
2003 C. Lyon
2004 S. McDonald
2005 D. Langley
2006 J. Fowl
2007 K. Saeed

Flyweight

1920 H. Groves
1921 W. Cuthbertson
1922 E. Warwick
1923 L. Tarrant
1924 E. Warwick
1925 E. Warwick
1926 J. Hill
1927 J. Roland
1928 C. Taylor
1929 T. Pardoe
1930 T. Pardoe
1931 T. Pardoe
1932 T. Pardoe
1933 T. Pardoe
1934 P. Palmer
1935 G. Fayaud
1936 G. Fayaud
1937 P. O'Donaghue
1938 A. Russell
1939 D. McKay
1944 J. Clinton
1945 J. Bryce
1946 R. Gallacher
1947 J. Clinton
1948 H. Carpenter
1949 H. Riley
1950 A. Jones
1951 G. John
1952 D. Dower
1953 R. Currie
1954 R. Currie
1955 D. Lloyd
1956 T. Spinks
1957 R. Davies
1958 J. Brown
1959 M. Gushlow
1960 D. Lee
1961 W. McGowan
1962 M. Pye
1963 M. Laud
1964 J. McCluskey
1965 J. McCluskey
1966 P. Maguire
1967 S. Curtis
1968 J. McGonigle
1969 D. Needham
1970 D. Needham
1971 P. Wakefield
1972 M. O'Sullivan
1973 R. Hilton
1974 M. O'Sullivan
1975 C. Magri
1976 C. Magri
1977 C. Magri
1978 G. Nickels
1979 R. Gilbody
1980 K. Wallace
1981 K. Wallace
1982 J. Kelly
1983 S. Nolan
1984 P. Clinton
1985 P. Clinton
1986 J. Lyon
1987 J. Lyon
1988 J. Lyon
1989 J. Lyon
1990 J. Armour
1991 P. Ingle
1992 K. Knox
1993 P. Ingle
1994 D. Costello
1995 D. Costello
1996 D. Costello
1997 M. Hunter
1998 J. Hegney
1999 D. Robinson
2000 D. Robinson
2001 M. Marsh
2002 D. Barriball
2003 D. Broadhurst
2004 S. Langley
2005 S. Langley
2006 P. Edwards
2007 M. Walsh

Bantamweight

1884 A. Woodward
1885 A. Woodward
1886 T. Isley
1887 T. Isley
1888 H. Oakman
1889 H. Brown
1890 J. Rowe
1891 E. Moore
1892 F. Godbold
1893 E. Watson
1894 P. Jones
1895 P. Jones
1896 P. Jones
1897 C. Lamb
1898 F. Herring
1899 A. Avent
1900 J. Freeman
1901 W. Morgan
1902 A. Miner
1903 H. Perry
1904 H. Perry
1905 W. Webb
1906 T. Ringer
1907 E. Adams
1908 H. Thomas
1909 J. Condon
1910 W. Webb
1911 W. Allen
1912 W. Allen
1913 A. Wye
1914 W. Allen
1919 W. Allen
1920 G. McKenzie
1921 L. Tarrant
1922 W. Boulding
1923 A. Smith
1924 L. Tarrant
1925 A. Goom
1926 F. Webster
1927 E. Warwick
1928 J. Garland
1929 F. Bennett
1930 H. Mizler
1931 F. Bennett
1932 J. Treadaway
1933 G. Johnston
1934 A. Barnes
1935 L. Case
1936 A. Barnes
1937 A. Barnes
1938 J. Pottinger
1939 R. Watson
1944 R. Bissell
1945 P. Brander
1946 C. Squire
1947 D. O'Sullivan
1948 T. Profitt
1949 T. Miller
1950 K. Lawrence
1951 T. Nicholls
1952 T. Nicholls
1953 J. Smillie
1954 J. Smillie
1955 G. Dormer
1956 O. Reilly
1957 J. Morrissey
1958 H. Winstone
1959 D. Weller
1960 F. Taylor
1961 P. Benneyworth
1962 P. Benneyworth
1963 B. Packer
1964 B. Packer
1965 R. Mallon
1966 J. Clark
1967 M. Carter
1968 M. Carter
1969 M. Piner
1970 A. Oxley
1971 G. Turpin
1972 G. Turpin
1973 P. Cowdell
1974 S. Ogilvie
1975 S. Ogilvie
1976 J. Bambrick
1977 J. Turner
1978 J. Turner
1979 R. Ashton
1980 R. Gilboy
1981 P. Jones
1982 R. Gilboy
1983 J. Hyland
1984 J. Hyland
1985 S. Murphy
1986 S. Murphy
1987 J. Sillitoe
1988 K. Howlett
1989 K. Howlett
1990 P. Lloyd
1991 D. Hardie
1992 P. Mullings
1993 R. Evatt
1994 S. Oliver
1995 N. Wilders
1996 L. Eedle
1997 S. Oates
1998 L. Pattison
1999 M. Hunter
2000 S. Foster
2001 S. Foster
2002 D. Matthews
2003 N. McDonald
2004 M. Marsh
2005 N. McDonald
2006 N. McDonald
2007 L. Campbell

Featherweight

1881 T. Hill
1882 T. Hill
1883 T. Hill
1884 E. Hutchings
1885 J. Pennell
1886 T. McNeil
1887 J. Pennell
1888 J. Taylor
1889 G. Belsey
1890 G. Belsey
1891 F. Curtis
1892 F. Curtis
1893 T. Davidson
1894 R. Gunn
1895 R. Gunn
1896 R. Gunn
1897 N. Smith
1898 P. Lunn
1899 J. Scholes
1900 R. Lee
1901 C. Clarke
1902 C. Clarke
1903 J. Godfrey
1904 C. Morris
1905 H. Holmes
1906 A. Miner
1907 C. Morris
1908 T. Ringer
1909 A. Lambert
1910 C. Houghton
1911 H. Bowers
1912 G. Baker
1913 G. Baker
1914 G. Baker
1919 G. Baker
1920 J. Fleming
1921 G. Baker
1922 E. Swash
1923 E. Swash
1924 A. Beavis
1925 A. Beavis
1926 R. Minshull
1927 F. Webster
1928 F. Meachem
1929 F. Meachem
1930 J. Duffield
1931 B. Caplan
1932 H. Mizler
1933 J. Walters
1934 J. Treadaway
1935 E. Ryan
1936 J. Treadaway
1937 A. Harper
1938 C. Gallie
1939 C. Gallie
1944 D. Sullivan
1945 J. Carter
1946 P. Brander
1947 S. Evans
1948 P. Brander
1949 H. Gilliland
1950 P. Brander
1951 J. Travers
1952 P. Lewis
1953 P. Lewis
1954 D. Charnley
1955 T. Nicholls
1956 T. Nicholls
1957 M. Collins
1958 M. Collins
1959 G. Judge
1960 P. Lundgren
1961 P. Cheevers
1962 B. Wilson
1963 A. Riley
1964 R. Smith
1965 K. Buchanan
1966 H. Baxter
1967 K. Cooper
1968 J. Cheshire
1969 A. Richardson
1970 D. Polak
1971 T. Wright
1972 K. Laing
1973 J. Lynch
1974 G. Gilbody

1975 R. Beaumont	1922 G. Renouf
1976 P. Cowdell	1923 G. Shorter
1977 P. Cowdell	1924 W. White
1978 M. O'Brien	1925 E. Viney
1979 P. Hanlon	1926 T. Slater
1980 M. Hanif	1927 W. Hunt
1981 P. Hanlon	1928 F. Webster
1982 H. Henry	1929 W. Hunt
1983 P. Bradley	1930 J. Waples
1984 K. Taylor	1931 D. McCleave
1985 F. Havard	1932 F. Meachem
1986 P. Hodkinson	1933 H. Mizler
1987 P. English	1934 J. Rolland
1988 D. Anderson	1935 F. Frost
1989 P. Richardson	1936 F. Simpson
1990 B. Carr	1937 A. Danahar
1991 J. Irwin	1938 T. McGrath
1992 A. Temple	1939 H. Groves
1993 J. Cook	1944 W. Thompson
1994 D. Pithie	1945 J. Williamson
1995 D. Burrows	1946 E. Thomas
1996 T. Mulholland	1947 C. Morrissey
1997 S. Bell	1948 R. Cooper
1998 D. Williams	1949 A. Smith
1999 S. Miller	1950 R. Latham
2000 H. Castle	1951 R. Hinson
2001 S. Bell	1952 F. Reardon
2002 D. Mulholland	1953 D. Hinson
2003 K. Mitchell	1954 G. Whelan
2004 D. Mulholland	1955 S. Coffey
2005 G. Sykes	1956 R. McTaggart
2006 S. Smith	1957 J. Kidd
2007 S. Smith	1958 R. McTaggart
	1959 P. Warwick

Lightweight

1881 F. Hobday	1960 R. McTaggart
1882 A. Bettinson	1961 P. Warwick
1883 A. Diamond	1962 B. Whelan
1884 A. Diamond	1963 B. O'Sullivan
1885 A. Diamond	1964 J. Dunne
1886 G. Roberts	1965 A. White
1887 J. Hair	1966 J. Head
1888 A. Newton	1967 T. Waller
1889 W. Neale	1968 J. Watt
1890 A. Newton	1969 H. Hayes
1891 E. Dettmer	1970 N. Cole
1892 E. Dettmer	1971 J. Singleton
1893 W. Campbell	1972 N. Cole
1894 W. Campbell	1973 T. Dunn
1895 A. Randall	1974 J. Lynch
1896 A. Vanderhout	1975 P. Cowdell
1897 A. Vanderhout	1976 S. Mittee
1898 H. Marks	1977 G. Gilbody
1899 H. Brewer	1978 T. Marsh
1900 G. Humphries	1979 G. Gilbody
1901 A. Warner	1980 G. Gilbody
1902 A. Warner	1981 G. Gilbody
1903 H. Fergus	1982 J. McDonnell
1904 M. Wells	1983 K. Willis
1905 M. Wells	1984 A. Dickson
1906 M. Wells	1985 E. McAuley
1907 M. Wells	1986 J. Jacobs
1908 H. Holmes	1987 M. Ayers
1909 F. Grace	1988 C. Kane
1910 T. Tees	1989 M. Ramsey
1911 A. Spenceley	1990 P. Gallagher
1912 R. Marriott	1991 P. Ramsey
1913 R. Grace	1992 D. Amory
1914 R. Marriott	1993 B. Welsh
1919 F. Grace	1994 A. Green
1920 F. Grace	1995 R. Rutherford
1921 G. Shorter	1996 K. Wing
	1997 M. Hawthorne

1998 A. McLean	1921 A. Ireland
1999 S. Burke	1922 E. White
2000 A. McLean	1923 P. Green
2001 S. Burke	1924 P. O'Hanrahan
2002 A. Morris	1925 P. O'Hanrahan
2003 S. Burke	1926 B. Marshall
2004 C. Pacy	1927 H. Dunn
2005 F. Gavin	1928 H. Bone
2006 A. Crolla	1929 T. Wigmore
2007 F. Gavin	1930 F. Brooman
	1931 J. Barry

L. Welterweight

1951 W. Connor	1932 D. McCleave
1952 P. Waterman	1933 P. Peters
1953 D. Hughes	1934 D. McCleave
1954 G. Martin	1935 D. Lynch
1955 F. McQuillan	1936 W. Pack
1956 D. Stone	1937 D. Lynch
1957 D. Stone	1938 C. Webster
1958 R. Kane	1939 R. Thomas
1959 R. Kane	1944 H. Hall
1960 R. Day	1945 R. Turpin
1961 B. Brazier	1946 J. Ryan
1962 B. Brazier	1947 J. Ryan
1963 R. McTaggart	1948 M. Shacklady
1964 R. Taylor	1949 A. Buxton
1965 R. McTaggart	1950 T. Ratcliffe
1966 W. Hiatt	1951 J. Maloney
1967 B. Hudspeth	1952 J. Maloney
1968 E. Cole	1953 L. Morgan
1969 J. Stracey	1954 N. Gargano
1970 D. Davies	1955 N. Gargano
1971 M. Kingwell	1956 N. Gargano
1972 T. Waller	1957 R. Warnes
1973 N. Cole	1958 B. Nancurvis
1974 P. Kelly	1959 J. McGrail
1975 J. Zeraschi	1960 C. Humphries
1976 C. McKenzie	1961 A. Lewis
1977 J. Douglas	1962 J. Pritchett
1978 D. Williams	1963 J. Pritchett
1979 E. Copeland	1964 M. Varley
1980 A. Willis	1965 P. Henderson
1981 A. Willis	1966 P. Cragg
1982 A. Adams	1967 D. Cranswick
1983 D. Dent	1968 A. Tottoh
1984 D. Griffiths	1969 T. Henderson
1985 I. Mustafa	1970 T. Waller
1986 J. Alsop	1971 D. Davies
1987 A. Holligan	1972 T. Francis
1988 A. Hall	1973 T. Waller
1989 A. Hall	1974 T. Waller
1990 J. Pender	1975 W. Bennett
1991 J. Matthews	1976 C. Jones
1992 D. McCarrick	1977 C. Jones
1993 P. Richardson	1978 E. Byrne
1994 A. Temple	1979 J. Frost
1995 A. Vaughan	1980 T. Marsh
1996 C. Wall	1981 T. Marsh
1997 R. Hatton	1982 C. Pyatt
1998 N. Wright	1983 R. McKenley
1999 D. Happe	1984 M. Hughes
2000 N. Wright	1985 E. McDonald
2001 G. Smith	1986 D. Dyer
2002 L. Daws	1987 M. Elliot
2003 L. Beavis	1988 M. McCreath
2004 J. Watson	1989 M. Elliot
2005 M. Grant	1990 A. Carew
2006 J. Cox	1991 J. Calzaghe
2007 B. Saunders	1992 M. Santini
	1993 C. Bessey

Welterweight

1920 F. Whitbread	1994 K. Short
	1995 M. Hall
	1996 J. Khaliq

1997 F. Barrett	
1998 D. Walker	
1999 A. Cesay	
2000 F. Doherty	
2001 M. Macklin	
2002 M. Lomax	
2003 D. Happe	
2004 M. Murray	
2005 B. Flournoy	
2006 D. Vassell	
2007 J. Selkirk	

L. Middleweight

1951 A. Lay	
1952 B. Foster	
1953 B. Wells	
1954 B. Wells	
1955 B. Foster	
1956 J. McCormack	
1957 J. Cunningham	
1958 S. Pearson	
1959 S. Pearson	
1960 W. Fisher	
1961 J. Gamble	
1962 J. Lloyd	
1963 A. Wyper	
1964 W. Robinson	
1965 P. Dwyer	
1966 T. Imrie	
1967 A. Edwards	
1968 E. Blake	
1969 T. Imrie	
1970 D. Simmonds	
1971 A. Edwards	
1972 L. Paul	
1973 R. Maxwell	
1974 R. Maxwell	
1975 A. Harrison	
1976 W. Lauder	
1977 C. Malarkey	
1978 E. Henderson	
1979 D. Brewster	
1980 J. Price	
1981 E. Christie	
1982 D. Milligan	
1983 R. Douglas	
1984 R. Douglas	
1985 R. Douglas	
1986 T. Velinor	
1987 N. Brown	
1988 W. Ellis	
1989 N. Brown	
1990 T. Taylor	
1991 T. Taylor	
1992 J. Calzaghe	
1993 D. Starie	
1994 W. Alexander	
1995 C. Bessey	
1996 S. Dann	
1997 C. Bessey	
1998 C. Bessey	
1999 C. Bessey	
2000 C. Bessey	
2001 M. Thirwall	
2002 P. Smith	

Middleweight

1881 T. Bellhouse	
1882 A. H. Curnick	
1883 A. J. Curnick	
1884 W. Brown	
1885 M. Salmon	

1886 W. King	1965 W. Robinson	1950 P. Messervy	1885 W. West	1965 W. Wells
1887 R. Hair	1966 C. Finnegan	1951 G. Walker	1886 A. Diamond	1966 A. Brogan
1888 R. Hair	1967 A. Ball	1952 H. Cooper	1887 E. White	1967 P. Boddington
1889 G. Sykes	1968 P. McCann	1953 H. Cooper	1888 W. King	1968 W. Wells
1890 J. Hoare	1969 D. Wallington	1954 A. Madigan	1889 A. Bowman	1969 A. Burton
1891 J. Steers	1970 J. Conteh	1955 D. Rent	1890 J. Steers	1970 J. Gilmour
1892 J. Steers	1971 A. Minter	1956 D. Mooney	1891 V. Barker	1971 L. Stevens
1893 J. Steers	1972 F. Lucas	1957 T. Green	1892 J. Steers	1972 T. Wood
1894 W. Sykes	1973 F. Lucas	1958 J. Leeming	1893 J. Steers	1973 G. McEwan
1895 G. Townsend	1974 D. Odwell	1959 J. Ould	1894 H. King	1974 N. Meade
1896 W. Ross	1975 D. Odwell	1960 J. Ould	1895 W. E. Johnstone	1975 G. McEwan
1897 W. Dees	1976 E. Burke	1961 J. Bodell	1896 W. E. Johnstone	1976 J. Rafferty
1898 G. Townsend	1977 R. Davies	1962 J. Hendrickson	1897 G. Townsend	1977 G. Adair
1899 R. Warnes	1978 H. Graham	1963 P. Murphy	1898 G. Townsend	1978 J. Awome
1900 E. Mann	1979 N. Wilshire	1964 J. Fisher	1899 F. Parks	1979 A. Palmer
1901 R. Warnes	1980 M. Kaylor	1965 E. Whistler	1900 W. Dees	1980 F. Bruno
1902 E. Mann	1981 B. Schumacher	1966 R. Tighe	1901 F. Parks	1981 A. Elliott
1903 R. Warnes	1982 J. Price	1967 M. Smith	1902 F. Parks	1982 H. Hylton
1904 E. Mann	1983 T. Forbes	1968 R. Brittle	1903 F. Dickson	1983 H. Notice
1905 J. Douglas	1984 B. Schumacher	1969 J. Frankham	1904 A. Horner	1984 D. Young
1906 A. Murdock	1985 D. Cronin	1970 J. Rafferty	1905 F. Parks	1985 H. Hylton
1907 R. Warnes	1986 N. Benn	1971 J. Conteh	1906 F. Parks	1986 E. Cardouza
1908 W. Child	1987 R. Douglas	1972 W. Knight	1907 H. Brewer	1987 J. Moran
1909 W. Child	1988 M. Edwards	1973 W. Knight	1908 S. Evans	1988 H. Akinwande
1910 R. Warnes	1989 S. Johnson	1974 W. Knight	1909 C. Brown	1989 H. Akinwande
1911 W. Child	1990 S. Wilson	1975 M. Heath	1910 F. Storbeck	1990 K. Inglis
1912 E. Chandler	1991 M. Edwards	1976 G. Evans	1911 W. Hazell	1991 P. Lawson
1913 W. Bradley	1992 L. Woolcock	1977 C. Lawson	1912 R. Smith	1992 S. Welch
1914 H. Brown	1993 J. Calzaghe	1978 V. Smith	1913 R. Smith	1993 P. Lawson
1919 H. Mallin	1994 D. Starie	1979 A. Straughn	1914 E. Chandler	1994 S. Burford
1920 H. Mallin	1995 J. Matthews	1980 A. Straughn	1919 H. Brown	1995 M. Ellis
1921 H. Mallin	1996 J. Pearce	1981 A. Straughn	1920 R. Rawson	1996 T. Oakey
1922 H. Mallin	1997 I. Cooper	1982 G. Crawford	1921 R. Rawson	1997 B. Stevens
1923 H. Mallin	1998 J. Pearce	1983 A. Wilson	1922 T. Evans	1998 N. Hosking
1924 J. Elliot	1999 C. Froch	1984 A. Wilson	1923 E. Eagan	1999 S. St John
1925 J. Elliot	2000 S. Swales	1985 J. Beckles	1924 A. Clifton	2000 D. Dolan
1926 F. P. Crawley	2001 C. Froch	1986 J. Moran	1925 D. Lister	2001 D. Dolan
1927 F. P. Crawley	2002 N. Perkins	1987 J. Beckles	1926 T. Petersen	2002 D. Dolan
1928 F. Mallin	2003 N. Perkins	1988 H. Lawson	1927 C. Capper	2003 M. O'Connell
1929 F. Mallin	2004 D. Guthrie	1989 N. Piper	1928 J. L. Driscoll	2004 T. Bellew
1930 F. Mallin	2005 J. Degale	1990 J. McCluskey	1929 P. Floyd	2005 T. Bellew
1931 F. Mallin	2006 J. Degale	1991 A. Todd	1930 V. Stuart	2006 T. Bellew
1932 F. Mallin	2007 G. Groves	1992 K. Oliver	1931 M. Flanagan	2007 Daniel Price
1933 A. Shawyer		1993 K. Oliver	1932 V. Stuart	
1934 J. Magill	**L. Heavyweight**	1994 K. Oliver	1933 C. O'Grady	**S. Heavyweight**
1935 J. Magill	1920 H. Franks	1995 K. Oliver	1934 P. Floyd	1982 A. Elliott
1936 A. Harrington	1921 L. Collett	1996 C. Fry	1935 P. Floyd	1983 K. Ferdinand
1937 M. Dennis	1922 H. Mitchell	1997 P. Rogers	1936 V. Stuart	1984 R. Wells
1938 H. Tiller	1923 H. Mitchell	1998 C. Fry	1937 V. Stuart	1985 G. Williamson
1939 H. Davies	1924 H. Mitchell	1999 J. Ainscough	1938 G. Preston	1986 J. Oyebola
1944 J. Hockley	1925 H. Mitchell	2000 P. Haymer	1939 A. Porter	1987 J. Oyebola
1945 R. Parker	1926 D. McCorkindale	2001 C. Fry	1944 M. Hart	1988 K. McCormack
1946 R. Turpin	1927 A. Jackson	2002 T. Marsden	1945 D. Scott	1989 P. Passley
1947 R. Agland	1928 A. Jackson	2003 J. Boyd	1946 P. Floyd	1990 K. McCormack
1948 J. Wright	1929 J. Goyder	2004 M. Abdusalem	1947 G. Scriven	1991 K. McCormack
1949 S. Lewis	1930 J. Murphy	2005 D. Pendleton	1948 J. Gardner	1992 M. Hopper
1950 P. Longo	1931 J. Petersen	2006 T. Jeffries	1949 A. Worrall	1993 M. McKenzie
1951 E. Ludlam	1932 J. Goyder	2007 O. Mbwakongo	1950 P. Toch	1994 D. Watts
1952 T. Gooding	1933 G. Brennan		1951 A. Halsey	1995 R. Allen
1953 R. Barton	1934 G. Brennan	**Cruiserweight**	1952 E. Hearn	1996 D. Watts
1954 K. Phillips	1935 R. Hearns	1998 T. Oakey	1953 J. Erskine	1997 A. Harrison
1955 F. Hope	1936 J. Magill	1999 M. Krence	1954 B. Harper	1998 A. Harrison
1956 R. Redrup	1937 J. Wilby	2000 J. Dolan	1955 D. Rowe	1999 W. Bessey
1957 P. Burke	1938 A. S. Brown	2001 J. Dolan	1956 D. Rent	2000 J. McDermott
1958 P. Hill	1939 B. Woodcock	2002 J. Dolan	1957 D. Thomas	2001 M. Grainger
1959 F. Elderfield	1944 E. Shackleton	2007 J-L Dickinson	1958 D. Thomas	2002 M. Grainger
1960 R. Addison	1945 A. Watson		1959 D. Thomas	2003 David Price
1961 J. Caiger	1946 J. Taylor	**Heavyweight**	1960 L. Hobbs	2004 J. Young
1962 A. Matthews	1947 A. Watson	1881 R. Frost-Smith	1961 W. Walker	2005 David Price
1963 A. Matthews	1948 D. Scott	1882 H. Dearsley	1962 R. Dryden	2006 D. Chisora
1964 W. Stack	1949 *Declared no contest*	1883 H. Dearsley	1963 R. Sanders	2007 David Price
		1884 H. Dearsley	1964 C. Woodhouse	

Irish Championships, 2006-2007

Senior Tournament

The National Stadium, Dublin 19, 26 & 27 January & 2 February

L.Fly: *semi-finals:* J.Moore (St Francis, Limerick) wo, P.Barnes (Holy Family, Belfast) w pts G.McDonagh (Kilcullen, Kildare); *final:* P.Barnes w pts J.Moore. **Fly:** *final:* C.Ahern (Balydoyle, Dublin) w pts S.Cox (Gorey, Wexford). **Bantam:** *quarter-finals:* C.Frampton (Midland White City, Belfast) wo, K.Fennessy (Clonmel, Tipperary) wo, R.Lindberg (Immaculata, Belfast) w pts S.Kilroy (Holy Family, Belfast), T.Doheny (Portlaoise, Laois) w pts S.Myers (Brosna, Westmeath); *semi-finals:* R.Lindberg w pts C.Frampton, K.Fennessy w pts T.Doheny; *final:* R.Lindberg w pts K.Fennessy. **Feather:** *semi-finals:* E.Donovan (St Michael's, Athy) w pts W.Casey (Our Lady of Lourdes, Limerick), D.O. Joyce (St Michael's, Athy) w pts R.Hickey (Grangecon, Kildare); *final:* D.O.Joyce w pts E.Donovan. **Light:** *quarter-finals:* J.J.Joyce (St Michael's, Athy) wo, J.Campbell (Edenderry, Offaly) wo, K.Crawley (Glasnevin, Dublin) w pts A.Sadlier (St Saviour's, Dublin), C.Bates (St Mary's, Dublin w pts S.Hickey (Brian Dillon's, Cork); *semi-finals:* J.J.Joyce w pts K.Crawley, C.Bates w pts J.Campbell; *final:* J.J.Joyce w pts C.Bates. **L.Welter:** *quarter-finals:* A.Carlyle (Golden Cobra, Dublin) wo, E.Touhey (Moate, Westmeath) wo, M.Wickham (St Anthony's/St Patrick's, Wexford), T.Dwyer (St Aidan's, Wexford) w pts M.McLoughlin (Holy Trinity, Belfast); *semi-finals:* A.Carlyle w rsc 3 E.Touhey, T.Dwyer w pts M.Wickham; *final:* A.Carlyle w pts T.Dwyer. **Welter:** *quarter-finals:* R.Sheehan (St Michael's, Athy) wo, F.Redmond (Arklow, Wicklow) w pts P.Walsh (St Colman's, Cork), T.Hamill (All Saints, Ballymena) w pts L.Keeler (St Matthew's, Dublin), D.Joyce St Michael's, Athy) w pts F.Turner (St Ibar's/Joseph's, Wexford; *semi-finals:* R.Sheehan w pts F.Redmond, D.Joyce w pts T.Hamill; *final:* R.Sheehan w pts D.Joyce. **Middle:** *semi-finals:* D.Sutherland (St Saviour's, Dublin) w rsc 3 E.Healy (Portlaoise, Laoise) , E.O'Kane (Immaculata, Belfast) w rsc 4 S.Shevlin (Dealgan, Louth); *final:* D.Sutherland w rsc 3 E.O'Kane. **L.Heavy:** *semi-finals:* K.Egan (Neilstown, Dublin) wo, W.Mitchell (Dromore, Tyrone) w pts S.Crudden (Enniskillen, Fermanagh); *final:* K.Egan w rsc 1 W.Mitchell. **Heavy:** *quarter-finals:* I.Tims (St Matthew's, Dublin) w rsc 4 P.Kearns (Golden Cobra, Dublin), James Sweeney (Drimnagh, Dublin) w pts M.Osun (Arklow, Wicklow), John Sweeney (Dungloe, Donegal) w pts J.Waldron Castlebar, Mayo), M.Mullaney (Claremorris, Mayo) w rsc 3 M.Stokes (Drimnagh, Dublin); *semi-finals:* I.Tims w pts James Sweeney, John Sweeney w pts M.Mullaney; *final:* I.Tims w pts John Sweeney. **S.Heavy:** *semi-finals:* A.Crampton (St Broughan's, Offaly) w pts M.Sweeney (Drimnagh, Dublin), C.McGonagle (Holy Trinity, Belfast) w pts S.Reilly (Drimnagh, Dublin); *final:* C.McGonagle w pts A.Crampton.

Intermediate Finals

The National Stadium, Dublin – 16 December

L.Fly: G.McDonagh (Killcullen, Kildare) wo. **Fly:** J.Nevin (Cavan) w pts C.McDonald (Golden Cobra, Dublin). **Bantam:** M.McCullagh (Cairn Lodge, Belfast) w pts M.Connors (Holy Family, Belfast). **Feather:** S.Upton (Westside, Dublin) w rsc 3 J.Keenan (Loughmahon, Cork). **Light:** S.Hickey (Brian Dillon's, Cork) w pts J.Murray (Gorey, Wexford). **L.Welter:** M.McLaughlin (Holy Trinity, Belfast) w pts N.McGinlay (Bishop Kelly, Tyrone). **Welter:** P.Ward (Galway) w pts S.McKeown (Sacred Heart, Newry). **L.Middle:** D.Ward (Loughglynn, Roscommon) w pts S.O'Reilly (Twintowns, Donegal). **Middle:** M.Ward (Galway) w pts P.McCrory (St John's, Belfast). **L.Heavy:** P.Corcoran (Galway) w rsc 3 P.Halligan (Midfield, Mayo). **Heavy:** N.Kennedy (Gorey, Wexford) w pts E.McDonagh (Crumlin, Dublin). **S.Heavy:** J.Power (St Francis, Limerick) w pts C.O'Donnell (Conamara, Galway).

Junior Finals (Under-21)

The National Stadium – 28 October

L.Fly: J.Nevin (Cavan) wo. **Fly:** J.Conlon (St John Bosco, Belfast) w pts G.McDonagh (Kilcullen, Kildare). **Bantam:** R.Lindberg (Immaculata, Belfast) w pts D.Thorpe (St Aidan's, Ferns). **Feather:** J.Upton (Westside, Dublin) wo S.Upton (Westside, Dublin). **Light:** P.Upton (Westside, Dublin) w pts J.Murray (Gorey, Wexford). **L.Welter:** T.Dwyer (St Aidan's, Ferns) w pts J.McDonagh (Dockers, Belfast). **Welter:** M.Collins (Darndale, Dublin) w pts D.Nevin (Cavan). **L.Middle:** S.O'Reilly (Twintowns, Donegal) w pts J.J. McDonagh (Brosna, Westmeath). **Middle:** T.McGrath (St Colman's, Cork) w pts F.Foley (St Michael's, Athy). **L.Heavy:** C.McAuley (Holy Family, Belfast) w rsc 2 A.Griffin (Conamara, Galway). **Cruiser:** D.Tourish (Twintowns, Donegal) wo. **Heavy:** E.McDonagh (Crumlin, Dublin) w pts J.Sweeney (Drimnagh, Dublin). **S.Heavy:** M.Stokes (Crumlin, Dublin) wo.

Under-19 Finals

The National Stadium – 12 May

L.Fly: K.O'Neill (Edenderry, Offaly) w pts C.Rice (Immaculata, Belfast), **Fly:** J.Nevin (Cavan) w rsc 4 P.Singh (Letterkenny, Donegal). **Bantam:** M.McCullough (Cairn Lodge, Belfast) w pts S.Kilroy (Holy Family, Drogheda). **Feather:** R.Moylett (St Annes, Westport) w pts E.Finnegan (Oliver Plunkett, Belfast). **Light:** A.Carace (Oliver Plunkett, Belfast) w pts J.Kavanagh (Crumlin, Dublin). **L.Welter:** P.Sutcliffe (Crumlin, Dublin) w pts D.Walsh (St John's, Antrim). **Welter:** A.Meli (Immaculata, Belfast) w pts B.Redmond (Golden Cobra, Dublin). **Middle:** D.Ward (Loughglynn, Roscommon) w pts I.Carmichael (Olympic, Galway). **L.Heavy:** D.Trainor (St Broughan's, Offaly) w pts C.McAuley (Holy Family, Belfast). **Heavy:** D.Nevin (Brosna, Westmeath) w pts C.Sheehan (Clonmel, Tipperary). **S.Heavy:** A.Griffin (Conamara, Galway) w rsc 1 K.Carey (Geesala, Mayo).

Scottish and Welsh Senior Championships, 2006-2007

Scotland ABA

High School, Lasswade – 3 & 23 March, Town Hall, Darvel – 9 March, Treetops Hotel, Aberdeen – 16 March

L.Fly: no entries. **Fly:** no entries. **Bantam:** *quarter-finals:* P.McElhinney (Noble Art) wo, D.King (Madison) wo, C.Thomson (Dennistoun) wo, R.Muncie (Granite City) w pts S.Tiffney (Gilmerton); *semi-finals:* P.McElhinney w pts D.King, R.Muncie w pts J.Thomson; *final:* R.Muncie w pts P.McElhinney. **Feather:** *quarter-finals:* D.Savage (Argo) wo, D.Traynor (Granite City) wo, J.McGregor (Four Isles) wo, J.Hastie (Gilmerton) w pts M.Roberts (Forgewood); *semi-finals:* D.Traynor w pts D.Savage, J.Hastie w pts J.McGregor; *final:* D.Traynor w disq 4 J.Hastie. **Light:** *semi-finals:* J.Kelso (Blantyre) w pts R.Barclay (Noble Art), J.Thain (Gilmerton) w pts P.Clark (Glenrothes); *final:* J.Kelso w pts J.Thain. **L.Welter:** *quarter-finals:* E.Gear (Kingswells) w pts E.Finney (Kingdom), M.McAllister (Granite City) w pts R.McMurdie (Newarthill), E.Doyle (Glenboig) w rsc 1 R.Love (Holyrood), J.Smith (Four Isles) w pts S.Hill (Bellahouston); *semi-finals:* M.McAllister w pts E.Gear, E.Doyle w pts J.Smith; *final:* E.Doyle w pts M.McAllister. **Welter:** *quarter-finals:* J.McLevy (Clydeview) wo, J.Nolan (Newarthill) w pts J.McCallum (Leith Victoria), D.Scott (Holyrood) w pts I.Ferguson (Holyrood), K.Carslaw (Paisley YMCA) w rsc 4 A.Barlow (Kingdom); *semi-finals:* K.Carslaw wo D.Scott, J.McLevy w rsc 3 J.Nolan; *final:* K.Carslaw w pts J.McLevy. **Middle:** *prelims:* J.McComiskey (Fauldhouse) wo, K.McDonald (Paisley) w pts M.Aniba (Barn), A.McKelvie (Discovery) w pts M.Mower (Stirling), D.Campbell (Denbeath) w rsc 1 L.Thomson (Holyrood), J.Lee (Madison) w rsc 3 K.Buchanan (Holyrood), R.Kaminski (Perth) w pts C.Kearney (Glenrothes), S.Morgan (Bonnyrigg) w pts P.Roy (Elgin), G.Thomson (Stirling) w pts S.Banks (Orbiston); *quarter-finals:* J.McComiskey w pts K.McDonald, D.Campbell w pts A.McKelvie, J.Lee w pts R.Kaminski, G.Thomson w pts S.Morgan; *semi-finals:* D.Campbell w pts J.McComiskey, J.Lee w pts G.Thomson; *final:* D.Campbell w pts J.Lee. **L.Heavy:** *quarter-finals:* J.Quigley (Port Glasgow) wo, J.Kubas (Sparta) w co 3 J.Cunningham (Dennistoun), J.Cook (Denbeath) w rsc 2 R.Caddow (Holyrood), C.Johnson (Newarthill) w rsc 1 A.Leishman (Dunfermline); *semi-finals:* J.Quigley w pts J.Kubas, C.Johnson w co 1 J.Cook; *final:* C.Johnson w pts J.Quigley. **Heavy:** *quarter-finals:* M.McDonagh (Clydeview) w rsc 1 S.Kerr (Holyrood), B.Nisbett (Orbiston) w pts C.Koo (Holyrood), D.Drummond (Kinross) w co 3 J.McAvoy (Stirling), Y.Pavlov (Glenrothes) w disq 3 J.Fowler (Port Glasgow); *semi-finals:* M.McDonagh w rsc 4 B.Nisbett, Y.Pavlov w pts D.Drummond; *final:* Y.Pavlov w pts M.McDonagh. **S.Heavy:** *semi-finals:* S.Scott (Forgewood) wo, J.Perry (Larkhall) w pts F.Thirde (Arbroath); *final:* S.Scott w disq 4 J.Perry.

Wales ABA

East Street Sports Centre, Tylorstown - 13 & 14 January & 17 February, Rhondda Leisure Centre, Ystradgynlais – 23 March

L.Fly: *final:* M.Nasir (St Joseph's, Newport) w rsc 3 G.Jones (Llay). **Fly:** *semi-finals:* K.Spong (Army) wo, A.Selby (Splott Adventure) w pts R.Harris (Penyrheol); *final:* A.Selby w rsc 3 K.Spong. **Bantam:** final: C.Jenkins (Cwmgors) wo. **Feather:** *quarter-finals:* B.Gillen (Prince of Wales) wo, K.Foley (St Joseph's Cardiff) wo, S.Davies (Carmarthen) wo, R.Turley (Fleur-de-Lys) w pts N.Ali (St Joseph's, Newport); *semi-finals:* B.Gillen w R.Turley, K.Foley w rsc 2 S.Davies; *final:* B.Gillen w pts K.Foley. **Light:** *quarter-finals:* C.O'Sullivan (Merlins Bridge) wo, L.Selby (Splott Adventure) wo, Z.Ummer (St Joseph's, Newport) wo, R.Griffiths (Merthyr Ex-Servicemen) w rsc 2 L.Quinn (Dyffryn); *semi-finals:* L.Selby w rsc 2 C.O'Sullivan, R.Griffiths w rtd 3 Z.Ummer; *final:* L.Selby w rsc 3 R.Griffiths. **L.Welter:** *quarter-finals:* J.Flynn (Triumph) wo, M.Evans (Red Dragon) wo, S.Jama (Cardiff YMCA) w pts R.Saunders (Victoria Park), R.Evans (Dowlais) w pts P.Davies (Diamond Gloves); *semi-finals:* J.Flynn w pts M.Evans, R.Evans wo S.Jama; *final:* R.Evans w pts J.Flynn. **Welter:** *prelims:* D.Richards (Heads of Valleys) wo, S.Scourfield (Clwyd) wo, J.Orchard (Tiger Bay) wo, D.Jones (Fleur-de-Lys) wo, J.Jevons (Merthyr Ex-Servicemen) wo, J.Todd (Bonymaen) wo, P.Chappell (Porthcawl/Pyle) wo, L.Trott (Cwmgors) w pts K.O'Sullivan; *quarter-finals:* D.Richards w pts S.Scourfield, J.Orchard w pts D.Jones, J.Jevons w pts J.Todd, P.Chappell w pts L.Trott; *semi-finals:* D.Richards w rsc 3 J.Orchard, J.Jevons w pts P.Chappell; *final:* D.Richards w pts J.Jevons. **Middle:** *prelims:* G.Staddon (Trostre) wo, S.Burnett (Ferndale) wo, L.Bunce (Merthyr Ex-Servicemen) wo, J.Mulhern (Carmarthen) wo, G.Jones (Army) wo, L.Bannister (Dyffryn) wo, E.Jodlowski (Cardiff YMCA) w pts J.Rees (Trostre), W.O'Sullivan (Merlins Bridge) w pts I.Jenkins (Cwmgors); *quarter-finals:* G.Staddon w pts S.Burnett, L.Bunce w co 2 J.Mulhern, G.Jones w rsc L.Bannister, W.O'Sullivan w pts E.Jodlowski; *semi-finals:* G.Staddon w pts L.Bunce, W.O'Sullivan w pts G.Jones; *final:* W.O'Sullivan w pts G.Staddon. **L.Heavy:** *prelims:* J.Hughes (St Joseph's, Newport) wo, T.Webb (Bonymaen) wo, R.Davies (Triumph) wo, J.Asare (Merthyr Ex-Servicemen) wo, J.Evans (Pontypool & Panteg) wo, O.Hardcastle (Dowlais) wo, I.Appleby (Gilfach Goch) wo, J.Morris (Fleur-de-Lys) w pts J.Gullan (Pembroke); *quarter-finals:* T.Webb w pts J.Hughes, R.Davies w rsc 4 J.Asare, J.Evans w rsc O.Hardcastle, I.Appleby w rtd 3 J.Morris; *semi-finals:* T.Webb w pts R.Davies, J.Evans w pts I.Appleby; *final:* T.Webb w rsc 3 J.Evans. **Heavy:** *quarter-finals:* O.Harries (Penyrheol) wo, J.Boland (Penarth) wo, R.Davies (Trostre) w pts J.Bunce (Merthyr Ex-Servicemen), K.Griffiths (Llangeni) w pts L.Milsjen (Rhoose); *semi-finals:* R.Davies w pts K.Griffiths, O.Harries w pts J.Boland; *final:* O.Harries w rsc 1 R.Davies. **S.Heavy:** *semi-finals:* J.Mitchell (St Joseph's, Newport) wo, A.Jones (Shotton) w pts G.Vincent (Clwyd); *final:* A.Jones w pts J.Mitchell.

British Junior Championship Finals, 2006-2007

National Association of Clubs for Young People (NACYP)

The Festival Hall, Kirkby in Ashfield – 4 December

Class A: 46kg: L.Gooding (Sunderland) w pts M.Joyce (Kingsthorpe). 48kg: D.Chapman (Gwynfi) w pts K.Farrell (Northside). 50kg: J.Quigley (Tower Hill) w pts L.Pettitt (Nemesis). 52kg: B.Morgan (West Ham) w rsc 3 L.Fielding (Tamworth). 54kg: R.Johnson (Tamworth) w pts M.McCarthy (Dagenham). 57kg: P.Gallagher (Tower Hill) w pts J.Baker (Repton). 60kg: J.Hughes (Malmesbury) w pts R.Heffron (Boarshaw). 63kg: J.Farrer (Sunderland) w pts C.Sewell (Eltham). 66kg: J.McClumpha (Plains Farm) w rsc 1 C.McGivern (Torfaen Warriors). 70kg: M.Nugent (West Ham) w pts L.Taylor (Steel City). 75kg: K.Garvey (Earlsfield) w pts M.Laws (Plains Farm).

Winter Gardens, Blackpool – 8 December

Class B: 48kg: D.Lawlor (Birmingham City) w pts D.Perry (Norwich Lads). 50kg: W.Hussain (Aston) w pts D.Boyle (Birtley Boys). 52kg: J.Gage (Cwmavon) w pts R.Jameson (South Bank). 54kg: M.Maguire (Kettering SoB) w rsc 2 D.Walton (Chelmsley Wood). 57kg: J.Rodgers (Parsons Cross) w pts J.Herbert (West Ham). 60kg: T.Coyle (St Paul's) w pts B.Clayden (Guildford City). 63kg: S.Cardle (Fleetwood Gym) w pts D.O'Shaughnessy (West Ham). 66kg: J.Innes (Cwmbran) w pts J.Binnie (Scarborough). 70kg: B.J.Saunders (Hoddesdon) w pts J.Armfield (Bolton Lads). 75kg: J.Gosling (Southend) w pts N.Tallon (Hall Green). 80kg: R.Pearce (South Normanton) w rsc 3 L.Darling (St Mary's). 86kg: L.Phillips (Cwmavon) wo. 92kg: J.Brown (Marsh Lane) w pts F.McDonagh (Splott Adventure).

Café Royal, Piccadilly, London – 5 December

Class C: 48kg: B.Fowl (Hoddesdon) wo P.Douglas (Phil Thomas SoB). 51kg: no final. 54kg: D.Burrell (Peacock) w pts D.Anderson (Priory Park). 57kg: M.Fagan (Vauxhall Motors) w pts S.Winson (Woking). 60kg: D.Rogers (Kettering SoB) w pts R.Ghent (Priory Park). 64kg: C.Groombridge (Burton) w pts J.Radford (Newham). 69kg: H.Burton (Egan's Academy) w pts C.Williamson (Lewsey). 75kg: T.Dickinson (Birtley Boys) w rsc 4 T.Jacobs (Harwich). 81kg: J.McCann (Kettering SoB) w pts K.Thompson (South Durham). 91kg: S.Jury (Thames Valley) wo C.Pollock (Phil Thomas SoB). 91+kg: A.Simpson (Grainger Park) w pts J.Mitchell (St Joseph's East).

Golden Gloves (Schools)

The Leisure Centre, Knottingley – 24 & 25 March

Class 1: 30kg: C.Coghill (St Paul's) w pts J.Coglan (Spennymoor). 32kg: J.Bateson (Burmantofts) w pts T.Wilson (Knowsley Vale). 34kg: B.Saunders (St Mary's) w pts P.Lovejoy (Earlsfield). 36kg: T.Ward (Birtley Boys) w pts Scott McNess (Repton). 38kg: T.Beaney (West Ham) w pts W.Crane (Croxteth). 40kg: A.Price (Cheshunt) w pts S.Bezzina (Ongar). 42kg: J.Kelly (Sunderland) w pts J.Holmes (Hull Boys). 44kg: F.Smith (Hastings West Hill) w pts A.Moulden (Bateson's). 46kg: M.Johnson (Kirkby) w pts Y.Javed (Danson Youth). 48kg: P.Miller (Lancaster Boys) w pts J.Lewis (Kingston). 50kg: T.Carr (Repton) w pts A.Preece (Guildford). 52: D.Preece (Guildford) w pts J.Gill (Chatteris). 54kg: B.Newman (Dagenham) wo. 57kg: R.Martin (Walcot Boys) w pts K.Jones (Heartlands). 60kg: G.Bannister (Grainger Park) w rsc 2 T.Buckley (Danson Youth).

Class 2: 34kg: C.Driscoll (West Ham) w pts J.J.Cooke (Triumph). 36kg: T.Halimond (Shildon) w pts H.Disson (Dale Youth). 38kg: C.Edwards (Earlsfield) w pts J.Dring (Gemini). 40kg: J.Austin (Newham) w pts R.McNamara (Hoddesdon). 42kg: Q.Ashfaq (Bateson's) w pts D.Canmore (Aycliffe). 44kg: H.Thomas (Darlington) w rsc 3 J.McDonagh (Stowe). 46kg: B.Jackson (Spennymoor) w pts R.Jackson (Fisher). 48kg: M.Lee (Guildford) w pts C.O'Riordan (Ongar). 50kg: B.Jones (Bateson's) w rsc 2 D.Codona (Bushey). 52kg: Z.Smith (Tower Hill) w pts D.Jones (Bateson's). 54kg: A.Doe (Bushey) w pts O.A.Baig (Rawthorpe). 57kg: E.Matthews (Guildford) w pts W.Ingram (Gloucester). 60kg: L.Coneley (Sporting Ring) w pts J.Smith (Repton). 63kg: S.Smith (Pinewood Starr) w pts R.Legg (Dagenham). 66kg: E.Frankham (Wisbech) w rsc 3 S.Long (Sandy).

Class 3: 38kg: B.Sykes (Chesterfield) w pts D.Painting (Bexley). 40kg: G.Veness (Newham) w pts T.J.West (Bridgefoot). 42kg: L.Coppin (Ongar) w pts T.Yates (Arrow). 44kg: C.Mbwakongo (Fisher) w pts C.Chadwick (Phoenix). 46kg: W.Dolan (Birtley Boys) w pts D.Beadon (Repton). 48kg: M.Hedges (West Ham) w pts M.Bradford (Plains Farm). 50kg: C.Quarmby (Hetton Town) w pts B.Smith (Bexley). 52kg: J.Ward (Repton) w pts T.Simpson (Stockbridge). 54kg: Sam McNess (Repton) w pts J.King (Hetton Town). 57kg: M.Cash (St Albans) w pts R.Yeo (Earlsfield). 60kg: L.Richards (Repton) w pts J.Kelly (Jimmy Egan's BA). 63kg: J.Docherty (Bushey) w rsc 3 A.Carolan (Doncaster Plant). 66kg: G.McCrory (Aston) w pts T.Marsden (Handsworth). 70kg: E.Duraku (Reading) w rsc 2 A.Lacey-Sheils (Dale Youth). 75kg: M.Watson (South Durham) w pts A.Kirby (Gold Star).

ABA Youth

The National Sports Centre, Crystal Palace – 5 May

Class 4: 46kg: M.Ward (Repton) w pts B.Joyce (Kingsthorpe). 48kg: J.Dickens (Golden Gloves) w pts L.Hunt (Chadd). 50kg: G.Yafai (Birmingham City) wo T.Baker (Repton). 52kg: P.O'Sullivan (Rotunda) w pts D.Fletcher (Kelly's). 54kg: J.McDonough (Dale Youth) w pts C.Ellenor (Sunderland). 57kg: S.Jenkins (St Michael's) w rsc 2 T.Aspell (Dale Youth). 60kg: S.Barnes (Manor) w pts T.Shinkwin (Bushey). 63kg: R.Aston (Priory Park) w pts A.Little (Kirkham). 70kg: J.Dennis (Brompton) w pts K.Haywood (Earl Shilton). 75kg: J.Cetaj (Walcot Boys) w co 3 D.Price (Skelmersdale). 80kg: D.Fusco (East Durham) w pts M.Joratt (All Stars). 85kg: N.Smith (Pinewood Starr) w rsc 3 F.Qualla (Trojan).

Class 5: 48kg: M.Joyce (Kingsthorpe) w pts K.Farrell (Boarshaw). 50kg: L.Pettitt (Nemesis) w pts S.McBride (Redcar). 52kg: B.Morgan (West Ham) w pts J.Warrington (Kelly's). 54kg: J.Barker (Northside) w pts J.Gardiner (Gloucester). 57kg: I.Weaver (Golden Ring) w pts D.Phillips (South Bank). 60kg: R.Heffron (Boarshaw) w pts T.Nurse (Parsons Cross). 63kg: C.Smith (Rotunda) w pts T.Shaw (Burton). 66kg: J.McClumpha (Plains Farm) w pts C.Betteridge (Larches & Savick). 70kg: M.Nugent (West Ham) w pts L.Taylor (Steel City). 75kg: K.Garvey (Earlsfield) w pts L.Knight (Plains Farm). 80kg: J.Pollock (Phil Thomas SoB) w pts L.Rennie (Kings). 85kg: N.Seager (Fulbourn) w pts S.Karamanoglu (Bexley). 91kg: L.Augustine (Marston) w rsc 1 P.White (King Alfred's).

Class 6: 50kg: L.Ward (Bridgefoot) w pts D.Lawlor (Birmingham City). 52kg: O.Webb (Repton) w pts L.O'Rourke (Consett). 54kg: B.Evans (Stevenage) w rsc 2 S.Costello (Kettering SoB). 57kg: M.Hadfield (Headland) w pts L.Gibb (Nemesis). 60kg: R.Davies (Knowsley Vale) w pts A.Townsend (White Rose). 63kg: D.O'Shaughnessy (West Ham) w pts T.Langford (Bideford). 66kg: S.Cardle (Kirkham) w rsc 2 S.McLean (Tamworth). 70kg: J.Armfield (Pool of Life) w rsc 2 C.Wallace (East Durham). 75kg: P.Smith (West Ham) w pts N.Tallon (Hall Green). 80kg: S.Griffiths (Shrewsbury & Severnside) w pts M.McDonough (South Norwood & Victory).

International Amateur Champions, 1904-2007

Shows all Olympic, World, European & Commonwealth champions since 1904. British silver and bronze medal winners are shown throughout, where applicable.

Country Code
ALG = Algeria; ARG = Argentina; ARM = Armenia; AUS = Australia; AUT = Austria; AZE = Azerbaijan; BE = Belarus; BEL = Belgium; BUL = Bulgaria; CAN = Canada; CEY = Ceylon (now Sri Lanka); CI = Channel Islands; CHI = China; CUB = Cuba; DEN = Denmark; DOM = Dominican Republic; ENG = England; ESP = Spain; EST = Estonia; FIJ = Fiji Islands; FIN = Finland; FRA = France; GBR = United Kingdom; GDR = German Democratic Republic; GEO = Georgia; GER = Germany (but West Germany only from 1968-1990); GHA = Ghana; GUY = Guyana; HOL = Netherlands; HUN = Hungary; IND = India; IRL = Ireland; ITA = Italy; JAM = Jamaica; JPN = Japan; KAZ = Kazakhstan; KEN = Kenya; LIT = Lithuania; MAS = Malaysia; MEX = Mexico; MOR = Morocco; MRI = Mauritius; NAM = Nambia; NKO = North Korea; NIG = Nigeria; NIR = Northern Ireland; NOR = Norway; NZL = New Zealand; PAK = Pakistan; POL = Poland; PUR = Puerto Rico; ROM = Romania; RUS = Russia; SAF = South Africa; SCO = Scotland; SER = Serbia; SKO = South Korea; SR = Southern Rhodesia; STV = St Vincent; SWE = Sweden; TCH = Czechoslovakia; THA = Thailand; TUR = Turkey; UGA = Uganda; UKR = Ukraine; URS = USSR; USA = United States of America; UZB = Uzbekistan; VEN = Venezuela; WAL = Wales; YUG = Yugoslavia; ZAM = Zambia.

Olympic Champions, 1904-2004

St Louis, USA - 1904
Fly: G. Finnegan (USA). **Bantam:** O. Kirk (USA). **Feather:** O. Kirk (USA). **Light:** H. Spangler (USA). **Welter:** A. Young (USA). **Middle:** C. May (USA). **Heavy:** S. Berger (USA).

London, England - 1908
Bantam: H. Thomas (GBR). **Feather:** R. Gunn (GBR). **Light:** F. Grace (GBR). **Middle:** J.W.H.T. Douglas (GBR). **Heavy:** A. Oldman (GBR).
Silver medals: J. Condon (GBR), C. Morris (GBR), F. Spiller (GBR), S. Evans (GBR).
Bronze medals: W. Webb (GBR), H. Rodding (GBR), T. Ringer (GBR), H. Johnson (GBR), R. Warnes (GBR), W. Philo (GBR), F. Parks (GBR).

Antwerp, Belgium - 1920
Fly: F. Genaro (USA). **Bantam:** C. Walker (SAF). **Feather:** R. Fritsch (FRA). **Light:** S. Mossberg (USA). **Welter:** T. Schneider (CAN). **Middle:** H. Mallin (GBR). **L. Heavy:** E. Eagan (USA). **Heavy:** R. Rawson (GBR).
Silver medal: A. Ireland (GBR).
Bronze medals: W. Cuthbertson (GBR), G. McKenzie (GBR), H. Franks (GBR).

Paris, France - 1924
Fly: F. la Barba (USA). **Bantam:** W. Smith (SAF). **Feather:** J. Fields (USA). **Light:** H. Nielson (DEN). **Welter:** J. Delarge (BEL). **Middle:** H. Mallin (GBR). **L. Heavy:** H. Mitchell (GBR). **Heavy:** O. von Porat (NOR).
Silver medals: J. McKenzie (GBR), J. Elliot (GBR).

Amsterdam, Holland - 1928
Fly: A. Kocsis (HUN). **Bantam:** V. Tamagnini (ITA). **Feather:** B. van Klaveren (HOL). **Light:** C. Orlando (ITA). **Welter:** E. Morgan (NZL). **Middle:** P. Toscani (ITA). **L. Heavy:** V. Avendano (ARG). **Heavy:** A. Rodriguez Jurado (ARG).

Los Angeles, USA - 1932
Fly: I. Enekes (HUN). **Bantam:** H. Gwynne (CAN). **Feather:** C. Robledo (ARG). **Light:** L. Stevens (SAF). **Welter:** E. Flynn (USA). **Middle:** C. Barth (USA). **L. Heavy:** D. Carstens (SAF). **Heavy:** A. Lovell (ARG).

Berlin, West Germany - 1936
Fly: W. Kaiser (GER). **Bantam:** U. Sergo (ITA). **Feather:** O. Casanova (ARG). **Light:** I. Harangi (HUN). **Welter:** S. Suvio (FIN). **Middle:** J. Despeaux (FRA). **L. Heavy:** R. Michelot (FRA). **Heavy:** H. Runge (GER).

London, England - 1948
Fly: P. Perez (ARG). **Bantam:** T. Csik (HUN). **Feather:** E. Formenti (ITA). **Light:** G. Dreyer (SAF). **Welter:** J. Torma (TCH). **Middle:** L. Papp (HUN). **L. Heavy:** G. Hunter (SAF). **Heavy:** R. Iglesas (ARG).
Silver medals: J. Wright (GBR), D. Scott (GBR).

Helsinki, Finland - 1952
Fly: N. Brooks (USA). **Bantam:** P. Hamalainen (FIN). **Feather:** J. Zachara (TCH). **Light:** A. Bolognesi (ITA). **L. Welter:** C. Adkins (USA). **Welter:** Z. Chychla (POL). **L. Middle:** L. Papp (HUN). **Middle:** F. Patterson (USA). **L. Heavy:** N. Lee (USA). **Heavy:** E. Sanders (USA).
Silver medal: J. McNally (IRL).

Melbourne, Australia - 1956
Fly: T. Spinks (GBR). **Bantam:** W. Behrendt (GER). **Feather:** V. Safronov (URS). **Light:** R. McTaggart (GBR). **L. Welter:** V. Jengibarian (URS). **Welter:** N. Linca (ROM). **L. Middle:** L. Papp (HUN). **Middle:** G. Schatkov (URS). **L. Heavy:** J. Boyd (USA). **Heavy:** P. Rademacher (USA).

Silver medals: T. Nicholls (GBR), F. Tiedt (IRL).
Bronze medals: J. Caldwell (IRL), F. Gilroy (IRL), A. Bryne (IRL), N. Gargano (GBR), J. McCormack (GBR).

Rome, Italy - 1960
Fly: G. Torok (HUN). **Bantam:** O. Grigoryev (URS). **Feather:** F. Musso (ITA). **Light:** K. Pazdzior (POL). **L. Welter:** B. Nemecek (TCH). **Welter:** N. Benvenuti (ITA). **L. Middle:** W. McClure (USA). **Middle:** E. Crook (USA). **L. Heavy:** C. Clay (USA). **Heavy:** F. de Piccoli (ITA).
Bronze medals: R. McTaggart (GBR), J. Lloyd (GBR), W. Fisher (GBR).

Tokyo, Japan - 1964
Fly: F. Atzori (ITA). **Bantam:** T. Sakurai (JPN). **Feather:** S. Stepashkin (URS). **Light:** J. Grudzien (POL). **L. Welter:** J. Kulej (POL). **Welter:** M. Kasprzyk (POL). **L. Middle:** B. Lagutin (URS). **Middle:** V. Popenchenko (URS). **L. Heavy:** C. Pinto (ITA). **Heavy:** J. Frazier (USA).
Bronze medal: J. McCourt (IRL).

Mexico City, Mexico - 1968
L. Fly: F. Rodriguez (VEN). **Fly:** R. Delgado (MEX). **Bantam:** V. Sokolov (URS). **Feather:** A. Roldan (MEX). **Light:** H. Ramos (MEX). **L. Welter:** J. Kulej (POL). **Welter:** M. Wolke (GDR). **L. Middle:** B. Lagutin (URS). **Middle:** C. Finnegan (GBR). **L. Heavy:** D. Poznyak (URS). **Heavy:** G. Foreman (USA).

Munich, West Germany - 1972
L. Fly: G. Gedo (HUN). **Fly:** G. Kostadinov (BUL). **Bantam:** O. Martinez (CUB). **Feather:** B. Kusnetsov (URS). **Light:** J. Szczepanski (POL). **L. Welter:** R. Seales (USA). **Welter:** E. Correa (CUB). **L. Middle:** D. Kottysch (GER). **Middle:** V. Lemeschev (URS). **L. Heavy:** M. Parlov (YUG). **Heavy:** T. Stevenson (CUB).
Bronze medals: R. Evans (GBR), G. Turpin (GBR), A. Minter (GBR).

Montreal, Canada - 1976
L. Fly: J. Hernandez (CUB). **Fly:** L. Randolph (USA). **Bantam:** Y-J. Gu (NKO). **Feather:** A. Herrera (CUB). **Light:** H. Davis (USA). **L. Welter:** R. Leonard (USA). **Welter:** J. Bachfield (GDR). **L. Middle:** J. Rybicki (POL). **Middle:** M. Spinks (USA). **L. Heavy:** L. Spinks (USA). **Heavy:** T. Stevenson (CUB).
Bronze medal: P. Cowdell (GBR).

Moscow, USSR - 1980
L. Fly: S. Sabirov (URS). **Fly:** P. Lessov (BUL). **Bantam:** J. Hernandez (CUB). **Feather:** R. Fink (GDR). **Light:** A. Herrera (CUB). **L. Welter:** P. Oliva (ITA). **Welter:** A. Aldama (CUB). **L. Middle:** A. Martinez (CUB). **Middle:** J. Gomez (CUB). **L. Heavy:** S. Kacar (YUG). **Heavy:** T. Stevenson (CUB).
Bronze medals: H. Russell (IRL), A. Willis (GBR).

Los Angeles, USA - 1984
L. Fly: P. Gonzalez (USA). **Fly:** S. McCrory (USA). **Bantam:** M. Stecca (ITA). **Feather:** M. Taylor (USA). **Light:** P. Whitaker (USA). **L. Welter:** J. Page (USA). **Welter:** M. Breland (USA). **L. Middle:** F. Tate (USA). **Middle:** J-S. Shin (SKO). **L. Heavy:** A. Josipovic (YUG). **Heavy:** H. Tillman (USA). **S. Heavy:** T. Biggs (USA).
Bronze medal: B. Wells (GBR).

Seoul, South Korea - 1988
L. Fly: I. Mustafov (BUL). **Fly:** H-S. Kim (SKO). **Bantam:** K. McKinney (USA). **Feather:** G. Parisi (ITA). **Light:** A. Zuelow (GDR). **L. Welter:** V. Yanovsky (URS). **Welter:** R. Wangila (KEN). **L. Middle:** S-H. Park (SKO). **Middle:** H. Maske (GDR). **L. Heavy:** A. Maynard (USA). **Heavy:** R. Mercer (USA). **S. Heavy:** L. Lewis (CAN).
Bronze medal: R. Woodhall (GBR).

Barcelona, Spain - 1992
L. Fly: R. Marcelo (CUB). **Fly:** C-C. Su (NKO). **Bantam:** J. Casamayor (CUB). **Feather:** A. Tews (GER). **Light:** O. de la Hoya (USA). **L. Welter:** H. Vinent (CUB). **Welter:** M. Carruth (IRL). **L. Middle:** J. Lemus (CUB). **Middle:** A. Hernandez (CUB). **L. Heavy:** T. May (GER). **Heavy:** F. Savon (CUB). **S. Heavy:** R. Balado (CUB).
Silver medal: W. McCullough (IRL).
Bronze medal: R. Reid (GBR).

Atlanta, USA - 1996
L. Fly: D. Petrov (BUL). **Fly:** M. Romero (CUB). **Bantam:** I. Kovaks (HUN). **Feather:** S. Kamsing (THA). **Light:** H. Soltani (ALG). **L. Welter:** H. Vinent (CUB). **Welter:** O. Saitov (RUS). **L. Middle:** D. Reid (USA). **Middle:** A. Hernandez (CUB). **L. Heavy:** V. Jirov (KAZ). **Heavy:** F. Savon (CUB). **S. Heavy:** Vladimir Klitschko (UKR).

Sydney, Australia - 2000
L. Fly: B. Aslom (FRA). **Fly:** W. Ponlid (THA). **Bantam:** G. Rigondeaux (CUB). **Feather:** B. Sattarkhanov (KAZ). **Light:** M. Kindelan (CUB). **L. Welter:** M. Abdullaev (UZB). **Welter:** O. Saitov (RUS). **L. Middle:** Y. Ibraimov (KAZ). **Middle:** J. Gutierrez Espinosa (CUB). **L. Heavy:** A. Lebziak (RUS). **Heavy:** F. Savon (CUB). **S. Heavy:** A. Harrison (ENG).

Athens, Greece - 2004
L. Fly: Y. Bartelemi (CUB). **Fly:** Y. Gamboa (CUB). **Bantam:** G. Rigondeaux (CUB). **Feather:** A. Tichtchenko (RUS). **Light:** M. Kindelan (CUB). **L. Welter:** M. Boonjumnong (THA). **Welter:** B. Artayev (KAZ). **Middle:** G. Gaiderbekov (RUS). **L. Heavy:** A. Ward (USA). **Heavy:** O. Solis (CUB). **S. Heavy:** A. Povetkin (RUS).
Silver medal: A. Khan (ENG).

World Champions, 1974-2005

Havana, Cuba - 1974
L. Fly: J. Hernandez (CUB). **Fly:** D. Rodriguez (CUB). **Bantam:** W. Gomez (PUR). **Feather:** H. Davis (USA). **Light:** V. Solomin (URS). **L. Welter:** A. Kalule (UGA). **Welter:** E. Correa (CUB). **L. Middle:** R. Garbey (CUB). **Middle:** R. Riskiev (URS). **L. Heavy:** M. Parlov (YUG). **Heavy:** T. Stevenson (CUB).

Belgrade, Yugoslavia - 1978
L. Fly: S. Muchoki (KEN). **Fly:** H. Strednicki (POL). **Bantam:** A. Horta (CUB). **Feather:** B. Herrera (CUB). **Light:** D. Andeh (NIG). **L. Welter:** V. Lvov (URS). **Welter:** V. Rachkov (URS). **L. Middle:** V. Savchenko (URS). **Middle:** J. Gomez (CUB). **L. Heavy:** S. Soria (CUB). **Heavy:** T. Stevenson (CUB).

Munich, West Germany - 1982
L. Fly: I. Mustafov (BUL). **Fly:** Y. Alexandrov (URS). **Bantam:** F. Favors (USA). **Feather:** A. Horta (CUB). **Light:** A. Herrera (CUB). **L. Welter:** C. Garcia (USA). **Welter:** M. Breland (USA). **L. Middle:** A. Koshkin (URS). **Middle:** B. Comas (CUB). **L. Heavy:** P. Romero (CUB). **Heavy:** A. Jagubkin (URS). **S. Heavy:** T. Biggs (USA).
Bronze medal: T. Corr (IRL).

Reno, USA - 1986
L. Fly: J. Odelin (CUB). **Fly:** P. Reyes (CUB). **Bantam:** S-I. Moon (SKO). **Feather:** K. Banks (USA). **Light:** A. Horta (CUB). **L. Welter:** V. Shishov (URS). **Welter:** K. Gould (USA). **L. Middle:** A. Espinosa (CUB). **Middle:** D. Allen (USA). **L. Heavy:** P. Romero (CUB). **Heavy:** F. Savon (CUB). **S. Heavy:** T. Stevenson (CUB).

Moscow, USSR - 1989
L. Fly: E. Griffin (USA). **Fly:** Y. Arbachakov (URS). **Bantam:** E. Carrion (CUB). **Feather:** A. Khamatov (URS). **Light:** J. Gonzalez (CUB). **L. Welter:** I. Ruzinkov (URS). **Welter:** F. Vastag (Rom). **L. Middle:** I. Akopokhian (URS). **Middle:** A. Kurniavka (URS). **L. Heavy:** H. Maske (GDR). **Heavy:** F. Savon (CUB). **S. Heavy:** R. Balado (CUB).
Bronze medal: M. Carruth (IRL).

Sydney, Australia - 1991
L. Fly: E. Griffin (USA). **Fly:** I. Kovacs (HUN). **Bantam:** S. Todorov (BUL). **Feather:** K. Kirkorov (BUL). **Light:** M. Rudolph (GER). **L. Welter:** K. Tszyu (URS). **Welter:** J. Hernandez (CUB). **L. Middle:** J. Lemus (CUB). **Middle:** T. Russo (ITA). **L. Heavy:** T. May (GER). **Heavy:** F. Savon (CUB). **S. Heavy:** R. Balado (CUB).

Tampere, Finland - 1993
L. Fly: N. Munchian (ARM). **Fly:** W. Font (CUB). **Bantam:** A. Christov (BUL). **Feather:** S. Todorov (BUL). **Light:** D. Austin (CUB). **L. Welter:** H. Vinent (CUB). **Welter:** J. Hernandez (CUB). **L. Middle:** F. Vastag (ROM). **Middle:** A. Hernandez (CUB). **L. Heavy:** R. Garbey (CUB). **Heavy:** F. Savon (CUB). **S. Heavy:** R. Balado (CUB).
Bronze medal: D. Kelly (IRL).

Berlin, Germany - 1995
L. Fly: D. Petrov (BUL). **Fly:** Z. Lunka (GER). **Bantam:** R. Malachbekov (RUS).

Feather: S. Todorov (BUL). **Light:** L. Doroftel (ROM). **L. Welter:** H. Vinent (CUB). **Welter:** J. Hernandez (CUB). **L. Middle:** F. Vastag (ROM). **Middle:** A. Hernandez (CUB). **L. Heavy:** A. Tarver (USA). **Heavy:** F. Savon (CUB). **S. Heavy:** A. Lezin (RUS).

Budapest, Hungary - 1997
L. Fly: M. Romero (CUB). **Fly:** M. Mantilla (CUB). **Bantam:** R Malakhbekov (RUS). **Feather:** I. Kovacs (HUN). **Light:** A. Maletin (RUS). **L. Welter:** D. Simion (ROM). **Welter:** O. Saitov (RUS). **L. Middle:** A. Duvergel (CUB). **Middle:** Z. Erdei (HUN). **L. Heavy:** A. Lebsiak (RUS). **Heavy:** F. Savon (CUB). **S. Heavy:** G. Kandelaki (GEO).
Bronze medal: S. Kirk (IRL).

Houston, USA - 1999
L. Fly: B. Viloria (USA). **Fly:** B. Jumadilov (KAZ). **Bantam:** R. Crinu (ROM). **Feather:** R. Juarez (USA). **Light:** M. Kindelan (CUB). **L. Welter:** M. Abdullaev (UZB). **Welter:** J. Hernandez (CUB). **L. Middle:** M. Simion (ROM). **Middle:** U. Haydarov (UZB). **L. Heavy:** M. Simms (USA). **Heavy:** M. Bennett (USA). **S. Heavy:** S. Samilsan (TUR).
Bronze medal: K. Evans (WAL).

Belfast, Northern Ireland - 2001
L. Fly: Y. Bartelemi (CUB). **Fly:** J. Thomas (FRA). **Bantam:** G. Rigondeaux (CUB). **Feather:** R. Palyani (TUR). **Light:** M. Kindelan (CUB). **L. Welter:** D. Luna Martinez (CUB). **Welter:** L. Aragon (CUB). **L. Middle:** D. Austin (CUB). **Middle:** A. Gogolev (RUS). **L. Heavy:** Y. Makarenko (RUS). **Heavy:** O. Solis (CUB). **S. Heavy:** R. Chagaev (UZB).
Silver medal: D. Haye (ENG).
Bronze medals: J. Moore (IRL), C. Froch (ENG).

Bangkok, Thailand - 2003
L. Fly: S. Karazov (RUS). **Fly:** S. Jongjohor (THA). **Bantam:** A. Mamedov (AZE). **Feather:** G. Jafarov (KAZ). **Light:** M. Kindelan (CUB). **L. Welter:** W. Blain (FRA). **Welter:** L. Aragon (CUB). **Middle:** G. Golovkin (KAZ). **L. Heavy:** Y. Makarenko (RUS). **Heavy:** O. Solis (CUB). **S. Heavy:** A. Povetkin (RUS).

Mianyang City, China - 2005
L. Fly: S. Zou (CHI). **Fly:** O-S Lee (SKO). **Bantam:** G. Rigondeaux (CUB). **Feather:** A. Tischenko (RUS). **Light:** Y. Ugas (CUB). **L. Welter:** S. Sapiyev (KAZ). **Welter:** E. Lara (CUB). **Middle:** M. Korobev (RUS). **L. Heavy:** Y. Dzhanabergenov (KAZ). **Heavy:** A. Alexeev (RUS). **S. Heavy:** O. Solis (CUB).
Bronze medal: N. Perkins (ENG).

World Junior Champions, 1979-2006

Yokohama, Japan - 1979
L. Fly: R. Shannon (USA). **Fly:** P. Lessov (BUL). **Bantam:** P-K. Choi (SKO). **Feather:** Y. Gladychev (URS). **Light:** R. Blake (USA). **L. Welter:** I. Akopokhian (URS). **Welter:** M. McCrory (USA). **L. Middle:** A. Mayes (USA). **Middle:** A. Milov (URS). **L. Heavy:** A. Lebedev (URS). **Heavy:** M. Frazier (USA).
Silver medals: N. Wilshire (ENG), D. Cross (ENG).
Bronze medal: I. Scott (SCO).

Santa Domingo, Dominican Republic - 1983
L. Fly: M. Herrera (DOM). **Fly:** J. Gonzalez (CUB). **Bantam:** J. Molina (PUR). **Feather:** A. Miesses (DOM). **Light:** A. Beltre (DOM). **L. Welter:** A. Espinoza (CUB). **Welter:** M. Watkins (USA). **L. Middle:** U. Castillo (CUB). **Middle:** R. Batista (CUB). **L. Heavy:** O. Pought (USA). **Heavy:** A. Williams (USA). **S. Heavy:** L. Lewis (CAN).

Bucharest, Romania - 1985
L. Fly: R-S. Hwang (SKO). **Fly:** T. Marcelica (ROM). **Bantam:** R. Diaz (CUB). **Feather:** D. Maeran (ROM). **Light:** J. Teiche (GDR). **L. Welter:** W. Saeger (GDR). **Welter:** A. Stoianov (BUL). **L. Middle:** M. Franek (TCH). **Middle:** O. Zahalotskih (URS). **L. Heavy:** B. Riddick (USA). **Heavy:** F. Savon (CUB). **S. Heavy:** A. Prianichnikov (URS).

Havana, Cuba - 1987
L. Fly: E. Paisan (CUB). **Fly:** C. Daniels (USA). **Bantam:** A. Moya (CUB). **Feather:** G. Iliyasov (URS). **Light:** J. Hernandez (CUB). **L. Welter:** L. Mihai (ROM). **Welter:** F. Vastag (ROM). **L. Middle:** A. Lobsyak (URS). **Middle:** W. Martinez (CUB). **L. Heavy:** D. Yeliseyev (URS). **Heavy:** R. Balado (CUB). **S. Heavy:** L. Martinez (CUB).
Silver medal: E. Loughran (IRL).
Bronze medal: D. Galvin (IRL).

San Juan, Puerto Rico - 1989
L. Fly: D. Petrov (BUL). **Fly:** N. Monchai (FRA). **Bantam:** J. Casamayor (CUB). **Feather:** C. Febres (PUR). **Light:** A. Acevedo (PUR). **L. Welter:** E. Berger (GDR). **Welter:** A. Hernandez (CUB). **L. Middle:** L. Bedey (CUB). **Middle:** R. Garbey (CUB). **L. Heavy:** R. Alvarez (CUB). **Heavy:** K. Johnson (CAN). **S. Heavy:** A. Burdiantz (URS).
Silver medals: E. Magee (IRL), R. Reid (ENG), S. Wilson (SCO).

Lima, Peru - 1990
L. Fly: D. Alicea (PUR). **Fly:** K. Pielert (GDR). **Bantam:** K. Baravi (URS).

Feather: A. Vaughan (ENG). **Light:** J. Mendez (CUB). **L. Welter:** H. Vinent (CUB). **Welter:** A. Hernandez (CUB). **L. Middle:** A. Kakauridze (URS). **Middle:** J. Gomez (CUB). **L. Heavy:** B. Torsten (GDR). **Heavy:** I. Andreev (URS). **S. Heavy:** J. Quesada (CUB).
Bronze medal: P. Ingle (ENG).

Montreal, Canada - 1992
L. Fly: W. Font (CUB). **Fly:** J. Oragon (CUB). **Bantam:** N. Machado (CUB). **Feather:** M. Stewart (CAN). **Light:** D. Austin (CUB). **L. Welter:** O. Saitov (RUS). **Welter:** L. Brors (GER). **L. Middle:** J. Acosta (CUB). **Middle:** I. Arsangaliev (RUS). **L. Heavy:** S. Samilsan (TUR). **Heavy:** G. Kandeliaki (GEO). **S. Heavy:** M. Porchnev (RUS).
Bronze medal: N. Sinclair (IRL).

Istanbul, Turkey - 1994
L. Fly: J. Turunen (FIN). **Fly:** A. Jimenez (CUB). **Bantam:** J. Despaigne (CUB). **Feather:** D. Simion (ROM). **Light:** L. Diogenes (CUB). **L. Welter:** V. Romero (CUB). **Welter:** E. Aslan (TUR). **L. Middle:** G. Ledsvanys (CUB). **Middle:** M. Genc (TUR). **L. Heavy:** P. Aurino (ITA). **Heavy:** M. Lopez (CUB). **S. Heavy:** P. Carrion (CUB).

Havana, Cuba - 1996
L. Fly: L. Hernandez (CUB). **Fly:** L. Cabrera (CUB). **Bantam:** P. Miradal (CUB). **Feather:** E. Rodriguez (CUB). **Light:** R. Vaillan (CUB). **L. Welter:** T. Mergadze (RUS). **Welter:** J. Brahmer (GER). **L. Middle:** L. Mezquia (CUB). **Middle:** V. Pletniov (RUS). **L. Heavy:** O. Simon (CUB). **Heavy:** A. Yatsenko (UKR). **S. Heavy:** S. Fabre (CUB).
Bronze medal: R. Hatton (ENG).

Buenos Aires, Argentina - 1998
L. Fly: S. Tanasie (ROM). **Fly:** S. Yeledov (KAZ). **Bantam:** S. Suleymanov (UKR). **Feather:** I. Perez (ARG). **Light:** A. Solopov (RUS). **L. Welter:** Y. Tomashov (UKR). **Welter:** K. Oustarkhanov (RUS). **L. Middle:** S. Kostenko (UKR). **Middle:** M. Kempe (GER). **L. Heavy:** H. Yohanson Martinez (CUB). **Heavy:** O. Solis Fonte (CUB). **S. Heavy:** B. Ohanyan (ARM).
Silver medal: H. Cunningham (IRL).
Bronze medal: D. Campbell (IRL).

Budapest, Hungary - 2000
L. Fly: Y. Leon Alarcon (CUB). **Fly:** O. Franco Vasquez (CUB). **Bantam:** V. Tajbert (GER). **Feather:** G. Kate (HUN). **Light:** F. Adzsanalov (AZE). **L. Welter:** G. Galovkin (KAZ). **Welter:** S. Ustunel (TUR). **L. Middle:** D. Chernysh (RUS). **Middle:** F. Sullivan Barrera (CUB). **L. Heavy:** A. Shekmourov (RUS). **Heavy:** D. Medzhydov (UKR). **S. Heavy:** A. Dmitrienko (RUS).
Bronze medal: C. Barrett (IRL).

Santiago, Cuba - 2002
L. Fly: D. Acripitian (RUS). **Fly:** Y. Fabregas (CUB). **Bantam:** S. Bahodirijan (UZB). **Feather:** A. Tichtchenko (RUS). **Light:** S. Mendez (CUB). **L. Welter:** K. Iliyasov (KAZ). **Welter:** J. McPherson (USA). **L. Middle:** V. Diaz (CUB). **Middle:** A. Duarte (CUB). **L. Heavy:** R. Zavalnyuyk (UKR). **Heavy:** Y. P. Hernandez (CUB). **S. Heavy:** P. Portal (CUB).
Silver medal: A. Lee (IRL).
Bronze medal: N. Brough (ENG).

Jeju Island, South Korea - 2004
L. Fly: P. Bedak (Hun). **Fly:** I. Rahimov (UZB). **Bantam:** A. Abdimomunov (KAZ). **Feather:** E. Ambartsumyan (RUS). **Light:** A. Khan (ENG). **L. Welter:** C. Banteur (CUB). **Welter:** E. Rasulov (UZB). **Middle:** D. Tchudinov (RUS). **L. Heavy:** I. Perez (CUB). **Heavy:** E. Romanov (RUS). **S.Heavy:** D. Boytsov (RUS).
Bronze medal: D. Price (ENG).

Agadir, Morocco - 2006
L.Fly: A.Collado Acosta (CUB). **Fly:** V.Lomachenko (UKR). **Bantam:** M.Ouatine (MOR). **Feather:** Y.Frometa (CUB). **Light:** R.Iglesias (CUB). **L.Welter:** B.Bacskai (HUN). **Welter:** J.Iglesias (CUB). **Middle:** L.Garcia (CUB). **L.Heavy:** I.Yandiev (RUS). **Heavy:** S.Kalchugin (RUS). **S.Heavy:** C.Ciocan (ROM).
Bronze medals: O.Mbwakongo (ENG), T.Fury (ENG).

European Champions, 1924-2006

Paris, France - 1924
Fly: J. McKenzie (GBR). **Bantam:** J. Ces (FRA). **Feather:** R. de Vergnie (BEL). **Light:** N. Nielsen (DEN). **Welter:** J. Delarge (BEL). **Middle:** H. Mallin (GBR). **L. Heavy:** H. Mitchell (GBR). **Heavy:** O. von Porat (NOR).

Stockholm, Sweden - 1925
Fly: E. Pladner (FRA). **Bantam:** A. Rule (GBR). **Feather:** P. Andren (SWE). **Light:** S. Johanssen (SWE). **Welter:** H. Nielsen (DEN). **Middle:** F. Crawley (GBR). **L. Heavy:** T. Petersen (DEN). **Heavy:** B. Persson (SWE).
Silver medals: J. James (GBR), E. Viney (GBR), D. Lister (GBR).

Berlin, Germany - 1927
Fly: L. Boman (SWE). **Bantam:** K. Dalchow (GER). **Feather:** F. Dubbers (GER). **Light:** H. Domgoergen (GER). **Welter:** R. Caneva (ITA). **Middle:** J. Christensen (NOR). **L. Heavy:** H. Muller (GER). **Heavy:** N. Ramm (SWE).

Amsterdam, Holland - 1928
Fly: A. Kocsis (HUN). **Bantam:** V. Tamagnini (ITA). **Feather:** B. van Klaveren (HOL). **Light:** C. Orlandi (ITA). **Welter:** R. Galataud (FRA). **Middle:** P. Toscani (ITA). **L. Heavy:** E. Pistulla (GER). **Heavy:** N. Ramm (SWE).

Budapest, Hungary - 1930
Fly: I. Enekes (HUN). **Bantam:** J. Szeles (HUN). **Feather:** G. Szabo (HUN). **Light:** M. Bianchini (ITA). **Welter:** J. Besselmann (GER). **Middle:** C. Meroni (ITA). **L. Heavy:** T. Petersen (DEN). **Heavy:** J. Michaelson (DEN).

Los Angeles, USA - 1932
Fly: I. Enekes (HUN). **Bantam:** H. Ziglarski (GER). **Feather:** J. Schleinkofer (GER). **Light:** T. Ahlqvist (SWE). **Welter:** E. Campe (GER). **Middle:** R. Michelot (FRA). **L. Heavy:** G. Rossi (ITA). **Heavy:** L. Rovati (ITA).

Budapest, Hungary - 1934
Fly: P. Palmer (GBR). **Bantam:** I. Enekes (HUN). **Feather:** O. Kaestner GER). **Light:** E. Facchini (ITA). **Welter:** D. McCleave (GBR). **Middle:** S. Szigetti (HUN). **L. Heavy:** P. Zehetmayer (AUT). **Heavy:** G. Baerlund (FIN).
Bronze medal: P. Floyd (GBR).

Milan, Italy - 1937
Fly: I. Enekes (HUN). **Bantam:** U. Sergo (ITA). **Feather:** A. Polus (POL). **Light:** H. Nuremberg (GER). **Welter:** M. Murach (GER). **Middle:** H. Chmielewski (POL). **L. Heavy:** S. Szigetti (HUN). **Heavy:** O. Tandberg (SWE).

Dublin, Eire - 1939
Fly: J. Ingle (IRL). **Bantam:** U. Sergo (ITA). **Feather:** P. Dowdall (IRL). **Light:** H. Nuremberg (GER). **Welter:** A. Kolczyski (POL). **Middle:** A. Raadik (EST). **L. Heavy:** L. Musina (ITA). **Heavy:** O. Tandberg (SWE).
Bronze medal: C. Evenden (IRL).

Dublin, Eire - 1947
Fly: L. Martinez (ESP). **Bantam:** L. Bogacs (HUN). **Feather:** K. Kreuger (SWE). **Light:** J. Vissers (BEL). **Welter:** J. Ryan (ENG). **Middle:** A. Escudie (FRA). **L. Heavy:** H. Quentemeyer (HOL). **Heavy:** G. O'Colmain (IRL).
Silver medals: J. Clinton (SCO), P. Maguire (IRL), W. Thom (ENG), G. Scriven (ENG).
Bronze medals: J. Dwyer (SCO), A. Sanderson (ENG), W. Frith (SCO), E. Cantwell (IRL), K. Wyatt (ENG).

Oslo, Norway - 1949
Fly: J. Kasperczak (POL). **Bantam:** G. Zuddas (ITA). **Feather:** J. Bataille (FRA). **Light:** M. McCullagh (IRL). **Welter:** J. Torma (TCH). **Middle:** L. Papp (HUN). **L. Heavy:** G. di Segni (ITA). **Heavy:** L. Bene (HUN).
Bronze medal: D. Connell (IRL).

Milan, Italy - 1951
Fly: A. Pozzali (ITA). **Bantam:** V. Dall'Osso (ITA). **Feather:** J. Ventaja (FRA). **Light:** B. Visintin (ITA). **L. Welter:** H. Schelling (GER). **Welter:** Z. Chychla (POL). **L. Middle:** L. Papp (HUN). **Middle:** S. Sjolin (SWE). **L. Heavy:** M. Limage (BEL). **Heavy:** G. di Segni (ITA).
Silver medal: J. Kelly (IRL).
Bronze medals: D. Connell (IRL), T. Milligan (IRL), A. Lay (ENG).

Warsaw, Poland - 1953
Fly: H. Kukier (POL). **Bantam:** Z. Stefaniuk (POL). **Feather:** J. Kruza (POL). **Light:** V. Jengibarian (URS). **L. Welter:** L. Drogosz (POL). **Welter:** Z. Chychla (POL). **L. Middle:** B. Wells (ENG). **Middle:** D. Wemhoner (GER). **L. Heavy:** U. Nietchke (GER). **Heavy:** A. Schotzikas (URS).
Silver medal: T. Milligan (IRL).
Bronze medals: J. McNally (IRL), R. Barton (ENG).

Berlin, West Germany - 1955
Fly: E. Basel (GER). **Bantam:** Z. Stefaniuk (POL). **Feather:** T. Nicholls (ENG). **Light:** H. Kurschat (GER). **L. Welter:** L. Drogosz (POL). **Welter:** N. Gargano (ENG). **L. Middle:** Z. Pietrzykowski (POL). **Middle:** G. Schatkov (URS). **L. Heavy:** E. Schoeppner (GER). **Heavy:** A. Schotzikas (URS).

Prague, Czechoslovakia - 1957
Fly: M. Homberg (GER). **Bantam:** O. Grigoryev (URS). **Feather:** D. Venilov (BUL). **Light:** K. Pazdzior (POL). **L. Welter:** V. Jengibarian (URS). **Welter:** M. Graus (GER). **L. Middle:** N. Benvenuti (ITA). **Middle:** Z. Pietrzykowski (POL). **L. Heavy:** G. Negrea (ROM). **Heavy:** A. Abramov (URS).
Bronze medals: R. Davies (WAL), J. Morrissey (SCO), J. Kidd (SCO), F. Teidt (IRL).

Lucerne, Switzerland - 1959
Fly: M. Homberg (GER). **Bantam:** H. Rascher (GER). **Feather:** J. Adamski (POL). **Light:** O. Maki (FIN). **L. Welter:** V. Jengibarian (URS). **Welter:** L. Drogosz (POL). **L. Middle:** N. Benvenuti (ITA). **Middle:** G. Schatkov (URS). **L. Heavy:** Z. Pietrzykowski (POL). **Heavy:** A. Abramov (URS).
Silver medal: D. Thomas (ENG).
Bronze medals: A. McClean (IRL), H. Perry (IRL), C. McCoy (IRL), H. Scott (ENG).

Belgrade, Yugoslavia - 1961
Fly: P. Vacca (ITA). **Bantam:** S. Sivko (URS). **Feather:** F. Taylor (ENG). **Light:** R. McTaggart (SCO). **L. Welter:** A. Tamulis (URS). **Welter:** R. Tamulis (URS). **L. Middle:** B. Lagutin (URS). **Middle:** T. Walasek (POL). **L. Heavy:** G. Saraudi (ITA). **Heavy:** A. Abramov (URS).
Bronze medals: P. Warwick (ENG), I. McKenzie (SCO), J. Bodell (ENG).

Moscow, USSR - 1963
Fly: V. Bystrov (URS). **Bantam:** O. Grigoryev (URS). **Feather:** S. Stepashkin (URS). **Light:** J. Kajdi (HUN). **L. Welter:** J. Kulej (POL). **Welter:** R. Tamulis (URS). **L. Middle:** B. Lagutin (URS). **Middle:** V. Popenchenko (URS). **L. Heavy:** Z. Pietrzykowski (POL). **Heavy:** J. Nemec (TCH).
Silver medal: A. Wyper (SCO).

Berlin, East Germany - 1965
Fly: H. Freisdadt (GER). **Bantam:** O. Grigoryev (URS). **Feather:** S. Stepashkin (URS). **Light:** V. Barranikov (URS). **L. Welter:** J. Kulej (POL). **Welter:** R. Tamulis (URS). **L. Middle:** V. Ageyev (URS). **Middle:** V. Popenchenko (URS). **L. Heavy:** D. Poznyak (URS). **Heavy:** A. Isosimov (URS).
Silver medal: B. Robinson (ENG).
Bronze medals: J. McCluskey (SCO), K. Buchanan (SCO), J. McCourt (IRL).

Rome, Italy - 1967
Fly: H. Skrzyczak (POL). **Bantam:** N. Giju (ROM). **Feather:** R. Petek (POL). **Light:** J. Grudzien (POL). **L. Welter:** V. Frolov (URS). **Welter:** B. Nemecek (TCH). **L. Middle:** V. Ageyev (URS). **Middle:** M. Casati (ITA). **L. Heavy:** D. Poznyak (URS). **Heavy:** M. Baruzzi (ITA).
Silver medal: P. Boddington (ENG).

Bucharest, Romania - 1969
L. Fly: G. Gedo (HUN). **Fly:** C. Ciuca (ROM). **Bantam:** A. Dumitrescu (ROM). **Feather:** L. Orban (HUN). **Light:** S. Cutov (ROM). **L. Welter:** V. Frolov (URS). **Welter:** G. Meier (GER). **L. Middle:** V. Tregubov (URS). **Middle:** V. Tarasenkov (URS). **L. Heavy:** D. Poznyak (URS). **Heavy:** I. Alexe (ROM).
Bronze medals: M. Dowling (IRL), M. Piner (ENG), A. Richardson (ENG), T. Imrie (SCO).

Madrid, Spain - 1971
L. Fly: G. Gedo (HUN). **Fly:** J. Rodriguez (ESP). **Bantam:** T. Badar (HUN). **Feather:** R. Tomczyk (POL). **Light:** J. Szczepanski (POL). **L. Welter:** U. Beyer (GDR). **Welter:** J. Kajdi (HUN). **L. Middle:** V. Tregubov (URS). **Middle:** J. Juotsiavitchus (URS). **L. Heavy:** M. Parlov (YUG). **Heavy:** V. Tchernishev (URS).
Bronze medals: N. McLaughlin (IRL), M. Dowling (IRL), B. McCarthy (IRL), M. Kingwell (ENG), L. Stevens (ENG).

Belgrade, Yugoslavia - 1973
L. Fly: V. Zasypko (URS). **Fly:** C. Gruescu (ROM). **Bantam:** A. Cosentino (FRA). **Feather:** S. Forster (GDR). **Light:** S. Cutov (ROM). **L. Welter:** M. Benes (YUG). **Welter:** S. Csjef (HUN). **L. Middle:** A. Klimanov (URS). **Middle:** V. Lemechev (URS). **L. Heavy:** M. Parlov (YUG). **Heavy:** V. Ulyanich (URS).
Bronze medal: J. Bambrick (SCO).

Katowice, Poland - 1975
L. Fly: A. Tkachenko (URS). **Fly:** V. Zasypko (URS). **Bantam:** V. Rybakov (URS). **Feather:** T. Badari (HUN). **Light:** S. Cutov (ROM). **L. Welter:** V. Limasov (URS). **Welter:** K. Marjaama (FIN). **L. Middle:** W. Rudnowski (POL). **Middle:** V. Lemechev (URS). **L. Heavy:** A. Klimanov (URS). **Heavy:** A. Biegalski (POL).
Bronze medals: C. Magri (ENG), P. Cowdell (ENG), G. McEwan (ENG).

Halle, East Germany - 1977
L. Fly: H. Srednicki (POL). **Fly:** L. Blazynski (POL). **Bantam:** S. Forster (GDR). **Feather:** R. Nowakowski (GDR). **Light:** A. Rusevski (YUG). **L. Welter:** B. Gajda (POL). **Welter:** V. Limasov (URS). **L. Middle:** V. Saychenko (URS). **Middle:** I. Shaposhnikov (URS). **L. Heavy:** D. Kvachadze (URS). **Heavy:** E. Gorstkov (URS).
Bronze medal: P. Sutcliffe (IRL).

Cologne, West Germany - 1979
L. Fly: S. Sabirov (URS). **Fly:** H. Strednicki (POL). **Bantam:** N. Khrapzov (URS). **Feather:** V. Rybakov (URS). **Light:** V. Demianenko (URS). **L. Welter:** S. Konakbaev (URS). **Welter:** E. Muller (GER). **L. Middle:** M. Perunovic (YUG). **Middle:** T. Uusiverta (FIN). **L. Heavy:** A. Nikolyan (URS). **Heavy:** E. Gorstkov (URS). **S. Heavy:** P. Hussing (GER).
Bronze medal: P. Sutcliffe (IRL).

Tampere, Finland - 1981
L. Fly: I. Mustafov (BUL). **Fly:** P. Lessov (BUL). **Bantam:** V. Miroschnichenko (URS). **Feather:** R. Nowakowski (GDR). **Light:** V. Rybakov (URS). **L. Welter:** V. Shisov (URS). **Welter:** S. Konakvbaev (URS). **L. Middle:** A. Koshkin (URS). **Middle:** J. Torbek (URS). **L. Heavy:** A Krupin (URS). **Heavy:** A. Jagupkin (URS). **S. Heavy:** F. Damiani (ITA).
Bronze medal: G. Hawkins (IRL).

Varna, Bulgaria - 1983
L. Fly: I. Mustafov (BUL). **Fly:** P. Lessov (BUL). **Bantam:** Y. Alexandrov (URS).

Feather: S. Nurkazov (URS). **Light:** E. Chuprenski (BUL). **L. Welter:** V. Shishov (URS). **Welter:** P. Galkin (URS). **L. Middle:** V. Laptev (URS). **Middle:** V. Melnik (URS). **L. Heavy:** V. Kokhanovski (URS). **Heavy:** A. Jagubkin (URS). **S. Heavy:** F. Damiani (ITA).
Bronze medal: K. Joyce (IRL).

Budapest, Hungary - 1985
L. Fly: R. Breitbarth (GDR). **Fly:** D. Berg (GDR). **Bantam:** L. Simic (YUG). **Feather:** S. Khachatrian (URS). **Light:** E. Chuprenski (BUL) **L. Welter:** S. Mehnert (GDR). **Welter:** I. Akopokhian (URS). **L. Middle:** M. Timm (GDR). **Middle:** H. Maske (GDR). **L. Heavy:** N. Shanavasov (URS). **Heavy:** A. Jagubkin (URS). **S. Heavy:** F. Somodi (HUN).
Bronze medals: S. Casey(IRL), J. Beckles (ENG).

Turin, Italy - 1987
L. Fly: N. Munchyan (URS). **Fly:** A. Tews (GDR). **Bantam:** A. Hristov (BUL). **Feather:** M. Kazaryan (URS). **Light:** O. Nazarov (URS). **L. Welter:** B. Abadjier (BUL). **Welter:** V. Shishov (URS). **L. Middle:** E. Richter (GDR). **Middle:** H. Maske (GDR). **L. Heavy:** Y. Vaulin (URS). **Heavy:** A. Vanderlijde (HOL). **S. Heavy:** U. Kaden (GDR).
Bronze medal: N. Brown (ENG).

Athens, Greece - 1989
L. Fly: I.Mustafov (BUL). **Fly:** Y. Arbachakov (URS). **Bantam:** S. Todorov (BUL). **Feather:** K. Kirkorov (BUL). **Light:** K. Tsziu (URS). **L. Welter:** I. Ruznikov (URS). **Welter:** S. Mehnert (GDR). **L. Middle:** I. Akopokhian (URS). **Middle:** H. Maske (GDR). **L. Heavy:** S. Lange (GDR). **Heavy:** A. Vanderlijde (HOL). **S. Heavy:** U. Kaden (GDR).
Bronze Medal: D. Anderson (SCO).

Gothenburg, Sweden - 1991
L. Fly: I. Marinov (BUL). **Fly:** I. Kovacs (HUN). **Bantam:** S. Todorov (BUL). **Feather:** P. Griffin (IRL). **Light:** V. Nistor (ROM). **L. Welter:** K. Tsziu (URS). **Welter:** R. Welin (SWE). **L. Middle:** I. Akopokhian (URS). **Middle:** S. Otke (GER). **L. Heavy:** D. Michalczewski (GER). **Heavy:** A. Vanderlijde (HOL). **S. Heavy:** E. Beloussov (URS).
Bronze medals: P. Weir (SCO), A. Vaughan (ENG).

Bursa, Turkey - 1993
L. Fly: D. Petrov (BUL). **Fly:** R. Husseinov (AZE). **Bantam:** R. Malakhbetov (RUS). **Feather:** S. Todorov (BUL). **Light:** J. Bielski (POL). **L. Welter:** N. Suleymanogiu (TUR). **Welter:** V. Karpaclauskas (LIT). **L. Middle:** F. Vastag (ROM). **Middle:** D. Eigenbrodt (GER). **L. Heavy:** I. Kshinin (RUS). **Heavy:** G. Kandelaki (GEO). **S. Heavy:** S. Rusinov (BUL).
Bronze medals: P. Griffin (IRL), D. Williams (ENG), K. McCormack (WAL).

Vejle, Denmark - 1996
L. Fly: D. Petrov (BUL). **Fly:** A. Pakeev (RUS). **Bantam:** I. Kovacs (HUN). **Feather:** R. Paliani (RUS). **Light:** L. Doroftei (ROM). **L. Welter:** O. Urkal (GER). **Welter:** H. Al (DEN). **L. Middle:** F. Vastag (ROM). **Middle:** S. Ottke (GER). **L. Heavy:** P. Aurino (ITA). **Heavy:** L. Krasniqi (GER). **S. Heavy:** A. Lezin (RUS).
Bronze medals: S. Harrison (SCO), D. Burke (ENG), D. Kelly (IRL).

Minsk, Belarus - 1998
L. Fly: S. Kazakov (RUS). **Fly:** V. Sidorenko (UKR). **Bantam:** S. Danilchenko (UKR). **Feather:** R. Paliani (TUR). **Light:** K. Huste (GER). **L. Welter:** D. Simion (ROM). **Welter:** O. Saitov (RUS). **L. Middle:** F. Esther (FRA). **Middle:** Z. Erdei (HUN). **L. Heavy:** A. Lebsiak (RUS). **Heavy:** G. Fragomeni (ITA). **S. Heavy:** A. Lezin (RUS).
Silver Medals: B. Magee (IRL), C. Fry (ENG).
Bronze medal: C. Bessey (ENG).

Tampere, Finland - 2000
L. Fly: Valeri Sidorenko (UKR). **Fly:** Vladimir Sidorenko (UKR). **Bantam:** A. Agagueloglu (TUR). **Feather:** R. Paliani (TUR). **Light:** A. Maletin (RUS). **L. Welter:** A. Leonev (RUS). **Welter:** B. Ueluesoy (TUR). **L. Middle:** A. Catic (GER). **Middle:** Z. Erdei (HUN). **L. Heavy:** A. Lebsiak (RUS). **Heavy:** J. Chanet (FRA). **S. Heavy:** A. Lezin (RUS).

Perm, Russia - 2002
L. Fly: S. Kazakov (RUS). **Fly:** G. Balakshin (RUS). **Bantam:** K. Khatsygov (BE). **Feather:** R. Malakhbekov (RUS). **Light:** A. Maletin (RUS). **L. Welter:** D. Panayotov (BUL). **Welter:** T. Gaidalov (RUS). **L. Middle:** A. Mishin (RUS). **Middle:** O. Mashkin (UKR). **L. Heavy:** M. Gala (RUS). **Heavy:** E. Makarenko (RUS). **S. Heavy:** A. Povetkin (RUS).

Pula, Croatia - 2004
L. Fly: S. Kazakov (RUS). **Fly:** G. Balakchine (RUS). **Bantam:** G. Kovalev (RUS). **Feather:** V. Tajbert (GER). **Light:** D. Stilianov (BUL). **L. Welter:** A. Maletin (RUS). **Welter:** O. Saitov (RUS). **Middle:** G. Gaiderbekov (RUS). **L. Heavy:** E. Makarenko (RUS). **Heavy:** A. Alekseev (RUS). **S. Heavy:** A. Povetkin (RUS).
Bronze medal: A. Lee (IRL).

Note: Gold medals were awarded to the Europeans who went the furthest in the Olympic Games of 1924, 1928 & 1932.

Plovdiv, Bulgaria - 2006
L. Fly: D. Ayrapetyan (RUS). Fly: G. Balakshin (RUS). Bantam: A. Aliev (RUS). Feather: A. Selimov (RUS). Light: A. Tishchenko (RUS). L. Welter: B. Georgiev (BUL). Welter: A. Balanov (RUS). Middle: M. Korobov (RUS). L. Heavy: A. Beterbiev (RUS). Heavy: D. Poyatsika (UKR). S. Heavy: I. Timurziev (RUS). Bronze medals: S. Smith (ENG), F. Mhura (SCO), K. Egan (IRL).

European Junior Champions, 1970-2007

Miskolc, Hungary - 1970
L. Fly: Gluck (HUN). Fly: Z. Kismeneth (HUN). Bantam: A. Levitschev (URS). Feather: Andrianov (URS). Light: L. Juhasz (HUN). L. Welter: K. Nemec (HUN). Welter: Davidov (URS). L. Middle: A. Lemeschev (URS). Middle: N. Anfimov (URS). L. Heavy: O. Sasche (GDR). Heavy: J. Reder (HUN).
Bronze medals: D. Needham (ENG), R. Barlow (ENG), L. Stevens (ENG).

Bucharest, Romania - 1972
L. Fly: A. Turei (ROM). Fly: Condurat (ROM). Bantam: V. Solomin (URS). Feather: V. Lvov (URS). Light: S. Cutov (ROM). L. Welter: K. Pierwieniecki (POL). Welter: Zorov (URS). L. Middle: Babescu (ROM). Middle: V. Lemeschev (URS). L. Heavy: Mirounik (URS). Heavy: Subutin (URS).
Bronze medals: J. Gale (ENG), R. Maxwell (ENG), D. Odwell (ENG).

Kiev, Russia - 1974
L. Fly: A. Tkachenko (URS). Fly: V. Rybakov (URS). Bantam: C. Andreikovski (BUL). Feather: V. Sorokin (URS). Light: V. Limasov (URS). L. Welter: N. Sigov (URS). Welter: M. Bychkov (URS). L. Middle: V. Danshin (URS). Middle: D. Jende (GDR). L. Heavy: K. Dafinoiu (ROM). Heavy: K. Mashev (BUL).
Silver medal: C. Magri (ENG).
Bronze medals: G. Gilbody (ENG), K. Laing (ENG).

Izmir, Turkey - 1976
L. Fly: C. Seican (ROM). Fly: G. Khratsov (URS). Bantam: M. Navros (URS). Feather: V. Demoianeko (URS). Light: M. Puzovic (YUG). L. Welter: V. Zverev (URS). Welter: K. Ozoglouz (TUR). L. Middle: W. Lauder (SCO). Middle: H. Lenhart (GER). L. Heavy: I. Yantchauskas (URS). Heavy: B. Enjenyan (URS).
Silver medal: J. Decker (ENG).
Bronze medals: I. McLeod (SCO), N. Croombes (ENG).

Dublin, Ireland - 1978
L. Fly: R. Marx (GDR). Fly: D. Radu (ROM). Bantam: S. Khatchatrian (URS). Feather: H. Loukmanov (URS). Light: P. Oliva (ITA). L. Welter: V. Laptiev (URS). Welter: R. Filimanov (URS). L. Middle: A. Beliave (URS). Middle: G. Zinkovitch (URS). L. Heavy: I. Jolta (ROM). Heavy: P. Stoimenov (BUL).
Silver medals: M. Holmes (IRL), P. Hanlon (ENG), M. Courtney (ENG).
Bronze medals: T. Thompson (IRL), J. Turner (ENG), M. Bennett (WAL), J. McAllister (SCO), C. Devine (ENG).

Rimini, Italy - 1980
L. Fly: A. Mikoulin (URS). Fly: J. Varadi (HUN). Bantam: F. Rauschning (GDR). Feather: J. Gladychev (URS). Light: V. Shishov (URS). L. Welter: R. Lomski (BUL). Welter: T. Holonics (GDR). L. Middle: N. Wilshire (ENG). Middle: S. Laptiev (URS). L. Heavy: V. Dolgoun (URS). Heavy: V. Tioumentsev (URS). S. Heavy: S. Kormihtsine (URS).
Bronze medals: N. Potter (ENG), B. McGuigan (IRL), M. Brereton (IRL), D. Cross (ENG).

Schwerin, East Germany - 1982
L. Fly: R. Kabirov (URS). Fly: I. Filchev (BUL). Bantam: M. Stecca (ITA). Feather: B. Blagoev (BUL). Light: E. Chakimov (URS). L. Welter: S. Mehnert (GDR). Welter: T. Schmitz (GDR). L. Middle: B. Shararov (URS). Middle: E. Christie (ENG). L. Heavy: Y. Waulin (URS). Heavy: A. Popov (URS). S. Heavy: V. Aldoshin (URS).
Silver medal: D. Kenny (ENG).
Bronze medal: O. Jones (ENG).

Tampere, Finland - 1984
L. Fly: R. Breitbart (GDR). Fly: D. Berg (GDR). Bantam: K. Khdrian (URS). Feather: O. Nazarov (URS). Light: C. Furnikov (BUL). L. Welter: W. Schmidt (GDR). Welter: K. Doinov (BUL). L. Middle: O. Volkov (URS). Middle: R. Ryll (GDR). L. Heavy: G. Peskov (URS). Heavy: R. Draskovic (YUG). S. Heavy: L. Kamenov (BUL).
Bronze medals: J. Lowey (IRL), F. Harding (ENG), N. Moore (ENG).

Copenhagen, Denmark - 1986
L. Fly: S. Todorov (BUL). Fly: S. Galotian (URS). Bantam: D. Drumm (GDR). Feather: K. Tsziu (URS). Light: G. Akopkhian (URS). L. Welter: F. Vastag (ROM). Welter: S. Karavayev (URS). L. Middle: E. Elibaev (URS). Middle: A. Kurnabka (URS). L. Heavy: A. Schultz (GDR). Heavy: A. Golota (POL). S. Heavy: A. Prianichnikov (URS).

Gdansk, Poland - 1988
L. Fly: I. Kovacs (HUN). Fly: M. Beyer (GDR). Bantam: M. Aitzanov (URS). Feather: M. Rudolph (GDR). Light: M. Shaburov (URS). L. Welter: G.

Campanella (ITA). Welter: D. Konsun (URS). L. Middle: K. Kiselev (URS). Middle: A. Rudenko (URS). L. Heavy: O. Velikanov (URS). Heavy: A. Ter-Okopian (URS). S. Heavy: E. Belusov (URS).
Bronze medals: P. Ramsey (ENG), M. Smyth (WAL).

Usti Nad Labem, Czechoslovakia - 1990
L. Fly: Z. Paliani (URS). Fly: K. Pielert (GDR). Bantam: K. Baravi (URS). Feather: P. Gvasalia (URS). Light: J. Hildenbrandt (GDR). L. Welter: N. Smanov (URS). Welter: A. Preda (ROM). L. Middle: A. Kakauridze (URS). Middle: J. Schwank (GDR). L. Heavy: Iljin (URS). Heavy: I. Andrejev (URS). S. Heavy: W. Fischer (GDR).
Silver medal: A. Todd (ENG).
Bronze medal: P. Craig (ENG).

Edinburgh, Scotland - 1992
L. Fly: M. Ismailov (URS). Fly: F. Brennfuhrer (GER). Bantam: S. Kuchler (GER). Feather: M. Silantiev (URS). Light: S. Shcherbakov (URS). L. Welter: O. Saitov (URS). Welter: H. Kurlumaz (TUR). L. Middle: Z. Erdie (HUN). Middle: V. Zhirov (URS). L. Heavy: D. Gorbachev (URS). Heavy: L. Achkasov (URS). S. Heavy: A. Mamedov (URS).
Silver medals: M. Hall (ENG), B. Jones (WAL).
Bronze medals: F. Slane (IRL), G. Stephens (IRL), C. Davies (WAL).

Salonika, Greece - 1993
L. Fly: O. Kiroukhine (UKR). Fly: R. Husseinov (AZE). Bantam: M. Kulbe (GER). Feather: E. Zakharov (RUS). Light: O. Sergeev (RUS). L. Welter: A. Selihanov (RUS). Welter: O. Kudinov (UKR). L. Middle: E. Makarenko (RUS). Middle: D. Droukovski (RUS). L. Heavy: A. Voida (RUS). Heavy: Vladimir Klitschko (UKR). S. Heavy: A. Moiseev (RUS).
Bronze medal: D. Costello (ENG).

Sifok, Hungary - 1995
L. Fly: D. Gaissine (RUS). Fly: A. Kotelnik (UKR). Bantam: A. Loutsenko (UKR). Feather: S. Harrison (SCO). Light: D. Simon (ROM). L. Welter: B. Ulusoy (TUR). Welter: O. Bouts (UKR). L. Middle: O. Bukalo (UKR). Middle: V. Plettnev (RUS). L. Heavy: A. Derevtsov (RUS). Heavy: C. O'Grady (IRL). S. Heavy: D. Savvine (RUS).
Silver medal: G. Murphy (SCO).
Bronze medal: N. Linford (ENG).

Birmingham, England - 1997
L. Fly: G. Balakshine (RUS). Fly: K. Dzhamoloudinov (RUS). Bantam: A. Shaiduline (RUS). Feather: D. Marciukaitis (LIT). Light: D. Baranov (RUS). L. Welter: A. Mishine (RUS). Welter: D. Yuldashev (UKR). L. Middle: A. Catic (GER). Middle: D. Lebedev (RUS). L. Heavy: V. Uzelkov (UKR). Heavy: S. Koeber (GER). S. Heavy: D. Pirozhenko (RUS).
Silver medal: S. Miller (ENG).
Bronze medals: S. Burke (ENG), M. Dean (ENG), P. Pierson (ENG), M. Lee (IRE).

Rijeka, Croatia - 1999
L. Fly: Kibalyuk (UKR). Fly: A. Bakhtin (RUS). Bantam: V. Simion (ROM). Feather: Kiutkhukow (BUL). Light: Pontilov (RUS). L. Welter: G. Ajetovic (YUG). Welter: S. Nouaouria (FRA). L. Middle: S. Kazantsev (RUS). Middle: D. Tsariouk (RUS). L. Heavy: Alexeev (RUS). Heavy: Alborov (RUS). S. Heavy: Soukhoverkov (RUS).
Bronze medal: S. Birch (ENG).

Sarejevo, Croatia - 2001
L. Fly: A. Taratokin (RUS). Fly: E. Abzalimov (RUS). Bantam: G. Kovaljov (RUS). Feather: M. Hratchev (RUS). Light: S. Aydin (TUR). L. Welter: D. Mikulin (RUS). Welter: O. Bokalo (UKR). L. Middle: M. Korobov (RUS). Middle: I. Bogdanov (UKR). L. Heavy: R. Kahkijev (RUS). Heavy: V. Zuyev (BE). S. Heavy: I. Timurziejev (RUS).
Bronze medal: K. Anderson (SCO).

Warsaw, Poland - 2003
L. Fly: P. Bedak (HUN). Fly: A. Ganev (RUS). Bantam: M. Tretiak (UKR). Feather: A. Alexandru (ROM). Light: A. Aleksiev (RUS). L. Welter: T. Tabotadze (UKR). Welter: Z. Baisangurov (RUS). Middle: J. Machoncev (RUS). L. Heavy: I. Michalkin (RUS). Heavy: Y. Romanov (RUS). S. Heavy: D. Arshba (RUS).
Bronze medal: S. Smith (ENG), F. Gavin (ENG), J. O'Donnell (ENG), T. Jeffries (ENG).

Tallinn, Estonia - 2005
L. Fly: S. Vodopyanov (RUS). Fly: S. Mamodov (AZE). Bantam: A. Akhba (RUS). Feather: M. Ignatev (RUS). Light: I. Iksanov (RUS). L. Welter: A.Zamkovoy (RUS). Welter: M. Koptyakov (RUS). Middle: S. Skiarov (RUS). L.Heavy: D. Chudinov (RUS). Heavy: S. Kalchugin (RUS). S. Heavy: A.Volkov (RUS).
Bronze Medal: J. Joyce (IRL).

Sombor, Serbia - 2007
L.Fly: M.Dvinskiy (RUS). Fly: M.Aloyan (RUS). Bantam: M.Maguire (ENG). Feather: B.Shelestyuk (UKR). Light: V.Shipunov (RUS). L.Welter: D.Lazarev (UKR). Welter: Y.Khytrov (UKR). Middle: N.Jovanovic (SER). L.Heavy:

E.Yakushev (RUS). **Heavy:** V.Kudukhov (RUS). **S.Heavy:** M.Babanin (RUS). **Silver medals:** K.Saeed (ENG), T.Fury (ENG).

Note: The age limit for the championships were reduced from 21 to 19 in 1976.

Commonwealth Champions, 1930-2006

Hamilton, Canada - 1930
Fly: W. Smith (SAF). **Bantam:** H. Mizler (ENG). **Feather:** F. Meacham (ENG). **Light:** J. Rolland (SCO). **Welter:** L. Hall (SAF). **Middle:** F. Mallin (ENG). **L. Heavy:** J. Goyder (ENG). **Heavy:** V. Stuart (ENG).
Silver medals: T. Pardoe (ENG), T. Holt (SCO).
Bronze medals: A. Lyons (SCO), A. Love (ENG), F. Breeman (ENG).

Wembley, England - 1934
Fly: P. Palmer (ENG). **Bantam:** F. Ryan (ENG). **Feather:** C. Cattarall (SAF). **Light:** L. Cook (WAL). **Welter:** D. McCleave (ENG). **Middle:** A. Shawyer (ENG). **L. Heavy:** G. Brennan (ENG). **Heavy:** P. Floyd (ENG).
Silver medals: A. Barnes (WAL), J. Jones (WAL), F. Taylor (WAL), J. Holton (SCO).
Bronze medals: J. Pottinger (WAL), T. Wells (SCO), H. Moy (ENG), W. Duncan (NIR), J. Magill (NIR), Lord D. Douglas-Hamilton (SCO).

Melbourne, Australia - 1938
Fly: J. Joubert (SAF). **Bantam:** W. Butler (ENG). **Feather:** A. Henricus (CEY). **Light:** H. Groves (ENG). **Welter:** W. Smith (AUS). **Middle:** D. Reardon (WAL). **L. Heavy:** N. Wolmarans (SAF). **Heavy:** T. Osborne (CAN).
Silver medals: J. Watson (SCO), M. Dennis (ENG).
Bronze medals: H. Cameron (SCO), J. Wilby (ENG).

Auckland, New Zealand - 1950
Fly: H. Riley (SCO). **Bantam:** J. van Rensburg (SAF). **Feather:** H. Gilliland (SCO). **Light:** R. Latham (ENG). **Welter:** T. Ratcliffe (ENG). **Middle:** T. van Schalkwyk (SAF). **L. Heavy:** D. Scott (ENG). **Heavy:** F. Creagh (NZL).
Bronze medal: P. Brander (ENG).

Vancouver, Canada - 1954
Fly: R. Currie (SCO). **Bantam:** J. Smillie (SCO). **Feather:** L. Leisching (SAF). **Light:** P. van Staden (SR). **L. Welter:** M. Bergin (CAN). **Welter:** N. Gargano (ENG). **L. Middle:** W. Greaves (CAN). **Middle:** J. van de Kolff (SAF). **L. Heavy:** P. van Vuuren (SAF). **Heavy:** B. Harper (ENG).
Silver medals: M. Collins (WAL), F. McQuillan (SCO).
Bronze medals: D. Charnley (ENG), B. Wells (ENG).

Cardiff, Wales - 1958
Fly: R. Davies (SCO). **Bantam:** H. Winstone (WAL). **Feather:** W. Taylor (AUS). **Light:** R. McTaggart (SCO). **L. Welter:** H. Loubscher (SAF). **Welter:** J. Greyling (SAF). **L. Middle:** G. Webster (SAF). **Middle:** T. Milligan (NIR). **L. Heavy:** A. Madigan (AUS). **Heavy:** D. Bekker (SAF).
Silver medals: T. Bache (ENG), M. Collins (WAL), J. Jordan (NIR), R. Kane (SCO), S. Pearson (ENG), A. Higgins (WAL), D. Thomas (ENG).
Bronze medals: P. Lavery (NIR), D. Braithwaite (WAL), R. Hanna (NIR), A. Owen (SCO), J. McClory (NIR), J. Cooke (ENG), J. Jacobs (ENG), B. Nancurvis (ENG), R. Scott (SCO), W. Brown (WAL), J. Caiger (ENG), W. Bannon (SCO), R. Pleace (WAL).

Perth, Australia - 1962
Fly: R. Mallon (SCO). **Bantam:** J. Dynevor (AUS). **Feather:** J. McDermott (SCO). **Light:** E. Blay (GHA). **L. Welter:** C. Quartey (GHA). **Welter:** W. Coe (NZL). **L. Middle:** H. Mann (CAN). **Middle:** M. Calhoun (JAM). **L. Heavy:** A. Madigan (AUS). **Heavy:** G. Oywello (UGA).
Silver medals: R. McTaggart (SCO), J. Pritchett (ENG).
Bronze medals: M. Pye (ENG), P. Benneyworth (ENG), B. Whelan (ENG), B. Brazier (ENG), C. Rice (NIR), T. Menzies (SCO), H. Christie (NIR), A. Turmel (CI).

Kingston, Jamaica - 1966
Fly: S. Shittu (GHA). **Bantam:** E. Ndukwu (NIG). **Feather:** P. Waruinge (KEN). **Light:** A. Andeh (NIG). **L. Welter:** J. McCourt (NIR). **Welter:** E. Blay (GHA). **Middle:** M. Rowe (ENG). **Middle:** J. Darkey (GHA). **L. Heavy:** R. Tighe (ENG). **Heavy:** J. Kini (NZL).
Silver medals: P. Maguire (NIR), R. Thurston (ENG), R. Arthur (ENG), T. Imrie (SCO).
Bronze medals: S. Lockhart (NIR), A. Peace (SCO), F. Young (NIR), J. Turpin (ENG), D. McAlinden (NIR).

Edinburgh, Scotland - 1970
L. Fly: J. Odwori (UGA). **Fly:** D. Needham (ENG). **Bantam:** S. Shittu (GHA). **Feather:** P. Waruinge (KEN). **Light:** A. Adeyemi (NIG). **L. Welter:** M. Muruli (UGA). **Welter:** E. Ankudey (GHA). **L. Middle:** T. Imrie (SCO). **Middle:** J. Conteh (ENG). **L. Heavy:** F. Ayinla (NIG). **Heavy:** B. Masanda (UGA).
Silver medals: T. Davies (WAL), J. Gillan (SCO), D. Davies (WAL), J. McKinty (NIR).
Bronze medals: M. Abrams (ENG), A. McHugh (SCO), D. Larmour (NIR), S. Oglivie (SCO), A. Richardson (ENG), T. Joyce (SCO), P. Doherty (NIR), J. Rafferty (SCO), L. Stevens (ENG).

Christchurch, New Zealand - 1974
L. Fly: S. Muchoki (KEN). **Fly:** D. Larmour (NIR). **Bantam:** P. Cowdell (ENG). **Feather:** E. Ndukwu (NIG). **Light:** A. Kalule (UGA). **L. Welter:** O. Nwankpa (NIG). **Welter:** M. Muruli (UGA). **L. Middle:** L. Mwale (ZAM). **Middle:** F. Lucas (STV). **L. Heavy:** W. Knight (ENG). **Heavy:** N. Meade (ENG).
Silver medals: E. McKenzie (WAL), A. Harrison (SCO).
Bronze medals: J. Bambrick (SCO), J. Douglas (SCO), J. Rodgers (NIR), S. Cooney (SCO), R. Davies (ENG), C. Speare (ENG), G. Ferris (NIR).

Edmonton, Canada - 1978
L. Fly: S. Muchoki (KEN). **Fly:** M. Irungu (KEN). **Bantam:** B. McGuigan (NIR). **Feather:** A. Nelson (GHA). **Light:** G. Hamill (NIR). **L. Welter:** W. Braithwaite (GUY). **Welter:** M. McCallum (JAM). **L. Middle:** K. Perlette (CAN). **Middle:** P. McElwaine (AUS). **L. Heavy:** R. Fortin (CAN). **Heavy:** J. Awome (ENG).
Silver medals: J. Douglas (SCO), K. Beattie (NIR), D. Parkes (ENG), V. Smith (ENG).
Bronze medals: H. Russell (NIR), M. O'Brien (ENG), J. McAllister (SCO), T. Feal (WAL).

Brisbane, Australia - 1982
L. Fly: A. Wachire (KEN). **Fly:** M. Mutua (KEN). **Bantam:** J. Orewa (NIG). **Feather:** P. Konyegwachie (NIG). **Light:** H. Khalili (KEN). **L. Welter:** C. Ossai (NIG). **Welter:** C. Pyatt (ENG). **L. Middle:** S. O'Sullivan (CAN). **Middle:** J. Price (ENG). **L. Heavy:** F. Sani (FIJ). **Heavy:** W. de Wit (CAN).
Silver medals: J. Lyon (ENG), J. Kelly (SCO), R. Webb (NIR), P. Hanlon (ENG), J. McDonnell (ENG), N. Croombes (ENG), H. Hylton (ENG).
Bronze medals: R. Gilbody (ENG), C. McIntosh (ENG), R. Corr (NIR).

Edinburgh, Scotland - 1986
L. Fly: S. Olson (CAN). **Fly:** J. Lyon (ENG). **Bantam:** S. Murphy (ENG). **Feather:** B. Downey (CAN). **Light:** A. Dar (CAN). **L. Welter:** H. Grant (CAN). **Welter:** D. Dyer (ENG). **L. Middle:** D. Sherry (CAN). **Middle:** R. Douglas (ENG). **L. Heavy:** J. Moran (ENG). **Heavy:** J. Peau (NZL). **S. Heavy:** L. Lewis (CAN).
Silver medals: M. Epton (ENG), R. Nash (NIR), P. English (ENG), N. Haddock (WAL), J. McAlister (SCO), H. Lawson (SCO), D. Young (SCO), A. Evans (WAL).
Bronze medals: W. Docherty (SCO), J. Todd (NIR), K. Webber (WAL), G. Brooks (SCO), J. Wallace (SCO), C. Carleton (NIR), J. Jacobs (ENG), B. Lowe (NIR), D. Denny (NIR), G. Thomas (WAL), A. Mullen (SCO), G. Ferrie (SCO), P. Tinney (NIR), B. Pullen (WAL), E. Cardouza (ENG), J. Oyebola (ENG), J. Sillitoe (CI).

Auckland, New Zealand - 1990
L. Fly: J. Juuko (UGA). **Fly:** W. McCullough (NIR). **Bantam:** S. Mohammed (NIG). **Feather:** J. Irwin (ENG). **Light:** G. Nyakana (UGA). **L. Welter:** C. Kane (SCO). **Welter:** D. Defiagbon (NIG). **L. Middle:** R. Woodhall (ENG). **Middle:** C. Johnson (CAN). **L. Heavy:** J. Akhasamba (KEN). **Heavy:** G. Onyango (KEN). **S. Heavy:** M. Kenny (NZL).
Bronze medals: D. Anderson (SCO), M. Edwards (ENG), P. Douglas (NIR).

Victoria, Canada - 1994
L. Fly: H. Ramadhani (KEN). **Fly:** P. Shepherd (SCO). **Bantam:** R. Peden (AUS). **Feather:** C. Patton (CAN). **Light:** M. Strange (CAN). **L. Welter:** P. Richardson (ENG). **Welter:** N. Sinclair (NIR). **L. Middle:** J. Webb (NIR). **Middle:** R. Donaldson (CAN). **L. Heavy:** D. Brown (CAN). **Heavy:** O. Ahmed (KEN). **S. Heavy:** D. Dokiwari (NIG).
Silver medals: S. Oliver (ENG), J. Cook (WAL), M. Renaghan (NIR), M. Winters (NIR), J. Wilson (SCO).
Bronze medals: D. Costello (ENG), J. Townsley (SCO), D. Williams (ENG).

Kuala Lumpar, Malaysia - 1998
L. Fly: S. Biki (MAS). **Fly:** R. Sunee (MRI). **Bantam:** M. Yomba (TAN). **Feather:** A. Arthur (CAN). **Light:** R. Narh (GHA). **L. Welter:** M. Strange (CAN). **Welter:** J. Molitor (CAN). **L. Middle:** C. Bessey (ENG). **Middle:** J. Pearce (ENG). **L. Heavy:** C. Fry (ENG). **Heavy:** M. Simmons (CAN). **S. Heavy:** A. Harrison (ENG).
Silver medal: L. Cunningham (NIR).
Bronze medals: G. Jones (ENG), A. McLean (ENG), C. McNeil (SCO), J. Townsley (SCO), B. Magee (NIR), K. Evans (WAL).

Manchester, England - 2002
L. Fly: M. Ali Qamar (IND). **Fly:** K. Kanyanta (ZAM). **Bantam:** J. Kane (AUS). **Feather:** H. Ali (PAK). **Light:** J. Arthur (WAL). **L. Welter:** D. Barker (ENG). **Welter:** D. Geale (AUS). **L. Middle:** J. Pascal (CAN). **Middle:** P. Miller (AUS). **L. Heavy:** J. Albert (NIG). **Heavy:** J. Douglas (CAN). **S. Heavy:** D. Dolan (ENG).
Silver medals: D. Langley (ENG), P. Smith (ENG), S. Birch (ENG).
Bronze medals: M. Moran (ENG), A. Morris (ENG), C. McEwan (SCO), A. Young (SCO), K. Evans (WAL).

Melbourne, Australia - 2006
L. Fly: J. Utoni (NAM). **Fly:** D. Broadhurst (ENG). **Bantam:** G. Kumar (FIJ). **Feather:** S. Smith (ENG). **Light:** F. Gavin (ENG). **L. Welter:** J. Cox (ENG). **Welter:** B. Mwelase (SA). **Middle:** J. Fletcher (AUS). **L. Heavy:** K. Anderson (SCO). **Heavy:** B. Pitt (AUS). **S. Heavy:** D. Price (ENG).
Silver medals: D. Langley (ENG), K. Evans (WAL).
Bronze medals: M. Nasir (WAL), D. Edwards (WAL), J. Crees (WAL), N. Perkins (ENG), J. Degale (ENG).

The Triple Hitters' Boxing Quiz: Part 12

Compiled by Ralph Oates

QUESTIONS

1. On 26 March 1914, Percy Jones made the first defence of his European and World flyweight titles when he outpointed Eugene Criqui over twenty rounds in Liverpool. What was the nationality of Criqui?
   A. Italian.   B. French.   C. Spanish.

2. Bob Marriott won the vacant British lightweight title on 23 June 1919 when he defeated Johnny Summers by a disqualification. In which round?
   A. Eighth.   B. Ninth.   C. Tenth.

3. In which weight division was Tom Gummer a British champion?
   A. Lightweight.   B. Welterweight.   C. Middleweight.

4. On 18 July 1929, James J. Braddock failed in his attempt to win the World light-heavyweight crown when he was outpointed over fifteen rounds by the defending champion, Tommy Loughran. Who was the referee for this contest?
   A. Leo Houck.   B. Eddie Forbes.   C. Harry Graham.

5. Jimmy Walsh won the British lightweight title on 24 April 1936 when he stopped the defending champion, Jack Kid Berg. In which round?
   A. Seventh.   B. Eighth.   C. Ninth.

6. Billy Conn retained the NY/NBA version of the World light-heavyweight title on 5 June 1940 when he outpointed Gus Lesnevich over fifteen rounds. Where did this contest take place?
   A. Miami.   B. Detroit.   C. New York.

7. On 27 August 1943, Sugar Ray Robinson met Henry Armstrong in a ten-round contest and won by which method?
   A. Fourth-round stoppage.   B. Eighth-round knockout.
   C. Points.

8. Future British, European and Commonwealth welterweight champion, Ralph Charles, made his professional debut on 29 October 1963, knocking out which opponent in round two?
   A. Johnny Brown.   B. Bill Rowan.   C. Maurice Lloyd.

9. On 28 May 1964, the former British and World middleweight champion, Terry Downes, outpointed Ed Zaremba over ten rounds. In which part of Scotland did this contest take place?
   A. Glasgow.   B. Edinburgh.   C. Dundee.

10. In which round did the future British, European and Commonwealth heavyweight champion, Jack Bodell, stop Bob Stallings on 13 December 1966?
    A. Fifth.   B. Sixth.   C. Seventh.

11. Billy Walker defeated Giulio Rinaldi by a disqualification in the opening round on 13 February 1967. This contest took place in Manchester. On how many occasions in the professional ranks had Walker boxed in Manchester at that point?
    A. Once.   B. Twice.   C. Three.

12. During his career, which boxer did the former British, European and WBC World featherweight champion, Howard Winstone, not meet in the professional ranks?
    A. Jimmy Henderson.   B. Jimmy Revie.
    C. John O'Brien.

13. On 14 September 1967, the future World lightweight champion, Ken Buchanan, stopped Al Rocca in round seven. At this stage of his career, Buchanan was undefeated in 22 professional bouts. How many had he won inside the distance?
    A. Six.   B. Seven.   C. Eight.

14. On 20 May 1969, the future British and Commonwealth middleweight king, Mark Rowe, met Doug Huntley in an eight-round contest. What was the result?
    A. Points win for Rowe.   B. Points win for Huntley.
    C. A draw.

15. The then reigning British featherweight champion, Vernon Sollas, defeated Arnold Taylor on 24 November 1976 by way of an eighth-round retirement. In which weight division had Taylor previously held a WBA world title?
    A. Flyweight.   B. Bantamweight.   C. Featherweight.

16. How many bouts did the Eurosport boxing commentator, Steve Holdsworth, have during his professional career?
    A. Ten.   B. Eleven.   C. Twelve.

17. Jim Watt won the vacant European lightweight championship on 5 August 1977 when he stopped Andre Holyk in the opening round. How many successful defences of the European title did Watt make before he relinquished the crown?
    A. One.   B. Two.   C. Three.

18. In which round did Johnny Owen stop Wayne Evans

in defence of his British bantamweight title on 6 April 1978?
A. Ninth.   B. Tenth.   C. Eleventh.

19. Alan Minter won the World middleweight title on 16 March 1980 when he outpointed the defending champion, Vito Antuofermo, over fifteen rounds in Las Vegas. At that stage of his career how many professional bouts had Minter taken part in?
A. 44.   B. 45.   C. 46.

20. On 20 October 1986, the future British featherweight champion, Gary De'Roux, stopped Nigel Lawrence. In which round?
A. First.   B. Second.   C. Third.

21. Chris Pyatt lost his European light-middleweight crown in his first defence, on 28 January 1987, when he was outpointed over twelve rounds by Gianfranco Rosi. In which country did this contest take place?
A. England.   B. Italy.   C. Spain.

22. Lloyd Honeyghan lost his WBC World welterweight title in Las Vegas on 5 February 1989 to the former WBA holder of the crown, Marlon Starling, when stopped. In which round?
A. Seventh.   B. Eighth.   C. Ninth.

23. On 14 February 1989, Billy Hardy retained his British bantamweight title when he defeated Ronnie Carroll. By which method?
A. Fourth-round stoppage.   B. Sixth-round knockout.
C. Twelve-round points decision.

24. James Toney retained the IBF version of the World middleweight championship on 29 June 1991 when he outpointed Reggie Johnson over twelve rounds. In which part of America did this contest take place?
A. Atlantic City.   B. Las Vegas.   C. Boston.

25. On 8 December 1995, Colin Dunne won the vacant Southern Area lightweight title when he stopped Jonathan Thaxton in round five. At this stage of his career, Dunne was undefeated. How many professional contests had he taken part in?
A. Fourteen.   B. Fifteen.   C. Sixteen.

26. In a final eliminator for the WBC World super-middleweight title, Glenn Catley stopped Eric Lucas in round twelve on 10 December 1999. In which country did this contest take place?
A. England.   B. Canada.   C. Australia.

27. Which version of the World middleweight title did Iran Barkley formerly hold?
A. WBC.   B. WBA.   C. IBF.

28. During his career, which opponent did the former European and WBO World featherweight champion, Steve Robinson, not box in the professional ranks?
A. Colin Lynch.   B. Brian Roche.   C. Gary De'Roux.

29. On 19 February 2000, Ian McLeod won the Commonwealth super-featherweight title when he stopped the defending champion, Mick O'Malley, in round six. Who was the referee for this contest?
A. Richie Davies.   B. Paul Thomas.   C. Roy Francis.

30. During her career, which opponent did Michelle Sutcliffe not box in the professional ranks?
A. Regina Halmich.   B. Cathy Brown.   C. Daisy Lang.

31. On 14 July 2001, Billy Schwer lost his IBO World light-welterweight title when Pablo Sarmiento stopped him. In which round?
A. Tenth.   B. Eleventh.   C. Twelfth.

32. Brian Coleman lost a four-round points decision to Ronnie Nailen on 8 June 2002. At this stage of his career, how many professional bouts had Coleman taken part in?
A. 134.   B. 135.   C. 136.

33. On 21 December 2002, David Walker and Jimmy Vincent met in a final eliminator for the British welterweight title. What was the result?
A. Eighth-round stoppage win for Vincent.   B. Ninth-round knockout win for Walker.   C. A draw.

34. In defence of his British super-featherweight title on 12 July 2003, in which round did Alex Arthur stop Willie Limond?
A. Sixth.   B. Seventh.   C. Eighth.

35. During his career, how many professional bouts did the former World flyweight and European bantamweight champion, Peter Kane, have?
A. 102.   B. 103.   C. 104.

36. On 19 November 2004, Michael Hunter retained the British super-bantamweight crown when he stopped Marc Callaghan in round ten. Hunter and Callaghan had previously boxed each other in a six-round contest on 18 March 2002. What was the result on that occasion?
A. Points win for Hunter.   B. A draw.
C. Points win for Callaghan.

37. Ross Minter won the Southern Area welterweight title when he stopped the holder, Chas Symonds, in round three on 29 April 2005. Ross is the son of the former World middleweight champion, Alan Minter.
True or False?

38. On 29 April 2005, Lee Haskins stopped Andrzej Ziora in the opening round. Who was Haskins' manager at the time?
A. Frank Maloney. B. Tania Follett. C. Chris Sanigar.

39. Nicky Cook became a triple champion when defending his European and Commonwealth titles at featherweight and challenging for the British crown against Dazzo Williams, whom he knocked out in two rounds on 16 June 2005. Who was the referee for this contest?
A. Phil Edwards. B. John Keane. C. Howard Foster.

40. In which weight division was Ross Hale a British and Commonwealth champion?
A. Lightweight. B. Light-welterweight.
C. Welterweight.

41. Peter Haymer retained his English light-heavyweight title on 19 June 2005 when he defeated Tony Oakey. By which method?
A. Fourth-round stoppage. B. Sixth-round knockout.
C. Ten-round points decision.

42. Which boxer started his professional career with a drawn decision over six rounds?
A. Colin Lynes. B. Junior Witter. C. Ricky Hatton.

43. Which of the following did not box in the southpaw stance?
A. Marvin Hagler. B. Jim Watt. C. Floyd Patterson.

44. Which former World flyweight champion was nicknamed 'The Ghost with a Hammer in his Hand'?
A. Charlie Magri. B. Jimmy Wilde.
C. Walter McGowan.

45. During his professional career how many World light-middleweight title bouts did the former WBC titleholder, Maurice Hope, participate in?
A. Four. B. Five. C. Six.

46. Arturo Gatti lost his WBC World light-welterweight title on 25 June 2005, when retiring in round six against Floyd Mayweather. In which part of America did this contest take place?
A. Boston. B. Atlantic City. C. Los Angeles.

47. On 21 October 2005, Junior Witter retained his British, European and Commonwealth light-welterweight titles when he defeated Colin Lynes. By which method?
A. Fifth-round stoppage. B. Eighth-round knockout.
C. Twelve-round points decision.

48. David Haye won the European cruiserweight title on 16 December 2005 when he knocked out the holder, Alexander Gurov, in the opening round. Prior to Haye, who was the last British fighter to hold this championship?
A. Terry Dunstan. B. Carl Thompson.
C. Johnny Nelson.

49. On 17 December 2005, Nicolai Valuev won the WBA World heavyweight title when he outpointed the holder, John Ruiz, over twelve rounds. What is Valuev's nickname?
A. Eastern Assassin. B. Beast from the East.
C. Eastern Beast.

50. The WBO World super-middleweight champion, Joe Calzaghe, met Jeff Lacy, the IBF and IBO king, in a unification match on 4 March 2006. By which method did Calzaghe win?
A. Fifth-round stoppage. B. Eighth-round knockout.
C. Twelve-round points decision.

Warmly Remembered

Mike Higgins

30th April 1961 – 6th August 2006

Once an amateur boxer, Mike had a real passion for the boxing game. He worked at Speedy Hire Plc – the UK's leading hirer of tools and equipment- for the last 19 years of his life helping to build the national accounts team into one of the most successful in the industry.

Mike was a man who really left a lasting impression on everyone who had the good fortune to meet him; the number of people who feel his loss is a true tribute to him.

From all of your friends and colleagues at Speedy, in the construction industry and within boxing circles.

Directory of Ex-Boxers' Associations

by Ray Caulfield

BOURNEMOUTH Founded 1980. HQ: The Cricketers, Windham Road, off Ashley Road, Bournemouth. Dai Dower MBE (P); Dave Fry (C); Peter Judge (VC); Percy Singer (T); Jack Streek (S), 38 St Leonard's Farm, Ringwood Road, Ferndown, Dorset BH22 0AG (0120 289 4647)

BRIGHTON Formed 2007. HQ: Southwick Football Club, Old Barn Way, off Manor Hall Way, Southwick, Sussex. Alan Minter (P); Ernie Price (C); Barry Noonan (VC); Mick Smith (PRO); Karen Knight (T & S), 1 Tall Trees, Penstone Park, Lancing, West Sussex BN15 9AG (0190 376 6893). E-mail: kazzie.knight@homecall.co.uk

CORK Founded 1973. HQ: Glen Boxing Club, Blackpool, Cork. William O'Leary (P & C); Phil Murray (VC); John Martin (S); John Donovan (T)

CORNWALL Founded 1989. HQ: Upper Tolcarne House, Burras, Wendron, Helston. Salvo Nucciforo (VC); Eric Bradshaw (T); Stan Cullis (P & PRO), Upper Tolcarne House, Burras, Wendron, Helston, Cornwall TR13 0JD (0120 983 1463). E-mail: stan@cullis1.freeserve.co.uk

CROYDON Founded 1982. HQ: Ivy House Club, Campbell Road, West Croydon. Gilbert Allnutt (P); Derek O'Dell (T); Barry Penny (C); Simon Euan-Smith (PRO); Paul Nihill MBE (S), 24 Walderslade Road, Chatham, Kent ME4 6NZ (0163 440 4240/0208 651 2742)

EASTERN AREA Founded 1973. HQ: Coach & Horses, Union Street, Norwich. Brian Fitzmaurice (P); Ron Springall (S & T); Clive Campling (C), 54 Robson Road, Norwich, Norfolk NR5 8NZ

HOME COUNTIES Founded 2005. HQ: Golden Lion Public House, High Street, London Colney, Herts. Terry Downes (P); Bob Williams (C); Ann Ayles (T); Dave Ayles (S), 144 Trident Drive, Houghton Regis, Dunstable, Beds LU5 5QQ

HULL & EAST YORKSHIRE Founded 1993. HQ: Crooked Billett, Holdens Road, Hull or Kings Arms, King Street, Bridlington. Don Harrison (C); Johnny Borrill (P); Len Storey (S); Bert Smith (T), 54 St Aidan Road, Bridlington, E. Yorks (0126 267 2573)

IPSWICH Founded 1970. HQ: Loco Club, Station Street, Stoke, Ipswich. Alby Kingham (P); Chris Collins (PRO); Vic Thurlow (C & T); Michael Thurlow (S), 147 Clapgate Lane, Ipswich, Suffolk IP3 0RF (0147 382 3042). E-mail: mickandjan1912@btinternet.com

IRISH Founded 1973. HQ: National Boxing Stadium, South Circular Road, Dublin. Val Harris (P); Martin Gannon (C); Tommy Butler (T); Paddy O'Reilly (VC); Willie Duggan (S), 175 Kimmage Road West, Dublin 6W

KENT Founded 1967. HQ: RAFA Club, Dock Road, Chatham. Harry Doherty (P); Bill Quinton (C); Paul Nihill MBE (S, PRO & T), 24 Walderslade Road, Chatham, Kent ME4 6NZ (0163 440 4240)

LEEDS Founded 1952. HQ: North Leeds WMC, Lincoln Green Road, Leeds. Alan Richardson (P); Kevin Cunningham (C); Peter Selby (S); Alan Alster (T); Frank Johnson (PRO), 82 Windmill Chase, Rothwell, Leeds, Yorks LS26 0XB (0113 288 7753)

LEICESTER Founded 1972. HQ: The Jungle Club, Checketts Road, Leicester. Mick Greaves (P & C); Fred Roberts (T), Alan Parr (S & PRO), 22 Hewes Close, Glen Parva, Leicester LE2 9NU (0116 277 9327/0791 332 3950). E-mail: alan.parr3@btinternet.com

LONDON Founded 1971. HQ; The Queen Mary College, Bancroft Road, Mile End, London E1. Stephen Powell (P); Micky O'Sullivan (C); Charlie Wright (VC); Ray Caulfield (T); Mrs Mary Powell (S), 36 St Peters Street, Islington, London N1 8JT (0207 226 9032). E-mail: marypowell@btconnect.com

MANCHESTER Founded 1968. HQ: Crown & Cushion, Corporation Street, Manchester M4 4DU. Tommy Proffitt (LP); Jack Edwards (P); Neville Tetlow (VC); Kenny Baker (T); John Redfern (PRO); Jimmy Lewis (C); Eddie Copeland (S), 9 Lakeside, Hadfield, Glossop, Derbys SK13 1HW (0145 786 8142). E-mail: edwin@edwin8.wanadoo.co.uk

MERSEYSIDE (Liverpool) Founded 1973. HQ: Arriva Club, Hockenhall Alley, Liverpool. Harry Scott (P); Terry Carson (C); Tony Smith (VC); Tommy Brown (PRO); Jim Jenkinson (S & T), 13 Brooklands Avenue, Waterloo, Liverpool, Merseyside L22 3XY (0151 928 0301). E-mail: mersey-wirralformerboxers@hotmail.com. Website: www.mfba.org.uk

MIDLANDS Founded 2002. HQ: The Portland Pavilion, Portland Road, Edgbaston, Birmingham. Bunny Johnson (P); Martin Florey (C); Paul Rowson (VC); Stephen Florey (T); Jerry Hjelter (S & PRO), 67 Abberley Avenue, Stourport on Severn, Warwicks DY13 0LY (0129 987 9907). E-mail: jerryhjboxing@hotmail.com. Website: www.midlandexboxersassociation.fortunecity.com/index.html

NORTHAMPTONSHIRE Founded 1981. HQ: Semilong Working Mens Club, 212 St Andrews Road, Northampton. Dick Rogers (P); Gil Wilson (C); Mick Doran (VC); George Ward (PRO); Mrs Pam Ward (S & T), 6 Derwent Close, Kings Heath, Northampton NN5 7JS (0160 458 3057)

NORTHERN FEDERATION Founded 1974. Several member EBAs. Annual Gala. Jimmy Lewis (P); Terry Carson (C); John Redfern (PRO); Eddie Copeland (S & T), 9 Lakeside, Hadfield, Glossop, Derbys SK13 1HW

NORTHERN IRELAND Founded 1970. HQ: Ulster Sports Club, High Street, Belfast. Gerry Hassett (P); Cecil Martin (C); S.Thompson (T); Terry Milligan (S), 32 Rockdale Street, Belfast BT12 7PA

NORTH STAFFS & SOUTH CHESHIRE Founded 1969. HQ: The Roe Buck, Wedgwood Place, Burslem, Stoke on Trent. Roy Simms (C); Larry Parkes (VC); Les Dean (S & PRO); John

Greatbach (T); Billy Tudor (P), 133 Springbank Road, Chell Heath, Stoke on Trent, Staffs ST6 6HW (0163 067 2484)

NORWICH Founded 1990. HQ: Wymondham Snooker Club, Town Green, Wymondham, Norfolk. Les King (P & C); Len Jarvis (T); Reg Harris (S) (0195 360 3997)

NOTTINGHAM Founded 1979. HQ: The Wheatsheaf, Sneinton Road, Nottingham. Len Chorley (P); Walter Spencer (C); Mick Smith (VC); Gary Rooksby (T); John Kinsella (PRO); Graham Rooksby (S), 42 Spinney Road, Keyworth, Notts NG12 5LN (0115 937 5242). E-mail: nebsa@rooksby.com

PLYMOUTH Founded 1982. HQ: Stoke Social Club, Devonport Road, Plymouth. Tom Pryce-Davies (P); Jimmy Ryan (C); Jimmy Bevel (VC); Arthur Willis (T); Pat Crago (S & PRO), 8 Hawkinge Gardens, Ernsettle, Plymouth, Devon PL5 2RJ (0175 236 6339). E-mail: crago@blueyonder.co.uk

PRESTON Founded 1973. HQ: Barney's Piano Bar, Church Street, Preston. John Allen (C & S); Eddie Monahan (P); Bobby Rhodes (T), 1 Norris Street, Preston, Lancs PR1 7PX

ST HELENS Founded 1983. HQ: Royal Naval Association, Volunteer Street, St Helens. Ray Britch (C); Tommy McNamara (T); Paul Britch (S), 16 Oxley Street, Sutton, St Helens, Merseyside WA9 3PE

SCOTTISH Founded 1997. HQ: Iron Horse Public House, West Nile Street, Glasgow. John McCluskey (P); Frank O'Donnell (LP); Al Hutcheon (C); Phil McIntyre (VC); Peter Baines (T); Liam McColgan (S), 25 Dalton Avenue, Linnvale, Clydebank, West Dunbartonshire G81 2SH (0141 562 5575). E-mail: p.baines20@ntlworld.com

SHEFFIELD & SOUTH YORKSHIRE Founded 1974. Reformed 2002. HQ: The Richmond Hotel, 443 Richmond Road, Sheffield. Billy Calvert (P & T); Harry Carnell (C); Eric Goodlad (VC); John Redfern (S & PRO), 33 Birch Avenue, Chapeltown, Sheffield, South Yorks S35 1RQ (0114 257 8326)

SQUARE RING (TORBAY) Founded 1978. HQ: Snooty Fox Hotel, St Marychurch. Ken Wittey (C); Johnny Mudge (S); Jim Banks (T); Paul King (P & VC), 8 Winchester Avenue, Torquay, Devon TQ2 8AR

SUNDERLAND Founded 1959. HQ: River Wear Social Club, Whitehouse Road, Hendon, Sunderland. George Martin (P); Ted Lynn (C); John Brown (VC); Andy Parkin (PRO); Les Simm (T & S), 21 Orchard Street, Pallion, Sunderland, Tyne & Wear SR4 6QL (0191 514 1809)

SUSSEX Founded 1974. Reformed 2003. HQ: British Legion Club, Shirley Street, Hove. Tommy Mellis (P); Mick Smith (PRO); John McNeil (C); Ian Hargie (T); Karen Knight (S), 1 Tal Trees, Penstone Park, Lancing, West Sussex BN15 9AG (0190 376 6893). E-mail: kazzie.knight@homecall.co.uk Website: www.sussexexboxers.com

SWANSEA & SOUTH WEST WALES Founded 1983. HQ: The Conservative Club, Swansea. Cliff Curvis (P); Gordon Pape (C); Len Smith (S), 105 Cockett Road, Swansea, Glamorgan SA2 0FG

TYNESIDE Founded 1970. HQ: The Pelaw Social Club, Heworth House, Kirkstone Road, Pelaw, Gateshead. Maxie Walsh (P, PRO & C); John Jarrett (VC); Malcolm Dinning (T); Maxie Walsh (P, C & S), c/o 9 Prendwick Court, Hebburn, Tyne & Wear NE31 2NQ (0191 483 4267)

WELSH Founded 1976. HQ: Rhydyfelin Labour Club, Pontypridd. Patron: Lord Brooks of Tremorfa. Wynford Jones (P); John Floyd (C); Peter Rogers (VC); Mark Warner (T); Don James (S), 5 Aeron Terrace, Twynyroyn, Merthyr Tydfil, South Wales C47 0LN

WIRRAL Founded 1973. Reformed 2003. HQ: RNA Club, Thornbury Park Road East, Birkenhead. Frank Johnson (P); Pat Garry (T); Terry Carson (C); Pat McAteer (VC); Alan Crowther (S), 15 Scythia Close, New Ferry, Wirral, Merseyside CH62 1HH (0151 645 0466). Website: www.lmu.livjm.ac.uk/inmylife/channels/sport/1116.htm

The above information is set at the time of going to press and no responsibility can be taken for any changes in officers or addresses of HQs that may happen between then and publication or changes that have not been notified to me.

ABBREVIATIONS

P - President. HP - Honorary President. LP - Life President. AP - Acting President. C - Chairman. VC - Vice Chairman. T - Treasurer. S - Secretary. PRO - Public Relations Officer and/or Press Officer.

Ray Caulfield (right) is seen here with Evan Armstrong, the former British & Commonwealth featherweight champion, prior to presenting Evan with a solid silver plaque to commemorate his Commonwealth title win in 1974

Obituaries

by Derek O'Dell

It is impossible to list everyone, but I have again done my best to include final tributes for as many of the well-known boxers and other familiar names within the sport who have passed away since the 2007 Yearbook was published. We honour them and remember them.

AGLAND Roy *From* Tir-y-Berth, Wales. *Died* 6 November 2006, aged 80. Geraint Richards informs me of the death of this former Welsh middleweight champion, who was a star amateur winner of the ABA title in 1947 and a man who represented Great Britain many times. He never defended his title because of synoritis of the hands – a problem that plagued him throughout his fighting years and one that eventually forced him out of the game when he was knocking on the championship door. Roy turned pro in 1950 and had a couple of wins but his hands were still sore. He took 18 months out, returning in 1952. Within a few fights he had the Welsh Championship belt around his waist after knocking out Jimmy Roberts. Only Michael Stack from the Turpin stable in Leamington Spa had beaten him. Against that sole loss were wins over Frank Duffy, Jimmy Redgewell and Tom Johnston. Wally caused a small sensation when he stopped Roy in 1953. It was a set back but Roy got a return, won it, and went on to beat Hector Constance, George Dilkes and Billy Ellaway. He was now top contender and was offered a shot at Pat McAteer's title. Alas, the fight never took place, Roy's hands being so painful that he was forced to retire. He didn't turn his back on the game after having such cruel luck but coached young boxers and gave them the benefit of his experience. With two good hands and a championship in the offing, who knows what he may have achieved?

AGOSTINO Rocco *From* Italy. *Died* December 2006, aged 75. Respected Italian boxers' manager, Rocco handled some of the best Italian boxers of post-war years and guided 18 men to World or European championships. Among them were Mauro Galvano, Massimiliano Duran, Patrizio Oliva and the great Bruno Arcari.

ARIAS Ramon *From* Cabimas, Venezuela. *Died* 17 June 2007, aged 71. Venezuelan flyweight Ramon fought twice for world titles and each time he was facing a champion with a claim to greatness. Pascual Perez outpointed him at flyweight level and three years later, Brazil's best-ever bantamweight had too many guns for the plucky Ramon. His was a spectacular rise to world class, winning the Venezuelan flyweight championship in his fourth fight and taking on Perez six fights later. It's important to note that he gave the champion a strong challenge. He was a force at world level with wins over Billy Peacock, Frankie Jones, Mimoun Ben Ali, Sadao Yaoita and Ray Pacheco. He never could score over Bernardo Caraballo, who beat him twice, and there was a hint that perhaps he was on the slide when he failed in a challenge for the Venezuelan bantamweight title. Nelson Estrada edged him out over 15 rounds and Risto Luukkonen beat him soon after. Although he regrouped, with wins over Ronnie DeCost and Manuel Moreno, he went to pieces after that. In 1963 he failed to win in four outings, with losses to Natalio Jiminez, Horacio Accavallo, Carlos Rodriguez and Raton Mojica hastening his retirement. He had plenty of good fights left in him, but his decision was wise. Smooth, tactically good and never easy to beat, in another era he may well have reached the pinnacle of his profession.

ARMSTEAD Paul *From* Los Angeles, California, USA. *Died* 30 November 2006, aged 69. Paul, a world-rated lightweight during the 50s and 60s, was a Texan based in Los Angeles, all his early fights taking place in Hollywood. He gave notice of his incipient class in his second year as a pro when he reversed a previous defeat by Tommy Tibbs and then beat former world champion, Lauro Salas, for the vacant Californian title. Wins over Kid Anahuac, Johnny Gonsalves and Len Matthews were all over the ten-round distance. It looked as if he was on the way. Then his career dipped in 1960 with only five outings recorded for that year. Stepping out of his home turf for the first time, he found Dave Charnley too strong for him, the latter and Kenny Lane being the only men to score stoppage wins over him. Between the Charnley and Lane fights Paul was undefeated in 16 outings against good opposition. Then he twice beat Joe 'Old Bones' Brown. In later appearances in Great Britain he beat Des Rea and Joe Tetteh, but blew a ten rounder to Johnny Cooke. After drawing in Helsinki with Oli Maki he then campaigned in South Africa, where he was unbeaten in three outings. In Italy he beat Angel Robinson Garcia and Massimo Consolati. He was now 33 and had had a long innings and following a year's break he wound up his career in Las Vegas.

BACILIERI Uber *From* Copparo, Italy. *Died* 29 January 2007, aged 73. An Italian, Uber was a good European heavyweight and a recurring winner of the Italian title without ever aspiring to title contention at world level. He was the first man to beat Henry Cooper, albeit via a cut-eye injury. Prior to that he had taken rising star, Ingemar Johansson, the distance in Stockholm. Cooper got his revenge five months later, but Bacilieri had proved that he could give European heavyweights a fight. He could best be described as a solid performer, ready to do battle and usually one who went the distance. Don Cockell beat him in 1953 when the Don was feeling his way into the heavyweight division and two other British champions in Joe Erskine and Jack Gardner also claimed his scalp. The Italian was on firmer ground on his home patch, winning the national title from Giorgio Milan and losing it two years later to Franco

Cavicchi. He regained the championship in 1956 and successfully defended it six times before Mario de Persio relieved him of it in 1958. This was at the end of his career in which he'd faced quality opponents in Hein ten Hoff, Joe Bygraves, Kitione Lave, Robert Eugene, Connie Rux, Ed 'Polly' Smith and Werner Wiegand. Usually he gave a good account of himself and would travel far to get work.

Uber Bacilieri

BACK Ken *From* Ashford, Kent. *Died* 4 August 2007, aged 90. Ken was a dedicated boxing enthusiast, training at the Sylvan ABC and cycling there from his home in Ashford. I opened my atlas to ascertain the distance between the two towns and estimate it to be between 17 and 25 miles! He first donned the gloves in 1931 and claimed 150 bouts as an amateur and professional. Dick Gutteridge, on convalescence in Kent following an operation, saw Ken shadow-boxing and was impressed by the way he shaped up. Ken took Dick to his home and showed him his collection of books and magazines on boxing, plus silver cups he'd won, having beaten everyone of his weight in Kent. Progression to the paid ranks, under the management of Dick and his brother followed and they took him to the NSC for his debut, which he won by a knockout. It was 1939. Before the year was out, he'd had 12 fights with two losses, one of which

was to Joe Kay of Horwich, who continued his career in America. There was a notable win over Dave Clemo that indicated Ken was going somewhere, but the man who really curtailed his career was Adolf Hitler. Soon, Ken found himself involved in a bigger fight when serving in the RAF and was too old for active boxing when hostilities ceased in 1945. In retirement, he became an excellent artist. Harold Alderman persuaded him to join the Kent EBA in the 1970s when the ex-boxers' movement was in its boom years.

BARKER Gary *From* London. *Died* 10 December 2006, aged 19. Repton ABC light-welterweight prospect Gary was killed when his car hit a crash barrier. He was travelling to visit his girl friend when the vehicle rolled over. The youngster seemed to have a bright future in boxing, being one of our hopes for a medal at the Beijing Olympics. His credentials were impressive: a junior Olympic gold medallist and a Commonwealth Youth Games champion. The brother of Darren, a promising pro, and the son of Terry, a former ABA champion, in 2005 he won the junior ABA lightweight title.

BAXTER Cornelius *From* Scotland. *Died* 29 August 2006, aged 15. Another death on the roads took the life of 15-year-old 'Neilly'. Big things were expected of the young Scot, who had become the Scottish Youth champion when the formbook was against him. The prospect of championship stature seemed to raise his game and throughout the championship tournament he showed sound defensive abilities, coupled with clever boxing, that presaged a promising future that was, alas, curtailed by tragedy.

BENDIG Brunon *From* Chelmno, Poland. *Died* 15 September 2006, aged 67. From a country that didn't allow pro boxing and produced world-class performers in the amateur ranks, Brunon became the Polish bantamweight champion from 1962 to 1964 and the national featherweight champion in 1965. He first came to prominence in 1960 at the Rome Olympics when winning a bronze medal after being outpointed by the eventual winner, Oleg Grigoryev. Although he went out in the second series in the 1964 Games, being outpointed by Nigeria's Karim Young, he came back strongly in the European Championships the following year. Fighting at featherweight, he reached the final where he was outpointed by the reigning Olympic champion, Russia's Stanislav Stepashkin. He boxed three times for Poland in Britain, outpointing Bobby Mallon (1964), Mickey Pye (1964) and Ron Russell (1965).

BENSON Tom *From* Preston. *Died* February 2007, aged 76. After an amateur career that lasted into his late 20s, Tom became a trainer for Bamber Bridge ABC and maintained his connection with the club up to his death. He boxed in the Far East when in the forces, before returning to civvy street in the 1950s.

BERBICK Trevor *From* Canada. *Died* 28 October 2006, aged 51. When I heard that this former world heavyweight champion had been murdered I wondered how he would be remembered. Would it be for his genuine claim to a share of the heavyweight championship, for being the last man to fight and destroy Muhammad Ali, or for the manner in which he lost to Mike Tyson. And what of his post-boxing life that, at times, seemed bizarre beyond belief? After reading his obituaries in national and specialist newspapers, the loss to Tyson came to the top ahead of his victory over the shell of Ali. He'd lost to Iron Mike in two rounds when a left hook turned his legs to rubber and put him squirming on the canvas, his WBC title lost after a brief reign. Nearly everyone except Trevor could see this coming. Going into the arena that night he was, perhaps, the only person with faith in his ability to halt the inexorable rise of Tyson. He was Commonwealth and Canadian heavyweight champion in the 1980s and WBC champion by dint of scoring a points win over Pinklon Thomas in 1986. Having lost that title to Tyson eight months later, his slide down the ratings began. Trevor took up boxing in 1972 and had only 11 amateur fights before representing Jamaica, where he was born, in the Montreal Olympics. He then emigrated to Canada and turned professional. Although he unsuccessfully challenged Larry Holmes for his WBC title, losing clearly on points, he gave the vastly more experienced champion plenty of problems. Trevor had been given the chance following a stunning knockout win over John Tate, who had lost his WBA title only three months earlier. He also beat Greg Page, Iran Barkley and David Bey, but did nothing of note after losing to Tyson. After becoming a church preacher, he ran into trouble with the law and served a term in prison for sexually assaulting his children's babysitter. Although violating his parole and being deported from the USA, Trevor eventually returned later and started to train boxers in Florida. Deported again, he was allowed to stay in Canada before returning to Jamaica, where he was brutally murdered by his nephew following a land dispute.

Trevor Berbick

BETTS Alex *From* Maidstone. *Died* January 2007, aged 79. Alex won the Kent County ABA light-welterweight title back in 1951 at the age of 23, having established himself as a good amateur fighter. After injuries forced him to finish with active boxing, he took up coaching the younger generation and gained high respect from the Kent boxing community.

BINI Dante *From* Bezons, France. *Died* March 2007, aged 79. Dante was a smooth-boxing bantamweight who came out of France to box all over Europe from 1949 to 1958. Scientific boxing was his forte. He was no power puncher and it's notable that all but four of his wins were over the full distance. When he lost, he was usually still standing at the final bell. Dante fought in Britain, Italy, Belgium, Morocco, Denmark, Switzerland and Finland, as well as in his native France. His record contains the names of most top-rated European boxers of his time: Peter Keenan, Robert Cohen, Theo Medina, Jean Sneyers, Pierre Cossemyns – all of whom held championships of a kind. Then there were world-rated Vic Herman, Tanny Campo and Piero Rollo. Later on a defeat by Alphonse Halimi hastened his retirement. Halimi was world champion at the time. On Britain's shores his best performance was a fine win over Jake Tuli. Without referring to my newspaper cuttings, I can clearly recall the headline: "Tuli slips on French polish". In London, Dante had also beaten Jimmy Cardew. He had two unsuccessful attempts to win the French title, losing to Andre Valignat and Emile Chemama, but was lucky on his third challenge against Stan Sobolak and emerging as the proud owner of the bantamweight championship. He defended it twice before losing it to Eugene le Cozzanet at the end of 1957. Dante's record contains many draws: Robert Tartari, Tino Cardinale, Gianni Zuddas, Gaetano Annaloro, Andre Younsi, Robert Meunier amongst minor opponents at the beginning of his career. He got out of the game once Halimi beat him. Halimi was at his peak and Dante was 31 and by no means a has-been. He is best remembered by those who followed boxing in the 1950s.

Dante Bini

BLAY Eddie *From* Accra, Ghana. *Died* 15 October 2006, aged 63. Eddie entered the paid ranks with impressive amateur credentials: All-African champion, Olympic bronze medallist and winner of two Commonwealth gold medals. It took a man of exceptional talent - Dick McTaggart - to beat him into the silver medal position in the 1960 Olympics. Born in Accra, Ghana, he fought out of Italy for his entire professional career. By his fourth outing, Eddie was in the eight-round class and winning his fights inside the scheduled distance. Only Ferdinand Ahumibe lasted the full course. Three draws followed before Silvano Bertini inflicted his first defeat of note, but the Ghanaian put this behind him and won all but one of his next 12 outings before getting his chance for fistic eminence against dangerous Dane, Jorgen Hansen. He capitalised on his opportunity, stopping the betting favourite and propelling himself into a Commonwealth title challenge against Canada's Clyde Gray. It went the full 15 rounds but Eddie lost and he also lost a return with Hansen before being defeated by Eddie Perkins. Although past his prime and in his 30s, he still had plenty of steam. He stopped Max Hebeisen, beat Tiger Quaye and drew with Salem Ouedrago. When Joseph Bessala beat him for the All-African championship, he knew that his career was nearing its end. Two more losses followed before he finished to take a less-demanding profession as a restauranteur. He was married to an Italian girl and together they ran an Italian restaurant in Ghana. She and three children survive him.

BOYLE Israel From Liverpool, but born in Abonnema, Nigeria. Died July 2007, aged 79. Israel settled in England in 1949, after starting out as a pro in his native Nigeria in 1946. A member of the Yaruba tribe, he used to tell people that he was really born in 1923 and started boxing much earlier than recorded. Harold Alderman can find 12 fights for him before he arrived in Liverpool and has him winning six and losing six, with Ray Folami (Young Panther), Billy Wells and Roy Ankrah beating him. The Ankrah fight involved the West African featherweight title. After losing his first two fights in England, to Mickey Flanagan and Harry Brangham, he soon acclimatised and went 16 undefeated before being outpointed by Billy Rattray. Only good men beat Israel, while he accounted for Brangham, Eric Billington, Roy Davies, Ginger Roberts, Terry Cullen, Les Rendle, Mosh Mancini, Johnny Downes, Danny McKay, Jimmy Molloy (2), Joe Baillie, Ernie Vickers (3), Eric Davies, Bob Frost, Tommy Hinson, Terry Ratcliffe (2), Wells, Giel de Roode, Duggie du Preez, Jeff Tite, Rees Moore, Leslie McKenzie and Vincent O'Kine. Israel had 24 fights in 1950, 13 in 1951, 14 in 1952 and was looking to hit 1953 running before being forced to retire with eye problems following a points loss against Hector Constance. Of his last fight, *Boxing News* reported: "How referee Davidson came to make Constance the winner at the end of eight rounds is hard to imagine. In our view there was only one man in it when it came to boxing and that man wasn't Constance". Jackie Braddock, Roy Baird, Frank Duffy, Billy Ambrose, Peter Fallon and Bunty Adamson were among those who defeated him, but a close look at Israel's record tells you all you need to know.

Who knows what he might have achieved had he been properly looked after.

BROUGHTON Ted *From* Gorton, Manchester. *Died* 6 June 2007. Harold Alderman provides details of the death of Ted, who boxed at the featherweight poundage from the mid 1930s up to 1949. Harold has traced 34 contests with 18 wins and a draw, pointing out that there is still a lot of work to do on his record. For instance, there is a huge gap from 1939 to 1947, but seven of those were wartime years. Ted had commenced boxing in 1935 and was just getting into his stride by 1939. Coming back in 1947, four fights have been traced with two wins and two losses, the last contest being a stoppage defeat by Ken Maynard. He was a clever boxer with an 'educated' left hand, but unfortunately lacked a big punch and his stamina over longer distances was suspect. His early years were his best, with only two losses in 17 starts, but from 1937 it becomes spotty. He was then in the ten-round class. There is a good win over Billy Cakewell and two knockout victories over Tommy Dempsey and Norman Ford. Apart from Cakewell, the most notable name on his record is that of Harry 'Kid' Silver, who beat him in 1938. A period of inactivity followed and the loss to Maynard in 1947 seems to be his last contest.

BRUZAS Ron *From* Blackwood. *Died* 12 July 2007. Geraint Richards, who is a most reliable informant of Welsh boxing affairs, writes in to report the death of Ron. I remember him well and am surprised, on checking his record, that he had only 18 contests, having turned pro after winning the Welsh amateur lightweight title in 1949. He was undefeated going into a challenge for the Welsh lightweight title, but found Reg Quinlan too good before being beaten in ten rounds. Emmett Kenny also beat him, but on the credit side are wins over Selwyn Evans, Hugh Mackie and Andy Blythe. There were also credible draws against Al Brown and Johnny Carrington. Following an arm injury sustained at work he was out of the ring for almost two years and called it a day after Jimmy Tippett beat him in October 1953. Rising to the post of Chairman, he and brother Harry were great assets to the Welsh Ex-Boxers' Association, especially when arranging concerts to raise funds that helped former boxers who'd fallen on hard times.

BURGOYNE Tommy *From* Halton. *Died* 2007, aged 68. Former Scottish bantamweight champion Tommy turned pro in 1960 and went to the well 47 times before retiring in 1965. He was one of Alan Rudkin's early opponents and won the vacant title in his next contest by stopping Lewie Mackay in eight rounds. His career spiralled downwards after that, wins were few and he was used as an 'opponent' for aspiring contenders. This didn't bother Tommy, who could look after himself, and he got plenty of work, while never being counted out. He beat Danny Wells, Johnny Lewis, Davey Whittaker, Brian Bissmire and Gerald Jones. Those who honed their skills at his expense were Evan Armstrong, Don Weller, Dai Corp, Alex Ambrose, Johnny Morrissey, Terry Crimmins, Mick Greaves, Billy Hardacre and Jackie Brown. Few of them had an easy time with

Tommy, he was a survivor. As an amateur he boxed for the Territorial Army and was in the same team as Geraint Richards, who sent me Tommy's record. He lived alone and was found dead sitting in his armchair. One of the first to be told was his old opponent and good friend over the years, Danny Wells, now a Board Inspector.

BYRNE Jim *From* Dublin. *Died* May 2007, aged 68. A former Irish amateur champion, Jim was the Irish junior light-middleweight champion in 1960, after which he won the senior middleweight title. Starting and finishing with Arbour Hill ABC, in 1963, he won the heavyweight title. Survived by daughter, Angela.

CAICEDO Fernando *From* Colombia. *Died* 19 June 2007, aged 38. Fernando was a southpaw who challenged for the IBF super-featherweight championship in 1992, but was stopped by John-John Molina. Prior to that he'd won 15 contests, 11 of them inside the distance and had defeated Tommy Valdez to win the WBC Continental Americas featherweight title. The most notable win on his record is one in which he beat Lupe Pintor, who was on a comeback after eight years out of boxing. The fight took place in 1994 when Pintor had three wins on his comeback sheet. Fernando fought from 1988 to 1995, winning 20 and losing two.

CAIN Sid *From* Watford. *Died* 1 June 2007, aged 74. Sid made his debut in 1953, beating Jim Lockwood of Deal, and his final fight was in 1961 when Ken Potter stopped him. A huge gap appears in his record from 1956, but it was during the following three years that he was most active. Sid took to booth fighting and seldom missed a day without donning the gloves, fighting for Alf Weston, Ronnie Taylor, Ma McKeown, Jack Gage and Mel Read, etc. He was no slouch as a licensed performer either, knocking out Jackie Abbott and Kwame Lokko and twice beat both Don Stoker and Bob Couttie. In his nine-year career, Sid shared the ring with Eddie Wright, Noel Trigg, Tony Dove, Ted Morgan, Dick Richardson (twice), Dave Ould, Abe Stanley, Ray Shiel, Ron Gray and Dennis Fewkes.

CASTELLANO Carol *From* Las Vegas, Nevada, USA. *Died* March 2007, aged 74. One of the first women boxing judges, Carol, whose one incursion into London was to judge at the second Jorge Vaca v Lloyd Honeyghan fight, died in her Las Vegas home.

CHIPPENDALE Danny *From* Putney. *Died* December 2006, aged 69. I never saw a stronger featherweight than Danny. It would have taken a hand grenade to have slowed his advance just a little when he was in his prime. He was an army champion and based in Germany where he took part in two paid fights boxing under assumed names of Danny Lyon and Danny Strong. Back home he got regular work on the unlicensed circuit, his style being suited to a professional career. On one occasion I recall him losing an amateur fight when knocking out his man with a borderline punch. The decision was harsh. Arthur Boggis saw it and approached Danny with the offer to turn professional under

his aegis. Boggis had Dave Charnley, who was an old club-mate at the Lynn ABC, but the army was beckoning and the offer wasn't taken up. I lost touch with him when I moved overseas and when we met in later years, I didn't, at first, recognise him, he was no longer a featherweight but tipped the scales several divisions higher. He was training young hopefuls then and ran a very busy gymnasium. This acted as a rudder for him after he lost his son in a tragic accident. Cancer got Danny in the end, but he fought it in the same manner that he fought in the ring. It was a cruel loss. He was a marvellous companion in the gym and a stylish, very tough fighter in the ring. His two pro fights, both in 1961, saw him beat Dave Chandler before a loss to Al Ceres convinced him to hang up the gloves.

CLARK Lamar *From* Cedar City, Utah, USA. *Died* November 2006, aged 71. Lamar fought 51 times between 1955 and 1961. There was a two-year hiatus from 1956 to 1958, so he was never short of fights. He kicked off with three that all went the distance and after that he ran up an amazing record of consecutive stoppages or knockouts. Most were scored inside a round – 44 of them, and this still stands today as a record unlikely to be beaten. Another extraordinary feature of Lamar's career is the number of times that he had multiple fights in the same night in 1958: two on 13 October, three on 10 November, followed by another two 18 days later, then six on 1 December, two on the 15th and finally two in May 1959. Eleven of these didn't last a round and in December 1958 he fought 11 times with only two going into round two. It's obvious that Lamar was a banger, but one searches in vain for a name fighter amongst his victims. Still, his manager Marv Jensen got his name indelibly stamped in the annals of boxing and it is a unique record. Lamar lost for the first time to Dominican Republic light-heavyweight, Bartolo Soni, in nine rounds. Soni was unable to cash in, Jerry Luedee and Babe Simmons both stopping him before he faded from the scene. Lamar also stepped up in class, but never won again. Pete Rademacher, Chuck Wilburn and a rising star called Cassius Clay all beat him and, as was usual, none of those went the distance. He was never a force at world level, but he was one of the power punchers of our time and his 32 outings in 1958 mark him as being one of the busiest fighters of the 50s.

CLAUS Bobby *From* Buffalo, New York, USA. *Died* 19 January 2007, aged 86. Having come through a successful amateur career in which he excelled in various Golden Glove tournaments, this New York welterweight, turned professional. He'd damaged a knee prior to the war and that, coupled with bad management, prevented him from attaining his boxing potentiality. It was 1941 and he started well against little-known men like Otis Cobb, Johnny Green and Pete Galiano, but was outclassed in a ten rounder by Jimmy Doyle. Over the next five years he was thrown in with Tony Zale (twice), Tippy Larkin and Rocky Graziano. Wins became fewer and fewer so Bobby quit in 1949 to follow his other interests as a horse-trainer. He also drove a taxi and was therefore a well-known figure in Buffalo. He died in an infirmary after a long illness.

CLAY Von *From* Philadelphia, Pennsylvania, USA. *Died* 27 April 2007, aged 67. In 1961, the world's number three rated light-heavyweight Chic Calderwood was unbeaten and looking for a 'safe' opponent before angling for a shot at the world title. Harry Levene brought this American to Britain for what was supposed to be a routine ten rounder. Calderwood was fresh from a win over Willie Pastrano and Von, after a solid start in the paid ranks, had been beaten by Doug Jones. It turned out to be a tough fight as Von stood up to everything that Calderwood threw at him and broke Chic's nose en-route to a points win. Significantly there were several knockdowns with the Scot being the recipient. Perhaps, following his shock win, Von could scent a world championship to put his future financially secure. He got his chance against Harold Johnson, who was the NBA champion, but unfortunately he was out of his depth and folded in two rounds. Von was then stopped in a return with Doug Jones and failed to go the course with Mauro Mina. Probably, it would have been better to have stopped then but he chose to fight on and slowly slid downhill, mostly against good opposition. Chic Calderwood got his revenge and Brian London beat him on points. Losses followed to Erich Schoeppner in Germany and to Piero Tomasoni in Rome. There were victories too, notably over Billy Hunter, Leroy Green and Dick Young, but they were rarities. Periods of inactivity followed and he returned in 1967 to stop Herman Harris, who was no world-beater. Three losses followed and he called it quits. His record doesn't do justice to his ability and perhaps he aimed too high too soon.

CLIFF Sugar *From* Nassau. *Died* 24 May 2007, aged 72. Sugar was a West Indies welterweight who mixed in good company but never won a title. His last fight, a loss to Elisha Obed, was for the Bahamas welterweight title, so his name still goes into the record books as a title challenger. His career kicked off in 1959 when he lived in Miami Beach and he went into his fourth year as a pro before tasting defeat at the hands of Bunny Grant. He got back on the winning trail against Ricky McMasters, who later continued his fighting in England. Cliff had already beaten Ike Vaughn twice before Grant blotted his record and in subsequent years he fought Brian Curvis, Jose Stable, Alessandro Mazzinghi and Percy Pugh. Sugar won plenty of fights – 30 in all out of 42 starts, but seemed to lose the important ones. He beat Les McFadden in New York, won one and lost two in Jamaica, drew with Luciano Piazza in Milan and was stopped by Mazzinghi in Rome. The one appearance on these shores was against Curvis who outpointed him in Cardiff and although both men were inside the welterweight limit, the contracted weight was in excess of 147lbs in order to protect the Welshman's British Empire title.

COHEN Ronnie *From* New Rochelle, New York, USA. *Died* 4 February 2007, aged 70. A welterweight who was active from 1958 to 1961, Ronnie (real name Ronald Cowell) carried a heavy dig that gained him 16 early wins out of 20. Had he retired in 1960 after stopping Eddie Antonetti his record would have stayed impressive, but after that fight he never won again and finished with seven straight losses. One was a credible points defeat by Stefan Redl, but he was favoured to win against Joe Salci and Gil Diaz. His career started with a loss to Vernon Lynch, then he went through 21 contests with only two defeats. In that time he had 12 consecutive stoppage wins. His was a brief career, quitting boxing when he was only 25.

CONNOLLY Hilary *From* Queensland, Australia. *Died* 25 July 2006, aged 61. A crowd-pleasing lightweight, Hilary was very popular in Australia because of his regularly televised fights. He was busy in the ring, seldom stopping his forward march and forever seeking a gap in his opponent's defence. In short, he was all-action. He boxed from 1968 to 1972 against men like Manny Santos (four times), Hector Thompson (twice) and Jeff White. Voted as 'TV Ringsider of the Year' in 1969 and a winner of the TV lightweight title two years later, he eventually he lost that crown to Andy Broome.

CONNOR Tommy *From* Glasgow. *Died* December 2006, aged 67. This Scottish bantamweight plied his trade in the mid 1960s. His most notable achievement was in holding the future world-title challenger, Johnny Clarke, to a draw in 1966. Johnny won the return and also the rubber match, but he was well on his way up the ladder by then. Another champion to beat Tommy was John McCluskey, who turned in the trick twice. There were some fine wins too on Connor's record. He twice beat Tommy Burgoyne, Henry Hoey, Sammy Abbey, Frank Fitzgerald and Sammy McIlvenney. In 1964 he also twice outpointed Johnny Coats, who had won and lost in two amateur contests against the Yearbook editor. On the debit side were losses to Patrick Mambwe and Brian Packer. In later years, a propensity for drink and gambling seriously affected his health.

CORRALES Diego *From* Sacramento, California, USA. *Died* May 2007, aged 29. Tragedy struck boxing in May when Diego hit a lorry when driving his motorcycle, being thrown into the path of a car and dying instantly. This came within two years of his sensational victory over Jose Castillo, when he twice climbed off the deck and fought back to stop his man after his cause seemed to be lost. Details are superfluous since the fight is within very recent memory. Corrales' demise is reminiscent of the death of Salvador Sanchez 20 years previously. Both men fought hard, lived hard and died very young. Instead of taking a rest after beating Castillo, Diego opted for a quick return. He was too much of a fighter for his own good and lost the fight by a knockout. The Mexican was well overweight but the fight went ahead at Diego's request. "What the hell", he said, "the customers have paid to see a fight". He could never match his previous form after those two career-shortening fights, but will be remembered with awe, having won one of the greatest victories ever seen in a boxing ring. The autopsy showed that he had high alcohol level in his bloodstream at the time of his death. In a 43-fight career, with just three losses on his record, he had been the undefeated WBO and IBF super-featherweight champion before going on to reign as the WBC and WBO lightweight titleholder. He was married twice, his second wife, seven months pregnant and four children survive him.

Diego Corrales

CORRO Hugo *From* Mendoza, Argentina. *Died* 15 June 2007, aged 53. In the 1970s, the middleweight division was dominated by Carlos Monzon and Rodrigo Valdez. These two great South American boxers were succeeded by this lesser known Argentinian, who came out of nowhere to usurp the champion, Valdez, and faded from the championship scene as quickly as he had arrived. Hugo's record prior to taking Valdez' title, was devoid of big names. On paper, Valdez was in no danger of losing his title, but Hugo had his number and it was no fluke victory. He then defended against Ronnie Harris, beat Valdez again and then lost his title to Vito Antuofermo. Like Valdez, he fought twice more after losing his title and announced his retirement. Unlike Valdez he came back twice, the second time after a six-year gap. Successive defeats by Juan Roldan and Hugo Corti convinced him to hang up his gloves for good, leaving him with an overall record of 47 wins and two losses prior to losing to Antuofermo. Hugo was unlucky against Antuofermo and his legacy is an upset but a deserving win against a dangerous man who put Carlos Monzon on the deck when challenging for a world title.

DAVENPORT John *From* New Jersey, USA. *Died* 2007, aged 67. A strict and successful trainer of boxers, John passed away after a long fight with cancer. Responsible for honing Lennox Lewis' skills, his no-nonsense approach to training matters and often prickly manner gained him enemies as well as admirers. Regardless of that, there is no denying his achievements and all fighters coming under his tuition had much for which to be grateful.

DE VOOGD 'Baby' Henk *From* Holland. *Died* 19 June 2007, aged 77. Dutch heavyweights have been thin on the ground since the retirement of Jan Klein. Henk found it difficult to get regular contests and never reached the level of his compatriot, despite being 15 and a half stone – a big heavyweight for men boxing in the 1950s. Considering the superior experience of many opponents, he did well. There were wins over Prosper Beck, Georges Rogiers and Pete Shetzoff in Rotterdam, but he was out of depth in his sole fight on British soil, Joe Erskine stopping him in under a round. Losses to Hans Friedrich, Werner Wiegand and Hans Kalbfell were no surprise, as Henk had been thrown in over his head. There was a good win over Lucien Touzard, but losses to fellow countrymen, Hennie Quentenmeier and Willie Schaagen, hastened his exit from boxing. He quit for good once Werner Walloschek beat him in Berlin in 1959.

Henk 'Baby' de Voogd

DISTON Ken *From* Hendon. *Died* aged 79. A popular small-halls scrapper, Ken began pro boxing in 1948 with a win over Bow's Billy Daniels on 14 September. Before the end of the year he'd racked up another six contests with just one loss. He saw the year out with a fine win over Peter Fay – a man he was destined to fight three more times. Ken lived in Hendon all his life and was a favourite with the fans at nearby Wembley Town Hall. Although he won only half of his fights at that venue, he gave the paying customers value for money. They always wanted him back. Ken beat Johnny O'Gara, Roy Ball, Johnny Kent, Tony Cummings, Alf Clarke, Mickey O'Sullivan and Terry Ward. Others he fought included Tommy Proffitt, Sid Band, Jimmy Cardew, Tommy Bramble, Harry Alley and Jimmy Webster, the first named being one of the very few men to beat Ken inside the scheduled distance. After retiring in 1953 following defeats by Johnny Barnham and Alley, he went on to train the boys of West Hendon ABC and was still there into the 1980s. A quietly spoken, unassuming and modest man, Ken stayed in touch in his post-boxing years as a long-standing member of the London Ex-Boxers' Association. His funeral was attended by ex-boxers and a host of old friends.

DITTMAR Len *From* Largo Bay, South Australia. *Died* 13 March 2007, aged 81. Len based himself in Melbourne during his boxing career and retired to Brisbane after his fighting days had gone. He was a protege of Ambrose Palmer who, in more recent years, guided Johnny Famechon to world fame. His early fights are difficult to trace, having turned pro at the age of 16 in 1942. Records weren't always kept scrupulously in wartime years. Len fought for ten years, upsetting the odds on many occasions. He was the archetypal hungry fighter, coming from a family of nine boys and being brought up in an orphanage. Not being a heavy puncher hardly diminished his chances in the ring and he won his fights with good boxing and fast footwork. Also he was dead game, showing real guts to twice climb off the canvas to upset the great Tommy Burns for the vacant Australian welterweight title. His losses, apart from one early in his career, came against really good fighters: Freddie Dawson, Wallace 'Bud' Smith, Dave Sands, Al Bourke and O'Neil Bell. Len got his chance with Burns by eliminating Mickey Tollis from the queue and after Burns, he beat wild, bar-room brawling Don 'Bronco' Johnson. That was his last win. Losing to the above mentioned Dawson and Smith made him realise that he wasn't going further at world level, so he got out when still at his peak at the age of 26. Popular in Brisbane earning a living as a bookmaker, in the last three years his health deteriorated after he injured himself in a fall and the onset of Alzheimer's disease speeded his demise. He is survived by his wife and five children.

DOBSON Freddie *From* Manchester. *Died* 25 March 2007, aged 68. Mankind's deadly foe, cancer, claimed the life of this Manchester featherweight boxer. In his heyday he was a contender for the British title, having had a good amateur career when winning a schools' championship and a junior ABA title. There are good wins on his record against rated men like Con Mount Bassie, Eddie Burns, Chris Elliott, Peter Lavery, Bobby Fisher and Al McCarthy. Freddie was confident that he'd give Howard Winstone plenty of problems when they met in 1962, but he was outboxed, outfought and stopped in three rounds by a man who had already begun his rise to world fame. Undeterred, Freddie came back with wins over Bobby Fisher and Johnny McKenna. He outpointed Mick Carney in 1963 but lost the return match when the vacant Central Area featherweight

championship was at stake. In retirement he returned to his former trade of welding, but retained his boxing links by training amateurs in the Oldham area.

DREWETT Keith *From* Battersea. *Died* 1 August 2006, aged 62. Keith Drewett's obsession with beating Johnny Frankham seems to be the main thrust of his career. Try as he did, Keith never scored a win over the man who'd edged him out in the ABAs in 1969. Ambitiously, he fought Frankham in his first two paid outings. Against Ray Brittle and Phil Watford he was on firmer ground, posting wins against both men. Watford was Southern Area light-heavyweight champion and Ray Brittle had lost only two out of 14 starts. Keith also performed well overseas where few favours are bestowed on visiting fighters. He licked Ralf Jensen in Copenhagen and Jean-Claude Capitolin in Paris, but was less fortunate in Johannesburg where he lost to Kosie Smith. Once upon a time, visiting fighters blamed Johannesburg's altitude for losing, but Keith would have none of that. He gave Smith a hard fight and took home the loser's purse without making excuses - that was his style. He was what is termed an 'honest fighter'. Between the Paris and Johannesburg outings he squeezed in four fights with his nemesis, Frankham, and closed his career with wins over Jeff Shaw and Kevin Madden before becoming a trainer for Rosehill ABC. That was after after eye injuries had forced him into retirement. He lost his fight with brain disease, leaving behind a wife and three children.

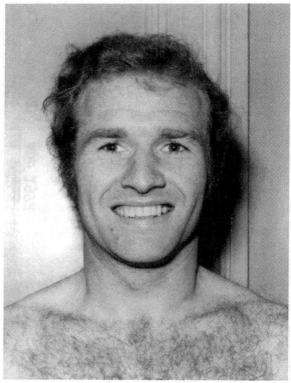

Keith Drewett

DUPAS Tony *From* New Orleans, Louisiana, USA. *Died* 8 December 2006, aged 68. Like his elder, world-rated brother Ralph, he was a welterweight. Starting boxing in 1954, soon after Ralph lost to Paddy DeMarco, Tony avenged his brother's defeat five years later when he outpointed DeMarco, who once held the world's lightweight title. Ralph returned the favour in 1961 when he licked Greg Sumlin, who held two wins over Tony. Following a famous brother into a boxing career gave Tony much to live up to. He started well with only one defeat in 19 starts, then won and lost to Paul Jorgensen, and dropped two decisions to Rocky Randell. Following that, he went two years without defeat and got a good win over Ramon Fuentes. There were other victories over Teddy Davis, Rocky Caballero and Billy DePriest, but these were interspersed with losses to Joey Archer, Denny Moyer and Stan Harrington. After beating Sugar Boy Nando and Walter Moerbe, he should have quit, but instead he went to Australia, failing to register a win there. Only five fights followed spread over two and a half years. A good record was spoiled by staying on too long – the old, sad story.

Yvon Durelle

DURELLE Yvon *From* Baie St Anne, Canada. *Died* January 2007, aged 77. The tough life of a fisherman tempered the steel that showed when giving both Archie Moore and Floyd Patterson tough fights. Moore, often rated as the best light-heavyweight fighter ever, remembered his first encounter with Yvon as being his hardest fight. Strangely, he never cut much ice in Europe, losing to Gerhardt Hecht and Art Henri in Berlin and Ron Barton, Yolande Pompey, Artie Towne and Arthur Howard in England. He performed far better on

his own patch and like some good wines, didn't travel well. Yvon won his first title when he beat Gordon Wallace for the Canadian light-heavyweight championship in 1953. At that stage he'd lost only five of 49 fights. Tiger Warrington was beaten twice and George Ross and Curtis Wade went home as losers. He again licked Wallace for the title in 1954, having previously lost it to Doug Harper. Much later he and Wallace fought for the Empire title, which Yvon won and would successfully defend against South Africa's Mike Holt. After his second loss to Archie Moore, he threw his hat in the ring against George Chuvalo, with the Canadian heavyweight as a prize, but was stopped in 12 rounds. He announced his retirement then changed his mind and fought four times more with three wins against a single loss. The *Ring Record Book* records 110 fights for him and against class opponents he seemed to be able to raise his game, as was evident in his first great fight with Moore. Moore should have been grateful to the Canadian, his 1958 victory cemented Archie's reputation as being one of the all-time greats. Yvon, who died of a stroke after suffering for years with Parkinson's disease, is survived by his wife, Theresa, and four children.

DURKIN Brian *From* Livingston, West Lothian. *Died* 20 July 2006, aged 47. Cancer claimed the life of this Scottish bantamweight, who boxed as an amateur for Leith Victoria ABC in the 1970s. One of the club's more successful members, he fought his illness with courage over a long period before eventually succumbing.

EASTHAM George *From* Preston. *Died* February 2007, aged 76. After being involved in boxing for all his adult life, George's sudden demise left a big void. He was an active fighter in his young days, especially during three years in service uniform when he boxed in the Far East. George turned pro in 1949, losing to Johnny Fitzpatrick, Vince Marshall and Ernie Vickers in his first three fights before taking time out and re-appearing in 1954. Winning two of three he retired again before coming back in 1958. After four wins, including revenge over Cliff Lawrence, he was beaten by Colin Moore and Tony Smith before lacing them up for good. George became a trainer for Bamber Bridge ABC at the age of 29 and also coached members of the Young England team.

FLANNERY Frankie *From* Footscray, Melbourne, Australia. *Died* 25 July 2006, aged 79. Frankie's boyhood ambition was to be a jockey, but fortunately for Australian boxing he matured into a boxer, or perhaps a more apt term is 'fighter'. He had that kind of style and was box-office magic as a result of his no-nonsense, aggressive and exciting mode of combat. He won the Australian lightweight title in 1951, stopping Jack Hassen in nine rounds and on his record are two world champions, Harold Dade and Wallace 'Bud' Smith. Other opponents are no less impressive: Pierre Montane, Andre Famechon, George Barnes, Bruno Visintin, Archie Kemp, Alex Sinnaeve, Mario Trigo, Ernesto Aguilla, et al. Outside the ring he was quick-tempered and often in trouble. The fans loved to boo, cat-call and throw missiles at him, but Frankie packed out the stadiums. Despite the torrent of abuse that the fans threw, they loved him and he was never in a dull fight. I never had the privilege of seeing him in action. On the only occasion we met he was approachable and friendly, with a cheeky grin, an out-thrust hand and a cheery greeting of "Ow yer going"? Frankie started boxing at 15 and became a main-event force three years later. He was then a featherweight and still growing. His best performances - and there were many - came as a lightweight and the title he won from Hassen was his until Pat Ford relieved him of it in 1953. Frank Johnson had shown that Frankie was slipping when stopping him in a contest where the vacant Empire title was the prize. The Ford loss followed. Slipping or not, Frankie came back with a great win in a slugfest over Darby Brown, then bowed out in 1954 with a loss to Trigo, having fought 70 contests, with 39 wins, 22 losses and nine draws. Twice married, he was a father of one boy and two girls.

Bernie 'Schoolboy' Friedkin

FRIEDKIN 'Schoolboy' Bernie *From* Brooklyn, NYC, New York, USA. *Died* 18 January 2007, aged 89. Like any other good fighter of 1930s vintage Bernie was busy, boxing from featherweight to lightweight between 1935 and 1940. Four names stand out on his long record - Petey Scalzo, Mike Belloise, Kid Chocolate and Al 'Bummy' Davis. He drew and lost to Scalzo, drew twice with Belloise and also drew with Chocolate when he was boxing over eight rounds for the first time. Davis, who was a local rival, knocked him out in four rounds in a fight that packed out Madison

Square Garden. Prior to that, he had twice drawn with Orville Drouillard, whom he'd previously beaten on points. A clever fighter with a sound defence, but not a puncher, most of his wins came on points. There were also 16 draws on his record. Bernie, nicknamed 'Schoolboy' because of his youthful appearance, died in a hospice, leaving a wife, Lenore, two children and three grandchildren.

GARCIA Manolo *From* Tarifa, Spain. *Died* 2007, aged 77. Even a half-decent Spanish featherweight active in the 1950s could get plenty of fights. The division was rife with men anxious to get on with their careers. In Manolo, Spain produced a man destined to become the nation's featherweight champion - one whose long career embraced fights with most of Europe's top fighters. I can trace 132 fights for him. According to what I have, he began in 1951 and went straight into the ten-round class. I suspect that he started a few years earlier and not at the age of 22. What I can confirm is that he had his last fight at the age of 39. For the first few years of his career, he fought exclusively in Morocco - a country where boxing records are poorly chronicled. What is notable though is the quality of opposition in his first two years of fighting - Theo Medina, Georges Mousse, Ali Ramdane, Luis Romero, Lucien Meraint, etc. Jose Hernandez defended the Spanish championship against him twice, the first fight being a draw with Hernandez winning the second. When the title became vacant in 1956, Manolo won it by knocking out Pedro Paris in Madrid. He then campaigned in Argentina from late 1957 to 1959. A full account of his career would take up pages, but it's worth listing some of his opponents, which include Mohamed Chickaoui, Roy Ankrah, Bobby Ros, Cherif Hamia, Sergio Caprari, Jaime Gine, Manuel Alvarez, Sergio Milan, Fred Galiana (who won the Spanish title from him in 1960), Andre Valignat, Charlie Douglas and Giordano Campari. The list goes on and on. Following an unsuccessful bid to win the European title in 1960, he began to lose more often than he won and announced his retirement when Paul Maolet beat him in Paris. He was then 32, but resurfaced, rather unwisely, seven years later when taking a few more fights with scant success. Overall, his record puts him in an exalted place in European boxing history.

GIOSA Eddie *From* Philadelphia, Pennsylvania, USA. *Died* 18 February 2007, aged 82. An Italian-American welterweight, Eddie had a good amateur career before turning to the paid ranks in 1943. When he retired in 1954 he had a distinguished record that included wins over four one-time world champions in Ike Williams, Sandy Saddler, Beau Jack and Paddy DeMarco. Eddie fought Willie Pep in his third year of boxing. It was 1945 and a year in which his long run of victories was spoiled by unexpected losses, Wesley Mouzon beating him twice with further defeats following at the hands of Jimmy McAllister and Archie Wilmer. After losing to Pep over ten rounds, Eddie got back on the winning trail when beating Pat Scanlon and Cleo Shans. Ike Williams beat him twice in great fights and the year closed with a clever victory over Lulu Constantino. Eddie fought and beat Charley Fusari, Rudy Cruz, Percy Bassett, Lew Jenkins,

Johnny Greco and Carmen Basilio. Other good names on his account are those of Bernard Docusen, Arthur King, Sonny Boy West, Enrique Bolanos, Jesse Flores, Charles 'Cabey' Lewis and Maxie Shapiro. With over 100 contests against such elite opposition, he can be remembered as a man who could mix with the very best men of his time. He is survived by his wife and 24 family members.

Johnny Gonsalves

GONSALVES Johnny *From* Oakland, California, USA. *Died* 17 January 2007, aged 76. A top lightweight contender of the 1950s and popular Oakland citizen, Johnny died at his Oakland home. He was National AAU lightweight champion in 1947 and 1948 and for many years as a professional he was knocking on the championship door, but his chance never came. He fought once on these shores and was unlucky to meet Dave Charnley at the top of his form. It was 1957 and a year in which he lost all four of his fights. Like all really good fighters, he put it behind him when regrouping with wins over Cisco Andrade, Paul Armstead, Paddy DeMarco and Bobby Scanlon. Purely a boxer with slick footwork and defensive skills, in his 12th fight he held Maxie Docusen to a ten-round draw. Those who know their 1940s boxing will have a line on Johnny's talent. Beau Jack and Philip Kim beat him in his learning years then

came a win over Tommy Campbell, which put him on the fringe of contendership. Victories came over Solly Cantor, George Araujo, Orlando Zulueta, Virgil Akins and Paddy DeMarco, while there were losses to a couple of top-class men in Ralph Dupas and Freddie Dawson before Johnny returned to winning form against Wallace 'Bud' Smith, Lulu Perez, Andrade and Armstead. When losses came against Len Matthews, Gaspar Ortega and Paolo Rosi, Johnny decided it was time to quit but the urge to box returned after a six-month sojourn. Beating Bobby Scanlon but falling foul of Luis Rodriguez, when Yoshinori Takahashi got a controversial decision over him in Tokyo he retired for good. The story goes that Johnny resisted attempts by the underworld characters in boxing to manipulate his career. Maybe there is credence to that. Yea or nay, he never once got a chance to challenge for the top title.

GONZALEZ DOPICO Jose *From* Ferrol, Spain. *Died* April 2007, aged 62. This tough Spanish welterweight boxed from 1964 to 1975, winning titular honours in 1971 when he beat Antonio Torres for the Spanish championship. It was his second attempt to gain a place on the role of champions and it began a purple patch in his career. As an encore he beat Jean Josselin, Robinson Garcia and then defended against his old foe, Torres. The hard-punching Dane, Jorgen Hansen, then halted his forward march, stopping him in five rounds in Copenhagen. The Spaniard came back to defend his title three times before challenging Roger Menetrey for the European title and in a close affair the world-rated Frenchman edged him out over 15 rounds. Successive defeats by Roger Zami and Germain le Maitre indicated that Jose's best days had passed, although he still retained enough ambition to see off Jose Luis Pacheco in a domestic title defence. The last contest I can find for him is a stoppage loss, due to facial cuts, against Ghanaian, Eddie Blay, whose death occurred six months prior to that of his.

GRIFFITHS Dave *From* Cardiff. *Died* March 2007, aged 43. A former ABA light-welterweight champion and Olympic representative, Dave was found dead in his flat at a young age. Following a distinguished amateur career, he turned professional in 1985, first under Eddie Thomas's management and later, Paddy Byrne's. His paid career kicked off with a quick win over George Jones and was followed by wins over Pascal Lorcy and Spain's Angel Gonzalez. Dave was selected to contest the vacant Welsh championship against Mark Pearce and after winning he defended it 18 months later against the same man. Between those two fights he beat Dean Bramhald and Lenny Gloster, but lost to Gary Logan. Finishing with a record of 10-1-8, of his losing fights, four came in overseas matches.

HALIMI Alphonse *From* Paris, France. *Died* 12 November 2006, aged 74. Considering his impressive amateur pedigree, it is not surprising the Alphonse's rise to the top of his profession was quick. He was, as a Simon-pure, French bantamweight champion in three consecutive years. Jewish-born in Algeria, as one of a large family, he moved to Paris and started boxing in the amateur ranks in 1949.

His prowess attracted Gilbert Benaim, who sponsored him as a professional and stayed with him all the way through. Alphonse beat Mario D'Agata for the New York version of the world title in 1957, it being his 17th paid fight - rapid strides indeed. He was soon to unify the title by beating Raton Macias. A consistent fighter, he'd reached the top with victories over Billy Peacock, Dante Bini, Al Asuncion, Stan Sobolak, Antonio Diaz and Andre Jasse. Jimmy Carson ended his winning streak when bad facial cuts forced the referee to send him back to his corner. It took three years for the pair to be re-matched and Carson never got past the ninth round. Peter Keenan was another who failed against Alphonse, before he lost his title to Jose Beccera when journeying to Los Angeles to defend when tempted by a pot of gold. He tried to regain his title from the hard-punching Mexican, but was spectacularly knocked out in nine rounds. Beccera's tenure was brief and he retired from boxing after losing to Eloy Sanchez. The European Boxing Union quickly matched Alphonse with Freddie Gilroy and recognised the winner as world champion after the Frenchman scored a late knockdown that swayed the points in his favour. Once again he held a championship and he went unbeaten until Johnny Caldwell took his title. Caldwell also won the return and gradually Alphonse faded from the scene. He won and lost to Piero Rollo for the European title, but a defeat by Victor Cano in distant Bogota, Colombia was his last fight. Retiring with no scars despite a long career, he proved to be a good businessman, investing much of his wealth and managing a Parisian restaurant. His later years were marred by health problems, having contracted Alzheimer's disease in the late 1900s and spending his final years in a clinic.

Alphonse Halimi

HALL Bernie *From* Sydney, Australia. *Died* May 2007, aged 79. That great American lightweight, Freddie Dawson, twice beat Bernie. The first time Bernie gave him such a tussle that a return was made on the spot, but once again the exceptional class of Dawson prevailed. Bernie was no stranger to opposition, that was, or went on to be, right up there with the best. Joe Brown beat him at the end of 1950 when Bernie had returned from an inactive period, then Jimmy Carter outpointed him in Melbourne. Perhaps it was his performance against that trio of greats that inspired Bernie to hit a winning streak. Only one of his following eight foes lasted the distance, with Clem Sands, one of the famous six fighting brothers from Burnt Ridge, losing three times, George Kapeen, Red Briggs, Jackie de Belin and Johnny Oldham failing to last the course. The winning run was halted by another of the Sands' clan, namely Alfie, who beat Bernie in 11 rounds, but the Sydney man had his best years ahead. After knocking out Alfie Clay and stopping Ivor 'Kid' Germain, one of his best performances was to beat Darby Brown. He fought for the vacant Australian welterweight title, but lost to Kapeen. In retirement, Bernie passed on the benefit of his talent to train boxers, taking Charkay Ramon to the Commonwealth light-middleweight championship. He also coached, amongst many others, Ken Salisbury and Ron Beekin.

HANSEN Paul *From* Sydney, Australia. *Died* March 2007. This former Australian lightweight passed away in March 2007. Active from 1976 to 1986, his most notable opponent was Wayne Mulholland, who outpointed him in 1979. Paul beat Patrick Young in 1981, which was his best win, having previously outpointed Roy Hughes and drawn with Rocky Warren.

HARE Harry *From* Leeds. *Died* May 2007, aged 77. An early 1950s welterweight, Harry turned pro in 1952, beating Peter Townsend and Johnny Spittle before a stoppage defeat at the hands of John Watson saw him call it a day.

HARMAN Harry *From* Chatham. *Died* in August 2007, aged 90. From a boxing family, Harry's full record cannot be fully ascertained as he fought under so many different names. However, we do know that when boxing as a lightweight between 1935 and 1939, he twice beat Alex Gurr and shared a ring with others such as Dave Penfield, Fred Colegrave and Tim Cole. Was related to Ron Harman, the well-known heavyweight from the 1950s.

HILL Doug *From* Stoke. *Died* 26 May 2007, aged 51. An active professional from 1978 to1981, Doug died at a young age from a brain tumour. He was a former Midlands-Area featherweight champion, having annexed the vacant title when beating Alec Irvine in his 11th contest. Doug kicked off his career under the management of Pat Brogan with a draw against Bobby Baker and a loss to Selvin Bell in his first two outings. He then beat John Singlewood, Shaun Durkin, Steve Enright, Baker, Andy Dane and Shaun Stewart before drawing with Eric Ragonesi. After avenging his loss to Bell, he beat Irvine for the Midland title, but four fights later he was overwhelmed by Jimmy Flint when he stepped up in class. He then took three months off before defending his title against Don Aagesen and beating Steve Farnsworth, but called it a day when Glyn Rhodes forced him to quit after six rounds. Doug kept physically active until the tumour developed to a stage that required his admission to hospital.

O'Grady, Bob Cleaver, Ron Cooper, Bert Sanders, Bert Hyland, Les Allen, Sammy Wilde, Gene Fowler, etc, etc. Formerly a Smithfield Meat Market employee prior to and in his boxing years, he became a publican once his fighting days were over. He served pints in the location where he'd lived and where he'd so often boxed – and was a member of the London Ex-Boxers' Association.

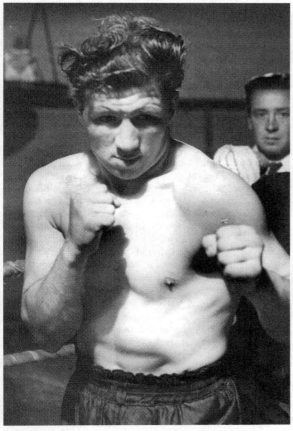

Alby Hollister

Bert Hyland

HOLLISTER Alby   *From* Islington. *Died* December 2006, aged 83. The popular Islington middleweight will be remembered for decking Randolph Turpin in the first round of their fight in Birmingham. Turpin got up to pound out an eight-round points win, but history of a sort had been made even though it took the passage of time to realise the importance of that punch. Turpin had been knocking out his opponents in jig time, but was years from making his mark at world level. In a six-year career, Alby mixed with most of the British middleweights of note and won just over a half of his fights. To call his record 'spotty' wouldn't take into account the fact that he never picked his opponent nor refused a fight. He was a promoter's dream and is remembered with affection by those who lived through the post-war boxing boom. Alby fought Alex Buxton, Albert Finch, Jimmy Davis, Mark Hart, Jack Lewis, Harry

HYLAND Bert   *From* Dublin. *Died* June 2007, aged 82. Ginger haired Bert was a fighter's fighter – prepared to trade blows at the drop of a hat and never querying who might be coming out of the opposite corner. Bert took 'em on as he was asked and never, as far as I know, refused a fight. Possibly it was an early-career win over Ernie Roderick at Marylebone's Seymour Hall that boosted his confidence to take on Jimmy Bray, Albert Finch and Randolph Turpin. He lost to all three but was made of stern stuff and a good win over New Zealand's tough Billy Coloulias put him back on track. He again lost to Finch much later in his career, but got another chance and won it - that was 1949, a good year for him. Now living in London after starting his boxing in Liverpool, Alby Hollister, Sammy Wilde, Joe Rood, Jimmy Ingle and Jackie Wilson were all the wrong end of the points tally. Bert slipped a bit in 1950, losing to good opponents in Jimmy Davis, Ron Pudney and Dick Langley. He took a rest and returned in 1952, but never reproduced his best form and his loss to Carshalton's Wally Beckett in Dublin was his last fight. In 43 contests he met the likes of Doug Miller of South Africa, Bert Sanders, Roy Peterson, George Howard, Lefty 'Satan' Flynn, Johnny Boyd, Harry Davis, Brian Anders, Reg Spring, Jim Laverick and Ron Cooper, et al. Bert's son married Peter Arnold's daughter but they separated later. Arnold was author of several boxing books, one of which he produced in conjunction with our editor, Barry Hugman.

INNOCENT Gene *From* Cardiff. *Died* September 2006, aged 61. Cardiff-born Gene fought from 1967 to 1973 under Benny Jacobs' management. He was a heavyweight who fought once for the Welsh title, but failed to bring home the prize he sought, fellow Cardiff fighter, Dennis Avoth, beating him on points. Gene made an auspicious start, going through 1967 unbeaten, scoring three wins over Jim McIlvaney. Others he beat included Mick Carter, Barry Rodney and Peter Thomas. His first defeat, which doesn't look demeaning to his record in retrospect, was against Joe Bugner, who stopped him in 1968. Gene had beaten Rocky James, Paul Brown and Ernie Field inside the distance that year but couldn't maintain the impetus against Bugner. Discouraged, he took a long break until 1972. His enthusiasm had returned and with it, some of his old form. A draw with Roger Barlow late in the year was a good result and this brought him the title contest with Avoth. He'd twice beaten Mal Isaacs, but following the Avoth fight came a further loss to Peter Freeman and he never fought again. He retired, having had only 17 fights, and left his fans with a feeling that with a little more luck he might have become a force at European level. He died of cancer and is survived by his wife and four children.

Gene Innocent

JACKSON Billy *From* Thornaby. *Died* 12 January 2007, aged 94. Harold Alderman reports the death of old-timer Billy Jackson, whose part-record he has compiled with some difficulty. There were dozens of Jacksons active in the 1930s, which often causes confusion to record compilers. There are 42 known fights with one victory standing out – a win over Willie Sharkey. Jackson also beat Bob Smart, Ted Carter and Mickey Rooney. It's possible that he had over 100 fights. That was nothing unusual for men of similar age, but most of his achievements never graced the sports' columns of national newspapers. Keith Robinson, a relative who writes for the Yearbook, has produced an article on Billy and his brother, which you will find within these pages.

JENSEN Marv *From* West Jordan, Utah, USA. *Died* 14 March 2007, aged 89. Utah's Marv described himself as a self-made boxers' manager, trainer and promoter, steering fellow-Mormon, Gene Fullmer, to middleweight fame and handling Lamar Clark and Rex Layne. Later, Fullmer's brother Don joined the stable. Boxing was not the sole interest of his multi-faceted life – as he owned a mink farm, was one-time mayor of West Utah's Jordan area, a local school-board chairman, a Salt Lake City commissioner and a director of a State park. A rare fever finished his own boxing career in the 1920s so he stayed on in the game as a trainer, opening the basement of his house as a gymnasium. It was there that Gene Fullmer learned the rudiments of his trade. The two remained friends right up to Marv's death, which shattered iron-man Fullmer. Marv was admitted to hospital following a spell of stomach flu, but at his age there is no such thing as a 'minor' illness and he just faded away just as his gym did. A school now stands on the site.

JIMINEZ 'Baba' Nestor *From* Cartagena, Colombia. *Died* March 2007, aged 59. World title challenger, Nestor, squeezed over 80 fights into a long career. At the bantamweight and super-bantamweight poundages he won and defended both Colombian and Central American titles, but was out of luck when challenging Wilfredo Gomez for the world 122lbs championship, the fight coming at the end of his career. Like many fighters from the South American continent, Nestor's form remained constant throughout most of his career. He was a busy professional who seldom had to step outside of his own country to get contests. Fights in Panama, Venezuela, Costa Rica and Managua were the only seven places found on his record that were outside of Colombia. He was world class and had a stylish approach to boxing, being a craftsman rather than a puncher. His technique helped him to last so long against the best opposition and he scored notable wins over Jaime Amaya, Ruben Valdez, Enrique Pinto, Ricardo Cardona and Juan Mayoral. Those who beat him were all rated fighters. Rodolfo Martinez stopped him in defence of his WBC title in 1975, in one of his worst years, and Carlos Zarate and old-foe Pinto beat him, but he was back on the winning side in 1977, going through to 1979 without tasting defeat. Then came the challenge to Gomez and a year's inactivity was followed by a stoppage win over Jose Patricio. He was now 33 and was starting to lose as many fights as he won. Slowly, he faded from the scene and nothing can be traced beyond 1981 in his boxing record.

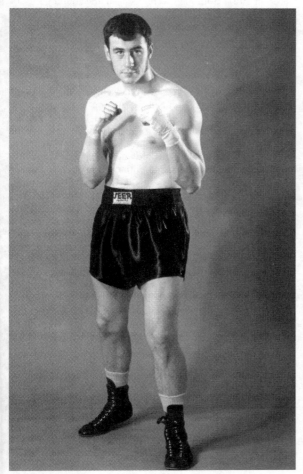

Roy John

JOHN Roy *From* Abercynon. *Died* 12 February 2007, aged 59. Roy was one of those unsung professional boxers with a penchant for upsetting the odds. Had he been based in London, he may well have had his name adorning the list of British light-heavyweight champions. As it was, he gave Chris Finnegan an extremely tough fight for the British and Commonwealth light-heavyweight championship in 1973, having won the right to challenge Chris by surprisingly outpointing Johnny Frankham. Frankham clowned and played to the gallery and John, who was so confident, got on with it and won clearly. He never did get the return match with Finnegan, who developed serious eye conditions and was forced to get out of boxing. Roy didn't have an easy ride to title contention. He lost to Kosie Smith in Johannesburg then returned to beat Arno Prick. Two losing fights came in Italy and then an excursion to France saw him drop a decision to Christian Poncelet, while in Rotterdam Bas van Duivenbode got a lucky decision over eight rounds. Roy had been given few favours overseas but was more fortunate at home, beating Guinea Roger, Jeff Shaw, Maxie Smith and Phil Matthews. After his stern challenge against Finnegan, John lost to Tom Bogs in Denmark and then courageously fought his way back with a series of victories, culminating in a title eliminator with Tim Wood. He beat Wood but never got the second chance to win the British title. He deserved it and would have been favoured, but the dangerous Mustapha Wassaja beat him in Denmark in January 1978. It was a big disappointment and Roy decided it was the time to quit.

JOHNSON 'Bronco' Don *From* Boojie, Queensland, Australia. *Died* 17 October 2006, aged 78. With his wild style of fighting that defied the tenets of boxing instruction manuals, Don drew in the fans at Stadiums in Sydney and Brisbane during the 1950s and early '60s. If he caught them with one of his haymakers, and he often did, then they'd wake up in the dressing room. An eccentric character, sometimes seen on Brisbane streets dressed in rodeo gear with a baby crocodile under his arm, he was, at one time, a rodeo rider and later owned his own rodeo show and boxing troupe. As an itinerant fairground entertainer, who'd travelled with Jimmy Sharman, he was popular on the eastern coast of Australia. Don was attracted to boxing when young, getting his brothers to train him, and there must have been some discipline in him then because he won the Queensland amateur middleweight championship. He turned professional under the aegis of Ern McQuillan and blew away his first 11 opponents in jig time. Amongst them were Pran Mikus and Alfie Sands, both of them technically superior but both being hit with the one punch that mattered. The great Aussie welterweight, Tommy Burns, stopped Don's progress when halting him in eight rounds, but described it as being by far his hardest fight. From such an experienced boxer, that was indeed, praise to be noted. Mikus fought Don four times with only one win, but Ricardo Marcos beat Don four times out of five. He hung his chin out once and paid the penalty and in their last encounter, won by Marcos, the Australian light-heavyweight crown was at stake. Five years previously, Al Bourke had beaten Don for the middleweight title, but Don beat Luigi Male, Carlo Marchini and Ernie Hughes. He forced Tiberio Mitri to go 12 rounds and never heard 'ten' counted over him in a 45-fight career.

JORDAN Bert *From* Bridlington. *Died* 9 December 2006, aged 86. Tracing the bulk of Bert's fights is an impossible task. His boxing achievements are typical of those of an itinerant pug of his era, a man who fought on unlicensed shows and on booths. He did so for ages and those activities went unreported in the press. Vic Hardwicke unearthed three results for 1938-39, which is when 17-year-old Bert took up boxing seriously. He lost his first licensed ten rounder to George Lake, but was young and had never fought over that distance. He simply ran out of gas, so back into the gym where he went to learn how to pace a fight. It paid off as he beat Percy Mattison then stopped Ken Mumby. Bert had been boxing since he was five without having the advantage of a local boxing club and what boxing he got was when sparring with anyone of his weight and age. Having been on the licensed circuit for a year when army service called, in uniform he reverted to amateur status since he was not allowed to earn money. The war ended, so back in civvy street in 1946 he resumed his career. He was a 26-year-old featherweight, who was short of experience but very fit and soon discovered that he could hurt his adversaries. Despite twice decking his first opponent he lost, but when Tony Vairo took over his management his career took off. He beat Jackie Lucraft, Tom Bailey, Stan Gossip and Jack Dougherty and although Ray Fitton beat him in four rounds he'd proved that he could hold his own with well-known names. Bert had done well, but the loss of those prime years in the early 1940s probably stopped him from making a bigger name for himself. By trade he was a joiner and this gave him a good living after his boxing days. He also stayed active in the game, coaching youngsters in his native Yorkshire.

JURIETTI Charles *From* Valence, France. *Died* 14 April 2007, aged 54. Charles was a former holder of both the lightweight and junior lightweight French titles. He also fought twice for the European junior lightweight title, forcing Natale Vezzoli to a draw on the first occasion and losing to Rodolfo Sanchez in Spain in his second attempt. After beating Maurice Apeang in the unusual location of Papeete, Tahiti, he was crowned French junior lightweight champion and proved that he had the Indian sign on his rival against whom he made his first defence. A good win over Sammy Meck followed, then another defence against Michel Leferbre. He then outgrew the division and won the lightweight title from Didier Kowalski in 1982, defending it three times before losing his crown to Frederic Geoffroy. One more fight followed before he bowed out in 1984 after being knocked out by Gert Bo Jacobsen. A glance at his record shows that he beat Rene Martin, Carlos Dos Santos and Aldo di Benedetto (twice), but was defeated by Elio Cotena.

KENNEDY 'Tiger' Paul *From* Yakima, Washington, USA. *Died* 7 July 2006, aged 81. Paul first donned gloves for fistic combat back in 1939 when he was ten. War in Europe had just been declared, tournaments were scarce but he got many fights while maturing into a welterweight. Having competed in the AAU National Championships before turning pro in 1948, Paul was an orthodox boxer with a sound technique, who fought as a middleweight for most of his pro career. In his baptismal year, he won two, lost two and drew one. This pattern continued into the early 1960s when a succession of defeats told him that it was time to sit back and let others vie for fame. He won, lost and drew with Dick Wolfe all over ten rounds and continued to fight frequently on Los Angeles and Hollywood undercards, with a notable stoppage victory over Rocky Finnegan in 1951. Paul was a frequent performer in Vancouver, Canada, where he fought eight times with just two losses.

LEONARD Jackie *From* Los Angeles, California. *Died* on 26 August 2007, aged 89. A promoter and matchmaker at the old Hollywood Legion Stadium who was involved in several world title bouts, Jackie is probably more famous for being the man who testified against Blinky Palermo and Frankie Carbo in 1961. Both men were accused and found guilty of muscling in on Don Jordan after the latter had twice beaten Virgil Akins for the world welterweight title. Following the trial, Jackie was forced to spend 20 years in the witness protection programme before returning to boxing in the 1980s.

LESTER Jimmy *From* San Francisco, California, USA. *Died* 9 September 2006, aged 61. At one time a top-rated fighter, Jimmy got out of the game too late and marred what had been an impressive record. He went through his first two years of fighting without tasting defeat then lost to Denny Moyer, a man he'd previously beaten. Thrown in as a huge underdog against Florentino Fernandez he caused a startling upset by taking out the Cuban in two rounds, but sustained a hand injury that kept him inactive for five months. Nine fights followed, in which he flattened six of his adversaries but lost two big ones to Andy Heilman and Stan Harrington and his record became spotty after this. There were good wins over Charlie Austin, Carl Moore and Tito Marshall, but he was in over his head against Charley Scott, Luis Rodriguez, Bennie Briscoe and Nate Collins. He continued into the 1970s with sparse success, losing on points to future light-heavyweight contender Jesse Burnett in 1973. His last win came in 1971 when he knocked out Al Mills in the opening round. After his ring days were over he worked for the Police Department, married and raised a son and daughter.

LIBEER Rene *From* Roubaix, France. *Died* November 2006, aged 72. This former French international amateur flyweight, who won a bronze medal at the 1956 Olympics when losing to Terry Spinks in England as a pro. He'd won the French title in his second year as a professional and was regarded as a man capable of extending British fighters without endangering their records. And so it proved. In those three fights he acquitted himself well and it is interesting that two of the men he fought, Walter McGowan and Johnny Caldwell, became world champions and the other one, Freddie Gilroy, just lost by a whisker when he challenged Alphonse Halimi. Gaining in experience, Rene fought on and rose to fight for European honours in 1965, beating Paul Chervet for the vacant title. On the way he'd won the French flyweight title, which he defended three times. His first shot at the European championship ended in failure when Salvatore Burruni beat him in 1963, but, again, he'd lost to a man destined to win world honours. When he did acquire the title, he defended it against Jo Horny, Dionisio Bisbal and Antoine Porcel, eventually surrendering it to the latter. He got a return and forced a draw. By then he was 33 and decided to retire when still able to give a good account of himself. He'd had ten title fights in 39 outings – a ratio of one in ten. That says it all. The cause of death was not stated.

KOKMEIJER Harko *From* Amsterdam, Holland. *Died* 6 May 2007, aged 71. Unlike today, there was a fair amount of boxing activity in Northern Europe when this Dutch middleweight plied his wares. He was successful on his own patch with 13 wins from 13 fights in Amsterdam and just one defeat in five outings in Rotterdam. On Dutch soil, he beat Jimmy Lygett, Theun Brommer, Edouard Delannoit and Mohamed le Noir, but in foreign territory he didn't always do so well. Although he beat Richard Bouchez in Ghent and held Bob Stevens to a draw at the same venue, he lasted less than a round against Fortunato Manca in Cagliari. Jo Janssens beat him in Liege and Leo Potesil stopped him in Vienna. By 1961 he'd fought back well to get a shot at the vacant European title in London. Although Harko had matured into a decent fighter by then he wasn't skilled enough to beat the Scottish southpaw, John 'Cowboy' McCormack, who finished with the points in his favour. Subsequent defeats by good European contenders in Peter Muller and Chris Christensen forced him to take a rest. Returning to the ring after a couple of years off, he fought well against lower-rated opposition, winning most of his fights before quitting at the age of 32.

McEWAN Bobby *From* Glasgow. *Died* April 2007. Having been told he would never box again after being injured in a 60-foot fall, 'Blondie' surprised everyone when coming back in 1954 to win the Western District of Scotland's amateur featherweight title. Later, he emigrated to Canada and won the all-Canadian title, which enabled him to represent the country in the 1958 British Empire Games. After being narrowly outpointed by England's Roy Beaman he eventually returned to Scotland and boxed for the Glasgow Transport club. He then became a coach and was instrumental in developing good amateurs such as Carlo Melucci.

McGUINNESS Tommy *From* Edinburgh. *Died* April 2007, aged 72. Brian Donald informs me of this former ABA lightweight finalist's death. Tommy learned his boxing at the famous Sparta club and won two Scottish titles before embarking on a three-year career as a professional, which started in 1957 with a knockout victory over Ken Scott. Tommy went through seven fights unbeaten before London taxi-driver, Barney Beale, halted his winning run. Although Tommy got a return he couldn't reverse the loss, but he did manage to beat Dave Stone and thereby took revenge for his defeat in the 1956 ABA finals. He then scored a credible victory over Brian Husband, but came unstuck against Paddington's Johnny Simmons and Johnny McLaren, the latter fight being for the Scottish lightweight title. The loss was a big disappointment because he'd earlier beaten Johnny clearly. Tommy and Peter Heath fought a draw, which is the only one on his record, and there were wins over Jimmy Cottrill, Arthur Murphy, Ronnie Rush, Johnny Bamborough and Tony McCrorey. In 1960 he lost a light-welterweight challenge for the Scottish title when his namesake, Jimmy McGuinness, from Wishaw, outpointed him. After that, he drifted away from active boxing and offered his talents to help train young Sparta ABC boxers, one of them being a youngster called Ken Buchanan. Tommy is survived by his wife, Freda, and three children.

Tommy McGuinness

McINNES Peter *From* Bournemouth. *Died* 7 February 2007, aged 80. Peter owned a boxing library that is unsurpassed. He was a boxing man right from his pre-teens and as a boy idolised his neighbour, Freddie Mills. It was Peter who wrote the Mills' biography *Twenty Years*. He also wrote another on Benny Lynch and ghost-wrote *Somebody Ring The Bell*, the life story of Willie Toweel. Under his own name, Peter produced several books a few of which were advertised in the trade journal until his death. He was a regular advertiser and reader of *Southern Ex-Boxer* when I was producing that bi-annual magazine. Peter always paid his subs and advertising bill on time and I doubt if he got, or expected, many sales of his books, but used the advertisement as an excuse to support the publication. In the McInnes' collection was a rare six-volume edition of *Boxiana* and I'm not including the volume of illustrations as part of that set. What Peter owned was a very rare collectors' item. There were also bound volumes of *Mirror Life*. A student of the game could glean most of its history through the impressive collection that he had acquired over the years. He was a university and army boxer in his day, his army boxing being done in a team that included Henry Cooper. In later years, he and his wife Jane were housebound, but he used the telephone as a means of communication and never became out of touch. Boxing has an exalted place in English literature and nearly all books on the subject passed through his hands at one time or other. I had known him since 1946 when collectors of boxing literature were part of a closely-knit group. His other hobby was dogs, of which he and his wife were very fond.

McNAIR John *From* Glasgow. *Died* 21 March 2007, aged 71. An amateur with 300 fights, and a man who fought Dick McTaggart, Jim Watt and Alan Richardson amongst others, John provided an invaluable service to the East of Glasgow when training youngsters at clubs such as Riverside, Glasgow Transport, Gallagher and Dennistoun. Boxing at featherweight and lightweight, John won a Western District title and was good enough to box for Scotland on several occasions. His son Alexander was an ex-Scottish amateur champion.

Maurice 'Mosh' Mancini

MANCINI 'Mosh' Maurice *From* Leamington. *Died* 1 March 2007, aged 80. Any fighter in the George Middleton stable got plenty of work in the 1950s. The Turpins were the stars, but good performers like Mosh got top-class sparring and this showed in the ring, especially when he scored six clean knockouts and four stoppages in the year of his debut. There were seven points' wins against three losses. Not a bad start at all and the trend continued until he'd fought his way into the top-ten ratings. I'm reminded of Vic Hardwicke's comment on boxing records. "Never mind the win-loss breakdown, look at the quality of the opponent". Mosh had knocked out Vic's protege, Fred Archer, in 1948

and went on to score wins over Hal Bagwell, Cliff Anderson, Bert Hornby, Bob Anderson, Roy Sharples, Chris Jenkins, Harry Hughes and that very experienced boxer from Covent Garden, Johnny Hudson. Other big names on an excellent record are Roy Coote, Tommy Hinson, Bert Middleton, Tommy Barnham, Owen Trainor, Tommy McGovern, Peter Fallon, Israel Boyle, Chris Jenkins and Dick Levers. He had over 60 fights squeezed into a five-year career and retired at the young age of 26 before returning to his old trade of spraying cars. Having joined the Navy in 1944 and started boxing when he was still in service uniform, his strong ties with the Turpin family were such that he wrote a piece of music dedicated to Randolph following his death in 1966. Mosh and I shared many an illuminating conversation at fights and boxing events when he remembered his fighting days with pride.

MARQUES Herman *From* Stocton, California, USA. *Died* 3 October 2006, aged 72. Mexican-born Herman made his mark as a bantamweight fighter in the 1960s after having had a good amateur grounding with a National AAU title to his name. His paid career ran from 1957 to 1962 and he retired when still at his fistic zenith. That great fighter, Eder Jofre, stopped him in a world title fight but had to come from behind to do so. Herman was a man with a fluid boxing style, but could turn fighter if the circumstances so demanded. He started in April 1957 with a stoppage win over Al Aguilar and within a year he'd beaten Billy Peacock and had drawn with Dwight Hawkins. This got him a shot at the Californian title, but his chance had come too early. Boots Monroe beat him and Herman had to wait three years before getting another opportunity. When it came, he beat Ronnie Perez on points and defended his newly won crown twice before the year was over. A win over Ignacio Pina secured his place as a challenger to Eder Jofre. He didn't linger in the game to become a trial-horse for up-and- coming fighters, taking a job in a cannery and then working on the docks in Stockton. He left behind a wife and four children.

MARTIN Young *From* Madrid, Spain. *Died* 17 June 2007, aged 71. A former Spanish and European flyweight champion, Young Martin, christened Marin Marco Voto, was brought to England to fight Dai Dower in 1955. The European title was on line and Dower, unbeaten at that stage, was confident of emerging victorious. Martin upset the Welshman, who spent as much time on the canvas as he did standing up. The hammering went on for 12 rounds before the Spaniard applied the knockout. Martin, who was the Spanish champion, lost his first shot at the title some three years earlier when Louis Skena stopped him in eight rounds. But Martin had an iron will and he came back to beat Theo Medina, Ogli Tettey, Andre Jasse and Robert Meunier. Obviously, Dower should have taken heed. After beating Dower, Martin defended his title four times before the lanky Finnish champion, Risto Luukkonen, deprived him of it. He never got past the third round when challenging for the world title against the great Pascual Perez, but he was still a very powerful force at European level. He defeated Alex Bollaert, Stan Sobolak and Robert Pollazon, but hit the slide after being beaten by Britain's George Bowes. Johnny Caldwell also beat him and his Spanish title went to Raton Osuna, a man he'd beaten previously. As his career was reaching its end, he dropped down to the eight-round class and piled up a few more wins, but the money wasn't there so he decided to call it a day.

Young Martin

MARTINEZ Jimmy *From* Glendale, Arizona, USA. *Died* 13 April 2007, aged 77. Jimmy's career lasted throughout the 1950s, with 153 fights in ten years of campaigning, and he was on the fringe of world class right up to the time he chose to quit boxing. His battling average - 15 fights per year - indicates that he was in demand. As well as fighting all over the USA, Jimmy travelled to South Africa, where he beat Mike Holt and Jimmy Elliott; to Berlin where he drew with Gustav Scholz; to Kitwe when knocking out Tenus Viviers; and in Australia where he beat Joe N'Gidi and Willie Vaughan. A durable middleweight, only two men stopped him – Danny Giovanelli and Ellsworth 'Spider' Webb. There are two world champions' names on his record in Carl 'Bobo' Olson and Willie Pastrano, whom he boxed twice. Then there are many world-rated men that Jimmy beat, such as Chu Chu Escobar, Allie Gronik, Del Flanagan, Bobby Dykes, Joe Miceli, Tony Dupas, Armando Muniz, Milo Savage, Jimmy Beecham and Ramon Fuentes. I'll list a few more of note: Pat Lowry, Peter Muller, Ernie Durando, Yama Bahama, Phil Moyer, Gomeo Brennan and Rudolf Bent, against whom he had his last fight when losing on points. He notched up 112 wins against nine draws and 32 losses – a very busy fighter, who was both consistent and reliable.

MARTINEZ Ruben *From* Spain. *Died* 17 November 2006, aged 68. In 1990, Ruben became First Executive Vice President of the World Boxing Council and in the same year he was appointed Chairman of the European Boxing Union. He was also the Chairman of the Spanish Boxing Federation and was a member of the Spanish Olympic Committee. An outstanding administrator, he was awarded the honour of being Commissioner of the Year by the WBC three times and will be sorely missed by those at the EBU, which remained strong throughout his reign.

MEAD Pete *From* Arkansas. *Died* July 2007, aged 80. Fight-goers who were around in the 1940s will remember this man for his two gallant fights at Harringay, where he met Dave Sands and Randolph Turpin. Promoter Jack Solomons was searching for an opponent for Sands, but wanted someone durable and capable of extending the Australian. Sands had recently won the Empire championship and followed it with one of his best-ever performances when beating France's Robert Villemain in a thriller. In choosing the American, Solomons got a man who would endear himself to British fans. We knew that he'd twice beaten Joey DeJohn, Sonny Horne, Cocoa Kid, Herbie Kronowitz and an aging Fritzie Zivic. A more recent guide to his form was that he too had fought Villemain. Pete didn't win, but gave the Frenchman a hard battle over the ten-round distance. He didn't beat Sands either, but what a thrilling, gutsy performance it was! No matter how hard Sands hit him, Pete marched forward and on the occasions that he got past Sands' left hand, meted out punishment to the body that the Aussie didn't relish. It was clearly Sands' fight, but it was never easy. Pete made him fight every inch of the way and at the final bell received one of the loudest ovations ever given to a loser. He was happy to have pleased the British public and one month later he was back in the same ring opposed to Turpin, who was one year the younger man and on the way up – a very formidable fighter. Once again, Pete stood up to tremendous punishment gamely, but had taken such a battering to the body that on leaving his corner for the fifth round he fainted. Taken to hospital, it was shown that the American had severely bruised ribs. That he wasn't hesitant in coming out for another round and that he'd never been off his feet, showed what a courageous and genuine fighter he was. Taking time out, Pete came back almost a year later, only to be knocked out in the third round by Rocky Graziano. Despite being just 23 years of age, Pete decided it was time to get out. Eighteen months later Turpin was middleweight champion of the world, but would never fight a tougher man.

MERRITT George *From* Silvertown. *Died* 1 June 2007, aged 93. When I heard of George's death I felt that one of the last links in a chain of boxers active in the 1930s had been broken. Sadly, there will be no more tales of his boxing experiences, no more of his jokes, and no more pearls of wisdom. George was so popular and was a member of both the London, Kent and Croydon Ex-Boxers' Associations. To still be part of the boxing community meant much to him. When his wife died a few years ago, George was distraught but turned up at the Croydon meeting the next day. He wanted us to know that he was determined to carry on. Despite being a sad man he was a proud one. I suggested that he should try the meals-on-wheels service but he refused outright, saying that he wanted to carry on as he usually did. I received a lovely letter from him thanking me for my concern. I still have it placed in a box with other treasures. He was a welterweight who took up boxing with no amateur experience. What he'd learned in spars with his brother Curly at the back of the family grocer's shop was enough to launch him on a long career. I can trace 131 fights, but I know there were more. Nobody ever put George down for ten and despite having many losses due to cuts, he had only one bad defeat when Ginger Ross tore out of his corner and swamped George with an avalanche of punches that caused the referee to halt it after only 45 seconds. Ross, George told me, was a banger – he later nearly succeeded in doing a similar job on Fred Bullions. Three days after the Ross debacle, George was back in action, stopping Dick Johnson in eight rounds at Euston. That's the way things were in George's day. He had six fights with Arnold 'Kid' Sheppard and won the lot. They had great respect for each other. In their last fight, when Sheppard was having difficulty in seeing, George stopped boxing to ask him what was the matter and let him remove grit from his eye. That was sportsmanship and George still smiled many years later when he told of how Sheppard responded with a right that gave him his 'cap badge' as he termed it, meaning his cauliflower ear of course. George had another series with Mike Sullivan, involving nine fights, with three to George, one to Sullivan and five draws. There were three fights with Billy Curran of Walton on Thames, George winning the first but losing the other two. He also met Harry Howard seven times. His biggest disappointment was in losing to Norman Snow when substituting for Derby's Tommy Jones just before Christmas in 1939, being ahead on points and in a strong position when facial cuts caused a halt. His record contains the names of Buster Osborne, Rabbit Ryan, Johnny Waples, Frank Meacham, Alf Paolozzi, Steve Fay, George Bissett and Billy Bird. Some of his best wins came over Dave Penfield, Harry Davis and George Bennett. After the war George turned his hand to promoting. He was always a good-humoured man and a pleasure to talk to. I usually commented on the size of his hands; mine are like shovels but looked like a baby's next to his. No wonder he was reputed as being a solid puncher! Admitted to hospital in January 2007 and dying of pneumonia nearly six months later, he is survived by two daughters and a grand daughter.

MIKUS Pran *From* Melbourne, Australia. *Died* 23 May 2007, aged 78. British fans got an inclination that Pran was no boxing fool when he stopped Eric Boon during the Englishman's not-too-successful Australian tour. Admittedly, Boon was well past his best at the time. Despite having a chequered career and at times looking as if he wouldn't reach championship heights, an examination of Pran's record reveals that he was thrown in with the lions far too early in his career. George Kapeen and Don Johnson stopped him, but the rot ended when Pran matured into a top-of-the-bill performer after outpointing Andre Famechon in only his second year as a professional. Although born in Lithuania, a country with a very limited boxing history,

residence in Australia gave him the opportunity to make a name for himself and he challenged for an Australian title twice before beating Carlo Marchini for the middleweight crown. Two years prior to that he'd lost to George Barnes for the vacant welterweight title. Having gone through the ranks from lightweight to middleweight before he retired in 1956, he never could beat Barnes, but did force a draw in their first fight when he was a 23-year-old lightweight. He was successful against British-based men like Ivor 'Kid' Germain, Al Wilburn and the aforementioned Boon. It took four attempts before Pran beat Johnson, but he was on firmer ground against Alfie Sands, with whom he fought a draw followed by two subsequent wins. Other names on his record are Luigi Coluzzi, Ricardo Marcos, Johnny Halafihi and Tommy Burns, who he pushed to the 12-round limit in a credible showing in 1953. Billy McDonnell took Pran's middleweight title in 1955, but he was nearing the end by then. He finished with more than 50 fights spread over four weight divisions.

MILANDRI Widmer *From* Forli, Italy. *Died* 3 August 2007, aged 85. Those who were following boxing in the 1940s will recall Widmer being brought here to face the British Champion, Vince Hawkins, in 1947. The Italian had been a pro for three years at that time and his fighting had been confined to Continental Europe. He was not an unknown quantity because he'd just lost to Cyril Delannoit, who was only the second man to beat him, but Hawkins was vastly experienced with one defeat, later avenged, in 70 fights. Widmer took Hawkins the distance and from that point on fought at top European level, taking on some of the best men around at the time with his win-loss record being marred as a result. He lost to Alex Buxton, Jacques Royer-Crecy, Alessandro D'Ottavio, Laurent Dauthille, Hans Stretz and Charles Humez, but obviously learned from his defeats. In a return with D'Ottavio he turned the tables. It was a domestic championship fight and he lost his title one year later, Bruno Tripoli beating him in two rounds to win the championship belt that Widmer had worn so briefly. Having drawn with Ivano Fontana and scored some good wins over Italian opposition, he was brought back to London to test Gordon Hazell. Widmer was past his prime and Hazell, who was on the way up, won in five rounds. Fights were infrequent after that, with just two wins before his career petered out in 1957 following losses to Giulio Rinaldi and Domenico Baccheschi. Among other top names on his record are Fernando Jannilli, Giovanni Manca and Bos Murphy.

MTHEMBU Theo *From* Newcastle, Natal, South Africa. *Died* 22 February 2007, aged 79. Theo's boxing career was curtailed by injuries sustained in a shooting incident. He'd fought his way into contention for a shot at the national South African featherweight title in 1952, but the points' score went against him. He'll be remembered more for his role as a trainer and manager, piloting Baby Jake Matlala to four world title fights. Matlala was a boy when he came under Theo's umbrella, but stayed with him to become one of the oldest active flyweights in boxing history. Theo also trained Anthony Morodi and later in life became a promoter. His contribution to South African boxing is a saga of dedication, hard work and a long love affair with fisticuffs.

OLVER Ron *From* Wood Green, London. *Died* 27 March 2007, aged 91. Ron was famous in the boxing world for being the man to introduce the 'Old Timers' column in *Boxing News* and also going on to help build up the ex-boxers movement, while giving the organisation much needed publicity on a national basis. The Ex-Boxers Associations, of which there are 34 in the UK and Ireland, are unique to our islands and acknowledge that without Ron their rise would never have happened on such a scale. At *Boxing News*, Ron wrote enthusiastically about retired boxers, trainers, managers and promoters and it was therefore a natural progression for him to become a Committee Member of the British Boxing Board of Control's Benevolent Fund. It is also no surprise that he was appointed a Vice President of several Ex-Boxers Associations from Scotland to Cornwall. He was also a member of the Yearbook team, having been with us from day one. Born in Plymouth, although he liked watching boxing, football, athletics and cricket were really Ron's sports and he played for many years. He even had a trial for Plymouth Argyll, but unfortunately a rule banning players who wore glasses meant he couldn't be signed – there were no contact lenses in those days! However, that did not deter Ron from playing, and when he joined the Army they issued him with metal rimmed glasses. He then went on to represent the Army football team in tournaments in Africa, Germany, Italy, and even played against an England team. When the war was finished, Ron, who was a chief clerk, was transferred to Germany from 1945 until 1949 to oversee the changes to the banking system. On returning to the UK in 1949 a good friend that he had corresponded with, Neville Buckley, gave him a letter of introduction to Gilbert Odd, the then editor of *Boxing News,* and when Ron went for an interview, after a few minutes Gilbert said: "There is a desk over there, get started, we have a deadline to meet". The rest is history. Unfortunately, having suffered a stroke a few years ago, he lost his mobility and became housebound after being left partially blind. It was then that Ron proved that he too was a fighter by nature. With the aid of his wife Phyllis of nearly 60 years and his daughter Pat, he gathered the information each week from letters, phone calls and reports from his many contacts and, like clockwork, the deadline was met. Ron's contacts in the boxing world were incredible, having met and interviewed many of the all-time greats from Joe Louis to Mohammad Ali, but his favourite boxer was Len Harvey, whom he knew very well. At *Boxing News* he became the assistant editor and covered so many shows (there were far more in the London area than today) that Phyllis rarely saw him. A real sportsman, Ron played cricket into his late 40s and liked nothing better than watching his 'second' favourite team, Arsenal, play every other week. He was over the moon when they went unbeaten for a whole season, something that was thought to be nigh impossible. Ron did lots of good work in boxing, but it was his efforts in keeping the retired fighters in the limelight for which he will be largely remembered and he will never be forgotten by the Ex-Boxers' Associations for as long as they last. The stories will be passed down from generation to generation. His book *The Professionals,* which detailed many a past career, showed where his heart was and the old fighters loved him for it. There were many other achievements and I have listed some of them here. Apart from *Boxing News*, he was a former assistant editor of *Boxing World*; was the British correspondent of *The Ring*; produced the boxing section within *Encyclopedia Britannica*; did specialist work on *Boxing* - Foyles' library service; and was the former co-editor of the *Boxing News Annual*. His honorary work, saw him as the Chairman of the BBBoC Charity Grants' Committee; the Public Relations Officer of the London Ex-Boxers' Association; among the membership of the Commonwealth Boxing Council as New Zealand's representative. In recent years, Ron was honoured by the Boxing Writers' Club, the BBBoC, and the Commonwealth Boxing Council. He was further honoured by the Boxing Writers' Club, who made him an Honorary Life Member. The *Yearbook* editor, Barry Hugman, knew Ron well and thought very highly of him. He can be quoted as saying: "When I was producing the *George Wimpey Amateur Boxing Annual*, Ron was most supportive and from then on we struck up a firm friendship. It was Ron who I always turned to first for advice on boxing matters and he went on to support my work with the *British Boxing Yearbook*, *Boxing Monthly* and *Boxing Weekly*. I will miss him very much. He was a terrific supporter of former boxers as he knew how tough it had been for them and in my opinion the ex-boxers movement as we know it today would never have got off the ground. A kind man, he always had a good word for all of those he came into contact with and was revered by the hard men in boxing. Rest in peace my friend".

O'SULLIVAN Dickie *From* Finsbury Park. *Died* 17 April 2007, aged 80. In boxing circles Dickie was known as 'The Toy Bulldog'. This monniker wasn't borrowed from the famous Mickey Walker, but was bestowed on him in Australia because he fought with the spirit of a British Bulldog. He was a tiny man who could fight. Strangely enough, although being world-rated, he never held a title but he did get very near. In 1948 he challenged Maurice Sandeyron for the European flyweight championship and got a draw after a hard-fought battle. Three months later Dickie beat the Frenchman in eight rounds to earn another title shot, but this time Sandeyron won a narrow victory. Dickie began pro boxing in Australia when serving as a cook in the Royal Navy, having five fights with four wins and a draw, beating Stumpy Butwell in one of them. He was a London ABA champion prior to enlisting and back in home rings he won an eliminator for the British title when beating Charlie Squire. Stoppage victories came over Jimmy Gill and Billy Davies, before Terry Allen beat him on a disqualification and won the return on points. But it wasn't all doom and gloom and he had good wins over Emile Famechon and Vic Herman of Scotland, but the latter win was his last victory of note. After Peter Keenan knocked him out in three rounds, Dickie later told me that he thought nobody could ever do that to him, and it sowed the seeds of retirement. Ten months later he was outpointed by Teddy Gardner, which hastened the end of his career. He emigrated to Australia where he gave boxing one more fling, losing to little-known Johnny Gleeson. That was it. Dickie stayed put for ten years, returned home and got a job in the printing trade. There were three fighting O'Sullivans active at one time, Danny, Dickie and Mickey. Their father was a boxer too and on their mother's side they were related to Bobby Fordham. Despite their Irish name, all were reared in Finsbury Park. Jim Pettengell trained them and Benny Huntman steered them up the ladder. Mickey O'Sullivan remains with us today. As chairman of the London Ex-Boxers' Association he is well liked and respected by all ex-boxers.

James Oyabola

OYEBOLA James   *From* Neasden. *Died* 27 July 2007, aged 46. The much publicised murder of James was the most tragic British boxing incidence in 2007, his death coming just as he was due to receive an award for services to African boxing. A Nigerian by birth, and having lived in England from the age of six, his simon-pure career started at 12. As a product of the All-Stars ABC in Paddington – a club to which he brought prestige by winning two ABA titles and a bronze medal in the super-heavyweight category at the 1986 Commonwealth Games. Oyebola was tall at 6ft 7in, superbly built and always in good physical condition. He could hit too. His defeats all came inside the scheduled distance and he often got off the deck to win. A dull fighter he definitely was not, very few of his fights being decided on points. En-route to the Southern Area title, which he won via a first-round knockout, he'd scored 11 stoppages in 14 outings. When he stopped Scott Welch in Atlantic City, he won the WBC International belt and in his next fight, which

was for the British title, he hammered the unbeaten Clifton Mitchell to defeat in four rounds. His career had reached its apex and it was downhill from thereon. James' British crown went to the man from whom he'd won it, Scott Welch, who got his revenge in an exciting fight in which he had to be rescued in round ten. The vacant Commonwealth and WBO Inter-Continental titles were also at stake. His final contest was an unsuccessful bid for the Southern Area title and a 23-fight career came to an end after he'd fought for eight championships. He then took out a manager's license and was building a good stable of fighters, including Ajose Olusegun and Tony Salam. All this was wiped out by gunshot wounds, which brought his life to a premature end. James leaves a wife and two children.

PALANCE Jack   *From* Los Angeles, California, USA. *Died* 10 November 2006, aged 87. The son of Russian immigrants and christened Palanuik, Jack was born at Lattimer Mines in Pennsylvanian coalmining country and eventually would become famous as a leading Hollywood actor after making his film debut in 1950. His acting career took off after playing the 'Baddie' in Shane (1953) and he made countless films before retiring in 2004, having won an Oscar. He is listed here not for his film prowess, but because he boxed professionally. The IMDB film entry has him winning 15 pro fights before being outpointed by Joe Baksi (1940), a future top-three heavyweight who blighted our own Bruce Woodcock's career. However, I can only trace four fights for him, all in New York. Known as Jack Brazzo when fighting Baksi, he had two wins as Jack Lansky before being stopped by Charley Harvey in March 1941. Excelling at sport, Jack won a football scholarship to the University of North Carolina before joining the Army Air Corps in 1942. Interestingly, his battered features came from a serious accident suffered during the war and not in a boxing ring.

PARKES George   *From* Dundee. *Died* January 2007, aged 86. A former flyweight, George was active in an era of good eight-stone men, with Jackie Paterson sitting at the top of the tree. A Great-Britain based flyweight could get plenty of fights in the 1940s even if a war was raging. George's career started in 1943 and up to the end of '44 he racked up ten fights. His bête noir was the Welshman, Norman Lewis, who won all four of their fights. Going into the ten-round class, George beat Hugh Cameron then lost to ill-fated Alex Murphy, drew with him in a return, and twice beat the experienced Sammy Reynolds. One of his best wins was over Frankie 'Kid' Bonsor up in Leicester and he also beat Barney McVeigh. George is survived by his wife, five children, nine grandchildren and one great grandchild.

PEP Willie   *From* Hartford, Connecticut, USA. *Died* 23 November 2006, aged 84. Willie was a master boxer and all-time great and nobody has ever disputed his claim to being one of the best of all time. Look at the statistics. He beat Chalky Wright for the world featherweight title before he was 21 and had won 61 straight before Sammy Angott, a bigger man, became the first to beat him. Then he went another 73 fights before losing sensationally to

Sandy Saddler. Then, in one of boxing's classic fights, Willie outpointed Saddler in a return. They were to meet twice more, each fight having an unsatisfactory end with Pep adjudged as loser. He was contracted to defend his title in England against Nel Tarleton in 1947, but barely survived an air crash that prevented the fight taking place. Pep was a modest man and when asked about the proposed fight in England, he said of Tarleton. "I'm glad I didn't have to fight him, he must have been good". Gracious comment from a man who was favoured to win easily, Tarleton being old while Willie was young and full of ambition. To assess Willie's achievements I must ask you to refer to the record books. He fought from 1940 to 1966 with 230 wins out of 242 fights. From the age of 19 he was in with the best men in the world – too long a record to review adequately in limited space. Just a few of the good man he beat were: Manuel Ortiz, Hogan 'Kid' Bassey, Charley Riley, Ray Famechon, Sal Bartolo, Willie Joyce, Phil Terranova, Jock Leslie, Paddy DeMarco, Humberto Sierra and Harold Dade. Four of Willie's losses came at the end of his career when he was in his 40s. Consider that when you assess his place in the pantheon of greats and also give thought to his guts in coming back from a plane crash, to his modest recollection of his achievements and his sportsmanship when ahead against Bassey before being stopped. Willie commented. "The kid had me cold". No excuses ever came from Willie's lips. He went through five divorces, which cost him most of his money and forced him to box well beyond the time when he should have retired. After being admitted to a nursing home suffering from Alzheimer's disease in 2001, he fought his illness for five years before losing the battle. The likes of him will never be seen again in a boxing ring.

Willie Pep

PRADA Alfredo *From* Buenos Aires, Argentina. *Died* 25 May 2007, aged 82. Alfredo was 19 when he turned professional in 1943 and when he retired in 1956 he'd never got a single shot at the Argentine lightweight championship. Competition was rife and dozens of men were scrambling over each other in hope of getting titles. Alfredo was a strong puncher in his prime years of 1950 to 1955 when 23 of his 38 victories came via the short route. On his whole record there is only one inside-the-distance loss and it took the great Sandy Saddler to perform that feat. Basking after a good win over Mario Salinas, the subsequent clash with Saddler was an ambitious attempt to crash into the world ratings. Early in his career there were losses to Arthur King and Sonny Boy West, but after that there were just five. Seven losses in a 99-fight career, fought almost entirely on the busy South American continent accentuated his fistic ability. He had five fights in New York in 1949 and was still fighting 12-rounders in his last year of activity.

PRIOR David *From* Newport Pagnell. *Died* 29 October 2006, aged 73. Boxing lost another fine servant with the death of David, who was a respected and knowledgeable student of the amateur game. Born on the Isle of Wight, but living in Teignmouth, Devon at the time of his passing, this man did nothing but good for a sport he clearly loved. By profession David was a chartered secretary, but he was also a boxing fan for over 50 years, starting out on the coaching side and working in the gym and corners with young amateurs. He then became a judge before turning to writing for *Boxing News*, *Amateur Boxing Scene* and, of course, the *British Boxing Yearbook*. In 1995 David compiled an excellent book called *Ringside with the Amateurs*, which was a meticulously researched and contained much well written material as well. For him it was a labour of love, once again putting something into the sport that he was devoted to. Such was his passion for the amateur code that he spent a lot of his time delving into old, mellowed newspapers and boxing magazines in an attempt to bring to life the achievements of many of the past heroes as well as giving credence to the current stars. It was a magnificent effort and one he could be extremely proud of, doing it not for financial gain but for his love of the sport. That was the story of David's life – always being helpful and always putting something back. Looking back at the introduction in his book, he can be summed up best in the last paragraph in which he states: "…if you are going to do something untoward concerning this book, please ask and write something nice about the sport". To me, that summed up the man perfectly. The National Association of Boys' Clubs also thought highly of David's work and presented him with a special award for services to boxing. Having retired to Teignmouth a few years ago, following a hip replacement his health went downhill and he passed away leaving his wife of over 45 years, Mary, his children Nicola and James, along with three doting grandchildren. Barry Hugman, the editor of the *Yearbook*, said: "I first met David some 20 years ago and was immediately impressed by him as a man of integrity. He was determined to get his project off the ground and ultimately succeeded, which was no surprise to me. He really knew his amateur boxing inside out and shortly afterwards I asked him to take over the amateur section in the *Yearbook*, a job he did with some relish. I cannot speak too highly of him as a fellow professional and it came as a shock when Mary rang me up to tell me of his passing. David really was one of boxing's good guys and I will miss him".

PUDGE Terry *From* Cardiff. *Died* 9 July 2007, aged 85. I last spoke to Terry at a function run by the now defunct Uppercut Club. He seemed delighted to talk boxing with Fred Snelling and me and pointed to his brothers who sat quietly in a row at the far side of the hall. "Everyone of my brothers was a boxer", he said. That was self-evident after a quick glance in their direction. Never have I seen a better collection of cauliflower ears in one family, but it struck me too how impeccably mannered, quietly spoken and neatly dressed they all were. They represented everything that is good about Welsh boxing. Our man in Wales, Geraint Richards, has kindly supplied me with details of Terry's career, for which I am grateful as I do not keep amateur records. He was the 1937 Senior eight-stone schoolboy champion of Great Britain; the runner-up at flyweight in the Welsh Championships in 1938; was a Welsh flyweight representative in 1939/40; was in the RAF and represented them against the Army in 1941; was posted to Northern Ireland in 1942, representing the Services against the American Forces; represented Belfast against Dublin in 1943; boxed in Dublin, Londonderry, Enniskillen, Coleraine and Belfast from 1944 to 1946; and was a semi-finalist in the 1947 Welsh featherweight championships before retiring in 1948. Out of 63 bouts, he won 49 and lost 14. Terry, who was a prominent member of the Welsh EBA and held the post of Chairman following the retirement of Vernon Ball, was a lovely man whose life was devoted to boxing.

PYLE Joey *From* Carshalton. *Died* February 2007, aged 72. Joey's non-sporting activities have been duly recorded in the daily newspapers over the years, but the public rarely heard about his charity work and those who benefited from his generosity. His name also appeared on the sports' pages during a brief professional career at the middleweight limit when he beat Joe Somerville, Fitzroy Lindo and Sammy Royals and lost to Paul Gormley and Maxie Beech, before he received a jail sentence for assault in 1958. His son, also named Joe, holds a current BBBoC promoters licence and has put on some pretty fair shows over the years.

ROBINSON 'Sugar' Bill *From* Melbourne, Australia. *Died* August 2006, aged 69. It is difficult to confirm the claim that Sugar Bill had 470 contests, but in his time there was hyper-activity in the amateur ranks. He was attracted to booth fighting too. Whatever are the true statistics, he was a fighter for a long period of time. Bill was born on an Indian reservation in Canada and took up boxing in England where he won two ABA titles and represented the UK in the 1964 Olympics. He also won a silver medal in the 1965 European Games. His main claim to fame prior to those successes was the fact that he was the last man who Terry Downes beat in the Simon-pure ranks before turning pro and rising

to world fame. Back home in Australia, Robinson fought professionally from the age of 33, scoring 11 wins in 19 fights as a light-heavyweight. He engaged in wars with Kahu Mahanga, John McCubbin and John Gorkom and his last fight, which he lost, was against Tony Mundine in May 1972. Bill was a talented musician who regularly played in a 26-piece orchestra under the name of Jackson McQuade, the name he had used for his Australian boxing career. When he finished with boxing he taught saxophone, guitar and flute to young musicians and also formed many jazz clubs in Victoria, especially in the Melbourne area.

'Sugar' Bill Robinson

ROWE Neville *From* Blackpool. *Died* May 2007, aged 75. An all-round sportsman, Neville left Australia to pursue a soccer career in England, but after trials with Preston North End and Blackpool brought no offers of regular work he turned his hand to boxing. In an 11-year career he fought some of the best light-heavyweights in Great Britain, with notable wins over Willie Armstrong, Redvers Sangoe, Colin Strauch and Eddie Wright. Neville also drew with Al Allotey, Sam Langford and Ron Redrup. He was inactive in 1961 and bowed out of the game in 1963 following a points win over Rupert Bentley. He had fought notables such as Arthur Howard, Ron Barton, Chic Calderwood, Billy Ellaway, Noel Trigg, Johnny Halafihi and Jack Whittaker. After boxing, he turned to wrestling and then to Rugby League with the Blackpool Borough Club. Later he became boxing coach firstly at Burn Naze and then Blackpool, a position he held until the onset of Parkinson's disease. Neville died at his Blackpool home and leaves a wife and family.

Neville Rowe

STANLEY Billy *From* Sydney, Australia. *Died* 16 January 2007, aged 71. Billy was a former Australian welterweight champion who started boxing in 1954. He was stylish and had a heavy punch. Bert Hornby beat him in 1956 and so did Augustin Argote, but these fights were preceded by a string of wins. After 1956 – a bad year – he beat Bill Riley and Tommy Evans. Billy fought Billy Todd three times and scored his best win in their second encounter, stopping Todd in 11 rounds. He couldn't give weight away to two of his antagonists, Clive Stewart and American Freddie Little, but gave a stern losing performance each time. Other men he fought were Harry Grogan, Johnny Nomura and Darby Brown, his last fight being in 1964.

SYKES Paul *From* Walefield. *Died* March 2007, aged 60. In recent years Paul was a sad figure, whose vagrant lifestyle brought on pneumonia that caused his death. It was

a sad end to a life that once saw him rise quickly through the ranks of British heavyweights to challenge for John L. Gardner's British and Commonwealth titles. His ambition seemed to dissolve after he lost to Gardner and he fought just once more, losing in one round to hard-punching Ngozika Ekwelum in distant Lagos. Paul had only ten professional fights, but his impact on the heavyweight scene was remarkable. Going into his match with Gardner he'd lost just once – on a disqualification to Neil Malpass. Four months later he forced the same opponent to a ten-round draw. Previously he'd beaten Tommy Kiely, Neville Meade and Dave Wilson. All this in his first year as a professional. Although a former prison inmate, Paul was an intelligent and gifted man and he wrote a book, mostly autobiographical, on his experiences and views, during which he revealed some remarkable tales of his private life. His career was short, but during the time that he fought for pay he brought colour and excitement to the game.

THOMPSON Trevor *From* Blackburn. *Died* 11 February 2007. Trevor, the father and trainer of Gary Thompson, a current heavyweight, was killed in a traffic accident on the way home from a boxing promotion at Wembley. His son was also injured in the accident. Such was the regard for him and his contribution to boxing that tributes were still pouring in some weeks later. He was a trainer to so many youngsters, most of them of school-going years. Keeping himself ultra fit and performing many feats of strength, Lancashire boxing in particular will miss this fine servant of the game.

TOLLIS Mickey *From* Newcastle, NSW, Australia. *Died* 23 May 2007, aged 79. A former Aussie welterweight champion, Mickey boxed in England during 1949 and was unbeaten in four contests here, his victims being Billy Exley, Jimmy Molloy, Frank Duffy and Billy Rattray. He was also successful on his own turf against European opposition, with wins over Pierre Langlois, Andre Famechon, Jean Mougin and Britain's Al Wilburn. His career peaked in 1948 when he held Vic Patrick to a draw in a match for the Australian lightweight crown and he continued to box at top level until 1951, having become Australia's welterweight champion. After defending his title twice, successive losses to Len Dittmar and Tommy Burns caused him to announce his retirement. Mickey was a stylish counter-puncher who fought off the back foot before surging forward throwing clusters of punches towards the end of a round. He was game to the core, but two knock-'em-down, drag-'em-out victories of Jack Hassen were won at a cost and although he had enough of his old form left to defend his title against Ken Bailey, the Burns fight in 1951 was his last.

TORTORICE Gene *From* Niagra Falls, New York, USA. *Died* 1 June 2006, aged 72. Pittsburgh-born Gene was a 1950s welterweight who graduated into the ten-round class after boxing six-rounders for the first four years of his career. He outpointed Pat Manzi over the longer distance, but inexplicably was thrown in with the 108-fights veteran, Joe Miceli. To his credit, Gene went the distance, but the loss made him aware of his own shortcomings and he decided to hang up his gloves at the age of 27. It's interesting to note that Miceli had been stopped by Manzi before fighting men like Ike Williams, Don Jordan, Johnny Saxton and Kid Gavilan, all holders of world titles. Following that, Gene returned to his old job in the construction industry and kept his boxing interests alive by coaching young amateurs.

TURMAN 'Buddy' Reagan *From* Tyler, Texas, USA. *Died* 1 April 2007, aged 72. The globe-trotting Buddy died from hepatitis and liver failure after a long battle with bad health. There were 62 fights and only 15 losses after Buddy began scrapping in 1954 and in the first five years of combat he lost only four times. He had a winning streak broken by Roy Harris and then won 14, all by stoppages, before losing to Art Swiden, having beaten Alvin Williams, Emil Brtko, Tommy Fields and Dean Bogany to put himself on the fringe of world-class. His first big win came when he beat Canada's Robert Cleroux and he then drew with Donnie Fleeman, who'd beaten him previously. In 1963, two losses to Archie Moore and another to Pete Rademacher decided him to take a break. He resumed boxing in 1964, first in South Africa and then on to Great Britain, Italy, Austria and Germany. Germany is where he performed best, beating Dave Bailey, Manfred Ackers, Lars Norling and in the last contest of his career, Rudolf Nehring.

VODDEN Bob *From* Islington, London. *Died* 23 September 2006. Bob first came to prominence when winning the NW Division of London lightweight title in 1954 while representing the Alexandra ABC. He then became a valued member of the RAF boxing team, but could never quite win the title with men such as Tex Woodward, Dick McTaggart and Johnny Kidd standing in his way. The June 1955 edition of the *Ring* magazine shows him ranked as Britain's number seven light-welterweight after giving Woodward a tremendous, but losing tousle for that year's RAF title.

WAGNER Dick *From* Portland, Oregon, USA. *Died* 8 September 2006, aged 79. Dick was one of Floyd Patterson's early opponents. That was back in 1953 when Patterson, still a light-heavyweight, was trying to establish his credentials as a contender. After beating Dick twice in back-to-back contests he was then on his way, but for the loser it signalled the tail end of a career that had started in 1945. People started to take note of him when he beat Dan Bucceroni in 1948, but up to that stage few well-known names had adorned his record. Dick twice beat Billy Fox by stoppages and then hit a losing patch, being defeated by very good opposition in Nick Barone, Jake LaMotta, Tiberio Mitri and Bob Murphy. He got wins against Lulo Sabotin, Jack Nelson and Joey DeJohn and kept fighting in good company until the losses to Patterson convinced him that he'd gone as far as he could.

WALTERS Jeff *From* Scarborough. *Died* January 2007, aged 76. Before Dave Charnley beat him, Jeff was gaining in experience with some demanding fights. He was a quick learner – Charlie Simpkins, Tommy Rushworth, and Jimmy Ford all beat him but lost in return bouts. Jeff couldn't

achieve the same against Syd Greb or Emrys Jones, the former beating him twice, although he did manage a draw with Jones. Boxing from 1950 to 1956, his better wins came over Tommy Mason, Brian Jelley and Colin Malone, but there were some real fighting men on his record such as Paddington's Tommy Ryan, Kurt Ernest, Darkie Hughes and, of course, one of Britain's best-ever lightweights in Charnley.

WASHINGTON George *From* Brooklyn, NYC, New York, USA. *Died* 11 June 2006, aged 79. In George's days New York City was the Mecca of boxing with plentiful gymnasiums and dozens of young men anxious to learn the rudiments of boxing. George trained hundreds of them in Brooklyn gyms and at Gleasons. There were notable successes and several of his proteges reached Olympic standard. Mark Breland is a prime example, yet George had no favourites and anyone who wanted to learn got his full attention. Beginners were as important to him as those getting to the top. He was in the USA Marine team as a heavyweight when serving his country, before turning pro in September 1947 when back in the States. In 42 fights up until 1956 George went in with some good men, beating Earl Walls, Charlie Norkus, Keene Simmons, while losing to Carmine Vingo (2), Norkus, Simmons, Coley Wallace, Howie Turner (2) and Garvin Sawyer. George was still coaching up to a month before his death.

WELLS George BEM *From* Newcastle on Tyne. *Died* 27 September 2006, aged 84. Harold Alderman has submitted details of fights for this former bantamweight and featherweight. George began boxing in 1946, beating Ken Hall at the New St James' Hall where he had the majority of his fights. Many are missing from his record, despite the trade paper's slogan: "A ringside seat at every fight", some squeezed through the net. Even today this happens, but fortunately such occurrences are very rare. In the mid-1940s press reporting was haphazard until the clouds of war had blown away for good. George boxed through to the end of the 1940s, when his last known fight ended in a defeat by Mark Harrison. Until then, it had been a positive year for him, as he'd beaten Bob Lloyd for the second time and had stopped Jack Grimley, who retired with an ear injury. In June, he took on Battling Jim Hayes as a late substitute and put up stern resistance before losing on points in a thriller, George hitting the deck in the fourth round and being saved by the bell. In a return, he dropped Hayes for a long count, but lost a disputed verdict at the close. He also beat Dennis Stansill, Billy Johnson, Roy Ashton and Billy Wells. In retirement he worked tirelessly for the Red Cross, raising thousand of pounds for the charity and in recognition of his work he received the BEM.

WENTON Terry *From* Liverpool. *Died* August 2007, aged 64. The father of Richie (the former British super-bantamweight champion) and Nigel, two top British pros who each contested a WBO version of the world title, Terry was a top amateur in his own right who boxed for England six times between 1966 and 1971. Although he reached the ABA semi-finals on four occasions while wearing the Golden Gloves ABC singlet, once at fly and three times as a light-fly, the main prize always eluded him. Boxing until he was 48 years of age, Terry made history when, along with Nigel and Richie, he boxed on the same bill in 1980. After retiring, Terry settled down to coach the boys at Wavertree before moving on to St Ambrose and then Rose Heath, where he worked with several international class boys.

WHEELER Johnny *From* Melbourne, Australia. *Died* 10 November 2006, aged 75. The website *BoxRec* lists 66 fights between 1948 and 1957 for Johnny, a lightweight based in Melbourne where many of his fights took place. Johnny beat Bluey Wilkins and Norm Foster and scored a draw with the Swiss boxer, Sigi Tennenbaum. Going up in class was, at first, tough, Johnny dropping two decisions to Trevor King before settling down with wins over Russell Sands, Sergio Milan, Colin Shanks and former New Zealand champ at two-weight divisions, Johnny Hanks. A rising star in George Bracken beat him in 1956 and his career fizzled out soon after. He was only a moderate puncher so he relied on skill to win, but was clever and had good footwork. After hanging up his gloves, he became a respected referee and his years as an arbiter lasted four times that of his ring career. As the third man when Jeff Fenech challenged Steve McCrory in 1986, he won himself a good reputation and was always in control of the action.

WILLIAMS Johnny *From* Rugby. *Died* 29 January 2007, aged 80. Early one Sunday morning I was glancing at a 1947 programme for one of Isidore Green's talent tournaments at Wembley Town Hall and noticed that on the bill was a cruiserweight match between Johnny Williams and Jimmy Carroll of Stockport. Johnny won it in five rounds. I then checked his record just before the telephone rang to inform me of Johnny's death. The news saddened me but didn't cause surprise as he'd been ill for some time and was being looked after by staff in a nursing home. Three years previously I'd put his picture on the front of the *Southern Ex-Boxer,* a magazine I was producing twice yearly, because I feared that his days were numbered. That he lasted so long is a tribute to his courage. Grit is a quality he had in abundance, having been slated so often by the press for being too timid in his pre-championship days, he dug his heels in and fought courageously against Jack Gardner. What Johnny's critics overlooked was that he came from the old boxing school where skill and sound technique were priorities. He was to show vast courage and determination when he was British heavyweight champion, his first fight with Gardner being one of the hardest in the division's history and both men were taken to hospital afterwards. They met three times, Jack winning the first but losing his title in the second, while the third was a grim struggle that saw Jack, 25 lbs heavier, winning. It was 1955. Three years earlier, Johnny had the Empire title to his name by virtue of a decision over South Africa's Johnny Arthur. There were wins over danger-man Kitione Lave, Don Cockell, Stephan Olek, Joe Weidin and Gerhardt Hecht, while losses to Pat Comiskey and Bill Weinberg were due to cuts and two drawn fights in

Germany, against Heinz Neuhaus and Willi Hoepner, would have gone Johnny's way in any other country. His best win was over America's Aaron Wilson, who'd been a thorn in the sides of British heavyweights. After packing in boxing when Joe Erskine and Joe Bygraves beat him Johnny returned to his farm in Rugby where he'd lived nearly all his life. He then took out a manager's license and steered Geo Aldridge to a British title. Johnny had taken up boxing as a young boy when he became friendly with Sam Minto, who used to give him lessons in his boxing booth. Sam's skills rubbed off on his impressionable pupil and they were friends right up to the latter's death. When Johnny quit boxing, his manager, Ted Broadribb, retired too. Later on, Johnny joined the ex-boxers' movement when it was formed and was always the epitome of grace and good manners. On parting he'd always say: "Please remember me to Mr Snelling". Fred and I had many enjoyable moments in Johnny's company. What times they were!

Johnny Williams

WILSON Terry *From* Australia. *Died* 2007, aged 62. The death is reported of this former Australian junior-lightweight champion, who turned professional in 1965 and boxed as Terry Ball for two years. He beat Trevor Ditton twice, Ron Stanford, Tony Lythgoe and Noel Kelly before reverting to his birth-name of Wilson. In 1967 he won his title by stopping Bobby Daldy in ten rounds, then lost to Ghana's Kimpo Amarfio, Terry being unlucky to receive a cut that forced the referee's intervention. He beat Arthur Thomas, Daryl Carrick and Jake Guilino but in his sole fight in Auckland, New Zealand, he lost to Toro George.

WILSON Tyrell *From* Newport. *Died* 12 July 2007, aged 48. Cancer claimed the life of Tyrell, a former sparring partner of Steve Sims. He had a record of 42 fights between 1979 and 1986 with just ten wins, but once again a win-loss record obscures the ability of a man who never picked an opponent and was talented enough to make them all sweat for their money. Tyrell was in there against Gary Jacobs, Andy Till, Colin Harrison, Trevor Smith and Nick Meloscia, while beating John Lindo, Phillip Morris, Mark Rusling and, in his last fight, Nick Lucas. Sims, the former British and Welsh featherweight champion, spoke highly of how Tyrell was always prepared to spar with him for as long as was required. "He would cram in as many fights as he could and was, in fact, a good boxer", said Sims. Tyrell ran his own plastering business after his ring days were over.

ZANNELLI 'Ripper' Ralph *From* Providence, New England, USA. *Died* 29 November 2006, aged 91. An Italian-American, Ralph's name may not be well-known to today's followers of boxing which is a pity because he was a classy performer whose record speaks volumes for his ability: In 147 contests as a pro, after having about the same amount as an amateur, 12 of them were against men who had been, or eventually would become, world champions. He fought Henry Armstrong three times, Fritzie Zivic twice, Sugar Ray Robinson, Kid Gavilan, Sammy Angott, Johnny Bratton, Ike Williams twice and Johnny Jadick. Okay, so the only ones he beat were Zivic and Jadick, but you can take it from me that Ralph was good enough to fight the best men around, beating Sammy Secreet, Al Priest, Johnny Greco, Berry Wright, Otis Graham, Anton Raadik, Joe Rindone, Sonny Horne, Saverio Turiello, Vic Cardell and Izzy Jannazzo. He also fought top contenders Billy Arnold, Laurent Dauthille, Coley Welch, Bernard Docusen, Bobby Dykes, Rocky Castellani, Steve Mamakos and Jimmy Doyle. In a record stretching from 1936 to 1952, he won 92, lost 48 and drew seven. He went through his first 32 fights unbeaten and served a solid apprenticeship before arriving on the world scene. After retiring from boxing at the advanced age of 37, he worked for a brewery and earlier for a construction company, while still retaining his interest in boxing.

Other pro boxers who have also passed away during the period, include **Kenny Berrios**, 36 (Puerto Rican bantam from 1991 to 2003 – 21 contests), **Johnny Brenda**, 85 (USA light in 1942 – 4 contests), **Wilfredo Brown** (Panamanian light from 1947 to 1955 – 20 contests), **Suzuki Cabato**, 38 (Japanese fly from 1988 to 1999 – 62 contests), **Joe Capocetto**, 79 (USA heavy from 1947 to 1949 – 3 contests), **Larry Crawley** (USA welter from 1952 to 1960 – 20 contests), **Tally Disolane** (South African super-feather from 2000 to 2006 – 14 contests), **Thamsanga Dubase** (South African feather in 2006 – 3 contests), **Curly Ray Fidler** (Canadian heavy from 1963 to 1968 – 9 contests), **Wyatt Frost**, 31 (USA welter from 2003 to 2006 – 5 contests), **Nelson Javier Galdamez**, 32 (Argentinian bantam from 2003 to 2007 – 13 contests), **Vincent Garcia**, 20 (USA welter from 2004 to 2006 – 18 contests), **Sandare Hamed** (Ivory Coast light from 1999 to 2003 – 7 contests), **Troy Harden**, 22 (USA light-welter from 2005 to 2007 – 6 contests), **Les Hardy** (Australian welter from 1943 to 1945 – 41 contests), **Jim Hegerle**, 71 (USA middle from 1954 to 1962 – 53 contests), **Stefan Hentschel**, 58 (German heavy in 1973 – 1 contest), **Leo Johnson** (USA heavy from 1952 to 1957 – 21 contests), **Carl Jordan**, 71 (USA welter from 1958 to 1968 – 37 contests), **Tetsuro Kawai**, 68 (Japanese bantam from 1962 to 1966 – 23 contests), **Deeden Kengkarun**, 28 (Thai light-fly from 1995-2005 – 36 contests), **Gyorgy Kincses** (Hungarian welter from 1991 to 1993 – 8 contests), **Kemal Kolenovic**, 28 (Montenegro welter from 1999 to 2006 – 18 contests), **Geoffrey Legrand** (French welter from 2006 to 2007 – 3 contests), **Hearn Marler**, 36 (USA heavy from 1991 to 2005 – 12 contests), **Frank Maybury** (Australian feather from 1946 to 1947 – 2 contests), **Asia Mays**, 24 (USA female light-welter from 2004 to 2005 – 3 contests), **Sandile Mentile**, 30 (South African bantam from 1996 to 1998 – 8 contests), **Johnny Mills** (USA welter from 1946 to 1953 – 13 contests), **Anis Dwi Mulya**, 23 (Indonesian feather from 2001 to 2007 – 6 contests), **Junji Murakami**, 30 (Japanese super-feather from 2000 to 2007 – 22 contests), **Max Murvanick**, 102 (USA feather from 1923 to 1924 – 3 contests), **Richard Nunez** (Peruvian light from 1997 to 2006 – 6 contests), **Joe O'Connell**, 76 (USA light-heavy from 1943 to 1954 – 35 contests), **Joey Olguin** (USA light from 1959 to 1968 – 28 contests), **Enrique Palau**, 27 (USA light-middle from 2005 to 2006 – 7 contests), **Gene Parker**, 76 (USA light from 1948 to 1955 – 60 contests), **Harry Poulton** (USA middle from 1945 to 1954 – 18 contests), **Teddy Quinn**, 76 (South African middle from 1951 to 1954 – 5 contests), **Kili Kili Rachman**, 32 (Indonesian feather from 2001 to 2005 – 12 contests), **Marcelo Ressurreicao** (Brazilian feather from 2003 to 2007 - 8 contests), **Lilly Rodriguez** (USA female feather in 1979 – 1 contest), **Lito Sisnorio**, 34 (Filipino super-fly from 2003 to 2007 – 17 contests), **Santos Solis**, 53 (Puerto Rican welter from 1972 to 1986 – 17 contests), **Basil Thomas**, 46 (South African light-welter from 1982 to 1986 – 11 contests), **Gianfranco Vantaggioli**, 37 (Italian light-middle from 1991 to 1992 – 6 contests), **Moses Varasikete**, 36 (Fijian heavy from 1959 to 1960 – 6 contests), **Doug Villarreal**, 44 (USA light-welter from 1992 to 2003 - 40 contests), **Benny Walker** (USA middle from 1947 to 1959 – 49 contests), **Shelby Walker**, 29 (USA female light from 2002 to 2006 – 14 contests), **Tommy Watts**, 78 (Australian light from 1939 to 1949 – 24 contests).

A Boxing Quiz with a Few Below the Belt: Part 12

Compiled by Les Clark

QUESTIONS

1. Can you name any British boxers who fought Duke McKenzie and who were still fighting as of June 2007?

2. Jimmy Lloyd (Liverpool) won the bronze medal in the 1960 Rome Olympics. Who beat him in the semi-final?

3. What did Cornelius Boza Edwards, Prince Naseem Hamed and Zolani Petola have in common?

4. His birthname was Manop Lamthuam and he had a fight record of 56 wins (32 inside) and two losses. Can you name the two men who beat him?

5. Can you name the former WBC champion who, in five consecutive fights, won a world title, lost it, won a non-title bout, regained his old title and then lost it again?

6. Can you name the man who defeated Ray Gilbody in the 1980 Moscow Olympics and who went on to be a world champion and a 'Hall of Famer'?

7. Do you know the name of the referee who controlled the fight between Kirkland Laing and Roberto Duran in Detroit?

8. What do Bobby Chacon and Fighting Harada have in common?

9. Who defeated Dai Dower for his European title?

10. Where and when did Terry Downes bow out of boxing?

11. Cruiserweight Imamu Mayfield once fought in the UK. Where did he appear?

12. Who was Duke McKenzie's last opponent?

13. Can you name the first Romanian boxer to win a world professional title?

14. What have John Cunningham, John Kidd and John Pritchett have in common?

15. Who fought both Horace McKenzie and Kirkland Laing on two occasions?

16. Who did Ruben Olivares beat for the vacant WBA featherweight title?

17. Terry Spinks won his Olympic gold in Australia. Can you name the men he beat?

18. Which heavyweight, who recently passed away, fought both Don Cockell and Jack Gardner on three occasions?

19. Can you name this British-based heavyweight who fought George Chuvalo, Gerhard Zech, Karl Mildenberger, Zora Folley, Willie Pastrano, Henry Cooper, Billy Walker, Joe Erskine, Dick Richardson and Johnny Williams?

20. Who did Nigel Benn defeat to gain the Commonwealth title?

21. Do you know the combined knockout win record of Alfonso Zamora and Carlos Zarate when they met in 1977 at the Inglewood Forum?

22. In the bout between Herol Graham and Vinny Pazienza one of the three judges was British. Can you remember his name?

23. What have Joe Frazier junior and Barry McGuigan got in common?

24. What was Tommy Pardoe's claim to boxing fame?

25. What welterweight belts did Lloyd Honeyghan relieve Donald Curry of in Atlantic City?

26. Terry Marsh retired in December 1987 with a record of 27 fights; winning 26 and drawing one. Name the man who drew with him?

27. Can you name an American boxer who beat Pipino Cuevas and Carlos Palomino over ten rounds, but lost to Dave 'Boy' Green?

28. What unusual thing happened in the 1990 bout between Jose Luis Ramirez and Juan Martin Coggi in France?

29. Who did Tommy Burns beat to claim the vacant heavyweight title?

30. The 2001 Will Smith film, ALI, showed events between 1964 and 1974. Name the man Ali fought during this period who was not depicted in the movie?

31. Can you name this true journeyman? He turned pro with Jimmy Gill and his first fight was a win against Mark Needham. During his career he won and lost a British Master's title, fought several area and national champions, and even has a world champion on his record. He finished with a tally of 21 wins, 70 losses and five draws in his 96 bouts.

32. Can you remember in which round Nigel Benn stopped Iran Barkley?

33. Who was the last man Ali beat before starting his three-year ban from boxing?

34. On how many occasions did Primo Carnera fight in the UK?

35. A Nottingham fighter from the Wally Swift stable lost his first five bouts. He also lost his last 18 contests in a 57-fight career. During his time in the ring, this brave journeyman fought British, Commonwealth, European and World champions in the making. Can you name him?

36. What was Tommy Burns' real name?

37. Upon his retirement in 1904, James J. Jeffries allegedly chose two men to fight for the vacant title. Can you name them?

38. Who was the first light-heavyweight champion to win the heavyweight crown?

39. In 1978 Ken Norton was awarded the WBC heavyweight title when the fighter nominated to contest the vacancy with him refused the fight. Name the fighter concerned?

40. Which fighter equalled Jack Dempsey's record of seven knockdowns in a single round of a world title fight?

41. Can you name this crowd-pleasing fighter who turned pro with Greg Steene? His first fight was a win against John Hargin and he fought many champions. In fact he twice fought a British and European champion.

42. Gene Fullmer had three draws in his career, Sugar Ray Robinson and Dick Tiger being two of those opponents. Who was the other one?

43. Ike Williams won NBA lightweight championship recognition with a second-round knockout win. Name the defending champion?

44. What year did boxing become an Olympic sport?

45. Who was the Detroit Kronk's first world champion?

46. Which was the first heavyweight championship bout to be decided in Las Vegas?

47. Carlos Monzon had seven knockouts on his record as well as a no-contest in his first eight professional fights before losing. Name the man who beat him?

48. Who was the first black African to win an Olympic gold medal?

49. Name the boxers who contested the WBC super-featherweight title in Monte Carlo in Aug 1986?

50. Who was the last heavyweight champion born in the 1800s?

Leading BBBoC License Holders: Names and Addresses

Licensed Promoters

A Force Promotions
PO Box 577
Waltham Cross
Herts EN8 1AP
0199 262 3062

Spencer Alton
(Contender Boxing
Promotions)
64 Glenmore Drive
Stenson Fields
Derby DE24 3HT
0133 223 2050

Bruce Baker
The Garden Flat
38 Lupus Street
London
SW1V 3EB
0207 592 0102

Mark Bateson
33 Springfield Road
Guisley
Leeds LS20 9AN
0777 860 1427

Jack Bishop
76 Gordon Road
Fareham
Hants PO16 7SS
0132 928 4708

Paul Boyce
79 Church Street
Briton Ferry
Neath SA11 2JG
0163 981 3723

(Braveheart
Promotions)
Barry Hughes
5 Royal Exchange
Square
Glasgow G1 3AH
0141 248 8899

Tony Burns
(TBS Promotions)
67 Peel Place
Woodford Green
Essex IG5 0PT
0208 550 8911

Scott Calow
18 Farnworth Grove
Huthwaite
Notts
NG17 2NL
0787 664 1055

George Carman
5 Mansion Lane
Mobile Home Site
Iver
Bucks S10 9RQ
0175 365 3096

Michael Carney
(Impact Boxing
Promotions)
Bradley Arms Farm
Alton Road
Cheadle
Staffs ST10 4RA
0797 049 5597

Paul Carpenter
(Leicester Sporting
Club)
42 The Willows
Bedworth
Warwickshire
CV12 0NX
0787 846 7401

Dave Coldwell
(Koncrete Promotions)
5 Penwood Walk
Bramley
Rotherham
Yorks S66 3XS
0170 951 0001

Annette Conroy
(North-East Sporting
Club)
144 High Street East
Sunderland
Tyne and Wear SR1 2BL
0191 567 6871

Coventry Sporting
Club
Les Allen
180 Longford Road
Longford
Coventry
0247 636 4237

Pat Cowdell
129a Moat Road
Oldbury, Warley
West Midlands
0121 552 8082

Dennis Cross
8 Tumbling Bank
Blackley
Manchester M9 6AU
0161 720 9371

David Currivan
15 Northolt Avenue
South Ruislip
Middlesex HA4 6SS
0208 841 9933

Wally Dixon
Littlemoss House
1 Wayne Close
Littlemoss
Droylsden
Manchester M43 7LQ
0161 223 8855

Jack Doughty
(Tara Promotions)
Lane End Cottage
Golden Street
Off Buckstone Road
Shaw
Oldham OL1 8LY
01706 845753

Carl Dunn
20 Fennel Grove
South Shields
Tyne & Wear
NE34 8TH
0787 299 7258

Jim Evans
(Evans-Waterman
Promotions)
Abgah
88 Windsor Road
Bray
Berks SL6 2DJ
0162 862 3640

Jonathan Feld
(World Sports
Organisation)
c/o Angel Media Group
Ltd
The Office Islington
338 City Road
London
EC1V 2PT
0207 239 8289

Joe Frater
The Cottage
Main Road
Grainthorpe
Louth
Lincs
0147 234 3194

Stephen Garber
(Premier SC)
PO Box 704
Bradford
West Yorks
BD3 7WU
0870 350 5525

Dave Garside
33 Lowthian Road
Hartlepool
Cleveland
TS26 8AL
0142 929 1611
07973 792588

Christopher Gilmour
Platinum House
120 Carnegie Road
Hillington Park
Glasgow
G52 4JZ
0773 041 5036

Tommy Gilmour MBE
(St Andrew's Sporting
Club)
Platinum House
120 Carnegie Road
Hillington Park
Glasgow G52 4JZ
0141 810 5700

Johnny Griffin
0798 921 5287
0116 262 9287

Jess Harding
c/o UK Industrial Pallets
Ltd
Travellers Lane
Industrial Estate
Travellers Lane
Welham Green
Hatfield
Herts AL9 7HF
0170 727 0440

(Harvey Sports
International)
Kevin Houston
216 Longford Road
Longford
Coventry
CV6 6BH
0779 067 3766

Tony Hay
Romilly House
201 First Avenue
Central Park
Petherton Road
Hengrove
Bristol
BS14 9BZ
0797 466 2968

Barry Hearn
(Matchroom)
'Mascalls'
Mascalls Lane
Great Warley
Essex CM14 5LJ
0127 735 9900

Michael Helliet
(Mayfair Sporting
Club)
Flat 1
102 Whitfield Street
London W1T 5EB
0207 388 5999
0784 363 6920

Mick Hennessy
(Hennessy Sports)
Ravensbourne
Westerham Road
Keston
Kent BR2 6HE
0168 986 8080

Dennis Hobson
(Fight Academy)
130 Handsworth Road
Sheffield
South Yorkshire
S9 4AE
0114 256 0555
07836 252429

Dennis Hobson Snr
(DVSA Promotions)
73 Darnall Road
Don Valley
Sheffield S9 5AH
0114 243 4700

Nicholas Hodges
Llys & Deryn
Cilcennin
Lampeter
Ceredigion
SA48 8RR
0157 047 0452

Jayson Hollier
(Shakespeare
Promotions)
21 Hillmorton Road
Rugby CV22 5DF
07766 644 0829

Hull & District
Sporting Club
Mick Toomey
24 Schubert Close
Rutherglen Drive
Hull HU9 3PL
0148 786 307

Alma Ingle
26 Newman Road
Wincobank
Sheffield S9 1LP
0114 281 1277

Errol Johnson
(EJKO Promotions)
36 Newton Street
West Bromwich
B71 3RQ
0121 532 6118

Thomas Jones
(Sports Management,
Hale, Ltd)
13 Planetree Road
Hale
Cheshire
WA15 9JL
0161 980 2661

Paul McCausland
1 Prospect Heights
Carrickfergus
Northern Ireland
BT38 8QY
0289 336 5942

M & J Promotions
Jane Couch & Sandra
Rowe
Spaniorum Farm Gym
Berwick Lane
Bristol
BS35 5RX
0772 504 5405

Malcolm McKillop
14 Springfield Road
Mangotsfield
Bristol
0117 957 3567

Frank Maloney
(Maloney Promotions)
Lord Clyde
9 Wotton Road
Deptford
London
SE8 5TQ
0208 691 4165

Rebecca Margel
10 Bentcliffe Lane
Leeds
LS17 6QF
0113 268 0681

John Merton
(John Merton
Promotions)
Merton Technologies
Ltd
38 Delaune Street
London SE17 3UR
0207 582 5200

Clifton Mitchell
42 Wiltshire Road
Derby DE 21 6EX
0797 032 8715

Alex Morrison
197 Swanston Street
Laird Business Park
Dalmarnock
Glasgow
G40 4HW
0141 554 7777

Katherine Morrison
197 Swanston Street
Laird Business Park
Dalmarnock
Glasgow
G40 4HW
0141 554 7777

Ian Pauly
1202 Lincoln Road
Peterborough
Cambs
PE4 6LA
0173 331 1266

Ken Purchase
(Ringside Promotions)
Allscott Mill
Allscott
Telford TF6 5EE
0195 225 0950

Joe Pyle
36 Manship Road
Mitcham
Surrey
CR4 2AZ
0208 646 2289
0208 646 7793

Glyn Rhodes
166 Oldfield Road
Stannington
Sheffield S6 6DY
0114 232 6513

Gus Robinson MBE
Stranton House
West View Road
Hartlepool
Cleveland TS24 0BB
0142 923 4221

Ian Robinson
(Anglo American
Sporting Club)
Tollbar House
1 Manchester Road
Droylsden
Manchester M49 6ET
0161 301 3799

Paul Rowson
(PJ Promotions)
Roughstones
75 Catholic Lane
Sedgley
West Midlands
DY3 3YE
0190 267 0007

Christine Rushton
20 Alverley Lane
Balby, Doncaster
Yorks DN4 9AS
0130 231 0919

John Rushton
20 Alverley Lane
Balby, Doncaster
Yorks DN4 9AS
0130 231 0919

Kevin Sanders
9 Moggswell Lane
Orton Longueville
Village
Peterborough
Cambs PE2 7DS
0173 337 1912

Chris Sanigar
Bristol Boxing Gym
40 Thomas Street
St Agnes
Bristol
Avon BS2 9LL
0117 949 6699

Jamie Sanigar
Bristol Boxing Gym
40 Thomas Street
St Agnes
Bristol
Avon BS2 9LL
0117 949 6699

Matt Scriven
(The Robin Hood
Executive Sporting
Club)
The Old One, Two
Fitness & Boxing Studio
2a Thoresby Street
Mansfield
Notts NG18 1QF
0783 399 5770

Kevin Spratt
8 Springfield Road
Guisley
Leeds LS20 8AL
0194 387 6229

Keith Walker
(Walkers Boxing
Promotions)
Headlands House
Business Centre
Suite 21-35
Spawd Bone Lane
Knottingley
West Yorks WF11 0HY
0197 766 2616

Frank Warren
(Sports Network)
Centurion House
Bircherley Green
Hertford
Herts SG14 1AP
0199 250 5550

Derek V. Williams
65 Virginia Road
Thornton Heath
Surrey CR7 8EN
0208 765 0492

Jane Wilton
(Belfast Boxing
Promotions)
The Bridge
42 Derryboy Road
Crossgar
Northern Ireland
BT30 9LH
0289 754 2195

(Sportslink
Promotions)
Unit 6
Drayton Business Park
Taversham
Drayton
Norwich
NR8 6RL
0160 386 8606

Stephen Wood
(C/O Viking
Promotions)
Edward Street
Cambridge Industrial
Area
Salford
Manchester M7 1RL
0161 834 9496

Note: Jane Couch, Neil Featherby and Mike Goodall, who promoted last season, no longer hold current Promoter's licenses, although Jane Couch is now promoting with Sandra Rowe under the M & J Promotions banner.

Licensed Managers

Babatunde Ajayi
2 Granville Square
Blakes Road
Peckham
London SE15 6DU
0207 732 1235

Isola Akay MBE
129 Portnall Road
Paddington
London W9 3BN
0717 119 8501

Michael Alldis
77 Buckswood Drive
Gossops Green
Crawley
West Sussex RH11 8HU
0773 435 1966

Chris Aston
54/56 May Street
Crosland Moor
Huddersfield
West Yorks HD4 5DG
0148 432 9112

Andy Ayling
Centurion House
Bircherley Green
Hertford
Herts SG14 1AP
0199250 5550

Bruce Baker
Garden Flat
38 Lupus Street
Pimlico
London SW1 U3EB
0207 592 0102

Robert Bannan
1c Thornton Street
Townhead, Coatbridge
North Lanarkshire
ML5 2NZ
0123 660 6736

Wayne Barker
1 Manchester Road
Droylsden
Manchester M43 6EP
0161 301 3799

Mark Bateson
33 Springfield Road
Guiseley
Leeds LS20 9AN
0777 860 1427

Jack Bishop
76 Gordon Road
Fareham
Hants
PO16 7SS
0132 928 4708

Adam Booth
57 Jackson Road
Bromley
Kent BR2 8NT
0779 382 5255

Peter Bowen
50 Newman Avenue
Lanesfield
Wolverhampton
West Midlands
WV4 6BZ
0190 282 8159

Jackie Bowers
36 Drew Road
Silvertown
London E16
0796 188 3654

Paul Boyce
Winstones
Church Street
Briton Ferry
Neath
West Glamorgan
SA11 2GJ
0783 637 72702

David Bradley
The Dovecote
Aston Hall
Claverley
WV5 7DZ
0174 671 0287

John Branch
44 Hill Way
Holly Lodge Estate
London NE6 4EP

John Breen
Cedar Lodge
589 Antrim Road
Belfast BT15
0289 077 0238

Steve Butler
107 Cambridge Street
Normanton
West Yorks
WF6 1ES
0192 489 1097

Roy Callaghan
158 Harwich Road
Little Clacton
Essex
CO16 9NL
0793 994 7807

Scott Calow
18 Farnsworth Grove
Huthwaite
Notts
NG17 2NL
0787 664 1055

Enzo Calzaghe
51 Caerbryn
Pentwynmawr
Newbridge
Gwent
0149 524 8988

George Carman
5 Mansion Lane
Mobile Home Site
Iver
Bucks
S10 9RQ
0175 365 3096

Michael Carney
Bradley Elms Farm
Alton Road
Threapwood
Cheadle
Stoke on Trent
Staffs
ST10 4RA
0797 049 5597

Paul Carpenter
42 The Willows
Woodlands Park
Bedworth
0787 846 7401

John Celebanski
5 Ling Park Avenue
Wilsden
Bradford
BD15 0NE
0127 482 4015

Nigel Christian
22 Spire Court
Efford
Plymouth
PL3 6HP
0175 225 1136

Azumah Cofie
Suite 130
Dorset House
Duke Street
Chelmsford
Essex
CM1 1TB
0786 797 7406

David Coldwell
5 Penwood Park
Bramley
Rotherham
Yorks S66 3XS
0779 945 6400

Brian Coleman
31 Gwernifor Street
Mountain Ash
Mid Glamorgan
CF45 3NA
0785 906 1911

William Connelly
72 Clincart Road
Mount Florida
Glasgow
G42
0141 632 5818

Tommy Conroy
144 High Street East
Sunderland
Tyne and Wear
0191 567 6871

Pat Cowdell
129aMoat Road
Oldbury
Warley
West Midlands
B68 8EE
0121 552 8082

David Cowland
3 Linkfield Court
78 Auckland Road
London SE19 2DQ
0208 771 5974

John Cox
68 Chilton Way
Duston
Northants NN5 6AR
0781 499 2249

Dave Currivan
15 Northolt Avenue
South Ruislip
Middlesex
0208 841 9933

David Davies
10 Bryngelli
Carmel
Llanelli
Dyfed SA14 7TL
0126 984 3204

John Davies
Unit 14, Rectors Yard
Rectors Lane
Penre Sandycroft
Deeside
CH5 2DH
0776 550 8683

Ronnie Davies
3 Vallensdean Cottages
Hangleton Lane
Portslade
Sussex
0127 341 6497

Gary De Roux
68 Lynton Road
Peterborough
PE1 3DU
0173 334 2975

Walter Dixon
Littlemoss House
1 Wayne Close
Littlemoss
Droylsden M43 7LQ
0793 170 0478

Jack Doughty
Lane End Cottage
Golden Street
Off Buckstones Road
Shaw
Oldham OL2 8LY
0170 684 5753

Mickey Duff
40 Bilton Towers
Great Cumberland Place
London
W1H 7LD
0207 724 8494

Tony Dunlop
3a Fianna House
Queens Parade
Belfast
BT15 2ES
0289 023 5874

Paul Dykes
7 Hadderidge
Burslem
Stoke on Trent
ST6 3ER
0783 177 7310

John Eames
83 Stokes Road
East Ham
London E6 3SF
0207 473 3173

Graham Earl
28 Talbot Road
Luton
Beds
LU2 7RW
0158 245 1117

Jim Evans
88 Windsor Road
Maidenhead
Berks SL6 2DJ
0162 862 3640

Graham Everett
7 Laud Close
Norwich NR7 0TN
0160 370 1484

Spencer Fearon
The Ring Boxing Club
70 Ewer Street
London SE1 0NR
0208 270 0759

Jonathan Feld
c/o Angel Media Group
Ltd
The Office Islington
338 City Road
London
EC1V 2PT
0785 420 9501

Chris Firth
14 Fisher Avenue
Whiston
Prescot
Merseyside
L35 3PF
0151 289 3579

Tania Follett
123 Calfridus Way
Bracknell
Berks
RG12 3HD
07930 904303

Philippe Fondu
1b Nursery Gardens
Birch Cottage
Chislehurst
Kent
BR7 5BW
0208 295 3598

Ali Forbes
14 Overdown Road
Catford
London
SE6 3ER
0794 075 8091

Steve Foster
7 Howclough Close
Worsley
M28 3HX
0784 250 8193

Winston Fuller
271 Cavendish Road
Balham
London
SW12 0PH
0793 917 7929

Joseph Gallagher
0161 374 1683

Dai Gardiner
13 Hengoed Hall Drive
Cefn Hengoed
Mid Glamorgan
CF8 7JW
0144 381 2971

Dave Garside
33 Lowthian Road
Hartlepool
Cleveland
TS26 8AL
0142 929 1611

Malcolm Gates
78 Cedar Drive
Jarrow
Tyne &Wear
NE32 4BG
0191 537 2574

Jimmy Gill
13 Thompson Close
Chilwell
Notts
NG9 5GF
0115 913 5482

Tommy Gilmour
Platinum House
120 Carnegie Road
Hillington Park
Glasgow
G52 4NY
0141 810 5700

Stephen Goodwin
Unit W1
Chester Enterprise
Centre
Hoole Bridge
Chester
0124 434 2012

Billy Graham
116 Stockport Road
Mossley
Ashton under Lyne
Manchester
0145 783 5100

Lee Graham
28 Smeaton Court
50 Rockingham Street
London SE1 6PF
0207 357 6648

Carl Greaves
62 Nelson Road
Balderton
Newark
Notts NG24 3EL
0163 661 2320

Carl Gunns
10 Edith Murphy Close
Goscote Hall
Birstall
Leics LE4 3DZ
0116 267 1494

Christopher Hall
38 Fairley Way
Cheshunt
Herts
EN7 6LG
0783 813 2091

Jess Harding
c/o UK Industrial Pallets
Ltd
Travellers Lane
Industrial Estate
Travellers Lane
Welham Green
Hatfield
Herts
AL9 7HF
0170 727 0440

Tony Harris
237 Stapleford Road
Trowell
Notts
NG9 3QE
0115 913 6564

Oliver Harrison
Farrington House
Auckland Drive
Salford
M6 6FW
0781 882 2522

Richard Hatton
25 Queens Drive
Gee Cross
Hyde
Cheshire
SK14 5LQ
0161 366 8133

Pat Healy
1 Cranley Buildings
Brookes Market
Holborn
London EC1
0207 242 8121

Barry Hearn
'Mascalls'
Mascalls Lane
Great Warley
Brentwood
Essex CM14 5LJ
0127 735 9900

Michael Helliet
Flat 1
Lower Ground Floor
102 Whitfield Street
London W1T 5EB
0207 388 5999

Martin Herdman
24a Crown Road
St Margarets
Twickenham
Middlesex TW1 3EE
0208 891 6040

Dennis Hobson
130 Handsworth Road
Sheffield S9 4AE
0114 256 0555

Dennis Hobson Snr
73 Darnall Road
Sheffield S9 5AH
0114 243 4700

Nicholas Hodges
Llys-y-Deryn
Cilcennin
Lampeter
Ceredigion
West Wales
SA48 8RR
0157 047 0452

Harry Holland
12 Kendall Close
Feltham
Middlesex
0208 867 0435

Jayson Hollier
21 Hillmorton Road
Rugby CV22 5DF
0779 089 6635

Lloyd Honeyghan
PO Box 17216
London SE17 1ZU
07956 405007

Barry Hughes
5 Royal Exchange
Square
Glasgow G1 3AH
0777 188 8844

Brian Hughes MBE
41 Fold Green
Chadderton
Lancs OL9 9DX
0161 620 2916

Geoff Hunter
6 Hawkshead Way
Winsford
Cheshire CW7 2SZ
0160 686 2162

Dominic Ingle
5 Eccles Street
Sheffield
S9 1LN
0114 281 1277

John Ingle
20 Rockmount Road
Wincobank
Sheffield S9
0114 261 7934

Steve James
c/o The Tool People
Barkers Yard
George Street
Wellingborough
Northants
NN8 4RD
0771 875 6677

Errol Johnson
36 Newton Street
West Bromwich
West Midlands
B71 3RQ
0121 532 6118

Thomas Jones
13 Planetree Road
Hale
Cheshire
WA15 9JL
0161 980 2661

Frank Joseph
29 Arlington Road
Ealing
London W13 8PF
0777 963 5783

Brian Lawrence
218 Millfields Road
London E5 0AR
0208 561 6736

Buddy Lee
The Walnuts
Roman Bank
Leverington
Wisbech
Cambs
PE13 5AR
0194 558 3266

Daniel Lutaaya
c/o Zaina Bukenya
41 Cresset House
Retreat Place
London E9 6RW
0795 162 7066

Pat Lynch
Gotherington
68 Kelsey Lane
Balsall Common
Near Coventry
CV7 7GL
0167 633374

Danny McAlinden
589 Antrim Road
Belfast BT15 4DX
0793 921 5235

Paul McCausland
1 Prospect Heights
Carrickfergus
Northern Ireland
BT38 8QY
0289 336 5942

Robert McCracken
Ravensbourne
Westerham Road
Keston
Kent BR2 6HE
0190 579 8976

Jim McDonnell
2 Meadway
Hillside Avenue
Woodford Green
Essex IG8 7RF
07860 770006

John McIntyre
123 Newton Avenue
Barrhead G78 2PS
0141 571 4393

Angel McKenzie
85e Herne Hill
London SE24 9NE
0207 737 2338

Owen McMahon
3 Atlantic Avenue
Belfast BT15
0289 074 3535

Colin McMillan
60 Billet Road
Chadwell Heath
Romford
Essex RM6 5SU
0208 597 4464

Patrick Magee
35 Deramore Park South
Belfast BT9 5JY
0289 043 8743

Frank Maloney
Lord Clyde
9 Wotton Road
Deptford
London SE8 5TQ
0776 869 8358

Lee Maloney
4 St Pauls Cottages
Wentlock Court
Halewood Village
Liverpool
L26 0TA
0797 102 4704

Rick Manners
5 Foundry Avenue
Harehills
Leeds LS9 6BY
0793 296 5863

Rebecca Margel
10 Bentcliffe Lane
Leeds
LS17 6QF
0113 268 0681

Michael Marsden
1 North View
Roydes Lane
Rothwell
Leeds
LS26 0BQ
0113 282 5565

Terry Marsh
60 Gaynesford
Basildon
Essex SS16 5SG
0207 0152207

Clifton Mitchell
42 Wiltshire Road
Derby DE21 6EX
01332 295380

Alex Morrison
197 Swanston Street
Laird Business Park
Dalmarnock
Glasgow G40 4HW
0141 554 7777

Katherine Morrison
197 Swanston Street
Laird Business Park
Dalmarnock
Glasgow
G40 4HW
0141 554 7777

Bert Myers
8 Thornhill Street
Burnley
Lancs BB12 6LU
0781 696 6742

Trevor Nerwal
Wayside Cottage
64 Vicarage Lane
Water Orton
Birmingham
B46 1RU
0121 730 1546

Paul Newman
12 Edgehill Way
Portslade
Brighton
BN41 2PU
0127 341 9777

Norman Nobbs
364 Kings Road
Kingstanding
Birmingham
B44 0UG
0121 355 5341

Stewart Nubley
94 Richmond Road
Kirkby in Ashfield
Notts NG17 7PW
0162 343 2357

Frankie O'Connor
48 Belhaven Terrace
Wishaw
North Lanarkshire
ML2 7AY
0169 884 1813

Terry O'Neill
48 Kirkfield View
Colton Village
Leeds
LS15 9DX
0113 225 6140

Ian Pauly
1202 Lincoln Road
Peterborough
PE4 6LA
0173 331 1266

Alek Penarski
4 Vale Coppice
Horwich
Bolton BL 6 5RP
0120 446 9692

Joseph Pennington
215 North Road
Clayton
Manchester
M11 4WQ
0161 223 4463

Brian Powell
138 Laurel Road
Bassaleg
Newport
Gwent NP10 8PT
0163 389 2165

Dean Powell
Sports Network
Centurion House
Bircherley Green
Herts
07956 905741

Paul Rees
11 Abbots Park
London Road
St Albans
Herts
AL1 1TW
0172 776 3160

Glyn Rhodes
166 Oldfield Road
Stannington
Sheffield S6 6DY
0114 232 6513

Gus Robinson MBE
Stranton House
Westview Road
Hartlepool
TS24 0BB
0142 923 4221

John Rooney
11 Cedar House
Erlanger Road
London
SE14 5TB
0788 407 7024

John Rushton
20 Alverley Lane
Balby
Doncaster
DN4 9AS
0130 231 0919

Kevin Sanders
9 Moggswell Lane
Orton Longueville
Village
Peterborough
Cambs PE2 7DS
0173 337 1912

Chris Sanigar
Bristol Boxing Gym
40 Thomas Street
St Agnes
Bristol BS2 9LL
0117 949 6699

Trevor Schofield
234 Doncaster Road
Barnsley
South Yorks
S70 1UQ
0122 629 7376

Matthew Scriven
The Old One, Two
Fitness &Boxing Studio
2a Thoresby Street
Mansfield
Notts NG18 1QF
0783 399 5770

Mark Seltzer
50 Valley Hill
Loughton
Essex IG10 3AL
0776 378 5226

Mike Shinfield
126 Birchwood Lane
Somercotes
Derbys DE55 4NE
0177 360 3124

Gurcharan Sing
165 St Giles Road
Ash Green
Coventry
CV7 9HB
0777 576 7815

Tony Sims
67 Peel Place
Clayhall
Ilford
Essex IG5 0PT
0208 550 8911

Les Southey
Oakhouse
Park Way
Hillingdon
Middlesex
0189 525 4719

Marvin Stone
4 Othello Court
3 Old Hospital Close
Tooting
London SW12 8SR
0781 503 5466

Glenroy Taylor
73 Aspen Lane
Northolt
Middlesex
U35 6XH
0795 645 3787

John Tiftik
2 Nuffield Lodge
Carlton Gate
Admiral Walk
London W9 3TP
0795 151 8117

Kevin Toomey
11 Ward Avenue
Bilton
Hull
HU11 4EE
0780 117 8528

Jack Trickett
Blossom Barn
Blossom Lane
Woodford
Cheshire
SK7 1RE
0161 439 8943

James Tugby
5 Burnside Close
Kirby in Ashfield
Notts
NG17 8NX
0777 022 6656

Louis Veitch
80 Sherborne Road
North Shore
Blackpool
FY1 2PQ
0125 362 8943

Keith Walker
Walkers Boxing
Promotions
Headland House
Suite 21-35
Spawd Bone Lane
Knottingley
West Yorks
WF11 0HY
0197 760 7888

Frank Warren
Centurion House
Bircherley Green
Hertford
Herts
SG14 1AP
0199 250 5550

Robert Watt
32 Dowanhill Street
Glasgow
G11
0141 334 7465

Delroy Waul
35 Gair Road
Reddich
Stockport
SK5 7LH
07796 271968

Derek V. Williams
65 Virginia Road
Surrey
CR7 8EN
0208 765 0492

Derek Williams
Pendeen
Bodiniel Road
Bodmin
Cornwall
PL31 2PE
0777 633 0516

John Williams
3a Langham Road
Tottenham
London
N15 3QX
0778 782 2245

Alan Wilton
The Bridge
42 Derryboy Road
Crossgar
BT30 9LH
0289 754 2195

Barry Winter
9 McNeill Avenue
Linnvale
Clydebank
G81 2TB
0141 952 9942

Stephen Wood
Edward Street
Cambridge Industrial
Area
Salford
Manchester
M7 1RL
0161 834 9496

Richie Woodhall
3 Leasowe Green
Lightmoor
Telford
Shropshire
TF4 3QX
0195 259 3886

Tex Woodward
Spaniorum Farm
Compton Greenfield
Bristol
BS12 3RX
0145 463 2448

Licensed Matchmakers

Neil Bowers
59 Carson Road
Canning Town
London
E16 4BD
0207 473 5631

Nigel Christian
22 Spire Court
Efford
Plymouth
PL3 6HP
0175 225 1136

Jim Evans
88 Windsor Road
Bray
Maidenhead
Berks SL6 2DJ
0162 862 3640

Jimmy Gill
13 Thompson Close
Chilwell
Notts NG9 5GF
0115 913 5482

Tommy Gilmour MBE
Platinum House
120 Carnegie Road
Hillington Park
Glasgow
G52 4NY
0141 810 5700

Roy Hilder
2 Farrington Place
Chislehurst
Kent BR7 6BE
0208 325 6156

John Ingle
20 Rockmount Road
Wincobank
Sheffield S9 1LP
0114 261 7934

Errol Johnson
36 Newton Street
West Bromwich
Birmingham
B71 3RQ
0121 532 6118

Michael Marsden
1 North View
Roydes Lane
Rothwell
Leeds LS26 0BQ
0113 282 2210

Ken Morton
3 St Quintin Mount
'Bradway'
Sheffield S17 4PQ
0114 262 1829

Jonathan Pegg
9 Finchmead Road
Tile Cross
Birmingham
B33 0LP
0781 731 3319

Dean Powell
Sports Network
Centurion House
Bircherley Green
Herts SG14 1AP
0199 250 5550

Richard Poxon
148 Cliffefield Road
Sheffield S8 9BS
0114 225 7856

John Rushton
20 Averley Lane
Balby
Doncaster
South Yorks
0130 231 0919

Chris Sanigar
Bristol Boxing Gym
40 Thomas Street
St Agnes
Bristol
BS2 9LL
0117 949 6699

Mark Seltzer
50 Valley Hill
Loughton
Essex
IG10 3AL
0776 378 5226

Mike Shinfield
126 Birchwood Lane
Somercotes
Derbys
DE55 4NE
0177 360 3124

Tony Sims
67 Peel Place
Clayhall Avenue
Ilford
Essex
IG5 0PT
0773 961 7830

John Wilson
1 Shenley Hill
Radlett
Herts
WD7 3AS

Licensed BBBoC Referees, Timekeepers, Ringwhips and Inspectors

Licensed Referees

Class 'B'
Michael Alexander	Central Area
Christopher Kelly	Central Area
Paul McCullagh	Northern Ireland
David Morgan	Welsh Area
Kenneth Pringle	Scottish Area
Bob Williams	Southern Area
Gary Williams	Northern Area

Class 'A'
Terence Cole	Northern Area
Mark Curry	Northern Area
Kenneth Curtis	Southern Area
Roddy Evans	Welsh Area
Keith Garner	Central Area
Paul Graham	Scottish Area
Stephen Gray	Central Area
Jeff Hinds	Southern Area
David Irving	Northern Ireland
Wynford Jones	Welsh Area
Shaun Messer	Midlands Area
Sean Russell	Northern Ireland
Grant Wallis	Western Area
Andrew Wright	Northern Area

Class 'A' Star
Richie Davies	Southern Area
Phillip Edwards	Central Area
Howard Foster	Central Area
Mark Green	Southern Area
Ian John-Lewis	Southern Area
John Keane	Midlands Area
Victor Loughlin	Scottish Area
Marcus McDonnell	Southern Area
Terry O'Connor	Midlands Area
Dave Parris	Southern Area
Mickey Vann	Central Area

Licensed Timekeepers
Arnold Bryson	Northern Area
Neil Burder	Welsh Area
Anthony Dunkerley	Midlands Area
Andrew East	Central Area
Robert Edgeworth	Southern Area
Dale Elliott	Northern Ireland
Harry Foxall	Midlands Area
Eric Gilmour	Scottish Area
Gary Grennan	Central Area
Brian Heath	Midlands Area
Greg Hue	Southern Area
James Kirkwood	Scottish Area
Jon Lee	Western Area
Roddy McAllister	Scottish Area
Michael McCann	Southern Area
Peter McCann	Southern Area
Norman Maddox	Midlands Area

Barry Pinder	Central Area
Raymond Rice	Southern Area
Colin Roberts	Central Area
David Walters	Welsh Area
Nick White	Southern Area
Graeme Williams	Northern Area

Licensed Ringwhips
Michael Burke	Scottish Area
Steve Butler	Central Area
David Clark	Scottish Area
Ernie Draper	Southern Area
Simon Goodall	Midlands Area
Mark Currivan	Southern Area
Lee Gostolo	Central Area
Edward Higgins	Scottish Area
Mervyn Lewis	Welsh Area
Stuart Lithgo	Northern Area
Tommy Miller (Jnr)	Central Area
Tommy Rice	Southern Area
Sandy Risley	Southern Area
Stephen Sidebottom	Central Area
Gary Stanford	Southern Area

Inspectors
Herold Adams	Southern Area
Alan Alster	Central Area
William Ball	Southern Area
Richard Barber	Southern Area
Don Bartlett	Midlands Area
Geoff Boulter	Midlands Area
Fred Breyer	Southern Area
Walter Campbell	Northern Ireland
Edward Cassidy	Northern Ireland
Michael Collier	Southern Area
Dai Corp	Welsh Area
Julian Courtney	Welsh Area
Maurice Cunningham	Northern Ireland
Robert Curry	Northern Area
Jaswinder Dhaliwal	Midlands Area
Christopher Dolman	Midlands Area
Will Downie	Scottish Area
Gordon Foulds	Scottish Area
Kevin Fulthorpe	Welsh Area
James Gamble	Northern Ireland
Paul Gooding	Welsh Area
Michael Hills	Northern Area
Alan Honnibal	Western Area
Wayne Hutton	Northern Ireland
James Ivory	Central Area
Philip Jones	Midlands Area
Francis Keenan	Northern Ireland
Nicholas Laidman	Southern Area
Kevin Leafe	Central Area
Denzil Lewis	Central Area
Eddie Lillis	Central Area

Fred Little	Western Area
Reginald Long	Northern Area
Bob Lonkhurst	Southern Area
Sam McAughtry	Northern Ireland
Dave McAuley	Northern Ireland
Liam McColgan	Scottish Area
Billy McCrory	Northern Ireland
Gerry McGinley	Scottish Area
Paul McKeown	Northern Ireland
Neil McLean	Scottish Area
Michael Madden	Northern Ireland
Pat Magee	Northern Ireland
Paddy Maguire	Northern Ireland
Andy Morris	Central Area
Daryl Neatis	Northern Area
Thomas Nichol	Northern Ireland
Phil O'Hare	Central Area
Ron Pavett	Welsh Area
Richard Peers	Central Area
Dave Porter	Southern Area
Fred Potter	Northern Area
Suzanne Potts	Midlands Area
Steve Ray	Central Area
Hugh Russell	Northern Ireland
Charlie Sexton	Scottish Area
Neil Sinclair	Southern Area
Glyn Thomas	Welsh Area
Nigel Underwood	Midlands Area
Richard Vaughan	Midlands Area
David Venn	Northern Area
Phil Waites	Midlands Area
Kevin Walters	Northern Area
Ron Warburton	Central Area
Mark Warner	Welsh Area
Danny Wells	Southern Area
Barney Wilson	Northern Ireland
Robert Wilson	Scottish Area
Fred Wright	Central Area

Terry O'Connor: Class "A" Star Referee
Les Clark

Robin Hood Boxing and Fitness
2a Thoresby Street, Mansfield
Nottinghamshire, NG18 1QF
Tel: 01623 476397
Mobile: 07833995770 / 07757821555
Email: Robinhoodboxing@hotmail.co.uk

Robin Hood Boxing Stable

Professional and Amateur
BBB of Control
Regular Promotions
Training

Manager/Trainer
Matt Scriven
11 years Army P.T.I.
10 years Pro Boxer

NEWCOMERS VERY WELCOME

Current Fighters

Andy Bell – Midlands Area & British Masters Bantamweight Champion
Matt Scriven – L.Middleweight
Alex Spitko – L.Welterweight
Mick Monaghan – S.Middleweight
Dennis Corpe – L.Middleweight
Karl Chiverton – Welterweight
Charlie Chiverton – Middleweight
Sergei Rozhakmens – S.Featherweight
Jon Foster – Middleweight
Nicki Taylor – L.Heavyweight
Radoslaw Wilkojc – L.Heavyweight
Daz Broomhall – Lightweight

Robin Hood A.B.C.

Director: P. Scriven
Secretary: T. Bell
Treasurer: R. Scriven
Trainers: Dave Pearson
                   Rob Sharpe

REGULAR SHOWS

VIP Promotions Ltd.

TAKING BOXING FORWARD

C/o Edward Street, Cambridge Industrial Area, Salford 7, Gtr Manchester M7 1RL
Tel: 0161-834 9496   Fax: 0161-832 8099   Email: swood@vip-ltd.co.uk

Manager & Promoter: Stephen Wood

Matchmaker: Ken Morton
Trainers: Oliver Harrison, Karl Ince, Joe Pennington, Bob Shannon
Bobby Rimmer, Nigel Hardman, Humphrey Harrison

Current List of VIP Boxers

Scott Mitchell – Heavyweight
Robin White – L.Heavyweight
Carl Dilks – S.Middleweight
Wayne Pinder – Middleweight
Sean Crompton – Middleweight
Nigel Travis – Middleweight
Martin Murray – Middleweight
Jamie Moore – L.Middleweight (British Champion)
Alex Matvienko – L.Middleweight
Jack Armfield – L.Middleweight
Chris Johnson – Welterweight
Ali Nuumbembe – Welterweight (Commonwealth Champion)
Mark Thompson – Welterweight
Thomas Mazurkiewicz – L.Welterweight
Gary O'Connor – L.Welterweight
Danny Harding – Lightweight
Michael Gomez – S.Featherweight
Gary Sykes – S.Featherweight
Stephen Foster Jnr – Featherweight
Mark Moran – S.Bantamweight
Stuart McFadyen – Bantamweight

NB All Above Fighters Are Managed By Ourselves. Other Boxers Are Available Through Our Associate Connections

Regular Promotions / Good Management / Top-Class Training
Any unattached boxer should contact us direct to discuss their future

Website: www.vipboxing.com

Fully Licensed by the British Boxing Board of Control

314

WINNING COMBINATION

Tel: (0191) 567 6871
Fax: (0191) 565 2581
Mobile: (07850) 434457

Tommy Conroy - Manager and Trainer
Annette Conroy - First North-East Lady Promoter
Matchmaker: Ken Morton
Trainers: Charlie Armstrong, Paul Fiske and Stan Williamson

144 High Street East,
Sunderland,
Tyne & Wear,
SR1 2BL, England.

Sunderland-Based Stable

David Ferguson Heavyweight (North Shields)
Danny 'Boy' Hughes Heavyweight (Sunderland)
Ryan Kerr Former Undefeated English & Northern Area Super-Middleweight Champion
(Sunderland, via Bannockburn)
Shaun Farmer Light-Middleweight (Sunderland, via Liverpool)
Martin Marshall Light-Middleweight (Sunderland)
Paul 'The Mackem' Holborn Light-Welterweight (Sunderland)
'John' George Watson Lightweight (Newcastle)

The North-East Executive Sporting Club is now into its 14th Year

NORTH-EAST EXECUTIVE SPORTING CLUB dates for 2008
Venue: Tavistock Roker Hotel

Friday   15 February
Thursday   15 May
Friday   3 October
Thursday   4 December

315

Boxers' Record Index